Pensions Law Handbook

Thirteenth Edition

Pensions Law Handbook

Thirteenth Edition

by the Pensions Department of Nabarro LLP

Joint Editors

Jennifer Bell BA (Hons)
Partner

Susan Jones LLB (Hons)
Solicitor

Bloomsbury Professional

Bloomsbury Professional

An imprint of Bloomsbury Publishing Plc

Bloomsbury Professional Ltd	Bloomsbury Publishing Plc
41–43 Boltro Road	50 Bedford Square
Haywards Heath	London
RH16 1BJ	WC1B 3DP
UK	UK

www.bloomsbury.com

**BLOOMSBURY and the Diana logo are trademarks of
Bloomsbury Publishing Plc**

© Bloomsbury Professional Ltd 2017

British Library Cataloguing-in-Publication Data

A catalogue record for this book is available from the British Library.

ISBN:	PB:	978 1 78043 852 8
	ePDF:	978 1 78451 244 6
	ePub:	978 1 78451 243 9

Typeset by Phoenix Photosetting Ltd, Chatham, Kent
Printed and bound by CPI Group (UK) Ltd, Croydon, CR0 4YY

To find out more about our authors and books visit
www.bloomsburyprofessional.com. Here you will find extracts, author information,
details of forthcoming events and the option to sign up for our newsletters.

Preface

We are delighted to introduce this 13th edition of the immensely popular *Pensions Law Handbook*. As always, the book has been written and revised entirely by pension lawyers who are members of the pensions team at Nabarro LLP, together with support from other specialised practitioners around the firm. We have also undertaken the detailed work of editing the book.

Nabarro is one of the largest independent law practices in the UK. Its pensions team has for many years been one of its strengths. Our pension lawyers have a deep technical knowledge of their subject and advise an impressive range of clients on the areas that the book covers. From 1 May 2017, Nabarro will combine with CMS and Olswang to create the sixth largest law firm in the UK, which will include one of the largest pensions practices in the UK.

We are sure that readers will find this new edition valuable. With the overwhelming volume of legislation that continues to swamp the pensions world and the constantly changing legal and economic environment within which trustees of pension schemes, sponsoring employers and their advisers operate, we hope this new edition will be helpful to all. As well as undertaking a full update of existing content, new material in this edition includes the benefit flexibilities introduced from April 2015, new requirements for DC governance, the abolition of contracting-out and changes to statutory transfer rights.

Our aim has been to state the law as at 6 April 2016. Where there have been later developments that we have been able to take into account, this is clearly stated in the text.

The impact on pensions law of the referendum vote for the UK to leave the EU is as yet unknown. From a legal perspective, there will be no immediate change. The initial impact has been on markets and currency. There has also been a fall in gilt yields which will affect the funding position of many pension schemes. Longer term, there are areas where UK legislation derives from EU law and could be subject to amendment or repeal. In the pensions context this includes scheme funding and investment, data protection and discrimination.

We are very grateful to all the members of the pensions team who have contributed to the book for their hard work and dedication. The contributors are (in alphabetical order) from the pensions team: Sarah Aldred, Jennifer Bell,

Preface

Michael Draper, Jayne Firth, Richard Gibson, Ian Greenstreet, John Hanratty, Susan Jones, Victoria Lee, Katie Lopez, Sharon Piert, Chris Ransom, Kate Richards and Alexander Waters, and, from other specialisms: Glen Flannery, Anoushka Gangji, Tracey Marsden, Chris Stewart and Sarah Verrecchia.

Jennifer Bell
Susan Jones
Editors
Nabarro LLP

Disclaimer

Contents

Contents

Contents

Contents

Table of Cases

[*All references are to paragraph number*]

A

Table of Cases

C

I

J

K

L

M

N

Q

R

T

U

V

W

Table of Cases

Table of Statutes

[All references are to paragraph number]

Table of Statutory Instruments

[All references are to paragraph number]

Abbreviations and References

Abbreviations

A-Day	6 April 2006
ADR	alternative dispute resolution
Age Exceptions Order	Equality Act (Age Exceptions for Pensions Schemes) Order 2010 (SI 2010/2133), as amended
Age Regulations	Employment Equality (Age) Regulations 2006 (SI 2006/1031) as amended
AML	additional maternity leave
APPS	Appropriate Personal Pension Scheme
AVC	additional voluntary contribution
APS P1	Actuarial Professional Standards P1
APS X2	Actuarial Professional Standards X2
Automatic Enrolment Regulations	Occupational and Personal Pension Schemes (Automatic Enrolment) Regulations 2010 (SI 2010/772)
BAU	business as usual
BIS	Department for Business, Innovation and Skills (previously BERR and DTI)
Business Order	Financial Services and Markets Act 2000 (Carrying on Regulated Activities by Way of Business) Order 2001 (SI 2001/1177)
CA 1985	Companies Act 1985
CA 2006	Companies Act 2006
CARE	Career Average Scheme
CETV	cash equivalent transfer value
CJEU	Court of Justice of the European Union
CN	contribution notice
COMB	contacted-out mixed benefit
COMP	contracted-out money purchase
Contracting-Out Regulations	Occupational Pension Schemes (Contracting-out) Regulations 1996 (SI 1996/1172) as amended

Contracting-out Regulations 2015	Occupational Pension Schemes (Schemes that were Contracted-out) (No 2) Regulations 2015 (SI 2015/1677)
COPE	contracted-out pension equivalent
COSR	contracted-out salary related
CPA 2004	Civil Partnerships Act 2004
CPI	Consumer Prices Index
CPR	Civil Procedure Rules 1998 (SI 1998/3132)
CVA	Company Voluntary Arrangement
CVL	Creditor's Voluntary Liquidation
DB	defined benefits
DC	defined contribution
DCLG	Department for Communities and Local Government
DDA 1995	Disability Discrimination Act 1995
Disclosure Regulations	Occupational and Personal Pension Schemes (Disclosure of Information) Regulations 2013 (SI 2013/2734)
DPA	Data Protection Act 1998
DRA	default retirement age
DWP	Department for Work and Pensions
EAT	Employment Appeal Tribunal
EFRBS	Employer-Financed Retirement Benefits Scheme
EFTA	European Free Trade Association
Employer Debt Regulations	Occupational Pension Schemes (Employer Debt) Regulations 2005 (SI 2005/678) as amended
EqA	Equality Act 2010
Equal Treatment Framework Directive	Council Directive 2000/78/EC establishing a general framework for equal treatment in employment and occupation
Equal Treatment Regulations	Occupational Pension Schemes (Equal Treatment) Regulations 1995 (SI 1995/3183) as amended
ERA 1996	Employment Rights Act 1996
ERPA	early retirement pivot age
EU	European Union
EWC	expected week of childbirth
FA 1921/1970/1986/2004/ 2005/2006/2007/2008/2011/ 2012/2013/2014/2016	Finance Act 1921/1970/1986/2004/2005/2006/2007/2 008/2011/2012/2013/2014/2016

FAS	Financial Assistance Scheme
FAS Regulations	Financial Assistance Scheme Regulations 2005 (SI 2005/1986) as amended
FCA	Financial Conduct Authority
Forfeiture Regulations	Occupational Pension Schemes (Assignment, Forfeiture, Bankruptcy etc) Regulations 1997 (SI 1997/785) as amended
FOS	Financial Ombudsman Service
FPC	Financial Policy Committee
FRC	Financial Reporting Council
FSA	Financial Services Authority
FSA 2012	Financial Services Act 2012
FSAVC	free-standing additional voluntary contributions
FSD	Financial Support Division
FSMA 2000	Financial Services and Markets Act 2000
FURBS	funded unapproved retirement benefit schemes
GAA	Governance Advisory Arrangement
GAD	Government Actuary's Department
GDPR	General Data Protection Regulation
GLO	group litigation order
GMP	guaranteed minimum pension
HMRC	Her Majesty's Revenue and Customs
IA 1986	Insolvency Act 1986
IA 2000	Insolvency Act 2000
ICE	initial cash equivalent
ICO	Information Commissioner's Office
ICTA 1988	Income and Corporation Taxes Act 1988
IDR	internal dispute resolution
IDRP	Internal dispute resolution procedure
IFA	Independent Financial Adviser
IGC	Independent Governance Committee
IGG	Investment Governance Group
IHTA 1984	Inheritance Tax Act 1984
IHTM	Inheritance Tax Manual
IMA	Investment Management Association

Investment Regulations	Occupational Pension Schemes (Investment) Regulations 2005 (SI 2005/3378) as amended
IORP	Directive 2003/41/EC of the European Parliament and Council on the activities and supervision of institutions for occupational retirement provision
IP	Insolvency Practitioner
IR 1986	Insolvency Rules 1986
IRPS	investment-regulated pension scheme
ITEPA 2003	Income Tax (Earnings and Pensions) Act 2003
ITTOIA 2005	Income Tax (Trading and Other Income) Act 2005
IWCSSS	Industry Wide Coal Staff Superannuation Scheme
IWMPS	Industry Wide Mineworkers' Pension Scheme
LEL	lower earnings limit
LET	lower earnings threshold
LGPS	local government pension scheme
LLP	limited liability partnership
LPA 1925	Law of Property Act 1925
LPI	limited price indexation
MCA 1973	Matrimonial Causes Act 1973
MFR	minimum funding requirement
MIR	minimum income requirement
MND	member-nominated director
MNT	member-nominated trustee
MNT Regulations	Occupational Pension Schemes (Member-nominated Trustees and Directors) Regulations 2006 (SI 2006/714) as amended
Modification Regulations	Occupational Pension Schemes (Modification of Schemes) Regulations 2006 (SI 2006/759) as amended
MVL	Members' Voluntary Liquidation
NAPF	National Association of Pension Funds
NCA	National Council on Ageing
NEST	National Employment Savings Trust
NISPI	National Insurance Services to Pensions Industry
NRD	normal retirement date
NSP	new State pension

Ombudsman Regulations	Personal and Occupational Pension Schemes (Pension Ombudsman) Regulations 1996 (SI 1996/2475) as amended
OML	ordinary maternity leave
Opra	Occupational Pensions Regulatory Authority
PA 1995/2004/2007/2008/ 2011/2014	Pensions Act 1995/2004/2007/2008/2011/2014
PADA	Personal Accounts Delivery Authority
PD	Practice Direction
PERG	Perimeter Guidance Manual
PIE	Pension Increase Exchange
PLSA	Pensions and Lifetime Savings Association
PMI	Pensions Management Institute
PNLD	Police National Legal Database
PO	Pensions Ombudsman
Power to Amend Regulations	Occupational Pension Schemes (Power to Amend Schemes to Reflect Abolition of Contracting-out) Regulations 2015 (SI 2015/118)
PPF	Pension Protection Fund
PPF Entry Rules	Pension Protection Fund (Entry Rules) Regulations 2005 (SI 2005/590)
PPFO	PPF Ombudsman
PRA	Prudential Regulation Authority
Preservation Regulations	Occupational Pension Schemes (Preservation of Benefit) Regulations 1991 (SI 1991/167) as amended
Protected Rights Regulations	Personal and Occupational Pension Schemes (Protected Rights) Regulations 1996 (SI 1996/1537) as amended
Provision of Information Regulations	Registered Pension Schemes (Provision of Information) Regulations 2006 (SI 2006/567)
PSA 1993/2015	Pension Schemes Act 1993/2015
PSPA 2013	Public Service Pensions Act 2013
PSO	pension sharing order
PTM	Pensions Tax Manual
QPSIPs	qualifying pension scheme indemnity provisions
QROPS	qualifying recognised overseas pension scheme
QTPIPs	qualifying third party indemnity provisions
RAA	regulated apportionment arrangement

RAC	retirement annuity contract
Regulated Activities Order	Financial Services and Markets Act 2000 (Regulated Activities) Order 2001 (SI 2001/544)
Regulator	Pensions Regulator (as established by PA 2004, s 1)
ROFR	regulatory own funds requirement
RPSM	Registered Pension Schemes Manual
RVF	Relevant Valuation Factor
S2P	State second pension
SAA	scheme apportionment arrangement
Scheme Administration Regulations	Occupational Pension Schemes (Scheme Administration) Regulations 1996 (SI 1996/1715) as amended
Scheme Funding Regulations	Occupational Pension Schemes (Scheme Funding) Regulations 2005 (SI 2005/3377)
SERPS	State Earnings-Related Pension Scheme
SFO	statutory funding objective
SFP	statement of funding principles
SIF	special investment fund
SIP	statement of investment principles
SIPP	self-invested personal pension
SMP	statutory maternity pay
SPA	State pension age
SRS	Scheme Reconciliation Service
SSCBA 1992	Social Security Contributions and Benefits Act 1992
TA 1925/2000	Trustee Act 1925/2000
TCGA 1992	Taxation of Chargeable Gains Act 1992
TFEU	Treaty on the Functioning of the European Union
TIA 1961	Trustee Investments Act 1961
TKU	trustee knowledge and understanding
TPA 2014	Taxation of Pensions Act 2014
TPAS	The Pension Advisory Service
Transfer Regulations	Occupational Pension Schemes (Transfer Values) Regulations 1996 (SI 1996/1847) as amended
Transitional Money Purchase Regulations	Transitional, Consequential and Supplementary Provisions) Regulations 2014 (SI 2014/1711)
TUPE	Transfer of Undertakings (Protection of Employment) Regulations 2006 (SI 2006/246)

UCTA 1977	Unfair Contract Terms Act 1977
UEL	upper earnings limit
UFLSDB	uncrystallised funds lump sum death benefit
UURBS	unfunded unapproved retirement benefit schemes
VAT	value added tax
WRPA 1999	Welfare Reform and Pensions Act 1999

References

AC	Appeal Cases (Law Reports)
All ER	All England Law Reports
Ch	Chancery (Law Reports)
CSIH	Court of Session Inner House (Scotland)
ECR	European Court Reports
ICR	Industrial Cases Reports
IRLR	Industrial Relations Law Reports
KB	King's Bench (Law Reports)
ONCA	Court of Appeal for Ontario
ONSC	Ontario Superior Court of Justice
OPLR	Occupational Pensions Law Reports
PBLR	Pension Benefits Law Reports
PLR	Pensions Law Reports
TC	Tax Cases
TLR	Times Law Reports
WLR	Weekly Law Reports

Chapter 1

Pension provision in the UK – an introduction

Introduction

1.1   'Pension' is defined in the Oxford English Dictionary as 'an annuity or other regular payment made to a retired employee, servant or citizen by right or in consideration of past services or the relinquishment of an emolument'.

A pension scheme is an arrangement for meeting these payments. Pension schemes may be either State schemes or private arrangements. Where a scheme is established by the Government, it will often be a 'pay as you go' arrangement with no advance provision being made for the funding of benefits. Private pension arrangements, whether established by an employer or arranged by an individual, will usually be funded; contributions will be made by the individual and/or his employer during his working life to ensure that, when he retires, sufficient money is available to provide his pension and any other benefits which are payable.

Private pension arrangements are governed by a mixture of trust, employment, fiscal, social security and family law, which together provide the framework within which such schemes must operate. Pension provision for the public sector tends to be governed more rigidly by legislation. Many public sector schemes, including the Local Government Pension Scheme and the National Health Service Pension Scheme, are governed and administered almost exclusively by statutory instruments. Such schemes are generally outside the scope of this book. As are personal pension schemes, although brief references are made to them from **1.50** below and in **Chapter 17**.

A brief history of pension legislation in the UK

1.2   The first arrangement to contain features which are recognisable in modern pension schemes was established in 1671 by HM Customs and Excise. Originally the arrangement provided for a retiring employee to be paid a pension by his successor. By 1686 employees were required to make

1

advance provision for their own retirement by paying contributions towards a retirement fund.

Pension protection was gradually extended to a broader range of civil servants but it was not until the *Civil Service Superannuation Act 1834* (the first enactment devoted solely to pensions) that any formal legislative framework was established. During the early nineteenth century the concept of pension provision was extended so that other employees, both in the public and private sectors, became eligible for membership of pension schemes. Insurance and life assurance schemes became available and actuarial methods for assessing risk gradually developed.

The beginning of the twentieth century saw the introduction of the first State pension scheme. In 1908 the *Old Age Pension Act* was passed, giving those over 70 a non-contributory, but means-tested, pension. General taxation paid for this early State scheme although that was changed following the passing of the *National Insurance Act 1911*. At the same time, there was a continuing increase in the establishment of pension funds by large private sector employers.

The growth in pension provision prompted pressure for change in the tax treatment of pension funds and in 1920 the Royal Commission on Income Tax recommended that investment income earned by pension funds should be tax-free. The *Finance Act 1921* provided a statutory right to tax relief on contributions made to pension funds by employers and employees and on the investment income of HMRC 'approved' pension funds. To gain HMRC approval, assets constituting pension funds had to be kept separate from an employer's other assets and consequently trust funds emerged as a natural vehicle for obtaining tax-approved status.

The *Finance Act 1970* established a new system of approval for occupational pension schemes. Although this was consolidated and amended in the *Income and Corporation Taxes Act 1988*, the basic underlying taxation principles for UK occupational schemes remained the same until the *Finance Act 2004* (*FA 2004*) (see **1.3** below).

In addition to tax legislation, various pieces of social security legislation affecting pension schemes were passed during the 1970s. These included the *Social Security Act 1973* which introduced provisions to protect members who left service or opted out of the scheme before retirement (known as 'early leavers') and the *Social Security Pensions Act 1975*. The 1980s saw the introduction of further legislation; the *Social Security Acts 1985* and *1986* extended the protection offered to early leavers and, in particular, gave them the right to transfer their benefits to another pension scheme. The various Acts passed in the 1970s and 1980s, together with the relevant provisions of the *Social Security Act 1990*, are now consolidated in the *Pension Schemes Act 1993 (PSA 1993)*. The protection of early leavers is considered in **Chapter 6**.

A major review of pension provision in the UK was undertaken in the early 1990s by the Pension Law Review Committee chaired by Professor Roy Goode. In its report, 'Pension Law Reform' (Cm 2342-1, September 1993), the Committee made many recommendations as to how the legislative framework for pension provision could be amended to provide greater protection for scheme members. Many of the recommendations were adopted in the *Pensions Act 1995 (PA 1995)*, the bulk of which came into force on 6 April 1997. Two further significant Acts followed, namely the *Welfare Reform and Pensions Act 1999 (WRPA 1999)* and the *Child Support, Pensions and Social Security Act 2000*. The most notable changes introduced by these Acts were the introduction of pension sharing on divorce provisions, stakeholder pension requirements and the State second pension.

From 2002, a number of consultations and reviews were undertaken which led to the introduction of the *Finance Act 2004* and the *Pensions Act 2004*.

Finance Act 2004 and Pensions Act 2004

1.3   (a)   *The Finance Act 2004 (FA 2004)*

The pensions tax simplification regime introduced by *FA 2004* follows, broadly, the proposals outlined in a consultation paper published in December 2002, 'Simplifying the taxation of pensions: increasing choice and flexibility for all'. On 6 April 2006 (known as 'A-Day'), the eight then-existing taxation regimes were replaced by a single set of rules, applicable to all 'registered schemes' (the equivalent of tax approved pension schemes under the previous regime), including defined benefit and defined contribution occupational pension schemes and personal pension schemes. The main features include:

- Removal of the pre-existing HMRC limits (including the earnings cap).

- Introduction of a single lifetime limit on the amount of pension saving that attracts favourable tax treatment (known as the 'lifetime allowance'). This was initially set at £1.5 million for the tax year 2006/2007 and at its peak rose to £1.8 million. However, under the Government's plans to restrict pensions tax relief the allowance has been falling and with effect from 6 April 2016 has dropped to £1 million.

- Introduction of an annual limit on the inflows of value to an individual's pension fund (both in the form of contributions and accrual) that attract favourable tax treatment (known as the 'annual allowance'). At its peak the annual allowance was £255,000. However, with effect from 6 April 2014, this dropped to £40,000.

- The possibility for members to draw pension benefits whilst continuing to work.

- Raising the minimum age for taking early retirement benefits from 50 to 55.

- Removal of the tax advantages for unapproved pension schemes.

- Increased flexibility in relation to the treatment of death benefits.

- Transitional provisions gave a level of protection to those who, as at 6 April 2006, had rights that were inconsistent with the new regime.

FA 2004 is considered further in **Chapter 17**.

(b) The Pensions Act 2004 (PA 2004)

The main provisions of *PA 2004* are:

- **The Pensions Regulator**: On 6 April 2005, the Pensions Regulator ('the Regulator') became the regulator of occupational pensions in the UK under *PA 2004, Part 1*, replacing the Occupational Pensions Regulatory Authority (Opra). The Regulator's main objectives (as set out in *PA 2004, s 5*) are to protect the benefits of members of occupational and personal pension schemes; to reduce the risk of situations arising which may lead to compensation being payable by the Pension Protection Fund (see below); to promote and improve understanding of the good administration of work-based occupational, personal and stakeholder schemes; and (from July 2014), in relation to scheme funding only, to minimise any adverse impact on the sustainable growth of an employer. The Regulator has a number of powers to enable it to achieve these objectives including power to collect data and demand information, to issue improvement notices where the security of members' benefits is under threat, to appoint and remove trustees, to impose civil penalties and to issue contribution notices and financial support directions where it believes that an employer is attempting to avoid its pension obligations.

- **The Pension Protection Fund**: The Board of the Pension Protection Fund ('PPF') was established under *PA 2004, Part 2*. The Board is responsible for holding, managing and applying the PPF and the Fraud Compensation Fund. Since 10 July 2009 the Board of the PPF has also been responsible for managing the Financial Assistance Scheme (see **Chapter 5**).

  The PPF is designed to give members of defined benefit schemes a measure of protection where their employers are insolvent. The Board will assume responsibility for eligible schemes where a 'qualifying insolvency event' has occurred in relation to the employer or where an employer of a prescribed description is unlikely to be able to continue as a going concern; the scheme is unable to secure its 'protected liabilities' and there is no possibility of a scheme rescue. Once the Board has assumed responsibility for a scheme, it must provide compensation to the scheme beneficiaries in the form of pension or lump sum payments. The assets from which such compensation payments are made derive from both the assets of the schemes for which it has assumed responsibility and the levy payable by eligible schemes. The 'pension protection levy' includes a risk-based and a scheme-based element meaning that schemes with poor funding positions and weak sponsoring employers are likely to be required to pay more.

- **Funding**: *PA 2004, Part 3* replaced the statutory minimum funding requirement for defined benefit schemes with a scheme-specific funding standard, requiring each scheme to have sufficient and appropriate assets to cover its liabilities or have a recovery plan in place to achieve that within a stated period (see **Chapter 11**).

- **Member-nominated trustees**: Unless the scheme is exempt, there must be arrangements in place to allow at least one-third of trustees to be member-nominated. All of the members and pensioners (or an organisation that adequately represents them) must be allowed to participate in the initial nomination stage of the process, and at least some of the members allowed to participate in the final selection (*PA 2004, ss 241, 243*) (see **Chapter 3**).

- **Trustee knowledge and understanding**: *PA 2004, ss 247–249* introduced a legal requirement for all trustees to be conversant with their scheme documentation and to have knowledge and understanding of pensions and trust law and of the principles underpinning investment and funding (see **Chapter 3**).

- **Business transfers**: *PA 2004, ss 257 and 258* have increased the protection of pension rights where there is a relevant transfer within the meaning of the *Transfer of Undertakings (Protection of Employment) Regulations 2006*. The protection applies to employees who are members of (or are, or would be, entitled to be members of) an occupational pension scheme to which the employer contributes (or would be required to contribute) before the transfer. In such situations the purchaser must ensure that, after the transfer, a minimum level of contributions or benefits is provided, depending on the type of scheme from which and to which the member transferred (see **Chapter 15**).

- **Consultation requirements**: Certain employers are required under *PA 2004, ss 259–261* to consult employees and/or their representatives before making prescribed changes to pension arrangements, including, for example, closing a scheme to future accrual, changing from a defined benefit scheme to a defined contribution scheme and reducing or removing the requirement for an employer to contribute to a defined contribution scheme (see **Chapter 7**).

- **Amendment power**: *PA 1995, s 67* was amended giving occupational pension schemes greater freedom to amend their rules (see **Chapter 13**).

- **Early leavers**: *PA 2004* amended *PSA 1993* to provide protection for the pension benefits of early leavers with between three months and two years' pensionable service. Members falling within this category have the right to opt for either a cash transfer sum (cash equivalent) or a contribution refund on leaving the scheme (see **Chapter 6**).

- **Winding up priority**: A new statutory priority order was introduced by *PA 2004, s 270* for schemes that commenced winding up on or after 6 April 2005. The priority order aligns the statutory winding-up priorities with the PPF provisions, the intention being to ensure that the benefits provided for members on the winding-up of a scheme are no less than would have been provided by the PPF had the Board assumed responsibility for the scheme (see **Chapter 12**).

- **Increases to pensions in payment**: The limited price indexation (LPI) requirement contained in *PA 1995, s 51* (which provides for statutory increases to be made to pensions in payment) was reduced from a revaluation percentage based on retail prices (RPI) capped at 5 per cent to RPI capped at 2.5 per cent in relation to defined benefits accrued on and after 6 April 2005. This section of the 1995 Act was amended again by the *Pensions Act 2011*: see **1.41** below. From January 2011 the index used to calculate the statutory revaluation percentage was changed from RPI to CPI. In relation to defined contribution benefits, the LPI requirement was removed for pensions coming into payment on or after 6 April 2005.

Retirement provision by the State

Types of State pension

1.4   State pension provision is based on an individual's National Insurance contribution record. Those reaching State pension age ('SPA') before 6 April 2016 will remain subject to the provisions of the *Social Security Contributions and Benefits Act 1992 (SSCBA 1992)* (as amended) and will receive (if they qualify) a basic and additional State pension. Those reaching SPA on and from 6 April 2016 will (if they qualify) receive the new State pension ('NSP'). This is a single-tier pension (with the distinction between basic and additional pensions removed) as provided for in the *Pensions Act 2014 (PA 2014)*.

Until recently, men had an SPA of 65 and women 60. This has now changed and the rules for determining SPA operate on the basis of a person's date of birth. The more recently a person was born, the higher his or her SPA will be. The detail is set out in tables in *PA 1995, Sch 4, Part 1* (as amended by the *Pensions Act 2007 (PA 2007)*, the *Pensions Act 2011 (PA 2011)* and the *PA 2014*). Women's SPA will increase to 65 by November 2018 and then, from

December 2018, SPA for both men and women will increase to reach 66 by October 2020. Under *PA 2014*, SPA will increase to 67 by 2028. Currently, SPA is due to increase to 68 by 2046, but this is subject to review.

State pension provision is considered in more detail in **Chapter 4**.

Occupational pension schemes

What is an occupational pension scheme?

1.5   One definition of occupational pension scheme is set out in *PSA 1993, s 1*, which describes it as a pension scheme:

'(*a*)   that—

   (i)   for the purpose of providing benefits to, or in respect of, people with service in employments of a description, or

   (ii)   for that purpose and also for the purpose of providing benefits to, or in respect of, other people, is established by, or by persons who include, a person to whom subsection (2) applies when the scheme is established or (as the case may be) to whom that subsection would have applied when the scheme was established had that subsection then been in force, and

(*b*)   that has its main administration in the United Kingdom or outside the EEA States;

or a pension scheme that is prescribed or is of a prescribed description; ...'

For the purposes of the definition, 'employment' means 'any trade, business, profession, office or vocation' and a person to whom *subsection (2)* applies means, broadly, the employer. 'Pension scheme' is defined in the same section as:

'a scheme or other arrangement, comprised in one or more instruments or agreements, having or capable of having effect so as to provide benefits to or in respect of people—

(*a*)   on retirement,

(*b*)   on having reached a particular age, or

(*c*)   on termination of service in an employment.'

The *PSA 1993* definition of an occupational pension scheme is therefore wide: it can relate to an entire workforce, a specified group of employees or a single individual; it can be established and governed by a single clause in a contract of employment or by a complex trust deed.

The tax regime established by *FA 2004* applies to all 'registered' schemes. *FA 2004, s 150* separately defines 'occupational pension scheme' as meaning:

'... a pension scheme established by an employer or employers and having or capable of having effect so as to provide benefits to or in respect of any or all of the employees of—

(*a*)   that employer or those employers, or

(*b*)   any other employer,

(whether or not it also has or is capable of having effect so as to provide benefits to or in respect of other persons).'

Traditionally, most occupational pension schemes have been able to benefit from tax privileges if correctly structured. Prior to 6 April 2006 (A-Day), schemes were either approved by HMRC or unapproved. Those schemes approved by HMRC received considerably more tax privileges than unapproved schemes but were, as would be expected, more heavily regulated with detailed restrictions on the form and amount of benefits which could be paid.

On A-Day, these restrictions were simplified, so that all types of registered pension schemes may make any payment to a member. Where it is an 'authorised member payment' under *FA 2004* the usual tax privileges will apply. Unauthorised payments will have adverse tax consequences, usually for both the member and the scheme (see **Chapter 17**).

Most occupational pension schemes, whatever their nature, are required to comply with the provisions of the *PSA 1993* and the regulations made under that Act. In particular, all schemes are required to comply with the provisions dealing with protection for early leavers (see **Chapter 6**). Schemes with a contracted-out component are also required to comply with the relevant provisions relating to contracting-out (see **Chapter 4**).

Occupational pension schemes are also subject to *PA 1995* and *PA 2004* which aim to improve the administration of pension schemes and increase security for members. The effects of *PA 1995* and *PA 2004* are considered throughout this book. *Section 252* of *PA 2004* requires that most UK based occupational pension schemes (other than public service pension schemes) cannot receive any funding unless they are established under irrevocable trust. The effect of this is that almost all private sector occupational pension schemes will be established under trust (see **1.12**).

Certain types of occupational schemes have been exempted from many of the provisions of *PA 1995* and *PA 2004* by regulations. Most notably, unregistered schemes are exempt from many, but not all, of the requirements.

Why establish a pension scheme?

1.6   No occupational pension scheme is cheap to run. Employers have to think carefully about the costs involved before establishing an occupational pension scheme. The Office for National Statistics Occupational Pension Schemes Survey 2014 (published in September 2015) recorded average private sector employer contributions of 2.9 per cent of payroll in defined contribution schemes and 15.8 per cent for defined benefit schemes (see **1.7** below). Contributions in the form of lump sum payments, life assurance premiums and the general day-to-day expenses of running the scheme can also add to the cost. Perhaps unsurprisingly, defined benefit schemes are generally perceived to be more expensive, and many have been closed in recent years.

A common reason for an employer to provide a pension scheme (other than where there is a legal requirement to do so) is to look after its employees after retirement (the paternalistic approach). Other reasons may include recruitment and retention and building a reputation as a responsible employer. Sometimes an employer may be required to establish a scheme as part of a commercial transaction or as a result of a public sector contracting-out exercise (although this is less likely now due to changes in pension requirements on public sector contracting-out introduced in October 2013).

Registered pension schemes benefit from a number of tax advantages (see **Chapter 17**) and so, although costly, the provision of an occupational pension scheme remains a relatively tax-efficient way of providing employee benefits.

From the employee's point of view, membership of an occupational scheme can be very attractive. The pension provided by the State is unlikely to be adequate for most people to maintain their standard of living during retirement; and although employees often have to contribute to an occupational pension scheme in order to build up their pension entitlement, they will also obtain the value of employer contributions made for their benefit and tax relief on their own contributions.

Types of benefits provided by occupational pension schemes

1.7   Traditionally, occupational pension schemes have been commonly described as either defined benefit (or final salary) schemes or defined contribution (or money purchase) schemes, depending on the type of benefits they provide. In a defined benefit scheme, the amount of pension which a member ultimately receives will be directly related to his remuneration, usually, at or around the date of his retirement (although schemes where benefits accrue on a 'career average' basis are becoming more popular). In a defined contribution or money purchase scheme, the amount of pension a member receives will be related to the contributions made and the investment

9

return on those contributions. Much of the pensions legislation differentiates between money purchase schemes and schemes which are not money purchase schemes (see **1.11** below). The most important difference between the two types of scheme, other than the benefits they provide (see **1.28** to **1.39** below), is the way in which they are funded and the resulting risks for the employer and the member. A new category of 'shared risk' scheme is defined in the *Pension Schemes Act 2015* (*PSA 2015*), but the relevant provisions are yet to come into force (see **1.10** below).

Defined benefit schemes

1.8   A member of a defined benefit scheme will generally be required to pay into the scheme a specific proportion of his remuneration by way of contributions (although in some schemes this can fluctuate and in others the member may not be required to contribute). The balance of the cost of providing scheme benefits will generally be met by the employer (hence these schemes can also be known as 'balance of cost' schemes). The exact cost of providing the benefits will not be known until the last beneficiary under the scheme dies, so a defined benefit scheme represents a very open-ended risk to the employer. The way in which the contributions of the employer are calculated is considered further in **Chapter 11**.

Money purchase schemes

1.9   The rules of a money purchase scheme (also referred to as a defined contribution scheme) will usually specify the contributions a member is required to pay to the scheme and the contributions the member's employer is required to make in respect of him. Usually the rules will provide for the member to have a notional 'individual account' which is credited with his contributions, the contributions made by his employer in respect of him and the investment growth attributable to those contributions. When the member retires, assets equal to the value of his account will be realised and usually the proceeds are used to purchase an annuity to provide him with an income (although a wider range of options have been available since April 2015) (see **1.40** below and **Chapter 17**).

The amount of pension the member receives will be dependent on the contributions made, the investment growth achieved and (for those who choose to purchase an annuity) the annuity rate obtained; it will not be directly related to the member's earnings before retirement. For many employers a defined contribution scheme represents an attractive proposition as the cost of financing the scheme can be predicted with some certainty. For an employee, such schemes are often less attractive because, if the investments perform poorly or annuity rates are high at the time of retirement, it is the employee upon whom this will impact.

There has been some dispute as to what exactly money purchase benefits and money purchase schemes are. In *Aon Trust Corpn Ltd v KPMG [2005] EWCA Civ 1004* the question arose, in relation to the obligation of the employer to fund a deficit, as to whether the scheme was a money purchase scheme (being one which provides only money purchase benefits) as defined in *PSA 1993, s 181* as it then stood. The Court of Appeal looked in some detail at the meaning of 'money purchase scheme' and held that the scheme in question did not, as the employer was asserting, fall within this category. The direct relationship between contributions and benefits required in a money purchase scheme was broken by the introduction of actuarial factors in the calculation of benefits.

This decision was distinguished by the High Court and the Court of Appeal in the case of *Bridge Trustees v Yates [2008] EWHC 964 (CH), [2010] EWCA Civ 179)*, where it was held that the use of actuarial factors was not inevitably fatal to a benefit being money purchase. The Court of Appeal held that the correct interpretation of the statutory definition of 'money purchase benefits' is to avoid a restrictive reading and to construe the definition in a 'fair and reasonable' way and apply it sensibly to the provisions of the particular scheme construed in their context. This decision was appealed to the Supreme Court which upheld the decision of the Court of Appeal and found that 'the equilibrium of assets and liabilities is not a requirement of the statutory definition of a money purchase scheme' and also concluded that the provision of internal annuities (ie the trustees paying a pension from scheme assets on the retirement of a money purchase member) is not incompatible with money purchase benefits.

Immediately following the decision of the Supreme Court on 27 July 2011, the DWP issued a statement. The DWP's view was that the judgment in *Bridge* would result in schemes which may previously have thought they were not money purchase schemes falling within the definition, placing them outside the scope of legislation protecting members including that governing:

- scheme funding,
- employer debt,
- the Pension Protection Fund, and
- the Financial Assistance Scheme.

In the view of the DWP, the judgment also introduced uncertainty about how the trustees of some schemes should distribute assets on winding up. There followed an amendment to the definition of 'money purchase benefit' by *PA 2011, s 29(1)*, which amended *PSA 1993, s 181* on 24 July 2014 with retrospective effect from 1 January 1997 to include within the definition of money purchase benefits, a benefit only if 'its rate or amount calculated solely by reference to assets which (because of the nature of the calculation) must necessarily suffice for the purposes of its provision to or in respect of the member'.

Two sets of transitional regulations were made which limit the retrospective effect of the new money purchase definition so that most decisions and actions taken before 24 July 2014 will not have to be revisited. The majority of the provisions are the *Pensions Act 2011 (Transitional, Consequential and Supplementary Provisions) Regulations 2014 (SI 2014/1711)* (the *'Transitional Money Purchase Regulations'*) with some consequential changes to primary legislation made by the *Pensions Act 2011 (Consequential and Supplementary Provisions) Regulations 2014 (SI 2014/1954)*.

Hybrid, CARE and other shared risk structures

1.10   As employers become more cost-sensitive and wish to minimise the scope for fluctuations in contribution rates, other benefit structures are being introduced, often aimed at sharing the risk more evenly between employer and member.

It is possible to have a hybrid scheme that provides pensions accrued on both a defined contribution basis and a defined benefit basis, usually by operating a defined contribution and a defined benefit section. A member will accrue benefits under one or other section and may be able to switch between the two upon satisfying a specified condition. A hybrid scheme may alternatively provide defined contribution benefits but with a defined benefit underpin (or vice versa) so that the member will receive the greater of the benefits provided by his individual account and a pension calculated by reference to his salary before retirement.

A career average scheme (CARE) provides defined benefits but instead of a proportion of the member's final pensionable salary at retirement, the member accrues a proportion of his salary (say 1/60th) for each year of pensionable service. At retirement, each year's accrual is added up (after being revalued from the year that it accrued to the year that the member retires) to provide the final benefit. The advantage for an employer of a career average benefit is that it provides the employer with some certainty regarding the cost of ongoing accrual as the funding risk relating to salary inflation over the working life of the member is contained (but not entirely eliminated) and the employer is still at risk from price inflation over the period and longevity.

CARE schemes tend to provide pensions that are less valuable to members with high earnings towards the end of their career because the pension is based on the members' earnings throughout their career. A CARE scheme can provide a better level of pension to those members whose earnings are steady or who wish to work part-time towards the end of their career.

Although defined benefit schemes present much higher risks for the employer, some paternalistic employers may be reluctant to put all the investment risk on employees. Some employers are choosing a cash balance arrangement which is a blend between a defined contribution and a defined benefit arrangement. Typically, it provides that the member and employer make contributions based on a percentage of salary and on retirement the member will receive a specified amount for each year of service. So, in effect, the employer is providing a guaranteed rate of return on the investment of the defined contribution monies. When the member retires, the member then purchases an annuity with the value of his accrued balance.

In November 2012 the Government published a strategy document called 'Reinvigorating Workplace Pensions' and in November 2013, the DWP published a consultation 'Reshaping Workplace Pensions for Future Generations' introducing the idea of a new 'defined ambition' pension scheme. The idea behind defined ambition is to remove some legislative and regulatory restrictions to 'enable industry innovation and development of new products including those which will give people more certainty about their pensions and encourage more risk sharing'.

Provision for defined ambition schemes, now renamed as 'shared risk', was included in the *PSA 2015*. It introduced a new legislative framework with three mutually exclusive scheme types (defined benefit, shared risk and defined contribution). The definitions are based on the type of promise about benefits the scheme offers members during the accumulation phase:

- A **defined benefits scheme** is one that provides a pre-determined retirement income to all members, beginning at pension age and continuing for life. There must be a 'full pensions promise' to members, which means that the level of benefit is determined solely by reference to that promise.

- A **shared risk scheme** is one that offers a 'pensions promise' but not a 'full pensions promise', to all members at some point during the accumulation phase in relation to at least some of the retirement benefit that members might receive.

- A **defined contributions scheme** is one that gives no promise during the accumulation phase in relation to any of the retirement benefits that may be provided to members.

PSA 2015 also includes new rules for 'collective benefit' schemes which will allow members to pool risk.

In October 2015, the then Pensions Minister, Baroness Altman, announced that shared risk and collective benefit schemes were being put on hold indefinitely and the relevant provisions of *PSA 2015* are yet to be brought into force.

Application of legislation to different types of occupational pension schemes

1.11   The legislation relating to occupational pension schemes generally applies equally to schemes which provide solely money purchase benefits (or money purchase benefits and insured death benefits) as to those which provide non-money purchase benefits. However, there are exemptions or modifications for money purchase schemes from some of the requirements of the legislation, as referred to in the table below.

Legislation relating to:	Applicability to occupational pension schemes:	
	Non-money purchase schemes	**Money purchase schemes (or schemes providing only money purchase benefits and insured death benefits)**
Protection for early leavers, (ie preservation, transfers and revaluation) (see **Chapter 6**)	All schemes are required to comply with the legislation relating to the protection of early leavers under *PSA 1993, Part IV* although the time limits for the payment of transfer values and ways in which benefits are calculated will vary.	
Equal treatment (see **Chapter 9**)	The equal treatment requirements set out in *Equality Act 2010, s 61* apply to all schemes.	
Independent trustees (see **Chapter 3**)	Where a scheme employer suffers an insolvency event, the Regulator may appoint an independent trustee under *PA 1995, ss 22–25*. The Regulator also has power to appoint an independent trustee if there is a Pension Protection Fund assessment period in relation to the scheme.	The independent trustee provisions also apply to money purchase schemes but provisions relating to PPF assessment periods will not be relevant.

Employer debt (see **Chapters 12** and **15**)	Where a scheme is being wound up, a 'relevant event' occurs or an employer ceases to participate in the scheme (whilst at least one other continues) and the value of the assets of the scheme is less than the value of its liabilities, a debt may become due to the trustees of the scheme from the employer.	The employer debt provisions apply only in limited circumstances where the general scheme levy has not been paid or assets of the scheme have been reduced due to criminal action. In most circumstances the employer debt provisions do not apply to employers in hybrid schemes whose liabilities relate only to money purchase benefits, although they can be liable for orphan liabilities.
Disclosure (see **Chapter 3** and **Appendix II**)	Trustees of all schemes are required to comply with the requirements of the *Occupational and Personal Pension Schemes (Disclosure of Information) Regulations 2013 (SI 2013/2734)*.	
Statutory pension increases (see **1.41** below)	Limited Price Indexation (LPI) applies where the pension is attributable to pensionable service accrued on or after 6 April 1997.	LPI does not apply to benefits coming into payment on or after 6 April 2005.
Investments (see **Chapter 10**)	All trustees must comply with the statutory requirements set out in *PA 1995, ss 33–36*. These requirements affect the choice of investments, the appointment of fund managers and the maintenance of a statement of investment principles amongst other things (unless the scheme has an appropriate exemption under the relevant regulations).	
Contracting-out (see **Chapter 4**)	Contracting-out on the basis of satisfying the reference scheme test was abolished with effect from 6 April 2016.	Contracting-out for money purchase schemes was abolished with effect from 6 April 2012.
Voluntary membership (see **1.14** below)	Membership of a scheme cannot be compulsory (*PSA 1993, s 160*) but see **Chapter 14** for automatic enrolment requirements.	

Registration	All occupational pension schemes may register with HMRC under *FA 2004, s 153* and were deemed registered if exempt approved as at 6 April 2006. All schemes with more than one member must also register with the Pensions Regulator in accordance with *PA 2004, s 62*.	
Dispute resolution (see **Chapter 3**)	Trustees of all occupational pension schemes (other than those exempted by regulations) must put in place a dispute resolution procedure in accordance with *PA 1995, s 50*.	
Pensions Ombudsman (see **Chapter 2**)	The Pensions Ombudsman has jurisdiction to investigate a wide range of complaints in relation to all occupational pension schemes.	
Appointment of professional advisers (see **Chapter 2**)	Under *PA 1995, s 47*, trustees must appoint an individual as scheme actuary and an individual or firm as scheme auditor. Where the assets include 'investments', an individual or firm must be appointed as fund manager unless the scheme is wholly insured. Trustees should not rely on the advice of any professional adviser they did not appoint.	As for defined benefit schemes except there is no requirement to appoint a scheme actuary.
Member-nominated trustees (see **Chapter 3**)	Trustees must arrange for the appointment of member-nominated trustees (or directors in the case of a trustee company) unless the scheme is exempt under regulations.	
Pension Protection Fund (see **Chapter 5**)	Most defined benefit schemes are eligible for the PPF and required to pay the levy	Not eligible for PPF entry.
Scheme Funding (see **Chapter 11**)	Must comply with the scheme funding requirements in *PA 2004, Part 3* (see **1.22** below).	Not required to comply with the statutory scheme funding requirements.

Winding up (see **Chapter 12**)	The order in which the liabilities of a tax approved defined benefit scheme must be secured in the event of a winding up is governed by *PA 1995, ss 73–76*.	The statutory winding-up priority order does not apply.
Payment of surplus (see **Chapter 11**)	*PA 1995, s 37* confers certain powers on trustees to make payments of surplus to an employer provided that conditions are satisfied.	The payment of surplus provisions do not apply to money purchase schemes.

How are occupational pension schemes established?

1.12   Before 6 April 2006, tax relief for occupational pension schemes was only available to schemes approved by HMRC and established under irrevocable trusts in accordance with *ICTA 1988, s 592*. Consequently, the vast majority of such schemes were established by trust deed or a declaration of trust and were known as 'exempt approved schemes'.

An equivalent requirement was introduced with effect from 22 September 2005 by *PA 2004, s 252*, whereby if an occupational pension scheme has its main administration in the UK, the trustees or managers of the scheme are prohibited from accepting any payment to fund benefits unless the scheme is established under irrevocable trusts.

With effect from A-Day, newly established pension schemes must make an application to HMRC to be registered in accordance with *FA 2004, s 153*. The application must contain any information reasonably requested by HMRC and must be accompanied by a prescribed declaration by the scheme administrator and any other declarations reasonably required by HMRC (*FA 2004, ss 153(2), 270*); see **Chapter 17**. Schemes with exempt approved status immediately prior to A-Day were automatically treated as registered with the Inland Revenue on 6 April 2006 unless they opted out.

The documentation governing a scheme will usually consist of a definitive trust deed and one or more sets of rules. There is no particular format for what should be contained in the trust deed and what should be in the rules. It is quite common for the trust deed to contain the administrative provisions of the trust and for the rules to detail the benefits payable under the scheme, but there are many variations on this theme.

The first trust deed will generally appoint the first trustees of the scheme and set out the purpose and terms of the trust. In particular it will be necessary for the trust deed to include or make provision for a power of amendment so that the scheme can be amended to account for future changes in legislation and/or practice. The trustees will also need to be given sufficient powers in the trust deed to be able to administer the trust.

When a scheme's documentation is first drafted, consideration needs to be given to the 'balance of power' between the trustees and the employer. It is necessary to decide which powers should be vested in the trustees, which powers should be vested in the employer and which powers should be vested jointly. As a general rule, if the exercise of the power could have financial implications for the scheme, the employer will usually wish to be involved in exercising that power; the power could be vested in the employer or it could be vested in the trustees, subject to the consent of the employer. Legislation has, in some instances, overridden this 'balance of power' in the trust documentation. For example, under the statutory funding regime established by *PA 2004, s 222*, trustees in many schemes have been given more power in the process of determining the level of the employer's contribution.

The rules of a scheme will generally detail the benefits payable under the scheme. Usually, they will also set out conditions for membership and specify the contributions (if any) that the members are required to pay. The exact details of the rules will, of course, depend on the benefit structure of the scheme. However, *FA 2004, s 164* defines the authorised payments that a registered pension scheme can make in respect of scheme members. These include pensions permitted under *ss 165* and *167*, lump sums permitted under *ss 166* and *168* and 'recognised transfers' as defined in *s 169*. Generally, any unauthorised payments are likely to have adverse tax consequences and many schemes will contain a rule restricting benefits to those which are authorised.

The taxation of pension schemes is considered further in **Chapter 17**.

Multi-employer schemes

1.13   It may be possible for an employer to participate in a 'centralised' or 'multi-employer' occupational pension scheme, rather than establish its own scheme, thus benefiting from lower administration costs. Such schemes generally have a principal employer, and a number of associated or participating employers on whose behalf the principal employer will act.

Before A-Day, the general rule was that a non-sectionalised occupational pension scheme had to restrict membership to employers of 'associated' employers to obtain and retain HMRC exempt approved status. However, under the *FA 2004* regime, a registered occupational pension scheme is now able to include employees of non-associated employers.

Participation is usually achieved by the trustees, the principal employer and the participating employer executing a deed of adherence or participation setting out the terms on which the employer can participate in the scheme.

In recent years a number of 'master trusts' (or 'relevant multi-employer schemes') have been established. They are generally money purchase schemes in which unconnected employers can participate. They have been widely used by smaller employers to satisfy their automatic enrolment obligations (see **Chapter 14**). The Regulator and the Government have expressed some concerns about the governance and security of master trusts. The Regulator maintains a list of master trusts which meet an independent assurance standard. In addition, they are subject to enhanced governance standards including:

- the scheme must have at least three trustees (or trustee directors) and a majority of these, including the chair, must be independent of any company that provides advisory, administration, investment or other services to the scheme ('non-affiliated trustees');

- non-affiliated trustees must be appointed in an open and transparent fashion;

- trustees must have a process in place to encourage scheme members to make their views known on matters that affect them.

The Queen's Speech in May 2016 included confirmation that, under a new Pensions Bill, master trusts will have to meet new criteria and be subject to closer supervision.

Membership of occupational pension schemes

Non-compulsory membership

1.14   Membership of an occupational pension scheme cannot currently be made compulsory and any term in a contract of employment or any rule in an occupational pension scheme to the effect that an employee must be a member of a particular pension scheme is void. Legislation relating to non-compulsory membership was introduced by the *Social Security Act 1986* and first became effective on 6 April 1988; it is now contained in *PSA 1993, s 160*. The only exception to this is that membership may be compulsory for a death in service only scheme if the benefit is provided on a non-contributory basis, as set out in *Pension Schemes (Voluntary Contributions Requirements and Voluntary and Compulsory Membership) Regulations 1987, reg 3*. In practice, it is permissible (as long as the matter is correctly handled) for employees to be included automatically as members of their employer's scheme unless they specifically request to opt out.

PA 2008 sets out the requirements for automatic enrolment which came into force on 1 October 2012. The provisions require all employers to automatically enrol their qualifying employees (those aged between 22 and State pension age and earning a threshold amount) into a qualifying scheme (see **Chapter 14** for details).

HMRC requirements

1.15   Until 6 April 2006 (A-Day), membership of an occupational pension scheme was confined to the employees of employers participating in the scheme. As from A-Day, an occupational pension scheme need not restrict membership to its own employees in order to remain registered.

In the past, save for limited exceptions, an employee could not be a member of an occupational pension scheme if he was also contributing to a personal pension scheme. This restriction was relaxed to a certain extent by the stakeholder legislation which allowed employees with earnings of less than £30,000 in 2004/2005 to pay up to £3,600 to a personal pension or stakeholder pension, whilst at the same time continuing to be eligible for concurrent membership of their occupational pension scheme.

Under the *FA 2004* regime, an individual may be a member of as many schemes or arrangements as he wishes. There is, however, a limit to the amount of tax privilege that will be allowed to an individual in respect of his pension savings in relation both to an annual and lifetime allowance.

The taxation of registered schemes is considered further in **Chapter 17**.

The Equality Act 2010

1.16   The majority of the provisions of the *Equality Act 2010* (*EqA 2010*) Act came into force on 1 October 2010. *EqA 2010* has two main stated purposes:

• to harmonise discrimination law; and

• to strengthen the law to support progress on equality.

Essentially, *EqA 2010* is a consolidation of discrimination law, with the previous statutes and regulations being repealed and a new statutory structure introduced.

EqA 2010 contains key concepts:

- a list of 'protected characteristics'; and

- definitions of discrimination, harassment and victimisation.

These key concepts are then applied in specific areas, including pensions.

The protected characteristics are:

- age – by reference to a particular age or to a range of ages (see **1.19** below);

- disability (a physical or mental impairment having a substantial and long-term adverse affect on the ability to carry out normal day-to-day activities) (see **1.18** below);

- gender reassignment – someone proposing to undergo, undergoing or who has undergone gender reassignment (no need for medical supervision);

- marriage and civil partnership;

- pregnancy and maternity;

- race;

- religion or belief;

- sex (see **1.17** below); and

- sexual orientation.

EqA 2010 is considered further in **Chapter 9**.

Sex discrimination

1.17   Sex discrimination claims relating to pensions tend to arise under two broad headings: equal benefits and equal access. Both are derived from *Article 157* of the *Treaty on the Functioning of the European Union ('TFEU')* (formerly *Article 119* and then *Article 141* of the *EC Treaty*) which requires that Member States apply the principle of equal pay for equal work or work of equal value. The decision of the CJEU in *Bilka-Kaufhaus Gmbh v Weber (C-170/84)* established that pensions were 'pay' for the purposes of the *TFEU*.

Claims relating to unequal benefits cases originally tended to arise out of the fact that defined benefit schemes typically provided different retirement dates for men and women, meaning that men had to work longer in order to receive their full pension entitlement. The *Coloroll* decision *(C-200/91)*, which was given in September 1994, established that equal treatment claims could be brought in relation to benefits payable in respect of periods of service on and after 17 May 1990 (which was the date of the *Barber* judgment *(C-262/88))*. However, there was great uncertainty on how to equalise benefits, and recent claims have arisen out of failures to do this correctly.

The principle of equal access is set out in the *EqA 2010, s 67* which provides that the terms on which employees may become members of an occupational pension scheme must be the same for both men and women. Historically, disputes in this area arose in the context of part-timer claims, due to the fact that, part-time workers were not given equal access to pension schemes. Since a greater proportion of women than men tended to work part-time, claims arose on the grounds of indirect discrimination. A key case in this area is *Preston v Wolverhampton Healthcare NHS Trust [2001] UKHL 5,* in which the House of Lords decided that, subject to the employee making back-payments in respect of the membership period claimed, pension benefits could be calculated by reference to periods of part-time service subsequent to 8 April 1976 (which was the date on which the ECJ decided in *Defrenne v Sabena (C-43/75)* that *Article 157* of the *TFEU* had direct effect).

It is worth noting in this context that the *Part-time Workers (Prevention of Less Favourable Treatment) Regulations 2000 (SI 2000/1551)* and the *Fixed-term Employees (Prevention of Less Favourable Treatment) Regulations 2002 (SI 2002/2034)* introduced measures to protect part-time and fixed-term workers from unjustified exclusion from pension schemes (alongside more general employment protection).

The issue of sex discrimination in relation to occupational pension schemes is considered further in **Chapter 9**.

Disability discrimination

1.18   It is unlawful for an employer to discriminate, without justification, against disabled employees in terms of the benefits provided to those employees, including the access to and benefits provided from, an occupational pension scheme. *EqA 2010, s 6* provides that a person has a disability 'if he has a physical or mental impairment and the impairment has a substantial and long term adverse effect on his ability to carry out normal day-to-day activities'. An employer discriminates against a disabled person if it treats that person unfavourably because of something arising in consequence of that person's disability and the employer cannot show that the treatment is a proportionate means of achieving a legitimate aim *(EqA 2010, s 15)*.

EqA 2010, s 61 incorporates an overriding 'non-discrimination rule' into the rules of every occupational pension scheme. Under the non-discrimination rule, trustees and managers may not, in relation to the scheme, discriminate against a disabled person in carrying out their functions (especially in relation to admission and treatment of members) and neither should they subject a disabled person to harassment. Trustees or managers must make 'reasonable adjustments', which may include altering scheme rules, to prevent any of their provisions, criterions or practices from putting a disabled person at a substantial disadvantage.

No obligation is placed on trustees to make reasonable adjustments if they do not know and could not reasonably be expected to know that a person is a disabled person for the purposes of *EqA 2010*, or that he has a disability and is likely to be disadvantaged (*EqA 2010, Sch 8, Part 3*).

Discrimination on the grounds of disability is considered further in **Chapter 9**.

Age discrimination

1.19   *EqA 2010* prohibits discrimination on the grounds of age. It is unlawful, in relation to rights accrued or benefits payable in respect of periods of service on or after 1 December 2006, for the trustees or employer in relation to an occupational pension scheme to discriminate on the grounds of age against a member or prospective member of the scheme in carrying out any of their functions (including in particular their functions relating to the admission of members to the scheme and the treatment of members of it).

EqA 2010, s 61 incorporates an overriding 'non-discrimination rule' into the rules of every occupational pension scheme. Under the non-discrimination rule, trustees and managers must refrain from unlawfully discriminating on the grounds of age. *EqA 2010, s 62* also confers a power on the trustees or managers to make alterations to the scheme in order to secure conformity with the non-discrimination rule.

The Equality Act (Age Exceptions for Pension Schemes) Order 2010 contains exemptions from the non-discrimination rule for occupational pension schemes which include:

- setting a minimum or maximum age for admission;

- using age criteria in actuarial calculations;

- making age-related contributions (subject to certain conditions);

- making reductions to pension levels where a dependant is a specified number of years younger than the member;

- setting a minimum age before which unreduced benefits cannot be taken.

Discrimination on the grounds of age is considered further in **Chapter 9**.

Procedure for becoming a member

1.20 The rules of a scheme will often set out the procedure which an employee must follow if he wishes to become a member of the scheme. The rules may provide for a minimum and maximum entry age, thus allowing an employer to exclude the very young (who may be likely to change jobs more frequently) and the very old (for whom the costs of benefits are particularly high). See **1.19** above and **Chapter 9** in relation to age discrimination.

It is not uncommon for the rules of a scheme to impose a 'waiting period' where an employee has to be employed for a certain period of time before being eligible to become a member (although this is becoming less common). A waiting period may correspond to an employee's 'probationary period' under his contract of employment; some rules will provide that an employee is only eligible once he is a 'permanent' employee. However, the *Fixed-term Employees (Prevention of Less Favourable Treatment) Regulations 2002 (SI 2002/2034)* provide that fixed-term employees should be provided with benefits on a pro-rata basis equivalent to those provided to their permanent counterparts, unless their exclusion can be objectively justified (see **Chapter 9**). There may also be difficulties for trustees under the age discrimination legislation in imposing a waiting period in excess of five years unless it can be justified. Waiting periods in excess of three months are not allowed under the automatic enrolment requirements (see **Chapter 14**).

Unless the automatic enrolment provisions apply, an employee may be required to complete an application form for membership of an occupational pension scheme; in the case of a contributory scheme, this form will normally authorise the employer to deduct contributions from the employee's salary. It is common for employers to ask employees who do not wish to join the scheme or who choose to opt out of the scheme to sign a waiver form confirming that they understand that they are giving up benefits.

Since 1 October 2012 (subject to a phasing in period) employers are required to automatically enrol many of their employees into a qualifying pension scheme. The employee will then be given the option to opt out. This, and other details of the regime established by the *PA 2008*, is dealt with in **Chapter 14**.

Making contributions to occupational pension schemes

Employer's contributions

1.21 Before *PA 1995* came into force, there was little in the way of statutory control over funding and contributions (see **Chapter 11**). *PA 1995* introduced provisions requiring trustees to maintain, in the case of defined benefit schemes, schedules of contributions and, in the case of money purchase schemes, payment schedules. With effect from 30 December 2005, *PA 2004* superseded *PA 1995* in relation to the funding of defined benefit schemes.

Defined benefit schemes

1.22   The trustees of a defined benefit scheme which is subject to the statutory funding objective under *PA 2004, 227* must prepare, and keep under review, a schedule of contributions. In accordance with the *Occupational Pension Schemes (Scheme Funding) Regulations 2005*, the schedule must be signed by the trustees or managers of the scheme and must make provision for signature by the employer in order to confirm its agreement to the matters included in it. The schedule must show:

(*a*)   the rates and due dates of all contributions (other than voluntary contributions) payable towards the scheme by or on behalf of the employer and active members of the scheme during the period of five years after the date on which the schedule is certified;

(*b*)   any contributions to cover expenses must be listed separately; and

(*c*)   additional contributions under a recovery plan must be shown separately.

The schedule must be certified by the scheme actuary (ie the actuary appointed under *PA 1995, s 47(1)(b)*). The schedule will not come into force until it has been so certified.

Where employer or employee contributions are not made on time in accordance with the schedule, a report to the Regulator may be required where there is reasonable cause to believe that the failure is likely to be of material significance in the exercise by the Regulator of any of its functions (*PA 2004, s 228*). The Regulator has issued a Code of Practice on Funding defined benefits, which states that trustees should ensure that there is a robust procedure for monitoring the receipt of contributions and investigate any failure by the employer to adhere to the schedule of contributions (the original Code was replaced in the summer of 2014 by a new Code of Practice which is considered in **Chapter 11**). If the failure is likely to be of material significance to the Regulator, a report should be made within ten working days of the end of the period in which the payment should have been made (*PA 1995, s 49(9)*). Members of the scheme should be informed within one month.

If there has been 'fraudulent evasion' in failing to pass employee contributions to the trustees or managers, criminal penalties may apply (*PA 1995, s 49(11), (12)*).

The statutory requirements relating to scheme funding and to schedules of contributions are considered further in **Chapter 11**.

Money purchase schemes

1.23   The trustees or managers of a money purchase scheme must (unless the scheme is exempt) ensure that a payment schedule is periodically prepared, maintained and revised in relation to the scheme. Any trustee who fails to comply with the requirement to maintain a payment schedule may be fined (see also **Appendix I**). *PA 1995, s 87* and *Scheme Administration Regulations (SI 1996/1715), regs 18, 19* provide that the schedule must show, for the year to which it relates:

(*a*)   the rates of contributions payable towards the scheme by or on behalf of the employer (or in the case of multi-employer schemes, each employer) and the active members of the scheme;

(*b*)   the amounts payable towards the scheme by the (or each) employer in respect of expenses likely to be incurred during the year in question; and

(*c*)   the dates on or before which these payments are to be made.

Where any amounts payable in accordance with a payment schedule by or on behalf of the employer have not been paid on or before the due date and the trustees and managers consider the failure to be material, then notice of the failure must be given to the Regulator and to the scheme members. The Regulator has issued a Code of Practice on Reporting Late Payment of Contributions to Occupational Money Purchase Schemes (revised in September 2013) which sets out the Regulator's views on which late payments are likely to be material. A reasonable period for a report would usually be within ten working days of the trustees having identified the late payment as material.

Failure to put in place a payment schedule or to make the appropriate reports to the Regulator and the members amounts to a civil offence under *PA 1995*, punishable by fine. If there has been 'fraudulent evasion' in failing to pass employee contributions to the trustees or managers, criminal penalties may apply (*PA 1995, s 49(11), (12)*).

Scheme Administration Regulations, reg 17 provides that trustees of the following schemes do not have to maintain a payment schedule:

• occupational pension schemes with fewer than two members;

• schemes with fewer than 12 members where all the members of the scheme are trustees or directors; and all decisions are made by the unanimous agreement of those trustees or directors or the scheme has an independent director or trustee;

- unregistered schemes with fewer than 100 members; and
- *s 615* schemes with fewer than 100 members.

HMRC requirements

1.24   Broadly speaking, employers can claim tax relief on the contributions they make to a pension scheme by deducting those contributions from their profits chargeable to UK tax. The tax treatment of contributions made by employers to registered occupational pension schemes is considered in **Chapter 17**.

Members' contributions

Ordinary contributions

1.25   The level of the contributions which members are required to make is a matter of scheme design. Contributory schemes typically require a contribution of between 4 and 7 per cent of salary. Contributions will generally be deducted from a member's salary by his employer through the payroll. The employee must specifically consent to contributions being deducted for this purpose (*Employment Rights Act 1996, s 13*) other than in relation to automatic enrolment (*PA 2008, s 33*) and consequently membership application forms will generally include provision for the necessary consent to be given.

Contributions deducted by a member's employer must be paid to the trustees of the scheme within 19 days (or 22 days where the payments are transferred electronically) of the end of the month within which the contribution is deducted in accordance with *PA 1995, s 49(8)* and the *Scheme Administration Regulations, reg 16(1)*. These time periods are extended to a period of up to three months in relation to automatic enrolment (*Scheme Administration Regulations, reg 16(2)*). Failure to pay the contributions over within these limits may give rise to a civil penalty under *PA 1995, s 10* or, where there is fraudulent evasion, a criminal offence under *PA 1995, s 49(11)* and a prison sentence of up to seven years.

Voluntary contributions

1.26   A member may wish to enhance his pension benefits by making additional voluntary contributions ('AVCs') in addition to any contributions he is required to make under the rules of a scheme. Generally, the benefits deriving from AVCs are money purchase benefits, irrespective of whether the scheme is money purchase or defined benefit but AVCs may sometimes be used to purchase added years of service which count toward the member's defined benefits.

Prior to April 2006, under *PSA 1993, s 111*, the rules of a scheme had to allow members to pay voluntary contributions, except to the extent necessary to comply with HMRC requirements and as prescribed. The requirement for schemes to provide an AVC facility was removed by *PA 2004, s 267* from 6 April 2006. Trustees cannot require members with existing AVCs to transfer out, so will still have to administer the AVC facility for existing members even if the rules are changed.

Instead of making voluntary contributions 'in-house' through an employer's scheme, individuals may choose to make contributions to their own personal pension arrangements. Prior to 6 April 2006 this was often through a 'free standing additional voluntary contributions' ('FSAVC') arrangement. Such arrangements have much in common with a personal pension scheme and were established by a provider in exactly the same way. Usually the provider is an insurance company, friendly society, bank or building society. The main disadvantage with a personal pension or FSAVC arrangement is that the member is generally obliged to meet the fees associated with the administration and management of the arrangement whereas, if voluntary contributions are paid 'in-house', the employer may bear these costs (and, even if it does not, the members may benefit, as costs will be spread between them).

HMRC restrictions

1.27 Prior to A-Day, the total amount of contributions (ordinary and voluntary) that could be made to a scheme by a member in any tax year was restricted by HMRC to 15 per cent of the member's remuneration in that year. (*ICTA 1988, s 592*).

Under the *FA 2004* regime, contributions to registered pension schemes are not subject to any limits as such. Members are given tax relief on their annual pension contributions up to the greater of £3,600 or 100 per cent of their UK earnings chargeable to income tax.

FA 2004, however, introduced an annual limit on the inflows of value to an individual's pension fund (both in the form of contributions and accrual) that attract favourable tax treatment (known as the 'annual allowance'). The annual allowance is set by Treasury Order. It was set at £215,000 per individual for the tax year 2006/2007; however, for the tax years 2014/2015 onwards it is only £40,000 (down from £50,000 in the tax years 2011/2012 and 2012/2013). A further reduction to £10,000 for future money purchase pension savings took effect from 6 April 2015 for those accessing their money purchase funds flexibly as a result of new rules introduced following the 2014 Budget announcement (see **1.40** below). There is also a tapering down of annual allowance for high earners.

Individuals will be taxed at their marginal rate on any pension input above the annual allowance (*FA 2004, s 227 as amended by FA 2011*).

FA 2004 also introduced a single lifetime limit on the amount of pension saving that attracts favourable tax treatment (known as the 'lifetime allowance'). The lifetime allowance is set by Treasury Order. It was set at £1.5 million per individual for the tax year 2006/2007 and at its peak reached £1.8 million. However, for the tax year 2016/2017 it has been reduced to £1 million.

Individuals will be liable to pay a lifetime allowance charge of 55 per cent, or 25 per cent on crystallised amounts greater that the lifetime allowance, depending on whether a lump sum is paid or the monies are retained within the scheme. There are transitional provisions allowing individuals protection, giving them a lifetime allowance in excess of the standard figures listed above.

There are further details of the annual allowance and lifetime allowance in **Chapter 17**.

Benefits payable from occupational pension schemes

HMRC requirements

1.28   Prior to A-Day, the benefits payable from an approved occupational pension scheme, whether defined contribution or defined benefit, were limited by HMRC.

The types of authorised payments that can now be made from a registered pension scheme are set out in *FA 2004, Part 4*. If a registered pension scheme makes unauthorised member payments or unauthorised employer payments, there may be adverse tax consequences for the employer, the member and for the scheme administrator (which will usually be the trustees). This is considered further in **Chapter 17**.

When are benefits payable?

1.29   Benefits will usually become payable under a scheme either on the death of a member or on the member's retirement, whichever is the earlier (although *FA 2004* does enable benefits to be taken while the member remains in service if the scheme rules allow). Benefits in a defined benefit scheme are usually calculated on the basis of the member's normal retirement date under the scheme, which will generally be between age 60 and 65. Under the

Pension Rules set out in *FA 2004, s 165*, benefits may not be paid before a member reaches normal minimum pension age (which was increased from age 50 to age 55 from 6 April 2010), other than where the ill-health condition is met. Members who had a prospective right on 5 April 2006 (deriving from the scheme rules as at 10 December 2003) to draw any benefit before age 55 may retain those rights and have a protected pension age (*FA 2004, Sch 36*).

Normal retirement date may differ for different categories of members, for example, directors may have a normal retirement date of age 60 while all other members have a normal retirement date of age 65. In the past, it was common to find schemes with a different retirement age for men and women (usually reflecting the State pension age); but, following the decision in *Barber v GRE Insurance Group [1990] ECR-I 1889*, this should no longer be the case (see **Chapter 9** for a fuller consideration of the equalisation of normal retirement dates).

Benefits payable on early retirement are considered further in **1.31** below. Benefits payable on late retirement are considered in **1.32** below.

Defined benefit schemes

Pension benefits at normal retirement

1.30   In the case of a final salary defined benefit scheme, a member's pension is calculated by reference to the remuneration he is receiving at or shortly before he retires or leaves service. The level of remuneration by which benefits are calculated is often referred to as 'final pensionable salary' or some similar expression. The definition of final pensionable salary is a matter of scheme design. It may be his earnings at the date on which he retires, his total earnings during the previous year or his earnings averaged over a certain period, such as the previous three years; it may include fluctuating emoluments such as commissions or bonuses or it may simply be basic salary. There may be offsets against final pensionable salary; for example, it is not uncommon for a deduction equal to the lower earnings limit to be made.

Typically, a scheme's rules will contain a formula for calculating the pension payable. This will generally be expressed as a fraction or percentage of final pensionable salary for each year of pensionable service (ie service whilst an active member and any service deemed, under the rules of the scheme, to be pensionable service); 1/60th or 1/80th are the most common annual accrual rates. A formula such as this gives the member some reassurance that, assuming that he has been a member of a scheme for much of his working life, his pension will be a reasonable proportion of the salary he was earning at the time he retired. For example, a person who has been a member of a scheme offering a 1/60th accrual rate for 30 years will receive a pension of 30/60ths, or one half of his final pensionable salary.

Pension benefits on early retirement

1.31   The rules of the scheme may allow members to retire on a pension at any time if retirement is due to incapacity, or at any time from age 55 for any other reason. Generally the rules will specify that either employer or trustee consent is required for early retirement and, in the case of incapacity retirement, that satisfactory medical evidence is produced. Where a member receives his pension early he is effectively receiving benefits as an alternative to a preserved benefit and consequently the preservation legislation must be complied with. This is considered further in **Chapter 6**.

It is often the case that the level of benefits payable on early retirement will depend on whether or not the retirement is due to incapacity. A non incapacity-related early retirement pension will generally be calculated using the same formula as for normal retirement but taking account of actual pensionable service and final pensionable salary at the date of retirement. The resulting pension will often be reduced to take account of early receipt (and may need to be reduced to comply with age discrimination requirements, see **Chapter 9**). This is usually done by applying a percentage reduction, for example, a member's pension may be reduced by 3 per cent for each year that actual retirement precedes normal retirement date.

Where the retirement is due to incapacity, the benefits provided will often be more generous. They may, for example, be calculated without reduction for early receipt or possibly on the basis of the pensionable service the member would have completed had he remained a member until his normal retirement date. Such pensions are obviously more expensive than non incapacity-related early retirement pensions and so the eligibility conditions are generally quite restrictive.

(a)   Defining incapacity

Pre A-Day, incapacity was defined in HMRC's Practice Notes as 'physical or mental deterioration which is sufficiently serious to prevent the individual from following his or her normal employment, or which seriously impairs his or her earning capacity'. The definition added that incapacity does not mean 'simply a decline in energy or ability'. The rules of many schemes go further than that definition (eg self-inflicted injuries or drug addiction may be excluded); employer and/or trustee consent will often be required before an individual can be said to fall within this category; and the member may have to be incapacitated to the extent that he is incapable of any full-time employment, not just of working for his current employer.

Under the Pension Rules set out in *FA 2004, s 165*, the ill-health condition is similar, but not identical, to the pre A-Day definition of 'incapacity'.

The ill-health condition will be met if:

(*a*) the scheme administrator has received evidence from a registered medical practitioner that the member is (and will continue to be) incapable of carrying on the member's occupation because of physical or medical impairment; and

(*b*) the member has in fact ceased to carry on the member's occupation (*FA 2004, Sch 28, Part 1, para 1*).

The ill-health condition is considered further in **Chapter 17.**

(b)   Determining incapacity

The fact that there are often many conditions relating to the payment of an incapacity pension and that an incapacity pension is generally more generous than an ordinary early retirement pension has given rise to a number of disputes between members and trustees as to whether such a pension should be paid. The decisions, to an extent, turn on the particular wording of the incapacity rule in question but generally an employer must act in good faith when considering any medical evidence provided in relation to an application for an incapacity pension. Trustees may be required to exercise a discretion in relation to the payment of benefits such as an incapacity pension. When exercising such a discretion, trustees should ensure that they take into account all relevant, but no irrelevant, factors; ask themselves the proper questions; adopt a correct construction of the rules of the scheme; and do not arrive at a perverse decision (ie one which no reasonable body of trustees could arrive at in the light of the same circumstances and evidence) (*Lee v Showman's Guild [1952] 2 QB 329*; *Harris v Lord Shuttleworth [1994] PLR 47*; and *Edge v Pensions Ombudsman [1999] 49 PBLR (36)*).

(c)   Early retirement or dismissal?

One area that has given rise to a number disputes is the question of whether a person can be said to have retired on grounds of incapacity when their employment has in fact been unilaterally terminated by their employer. Cases dealing with early retirement pensions in the context of dismissals have also turned on the rules of a particular scheme, but the courts have set out a number of principles that should assist trustees in deciding whether or not there has been a retirement for the purposes of the rules and consequently the relevant level of pension benefit. In *AGCO Ltd v Massey Ferguson Works Pension Trust Ltd [2003] EWCA Civ 1044, [2003] 57 PBLR*, the Court of Appeal considered the difference between retirement and dismissal in the context of redundancy. The rules provided more generous benefits on early retirement when an employee 'retire(d) from Service at the request of the Employer' and the question arose as to whether these words included voluntary and/or compulsory redundancy.

The Court held that in employment terms retirement is an entirely consensual event and comes about by 'effluxion of time and the expiry of the contract of employment'. 'Retire' therefore naturally covers situations distinct from dismissal and is different from the expression 'leaving Service' which covers broader circumstances. However, while voluntary and compulsory redundancy both involve an element of dismissal, voluntary redundancy (within the proper meaning of that term) occurs as a result of prior consent by the employee to such a dismissal. Consequently, the words 'retires from Service at the request of the Employer and after his fiftieth birthday' did encompass voluntary redundancy as they were designed to enable the employer to offer early retirement to certain employees, subject to the employee's acceptance. Compulsory redundancy did not however fall within the wording of the rule.

The High Court in *Minter v Julius Bear Investment Management [2004] EWHC 2472 (Ch)* further considered the question of whether a person can be said to have retired with the consent of his employer. Rimer J stated that 'All the circumstances of the dismissal need to be examined in order to identify the true nature of the employee's departure'. The essence of 'retirement with the consent of the employer' is that 'the initiative to leave service comes from the employee and the employer (in effect) agrees to his premature release from the service agreement'. Although Mr Minter had negotiated the terms of his redundancy with the employer, the judge found on the facts that the termination of his employment was decided by his employer.

Pension benefits on late retirement

1.32 The rules of a scheme may permit a member to remain in service after his normal retirement date.

Under the pre A-Day tax regime, where a member of an approved scheme postponed his retirement his pension did not become payable until he actually left service (except that all his benefits had to be taken on or before his 75th birthday, even if he had not retired). However, if the member had accrued (or was deemed to have accrued) benefits under the scheme before 1 June 1989, he was able to take his benefits at any time after attaining normal retirement date even though he was continuing in service.

Post A-Day there is nothing to prevent the member taking some or all of his benefits once he has reached 'normal minimum pension age', even if he remains in employment, as long as the scheme rules permit this.

The benefits payable on late retirement will be greater than the benefits payable on normal retirement. Depending on the scheme rules, a member may continue to accrue pensionable service after his normal retirement date or alternatively his benefits may be calculated as at his normal retirement date and then increased by actuarial factors to take account of late receipt. The age discrimination provisions effectively require schemes to offer continued accrual (see **Chapter 9**).

As with early retirement benefits, the provision of late retirement benefits is considered to be an alternative to a preserved benefit and so the legislation relating to preservation of benefits must be complied with (see **Chapter 6**).

Tax-free lump sum on retirement

1.33   A member may choose to take part of his retirement benefits in the form of a tax-free cash lump sum if the rules of the scheme allow. Under *FA 2004* the general position is that up to 25 per cent of the value of an individual's fund or benefits crystallised on that date may be taken as tax-free cash.

If a higher amount is paid then it will be an unauthorised payment, and adverse tax consequences will arise unless the individual is entitled to benefit from the transitional protection provisions, under *FA 2004, Sch 36*, where the entitlement to maximum tax-free cash for service accrued up to 6 April 2006 exceeds the entitlement to tax-free cash under the new regime.

Full commutation of benefits may be permissible where the member is in serious ill-health (life expectancy of less than one year) or where the benefits payable are classed as trivial (see **Chapter 17**).

Lump sum death benefits

1.34   An occupational pension scheme will usually provide a life assurance benefit in the event of the death of an active member. This benefit is usually calculated by multiplying a member's salary (which can be pensionable salary, annual salary or final pensionable salary) by a specified figure, but occasionally it is a fixed sum.

In the event of a member's death, the life assurance benefit will usually be payable under 'discretionary trust' in order to mitigate inheritance tax liability. If a payment is made through a discretionary trust, it will not form part of the member's estate and consequently will not be taken into account when assessing liability for inheritance tax. A scheme's governing rules will usually contain an appropriate discretionary trust provision. When a member joins the scheme he may be asked to complete a 'statement of wishes' form to indicate to the trustees the person he would wish to receive a lump sum death benefit in the event of his death. This statement of wishes does not bind the trustees but simply acts as guidance for them. Irrespective of whether the member has completed a statement of wishes form, the trustees should make proper inquiries to establish whether or not they are paying the benefits to the most appropriate person. This is particularly true where there has been a change in the member's personal circumstances, such as a remarriage or death in the family. The trustees should tread carefully, as they will be exercising their discretion and so must take into account all relevant, but no irrelevant, factors; ask themselves the proper questions; adopt a correct construction of the rules of the scheme; and do not arrive at a perverse decision (ie one which no reasonable body of trustees could arrive at in the light of the same circumstances and evidence). (See **1.31** above; and *Wild v Smith [1996] PLR 275.*)

Lump sum death benefits are usually insured. Only the largest occupational schemes are likely to be able to afford the risk of paying death benefits directly out of the fund.

Spouse's/dependant's pension

1.35   In addition to the lump sum life assurance benefit payable in the event of the death of a member, a pension is often payable to his surviving spouse or civil partner. The amount of the benefit payable will generally vary depending on whether the member died before or after retirement.

If a member dies whilst an active member, the amount payable will usually be a percentage (often 50 per cent) of the member's prospective pension. This will be calculated on the basis of either his actual pensionable service at the date of death or the pensionable service he would have completed had he remained an active member until his normal retirement date and had his pensionable salary remained static.

In the case of the death of a member following his retirement, the spouse's pension is often calculated as a percentage of the member's pension at the date of his death. A spouse's pension of 50 per cent of the pension the member was receiving at the date of his death is common.

The rules of the scheme may also permit a child or dependant's pension to be paid either where the member dies leaving no spouse or civil partner (or a spouse or civil partner who subsequently dies) or in addition to any spouse or civil partner's pension which is payable. *FA 2004, s 167* sets out who may qualify for a dependant's pension and a child may fall within that category if he is under the age of 23 or has reached that age but, in the opinion of the scheme administrator, was dependent on the member at the date of the member's death because of physical or mental impairment (see **Chapter 17** for further details).

Note that, in accordance with the *Civil Partnership Act 2005*, with effect from 5 December 2005, the surviving civil partner of a member of a pension scheme is entitled to an equivalent pension to a surviving spouse based on the pension rights accrued by the deceased civil partner in respect of service from that date. Similar provisions apply in respect of same-sex marriages from 13 March 2014 relating to pensionable service from 5 December 2005. Further details are in **Chapter 9**. Schemes that were contracted out are also required to pay a civil partner a pension in respect of contracted out employment from 6 April 1988 to 5 April 2016 (in the same way that they are required to pay a pension to a member's widower). As the contracting-out requirements are not overriding, rule amendments may need to be made to give effect to this, in which case *PA 1995, s 67* must be complied with by trustees. Alternatively, the *Occupational Pension Schemes (Modification of Schemes) Regulations 2006 (SI 2006/759), regs 7* and *7ZA* allow trustees to make appropriate modifications under *PA 1995, s 68*.

Benefits on leaving service other than on retirement

1.36 A member is entitled to a preserved benefit within a scheme if his pensionable service under that scheme is terminated before his normal pension age and he has at least two years' qualifying service. Broadly speaking, qualifying service is pensionable service under the scheme, service in employment which was contracted out by reference to the scheme or service which is deemed to be qualifying service by virtue of a transfer payment received by the scheme in respect of the member. A member's normal pension age is the earliest date on which he has an unqualified right to retire on an unreduced pension, other than on special grounds, such as ill-health or redundancy.

PSA 1993, Part IV sets out the minimum requirements with which schemes must comply in the context of preservation. If a member has a preserved benefit under a scheme, he has a statutory right to have that benefit calculated on the same basis as if he had remained in the relevant employment and rendered service so as to qualify for benefits until normal pension age. Once calculated, the preserved amount must then be revalued in order to protect it from the impact of inflation.

Alternatively, the individual may choose to transfer the 'cash equivalent' of his benefits to a registered pension scheme, qualifying recognised overseas pension scheme or buy-out policy. Transfer values from defined benefit schemes are calculated by the trustees, who must determine the assumptions to be used on a 'best estimate' basis after obtaining actuarial advice.

Members who leave a scheme without having completed at least three months' qualifying service but who do not have vested rights under the scheme have the right to elect for a 'cash transfer sum' which they may take as an alternative to a refund of their contributions. In contrast to a refund, a cash transfer sum includes the value of the employer's contributions as well as those of the member.

The protection afforded to early leavers is considered in detail in **Chapter 6.**

Money purchase schemes

Pension benefits

1.37   The benefits paid to a member of a money purchase scheme have traditionally been determined by two factors, namely:

(*a*)   the amount of money held by the trustees on behalf of the member at retirement; and

(*b*)   the annuity rates applicable at the time when the member's benefits become payable.

The amount of money held by the trustees under (*a*) will be determined by the level of contributions paid by the member's employer and the member himself, and the investment return realised in respect of those contributions. The total amount is generally referred to as the member's 'individual account' or, more colloquially, his 'pot'.

It is becoming increasingly common for members to be given some discretion over the way in which their individual account is invested. Often members will be given a choice of funds and are required to indicate to the trustees of the scheme what percentage of their individual account they wish to invest in each fund. The scheme must be carefully structured to ensure that the arrangements put in place, whilst offering the member choice, do not expose the trustees to potential claims from members whose investment choices do not perform as well as expected.

A member will not have any claim to any particular asset, even if he is given some power in relation to how his account is invested. All the assets of the scheme will be invested together so that, although the member's account will be credited with interest or investment growth, no specific scheme asset will be attributable to his account.

On the member's retirement, whether at, before or after normal retirement date, assets equal in value to his individual account will be realised and the proceeds will be used to provide the member with a pension. Some defined contribution schemes provide additional benefits on the retirement of a member due to incapacity, but this will almost certainly be at the discretion of the employer.

Under the *FA 2004* tax regime, money purchase schemes (which include schemes providing cash balance benefits) may pay retirement income as a scheme pension, lifetime annuity or income withdrawal.

A scheme pension can only be paid if the member has first been given the opportunity to select a lifetime annuity (*PA 2004, s 165*).

Scheme pensions are either pensions paid directly from the scheme out of its own resources, or by an insurance company selected by the scheme administrator (*FA 2004, Sch 28, para 2*). A lifetime annuity is an annuity payable by an insurance company which meets certain specified requirements (*FA 2004, Sch 28, para 3*). Income withdrawal is income payable from a drawdown arrangement (*FA 2004, Sch 28, paras 4–10B* (as amended).

Fundamental changes to the payment rules for money purchase benefits came into effect on 6 April 2015. This includes the flexible payment of lump sums as 'uncrystallised funds pension lump sums', which effectively allow members to control what they draw and when (see **1.40** below and **Chapter 17**).

Death benefits

1.38   Most money purchase schemes provide lump sum death-in-service benefits in much the same way as defined benefit schemes (see **1.34** above).

The benefits provided to the spouse and/or dependants of a member of a money purchase scheme may be a proportion of the member's salary or may be such level of pension as can be secured by the proceeds of the member's account. If the scheme provides a percentage of salary, there will usually be some form of insurance as it is possible (and in the case of young or new members, likely) that the member's account will be insufficient to provide the necessary funds to secure the benefit.

Benefits on leaving service

1.39   A member of a money purchase scheme who terminates his pensionable service before his normal retirement date is entitled to benefits in much the same way as a member of a defined benefit scheme. The same statutory criteria determine whether the member has a right to preserved benefit or not, although the method of calculating the preserved benefit will, of course, be different.

A member of a money purchase scheme who has at least three months' qualifying service (30 days once *PA 2014, s 36* comes into force) will also generally have a statutory right to require that the cash equivalent of his benefits be transferred to a registered pension scheme, qualifying recognised overseas pension scheme or buy-out policy (see **Chapter 6**).

Budget 2014 and the new flexible pensions regime

1.40 In the March 2014 Budget, the Chancellor announced that from 6 April 2015 anyone over age 55 will be able to take their entire money purchase pension pot without any requirement to purchase an annuity or be subject to income drawdown.

HM Treasury issued consultation on the Budget proposals in March 2014 ('Freedom and choice in pensions'). The response to that consultation, published on 21 July 2014, provided more details on the new regime. This was followed by the draft *Taxation of Pensions Bill*, published on 6 August 2014, which gives some detail on how the new pension flexibilities will work in practice, followed by the *Taxation of Pensions Act 2014 (TPA 2014)*, which came into force on 6 April 2015. The new provisions apply to 'money purchase arrangements' as defined in *FA 2004*. This is much wider than the new definition of 'money purchase benefit' in the pensions legislation (see **1.9** above) and includes cash balance arrangements as well as 'pure' money purchase.

Essentially there will be two options for individuals with money purchase arrangements. Take a tax-free lump sum and designate an associated amount for drawdown (flexi-access drawdown) or, take a lump sum, 25 per cent which will be tax-free and the remainder taxed as income (uncrystallised funds pension lump sum). This gives members significantly greater flexibility as to when and how they access money purchase funds. The provisions are enabling. Schemes are not required to offer the new flexibilities.

Members taking flexi-access drawdown or an uncrystallised funds lump sum will be subject to new annual allowance rules. These are intended to prevent individuals diverting their salary into a pension scheme with tax relief and then immediately withdrawing 25 per cent tax-free. Where the money purchase annual allowance is triggered, the individual will broadly have an annual allowance of £10,000 for money purchase savings and £30,000 for other pension savings. Any carry-forward from previous years can only be used for non-money purchase savings. There is no carry forward of unused money purchase annual allowance.

The new flexibilities come with a guidance guarantee. Trustees are required, when communicating with members about retirement options, to inform them of the availability of the Pension Wise guidance service. The guidance is not intended as advice, but should equip individuals to make informed choices about how they use their pension savings. HM Treasury is responsible for designing and implementing Pension Wise. It is currently being delivered by the Pensions Advisory Service ('TPAS') and Citizens Advice. Those offering guidance do not have to be authorised by the Financial Conduct Authority ('FCA'), but are subject to a standards regime operated by the FCA.

Members of defined benefit schemes will be largely unaffected by the changes. Safeguards have been introduced to the cash equivalent transfer legislation due to concerns that individuals may be tempted to transfer to a money purchase arrangement and 'cash out' their benefits without fully appreciating the impact on their retirement income. Trustees of defined benefit schemes are required to check that the member has taken appropriate independent financial advice before allowing the transfer to be paid where the defined benefits are valued at £30,000 or more.

The Budget 2014 changes are considered in more detail in **Chapter 17** and transfer rights in **Chapter 6**.

Increasing pensions in payment

1.41   *PA 1995, s 51* (which was amended with effect from 6 April 2005 by *PA 2004* and from 3 January 2012 by *PA 2011*) applies to any part of a pension under an occupational pension scheme that is:

(*a*)   a defined benefit attributable to pensionable service on or after 6 April 1997; or

(*b*)   a money purchase benefit in respect of employment carried out on or after 6 April 1997 but in payment before 6 April 2005.

(*c*)   a cash balance benefit in respect of employment carried out on or after 6 April 1997 but in payment before 3 January 2012.

The above pensions must be increased annually by a minimum amount referred to in *s 51* as the 'appropriate percentage'. The 'appropriate percentage' is defined in *PA 1995, s 51ZA* and is derived from the same statutory revaluation orders as are used for revaluing pensions in deferment (see **Chapter 6**).

Until January 2011 the relevant increases for defined benefits were:

(*a*)   RPI capped at 5 per cent for benefits accrued through service between 6 April 1997 and 5 April 2005; and

(*b*)   RPI capped at 2.5 per cent for benefits accrued on and after 6 April 2005.

Since 1 January 2011, the Secretary of State has used CPI rather than RPI in the statutory revaluation order. In the long term, CPI, which does not include mortgage interest repayments, is likely to be a lower rate than RPI resulting in lower benefits for pensioners. The impact of this change on a pension scheme will depend on the precise wording of the pension increase rule in its governing trust deed. Broadly:

- in schemes which refer directly to statutory increases, the CPI formula will feed through automatically and could have an immediate positive funding impact;

- in schemes which 'hard code' RPI (or other more generous) increases into the rules the changes can only affect future accrual and then only if a rule amendment is made, so will have no immediate funding impact.

Consequential amendments were made to *PA 1995, s 51* under the *Pensions Act 2011* to reflect the replacement of RPI with CPI as the basis for calculating pension increases. One amendment provides that for schemes which have 'hard coded' RPI increases into their governing rules, there will not be a requirement to provide a CPI underpin in years where CPI is higher than RPI, if the pension increase rule satisfies certain criteria (see PA 1995, *ss 51(4ZA)–(4ZG)*).

If an increase in excess of the statutory minimum is given in a particular tax year, the excess may be offset against the following year's increase (*PA 1995, s 53*). Statutory increases do not have to be given in respect of pensions which derive from a member's voluntary contributions (*PA 1995, s 51(6)*). Neither do increases have to be given in respect of a pension paid to a member who has not attained the age of 55 unless he retired on account of incapacity (*PA 1995, s 52*) nor in respect of benefits derived from a pension credit awarded as a result of a pension sharing order on the divorce of a member (*PA 1995, s 51(6)*).

Forfeiture and suspension of benefits

1.42   Generally, a member's entitlement or accrued right to a pension under an occupational pension scheme cannot be assigned, commuted, surrendered, charged or set off (*PA 1995, s 91*). However, there are various exceptions to this general rule (see below). Where a pension is prevented from being assigned under *s 91*, a court is not able to make an order, other than an attachment of earnings order or an income payments order, that would restrain a member from receiving that pension (although unregistered schemes, apart from public service pension schemes and the Armed Forces Pension Scheme are excepted from this restriction).

Exceptions to inalienability

Commutation of pension

1.43   The rules of an occupational pension scheme may, and generally do, allow a member to commute part or, in some circumstances, all of his pension for a lump sum (see **1.33** above). The situations in which such commutation will fall within an exception to the inalienability rule are set out in *PA 1995, s 91(5) (c)* and *Occupational Pension Schemes (Assignment, Forfeiture, Bankruptcy etc) Regulations 1997 (the 'Forfeiture Regulations'), reg 2.*

Surrender in favour of a spouse and/or dependant

1.44 The rules of a scheme may allow a member to assign to, or surrender part of his pension to provide a pension for, his widow, widower, surviving civil partner and/or dependants. A person may also surrender part of his pension in order to acquire an entitlement to further benefits under the scheme (*PA 1995, s 91(5)(a), (b)*).

Charge, lien or set-off

1.45 *PA 1995, s 91(5)(d) and (e)* provide that the rules of a scheme may allow for a charge or lien on, or a set-off against, an individual's pension benefits to be made for the purposes of:

(*a*) enabling the individual's employer to discharge a monetary obligation due to the employer arising out of the individual's criminal, negligent or fraudulent act or omission (although only certain transfer credits may be used in this context); and

(*b*) discharging a monetary obligation due to the scheme arising out of:

    (i) the individual's criminal, negligent or fraudulent act or omission; or

    (ii) a breach of trust by the individual where he is a trustee (unless the court has relieved him, wholly or partly, from personal liability under *Trustee Act 1925, s 61*) (*Forfeiture Regulations, reg 4*).

PA 1995, s 91(5)(f) allows trustees to reduce or suspend pensions in payment in order to recoup overpayments of benefits.

The amount of any charge, lien or set-off (including a suspension or reduction under *s 91(5)(f)*) is restricted to the amount of the monetary obligation in question or, if less, the value of the member's entitlement or accrued right. The member must be given a certificate showing the amount of the charge, lien or set-off and its effect on his benefits under the scheme. If the member disputes the amount, the charge, lien or set-off cannot be effected unless the obligation becomes enforceable by a court order or an arbitrator's award. It is questionable whether silence on the part of the member concerned amounts to consent to the amount of the charge, lien or set-off, even if the certificate specifies that any dispute must be raised within a certain time limit. In effect, unless the member agrees to the charge, lien or set-off being exercised, the safest course of action is to obtain a court order or arbitrator's award.

A member's accrued right to a guaranteed minimum pension cannot be assigned or charged (*PSA 1993, s 159*). Neither can a charge, lien or set-off be exercised against a transfer payment received by the scheme in respect of a member (in the context of discharging a monetary obligation due to the employer) unless it is attributable to employment with the same or a financially associated employer, and the benefits transferred could have been subject to a charge, lien or set-off under the transferring scheme (*Forfeiture Regulations, reg 3*).

Forfeiture

1.46   Forfeiture is defined under *PA 1995, s 92* to include any manner of deprivation or suspension of an entitlement, or accrued right, to a pension under an occupational pension scheme. Such an entitlement or right cannot be forfeited other than as a consequence of:

(*a*)   an actual or purported assignment, commutation, surrender, charge, lien or set-off which under *s 91* is of no effect;

(*b*)   the member being convicted of certain offences such as treason before the pension becomes payable;

(*c*)   the failure of the member to make a claim within a limitation period or within six years of the benefit becoming due; or

(*d*)   prescribed circumstances.

Where a member's benefits are forfeited under the circumstances in paragraph (*a*) above, the trustees have a discretion under *PA 1995, s 92(3)* to pay any pension or benefit which was, or would but for the forfeiture have become payable, to all or any of the following:

•   the member of the scheme to, or in respect of whom the pension was, or would have become, payable;

•   the spouse, civil partner, widow, widower, surviving civil partner or any dependant of the member;

•   any other person to whom, under the rules of the scheme, the pension was or could have been paid.

The prescribed circumstances in paragraph (*d*) above include the situation where a pension is payable to a person nominated by the member and that person is convicted of the murder, manslaughter or an offence relating to the unlawful killing of the member; and where a potential beneficiary has caused a monetary loss to the scheme arising out of a breach of trust as trustee or as a result of a criminal, negligent or fraudulent act or omission. In each case an entitlement, or accrued right, to a pension under an occupational pension scheme may be forfeited. *PA 1995* also makes separate provision for public service pension schemes and the Armed Forces Pension Scheme.

A person's benefits may also be forfeited if he has incurred some monetary obligation due to the employer arising out of a criminal, negligent or fraudulent act or omission. The conditions are similar to those that apply when exercising a charge, lien or set-off, in respect of the amount of the monetary obligation and the requirements concerning disputes and certification. If a member's benefits are forfeited in these circumstances, the trustees have power to determine that the amount forfeited is paid to the employer (*PA 1995, s 93(5)*).

Pension rights following a member's bankruptcy

1.47   When an individual is declared bankrupt the general rule is that his estate automatically vests in the trustee in bankruptcy (*Insolvency Act 1986 (IA 1986), s 306*). The bankrupt's estate is defined as all property belonging to or vested in the bankrupt at the commencement of the bankruptcy, except for items for the bankrupt's personal use in his employment, and items for the basic domestic needs of the bankrupt and his family (*IA 1986, s 283*).

It was previously established that a trustee in bankruptcy was entitled to claim the entire pension benefits of a scheme member, not just pensions in payment (see *Re Landau [1997] 3 All ER 322*). In order to protect scheme members, many pension schemes included forfeiture clauses – these will all be slightly different but the purpose of them was automatically to forfeit the member's entitlement to scheme benefits on his bankruptcy and for the trustees to have a discretion to distribute payments, up to the value of those benefits, to the member or his family (commonly known as 'protective trusts').

As a result of the *Welfare Reform and Pensions Act 1999* (*WRPA 1999*), in relation to bankruptcy petitions presented on or after 6 April 2002, forfeiture clauses are no longer effective. Pension benefits do not vest in the trustee in bankruptcy on his appointment and are payable from the scheme under the provisions of the trust deed and rules.

If a member is in receipt of a pension during the period of his bankruptcy (between the date of bankruptcy order and the date of discharge), it is open to the trustee in bankruptcy to apply to the court for an income payments order under *IA 1986, s 310* requiring the pension to be paid to the trustee in bankruptcy rather than the member. This would equally apply if a lump sum payment was made from the scheme during the period of bankruptcy. The court will only make such an order where it would not have the effect of reducing the income of the bankrupt below what appears to the court to be necessary for meeting the reasonable domestic needs of the bankrupt and his family.

In *Raithatha v Williamson [2012] EWHC 909 (Ch)* the High Court held that a trustee in bankruptcy could apply for an income payments order in respect of the member's personal pension and require the member to draw his pension for the benefit of his creditors. The bankrupt's right to draw his pension represented income which could be the subject of an income payments order under *IA 1986*. In contrast, in *Horton v Henry [2014] EWHC 4209 (Ch)* it was held that the trustee in bankruptcy could not obtain an income payments order over a personal pension where the pension was not yet in payment as there was no 'entitlement' on which the order could bite. *Horton v Henry* has been heard by the Court of Appeal but, at the time of writing, judgment is still awaited. In the meantime, in May 2016, the High Court in *Hinton v Wotherspoon [2016] EWHC 621 (Ch)* found, in relation to a drawdown arrangement, that the income the member had elected to take could be made subject to an income payments order. However, the court commented to the effect that had he not elected to take specific income then the order could not have been made. The court in *Hinton* preferred the *Horton v Henry* decision to *Raithatha*.

The flexibilities introduced from 6 April 2015 (see **1.40** above) may make money purchase savings more vulnerable to applications from the trustee in bankruptcy as members will have almost unrestricted rights to draw on their funds from age 55.

The *Enterprise Act 2002* introduced an alternative to the income payments order, in the form of an income payments agreement (as set out in *IA 1986, s 310A*). An income payments agreement is a written agreement between the bankrupt and his trustee in bankruptcy or official receiver. The agreement provides for the bankrupt or a third party (which can include the trustees of a pension scheme) to pay to the trustee in bankruptcy or official receiver an amount equal to a specified part or proportion of the bankrupt's income for a specified period. An income payments agreement avoids the requirement of a court hearing, but the terms of the agreement can be enforced as if they were provisions of an income payments order. An income payments agreement must specify the period for which it is to have effect and it can continue in force past the date of the discharge of the bankrupt for up to a maximum period of three years from the date of the agreement.

The effect on unregistered schemes

1.48   The benefits provided by an unapproved pension scheme (within the meaning of *WRPA 1999, Part II*) will vest automatically in the trustee in bankruptcy. However, the Secretary of State is able to make regulations that define what constitutes an unapproved pension scheme and how that might, in prescribed circumstances, be excluded from his estate (see *WRPA 1999, s 12*). The member is able to apply to the Court for an order excluding all or part of his entitlement under the scheme, or he may reach a formal agreement to that effect with the trustee in bankruptcy (see *Occupational and Personal Pension Schemes (Bankruptcy) (No 2) Regulations 2002, reg 4*).

Excessive contributions

1.49 *IA 1986, ss 342A–342C* enables the trustee in bankruptcy to seek an order from the court, where excessive contributions have been made to a registered pension scheme and the court is satisfied that the contributions:

(a)   have unfairly prejudiced individual creditors; and

(b)   have been made in an effort to keep them beyond the reach of creditors; and

(c)   were excessive when looking at the individual's personal circumstances at the time.

Any order will restore the position to what it would have been, had the excessive contributions not been made (and the trustees of the scheme will be ordered to pay an amount to the trustee in bankruptcy).

Personal pension schemes

Background

1.50   The forerunner to the personal pension scheme was the retirement annuity contract ('RAC') first introduced in the 1950s. They subsequently became governed by *Income and Corporation Taxes Act 1970, s 226* and consequently are often referred to as '*s 226* policies'. The most significant distinctions between RACs and personal pension schemes are:

(a)   RACs were only available to the self-employed and those in non-pensionable employment;

(b)   an individual's employer was not permitted to contribute to a RAC but could contribute to a personal pension scheme (*ICTA 1988, s 620*, now repealed); and

(c)   up until 6 April 2012, personal pension schemes allowed individuals to contract out of the second-tier State scheme via an appropriate personal pension scheme ('APPS') – there was no such facility under an RAC (*PSA 1993, s 43(1)*).

Although RACs are still in existence and contributions can still be made to them, it has not been possible to establish a new RAC since 1 July 1988.

The concept of personal pensions was introduced by the *Social Security Act 1986* and they first became available on 1 July 1988. The main reason for the introduction of personal pensions was to allow individuals who did not have access to an occupational scheme (or who wanted to leave such a scheme whilst still employed by the sponsoring employer (ie to 'opt out')) the opportunity of building up their own pension entitlement. The ability of an employee to opt out of their occupational scheme was one of the major factors in the pensions mis-selling scandal and resulted in many providers of personal pension schemes having to pay substantial compensation to individuals. Personal pension schemes were also designed to give individuals the opportunity to contract out of SERPS on an individual basis.

The introduction of the Self-Invested Personal Pension Scheme ('SIPP') in the 1989 Budget led to even more choice in retirement provision by giving the member the opportunity to become involved in decisions about the investment of contributions. SIPPs have tended to attract higher earners because of the higher costs of administration and the general complexity of such arrangements. SIPPs and other 'investment-regulated Pension Schemes' (see *FA 2004, s 174A, Sch 29A*) are effectively limited in the investments that they can make; this is discussed in more detail in **Chapter 17**.

Establishing a personal pension scheme

1.51   An application to register a personal pension scheme can only be made if the scheme has been established by a person with permission under *FSMA 2000* 'to establish in the United Kingdom a personal pension scheme' (*FA 2004, s 154(1)*).

The FCA, in its Perimeter Guidance Manual ('PERG'), describes what it considers to be involved in 'establishing', 'operating' and 'winding-up' a personal pension scheme. In particular, PERG 12 states that in a trust-based scheme the establisher will 'usually be the person who executes the trust as Provider'. It goes on to highlight that 'there will usually only be one person who establishes the scheme', and that 'the activity of establishing a personal pension scheme ceases once the scheme is established'.

PERG 12 also describes what is involved in operating a personal pension scheme. It states that the operator 'is the person responsible to the members for managing and administering the assets and income of, and the benefits payable under, the scheme in accordance with the relevant pensions and tax legislation, the scheme's constitution and the regulatory system'. It is likely that, in most instances, this will be the scheme administrator under *FA 2004, s 270*. However, this may not always be the case, especially in SIPPs where a separate scheme administrator is appointed alongside a trustee. In such a situation, PERG 12 states that 'it may be the case that [the trustees] are operating a scheme jointly with the scheme administrator by virtue of the responsibilities they assume under the trust deed for the management and administration of the scheme assets'. This means that there can be more than one operator of a personal pension scheme but generally this will not be the case if the trustee is nothing more than a bare trustee. An examination of the trustees' duties and powers under the scheme rules may be necessary to decide whether authorisation as an 'operator' is required.

PERG 12 also clarifies that, despite the fact that a member of a SIPP may have the right to direct where the assets of that scheme will be invested, it will not result in him being considered an 'operator'.

Permission from the FCA is only available where the person establishing, operating or winding up the scheme does so by way of business. This means that a person seeking to establish a personal pension scheme other than as part of its business would be unable to gain permission under *FSMA 2000* (as it would not be a regulated activity) which would mean it could not be a registered scheme under *FA 2004, s 154*. Someone operating or winding up a personal pension scheme could do so other than by way of business without being in breach of *FSMA 2000*. PERG 12 confirms that, in very broad terms, it is likely that any corporate body (including a corporate trustee) that operates a personal pension scheme would be carrying on that activity by way of business and so would need to be authorised.

Registering a personal pension scheme

1.52   Schemes established on or after A-Day must be registered under *FA 2004, s 153* (see **Chapter 17**). Prior to A-Day, approval for a personal pension scheme was granted under *ICTA 1988, Part XIV, Chapter IV*. On A-Day approved schemes were automatically treated as registered schemes unless they opted out (*FA 2004, Sch 36, para 1*).

The Regulator

1.53   *PA 2004, s 4* provides that workplace personal pension schemes (where direct payment arrangements are made by the employer) are included within the remit of the Regulator. The Regulator's powers are discussed in **Chapter 2**.

Benefits payable

1.54   A personal pension scheme is a money purchase scheme. The benefits it can provide are determined by the level of contributions paid into it and the amount of investment growth achieved on those contributions. The main legislative control on funding is the tax treatment of contributions and benefits by reference to the Annual Allowance and Lifetime Allowance (see **1.27** above and **Chapter 17**). However, the rules of a scheme may contain further restrictions on benefits and contributions.

Date of commencement of pension

1.55   The rules of a personal pension scheme will usually allow the member to choose the date on which he retires but, in most cases, it must not be before age 55 which is the normal minimum pension age (*FA 2004, s 279*).

HMRC used to allow a pension to commence early if it was satisfied that the member's occupation was one in which people usually retired before the age of 50. A list of occupations where HMRC permitted an earlier pension date is set out in the *Registered Pension Schemes (Prescribed Schemes and Occupations) Regulations 2005 (SI 2005/3451)*).

Where an individual had an existing actual or prospective right to take their benefits earlier than age 55, they may have a lower protected pension age subject to fulfilling certain conditions. The detailed conditions are set out in *FA 2004, Sch 36, paras 19–23A*, and can be summarised as follows:

- the scheme must have been approved by HMRC immediately prior to A-Day; and

   - as at 10 December 2003, the member must have been entitled under the rules of the scheme to a pension from an age earlier than 55; or

   - as at 5 April 2006, the member had an actual or prospective right under the pension scheme to a pension from an age of less than 50 and the member was in a prescribed occupation.

The age at which the member has the right to take a pension on 10 December 2003 or 5 April 2006 (as applicable), will be their 'protected pension age' (subject to all the statutory requirements being met).

Transfer values

1.56   A member of a personal pension scheme has a statutory right to a cash equivalent transfer value, subject to the provisions of *PSA 1993, Chap IV*. The *FA 2004* rules regarding transfers apply to personal pension schemes and these are discussed in more detail in **Chapter 17**.

Disclosure of information

1.57   The trustees (or the provider) are responsible for disclosing certain information to the member under the *Disclosure Regulations 2013*. In particular they must provide certain basic information about the scheme to every new member within two months of joining.

Information relating, in particular, to the amount of contributions credited to the member and the value of the member's accrued rights must be given to the member annually. In addition, further specified information must be given to each member shortly before his retirement.

Stakeholder pension schemes

1.58   Stakeholder schemes were introduced by the Government in an attempt to increase pension coverage for the UK working population. One of the main driving forces was that stakeholder schemes were to be low cost. They were originally introduced by the *Welfare Reform and Pensions Act 1999 (WRPA 1999)* and the first stakeholder schemes were available from April 2001.

On 1 October 2012, to coincide with the start of the automatic enrolment requirements (see **Chapter 14**), the duty on employers to designate a stakeholder scheme for employees was abolished (*The* Pensions *Act 2008 (Commencement No 14 and Supplementary Provisions) Order 2012 (SI 2012/2480)*). The *Order* brought into force *PA 2008, s 87*, which amends *WRPA 1999* (duty of employers to facilitate access to stakeholder pension schemes).

From that date employers are not required to provide access to a stakeholder scheme, except in relation to any employee who, before 1 October 2012, made a request to join a stakeholder scheme, had not withdrawn that request, and in relation to whom at least one employee contribution had been deducted. Under *Clause 3* of the *Order*, if he subsequently withdraws a request to the employer to make deductions, the employer must notify the person (a) that the employer is no longer required to make deductions from the person's remuneration and pay contributions to the trustees or managers of the stakeholder pension scheme; and (b)that the person may still be able to make payments directly to the stakeholder pension scheme, subject to the rules of that scheme or the terms and conditions of any contract governing that scheme.

United Kingdom's withdrawal from the European Union

1.59   On 23 June 2016, the UK voted to leave the European Union. The consequences of the outcome of the referendum ultimately depend on the type of exit model adopted and any transitional provisions that are agreed in the meantime.

Article 50 of the Treaty on European Union allows a member state to withdraw from the EU 'in accordance with its own constitutional requirements'. Once the article 50 notice is delivered, the formal negotiation procedure commences and the start of the two-year exit period begins.

The immediate impact on pension schemes is expected to be financial in relation to market volatility and the ramifications this has on scheme funding. The legal and day-to-day operational implications are likely to be minimal. However, in the longer term there are areas where UK pensions legislation and regulation derives from EU law and could therefore be subject to amendment or repeal.

As a result of the referendum outcome there exists considerable volatility in relation to share prices, interest rates and inward investment to the UK, all of which have an impact on pension scheme funding. Pension schemes are long-term investment vehicles and typically investment strategies account for short-term market volatility and uncertainty.

A significant body of EU pensions law has already been incorporated into UK domestic legislation (for example, the scheme funding provisions in *PA 2004*, which are considered in **Chapter 11**). Although the UK would no longer be bound by EU law following the withdrawal, it seems unlikely that provisions which protect pension savings and are generally considered to be working reasonably well would be repealed. However, the UK will have the opportunity to deviate from EU requirements and adopt its own domestic direction. Over time we may see the UK Parliament repealing some existing provisions in an attempt to cut EU red tape.

In the longer term, there are some areas where UK law may diverge from EU regulations. Financial services legislation is heavily regulated by the EU, but it is likely that financial service institutions will continue to comply with most EU regulations in order to continue participating in the European market. Below are some areas of UK pension law which are currently subject to EU law.

Scheme funding	The current technical provisions funding regime derives from the IORP Directive. There is unlikely to be any major change in the short or medium term but there would be scope for relaxing some of the more technical detail in future if desired. See **Chapter 11**.

Investment	Some of the investment requirements (including limits on employer-related investments and the requirement to diversify) derive from IORP. There are unlikely to be major changes to the current requirements in the foreseeable future. Many of the rules governing the financial services industry more generally also derive from the EU – it is unlikely there will be major changes here as the UK industry will need to continue to comply in order to operate in the European market. Once the position is clearer, a review of specific investment documents may be advisable. See **Chapter 10**.
Equal treatment	There are unlikely to be major changes here on policy grounds. There may be an opportunity to relax some of the age discrimination provisions in order to allow pension schemes to operate with more certainty and not have to rely on justification arguments. See **Chapter 9**.
TUPE transfers	There will be scope for the Government to amend or relax the TUPE requirements and to give more clarity on early retirement (*Beckmann*) issues. See **Chapter 8**.
PPF	The PPF was established to fulfil the UK's obligations under the EU Insolvency Directive. It is unlikely there will be any major changes to the PPF in the current climate. See **Chapter 5**.
Data protection	It is likely that current data protection legislation will remain in place (as well as new requirements equivalent to those under the EU General Data Protection Directive) so that UK business can continue to transfer data to the EU.

Chapter 2

People involved with pensions

Introduction

2.1   This Chapter considers the roles of the individuals and organisations involved in the administration, management and regulation of pension schemes. The people involved in pensions fall within four main categories:

(*a*)   those whose involvement is specific to the scheme in question; this group includes the trustees of the scheme and the professional advisers they appoint (ie the actuary, auditor and fund manager) to assist them in carrying out their functions;

(*b*)   those which can broadly be termed the regulatory bodies; this group includes the Pensions Regulator ('the Regulator'), Her Majesty's Revenue and Customs ('HMRC'), National Insurance Services to Pensions Industry ('NISPI'), which is a directorate within the National Insurance Contributions Office operated by HMRC and the Board of the Pension Protection Fund ('PPF');

(*c*)   the Pensions Advisory Service ('TPAS') (formerly OPAS) and the Pensions Ombudsman, both of whom may have a role to play when disputes arise; and

(*d*)   various industry bodies, the most important of which are the Pensions Management Institute ('PMI') and the Pensions and Lifetime Savings Association ('PLSA').

Trustees

2.2   Where a pension scheme is established by an employer under trust, the role of the trustees is to hold the scheme's assets separately from the employer's assets and to apply them for the benefit of scheme members in accordance with the trust documents, general trust law and overriding legislation. If the scheme's liabilities are funded in advance over a period of time by employers' and employees' contributions, the use of a trust creates a degree of security for scheme members by placing the scheme's assets beyond the reach of the employers' creditors. Any UK-based occupational pension scheme wishing to

53

accept payments to the scheme to fund benefits must be established under trust (*PA 2004, s 252*).

In the past, there were few restrictions as to who could be a pension scheme trustee: for example, a trustee could be an individual, the scheme's principal employer, a company, an elected employee or a member representative. For practical reasons, however, a scheme's trustees would usually be either at least two individuals or a company, whose board of directors would take the relevant decisions. *PA 1995* imposed requirements as to who may and may not be a pension scheme trustee (see **3.2** below) and, in broad terms, entitled scheme members to nominate at least one third of the trustees (see **Chapter 3**).

Trustees must act in the best interests of the beneficiaries (generally considered to mean their best financial interests) and in accordance with trust law and the scheme's trust deed and rules. **Chapter 3** takes a more detailed look at trustees' duties and responsibilities.

PA 2004 requires trustees to be conversant with their scheme's documents and to have knowledge and understanding of pensions and trust law and of the principles relating to pension scheme funding and investment (*PA 2004, ss 247–249*). This is considered further in **Chapter 3**.

PA 1995 introduced civil and criminal penalties for trustees in respect of breaches of certain sections of *PA 1995* (and *PSA 1993*, as amended) and the prohibition or suspension of trustees in certain circumstances. Certain breaches of *PA 2004* are also subject to penalties under *PA 1995*. Details of these appear throughout this book and are summarised in **Appendix I**.

Actuaries

The role of the actuary

2.3   Actuaries assess financial problems, using mathematical and statistical methods, specialising, in particular, in problems concerning uncertain future events. In the context of pension schemes this most often involves predicting movements in the scheme (deaths, retirements and withdrawals) and estimating the costs of providing the benefits due and accruing in the future.

Previously, the actuary to a scheme would have recommended the assumptions and methods to be used to value the scheme's assets and liabilities, would periodically value these and would have recommended the rate of contribution which was necessary to provide those benefits (see **Chapter 11**). The actuary's role changed for all valuations with effect from 22 September 2005. The trustees (in most cases with the consent of the employer) must now choose the assumptions to be used in the valuation, adopt a statement of funding principles and set the contribution rate. However, they are required by *PA 2004* to take advice from the actuary before making any decisions on these matters.

The actuary will also advise on a day-to-day basis on benefit issues, such as the calculation of cash equivalents and early retirement factors (for example, the extent to which an early retirement pension should be discounted to take account of early payment). An actuary may also advise the trustees on strategic investment decisions.

The appointment of the actuary under PA 1995

2.4 Under *PA 1995, s 47* (subject to the exemptions listed below), the trustees of each occupational pension scheme must appoint an actuary. The actuary must be a named individual, even if working in an actuarial firm (*PA 1995, s 47(1)(b)*). The individual actuary appointed under this provision ('the scheme actuary') has specific functions to perform under *PA 1995* and *PA 2004*. In particular, it is the scheme actuary who is responsible for signing valuations (see **Chapter 11**).

Under the *Scheme Administration Regulations 1996 (SI 1996/1715), reg 3(2)*, as amended, the requirement for a scheme actuary does not apply to:

(*a*)   money purchase schemes;

(*b*)   statutory schemes, or schemes with a Crown guarantee;

(*c*)   unfunded occupational pension schemes;

(*d*)   occupational schemes with less than two members;

(*e*)   unregistered schemes with fewer than 100 members;

(*f*)   expatriate occupational pension schemes with a superannuation fund under *ICTA 1988, s 615(6)* with fewer than 100 members;

(*g*)   schemes with fewer than 12 members where all the members are trustees and either all decisions must be made unanimously by the trustees, or a statutory independent trustee has been appointed; and

(*h*)   schemes with fewer than 12 members where all the members are directors of a company which is the sole trustee of the scheme and either the provisions of the scheme provide that any decisions made by the company in its capacity as trustee are made by the unanimous agreement of all the directors who are members of the scheme, or a statutory independent director has been appointed.

The *Scheme Administration Regulations 1996, reg 4(1)(b)* sets out the qualifications and experience or approval required for appointment as the scheme actuary. An actuary must be a Fellow of the Institute and Faculty of Actuaries or must be approved by the Secretary of State. Additionally, an actuary cannot be a trustee of the pension scheme nor must he be connected with or an associate of a trustee of that scheme (see **2.6** below).

Any actuary can perform functions which do not have to be performed by the scheme actuary, but if the trustees rely on the skill or judgement of an actuary they have not appointed, they will risk incurring civil penalties. Consequently, whenever trustees of a pension scheme (even one that is exempt from having to appoint a scheme actuary) seek advice from an actuary, they should ensure that the actuary has been properly appointed in accordance with the requirements of *PA 1995*.

There are specific requirements for trustees to observe in making the necessary appointments (see *Scheme Administration Regulations 1996, reg 5*). The notice of appointment must be in writing, must specify the date of the appointment, and must set out whom the actuary should report to and take instructions from (*Scheme Administration Regulations, reg 5(1)*). The actuary must acknowledge the notice in writing within one month of receipt (*Scheme Administration Regulations 1996, reg 5(2)(a)*). In addition, the actuary must confirm in writing that he will notify the trustees of any conflict of interest to which he is subject in relation to the scheme immediately on becoming aware of the existence of the conflict (*Scheme Administration Regulations 1996, reg 5(2)(b)(ii)*). If the actuary resigns from the appointment or is removed by the trustees, he is required to certify whether the circumstances of the resignation or removal are likely to affect the members (*Scheme Administration Regulations, reg 5(4)*). Subject to these requirements, the trustees are free to determine the terms of the appointment and, where an actuary resigns or is removed from the appointment, the trustees are required to appoint a replacement within three months (*Scheme Administration Regulations 1996, reg 5(8)*).

Actuarial appointments are also subject to the requirements contained in Actuarial Professional Standards APS P1: 'Duties and Responsibilities of Members Undertaking Work in Relation to Pension Schemes' (version 2.0) ('APS P1') which came into effect on 1 July 2013. In particular, the actuary must have a written agreement with the trustees covering the information that the trustees need to provide, or allow access to, so that the actuary can perform his duties properly and allow him to share information with other advisers as appropriate (paragraph 3.1).

APS P1 recognises that the specific matters to be covered in the agreement will vary from scheme to scheme. However, the agreement should include the matters set out in Appendix 1 to APS P1 unless there is a justifiable reason not to include these (eg where the matter is not deemed to be sufficiently significant to justify amending an already-existing agreement).

Whistleblowing

2.5   The scheme actuary is required by *PA 2004, s 70* to be a whistleblower (see **2.14** below).

The actuary's professional obligations are set out in APS P1 and APS X2: 'Review of Actuarial Work' (version 1.0) ('APS X2'), the latter of which came into effect on 1 July 2015. APS X2 sets out the circumstances in which an actuary is required to seek a review of his work and governs the conduct of such reviews.

APS P1 recommends that the actuary should inform the trustees where he becomes aware of any significant matter relating to his regulatory, contractual or other professional responsibility which might impact upon the scheme's funding, where the actuary considers (further) advice may be required either from the scheme actuary or another adviser. The actuary is not under a duty to do so where he believes that another person (such as the trustees' legal adviser) has appropriately informed or will inform the trustees.

Where the scheme actuary has material concerns that:

- a course of action is not appropriate;

- the trustees have failed or are failing to carry out an appropriate action; and/or

- the trustees might be unaware of a duty or responsibility, or of relevant legislation or guidance relating to a duty or responsibility,

he should share these with the trustees and take such action as is appropriate in the circumstances. Depending on the circumstances, appropriate actions might include making a report to the Regulator under *PA 2004, s 70* and/or resigning his appointment.

Ineligibility to act if a trustee

2.6   Under *PA 1995, s 27* a trustee of a pension scheme (and any person connected or associated with such a trustee) may not be an actuary to the same scheme. (The terms 'connected' and 'associated' are defined in *PA 1995, s 123* by reference to *Insolvency Act 1986, ss 249* and *435*.)

However, a director, partner or employee of a firm of actuaries may act as a scheme's actuary even though another director, partner or employee of the firm is a trustee of that scheme (*PA 1995, s 27(2)*), or a company with which he is associated with is the trustee (*Scheme Administration Regulations), reg 7*).

Breach of *PA 1995, s 27* is a criminal offence (*PA 1995, s 28*), punishable by a £5,000 fine and/or a custodial sentence.

Auditors

2.7   Trustees of occupational pension schemes must appoint an individual or a firm as auditor under *PA 1995, s 47*. That individual or firm must be eligible for appointment as a statutory auditor under *Companies Act 2006, Part 42* or otherwise approved by the Secretary of State. Under the *Scheme Administration Regulations, reg 3(1)*, this requirement does not apply to:

(*a*)   unregistered schemes;

(*b*)   unfunded occupational pension schemes;

(*c*)   occupational schemes with fewer than two members;

(*d*)   overseas schemes under *ICTA 1988, s 615(6)*;

(*e*)   schemes with fewer than 12 members where all the members are trustees and either all decisions must be made unanimously by the trustees, or a statutory independent trustee has been appointed under *PA 1995, s 23*;

(*f*)   schemes with fewer than 12 members where all the members are directors of a company which is the sole trustee of the scheme and either the provisions of the scheme provide that any decisions made by the company in its capacity as trustee are made by the unanimous agreement of all the directors who are members of the scheme, or a statutory independent director has been appointed; and

(*g*)   certain schemes established by statute or protected by Crown guarantee.

Rules similar to those applying to the appointment of actuaries apply to the appointment of auditors under *PA 1995* (see **2.4** above). However, the bar on a trustee (or anyone connected or associated with a trustee) acting as auditor (see **2.6** above) is arguably wider, in that there is no specific provision enabling a director, partner or employee of a firm of auditors to act as auditor where another director, partner or employee of that firm is a trustee of the scheme. The same sanction as referred to in **2.6** above applies to any auditor who breaches the provisions of *PA 1995, s 27*. The auditor is also required to whistleblow in the circumstances set out in **2.5** above under *PA 2004, s 70*.

The *Occupational Pension Schemes (Requirement to obtain Audited Accounts and a Statement from the Auditor) Regulations 1996 (SI 1996/1975)* (as amended), apply to all schemes which are required to appoint an auditor under *PA 1995, s 47*, except insured schemes which earmark insurance policies for each member, and require:

(*a*)   the trustees to obtain audited accounts and the auditor's statement regarding payment of contributions within seven months of the end of the scheme year; and

(*b*)   the accounts to contain a statement that they have been prepared and audited in accordance with the regulations.

In particular, the auditor will be required to express an opinion as to whether or not the accounts show a true and fair view of the financial transactions of the scheme during the scheme year, details of any dispositions of scheme assets (including the amount) during the scheme year and liabilities of the scheme, other than those relating to the payment of pensions and benefits after the end of the scheme year (*The Occupational Pension Schemes (Requirement to obtain Audited Accounts and a Statement from the Auditor) Regulations 1996, reg 3*).

In addition, occupational pension schemes with 100 or more members which are unregistered or overseas schemes under *ICTA 1988, s 615(6)* are required to produce audited accounts (despite the fact they are exempt from the requirements to appoint an auditor). This provision was introduced by the *Occupational Pension Schemes (Administration and Audited Accounts) (Amendment) Regulations 2005 (SI 2005/2426)* as a result of the European *Directive 2003/41/EC on the Activities and Supervision of Institutions for Occupational Retirement Provision* ('IORP').

Further guidance for auditors can be found in the Auditing Practices Board's ('APB') Practice Note 15: 'The Audit of Occupational Pension Schemes in the United Kingdom' which was revised in January 2011.

Investment managers

2.8   A scheme's trust deed and rules will usually give the trustees wide investment powers to enable them to deal with trust assets as if they were the beneficial owners. In addition, *PA 1995, s 34* confers on occupational scheme trustees (including trust-based stakeholder scheme trustees registered in accordance with *WRPA 1999, s 2*) an investment power which is the same as if they were absolutely entitled to the scheme's assets themselves and which is subject only to any restrictions imposed by the scheme. *PA 2004* introduced amendments to *PA 1995, ss 34* and *36* which required trustees to exercise their powers of investment in accordance with regulations. The *Occupational Pension Schemes (Investment) Regulations 2005 (SI 2005/3378)* require trustees to exercise their powers of investment in a manner calculated to ensure the security, quality, liquidity and profitability of the portfolio as a whole and include some specific restrictions on investment and borrowing.

The Financial Services and Markets Act 2000 (*FSMA 2000*) prohibits a person from carrying on a regulated activity unless they are authorised or exempt.

Trustees will generally delegate their investment power to a fund manager who is authorised rather than seek authorisation themselves. This is usually achieved by way of an investment management agreement ('IMA'). The IMA must contain certain information as prescribed by *PA 1995*, which includes dealing with any conflicts of interest that may arise.

Trustees are required under *PA 1995, s 47(2)* to appoint a fund manager if their scheme has 'investments', which include 'any asset right or interest' as defined in *FSMA 2000, s 22*. The regulated activities are described more fully under *FSMA 2000, Sch 2* and separated into the following headings:

- dealing in investments;
- arranging deals in investments;
- deposit taking;
- safekeeping and administration of assets;
- managing investments;
- investment advice; and
- establishing collective investment schemes.

The *Scheme Administration Regulations 1996* (as amended) exempt (amongst others) unfunded schemes, schemes with fewer than two members, wholly insured schemes and schemes with no more than 12 members in which all members are trustees and all investment decisions are made by all or a majority of the trustees (further exemptions are provided for under the *Scheme Administration Regulations, reg 3(3)* and *Financial Services and Markets Act 2000 (Carrying on Regulated Activities by Way of Business) Order 2001 (SI 2001/1177), art 4(4)*, as amended by the *Financial Services and Markets Act 2000 (Carrying on Regulated Activities by Way of Business) (Amendment) Order 2005 (SI 2005/922))*.

Investment is dealt with in more detail in **Chapter 10**.

Pension Schemes Services of Her Majesty's Revenue and Customs

2.9   Responsibility for pension schemes within Her Majesty's Revenue and Customs ('HMRC') lies with the Pension Schemes Services ('PSS'). PSS's main responsibility is to oversee the requirements placed on pension schemes claiming tax relief, as well as related implications for members, their employers and other parties.

HMRC's main guidance relating to pension schemes is the Pensions Tax Manual. This replaced the Registered Pension Schemes Manual from 15 April

2016. The tax treatment of registered pension schemes is dealt with further in **Chapter 17**.

The PSS can be contacted at HM Revenue and Customs – Pension Scheme Services, FitzRoy House, Castle Meadow Road, Nottingham NG2 1BD. Tel: 0300 123 1079; website: www.hmrc.gov.uk.

National Insurance Services to Pensions Industry

2.10   National Insurance Services to Pensions Industry ('NISPI') (formerly the Contracted-Out Employments Group ('COEG')) is a directorate within the HMRC National Insurance Contributions Office and is responsible for ensuring that the pension rights of employees who were contracted out of the State second pension (S2P) are maintained and safeguarded (see **Chapter 4**). In particular, NISPI is responsible for:

(*a*)   dealing with the termination of contracted-out employment;

(*b*)   communicating with scheme authorities about the facility for checking National Insurance numbers, dates of birth etc for funding purposes; and

(*c*)   answering general queries regarding contracted-out arrangements.

In the run-up to 6 April 2016, NISPI's key focus has been on assisting contracted-out schemes to prepare for the abolition of contracting-out. Since March 2014, it has published a series of Countdown Bulletins for scheme administrators to explain the abolition process and to provide guidance on what actions contracted-out schemes need to take.

One particular service that contracted-out schemes have been encouraged (but not obliged) to make use of has been the Scheme Reconciliation Service ('SRS'). This service, which allows pension scheme administrators to reconcile their data regarding scheme membership and GMPs with HMRC's data was previously only available for schemes that were winding up, but was extended to all contracted-out schemes from April 2014. Crucially, schemes wishing to make use of the service were required to register with HMRC by submitting an expression of interest before 5 April 2016. HMRC's website does, however, state that in any event it will continue to offer support to deal with queries relating to contracting-out until December 2018.

NISPI can be contacted by email at nispi.magmedia@hmrc.gsi.gov.uk. The SRS can be contacted by email at mailbox.newstatepensionenquiries@hmrc.gsi.gov.uk or by phone on 0300 200 3507.

The Pensions Regulator

Objectives and functions

2.11   The Pensions Regulator ('the Regulator') was established under *PA 2004, Part 1*, and replaced the previous regulatory body, the Occupational Pensions Regulatory Authority ('Opra'), from April 2005. Lesley Titcomb is the current Chief Executive.

The role of the Regulator is defined by its objectives and functions as laid down by *PA 2004, s 5*. The six main objectives are:

- to protect the benefits of scheme members under occupational pension schemes;

- to protect the benefits of scheme members under personal pension schemes;

- to reduce the risk of situations arising which may lead to compensation being payable from the Pension Protection Fund;

- (in relation to the exercise of its functions in relation to scheme funding), to minimise any adverse impact on the sustainable growth of DB scheme employers;

- to maximise employer compliance with their automatic enrolment schemes; and

- to promote, and improve the understanding of, good administration of work-based pension schemes.

In addition to these objectives, the Regulator also has responsibilities as regards the regulation of public service pension schemes. These are defined in *PA 2004* as:

- a scheme under the *Public Service Pensions Act 2013 (PSPA 2013), s 1* – very broadly, schemes established for and in respect of a variety of public sector workers, such as civil servants, teachers and health service workers;

- a new public body pension scheme (within the meaning of *PSPA 2013);* or

- any statutory pension scheme which is connected with a scheme under *PSPA 2013* or a new public body pension scheme within the meaning of *PSPA 2013*.

The Regulator's responsibilities and powers relating to the oversight of public service schemes were introduced into *PA 2004* by a series of amendments made under *PSPA 2013*. Subsequently, the Regulator published a new Code of

Practice (Code 14: 'Governance and administration of public service pension schemes'), which came into force from April 2015.

The Regulator operates in part through the Non-Executive Committee and the Determinations Panel, both of which the Regulator is under a duty to establish and maintain.

The *Non-Executive Committee* is essentially an internal regulatory body, established pursuant to *PA 2004, s 8* to monitor, assess and report on the functions carried out by the Regulator. Its role includes:

• monitoring the extent to which objectives and targets are being met;

• preparing a report on the discharge of its functions, to be included in the Pensions Regulator's annual report;

• reviewing the Regulator's internal financial controls; and

• setting the terms and conditions of remuneration of the Chief Executive.

The *Determinations Panel* is the body established pursuant to *PA 2004, s 9* to determine and exercise the 'reserved regulatory functions' on behalf of the Regulator (which can be extended or modified by regulations). These functions are listed in *PA 2004, Sch 2*. It is worth highlighting a few as follows:

Those powers transferred from *Opra* (retained in relevant sections of *PA 1995*):

• to issue trustee prohibition and suspension orders (*ss 3, 4*);

• to appoint trustees (*s 7*);

• to impose civil penalties (*s 10*);

• to direct a winding up (*s 11*);

• to give directions to trustees (*s 15*);

• to authorise modifications to schemes (*s 69*).

The powers established by *PA 2004* include:

• to issue and extend freezing orders (*s 23*);

• to issue contribution notices and financial support directions (*ss 38, 43*);

• to issue restoration orders where there has been a transaction at an undervalue (*s 52*);

• to issue notices requiring a report to be made to the Regulator (*s 71*); and

• to issue an order modifying a scheme, giving directions or imposing a schedule of contributions (*s 231*).

2.12   *People involved with pensions*

The Regulator may also delegate to the Determinations Panel other regulatory functions pursuant to *PA 2004, s 10*.

The Regulator has shown an increased willingness to exercise its moral hazard powers, beginning in June 2007 when it issued a financial support direction in relation to the Sea Containers Schemes. Since then, it has issued several financial support directions and contribution notices, most recently in April 2015 when the Determinations Panel determined to issue a contribution notice in relation to the Carrington Wire Defined Benefit Pension Scheme. The Regulator's moral hazard powers are considered in greater depth in **Chapter 11**.

In addition to these and other specific functions the Regulator has supplementary powers under *PA 2004, s 6* to do anything, except borrow money, which 'is calculated to facilitate the exercise of its functions or which is incidental or conducive to their exercise'.

Codes of Practice (ss 90 and 90A)

2.12   The Regulator may issue practical guidance in relation to the exercise of its functions under pensions legislation and with regard to standards of conduct and practice in relation to the exercise of those functions.

The Regulator is required to issue codes on a number of matters including what constitutes a 'reasonable period' for the purposes of any pensions legislation, the whistleblowing requirements under *PA 2004*, compliance with scheme specific funding requirements, member-nominated trustee requirements, knowledge and understanding requirements, requirements to report with regard to failure to pay contributions and other matters.

If any Code of Practice is not observed, this is not in itself a breach of a legal requirement. However, the Codes of Practice will be admissible in evidence in legal proceedings, including proceedings before the Pensions Ombudsman. *PA 2004* specifies a procedure to be followed for the issuing and publication of Codes of Practice, including the publication of a draft for consultation. Before a Code of Practice can come into force, the draft must have been laid before Parliament for at least 40 sitting days (*PA 2004, s 91*).

Set out below is a list of the Code of Practices that have been issued by the Regulator.

Code of Practice	Summary of scope	Date in force
Code 1 Reporting breaches of the law	Reporting by statutory whistleblowers of certain breaches of the law which affect pension schemes to the Regulator.	6 April 2005
Code 2 Notifiable events	Notifying the Regulator of prescribed events which occur in respect of pension schemes, and in respect of employers who sponsor pension schemes.	April 2005
Code 3 Funding defined benefits	Implementation of the funding arrangements that apply to most private sector occupational pension schemes that provide defined benefits.	July 2014 Revised version
Code 4 Early leavers	Trustees' or managers' duty to provide members who leave schemes after a short period of membership with a statement of their entitlements. Definition of reasonable period within which specified steps must be taken.	May 2006
Code 5 Reporting late payment of contributions to occupational money purchase schemes	Trustees or managers of occupational defined contributions schemes to report late payments to the Regulator in certain circumstances.	September 2013 Revised version
Code 6 Reporting late payment of contributions to personal pension schemes	Managers of personal pension schemes to report late payments to the Regulator in certain circumstances.	September 2013 Revised version
Code 7 Trustee knowledge and understanding	Trustees of relevant schemes to have an appropriate body of knowledge and understanding of the law relating to pensions and trusts and the principles relating to the funding of occupational pension schemes and investment of scheme assets.	November 2009 Revised version

Code of Practice	Summary of scope	Date in force
Code 8 Member-nominated trustees and directors – putting arrangements in place	Implementation of arrangements to ensure that at least one third of the trustees or trustee directors are member-nominated. Definition of reasonable period within which specified steps must be taken.	November 2006
Code 9 Internal controls	Implementation of the requirement for trustees and managers to have adequate internal controls to ensure that an occupational scheme is managed and administered correctly.	November 2006
Code 10 Modification of subsisting rights	Exercise of power to make limited modifications to subsisting rights to benefits under occupational pension schemes whilst protecting the accrued rights of members.	January 2007
Code 11 Internal dispute resolution ('IDR') – reasonable periods	Practical Guidance on what the Regulator expects would satisfy the 'reasonable time period' in relation to the period within which trustees and managers must make and communicate a decision via a scheme's internal dispute resolution procedure.	July 2008
Code 12 Circumstances in relation to the material detriment test	Outlines the circumstances in which the Regulator would expect to issue a contribution notice under the 'material detriment' test introduced by the *Pensions Act 2008.*	June 2009
Code 13 Governance and administration of occupational DC trust-based schemes	Sets out the standards of governance and administration that trustees of occupational DC trust-based schemes need to attain.	November 2013 (NB. revised version published in July 2016)

Code of Practice	Summary of scope	Date in force
Code 14 Governance and administration of public service pension schemes	Outlines the standards of governance that scheme managers of public service schemes within the meaning of the *Pensions Act 2004* need to attain.	April 2015

Reporting breaches of the law

The duty to report

2.13 *PA 2004, s 70* imposes a duty to report to the Regulator 'materially significant' breaches of the law relating to pension scheme administration on anyone who is involved in the running and administration of a scheme. This includes trustees and managers, employers, professional advisers and anyone otherwise involved in the administration of a scheme, eg anyone providing services or advice in relation to a scheme.

The decision to report

2.14 As set out in the Regulator's Code of practice and guidance on reporting breaches of law, the decision to report requires two key judgments:

- Does the reporter have **reasonable cause to believe** there has been a breach of the law?

  The reporter must have a tangible reason to want to make a report, not merely a suspicion which cannot be substantiated.

- If so, does the reporter believe the breach **likely to be of material significance** to the Regulator?

  What will be of material significance will depend on various factors, including the cause, effect, reaction to and wider implications of the breach. Examples of material and non-material points relating to each of these factors can be found in the Regulator's Code of Practice and guidance.

Making a report

2.15 All reporters should have effective procedures in place to identify breaches and to determine whether they are likely to be of material significance to the Regulator.

Reports detailing the particulars of the scheme, the purported breach and the reporter must be submitted in writing and, wherever practicable, use the standard format available on the Regulator's website at www.thepensionsregulator. gov.uk. Alternatively, a report can be submitted to the Regulator online using Exchange.

Failure to comply with the obligation to report a breach is a civil offence.

The Regulator's response to a breach

2.16   According to the Code of Practice, the Regulator has a wide range of measures it can use in reacting to a report of a breach, including:

- assisting or instructing trustees and others to achieve compliance;
- removing trustees from office and/or appointing trustees to help run the scheme;
- freezing the scheme;
- imposing special measures where the scheme funding requirements of *PA 2004* are not complied with;
- ordering that the scheme's funding position be restored to the level before a breach or other detrimental events occurred; and
- imposing fines where appropriate.

Reporting notifiable events

Notifiable events duty

2.17   Trustees, employers and, where applicable, guarantors of schemes eligible for PPF entry are required by *PA 2004, s 69* to notify certain events to the Regulator. The purpose of notification is to reduce the risk of circumstances arising which may lead to compensation being payable from the PPF, as well as providing the Regulator with an early warning of problems which might give rise to a claim on the PPF.

Details of events which are notifiable are set out in the *Pensions Regulator (Notifiable Events) Regulations 2005 (SI 2005/900)*, as amended. The Regulator has also issued a Code of Practice and Directions dealing with the notifiable events duty.

Events to be notified

2.18   The duty to notify requires written notice to be given to the Regulator of the following types of events:

- in respect of employers, in relation to their pension schemes (see **2.19** below);

- in respect of pension schemes (see **2.20** below); and

- in respect of certain events under the *Occupational Pension Schemes (Employer Debt) Regulations 2005 (SI 2005/678)*. These are discussed further at **15.72** below.

Employer-related events

2.19   Employers must notify the following events:

- any decision by the employer to take action which will, or is intended to, result in a debt which is or may become due to the scheme not being paid in full;

- a decision by the employer to cease to carry on business in the UK, or cessation of business in the UK without such a decision having been taken;

- receipt by the employer of advice that it is trading wrongfully or a director or former director of the company knows that there is no reasonable prospect that the company will avoid going into insolvent liquidation;

- any breach of a banking covenant by the employer, other than where the bank or other institution agrees with the employer not to enforce the covenant *unless* the conditions in A and B below are satisfied;

- a decision by a controlling company to relinquish control of the employer, or the controlling company relinquishing control without a decision to do so having been taken, *unless* the conditions in A and B below are satisfied; and

- the conviction of an individual for an offence involving dishonesty, if the offence was committed while the individual was a director or partner of the employer.

Scheme-related events

2.20   Trustees must report the following events:

- any decision by the trustees or managers to take action which will, or is intended to, result in any debt which is or may become due to the scheme not being paid in full *unless* the conditions in A, B and C below are satisfied;

- a decision by the trustees to make or accept a transfer value from another scheme, or making or accepting such a transfer where no decision is required, the value of which is more than the lower of 5 per cent of the value of the scheme assets or £1.5 million *unless* the conditions in A and B below are satisfied;

- a decision by the trustees to grant benefits (or a right to benefits) on more favourable terms than those provided for by the scheme rules without either seeking advice from the actuary or securing additional funding where so advised; and

- a decision by the trustees to grant benefits (or a right to benefits) to a member, or granting such benefits where no decision is required, the cost of which is more than the lower of 5 per cent of the scheme assets and £1.5 million *unless* the conditions of A and B below are satisfied.

The conditions

2.21   The conditions are set out in Directions, which were last updated by the Regulator in April 2009:

- *Condition A*: Scheme funding must be at least at the PPF level at the most recent *s 179* valuation (see **Chapter 5**).

- *Condition B*: The trustees have not needed to report to the Regulator in the previous 12 months any failure of non-payment under the schedule of contributions.

- *Condition C*: The debt not collected is less than 0.5 per cent of the scheme assets (as valued at the most recent valuation mentioned at condition A above).

When and how to make a notification

2.22   Notifiable events must be notified to the Regulator *as soon as reasonably practicable*. While dependant on the circumstances, this implies urgency in all cases (hence the need to ensure schemes put in place proper notification procedures). As an example, the Regulator suggests that where a trustee learns of a notifiable event on a Sunday, he should notify the Regulator on the Monday (in the Regulator's view, seeking professional advice first is not necessary).

Notifications setting out the details of a notifiable event must be made in writing and, where practicable, use the standard for available on the Regulator's website at www.thepensionsregulator.gov.uk. Reports may be sent by post, e-mail or fax. A notification may also be submitted to the Regulator online using Exchange.

Failure to notify

2.23 Trustees are required to take all reasonable steps to comply with the notifiable events requirements. This means considering whether, where a failure to notify a notifiable event occurs, an objective person would consider that the trustees nevertheless took all reasonable and expected steps in order to comply.

Employers must comply with the notifiable events regime unless they have a reasonable excuse for not doing so. Where a failure to comply occurs, it will be assessed on the basis of whether an objective person would consider that there was a reasonable basis for the failure.

A failure by itself will not lead to a transaction being void. However, the Regulator will seek an explanation for the failure and, where appropriate, a civil penalty may be imposed.

In practice, trustees and employers should ensure that they are aware of what the notifiable events are, who is required to notify and the exceptions to the requirement, and put in place an appropriate procedure for identifying and notifying.

The Register

2.24 The Regulator is charged by *PA 2004, s 59* with maintaining a register of 'registrable' occupational and personal pension schemes which records 'registrable information' about those schemes and any notifications that a scheme has been wound up or transferred to the PPF.

As prescribed in the *Register of Occupational and Personal Pension Schemes Regulations 2005 (SI 2005/597)* ('*Register of Schemes Regulations 2005*'), registrable schemes include all registered pension schemes with more than one member, and any scheme with a superannuation fund as is mentioned in *ICTA 1988, s 615(6)* which is undertaking cross-border activities.

Registrable information is defined in *PA 2004, s 60* and covers basic details of the scheme and the benefits it provides, its trustees or managers and, for occupational schemes, its relevant employers and number of members. The *Register of Schemes Regulations 2005* require further information, including the category of the scheme, the nature of the business of any relevant employer and whether the scheme has commenced winding up.

The Regulator may obtain the information required for the register by issuing scheme return notices under *PA 2004, s 63*. Where a new registrable scheme is established or a scheme becomes registrable, the trustees or managers must notify the Regulator and provide the registrable information within three months. Where there is a change in registrable information or a scheme ceases to be registrable or is wound up, the trustees or managers must notify the Regulator as soon as reasonably practicable. Failure to do so could give rise to civil penalties under *PA 1995, s 10* (*PA 2004, s 62*).

The Department for Work and Pensions runs a pensions tracing service which allows individuals who think they are entitled to benefit under a scheme to make an application for information. The *Register of Schemes Regulations 2005* allow the Secretary of State access to information from the register and the right to inspect the register for the purposes of operating the tracing service.

Appeals from decisions of the Regulator

2.25   In accordance with the *Transfer of Tribunal Functions Order 2010 (SI 2010/22)*, appeals against decisions made by the Regulator have, since 6 April 2010, been heard by a two-tier system which is part of the Tax and Chancery Chamber of the Upper Tribunal. These appeals are now governed by the procedural rules that apply to all Upper Chamber disputes (the *Tribunal Procedure (Upper Tribunal) Rules 2008 (SI 2008/2698)*, as amended by the *Tribunal Procedure (Upper Tribunal)(Amendment) Rules 2010 (SI 2010/747)*.

Any appeal by a party affected by a determination or a notice of the Regulator should generally be referred within 28 days of the Regulator's determination or notice. Late reference applications may still be made to the Upper Tribunal (*Tribunal Procedure (Upper Tribunal) Rules 2008, r 21*).

When considering a reference, the tribunal may consider any evidence relating to the subject matter of the reference, whether it was before the Regulator or not, and regardless of whether it would be admissible in a court of law. On determining a reference, the Tribunal must remit the matter to the Regulator with appropriate directions for giving effect to its determination. This may include directions to vary or revoke the Regulator's original determination or to substitute a different determination. The Upper Tribunal may also strike out a case on the basis that it has no reasonable prospect of success (*Tribunal Procedure (Upper Tribunal) Rules 2008, r 8(3)*).

On 17 January 2011, Mr Justice Warren, the then President of the Upper Tribunal: Tax and Chancery Chamber, gave his decision on a number of preliminary issues in a reference concerning the Bonas Group Pension Scheme (*Re the Bonas Group Pension Scheme [2011] UKUT (FS)*). The reference related to a decision by the Regulator's Determinations Panel to issue a Contribution Notice. In his decision Warren J confirmed his understanding of the role of the Tribunal when considering references relating to decisions of the Determinations Panel. He confirmed that the role of the Tribunal was to undertake its own assessment of the evidence (including new evidence) before making its own decision. It does not sit as an appellate body (ie it was not limited to deciding whether the Determinations Panel had acted reasonably or was in error).

The Tribunal will use its case-management powers to determine how a hearing will be conducted. Matters should usually be decided following an oral hearing but this may be dispensed with in certain circumstances including where:

- the parties agree in writing;

- the Regulator does not oppose the reference;

- the Regulator does not properly respond to the reference; or

- the reference is for directions only (*Tribunal Procedure (Upper Tribunal) Rules 2008, r 34*).

Appeals from the Tribunal may be made to the Court of Appeal (Court of Session in Scotland) on a point of law only, with the permission of the Tribunal (*Tribunals, Courts and Enforcement Act 2007, s 13*). Only those party to a Tribunal reference may appeal. Permission may be requested at the end of the hearing or in writing within 14 days of notification of the decision (*Tribunal Procedure (Upper Tribunal) Rules 2008, r 44*).

Cost of the Regulator

2.26   For the purposes of meeting the expenditure of the Regulator, regulations under *PSA 1993, s 175* (as amended by *PA 1995, s 165* and *PA 2004, s 174*) make provision for imposing a levy. The levy is payable to the Secretary of State by or on behalf of the administrator of public service schemes or the trustees or managers of occupational or personal pension schemes.

The Regulator can be contacted at The Pensions Regulator, Napier House, Trafalgar Place, Brighton BN1 4DW. Tel: 0845 6000707; e-mail: customersupport@tpr.gov.uk; website: www.thepensionsregulator.gov.uk.

The Pension Protection Fund ('PPF')

Establishment of the PPF

2.27

'The Pensions Act 2004 has established the Pension Protection Fund to protect members of private sector defined benefit schemes whose firms become insolvent with insufficient funds in their pension scheme.

'We will make sure that in future individuals in final salary schemes will never again face the injustice of saving throughout their lives only to have their hard-earned pension slashed just before they retire. The Pension Protection Fund will allow individuals to save with confidence.'

Andrew Smith, the then Secretary of State for Work and Pensions, 12 February 2004.

The aim of the PPF

2.28   The main purpose of the PPF is to ensure that where an employer in relation to a UK-based defined benefit scheme becomes insolvent and its pension scheme is not sufficiently funded, members will still receive the majority of the benefits to which they are entitled. The PPF will, where it has assumed responsibility for the scheme, provide benefits in accordance with the '*pension compensation provisions*' which are:

- where a member has attained normal pension age at the date of insolvency, they will receive 100 per cent of their entitlement;

- for members who have yet to reach normal pension age at the date of insolvency, they will receive 90 per cent of their entitlement subject to an annual cap. From 1 April 2016 the effective cap is £33,678.38 at age 65 (90 per cent of £37,420.42), with a sliding scale for younger members;

- dependants' pensions payable on the future death of the member are limited to 50 per cent of the member's pension; and

- pensions in payment built up from 5 April 1997 increase in line with the Consumer Price Index ('CPI').

Eligibility for the PPF

2.29   Most private sector registered defined benefit or hybrid occupational pension schemes will be eligible for the PPF. Money purchase schemes are not eligible (*PA 2004, s 126*). Any scheme which commenced winding up before 6 April 2005 will not be eligible (although some members of such schemes may be eligible for the Financial Assistance Scheme). Schemes excluded from the PPF include those with fewer than two members, schemes with fewer than 12 members who are all trustees and unanimous decisions are required or there is a statutory independent trustee, and schemes providing death benefits only. The *Pension Protection Fund (Entry Rules) Regulations 2005 (SI 2005/590), reg 2* (as amended) lists those schemes which are not eligible.

An otherwise eligible scheme may be rendered ineligible if the trustees compromise a *s 75* debt without actuarial advice or the consent of the Board (*reg 2(2)*).

When will the PPF get involved?

2.30   In broad terms, the PPF will become involved in a scheme if an insolvency event (as defined in *PA 2004, s 121*) occurs in relation to the employer or, where the employer is a non-corporate organisation such as a trade union or charity, it appears to the trustees or the Regulator that the employer is likely to cease to continue as a going concern (*PA 2004, s 129*).

In relation to this latter category, it should be noted that the legislation regarding PPF eligibility has been amended with effect from 6 April 2016 to cover off a gap in the eligibility criteria that was brought into focus by the long-running Olympic Airlines litigation, which culminated in 2015 with a decision in the Supreme Court (*Olympic Airlines Pension Scheme v Olympic Airlines [2015] UKSC 27*). The amendments aim to address the issue faced by schemes which are nominally eligible to enter the PPF but which find that they are unable to do so as they have an overseas sponsoring employer who does not have an 'establishment' in the UK.

Where a qualifying insolvency event occurs, there then follows an assessment period during which the Board will determine whether the PPF will take responsibility for the scheme. The PPF must take responsibility for the scheme where:

- the value of the assets of the scheme were less than the amount of the *protected liabilities* immediately before the qualifying insolvency event occurs; and

- a 'scheme rescue' has been deemed impossible by the insolvency practitioner.

The protected liabilities are the liabilities for benefits up to the level of PPF compensation, plus scheme liabilities other than for benefits and the estimated winding-up expenses.

During this period of assessment, the scheme is effectively frozen. No new members may be admitted, contributions are suspended (other than those due to be paid before the beginning of the assessment period), no benefits accrue under the scheme in respect of the members and benefits in payment will be reduced to the PPF protection level. In addition, the PPF may also give directions to ensure that the scheme's protected liabilities do not exceed its assets or keep the excess to a minimum.

In addition to the above, during an assessment period, the winding up of a scheme cannot begin, no transfers or transfer payments in respect of member's rights are to be made from the scheme and no other steps may be taken to discharge any liability to the scheme in respect of pensions or other benefits or such other liabilities as may be prescribed. Civil penalties will apply to any trustee or manager who fails to take all reasonable steps to ensure compliance.

In order to assist with its assessment, the PPF must obtain an actuarial valuation of the scheme. This is referred to as a *s 143* valuation. Regulations set out how the assets and protected liabilities are to be determined and the Board has issued guidance to assist actuaries undertaking *s 143* valuations.

If the valuation reveals a deficit between the value of scheme assets and protected liabilities, the PPF will issue a transfer notice to the trustees or the managers and assume responsibility for the scheme. The effect of the Board assuming responsibility for a scheme is that:

- the property, rights and liabilities of the scheme are transferred to the PPF;

- the trustees or managers of the scheme are discharged from their pension obligations;

- the PPF assumes responsibility for securing that compensation is paid in accordance with the compensation provisions; and

- the scheme is to be treated as having been wound up immediately after that time.

If the PPF determines that the valuation does not disclose a deficit, it must refuse responsibility for the scheme and issue a notice to that effect to the Regulator, the trustees/managers and to any insolvency practitioner (a 'determination notice'). The trustees or manager can make an application to the PPF asking them to reconsider their decision. Where the PPF refuses responsibility the trustees will be required to wind up the scheme, unless a 'scheme rescue' has occurred and the scheme has been taken over by another employer or the PPF has given permission for it to be run as a closed scheme (this will be where the assets are not sufficient to actually buy out the protected liabilities).

The PPF is dealt with in more detail in **Chapter 5**.

The Board of the PPF

2.31   The legal embodiment of the PPF is its Board, established under *PA 2004, s 107*. Functions of the Board include paying compensation, calculating annual levies and setting and overseeing the investment strategy of the PPF. Membership of the Board consists of a Chairman (Arnold Wagner OBE is the current Chairman), the Chief Executive of the Board (Alan Rubenstein), and a mix of executive and non-executive members. To ensure independence, the Chairman cannot be appointed from the staff of the Board or be the chairman of the Regulator.

The Board has a Non-Executive Committee, consisting only of non-executive members of the Board. Its role is to keep under review the question of whether the Board's internal financial controls secure the proper conduct of its financial affairs; and it determines the terms and conditions as to remuneration of the Chief Executive and any member of staff who is also to be an executive member of the Board. As part of its functions, the Board must submit an annual report and accounts to the Secretary of State who, in turn, presents them to Parliament.

The PPF can be contacted at:

- PO Box 128, Mowden Hall, Darlington DL1 9DA. Tel. 0845 603 7224; e-mail: members@ppfonline.org.uk (for schemes which have transferred); or

- the Pension Protection Fund, Renaissance, 12 Dingwall Road, Croydon CR0 2NA. Tel. 0345 600 2541; e-mail: information@ppf.gsi.gov.uk (for schemes which have not transferred).

Funding the PPF

2.32   The PPF is funded primarily by the pension protection levy, a charge paid annually by the trustees or managers (or such other persons as may be prescribed in regulations) of eligible pension schemes. It comprises:

- *a risk-based levy* – a charge which takes into account the risk of a scheme's sponsoring employer becoming insolvent and the amount of compensation that the PPF may have to pay in such a situation. This levy must comprise no less than 80% of the total pension protection levy; and

- *a scheme-based levy* – a charge that considers the number of members in an eligible scheme and the extent of that scheme's liabilities as compared against the amount of its protected liabilities. This cannot make up more than 20% of the total pension protection levy.

All eligible schemes, as defined in *PA 2004, s 126* and the *Pension Protection Fund (Entry Rules) Regulations 2005*, must pay the scheme-based element of the pension protection levy. All eligible schemes are liable to be charged the risk-based element of the pension protection levy. The risk-based element can be reduced to zero where the underfunding risk is zero (ie the value of assets equals or exceeds the value of liabilities on the basis determined by the Board).

Before the beginning of each financial year, the Board must determine the factors with which to assess the levies, the timing of the assessments, the rate and when the levies will become payable. In recent years, the Board has engaged in a series of consultations on the levy. The consultations focus on taking into account several long-term factors in individual scheme calculations, including the probability that a scheme employer may become insolvent over a five-year period, and the risk a scheme's investment strategy poses to the PPF.

The levy imposed by the Board is subject to a ceiling set by the Secretary of State before the beginning of each financial year and increased annually in line with the general level of earnings (£981,724,264 for 2016/2017). The 2016/17 cap on the risk-based levy is 0.0075 of the scheme's liabilities and the Board has set a pension protection levy estimate (ie the total which will be collected) for 2016/2017 of £615 million.

Since the 2015/2016 levy year, the Board has worked with Experian to obtain insolvency risk scoring for employers, who are ranked into different employer groups based on the available data for each employer. Each group is associated with a separate 'scorecard' that is used to estimate the probability of employers in that group failing in each of the next 12 months. The monthly scores for each employer are then adjusted to produce an average score which is used to distribute employers between ten levy bands with their own insolvency risk rates (ie the levy rate).

The Board recognises the following types of contingent assets which will be taken into account when considering the underfunding risk:

- guarantees given by associated companies (Type A);
- security over cash, securities or UK real estate (Type B); and
- letters of credit and bank guarantees (Type C).

The Board sets down strict requirements for the form of a contingent asset if it is to be recognised and publishes annual guidance which must be followed.

In the last two years, the PPF has allowed schemes to use asset backed contribution funding structures ('ABCs') as contingent assets for the purpose of reducing their levy rates. The focus in relation to these arrangements is on their value for a scheme in the event of the employer's insolvency, and there is a strict reporting and information procedure that has to be followed if schemes are to use ABCs successfully for PPF levy purposes.

The PPF published its final determination for the 2016/17 levy on 17 December 2015.

In addition to the pension protection levy, there is also an administration levy which will be applied for the purpose of meeting the ongoing costs of the PPF. Schemes pay an amount per scheme member, which varies depending on the size of the scheme.

The PPF has the power to charge interest on late payment of levies or otherwise charge interest in certain circumstances (*PA 2004, s 181A*, as inserted by *PA 2008, Sch 10*).

Information to be provided to the Board

2.33   The Board may issue a notice to persons including the trustees or manager of the scheme, the employer, a professional adviser to the scheme and an insolvency practitioner, amongst others. The notice may require the recipient to produce any document or provide any other information which is relevant to the exercise of the Board's functions in relation to an occupational pension scheme. When such a notice is received, the information must be provided in the form prescribed, at such a place and within timescales specified in the notice.

The Board's powers are such that it can enter premises at any reasonable time and whilst there, make inquiries as necessary, request any person on the premises to produce or secure the production of any relevant document, take copies of such documentation and may even remove them from the premises if it is necessary to prevent their interference.

Where a person (without reasonable excuse) neglects or refuses to provide information, he will be guilty of an offence and is liable on conviction to a fine not exceeding £5,000. If a person intentionally and without reasonable excuse alters, suppresses, conceals or destroys any document which is liable to be produced, a higher fine or a custodial sentence, not exceeding two years, could be imposed. The same penalties would be imposed on someone who knowingly or recklessly provides information which is false or misleading (*PA 2004, Part 2, Chapter 5*).

The Fraud Compensation Fund

2.34   The Board of the PPF manages the Fraud Compensation Fund. It is a fund from which compensation may be paid to occupational pension scheme members where there has been a misappropriation of assets or fraud in a scheme with an insolvent employer. This covers PPF eligible schemes and some schemes that are not covered by the PPF, including defined contributions schemes. Compensation may be payable where:

- the value of the assets of an eligible scheme has been reduced as a consequence of an act or omission which constitutes an offence of dishonesty, including an intention to defraud; and

- a qualifying insolvency event in relation to the employer has occurred and a scheme failure notice has been issued.

The Fraud Compensation Fund is paid for by way of a fraud compensation levy. It is determined by the Board and must be paid by the trustees or managers of a scheme. The Board determines which schemes will be required to pay the levy, calculates the amount of the levy in relation to those schemes and notifies any person liable to pay the levy in respect of the scheme as well as when it becomes payable. The levy is to cover all payments made from the Fraud Compensation Fund to ensure that the Fund's assets are sufficient to cover its liabilities.

The Board determines the amount of any fraud compensation payment to be made in accordance with the *Occupational Pension Schemes (Fraud Compensation Payments and Miscellaneous Amendments) Regulations 2005 (SI 2005/2184)*, as amended.

PPF Ombudsman

2.35   The office of PPF Ombudsman was established with effect from 6 April 2006 by *PA 2004, s 209*. The PPF Ombudsman is Anthony Arter, who is also the current Pensions Ombudsman. 'Reviewable matters' may be referred to the PPF Ombudsman following a reconsideration by the Board under *PA 2004, s 207*. 'Reviewable matters' include the issuing of a determination notice under *PA 2004, s 123*. Any person who is sent, or is required to be sent, a notice of the reconsideration decision is entitled to refer the matter to the PPF Ombudsman (*Pension Protection Fund (Reference of Reviewable Matters to the PPF Ombudsman) Regulations 2005 (SI 2005/2024), reg 2*). The referral must be made within 28 days from the date on which that person was sent a notice of the reconsideration decision.

Following the 2010 Cabinet Office Review of Public Bodies, the *Public Bodies Act 2011* provided for the merger of the PPF Ombudsman and the Pensions Ombudsman. The timing of the actual merger has yet to be announced but as at April 2016 had still not taken place.

The PPF Ombudsman's Office can be contacted at the Office of the Pension Protection Fund Ombudsman, 11 Belgrave Road, London SW1V 1RB. Tel: 020 7630 2200; e-mail: enquiries@pensions-ombusman.org.uk; website: www.ppfo.org.uk.

Financial Assistance Scheme

2.36   The Financial Assistance Scheme ('FAS') was introduced at a late stage of the *Pensions Bill 2004* as a result of sustained lobbying by and on behalf of members of defined benefit pension schemes who had lost some or all of their benefits when their schemes wound up in deficit but would not be able to qualify for the PPF (because the winding up had commenced before 6 April 2005). The provisions of *PA 2004, s 286* allowed for the establishment of the FAS but provided very little detail. The *Financial Assistance Scheme Regulations 2005 (SI 2005/1986)* came into force for most purposes on 1 September 2005. The Regulations set out which members of which schemes would qualify for assistance. Initially, schemes which qualified for the FAS included most occupational pension schemes (other than money purchase or public sector schemes) which commenced winding up between 1 January 1997 and 5 April 2005 and where the employer had become insolvent by a specified date. The initial coverage of FAS was very narrow (limited to those members at or very near to retirement when their schemes wound up). Since the original Regulations, there have been substantial amendments both to the level of assistance payable and the organisation and structure of FAS. The improvement to the level of assistance was partly in response to political pressure and the decision of the CJEU in *Robins and Others v Secretary of State for Work and Pensions (C-278/05)* which found that the UK Government had failed to properly protect pensions on the insolvency of an employer.

PA 2007, s 18 included amendments to *PA 2004, s 286* requiring the Secretary of State to make provision for all qualifying members to receive benefits totalling 80 per cent of their expected scheme pension subject to a cap of £26,000 and for initial payments of up to 80 per cent to be made during the winding up of a scheme. This benefit level has been modified by the *Financial Assistance Scheme (Miscellaneous Amendments) Regulations 2007 (SI 2007/3581)* which came into force on 19 December 2007, *PA 2008* and the *Financial Assistance Scheme (Miscellaneous Provisions) Regulations 2009 (SI 2009/1851)*.

The key provisions include:

- All members of qualifying pension schemes will receive 90 per cent of their accrued pension entitlement at the date their scheme began to wind up, subject to a compensation cap of £33,890 (for people whose entitlement begins between 1 April 2016 and 31 March 2017). The cap will be revalued on an annual basis according to the Consumer Prices Index ('CPI').

- Compensation payments deriving from service after 1997 will be index-linked, subject to an increase of 2.5 per cent per year capped at CPI.

- Compensation will be payable from each scheme's normal retirement age (subject to a minimum age of 60) or from 14 May 2004, whichever is later.

- Ill-health benefits are payable to those below normal retirement age.

- Schemes that began winding up between 1 January 1997 and 5 April 2005, where the employer is still trading but a compromise agreement is in place and there is evidence that enforcing the debt against the employer would have forced the employer into insolvency are included.

- The time period by which an employer must have an insolvency event in order for its scheme to be eligible for FAS assistance is extended indefinitely, provided that the scheme manager is of the opinion that the insolvency event of the employer and the winding-up of the scheme were linked.

PA 2008, s 125(1) inserted *s 286A* into the *PA 2004*, with effect from 26 June 2008. This provides that the trustees of any qualifying pension scheme must not purchase or agree to purchase annuities without the permission of the FAS manager. On 10 July 2009 the Board of the PPF became the manager of the FAS.

From 1 April 2010, the *Financial Assistance Scheme (Miscellaneous Amendments) Regulations 2010 (SI 2010/1149)* have enabled the assets remaining in FAS qualifying schemes to be transferred to the PPF (to be held separately to main PPF assets). This means that all benefit payments will be made by FAS rather than it providing payments to top up the benefits paid by the pension scheme.

Plans to consolidate and simplify the existing legislative and regulatory structure of FAS have been in development since 2011, when the DWP began a consultation in this regard. However, as yet the consolidation has not taken place. The explanatory memorandum to a new set of regulations which widened the eligibility criteria for FAS with effect from 28 March 2014, the *Financial Assistance Scheme (Qualifying Pension Scheme Amendment) Regulations 2014,* suggests that the delay has been the result of the task providing to be 'a more complex operation that previously thought', although it also notes a continued intention to publish consolidating regulations in the future.

The *Financial Assistance Scheme (Internal Review) Regulations 2005 (SI 2005/1994)* allow for beneficiaries and potential beneficiaries under a scheme, or their representative, to apply for a review of a decision in relation to the FAS. The *Financial Assistance Scheme (Appeals) Regulations 2005 (SI 2005/3273)* allow for the appeal to the PPF Ombudsman of a decision which had been subject to internal review (see **2.35** above).

In early 2016, the PPF announced that the FAS would stop accepting new notifications from 1 September 2016. The announcement called for schemes which believe they might be eligible for assistance from the FAS to get in contact with them as soon as possible before this deadline.

FAS can be contacted at:

- PO Box 128, Mowden Hall, Darlington DL1 9DA. Tel. 0845 603 7224; e-mail: members@ppfonline.org.uk (for schemes which have transferred); or

- the Pension Protection Fund, Renaissance, 12 Dingwall Road, Croydon CR0 2NA. Tel. 0345 600 2541; e-mail: information@ppf.gsi.gov.uk (for schemes which have not transferred).

FAS is dealt with in more detail in **Chapter 5**.

NEST Corporation

2.37   The Pensions Commission, in its 2005 report to the Government, called for fairer and wider pension provision. The report suggested that automatic enrolment into a workplace pension scheme with employer contributions should form the bedrock of any Government initiative to tackle the issue of under-saving for retirement.

It was with this in mind that the *Pensions Act 2007 (PA 2007)* established the Personal Accounts Delivery Authority ('PADA'), which was originally given responsibility for designing and introducing the infrastructure for the National Employment Savings Trust (or 'NEST'). The new scheme is a trust-based occupational defined contribution scheme, operational since July 2012. It is regulated by HMRC and the Pensions Regulator.

Employers will need to choose whether to enrol most of their employees into NEST or into an alternative qualifying scheme. Under either option, employers must make contributions on an employee's behalf unless the employee elects to opt out. Further details about the workings of the automatic enrolment regime can be found in **Chapter 14**.

PADA was wound up on 5 July 2010 and replaced by NEST Corporation as the trustee body which has assumed responsibility for NEST. NEST Corporation is a non-departmental public body that operates at arm's length from the Government but remains accountable to Parliament through the Department for Work and Pensions. NEST Corporation has a chairman and up to 14 trustee members responsible for setting the strategic direction and objectives for NEST. NEST Corporation's trustee members are selected currently by the Secretary of State based on their experience, skills and knowledge of the pensions industry.

The Regulator has responsibility for enforcement of, and compliance with, the employer duties set out in *PA 2008* regarding automatic enrolment. It has the power to issue compliance notices (where the requirements are breached) and unpaid contribution notices. Where the employer continues to fail to comply with either of these notices, the Regulator is able to take further action (including issuing a fixed penalty notice imposing a fine of up to £50,000). A wilful failure to comply with employer duties is a criminal offence punishable by a fine or a two-year prison sentence.

NEST Corporation can be contacted at NEST Corporation, Riverside House, Southwark Bridge Road, London SE1 9HA. Tel: 0300 020 0393; e-mail: enquiries@nestcorporation.org.uk; website: www.nestpensions.org.uk.

The Pensions Advisory Service

2.38   The Pensions Advisory Service ('TPAS') (formerly 'OPAS') is an independent, grant-aided, non-profit making company limited by guarantee with a network of local volunteer advisers, who are experienced pensions professionals. The aim of TPAS is to provide free assistance to members of the public with difficulties which they have failed to resolve with the trustees, administrators or pension provider of their pension scheme. The TPAS service is available to anyone who believes he has pension rights. This includes active members of pension schemes (including company, personal and stakeholder arrangements), pensioners, those with deferred pensions from previous employment, and dependants. TPAS can be contacted directly.

TPAS's remit is to explain pension scheme benefits to members and liaise directly with trustees or administrators to provide further information to members or to assist a member in obtaining his correct legal entitlement from a pension scheme.

If TPAS is unable to resolve the problem but believes that the complaint is valid, it may assist a member in making a formal complaint to the appropriate Ombudsman (the Pensions Ombudsman or the Financial Ombudsman Service). TPAS cannot:

(*a*)   initiate legal action on a member's behalf;

(*b*)   give financial advice;

(*c*)   act as a lobbying force for any improvement in pension scheme benefits;

(*d*)   offer advice on State pension benefits; or

(*e*)   assist if legal proceedings have been initiated or if the Pensions Ombudsman (see **2.39** below) has already investigated a complaint.

TPAS has been named by the Government as one of its delivery partners for the Guidance Guarantee (a requirement from April 2015 that each individual will be entitled to free guidance on access to their DC pension savings in the lead up to retirement). This is provided under the Pension Wise service. This follows on from the changes announced in the 2014 Budget which are dealt with in more detail in **Chapter 17**.

TPAS can be contacted at The Pensions Advisory Service, 11 Belgrave Road, London SW1V 1RB. National telephone helpline: 0300 123 1047; e-mail: through an online form available on the organisation's website, www. pensionsadvisoryservice.org.uk.

The Pensions Ombudsman

The role of the Pensions Ombudsman

2.39   The Pensions Ombudsman's office was established on 1 October 1990. The Ombudsman is appointed by the Secretary of State under *PSA 1993, s 145* which also sets out his role. Anthony Arter is the current Ombudsman.

Under *PA 1995* the Ombudsman has power to appoint his own staff (with the approval of the Secretary of State for Work and Pensions) and has taken advantage of this by seeking to appoint professional staff from the pensions industry and legally qualified pensions experts. The Ombudsman's budget is paid for out of the levy imposed on all occupational pension schemes.

The role of the Pensions Ombudsman is to investigate and decide complaints and disputes about the way that pension schemes are run. He is completely independent and acts as an impartial adjudicator.

PA 2004, s 274 inserted *s 145A* into *PSA 1993* which makes provision for the appointment of a Deputy Pensions Ombudsman to be appointed by the Secretary of State. Karen Johnston is the current Deputy Pensions Ombudsman, appointed on 1 July 2015.

Jurisdiction

2.40   The complaints and disputes which the Ombudsman may investigate are described in *PSA 1993, s 146* (as amended by the *Child Support, Pensions and Social Security Act 2000*) and are summarised in the following table:

Type of scheme	Who may complain or refer a dispute to the Ombudsman	Parties against whom a complaint may be made or a dispute may be referred to the Ombudsman	Nature of complaint or dispute
Complaints of maladministration			
Occupational or personal	By or on behalf of any actual or potential beneficiary.	Trustees, managers, employers and/or administrators.	Complaint of injustice in consequence of maladministration.
Occupational	By or on behalf of any trustee or, manager of a scheme.	Trustees, employers.	Complaint of maladministration.

Type of scheme	Who may complain or refer a dispute to the Ombudsman	Parties against whom a complaint may be made or a dispute may be referred to the Ombudsman	Nature of complaint or dispute
Occupational	An employer in relation to a scheme.	Trustees or managers of that scheme.	Complaint of maladministration.
Occupational	By or on behalf of any trustee or manager of a scheme.	Trustees or managers of another scheme.	Complaint of maladministration.
Trust scheme	By or on behalf of an independent trustee.	Trustees or former trustees who are/were not independent trustees of that scheme.	Complaint of maladministration.
Disputes of fact or law			
Occupational or personal	By any actual or potential beneficiary.	Trustees, managers and/or employers.	Dispute of fact or law.
Occupational	By or on behalf of any trustee or manager of a scheme.	Trustees, managers or employers of that scheme. (Note that trustees/managers cannot refer disputes with managers; and employers cannot refer disputes with other employers.)	Dispute of fact or law.
Occupational	An employer in relation to a scheme.	Trustees or managers of that scheme.	Dispute of fact or law.
Occupational	By or on behalf of any party to the dispute.	Trustees or managers of another scheme.	Dispute of fact or law in relation to the other scheme.
Complaints or disputes			
Occupational	By or on behalf of at least half the trustees of the scheme.	Different trustees of the same scheme.	Dispute of fact or law or maladministration.

86

Type of scheme	Who may complain or refer a dispute to the Ombudsman	Parties against whom a complaint may be made or a dispute may be referred to the Ombudsman	Nature of complaint or dispute
Occupational subject to insolvency procedures	By or on behalf of the independent trustee who is a party to the dispute.	Trustees or former trustees of the scheme who are not independent.	Any dispute (in relation to a time when PA 1995, s 22 applies).
Occupational	By or on behalf of the sole trustee.		Any question relating to the carrying out of functions of that trustee.

The word 'maladministration' is not defined in the legislation, although the Pensions Ombudsman describes it as including bias, neglect, inattention, delay, incompetence and arbitrariness. The complaint must include behaviour which constitutes maladministration which in turn has led to injustice. Again, this is not defined but is described by the Pensions Ombudsman as not only including a financial loss, but incorporating distress, delay or inconvenience. In November 2005 the Pensions Ombudsman issued a guide 'How to Avoid the Pensions Ombudsman'. It contains guidance for those running pension schemes, based on actual cases which have been determined by the Pensions Ombudsman, on how they might operate schemes and manage disputes in order to avoid complaints being made. It is available on www.pensions-ombudsman.org.uk.

The *Personal and Occupational Pension Schemes (Pensions Ombudsman) Regulations 1996 (SI 1996/2475)* ('the *Ombudsman Regulations*'), introduced under *PA 1995*, provide that the Ombudsman may not investigate or determine a complaint unless the internal dispute resolution procedure has first been followed (*Ombudsman Regulations, reg 3*). (The internal dispute resolution procedure is discussed in **Chapter 3**.) The only exception to this is where a complaint has been referred to the internal dispute procedure and the Ombudsman is satisfied that there is no prospect of a decision being reached within a reasonable period (*Ombudsman Regulations, reg 3(2)*).

Ombudsman Regulations, reg 5 covers the time limits for referring a dispute to the Ombudsman's office. The Ombudsman is not permitted to investigate a complaint if it is received by him more than three years after the date on which the act or omission complained of occurred, or three years after the date on which the complainant knew or ought to have known of its occurrence. However, this period can be extended where the Ombudsman believes it was reasonable for a complaint not to be made before the end of this period, in which case the time limit may be extended to such further period as he considers reasonable (*Ombudsman Regulations, reg 5(3)*).

Where the Pensions Ombudsman is asked to determine a dispute of law, he cannot take a more liberal approach than a court of law could take, for example, where the Limitation Act 1980 would time bar the complaint (*Arjo Wiggins Limited v Ralph [2009] EWHC 3198 (Ch)*). However, where the Ombudsman is asked to determine on pure maladministration complaints which are not bound by statutory time limits, the Ombudsman has greater freedom to determine applicable timescales for bringing the complaint as a court of law is unable to consider such issues.

Investigating a complaint

2.41   The procedure which the Ombudsman follows during his investigations is set out in the *Personal and Occupational Pension Schemes (Pensions Ombudsman) (Procedure) Rules 1995 (SI 1995/1053)* ('the *Procedure Rules*' (as amended)); it is summarised in the booklet accompanying the complaint form. Upon receipt of the complaint form a caseworker at the Ombudsman's office will make an initial review of the case to decide whether it should be accepted for formal investigation. Then the complaint form and accompanying papers, if any, are copied to the respondent (ie the employer, trustees, managers or administrators) and any other person against whom allegations are made in order to allow them an opportunity to respond in writing to the allegations (*Procedure Rules, r 5(2)*).

The Ombudsman has powers to demand papers from parties (*PSA 1993, Part X, s 150(1)*) who may hold them and can also hold oral hearings if he considers this necessary (although to date, these have been rare (*Procedure Rules, r 10(1)*). Both the complainant and the respondent have an opportunity, with leave of the Ombudsman, to submit a supplementary statement and/or amend details of their original complaint/response (*Procedure Rules, rr 3 and 7*).

In conducting the investigation, the Ombudsman must comply with the statutory rules to ensure fairness and must also comply with the principles of natural justice (*Duffield v Pensions Ombudsman [1995] PLR 285*). In particular, he must:

(*a*)   make clear to the respondent the specific allegation(s) to be investigated;

(*b*)   express the substance of the allegation(s) in plain and simple language; and

(*c*)   disclose to the respondent all potentially relevant information obtained by him (particularly all evidence and representations made by the complainant).

The Court of Appeal's 1999 decision in *Edge v Pensions Ombudsman [1999] PLR 215* emphasised the need for the Ombudsman to observe the principles of natural justice. In particular, it was decided that he could not consider complaints which could only be remedied by steps which would adversely affect someone who was not a party to the investigation. Turning this the other way, in the case of *Marsh Mercer Pension Scheme v Pensions Ombudsman [2001] 16 PBLR (28)* (the *Williamson Case*) heard in the High Court, the Ombudsman's decision that a pension scheme should equalise all GMPs between men and women was set aside. Principally, it was held that the Pension Ombudsman had affected all members of the scheme, not only the complainant. Accordingly, he should have either declined jurisdiction or made a decision which would only affect the complainant.

After receiving a copy of the complaint the respondent has 21 days within which to produce a written reply (*Procedure Rules, r 6(3)*), although time extensions can be requested (*Procedure Rules, r 16(1)*). The reply can include a reference to any other person (such as a manager or administrator of the scheme) who, in his opinion, has a direct interest in the subject matter of the complaint (*Procedure Rules, r 6(2)*). It is not, however, possible for the respondent to join a third party as a second respondent. The Ombudsman will then issue a written provisional determination of his decision, which will be sent out to both the respondent and the complainant in draft form for their comments. At this stage, changes to the determination can still be made.

Although not stated in the *Procedure Rules*, in practice the Ombudsman operates a 'fast-track' procedure for those complaints which he thinks have no merit. In these instances, the investigator will inform the complainant who will then have 14 days in which to make a further submission which would make the Ombudsman change his mind. Equally, the Ombudsman can fast track to success those complaints where he considers the complainant to have a winning case.

After investigating the complaint, and examining the comments of both parties, the Ombudsman will issue a final written determination. This determination will direct any person responsible for the management of the scheme concerned 'to take or refrain from taking' such action as the Ombudsman considers appropriate (*PSA 1993, Part X, s 151(2)*). It is generally accepted that the Pensions Ombudsman can award compensation for distress and inconvenience to a complainant, although this is not beyond doubt. In *Westminster City Council v Haywood [1996] PLR 161* the court considered that the Ombudsman's powers under *s 151(2)* included the payment of reasonable compensation for distress and inconvenience. However, the court ruled in *City and County of Swansea v Johnson [1999] PLR 187* that such compensation must be modest, not exceeding £1,000 other than in exceptional circumstances. The Ombudsman released a guidance factsheet on this topic in June 2015 setting out the kinds of redress that are available for 'non-financial injustice' and how the Ombudsman will assess this.

The Ombudsman's determination is final and binding on the parties, subject only to an appeal to the High Court on a point of law (with permission of the High Court) under the High Court's general jurisdiction to hear appeals from any court, tribunal or person. This is referred to in *Civil Procedure Rules 1998, Part 52*. Determinations can be enforced through the county court. Costs cannot be awarded against a complainant, even if the complaint is not upheld.

The Pensions Ombudsman website can be found at www.pensions-ombudsman.org.uk, and determinations issued from 1 April 2001 (and frequently requested determinations issued before 1 April 2000) are available for review. The Pensions Ombudsman can be contacted at the Office of the Pensions Ombudsman, 11 Belgrave Road, London SW1V 1RB. Tel: 020 7630 2200; e-mail: enquiries@pensions-ombudsman.org.uk.

Other bodies

Pensions Management Institute (PMI)

2.42 The PMI was established in 1976 to promote professionalism amongst those working in the field of pensions. It is an independent non-political organisation which establishes, maintains and improves professional standards in every aspect of pension scheme management and consultancy. There are a number of different grades of membership including student membership, which is the introductory level for those wishing to study the Institute's examinations. Other grades include Associate Member (someone who has passed the Institute's examinations and has three years' experience in pensions management or administration) and Fellowship (an individual who has five years' experience as an Associate of the PMI, five years continuous CPD recorded and has 'contributed and achieved in the wider pensions industry'). The PMI is directed by a Council of 16 elected fellows, who are actively involved in pension schemes.

The PMI also offers examinations for trustees including an Award in Pensions Trusteeship.

The PMI can be contacted at PMI House, 4–10 Artillery Lane, London E1 7LS. Tel: 020 7247 1452; fax: 020 7375 0603; e-mail: enquiries@pension-pmi.org.uk; website: www.pensions-pmi.org.uk.

The Pensions and Lifetime Savings Association (PLSA)

2.43 The PLSA (previously the National Association of Pension Funds or NAPF) provides representation and other services for those involved in designing, operating, advising and investing in all aspects of pensions and other retirement provision. Among its members are large and small companies, local authority and public sector bodies. PLSA members also include corporate trustees and other organisations providing professional advice to schemes. The PLSA also allows individual trustees, trustee directors and chairmen of trustee boards of PLSA member funds to join. The PLSA's principle aim is to encourage pension provision by employers by representing the interests of members to the UK Government, Europe, regulators and other professional bodies (including the media). It seeks to achieve this by:

(*a*)   influencing public opinion;

(*b*)   consulting Government bodies;

(*c*)   collecting and disseminating information on best practice and trends involving schemes;

(*d*)   publishing guidelines and information; and

(*e*)   providing education in the form of seminars and conferences.

The PLSA can be contacted at the Pensions and Lifetime Savings Association, Cheapside House, 138 Cheapside, London EC2V 6AE. Tel: 020 7601 1700; fax: 020 7601 1799; e-mail: through an online form on the organisation's website, www.plsa.co.uk.

Information Commissioner

2.44   Although not a pensions body as such, the Information Commissioner's Office regulates the holding, use and protection of personal information relating to living individuals by data controllers. The Information Commissioner enforces and oversees the *Data Protection Act 1998* and the *Freedom of Information Act 2000*. The Commissioner is a UK independent supervisory authority.

The Information Commissioner maintains a public register of data controllers. Each register entry contains the name and address of the data controller and a general description of the processing of personal data by a data controller. The public register is updated weekly, but new notifications, renewal and amendments may take several weeks to appear during busy periods. The Information Commissioner can, in certain circumstances, serve an information notice and assess compliance and, where there has been a breach, serve an enforcement notice ordering compliance or (since April 2010) impose a monetary penalty of up to £500,000. The impact of the data protection legislation and in particular, the *Data Protection Act 1998* is considered further in **Chapter 3**.

The Information Commissioner's Office can be contacted at Wycliffe House, Water Lane, Wilmslow, Cheshire SK9 5AF. ICO Helpline: 0303 123 1113 or 01625 545 745; fax: 01625 524 510; website: www.ico.org.uk.

The Department for Work and Pensions

2.45   The Department for Work and Pensions (DWP) is responsible for employment, equality, benefits, pensions and child support.

The DWP's priorities include (amongst others) delivering the Government's pension reform agenda. As of July 2016 (and the Cabinet reshuffle under the new Prime Minister Theresa May), Damian Green MP was appointed Secretary of State for Work and Pensions and he has overall responsibility for all work and pension matters. Baroness Ros Altmann CBE held the position of Minister for Pensions until July 2016, but is expected to be replaced in the role in due course.

To contact the DWP or any minister write to Caxton House, Tothill Street, London SW1H 9NA or via their website: www.gov.uk/dwp.

Chapter 3

Trustees

Introduction

3.1   The role of a pension scheme trustee is to apply the scheme assets for the benefit of scheme members and other beneficiaries in accordance with the scheme's trust documents, relevant legislation and general trust law.

Where trustees fail to comply with their duties, they may be held personally liable for any loss which is suffered by the fund as a result. Therefore trustees have a personal interest in ensuring that they are operating their scheme in accordance with the relevant legal requirements. It is common for a pension scheme's governing documentation to contain various protections for the trustees, including exoneration provisions, indemnities and the power to take out insurance.

Who can be a trustee?

3.2   Anyone who is legally capable of holding property can act as a trustee. In effect, this means that anyone aged 18 or over, whether based in the UK or overseas, can be appointed as a trustee. There are, however, circumstances where an individual may be disqualified. Under *PA 1995, s 29*, a person is disqualified from acting as a trustee if, for example:

(*a*)   he is or has been convicted of an offence involving dishonesty or deception;

(*b*)   he is an undischarged bankrupt;

(*c*)   he has made an arrangement with his creditors and has not been discharged in respect of it;

(*d*)   he is disqualified as a company director;

(*e*)   a moratorium period under a debt relief order applies in relation to him or he is the subject of a debt relief restrictions order; or

(*f*)   in the case of a trustee which is a company, any director of the company is disqualified for any of the reasons set out in *s 29*;

Further, the Regulator may prohibit any person from being a pension scheme trustee if it is satisfied that he is not a fit and proper person (*PA 1995, s 3*). In June 2013, the Regulator issued a statement setting out how it will exercise its powers in relation to trustee prohibition. The statement contains a non-exhaustive list of the criteria it will take into account when considering whether someone is a 'fit and proper person', including:

(*a*) any attempt to deceive;

(*b*) any misuse of trust funds;

(*c*) any breaches of trust or pensions law, particularly if these are significant, persistent, deliberate or contrary to legal advice received;

(*d*) if a trustee's professional charges constitute a breach of trust or demonstrate a lack of internal controls;

(*e*) criminal convictions (other than those under section 29 of the Pensions Act 1995) so far as these are not spent under the Rehabilitation of Offenders Act 1974. These convictions are not limited to those involving dishonesty or deception and could involve convictions for money laundering, violence or substance abuse.

The Regulator also has the power to suspend a person from acting as a trustee (*PA 1995, s 4*). Anyone who tries to act as a trustee while prohibited or suspended from doing so is liable to a fine and/or imprisonment (*PA 1995, s 6*).

A trustee, and any person connected or associated with him, is not allowed to be the actuary or auditor for the scheme of which he is trustee, but this does not prevent another person in the same firm of actuaries from being the scheme actuary (*PA 1995, s 27* and *Scheme Administration Regulations (SI 1996/1715), reg 7*).

Type of trustee

Individual trustees and corporate trustees

3.3 A trustee will either be an individual, acting in a personal capacity, or a corporate body such as a limited company (a 'corporate trustee'). A company will often be specifically formed to act as a trustee, but any company may act as a trustee unless restricted from doing so by its constitution. Although it is the company itself which is the trustee, in practical terms the directors will take all the relevant trustee decisions. Whilst the exposure to liability of a director of a corporate trustee is reduced (as compared with the position of an individual trustee) because of the 'corporate veil', the director concerned may not escape all liability to the beneficiaries. For further discussion of this topic, see **3.43** onwards.

A director (or other officer) of a trustee company is also subject to the same civil penalties as individual trustees under *PA 1995* where it can be shown that a breach took place with his consent or connivance or was attributable to neglect on his part (*PA 1995, s 10(5)*).

Trust corporations

3.4   A trust corporation is either the Public Trustee, or a corporation:

(*a*)   appointed by the court to be a trustee; or

(*b*)   entitled by rules made under the *Public Trustee Act 1906* to act as a custodian trustee (a special type of trustee with a role limited to holding trust assets) (*TA 1925, s 68*).

The main advantage of a trust corporation over individual trustees or a trustee company is that a trust corporation can give a valid receipt for the proceeds of a sale of land on its own. Otherwise, two trustees are needed to give a valid receipt (*TA 1925, s 14*). In practice this does not pose a problem for most sole corporate trustees, as they usually hold land in the name of a nominee.

Independent trustees

Non-statutory appointments

3.5   Although there is no statutory requirement to appoint one, some schemes may have a trustee who is independent of the employer (whether as the sole trustee or a director of the trustee company or one of the individual trustees). The reason may be to manage conflicts of interest within the trustee body and/or between the employer and the trustees, or to have a professional independent trustee with particular skills or experience.

Statutory appointments

3.6   Where an insolvency practitioner or official receiver has been appointed in relation to the scheme employer, or during a PPF assessment period, an independent trustee may be appointed by the Regulator: *PA 1995, ss 22–26* (as amended by *PA 2004* with effect from 6 April 2005) and the *Occupational Pension Schemes (Independent Trustee) Regulations 2005 (SI 2005/703)* (the '*Independent Trustee Regulations 2005*').

While there is an independent trustee of the scheme appointed under *PA 1995, s 23*, only the independent trustee may exercise any discretionary power vested in the trustees of the scheme and any discretionary power which the scheme confers on the employer as trustee of the power.

3.6 *Trustees*

The Regulator must appoint independent trustees only from the register of eligible trustees which it maintains. To be eligible, a person must satisfy various conditions set out in the *Independent Trustee Regulations 2005, reg 3*, including not being subject to a prohibition order or suspension order or being disqualified from being a trustee. The Regulator must be satisfied that the applicant has sufficient relevant experience of occupational pension schemes, is a fit and proper person to act as a trustee of an occupational pension scheme, operates sound administrative and accounting procedures and has adequate indemnity insurance cover. Further, the applicant must have premises in the UK from which he conducts his business as a trustee and he must disclose the address to the Regulator. The applicant must agree to have his fees and costs scrutinised by an independent adjudicator, must agree to the Regulator disclosing his name, address and areas of trustee work on the version of the trustee register which is to be publicly available, must comply with the reasonable requests of the Regulator to provide it with information, and must inform the Regulator as soon as is reasonably practicable if he becomes disqualified under *PA 1995, s 29*.

The *Independent Trustee Regulations 2005* also include provisions on refusal by the Regulator to register an applicant in the trustee register and on removal from the trustee register.

PA 1995, s 25 provides that an order appointing an independent trustee may make provision for its fees and expenses to be paid by the employer or out of the scheme's resources or by a combination of both. Where an appointed trustee's fees are to be met out of a scheme's resources, those fees will take priority over all other claims to be met.

Where a trustee has been appointed by the Regulator under *PA 1995, s 7(1) or (3)* (to replace a prohibited or disqualified trustee or because the Regulator considers it reasonable to appoint a trustee) or under *PA 1995, s 22*, it is the responsibility of that appointed trustee to supply in writing its name and address to every member (excluding deferred members whose address is not known to the trustees) or relevant trade union within a reasonable period following his appointment.

The appointed trustee must also provide on request:

(*a*)   the scale of fees that will be chargeable by him and payable by the scheme; and

(*b*)   details of the amounts he has charged to the scheme in the past 12 months (*Independent Trustee Regulations 2005, reg 13*).

PA 1995, s 25 provides that, where an appointed independent trustee ceases to be independent, he must, as soon as reasonably practical, notify the Regulator in writing and step down (or, if he is the only trustee, be replaced as trustee). Any failure to give such notice will result in civil penalties under *PA 1995, s 10*.

Member-nominated trustees

3.7 The statutory requirements for the appointment of member-nominated trustees and directors are to be found in *PA 2004, ss 241–243*. This is dealt with in **3.29** onwards.

Constructive trustees

3.8 In certain circumstances, a person (although not formally appointed as such) may find that he is treated in law as being a trustee of the assets of a scheme. This will usually happen because the person has, by his conduct, assumed trustee-like responsibilities. For example, where a person has never validly been appointed as a trustee but has nevertheless acted as one, he could at law be regarded as a constructive trustee.

Employment protection for trustees under the Employment Rights Act 1996

3.9 The *Employment Rights Act 1996 (ERA 1996)* offers protection for employees who are trustees of their employer's occupational pension scheme, whether as individuals or directors of a trustee company (see also **Chapter 7**). In particular *ERA 1996*:

(*a*) gives an employee the right not to be subjected to any detriment by any act, or any deliberate failure to act, done by his employer on the ground that, being a trustee of an occupational pension scheme which relates to his employment, the employee performed (or proposed to perform) any functions as a trustee (*ERA 1996, s 46*).

(*b*) entitles an employee trustee to reasonable time off during working hours to perform his trustee duties or undergo trustee training (*ERA 1996, s 58*);

(*c*) entitles an employee trustee to payment for that time taken off (ERA 1996, s 59);

(*d*) permits an employee trustee to complain to an employment tribunal if he has suffered any detriment under (*a*) above (*ERA 1996, s 48*) or the employer has failed to comply with (*b*) or (*c*) above (*ERA 1996, s 60*) (generally, such a complaint must be made within three months); and

(*e*) provides that an employee trustee is to be regarded as unfairly dismissed if the reason, or the principal reason, for the dismissal is that he performed (or proposed to perform) any functions as a trustee (*ERA 1996, s 102*).

Appointment, removal and discharge of trustees

3.10   Generally, a scheme's documentation will contain a specific provision setting out the power to appoint and remove trustees, such power most frequently being vested in the principal employer. An employer's power to remove or appoint trustees is generally (although not universally) regarded as a fiduciary power and so must be exercised in the interests of the scheme's beneficiaries. There are, in addition, statutory provisions governing the appointment and removal of trustees contained in *TA 1925* and, in relation to member-nominated trustees, in *PA 2004* (see **3.29** to **3.38**). The Regulator must be informed of changes of individual trustees and corporate trustees (but not changes to the directors of a trustee company) as soon as reasonably practicable after the change taking place (*PA 2004, s 62(4)*). In the majority of schemes, the power of appointment should be sufficiently widely drawn that reliance need not be placed on *TA 1925*.

TA 1925, s 36 deals with the power of appointing new or additional trustees where a trustee:

(a)   is dead;

(b)   remains out of the UK for more than 12 months;

(c)   desires to be discharged;

(d)   refuses or is unfit to act;

(e)   is incapable of acting; or

(f)   is an infant.

In such a situation, the power of appointment is exercisable by the person specified in the governing documentation as having the power of appointment. If there is no-one in whom such a power is vested (eg because the employer has been liquidated) or no-one who is able and willing to act, then the surviving or continuing trustee or trustees or the personal representatives of the last surviving or continuing trustee may make the appointment. The court also has power to appoint trustees, either in addition to or in substitution for any existing trustees, where it is otherwise difficult or impracticable to do so (*TA 1925, s 41*).

TA 1925, s 39 allows the retirement of an individual trustee without a new appointment being made, provided that, after the trustee's retirement, there remains either a trust corporation (see **3.4**) or at least two individual trustees. In such circumstances, the retiring trustee is discharged from the trust, provided that the retiring trustee, the remaining trustees and the person with power of appointment execute a deed in which the retiring trustee declares that he is desirous of being discharged from the trust.

Whenever there is a change in the trustees of a pension scheme, it is important to ensure that the ownership of the assets of the pension fund is transferred accordingly. Most trust assets vest automatically in the new and continuing trustees if the appointment is by way of a deed (*TA 1925, s 40*), with certain exceptions, including land and stocks and shares. A change of sole corporate trustee may also require agreements to be novated or assigned.

In addition to the powers to disqualify, prohibit and suspend trustees referred to in **3.2**, the Regulator also has power to appoint a trustee or trustees to a scheme in circumstances other than those set out in **3.6** (*PA 1995, s 7*). Such an appointment may be made following the prohibition or disqualification of a former trustee or where the Regulator is satisfied that it is reasonable to make an appointment:

(*a*)   to secure that the trustees as a whole have, or exercise, the necessary knowledge and skill for the proper administration of the scheme;

(*b*)   to secure that the number of trustees is sufficient for the proper administration of the scheme;

(*c*)   to secure the proper use or application of the assets of the scheme; or

(*d*)   otherwise to protect the interests of the generality of the scheme members.

The employer, existing trustees and scheme members can all apply to the Regulator for the appointment of a trustee under grounds (*a*) or (*c*) above.

When making an order, the Regulator may also determine the appropriate number of trustees for the proper administration of the scheme; require a trustee appointed by it to be paid fees and expenses by the employer, out of the scheme's resources, or a combination of both; and provide for the removal or replacement of such a trustee (*PA 1995, ss 7(5)* and *8(1)*). Finally, in most cases, unlike a statutory independent trustee, a trustee appointed by the Regulator under *s 7* has the same powers and duties as the other trustees of the scheme, unless the order appointing the trustee restricts those powers and duties or provides that those powers and duties are to be exercised by that trustee to the exclusion of the other trustees (*PA 1995, s 8(3), (4)*).

The Regulator's actions in the *Telent* case are an interesting example of the use of these powers. In October 2007 the Regulator used its special procedure to appoint three independent trustees to the GEC 1972 Plan under *s 7*, as it was satisfied that it was 'necessary to do so in order to ... secure the proper use or application of the assets of the scheme'. That decision was subsequently confirmed by the Determinations Panel (see *[2008] 05 PBLR*).

In brief, the facts were that, when Pension Corporation made a bid for Telent, the principal employer, the scheme trustees were concerned that it would appoint a majority of its own nominees as trustees in order to determine the scheme's investment strategy. The main concern was that the proposed trustees (who it was suggested would also be executive shareholders of Pension Corporation with a personal interest in the funding of the scheme) would operate an excessively risky investment policy, with the aim of achieving profit for its investors, which would conflict with the interests of scheme members. The Determinations Panel found that the *s 7* power was not restricted to situations in which a breach of trust had either occurred or was about to occur. Pension Corporation did not yet have control of Telent, but it had shown no real recognition of the potential conflicts, and the threat to the scheme's assets was sufficiently proximate to justify the use of the *s 7* power.

Trustees' duties

3.11   The following are some of the general duties with which trustees must comply. Except where those duties are stated as arising under a particular piece of legislation, they are general trust law duties, although there may be some overlap. Trust law duties are fiduciary. This means that they must be exercised for a proper purpose and generally in what the trustees consider to be the best interests of the scheme's beneficiaries.

In *Merchant Navy Ratings Pension Fund v Stena Line [2015] EWHC 448 (Ch)*, Asplin J considered that when exercising a power under a pension scheme, the trustees' primary duty was to promote the purpose for which the trust was created. In most pension schemes this purpose will be securing the benefits due under the rules. When exercising their powers, trustees must first decide what is the purpose of the trust and what benefits were intended to be received by the beneficiaries and then consider whether the proposed course is for the benefit of the beneficiaries or in their best interests.

Whilst there is argument as to what may or may not be in the best interests of the members, it is an established principle that the best interests of the beneficiaries of a scheme are usually their best financial interests. In *Cowan v Scargill [1984] 2 All ER 750*, Megarry V-C stated: '... under a trust for the provision of financial benefits, the paramount duty of the trustees is to provide the greatest financial benefits for the present and future beneficiaries.'

'Beneficiaries' has a wide meaning. It can include active, deferred and pensioner members, recipients of death benefits (such as spouses, civil partners, dependants and children) and, in some circumstances, the employers participating in the scheme.

The Law Commission report on Fiduciary Duties of Investment Intermediaries, published in July 2014, contains specific guidance on pension trustee investment duties. The report concludes that trustees may take certain non-financial factors (being environmental, social or governance concerns) into account when exercising their investment powers where the trustees have a good reason to think members would share the concern and the decision should not involve a risk of significant financial detriment to the scheme. This is considered in more depth in **Chapter 10**.

Trustees have to take care to identify, monitor and manage potential and actual conflicts of duty and conflicts of interest. A conflict of duty can arise where a trustee also owes a duty to a third party, which may conflict with the duties owed to the scheme beneficiaries, ie the trustee is 'wearing two hats'. The most common example of this is when senior staff of the sponsoring employer are appointed as trustees. A conflict of interest can arise when a trustee's personal interest conflicts with the duty owed as a trustee to the beneficiaries of the scheme.

The general rule is that a trustee should not put himself in a position where his duty conflicts with his personal interests or where a duty he owes to one party conflicts with a duty owed to another, without the informed consent of the parties affected. Against this however is the desire to have relatively senior and experienced individuals acting on the trustee board, given the knowledge and experience they can bring to the role.

In its guidance dealing with conflicts of interest, the Regulator states that such conflicts are of real concern and, if not managed effectively, decisions may be taken that put the interest of beneficiaries at risk or subsequently prove to be invalid. The Regulator recognises that it can be beneficial to appoint senior staff from the sponsoring employer as trustees but notes that conflicts are inherently likely to arise when appointing such individuals.

The Regulator's guidance states that the consideration of conflicts should be a three-stage process – identification, monitoring and managing, with the third stage highlighted as being particularly difficult. The guidance sets out a number of possible options for managing a conflict, ranging from the resignation of a trustee where the conflict is particularly acute, to the use of sub-committees arranged so that the conflicted trustee does not take part in certain discussions or vote in the decision-making process.

On a practical level, schemes should have a register of trustee's interests to record any interests which could lead to a conflict in the future and this should be kept updated. Schemes ought also to have conflicts as a standing agenda item at trustee meetings to ensure it is considered at the outset of each meeting. The Regulator's guidance also states that trustees should agree and document their policy for identifying, monitoring and managing conflicts and that this policy should be kept under regular review.

Directors of corporate trustees also need to comply with *Companies Act 2006, s 175*. A director has a statutory duty to 'avoid a situation in which he has, or can have, a direct or indirect interest that conflicts, or possibly may conflict, with the interests of the company'. There are exemptions where, broadly:

- the situation cannot reasonably be regarded as likely to give rise to a conflict of interest; or
- the matter has been authorised by the directors (but only those with no interest in the subject of the conflict), by shareholders' ordinary resolution or by the company's articles.

Even where authorisation is in place, the trustee may still need to take steps to manage any actual conflict which arises on a case-by-case basis.

The provisions of the *Bribery Act 2010*, which require commercial organisations to ensure that they have adequate anti-corruption policies, procedures and training in place, are generally accepted to apply to corporate trustees. An offence is also committed under the *Bribery Act 2010* if a bribe is offered or accepted by any trustee (individual or corporate) in return for the improper performance of the trustee's role. In addition to the statutory offences, arguably trustees have a general duty to take active steps to eradicate bribery and corruption, both to comply with good practice and as an aspect of good governance. In addition, in the event of an investigation by the authorities under the *Bribery Act 2010*, a defence may be available if it can be shown that a person took 'adequate procedures' to prevent bribery.

Duty not to profit from position as a trustee

3.12   As a general principle, a trustee may not receive any benefit from the scheme or exercise his powers in a way which creates a conflict between his personal interests and his duties to the scheme's beneficiaries. However, *PA 1995, s 39* provides that this principle does not apply to a trustee who is also a member of the scheme if, on exercising his powers in any manner, he benefits merely because the exercise of a power in that manner benefits (or may benefit) him as a scheme member. Despite this provision of *PA 1995*, a trustee may still not profit in other ways: for example, a trustee cannot buy assets from or sell assets to the scheme.

A trustee may, if the trust documents expressly permit it, be paid for acting as a trustee out of the trust fund. An independent trustee appointed under *PA 1995* (see **3.6**) may be paid his reasonable fees and expenses out of the trust fund regardless of whether this is permitted by the trust instrument (*PA 1995, s 25(6)*). Under *PA 1995, s 7(5)(b)*, the Regulator has the power to order that the fees and expenses of a trustee appointed by it are paid out of the scheme's resources.

In its statement on the prohibition of trustees issued in June 2013 (see **3.2**), the Regulator also addressed fees charged for trustee services. The Regulator states that it would be concerned if fees charged were not reasonable for the work carried out or where the work charged for was not done or was not actually necessary. The Regulator would also be concerned where there is any attempt to hide the real amount being charged by the trustee. For example, where the trustee uses a service company to do work which is charged to the scheme, but hides the fact that the company is owned by the trustee.

Duty of prudence

3.13   Each trustee has an obligation to act as a prudent person would, not only in the conduct of his own affairs, but also in looking after the affairs of third parties. In doing so, trustees must also use any skills or expertise which they possess (so a higher standard will be required of professional trustees). *Bartlett v Barclays Bank Trust Company Limited [1980] Ch 515* illustrates this point.

Under the *PA 2004* requirement for trustee knowledge and understanding trustees must be conversant with a number of issues. For an outline of these, see **3.22** onwards.

Duty to act in accordance with the trust deed and rules

3.14   Decisions and actions of trustees must be taken in accordance with the scheme's trust documents, and will be open to challenge if they are not. Trustees must therefore familiarise themselves and be conversant with the scheme's documentation and, if they are unsure as to the interpretation of any trust documentation (which may not be written in a particularly user-friendly manner) and any announcement which has not been incorporated into the trust documentation, suitable professional advice should be sought. Trustees should bear in mind that the effect of the trust deed and rules may be qualified or even contradicted by overriding legislation and decisions of the UK courts and the Court of Justice of the European Union and should, therefore, ensure that scheme documents are kept up to date.

Duties relating to investment decisions

3.15   All trustees should familiarise themselves and be conversant with their investment powers. This is one of the most fundamental duties of a trustee and must be exercised within the parameters of the trust deed, legislation and case law. *PA 1995, s 34(1)* reflects the general legal principle that trustees of occupational pension schemes have the power 'to make an investment of any kind as if they were absolutely entitled to the assets of the scheme', subject only to any specific restrictions imposed by their scheme documents. If trustees disregard any such restrictions, they may find themselves liable for any resulting loss to the value of the fund as a breach of trust.

If trustees do not wish, or do not have the skills, to take investment decisions, they may delegate responsibility for these decisions to someone who does have the skills and knowledge to take them effectively, whether a sub-committee of the trustees or a fund manager appointed in accordance with *PA 1995, s 34*.

The fact that trustees have power to make a particular investment does not necessarily mean that it is an appropriate investment for them to make; for instance, a high proportion of investment in property would be inappropriate in a fund where liquidity was required to pay pensions. Similarly, trustees would generally diversify their investments so as to maintain a balance between achieving good returns and protecting the fund against unnecessary risk.

PA 1995 contains specific provisions relating to the delegation by trustees of their investment discretions. In particular, for every occupational pension scheme whose assets include 'investments', the trustees must appoint a fund manager (*PA 1995, s 47(2)*). The *Occupational Pension Schemes (Investment) Regulations 2005 (SI 2005/3378)* make provision as to how trustees must exercise their power of investment (see further **Chapter 10**).

Duty to act impartially between the different classes of beneficiaries

3.16   A trustee must act fairly between different classes of beneficiary (such as pensioners, active members, deferred members, contingent beneficiaries and, in some cases, prospective members) and must also act fairly as between individuals. In some cases the employer may also be regarded as a beneficiary. This issue could arise where trustees are considering the allocation of surplus on the winding-up of a scheme.

That is not to say that all classes of beneficiary must be treated in an identical manner. In the Court of Appeal in *Edge v Pensions Ombudsman [1999] 4 All ER 546*, Chadwick LJ confirmed that the duty to act impartially:

> '... is no more than the ordinary duty which the law imposes on a person who is entrusted with the exercise of a discretionary power: that he exercises the power for the purpose for which it is given, giving proper consideration to the matters which are relevant and excluding from consideration matters which are irrelevant. If pension fund trustees do that, they cannot be criticised if they reach a decision which appears to prefer the claims of one interest – whether that of employers, current employees or pensioners

– over others. The preference will be the result of a proper exercise of the discretionary power.' (paragraph 50)

The *Edge* case also sets out the duty, when taking decisions, for trustees to take into account relevant factors and ignore irrelevant factors. The Supreme Court in the combined appeals of *Pitt v Holt* and *Futter v Futter [2011] EWCA Civ 197* confirmed, upholding the Court of Appeal's judgment, that this duty is a fiduciary one, so an act done as a result of a breach of that duty may be voidable. It also noted that, if the trustees seek and follow advice from apparently competent advisers then, in the absence of any other basis for a challenge, they are not in breach of their fiduciary duty if that advice turns out to be wrong.

Duty to seek appropriate professional advice on matters which a trustee does not understand

3.17   This duty is self-explanatory and should be complied with in areas where a trustee is not an expert. A trustee's decision will generally be harder to challenge if it can be shown to have been based on appropriate professional advice (see **3.16**). Specific requirements as to the use and appointment of professional advisers were introduced by *PA 1995* (see **Chapter 2**).

Delegation

3.18   Trustees must not generally delegate their powers or discretions unless they are authorised to do so by the trust deed and rules (although there are some statutory powers of delegation, most notably the limited general power to delegate under *TA 1925, s 25*, the narrow powers contained in *TA 2000* and the power to delegate investment discretions under *PA 1995, s 34* – see **Chapter 10**).

It may be appropriate for the trustees (provided there is power under the scheme's documentation), to appoint a person (whether one of the trustees or an external person) as pensions manager with delegated authority to administer the scheme and deal with member enquiries on a day-to-day basis. The person so appointed should be fully informed of the duties and responsibilities which the trustees have delegated to him. This person will often be in the employment of the sponsoring company. The trustees may also appoint an outside party to provide other administration services such as payment of pensions, retention of their membership records and other services. There should be a written agreement between the trustees and the administrator, not least because the trustees are required to ensure that the external administrator has appropriate systems in place to ensure the security and proper processing of members' personal data (see **3.54**), and the trustees should receive undertakings to that effect in the agreement. Some schemes use the employer's in-house staff to provide these services. The trustees must act prudently in choosing any person to whom they delegate any of their duties or responsibilities. Trustees remain ultimately responsible for the actions of those to whom they have delegated their functions (subject to a limited exception in relation to delegation to a fund manager (*PA 1995, s 34(4)*).

Note that the exercise of discretions by the trustees cannot be delegated unless the trust deed and rules and relevant legislation specifically permit this.

Duty to collect contributions

3.19   Trustees must arrange for the preparation of a schedule of contributions (under *PA 2004, s 227* in the case of a final salary scheme) or a schedule of payments (under *PA 1995, s 87* in the case of a money purchase scheme). In either case the schedule must show the rates of contributions payable and the dates on or before which such payments are due. Failure by the employer or members to make payments due may be reportable by the trustees to the Regulator (see **3.57** onwards). Trustees' duties generally in relation to scheme funding increased very significantly with the introduction of the overriding statutory funding requirement as set out in *PA 2004, ss 221–233* (see **Chapter 11**).

Duty to keep receipts, payments and records

3.20   *PA 1995, s 49* requires trustees to keep any money received by them in a separate bank account kept at an authorised deposit-taking institution. Trustees may instead arrange to keep money in an account operated by a third party and separate from the employer's bank account if they have entered into a suitable arrangement or contract with the third party. Any such arrangement or contract must ensure that records (including details of the amount paid in or out, date of payment, from or to whom it was paid, and interest earned) are kept for at least six years and that all interest is credited to the scheme (*Scheme Administration Regulations, reg 11*).

Trustees are required by *PA 1995, s 49* and *Scheme Administration Regulations, regs 12–14* to keep written records of their meetings (including meetings of any of their number, for example, sub-committees of the trustees) for at least six years from the end of the scheme year to which they relate, stating:

(*a*)   the date, time and place of the meeting;

(*b*)   the names of all the trustees invited to the meeting;

(*c*)   the names of the trustees who attended the meeting and those who did not attend;

(*d*)   the names of any professional advisers or other persons who attended the meeting;

(*e*)   any decisions made at the meeting; and

(*f*)   whether since the previous meeting there has been any occasion when a decision has been made by the trustees and if so the time, place and date of such a decision, and the names of the trustees who participated in the decision.

Trustees are also required by *PA 1995, s 49* and the *Scheme Administration Regulations, regs 12* and *14* to keep, for at least six years from the end of the scheme year to which they relate, books and records relating to certain transactions including records of:

(i)   any amount received in respect of any contribution payable in respect of an active member of the scheme;

(ii)   the date on which a member joins the scheme;

(iii) payments of pensions and benefits;

(iv)   payments made by or on behalf of the trustees to any person, including a professional adviser, including the name and address of the payee and the reason for that payment;

(v)   any movement or transfer of assets from the trustees to any person including a professional adviser, including the name and address of the person to whom the assets were moved or transferred and the reason for that transaction;

(vi)   the receipt or payment of money or assets in respect of the transfer of members into or out of the scheme along with certain prescribed details about the transfer;

(vii) payments made to a member who leaves the scheme other than on a transfer, including the name of that member, the date of leaving, the member's entitlement at that date, the method used for calculating any entitlement under the scheme and how that entitlement was discharged;

(viii) payments made to the employer; and

(ix)   other payments to, and withdrawals from, the scheme, including the name and address of the payee or payer.

In accordance with the *Employers' Duties (Registration and Compliance) Regulations 2010, reg 7*, trustees of a scheme being used for automatic enrolment must keep the information listed below for a period of six years (item (iii) for four years). On ceasing to act as a trustee the obligation to keep the records will cease, as long as they have been transferred to a successor.

(i)   the employer pension scheme reference;

(ii)   the date on which each jobholder or worker became an active member of the scheme;

(iii)   the name of any jobholder in relation to whom they have received an opt-out notice and the date of receipt;

(iv)   the date on which a jobholder ceases to be an active member of the scheme;

(v)   in relation to all members of a qualifying scheme:

- name, date of birth, gender and NI number (if received);

- last known residential address with UK postcode (if relevant);

- whether he is an active member or not.

In addition, the *Registered Pension Schemes (Provision of Information) Regulations 2006 (SI 2006/567), reg 18* requires the scheme administrator for HMRC purposes (which will usually be the trustees) and the trustees to retain certain records for a period of six years from the end of the relevant tax year.

Disclosure of information to members

3.21   Trustees are obliged to disclose certain documents and information to scheme members, prospective members (provided that the employer has told the trustees that the person is a member or prospective member), spouses and civil partners, other beneficiaries and recognised trade unions (but only if the employer has told the trustees that the union is recognised) under *PA 1995, s 41, PSA 1993, s 113* and the Occupational and Personal Pension Schemes (Disclosure of Information) Regulations 2013 (the 'Disclosure Regulations'). The requirements do not apply to schemes with only one member nor to schemes which provide only death benefits.

The Disclosure Regulations came into force on 6 April 2014 with the aim of simplifying and streamlining the disclosure regime for occupational and personal pension schemes. The provisions of the Occupational Pension Schemes (Disclosure of Information) Regulations 1996 and the Personal Pension Schemes (Disclosure of Information) Regulations 1987 have been revoked and their principal requirements consolidated into the Disclosure Regulations.

There are other regulations which also require disclosure of information to members in certain situations, for example, in relation to automatic enrolment and to pension sharing or earmarking on divorce. These are referred to in the context of the relevant chapter in this book, and a general summary of the information which must be disclosed is given at **Appendix II**.

Under the legislation, trustees are obliged to disclose, amongst other things, details of benefits payable, details of the scheme's governing documentation, basic scheme information (which is usually contained in the scheme's explanatory booklet), an annual report and accounts, the latest actuarial valuation and documents relating to the funding of the scheme. From 6 April 2014 there is an obligation for trustees to disclose information about lifestyling if they operate or introduce a lifestyling strategy.

Most information need only be disclosed at the request of the member, prospective member, spouse, civil partner, other beneficiary or trade union, although some information – most notably the basic scheme information and certain scheme-wide information – must be provided as a matter of course, regardless of whether or not a request is made. The legislation does not entitle a person to receive information which is not relevant to his own rights or entitlements under the scheme.

In practice, the issue of an annual report, a scheme booklet and individual benefit statements will satisfy many of the disclosure of information requirements.

The general trust law principle is that trustees are entitled to exercise their discretionary powers in a confidential manner. Case law, however, has set out circumstances in which a beneficiary may be able to have access to information about the administration of the trust (which may include information on how the trustees have reached their decisions).

The right of a beneficiary to have access to certain trust documents was considered in the case of *Re Londonderry's Settlement; Peat v Walsh [1964] 3 All ER 855*. The Court of Appeal held that, whilst a beneficiary is entitled to see trust documents, this rule did not extend to requiring trustees to disclose documents (such as minutes of a meeting) recording the reasons behind the exercise of a discretion.

The later case of *Wilson v Law Debenture Trust Corporation plc [1995] 2 All ER 337* applied the position in *Londonderry* more directly to a pensions context. It showed that it is only in exceptional circumstances that trustees should be compelled to give reasons for the exercise of a discretion, for example, where there was evidence that the trustees had failed to take into account a relevant consideration when exercising that discretion. However, the general presumption was that 'in the absence of evidence to the contrary a trustee has exercised his discretion properly'.

However, this long-held position has come under attack both in the courts and in front of the Pensions Ombudsman. In his 2002 decision in *Allen v TKM Group Pension Trust Ltd (L00370)*, the Pensions Ombudsman took a different view from the established position at law concerning the disclosure of trustees' reasons. He decided in this case that it was maladministration (but not a breach of the law) for the trustees not to provide reasons for their decisions, not to have disclosed in full the minutes of their meetings, and not to provide copies of the material they considered in taking their decision to those with a legitimate interest in the matter. This case illustrates the importance of trustees keeping clear records of decisions and it would appear that, when making decisions, trustees could be expected by the Pensions Ombudsman to give their reasons or be at risk of a finding of maladministration, in particular where a decision adverse to the interests of a member is taken.

Further, in *Schmidt v Rosewood Trust [2003] 2 WLR 1442, [2003] 3 All ER 76*, a case before the Privy Council, the belief that a beneficiary's right to view trust documents was based on the sort of proprietary interest put forward in *Londonderry* (ie a right to access documents that are your own) was dismissed. Instead, a beneficiary's right to see trust documents was viewed as a part of the court's inherent powers of supervision over trusts. This is a difficult concept for a trustee to consider in practice, as it would seem to be at the court's discretion which documents ought to be disclosed to a beneficiary where there is no statutory duty to disclose information. Especially where there are issues of personal or commercial confidentiality, the court may have to balance the competing interests of different beneficiaries, the trustees and third parties when considering what ought to be disclosed.

Members may also have a right, by invoking a subject access request under the *Data Protection Act 1998, s 7*, to the disclosure of data referring to themselves. This could include not only the basic records held by the trustees but also minutes of trustee meetings where decisions concerning that individual member were made.

The Pensions Act 2004

Trustee knowledge and understanding ('TKU')

3.22   *PA 2004, ss 247–249* created a new statutory requirement for knowledge and understanding for trustees of occupational pension schemes (whether individuals or directors of a corporate trustee). Trustees must be 'conversant' with key scheme documents and must have knowledge and understanding of the law relating to pensions and trusts and other matters including occupational pension scheme funding and investment. These requirements are dealt with in more detail in **3.23**. The degree of knowledge and understanding is that appropriate for enabling the person properly to exercise his functions as trustee (including as a member of any sub-committee of the trustees, such as one dealing with investment).

The requirements apply to 'every individual who is a trustee of an occupational pension scheme' and 'any company which is a trustee of an occupational pension scheme'. A trustee company has a duty to ensure that any individual who exercises any function which the company has, as trustee, satisfies the knowledge and understanding requirements.

Requirements of PA 2004, ss 247 to 249

3.23 *Sections 247* (individual trustees) and *248* (corporate trustees) state that trustees must be 'conversant' with the following scheme documents:

- the trust deed and rules;
- any statement of investment principles (SIP);
- any statement of funding principles (SFP);
- any other document recording the policy adopted in relation to scheme administration. This would include the scheme booklet, announcements, member communications, trustee minutes and the annual report.

The Regulator interprets being 'conversant with' scheme documents to mean that a trustee should have a working knowledge of those documents such that he is able to use them effectively when carrying out his duties as a trustee. The Regulator's revised Code of Practice (see **3.25**) states that 'Knowing the essential elements of the scheme's trust documentation will require every trustee to read it through thoroughly'; the original Code stated that every trustee did 'not necessarily' have to do this.

In addition to being 'conversant' with the above, trustees must have 'knowledge and understanding' of the following:

- the law relating to pensions and trusts;
- the principles relating to the (DB) funding of occupational pension schemes;
- the principles relating to the investment of the assets of occupational pension schemes; and
- such other matters as may be prescribed.

The degree of knowledge and understanding is that appropriate for the purposes of enabling an individual trustee properly to exercise his functions as a trustee or, in relation to a corporate trustee, of enabling an individual director properly to exercise his functions in relation to the trustee company (*PA 2004, ss 247(5)* and *248(6)*).

However, under the *Occupational Pension Scheme (Trustees' Knowledge and Understanding) Regulations 2006 (SI 2006/686)*, there is an exemption from these requirements where

- the scheme has fewer than 12 members;

- all the members are individual trustees (or directors of the sole corporate trustee); and

- either all trustee decisions must be made by the unanimous agreement of all the trustees (or directors), or one of the trustees (or directors) is independent.

Those Regulations also disapply the requirements for individual trustees and directors of corporate trustees of all occupational schemes for six months from the date on which they are appointed. However, as the Regulator notes in its Code of Practice, even a new trustee is accountable in law and must be equipped to make the decisions with which he or she might be faced, so the actual time allowed and priority given to acquiring different aspects of TKU may well be determined by the agendas of early trustee meetings and the precise role of the individual.

The six-month period of grace does not apply to independent trustees, or to trustees or directors who hold themselves out as having expertise in the law relating to pensions and trusts and the principles of funding and investment. The Code of Practice also excludes the chairman of the trustees from the six-month grace period.

The Regulator's powers

3.24 Under *PA 2004, s 13* the Regulator has the power to issue an improvement notice where it is of the opinion that a person is contravening pensions legislation or has contravened pensions legislation in circumstances that make it likely that the contravention will be continued or repeated. Therefore, it is within the Regulator's power to issue an improvement notice where trustees have not complied with the knowledge and understanding requirements. Under *s 13*, where a trustee has failed to comply with an improvement notice, civil penalties may be applied.

In its statement on the prohibition of trustees issued in June 2013 (see **3.2**), the Regulator stated that trustees who repeatedly fall below the appropriate standards of knowledge and understanding may be prohibited from being a trustee using the Regulator's power under *PA 1995, s 3*, particularly if no attempt has been made to attain the relevant learning. The Regulator also stated that professional trustees are expected to show a higher standard of expertise than lay trustees and an independent trustee or firm of trustees, could also be prohibited if it consistently fall short of the standards the Regulator reasonably expects.

Code of Practice

3.25   The Regulator's Code of Practice No 7 on the trustee knowledge and understanding requirements, revised in November 2009, aims to help trustees by setting out:

- the meaning and scope of the knowledge and understanding requirements in the legislation;

- how trustees might approach the task of determining the elements of knowledge and understanding which are appropriate for them;

- how they might acquire, update and demonstrate knowledge and understanding; and

- the scope of the requirement to be conversant with scheme documents and how trustees might become and remain conversant with them.

The Code is accompanied by Scope Guidance, which the Regulator describes as 'broadly speaking a list of items that the pensions industry considers that trustees need to know and understand and a list of the documents containing policy with which trustees may need to be familiar'.

Scope Guidance

3.26   Updated in November 2009, the Scope Guidance consists of three documents, for trustees of:

- DB schemes with associated DC arrangements;

- DC schemes with no link to DB arrangements; and

- Small (12–99 members) fully insured DC schemes.

In all three Scope documents, the areas of which trustees are required to have knowledge are divided into 'Units'. Summarised below are some of the areas covered in the Scope Guidance for DB schemes with associated DC arrangements:

- *Unit 1 – The law relating to trusts*, including the definition and nature of a pension trust, fiduciary duties, professional advice, conflicts of interest, fitness and properness to act as trustees;

- *Unit 2 – The law relating to pensions*, including key provisions of pensions legislation and *FA 2004*, Codes of Practice, dispute resolution, member-nominated trustees and the automatic enrolment requirement;

- *Unit 3 – Basic principles relating to* investment, including capital markets, the major asset classes and the balance between risk and reward;

- *Unit 4 – Funding (DB occupational arrangements),* including how liabilities are valued, potential risks to the ability of the scheme to pay benefits, transfers and bulk transfers and the impact of trustee powers;

- *Unit 5 – Contributions (DB occupational arrangements),* including the role of the sponsoring employer in the calculation and collection of contributions and the effect of the employer covenant;

- *Unit 6 – Strategic asset allocation (DB occupational arrangements);*

- *Unit 7 – Funding (DC occupational arrangements, including AVCs),* including how occupational DC arrangements work, the role of the employer, risks borne by members and the implications of contracting-out;

- *Unit 8 – Investment choice (DC occupational arrangements, including AVCs),* including investment strategy and the importance of member understanding of investment risk;

- *Unit 9 – Fund management,* including measuring performance using indices, the selection of fund managers and the structure of investment portfolios;

- *Unit 10 – Working knowledge of the scheme's trust documentation,* including duties, powers and discretions of trustees, the balance of powers and DB benefits offered;

- *Unit 11 – Working knowledge of the scheme's statement of investment principles,* including investment objectives, contents of the SIP and monitoring and updating the SIP;

- *Unit 12 – Working knowledge of the scheme's statement of funding principles (DB),* including responsibilities for preparing the SFP, contents of the SFP and review of the SFP;

- *Unit 13 – Working knowledge of the scheme's other relevant documents,* including the scheme booklet, announcements, actuarial valuations, annual reports and accounts, insurance policies, significant contracts, the internal dispute resolution procedure, memorandum and articles of association of a trustee company and minutes of meetings. Trustees should also know where the original documents are kept.

The Regulator strongly recommends that trustees regularly (at least annually) review their own knowledge and understanding against the published Scope documents and carry out learning or training to fill any gaps. Trustees may need to acquire new knowledge in relation to specific scheme changes or events (such as a buy-in or buy-out of liabilities).

Formal qualifications

3.27   The Regulator's free online modular course called the 'Trustee Toolkit' is intended to help trustees meet the required standards of knowledge and understanding. It is accessible from the trustee pages of the Regulator's website (www.thepensionsregulator.gov.uk). In addition, the Pensions Management Institute has developed the Awards in Pension Trusteeship providing formal recognition of TKU. There are no current plans for a mandatory qualification. However, the Code of Practice notes that professional trustees should be able to demonstrate that they are appropriately experienced and qualified from the date of appointment, and 'it is likely that a formal qualification will be expected'.

Trustee meetings

3.28   Specific provisions relating to the conduct of trustees' meetings are sometimes included in the trust documents (or, in the case of a corporate trustee, its articles of association) and will typically cover such matters as how and when notice of meetings is to be given, the number of trustees that will constitute a quorum (so that decisions can validly be made), how/if a chairman of the trustees is to be appointed and, if so, whether he has a casting vote. If these details are not set out in the trust documents (or articles), there should be some written record of them, for example in a minute or resolution passed at a trustees' meeting.

It is important to comply with these requirements. If, for example, notice has not been given to all of the trustees of a forthcoming meeting, then the validity of the decisions made at that meeting may subsequently be open to challenge.

Since 6 April 2015, most schemes holding money purchase benefits (other than where the only money purchase benefits are AVCs) are required to appoint a chair of trustees. The chair is then responsible for signing an annual governance statement. See **Chapter 14** for more details.

Under *PA 1995, s 32*, unless the scheme provides otherwise, decisions of trustees may be made on the basis of a majority vote and trustees may set their own quorum for meetings at which majority decisions may be taken. However, in certain situations, specific decision-making requirements apply (*PA 1995, s 32(4)*). For example the removal of a member-nominated trustee requires the agreement of all the other trustees (*PA 2004, s 241*). Notice of occasions where decisions may be taken by majority must be given to each trustee to whom it is reasonably practicable to give such notice, and must, unless the trustees agree otherwise, state the date, time and place of the meeting and be sent at least ten business days before the meeting to the last known address of each trustee (*Scheme Administration Regulations, reg 10*). However, notice of such a meeting does not have to be given in the manner described above where it is necessary, as a matter of urgency, for the trustees to make a decision (*Scheme Administration Regulations, reg 9*).

Member-nominated trustees

The MNT regime

3.29 Under *PA 2004* and the *Occupational Pension Schemes (Member-nominated Trustees and Directors) Regulations 2006 (SI 2006/714)* (the *'MNT Regulations'*) the trustees of occupational pension schemes are under a duty to secure that arrangements for at least one-third of the total number of trustees to be member-nominated trustees ('MNTs') are put in place and implemented unless the scheme is exempt. There is a parallel duty upon the directors of a corporate trustee to appoint member-nominated directors ('MNDs').

The *PA 2004* regime replaced the more prescriptive and less flexible *PA 1995* regime from 6 April 2006 and removed the facility for employers to 'opt out' of the MNT requirements. It also allows for the proportion of MNTs/MNDs to be increased from one-third to one-half (*PA 2004, s 243(1)*), but to date no regulations have been issued to make this change.

Who has to comply with the MNT/MND provisions?

3.30 *PA 2004, s 241(1)* provides that the trustees of an occupational trust scheme (other than those schemes exempted by regulations) must secure that the MNT requirements are complied with. For MNDs, *PA 2004, s 242(1)* provides that it is the trustee company which is responsible for securing compliance.

PA 2004, s 241(8) exempts from the MNT requirements schemes where every member of the scheme is a trustee of the scheme and no other person is a trustee.

Schemes where every trustee of the scheme is a company must appoint MNDs under *PA 2004, s 242(1)* except for any company which only has independent directors (*MNT Regulations, reg 5(7)*).

A company which is a trustee of more than one scheme may choose to apply the MND requirements to all schemes as if they were a single scheme; or separately in respect of each scheme; or a combination of both: *PA 2004, ss 242(8)* and *242(9)*. The Regulator's Code of Practice No 8 recommends that any corporate trustee intending to treat some or all of the schemes as a single scheme should consider seeking the views of the schemes' employers and, if appropriate, other trustee companies.

PA 2004, ss 241(8) and *242(10)* both exempt schemes of a 'prescribed description'. The prescribed scheme exemptions in the *MNT Regulations* include:

- a scheme with fewer than two members;

- a relevant small occupational pension scheme (broadly, with fewer than 12 members, all members are trustees and either decisions must be unanimous or there is a statutory independent trustee);

- a small insured scheme (fewer than 12 members);

- a scheme which is not registered;

- a relevant centralised scheme (non-associated employers);

- a stakeholder scheme;

- a scheme to which *PA 1995, s 22* applies (conditions for a statutory independent trustee);

- a scheme where the sole trustee or all the trustees are independent of the employer (but not necessarily a statutory independent trustee); it has been suggested that for some schemes this will effectively still allow the employer to opt out of the MNT requirements by appointing a sole professional trustee; and

- the National Employment Savings Trust (the Government's automatic enrolment default scheme: see **Chapter 14**).

Time limit for compliance

3.31 Under *PA 2004, s 241(1)* the MNT requirements must be satisfied within a reasonable period of the date on which a scheme becomes subject to them. The Code of Practice proposes six months as the maximum 'reasonable period', but recognises that what is reasonable will depend on the circumstances of each scheme.

What are the requirements?

Number of member-nominated trustees

3.32 Under *ss 241(1)* (MNTs) and *242(1)* (MNDs), trustees must secure that arrangements are in place and implemented which provide for at least one third of the total number of trustees/directors to be member nominated. Note that if scheme rules require a higher proportion to be member nominated or if the employer approves a higher proportion, that higher proportion will apply (*ss 241(4)* (MNTs) and *242(4)* (MNDs) and *MNT Regulations 2006, reg 5(2)*).

Nomination and selection

Who nominates and selects?

3.33 Under *ss 241(2)* (MNTs) and *242(2)* (MNDs), the nomination process has to include all the active members of the scheme (or an organisation which adequately represents them) and all the pensioners of the scheme (or an organisation which adequately represents them). The representative organisations might be trade unions, staff committees, pensioner groups or any other organisation considered by the trustees adequately to represent the relevant members. Deferred and pension credit members can, but do not have to, be included in the process. Where a scheme has no active or pensioner members, the nomination process must include such deferred members as the trustees determine are eligible to participate (*MNT Regulations, reg 5(6)*).

MNTs are to be selected as a result of a 'process which involves some or all of the members of the scheme'. This could be a selection panel or ballot.

Neither *PA 2004* nor the Code of Practice specifies any particular process which must be adopted for nomination or selection. However, the Regulator does expect the process to be 'proportionate, fair and transparent' and notes that the selection arrangements should provide for a combination of methods to be used if this is more effective.

Sections 241(5)(c) and *242(5)(c)* provide that a person who is not a member of the scheme must have the employer's approval to qualify for selection as an MNT or MND, if the employer so requires. Subject to that proviso, the arrangements may provide that, where the number of nominations received is equal to or less than the number of appointments required, the nominees are deemed to be selected (*PA 2004, ss 241(5)(d)* and *242(5)(d)*).

The appointment process

3.34 The MNT legislation does not override a scheme's own provisions relating to the appointment of trustees: it requires arrangements for nomination and selection and the subsequent implementation of those arrangements. The final stage of implementation would be effected under the scheme rules (eg by a deed of appointment of a new trustee or, in the case of a corporate trustee, the appropriate formalities under its articles of association and completion of the relevant Companies House form).

Vacancies

3.35 *Sections 241(5)(b)* and *242(5)(b)* require that the MNT/MND arrangements must provide that, where a vacancy is not filled because insufficient nominations are received, the nomination and selection process is to be repeated at reasonable intervals until the vacancy is filled. The Code of Practice suggests this period should be no longer than three years, and that trustees should consider shortening it if a significant change occurs to the scheme membership, such as a bulk transfer in of new members.

Removal of MNTs/MNDs

3.36 Under *ss 241(6)* and *242(6)* the MNT/MND arrangements must provide that the removal of the member-nominated trustee requires the agreement of all the other trustees or directors, except in the case of MNTs (but not MNDs) where the scheme rules provide that trustees may be removed by a vote of the membership: *MNT Regulations, reg 5(3)*.

Functions of MNTs

3.37 *Sections 241(7)* and *242(7)* provide that the arrangements must not exclude MNTs/MNDs from the exercise of any of the functions exercisable by the other trustees by reason only of the fact that they are member nominated. The principle is that all trustees are equal and have the same duties (unless otherwise ordered by the Regulator).

Penalties for failure to comply

3.38 *Sections 241(9)* and *242(11)* provide for the imposition of civil penalties where the MNT/MND requirements have not been complied with.

Internal dispute resolution ('IDR')

Introduction

3.39 *PA 1995, s 50* (subsequently amended by *PA 2004, s 273*, itself amended by *PA 2007*) requires trustees of occupational pension schemes to secure that arrangements are made and implemented for the resolution of disagreements about matters relating to the scheme of 'any person with an interest in the scheme' (defined in *s 50A*) or his estate or representative.

Schemes of which all the members are trustees, or which have only one member, or of which there is a sole corporate trustee and every member is a director of that company, are exempt from the requirements (*s 50(8)*).

The aim is to provide a flexible, low-cost way to resolve disputes about an occupational pension scheme. Note that not every member or beneficiary query necessarily needs to be treated as an IDR dispute.

Details of the IDR procedure, including the address and job title of the person to contact, must be set out in writing and given as part of the 'basic information about the scheme' under the *Disclosure Regulations*.

Ideally, the IDR procedure should be in addition to other efforts to resolve the matter and should be operated to provide an opportunity to resolve misunderstandings before they escalate to the Pensions Ombudsman. Bearing this in mind, it is useful to provide a simple form to assist individuals who have a complaint. Failing to help individuals with a grievance may, in some situations, amount to 'maladministration' and lead to criticism of the trustees. An IDR complaint can be compromised by the parties, possibly with a payment by the trustees in full and final settlement of the dispute.

Who can make a complaint?

3.40   Under *PA 1995, s 50* (as amended) the IDR procedure must cover disagreements between the trustees and any 'person with an interest in the scheme' as set out in *PA 2005, s 50A*. This means:

(*a*)   a member (ie active members, deferred pensioners, pensioners and pension credit members);

(*b*)   the widow, widower, surviving civil partner or dependant of a deceased member;

(*c*)   any other person entitled to benefits on the death of a member;

(*d*)   a prospective member of the scheme (ie any person who, under the terms of his contract or the scheme rules:

    (i)   is able at his own option to become a member or will be able if he remains in the same employment for long enough;

    (ii)   will automatically become a member unless he elects otherwise; or

    (iii)   may become a member if his employer consents);

(*e*)   someone who has ceased to be in one of the categories (*a*) to (*d*) above;

(*f*)   someone claiming to be within one of the categories (*a*) to (*e*) above.

Any claim by someone in category (*e*), or someone in category (*f*) claiming to be in category (*e*) must be made within a period of six months beginning immediately after the date on which he ceased to be, or claims he ceased to be, a person with an interest in the scheme (*PA 1995, s 50B(3)* and the Regulator's

Code of Practice No 11, 'Dispute Resolution – reasonable periods'). The trustees may include a reasonable time limit of their choosing for claimants in any of the other categories (*PA 1995, s 50B(3)(b)*).

A claimant can nominate a representative to make or continue the complaint on his behalf. If the claimant is incapable of acting for himself or is a minor, a family member or other suitable person can bring or continue a claim. In the case of a deceased member, his personal representatives can bring or continue a claim (*PA 1995, s 50B*).

IDR procedures

3.41　The IDR procedure can be either two-stage (involving a specified decision-maker and then the trustees) or single-stage (involving the trustees alone).

Decisions must be made and notified within 'reasonable periods', which are set out in the Regulator's Code of Practice No 11. The Regulator expects that a decision on a dispute will be made within four months of receiving the application, and complainants should be notified within 15 working days of a decision being made. The same time periods apply to each stage if a two-stage IDR procedure is in place. If it is likely that any specified deadlines are not going to be met, it would be good practice to let the complainant know.

Whether the IDR procedure is one stage or two stage, the (initial) decision maker must inform the complainant as soon as reasonably practicable on receipt of an IDR complaint of the availability of The Pensions Advisory Service ('TPAS') to assist with any difficulty with the scheme, and provide its contact details. The notification of a final decision must include a statement that the Pensions Ombudsman may investigate and determine any complaint or dispute of fact or law in relation to a scheme and provide his contact details: *The Occupational Pension Schemes (Internal Dispute Resolution Procedures Consequential and Miscellaneous Amendments) Regulations 2008 (SI 2008/649), reg 2*).

Exempted disagreements

3.42　Under *PA 1995, s 50(9)* the IDR procedure cannot be used where proceedings have begun in a court or tribunal, or where the Pensions Ombudsman has commenced an investigation in respect of the dispute. The *Ombudsman Regulations* provide that the Pensions Ombudsman will generally refuse to investigate a complaint unless the complainant has first made full use of the IDR procedure and has received a final decision, unless he is satisfied that:

(*a*)   there is no real prospect of notice of a decision under the IDR procedure being issued within a reasonable period from the date on which he received a complaint; and

(*b*)   it is reasonable in the circumstances that he should investigate and determine the complaint.

Protection from liability

General

3.43   Trustees who act outside their powers, or who act in a way which is in breach of their trust law duties to scheme beneficiaries, may find themselves personally liable to the beneficiaries for breach of trust. Alternatively, where they are in breach of a statutory duty, they will usually be liable as stated in the relevant Act (see **Appendix I** for examples). In practice, directors of a trustee company may have more protection than they would if they were individual trustees through the 'corporate veil', although the position is not straightforward. The extent to which directors of a trustee company can be held directly liable to scheme beneficiaries (ie where the corporate veil is pierced) was considered in the case of *HR v JAPT [1997] PLR 99*, where the court found that directors of a trustee company do not normally owe a direct fiduciary duty to beneficiaries of a trust. The exception to this principle is where a director is found guilty of 'accessory liability'. In order to be found liable as an 'accessory' to a breach of trust, the director must have acted dishonestly in the sense described in the case of *Royal Brunei Airlines v Tan [1995] 2 AC 378* and referred to in the case of *JAPT* as follows:

'It is *Royal Brunei* dishonest for a person, unless there is a very good and compelling reason, to participate in a transaction if he knows it involves a misapplication of trust assets to the detriment of the beneficiaries or if he deliberately closes his eyes and ears or chooses deliberately not to ask questions so as to avoid his learning something he would rather not know and for him then to proceed regardless.' (paragraph 61).

JAPT was followed in the High Court case of *Gregson v HAE Trustees and Others [2008] EWHC 1006 (Ch)* which confirmed that trustee directors do not owe a duty directly to the scheme's beneficiaries.

There are, however, some protections from liability available to trustees. These are considered below.

Exoneration clause in the trust deed

3.44   Most pension schemes' trust deeds will contain a provision under which the trustees (or directors of a trustee company) will not be liable except in limited circumstances. This is known as an exoneration (or exclusion) clause. These circumstances will typically be conduct which involves some degree of bad faith or negligence on the part of the person sought to be made liable. 'Wilful neglect or default' is a phrase commonly used in exoneration clauses; 'deliberate and knowing breach of trust' is another. Clauses of this nature have been upheld by the courts in relation to trustees' liabilities to beneficiaries, for example, *Armitage v Nurse [1998] Ch 241* and the Privy Council decision in *Spread Trustee v Hutcheson [2011] UKPC 13*. However, under *PA 1995, s 33* an exoneration clause cannot exclude liability for breach of the trustees' duty of skill and care in the performance of any investment functions. Nor would such wording in a trust deed be sufficient to exclude penalties imposed by *PA 1995* and other statutes (see **Appendix I**), which cannot be met from the assets of the scheme, or liabilities to third parties (ie persons who are not beneficiaries or parties to the trust deed), which will usually arise under the terms of a contract rather than under the terms of the trust deed (*PA 2004, s 256*).

UCTA 1977, s 2(2) restricts the validity of certain clauses which seek to exclude liability for negligence. However, this restriction applies only to business liability, and so (in the context of actions brought by beneficiaries) is likely only to apply to professional trustees who charge for acting as such; it is for this reason that some exoneration clauses in trust deeds specify that liability for the negligence of a professional trustee is not excluded.

PA 1995, s 33(1) prohibits the exclusion or restriction of any liability for breach of an obligation under any rule of law to take care or exercise skill in the performance of any investment functions which is exercisable by a trustee of the scheme or by a person to whom the function has been delegated under *PA 1995, s 34* (see *Independent Trustee Services v GP Noble Trustees [2010] EWHC 1653 (Ch)*). However, where the trustees have delegated discretion to make investment decisions to a fund manager under *s 34, s 34(4)* relieves them of responsibility for any act or default of that fund manager in the exercise of any discretion delegated to him, so long as they (or anybody else making the delegation on their behalf) have taken all reasonable steps to satisfy themselves that the fund manager has the appropriate knowledge and experience for managing the investments of the scheme and that he is carrying out his work competently and complying with the requirements of *PA 1995, s 36* (see **Chapter 10**).

The Law Commission's January 2003 consultation paper CP171, 'Trustee Exemption Clauses', proposed that professional (but not lay) trustees should no longer be able to rely on clauses which excluded their liability for breach of trust arising from negligence, nor should they be indemnified from the trust fund in respect of such breaches. However, the Commission concluded that the proposed statutory intervention faced a number of obstacles and could lead to adverse consequences more damaging than anticipated. Its July 2006 report instead recommended the adoption of a non-statutory rule of practice that any paid trustee proposing the inclusion of such a clause in a trust instrument should before the creation of the trust take reasonable steps to ensure that the settlor is aware of the meaning and effect of the clause. Importantly, the report recognised that the rule should be of no application to pension trusts.

Indemnity clause in the trust deed

3.45   A scheme's trust deed will often provide for the trustees to be indemnified against liability. The clause may entitle them to be indemnified by the sponsoring employer or from the trust fund in the event of default on the indemnity by the employer. In any case, any kind of liability which is not covered by the trust deed's exoneration clause will typically also not be covered by the indemnity clause. *PA 2004, s 256* prevents trustees from being indemnified out of the fund in respect of fines or certain civil penalties (see **Appendix I**).

Care needs to be taken with corporate trustees as some statutory restrictions apply on indemnities given from one company to directors of another in the group (assuming here that the shareholder of the corporate trustee is a company in the employer's group).

Employer indemnity – position before 1 October 2007

3.46   The pre-October 2007 position remains relevant where older indemnities are still in place. Under *Companies Act 1985 (CA 1985), s 310*, any indemnity given by a company to its directors was void to the extent that it was in connection with any breach *in relation to the company*. This meant that individual trustees and directors of a corporate trustee (assuming the corporate trustee to be associated with the employer) who were also directors of the employer could not benefit from any indemnity in respect of liabilities in relation to the company. However, it was strongly arguable that this would not prevent such individuals from being indemnified against liability *in relation to the pension scheme*. These provisions did not impact on individual trustees or trustee directors who were not also directors of the employer and they could benefit from a full employer indemnity.

CA 1985, ss 309A–309C (introduced with effect from 6 April 2005 and repealed on 1 October 2007) then provided that any attempt by a company to indemnify a director of the company *or an associated company* in respect of any liability in relation to the company of which he was director was void, unless it was a 'qualifying third party indemnity provision', under which indemnity was given for liability incurred by the director to a person other than the company or associated company.

Qualifying third party indemnity provisions (QTPIP) must not allow indemnity against:

- liability by the director to the company or associated company;
- liabilities for criminal or regulatory fines or penalties; and/or
- (broadly) the cost of defending criminal or civil proceedings.

Individual trustees who were also directors of the employer could not be indemnified in respect of liabilities in relation to the company, unless the indemnity was a QTPIP. Similarly, trustee directors who were also directors of the employer could not benefit from an indemnity in relation to the trustee company or the employer unless it was a QTPIP. Crucially, this meant that (even where a QTPIP was in place) they could no longer be indemnified in respect of liabilities to the trustee company. This opened up the possibility of claims in relation to pension scheme liabilities (as, potentially, the trustee company could be found liable for losses to the scheme and then itself seek to recover that from individual directors).

Transitional provisions provided that *s 309A* had no effect on indemnities which were in place before 29 October 2004 and were valid under the old *s 310*. So directors with indemnities in place before that date could keep them. However, for certainty, incoming directors wishing to take advantage of an existing indemnity (eg one in a trust deed executed before 29 October 2004) could have been given a QTPIP which was only operative if they were found to be unable to rely on the existing indemnity.

Employer indemnity – position from 1 October 2007

3.47 The provisions of the *CA 1985* are repealed and restated in the *Companies Act 2006 (CA 2006)*. In addition to restating the requirements in relation to QTPIPs, *CA 2006* also introduced new provisions (*s 235*) in relation to 'qualifying pension scheme indemnity provisions' (QPSIPs). These provisions apply to any indemnity given on or after 1 October 2007 (to both new and existing directors).

A QPSIP allows a director of a corporate trustee of an occupational pension scheme to be indemnified by an associated company against liability incurred in connection with the company's activities as a trustee of the scheme. A QPSIP must not provide any indemnity against:

- liabilities for criminal or regulatory fines or penalties; or
- the cost of defending criminal proceedings in which the director is convicted.

The QPSIP permits a much wider indemnity than the QTPIP provisions as it allows for an indemnity against liabilities to the trustee company itself. This represents a relaxation of the position imposed by *CA 1985, s 309A*.

QTPIPs continue to be allowed under *CA 2006, s 234.*

Employer indemnity – transitional provisions

3.48 *Companies Act 2006 (Commencement No 3, Consequential Amendments, Transitional Provisions and Savings) Order 2007 (SI 2007/2194), Sch 3, para 15* provides transitional protection for pre-existing indemnities. It provides that the *CA 2006* sections apply to 'any provision made on or after 1 October 2007'. It also provides that *CA 1985, ss 309A* and *309B* will continue to apply 'in relation to any provision to which they applied immediately before that date'.

This means that existing indemnities and QTPIPs made under *s 309A* before 1 October 2007 remain valid (although consideration should be given to replacing them with a QPSIP where appropriate). The transitional provisions also appear to save pre-October 2004 indemnities which were previously expressly protected and exempt from *s 309A* (although the safest approach would be to put in place a QPSIP which is operative only if the previous indemnity is found not to be saved by the transitional provisions). It is still not entirely clear whether newly appointed directors can take advantage of existing indemnities under the transitional provisions. The safest course again might be to put in place a new indemnity (with a QPSIP if appropriate) which is operative only if the director is found not to be able to rely on the existing indemnity.

Court's discretion

3.49 Under *TA 1925, s 61*:

> 'If it appears to the court that a trustee … is or may be personally liable for any breach of trust…but has acted honestly and reasonably, and ought fairly to be excused for the breach of trust … the court may relieve him either wholly or partly from personal liability for the same.'

This is only a discretion of the court, and trustees should be reluctant to place too much reliance on it. In most situations the trustees are likely to rely on any exoneration and/or indemnity in the trust deed and rules, and only where none exists would the trustees seek an order under the provisions of this section.

Insurance

3.50 Trustees may wish to take out insurance against liability but should be mindful as to how far the terms of the policy restrict the circumstances in which they could make a claim. If it is intended that the premiums be paid from the trust fund, advice should be sought as to whether the circumstances and the terms of the scheme will permit this (eg see *Kemble v Hicks (No 2) [1999] PLR 287* on whether trustees can use scheme funds to pay for winding-up insurance). In any event, *PA 2004, s 256* prohibits the payment of premiums from a scheme's assets to insure against the imposition of fines or civil penalties (see **Appendix I**). More commonly, insurance tends to be used to protect the trustees against claims by 'missing beneficiaries' on the winding up of a scheme, rather than liabilities generally in relation to their actions (eg see *NBPF Pension Trustees Ltd [2008] EWHC 455 (Ch)*).

Data protection

3.51   Pension scheme trustees must comply with the *Data Protection Act 1998 (DPA 1998)*. In most cases, trustees will be 'data controllers' since they determine the purpose for which and the manner in which personal data is held and processed. The emphasis of *DPA 1998* is on compliance with the data protection principles and the rights of individuals (the data subjects) in respect of whom personal data is processed.

Personal data is data from which a living individual can be identified (either from that data alone or from that data and personal data that is likely to come into the possession of the data controller), including any expression of opinion. For example, this may include names, addresses and policy numbers relating to an individual. 'Processing' in relation to personal data covers almost all types of activity in relation to personal data, from obtaining to deletion, and includes all manner of activities in between, from retrieval to consultation.

The eight data protection principles, in summary, require that personal data must be:

(i)   processed fairly and lawfully;

(ii)   obtained and processed only for specified and lawful purposes;

(iii)   adequate, relevant and not excessive;

(iv)   accurate and, where necessary, kept up to date;

(v)   kept for no longer than necessary;

(vi)   processed in accordance with the rights of data subjects;

(vii)   kept secure, by ensuring appropriate technical and organisational measures are in place; and

(viii)   not transferred outside the European Economic Area unless adequate data protection safeguards are in place in the relevant territory.

For personal data to be processed 'fairly and lawfully', one or more of the conditions in *DPA 1998, Sch 2* must apply. One of these is that the data subject has given his or her consent to the processing. For 'sensitive personal data' to be processed 'fairly and lawfully', one or more of the conditions in *DPA 1998, Sch 3* must apply; here too one of the conditions is that the data subject has given his or her 'explicit' consent to the processing. 'Sensitive personal data' is defined in *DPA 1998* and includes data on a living individual's health condition, racial or ethnic origin, religious beliefs, offences or alleged offences, sexual life and whether he or she is a member of a Trade Union.

DPA 1998 gives the following rights to data subjects:

(a)   rights of access to information;

(b)   express rights to prevent direct marketing;

(c)   rights to rectify and erase inaccurate data;

(d)   rights relating to decisions taken by computer;

(e)   certain rights to prevent processing of data; and

(f)   rights to compensation.

Paper records as well as computerised data are covered by *DPA 1998*. Paper records will be covered if they are part of a 'relevant filing system' where specific information relating to a particular individual can be readily accessed. Manual files organised by reference to individual policy holders will, therefore, be caught.

Notification of pension scheme trustees

3.52   *DPA 1998* is regulated and enforced by the Information Commissioner's Office (ICO). Under *DPA 1998*, data controllers who process personal data – except where certain limited exemptions apply – must submit an annual notification to the ICO describing, amongst other matters, the purposes for which the personal data is processed. Notification can be done online; further information is available on the ICO web site (www.ico.gov.uk). Failure to notify when required to do so is a criminal offence.

Data controllers and data processors

3.53   Under *DPA 1998*, data processors (ie third parties who process personal data on behalf of a data controller) do not need to notify in that capacity. This means that pension scheme administrators (who often act as agents on behalf of pension scheme trustees in terms of processing data), advisers and annuity providers will not need to notify in that capacity. However, they may well need to notify in respect of personal data they process in their own right as data controller.

In some circumstances, a person holding data on behalf of a data controller can himself become a data controller (rather than merely a data processor). Guidance from the ICO ('Data controllers and data processors: what the difference is and what the governance implications are') provides that whether a person or organisation is a data controller or processor would depend on their roles and responsibilities in relation to the processing. If a professional service provider controls the information it obtains and processes, and also has its own professional standards, then the professional service provider could be a data controller in its own right. For example, if a pension scheme trustee engages a lawyer to write a report, the lawyer may also be a data controller along with the trustee. The lawyer, as a professional, will decide what information he needs to produce the report. Regardless of whether or not the client follows the lawyer's advice, the lawyer will not amend his advice as he alone decides the purposes for, and the way in which the data is used. The Scheme Actuary could in some circumstances also become a data controller where their work means that they are determining the purposes for which the data is used.

Pension scheme trustees acting as data controllers have various obligations under the seventh data protection principle of *DPA 1998* with respect to personal data processed by their data processors. Firstly, they must choose a data processor that provides sufficient guarantees in respect of technical and organisational measures governing the processing. This will require a certain amount of prior due diligence. Secondly, the data controller will need to have a contract in writing with each of its data processors under which they agree only to act on the instructions of the data controller and to put in place sufficient technical and organisational measures to keep personal data secure. Pension scheme trustees may also, as good practice, require in the data processing contract that the data processor immediately notify the pension scheme trustee upon becoming aware of any personal data breach or loss.

The ICO takes data controllers' obligations under the seventh data protection principle very seriously. In September 2012, Scottish Borders Council was fined £250,000 for a breach of the seventh data protection principle. Scottish Borders Council had engaged an outside company to digitise its pensions records but failed to seek appropriate guarantees about data security and failed to put a written contract in place. This came to light after a member of the public found copies of the pension records in a supermarket recycling bin and reported the matter to the police. Although, in this case, the fine was subsequently overturned on appeal in 2013, the issue of data security will continue to be a key issue for pension scheme trustees.

Practical steps to ensure compliance

3.54 Pension scheme trustees can take a number of practical steps to show that they are complying with *DPA 1998*:

(a)   appoint one person to take overall responsibility for data protection (commonly known as a 'data protection officer');

(b)   periodically carry out audits of processing activities, key risks and key risk management measures;

(c)   regularly update the forms used to collect personal and sensitive personal data;

(d)   ensure that suitable agreements are in place with all data processors;

(e)   address security issues both technical and organisational;

(f)   have procedures in place to deal with data subjects' requests;

(g)   have procedures in place to deal with data security breaches and train staff accordingly (including, but not limited to, initial reporting through to incident mitigation and management); and

(h)   review how necessary it is to collect data, especially 'sensitive' data as defined under *DPA 1998*.

Of particular relevance to pension scheme trustees will be:

(i)   data protection notices which need to be given to scheme members;

(ii)   the requirement to obtain express member consent for the processing of sensitive personal data;

(iii)   the security obligations, particularly with regard to data held by third parties; and

(iv)   restrictions on transferring data outside Europe.

Data protection developments

3.55 Data protection law and practice is developing rapidly, at both national and international level. It is vital from a risk management perspective that pension scheme trustees keep up to date with the latest developments and amend their policies and practices accordingly. In addition to consulting *DPA 1998*, pension scheme trustees should be aware of the various statutory instruments which supplement the *DPA 1998* provisions, together with the increasing number of guidance notes and codes of practice issued by the ICO.

In 2012 the ICO issued guidance on matters including data protection risk management with regard to cloud computing and anonymisation of personal data. In 2013, the ICO issued a new code of practice on dealing with subject access requests in addition to guidance on issues relating to Bring Your Own Device (the use of staff mobile devices for their work). More recently, in 2014 the ICO published a new code of practice on privacy impact assessments, which as their name suggests, are a tool for identifying and managing data protection/data privacy risks. These developments have occurred together with a steady stream of enforcement activity and fines from the ICO.

At EU level, the European Commission published a package of legal reforms in January 2012. These included a draft General Data Protection Regulation ('GDPR'). The official text of the GDPR (Regulation (EU) 2016/679) was published in the Official Journal of the European Union on 4 May 2016. It will replace the current Data Protection Directive (on which *DPA 1998* is based) and apply in all member states from 25 May 2018. The GDPR introduces much more extensive data protection regulation including more stringent data controller obligations, new data subject rights and mandatory data breach notification with fines of up to five per cent of annual worldwide turnover for breaches.

In view of the result of the UK referendum on 23 June 2016, it remains to be seen the extent to which, if at all, any provisions equivalent to those in the GDRP will be adopted by the UK Government. There would, on exit from the EU, be scope for *DPA 1998* to be amended or repealed as it is itself based on an EU Directive. However, it seems likely that the UK will maintain robust data protection legislation in order to allow international data transfer to continue. If the UK joins the European Free Trade Association (EFTA) then it is likely that the GDRP would apply. If some other model of trade agreement is reached then either the UK would need to have sufficient protections in place to qualify as a 'safe third country' or data transfers to the UK would be subject to stricter specific controls (such as those which currently apply on transfers to the US).

Trustees' duties to the employer

3.56   As considered in **3.11**, trustees must act to promote the proper purposes of the scheme. This will almost always mean acting in the best financial interests of the members and other beneficiaries. Case law allows trustees in certain circumstances to take into consideration the interests of the sponsoring employer (as an employer can in certain circumstances be a beneficiary of the scheme). This follows on from the trustees' fundamental duty to give effect to the trust deed and rules, which in turn is a reflection of the employer's promise (contractual or otherwise) to its employees to provide pension benefits. The trust deed and rules will confer a variety of powers, duties and discretions on the trustees to enable them to give effect to the promise of the employer to the employees. How the trustees exercise their powers, duties and discretions can have a significant impact on the ultimate costs borne by the employer.

An employer's interests in the occupational pension scheme which it sponsors are varied. One particular example of a trustee power which can significantly affect the interests of the employer is the trustee's power of investment. In a balance of cost scheme (such as a final salary or career average scheme) any failure by the trustees to obtain reasonable returns on the investment of the pension fund will result in the employer having to make greater contributions to the scheme to fund the promised benefits. In support of this are *PA 1995, s 35* and the *Investment Regulations, reg 2*, which oblige trustees to consult the employer when preparing or revising the statement of investment principles. Whilst the consultation process does not require the consent of the employer (indeed, this is prohibited by *s 35(5)*), the employer nevertheless may have rights against the trustees should they cause loss to the employer by exercising their powers in an imprudent manner.

Another example where the employer's interests are evident is in the case of the distribution of any surplus (less common in recent times), especially upon the winding-up of a scheme. There is a significant body of case law on this subject. In *Thrells Limited v Lomas [1993] 1 WLR 456* the scheme was winding up and was in surplus with an insolvent employer. The ultimate beneficiaries of any refund of surplus to the employer would be its creditors. The case set out factors that trustees should take into account in deciding how to exercise their discretion on allocation of surplus monies. The principal factors to consider are the scope of the discretion and its purpose, the source and size of the surplus, the financial position of the employer and the needs of members of the scheme. The usual duties of trustees will also apply when exercising their powers and they should, therefore, give proper consideration to all matters relevant to the exercise of the discretion.

This duty to the employer was noted by the High Court in *Edge v Pensions Ombudsman [1998] 2 All ER 547* where it stated:

> '... the proposition that the trustees were not entitled, when deciding how to reduce the £29.9 million surplus, to take any account of the position of the employers is one with which I emphatically disagree. The Employers play a critical part in this Pension Scheme. They have to pay contributions sufficient to keep the Scheme solvent.'

In *Merchant Navy Ratings Pension Fund v Stena Line [2015] EWHC 448 (Ch)*, the High Court was asked to consider a proposed rule amendment which would provide for deficit repair contributions to be paid by a wider group of former employers than the existing rules allowed. The effect of the amendment, if passed, would be likely to reduce the liability of certain existing employers. Asplin J held that this was a proper exercise of the trustees' powers. As long as the primary purpose of securing benefits was furthered, it was reasonable and proper, should the trustees consider it appropriate to do so, to take into account the interests of the participating employers. There was nothing improper when furthering the purposes of the scheme if some employers may ultimately pay less. The possibility of a reduction in liability for any employer was, at best, a side effect of the purpose for which the power was being exercised.

It is clear from the above that it would be wrong for the trustees blindly to ignore the interests of the employer when exercising their powers. On those occasions where trustees enter into negotiations with the employer about benefit changes or cessation of accrual, the trustees should be mindful that any extra financial burden which is placed (or continues to be placed) on the employer could ultimately jeopardise the ability of the employer to continue sponsoring the scheme. The circumstances of each exercise of the trustees' powers should be carefully examined and the interests of the employer taken into consideration.

Reporting breaches of the law

3.57   *PA 2004* imposes on trustees, employers, advisers and anyone involved in the administration of a scheme a duty to report to the Regulator breaches of law in relation to the administration of the scheme which are likely to be of material significance to the Regulator (*PA 2004, s 70*). The Regulator's Code of Practice No 1 'Reporting breaches of the law' sets out the requirements.

Who has a duty to report?

3.58   A legal duty to report falls on:

- trustees of trust-based pension schemes: each individually appointed trustee or, in the case of a corporate trustee, the trustee company;

- managers of schemes not established under trust (ie managers of personal pension schemes, including stakeholder schemes);

- persons otherwise involved in the administration of a scheme; this would include insurance companies and third party (as well as in-house) administrators;

- any employer participating in an occupational pension scheme;

- professional advisers – scheme actuaries, scheme auditors, legal advisers, fund managers and custodians of scheme assets; where the appointment is of a firm rather than an individual, the firm must put in place suitable systems to ensure that it meets this duty;

- persons otherwise involved in advising trustees or managers of a scheme in relation to the scheme; this could include IFAs, pensions consultants, investment consultants and auditors.

Whistleblowing protection and confidentiality

3.59 *PA 2004* makes clear that the duty to report overrides any other duties a reporter may have such as confidentiality and that any such duty is not breached by making a report. The Regulator expects reporters to act conscientiously and honestly and to take account of expert or professional advice where appropriate.

The duty to report does not, however, override legal privilege. The Regulator will, if asked, try to keep the identity of the reporter confidential.

When does the duty to report arise?

3.60 The requirement to report breaches of the law arises when a duty has not been or is not being complied with and that duty is:

- imposed by or by virtue of an enactment (ie an Act of Parliament) or rule of law (ie decisions of the courts and general trust law); and

- relevant to the administration of a scheme (ie anything which could potentially affect members' benefits or their ability to access information to which they are entitled).

Not every breach should be reported. In particular, the Regulator does not normally regard a breach as materially significant where prompt action is taken to remedy the breach and its cause and to notify any affected members.

The decision to report

3.61 The decision to report requires two key judgements:

(i) Does the reporter have reasonable cause to believe there has been a breach of the law relevant to the administration of the scheme?

(ii) If so, does the reporter believe the breach is likely to be of material significance to the Regulator?

A reasonable cause to believe means more than a suspicion that cannot be substantiated. If all the facts are not known, the reporter is expected to investigate further; if he still has reasonable cause to believe that a breach has occurred he need not then gather all the evidence which the Regulator would require before taking legal action.

What is of material significance to the Regulator will depend on:

- the cause of the breach;

- its effect;
- the reaction to it (whether prompt and effective action is taken to remedy the breach and prevent a recurrence and to notify affected members); and
- its wider implications (eg effect on DB funding, likelihood of similar breaches occurring because trustees lack the appropriate knowledge and understanding).

The cause of the breach

3.62   Where a contributory cause of the breach is:

- dishonesty;
- poor governance or inadequate controls resulting in deficient administration or slow or inappropriate decision-making practices;
- incomplete or inaccurate advice; or
- acting (or failing to act) in deliberate contravention of the law,

then the breach is likely to be of material significance to the Regulator. However, the Regulator will not consider as materially significant a breach arising from an isolated incident.

The effect of the breach

3.63   The Regulator considers that breach of the following is likely to be of material significance to it in the context of its statutory objective to protect members' benefits:

- substantially the right money is paid into the scheme at the right time;
- assets are appropriately safeguarded;
- payments out of the scheme are legitimate and timely;
- defined benefit schemes are complying with the legal requirements on scheme funding;
- trustees of occupational pension schemes are properly considering their investment policy and investing in accordance with it; and
- contributions in respect of money purchase members are correctly allocated and invested.

The Regulator also has a statutory duty to reduce the risk of compensation being payable from the PPF, and so is concerned that notifiable events (see **3.66** onwards) are reported to it and that PPF requirements are complied with during an assessment period.

3.64 *Trustees*

Finally, the Regulator has a statutory duty to promote the good administration of pension schemes and so is concerned to hear that schemes are administered properly, appropriate records are maintained and members receive accurate, clear and impartial information without delay.

Making a report

3.64 All reporters should have effective arrangements in place to identify and report breaches that occur in areas relating to their functions and any other breaches they become aware of in the course of their work. Reports must be submitted as soon as reasonably practicable (depending on the circumstances). Each report should be dated and include as a minimum the name of the scheme; description of the breach; any relevant dates; name of the employer; name, position and contact details of the reporter; and the role of the reporter. Joint reports are possible. Reports can be sent by post or electronically, including by email or by fax, but the Pensions Regulator's preferred method is via its online Exchange system, accessible from its website (www.thepensionsregulator.gov. uk). Additional information is available on the website and in the Code of Practice.

Trustees must be aware of these reporting requirements and should put in place a formal policy for identifying, investigating and reporting breaches. Any policy should include arrangements for liaising with other reporters and ensuring that systems are in place to identify and, where appropriate, investigate suspected breaches at an early stage so that timely reports may be made where judged to be of material significance to the Regulator.

Civil penalties apply for failure to comply with the obligation to report a breach without reasonable excuse.

The Regulator's response

3.65 The Regulator has a wide range of measures it can use in reacting to a report of a breach, including:

- assisting or instructing trustees and others to achieve compliance;

- providing education or guidance;

- appointing trustees to help run the scheme;

- removing trustees from office;

- freezing the scheme;

- imposing special measures where the scheme funding requirements of *PA 2004* are not complied with;

- ordering that the scheme's funding position be restored to the level before a breach or other detrimental event occurred; and

- imposing fines where appropriate.

Reporting notifiable events

3.66   *PA 2004* introduced, with effect from 6 April 2005, a duty on the employer and the trustees to notify the Regulator of certain events (*PA 2004, s 69*), which are laid out in the *Pensions Regulator (Notifiable Events) Regulations 2005 (SI 2005/900)* (the *'Notifiable Events Regulations'*), as amended. The purpose of these is to give the Regulator an early warning of problems which might give rise to a claim on the PPF. The Regulator's 'Code of Practice No 2 – Notifiable Events' (first issued in June 2005) and related Directions (April 2005) provide exceptions to the duty to notify (broadly, fewer events need be notified if the scheme is funded above a certain level: see below). The notifiable events regime does not apply to money purchase schemes as they are not eligible for PPF protection. Further notifiable events have also been introduced as part of the employer debt regime (see **Chapter 15**).

Notifiable events duty

3.67   There are two main types of notifiable events:

- scheme-related events (*s 69(2)(a)*) notifiable by trustees (individually and collectively); and

- employer-related events (*s 69(2)(b)*) notifiable by employers.

Timing of notification

3.68   An event must be notified in writing to the Regulator as soon as reasonably practicable after the person becomes aware of it. The events themselves are worded to make clear when they should be notified. This will depend on the circumstances, though the Regulator states that 'In all cases … it implies urgency'. For example, where a trustee is made aware of a notifiable event on a Sunday, the Regulator expects to be notified on the Monday. It is not necessary to seek professional or expert advice on whether an event has occurred, but ideally trustees and employers should put in place a system for identifying and reporting notifiable events.

Trustees may be advised to enter into a dialogue with the employer with a view to agreeing a process for exchanging relevant information about potential notifiable events (on a confidential basis, if required by the employer).

How to notify

3.69 All notifications must be in writing. Reports can be sent by post or electronically, including by email or by fax, but the Pensions Regulator's preferred method is via its online Exchange system, accessible from its website (www.thepensionsregulator.gov.uk). The minimum information that should be included in a notification is the:

- description of the notifiable event;
- date of the event;
- name of the pension scheme;
- name of the employer; and
- name, position and contact details of the notifier.

Further additional information that the Regulator would find useful is also set out in the Code of Practice. The duty on trustees and employers to notify overrides any other duty of confidentiality except legal privilege.

Failure to notify

3.70 Trustees must take all reasonable steps to comply with the notifiable events duty and employers must comply unless they have a reasonable excuse for not doing so. Failure to comply is reportable as a breach of the law under *PA 2004, s 70*. In the event of a failure to notify, the Regulator will in the first instance seek an explanation. Following this it will have a range of actions it can take, including requiring training or other assistance – although the Regulator does not have the power to unwind any particular transaction. Where appropriate, however, civil penalties can be imposed, and failure to notify will be taken into account by the Regulator in deciding whether or not to impose a contribution notice.

Events to be reported

3.71 The *Notifiable Events Regulations* confirm which events will need to be reported to the Regulator. The Directions (see **3.66** and **3.74**) set down Conditions in which no report is required.

Trustee events

3.72 Subject to the Conditions, trustees must notify the following events:

(*a*)   any decision by the trustees to take action which will, or is intended to, result in any debt which is or may become due to the scheme not being paid in full *unless* the Conditions in A, B and C (set out below) are satisfied;

(*b*)   a decision by the trustees to make or accept a transfer payment to or from another scheme, or the making or acceptance of such a transfer payment where a decision is not required, the value of which is more than the lower of five per cent of the value of the scheme assets and £1.5 million *unless* the Conditions in A and B are satisfied;

(*c*)   a decision by the trustees to grant benefits, or a right to benefits, on more favourable terms than those provided for by the scheme rules, without either seeking advice from the scheme actuary or securing additional funding where such funding was advised by the actuary;

(*d*)   a decision by the trustees to grant benefits or rights to benefits to a member, or the granting of such benefits or rights where a decision is not required, the cost of which is more than the lower of five per cent of the scheme assets and £1.5 million *unless* the Conditions in A and B are satisfied.

Employer events

3.73   Subject to the Conditions, employers must notify the following events:

(*a*)   any decision by the employer to take action which will, or is intended to, result in a debt which is or may become due to the scheme not being paid in full;

(*b*)   a decision by the employer to cease to carry on business in the UK or, where the employer ceases to carry on business in the UK without such a decision being taken, the cessation of business in the UK by that employer;

(*c*)   receipt by the employer of advice that it is trading wrongfully or circumstances being reached where a director or former director of the company knows that there is no reasonable prospect that the company will avoid going into insolvent liquidation;

(*d*)   any breach of a banking covenant by the employer, other than where the bank agrees with the employer not to enforce the covenant, *unless* the Conditions in A and B are satisfied;

(*e*)   a decision by a controlling company to relinquish control of the employer or, where the controlling company relinquishes such control without a decision to do so having been taken, the relinquishing of control of the employer company by the controlling company, *unless* the Conditions in A and B are satisfied;

(*f*) the conviction of an individual, in any jurisdiction, for an offence involving dishonesty if the offence was committed while the individual was a director or partner of the employer.

The Directions

3.74

- *Condition A:* The value of the scheme's assets is equal to or greater than the value of the scheme's liabilities calculated on the basis of the most recent PPF risk-based levy valuation under *s 179 PA 2004.*

- *Condition B:* The trustees have not incurred a duty to make a report in the previous 12 months for:

  – the employer's failure to make a payment to the scheme of material significance to the Regulator in accordance with the most recently agreed schedule of contributions under *PA 2004*; or

  – the employer's failure to pay contributions due under a schedule of contributions in force under *PA 1995* on or before the due date.

- *Condition C:* The decision by the trustees to compromise a debt where the full amount is less than 0.5 per cent of the scheme's assets calculated on the relevant basis (see Condition A).

Internal controls

Requirement for internal controls

3.75 *Article 14* of the EC *Directive on Institutions for Occupational Retirement Provision* requires that occupational pension schemes have adequate internal control mechanisms. The *Occupational Pension Schemes (Internal Controls) Regulations 2005 (SI 2005/3379)* came into force on 30 December 2005. These Regulations inserted a new *s 249A* into *PA 2004*, which requires trustees or managers of occupational pension schemes to establish and operate internal controls which are adequate for the scheme to be administered and managed in accordance with the scheme rules and in accordance with pensions and other relevant legislation. Internal controls are defined as arrangements and procedures for administering and managing the scheme, systems and arrangements for monitoring that administration and management, and arrangements and procedures to be followed for the safe custody and security of the scheme's assets.

Code of Practice

3.76   The Regulator's 'Code of Practice No 9, Internal Controls', and related Guidance sets out the Regulator's expectations of how occupational pension schemes should comply with the requirement to have adequate internal controls, in particular as to the implementation of a risk management process by the trustees to identify, assess and manage risk in a proportionate manner. Specific types of risk identified by the Regulator are operational, financial, funding, regulatory and compliance risk. The revised and expanded Guidance, in force from June 2010, states that the Regulator sets out a non-exhaustive list of seven key areas of risk and suggests control procedures for each:

- lack of knowledge and understanding;
- conflicts of interest;
- ineffective relations with advisers;
- poor record keeping;
- deterioration in employer covenant;
- investment risk; and
- ineffective retirement processes.

The Regulator expects trustees to maintain a risk register, to identify risks in order of priority and to address all these risk areas over a reasonable period of time.

Chapter 4

State pension provision and contracting-out

Introduction

4.1 State pension provision is based on an individual's national insurance contribution ('NIC') record. Those reaching State pension age ('SPA') before 6 April 2016 will remain subject to the provisions of the *Social Security Contributions and Benefits Act 1992* (*SSCBA 1992*) (as amended) and will receive (if they qualify) a basic and additional State pension (see **4.3** to **4.6** below).

Those reaching SPA on and from 6 April 2016 will (if they qualify) receive the new State pension ('NSP'). This is a single-tier pension (with the distinction between basic and additional pensions removed) as provided for in the *Pensions Act 2014* (*PA 2014*) (see **4.7** to **4.9** below).

Historically, it was possible for occupational pension schemes to be contracted-out of the additional State pension. In order to have been contracted-out, a contracting-out certificate must have been issued in relation to a scheme, and the scheme must have satisfied, amongst other things, the requirements set out in *PSA 1993, Part III* (as amended) and the *Occupational Pension Schemes (Contracting-out) Regulations 1996 (SI 1996/1172)* (as amended) ('the *Contracting-out Regulations 1996*'). Contracting-out allowed both employers and employees to pay lower NICs during periods of contracted out employment.

Contracting-out on a money purchase basis ceased with effect from 6 April 2012 and contracting-out was abolished altogether under *PA 2014* with effect from 6 April 2016. Individuals who have been in contracted-out employment receive their basic State pension on reaching SPA before 6 April 2016, but payments representing their additional State pension relating to periods of contracted-out employment are made from the contracted-out scheme. For those reaching SPA on or after 6 April 2016, periods of contracted-out employment will be factored into the level of their NSP (see **4.9** below).

State pension provision

State Pension Age

4.2   Until recently, men had an SPA of 65 and women 60. This has now changed and the rules for determining SPA operate on the basis of a person's date of birth. The more recently a person was born, the higher his or her SPA will be. The detail is set out in tables in *PA 1995, Sch 4, Part 1* (as amended by the *Pensions Act 2007 (PA 2007)*, the *Pensions Act 2011 (PA 2011)* and *PA 2014*).

Following the amendments made by *PA 2011*, women's SPA will increase to 65 by November 2018 and then, from December 2018, SPA for both men and women will increase to reach 66 by October 2020. Under *PA 2014*, SPA will increase to 67 by 2028. Currently, SPA is due to increase to 68 by 2046, but this is subject to review as outlined below.

In the March 2012 Budget, the Chancellor announced that an automatic review of SPA would be introduced to take account of increases in longevity. This resulted in *PA 2014, s 27*, which requires a review of SPA at least every six years, with the first one taking place before 7 May 2017. The review must take into account life expectancy and other matters which the Secretary of State considers relevant, including whether a person should be expected to spend a specified proportion of his adult life in retirement. In December 2013, in his Autumn Statement, the Chancellor announced that the Government's position is that people should spend, on average, up to one-third of their adult life drawing a State pension. In March 2016, John Cridland CBE was appointed to undertake the first review, looking at SPA from 2028. The terms of reference for the review provide that the recommendations should be affordable in the long term, fair to current and future generations of pensioners and consistent with supporting fuller working lives. The terms of reference do not mention the one-third of adult life criteria previously announced.

An individual must apply to receive the State retirement pension. The Department for Work and Pensions sends the appropriate forms to those who are eligible shortly before they reach SPA.

Pensions for those reaching SPA before 6 April 2016

Categories of pension

4.3   For those reaching SPA before 6 April 2016 there are four categories of State retirement pension: A, B, C and D. Entitlement to State retirement provision for those individuals is governed principally by *SSCBA 1992* (as amended).

4.4   *State pension provision and contracting-out*

Category A and Category B pensions are contributory and are made up of the basic State pension and any additional element payable from the State Earnings Related Pension Scheme ('SERPS') or the State second pension ('S2P') (see **4.6** below). The Category A pension payable to an individual is derived from his NIC record. The Category B pension is payable in certain circumstances by virtue of the contribution record of an individual's spouse or civil partner.

Category C and Category D pensions are non-contributory and are payable only in very restricted circumstances. Category C pensions are payable to men and women who were over SPA on 5 July 1948 and to the spouses of those men who qualified (it seems unlikely that any Category C pension is still in payment). Certain individuals who are over age 80 may receive a Category D pension if they are not entitled to any other category of State pension or if the pension they are entitled to is less than the Category D pension.

For those reaching SPA on or after 6 April 2016 there is one category of State retirement pension: the NSP.

National Insurance contribution record

4.4   Generally, in order for an individual to qualify for a Category A or Category B State retirement pension, sufficient Class 1, Class 2 or Class 3 NICs must have been paid or credited to him or sufficient earnings must have been credited to him (in accordance with *SSCBA 1992, Sch 3, Part 1*). From 26 September 2007 (the date on which *PA 2007* came into effect), where the contributor attains SPA before 6 April 2010, in order to qualify for a full basic State pension, those payments or credits must have been made for 44 years for a man and 39 years for a woman. Where the contributor attains SPA on or after 6 April 2010, those payments or credits must have been made for not less than 30 years of his or her working life. Where the individual's NIC record falls short of these requirements, a reduced basic State pension may still be payable. From 6 April 2016, 35 years of NICs or contribution credits will be required for a full NSP, with a minimum of ten years for any NSP at all (see **4.7** below).

An individual's 'working life' starts on 6 April immediately preceding his 16th birthday and ends on 5 April immediately preceding his attaining SPA or his death. Usually, the working life of an individual born before 6 April 1959 will therefore be 49 years in the case of a man and between 44 and 49 years in the case of a woman (depending on her SPA). Individuals born on or after 6 April 1959 will usually have a working life of between 49 and 52 years depending on their SPA.

The level of NICs to be paid in respect of a person's earnings is set out in *SSCBA 1992, Part 1* and the *Social Security (Contributions) Regulations*

2001. The Class 1 National Insurance contributions payable depend on a person's earnings in relation to the primary and secondary thresholds and the lower and upper earnings limits. These are statutory measures which are prescribed each year. For the tax year 2015/2016, the annual primary threshold is £8,060 and the annual secondary threshold is £8,112, the lower earnings limit ('LEL') (or qualifying earnings factor) is £5,824 and the upper earnings limit ('UEL') is £43,004 for 2016/2017. Class 1 NICs are collected through the PAYE system.

Primary Class 1 NICs are payable by employees in respect of earnings during their working lives (as described above). For the tax years 2015/2016 and 2016/2017, employees are liable to pay Primary Class 1 NICs at the rate of 12 per cent on earnings in excess of the primary threshold but below the UEL. Additional NICs at the rate of two per cent are payable by employees on earnings in excess of the UEL. Employees earning between the LEL and the primary threshold do not pay primary Class 1 NICs, but are treated as having done so for contributory benefit purposes.

Secondary Class 1 NICs at the rate of 13.8 per cent are payable by employers in respect of those employees whose earnings are in excess of the secondary threshold for the year 2014/2015. There is no upper limit on secondary Class 1 NICs.

Class 2 NICs are flat-rate contributions payable by the self-employed. Class 3 NICs are voluntary contributions. They can be made by an individual to boost his contribution record so as to ensure that he has sufficient contributions to entitle him to a particular benefit. Class 4 NICs are paid by the self-employed on profits in excess of the lower profit limit. For the tax year 2016/2017, Class 4 NICs are payable at nine per cent on profits between the lower profit limit and upper profit limit (£8,060 and £43,000 respectively) and at two per cent on profits in excess of the upper profit limit.

Basic State pension

4.5   The basic State pension is payable to all individuals who have:

(*a*)   reached SPA before 6 April 2016;

(*b*)   made sufficient National Insurance contributions (see **4.4** above); and

(*c*)   made a claim for a State retirement pension.

The rate of the basic State pension is increased each year. From April 2016, the full rate of the basic State pension is £119.30 per week for an individual (this is the basic Category A pension and the basic Category B pension).

Additional State pension

4.6   The second element of a Category A or Category B pension is the additional State pension. This was first brought into force in 1978 under SERPS, which applied to certain earnings by employees from 6 April 1978 to 5 April 2002 (see **4.10** below). SERPS was replaced by S2P from 6 April 2002, aimed at providing a more generous additional State pension for certain categories of people. In order to receive an additional State pension the claimant must have reached SPA before 6 April 2016.

Where an individual was contracted-out, no additional pension would be payable from the State relating to the period during which he was contracted-out.

An individual could build up entitlement to SERPS in any tax year from 6 April 1978 to 5 April 2002 that fell within his working life (see **4.4** above). The entitlement would be based on the extent to which a proportion of earnings exceeded the LEL in any tax year during that period. Consequently, those individuals earning less than the LEL would not build up any entitlement to SERPS.

S2P was introduced by the *Child Support, Pensions and Social Security Act 2000* and was intended to provide a bigger pension than SERPS by boosting the additional State pension of low and moderate earners, carers and the long-term disabled.

In the tax years from 6 April 2002 to 5 April 2016, the S2P regime operated automatically to provide a yearly earnings factor for people who fall within one of the prescribed categories described below. The factor is based on the 'LET' (Low Earnings Threshold), which was set at £15,300 for the tax year 2015/2016 (but varies each year in line with the general level of earnings in Great Britain). The earnings factor is used as the basis on which to calculate the individual's annual rate of additional pension.

S2P applied to those who were:

(*a*)   employed and earning above the LEL;

(*b*)   claiming child benefit for a child under 12;

(*c*)   carers (for at least 20 hours per week); or

(*d*)   receiving specified illness or disability benefits.

Individuals earning less than the LET, but equal to or in excess of the LEL for the year, were treated for S2P calculation purposes as if they had earnings equal to the LET.

Pensions for those reaching SPA on or after 6 April 2016

New State pension

4.7   On 14 May 2014 *PA 2014* received Royal Assent. It introduced the new State pension ('NSP'), a single-tier pension for individuals who reach their SPA on or after 6 April 2016 (*PA 2014, ss 1* and *56(4)*).

The basics of the NSP are as follows:

- The starting level from 6 April 2016 is £155.65 per week. This will be increased annually. The current Government commitment is that annual increases will be based on a 'triple-lock' being the highest of increases in prices (currently measured using the Consumer Prices Index), earnings and 2.5 per cent.

- An individual will need 35 qualifying years of NICs (or credits to that effect) to be eligible to receive the full rate. For individuals who fall short of 35 qualifying years, a pro-rated amount will be paid provided they have at least ten qualifying years (*State Pension Regulations 2015, reg 13*) (see **4.4** above). Voluntary NICs can be paid to cover years where the individual's NIC record was not sufficient to count as a qualifying year.

- A deduction will be made for any period of contracted-out employment, the 'contracted-out pension equivalent' ('COPE') (see **4.9** below).

- It will be based solely on an individual's own NIC record, and it will not be possible to inherit or derive a pension from a spouse or civil partner.

Calculation of new State pension

4.8   Individuals who do not have a 'qualifying year' until after 5 April 2016 will have their pension calculated entirely under the NSP rules. A qualifying year is a year in which an individual's earnings factors equal or exceed the qualifying earnings factor (ie the LEL) for that year (*PA 2014, s 2*).

Individuals who are not working can obtain qualifying years through National Insurance credits. These apply to those who cannot work because of illness or disability, are carers or are unemployed. It includes those who could claim Child Benefit for a child under 12 or receive Jobseeker's Allowance, Employment and Support Allowance or Carer's Allowance (*SSBCA 1992, s 22* and the *State Pension Regulations 2015, SI 2015/173, Part 8*). Voluntary NICs can also be made in some circumstances to increase an individual's qualifying years.

The calculation of NSP is based on the number of qualifying years. For example, an individual who has 32 qualifying years (all falling after 5 April 2016) would have an NSP of 32/35 of the full amount when they reach SPA.

4.9 *State pension provision and contracting-out*

There are transitional calculation provisions for those whose working life started before 6 April 2016 (*PA 2014, ss 4* and *5* and *Sch 1*).

Each individual has a 'starting amount' as at 6 April 2016 which is the higher of:

(*a*)   the amount they would get under the old basic State pension and additional State pension as if they had reached SPA on 6 April 2016; and

(*b*)   the amount they would get had the NSP been in place for the whole of their working life. Where an individual has been in contracted-out employment, a deduction is made relating to those periods (see **4.9** below).

If the starting amount is more than the full rate of NSP on 6 April 2016 then this is what the individual will receive at SPA, subject to revaluation. The amount up to the value of NSP is revalued in line with increases in NSP. The amount in excess of NSP is revalued in line with prices (currently measured using the Consumer Prices Index). If the starting amount is lower than the NSP then the individual will get that amount (revalued to SPA in line with increases in NSP) plus additional pension up to the full NSP in relation to any qualifying years achieved between 6 April 2016 and SPA.

Contracted-out pensions equivalent ('COPE')

4.9   Where an individual has a period of contracted-out employment then this must be taken into account in the calculation of the 'starting amount' for the NSP under the transitional rules (see **4.8** above) (*PA 2014, Sch 1, para 5*).

The COPE is the difference between:

(*a*)   the amount of any additional State pension taken into account in step (*a*) of the calculation in **4.8** above; and

(*b*)   the amount of any additional State pension that would have been included if the employment had not been treated as having been contracted-out.

The COPE amount will not necessarily be exactly the same as the amount of additional pension the member will receive from his formerly contracted-out pension scheme. In defined benefit schemes it may be difficult to identify the amount of the 'additional' contracted-out element in relation to reference scheme test benefits (see **4.27** below) and in defined contribution schemes the actual amount of the pension received will depend on investment returns and the manner in which the benefit is taken rather than directly relating to the value of the additional State pension given up.

A brief history of contracting-out

Background

4.10 On 6 April 1978, the State Earnings Related Pension Scheme ('SERPS') was created, which introduced a mandatory, earnings-related top up to the basic State pension to supplement individuals' retirement pensions.

From the outset, it was possible for occupational pension schemes to be contracted-out of SERPS. Contracted-out schemes had to satisfy certain statutory requirements (originally in the *Social Security Pensions Act 1975* and, since 7 February 1994, in *PSA 1993*) and hold a contracting-out certificate. Members benefited from NIC rebates, and the intention was that they would receive pensions from their scheme that were at least equal to what they would have received from SERPS. Meanwhile, the State received a lower immediate NIC income but would no longer be required to pay for additional State pension out of future tax or NICs.

Initially, it was possible for schemes to contract out of SERPS only on a salary related basis and members were able to accrue rights to a Guaranteed Minimum Pension ('GMP'). From 6 April 1988, schemes could instead be contracted-out out on a money purchase basis, and members were able to accrue protected rights.

The legislation changed on 6 April 1997 (through amendments to *PSA 1993* made by *PA 1995*), following which GMPs could no longer accrue but the scheme could still contract out on a salary-related basis provided that it met an overall scheme quality test. The legislation also made it possible for schemes to be contracted-out on both a salary-related and a money purchase basis at the same time: see **4.13** below.

On 6 April 2002, SERPS was replaced by the State Second Pension (S2P). S2P was designed to boost the additional State pension of low and moderate earners and also to extend the category of people who would qualify. These changes were not intended to have a significant impact on the way in which occupational pension schemes were contracted-out. Certain other simplification measures, such as increasing the options available for discharging contracted-out rights and increasing members' transfer options, were also introduced (*Child Support, Pensions and Social Security Act 2000*).

The whole concept of contracting-out has been subject to Government review. This has led to various changes, including from 6 April 2009 (under *PA 2007*) a fixed cap on the earnings used to calculate S2P, the ability for schemes to convert GMPs into main scheme benefits, the abolition of contracting-out on a money purchase basis from 6 April 2012, and from 6 April 2016, the abolition of contracting-out entirely.

4.11 *State pension provision and contracting-out*

The requirements for the treatment of benefits accrued during periods of contracted-out employment are now set out in *PSA 1993, Part III* and the *Occupational Pension Schemes (Schemes that were Contracted-out) (No 2) Regulations 2015 (SI 2015/1677)* ('the *Contracting-out Regulations 2015*').

Defined benefit schemes

4.11   Although members of contracted-out salary related ('COSR') schemes ceased accruing GMPs on 5 April 1997, GMPs are retained in respect of service completed before that date. Even after they cease to be contracted-out, schemes must continue to comply with the requirements relating to GMPs. Between 6 April 1997 and 5 April 2016, COSR schemes had to satisfy the reference scheme test, a scheme quality test introduced by *PA 1995*. This aimed to ensure that a certain overall level of benefits would be provided for members of the scheme.

Money purchase schemes

4.12   It was possible, from April 1988 to April 2012, for members of money purchase arrangements, including personal pension schemes and freestanding additional voluntary contribution schemes, to contract out of SERPS. In the case of an employer-sponsored arrangement, generally a contracted-out money purchase ('COMP') scheme, each member had to be provided with benefits based on contributions actually made and the investment return on those contributions. The employer's contributions had to be at least equal to the contracted-out rebate (see **4.14** below).

In order to promote contracting-out for new arrangements, the Department of Social Security (now DWP) paid an 'incentive' of 2 per cent of earnings between the upper and lower earnings limit. This payment ceased in April 1993. From 6 April 1997, age-related rebates were payable in addition to the flat-rate contracted-out rebate (see **4.36** below).

Since 6 April 2012, it has not been possible to contract out on a money purchase basis.

Mixed benefit schemes

4.13   Prior to 6 April 1997, a scheme could only be contracted-out on either a salary related or a money purchase basis. A scheme could not contract out by both methods simultaneously, nor could it elect to convert from one to the other, unless it first ceased to contract out on the original basis and discharged its liability to pay contracted-out benefits on that basis.

From 6 April 1997, it became possible for schemes to contract out via both the money purchase and salary-related routes at the same time. Initially, only schemes which were contracting-out for the first time, and COSR schemes subject to a re-election to contract-out on or after 6 April 1997, were able to become contracted-out mixed benefit ('COMB') schemes. This flexibility was extended to COMP schemes from 6 April 1998.

The changes introduced with effect from 6 April 2012 mean that contracting-out on a COMB basis has not been possible since that date.

The contracted-out rebate

4.14   An individual's entitlement to a State pension will generally depend on the NICs that have been paid or credited to him. Primary Class 1 NICs are payable by employees, and secondary Class 1 NICs are payable by employers. When a person was in contracted-out employment, the Class 1 contributions were reduced and that reduction was known as the 'contracted-out rebate'.

The contracted-out rebate was originally intended to be equivalent to the cost of providing the additional State pension benefit being given up (which increases with the age of the person in respect of whom the benefit is provided). The contracted-out rebate was historically been based on the cost of providing the benefit for a person of 'average' age. Broadly, it was financially advantageous for those younger than the average age to contract out, and for those older than the average age to remain in the additional State pension.

The aggregate employer and employee contracted-out rebate on Class 1 NICs for COSR schemes 6 April 2012 to 5 April 2016 was 4.8 per cent of band earnings (ie earnings between the LEL and the upper accrual point). The employee benefited from a reduction in his Class 1 NICs equal to 1.4 per cent of his band earnings and the employer from a reduction equal to 3.4 per cent of band earnings. These rates were set out in the *Social Security (Reduced Rates of Class 1 Contributions, Rebates and Minimum Contributions) Order 2011 (SI 2011/1036)*.

The contracting-out certificate

4.15   Contracting-out certificates were issued to employers, stating that the employment of earners (or a category or description of earners) in a particular trade, business, profession, office or vocation was contracted-out employment by reference to a named contracted-out scheme. An employer must have had a valid contracting-out certificate in order to deduct and pay NICs at the reduced rate. All money purchase contracting-out certificates for COMP schemes and

COMB schemes were cancelled with effect from 6 April 2012 and for COSR schemes from 6 April 2016.

A person would have been in contracted-out employment in any period during which he was under SPA, where there was a contracting-out certificate in force in relation to his employment, and where his service qualified him for a pension provided by a contracted-out scheme (*PSA 1993, s 8*).

A COSR scheme would have been a contracted-out scheme in relation to an earner's employment if it was specified in a contracting-out certificate in relation to that employment. Certain conditions must have been satisfied by the scheme in order for it to be contracted-out (see **4.16** below).

Schemes contracting-out for the first time would have been required to comply with the election procedure set out in the *Contracting-out Regulations 1996, regs 2–16* (as they stood at the time the election was made).

Defined benefits schemes

Requirements for contracting-out

4.16   A salary related scheme could have been contracted-out in relation to an earner's employment only if:

(*a*)   in relation to service completed before 6 April 1997 (*PSA 1993, s 9(2A)*):

    (i)   the scheme complied with the requirements of *PSA 1993* relating to the provision of GMPs (as set out in *PSA 1993, ss 13 to 24E* and the *Contracting-out Regulations 1996*); and

    (ii)   the rules of the scheme applying to GMPs are framed so as to comply with any requirements relating to the form and content of contracted-out schemes as may be prescribed in regulations or imposed by HMRC; and

(*b*)   in relation to service completed on or after 6 April 1997 but before 6 April 2016 (*PSA 1993, s 9(2B)*), HMRC was satisfied that:

    (i)   the scheme satisfied the reference scheme test (see **4.28** to **4.30** below);

    (ii)   unless the scheme was a public service pension scheme, it was subject to, and complied with, the provisions of *PA 1995* relating to employer-related investments (as set out in *PA 1995, s 40*, see **Chapter 10**);

    (iii)   all parts of the scheme met the statutory funding objective or the actuary had certified that, in his opinion, the statutory funding objective could be expected to be met by the end of the period specified in the recovery plan (see **Chapter 11**);

(iv) the scheme did not permit the payment of a lump sum instead of a pension unless the payment was an authorised lump sum under *FA 2004* and satisfied certain other conditions (see **Chapter 17**);

(v) the scheme rules satisfied the requirements set out in *Contracting-out Regulations 1996, reg 20A* in relation to payments in respect of a person who was, in the opinion of the trustees, unable to act by reason of mental disorder;

(vi) the scheme provided for benefits to be payable by reference to an age equal for men and women and permitted by *FA 2004* (see **Chapter 17**); and

(vii) the rules of the scheme were framed so as to comply with any requirements relating to the form and content of contracted-out rules as prescribed in regulations or specified by HMRC.

(*PSA 1993, s 9* and *Contracting-out Regulations 1996, Part III* as they stood immediately before 6 April 2016).

Generally, schemes that are not registered (see **Chapter 17**) were not permitted to contract out (*Contracting-out Regulations 1996, reg 29*).

The abolition of contracting-out

4.17 Concurrent with the abolition of the additional State pension and the coming into effect of the new State pension (see **4.1** to **4.9** above) was the abolition of contracting-out for salary-related schemes. *PA 2014 s 24*, which received Royal Assent on 14 May 2014, abolished contracting-out with effect from 6 April 2016.

PA 2014 Sch 13 makes amendments to contracting-out legislation, principally *PSA 1993*, to achieve abolition and to provide safeguards for contracted-out rights. This includes the addition of a new *s 12E* to the *PSA 1993* which requires formerly contracted-out schemes to continue to meet GMP requirements and the requirements of the *Contracting-out Regulations 2015 (SI 2016/1677)*. Certain provisions of *PSA 1993* relating to the issue, variation and surrender of contracting-out certificates will remain in force after 6 April 2016 to allow HMRC to issue certificates relating to a period before the abolition date, and to deal with any variation or surrender which takes effect before that date.

PA 2014, Sch 13 also provides that the Secretary of State must give such guidance as he or she thinks appropriate about GMP conversion although DWP guidance on this topic has not yet been published.

4.17 *State pension provision and contracting-out*

In light of the removal of the contracting-out rebate (see **4.14** above), an overriding power was inserted by *PA 2014, Sch 14* enabling employers to amend scheme rules to increase member contributions and/or modify the rate of accrual, without the need for trustee consent where it would otherwise be required, in order to offset the additional cost of providing benefits. The power is available for a five-year period effective from 6 April 2016, and may be exercised in relation to current as well as future scheme members. Other conditions apply to the power, including that:

(*a*)   it cannot be used to reduce the value of members' benefits that accrue each year by more than the annual increase in employer NICs relating to those members;

(*b*)   it cannot have the effect of increasing the total employee contributions payable annually beyond the annual increase in employer NICs relating to those employees;

(*c*)   the power only applies to future benefits such that it cannot be used in a manner which would or might affect subsisting rights (see **Chapter 13**);

(*d*)   it may be used to amend scheme rules on more than one occasion in relation to the same member;

(*e*)   it cannot take effect before 6 April 2016 (although it may be exercised before or after that date); and

(*f*)   it cannot be used in relation to public sector schemes, or in relation to a 'protected person', ie persons who have protected person status due to their employment in nationalised industries which have subsequently become privatised (including the electricity, rail, coal and nuclear energy industries), and who continue to retain such statutory protection.

Certification is required from an actuary appointed by the employer that the value to the employer attaching to the amendment is not greater than the increase to the employer NICs. Details of the certification process, including details as to the actuarial assumptions which may be used for calculations and circumstances where discretion may be exercised when making amendments, are set out in the *Occupational Pension Schemes (Power to Amend Schemes to Reflect Abolition of Contracting-out) Regulations 2015 (SI 2015/118)* ('the *Power to Amend Regulations*').

Regulation 8 of the *Power to Amend Regulations* requires the actuary to calculate the increase in employee contributions, the increase in employer NICs and the reduction in scheme liabilities in relation to a 12-month period from a date selected by the employer falling on or after 31 December 2011, using the assumptions contained in the scheme's Statement of Funding Principles (see **Chapter 11**) as adjusted to remove any margin for prudence.

Employers will not be obliged to consult with employees about the change to contracting-out status itself, but will be required to consult in relation to any 'listed change' (as defined in the *Pension Consultation Regulations:* see **Chapter 7**) which is made pursuant to the new statutory amendment power. This will include any change to reduce the accrual rate or to require higher employee contributions.

Pre-6 April 1997 – guaranteed minimum pensions

4.18   GMPs could accrue in respect of service from 6 April 1978 to 5 April 1997. Although it has not been possible to accrue GMPs since that time, if a scheme was contracted-out of SERPS on a salary-related basis prior to 6 April 1997, or if a scheme wishes to be able to accept transfers of GMPs from a former COSR scheme, it must still comply with the requirements of *PSA 1993* relating to the provision of GMPs. The relevant requirements are contained in *PSA 1993, ss 13–24H* and the *Contracting-out Regulations 2015, regs 20–27A*. Prior to 6 April 2015 the relevant regulations were the *Contracting-out Regulations 1996, regs 55–69B*.

Conditions relating to members' GMPs

4.19   A member will be entitled to a GMP under a scheme if, in any week in the period from 6 April 1978 to 5 April 1997, earnings in excess of the lower earnings limit were paid to or in respect of him while he was in contracted-out employment by reference to that scheme (*PSA 1993, s 14*).

In order to satisfy the requirements of *PSA 1993* in relation to GMPs, the rules of the scheme must have provided for the member to be entitled to a pension of not less than the guaranteed minimum (*Contracting-out Regulations 1996, reg 55* (repealed from 6 April 2016)) unless the scheme has become exempt from these requirements by satisfying the conversion conditions (see **4.26** below). Although the *Contracting-out Regulations* do not contain an equivalent to *reg 55,* post-6 April 2016, restrictions on the ability to modify GMP provisions should protect accrued GMPs.

Scheme rules must also provide that a GMP will commence no later than 'pensionable age' which is 60 for women and 65 for men (*PSA 1993, ss 13 and 181*) (unless it is postponed) and be payable for life.

A scheme can provide for the commencement of the GMP to be postponed for any period during which a member continues in employment after attaining age 60 (women) or 65 (men). The consent of the member must be obtained if the period of postponement exceeds five years from 60/65, or if the postponement relates to employment which is not contracted-out by reference to the scheme

(PSA 1993, s 13). Where payment of a GMP is postponed until after 60/65, it must be increased by a specified amount to take account of late receipt *(PSA 1993, s 15).*

All GMPs in payment which are attributable to service in the period from 6 April 1988 to 5 April 1997 must be increased each year by at least the lesser of 3 per cent per annum and the increase in the general level of prices in Great Britain *(PSA 1993, s 109).* Until recently the price index used by the Secretary of State for this purpose was the Retail Prices Index but since 6 April 2011 this has been the Consumer Price Index (see **Chapter 1**).

Schemes are not required to provide increases on GMPs earned through service before 6 April 1988. For those members reaching SPA before 6 April 2016, such increases are effectively picked up by the State through increases to the additional State pension. The Government has committed, at least until December 2018, to continue to fund full GMP increases for former public sector employees. However, increases on pre-1988 GMPs for former private sector employees reaching SPA from 6 April 2016 will no longer be provided through the additional State pension.

Scheme rules should require that GMPs are to be accorded priority over other liabilities on a winding up *(PSA 1993, s 23),* although this provision is effectively overridden for those schemes which are subject to *PA 1995, s 73,* which sets out statutory priorities on winding up (see **Chapter 12**).

Conditions relating to survivors' GMPs

4.20 If a member who is entitled to a GMP dies leaving a widow, widower or surviving civil partner, the scheme must provide that the widow, widower or surviving civil partner will be entitled to a GMP under the scheme *(PSA 1993, s 17).* However, this requirement will not apply if the scheme has become exempt by satisfying the conversion conditions (see **4.26** below).

Scheme rules must set out the minimum rates of pension payable to any widow, widower or surviving civil partner *(Contracting-out Regulations 1996, reg 55* as it stood before 6 April 2016). Although the *Contracting-out Regulations 2015* do not contain an equivalent to *reg 55,* post-6 April 2016, restrictions on the ability to modify GMP provisions should protect accrued survivors' GMPs.

The GMP payable to a widow (other than the widow of a female member) must be at least one half of the GMP payable to the member. The GMP payable to a widower, surviving civil partner or surviving same sex spouse (of either sex) must be at least one half of that part of the member's GMP which is attributable to earnings in the period 6 April 1988 to 5 April 1997.

The scheme must also provide for the widow, widower or civil partner's pension to be payable for the periods and in the circumstances set out in the legislation (see *PSA 1993, s 17* and *Contracting-out Regulations 2015, regs 21* and *22*).

Calculating the GMP

4.21   The GMP payable to a member is based on the level of his earnings in excess of the lower earnings limit while in contracted-out employment on which primary Class 1 NICs have been paid or treated as paid. It is calculated according to the appropriate percentage of the member's 'earnings factors' derived from those earnings during the tax years from 6 April 1978 to 5 April 1997 (*PSA 1993, s 14*).

A member's earnings factors are derived from his earnings up to the upper earnings limit each year and are revalued in accordance with a statutory revaluation order made under the *Social Security Administration Act 1992, s 148*. The basis on which earnings factors were calculated changed on 6 April 1987, so separate calculations must be made in respect of pre- and post-April 1987 service.

The appropriate percentage also depends on the age of the member at 6 April 1978. Different calculations apply for men born before 6 April 1933 and women born before 6 April 1938 from those which apply for those born on or after each of those dates.

Different methods of revaluing a member's earnings factors may also be used by a scheme according to whether or not the member is an early leaver and whether or not a transfer of the member's accrued rights is taking place (see *Contracting-out Regulations 1996, regs 65* and *66* for those who ceased contracted-out employment before 6 April 2016, and the *Contracting-out (Transfer and Transfer Payment) Regulations 1996 (SI 1996/1462)* (the '*Contracting–out Transfer Regulations*'), *reg 13B* for schemes which ceased contracting-out on 6 April 2016).

A member's GMP must be reduced by the appropriate percentage where it becomes subject to a pension debit (*PSA 1993, s 15A*).

Revaluing early leavers' GMPs

4.22   GMPs of early leavers must be revalued from the date of leaving contracted-out employment (before 6 April 2016) up to age 60 for women and 65 for men (*PSA 1993, s 16*). The two methods currently available to revalue GMPs are:

(*a*)   *s 148* orders – this involves increasing the earnings factors used for calculating the GMP by the percentage prescribed by the last earnings factor order to come into force in the final tax year of the member's working life (in the same way as for active members); and

(*b*)   fixed rate revaluation – this involves:

(i)   increasing the earnings factors used for calculating the GMP by the percentage prescribed by the last earnings factor order in force before the end of tax year in which the member's contracted-out service ends; then once the guaranteed minimum has been calculated,

(ii)   for each subsequent tax year in the member's working life, revaluing the guaranteed minimum by a fixed percentage as prescribed by *Contracting-out Regulations 1996, reg 62*. The rate ranges from 4.0 to 8.5 per cent compound according to when the member's period of contracted-out service ended.

Revaluation will be based on *s 148* orders unless the scheme provides otherwise.

For schemes ceasing to be contracted-out on 6 April 2016, the scheme may provide for the revaluation of GMPs from the date the member leaves pensionable service (rather than contracted-out employment) to age 60/65 to be either on the basis of *s 148* orders or on the fixed-rate basis (*PSA 1993, s 16(2)* as amended). Most schemes will require an amendment to achieve this and if no amendment is made revaluation will have to be by *s 148* order. The *Occupational Pension Schemes (Modification of Schemes) Regulations 2006 (SI 2006/759), reg 7C* allows trustees to amend their scheme by resolution to achieve this (any such resolution must be passed before 6 April 2017).

To a limited extent, it is possible to revalue GMPs for those leaving before 6 April 1997 by what is known as limited rate revaluation (*PSA 1993, s 16(3)*, as preserved by *Pensions Act 1995 (Commencement No 10) Order 1997, art 3*). Using this method, GMPs must be increased by the lesser of:

(i)   five per cent compound for each complete tax year in the earner's working life after that in which contracted-out service terminated; and

(ii)   the increase which would apply using the last order made under *s 148* in the tax year before the member reaches SPA.

If limited rate revaluation is used, a Limited Revaluation Premium has to be paid.

Discharge of liability in respect of GMPs

4.23   If a member's GMPs are not paid from the scheme, they may be discharged by taking out a policy or policies of insurance, entering into an annuity contract or contracts, or transferring the benefit of such a policy or policies or such contract or contracts *(PSA 1993, s 19)*. The transaction must take place after the member's pensionable service has terminated, the GMPs must be appropriately secured and the requirements of *PSA 1993, s 19* must be satisfied. Further provision about the discharge of such liability is made in the *Occupational Pension Schemes (Discharge of Liability) Regulations 1997 (SI 1997/784)*.

It is also possible to transfer the rights to and liability for GMPs to another occupational pension scheme, personal pension scheme or overseas arrangement *(PSA 1993, s 20* and the *Contracting-out (Transfer and Transfer Payment) Regulations 1996 (SI 1996/1462), Part II)*.

Commutation, suspension and forfeiture

4.24   A member's or survivor's GMP may generally be commuted for a lump sum once it has become payable, provided that the payment would be authorised for the purposes of *FA 2004* and the payment would be permitted as a trivial commutation lump sum, trivial commutation lump sum death benefit, winding-up lump sum or winding-up lump sum death benefit (paid before 6 April 2015) or is a payment prescribed in *Part 2* of the *Registered Pension Schemes (Authorised Payments) Regulations 2009 (SI 2009/1171)*. It is also possible to commute GMPs in certain other circumstances including ill-health *(PSA 1993, s 21* and *Contracting-out Regulations 2015, reg 25)*, in which case a survivor's pension must continue to be payable if provided under the scheme rules.

A scheme may provide for a member's or survivor's GMP to be suspended where the person entitled to the payments is, in the opinion of the trustees, unable to act by reason of mental disorder, is in prison or detained in legal custody, or the earner is re-employed in contracted-out employment by reference to the scheme. In each case, the scheme rules must be in line with *Contracting-out Regulations 2015, reg 26* to permit the suspension.

A scheme may provide for a member's or survivor's GMP to be forfeited where the person entitled to the payments has committed a serious offence such as treason, the survivor is convicted of the murder or manslaughter of the member or where no claim has been made for payment and at least eight years have elapsed since payment was due *(Contracting-out Regulations 2015, reg 26)*.

Equalisation of GMPs

4.25   In January 2000, the then Pensions Ombudsman concluded (in *Williamson [H00177]*) that GMPs for men and women should be equalised (ie based on the same retirement age), on the basis that *PA 1995, s 62(1)* (subsequently revoked, but an equivalent provision is now set out in the *Equality Act 2010 ('EqA 2010'), s 67*), was overriding and required occupational pension schemes to be treated as including a sex equality rule. He ruled that the scheme in question should therefore ensure that GMPs were equalised. On 23 February 2001, in *Marsh Mercer Pension Scheme v Pensions Ombudsman [2001] 16 PBLR*, Rimer J decided that the Ombudsman did not have jurisdiction to make that ruling but left open the question of whether legislation requires GMPs to be equalised and, if so, how.

A written statement on 28 January 2010 by the then Pensions Minister declared that GMPs accrued since 17 May 1990 should be equalised and announced the Government's intention 'to bring forward amending legislation when Parliamentary time allows'.

Draft legislation was published by the DWP in a consultation document in January 2012. This included proposals to amend the *EqA 2010* so that certain requirements of that Act would apply without the need to find an opposite sex comparator where the difference in treatment between a man and a woman is a result of the GMP requirements and included a proposed method of equalisation. The proposed methodology was complex, effectively requiring annual benefit comparison calculations. Consultation on the proposals closed in April 2012. In April 2013, the DWP published an interim response, which although it confirmed that the proposed legislation would be finalised in the same form as set out in the consultation paper, also provided that the method for achieving equalisation set out in the consultation paper would not, but that this would be the subject of further guidance. No date has yet been given for finalisation of the legislation or for publication of the guidance.

Thus although there has been some movement since the Minister's 2010 statement, the issue of GMP equalisation generally remains unresolved and members could still bring claims on this point. Trustees and employers should consider reserving funds to cover the issue if it is raised in the future and should also think about who is to bear the risk on a transfer-in and in the context of share acquisitions and transfers of past service rights. Trustees may also wish to consider whether, and if so how, GMPs could be equalised in the context of a scheme wind up. In July 2015, the Pensions Ombudsman determined in the case of *Kenworthy* (PO 4579) that it was not maladministration for the trustees to defer taking action to equalise GMPs until the issue has been resolved by the enactment of legislation requiring equalisation.

In January 2011 the PPF issued a consultation paper on the calculation of PPF compensation and FAS assistance in the context of the equalisation of GMPs, followed by a detailed statement published in November 2011, the 'Statement on equalisation for GMPs and the application of a Statutory Minimum to PPF compensation for schemes in a PPF Assessment Period', under which the PPF announced that it would be undertaking a pilot study of a number of selected schemes within assessment periods which will equalise benefits on the PPF's favoured underpin method. In December 2012 the PPF announced that it will be requiring schemes to equalise GMPs in accordance with the method published in November 2011. Schemes transferring to the PPF are now required, before transfer, to complete their own GMP equalisation calculations using the PPF methodology.

The Government's view that GMPs must be equalised is based on its interpretation of EU law. The requirement to equalise may therefore be something which falls away, depending on the terms on which the UK leaves the EU following the 23 June 2016 referendum.

Sex equality of scheme benefits generally is dealt with in **Chapter 9**.

Conversion of GMPs

4.26   Since 6 April 2009, it has been possible for a scheme to convert GMPs into ordinary scheme benefits and become exempt from the requirement to guarantee a minimum pension. In order to become exempt, the scheme must satisfy the five conditions set out in *PSA 1993, s 24B*, which are as follows:

- the post-conversion benefits must be actuarially at least equivalent to the pre-conversion benefits; the trustees are responsible for determining actuarial equivalence, having considered the advice of the actuary (*Contracting-out Regulations 2015, reg 27*);

- there must be no reduction in pension for those entitled to payment of a pension immediately before the conversion;

- the post-conversion benefits must not include money purchase benefits (other than money purchase benefits provided under the scheme immediately before the conversion) (ie GMPs cannot be converted to money purchase benefits);

- the scheme must provide survivors' benefits in the circumstances and during the periods prescribed by *Contracting-out Regulations 2015, reg 28;* benefits must be at least 50 per cent of the pension to which the member would have been entitled up to 5 April 1997, from 6 April 1978 in the case of widows and from 6 April 1988 in the case of widowers and surviving civil partners (*PSA 1993, s 24D*); and

- the procedural requirements of *s 24E* must have been met.

The procedural requirements are:

- the employer must consent to the GMP conversion in advance;

- the trustees must take all reasonable steps to consult the earner in advance and to notify all affected members and survivors before or as soon as is reasonably practicable after the conversion date; and

- HMRC must be notified on or before the conversion date that the conversion will occur or has occurred and that it affects the earner (*PSA 1993, s 24E*).

In future, regulations may impose conditions or restrictions on transfers out of benefits from a converted scheme (*PSA 1993, s 24F*). Meanwhile, where a member applies to take his cash equivalent, the trustees may, with his consent, adjust any guaranteed cash equivalent so as to reflect rights that would have accrued if the scheme had been converted.

PSA 1993, s 24G gives trustees the power to amend their scheme by resolution to give effect to GMP conversion in accordance with the *s 24B* conditions. Furthermore, if the trustees choose to effect the conversion using the existing scheme amendment power, *PA 1995, s 67* will not apply insofar as the power enables the conversion in accordance with the *s 24B* conditions. Trustees may also include other amendments which they think are necessary or desirable as a consequence of, or to facilitate, the GMP conversion.

Where a scheme is winding up, the trustees may adjust rights under the scheme so as to reflect what would have happened if the scheme had been subject to GMP conversion.

The Regulator has certain powers in relation to the conversion process which may be exercised where it thinks that the *s 24B* conditions have not been satisfied in relation to any guaranteed cash equivalent or scheme amendment. The Regulator may make an order declaring the amendment, modification or adjustment void (*PSA 1993, s 24H*) and may require the trustees to take specified steps and declare that other steps are permissible. The Regulator may also intervene during the conversion process and give specific directions to trustees.

There has been a very low uptake of the GMP conversion process, not least due to the requirement to provide survivor benefits after the conversion and the fact that many schemes have not equalised GMPs.

PA 2014, Sch 13 includes a provision which, from 6 April 2016, requires the Secretary of State to give such guidance (if any) as he or she thinks appropriate about GMP conversion. Further consultation is awaited on DWP guidance to simplify GMP conversion, but no guidance has yet been given.

Post-6 April 1997 – the reference scheme test

4.27   Before 6 April 2016, in order for a COSR scheme to contract out of SERPS on a salary-related basis from 6 April 1997, to contract out of S2P from 6 April 2002, or to be able to accept transfers of post-1997 COSR scheme rights from another COSR scheme, it must have complied with the requirements of *PSA 1993* relating to the reference scheme test.

Reference scheme test benefits do not form any kind of underpin; they are simply a benchmark against which a scheme's benefits are measured. A scheme could be designed to incorporate an underpin based on the reference scheme test, with the rules being drafted to ensure that those benefits are provided as a minimum. Such a scheme would clearly be more complicated to administer and more costly to provide than a scheme based on a single benefit structure, as additional records would have to be maintained and checks made whenever a benefit became payable. However, an underpin might be attractive to employers, particularly in circumstances where a scheme generally provides benefits greater than the reference scheme but has difficulty demonstrating that it meets the reference scheme test.

The reference scheme test requirements are contained in *PSA 1993, ss 12A–12D* (which have been saved for three years from 6 April 2016 by the *Pensions Act 2014 (Savings) Order 2015, art 2(2)(d)* while the Government considers how best, after the abolition of contracting-out, to deal with schemes with reference scheme test underpins) and *Contracting-out Regulations 1996, regs 22–29*.

The reference scheme

4.28   The reference scheme test aimed to ensure that the pensions to be provided for most members and their widows, widowers or surviving civil partners satisfy the statutory standard. In other words, they must be broadly equivalent to, or better than, the pensions which would be provided to them under the 'reference scheme'.

Details of the reference scheme are set out in *PSA 1993, s 12B* and *Contracting-out Regulations 1996, regs 25* and *26* (at least until 5 April 2019). Essentially, the reference scheme is an occupational pension scheme which:

(*a*)   has a normal pension age of 65 for both men and women;

(*b*)   provides a pension for life at normal pension age based on 1/80th (per year of pensionable service) of average qualifying earnings in the last three tax years preceding the end of service, subject to a maximum of 40 years;

(c) provides that, the day following the death of a member, a pension is payable to the member's widow, widower or surviving civil partner unless:

- the member married or formed a civil partnership after having received benefits under the scheme; or

- the widow, widower or surviving civil partner marries, forms a civil partnership or cohabits with another person as a married couple after having received benefits under the scheme; or

- the widow, widower or surviving civil partner is cohabiting with a person as a married couple other than the member at the time of the member's death;

(d) provides that on the death of a member before normal pension age, any pension payable to a widow, widower or surviving civil partner is equal to 50 per cent of the pension the reference scheme would have provided to the member if his pension had become payable on the date of his death;

(e) provides that on the death of a member on or after normal pension age, any pension payable to a widow, widower or surviving civil partner is equal to 50 per cent of the pension the reference scheme was required to provide to the member immediately before his death;

(f) provides annual pension increases in accordance with *PA 1995, s 51* (see **Chapter 1**); and

(g) revalues deferred pensions between the date of leaving and normal pension age in accordance with *PSA 1993* (see **Chapter 6**).

For the purposes of the reference scheme test, qualifying earnings in any tax year before 2009/10 means 90 per cent of earnings between the lower and upper earnings limits for NICs and, in relevant tax years including and after 2009/10, means 90 per cent of earnings between the lower earnings limit and the upper accrual point.

The test – actuarial certification

4.29 A scheme meets the reference scheme test only if the scheme actuary (or, if the trustees are not required to appoint a scheme actuary, an actuary appointed for the purpose) certifies that pensions to be provided to the members and their widows, widowers or surviving civil partners are to be treated as broadly equivalent to, or better than, those payable under the reference scheme.

In order to provide the necessary certification, the actuary must comply with *Contracting-out Regulations 1996, reg 23* and *Sch 3* (as amended and added by the *Occupational Pension Schemes (Contracting-out) Amendment Regulations 2011, SI 2011/1294*).

Schemes with more than one benefit structure

4.30   For schemes with different sections relating to different categories of employment, or which offer different benefit structures for earners in the same category of employment, each section which was to be contracted-out needed to satisfy the reference scheme test independently (*Contracting-out Regulations 1996, reg 22*). If a scheme with multiple sections had one section which did not satisfy the reference scheme test, that section could not be contracted-out, even if, overall, the scheme would have satisfied the reference scheme test.

Amending COSR schemes

4.31   *PSA 93, s 37* prohibits changes to the rules of schemes which were COSR schemes unless the change is permitted by *Contracting-out Regulations 2015, regs 17* and *20* (prior to 6 April 2016, the relevant provision was *Contracting-out Regulations 1996, reg 42*).

In summary:

(*a*)   the rules of a scheme may be altered in relation to GMPs only if the alteration would not:

   (i)   affect any of the matters dealt with in *PSA 1993, Part III* (schemes that were contracted-out), or any regulations made under that Part, that relate to GMPs, in a manner that would or might adversely affect any entitlement or accrued rights of any member of the scheme acquired before the alteration takes effect; or

   (ii)   affect any of the matters dealt with in *PSA 1993, ss 87–92* (protection of increases in GMPs) or *ss 109* and *110* (annual increases of GMPs) or any matters dealt with in regulations made under any of those provisions;

(*b*)   the rules of a COSR cannot be altered in relation to any *PSA 1993 s 9(2B)* rights unless:

   (i)   following the alteration, the scheme provides benefits for the member and the member's widow, widower or surviving civil partner in respect of the pensionable service to which the alteration relates which are at least equal to the benefits which would be provided under the reference scheme as it had effect immediately before 6 April 2016 (see **4.28** above);

(ii)   the alteration is one to which *PA 1995 s 67* (see **Chapter 13**) does not apply;

(iii)   the alteration is one which is not a protected modification or a detrimental modification within the meaning of *PA 1995 s 67A* (see **Chapter 13**); or

(iv)   if the alteration is a detrimental modification, the actuarial equivalence requirements provided for *in PA 1995 s 67C and s 67D* (see **Chapter 13**) are met in relation to the proposed modification;

(*c*)   in the case of alterations falling under *(b)*(iii) or (iv) above, but not within (i) or (ii), the altered scheme must provide for a pension to be paid to the member's widow, widower or surviving civil partner which is at least as generous either as regards the amount of pension or the circumstances in which it will be paid, as it would have been before the alteration. In relation to a member who is in pensionable service immediately before the alteration takes effect, this requirement is satisfied if the survivor's pension which the scheme would provide if the member left pensionable service immediately after the alteration is at least as generous as the survivor's pension which the scheme would have provided had the member left service immediately before the alteration.

Where a scheme was subject to *PSA 1993, s 37* immediately prior to 6 April 1997, any requirements under its rules for the consent of the Occupational Pensions Board to such change ceased to have effect on 6 April 1997 (*Contracting-out Regulations 1996, reg 76B* (repealed)).

Defined contribution schemes and mixed benefit schemes

4.32   From April 1988, when the relevant provisions of the *Social Security Act 1986* first came into force, it became possible for employers and individuals to contract out of the additional State pension by way of money purchase arrangements. Employers and employees received a rebate on their Class 1 NICs based on the flat-rate rebate and the age-related rebate.

However, contracting-out for money purchase pension schemes (both occupational and personal pension schemes) was abolished on 6 April 2012. Neither has it been possible since that date to contract out via the defined contribution section of a COMB scheme.

The position before 6 April 2012

4.33   Prior to 6 April 2006, an occupational pension scheme (including a stakeholder scheme) could contract out of S2P on a money purchase basis if certain conditions were met. Those conditions were set out under *PSA 1993, s 9(3)* and *Contracting-out Regulations 1996, reg 30* (both now repealed).

It was also possible for a COSR scheme to contract out of the additional State pension on a money purchase basis by opening up a COMP section, and for a COMP scheme to contract out on a salary-related basis by opening up a COSR section. The separate sections of such COMB schemes were essentially treated as two different schemes, so that the requirements of *PA 1993* relating to a COSR scheme applied to the salary-related part, and those relating to a COMP scheme applied to the money purchase part, and the schemes were given two scheme contracting-out numbers (see **4.15** above).

Schemes which were not registered (see **Chapter 17**) were not permitted to contract-out on a money purchase basis.

Minimum payments and protected rights

4.34   Occupational pension schemes could contract out of S2P on a money purchase basis by providing 'protected rights'. These were the rights derived from the 'minimum payments' made to the scheme in respect of a member and certain other payments, including age-related rebates and transfers to the scheme of rights accrued in another contracted-out arrangement.

Identification of protected rights

4.35   Unless the scheme rules provided otherwise, a member's protected rights were all his rights to money purchase benefits under the scheme. It was possible for the rules of an occupational pension scheme instead to provide that a member's protected rights were:

(*a*)   the rights derived from the payment of minimum payments and age-related rebates (see **4.36** below) and incentive payments made in respect of the member; and

(*b*)   money purchase benefits derived from protected rights which have been transferred to the scheme from another arrangement; and

(*c*)   money purchase benefits derived from a GMP or post-1997 COSR rights which have been transferred to the scheme from another arrangement.

Where the rules of a scheme limited a member's protected rights as outlined above, there were also requirements to make provision for the identification of those rights.

167

Flat-rate rebates and age-related rebates

4.36   Before 6 April 2012, under COMP schemes, both the employer and the employee paid reduced rates of NICs, based on a percentage of band earnings. This was known as the 'flat-rate rebate', with rates being altered from time to time by order on the recommendation of the Secretary of State. Provisions of the *Contracting-out Regulations 1996* prescribed how the employer was to pay amounts equal to the value of the flat-rate rebate to trustees (ie the 'minimum payments'), and when the trustees had to invest such payments on behalf of the member.

Separate statutory provisions related to a second rebate, known as the 'age-related rebate', with a range of rates based prescribed on the age of the earner immediately before any tax year. An amount was payable by HMRC to the COMP scheme bank account annually, equal to the amount by which the age-related rebate exceeded the flat-rate rebate. As the age-related payment was effectively paid a year in arrears on submission of the end-of-year return, the amount due had to be taken into account on transfers and on the death or retirement of a member.

Giving effect to protected rights

4.37   Protected rights could only be discharged under a scheme's rules by providing a pension from the scheme, a transfer payment, a lump sum or purchasing an annuity. The *PSA 93* and the *Personal and Occupational Pension Schemes (Protected Rights) Regulations 1996, SI 1996/1537 (the 'Protected Rights Regulations')* set out requirements as to how these rights could be discharged, including how a pension was to be provided or an annuity was to be purchased for these purposes, and how scheme rules were to provide for effect to be given to a member's protected rights where this had not happened at the date of a member's death. In particular, the requirements included that:

- the pension or annuity needed to be offered and its rate calculated on a basis which did not discriminate on the basis of sex or (unless the member was neither married nor in a civil partnership and agreed to his pension rate being determined on his life only) marital or civil partnership status;

- scheme rules had to provide for effect to be given to a member's protected rights by payment to a surviving spouse or civil partner, where the member died before giving effect to his or her protected rights;

- on the death of the member while a pension or annuity was payable, specific provision needed to be made for the member's widow, widower or surviving civil partner;

- in certain circumstances, effect could be given to protected rights in an occupational pension scheme by the making of a transfer payment from that scheme to another occupational pension scheme, a personal pension scheme or an overseas arrangement, where the scheme to which the payment was to be made satisfied prescribed requirements;

- from 6 April 2006, protected rights could be paid as a lump sum equal to the value on that date of those protected rights, where the lump sum satisfied prescribed requirements; and

- scheme rules could not in general permit either the suspension or forfeiture of a person's protected rights other than as set out in the *Protected Rights Regulations.*

The position from 6 April 2012 onward

4.38   Under *PA 2007 (s 15* and S*chedule 4* and regulations made under them) contracting-out for defined contribution pension schemes (both occupational and personal pension schemes, including stakeholder schemes) was abolished from 6 April 2012. All contracting-out certificates for COMP schemes and the COMP sections of COMB schemes (and appropriate scheme certificates for personal pension schemes) ceased to have effect immediately before that date.

The amendments to *PSA 1993* inserted by the above provisions were then immediately repealed by *PA 2008, s 106,* removing the restrictions that applied to protected rights which had accrued before the abolition date.

Further detail is set out in the *Pensions Act 2007 (Abolition of Contracting-out for Defined Contribution Pension Schemes) (Consequential Amendments) Regulations 2011 (SI 2011/1245)* and the *Pensions Act 2007 (Abolition of Contracting-out for Defined Contribution Pension Schemes) (Consequential Amendments) (No 2) Regulations 2011 (SI 2011/1724).*

The combined effect of these changes is that, from 6 April 2012:

- former COMP scheme members or members of the COMP section of a former COMB scheme have been contracted back in to accrue rights under S2P, and it is no longer possible to build up protected rights. For tax years after the 2011/2012 tax year, such schemes no longer receive contracting-out rebates or minimum payments;

- references in the relevant legislation to 'contracted-out money purchase schemes', 'appropriate personal pension schemes' and 'protected rights' are removed. Former protected rights must be treated in the same way as other rights, there is no requirement for former protected rights to be separately identifiable from other rights and HMRC will not track former protected rights;

- most of the provisions of *PSA 1993* dealing with protected rights (including ss *25A, 27A* and *32A*) are repealed, meaning that all remaining conditions applying to protected rights (such as the requirement to provide survivors' benefits) no longer apply to former protected rights;

- although contracting-out certificates for COMP schemes were cancelled with immediate effect (from 6 April 2012), contracting-out certificates for COMB schemes remained valid for the salary-related sections until 5 April 2016;

- amendments are made to the *Insolvency Act 1986*, making it possible (subject to various requirements) for the trustee in bankruptcy (see **Chapter 1** above) to apply for an income payments order in relation to former protected rights where those rights come into payment on or after 6 April 2012; and

- for ease of scheme administration there is a transitional period of three years to allow adjustments to be made to minimum payments (see **4.39** below).

Where members of former COMP schemes ceased to be contracted-out of S2P on 6 April 2012, there was a requirement to inform 'affected members' of this fact within one month of 6 April 2012 under the *Pensions Act 2007 (Abolition of Contracting-out for Defined Contribution Pension Schemes) (Consequential Amendments) Regulations 2011*. Schemes were also required to explain to affected members the effect of the changes to protected rights by providing other prescribed information within four months of 6 April 2012.

HMRC and the Transitional Period

4.39   The statutory changes which came into effect on 6 April 2012 included provision for a transitional period lasting until 5 April 2015, in which rebates relating to the period before 6 April 2012 may still be paid to schemes, and during which HMRC may make any necessary amendments to the records of scheme members' NICs.

PA 2007, Schedule 4 made various amendments to *PSA 93* in relation to this transitional period, with the effect that since 6 April 2012, there is no further tax relief on rebates due to members individually, and all rebate adjustments will be paid directly to the members affected. In addition, a limit is set annually below which rebates will not be paid where the cost of administering the rebate exceeds the value of the rebate itself.

In relation to the 6 April 2012 changes, HMRC issued various information pages, including a series of 'Countdown bulletins' published on the HMRC website, setting out HMRC's requirements about how certain benefits must be administered in light of the changes taking place on the abolition date.

This includes confirmation by HMRC that survivors of members who died before 6 April 2012 were entitled to benefits under the pre-6 April 2012 protected rights regime, and this included instances where the survivor's benefit comes into payment on or after that date (*Countdown bulletin edition 5*). By contrast, where a member dies on or after 6 April 2012, there is no legal requirement for schemes to provide a survivor's pension for former protected rights (although a scheme's rules may require such a benefit to be paid). On the death of a member after 6 April 2012, trustees may also be able to apply former protected rights to pay a dependant's pension under discretionary trusts. This was not possible in relation to deaths occurring before that date.

Since 6 April 2012, pension schemes are no longer required to provide a survivor's pension out of former protected rights on the member's death following serious ill health. In *Countdown bulletin edition 6*, HMRC stated that where a serious ill health lump sum had been paid to a member before 6 April 2012, and the member is still alive after that date, it is possible for the remaining value of the former protected rights to be paid out as a second lump sum, where this option is available under the scheme rules.

HMRC also published confirmation that, subject to the requirements of *FA 2004* (see **Chapter 17**) and scheme rules, it is possible for a second short service refund lump sum to be paid out of former protected rights, where members had left schemes before 6 April 2012 and received an initial short service refund lump sum but the value of their protected rights has been retained in the scheme (*Countdown bulletin edition 6*). In cases where scheme rules have not yet been amended to allow former protected rights to be paid out under the short service refund lump sum, the *Registered Pension Schemes (Authorised Payments) Regulations 2009* have been amended by the *Registered Pension Schemes (Authorised Payments) (Amendment) (No 2) Regulations 2012 (SI 2012/1881)* to provide that a partial short-service refund may be paid out from a former COMP scheme as an Authorised Member Payment, even though: (i) the payment would not extinguish the member's entitlement to scheme benefits; and (ii) since 6 April 2012, there is no statutory exclusion for this. With effect from 6 April 2013, the easement has been modified by the *Registered Pension Schemes (Authorised Payments (Amendment) Regulations 2013 (SI 2013/1818)* to confirm that incentive payments (paid to schemes that became contracted-out on a money purchase basis between 1986 and 1993), age related rebates paid by HMRC and amounts recovered from minimum employer payments made to the scheme before 6 April 2012, are all 'member contributions' for the purpose of the part refund payments relating to short service provisions.

Transfers involving former COMP schemes

4.40   Before 6 April 2012, statutory provisions imposed detailed restrictions on transfers from COMP schemes under the *Protected Rights (Transfer Payment) Regulations 1996 (SI 1996/1461)*. Those regulations have been revoked and the restrictions no longer apply.

Since 6 April 2012, transfers of accrued benefits from a former COSR scheme to a former COMP scheme may be made subject to certain requirements being met. The requirements apply by reason of the *Pensions Act 2007 (Abolition of Contracting-out for Defined Contribution Pension Schemes) (Consequential Amendments) Regulations 2011*. These include the member having consented to the transfer in writing, the payment must be at least equal to the cash equivalent transfer value (see **Chapter 6**) and written confirmation from the member that:

- he or she has received a statement from the receiving scheme setting out the details of the transfer payment; and

- he or she accepts that the expected benefits may be different to those which he or she would have received from the transferring scheme and the receiving scheme will not be required to provide a survivor's pension.

Amending protected rights under scheme rules

4.41   One of the effects of the amendments made by *PA 2007, s 106* to *PSA 93* is that since 6 April 2012, there has been no statutory requirement for schemes to make special provisions within their rules for former protected rights. However, the removal of the requirement under statute is not overriding, and therefore amendments may be needed to scheme rules in order to disapply existing scheme restrictions in relation to former protected rights. The previous restrictions on making changes to protected rights provisions within scheme rules were removed by the *Pensions Act 2008 (Abolition of Protected Rights) (Consequential Amendments) (No 2) Order 2011*. Consequently, protected rights restrictions in scheme rules may be removed or amended by use of (and subject to) the scheme amendment power.

Some schemes contain protected rights rules which cannot be readily amended or removed in light of the restrictions of *PA 1995, s 67* (see **Chapter 13**). A statutory modification power has therefore been introduced under *PA 1995, s 68*, permitting trustees to amend scheme rules by resolution in light of the changes to contracting-out on a money purchase basis. This modification power will be available to trustees until 6 April 2018 (the *Occupational Pension Schemes (Modification of Schemes) Regulations 2006 (SI 2006/759), reg 7A*).

Termination of contracted-out employment

Securing contracted-out rights when a member leaves a scheme

4.42   Where a member's pensionable service terminates after he has completed two years' qualifying service, he is entitled to a preserved benefit under the scheme (see **Chapter 6**). In the case of a contracted-out scheme, the member's GMP and post-1997 COSR rights, as appropriate, will form part of the preserved benefit and must be appropriately revalued and secured. In each case, a member's rights may be secured by means of a scheme pension, transfer payment, lump sum or annuity purchase (see, in particular, **4.23** and **4.24** above in relation to GMPs).

A member who leaves pensionable service with more than three months' but less than two years' qualifying service and no vested rights will be entitled to a refund of his contributions or a transfer payment to another scheme. Anyone leaving with less than three months' pensionable service (for defined benefit entitlements, and since 1 October 2015, 30 days' pensionable service for defined contribution entitlements) would usually be entitled only to a refund of contributions. See **Chapter 6** for further on protection for early leavers.

In circumstances where the member has less than two years' contracted-out service in a COSR scheme, it may be possible to reinstate his rights into the State scheme by the trustees of the scheme paying to HMRC a 'contributions equivalent premium' (*PSA 1993, ss 55–58* and *Contracting-out Regulations 1996, regs 51* and *52*). The consequence of paying such a premium is that the member is treated as if he had not contracted-out for the period in respect of which the premium was paid. The member's accrued GMP and post-1997 COSR rights, as appropriate, are extinguished (*PSA 1993, s 60*).

Anti-franking

4.43   The GMPs of early leavers are protected by the principle of 'anti-franking'. The legislation relating to anti-franking is contained in *PSA 1993, ss 87–92*. The purpose of this legislation is to prevent the relevant pension benefits, broadly those in excess of GMP, from being eroded by financing the cost of providing for the revaluation of GMP rights out of that excess (ie by 'franking' that cost).

The legislation principally applies where the member ceases to be in contracted-out employment (on a salary related basis) before the date on which his GMP under that scheme commences. It will be relevant where, immediately after ceasing to be a member of the scheme, the value of his pension in payment or his revalued deferred pension exceeds the value of his GMP rights at that time and the GMP, when it comes into payment, is greater than it was when contracted-out employment ceased (which it generally will be).

PSA 1993, s 87(3) prescribes a minimum level of benefits which must be provided when the pension is required to be paid:

(*a*)   where the pension has been provided as a substitute for short service benefit, the value of the deferred pension; and (*b*)   in any other case, the aggregate of:

- the value of his pension in payment or his revalued deferred pension;

- the amount by which the value of his pension in payment or his revalued deferred pension exceeded the value of his GMP rights immediately after he ceased to be in the scheme;

- an additional amount comprising the member's pension, if any, accrued after he ceased to be contracted-out on a salary related basis, together with any increases due to postponement on the non-GMP part of his pension accrued before that time; and

- a further additional amount in respect of any pension accrued after the member ceased to be contracted-out on a salary related basis, based on the amount by which the non-GMP element of his pension would have increased from the date he ceased to be contracted-out on a salary related basis to the earlier of the date he took his pension or left the scheme.

The legislation provides equivalent protection in relation to GMPs for surviving spouses and civil partners.

Chapter 5

Employer insolvency: the implications for pension schemes

Introduction

5.1 The insolvency of an employer may have a number of implications for its occupational pension scheme.

From a statutory perspective, the insolvency may trigger a debt on the employer calculated on the buy-out basis (a '*section 75* debt') if the scheme is underfunded. The insolvency may cause the scheme to enter into an assessment period for the Pension Protection Fund ('PPF') or give rise to eligibility for the Financial Assistance Scheme ('FAS'). From the perspective of the scheme rules, the insolvency may trigger a full or partial wind up of the scheme.

The following are typical considerations for the pension scheme trustees:

(*a*)   Is the pension scheme eligible for the PPF?

(*b*)   Does the scheme have to go into a full or partial winding up?

(*c*)   Is there a deficit? How is it calculated and where does it rank in the insolvency?

(*d*)   Are there unpaid contributions? If so, how do they rank in the insolvency? Can they be claimed from elsewhere?

(*e*)   What happens if there is a surplus in the pension scheme?

This chapter considers the statutory meaning of 'insolvency event' and looks in detail at the PPF and FAS regimes. It also looks at the wider implications of insolvency events bearing in mind the questions set out above and the role of the Regulator. The majority of the issues covered in this chapter are not relevant to money purchase schemes.

Insolvency events

5.2 The statutory definition of 'insolvency event' is set out at *PA 2004, s 121*. The legislation lists various events relating to individuals, companies and partnerships that satisfy the definition.

5.2   *Employer insolvency: the implications for pension schemes*

In relation to companies, the list is fairly wide-ranging and essentially seeks to catch most insolvency events other than solvent liquidations (such as a members' voluntary liquidation). These are:

(*a*)   the nominee in relation to a proposal for a voluntary arrangement under *Part 1* of the *Insolvency Act 1986 (IA 1986)* submits a report to the court under *IA 1986, s 2* which states that, in his opinion, meetings of the company and its creditors should be summoned to consider the proposal (see **5.52** below);

(*b*)   the directors of the company file with the court documents and statements in accordance with *IA 1986, Sch A1, para 7(1)* (moratorium where directors propose voluntary arrangement) (see **5.52** below);

(*c*)   an administrative receiver within the meaning of *IA 1986, s 251* is appointed in relation to the company (see **5.56** below);

(*d*)   the company enters administration as per *IA 1986, Sch B1, para 1(2)(b)* (see **5.58** below);

(*e*)   a resolution is passed for a voluntary winding up of the company without a declaration of solvency under *IA 1986, s 89* (see **5.65** below);

(*f*)   a meeting of creditors is held in relation to the company under *IA 1986, s 95* (creditors' meeting to convert a members' voluntary winding up into a creditors' voluntary winding up) (see **5.64** below); and

(*g*)   an order for the winding up of the company is made by the court under *IA 1986, Part 4 or 5 (PA 2004, s 121(3))* (see **5.65** below).

The definition of insolvency event is extended by both the *Pension Protection Fund (Entry Rules) Regulations 2005 (SI 2005/590)* (the *'PPF Entry Rules'*) and the *Financial Assistance Scheme Regulations 2005 (SI 2005/1986)* (the *'FAS Regulations'*).

In relation to a company, the *PPF Entry Rules* provide that the following will also constitute an insolvency event in respect of a company:

(i)   an administration order is made by the court in respect of the company by virtue of any enactment which applies under *IA 1986, Part 2*;

(ii)   a notice from an administrator under *IA 1986, Sch B1, para 83(3)* (moving from administration to creditors' voluntary liquidation) in relation to the company is registered by the registrar of companies;

(iii) the company moves from administration to winding up pursuant to an order of the court under *Rule 2.132* of the *Insolvency Rules 1986 (IR 1986)*; or

(iv)   an administrator or liquidator of the company, being the nominee in relation to a proposal for a voluntary arrangement under *IA 1986, Part*

I, summons meetings of the company and its creditors, to consider the proposal, in accordance with *IA 1986, s 3(2)* (summoning of meetings) (*PPF Entry Rules, reg 5*).

The *PPF Entry Rules* were amended with effect from 21 July 2014 to include a new 'European insolvency event'. This is very narrowly drawn and is likely to be relevant only to the Olympic Airlines pension scheme (see **5.33** below) (*PPF Entry Rules, reg 5A*).

The *PPF Entry Rules* also extend the definition of insolvency event in relation to partnerships and set out insolvency events for other 'relevant bodies' (eg building societies and friendly societies) (*PPF Entry Rules, reg 5*).

The *FAS Regulations* adopt the *PA 2004, s 121* definition of insolvency event, with the exception of a meeting of creditors held in relation to the company under *IA 1986, s 95* (see paragraph (*f*) above). The definition is extended in relation to a company to include where:

(i)   an administration order is made by the court in relation to the company under, or by virtue of, any enactment which applies under *IA 1986, Part 2*;

(ii)   a resolution is passed for a voluntary winding up of the company with a declaration of solvency under *IA 1986, s 89*; and

(iii)   notice is published in the *London Gazette* that the company has been struck off the companies register.

Again, the definition of insolvency event is extended in relation to various different types of entity (*FAS Regulations, reg 13*).

All of these insolvency events, other than the recent easement for Olympic Airlines mentioned above, are those available under the laws of England and Wales (*PA 2004* also includes some Scottish insolvency events). This can create practical problems in dealing with foreign registered employers. Please see **5.33** below for a further discussion of the issues which can arise. More details about company voluntary arrangements ('CVAs'), liquidation, receivership and administration are set out from **5.51** below.

The appointment of an insolvency practitioner: communication with the trustees

5.3   Where an insolvency practitioner ('IP') is appointed in relation to a pension scheme employer, he must inform the trustees of the scheme of his appointment within one month. This requirement arises because every employer in relation to a pension scheme is under a duty to notify the trustees within one month of the occurrence of an event relating to the employer which will be of material significance to the trustees or their advisors in the exercise of any of their functions *(PA 1995, s 47(9)(a)* and *Occupational Pension Schemes (Scheme Administration) Regulations 1996 (SI 1996/1715), reg 6(1) (b))*. Under *PA 1995, s 49(10)*, the Regulator can levy a civil penalty if there is failure by an employer to comply with these requirements. The maximum penalty is £50,000 for a company and £5,000 for an individual *(PA 1995, s 10)*.

There are further notification requirements where an IP acting in relation to a scheme employer or the official receiver becomes (i) the liquidator or provisional liquidator of a company which is a scheme employer, or (ii) the interim receiver of the property of a scheme employer. In these circumstances, the IP or official receiver must provide the trustees of the scheme, as soon as practicable after the receipt of the request, with any information the trustees may reasonably require for the purpose of the scheme *(PA 1995, s 26(1))*. Any expenses incurred by the IP or official receiver in complying with a request for information are recoverable by him as part of his expenses incurred in the discharge of his duties *(PA 1995, s 26(2))*. The IP or official receiver is not required to take any action which involves expenses which cannot be recovered, unless the trustees of the scheme undertake to meet them *(PA 1995, s 26(3))*.

The appointment of an insolvency practitioner: communication with the Regulator and independent trustee requirements

5.4   Where an IP or the official receiver is appointed in relation to a scheme employer, he must report his appointment to the Regulator (as well as to the PPF and the trustees) *(PA 1995, s 22)*. It is then open to the Regulator to consider whether the appointment of a statutory independent trustee is appropriate *(PA 1995, s 23)*. Where any appointment is made, it must involve a trustee taken from the register maintained by the Regulator *(PA 1995, s 23(1) (b))*.

An order from the Regulator to appoint an independent trustee may provide for any of his fees and expenses to be paid: (a) by the employer; (b) out of the scheme's resources; or (c) partly by the employer and partly out of the scheme's resources *(PA 1995, s 25(6))*. Such an order may also provide that an amount equal to the amount paid out of the scheme's resources is to be treated as a debt due from the employer to the trustees of the scheme *(PA 1995, s 25(7))*. Where an order makes provision for any such fees or expenses to be paid out of the scheme's resources, the trustee is entitled to be paid in priority to all other claims falling to be met out of the scheme's resources *(PA 1995, s 25(8))*.

Where *PA 1995, s 22* applies to the scheme and there is an independent trustee appointed by the Regulator, all discretionary powers of the trustees and all powers of the employer which are of a fiduciary nature are exercisable by the independent trustee alone (*PA 1995, s 25(2)*. The independent trustee may not be removed from being a trustee by virtue only of any provision of the scheme (*PA 1995, s 25(3)*).

The role of pension scheme trustees in insolvency proceedings

5.5 In this section, we consider the role of the pension scheme trustee as a creditor or debtor in insolvency proceedings. Where trustees are creditors, their status will depend on whether they have security or a preferential debt or are just ordinary creditors. Broadly, a secured creditor will rank higher in an insolvency than an unsecured creditor, and amongst the unsecured creditors, anyone with a preferential debt will have priority.

Section 75 debts

Triggering a section 75 debt

5.6 In certain circumstances, the liabilities of the scheme may crystallise, resulting in a debt due from the employer to the scheme under *PA 1995, s 75*. Such a debt is typically known as a 'debt on the employer' or a '*section 75* debt' (see **Chapter 12**).

Section 75 debts can be triggered on the insolvency of the employer, the occurrence (in a multi-employer scheme) of an employment-cessation event, in a frozen multi-employer scheme if active steps are taken to trigger the debt or on the winding up of the scheme. The legislation in this area has been amended several times and it is always necessary to carefully consider which provisions apply in order to ascertain whether or not a debt has fallen due and the basis on which it will be calculated.

In this section, we will focus on the legislation in force as at 6 April 2016, which is closely tied to the PPF regime.

Single employer schemes

If a 'relevant event' occurs in relation to the participating employer in a scheme and immediately before that time, the value of the scheme's assets is less than the amount at that time of its liabilities, this may trigger a contingent employer debt under *PA 1995, s 75(4)*. The relevant event may be (a) an insolvency event in relation to the employer (as defined in *PA 2004, s 121*) (see **5.2** above), (b) a *section 129* application or notice (see **5.19** below) or (c) the passing of a resolution for a voluntary winding up of the employer where a declaration of solvency has been made under *IA 1986 s 89* (members' voluntary winding up) (*PA 1995, s 75(6A)*).

It is important to note that where the 'relevant event' is an insolvency event or a *s 129* notice/application, the debt will not immediately fall due, but will be contingent on one of two alternative sets of events taking place (*PA 1995, s 75(4C)*). Broadly, the first set of events is that:

(*a*)   after the relevant event, a scheme failure notice is issued and becomes binding (see **5.21** below);

(*b*)   after the relevant event but before the issuing of the scheme failure notice, no withdrawal notice has been issued and become binding (see **5.21** below) and this is not a possibility; and

(*c*)   before the scheme failure notice became binding, no members' voluntary winding up resolution was passed in relation to the employer (see also *PA 1995, s 75(6D)*).

The second set of events is that the winding up of the scheme commences before a scheme failure notice or withdrawal notice is issued and becomes binding or before a members' voluntary winding up resolution is passed.

Once the debt has ceased to be contingent, it will be treated as arising immediately before the relevant event (*PA 1995, s 75(4A)*). The debt will be equal to the difference between the value of the scheme's assets and the amount of its liabilities (*PA 1995, s 75(4)*), calculated on a buy-out basis (*The Occupational Pension Schemes (Employer Debt) Regulations 2005 ('the Employer Debt Regs'), reg 5(11)*).

Multi-employer schemes

As with a single employer scheme, if a 'relevant event' occurs in relation to a participating employer in a multi-employer scheme and immediately before that time, the value of the scheme's assets is less than the amount at that time of its liabilities, this may trigger a contingent employer debt under *PA 1995, s 75(4)* as modified by the *Employer Debt Regs, reg 6(1)*. Broadly, the debt will be equal to the employer's share of the difference as defined in the *Employer Debt Regs, reg 6(2)* (see **Chapter 15** for more details).

It is important to note that due to the contingent nature of the debt, in circumstances where there is a scheme rescue (see **5.21** below), the debt will not fall due.

Role as a creditor

5.7   Since 6 April 2005, the occurrence of an insolvency event in relation to an employer typically triggers not only a section 75 debt but also a PPF assessment period in relation to the scheme or part of the scheme (see **5.21** below). During a PPF assessment period, the rights and powers of the trustees in relation to any debt (including any contingent debt) due to them by the employer, are exercisable by the PPF to the exclusion of the trustees (*PA 2004, s 137*).

Typically, a trustee or the PPF claiming a debt under *PA 1995, s 75* against the employer in a liquidation will be claiming as an unsecured creditor. The trustees/PPF must lodge a 'proof of debt' with the liquidator in order to seek recovery of the deficit, or at least a share in what is available for distribution to the creditors.

A debt due solely by virtue of *s 75* is not preferential (*PA 1995, s 75(8)*). However, as *s 75* debts are calculated on a buy-out basis they can be very large and the PPF may have a significant influence over proposals put forward as part of an administration (see **5.58** below) and whether the required 75 per cent majority of unsecured creditors can be obtained to approve any proposals under a CVA (see **5.53** below). The PPF, exercising the powers of the trustees during the PPF assessment period, will generally be able to prove for voting purposes on the basis of the estimate of the contingent *s 75* debt payable.

For the purposes of any dividend due to unsecured creditors in a liquidation, or under an administration where a dividend is paid out without first appointing a liquidator, the PPF/trustees will be able to prove for dividend purposes the amount of any certified *s 75* debt due to the scheme. The PPF/trustees will need to put in a proof of debt (see **5.65** below).

The trustees of an occupational pension scheme may have security over an employer's assets, perhaps negotiated as part of a recovery plan or clearance application. Accordingly, they may have security for some or all of their debt which will be payable in priority to unsecured creditors (see **5.65** below).

Pre-insolvency pension scheme contributions

Recovery by the trustees of unpaid contributions

5.8   It is unlikely that on the insolvency of an employer, there will be significant unpaid employee and employer contributions. Employee contributions to an occupational pension scheme that have been deducted from salary generally have to be paid over to the trustees within 19 days (or 22 days where contributions are paid by electronic means) of the end of the calendar month in which they were deducted (*PA 1995, s 49(8)* and *Occupational*

Pension Schemes (Scheme Administration) Regulations 1996 (SI 1996/1715), reg 16). Employer contributions have to be paid over within the time limits specified in the schedule of contributions or payment schedule.

If there are arrears of contributions on the insolvency of an employer an element of those contributions may count as preferential debts within the meaning of *IA 1986, s 386 (IA 1986, Sch 6, paras 8, 9; PSA 1993, s 128, Sch 4)*:

(*a*)   employee contributions deducted from earnings of the employee in the four months before the employer's insolvency and not yet paid over to the scheme (*PSA 1993, Sch 4, para 1*);

(*b*)   certain unpaid employer contributions owed to a defined benefit contracted out scheme that were payable in the 12 months before the insolvency event. The appropriate amount of employer contributions that count as preferential for contributory earners is 3 per cent and 4.8 per cent for non-contributory earners (*PSA 1993, Sch 4, para 2(1)(A) and 2(3)(A))* and the *Social Security (Reduced Rates of Class 1 Contributions) (Salary Related Contracted-out Schemes) Order 1996 (SI 1996/1054)*). Contracting-out on a salary-related basis ceased with effect from 6 April 2016 so the preferential status of the debt will fall way over the following 12 months (and will be nil for insolvencies commencing after 5 April 2017).

To the extent that any unpaid contributions are not preferential they will count as an unsecured debt.

Recovery by the insolvency practitioner of paid contributions

5.9   There are circumstances in which paid contributions may be recoverable from the pension scheme.

Administrators and liquidators have the power to make applications to the court for certain transactions entered into by the company prior to administration or liquidation to be set aside. In the context of a pension scheme, the most obvious vulnerability is under *IA 1986, s 239*, which deals with preferences. A preference is given if a company's actions at a time when it is unable to pay its debts (or as a consequence of which it becomes unable to pay its debts) put a creditor or surety of the company's debts into a better position in an insolvent liquidation than the creditor or surety would have been if that action had not taken place and the company was influenced by a desire to put the creditor or surety into such better position.

This means that, at least in theory, an administrator/liquidator could make a claim in respect of contributions made into the scheme by the employer if it can be shown that the employer was influenced by a desire to prefer the scheme. For example, the administrator/liquidator may argue that a preference was shown where benefit enhancements occurred or substantial contributions were made into the scheme when the company was in financial difficulties.

Administrators can generally exercise the company's non-fiduciary powers in relation to the scheme using their general powers (to do all things necessary to manage the affairs of the company) (*Polly Peck International plc (in administration) v Henry [1998] All ER (D) 647*). There are also a number of cases which suggest that administrative receivers can exercise the company's powers in relation to the pension scheme on the basis that it forms part of the affairs of the company (*Simpson Curtis Pension Trustees Ltd v Readson Limited and others [1994] PLR 289, [1994] OPLR 231*).

The decision in *Simpson Curtis* should be contrasted with another case, *Buckley v Hudson Forge [1999] OPLR 249,* where the employer which was first in receivership and then liquidation was also a trustee of the scheme. A surplus arose and the court had to consider whether the receiver could exercise a discretion to augment benefits. The court held that the receiver could not exercise a fiduciary power of an employer. Even if he had the power, he could not exercise it because of the potential for conflict.

In cases where an independent trustee has been appointed, all fiduciary powers will in any event now vest in him, so this should no longer be an issue in most cases (see *PA 1995, s 25(2)*).

Pension scheme contributions paid or due during insolvency

Liquidations

5.10 If an employer goes into liquidation, this will generally trigger the termination of the employees' contracts of employment. The liquidation will also often be a trigger event giving rise to the winding up (or the potential winding-up) of the occupational pension scheme or, in a multi-employer occupational pension scheme, the partial wind-up of the scheme (see **5.43** below). Accordingly in liquidations, active members will usually be treated as having ceased to be in pensionable service, no further benefits will accrue and no ongoing employer and employee contributions will be due.

Administration and receivership – contracts of employment

5.11 Contracts of employment do not automatically come to an end in an administration, administrative receivership or receivership (see **5.55–5.58** below). The administrator, administrative receiver or receiver, as the case may be, has 14 days from his appointment to decide whether or not to adopt the contracts of employment.

5.12   *Employer insolvency: the implications for pension schemes*

The statutory provisions relating to the payment of employer and employee contributions differ slightly depending on the type of insolvency procedure. The relevant statutory provisions are as follows:

(*a*)   administrations – *IA 1986, Sch B1, para 99*, which applies to employment contracts that have been adopted;

(*b*)   administrative receiverships – *IA 1986, s 44*;

(*c*)   receiverships – *IA 1986, s 37*.

If a contract of employment is adopted by an administrator, any liability to pay wages or salary (including a sum payable in lieu of holiday entitlement or in respect of an occupational pension scheme contribution) is paid in priority to the administrator's own remuneration and expenses, except insofar as it arises by reference to anything done or which occurs before the adoption of the contract of employment (*IA 1986, Sch B1, para 99*).

In an administrative receivership, the administrative receiver is personally liable, to the extent of any qualifying liability, on any contract or contract of employment that he adopts in carrying out his functions. The administrative receiver is obliged to pay any wages and salary or contribution to an occupational pension scheme to the extent that the contributions relate to services rendered after the adoption of the employment contract (*IA 1986, s 44*).

In the case of an ordinary receiver appointed under powers contained in a charge (ie not by the court), he is also personally liable on any contract or employment contract that he adopts in carrying out his functions (*IA 1986, s 37*). However, unlike the position in relation to an administrative receiver, there is no specific provision expressly limiting the obligation to make contributions that relate to services rendered after the adoption of the employment contract (see *Powdrill v Watson [1995] 2 AC 394*).

It would appear to be difficult to argue that an administrator or receiver who adopts a contract of employment is personally liable to meet any debt under *PA 1995, s 75* or any employer contribution needed to meet enhanced early retirement/redundancy benefits due under the scheme. This is due to the fact that where a debt on the employer is triggered by an insolvency event under *PA 1995, s 75*, subsection *(4A)* provides that it is to be taken, for the purposes of the law relating to employer insolvency, to arise immediately before the occurrence of the insolvency event.

Administration and receivership – scheme membership

5.12   In most situations, it is unlikely that there will be any further ongoing employer and employee contributions due to any occupational pension scheme.

First, it is often the case that an insolvency event is a winding-up trigger under the scheme's rules. Where winding up is triggered, any active members will cease to be in pensionable service under the scheme and will become deferred members. Second, the insolvency event will often lead to the commencement of a PPF assessment period (see **5.21** below). During a PPF assessment period, generally no further benefits may accrue or contributions may be paid (other than those due to be paid before the beginning of the assessment period) (*PA 2004, s 133(3)–(5)*).

Where an assessment period comes to an end by virtue of the PPF ceasing to be involved with an eligible scheme following the issue of a withdrawal notice under *PA 2004, s 122(2)*, then in certain circumstances, members may accrue benefits in respect of any period of service in employment during the assessment period (*PA 2004, s 150(6); PPF (Entry Rules) Regulations 2005, reg 20(1)*). Broadly, where back employee contributions are paid, the employer is then obliged to pay back employer contributions and the members will be granted the benefits they would have accrued if the scheme had not entered the assessment period (subject to any scaling down under *PA 1995, s 73* if the scheme is wound up).

IPs who adopt contracts of employment may therefore need to make provision for any potential arrears of employer and employee contributions that may become due if the scheme or section of the scheme does not enter the PPF. This is only relevant, however, if employees are not automatically treated as deferred members on the insolvency event occurring under the rules of the scheme.

Recovering arrears of contributions from the National Insurance Fund

5.13   An application can be made to the Secretary of State to recover 'relevant contributions' where the employer has become insolvent (as defined in *PSA 1993, s 123*) and there are unpaid 'relevant contributions' falling to be paid by the scheme's employer (*PSA 1993, ss 123–125*). Any application to recover 'relevant contributions' is made by the persons competent to act on behalf of the scheme (ie generally the trustees (*PSA 1993, s 124(1)*)).

'Relevant contributions' include contributions payable to an occupational pension scheme or personal pension scheme by an employer both on its own account and on behalf of an employee, where the employee contributions have been deducted from salary but have not been paid over by the employer to the scheme (*PSA 1993, s 124(2)*).

The maximum amount of employer contributions recoverable from the National Insurance Fund in relation to an occupational pension scheme is limited to the smallest of the following:

(a)   the amount unpaid in respect of the 12 months preceding the date that the employer became insolvent *(PSA 1993, s 124(3)(a))*;

(b)   in the case of a scheme which is not a money purchase scheme, the amount certified by an actuary as necessary to meet the scheme's liabilities on dissolution to pay the benefits provided to or in respect of workers of the employer *(PSA 1993, s 124(3)(b))*; and

(c)   10 per cent of the total amount of remuneration paid or payable to those workers in the 12 months preceding the date of insolvency *(PSA 1993, s 124(3)(c))*.

The maximum amount recoverable in relation to a defined contribution scheme is the smaller of amounts (a) and (c) *(PSA 1993, s 124(3A))*.

The maximum amount recoverable in relation to unpaid contributions on behalf of a worker that are relevant contributions is limited to the amounts deducted from pay during the 12 months preceding the date of insolvency *(PSA 1993, s 124(5))*.

Before any payment is made, a statement will generally be required by the Secretary of State from the IP of the amount of relevant contributions which appear to have been unpaid on the date of insolvency and remain unpaid *(PSA 1993, s 125)*.

If the Secretary of State makes a payment out of the National Insurance Fund, he has subrogated rights against the employer in relation to these amounts, and stands in the shoes of the employee or pension scheme in relation to the recovery of these amounts in any insolvency proceedings *(PSA 1993, s 127)*.

The Pension Protection Fund

5.14   The PPF is a statutory fund designed to give members of eligible defined benefit pension schemes a measure of protection where the sponsoring employer suffers a qualifying insolvency event (on or after 6 April 2005) and there are insufficient assets in the pension scheme to cover PPF levels of compensation. It is funded by a charge levied on all eligible schemes and provides a minimum level of payment, known as compensation, to beneficiaries of schemes for which it has assumed responsibility.

To enter the PPF:

(a)   the scheme must be 'eligible' (see **5.15** onwards below);

(b)   a 'qualifying insolvency event' must occur in relation to the employer (or the employer must be unlikely to continue as a going concern) (see **5.19** below); and (*c*)   the assets of the scheme must be less than the protected liabilities (see **5.20** below).

Each of these concepts is discussed in more detail below.

Eligible schemes

5.15   *PA 2004* does not itself specify many conditions that must be satisfied for a scheme to be an 'eligible scheme'. It merely states, at *s 126*, that an eligible scheme is an occupational pension scheme which is not a money purchase scheme and is not a 'prescribed scheme' or a scheme of a 'prescribed description'. Subsection *(2)* also specifies that the scheme must not have commenced winding up prior to 6 April 2005 (*PA 2004, s 126(2); Pension Protection Fund (Eligible Schemes) Appointed Day Order 2005 (SI 2005/599)*). These conditions are supplemented by the voluminous *PPF Entry Rules* which set out several specific circumstances where a scheme will not be eligible.

Excluded schemes

5.16   The list of 'prescribed' or excluded schemes, contained in the *PPF Entry Regs, reg 2*, is fairly predictable. Local government schemes and many other public sector schemes are excluded. Unregistered schemes that are not statutory schemes also fall outside the PPF's remit, along with schemes that are administered outside the UK. Schemes which only provide death benefits or, in the case of a non contracted-out centralised scheme, provide only lump sum benefits, are also excluded.

The number of members in a scheme can also be grounds for its exclusion from the PPF. A scheme with fewer than two members, or where there are fewer than 12 members and all are trustees making unanimous decisions (or there is a registered independent trustee), will not be able to enter the PPF.

A scheme which did not have an employer as at 6 April 2005 will also be ineligible (owing to the need for a qualifying insolvency event).

However, after a PPF assessment period begins, if a scheme becomes unregistered or it ceases to have a sufficient number of members as a result of members dying, it will still be eligible for the PPF (*PPF Entry Rules, reg 3*).

Previous status of the scheme

5.17   If a scheme has not been eligible for the three years preceding the beginning of a PPF assessment period (see **5.21** below), or was established within that period and has not been eligible since the date of its inception, the PPF must refuse to assume responsibility for it (*PA 2004, s 146(1), PPF Entry Rules, reg 21*). Likewise, if the scheme was established to replace an existing non-eligible scheme within the three years preceding the beginning of a PPF assessment period, it will not be taken into the PPF (*PA 2004, s 147; PPF Entry Rules, reg 22*).

Other potential bars to PPF entry

5.18   Perhaps one of the most significant bars to PPF entry in practice is the existence of a *Bradstock* compromise agreement.

Before 6 April 2005 it was not uncommon for employers to enter into an agreement with trustees to compromise a debt due under *PA 1995, s 75*. This would enable the company to free itself of its pension liabilities without going through any insolvency process and the trustees to secure a better return for the scheme than if they had had to prove as an unsecured creditor in the insolvency. These compromises are commonly referred to as 'Bradstock agreements', named after a case where it was confirmed that it was legally possible to enter into such an arrangement (*Bradstock Group Pension Scheme Trustees Ltd v Bradstock Group plc & ors [2002] PLR 327*). *Bradstock* confirmed that it was possible to compromise a debt once it was triggered and that from a trust law perspective the trustees would need to *'honestly and reasonably believe'* that entering into the agreement would secure *'the largest amount towards the shortfall'*.

Under the *PPF Entry Rules, reg 2(2)*, if the trustees enter into a legally enforceable agreement the effect of which is to reduce the amount of any debt due to the scheme under *PA 1995, s 75* this will generally now prevent the scheme from being an eligible scheme for PPF entry purposes. As the legislation applies to agreements entered into 'at any time' this can be of great concern to schemes which entered into such agreements before the legislation came into force (although a purposive view may be to assume that the legislation only catches agreements entered into on or after that date (ie 6 April 2005)). There are some exceptions to the general rule.

Validation

Prior to the start of a PPF assessment period, trustees can compromise a *section 75* debt without preventing PPF entry if the scheme's assets at that time would be sufficient to meet the level of compensation that the PPF would provide (see **5.24** below). The scheme actuary has to provide the PPF with a written estimate of the scheme's current assets and protected liabilities (see **5.20** below), together with a statement about the effect the compromise agreement would have on the value of the assets. The PPF will then determine whether to validate the estimate and the statement (*PPF Entry Rules, reg 2(3)*).

The trustees are only likely to agree to a compromise, however, if it could potentially result in greater recovery than the alternatives. For example, the trustees would need to bear in mind that in an insolvency, they are likely to be a creditor for the full annuity buy-out costs of the scheme under *PA 1995, s 75*.

Scheme of arrangement

Prior to the start of a PPF assessment period, it is also possible (without jeopardising PPF entry) for a *section 75* debt to be compromised as part of an arrangement under *Companies Act 2006, Part 26* (formerly *CA 1985, s 425*) (power of company to compromise with creditors or members). The effect of such arrangements is to reduce the amount of the debt due to the scheme under *PA 1995, s 75* which may be recovered by, or on behalf of, those trustees.

Apportionment

A scheme apportionment arrangement, flexible apportionment arrangement, regulated apportionment arrangement ('RAA'), withdrawal arrangement, approved withdrawal arrangement or restructuring under the *Occupational Pension Schemes (Employer Debt) Regulations 2005* may be put in place in relation to the scheme prior to the start of the a PPF assessment period without prejudicing PPF entry. These arrangements are exceptions to the general prohibition on legally enforceable agreements to reduce debts due (*PPF Entry Rules, reg 2(4)*).

PPF powers

The PPF can itself compromise a *section 75* debt after the commencement of an assessment period without preventing the scheme entering the PPF (*PPF Entry Rules, reg 2(3)(c)*). During a PPF assessment period, the trustees' rights and powers in relation to any debts (including the power to compromise) are exercisable by the PPF (*PA 2004, s 137*).

Clearance

The directors of the company compromising the debt are likely to want to obtain clearance from the Regulator to confirm that they are not exposed to contribution notice liability. If the compromise happens in the context of the sale of the company, any purchaser will want clearance to confirm that a financial support direction will not be made (see **Chapter 15** and **5.48** to **5.50** below for more on clearance, contribution notices and financial support directions).

Regulator and PPF guidance on compromises

The Regulator has issued guidance on when it may be willing to grant clearance for and approve an RAA or to grant clearance for the compromise of a *section 75* debt as part of a company restructuring.

The PPF has also issued guidance on when it may be willing to exercise its creditor rights and agree to a compromise of a *section 75* debt in an insolvency process or not object to an RAA. See **5.45** to **5.48** below for more details.

Qualifying insolvency events and ceasing to continue as a going concern

5.19 In order for a scheme to enter the PPF, an employer must either suffer a 'qualifying insolvency event' (for the purposes of *PA 2004, s 127*) or be unlikely to continue as a going concern and meet the prescribed requirements (for the purposes of *PA 2004, ss 128–129*). These events will also trigger the start of a PPF assessment period (see **5.21** below).

An insolvency event (as defined by *PA 2004, s 121* and the *PPF Entry Rules, reg 5*) will only be a 'qualifying insolvency event', in accordance with *PA 2004, s 127(3)*, if it occurs on or after the day appointed under *s 126(2)* (6 April 2005) and is either the first insolvency event to occur in relation to the employer on or after that date or it does not occur within an earlier assessment period in relation to the scheme. See **5.2** above for more on the meaning of insolvency event.

The legislation does not specify when the trustees (or the Regulator) can conclude that they have become aware that the employer is unlikely to continue as a going concern. This is likely to depend on the facts. The *PPF Entry Rules* now provide that the trustees should make an application (a '*section 129 application*') to the PPF to assume responsibility for the scheme within 28 days of becoming aware that the employer is unlikely to continue as a going concern or such longer period of not more than three months as the PPF may determine is reasonable in the circumstances of a particular case (*PPF Entry Rules, reg 8(1)* as amended by the *Pension Protection Fund and Occupational and Personal Pension Schemes (Miscellaneous Amendments) Regulations 2016 (SI 2016/294)* with effect from 6 April 2016).

Before 6 April 2016 generally an application could only be made to the PPF under *PA 2004* in circumstances where the employer was a public body (where there was no government guarantee) or a charity, a trade union, an EEA credit institution or an EEA Insurer (*PPF Entry Rules, reg 7*). The route was intended to allow specific types of employers that could not suffer a qualifying insolvency event in the UK to enter the PPF. Following the *Olympic Airlines* case, where there were problems obtaining PPF entry for a non-UK employer which no longer had an establishment in the UK (see **5.33** below) the requirements for the use of the *section 129* route were amended to make them more principles based (*The Pension Protection Fund and Occupational Pension Schemes (Miscellaneous Amendments) Regulations 2016 (SI 2016/294)*) amending *PPF Entry Rules, reg 7*). Under revised legislation the *s 129* route is now capable of applying more generally in cases where it is not possible to trigger a qualifying insolvency event (*PA 2004, s 127*).

Under the reworked *section 129* requirements, the *section 129* route for PPF entry can be used where, one or more of the following paragraphs *7(2), (4)* and *(5)* apply to the employer.

'7(2) It is **not**:

(a) an individual;

(b) a company as defined in section 1(1) of the Companies Act 2006 [where generally it is possible to use the section 127 route to achieve PPF entry];

(c) a company which may be wound up under Part 5 of the Insolvency Act 1986 (unregistered companies) [*where generally it is possible to use the section 127 route to achieve PPF entry*];

(d) a partnership;

(e) a relevant body as defined in regulation 5(2). [Relevant bodies for this purpose include the following bodies where generally it is possible to have a qualifying insolvency event under the section 127 route ie (a) a credit union, (b) a limited liability partnership, (c) a building society, (d) a person who has permission to act under Part 4A of the FSMA (permission to carry out regulated activities), (e) the society of Lloyd's and Lloyd's members who have permission under Part 19 of the FSMA (Lloyd's), (f) a friendly society within the meaning given in the Friendly Societies Act 1992 and a co-operative or community benefit society.]

(3) For the purposes of paragraph (2)(c), an employer which is a company incorporated outside the United Kingdom is to be regarded as a company which may be wound up under Part 5 of the Insolvency Act 1986.

(4) This paragraph applies to an employer which is an EEA insurer or EEA Credit institution.

(5) This paragraph applies to an employer if–

(a) the employer's centre of main interests is situated within the territory of a member State other than the United Kingdom;

(b)   insolvency proceedings have been opened against the employer in a member State in accordance with Article 3 of the Insolvency Regulation; and

(c)   the employer does not have an establishment in the United Kingdom.'

The revised *para 7(2)* means that if a body is of a type which does not fall within *para 7(2)* the *section 129* route can be used.

Paragraph 7(5) is intended to assist in similar situations to the *Olympic Airlines* case where the non-UK employer no longer has an establishment in the UK so it is not possible to bring secondary insolvency proceedings in the UK. However, concerns were expressed by some commentators in response to the consultation about these changes, that there could still be circumstances in which the UK courts might refuse to exercise their discretion to order the winding up of non-UK employers based outside the UK where they have no business operations in the UK. Some commentators also expressed concerns that, in relation to employers based in other EU member states, the courts might still refuse to grant a winding-up order in the UK even if the employer did have an establishment in the UK, or that an employer without an establishment in the UK might effectively be insolvent but without insolvency proceedings in its centre of main interests, so the conditions for an application to the PPF under *section 129* may not be satisfied.

Protected liabilities

5.20   In order to achieve PPF entry the value of the scheme's assets immediately before the qualifying insolvency event (or *section 129 application*) (the 'relevant time'), must be less that the amount of the protected liabilities.

The term protected liabilities is defined at *PA 2004, s 131*. It includes:

(*a*)   the cost of securing benefits for and in respect of members of the scheme which correspond to the compensation that would be payable, in relation to the scheme, if the PPF assumed responsibility for it (see **5.24** below);

(*b*)   the liabilities of the scheme which are not liabilities to, or in respect of, its members; and

(*c*)   the estimated cost of winding up the scheme.

During the assessment period, the PPF is required to obtain a valuation of or make an assessment of the scheme's assets and protected liabilities at the relevant time (*PA 2004, s 143*) (see **5.21** below).

PPF assessment periods and entry into the PPF – single employer schemes

5.21   A scheme can only enter the PPF once it has been through an assessment period (*PA 2004, s 132*). This begins when a 'qualifying insolvency event' occurs or a *section 129 application* is made (see **5.19** above) in relation to the employer of an eligible scheme (see **5.15** above), and ends when:

(*a*)   the PPF ceases to be involved with the scheme (*PA 2004, s 149*); or

(*b*)   the trustees receive a transfer notice under *PA 2004, s 160*; or

(*c*)   the conditions in *PA 2004, s 154(2)* have been met (no scheme rescue has occurred but there are sufficient assets to meet the protected liabilities of the scheme etc.).

During the assessment period, the PPF will assess whether the value of the scheme's assets is less than the amount of its protected liabilities (see **5.20** above) and whether a scheme rescue can be effected (see below). Various restrictions will apply to the scheme and these are dealt with in **5.22** below.

The basic sequence of events during an assessment period is as follows.

(1)   The employer undergoes a qualifying insolvency event (*PA 2004, s 132(2)(a)*).

(2)   The insolvency practitioner ('IP') issues a *s 120* notice to the PPF, the Regulator and the trustees, to the effect that the insolvency event has occurred in relation to the employer. Notification must be given within 14 days beginning on the later of the insolvency date and the date on which the IP becomes aware of the existence of the scheme (*PPF Entry Rules, reg 4*).

(3)   The PPF confirms the assessment period has begun (*The Pension Protection Fund (Provision of Information) Regulations 2005 (SI 2005/674, reg 3)*).

(4)   The IP issues a *s 122* notice to the PPF, the Regulator and the trustees, to the effect that a scheme rescue is not possible (a 'scheme failure notice') (*PA 2004, s 122(2)(a)*). In order to issue the notice in relation to a company, the IP must be able to confirm, for the purposes of *s 122(5) (b)*, that:

(*a*)   after the beginning of an assessment period, the PPF has entered into a legally enforceable agreement on behalf of the trustees the effect of which is to reduce the amount of the debt due to the scheme under *PA 1995, s 75* which may be recovered by, or on behalf of, those trustees (see **5.18** above); or

(*b*)   the employer is not continuing as a going concern, no other person has assumed responsibility for meeting the employer's pension liabilities under the scheme and the IP is of the opinion that this will not take place (*PPF Entry Rules, reg 9(2)*).

Notices may also be given under *PA 2004, s 122* that a scheme rescue has occurred (a 'withdrawal notice') (*PA 2004, s 122(2)(b)*) or that confirmation of either the impossibility of or the occurrence of a scheme rescue cannot be given (*PA 2004, s 122(4)*).

If a withdrawal notice is issued and becomes binding, the PPF will cease to be involved with the scheme (*PA 2004, s 149*) and the assessment period will come to an end (*PA 2004, ss 132* and *150*). A withdrawal notice may only be issued in relation to a company if the IP can confirm that it has been rescued as a going concern; the employer retains responsibility for meeting the pension liabilities and has not entered into a legally enforceable agreement as mentioned above; or that another person has assumed responsibility for meeting the employer's pension liabilities under the scheme (*PPF Entry Rules, reg 9(1)*).

(5)   The PPF issues a determination notice upon deciding to approve the *s 122* notice. This will only happen if the PPF is satisfied that the IP was required to issue the notice and that it complies with the statutory requirements (*PA 2004, s 123*).

(6)   The PPF issues a notice confirming the status of the scheme. It will only give the notice once any period for reviewing the determination notice has expired (after 28 days (*PPF (Review and Reconsideration of Reviewable Matters) Regulations 2005 (SI 2005/669), reg 3*) (and any reviews having been disposed of) causing the *s 122* notice to become binding. The PPF will give the notice to the Regulator, trustees and IP (*PA 2004, s 125*). The PPF assessment period will then continue.

(7)   The PPF generally obtains an actuarial valuation of the scheme as at the relevant time (the time immediately before the qualifying insolvency event) (*PA 2004, s 143(2)(b)*). The purpose of the valuation is to establish whether the value of the scheme's assets at the relevant time was less than the amount of the protected liabilities (*PA 2004, s 143(2)*). The scheme actuary will carry out the actuarial valuation for the PPF, but where there is more than one employer it may require assistance from the scheme's legal advisers in determining how to split the asset value of the scheme into the relevant 'segregated parts'. From 23 July 2012 in certain circumstances the PPF can now make a determination whether the value of the scheme's assets at the relevant time was less than the amount of the protected liabilities without obtaining a formal valuation (*PA 2004, s 143(2A)* and *(4)*).

(8)   The PPF approves the valuation where it is satisfied that it has been prepared in accordance with *PA 2004, s 143*. A copy is given to the Regulator, the trustees and any IP (*PA 2004, s 144*). If the PPF is not satisfied, it will obtain another valuation under *PA 2004, s 143*.

(9) The PPF gives notice that the valuation is binding. It will only give the notice once any period for reviewing the approval of the valuation has expired (two months after the date of the valuation summaries being issued to members) (*PA 2004, Sch 9, para 9*; *PPF (Review and Reconsideration of Reviewable Matters) Regulations 2005 (SI 2005/669), reg 3*) (and any reviews having been disposed of) causing the *s 143* valuation to become binding. The PPF will give notice of this fact, together with a copy of the binding valuation, to the Regulator, trustees and IP(s). A binding valuation is conclusive in determining whether or not the scheme assets are less than the protected liabilities (*PA 2004, s 145*).

(10) The PPF gives a transfer notice where it is required to assume responsibility for the scheme under *PA 2004, s 127*. It must be given to the trustees, the Regulator and any IP (*PA 2004, s 160*). The PPF then assumes responsibility for the scheme (*PA 2004, s 161*). The effect of this is that:

(*a*) the property, rights and liabilities are transferred to the PPF with effect from the time the trustees receive the transfer notice;

(*b*) the trustees are discharged from their pension obligations from that time; and

(*c*) from that time, the PPF is responsible for securing that compensation is (and has been) paid in accordance with the pension compensation provisions.

The scheme is treated as having been wound up immediately after that time (*PA 2004, s 161(2)*).

Restrictions and PPF powers during the assessment period

5.22 During the assessment period, *PA 2004* imposes a number of restrictions on the scheme including:

(*a*) no new members of any class may be admitted (*PA 2004, s 133(2)*);

(*b*) no further contributions may be paid towards the scheme, other than those due to be paid before the assessment period began or in relation to an undischarged *PA 1995, s 75* debt, or obligations arising by virtue of a contribution notice, financial support direction or restoration order (*PA 2004, s 133(3)*; *PPF Entry Rules, reg 14*);

(*c*) no benefits may accrue (although this does not prevent any statutory increases in benefits or the accrual of money purchase benefits to the extent that they are derived from income or capital gains arising from investments) (*PA 2004, s 133(5)–(7)*);

(*d*) the winding up of the scheme must not begin (unless ordered by the Regulator) (*PA 2004, s 135(2), (3)*);

(*e*)   no transfers or transfer payments are to be made from the scheme and no steps may be taken to discharge any other member liabilities (excluding pension credits), except in prescribed circumstances (*PA 2004, s 135(4) to (8)*). There are some significant exceptions set out in *PPF Entry Rules, reg 16*, relating to entitlements which arose before the assessment period and in *PPF (Hybrid Schemes) (Modification) Regulations 2005 SI 2005/449 (the 'Hybrid Schemes Regs'), reg 2*, relating to money purchase benefits;

(*f*)   benefits payable to a member (excluding money purchase benefits) must be reduced in line with PPF compensation levels and, where relevant, as if the scheme were not winding up (*PA 2004, s 138*). *Section 138* also contains a number of other restrictions and powers available to the trustees, including the curtailment of early leaver payments and the ability to recover overpayments.

During the assessment period, the PPF may also make certain directions to any 'relevant person' in relation to the scheme (including the employer, the trustees and the scheme administrator). The power must be exercised with a view to ensuring that the scheme's protected liabilities do not exceed its assets (or, if they do exceed its assets that any excess is kept to a minimum). This is to reduce the burden on the PPF. Such directions may be given in respect of:

(*a*)   the investment of the scheme's assets (*PA 2004, s 134(2)*);

(*b*)   the incurring of expenditure (*PA 2004, s 134(2)*);

(*c*)   the instigation or conduct of legal proceedings (*PA 2004, s 134(2)*);

(*d*)   the amendment of scheme rules (*PPF Entry Rules, reg 15(2)*); and

(*e*)   discharging any money purchase liabilities (*Hybrid Schemes Regs, reg 3*).

Other important powers are conferred on the PPF during the assessment period. Aside from reviewing ill-health pensions (see **5.23** below) and obtaining an actuarial valuation (see **5.21** above), these are that:

•   The rights and powers of the trustees in relation to any employer debt (including any contingent debt) due to them, transfer to the PPF (*PA 2004, s 137*). This includes the power to make compromises (*PPF Entry Rules, reg 2(3)(c)*). Practically speaking this means that the trustees do not need to deal with any claims in the insolvency of the employer(s). The PPF must pay any amounts it receives to the trustees.

•   The PPF may, on application, make a loan to the trustees if they are not able to pay benefits as they fall due, though this will have to be repaid with interest at specified times (*PA 2004, s 139(2)*). This is not a personal liability on the trustees.

Paying benefits during a PPF assessment period: admissible rules

5.23   The payment of benefits will be one of the key issues for trustees to consider during a PPF assessment period. As highlighted at **5.22** above, benefits payable to a member during an assessment period (excluding money purchase benefits) must be reduced in line with PPF compensation levels (*PA 2004, ss 138, 161, 162*). Compensation is based on the scheme's 'admissible rules'. Accordingly, the trustees will need to review their scheme rules to determine which are admissible.

Broadly speaking, the 'admissible rules' are the scheme rules disregarding (a) 'recent rule changes' made or taking effect in the three years ending with the assessment date if these increase the protected liabilities (see **5.20** above) and (b) rules that operate by reference to the winding up of the scheme or any associated event (*PA 2004, Sch 7, para 35* and see also the *Pension Protection Fund (Compensation) Regulations 2005 (SI 2005/670)*).

The question of whether the settlement of a dispute relating to the sex equalisation of benefits could be a 'recent rule change' was considered in the case of *Capita v Zurkinskas [2010] EWHC 3365*. It was held that the settlement was not to be disregarded from the 'admissible rules' as changes attributable to overriding legislation (such as applies to equalisation (see **Chapter 9**)) are excluded from the definition of 'recent rule changes'. This decision does not rule out the possibility that a settlement or compromise could, where resolution of the dispute in a particular way is not a result of overriding legislation, be a 'recent rule change' and as such be excluded from the 'admissible rules'.

Recent discretionary increases in the three previous years are also disregarded if broadly they exceed the general level of prices when determining the amount of periodic compensation payable to pensioners and postponed pensioners (PA 2004, Sch 7, paras 35(7)–(10)).

The PPF may also review certain ill-health pensions made under the scheme prior to the beginning of the assessment period (*PA 2004, ss 140–142* and the *Pension Protection Fund (Reviewable Ill Health Pensions) Regulations 2005 (SI 2005/652)*).

The trustees will be asked to produce a project plan by the PPF setting out a plan to deal with all the various steps to achieve PPF entry which they will prepare in consultation with their PPF caseworker.

PPF compensation

5.24   The compensation that will be paid by the PPF (and in line with which the trustees must pay benefits during an assessment period) will depend on the age and status of the member immediately before the assessment date and the admissible rules (see **5.23** above) of the scheme (*PA 2004, Sch 7*). Broadly speaking:

(*a*)   individuals who have already reached the scheme's normal retirement date, or are already in receipt of a survivor's or ill-health pension, will be paid at the 100 per cent level of compensation;

(*b*)   individuals who have not reached the scheme's normal retirement date will be paid at the 90 per cent level of compensation. This will include those members who are still below the scheme's normal retirement date but have taken early retirement.

For those limited to 90 per cent under (*b*) above, there is also a compensation cap which varies with age (from 1 April 2016 it is £37,420.42 for a 65-year-old, giving an effective cap of £33,678.38) (*Pension Protection Fund and Occupational Pension Schemes (Levy Ceiling and Pension Compensation Cap) Order 2016 (SI 2016/82)*). Annual pension increases of CPI (RPI before 1 January 2012), limited to 2.5 per cent, are made on pensions attributable to service on and after 6 April 1997 (*PA 2004, Sch 7, para 28*).

In December 2012, the Pensions Minister Steve Webb announced plans to make revisions to the PPF compensation cap to better compensate those with long service. Further detail was given in a written ministerial statement on 25 June 2013. Under these plans the compensation cap will be increased by 3 per cent for every full year of pensionable service over 20 years. PPF compensation received by the member cannot, however, be more than double the 'standard' PPF compensation cap. The changes to the PPF compensation cap will apply to anyone already receiving PPF compensation (for future payments) as well as members of schemes entering the PPF on and after the date the provisions come into force. These changes are in *Schedule 20* of *PA 2014*. They are not yet in force but will be inserted as new *regulation 25A* of the *Pensions Protection Fund (Compensation) Regulations 2005 (SI 2005/670)*.

Compensation will be applied differently in respect of dependants where the member has died after the assessment period has begun. In many cases the dependant will only be able to receive 50 per cent of the member's compensation under the PPF (*PA 2004, Sch 7* and see also the *Pension Protection Fund (Compensation) Regulations 2005 (SI 2005/670)*).

Generally, money purchase benefits will be secured outside the to the statutory definition of 'money purchase benefits' in *PSA 1993, s 1* (see **Chapter 1**), there are transitional provisions to deal with the situation where trustees have treated benefits as money purchase but, because of the new definition, they no longer fall into that category.

Cessation of involvement/no requirement to assume responsibility

5.25   The PPF will cease to be involved with an eligible scheme on the occurrence of the first withdrawal event after the assessment period begins (*PA 2004, s 149*).

A withdrawal event may occur where:

- there is a scheme rescue (see **5.21** above); or

- the PPF is not satisfied that the scheme was eligible throughout the relevant period or was established simply in order to gain PPF entry; or

- no insolvency event has occurred or is likely to occur.

In these circumstances, benefits which were not paid during the assessment period owing to the requirement to pay benefits in line with PPF compensation levels will fall due (*PA 2004, s 150(1)*). Such benefits may be subject to *PA 1995, ss 73 to 73B*, where the winding up of the scheme has begun. Meanwhile, any overpayments may be recovered (*PA 2004, s 150(3)*). In certain circumstances, benefits may be treated as having accrued during the assessment period (see **5.12** above).

The PPF is not required to assume responsibility for an eligible scheme if the value of the scheme's assets at the relevant time was equal to or more than the amount of the protected liabilities at that time (*PA 2004, s 127(2), s 128(2)*). Where this is the only reason for the PPF not assuming responsibility:

(1)   The trustees may make a further application to the PPF under *PA 2004, s 151*. In these circumstances, the PPF must assume responsibility for the scheme if it is satisfied that the value of the scheme's assets at the reconsideration time is less than the aggregate of:

   (*a*)   the amount quoted in the protected benefits quotation accompanying the application;

   (*b*)   the amount at that time of the scheme's liabilities which are not liabilities to, or in respect of, members of the scheme; and

   (*c*)   the estimated costs of winding up the scheme at that time (*PA 2004, s 152(2)*);

If trustees or managers of the scheme have taken all reasonable steps to obtain a protected benefits quotation but were unable to do so and the PPF is satisfied that this is the case, the PPF must assume responsibility for the scheme if it is satisfied that the value of the assets of the scheme at the reconsideration time is less than the amount of the protected liabilities at that time (*PA 2004, s 152(2A) and (2B)*).

(2)   If the trustees are satisfied the scheme has sufficient assets to meet its protected liabilities but have taken all reasonable steps to obtain a full buy-out quotation, the trustees must apply to the PPF for authority to continue as a closed scheme (*PA 2004, s 153*). A closed scheme must be run in accordance with *PA 2004, s 155–159* which allows for further applications to be made for the PPF to assume responsibility for the scheme (*PA 2004, s 157*).

Where, broadly, following a *s 151* or *s 157* application the scheme has sufficient assets to meet the protected liabilities, the trustees must wind up (or continue winding up) the scheme (*PA 2004, s 154*). See **5.43** and **Chapter 12** for further details.

Appeals

5.26   The legislation requires the PPF to review certain 'reviewable matters' on which it has made a decision (*PA 2004, s 206, Sch 9*). Reviewable matters include things such as making a determination, or issuing a notice. The timescales for this process are set out in the *Pension Protection Fund (Review and Reconsideration of Reviewable Matters) Regulations 2005 (SI 2005/669)*.

There is also a PPF Ombudsman (*PA 2004, s 213*). He may investigate decisions reconsidered by the PPF, and then determine what action it should take. Regulations set out the mechanics of this (*The Pension Protection Fund (Reference of Reviewable Matters to the PPF Ombudsman) Regulations 2005 (SI 2005/2024)*). The PPF Ombudsman has many of the powers of the Pension Ombudsman, such as being able to hold oral hearings and compel the disclosure of documents. The current PPF Ombudsman is Anthony Arter, who is also the Pensions Ombudsman.

Application of PPF entry requirements to multi-employer schemes

Meaning of multi-employer schemes

5.27   The PPF entry requirements relating to single employer schemes (see **5.21** above) are modified in relation to multi-employer schemes.

A 'multi-employer scheme' is defined as 'an occupational pension scheme in relation to which there is more than one employer' (*PA 2004, s 307(4)*). As a consequence, when analysing the legislation relating to the PPF it will always be necessary to establish who is an employer within the meaning of *PA 2004*. The definition of employer is considered in **5.29** below.

First, it is helpful to understand the structure of the *PPF (Multi-employer Schemes) (Modification) Regulations 2005 (SI 2005/441)* (the '*PPF Multi-employer Regs*') and how they categorise different schemes.

PPF Multi-employer Regulations

5.28   The *PPF Multi-employer Regulations* are divided into a number of different parts, and the relevant ones are set out below for ease of reference:

Part 2	Segregated schemes: single employer sections
Part 3	Segregated schemes: multi-employer sections without a requirement for partial wind up on the withdrawal of a participating employer
Part 4	Segregated schemes: non-segregated multi-employer sections of segregated schemes with a requirement for partial wind up on the withdrawal of participating employer
Part 5	Non-segregated schemes: with a requirement for partial wind up on the withdrawal of a participating employer
Part 6	Non-segregated schemes: without provision for partial wind up on the withdrawal of a participating employer
Part 7	Non-segregated schemes: with an option to segregate on the withdrawal of a participating employer
Part 8	Segregated schemes: multi-employer sections of segregated schemes with an option to segregate on the withdrawal of a participating employer

As is clear from the headings of the different parts, these can be divided into those relating to:

(1)   Segregated schemes (*Parts 2, 3, 4* and *8*); and

(2)   Non-segregated schemes (*Parts 5, 6* and *7*).

A segregated scheme is:

'a multi-employer scheme which is divided into two or more sections where—

(*a*)   any contributions payable to the scheme by an employer in relation to the scheme or by a member are allocated to that employer's or that member's section; and

(*b*)   a specified proportion of the assets of the scheme is attributable to each section of the scheme and cannot be used for the purposes of any other section.' (*PPF Multi-employer Regs, reg 1.*)'

Segregated schemes

Each section in a segregated scheme is regarded as a separate scheme for the purposes of the *PPF Multi-employer Regs*. As discussed in **5.14** above, the key factors for achieving PPF entry in relation to a single employer scheme are that the scheme is eligible, the employer has suffered a qualifying insolvency event (or can no longer continue as a going concern), and the value of the assets is less than the protected liabilities. The same principles apply to a section of a multi-employer scheme.

Non-segregated schemes

In practice, the multi-employer schemes most commonly encountered are the non-segregated *Part 5, 6* and *7* schemes, and these are the ones discussed below. When considering entry to the PPF, the same principles apply as for single employer schemes, but with the key difference that there is more than one employer in relation to which an insolvency event may occur.

The *PPF Multi-employer Regs* deal with the existence of multiple employers in non-segregated schemes in different ways according to the provisions of their scheme's partial wind-up rule. It is on this basis that schemes are categorised into the different parts. Broadly speaking, upon the occurrence of an insolvency event in relation to a participating employer:

- *Part 5* schemes will segregate, and the part relating to the insolvent employer will enter a PPF assessment period.

- *Part 7* schemes will segregate, and the part relating to the insolvent employer will enter a PPF assessment period unless and until the trustees of the scheme decide to retain the segregated part.

- *Part 6* schemes will not segregate and will not enter a PPF assessment period until an insolvency event occurs in relation to the last employer (or the '*Rover* exemption' applies – see **5.32** below). These are often referred to as 'last man standing' schemes.

When assessing which *Part* of the *PPF Entry Rules* a scheme falls into, it is necessary to establish whether it has multiple employers (within the meaning of the legislation), whether it is segregated (see above), and what the rules of the scheme require the trustees to do in circumstances where an employer ceases to participate in the scheme.

What is an employer for the purposes of PPF entry?

5.29   *PA 2004, s 318* defines 'employer', in relation to an occupational pension scheme, as 'the employer of persons in the description of employment to which the scheme in question relates'. This is subject to any regulations extending the meaning of 'employer' to include 'persons who have been the employer in relation to the scheme'.

The meaning of employer is extended, in an almost identical way, by both the *PPF Multi-employer Regs* and the *PPF Entry Rules*. The extended definition is relevant both to PPF entry but also (by virtue of the *PPF Multi-employer Regs, reg 1(3)*) in relation to someone who is an employer for the purposes of calculating the PPF levy. In summary:

(1)   In relation to a single employer scheme or single employer section of a segregated scheme which, in either case, has no active members, 'employer' includes the person who was the employer of persons in the description of employment to which the scheme or section relates immediately before the scheme or section ceased to have any active members (*PPF Entry Rules, reg 1(4); PPF Multi-employer Regs, reg 1(2)*).

(2)   In relation to a non-segregated multi-employer scheme or a multi-employer section of a segregated scheme, 'employer' includes any person who before the assessment date has ceased to be the employer of persons in the description of employment to which the scheme or section relates unless one of a number of conditions is satisfied (*PPF Multi-employer Regs, reg 1(3)*). The *PPF Entry Rules* adopt a virtually identical definition.

In summary, the conditions relevant to a multi-employer scheme or section provide that a person will not be deemed to be an employer if, before the assessment date:

A   a *section 75* debt became due and has been paid;

B   a *section 75* debt became due but was reduced by means of a legally enforceable agreement and the reduced amount has been paid;

C   a *section 75* debt became due but was excluded from the value of the assets because it is unlikely to be recovered without disproportionate costs or within a reasonable time;

D   at the time the person ceased to be an employer (of persons in the description of employment to which the scheme or section relates), the value of the assets of the scheme or section was such that no *section 75* debt was treated as becoming due; or

E   a restructuring under *regulation 6ZB* or *6ZC* of the *Occupational Pension Schemes (Employer Debt) Regulations 2005* occurs, the employer was the exiting employer and neither *reg 6ZA(3)* nor *(4)* applies in relation to that restructuring.

F   a flexible apportionment arrangement has taken effect in accordance with *regulation 6E of the Occupational Pension Schemes (Employer Debt) Regulations 2005.*

5.30 *Employer insolvency: the implications for pension schemes*

The *PPF Entry Rules* adopt the same conditions save that, when determining who is an employer when a scheme is not in an assessment period, there is no requirement that these conditions should have been satisfied before the assessment date.

It is not entirely clear from the legislation exactly when a debt should be treated as becoming due, and this point, although discussed, was not decided in the case of *L v M Ltd [2007] 01 PBLR*. Sir Andrew Morritt VC had expressed the view in *Phoenix Venture Holdings Ltd [2005] 38 PBLR* (at paragraph 26) that, for the purposes of *PA 1995, s 75(2)*:

> 'There cannot be a debt until a sum certain has been ascertained. The designation of the time is so that the Actuary may know as of what date his calculations should be made. But until those calculations have been made in the prescribed manner the difference between the value of the assets and the amount of the liabilities cannot be ascertained and an amount equal to that difference remains uncertain.'

However, Warren J commented (at paragraph 98 of *L v M*):

> 'Whether a debt is due before it is quantified is not a question I need to answer, nor therefore do I need to say whether the decision in *Phoenix* governs the meaning of Regulation 2(2) (PPF Entry Rules).'

Our view is that it is possible for a debt to have fallen due even if it has not been certified. However, we recognise that it is an open point.

The definition of employer for the purposes of PPF entry is not the same as the definition used for the purposes of the employer debt legislation. The key point to note is that an employer may have ceased to be an employer for *section 75* debt purposes but still be an employer for PPF entry purposes.

Partial wind up rules – general

5.30 Having established that a non-segregated scheme has multiple employers, it is then necessary to look at the rule governing the situation when an employer ceases to participate in the scheme (the 'partial wind up rule'). In this way, it can be determined whether the scheme falls into *Part 5, 6 or 7* of the *PPF Multi-employer Regulations*.

Many schemes will have a partial wind up rule requiring a segregation of assets when an employer ceases to participate and indeed it used to be a requirement for Inland Revenue Approval that a scheme provided for a partial wind up in these circumstances. In recent years such a requirement was not always considered appropriate therefore provisions permitting retention of liabilities with the consent of the trustees or the principal employer were inserted.

For PPF entry (and levy) purposes, the categorisation of a non-segregated scheme will depend on whether, when an employer ceases to participate, the trustees are required to segregate the scheme; there is an option to segregate the scheme; or there is no provision to partially wind up the scheme. These are set out as follows:

> 'the requirement in the scheme rules for the trustees or managers of the scheme to segregate such part of the assets of the scheme as is attributable to the scheme's liabilities to provide pensions or other benefits to or in respect of the pensionable service of some or all of the members by reference to an employer in relation to the scheme ... would be triggered when an employer in relation to the scheme ceases to participate in the scheme' (*reg 45 (Part 5)*)

> 'the rules ... do not provide for the partial winding up of the scheme when an employer in relation to the scheme ceases to participate in the scheme' (*reg 61 (Part 6)*)

> 'under the rules of the scheme, the trustees or managers have an option, in circumstances where an employer in relation to the scheme ceases to participate in the scheme, to segregate such part of the assets of the scheme as is attributable to the scheme's liabilities to provide pensions or other benefits to or in respect of the pensionable service of some or all of the members by reference to that employer' (*reg 71 (Part 7)*).

Many scheme rules do not fit easily within the categories available and there has been legal debate about whether every scheme can be made to fit into one of the categories.

Partial wind up rules – practical difficulties

5.31   If a non-exhaustive interpretation of the classification is taken, it would mean that certain schemes might never be able to obtain PPF entry. For example, there are schemes with partial wind up rules where the principal employer alone has a right to determine when a partial wind up has been triggered. Arguably, this type of scheme is not a *Part 5* or a *Part 7* scheme, as there is no requirement for the trustees to segregate part of the scheme assets, but it is also not a *Part 6* scheme as there is a requirement for a partial winding up.

It is arguable that a court would seek to interpret the classification exhaustively. Otherwise it would mean that not all schemes could achieve PPF entry (notwithstanding their employer would have paid the PPF levy). This would not be consistent with the purpose for which the PPF compensation was established ie to provide a safety net for pension benefits of schemes of insolvent employers.

5.32 *Employer insolvency: the implications for pension schemes*

The PPF compensation scheme is an integral part of the overall system of protection under UK law designed to give effect to the UK's obligations, pursuant to *Directive 2008/94/EC* on the protection of employees in the event of the insolvency of their employer. Under *Article 8* of this directive:

> 'Member states shall ensure that the necessary measures are taken to protect the interests of employees and of persons having already left the employer's undertaking or business at the date of the onset of the employer's insolvency in respect or rights conferring on them immediate or prospective entitlement to old-age benefits, including survivors' benefits, under supplementary company or intercompany pension schemes outside national statutory social security systems.'

Under the *Marleasing* principle (*Marleasing SA v La Comercial International de Alimintacion SA (Case C-106/89 [1990] ECR I-04135*) a court should generally prefer a construction of legislation which avoids infringement or possible infringement of EU obligations. An exhaustive classification avoids any possible infringement of EU obligations.

It is to be hoped that a UK court would strive to interpret the PPF entry legislation in a way which would not result in certain schemes being in-eligible for entry into the PPF merely because of the manner in which the partial wind up rule is drafted.

Impact of categorisation

5.32   Having classified a scheme into the relevant *Part*, the *PPF Multi-employer Regulations* then determine what happens next. In this section, we consider the impact of that categorisation on orphan liabilities. These comprise any liabilities (other than those which have already entered the PPF) which relate to entities that are no longer employers at the commencement of a PPF assessment period.

Part 5 Schemes: Requirement to segregate

As indicated above, *PPF Multi-employer Regs, Part 5* applies where there is a requirement to segregate the portion of the scheme's assets attributable to its liability to provide benefits in respect of pensionable service with a particular employer (the 'segregation requirement'). When an insolvency event occurs in relation to that employer, the segregation requirement is deemed to have been triggered immediately and a segregated part deemed to have been created. This is the case whether or not the relevant triggering event in the partial wind up rule has in fact occurred (*PPF Multi-employer Regs, reg 45(2)*).

The 'segregated part' is defined as the section of the scheme which is created when a segregation requirement in the scheme rules has been triggered.

This part is then treated as a separate eligible scheme for the purposes of the *PPF Entry Rules* and *PA 2004*, and all references to the employer are treated as references to the employer in relation to the segregated part (*PPF Multi-employer Regs, regs 45(4)(b), 47*).

Our understanding of PPF practice is that, in a *Part 5* scheme, the orphan liabilities cannot enter an assessment period until there is only one employer remaining for *PPF Entry Rules* purposes, and a qualifying insolvency event occurs in relation to that employer. The scheme will then no longer be treated as a multi-employer scheme, and the orphan liabilities will be able to enter the PPF when the remaining employer does so under the procedure for a single employer scheme.

Part 7 Schemes: Option to segregate

PPF Multi-employer Regs, Part 7 applies where there is an option to segregate the portion of the scheme's assets attributable to the scheme's liability to provide benefits in respect of pensionable service with a particular employer. When an insolvency event occurs in relation to that employer, the trustees are deemed to have exercised the option to segregate under the scheme rules unless and until they decide not to exercise it and have given the PPF a notice to this effect (*PPF Multi-employer Regs, reg 71(2)(a)*).

Consequently, if the trustees do nothing, the scheme will broadly be treated in the same way as a *Part 5* scheme. If, however, the trustees decide not to exercise the option and give the PPF a non-segregation notice under *PA 2004, s 120(3A)*, the IP must issue a withdrawal notice as soon as practicable (*PA 2004, s 122(2A)* as inserted by *PPF Multi-employer Regs, reg 71(3)*). Once the withdrawal notice has become binding, the PPF will cease to be involved with the segregated part and the assessment period will come to an end (see **5.25** above).

Our understanding of PPF practice is that, in a *Part 7* scheme (as with a *Part 5* scheme), the orphan liabilities cannot enter a PPF assessment period until there is only one employer remaining for the purposes of the *PPF Entry Rules* and a qualifying insolvency event occurs in relation to that employer.

Part 6 Schemes: No partial wind-up

Part 6 applies where the rules do not provide for the partial winding up of the scheme. Take, for example, the following rule:

'An Employer may cease to participate in the Fund at any time by written notice to the Trustee, and will cease to participate if required to do so by the Principal Employer.

5.33   *Employer insolvency: the implications for pension schemes*

When an employer ceases to participate in the Fund, any Members who are then in employment with that employer will become entitled to benefits as if they had then left Service.'

This rule does not provide for partial wind-up, but provides for the departing employer's employees to be treated as deferred members.

In a *Part 6* scheme, an insolvency event will not be a 'qualifying insolvency event' and the scheme will not therefore be able to enter a PPF assessment period, unless:

(*a*)   insolvency events have occurred simultaneously in relation to all the other employers; or

(*b*)   it occurs in relation to the last remaining employer at a time when insolvency events have occurred (and IPs are still required), or *s 129* notices have been given in relation to all the other employers;

and it occurs on or after 6 April 2005 and is either the first insolvency event to occur in relation to that employer or does not occur within an earlier assessment period (*PA 2004, s 127(3)* as modified by *PPF Multi-employer Regs, reg 64*).

Similar provision is made in relation to entities that cannot continue as going concerns (*PA 2004, ss 128, 129* as modified by *PPF Multi-employer Regs, reg 64, 65*). However, there is also a specific exemption (the '*Rover* exemption') which was inserted in *Part 6*.

The *Rover* exemption provides for circumstances where the trustees become aware that a person is (or persons are) no longer employer(s) in relation to a scheme at a time when all the other employers have suffered insolvency events (and an IP is still required by law to be appointed to act in relation to them) or *s 129* notices have been given in respect of them. At least one such insolvency notice or event must have happened on or after 6 April 2005. In practice, this situation could arise if a solvent employer paid its debt in full after insolvency events had taken place in relation to all the other employers. In such cases, except where a PPF assessment period has already begun in relation to that scheme, the trustees can make an application to the PPF to assume responsibility for the scheme (*PPF Multi-Employer Regs, Reg 65(1)(a)*).

The existence of this exemption avoids many, but not all, of the problems with PPF entry for orphans in *Part 6* schemes. However, there is no comparable provision in place for *Part 5* or *Part 7* schemes.

Technical bars to PPF entry

5.33   There are a number of technical problems to achieving PPF entry under the *PPF Entry Rules*.

Non-UK insolvency proceedings are not generally insolvency events for the purposes of the *PPF Entry Rules*. This has in the past created issues in some cases in achieving PPF entry where there are non-UK registered employers who employ or have employed UK employees participating in a UK occupational pension scheme.

In many cases the lack of an insolvency event in relation to a non-UK employer can be overcome by instituting secondary insolvency proceedings in the UK. However, instituting secondary insolvency proceedings in the UK may not always be an option because the conditions or grounds for opening parallel proceedings may not exist. If parallel proceedings cannot be opened, this may mean that in the case of a *Part 5* or *Part 7* scheme, the liabilities relating to the non-UK company and the orphans cannot enter the PPF and, in relation to a *Part 6* scheme or a single employer scheme, the whole scheme cannot enter.

The problems with achieving entry for a scheme with a non-UK employer were illustrated by the Olympic Airlines case (*The Trustees of the Olympic Airlines SA Pension and Life Insurance Scheme v Olympic Airlines SA [2013] EWCA Civ 643*). The Court of Appeal held that Olympic Airlines did not have an 'establishment' in the UK at the relevant time (being the time immediately before the secondary petition was presented) as required in order to initiate the secondary insolvency proceedings. Having an 'establishment' required more economic activity than the mere process of winding up the business. The company had to have a place of operations', where non-transitory economic activity was carried on with human and physical resources. In this case, by the date on which the secondary petition was presented, Olympic Airlines had already been in liquidation in Greece for 10 months, had ceased all commercial operations and had dismissed and paid off most of its employees. Only a skeleton staff was maintained for the purposes of the winding-up. The London office had no assets of real value and at the relevant date had no economic function other than as part of the liquidation. In its judgment the Court of Appeal acknowledged (with regret) that 'this conclusion would leave the beneficiaries of the scheme unprotected under the PPF'.

Following the judgment in *Olympic Airlines*, the *PPF Entry Rules* were amended with effect from 21 July 2014 to assist the *Olympic Airlines* pension scheme achieve PPF entry and to enable the scheme members to benefit from PPF compensation (see *Regulation 5A* of the *PPF Entry Rules* as inserted by *Regulation 2 of the PPF (Entry Rules) (Amendment) Regulations 2014*). The amendment was very tightly drafted, time-limited and unlikely to be of relevance to other employers in the same situation. However, with effect from 6 April 2016, a more general amendment has now been made to enable employers in other EU states to achieve PPF entry in similar situations under the *section 129* route (see **5.19** above). Commentators are still concerned, however, that there could still be situations where non-UK employers may not be able to achieve PPF entry (see **5.19** above).

There can also be problems with multi-employer schemes achieving PPF entry if Conditions A to F cannot be satisfied in relation to all the employers (see **5.29** above). In a *Part 5* or *Part 7* scheme, this could mean that the liabilities relating to the employers in respect of whom Conditions A to F do not apply cannot be met and any orphan liabilities cannot enter the PPF. In the case of a *Part 6* scheme (unless the *Rover* exemption applies (see **5.32** above), the whole scheme may not be able to achieve PPF entry.

Levies and multi-employer schemes

5.34   One of the most controversial issues that emerged from the PPF was how it would be funded. The Government does not guarantee the solvency of the PPF and, by extension, the solvency of the schemes it seeks to support. Instead, it is funded in part by compulsory levies on all eligible schemes, with the balance of funding coming from the remaining assets of the schemes that the PPF takes on. Details are contained in **Chapter 2**.

To date, both the identity of the employers and the nature of the scheme's partial wind up rule have had an impact on the levy in relation to a multi-employer scheme, as both are relevant to the level of risk to the PPF associated with a particular scheme. The levy has been calculated by reference to:

(*a*)   the assumed probability of insolvency of those entities which are employers within the meaning of *PA 2004, s 318* (it is the insolvency of these employers which will give rise to assessment periods).

(*b*)   whether the scheme falls within *Part 5, 6* or *7* of the *PPF Multi-employer Regs*. Theoretically, *Part 6* schemes represent less risk to the PPF in comparison to *Part 5* and *7* schemes as insolvency events are generally required in relation to all the employers in such schemes before an assessment period will start. In the intervening period, the scheme will be supported by the solvent employers. In the 2012/13 determination, this reduction in risk was reflected by applying a reduced (0.9 as opposed to 1.0) insolvency probability factor in relation to Part 6 scheme employers. For the period 2015/2016–2017/2018 the continued availability of the full saving for Part 6 schemes will be linked to the concentration of employees amongst the individual employees participating in the Part 6 scheme. The reduction varies between 0.9 and 1.00 depending on how concentrated the employees are, the more concentrated the lower the saving.

The Financial Assistance Scheme

5.35   The Financial Assistance Scheme ('FAS') is a statutory scheme that is designed to give qualifying members of qualifying schemes a measure of protection where the scheme is underfunded, their employer is insolvent or has discharged its debts, and the scheme commenced winding up before 6 April 2005 (or in some cases 22 December 2008).

FAS started life as a top-up arrangement but it has since evolved. Since it was first established, the circumstances in which applications for entry can be made have been widened and the compensation to be provided has been improved several times. Qualifying schemes will now transfer to the FAS once they have satisfied the appropriate conditions and the FAS scheme manager will take over responsibility for making all payments. The FAS is managed by the Board of the PPF (*FAS Regulations, reg 5*) and is principally funded by the government (*FAS Regulations, reg 6*).

The PPF has announced that FAS will close to notification and qualification of new schemes from 1 September 2016.

Eligibility

5.36   FAS provides for annual payments to be paid to, or in respect of, qualifying members of qualifying schemes (*FAS Regulations, reg 17*).

Qualifying scheme

5.37   Broadly speaking, a qualifying scheme is an occupational pension scheme which:

(*a*)   immediately before the time it began to wind up, was neither a money purchase scheme nor a scheme of a prescribed description;

(*b*)   began to wind up during the period beginning on 1 January 1997 and ending on 5 April 2005 and in limited circumstances after that date;

(*c*)   the employer has:

   (i)   suffered an insolvency event (see **5.2** above) or, where specified, was unlikely to continue as a going concern and there was, in the opinion of the PPF, a relevant link between that event and the commencement of the winding up of the scheme, or

   (ii)   discharged any employer debt due or no debt was due; and

(*d*)   the prescribed details were notified to the PPF between 1 September 2005 and 28 February 2006 (or such later time as the PPF allows) (*FAS Regulations, reg 9*).

Slightly different conditions apply in relation to multi-employer schemes where broadly, either the principal employer or all of the employers must have suffered an insolvency event, or all of the employers must have discharged any employer debts due.

Prescribed schemes

As with the PPF, the list of excluded schemes referred to in paragraph (*a*) is fairly predictable: it can be found in the *FAS Regulations, reg 10*. Many public sector schemes are excluded, as are unregistered schemes that are not statutory schemes and schemes that are administered outside the UK. Schemes which only provide death benefits or, in the case of a non contracted-out centralised scheme, provide only lump sum benefits, are also excluded. Furthermore, a scheme with fewer than two members, or where there are fewer than 12 members and all are trustees making unanimous decisions (or it has a registered independent trustee), will not be able to enter the FAS.

Winding up

In addition to the schemes which began to wind up as per paragraph (*b*), schemes which began to wind up during the period beginning on 6 April 2005 and ending on 22 December 2008 where the employer suffered an insolvency event before 6 April 2005 may also qualify where they would not be eligible for the PPF (*FAS Regulations, reg 9(1B)*).

Also a further limited extension which may permit FAS entry where broadly:

(*a*)   a scheme commenced winding up on or after 23 December 2008 and before 27 March 2014;

(*b*)   a scheme winds up underfunded due to an insolvency event which occurred before 6 April 2005;

(*c*)   there has been a qualifying insolvency event; and

(*d*)   the relevant employer ceased to be an employer prior to 10 June 2011(*FAS Regulations, reg 9(1D)*).

Employers

As with the PPF, the FAS adopts a modified version of the term 'employer' but this does not differ as between single and multi-employer schemes. For the purposes of paragraph (*c*) above, the employer is: (a) the person who employed persons in the description or category of employment to which the scheme relates or related immediately before the time when the scheme began to wind up; or (b) where the scheme had no active members immediately before that time, the person who employed persons in the description or category of employment to which the scheme relates or related immediately before it ceased to have any active members (*FAS Regulations, regs 11(2), 12(3)–(4)*).

Relevant link

Paragraph (*c*) above highlights that the PPF must find a relevant link between the insolvency event and the commencement of winding up. Broadly speaking, such a link is deemed to be established in relation to any employer which has suffered an insolvency event or was unlikely to continue as a going concern before 1 January 2009 (*FAS Regulations, reg 9(1A)*).

Discharging debts

In order to satisfy the condition that a debt has been discharged for the purposes of paragraph (*c*), the FAS Regulations distinguish between schemes which began to wind up before 6 April 1997 (where the debt must have been discharged under *Pension Schemes Act 1993, s 144*) and those which began to wind up between 6 April 1997 to 10 June 2003 (where the debt must have been discharged under the *Pensions Act 1995 (PA 1995), s 75*). In either case, the condition is satisfied where no such debt was due when the scheme began to wind up. Furthermore, the PPF may treat the condition as having been satisfied where (a) it is satisfied that an appropriate proportion of the debt was discharged or is likely to be discharged, or (b) in its opinion, it was reasonable for it not to be so discharged (*FAS Regulations, regs 12A, 12B*).

Notifications

The information to be notified to the PPF is set out in, *FAS Regulations, reg 14* and includes the name of the scheme, its registration number and details of an employer and at least one trustee. It must be submitted in writing and a number of different people, including trustees, members and professional advisers may supply it.

Qualifying member

5.38   Broadly speaking, a qualifying member is a member or former member of a qualifying pension scheme:

(*a*)   who has an accrued right to a benefit under the scheme;

(*b*)   who was a member of the scheme immediately before it began to wind up or who subsequently became a pension credit member; and

(*c*)   in respect of whom the scheme's pension liabilities have not been satisfied in full (*FAS Regulations, reg 15*).

A person will also be included within the definition if he (a) would have satisfied the conditions had he not died before the coming into force of the FAS Regulations, or (b) was entitled to present payment from a qualifying pension scheme immediately before it began to wind up; the payment was attributable to the pensionable service of a former member who had died; and the scheme's pension liabilities in respect of that person have not been satisfied in full.

The *FAS Regulations* also define who is a survivor of a qualifying member in *reg 16A* and who is a surviving dependant in *reg 16B*.

Administering the scheme

The role of the trustees

5.39   Qualifying pension schemes must be administered in accordance with the restrictions set out in *PA 2004, ss 135* and *136* as modified by *Schedule 1* of the *FAS Regulations* until a transfer notice is issued.

The principal restriction is that during this time, no transfers or transfer payments are to be made from the scheme and no steps may be taken to discharge any other liabilities (excluding pension credits) which would be winding-up lump sums or trivial commutation lump sums (*PA 2004, s 135(4), FAS Regulations, Sch 1, para 3B*). However, exceptions are made in a number of circumstances as set out in *PA 2004, s 135(4A)* (inserted by *FAS Regulations, Sch 1, para 3B(d)*). These include where the trustees entered into a binding commitment to purchase an annuity for a qualifying member before 26 September 2007; they offered the qualifying member a trivial commutation lump sum before 2 April 2010; or the purchase of an annuity, transfer or discharge of liability has been approved by the PPF (and any necessary conditions satisfied). There are no restrictions on the transfer or discharges of money purchase benefits.

As is the case in PPF assessment periods, until the scheme is fully wound up, the PPF may make certain directions to any 'relevant person' in relation to the scheme (including the employer, the trustees and any professional advisers) (*PA 2004, s 134; FAS Regulations, Sch 1, para 3A*). The power must be exercised with a view to ensuring either that any reduction in the scheme's assets is kept to a minimum, or that the scheme's assets are invested in a way which, in the opinion of the PPF, is appropriate. Such directions may be given in respect of (a) the investment of the scheme's assets; (b) the incurring of expenditure; (c) the instigation or conduct of legal proceedings; and (d) the determination of interim pensions.

Payments

5.40   The level of benefits to be provided by the FAS, if the asset share applicable to the individual under the wind up priority order is not sufficient to provide a higher benefit, is set out in *Part 5* of and *Schedules 2, 3* and *4* to the *FAS Regulations*. Broadly, the benefits/compensation to be provided are as follows:

- all qualifying members of FAS qualifying pension schemes will receive 90 per cent of their accrued pension at the start of the wind up, revalued and indexed in accordance with the FAS rules (see *FAS Regulations, Sch 2, paras 3, 4*);

- this pension will be subject to a FAS cap of £37,420.42 (£33,678.38 after the 90% limit is applied) a year at age 65 for anyone whose entitlement begins between 1 April 2016 and 31 March 2017 (see *FAS Regulations, Sch 2, para 7*). A different cap applies where the pension commences from a different date. The amount of the cap is indexed each year;

- payments derived from post-1997 service are increased in line with inflation (CPI from 31 December 2011 and RPI before that date), subject to a 2.5 per cent limit (see *FAS Regulations, Sch 2, para 9*);

- assistance is generally paid from the later of 14 May 2004 and the scheme's normal retirement age (NRA), subject to a lower limit of age 60 and upper age of 65 (*FAS Regulations, reg 17(2)*);

- those who are unable to work due to ill-health are able to apply for earlier access from a date which falls five years before NRA subject to actuarial reduction (*FAS Regulations, reg 17A*). Severe ill-health payments are also payable in certain circumstances from age 55 without reduction (*FAS Regulations, reg 17C*);

- members in respect of whom a transfer notice has been given and who have not started taking a scheme pension at that time will be able to take 25 per cent of their FAS payment as a tax-free lump sum (*FAS Regulations, reg 17D*);

- a surviving spouse or civil partner (and, in certain circumstances, a surviving partner) of a qualifying member may be eligible for a payment (FAS *Regulations, Sch 2, para 5*). A survivor becomes eligible for payments from the day after the date the qualifying member dies, but not before 14 May 2004 (*FAS Regulations, reg 17(4)*). Broadly, the assistance is equal to one half of 90 per cent of the member's expected pension (see *FAS Regulations, Sch 2, para 5*);

- a surviving child of a deceased member can also qualify for assistance where, broadly, they were financially dependent on the deceased member and are under 18, or are under 23 and attending a qualifying course; or are disabled (*FAS Regulations, reg 16B*);

Higher payments may be made to members whose asset share would have produced more than 90 per cent of the expected pension, had their scheme continued to wind up in the normal manner (*FAS Regulations, regs 27 and 28*).

Transferring to the FAS

Valuation and subsequent calculations

5.41   Where a qualifying pension scheme has not been fully wound up and its liabilities to or in respect of all members and former members have not been discharged and are, in the opinion of the PPF, unlikely to be discharged by annuities, transfers, state scheme premiums or any other approved means, the PPF must obtain a valuation. Accordingly, the PPF must, when it considers it appropriate, instruct the trustees to obtain a valuation of the scheme's assets and liabilities. The calculation or 'as at' date of the valuation will be the last day of the month in which the instruction is given (*FAS Regulations, regs 21, 22*). Details about the valuation process are set out in *FAS Regulations, regs 22 to 24*.

Where the PPF is satisfied that the valuation has been prepared in accordance with *Part 7* of the *FAS Regulations*, it must approve the valuation and notify the trustees. Once approved, the valuation will become binding when the review period has expired and any review process finally disposed of (*FAS Regulations, regs 25, 26*). Further calculations must then be carried out by the PPF to determine the notional pensions and survivors' pensions which could have been purchased on the calculation date with the assets then available to discharge the liability (*FAS Regulations, regs 27, 28*).

Transfer notice

5.42   Where a valuation has become binding and the PPF is satisfied that the time is appropriate, it must give a transfer notice to the trustees (and send a copy to the Regulator) (*FAS Regulations, reg 29*).

Where the transfer notice is given, (a) the property, rights and liabilities of the scheme are transferred to the government with effect from the time the trustees are given the transfer notice; (b) the trustees are discharged from their pension obligations from that time; and (c) any liabilities other than those transferred or those in respect of certain money purchase benefits are discharged (*PA 2004, s 161* as modified by *FAS Regulations, Sch 1, para 3D*).

Winding up

Insolvency of the employer and the winding up of a pension scheme

5.43   It is common for occupational pension schemes to include provisions that require the scheme to be wound up (see **Chapter 12**) in circumstances involving the 'insolvency' of the employer or principal employer. Triggering events often include:

- the appointment of an IP to the principal employer;
- the principal employer ceasing to trade;
- the winding up or liquidation of the principal employer; and
- a company going from administration to winding up by way of a notice from the administrator.

Some schemes may simply refer to the company going into 'insolvency'. Unless the context of the pension scheme would infer a meaning otherwise, 'insolvency' can probably be read widely enough to include all of the regimes, particularly given *IA 1986, s 247*. Under *IA 1986, s 247(1)*, 'insolvency', in relation to a company, includes the approval of a voluntary arrangement, or the appointment of an administrator or administrative receiver.

'Liquidation', on the other hand, has a specific and narrower meaning and so would probably only be capable of referring to the employer going into formal liquidation (see **5.63** onwards below). A company 'goes into insolvent liquidation' if it passes a resolution for voluntary winding up ('CVL') or an order for its winding up is made by the court at a time when it has not already gone into liquidation by passing such a resolution (*IA 1986, s 247(2)*). In the case of a CVL (see **5.65** below), the liquidation will be from the date of the passing of the shareholders' resolution. In the case of a compulsory liquidation, the company will be in liquidation from the date of the passing of the order for its winding up, although for some purposes in the legislation the date of commencement of the winding up is deemed to be the date of the petition for winding up.

Even if the appointment of an IP has not triggered the winding up of the scheme, it may result in the termination of the contracts of employment of all or most of the employees which may in turn trigger the scheme's winding up. The failure on the part of the principal employer to pay contributions may also be a triggering event.

Where winding up has not automatically been triggered as a result of these events, the trustees may wish to use any alternative powers in the scheme rules to wind the scheme up or to continue the scheme as a closed scheme for the future.

As discussed above (see **5.22**), notwithstanding the provisions of the rules, generally, the winding up of the scheme must not begin during a PPF assessment period (*PA 2004, s 135(2)*) and during that period, no steps can generally be taken to transfer members' benefits from the scheme or secure them (*PA 2004, s 135(4)*). Where the winding up of the scheme commenced prior to the assessment period, the benefits payable during the assessment period must, subject to any adjustment to bring the benefits down to PPF compensation levels, be based on the benefits that would have been so payable in the absence of the winding up of the scheme (*PA 2004, s 138(6)*). In cases where benefits have been scaled down below PPF compensation levels in a wind up period which commenced before the start of the PPF assessment period this may result in an increase in benefits once a PPF assessment period begins.

However if a scheme is ineligible for the PPF or an assessment period comes to an end because: (a) the PPF ceases to be involved with a scheme (*PA 2004, s 150*); or (b) the scheme has sufficient assets to meet the protected liabilities (*PA 2004, s 154*), its winding up may take place. In certain circumstances, the winding up of the scheme may be backdated (*PA 2004, s 219*).

More detail about the winding up of pension schemes can be found in **Chapter 12**.

Surplus of scheme on employer insolvency

5.44   If a surplus becomes available on the winding up of a pension scheme, the IP may seek to have it returned to the employer (if the rules permit this) for distribution to creditors. Many rules require, or give trustees discretion as to, the use of surplus to augment members' benefits on wind up. The case of *Thrells Limited (1974) Pension Scheme v Lomas [1993] 2 All ER 546* gives guidance on some of the factors trustees may wish to consider when deciding how to allocate surplus where they have discretion.

PA 1995, s 76 governs the return of surplus on winding up in schemes whose rules confer power on the employer or the trustees to return assets to the employer in these circumstances. The surplus in the scheme can be returned to the employer, subject to a 35 per cent tax charge (*FA 2004, s 207*), provided that:

(*a*)   all the scheme liabilities have been discharged in full;

(*b*)   any power to distribute surplus assets to persons other than the employer has been exercised or a decision has been taken not to exercise it; and

(*c*)   the appropriate notice has been given to the scheme members.

Under *The Occupational Pension Schemes (Payments to Employers) Regulations 2006 (SI 2006/802), reg 15*, notice must be given to the members of the proposal to return the surplus to the employer. Any member dissatisfied with the proposal can make representations to the trustees or the employer or, ultimately, the Regulator on whether the correct procedure has been followed.

Compromising pension liabilities where insolvency is likely or as part of an insolvency process

5.45   As mentioned in **5.18** above, it is possible in certain circumstances, with agreement of the Regulator and with buy-in from the Trustees and PPF, to restructure a business to separate the pension liabilities from an employer and transfer them to the PPF so the restructured business can trade going forward free of those liabilities. These are as follows:

(1)   compromising all or a significant part of the pension liabilities as part of an insolvency process (eg a CVA or a pre-pack business sale by an administrator to a new entity) with the pension scheme entering the PPF. In this situation the PPF exercises the trustees' creditor rights once an insolvency event has occurred in relation to the company (*PA 2004, s 137*);

(2)   entering into a Regulated Apportionment Arrangement ('RAA') (see **Chapter 15**) without putting the trading company into an insolvency process under which all or a significant part of the pension liabilities are 'apportioned' to a sacrificial company which is then made insolvent so that the pension scheme can enter a PPF assessment period. An RAA can only be entered into where insolvency is likely to occur within 12 months or an insolvency event has already occurred and the scheme is already in a PPF assessment period.

In either case, the PPF typically seek an equity stake in the company owning the restructured business (one third if a connected or associated party remains in control and 10 per cent for a sale to a non associated party) plus immediate additional cash and loan note consideration which will result in it receiving a greater return than under insolvency. This type of deal is also only likely to be achievable where, what is proposed, is consistent with the relevant Regulator and PPF guidance (see **5.46** below).

The RAA option is often preferred where putting the trading company through an insolvency process and/or a business sale may have a detrimental effect on the business.

If a pension scheme has more than sufficient assets to secure liabilities at least equal to PPF compensation levels but insufficient to secure all its liabilities by purchasing annuities on wind-up it may still be possible to negotiate a deal directly with the trustees to compromise the pension liabilities under what is known as a 'Bradstock Agreement' if it can be demonstrated that insolvency is inevitable and the deal offers a greater prospect of recovery to the pension scheme as creditor than the alternative insolvent wind up of the company (see **5.18** above).

Regulator and PPF guidance on pre-packs and RAAs

5.46 The Regulator has issued guidance on when it will consider granting clearance to an arrangement under which the pension liabilities are compromised and the scheme will enter the PPF and also on the circumstances it will consider when deciding whether it is reasonable to approve an RAA and grant clearance to entering into such an arrangement (*Regulated Apportionment Arrangements and Employer Insolvency – 12 August 2010*).

These include:

(*a*)   whether the insolvency of the employer would otherwise be inevitable or whether there are other solutions which would avoid insolvency;

(*b*)   whether the scheme might receive more from an insolvency;

(*c*)   whether a better outcome for the scheme could be achieved by other means;

(*d*)   the position of the rest of the employer's group;

(*e*)   the outcome of the proposals for other creditors.

The PPF exercises the powers of the trustees as creditor in relation to any *section 75* debt triggered on the insolvency of the employer and so will need to be party to any compromise of pension liabilities as part of an insolvency process and must not object to an RAA for it to take effect. The principles the PPF applies in both these situations are most recently set out in its guidance (*Restructuring and insolvency – the PPF approach – 16 August 2016*) and are broadly as follows:

(*a*)   insolvency has become inevitable – this means that the PPF will have to take on the debt whatever happens;

(*b*)   the pension scheme will receive money or assets which are significantly better than it would have received through an otherwise inevitable insolvency;

(*c*)   what is offered to the pension scheme in the restructure or rescue is fair compared to what other creditors and shareholders will receive as part of the deal;

(*d*)   the PPF will seek at least a ten per cent equity in the new company if the future shareholders are not currently involved with the company. The PPF will seek 33 per cent if the future shareholders are parties currently involved;

(*e*)   the PPF needs to be sure the pension scheme would not be better off if the Regulator were to issue a contribution notice or financial support direction (see **5.48** below);

(*f*)   where the deal involves a refinancing, the fees charged by the bank(s) are reasonable; and

(*g*)   the party seeking the restructuring pays the costs incurred both by the PPF and the trustees in delivering the restructuring. These will include any fees for legal and financial advice and other costs incurred by the PPF as a result of the transaction, such as TUPE liability relating to the staff costs of the pension scheme.

Examples of restructuring arrangements

5.47   In December 2013, the former head of restructuring at the PPF was reported as stating that there had been about 50 cases where restructuring arrangements had been entered into since the establishment of the PPF. Examples reported in the press include *Heath Lambert* (the very first one) *and Sheffield Forgemasters International.*

It does not follow that the Regulator and the PPF will necessarily take the same view on a proposed arrangement. The widely reported case of *Reader's Digest* (in February 2010) gives an example of the type of pre-insolvency restructuring deal where approval to a restructuring and compromise was not given by the Regulator. It is understood that the PPF had agreed a deal whereby the US parent of the UK company (and sponsoring employer of the pension scheme) would make a lump sum payment into the scheme and would grant the PPF an equity stake in the UK company itself. The intention would then presumably have been to carry out a pre-pack insolvency (see **5.62** below) further to which a *section 75* debt would trigger and a PPF assessment period begin. The PPF would compromise the debt in line with the pre-agreed deal and the UK company would emerge from insolvency, free from its pension liabilities. However, in this case, the Regulator did not support the agreement. The UK company directors placed the company into insolvency on the basis that it was financially unable to meet its obligations towards the scheme and to sustain its operations. The PPF took responsibility for the pension scheme in December 2011 and would have had to claim in the insolvency process for the *section 75* debt with no stake in any emerging company.

On the other hand in the *Lufthansa* case (*British Midland Airways Pension and Life Assurance Scheme Report under s 89 of the Pensions Act 2004*), the Regulator issued a clearance notice in relation to an RAA under which Lufthansa withdrew support from its subsidiary, British Midlands Airways, in return for appropriate unspecified mitigation being received by the PPF. There had been earlier discussions in this case whether alternative funding solutions were viable. It was also significant that the British Midland Airways Group had been loss making over the last four years and Lufthansa had provided significant financial support in the past. As part of the solution ultimately arrived at an additional £84 million was paid by Lufthansa on a voluntary basis, in order to provide members with additional benefits to help address the reduction in the level of payments to members on the PPF assuming responsibility for the scheme. Although the Regulator was aware of this proposed voluntary payment it did not form part of its consideration as to whether approval of the RAA was appropriate.

The Regulator has also issued a clearance notice in a couple of innovative restructuring arrangements which are both described in *section 89* reports issued by the Regulator. In the *UK Coal* reconstruction the UK Coal Group participated in UK Coal sections of the Industry Wide Mineworkers' Pension Scheme ('IWMPS') and the Industry Wide Coal Staff Superannuation Scheme ('IWCSSS'), both of which had significant deficits. The IWMPS and IWCSSS were dependent on the UK Coal group continuing to trade to support the pension scheme liabilities. UK Coal wanted to restructure the group to mitigate the operating risks inherent in the mining business and to facilitate raising funds required by the group. In 2012 a restructuring was agreed and cleared by the Regulator under which:

(*a*)   the business was split into two ring-fenced businesses: mining, incorporating the group's three deep mines and its surface mines (Mineco); and property (Propco);

(*b*)   substantially all the economic interest in the group passed from the existing shareholders to the trustees via the trustees' acquisition of a 75.1% stake in Propco and their entitlement to substantially all the cash generated by Mineco (which would be free of bank debt).

The Trustees concluded that the plan offered a better potential outcome for the UK Coal sections of the IWMPS and IWCSSS.

Unfortunately, following the first UK Coal restructuring a fire broke out at the largest deep mine operated by UK Coal at Daw Mill. The mine needed to be closed permanently for health and safety reasons. This had two serious effects on the prospects for the Mineco business:

(*a*)   the costs of closing the mine (including the cost of making the mine safe and providing redundancy payments) would cause cash flow problems, risking insolvency;

(*b*)   even if insolvency in the short term could be avoided, the Mineco business would face a significant loss of revenue and profits. As a result, the funding that UK Coal could provide for the UK Coal sections of the IWCSSS and IWMPS would be significantly reduced.

The Propco business was not at risk of insolvency due to the ring-fencing introduced in the 2012 restructuring. However, due to ongoing arrangements between Propco and Mineco, the value of the Propco business was potentially adversely affected by an insolvency of the mining business.

UK Coal's management entered into immediate discussions with the trustees, the Regulator and the PPF. A restructuring proposal was put forward under which Mineco would be hived down to a new group. By leaving Daw Mill in Mineco this would avoid closure costs which would otherwise be unaffordable. It was proposed that the UK Coal sections of IWCSSS and IWMPS would remain with the hived down group. The Regulator was not convinced, however, that the hived down group could support the UK Coal sections and was concerned that the PPF would be exposed to continuing risk that the UK Coal sections could enter the PPF at a future date. The Regulator would therefore not support the proposal, but encouraged UK Coal's management to continue discussions with the trustees to explore alternative options.

A revised proposal was put forward by UK Coal. Under this arrangement, assets of Mineco would be hived down to a new group but the UK Coal sections of the IWCSSS and IWMPS would enter the PPF (following an assessment period triggered by insolvency of UK Coal). In order to facilitate the restructuring, the trustees agreed to release part of their claim against UK Coal as an unsecured creditor. In return the trustees (and ultimately the PPF on PPF entry) would secure significantly all the economic interest and value in the new group through a series of debt instruments held in the new group's operating company. The interest in the new groups was forecast to be more valuable than the portion of the claim given up. Ultimately the new UK Coal group did not survive due, among other things, to worldwide movements in the coal price, but the restructuring had the potential again to offer a significantly greater recovery to the PPF than the alternatives.

Both UK Coal restructurings illustrate that the Regulator and the PPF (where it is exercising the trustees powers in an insolvency process) will consider more innovative solutions (where there is sufficient money at stake to justify the arrangement) which may involve taking a significantly greater economic interest than the one-third anti-embarrassment stake referred to in its guidance.

Kodak was an even more innovative restructuring solution which is described in a *section 89* report issued by the Regulator in November 2014. In this case Kodak Ltd (Kodak UK) was the sole sponsoring employer of the Kodak Pension Plan ('KPP'). The KPP had approximately 15,000 members.

As part of past valuation negotiations the trustees secured a parent guarantee from Eastman Kodak Company ('EKC'), the parent company of the multi-national Kodak Group. In January 2012, EKC filed for Chapter 11 bankruptcy protection in the US along with other group entities not including Kodak UK. The trustees of KPP filed a claim in the bankruptcy proceedings for $2.837 billion (the buy-out deficit) on the basis of the guarantee. The Chapter 11 proceedings could potentially have resulted in the guarantee becoming worthless. There was also a risk that if EKC and the other group entities subject to Chapter 11 did not emerge from Chapter 11 this would potentially prevent the scheme receiving any further deficit repair contributions and/or a lower return on any potential insolvency of Kodak UK.

EKC, however, did not have sufficient cash to emerge from Chapter 11. Even if EKC was able to generate sufficient liquidity to exit Chapter 11 it would not be able to settle KPP's claim for cash.

Various alternative solutions were explored with support from the Regulator. Eventually a solution was arrived at under which KPP would acquire the Alaris businesses (which were profitable and cash-generative businesses). These potentially could generate cashflows which would be a good match of much of the KPP pension liabilities. The Trustees agreed to pay $325 million in cash (substantially lower than third-party bids which had previously been rejected) release their claim against EKC in Chapter 11, and, subject to the Regulator's approval and non-objection by the PPF, release Kodak UK's liability to the scheme by way of an RAA.

In reaching its decision to approve the RAA, the Regulator considered various factors including:

- whether the insolvency of the scheme's sponsoring employer Kodak UK was otherwise inevitable;

- whether the scheme might receive more from an insolvency; and

- whether a better outcome might otherwise be attained for the scheme by other means including the use of the Regulator's moral hazard powers.

The Regulator concluded that the potential recovery by KPP on insolvency in the event of global insolvency of Kodak Group would be minimal and PPF levy payers would have ended up taking over responsibility for a significant proportion of pension liabilities. The proposed mitigation was unusual in that it required part payment by the trustees but the trustees' advisers' analysis demonstrated that the value of the Alaris business significantly exceeded $325 million.

The effect of the RAA (and the release of the guarantee) was to leave KPP with no sponsoring employer covenant. The scheme would be wholly reliant on the assets of the scheme (including Alaris). While the trustees concluded that the scheme's assets including Alaris could not support all of the KPP liabilities they considered the assets could support a significant proportion of the liabilities.

Under the finalised proposal members were given the choice of remaining in KPP, which would transfer to the PPF (the default option), or members could elect to transfer to a new scheme (KPP2), which would offer benefits better than the PPF, but lower than the KPP. Following extensive consultation with the members, about 94 per cent opted to transfer to KPP2 and the liabilities of those members and a proportionate share of the assets transferred to the new plan along with a proportionate share of the KPP assets (including Alaris) and the KPP entered into a PPF assessment period.

The Kodak *section 89* report explains that the Regulator did have concerns about the ability of KPP2 to continue following the RAA without a sponsor because of the ongoing risk that KPP2 may still enter the PPF in the future with an increased deficit. To address these issues various protections were agreed under the new governance framework for KPP2. This involved:

- regular, scheduled monitoring of the performance of the Alaris businesses and the scheme's funding position;

- restrictions on the augmentation of benefits;

- restrictions on investments; and

- triggers for the winding up of the scheme.

The Regulator was satisfied that the governance framework provides a level of protection for the PPF and members by limiting the potential deterioration of the scheme's position.

The Kodak restructuring, was again a very bespoke solution, but illustrates that where appropriate (and there is enough money involved) the Regulator may be willing to work with all parties to obtain the greatest value for the scheme. It is unlikely, however, that in most cases the Regulator will be willing to agree a solution which results in the scheme losing its employer covenant and continuing without the support of the covenant because of the investment risk to the PPF.

Since Kodak various employers have sought to use elements of a Kodak-type restructuring solution to seek to reduce pension liabilities and to avoid the sponsor entering an insolvency process in situations which fall within the PPF's guidance for approving a RAA. It is public knowledge that a Kodak style solution was proposed twice unsuccessfully in the BHS case and also in the Halcrow case (see below).

Under this type of solution under the PPF guidance (see above) the insolvency of the employer has to be inevitable within 12 months and a mirror scheme is set up with PPF plus benefits for existing scheme members. The liabilities to fund the scheme are transferred to a sacrificial employer by using an RAA. Members can then transfer to the new pension scheme providing PPF-plus benefits (but lower than the current benefits) with a view to reducing the deficit or can enter the PPF when the sacrificial company is made insolvent. Generally, the main change to the benefits is the removal of increases other than PPF minimum increases in respect of post-5 April 1997 accrual. Under the PPF and Regulator's guidance if an RAA is used the PPF will generally still insist on anti-embarrassment equity stake and usually loan notes and cash consideration and will want to be satisfied that the potential recovery is greater than may be recovered by the Regulator using its moral hazard powers. This often meets resistance from employers who wish to explore this type of solution.

In *Pollock v Reed (Halcrow Pension Scheme) [2016] 041 PBLR (043)*, the Halcrow Scheme had a deficit of £600 million. The scheme's sponsor's American parent was no longer willing to provide adequate support, meaning that the scheme was likely to enter the PPF. The trustees sought to obtain a better deal by transferring without consent the members' benefits to a new scheme that would provide lower benefits than the existing scheme but at least as good as the PPF. The employer's US parent would then provide a capped guarantee. The approval of the court was sought to the transfer. Generally a transfer without consent can only be made under *regulation 12* of the *Occupational Pension Schemes (Preservation) Regulations 1991* if the actuary can certify to the transferring scheme trustees that the transfer credits to be acquired in the receiving scheme are at broadly no less favourable to the value of the rights being transferred. It was argued that as the transferring scheme would otherwise enter the PPF and only PPF benefits would be provided the certificate could be given. In other words, security could be taken into account when giving the certification. The court held that this was not the case and ruled that there was no power to make a bulk transfer without consent if the benefits were being reduced even if it was likely that they would have been scaled down if the restructuring had not proceeded. However, if there had been power to make the transfer the judge said she would have approved the trustees' decision to enter the transaction. Following the judge's ruling an alternative solution Kodak-style RAA was proposed and approved by the Regulator and the PPF has confirmed that it does not object. This means that the benefits of members who do not consent to the transfer of their existing benefits to the new scheme will enter the PPF and be scaled back to PPF compensation levels (see the Regulator's regulatory intervention report issued under *PA 1995, s 89* in relation to the Halcrow Pension Scheme (July 2016)).

Moral hazard powers

5.48   The Regulator has two key powers at its disposal to police the risk to the PPF: contribution notices ('CN's) and financial support directions ('FSD's). Both are designed to ensure that sponsoring employers and those connected and associated with them do not walk away from their pension liabilities. They are also discussed in **Chapter 16** in the context of corporate transactions. Generally, an IP will have no exposure in relation to an act or omission which would otherwise give rise to a CN risk as long as he was acting in accordance with his functions as an insolvency practitioner (*PA 2004, s 38(3)(c)*).

A CN is a notice issued to a person stating that he is under a liability to pay the sum specified in the notice (*PA 2004, s 38(2)*). An FSD is a direction which requires the person to whom it is issued to secure that financial support is put in place for the scheme within the period specified, that it remains in place and that the Regulator is kept notified of prescribed events (*PA 2004, s 43(3)*). If there is non-compliance with an FSD, the Regulator may then issue a CN under *PA 2004, s 47*. One of the key advantages of these powers is that they extend to companies and in some cases individuals who are not sponsoring employers of the pension scheme in question.

The Regulator will issue a warning notice of its intention to issue a CN. In many cases this will be an effective way of persuading an employer to contribute to a deficit under a solution involving a clearance application. There are, however, reported cases concerning the Regulator's powers to issue a CN, one in relation to the *Bonas Group Pension Scheme* and one in relation to the *Desmond & Sons Pension & Life Assurance Scheme*.

In *Bonas* the Regulator's Determinations Panel found that a pre-pack insolvency had been carried out in relation to the sponsoring employer: in this case, administration followed by a swift sale to another group company. As a consequence, a PPF assessment period began and the PPF ultimately assumed responsibility for the scheme. The Panel considered that the intention of the withdrawal of support by the parent company and the pre-pack was to retain the company's business and assets in another group company that had no liability towards the scheme and that the parent company had deliberately avoided telling the trustees. The Panel issued a Determination Notice on May 2011 confirming an intention to issue a CN against the parent company for £5.089m. The Panel concluded it would not be reasonable to issue a CN against the Bonas managing director on the basis that he was personally concerned with ensuring the continuation of employment of the Bonas staff.

The parent company appealed this decision to the Upper Tribunal which found among other things that generally (other than in exceptional circumstances) it would not be appropriate to issue a CN for a greater amount than the amount by which the act or failure to act has prejudiced recoverability of a *s 75* debt. The Tribunal considered that, on the facts, the most the act or omission had prevented from being paid was the greater of:

(*a*)   the amount by which the sum which should have been available in the administration but for the act or omission complained of exceeded the amount actually available. The Tribunal considered on the evidence that this would not be greater than £100,000; and

(*b*)   the amount of future contributions which would have been met by the parent company if it had acted openly and Bonas had not gone into a pre-pack administration. This figure could only be determined after a detailed factual enquiry.

The Tribunal also confirmed that it could consider new arguments which had not been raised before the Determinations Panel. The matter was settled in June 2011 with the Regulator issuing a CN against the parent company for £60,000 on the basis that the correct level of contributions to be imposed under a notice cannot exceed the amount that would have been payable had the parties not taken the steps complained of.

Desmond & Sons Ltd was a clothing manufacturer and the sponsor of the Desmond & Sons Ltd Pension & Life Assurance Scheme. In February 2004, Marks & Spencer (its sole customer) announced that it no longer wished to deal with the company. The company's shareholders (including the two main shareholders against whom the CN was to be issued) took advice from professional advisers and the company was put into members' voluntary liquidation (MVL) on 3 June 2004. The effect of the MVL was that, under the then legislation, the debt was calculated on a minimum funding requirement ('MFR') basis instead of a higher buy-out basis. The scheme had a deficit of £10.9 million on a buy-out basis but had no deficit on an MFR basis. As a consequence, the shareholders were able to realise more than if the scheme buy-out deficit of £10.9 million had been met. The Regulator argued that the shareholders acted to put the company into MVL with the main purpose of ensuring that the employer debt would be calculated on an MFR basis. The Regulator's Determination Panel issued a Determination Notice confirming its intention to issue a CN for £900,000 against one shareholder and £100,000 against the second on the basis that a fair and reasonable employer would have engaged in negotiation with the trustees and the most likely outcome would have been a larger payment than was actually paid to the scheme.

The trustees of the scheme referred the matter to the Upper Tribunal, challenging the Determination Notice on the basis that the CN should be for the full buy-out deficit in the scheme and seeking to require the Regulator to issue a CN against a third shareholder. The shareholders made an application to the Upper Tribunal seeking to strike out the trustees' reference on various grounds. The Upper Tribunal found among other things that it could increase the amount of a CN as part of its role to determine appropriate regulatory action. It could also reach its own decision which could involve departing from the Determination Panel's finding. It confirmed that no CN could be issued against the third shareholder as Regulator's six-year look-back period had ended on 2 June 2010. It is understood that the substantive issues in the case will now be considered by the Upper Tribunal.

More recently, there has been another notable case where the Regulator sought to use its CN powers to require the former parent company of Carrington Wire Limited ('CWL') to stand behind the pension liabilities of CWL. The background is described in a *section 89* report issued by the Regulator in May 2015 and also an associated determination (see below).

CWL was a manufacturing company based in Yorkshire. It was the sole sponsoring employer in relation to the Carrington Wire Defined Benefit Pension Scheme, which had around 500 members. In 2006 CWL was acquired by a subsidiary of PAO Severstal, the Russian parent company of the Severstal Group. CWL was loss-making at the time Severstal acquired it. As a condition of the acquisition the seller required Severstal to provide a guarantee to the scheme covering all payments to the scheme including payments due under *PA 1995, s 75*. However, Severstal negotiated a clause in the guarantee which provided it would fall away if Severstal ceased to be associated with CWL.

In 2008 Severstal explored various options to exit the business including a solvent wind-down of CWL. Severstal assured the trustees that it would continue to honour its guarantee following the wind down. In February 2008 the wind down was virtually complete and all the plant and machinery transported to Russia. CWL was left with only one asset (a property) and no on-going business, but a substantial liability to the scheme. Without informing the trustees or the regulator, Severstal entered into negotiations with Mr Richard Williams, sole director and shareholder of a company called Gillico, for the sale of CWL.

In June 2010 Severstal sold the entire shareholding of CWL to Gillico for one pound with a purported working capital adjustment of £400,000. The sale meant that the scheme lost the benefit of the guarantee and became solely reliant on Gillico. CWL entered liquidation in December 2012 and the PPF assessment period on the same date.

The Regulator issued a warning notice seeking to impose Contribution Notices on two Severstal companies and Mr Williams. The warning notice argued that the three targets were party to a series of acts which were materially detrimental to the likelihood of benefits being received and/or which had the main purpose of preventing the recovery of the whole or any part of the debt which might become due under *PA 1995, s 75*. The warning notice sought recovery of £17.1 million against the Russian targets (which was the estimated *section 75* debt at the time of the sale of CWL less certain funds the scheme had received after that date). The Regulator argued that it was reasonable to provide these sums despite the fact that CWL had received considerable support from Severstal during its period of ownership.

Settlement negotiations resulted in the Russian targets making various offers culminating in an offer of £8.5 million. In considering whether to accept the offer the Regulator had regard to the fact that the Russian targets had no UK assets and that any enforcement action would need to proceed through the Russian courts.

A hearing was later heard in relation to Mr Williams in March 2015. Following the hearing the determinations panel decided to issue a CN to Mr Williams for £382,136. Various points were made by the determination panel including:

(*a*) the Panel held that the 'main purpose test' in the *Pensions Act 2004 (PA 2004), s 38(5)(a)(i)* extends to acts which prevent recovery under a guarantee. This includes situations where the acts take place prior to the liability under the guarantee being established;

(*b*) the material detriment test in *PA 2004, s 38A* was met because of the effect of the acts on the scheme 'obligations' under the guarantee;

(*c*) the fact that when considering the reasonableness of issuing a contribution notice the reference to the targets financial circumstances in *PA 2004, s 38(7)(f)* is not limited to the target's financial worth, but also includes how the target has ended up in the financial position in which he finds himself. This includes taking into account the target's receipt of monies and how they have been used. In this case the £382,136 had already been applied for Mr Williams' purposes;

(*d*) the Panel accepted that it was correct to draw a distinction between the issuing of a CN and its enforcement. Questions about the ability to recover and the costs and proportionality of so doing are far less relevant to the decision to issue a CN than to decisions over whether and how it should enforced.

Different principles apply in relation to FSDs as there is no requirement for an act or omission the purpose of which is to prevent the recovery of a *s 75* debt or which is materially detrimental to the pension scheme (see **Chapter 15**). There does not need to be any evidence of fault on the part of a target in order for the Regulator to issue an FSD, although the presence or absence of fault may be relevant to the issue of reasonableness (paragraph 127 of the Determinations Panel decision in *Box Clever [2012] 014 PBLR*).

Generally an FSD cannot be issued against an individual. FSDs can only be issued against an employer or persons connected or associated with an employer if the various statutory requirements are satisfied including a finding that the employer in question is either insufficiently resourced or a service company. FSDs can only be issued to the extent it is reasonable to do so having regard to the various statutory factors laid down in the legislation. The Determinations Panel will consider all relevant matters in the round and then decide whether it is reasonable to issue an FSD against a target (paragraph 127 of the Determinations Panel decision in *Box Clever [2012] 014 PBLR*).

There have been various reported cases where the Regulator has issued (or considered issuing) an FSD including the *Sea Containers* case, *Box Clever*, *Lehman* and *Nortel* which all give an indication of how the Regulator approaches the exercise of its powers. There have also been a number of other cases where the Regulator has decided not to issue an FSD which are relevant to a consideration of how in practice the Regulator will exercise its powers including the *Lufthansa* case (*see* **5.47** below).

A helpful starting point in understanding the Regulator's stance on issuing FSDs in insolvency scenarios is perhaps the observation made by the Determinations Panel in its reasons in relation to the Determination Notice issued on 13 September 2010 regarding the *Lehman Brothers Pension Scheme*. The Panel stated at paragraph 122:

'In our view the insolvency of a target does not, in and of itself, go against the imposition of an FSD. There may well be situations where the particular circumstances of an insolvency do so, such as where there are no assets whatsoever available. In general and in principle we consider that insolvency is a situation where an FSD might be necessary and appropriate in order to protect the interests of members. In the case of the Lehman group, given its complexity and multi-jurisdictional nature with consequential uncertainties as to outcomes, we consider that if anything it is more reasonable to impose an FSD on an insolvent target.'

It is therefore clear that insolvency will not of itself be a reason for the Regulator to avoid exercising its powers. However, this gives rise to the question of how the CN or FSD will be treated in the insolvency proceedings (see **5.49** and **5.50** below).

In other related proceedings (the '*Storm Funding*' proceedings) it was also determined by the High Court that a CN requiring a contribution in respect of an FSD could make a number of companies jointly and severally liable for an aggregate amount in excess of the *section 75* debt although the total amount recovered could not exceed scheme deficit. As part of the consent order entered into in the *Lehman* case it was agreed that appeal on this point in *Storm Funding* would not be pursued. This case therefore remains good law.

Enforcement in the UK

5.49   The question of enforcing an FSD was considered in detail in a case concerning both the Nortel and Lehman Brothers schemes (*In the Matter of Nortel GMBH & Ors [2010] EWHC 3010 (Ch), [2011] EWCA Civ 1124, [2013] UKSC 52*).

In both cases, FSDs had been issued following the insolvency and entry into administration of the sponsoring employers. Mr Justice Briggs stated at first instance at paragraph 4:

'The question for determination is whether, in circumstances where an FSD or a CN is first issued after the target company has gone into administration or liquidation, it imposes any and if so what obligation on the target company and its office-holders. The critical issue is whether the cost of complying with an FSD, or the monetary obligation imposed by a CN, ranks in the administration or liquidation of the target as a provable debt, or as an expense, or neither of those, so that it is recoverable only in the very unlikely event that there is a surplus otherwise available for distribution to members after all creditors have been paid in full.'

If the obligation was a provable debt, it would rank equally with other unsecured debts and liabilities. Generally speaking, *'provable debts arise only out of matters which have occurred, or have begun to occur, prior to the cut-off date'* (ie the date of entering into administration or liquidation). If the obligation was an expense (which could arise after the cut-off date), it would have 'super-priority' over provable debts.

After a detailed consideration of pensions and insolvency law, the judge concluded at first instance that the financial obligations flowing from the FSD process created administration or liquidation expenses and so have priority over ordinary debts: a conclusion which is likely to benefit the pension scheme members/PPF to the detriment of the wider body of company creditors.

The *Nortel* case caused significant consternation amongst insolvency practitioners and was eventually appealed all the way to the Supreme Court (*[2013] UKSC 52*). The Supreme Court ruled, overturning the decision in the Court of Appeal which had considered itself bound by earlier case law, that the liability arising under the FSD regime, arising pursuant to an FSD issued after the company had gone into administration, ranked as a provable debt of the company and not as an expense of administration.

The *Lehman* case was ultimately resolved by the parties to the Upper Tribunal proceedings entering into a pensions settlement deed containing terms of settlement (see the *section 89* report published by Regulator in August 2014). The parties filed an agreed consent order to the Upper Tribunal withdrawing and/or staying proceedings indefinitely. The consent order was approved by the Upper Tribunal on 18 August 2014 and it is expected that the amount payable should be sufficient to buy-out members' benefits in full.

Finally, it is worth noting in the context of the issue of CNs or FSDs that where there is simply a risk of a CN or FSD being issued, the court has held that pension scheme trustees should not be considered as 'creditors' (*Re Liberty International plc [2010] EWHC 1060 (Ch)*). The question arose in relation to a proposed reduction of capital in the UK branch of Liberty International plc, parent of two sponsoring employers of UK defined benefit pension schemes.

Enforcement overseas

5.50 The status of CNs and FSDs has been considered in jurisdictions outside the UK as well as by the courts of England and Wales.

Initially, prospects for enforcement overseas looked positive. In the case of *Sea Containers*, the sponsoring employer (a UK incorporated company) and other overseas companies within its group had filed for *Chapter 11* bankruptcy proceedings in Delaware, USA. FSDs were subsequently issued and the US court admitted the trustees' claims against the parent company. It found that the issue of FSDs did not violate the automatic stay under the *US Bankruptcy Code* and that it was reasonable to calculate the claims made by the trustees as though the FSDs were valid and using the *section 75* buy-out basis.

However, in the case of *Nortel*, the Delaware and Ontario courts did not prove so compliant, both concluding that the FSD process breached the stay on legal proceedings and actions in their respective insolvency processes. In an order dated 26 February 2010, the Delaware court enforced the automatic stay in relation to the *Chapter 11* bankruptcy proceedings and held that it was fully applicable to the trustees and the PPF. The court distinguished *Sea Containers* and stated that it was confined to its facts. The court noted that the earlier ruling that the FSD proceeding did not violate the automatic stay *'was issued in an entirely different procedural context'* and that the objecting creditors in that case had never sought to enforce it nor had they formally objected to the proceedings in the UK. By contrast, in *Nortel*, there were objections to the UK proceedings and a dispute over the Regulator's right to proceed in the absence of relief from the stay. In June 2012 the US Supreme Court declined an application by trustees of the Nortel scheme to lift the stay on legal proceedings.

As mentioned in **5.48** above, in the *Carrington Wire* case the Regulator was able to reach a settlement with a Russian company with no assets in the UK of a potential FSD claim. In deciding whether to accept the settlement on offer the Regulator has regard to the fact it would have to enforce the FSD in the Russian courts although it maintained the position in this case that it was open to the Regulator to take such enforcement action.

Consequences of corporate insolvency under English law – the regimes

5.51 There are a number of corporate insolvency regimes ('regimes') under the *Insolvency Act 1986 (IA 1986)* (as amended) supplemented by the *Insolvency Rules 1986 (SI 1986/1925) (IR 1986)* (as amended) that may affect pension schemes. This section of the chapter aims to be a general introduction to those regimes, and the relevant persons appointed under them. It is restricted to the application of the regimes in relation to English and Welsh formed and registered companies. However, it should be noted that foreign entities can become subject to a regime if they have a connection with England and Wales.

Company voluntary arrangement

5.52 A company voluntary arrangements ('CVA'), under *IA 1986, ss 1–7 and Sch A1* and *IR 1986, Part 1*, is where a company enters into what is effectively a contract with its creditors for either a composition in satisfaction of its debts (an agreement that a debt is to be discharged by payment of a proportion of it), or a scheme of arrangement of its affairs (*IA 1986, s 1*). They are typically initiated by the directors of the company, but can also be initiated by a liquidator or administrator.

A CVA is initiated by the circulation of a proposal which is voted upon by the company's creditors and shareholders. If approved (with or without modifications), the proposal becomes the CVA; that is, the contract between the company and its creditors.

There are presently two broad types of CVA available:

(1) All companies – this is one where a proposal is put together without the benefit of any moratorium against creditor claims/actions. The provisions regulating this type of CVA are found in the main body of *IA 1986, ss 1–7*. See **5.2** for details of when the insolvency event is deemed to occur within the meaning of *PA 2004, s 121*.

(2) Small companies – this type allows for a moratorium against creditor claims/actions while the proposal is being formulated and put out for approval. It is, however, only available to a 'small company' within the meaning of that term in *Companies Act 2006, s 382*, provided certain other prescribed criteria are also satisfied. This type of CVA was introduced into *IA 1986* by the *Insolvency Act 2000* (*IA 2000*). The moratorium provisions are found in *IA 1986, s 1A* and *Sch A1*. See **5.2** for details of when the insolvency event is deemed to occur within the meaning of *PA 2004, s 121*.

The primary difference between the two types of CVA is that, under the former, the company has no protection from its creditors when formulating the proposal, but under the latter, it does. Accordingly, there is no bar against creditor enforcement action under the all company type, until and unless (typically) the proposal is approved.

The provisions regulating the content and procedure for approval and implementation of both types of CVA are broadly the same, despite the fact that they are separately provided for in *IA 1986*.

Voting on the proposal

5.53 The terms of either type of CVA will depend entirely on what is proposed and accepted (creditors can propose modifications to the proposal put to them) by at least 75 per cent in value of the company's unsecured creditors present and voting at the creditors' meeting. Accordingly, the size of a pension scheme's claim against an employer by comparison with the claims of other unsecured creditors will directly affect its influence on the CVA.

Certain votes will not be taken into account in approving a proposal, and/ or may render invalid a resolution which has been passed (*IR 1986, rr 1.19, 1.52*). For example, a resolution will be invalid if without taking into account the votes of connected creditors, the unconnected unsecured creditors have voted against the proposal. For the definition of 'connected' in this context, see *IA 1986, ss 249* and *435*.

In addition, the proposal may not affect the claims of secured or preferential creditors without their consent. For this reason, while secured creditors are entitled to vote, their votes are not taken into account to the extent that their claim is secured.

A secured creditor is one who has a valid right of recourse to the assets of the company, as opposed to only a right of action against the company – the latter is an unsecured creditor. Priority issues for secured creditors will be governed either by law, or if negotiated, by contract – if there is more than one secured creditor, a deed of priority may be entered into, governing not only which creditor has priority to the assets, but also enforcement rights. Meanwhile, a preferential creditor is one whose claim is preferential as defined in *IA 1986, s 386 and Sch 6*.

There is a right for creditors to challenge a decision taken in the meetings held to approve the proposal by application to court within a 28-day period after the approval of the CVA (the precise starting date of the appeal window depends on the circumstances). There are two grounds for such a challenge:

(*a*)   the CVA unfairly prejudices the interests of a creditor; and/or

(*b*)   there has been some material irregularity at or in relation to the meeting at which the proposal was voted upon.

Company shareholders are also required to vote. Subject to any express provision in the company's articles, approval is by more than one half in value of those voting, in person or by proxy, in favour of the proposal (and any proposed modifications). If the meetings disagree, the decision taken by the creditors will prevail, although an aggrieved shareholder can challenge the creditors' decision by application to court within 28 days of the last meeting held.

If approved, the CVA binds all persons:

(*a*)   who were entitled to vote on the proposal whether or not they did so; and

(*b*)   who would have been entitled to vote on it if they had had notice of the meeting at which the proposal was voted upon.

Terms of the proposal

5.54   The proposal will nominate a person to be the supervisor of the CVA. A licensed insolvency practitioner ('IP') is typically nominated. However, since the introduction of the *IA 2000*, a supervisor can now (subject to certain restrictions) also be any individual who, although not an IP, is a member of a body recognised by the Secretary of State (*IA 1986, s 389A(1)*) and is satisfactorily insured.

To be qualified to act as an IP, an individual must be authorised by a specified competent authority or by virtue of his membership of a specified professional body (*IA 1986, s 390*) and be properly insured. If an individual purports to act as an IP without being so qualified, he commits a criminal offence (*IA 1986, s 389*). Authorisation and membership requires the individual to be generally fit and proper, to meet acceptable levels of education and to have sufficient practical experience in the field. An undischarged bankrupt or a person who has been subject to a disqualification order under the *Company Directors Disqualification Act 1986* is not qualified to act as an IP (*IA 1986, s 390(4)*).

The extent of the supervisor's powers and obligations will be as prescribed in the CVA.

In a CVA initiated by the directors of the company, it is typical for the company to continue trading as normal (with its own management), its obligations being simply to make contributions into the CVA from its trading ultimately to satisfy (or part satisfy) creditors' claims. In such a CVA, the supervisor's powers and obligations will typically be limited to monitoring the company's compliance with the CVA terms, agreeing creditors' claims and making distributions in accordance with the CVA. It is rare for a supervisor's powers and obligations to extend to 'running' the company. This means that the directors remain in office, although subject to any restrictions imposed on them by the CVA. This can lead to some confusion for those dealing with the continuing company.

Typically, the terms of the CVA will prohibit action being taken against the company in connection with debts and liabilities bound by the CVA. However, action in respect of debts and liabilities outside the CVA will not be prohibited. This means that if the company is continuing to trade, a creditor will be entitled to take such steps as it deems appropriate against the company for a debt incurred post-CVA, including steps to wind up the company. What effect such steps (and indeed, any actions taken by the company post CVA) will have on the CVA and the funds realised in it will depend on the terms of the CVA.

By way of example, presentation of a winding-up petition could lead to the default of the CVA, resulting in its termination. Typically, CVAs will provide that funds realised in the CVA are held on trust for the CVA creditors meaning that even if it fails, the funds already realised can be paid to these creditors and do not need to be shared with all of the company's creditors. Furthermore, the CVA creditors are not in principle prevented from also claiming in any liquidation of the company for the full amount of their debts, less the amount received in the CVA.

The inter-relationship between CVAs and liquidation has been the subject of a number of cases and is a difficult area. In *Re NT Gallagher & Son Ltd, Shierson v Thompson [2002] 1 WLR 2380, [2002] 3 All ER 474* the Court of Appeal considered whether the trusts created by a CVA were brought to an end by the termination of the CVA because of the company's liquidation. The court held that the liquidation of the company, although bringing the CVA to an end, would not terminate the trust created under it unless there was specific provision in the arrangement for such termination. The case therefore confirms the basic principle that the terms of the CVA are key and should be respected. Even if the CVA terms do not expressly refer to a trust being created in respect of CVA funds, wording that implies that to be the intention should be given effect.

A well-drawn CVA will contain clear and specific terms about how it will come to an end and in what circumstances, including what happens if the CVA terms are breached.

Employment contracts

What happens to the employment contracts will depend upon the circumstances. The company may decide to retain its employees if it continues to trade, or it may seek to terminate some employment contracts, leaving the employees with claims bound by the CVA.

Receivership

5.55   Secured creditors can typically enforce their security by appointing a receiver or receiver and manager over the assets secured in their favour.

In an enforcement context, a receiver is a person appointed by a creditor who holds security over a company's assets. The receiver's primary function is to use the powers given to him to deal with those assets, with the aim of satisfying the debt owed to that secured creditor. A receiver is not directly concerned with the general body of creditors of the company. It is currently accepted that, at best, the receiver owes only limited duties to obtain the best price reasonably obtainable for the realised assets at the time of sale, in all the circumstances (see, for instance, *Standard Chartered Bank v Walker [1982] 1 WLR 1410, [1982] 3 All ER 938*).

Types of receivership

5.56   There are broadly three types of receiver:

(*a*)   Administrative receivers: these are appointed by floating charge holders over all or substantially all of the assets of the company, which typically means that they are appointed over businesses. *IA 1986* does not contain a right to appoint an administrative receiver. The floating charge must contain that right. The appointee must be an IP. The appointment of an administrative receiver is an insolvency event within the meaning of *PA 2004, s 121* (see **5.2** above). The IA 1986 provisions which regulate these appointments are found in *sections 28–49, 72, 72A–72H*. Unless the floating charge was created before 15 September 2003 or otherwise falls into the list of exceptions (*IA 1986, ss 72B–72H*), a floating charge holder, who prior to these changes would have had an unrestricted right to appoint an administrative receiver, no longer has that right. Consequently, the appointment of an administrative receiver has become increasingly rare.

(*b*)   LPA 1925 receivers: these are receivers appointed under statutory powers under the *Law of Property Act 1925* (*LPA 1925*), where the security is a mortgage created by deed. The powers of an LPA receiver are limited to collecting in income and applying it against the outstanding debt. An LPA receiver need not be a licensed insolvency practitioner. The provisions which regulate *LPA 1925* receiverships are found *sections 99–109*.

(*c*)   Fixed charge receivers: these are appointed pursuant to an express power in the security document creating the fixed charge. As the circumstances in which an *LPA 1925* receiver can be appointed are restricted under *LPA 1925*, most modern security documents contain provision permitting the secured creditor to appoint a receiver over the secured assets after the security has become enforceable. The security will also typically afford the receiver all of the powers of an *LPA 1925* receiver under the *LPA 1925* plus the additional powers expressly set out in the security document, which is why the terms 'LPA receiver' and 'fixed charge receiver' are sometimes used interchangeably. A fixed charge receiver need not be a licensed insolvency practitioner.

The ability to appoint an *LPA 1925* receiver has not been affected by the legislative changes to *IA 1986* as introduced by the *Enterprise Act 2002*; only the ability to appoint an administrative receiver is affected (*IA 1986, s 72A*).

Role of the receiver and the secured creditor

5.57   Once a receiver is appointed, it is up to him to exercise his powers over the secured property as he deems appropriate to achieve the purpose for which the appointment has been made.

Once appointed, a receiver typically acts as the agent of the company over whose assets he is appointed. Consequently, the company is generally responsible for the receiver's acts or defaults – unless the security document provides otherwise. The agency relationship ends once the company is placed into liquidation. However, the receiver can continue to deal with the company's property either as principal or (only if the secured creditor agrees) as its agent.

Following appointment, the receiver will typically report to the secured creditor during the remainder of the enforcement process. The secured assets are usually managed and sold by the receiver in the company's name. The directors of the company remain in office notwithstanding the appointment, but they cannot exercise any powers over the assets over which the receiver is appointed unless the receiver authorises them to do so.

The receiver is given powers to deal with the assets over which he is appointed. The powers given and where they can be found depend upon the type of appointment. They will often include a power to sell the assets. There are some restrictions to the exercise of that power, prohibiting a sale to the receiver and qualifying the right to sell to associated parties. An *LPA 1925* receiver will not have the power to sell, or indeed any powers other than to receive rent, and possibly insure, issue and accept lease surrenders, unless other powers are given to him in the security. The assets do not vest in the receiver, nor do they vest in the secured creditor, but the receiver is able to exercise those powers using the company's name, enabling him to pass title to the assets where necessary.

The receivership process does not prevent action being taken against the company by an aggrieved creditor. Indeed, such a creditor could issue a petition to wind up the company and it could go into liquidation, while still being in receivership. A liquidation will affect the capacity in which the receiver acts (he will no longer act as the company's agent) but it will not affect his powers over the secured assets.

If the secured assets are the only assets of the company and they are insufficient to pay in full the secured creditor's debt, then there may be nothing left for the unsecured creditors. The unsecured creditors will then be reliant on recovery from either:

(*a*)   the prescribed part (see above), if applicable; or

(*b*)   successful proceedings within the liquidation, in actions which lead to recoveries that do not form part of the company's secured asset pool.

There are certain actions that only a liquidator can bring, which if successful may result in recoveries which go into the 'pot' available for unsecured creditors, and may not fall into the assets secured by the secured creditor's security.

Ultimately, the level of any recovery will depend on the level of costs incurred and of any unpaid preferential creditors.

Employment contracts

Employment contracts do not automatically terminate when a receiver is appointed. The receiver has 14 days' grace after appointment (*IA 1986, ss 37, 44*) to decide whether or not to adopt any employment contract. If he fails to take any steps in connection with any such contract within that period, he will (on the basis of current case law) be taken to have adopted it (see *Powdrill v Watson [1995] 2 AC 394*). The liability that the receiver becomes subject to under the adopted employment contracts depends on the nature of the receivership. If the receiver decides not to adopt an employment contract, the contract will be terminated and the employee will be an unsecured creditor of the company (albeit some parts of the employee's claim may be a preferential debt). See **5.11** above for further discussion of this issue.

Administration

5.58   Administration (see *IA 1986, Sch B1*) was introduced into *IA 1986* as an alternative process to liquidation where there is a chance of the company or its business surviving. It is presently the primary formal rescue process available in England and Wales. Administration as an insolvency procedure was overhauled on 15 September 2003 following changes introduced to the *IA 1986* by the *Enterprise Act 2002*. This section deals only with the procedure post-15 September 2003.

Administration involves the appointment of an IP to the company (called an administrator), whose purpose is to manage the company while putting together proposals for the creditors to vote on which achieve the objectives for which the administrator is appointed.

In an administration, there is a sliding scale of objectives. First, the administrator must try to rescue the company as a going concern. Second, if the administrator concludes that the company cannot be rescued as a going concern or that the following objective would achieve a better result for all the creditors, his next objective is to get a better realisation of the company's assets than would be the case if the company had been immediately wound up instead of going into administration. Third, if he concludes that this cannot be done and achieving the following objective will not 'unnecessarily harm' the interests of all creditors, the administrator's third objective is simply to sell the company's assets and distribute the realisations to the company's secured creditors and preferential creditors under *IA 1986*.

The administrator effectively replaces the directors, who remain in office but neither they nor the company can exercise a management power without the administrator's consent. Entering into administration is an insolvency event within the meaning of *PA 2004, s 121* (see **5.2** above).

Administrators have very wide powers (principally set out in *IA 1986, Sch 1*), which include power to manage the business and to sell the company's assets. An administrator is an officer of the court and acts as agent on behalf of the company. When an administrator is pursuing the first and second objectives above, he must act in the best interests of the company's creditors as a whole. Where the third objective is being pursued, the administrator must not unnecessarily harm the interests of unsecured creditors.

An administrator may be appointed:

- by an administration order made by the court on the application of the company, its directors, one or more creditors of the company, the designated officer for a magistrates' court or any combination of them (*IA 1986, Sch B1, para 12*). In addition, the supervisor of a voluntary arrangement (*IA Sch B1, para 12(5) and s 7(4)(b)*), a liquidator (*IA 1986, Sch B1, para 38*), the Financial Conduct Authority and the Prudential Regulation Authority (*Financial Services and Markets Act 2000, s 359 (as amended)*) have standing to apply.

- out of court by the holder of a qualifying floating charge (*IA 1986, Sch B1, para 14*); or

- out of court by the company or its directors (*IA 1986, Sch B1, para 22*).

An administration will end automatically after a year, unless extended by the creditors or the court (*IA 1986, Sch B1, para 76*).

Voting on the proposal

5.59   Unless (a) the company has sufficient property to enable all creditors to be paid in full, (b) there is no prospect of a return to unsecured creditors or (c) neither of the first two objectives can be achieved, the administrator must hold a meeting of the company's creditors no later than ten weeks after the date the company entered administration (*IA 1986, Sch B1, para 51(2)*). The creditors will consider and vote on whether to approve the administrator's proposals. The proposals will be approved if they are voted for by a majority in value of those persons voting, in person or by proxy, and entitled to vote. Accordingly, the size of a pension scheme's claim against an employer by comparison with the claims of other creditors will directly affect its influence on the administration.

Certain votes will not be taken into account, and/or may render invalid a resolution passed (see *IR 1986, Part 2*). For example, a resolution will be invalid if, without taking into account the votes of connected creditors, the unconnected unsecured creditors have voted against the proposal (*IR 1986, rule 2.43(2)*). For the definition of 'connected' in this context, see *IA 1986, ss 249* and *435*.

Terms of the proposal and actions of the administrator

5.60   The proposal will depend entirely on the facts and circumstances. The proposal should be put to creditors within a short period after the administration is commenced (ten weeks (*IA 1986, Sch B1, para 51*) – this period can be extended), the intention being that the administration process should be creditor driven. That is, the ultimate fate of the company should be in the creditors' hands. The administrator may, however, before the proposal is put to the creditors, do such things as he thinks necessary and appropriate (including selling the company's business) if he is of the view that it is in the best interests of the company and its creditors to do so (see, for example, pre-packs below at **5.62**).

Administrators can make distributions to secured and preferential creditors within the process (*IA 1986, Sch B1, para 65(1)*), and with court leave, may also be able to make distributions to the company's unsecured creditors (*IA 1986, Sch B1, para 65(3)*), effectively making it possible for administration to be a 'one-stop shop'. The general order of priority of payment of creditors in an insolvency applies. See **5.65** below and the following in this section.

Moratorium and protection of creditors

5.61   A key feature of the administration process is that the company has the benefit of a statutory moratorium for the duration of the administration.

Without the administrator's consent or leave of the court:

- no steps may be taken to enforce security over the company's property or to repossess goods in the company's possession under a hire purchase agreement;

- a landlord may not exercise a right of forfeiture in relation to premises let to the company; and

- no legal process may be commenced or continued against the company or its property.

Where an application is made to the court for leave to take any of the steps listed above, it is for the person making the application to persuade the court that leave should be granted. In the leading case of *Re Atlantic Computer*

Systems Plc [1992] Ch 505, the Court of Appeal held that leave will normally be given where the court is persuaded that granting the application is unlikely to impede the achievement of the purpose of the administration. In other cases, the court will balance the interests of the applicant against the interests of the other creditors of the company.

Once the company goes into administration, the secured creditors' position as regards a fixed charge is, in very general terms, protected because the net proceeds of disposal must be paid to the secured creditor. The position of a floating charge creditor is less satisfactory. Floating charge realisations are first made available to meet the administration costs, expenses and liabilities and preferential creditors. In addition, for charges created after 15 September 2003, a prescribed part of the net floating charge realisations must be deducted and paid to unsecured creditors.

Employment contracts

Like administrative receivers, administrators have 14 days after appointment within which to decide which employment contracts, if any, they want to adopt (see **5.11** and **5.57** above). The meaning of adoption of contracts was considered in the House of Lords decision in *Powdrill v Watson [1995] 2 AC 394*, where it was held:

> 'The word "adopt" is not a term of art but takes its colour from the context in which it is used ... If the employment is continued for more than 14 days after the appointment of the administrator or receiver, there seems to be no escape from the conclusion that the whole contract has been adopted.'

To the extent that a qualifying liability is incurred after the adoption of any contract (such as a liability in respect of wages or salary including a sum payable in lieu of holiday entitlement or in respect of an occupation pension scheme contribution), such sum will have priority and rank ahead of the administrator's own remuneration and expenses (*IA 1986, Sch B1, para 99(5)*). See also **5.11** above.

Pre-packs

5.62   A pre-pack (short for 'pre-packaged') is a deal for the sale of an insolvent company's assets which is devised in advance of it entering into a formal insolvency process. It is frequently used in conjunction with administration. In most cases, the deal will have been agreed before the IP is appointed and will usually be executed by the IP shortly after appointment.

In certain circumstances, a pre-pack may be the best method of maximising realisations for a financially distressed company to the advantage of all stakeholders. By agreeing the deal in advance of a formal insolvency, the business is often sold without the negative publicity and business disruption that there would be if the company entered the insolvency process before the sale was arranged. A common justification for a pre-pack is that a formal insolvency process followed by a period of trading may destroy value and lead to a loss of business and staff. It is frequently used in the case of 'people' businesses or other businesses which cannot easily be traded in insolvency. It has become increasingly common in recent years in situations where there is a lack of available funding to keep a business trading through an insolvency process.

There are no specific provisions in insolvency legislation which deal with pre-packs. IPs who execute pre-packs are regulated by both statute and the codes of practice of their professional bodies. If a court subsequently found an insolvency officeholder had acted improperly in entering into a pre-pack, he might be liable for misfeasance. Equally, he could be subject to disciplinary proceedings.

The 'Statement of Insolvency Practice 16' which was introduced in January 2009 and updated in November 2013, sets out guidelines for IPs who are involved in pre-pack sales. It is intended to provide greater transparency for creditors, by providing them with detailed information about the terms of the sale, the buyer of the business and with more visibility into the formal insolvency process generally.

Liquidation

5.63   Liquidation is a regime that can either be initiated by the company voluntarily, or against the company by, among others, its creditors. It provides for the appointment of an IP to the company as a 'liquidator', who takes control of the company's assets, replacing, in effect, the directors, whose powers cease. It represents the 'beginning of the end' for a company and, except in exceptional circumstances, its business, because once the liquidation ends, the company will be automatically dissolved (unless an appeal against dissolution is lodged). It will therefore cease to be a legal entity after the liquidation is completed.

Solvent liquidations

5.64   Solvent liquidations (members' voluntary liquidations ('MVL')) are used where, for example, a company was incorporated for a particular purpose which it has achieved and it is, therefore, no longer required. The aim of an MVL is to realise all remaining assets in the company and to settle all outstanding claims against it (with interest), with a view to realising whatever surplus there is in the company so that it can be distributed to the company's members. As a consequence, an MVL is not an insolvency event within the meaning of *PA 2004, s 121* (as extended by regulations).

The MVL process is initiated by the company's directors swearing a statutory declaration of solvency (under the threat of criminal liability if they do not do so reasonably) to the effect that they have made a full inquiry into the company's affairs and that having done so, they have formed the view that the company can pay all of its debts and liabilities, including contingent and prospective liabilities, in full within a period not exceeding 12 months (*IA 1986, s 89*). Once they have done this, they then call a meeting of the company's members (shareholders) to pass a special resolution (a majority of 75 per cent in value of those voting, in person or by proxy) (*CA 2006, s 283*) to put the company into liquidation (*IA 1986 s 84(1)(b)*). The MVL takes effect from the time of the passing of this resolution.

If the company is later found to be insolvent by the liquidator appointed, he has a duty to convert it into a creditors' voluntary liquidation ('CVL'), which is an insolvent liquidation (*IA 1986, s 95*). At this stage, an insolvency event within the meaning of *PA 2004, s 121* will occur (see **5.2** above for more details). However, unless the company turns out to be insolvent, creditors of companies that go into MVL should be paid in full for their debts.

Insolvent liquidations

5.65   Insolvent liquidations can be either voluntary (CVLs) or compulsory, the latter initiated by a petition to the court. These will usually occur where there is no prospect of the company being able to continue trading or of its business surviving in any form, and there is no option but to appoint a liquidator to collect in all the company's assets to distribute them fairly among the company's creditors in the order prescribed in *IA 1986*. Both types of insolvent liquidation are insolvency events within the meaning of *PA 2004, s 121*.

The company's business will typically cease on the company going into any form of liquidation. It will only ever continue after liquidation in exceptional circumstances (where it would be beneficial to the winding up). The liquidator's powers are very wide (*IA 1986, Sch 4*), albeit not all of them can be actioned without the prior sanction of the creditors or the court.

Commencement

A CVL commences when the shareholders of the company resolve, by special resolution (75 per cent in value of those voting, in person or by proxy (*CA 2006, s 283 and IA 1986, s 84*)) to put it into liquidation. Five business days' notice of the proposed liquidation must be given to any chargee having a floating charge over the company's assets (*IA 1986, s 84(2A)*). This notice period can be shortened with the consent of the charge-holder (*IA 1986, s 84(2B)*).

In a CVL, the creditors and the shareholders at their respective meetings may each nominate a person to be the liquidator (*IA 1986, s 100(1)*). IA 1986 provides that the creditors' choice of liquidator shall prevail or, if no person has been nominated by the creditors, the liquidator shall be the person nominated by the shareholders (*IA 1986, s 100(2)*). The appointment takes effect on the passing of the resolution for the appointment (*IR 1986, rule 4.101(2)*).

In a compulsory liquidation, when a winding-up order is granted, the liquidation is deemed to have commenced on the date of the presentation of the petition pursuant to which the company is wound up (*IA 1986, s 129*). This, among other things, makes vulnerable actions taken by the company between presentation of the petition and the making of an order on that petition (*IA 1986, s 127*). If the company disposes of any of its property in that period, that disposition will be void unless it is authorised or ratified by the court. Even a payment by the company to a creditor during that period could be void on this basis. Generally, such a disposition will only be authorised or ratified if the disposition is likely to benefit all of the company's creditors, or at least not disadvantage them (*Re Gray's Inn Construction Co Ltd [1980] 1 WLR 711, [1980] 1 All ER 814*).

The first liquidator appointed to a company in a compulsory liquidation is typically the 'Official Receiver'. The Official Receiver is a person appointed to the office by the Secretary of State to carry out functions conferred upon him by the *IA 1986*. The Official Receiver then has 12 weeks within which to investigate the company's affairs (*IA 1986, s 132* explains his duties). He must also call meetings of, amongst others, the creditors of the company for the purpose of their choosing an IP to become the liquidator of the company in his place, or to give them notice that he will not be doing so, in which case he will continue as the liquidator (*IA 1986, s 136*). He will typically only call such meetings if there are assets in the company.

Moratorium and claims

Actions and proceedings against the company and its property are prohibited without court leave in a compulsory liquidation (*IA 1986, s 130*). This means that no actions already commenced against it can be proceeded with, and no new actions can be commenced, unless the court gives leave. The court will typically only give leave in cases where the normal process of making a claim in the liquidation is not seen as sufficient.

There is no such automatic prohibition on proceedings in a voluntary liquidation. That said, the liquidator may apply to court for a stay of any proceedings commenced for the same reasons as outlined above. A liquidator is likely to do so if proceedings for recovery of a simple debt claim are commenced.

The process of making a claim in a liquidation is called 'proving' and the claim is called a 'proof' – the rules as to proofs can be found in *IR 1986, rr 4.73–4.85, Chapter 9.* The proving process enables unsecured creditors to make their claim in the liquidation as fully as they wish (providing such supporting evidence as they deem appropriate), which the liquidator considers in a quasi-judicial capacity. If the liquidator needs more information in order to reach a decision on the claim, he can ask for it.

A secured creditor may prove for any unsecured balance of its debt or voluntarily surrender his security for the general benefit of creditors and prove for the whole debt as if it were unsecured (*IR 1986, rule 4.88*).

If the creditor is ultimately unhappy with the liquidator's decision on their proof (the liquidator can reject all or part of it). The creditor has a right to appeal by making an application to court within 21 days of receiving the liquidator's notice of the rejection (*IR 1986, rule 4.83*).

The order of priority of payment of creditors in an English insolvency is broadly as follows:

(1) Fixed charge asset realisations: used to pay (in the following order): (i) costs; (ii) fixed charge-holder.

(2) Floating charge asset realisations: used to pay (in the following order): (i) expenses of the insolvency process; (ii) preferential creditors; (iii) prescribed part or 'ring-fenced' fund for unsecured creditors (this is a percentage of net floating realisations up to a maximum of £600,000) (if applicable); (iv) floating charge-holder.

(3) Uncharged/surplus asset realisations: used to pay (i) costs and expenses of the insolvency process; (ii) preferential debts and (iii) unsecured claims (on a 'pari passu' or pro rata basis).

The general order of priorities can be modified by inter-creditor agreements, whereby parties agree to contractually alter the order of priorities as between themselves.

Employment contracts

The effect of liquidation on employment contracts is not prescribed in *IA 1986* (as it is in administration and receivership). As a consequence, there is some uncertainty as to the effect. It is generally accepted, although there is little firm authority on the point, that in a CVL and MVL, the employees' contracts typically terminate on or shortly after liquidation, but not because of the liquidation, rather because the company's business has ceased and so their contracts are effectively repudiated. If the liquidator carries on the business he may retain some employees during the period of trading. In a compulsory liquidation, on the other hand, it is thought that the employees' contracts automatically terminate because of the making of the winding-up order against the company (*Measures Brothers Ltd v Measures [1910] 2 Ch 248*).

Chapter 6

Protection for early leavers

Introduction

General

6.1 Historically, one of the main sources of dissatisfaction with occupational pension schemes had been the treatment of members who leave such schemes (usually because they left employment) before normal pension age. (The meaning of 'normal pension age' is discussed in **6.23** below.)

Consequently, legislation was introduced to provide a range of protections for early leavers relating to preservation (see **6.2** below), revaluation (see **6.3** to **6.5** below) and transfer values (see **6.6** below).

Preservation requirements

6.2 The preservation requirements set out the benefits which occupational pension schemes are required to provide for early leavers. These requirements are considered in **6.10** to **6.29** below.

The preservation requirements were first introduced by the *Social Security Act 1973* with effect from 6 April 1975, but have since been amended to give increased protection to leavers. They are now consolidated in *PSA 1993, Part IV, Chapter 1 (ss 69–82)* (as amended by *PA 1995, WRPA 1999, PA 2004, PA 2014* and *PSA 2015*) and the *Occupational Pension Schemes (Preservation of Benefit) Regulations 1991 (SI 1991/167)* (the '*Preservation Regulations*') (as amended).

Revaluation

6.3 An early leaver's scheme entitlement under the preservation requirements (see **6.2** above) will most typically take the form of a deferred pension from the scheme (commonly referred to as vested rights), prospectively payable from his normal pension age (see **6.23** below).

249

6.4 *Protection for early leavers*

Legislation requires the calculation of any such pension to include an element of revaluation in respect of the period of deferment.

Revaluation of benefits other than guaranteed minimum pensions

6.4   The revaluation of benefits other than guaranteed minimum pensions is governed by *PSA 1993, Part IV, Chapter II (ss 83–86)*. These requirements were first introduced by the *Social Security Act 1985*, but have since been revised by *PA 1995, WRPA 1999, the Civil Partnership Act 2004, PA 2004* and the *Public Service Pensions Act 2013*; they are discussed in **6.30** to **6.42** below.

Revaluation of guaranteed minimum pensions

6.5   The revaluation of guaranteed minimum pensions is governed by *PSA 1993, Part IV, Chapter III (ss 87–92)*. These requirements were originally introduced by the *Health and Social Security Act 1984* and have since been revised by the *Civil Partnership Act 2004, PA 2004, PA 2007* and *PA 2014*; they are summarised in **Chapter 4**.

Transfer values

6.6   *PSA 1993, Part IV, Chapter IV (ss 93–101)* as amended sets out certain statutory entitlements for an early leaver with vested rights to require a sum of money representing the value of his rights under the scheme to be used in one of a number of ways (for example, transferred to another scheme or used to buy an annuity). This right (first introduced by the *Social Security Act 1985*) is covered further from **6.43** below.

PSA 1993, Part IV, Chapter IVA (ss 101AA–101AI) was inserted by *PA 2004, s 264* with effect from 6 April 2006. These provisions give those leaving service with at least three months' pensionable service, but without any vested rights, the opportunity to take a cash transfer sum as an alternative to a refund of contributions. This is covered further in **6.66** below.

Scope of early leaver legislation

Schemes affected

6.7   The legislation referred to in **6.1** to **6.6** above applies to occupational pension schemes (as now defined in *PSA 1993*). The High Court, in the case of

Royal Masonic Hospital v Pensions Ombudsman [2001] 1 PBLR (9) held that *PSA 1993, s 69* did not cover unfunded private sector schemes as the pension promise was merely a contractual one that would be met in the future from the general assets of the employer rather than from an accrued fund.

Relationship of early leaver legislation to scheme rules

6.8   *PSA 1993, Part IV, Chapter I* (which relates to preservation) requires scheme rules to contain provisions which comply with the preservation requirements (summarised in **6.10** to **6.29** below). However, *Chapter I* does not actually go so far as to override the scheme rules if they do not comply (*PSA 1993, s 131*). Nevertheless, employers and trustees can still be challenged by members and beneficiaries for operating a scheme whose rules do not comply with the preservation requirements (see **6.9** below). In particular, it should be noted that *PSA 1993, s 132* requires trustees, where their scheme's rules do not meet the preservation requirements, to take such steps as are open to them for rectifying this. However there is no corresponding obligation on employers (see also **6.9** below). By contrast, *PSA 1993, Part IV, Chapters II, III, IV* and *V* and *Part 4ZA* (all of which relate to revaluation and transfer values) do override the scheme rules (subject to limited exceptions) (*PSA 1993, s 129*).

The legislation prescribes the minimum protections to be given to early leavers. A scheme's rules may apply the protection on a more generous basis.

Enforcement of preservation legislation

6.9   The Regulator has been responsible for ensuring that schemes complied with preservation since 6 April 2006. The Regulator has power to issue an improvement or third party notices where it is of the opinion that a provision of pensions legislation (including *PSA 1993*) is not being complied with. A trustee or employer not complying with such a notice could be subject to penalties under *PA 1995, s 10*. Otherwise the High Court has held, in the case of *IBM United Kingdom Pensions Trust v IBM United Kingdom Holdings Limited [2012] 118 PBLR (133)* that there is no power to require any person who is not the trustee or manager of the scheme to exercise their powers to ensure that the scheme complies with the preservation requirements. Alternatively, a member who is not satisfied that his scheme complies with preservation could seek recourse against the employer and/or the trustees through an application to the Pensions Ombudsman or through the courts.

Further, in the same *IBM* decision, the High Court decided that the Regulator may only require compliance with the current preservation requirements, and not with the preservation requirements as they may have applied at some past time when the non-compliance first occurred.

Preservation

Defined terms

6.10 *PSA 1993* uses a number of defined terms in relation to the preservation requirements. These are summarised below.

'Two years' or '30 days' qualifying service'

6.11 This is defined in *PSA 1993, s 71(7)*. It means two years (whether a single period of that duration or two or more periods, continuous or discontinuous, totalling two years) in which the member was at all times employed either:

(*a*) in 'pensionable service' (see **6.12** below) under the scheme; or

(*b*) in service in employment which was contracted out by reference to the scheme; or

(*c*) in 'linked qualifying service' (see **6.13** below) under another scheme.

There are special provisions in relation to periods of service previously terminated (*PSA 1993, s 71(9)* and *Preservation Regulations, reg 21*).

Where a member is entitled to money purchase benefits only, references to 'two years' qualifying service' should be read as references to '30 days' qualifying service' from 1 October 2015 (*PA 2014, s 36*).

'Pensionable service'

6.12 This is defined in *PSA 1993, s 70(2)*. In effect, pensionable service means actual service in employment to which the scheme relates which qualifies the member (assuming it continues for long enough) for retirement benefits at normal pension age.

There are detailed regulations regarding breaks in pensionable service (*Preservation Regulations, reg 21*). In particular, the service before and after the break must be added together (in ascertaining whether there is two years' qualifying service – see **6.11** above) where one or more of the following conditions are satisfied:

(*a*) the break does not exceed one month; or

(*b*) the break corresponds to the member's absence from work wholly or partly because of pregnancy or confinement and the member returns to pensionable service no later than one month after returning to work in exercise of her statutory right to return to work; or (*c*)   the break corresponds to the member's absence from work in furtherance of a 'trade dispute' as defined in the *Social Security Act 1975*.

Whether or not the break counts towards pension benefits is determined not only by the rules of the scheme, but also by any relevant employment and pensions legislation – particularly where the period is a period of maternity, adoption, paternity or family leave (see **Chapter 9**).

'Linked qualifying service'

6.13   Linked qualifying service is relevant where the scheme has accepted a transfer payment from another occupational pension scheme or a buyout policy. The qualifying service under the transferring scheme or secured by an insurance policy or annuity, is added to qualifying service in the scheme receiving the transfer payment. The trustees will be given certified details of the qualifying service as part of the conditions for accepting the transfer payment. The detailed definition of linked qualifying service is contained in *PSA 1993, s 179*. It includes restrictions on what can and cannot count as linked qualifying service, for example, regard can only be had to 'actual service'.

'Normal pension age'

6.14   Normal pension age is defined in *PSA 1993, s 180* and is discussed in detail in **6.23** below. The term is relevant to the questions as to whether a member is an early leaver and when a preserved pension for him becomes payable.

Members of schemes that are subject to the *Public Service Pensions Act 2013* have a normal pension age that is the same as their SPA or age 65, if higher (*PSPA 2013, s 10*).

'Long service benefit'

6.15   Long service benefit is defined in *PSA 1993, s 70(1)*. Broadly, it is:

(*a*)   retirement benefits for a member at normal pension age; and

(*b*)   benefits for his spouse, civil partner, dependants or others on his attaining normal pension age or, if later, death,

which would have been payable under the scheme had the member remained in pensionable service until normal pension age.

'Short service benefit'

6.16   Short service benefit is the benefit which a scheme may be required to provide in respect of an early leaver unless one of the prescribed 'alternatives to short service benefit' (see **6.24** to **6.29** below) applies instead. The definition is contained in *PSA 1993, s 71*. Short service benefit must be paid directly from scheme resources or assured to the member in accordance with the requirements of *Preservation Regulations, reg 6 (PSA 1993, s 73(1))*.

Qualifying for short service benefit

6.17   Under *PSA 1993, s 71(1)* a scheme must provide short service benefit (that is, benefit of any description which would otherwise have been payable as long service benefit) where a member's pensionable service is terminated before normal pension age and:

(*a*)   he has at least two years' qualifying service; or

(*b*)   a transfer payment in respect of his rights under a personal pension scheme has been made to the scheme.

In the case of a member with only money purchase benefits, *PA 2014, s 36* amended *PSA 1993, s 71(1)* with effect from 1 October 2015 to provide that such a member qualifies for short service benefit on completion of 30 days' qualifying service.

The short service benefit is generally payable from the member's normal pension age or age 65 if later (see **6.23** below).

Calculating the short service benefit – an overview

6.18   The method of calculating short service benefit is set out in *PSA 1993, s 74*.

Same basis as long service benefit

6.19   *PSA 1993, s 74(1)* requires that, except where the principle of 'uniform accrual' applies (see **6.20** below), 'a scheme must provide for short service benefit to be computed on the same basis as long service benefit'.

The application of this requirement to money purchase benefits is relatively simple. If a scheme provides long service benefit on a money purchase basis, the corresponding short service benefit should also be computed on the same basis (ie on a money purchase basis). Further details regarding money purchase benefits are contained in *Preservation Regulations, reg 10* (as amended).

Where long service benefits are calculated by reference to a member's salary at normal pension age, short service benefits must also be calculated in a corresponding manner by reference to the member's salary at the date of termination of pensionable service. Similarly, if the member's salary is averaged over a specified period before normal pension age when calculating his long service benefits, a period of the same duration must be used to average the member's salary for the purpose of calculating short service benefits (*PSA 1993, s 74(7)*).

The calculation of short service benefit in relation to defined benefits can be illustrated by the following example:

A member's pension, calculated at normal pension age, is 1/60th of final pensionable salary for each year of pensionable service. Final pensionable salary is defined as the average of the member's salary over the three years immediately preceding normal pension age. The member joins the scheme at age 30 and his normal pension age is 65. The calculation of his pension will be as follows:

(*a*) if the member stays to normal pension age, and so completes 35 years of pensionable service, his long service benefit will be a pension of 35/60ths of final pensionable salary, calculated by averaging his salary over the three years immediately preceding normal pension age; but

(*b*) if the member leaves pensionable service, say, at age 40, having completed ten years of pensionable service, his short service benefit will be a pension of 10/60ths of final pensionable salary, calculated by averaging his salary over the three years immediately preceding the date of leaving pensionable service. This pension will be payable from the scheme at the normal pension age of 65.

Uniform accrual

6.20   There are a number of circumstances where the legislation requires that short service benefits be computed on the basis of 'uniform accrual' rather than as set out in **6.19** above (*PSA 1993, s 74(6)*). In particular, uniform accrual must be applied where the following situations arise:

(*a*) the long service benefit formula is not related to the length of pensionable service or the number or amount of contributions paid (*PSA 1993, s 74(4)*); or

(*b*) the long service benefit accrues at a higher rate or otherwise more favourably if the member's pensionable service is of some specified minimum length or if he remains in pensionable service up to a specified minimum age *(PSA 1993, s 74(3))*.

In effect, uniform accrual is required where there is no obvious accrual rate in the scheme rules or the only accrual rate available would give an anomalous result. The principle of uniform accrual is that benefits accrue evenly over the period of pensionable service (thus creating a notional accrual rate). This is best illustrated by way of an example:

A member joins a scheme at age 30 and is promised a pension of two-thirds of his salary on retirement at age 60. This formula is not related to his length of pensionable service and so, under *PSA 1993, s 74(4)* and *(6)*, uniform accrual applies. The principle of uniform accrual treats the 'two-thirds' pension, which he will receive at age 60 if he remains in pensionable service, as accruing uniformly throughout the 30 years of his pensionable service (ie from age 30 to age 60). If the member leaves at age 45, he will have completed one half of this 30 year period (ie 15 years), so his short service benefit will be one half of the 'two-thirds' pension which he would have received had he stayed to age 60 (ie one-third of his salary at the date of termination of pensionable service).

Uniform accrual also applies (in a slightly different way) to any part of a member's long service benefit which derives from a benefit improvement granted in relation to previous pensionable service. In these circumstances, the benefit improvement is treated as accruing uniformly over the period from the date when the improvement was granted to the attainment of normal pension age *(PSA 1993, s 75(5))*.

Lump sum death benefits before normal pension age

6.21   It should be noted that the definition of 'long service benefit' contained in *PSA 1993, s 70* does not cover benefits payable on the death of an early leaver before his normal pension age. Consequently, a scheme is not required by the preservation laws to provide death benefits where an early leaver subsequently dies before normal pension age (although many schemes do provide some level of benefit in these circumstances).

Discretionary benefits

6.22   A further question which arises is how far discretionary benefits must be preserved. *PSA 1993, s 72(1)* provides that a scheme must not contain any rule which could result in an early leaver being treated less favourably for any purpose relating to short service benefit than he would have been treated for the same purpose relating to long service benefit if he had stayed in service. However, this does not apply to a rule which merely confers discretion on the trustees or some other person, so long as the rule does not specifically require the discretion to be exercised in any discriminatory manner against members in respect of the short service benefit (*PSA 1993, s 72(3)*). It is arguable that a scheme rule relating to discretionary augmentation which provides that the trustees cannot consider deferred members is discriminatory.

Date of payment of preserved benefits

6.23   Short service benefits are payable from an age no greater than 65, or 'normal pension age' if greater than 65 (*PSA 1993, s 71(3)* as amended by *PA 2004, s 263(1)* and the *Public Service Pensions Act 2013, s 27,* which introduces a new definition of 'normal pension age' with effect from 1 April 2014 for members of schemes which are subject to that Act). The change introduced by *PA 2004* from 6 April 2005 was significant. Previously, short service benefits were payable at normal pension age or age 60 if normal pension age was earlier than age 60. It is worth noting that in *IBM United Kingdom Pensions Trust Limited v IBM United Kingdom Holdings Limited & Others [2012] EWHC 2766 (Ch)* Warren J held that 'As a matter of construction, there is, in my judgment, no temporal limitation in relation to the changes to *s 71* and *72* introduced by the *Pensions Act 2004*. They apply to the entirety of the deferred pension of a member leaving service before normal retirement age.'

A member's 'normal pension age' is defined in *PSA 1993, s 180* as the earliest age at which the member is entitled to receive benefits (other than guaranteed minimum pension) on his retirement from any employment to which the scheme applies. Where the scheme only provides a guaranteed minimum pension, the normal pension age is the earliest age at which the member is entitled to receive the guaranteed minimum pension on retirement from such employment. An entitlement would arise where the member can call for his benefit without employer or trustee consent.

For the purposes of determining a member's normal pension age, any special provision as to early retirement on grounds of ill-health or otherwise must be disregarded (*PSA 1993, s 180(2)*).

Alternatives to short service benefit

6.24   *PSA 1993, s 73(2)* permits the rules of a scheme to provide one or more of a number of alternatives to short service benefit. The alternatives may be provided as a complete or partial substitute for the early leaver's short service benefit (*Preservation Regulations, reg 7(2)*).

Transfer payments

6.25 A member's accrued rights may be transferred to another occupational pension scheme, or to a personal pension scheme, with a view to acquiring rights for the member under the receiving scheme (*PSA 1993, s 73(2)(a)*). Furthermore, a scheme may provide for the member's accrued rights to be transferred, if the member consents, to an overseas arrangement. 'Overseas arrangement' means a scheme or arrangement, other than an occupational pension scheme, which:

(*a*)   has effect, or is capable of having effect, so as to provide benefits on termination of employment or on death or retirement to or in respect of earners; and

(*b*)   is administered wholly or primarily outside the UK (*Preservation Regulations, reg 11A*).

From 6 April 2013, it is possible to transfer the member's accrued rights to a 'European pensions institution' (as defined in *PA 2004, s 293(8)*) without the member's consent if the conditions in *reg 12(2)* and *(3)* are satisfied (*Preservation Regulations, reg 11B*).

Except in limited circumstances (see **6.28** below), the consent of the member must be obtained if a transfer is to be made as an alternative to providing short service benefits within the scheme (*PSA 1993, s 73(4)*).

Early retirement

6.26 The rules of a scheme may permit payment of benefits to commence before normal pension age. In such a situation, the benefits payable may be of different amounts, and be payable to different recipients, than applies in relation to short service benefit (*Preservation Regulations, reg 8(1)*).

However, where a scheme provides an early retirement pension as an alternative to short service benefits, the following requirements will apply:

(*a*)   the benefits must include a benefit payable to the member (*Preservation Regulations, reg 8(1)*);

(*b*)   it must be the case that either:

•   the member meets the ill-health condition in *FA 2004, Sch 28, para 1*; or

•   the member has attained normal minimum pension age as defined in *FA 2004, s 279*;

(*c*)   the member's consent must be obtained unless:

- his earning capacity is destroyed or seriously impaired because of physical or mental infirmity; and

- in the opinion of the scheme's trustees, he is incapable of deciding whether it is in his interests to consent (*Preservation Regulations, regs 7(2), 8(3)*); and

(*d*)   the relevant scheme rule must require the trustees to be reasonably satisfied that the total value of the benefits when they become payable is at least equal to the value of the accrued benefits which they replace (*Preservation Regulations, regs 8(4), 11*).

Late retirement

6.27   The rules of a scheme may also permit payment of benefits to commence after normal pension age as an alternative to short service benefit. The benefits payable may be of different amounts, and be payable to different recipients (but must include the member), than applies in relation to short service benefit (*Preservation Regulations, reg 8(1)*).

In this situation, the following requirements will apply:

(*a*)   the benefits must include a benefit payable to the member (*Preservation Regulations, reg 8(1)*);

(*b*)   the member's consent to this alternative must be obtained (except in limited circumstances; see **6.26**(*c*) above) (*Preservation Regulations, reg 7(2)*); and

(*c*)   the relevant scheme rule must require the trustees to be reasonably satisfied that the total value of the benefits when they become payable is at least equal to the value of the accrued benefits which they replace (*Preservation Regulations, regs 8(4), 11*).

Bought-out benefits

6.28   A scheme may provide for a member's benefits to be appropriately secured or 'bought out' by the purchase of an annuity contract or insurance policy from an insurance company. The benefits provided may be different from those required to constitute short service benefit. If this option is to be exercised the trustees must be reasonably satisfied that the payment made to the insurance company is at least equal to the value of the benefits that have accrued to or in respect of the member under the rules (*Preservation Regulations, regs 9 and 11*).

6.29 *Protection for early leavers*

Generally the consent of the member is required before benefits can be bought out (*Preservation Regulations, reg 7(2)*). However, consent is not required if the insurance policy or annuity contract to be purchased satisfies certain prescribed conditions (set out in the *Preservation Regulations, reg 9(4)*) and:

(*a*)   the scheme is being wound up; or

(*b*)   the member has less than 'five years qualifying service' (as defined in *Social Security Act 1973, Sch 16, para 7* immediately before the coming into force of *Social Security Act 1986, s 10* (changes to preservation requirements)); or

(*c*)   the trustees consider that, in the circumstances, it is reasonable for the benefits to be bought out without member consent (*Preservation Regulations, reg 9(4)(b), (5)*).

In the case of (*b*) and (*c*) above, the following further requirements must be satisfied:

(i)   at least 12 months must have elapsed between the termination of the member's pensionable service and the purchase of the insurance policy or annuity contract;

(ii)   the trustees give the member at least 30 days' written notice of their intention to take out the policy or enter into the annuity contract unless the member exercises the right to a cash equivalent (see **6.45** below); and

(iii) when the trustees actually take out the policy or enter into the annuity contract there must be no outstanding application by the member for a cash equivalent (see **6.45** below) (*Preservation Regulations, reg 9(6)*).

Money purchase benefits

6.29   A scheme may provide money purchase benefits as an alternative to short service benefit. The relevant scheme rule must require the trustees to be reasonably satisfied that the total value of the benefits when they become payable is at least equal to the value of the accrued benefits which they replace (*Preservation Regulations, regs 10, 11*). The member's consent is required if this alternative is to be provided (*Preservation Regulations, reg 7(2)*). In practice, this alternative is not widely used.

The alternatives to short service benefit discussed above may not include a return of contributions except in limited circumstances relating to service completed before 6 April 1975 (*PSA 1993, s 73(5)*).

Revaluation

Background

6.30   *PSA 1993, Part IV, Chapters II* and *III* provide for an element of revaluation to protect members' preserved pensions from the impact of inflation in respect of the period from leaving pensionable service to normal pension age. Effectively, two separate systems of revaluation apply:

(*a*)   guaranteed minimum pensions accrued by reference to contracted-out employment before 6 April 1997 are subject to revaluation under *Part IV, Chapter III* (this is summarised in **Chapter 4**);

(*b*)   revaluation of other benefits is as set out in *PSA 1993, Part IV, Chapter II* and *Sch 3*. It is these provisions which are summarised in **6.31** to **6.42** below.

General application of the revaluation requirements

6.31   Under *PSA 1993, s 83(1)(a)* the revaluation requirements of *Chapter II* apply where benefits are payable to or in respect of a member of an occupational pension scheme and:

(*a*)   his pensionable service ends on or after 1 January 1986;

(*b*)   when his pensionable service ends, he has accrued rights to benefits under the scheme;

(*c*)   there is a period from his date of leaving to his normal pension age of at least a year (see **6.23** above for meaning of 'normal pension age'); and

(*d*)   in the case of benefits payable to any other person in respect of the member, the member dies after normal pension age.

However, revaluation is not required to be applied in respect of any pension or other benefit (*PSA 1993, s 85; Preservation Regulations, regs 8–10; Pension Sharing (Pensions Credit Benefit) Regulations 2000 (SI 2000/1054), regs 7–9*) provided in accordance with the alternatives to short service benefit (*PSA 1993, s 73(2)(b)*) or pension credit benefit (*PSA 1993, s 101D(2)*).

For the purposes of the revaluation requirements, where 'normal pension age' is before the age of 60, it is taken to mean the age at which short service benefit is made payable under the scheme rules (see **6.23** above) (*Occupational Pensions Schemes (Revaluation) Regulations 1991 (SI 1991/168), reg 3*). 'Normal pension age' also has a different meaning for members of those public service pension schemes which are subject to the *Public Service Pensions Act 2013*.

Determining which method of revaluation applies

6.32   There are five methods of revaluation:

(*a*)   the 'average salary method';

(*b*)   the 'flat rate method';

(*c*)   the 'money purchase method';

(*d*)   the 'cash balance method'; and

(*e*)   the 'final salary method' (*PSA 1993, s 84* and *Sch 3* as amended).

The first step in revaluing a particular benefit is to decide which method is to apply. If none of methods (*a*) to (*d*) above apply, then the trustees must use the final salary method.

The average salary method

6.33   The average salary method applies where the benefit is an average salary benefit (ie one whose rate or amount is calculated by reference to a member's average salary over the period of service on which the benefit is based, such as a career average scheme) and the trustees consider it appropriate to use the average salary method (*PSA 1993, s 84(2)*).

The average salary method itself is set out in *PSA 1993, Sch 3, para 3*.

The flat rate method

6.34   The flat rate method applies where the benefit is a flat rate benefit (ie one whose rate or amount is calculated by reference solely to the member's length of service) and the trustees consider it appropriate to use the flat rate method (*PSA 1993, s 84(2)*).

The flat rate method will rarely apply in practice. The method itself is set out in *PSA 1993, Sch 3, para 4*.

The money purchase method

6.35   Where the benefit is a money purchase benefit, the money purchase method must be used.

The money purchase method is set out in *PSA 1993, Sch 3, para 5*. Effectively, the money purchase method requires the trustees to apply investment yield and bonuses arising from contributions paid by and on behalf of the member towards the provision of benefits, in the same way which would have applied had the member not left pensionable service.

The cash balance method

6.36   The cash balance method was introduced with effect from 24 July 2014 by the *Pensions Act 2011 (Transitional, Consequential and Supplementary Provisions) Regulations 2014 (2014/1711)* as a consequence of the amendment to the definition of 'money purchase benefits' in *PSA 1993, ss 181* and *181B* by *PA 2011* (see **Chapter 1**). The cash balance method is set out in *PSA 1993, Sch 3, para 3A*.

The cash balance method can only be used where benefits are not calculated by reference to final salary. Cash balance benefits accrued before 24 July 2014 can, if the trustees think appropriate, and if they have been treated as money purchase benefits prior to 24 July 2014, be revalued instead using the money purchase method. Trustees can choose, if they think appropriate, to apply the cash balance method in relation benefits accrued by reference to periods of service both before and after 24 July 2014 (*PSA 1993, s 84(3A)* and *(3B)*).

The final salary method

6.37   In all other cases, the final salary method applies. This is described in **6.38** to **6.42** below (*PSA 1993, s 84(1)*).

The final salary method

General

6.38   The final salary method is set out in *PSA 1993, Sch 3, paras 1, 2*. This method introduces the concept widely known as limited price indexation or 'LPI'. The effect of applying LPI to a benefit is to increase it in line with cost of living increases over a given period, subject to a maximum of 5 per cent or 2.5 per cent per annum, depending on when the member left pensionable service and whether the scheme has or is able to take advantage of the lower revaluation cap introduced by *PA 2008* (see **6.42** below). Precisely how LPI applies in this context is dealt with in the following paragraphs.

The 'revaluation percentage'

6.39   *PSA 1993, Sch 3, para 2* requires the Secretary of State to specify by order, in each calendar year, a 'higher revaluation percentage' and a 'lower revaluation percentage' for each period which is a 'revaluation period' in relation to that order.

A 'revaluation period' is a period which:

(*a*)   begins with 1 January 1986 or with an anniversary of that date falling before the making of the order; and

(*b*)   ends with the next day after the making of the order which is 31 December.

The 'higher revaluation percentage' in relation to a given revaluation period is the lesser of:

(*a*)   the percentage which appears to the Secretary of State to be the percentage increase in the general level of prices in Great Britain during that revaluation period; and

(*b*)   5 per cent per annum.

The 'lower revaluation percentage' in relation to a given revaluation period is the lesser of:

(*a*)   the percentage which appears to the Secretary of State to be the percentage increase in the general level of prices in Great Britain during that revaluation period; and

(*b*)   2.5 per cent compound per annum.

Calculating the appropriate revaluation percentage

6.40   The 'appropriate higher revaluation percentage' is the higher revaluation percentage (see **6.39** above) specified in the last calendar year before the date on which the member reaches normal pension age for a period of the same length as the number of complete years from the member's leaving pensionable service to his reaching normal pension age. Conversely, the 'appropriate lower revaluation percentage' is the lower revaluation percentage (see **6.39** above) specified in the last calendar year before the date on which the member reaches normal pension age for a period of the same length as the number of complete years from the member's leaving pensionable service to his reaching normal pension age (*PSA 1993, Sch 3, para 2(7)*).

Applying the appropriate revaluation percentage

6.41   The final salary method of revaluation is to add to the amount that would otherwise be payable, an amount equal to the whole or part of the appropriate revaluation percentage (see **6.40** above) of the benefit which has accrued on the date when pensionable service ends (*PSA 1993, Sch 3, para 1*).

Where pensionable service ends on or after 1 January 1991 or all pensionable service falls on or after 1 January 1985 the whole amount is added (*PSA 1993, Sch 3, para 1(1)(a)*). In any other case, a proportionate amount is added. The proportion is calculated by reference to the proportion which the member's post-31 December 1984 pensionable service bears to his total pensionable service (*PSA 1993, Sch 3, para 1(1)(b)*).

The higher revaluation percentage will apply to benefits accrued in relation to service prior to 6 April 2009 and may continue to apply after that date unless the scheme provisions allow the lower revaluation percentage introduced by *PA 2008* to be used (see **6.42** below).

Guaranteed minimum pensions are excluded from the benefit for the purpose of this calculation. These are revalued separately (see **Chapter 4**).

Revaluation in accordance with PA 2008

6.42   *PA 2008, s 101* introduced the lower revaluation percentage, meaning that the cap on LPI revaluation may be reduced from 5 per cent to 2.5 per cent with effect from 6 April 2009. The lower cap can only apply to benefits accrued in respect of pensionable service on or after 6 April 2009 (*PA 2008, s 101(2)* and *Sch 2, Part 1*).

The lower rate of revaluation is not obligatory. Schemes may continue (if the rules permit) providing revaluation by reference to LPI capped at 5 per cent. Depending on how the scheme's rules are written, it may well be that the new lower cap will apply automatically or that the old cap will continue to apply unless specific amendment is made.

Where the scheme's rules incorporate the revaluation requirements by reference to the applicable statutory requirements, the lower cap of 2.5 per cent on LPI will apply automatically. On the other hand, if the revaluation rule specifically provided for LPI with an express reference to 5 per cent, revaluation would continue at the rate of LPI capped at 5 per cent unless and until action was taken to change it.

The table below summarises the statutory revaluation requirements applying to different periods of service.

Date of leaving service	Period of accrual	Statutory revaluation
Before 1 January 1986	Any	None
1 January 1986 to 31 December 1990	Some before 1 January 1985, some after	5% LPI on accrual from 1 January 1985
1 January 1986 to 31 December 1990	On or after 1 January 1985	5% LPI
1 January 1991 to 5 April 2009	Any	5% LPI
On or after 6 April 2009	Any	5% LPI on pre-6 April 2009 accrual 2.5% LPI on post-5 April 2009 accrual

The move to CPI for revaluation

6.43   Since 1 January 2011, the Government has used the Consumer Price Index (CPI) rather than the Retail Prices Index (RPI) for the purposes of statutory revaluation (LPI for statutory revaluation purposes now being CPI capped at 5 per cent or 2.5 per cent as appropriate (as prescribed in the *Occupational Pensions (Revaluation) Order 2010 (SI 2010/2861)* and subsequent annual orders)).

The *Pensions Act 2011* amended *PSA, s 84* to remove the reference to the Retail Prices Index in *s 84* and refer in *s 84(5)* to 'the rise in the general level of prices in Great Britain' (ie CPI) with effect from 3 January 2012.

The extent to which the change from RPI to CPI affects the revaluation of deferred benefit entitlements in a defined benefits occupational pension scheme depends on the wording of that scheme's revaluation provisions.

Defined benefit schemes with rules referring to the statutory revaluation requirements or no express reference to revaluation of deferred pensions must revalue deferred pensions by reference to the revaluation orders published annually which now use CPI to calculate the revaluation percentages.

If the defined benefit scheme's rules refer expressly to revaluation on the basis of RPI then deferred pensions will have to be revalued in line with increases in RPI (provided that this is more than CPI). If CPI is greater than RPI, then the deferred pension will have to be revalued in line with CPI (even though this will mean revaluation in excess of that required by the scheme's rules). This however is subject to the precise terms of the rules referring to RPI, which may expressly refer to the trustees and/or the employer or another person (eg the scheme actuary) selecting (or, in the case of the scheme actuary, advising or recommending the use of) a different index for revaluation purposes.

In *QinetiQ Trustees v QinetiQ Holdings Limited [2012] EWHC 570 (CH)* the scheme's provisions referred to RPI or 'any other suitable cost of living index selected by the Trustees'. The High Court held that where the scheme's provisions gave the trustees power to change or select the index, the trustees could exercise that power in relation to periods of accrual both before and after the change, without infringing *PA 1995, s 67*. The High Court also confirmed that revaluation is calculated only once, when the pension commences payment and revaluation is on the basis of the index chosen by the trustees (where they have a choice) as it applies on the date the calculation is undertaken. This decision was approved in *Arcadia Group v Arcadia Group Pension Trust [2014] EWHC 2683 (Ch)* where it was held that a scheme provision providing for RPI or 'or any similar index satisfactory for the purposes of HM Revenue and Customs' allowed the trustees and employer jointly to select CPI as an alternative index.

In contrast, in *Buckinghamshire v Barnado's [2015] EWHC 2200 (Ch)* the High Court held that the trustees did not have the power to switch from RPI to CPI. Very broadly, in this case, the Rules provided for revaluation and indexation by reference to RPI 'or any replacement adopted by the Trustees without prejudicing approval'. The key issue was if this meant RPI or any index that replaces RPI and is adopted by the trustees or RPI or any index which is adopted by the Trustees as a replacement for RPI.

The court held that the scheme's rules only allowed the trustees to adopt a different index once RPI had been 'replaced' and RPI could only be replaced once it has ceased to be published. The fact that RPI is no longer recognised as a national index does not mean it has been 'replaced'. The court also noted that the wording in the *Arcadia* decision mentioned above was materially different because rule in that case did not refer to a replacement index.

In January 2015, a review by the UK Statistics Authority was published. It stated that RPI could not be discontinued at this time but did recommended that the government should work towards the ending of RPI.

Transfer values – introduction

6.44   Occupational pension schemes have always been able to offer a transfer payment as an alternative to providing benefits from the scheme. However, the *Social Security Act 1985* introduced legislation giving early leavers a statutory right to have the 'cash equivalent' of their benefits transferred to another pension arrangement. This statutory right overrides any inconsistent provisions in the scheme's governing documentation (other than those relating to the winding up of the scheme), but this does not prevent a scheme from being more generous.

A scheme-specific approach to the calculation of cash equivalent transfer values, and a shift in the responsibility from the actuary to the trustees for the calculation and verification of cash equivalent transfer values, was introduced with effect from 1 October 2008.

The legislation is now consolidated in *PSA 1993, ss 93–101* (as amended by *PA 1995, ss 152–154, WRPA 1999, s 84, PA 2004, s 319, PA 2007, ss 15, and 27, PA 2008, s 134* and *PA 2015, s 67*) and the *Occupational Pension Schemes (Transfer Values) Regulations 1996 (SI 1996/1847)* (the '*Transfer Regulations*'), as amended, in particular by the *Occupational Pension Schemes (Transfer Values) (Amendment) Regulations 2008 (SI 2008/1050)* (the '*2008 Transfer Regulations*').

The right to a cash equivalent

When does a member acquire a right to a cash equivalent?

6.45   Broadly speaking, before 6 April 1997 a member of an occupational pension scheme acquired a statutory right to a cash equivalent if he terminated pensionable service on or after 1 January 1986 and at least one year before normal pension age (see **6.23** above). The ambit of the legislation was extended by *PA 1995* to include members who terminated pensionable service before 1 January 1986 (*PA 1995, s 152*). However, the legislation does not apply to a member of a salary-related scheme who terminated his membership before 1 January 1986, if all his pension benefits have been revalued by at least the rate of inflation (*Transfer Regulations, reg 2(b)*).

PA 1995 introduced the concept of a 'guaranteed cash equivalent'. As from 6 April 1997, the cash equivalent of the benefits to which a member of a salary-related occupational pension scheme is entitled must be guaranteed for a certain period. A salary-related scheme is a scheme which is not a money purchase scheme or a scheme where the only benefits provided other than money purchase benefits are death benefits (*PSA 1993, s 93(1A)*).

A member of a money purchase occupational pension scheme acquires a right, when his pensionable service terminates, to the cash equivalent of any benefits which have accrued to or in respect of him under the rules of the scheme or any overriding legislation (*PSA 1993, s 94(1)(a)*).

Following the introduction of DC flexibilities (see **Chapters 1** and **17**), the legislation relating to transfer values was amended with effect from 6 April 2015 by *PSA 2015*.

PSA 2015 introduced the concept of 'transferable rights' and three categories of benefits. A member has a separate statutory right to transfer each category of benefit independently (*PSA 1993, s 100A*). A member may have more the one category of benefit in a scheme. The categories of benefit are as follows:

(*a*)   money purchase benefits;

(*b*)   flexible benefits other than money purchase benefits; and

(*c*)   benefits that are not flexible benefits.

A flexible benefit is defined as a money purchase benefit, a cash balance benefit (defined in *PSA 2015, s 75*) or a benefit other than a money purchase or cash balance benefit which is 'calculated by reference to an amount available for the provision of benefits to or in respect of the member (whether the amount so available is calculated by reference to payments made by the member or any other person in respect of the member or any other factor)' (*PSA 2015, s 74*).

A member may have 'transferable rights' in respect of each category of benefits if three conditions are met. The conditions are:

(*a*)   the member has accrued rights to any category of benefits under the scheme;

(*b*)   no crystallisation event has occurred in relation to the member's accrued rights in that category; and

(*c*)   the member has ceased accruing benefits in that category and in the case of benefits that are not flexible benefits, the member stopped accruing those benefits at least one year before his normal pension age ('NPA') (*PSA 93, s 93*).

A crystallisation event occurs in relation to a member's accrued rights to benefit in a category when:

(*a*)   pension payments in respect of any of the benefits have commenced; or

(*b*)   money purchase benefits are designated as available for drawdown.

PSA 2015 also introduced a definition of NPA for the purposes of the transfer value provisions set out in *PSA 1993, Chapter 1, Part 4ZA (PSA 1993, s 100C)*. Broadly, this is the earliest date on which the member is entitled to benefits from the scheme other than on the grounds of ill-health.

Members of unfunded public service defined benefit schemes may not use their CETV to acquire flexible benefits in another scheme (*PSA 1993, s 95(2A)*).

PA 2014 contains provisions (*s 33* and *Schedule 17*) for a system of automatic transfers of benefits in certain circumstances, including where the member's entitlements are worth less than a prescribed amount. These provisions have not yet been brought into force.

Statement of entitlement

6.46 On the application of a member with transferable rights other than money purchase benefits, the trustees must provide a written statement of entitlement, as at a 'guarantee date', of the amount of the cash equivalent in relation to each category of benefit (unless the application related to only one category of benefit) (*Transfer Regulations, reg 6(1)(c)*). This statement is referred to in the legislation as a 'statement of entitlement' (*PSA 1993, s 93A(1)*).

The guarantee date specified in the statement of entitlement must generally be within three months of the date of the member's application. However, this period can be extended (to a period which may not exceed six months) if the trustees are unable to provide the statement of entitlement within the three-month period for reasons beyond their control (*Transfer Regulations, reg 6(1)*). If the scheme is or becomes subject to a freezing order under *PA 2004, s 23*, the guarantee date must be within three months (or, if applicable, up to six months) of the member's application for the statement of entitlement or, if later, within three months of the date on which the direction prohibiting the issue of statements of entitlement no longer applies (*Transfer Regulations, reg 6(1A)*).

The statement of entitlement must be given to the member within ten days (excluding weekends, Christmas Day, New Year's Day and Good Friday) of the guarantee date (*Transfer Regulations, reg 6(2)*).

A member cannot make more than one request for a statement of entitlement within any 12-month period unless the rules of the scheme specifically provide for this or the trustees otherwise allow it (*Transfer Regulations, reg 6(3)*). Any trustee who fails to take all reasonable steps to provide a statement of entitlement to any member who requests it can be fined up to £1,000 in the case of an individual or £10,000 in any other case (*PSA 1993, s 93A(4); Transfer Regulations, reg 20*). See **Appendix I** regarding penalties generally.

The 'appropriate independent advice' requirement

6.47 Where a member has rights to 'safeguarded benefits' trustees must check that the member has received 'appropriate independent advice' before making a transfer payment with a view to requiring 'flexible benefits' under another pension scheme (*PSA 2015, s 48*) and the *Pension Schemes Act 2015 (Transitional Provisions and Appropriate Independent Advice) Regulations 2015 (SI 2015/742)* ('the *Appropriate Independent Advice Regulations*').

Safeguarded benefits are benefits other than money purchase benefits and cash balance benefits (*PSA 2015, s 48(8)*). Flexible benefits are defined in *PSA 2015, s 74* (see **6.45** above). The DWP issued guidance in January 2016 setting out its view on which benefits fall in the safeguarded category. In accordance with the guidance, the following are safeguarded benefits:

- a promised level of income by reference to pensionable service (ie DB/CARE);

- a promised level of income by reference to contributions (some old-style personal pensions have this);

- a promised minimum rate at which the member can convert their fund into income (GAR). It will remain a safeguarded benefit until the GAR expires (which some may do at, eg, age 65). If a plan has multiple GARs with multiple expiry dates then it will remain a safeguarded benefit until all GARs have expired;

- benefits representing or including GMPs and contracted-out benefits accrued between April 1997 and April 2016 which are subject to the reference scheme test; and

- pension review top-up plans (put in place to compensate for personal pension mis-selling).

The following (according to the DWP guidance) may be safeguarded benefits depending on their terms:

- retirement annuity contracts, if they include a minimum income guarantee or conversion rate;

- buy-out policies where an amount of pension income is secured or guaranteed; and

- income guarantees on drawdown plans.

The requirement for advice does not apply where the total value of the member's safeguarded benefits under the scheme is £30,000 or less (*Appropriate Independent Advice Regulations, reg 5*).

Trustees must provide members who have safeguarded rights with information about the requirement for the trustees to check that appropriate independent advice has been received before making a transfer (*Appropriate Independent Advice Regulations, reg 6*). This information must be provided at the point a relevant member makes an initial enquiry about how to transfer his benefits, makes an application for a statement of entitlement or makes a written request for a valuation of his safeguarded benefits; and where a pension credit member makes an application for a transfer of pension credit rights (*reg 8*). Unless the member confirms otherwise, trustees should assume that the purpose of the transfer is to provide flexible benefits under another pension scheme (*reg 6(c)*).

The member must provide the trustees with confirmation that he has taken appropriate independent advice within three months of the day on which the statement of entitlement is provided (*reg 6(b)*). The confirmation must be in the form of a statement in writing from the authorised independent adviser confirming that:

- advice has been provided to the member on the transfer;

- the adviser has permission under *FSMA 2000* to carry on the regulated activity of advising on safeguarded benefits under the *Regulated Activities Order, article 53E*;

- the firm reference number of the business in which the adviser works for the purposes of FCA authorisation; and

- the member's name and the name of the scheme (*Appropriate Independent Advice Regulations, reg 7*).

When the trustees receive confirmation that appropriate independent advice has been taken then they must check that the adviser does have permission under the *Regulated Activities Order, article 53E* (*Appropriate Independent Advice Regulations, reg 11*). The trustees are not required (or entitled) to actually see the advice and there is nothing to prevent the member continuing with the transfer even if the advice did not support it.

Where trustees have been unable to carry out the check required by *PSA 2015, s 48* by reason of factors outside their control, or have carried out the check but not received confirmation that the member had received appropriate independent advice, then the six-month time limit for making the transfer (see **6.59** below) will not apply (*PSA 1993, s 99(2A)*) and the member loses his right to take a cash equivalent on that occasion (see **6.48** below).

The Regulator issued guidance on DB to DC transfers and conversions in April 2015 which considers the issues of appropriate independent advice.

Losing the right to a cash equivalent

6.48   *PSA 1993, s 98* provides that the right to a cash equivalent is lost if:

(*a*)   the member does not make an application to take the cash equivalent within three months beginning with the guarantee date and, if the cash equivalent relates to benefits that are not flexible benefits, by no later than the one year before the member's normal pension age;

(*b*)   the transfer relates to safeguarded rights and the trustees have been unable to carry out the check required by *PSA 2015, s 48* by reason of factors outside their control, or have carried out the check but not received confirmation that the member had received appropriate independent advice; or

(*c*)   the scheme is wound up (ie the completion of the winding up process).

Calculating the cash equivalent from 1 October 2008

6.49   In June 2006, the DWP published a consultation document 'Approaches to the Calculation of Pensions Transfer Values'. Following that consultation, the *2008 Transfer Regulations* came into force on 1 October 2008. The *2008 Transfer Regulations* amend the *Transfer Regulations* by inserting new *regs 7–7E*, removing the former *reg 8*, and adding *Schs 1A* and *1B*.

The *2008 Transfer Regulations* introduce a new minimum transfer value, although trustees have the option to calculate and verify a cash equivalent 'in such manner' as they determine, provided that it is higher than the cash equivalent that would otherwise be calculated under the *Transfer Regulations* (*Transfer Regulations, reg 7E(3)*).

Calculating the initial cash equivalent transfer value

Salary-related benefits

6.50   The trustees must calculate and verify the initial cash equivalent (ICE) in accordance with the requirements of *Transfer Regulations, regs 7, 7A and 7B* (and *7C*, only in relation to cash balance benefits which are not calculated by reference to final salary). The ICE should be the trustees' best estimate of the amount 'at the guarantee date which is required to make provision within the scheme for a member's accrued benefits, options and discretionary benefits' (*Transfer Regulations, reg 7A(2)*).

Only those options which would increase the value of the member's ICE may be taken into account, and the trustees may take account of the proportion of members likely to exercise the various options. The trustees must have regard to any established custom or consent requirements when deciding which discretionary benefits, if any, should be taken into account (*Transfer Regulations, reg 7A(3)*).

The Regulator has published guidance (primarily intended for trustees) on calculating transfer values in defined benefit schemes.

The trustees calculate the ICE on the basis of various assumptions which are chosen with a view to making the best estimate of the ICE. *Transfer Regulations, reg 7B* requires the trustees to determine:

6.51 *Protection for early leavers*

(*a*)   the financial, economic and demographic assumptions used to calculate the initial cash equivalent (after taking actuarial advice on the assumptions from the scheme actuary (ie the actuary appointed in accordance with *PA 1995, s 47(1)(b)*);

(*b*)   when the trustees determine the demographic assumptions, they must have regard to the main characteristics of the scheme members or, if the scheme members are not a large enough group, then the characteristics of a wider population sharing similar characteristics to the members;

(*c*)   the scheme's investment strategy must be taken into account when setting the discount rate unless the scheme is a public service pension scheme for which the Treasury has prepared guidance on calculating the discount rates.

The Regulator in its guidance suggests that the trustees should review the assumptions from time to time (for example, following a scheme valuation) and take account of changes, if any, to the policy on discretionary benefits, the scheme's investment strategy and the impact of external changes, such as increases in longevity.

Pensions Act 2011 (Transitional, Consequential and Supplementary Provisions) Regulations 2014, reg 31 amends the *Transfer Regulations* to include a new category of 'cash balance benefits'. The cash equivalent transfer value for these, where they are not calculated by reference to final salary, is to be calculated as the 'realisable value' which can take into account interest, guarantees, options or customary discretions (*Transfer Regulations, reg 7C*) (see **6.53** below).

Alternative calculation of the initial cash equivalent

6.51   The trustees may choose an alternative manner to calculate and verify the initial cash equivalent. The alternative must result in an amount that is greater than the ICE calculation based on the trustees' best estimate of the cost of providing the same benefits in the scheme *(Transfer Regulations, reg 7E)*.

Reducing the initial cash equivalent – salary-related benefits

6.52   The ICE may be reduced if the trustees have an insufficiency report the insufficiency conditions are met and the guarantee date is at least one year before the member's normal pension age. Also, the trustees may reduce it to reflect reasonable administration costs, but these must be offset by any reasonable administrative savings (*Transfer Regulations, reg 7D, Sch 1A*).

The insufficiency report must be prepared by the scheme actuary in accordance with the detailed requirements of *Transfer Regulations, Sch 1B*.

The insufficiency conditions are described in *Transfer Regulations, Sch 1A, para 3* and, in order to be satisfied, the insufficiency report must show (at the effective date of the report) that the scheme's assets were less than its liabilities, in respect of all of the members and any category of member. The scheme's assets are measured by reference to the market value of those assets, and the liabilities are measured by reference to the ICE value calculated in accordance with the requirements of the *Transfer Regulations* (as varied by *Transfer Regulations, Sch 1B*).

There is no requirement for the trustees to reduce ICEs, and the Regulator has suggested that trustees should not rely on the insufficiency report itself as a reason to reduce. However, trustees need to be cautious about deciding not to reduce ICEs where there is a deficiency report because they could, for example, be criticised for continuing to pay full transfer values if the deficit increased significantly (which could partly be attributable to the payment of full cash equivalents) or the scheme went into winding up. In addition to the insufficiency report, the Regulator suggests that the trustees should take other factors into account, such as:

(*a*)   the level of underfunding in the scheme;

(*b*)   the strength of the employer covenant;

(*c*)   length and structure of any recovery plan;

(*d*)   any contingent assets that might be in place and the form of contingent asset;

(*e*)   any compensation payments from the employer to the scheme when a transfer is paid at an unreduced level.

(Pensions Regulator Guidance, Transfer Values, paras 34–37)

The insufficiency report will include a statement as to the maximum percentage by which a member's ICE may be reduced, known as the deficiency percentage.

Money purchase benefits and cash balance benefits

6.53   The ICE of any money purchase benefits and, from 24 July 2014, any cash balance benefits not calculated by reference to final salary, is the realisable value at the date of the calculation of the member's benefits. The realisable value is calculated by the trustees, in accordance with the scheme rules, and will also include any interest payments which are payable under the scheme's rules (*Transfer Regulations, reg 7C*). Generally, the ICE transfer value available in respect of money purchases benefits will simply be the accumulated value of the contributions made by and in respect of the member plus the investment growth of those contributions.

Taking account of customary discretionary benefits

6.54   As already mentioned (see **6.50** above), the trustees of salary-related occupational pension schemes must take into consideration those discretionary benefits in respect of which there is an established custom for the purposes of calculating a member's ICE.

A common discretionary benefit for which allowance should be made is where early retirement is permitted without actuarial reduction but subject to employer consent. If it would be usual for the employer to consent to any such retirement after, say, age 62, there would be an established custom of granting the additional benefits. The calculation of any cash equivalent should therefore reflect this, unless the trustees determine otherwise.

Reduction of cash equivalents

6.55   It is only possible to reduce the cash equivalent shown in the statement of entitlement for transferable rights in relation to cash balance and salary-related rights. A cash equivalent generally cannot be reduced unless either the scheme begins to be wound up or benefits have been surrendered, commuted or forfeited (see **6.52** above).

A cash equivalent of a member of a salary-related scheme can be recalculated and either increased or reduced, as appropriate, if it transpires that it was not originally calculated in accordance with the statutory requirements (*Transfer Regulations, reg 9*).

Exercising the right to a cash equivalent

Making a relevant application

6.56   The right to a cash equivalent can be exercised at any time after termination of pensionable service; it does not have to be exercised coincident with, for example, the date on which the member leaves service. A member exercises his right to a cash equivalent by making a relevant application, ie an application, in writing, to the trustees requiring them to use the cash equivalent by transferring it to a specified arrangement (*PSA 1993, s 95; Transfer Regulations, reg 12*). The legislation provides that an application is taken to have been made if it is delivered to the trustees personally or sent by post in a registered letter or by recorded delivery (*PSA 1993, s 95(9)*). However, in practice this requirement is often waived.

Broadly speaking, in the case of a registered pension scheme, a member can ask for his cash equivalent to be paid to any other suitable registered arrangement or a qualifying recognised overseas pension scheme ('QROPS') which is able and willing to accept a transfer. However, some restrictions apply, particularly in relation to transfers from unfunded public service defined benefits scheme (*PSA 1993, s 95 (2A)*) (the detail of which is outside the scope of this book) or a contracted-out scheme (see **Chapter 4**) (*PSA 1993, s 95; Transfer Regulations, reg 12*). See also **6.64** below if the trustees suspect that there is a risk of pensions liberation. Generally, a transfer will be used to:

(*a*)   acquire transfer credits under the rules of a registered occupational pension scheme;

(*b*)   acquire rights under the rules of a registered personal pension scheme;

(*c*)   purchase an annuity from an insurance company chosen by the member; or

(*d*)   acquire rights under a QROPS.

The application must specifically identify the receiving arrangement. An application which does not do this will simply be treated as an enquiry (or possibly a request for a statement of entitlement) and not a relevant application.

In the case of a salary-related scheme, a member must make a relevant application within three months of the guarantee date (*PSA 1993, s 95(1A)*). As not more than one request for a statement of entitlement can be made within any 12-month period unless the rules of the scheme specifically provide for this (or the trustees otherwise allow it (see **6.46** above)), a member who fails to make a relevant application within the three-month period could find that he cannot require the trustees to take any action for another nine months.

A member may withdraw an application for a cash equivalent at any time before the trustees are committed to complying with the member's request (*PSA 1993, s 100*). A member could not, therefore, withdraw his application if the trustees have already made a transfer or entered into a binding agreement with a third party, such as an insurance company. A member who withdraws an application is not prevented from making another application at some future date.

'Splitting' a cash equivalent

6.57   A cash equivalent can be 'split' between a number of arrangements. For example, a member can transfer part of his cash equivalent to an occupational pension scheme and part to a personal pension scheme (*PSA 1993, s 96(1)*). This is most commonly done where the transfer is from a formerly contracted-out scheme to a scheme which cannot accept assets representing the member's contracted-out rights (see **Chapter 4**).

Although a cash equivalent can be split between different arrangements, a member must generally take his whole cash equivalent in relation to a category of benefit (see **6.45** above) at one time (*PSA 1993, s 96*). There is one exception to this: where his cash equivalent includes contracted-out rights which the receiving arrangement is unable or unwilling to accept (*PSA 1993, s 96(1) (b), (2)*). This does not prevent a member taking a partial transfer value in other circumstances if the scheme rules allow, but this will be outside the cash equivalent regime and the trustees will not benefit from the statutory discharge (see **6.63** below).

Benefits to be provided by the receiving arrangement

6.58   The benefit which the receiving arrangement provides in respect of a cash equivalent will depend on the rules of that arrangement. A defined benefits scheme may provide a fixed amount of pension, similar to a revalued preserved pension. Alternatively the money may be invested in the same way as a member's additional voluntary contributions, or it may be translated into 'added years'. In the case of a money purchases scheme, a transfer value will usually simply be invested along with other contributions.

The *Transfer Regulations* do not regulate how the receiving arrangement treats the transfer payment. The Regulator has issued Transfer Value Guidance, which sets out a number of principles that the Regulator expects trustees to follow when calculating the transfer credit, and recommends that the trustees should take account of the following principles:

(*a*)   the transfer credit, from the member's perspective, should give fair value for the amount of the transfer payment;

(*b*)   the transfer credit should not prejudice the security of existing members' benefits;

(*c*)   the transfer credit should not require additional funding from the employer unless the employer has agreed to such funding in advance; and

(*d*)   it would be appropriate for the assumptions applied to transfers in to be consistent with the assumptions used for calculating transfers values out of the scheme.

Trustees' duties after member exercises his right

Complying with the member's request

6.59   In the case of a salary-related scheme the trustees must do what is necessary to carry out the member's request within six months of the guarantee date unless *PSA 2015, s 48* applies, the trustees have been unable to check that the member obtained independent financial advice for reasons outside their control, or the trustees have checked but have not had confirmation that the member received appropriate independent financial advice (*PSA 1993, s 99(2A)*) (see **6.47** above).

As the six-month period is from the guarantee date the trustees will have a minimum period of three months and a maximum period of six months in which to make the transfer payment (depending on how quickly the member requests the cash equivalent).

If the application relates to money purchase benefits, the necessary action must be taken within six months of the date on which the trustees received the application.

The Government announced February 2016 that new guidance would be issued by the Regulator on 'speeding up pensions transfers' and that from summer 2016, there would be a new requirement for schemes to report to the Regulator as the speed at which they are processing transfers against possible benchmarks or targets. This had not been introduced as of September 2016.

See **6.64** below if pensions liberation is suspected.

HMRC requirements

6.60   Broadly speaking, in the case of a registered pension scheme, a member can ask for his cash equivalent to be paid to any other suitable registered arrangement or a QROPS which is able and willing to accept a transfer. However some restrictions apply, particularly in relation to transfers from unfunded public service defined benefit schemes or a contracted-out scheme (see **Chapter 4**) (*PSA 1993, s 95; Transfer Regulations, reg 12*).

From 6 April 2006, in addition to the detailed rules governing transfer payments found in the *PSA 1993* and the *Transfer Regulations*, the trustees (in their capacity as scheme administrator) must also have regard to various provisions of the Pensions Tax Manual.

Before making the transfer, the scheme administrator should make sure that the person to whom they are transferring monies is someone with a position of responsibility in the receiving scheme' (*Pension Tax Manual PTM10001C*). In addition, where the receiving scheme is an insured scheme the scheme administrator will be liable to a penalty of up to £3,000 if the transfer payment is not made directly to the scheme administrator or an insurance company issuing policies under the receiving scheme. Only transfers made to other registered schemes or qualifying recognised overseas schemes will be 'recognised transfers', a transfer to any other arrangement will incur a tax penalty. See **Chapter 17**.

Variations and extensions of time limits

6.61   Under *PSA 1993, s 99(4)* and *Transfer Regulations, reg 13*, the Regulator may grant an extension of the time limits for making the transfer payment in certain circumstances, including where:

(*a*)   the scheme is being wound up or is about to be wound up;

(*b*)   the scheme is ceasing to be a contracted-out scheme;

(*c*)   the interests of the members of the scheme generally would be prejudiced if the trustees acted on a member's request within the statutory time limit;

(*d*)   the trustees have not been provided with the information they reasonably require to carry out properly what the member requires;

(*e*)   the guaranteed cash equivalent has been increased or reduced in accordance with *Transfer Regulations, reg 9*; and

(*f*)   the member has disputed the amount of the cash equivalent.

An application for an extension must be made during the period within which the trustees should have complied with the member's request.

The time limits may also be extended where the scheme is or has, within three months of the end of the guarantee period, become subject to a freezing order under *PA 2004, s 23*, which includes a direction that no transfers may be made or if the scheme is a former contracted-out scheme and HMRC have made a direction in relation to the scheme under *PSA 1993, s 53*.

If disciplinary or court proceedings are brought against a member within 12 months of the termination of his pensionable service and there is a likelihood that his benefits may be forfeited as a result, the period within which the trustees are required to comply with the member's request is extended to three months after conclusion of the disciplinary or court proceedings (*PSA 1993, s 99(3)*).

The Government wants pensions transfers speeded up (see **6.59** above). In addition, the Ombudsman has taken a hard line on delays and has found trustees guilty of maladministration for delays in making transfer payments despite them being completed well within the statutory six-month timeframe (*Kodak Pension Plan, PO-12720 and Optimum Internal Pension Plan, PO-3658*).

The appropriate timeframe for a transfer payment will depend on the facts of each case. In another decision the Ombudsman found that it was not maladministration for trustees to breach the statutory time limit (*Travel Automation Systems Retirement Benefits Scheme, PO-5688*).

Consequences of delay

6.62   If the trustees fail to do what is needed to carry out the member's request within the appropriate time frame, and cannot establish grounds for an extension, they must notify the Regulator of the failure to comply. In making their notification to the Regulator the trustees should give an explanation. The Regulator has power to impose a financial penalty (of up to £1,000 in the case of an individual or £10,000 in any other case) if the trustees have failed to take reasonable steps to ensure compliance (*PSA 1993, s 99(7)*; *Transfer Regulations, reg 20*).

A member's cash equivalent must be increased if the trustees delay implementing the member's request for more than six months. If there is a reasonable excuse for the delay, the cash equivalent must be recalculated, and increased as appropriate, as if the date on which the trustees carry out the member's request had been the guarantee date (in the case of a defined benefits scheme) or the date on which the trustees received the member's application for a cash equivalent (in any other case).

If there is no reasonable excuse for the delay, either the cash equivalent must be recalculated as above, or interest must be added to the original cash equivalent at one per cent above base rate if this would produce a greater amount (*Transfer Regulations, reg 10*).

Trustees are also at risk of members being able to successfully complain to the Ombudsman about delay, even if they meet the statutory timeframe (see **6.68** above).

Discharge of trustees

6.63   Once the trustees have done what is needed to carry out the member's request, they are discharged from any obligation to provide benefits to which the cash equivalent relates (*PSA 1993, s 99(1)*).

Pension liberation

6.64   Pension liberation schemes are becoming increasingly common. Typically a member will be invited to transfer his pension rights into a new pension scheme with the promise of being able to take lump sum benefits before normal minimum pension age (sometimes through a complex loan arrangement) or take a higher proportion of benefits as tax-free cash and with the expectation of high investment returns on any remaining assets. The result can be a large tax liability for the member with the remaining assets moved offshore and difficult or impossible to access.

Members who transfer pension benefits to an arrangement which then 'liberates' the transfer payment are potentially liable for tax charges of up to 55 per cent of the value of funds transferred (comprising an unauthorised payments charge of 40 per cent and an unauthorised payments surcharge of 15 per cent).

A major problem for trustees is the tension between the member's right to transfer (whether statutory or under the scheme rules) and their obligations to ensure scheme assets are used for a proper purpose.

In *Pi Consulting (Trustee Services) Ltd v the Pensions Regulator and others [2013] EWHC 3181 (Ch)* the High Court considered whether particular pension liberation schemes fell within the definition of 'occupational pension scheme' in *PSA 1993, s 1* as, if they did not, the Regulator would have no powers to intervene, for example to replace the trustees. It held that the schemes under consideration were, on the facts, occupational pension schemes. This finding was based on a two-pronged test looking at the purpose for which the schemes were established and whether the founders of the schemes employed a relevant person at the point of establishment.

A common device used for pension liberation is the establishment of an occupational pension scheme with a shell employer. Trustees have generally approached requests for transfers to such arrangements with caution and have in some cases refused transfers where the member was not able to evidence earnings with the 'employer' on the basis of the test set out in *Pi Consulting*. This approach has also been supported by the Ombudsman in some of his determinations. The recent decision of the High Court in *Hughes v The Royal London Mutual Insurance Society Ltd [2016] EWHC 319 (Ch)* may make it easier for individuals to insist on transfers to such arrangements.

Miss Hughes requested a transfer to an occupational pension scheme from her personal pension. The employer in relation to the new scheme did not appear to be trading and although Miss Hughes had an agreement to receive remuneration there was no evidence she had actually received any. Miss Hughes appealed from the Ombudsman's determination that she did not have a statutory right to transfer as she was not an 'earner' in a relevant employment for the purposes of the receiving scheme and the provider was correct in refusing to make the payment. The crux of the case was whether 'earner' in this context required Miss Hughes to have earnings from the scheme employer, or merely earnings from any source. On appeal, the High Court held that the legislation does not require the individual to be an 'earner' in relation to an employer under the rules of the receiving pension scheme but merely to be an 'earner' in any context.

Miss Hughes was an 'earner', as she had earnings from another source. This meant that she did have a statutory right to transfer.

Complaints to the Ombudsman have been made where the trustees have delayed or not implemented the member's request for a transfer payment and where members have transferred to a pension liberation arrangement and suffered loss. The Ombudsman clearly puts the onus on scheme trustees to make detailed enquiries of the receiving scheme where they have suspicions that a transfer might be being used for pension liberation. The starting point must always be to establish whether a right to transfer exists and, if it does, the transfer payment must be made. If it is established that no right exists (because the statutory requirements or any alternative requirements under the scheme rules are not met) then the trustees can and should refuse to make the transfer. It is up to the trustees to be satisfied that a right to transfer does not exist, rather than for the member to prove that it does. If the trustees refuse to make a transfer, they should provide a full explanation to the member concerned as to why the right to transfer does not exist in the circumstances.

HMRC and the Regulator, in conjunction with other bodies including TPAS and Action Fraud, have produced a range of material to help trustees identify potential pension liberation and an industry code of good practice was published in March 2015.

HMRC updated its registration procedures with effect from 21 October 2013 in order to reduce the risk of pension liberation. HMRC will undertake a detailed investigation before deciding whether or not to grant a scheme registered status. A 'fit and proper' person test was introduced for new applications to register a pension scheme on and after 1 September 2014. HMRC has power to request documents to enable it to consider if the 'fit and proper person' test is satisfied.

When trustees of transferring schemes ask HMRC to confirm a scheme's status as a registered pension scheme, HMRC will only provide this confirmation if it is satisfied that the scheme is registered at the relevant time and that it does not have any information suggesting that the scheme has been set up for or is being used for pension liberation. If HMRC is not satisfied, then it will, without obtaining the consent of the receiving scheme trustees, inform the transferring scheme trustees that it cannot confirm the registered pension scheme status of the transferring scheme. This puts the trustees on notice that there may be a risk of pension liberation if a transfer is made.

The Regulator published its first pension liberation materials in July 2014 and these were refreshed in March 2016. Trustees are encouraged to provide these materials to members. There is also a checklist for trustees to assist with due diligence when a member makes a transfer request. If trustees are concerned about pension liberation fraud and decide not to comply with the member's request, or delay while they seek further information, then this is potentially a breach of law which should be reported to the Regulator. The Regulator has said that it is for the trustees to decide whether or not to pay the transfer but if the trustees have delayed or refused a transfer value because of concerns about potential pension liberation, then it will be a factor that the Regulator will take into account when considering any regulatory action it may take.

The voluntary code of practice, which sets out 'industry standard due diligence' for trustees, providers and administrators to follow when dealing with pension transfer requests sits beside the existing legal and regulatory framework. The code highlights, but does not resolve, the difficulty for trustees where they believe that a scam is being committed but the member appears to have a legal right to demand the transfer.

The code has three main principles:

(*a*)   trustees should raise awareness of pension scams amongst members and beneficiaries in their scheme;

(*b*)   trustees should have robust, but proportionate, processes for assessing whether a receiving scheme may be operating as part of a pension scam, and for responding to that risk; and

(*c*)   trustees should generally be aware of the known current strategies of perpetrators of pension scams in order to inform their due diligence.

Trustees should conduct proper due diligence when dealing with a transfer request and carefully consider whether the transfer can and should proceed. Appropriate due diligence will vary but the code includes steps trustees should take including sample letters, standard information to request, additional information to consider when the transfer request is to a SIPP, SSAS or QROPS and how to report suspicious cases. It also includes checklists for recording the process and decisions made. The code also sets out some key risk indicators and lists questions plus possible follow-up actions that trustees should ask if they are concerned that there is a risk of pension liberation. It also includes checklists for recording the process and decisions made. If the trustees decide that there is no material risk of pension liberation, the transfer should be processed quickly and efficiently. If, on the other hand, the trustees conclude that there is a material risk, the trustees should check if the member has a legal right to transfer. If the member does have a right to transfer, then the transfer should be made but the trustees should obtain a suitably robust discharge.

The Regulator has certain powers to recover assets where pension liberation has occurred. Where money has been transferred out of a pension scheme on the basis that it would be used in an 'authorised way' and it has not or is not likely to be used in that way, the Regulator may apply to the court for an order of restitution to recover the money, or assets of an equivalent value, from the recipient (*PA 2004, s 19*). An 'authorised way' means, where it is a statutory transfer such as the exercise of the right to take a cash equivalent, a way authorised under the relevant statutory provisions. Where the transfer is made pursuant to the scheme rules or by exercising a statutory right to a transfer value, then an 'authorised way' is as allowed under the scheme rules or in accordance with the relevant statutory provision.

As an alternative to applying to the court for a restitution order, the Regulator has power to take action itself. *PA 2004, s 20* allows the Regulator to make a restraining order over any account which it is satisfied contains money which has been liberated, pending consideration of a repatriation order. *PA 2004, s 21* provides that, where a restraining order is in place and the Regulator is satisfied that the restrained account contains money liberated from a pension scheme, it may direct the person holding the account to pay the money to another pension scheme, towards an annuity or to the scheme member affected.

Transfer incentive exercises

6.65   In recent years employers have been looking to reduce the cost and risk in defined benefit schemes by encouraging members (or particular groups of members) to transfer out. In order to encourage take-up, members have in the past been offered transfer payments in excess of their cash equivalent and often accompanied by a cash incentive.

Government concern that individuals were giving up valuable defined benefit rights for much less certain personal pensions without being fully aware of the possible consequences led to the introduction in June 2012 of an industry voluntary code of practice on incentive exercises (the 'code'). The code also covers modifications to benefits, including pension increase exchanges which are dealt with in **Chapter 13**. A revised code was published February 2016. If the code is not complied with on a voluntary basis then legislation may follow and *PA 2014, s 34* contains a power to introduce regulations which would prohibit incentive exercises. This power came into force on 14 July 2014 and if no regulations are made under this provision before 14 July 2021 it will be repealed.

The key objectives of the code are to enable members to make informed decisions by making sure incentive exercises are:

(*a*)   carried out fairly and transparently;

(*b*)   communicated in a balanced way and in terms that members can understand;

(*c*)   available with appropriate financial advice (or in some limited circumstances, financial guidance) that is paid for by the party initiating the exercise (typically the employer);

(*d*)   able to achieve high levels of member engagement; and

(*e*)   provided with access to an independent complaints and compensation process.

The first principle of the code is that no cash incentive should be offered which is contingent on the member's decision to accept the offer. Employers may offer a modest incentive to the member (for example a shopping voucher) in return for engaging in the process, but it must not be dependent on the member deciding to transfer.

A key principle of the code is that the employer should provide each member faced with a transfer offer with impartial financial advice and that the member should be required to take advice before the offer can be accepted. The adviser should be suitably qualified and experienced and comply with FSA requirements and his qualifications and experience should be disclosed to the member. The employer should pay for the advice and the adviser's remuneration must not be related to take-up rates or involve commission. The advice should be tailored to the individual and his circumstances and should include at least one face-to-face or telephone meeting and result in a written, tailored recommendation to each member that is in his best interests.

Other principles of the code include fair, clear, unbiased and straightforward communications with members. Exercises should allow sufficient time for members to reflect on the issues and all parties must be aware of their roles and responsibilities and act in good faith.

The revised code applies in any case where an offer is made to a member after the date of publication (1 February 2016) and it included new boundary guidance with examples of when the code does and does not apply in certain situations.

The code sets out industry good practice and is relevant in situations where there is an invitation or inducement (usually initiated by the employer) to a member to change the form of their accrued DB pension rights where:

(*a*)   one objective is to reduce cost or risk to the scheme; and

(*b*)   the offer is not ordinarily available to members of the scheme (ie not business as usual (BAU)).

The code splits incentive exercises into two broad categories:

(*a*)   *transfer exercises* (where one of the requirements is for financial advice to be provided and paid for). These include enhanced transfer value exercises, total pension increases exchanges and the conversion of DB benefits into DC; and (*b*)   *modification exercises* (where financial advice must be provided unless certain value criteria are met, in which case guidance may be offered instead). These include full commutation exercises and partial pension increase exchanges.

There is a proportionality threshold which removes the requirement to provide advice (although guidance should still be made available). This applies to transfers or commutations of £10,000 or less or modification of a pension of £500 per annum or less.

The boundary guidance looks at the BAU threshold in various circumstances. This will determine whether the code applies at all. For an exercise to fall outside the scope of the code on the basis it was BAU, it should include the following features:

(*a*)   not time limited;

(*b*)   the same options, on consistent terms, being offered as is usual for the scheme;

(*c*)   the same access to, and level of payment for financial advice, being offered as is usual for the scheme;

(*d*)   consistent communications in style, content, balance etc. to those usually published; and

(*e*)   communications coming from the same party (or parties) as would be usual for the scheme.

Cash transfer sums

6.66   Employees leaving service on or after 6 April 2006 before normal retirement age with at least three months' pensionable service and linked qualifying service but no vested rights (usually less than two years' pensionable service) may choose a 'cash transfer sum' as an alternative to a refund of their contributions. The provisions were introduced by *PA 2004, s 264*, which inserted new *ss 101AA–101AI* into *PSA 1993*.

The cash transfer sum is defined in *PSA 1993, s 101AB* as being the cash equivalent value of the benefits that would have accrued for the member had there not been a rule requiring a minimum period of service before vesting of those rights. The *Occupational Pension Schemes (Early Leavers: Cash Transfer Sums and Contribution Refunds) Regulations 2006 (SI 2006/33)* (the '*Early Leaver Regulations*') provide for the cash equivalent to be reduced in certain circumstances including scheme underfunding based on an insufficiency report (see **6.52** above).

If the member wishes to exercise his right to a cash transfer sum, he must, by the reply date, make a written application to the trustees (*PSA 1993, s 101AD*). The reply date is not fixed in *PSA 1993* and trustees have a discretion to accept a response from the member after the reply date. The Regulator's *Code of Practice No 4, Early leavers – reasonable periods* suggests that three months is a reasonable period. A member loses his right to a cash transfer sum if he does not exercise his rights on or before the reply date or the scheme is wound up.

A member may use a cash transfer sum to acquire rights under another occupational pension scheme or a personal pension scheme or for purchasing one or more appropriate annuities (*PSA 1993, s 101AE*).

PSA 1993, s 101AC requires trustees to provide relevant departing members with information regarding the nature and amount of the rights acquired and details of what he must do to exercise those rights. *Early Leaver Regulations, reg 7* requires other information to be given to relevant members including the details and reasons for any reduction, details of any tax liability and the possibility of any reduction if the scheme were to commence winding up before payment is made.

The Regulator's Code of Practice includes suggested time limits for the various stages of the process:

(*a*)   the trustees should notify a member of his rights as soon as reasonably possible, normally within three months of leaving pensionable service;

(*b*)   the member should usually be given at least three months from the date the statement is given to him in which to make his election;

(*c*)   the trustees should complete the transfer or refund without unjustifiable delay and usually within three months of receiving the election.

Calculating the cash transfer sum

Salary-related schemes

6.67   The trustees must calculate and verify the initial cash transfer sum in accordance with *Early Leaver Regulations, regs 2A* and *2B* or, alternatively, in accordance with *reg 2D*, which reflect the provisions contained in the *Transfer Regulations* (see **6.50** above). The *Early Leaver Regula*tions are amended with effect from 24 July 2014 to reflect the distinction between salary-related benefits other than cash balance benefits not calculated by reference to final salary and money purchase benefits and cash balance benefits not calculated by reference to final salary as a consequence of the revised definition of 'money purchase benefits'.

The initial cash transfer sum should be the trustees' best estimate of the initial cash transfer sum which is the amount 'required to make provision within the scheme for a member's accrued benefits, options and discretionary benefits' (*Early Leaver Regulations, reg 2A(2)*). Only those options which would increase the value of the member's initial cash transfer sum may be taken into account, and the trustees may take account of the proportion of members likely to exercise the various options. The trustees must have regard to any established custom or consent requirements when deciding which discretionary benefits, if any, should be taken into account (*Early Leaver Regulations, reg 2A(3)*).

Early Leaver Regulations, reg 2B requires the trustees:

(*a*)   to determine the financial, economic and demographic assumptions used to calculate the initial cash equivalent (after taking actuarial advice on the assumptions from the scheme actuary (ie the actuary appointed in accordance with *PA 1995, s 47(1)(b)*);

(*b*)   when determining the demographic assumptions, to have regard to the main characteristics of the scheme members or, if the scheme members are not a large enough group, then the characteristics of a wider population sharing similar characteristics to the members; and

(*c*)   to take into account the scheme's investment strategy when setting the discount rate.

The trustees have the option of choosing an alternative manner of calculating and verifying the initial cash transfer sum. The alternative must result in an amount that is greater than the initial cash transfer sum calculation based on the trustees' best estimate of the cost of providing the same benefits in the scheme (*Early Leaver Regulations, reg 2D*).

The Regulator's guidance on transfer values states that the trustees should use the same basis for calculating initial cash transfer sums as they use for calculating cash equivalents (Pensions Regulator Guidance, Transfer Values, para 53).

Reducing the initial cash transfer sum

6.68   The initial cash transfer sum may be reduced if the trustees have an insufficiency report and the insufficiency conditions are met. Also, the trustees may reduce it to reflect reasonable administration costs but these must be offset by reasonable administrative savings (*Early Leaver Regulations, reg 4(12)*).

The insufficiency conditions and insufficiency report for the purposes of the initial cash transfer sum are the same conditions and the report prepared in accordance with the requirements of the *Transfer Regulations* (see **6.52** above) (*Early Leaver Regulations, regs 1(2), 4(2)*).

6.69   *Protection for early leavers*

The trustees may reduce the initial cash transfer sum by no more than the deficiency percentage (*Early Leaver Regulations, reg 4(3)*).

Money purchase benefits

6.69   The initial cash transfer sum in respect of any money purchase benefits (and cash balance benefits not calculated by reference to final salary) is the realisable value at the date of the calculation of the member's benefits. The realisable value is calculated by the trustees, in accordance with the scheme rules and which also includes any interest payments which are payable under the scheme rules (*Early Leaver Regulations, reg 2C*). Generally, the initial cash transfer sum in respect of money purchases benefits will be the accumulated value of the contributions made by and in respect of the member plus the investment growth of those contributions.

Disclosure requirements

6.70   Active members of any scheme and deferred members of money purchases schemes are entitled to certain information regarding cash equivalents and transfer values (*Transfer Regulations, reg 11, Sch 1*). In particular, a statement of whether or not a cash equivalent or other transfer value is available, or would be available if the member terminated pensionable service, must be provided. Members must also be given information about:

(*a*)   help available from the FCA, the Regulator and TPAS on transfers;

(*b*)   if the scheme is eligible to enter the PPF;

(*c*)   the need to consider taking financial advice before transferring.

(*Transfer Regulations, Sch 1*)

Trustees must also supply the following information as soon as practicable, and in any event within three months of the request being made:

(*a*)   an estimate of the amount of the cash equivalent (calculated on the basis that the member's service terminated or will terminate on a particular date);

(*b*)   details of the accrued rights to which the cash equivalent relates;

(*c*)   details of any additional discretionary benefits that have been taken into account when giving the estimate of the cash equivalent (or any part of it); and

(*d*)   if the initial cash equivalent was reduced in accordance with *Transfer Regulations, Sch 1A*, the fact of the reduction must be disclosed, together with information about why there has been a reduction and the amount of the reduction. The member must also be given an estimate of when an unreduced payment would be available and a statement of his right to obtain further estimates.

A member is only entitled to request this information once in every 12-month period. Similar information must be given in respect of any non-statutory transfer value that may be available to the member (*Transfer Regulations, reg 11*).

When a member is given a statement of entitlement to a guaranteed cash equivalent transfer value, certain additional information must also be given. In particular, the member must be given a statement explaining:

(*a*)   that the member can only request a statement of entitlement once in every 12-month period unless the trustees allow otherwise or the scheme rules permit more frequent requests;

(*b*)   that if the member wishes to exercise his right to take the guaranteed cash equivalent he must submit a written application to that effect within three months of the guarantee date; and

(*c*)   in exceptional circumstances the guaranteed cash equivalent may be reduced and the member will be informed if his cash equivalent is reduced.

Any trustee who fails to take all reasonable steps to comply with these disclosure requirements can be fined up to £1,000 in the case of an individual or £10,000 in any other case (*PSA 1993, s 93A; Transfer Regulations, reg 20*). See **Appendix I** regarding penalties generally and **Appendix II** regarding disclosure.

Chapter 7

Employment issues

Introduction

7.1   Traditionally, lawyers attempted to keep pension schemes and employment issues entirely separate, but the distinction between pension rights deriving from a trust and contractual employment rights has become more blurred.

Pension provision is now an integral part of the total remuneration package offered by employers and can often be a key recruitment and retention issue. Until relatively recently, employers had no statutory obligation to offer its employees access to a pension scheme (except in limited circumstances for ex-public sector employees). Since 2001 there has been a gradual improvement in employees' entitlements.

- From 8 October 2001, employers with five or more employees were required to designate a stakeholder pension scheme which their employees could elect to join, and to arrange for salary deductions to be made and contributions paid directly to the provider on behalf of employees (*Welfare Reform and Pensions Act 1999, s 1* (as amended by *PA 2004*)).

- Since 6 April 2005, on a transfer of a business or a service provision change, within the meaning of the *Transfer of Undertakings (Protection of Employment) Regulations 2006 (SI 2006/246)* ('*TUPE*'), if the transferor operates an occupational pension scheme, the transferee employer must offer membership of the transferee employer's occupational pension scheme or a stakeholder scheme to transferring employees who are either members of or eligible to join the transferor's scheme, and either provide benefits of a specified minimum level or make contributions at the prescribed level. For details, see **7.23** below.

- Most recently, as a result of the introduction of the automatic enrolment pension regime in 2012, all employers will be subject to a requirement to make minimum contributions into a pension scheme on behalf of 'eligible jobholders' who do not opt out (*PA 2008*, as amended by *PA 2011*). The new requirements are being phased in, starting with the largest employers. Broadly speaking, the automatic enrolment regime applies to employees aged between 22 and the state pension age, who reach a certain level of earnings. Employees outside these age bands are able to opt into a scheme and receive employers' contributions if they fall within the qualifying earning bands. More detail on automatic enrolment can be found in **Chapter 14**.

The automatic enrolment regime and some limited protection on business transfers aside, there is currently no minimum or maximum level of benefit that should by law be provided under a pension scheme. For pensionable service prior to 6 April 2016, contracted-out schemes had to provide certain minimum benefits required by statute (see **Chapter 4**); and before 6 April 2006 an exempt approved scheme was not permitted to provide benefits which exceeded HMRC limits, although this was changed by *FA 2004* to a restriction on the amount of tax-advantaged pension saving which may be made in a registered pension scheme (see **Chapter 17**). None of the tax, preservation, revaluation or contracting-out legislation requires the contract of employment to contain any pension rights for the employee as against the employer. The employee's pension rights are primarily against the trustees of the pension scheme alone. However, as of 1 October 2012, jobholders and prospective jobholders benefit from a range of measures that are designed to protect their employment rights under the automatic enrolment regime. Enforcement of these rights is against the employer. In relation to some rights, jobholders can seek redress directly against the employer at the employment tribunal (see **Chapter 14**).

An employee does have specific statutory rights against his or her employer in the areas of discrimination on grounds of age, disability, gender reassignment, marriage and civil partnership, pregnancy and maternity, race, religion or belief, sex and sexual orientation (covered in **Chapter 9**), and also rights to paternity, adoption and parental leave. *Barber v Guardian Royal Exchange [1990] 2 All ER 660* (as subsequently clarified by *Coloroll Pension Trustees Ltd v Russell [1995] All ER (EC) 23*) confirmed that pensions are pay, but only in the context of the equality provisions of *Article 157* of the *Treaty on the Functioning of the European Union* (formerly *Article 119* and then *Article 141* of the *EC Treaty* – see **Chapter 9**), as regards access to pension schemes and the benefits to be provided for men and women. Although pension contributions and benefits were also recognised as pay by the Central Arbitration Committee, this was only in respect of trade union recognition for collective bargaining purposes (*UNIFI v Union Bank of Nigeria plc [2001] IRLR 712*). Neither *Barber* nor *UNIFI* answer the more fundamental question of whether (and if so, to what extent) pensions are an employment right, and neither does *PA 1995*. *PA 2004* does so to a limited extent, in that it includes provisions regarding pension protection on transfer of employment (see **7.23** below).

The automatic enrolment regime prohibits an employer from contracting out of its liabilities or otherwise excluding any of its new duties, except under a settlement agreement or an Acas conciliated agreement but, even then, the exemption is limited to the range of employment protections during the course of recruitment, employment and termination, but not to the basic duty to automatically enrol a jobholder.

What is the employee promised?

Wording of the employment contract

7.2   In many cases the wording of the employment contract is unlikely to be of assistance in analysing pension rights, as it will usually be drafted to comply with statutory minimum requirements. The only contractual right likely to be specified in the contract will be the right to join the scheme.

Under the *Employment Rights Act 1996, s 1 (ERA 1996)*, within two months of the commencement of employment, the employer must provide a written statement of the essential terms of the employment and must include any terms and conditions relating to 'pensions and pension schemes' *(ERA 1996, s 1(4) (d)(iii))*. The information that has to be given is limited to access to a pension scheme, as opposed to the benefits which will be provided if an employee joins the pension scheme. It would be particularly risky for an employer to give express commitments in the employment contract as to the benefits to be provided under a final salary scheme as, until the winding up of a pension scheme and the crystallisation of its liabilities occur, an employer cannot be certain that there will be sufficient funds to meet the pension promise.

Usually the contract will merely state that an employee may join the pension scheme if eligible to do so, subject to the provisions governing the scheme from time to time, as summarised in the scheme booklet. The contract may also reserve to the employer the right to amend or terminate the pension scheme, or alternatively an employer may rely on a reference to the scheme booklet (which should, if properly drafted, contain such a caveat). In most instances, and as clarified by the High Court in *ITN v Ward [1997] PLR 131*, the trust deed will override the booklet in cases of inconsistency. This principle has been confirmed by the Court of Appeal (reversing the High Court judgment) in *Steria Ltd v Hutchison [2006] EWCA Civ 1551* and by the High Court in *Bainbridge v Quarters Trustees Ltd [2008] EWHC 979 (Ch)*.

The contracts of senior executives may contain more specific details about pension benefits provided where these do not follow a standard form, for example because they offer targeted benefits or contributions to individual pension arrangements. The specific wording used will depend on the pension provision offered.

In reality, an employee will obtain clearer information from the trustees of the occupational scheme, pursuant to the trustees' obligations under the disclosure requirements of *PA 1995* and *PA 2004* (for further details see **Chapter 3** and **Appendix II**), than he will from his employer. Basic information about the scheme (*Occupational Pension Schemes (Disclosure of Information) Regulations 2013 (SI 2013/2734), reg 6* (the '*Disclosure Regulations*')) must be provided as a matter of course to each prospective member or, if this is not practicable, within two months of him becoming a member.

Pension scheme documentation

7.3   The explanatory booklet or announcement will usually be designed to comply with the disclosure requirements of *PSA 1993*, *PA 1995*, *PA 2004* and the *Disclosure Regulations*. It will usually state that the scheme is established under a trust and is managed by trustees, that the booklet is explanatory only, and that the employee's rights are set out in the trust deed and rules, which are available for inspection or copies of which are available on application to the trustees. In practice it is uncommon for employees to exercise their rights to inspect the deed.

In addition, a statement will usually be incorporated to the effect that whilst the employer has every intention of continuing the scheme it reserves the right to modify or discontinue it at any time.

The application for membership will usually authorise the employer to deduct any contributions payable by the employee from his remuneration and to remit these contributions to the trustees. This authority (which must be in writing and precede the first deduction) is required under *ERA 1996, s 13* and may be specifically incorporated within the contract of employment or in a separate agreement. It is important to remember this upon the merger of two or more schemes or the transfer of a group of employees into a new scheme. The authority to deduct contributions may be specific to the former scheme and may have to be renewed for the new scheme before any deductions are made. There is an exception to this requirement in relation to deductions made pursuant to automatic enrolment arrangements (*PA 2008, s 33*).

The trust deed and rules will generally establish that an employee who joins the scheme will become entitled to benefits in defined circumstances. The formal documentation will contain a power of amendment, exercisable by the employer with the consent of the trustees, or vice versa, or (less commonly) by one party solely. Rights already accrued may also be expressly protected.

The employer will usually have power to discontinue contributions, following which the scheme will normally be wound up, although the trustees may have power to continue it as a closed scheme (see **Chapter 12** for further details regarding the winding up of pension schemes and the priority order in which scheme assets are to be applied among the various classes of members). The benefits provided on winding up will depend on the liabilities at that date, the value of the assets and the cost of purchasing annuities.

If a defined benefit scheme is underfunded, an employee will be looking to the employer to make good his loss, and *PA 1995, s 75* and the *Occupational Pension Schemes (Employer Debt) Regulations 2005 (SI 2005/678)*, as amended, will apply. If the scheme began to wind up before 6 April 2005 or, unless the scheme is a money purchase scheme, if a debt arose under *PA 1995, s 75* before that date, the *Occupational Pension Schemes (Deficiency on Winding Up etc) Regulations 1996 (SI 1996/3128)* (the *'Deficiency Regulations'*) will instead apply. These two sets of Regulations value benefits on different bases, depending on the date of winding up and the status of the employee; therefore, in certain circumstances, employees will not receive their full entitlement. In addition, the employer's debt under these Regulations is an unsecured debt owed to the trustees from the employer; so, if the employer is insolvent, the employee may receive reduced benefits. However, the employee does have some security on an ongoing basis as a result of the scheme-specific funding regime (see **Chapter 11**) and the statutory priorities on wind up (see **Chapter 12**) and from the Pension Protection Fund ('PPF') (see **Chapter 5**).

For a pension scheme established under trust, the security of the employee's benefits therefore depends on a number of factors including the continued payment of contributions by the employer to ensure sufficient funding and the fund's investment performance. It is in some circumstances difficult to ascertain what the employee's 'rights' against an employer are. His pension entitlement is enforceable against the trustees, who will look to the employer for additional funding, if required. If the scheme is in deficit, the trustees' enforceable rights against the employer are usually statutory, and statute does not guarantee that a full pension (ie as promised under the trust documentation) will be paid.

What are the employer's obligations in relation to the pension scheme?

General

7.4   The employer must comply with the rights and obligations set out in the trust deed and rules governing the scheme. However, these do not cover every eventuality and it is often necessary to look to case law for guidance.

Fiduciary duties – Mettoy and Icarus

7.5   *Mettoy Pension Trustees Ltd v Evans [1990] 1 WLR 1587* acknowledged (although the case did not hinge on this) that an employee's rights under a pension scheme trust are of a commercial and contractual origin;

they derive from the contract of employment, with benefits being earned by virtue of service with the employer under that contract and, where the scheme is contributory, by virtue of those contributions. Employees therefore benefit from an occupational pension scheme by virtue of their employment, which in turn is governed by the employment contract. Similar issues were previously raised in *Kerr v British Leyland (1986) CA, reported [2001] WTLR 1071* and *Mihlenstedt v Barclays Bank International [1989] IRLR 522*, in which the judge stated that the scheme was 'established against the background of such employment and falls to be interpreted against that background'.

In *Mettoy*, the Judge concluded that the power apparently vested in the employer to decide what to do with a surplus on winding up was a fiduciary power (effectively one which had to be exercised in the best interests of the members and putting the employer in the same position as a trustee as regards the duties owed to members).

A similar decision was made in *Icarus (Hertford) v Driscoll [1990] PLR 1*, where the employer remained as trustee of the scheme following its insolvency (this was prior to the legislation requiring an independent trustee to be appointed in such a situation). It is therefore logical that the judge held the employer to be in a fiduciary position, as the employer was the actual, as opposed to a quasi, trustee. There was held to be a fiduciary power which the employer had to exercise in good faith, 'in the sense that he cannot act for reasons which are irrelevant or perverse'.

Employers should, therefore, bear in mind that the powers which they exercise may be those which a court would consider fiduciary in nature and should seek to ensure compliance with the associated duties.

Duty of good faith – the Imperial case

7.6   It is well established that under the contract of employment there exist reciprocal duties of good faith, trust and confidence on the part of both employers and employees. This principle extends to the exercise of the employer's powers and obligations under a pension scheme (*Imperial Group Pension Trust v Imperial Tobacco [1991] 2 All ER 597*). The decision in *Imperial* is an example of the judiciary importing employment law concepts into the pensions arena. It was held that the employer was under an implied obligation of good faith in the exercise of its rights and powers under the pension scheme. The court also established the principle that the trust deed and rules were subject to the implied limitation that any rights or powers of the employer should only be exercised in accordance with the obligation not to seriously undermine the relationship of trust and confidence existing between the employer and the employee. This duty of good faith is not the same as a fiduciary duty (see **7.5** above); the judge (then Sir Nicolas Browne-Wilkinson

V-C) explained that the employer can have regard to its own interests (financial and otherwise) but only to the extent that in doing so it does not breach the obligation of good faith to its employees.

Post-Imperial

7.7 The *Imperial* duty continues to be an extremely important legal principle, in both High Court cases and in the Ombudsman's jurisdiction. For example in *Hillsdown Holdings plc v Pensions Ombudsman [1997] 1 All ER 862* Knox J found that the employer had been in breach of the duty of good faith by threatening to suspend contributions and flood an overfunded scheme with new entrants if the trustees did not agree to merger proposals put forward by the employer. In *National Grid* the Ombudsman determined that the power vested in an employer to distribute surplus had to be exercised in good faith and that, as the power was vested solely in the employer, the obligation approached a fiduciary duty, calling for the power to be exercised in the best interests of the scheme as a whole, without preferring the employer's interests. Given the financial significance of the Ombudsman's determination, National Grid appealed the decision. The appeal (*[1997] PLR 157*) was heard by the High Court simultaneously with a summons taken out by National Power, upon whom the *National Grid* determination would have impacted. Part of the appeal hinged on the Ombudsman's view that the duty to distribute surplus approached a fiduciary duty. Walker J concluded that there is an essential distinction between the duty of good faith and a fiduciary duty, being the right of the employer to look at its own interests. He stated that the Ombudsman had 'lost sight of that essential distinction', and felt that if the *Imperial* case had been heard before the *Mettoy* case, the judge in *Mettoy* could have come to a different conclusion. Although the duty of good faith may have aspects in common with a fiduciary duty, Walker J saw no reason to blend them together; he concluded that as no evidence had been put before the Ombudsman to suggest that National Grid was in breach of its duty of good faith, the Ombudsman had therefore erred in law. The Ombudsman's directions were consequently set aside by the High Court, but this decision was reversed by the Court of Appeal judgment (*[1999] PLR 37*) which, in turn, was reversed in the House of Lords in favour of the employers. However, these appeals were not concerned with the distinction between the duty of good faith and fiduciary duties, so the judgment of Walker J in that regard still stands.

Later decisions emphasise the limits of the *Imperial* principle. In *University of Nottingham v Eyett [1999] 2 All ER 437* an employer was not obliged to warn an employee that he had not chosen the most advantageous course of action. In *Outram v Academy Plastics [2000] IRLR 499*, the Court of Appeal struck out a claim that an employer owed a duty of care to an employee who had resigned after 20 years' service and later re-joined the employer to advise him that it would have been beneficial to rejoin the pension scheme. Employers, it was held, do not owe a duty of care to advise scheme members faced with choices about pension matters, nor do they owe a wider duty in tort than in contract. If, however, an employer voluntarily undertakes to provide such advice, an implied duty not to give inaccurate, negligent or misleading advice may apply. *Outram* was cited in *Wirral Metropolitan Borough Council v Evans and another [2001] OPLR 73* and the judgment was followed. It was held that there was no duty on the administrators to give advice to Mr Evans which might have prevented him from transferring his pension benefits to the scheme on unfavourable terms.

In *Crossley v Faithful & Gould Holdings Limited [2004] EWCA Civ 293, [2004] 4 All ER 447,* Dyson LJ, presiding, usefully analysed previous cases and concluded in paragraph 44 of the judgment that:

'The employer is not required to have regard to the employee's financial circumstances when he takes lawful business decisions which may affect the employee's economic welfare. There is no reason to suppose that he will even be aware of the details of those circumstances. Nor is it the function of the employer to act as his employee's financial adviser, that is simply not part of the bargain that is comprised in the contract of employment. There are no obvious policy reasons to impose on an employer the general duty to protect his employee's economic wellbeing. The employee can obtain his own advice, whether from his union or otherwise.'

Nevertheless, if an employer assumes the responsibility for giving financial advice to its employee, it is under a duty to take reasonable care in the giving of that advice. This principle was confirmed in *Lennon v Metropolitan Police Commissioner [2004] EWCA Civ 130, [2004] 2 All ER 266,* and cited in the *Crossley* case.

The High Court decision in *Prudential Staff Pensions Ltd v The Prudential Assurance Company Ltd & Ors [2011] EWHC 960 (Ch)* looked again at the employer's duty of good faith in relation to the exercise of a discretionary power to grant pension increases. In the context of a long history of awarding inflation-linked pensions increases for pre-1997 benefits, the beneficiaries argued that the Prudential breached its duty of good faith both in adopting a 2.5 per cent LPI cap and in the manner in which it applied the new policy.

Mr Justice Newey did not make any new statements of law in respect of an employer's duty of 'good faith' but merely relied upon the classic statement of good faith from the *Imperial* case:

'The employers will not, without reasonable and proper cause, conduct themselves in a manner calculated or likely to destroy or seriously damage the relationship of confidence and trust between employer and employee. [This obligation] applies as much to the exercise of his rights and powers under a pension scheme as they do to the other rights and powers of an employer ... the relevant question is not whether the company is acting reasonably ... It must be open to the company to look after its own interests, financially and otherwise, in the future operations of the scheme in deciding whether or not to give its consent.'

Newey J then went on to consider other pensions and employment cases dealing with good faith (including *Stannard v Fisons*, *National Grid*, *Hillsdown*, *Air Jamaica*, *Malik v BCCI*, *Johnson v Unisys* and *Clark v Nomura*). He concluded that the power to exercise the discretion to award pension increases was not fiduciary – this means that Prudential was entitled to have regard to its own interests. The question for the Court to consider was whether, overall, the decision was irrational or perverse. A breach of the obligation of trust and confidence required conduct of 'some seriousness' – an irrational decision on a trivial matter might not be enough to involve the breach of the obligation. Further, the manner in which a decision is communicated to members cannot affect its validity. He confirmed that the question of breach of good faith has to be approached on an objective basis and concluded that the decision made in 2005 to move to capped pension increases did not breach an obligation of good faith. One point dealt with was whether the 'very strong expectations of members' made Prudential's decision irrational. The conclusion was that they did not – the rule contained an unfettered discretion.

In the case of *IBM v Dalgleish [2014] EWHC 980 (Ch)*, Warren J considered in some detail the distinction between the contractual duties an employer owes its employees arising under the employment relationship and the duty of good faith required in the exercise of discretionary powers under the pension scheme (the *Imperial* duty). He summarised his findings at para 1507 of the judgment as follows:

'So far as concerns the law, I have addressed the nature of the *Imperial* duty as it applies to the exercise of discretionary powers by an employer and reached the conclusion that the test is one of irrationality and perversity in the sense that no reasonable employer could act in the way that Holdings has acted in the present case. The contractual duty can be expressed differently: an employer must treat his employees fairly in his conduct of his business, and in his treatment of his employees, an employer must act responsibly and in good faith; he must act with due regard to trust and confidence (or fairness): see paragraph 407 above. But as I have explained, to confound a Reasonable Expectation may, on the facts, be something that no reasonable employer would do in the way that is has been done. There may, accordingly, be no significant difference in the application of the two different tests to a particular set of closely related facts.'

He found that IBM had breached these duties by confounding members' 'reasonable expectations', ie expectations generated by the employer's own acts which go beyond 'mere expectations'. See **7.11** below. This case is subject to appeal.

In another recent case, *Bradbury v BBC [2015] EWHC 1368*, the High Court (Warren J) found that the overall conduct of the BBC when it imposed a one per cent cap on increases to pensionable salary did not give rise to a breach of its implied duties. The High Court held that the correct approach is to undertake an objective assessment in relation to the implied term read as a whole:

'... the conduct must be such as, objectively, is calculated or likely to undermine the duty of trust and confidence and must be conduct for which there is, objectively, no reasonable and proper cause.'

The *Bradbury* decision confirms that changes to a defined benefits scheme may legitimately be made without breaching implied contractual duties to employees, so long as the employer carries out such changes in a manner which could not be considered irrational or perverse.

Can an employer contract out of the Imperial duty?

7.8   This issue was considered by the Ombudsman in a determination issued in May 1997 (*Poole v Trustees of the Cytec Industries (UK) Limited, Case reference F00088*). The Interim Trust Deed of the Cytec Scheme contained a provision which stated that 'in exercising any discretion, or power, or giving its agreement or consent under the Plan, an Employer may act in its absolute unfettered discretion and in its sole and exclusive interests'.

The Ombudsman determined that this provision could not operate to nullify the implied obligation of good faith, particularly as it appeared in an agreement made between two parties (the employer and the trustees), to the exclusion of the complainant. Additionally the Ombudsman held that the provision could not be allowed to operate so as to enable the employer to contract out of the Ombudsman's jurisdiction in respect of injustice caused by maladministration. He also commented that the exclusion was unusual and oppressive.

Would the Ombudsman's decision have been different if the offending provision had been printed in the booklet? Probably not, for the reasons set out in **7.18** below.

Termination and reduction of benefits

7.9   Although it is now beyond doubt, following *Barber* and *Coloroll*, that pensions are deferred pay, the question of whether or not the employer has obligations (whether fiduciary or contractual, or arising from the duty of good faith) not to restrict, reduce or terminate the possibility of earning that future pay was not tested in the courts until recently (see **7.11** below). However, in certain circumstances resulting from the particular drafting of scheme documents, such as highlighted in the *Lloyds Bank* case (see **7.10** below) or the engendering 'reasonable expectations' in employees as to what the future would hold for their pension benefits as discussed in *IBM* (see **7.11** below), nothing can be taken for granted. These cases indicate how careful the employer must be in its communications with members and how carefully scheme documents have to be drafted and construed by trustees and employers, as a narrow interpretation is likely to be imposed by a court or the Ombudsman in the event of a dispute.

In ascertaining the crossover between pension and employment rights it is useful to focus on a scenario whereby the employer wishes to alter the level of benefits, either by terminating the pension scheme or by providing less beneficial benefits for future (or past) service. From a pure pensions viewpoint, the employer would have to consider the terms of the power of amendment (which may be jointly vested in the trustees and the employer and may have certain restrictions on how the power can be exercised) and the limitations imposed by *PA 1995, ss 67–67I*. In addition to these aspects, an employer would have to act in accordance with case law, in particular with the *Imperial* duty of good faith, and with the procedural requirements of *PA 2004* as to consultation with employees on the proposal (see **7.12** below). From an employment law perspective, both statutory and contractual issues may arise. See **Chapter 13** for more detail on the use of extrinsic contracts to modify pension rights.

The issues that arise when the employer wishes to terminate the scheme are much the same as those which arise where it wants to reduce future benefits under an on-going scheme, since termination of a scheme may be regarded as the ultimate reduction in future accrual. Different considerations apply where the employer wants to reduce past service benefits.

Reduction of past service benefits

7.10   In many cases the reduction of an employee's past service benefits will be prevented by the scheme's documentation and it is arguably precluded by general trust law principles. In addition, 'accrued rights and entitlements' have been protected (from 6 April 1997) by *PA 1995, s 67–67I*, as amended from 6 April 2006 by *PA 2004*, which replaced the original *s 67* with new *ss 67–67I*; these new sections refer to 'subsisting rights' rather than the original 'accrued rights and entitlements', though the two expressions cover much the same ground. This is considered in more detail in **Chapter 13**.

Section 67 allows rule changes which modify members' subsisting rights, provided certain conditions are met. Protected modifications are those which would or might either convert defined benefit (DB) subsisting rights to defined contribution (DC) rights; or reduce a pension in payment; the written consent of all affected members (and survivors) must be obtained to these major changes.

Detrimental modifications are those which are not protected modifications and which would or might adversely affect any subsisting right of an affected member (or survivor) (ie which would or might alter the nature or extent of the entitlements or rights in a way that would or might result in less generous benefits for the affected member). To effect a detrimental modification, the trustees must obtain the written consent of affected members or obtain a certificate of actuarial equivalence or use a combination of both methods. The trustees must formally approve the modification, no matter who has power to make amendments under the scheme rules. Before giving approval, they must ensure that all the requirements of *s 67* have been satisfied.

The issue of reduction of accrued rights was considered by the High Court in *Lloyds Bank Pension Trust Corporation v Lloyds Bank plc [1996] PLR 263*. In that case the power of amendment was vested jointly in the trustee and the employer, but precluded (*inter alia*) alterations which would in the opinion of the actuary decrease 'the pecuniary benefits secured to or in respect of ... members under the scheme'. The trustee and the employer brought the court application to determine whether the trustee could agree to equalise benefits in accordance with a proposal put forward by the employer. The proposal effectively equalised male benefits up to the female level for the period 17 May 1990 to 30 April 2000 (at a cost of £100 million), but equalised female benefits down to the previous male level for the period 1 May 2000 onwards. The scheme also contained express provisions requiring member consent to any alterations. Although this case turns on its own facts and the peculiarity of the amendment power, the legal reasoning is of interest. The judge considered that, except with the requisite level of member consent, no amendment could be made either affecting accrued rights or future benefits and, accordingly, the court would not endorse the amendment.

The case of *Walker Morris Trustees Ltd v Masterson [2009] EWHC 1955 (Ch)* is a useful reminder about the importance of properly applying the power of amendment. Most of the amendments which the trustees purported to make over a 30-year period were struck down (including *Barber* equalisation) because the trustees had failed to comply with the requirement of the amendment power to obtain a written opinion from the actuary that members' accrued rights would not be substantially prejudiced. The court held that the amendment rule clearly required the trustees always to seek the actuary's opinion, even where there could not possibly be any prejudice to members' benefits; and that *s 67* certificates issued by the actuary did not constitute the required written opinion, as *s 67* certificates are designed for a different purpose.

More recently, in *HR Trustees v German (IMG Pension Plan) [2009] EWHC 2785 (Ch)*, the Court looked at the conversion of the benefits in the scheme from final salary to money purchase in respect of both future and past service. The change was made in the context of a restrictive amendment power which provided that '*no amendment shall have the effect of reducing the value of benefits secured by contributions already made'*. It was held that the restriction on the amendment power required final salary linkage be maintained for the past service benefits so that, although the amending deed was effective to convert such benefits from a final salary entitlement to a money purchase entitlement this was subject to an underpin which preserved the future monetary value of the proportion of final pensionable pay which the member had accrued in respect of service prior to the date of the deed.

For other cases relating generally to the exercise of the amendment power, see **Chapter 13**.

Termination of a scheme or reduction of future accrual

7.11 Arguably, termination of a pension scheme (other than cases of insolvencies, where a winding up would often be automatically triggered) is the real test as to how far an employee has contractual rights against the employer, in addition to the established rights against the trustees under the trust deed and the employee's statutory rights.

As a point of employment law, the key question is whether the employer would be in breach of contract by deliberately discontinuing the scheme, or whether it can rely on the express enabling power to terminate, contained in the trust deed and (generally) referred to in the booklet. In practice, an employer can terminate a pension scheme, provided it acts in accordance with the termination procedures contained in the governing documentation. Employers must, however, act very carefully to minimise the risk of any claims by employees and must have a valid reason for wishing to terminate the pension scheme. The most compelling reason will be that the employer simply cannot continue to operate the scheme because of its cost and open-ended risk (a reason which has become more commonplace due to the additional costs arising as a result of *PA 1995* and then *PA 2004* and increased longevity).

In *IBM* (see **7.7** above), one of the key changes the court was asked to consider was the closure of the DB sections of the IBM schemes to future accrual. The closure to accrual could only be achieved unilaterally by the exercise of an 'exclusion power' which allowed IBM by notice to determine that individuals would cease to be active members. There had been two earlier benefit change exercises and some of the information and statements given to members by IBM during those earlier exercises were relevant to Warren J's findings insofar as they had given rise to members' 'reasonable expectations' as to their future pension benefits. A 'reasonable expectation' was found to be 'an expectation as to what will happen in the future engendered by the employer's own actions, which gives employees a positive reason to believe things will take a certain course'. Warren J found that the exercise of the exclusion power in the manner that it was exercised was within the scope of that power (thus enabling the decision to stop future accrual for DB members in principle) but that IBM was in breach of its *Imperial* duty in ceasing DB accrual in the manner in which it did. He held that it was not something a reasonable employer would have done given his finding that IBM had engendered amongst the members certain 'reasonable expectations' relating to future benefit accrual. The change was inconsistent with those 'reasonable expectations' and this went to the heart of the relationship between IBM and its employees. In Warren J's view, alternative proposals could have been adopted which would have met both IBM's commercial needs and the members' 'reasonable expectations'. The key factor in leading the judge to make findings that IBM had breached its duties was his conclusion that IBM had by its own acts engendered in its employees 'reasonable expectations', in contrast with mere expectations, as to what the future would hold for their pension benefits and then introduced changes which were inconsistent with those expectations. Not every breach of a 'reasonable expectation' will necessarily give rise to a breach of duty – the employee must then go on to show that the confounding of that expectation was sufficiently serious to constitute a breach of the contractual or *Imperial* duty (or both). This case is currently subject to appeal.

One method which has been used by employers wishing to terminate or reduce future benefit accrual is by seeking to terminate all existing contracts of employment (by giving the appropriate notice) and issuing new contracts reflecting the less favourable pension provision. This rather aggressive tactic carries the risk of employees arguing that they have been unfairly dismissed and/or that the unilateral change in their terms of employment constituted a fundamental breach of contract by the employer which would entitle them to resign and claim constructive dismissal. In either case, the employer would have to have a good and substantial reason for wishing to act in this way, the method of implementation would have to be fair. In addition, where more than twenty contracts of employment are terminated in such a manner in the same establishment, within a 90-day period, the employer would also be required to engage in a collective redundancies exercise.

Consultation by employers

7.12 Where the employer proposes to terminate the scheme or make changes to contributions or benefits it may be impracticable to seek the consent of all of the employees who are active scheme members, although this option may sometimes be chosen where the scheme has very few members. A period of consultation with employees or their trade union or employee representatives (with consent to the change being sought where reasonably practicable) is however advisable to demonstrate that the employer had complied with the *Imperial* duty of good faith.

Employment law obligations to provide information to, and consult with, trade unions or employee representatives may arise under *TUPE* in the case of a business transfer (see **7.23** below); under the collective redundancies legislation (*TULRCA*) in the case of large-scale redundancies; or under the *Information and Consultation of Employees Regulations 2004 (SI 2004/3426)* (the '*ICE Regulations*') in the case of other employment matters such as threats to employment, changes to terms and conditions of employment and the economic prospects of the business, but not where the *Pension Consultation Regulations* apply (see below).

The *Occupational and Personal Pension Schemes (Consultation by Employers and Miscellaneous Amendment) Regulations 2006 (SI 2006/349)* (the '*Pension Consultation Regulations*'), made under *PA 2004, ss 259–261*, introduce a statutory requirement for employers to consult with employees in respect of 'listed changes' to occupational and personal pension schemes, including the cessation or reduction of future accrual.

Although the obligation under the *Pension Consultation Regulations* is in addition to any of the other consultation requirements referred to above, the *ICE Regulations*, as amended, provide that employers are not obliged to consult about the same issues twice under the *ICE Regulations* and the *Pension Consultation Regulations*. However, if the proposed diminution of benefits is just one of a range of proposals by the employer, it may also be necessary to consult about those other proposals under the other requirements.

The *Pension Consultation Regulations* require employers to consult with affected active and prospective members of most occupational and personal pension schemes before certain changes may be made to a scheme in relation to future service benefits. The *Pension Consultation Regulations* apply to employers of 50 or more employees (whether or not they are scheme members). Entirely excluded from the pensions consultation requirement are:

- in the case of occupational pension schemes, any employer in relation to:

    – a public service scheme;

    – a 'small scheme';

    – a scheme with fewer than two members;

    – an employer-financed retirement benefits scheme;

    – an unregistered overseas scheme (having its main administration outside the EEA); and

- any employer in relation to a personal pension scheme where direct payment arrangements exist but no employer contributions fall to be paid towards the scheme.

The employer must give specified written information to all affected members and their representatives at least 60 days before the date on which it intends to take any decision (or series of decisions) to make a 'listed change'. The required information includes details of the listed change, its likely effects on the scheme and its members, and the timescale for implementation and it must be accompanied by any relevant background information. The information must be clear and comprehensive enough to enable members' representatives to consider the effect of the proposed change. If there are no existing employee representatives, employers will have to arrange for their appointment or election. If the employees do not appoint or elect representatives, employers will have to consult with all affected employees directly.

Listed changes are set out in *Pension Consultation Regulations, regs 8* and *9*, and include increasing the normal pension age; closing the scheme to new members; preventing or changing future accrual of benefits; changing some or all of the benefits provided under a defined benefit scheme to money purchase benefits; or changing (broadly, to the detriment of the members) the contributions required from members or provided by the employer. A new listed change was introduced with effect from 6 April 2010 by the *Occupational and Personal Pension Schemes (Miscellaneous Amendment) Regulations 2010 (SI 2010/499)* which catches any proposal to change what elements of pay constitute pensionable earnings, or to change the proportion of or limit the amount of any element of pay that forms part of pensionable earnings. This was in response to a number of schemes introducing caps on the level of pay which would in future be pensionable (thus effectively decreasing accrual rates).

Consultation 'in a spirit of co-operation, taking account the interests of both sides' must then take place with at least one of the specified employee representatives. The employer must consider the responses received and, if the listed changes were proposed by a third party (eg the trustees or the principal employer), notify the third party in writing of the responses. The third party must then satisfy itself that consultation was carried out in compliance with the regulations. If no responses are received, the consultation is deemed complete at the end of the consultation period.

The Regulator has power to impose a civil penalty on an employer who has failed, without reasonable excuse, to comply with the consultation requirements (up to £5,000 on an individual and £50,000 on a company).

In *IBM v Dalgleish [2014] EWHC 980 (Ch)* the High Court found that, although IBM had purported to consult under the *Pension Consultation Regulations* in relation to future benefit changes, it had not done so in an open or transparent way and deliberately provided misleading information as to the proposed changes. IBM was found to be in breach of its contractual and *Imperial* duties of good faith (see **7.7** above) in the manner in which it carried out the consultation. The judge rejected IBM's argument that the penalty under the *Pension Consultation Regulations* was the only remedy which could apply where there had been a breach of duty in relation to the consultation requirements.

How do the trustees fit in?

General

7.13 The trustees of a pension scheme have an overriding duty to exercise their powers for a proper purpose and generally in what they consider to be the best interests of the scheme's beneficiaries (see **Chapter 3**). If the power of amendment is vested solely in the employer, the trustees cannot control the outcome, save to ensure that the amendment complies with the requirements of *PA 1995, ss 67–67I* (except perhaps by way of court application in extreme circumstances, which could either be an injunction to prevent an amendment being made or an application for directions). When the power of amendment is vested in the trustees (or the trustees have to consent to the exercise of a power vested in the employer), the trustees must confine their considerations to the implications for the beneficiaries which includes existing active members, deferred members and pensioners, recipients of death benefits and may, in some circumstances, include participating employers. Depending on the particular circumstances, the trustees may also wish to take into account the position of prospective beneficiaries (eg if there was a waiting period before employees could join the scheme).

Whatever action the trustees take will depend very much on the facts of the individual case. This was highlighted in *Re Courage Group Pension Schemes [1987] 1 All ER 528*, where the judge stated that 'it is important to avoid fettering the power to amend the provisions of the scheme, thereby preventing the parties from making those changes which may be required by the exigencies of commercial life'.

The trustees may often find themselves in the position of arbitrators between an employer and employee if a dispute over a pension issue arises. Often trust deeds confer upon the trustees the power to reach decisions on any matter of doubt arising under the scheme documentation. Under *PA 1995, ss 50–50B* (as inserted by *PA 2004, s 273*, as amended by *PA 2007, s 16*), trustees of most occupational pension schemes have to put in place an internal dispute resolution (IDR) procedure, which can be either single-stage, where the decision is made by the trustees, or two-stage, where a dispute may not be referred to the trustees until it has first been considered, and a decision made, by a 'specified person'. The final decision rests with the trustees. The Regulator has issued a Code of Practice on the subject. This requirement for a dispute resolution procedure does not, however, extend to disputes between a member and an employer. For further details of IDR, see **Chapter 3**.

Cases of dismissal or leaving service

7.14   When an employment contract is terminated, the leaving service rules of the scheme will apply and the employee will, if his rights have vested, become a deferred member. The trustees will be obliged, if the ex-employee so requests, to provide details of his options under the trust deed in accordance with the requirements of the *Disclosure Regulations* and the *Preservation Regulations*. If the employee takes no action to exercise an option available to him, he will simply continue to be treated as a deferred member.

Depending on whom the power to augment is vested in, the trustees may have to liaise with an employer on dismissal or redundancy packages (see **7.15** below).

Entitlements in cases of dismissal or redundancy

Redundancy

7.15   If an employee is entitled to a statutory redundancy payment, it will be based upon his age, length of continuous employment and his gross average weekly pay (subject to a week's pay being capped at £479 a week with effect from 6 April 2016). For the purposes of *ERA 1996*, pay means either the remuneration payable under the contract of employment or, alternatively, pay based on the employee's average hourly rate.

The *ERA 1996* definition of 'a week's pay' does not include any element relating to an employer's contributions to a pension scheme. Therefore, an employee's pension entitlement on redundancy will depend upon the wording of the scheme documentation.

Generally, if the employee has been a member for less than three months (less than 30 days for those joining a DC scheme on or after 1 October 2015) he will be entitled to a refund of his contributions (less tax). If he has at least three months', but less than two years', pensionable service, and no vested rights then he will be entitled to either a refund of his contributions (less tax) or a cash transfer sum, which the trustees must pay to another registered pension scheme. Those with two years' pensionable service (or a shorter period of pensionable service but with vested rights) will become deferred members. It is also worth bearing in mind that some schemes, particularly ex-public sector ones, retain beneficial redundancy/early retirement provisions.

Unfair dismissal

7.16 Unfair dismissal is the dismissal of an employee entitled to protection under *ERA 1996* without a potentially fair reason or without following a fair procedure.

If an employment tribunal determines that an employee has been unfairly dismissed an award of compensation will usually be made, comprising: a basic award, based on his weekly pay (subject to the statutory cap mentioned at **7.15** above), age and length of service; and a compensatory award, calculated by reference to loss. Less common remedies include reinstatement or re-engagement. The effect of a reinstatement or re-engagement order is that the previous terms and conditions remain in force so, for pension purposes, the employer and employee will simply have to pay arrears of contributions. This, of course, presupposes that the rules of the scheme allow the employee to re-join.

The maximum basic award for claims where the effective date of termination is on or after 6 April 2015 is £14,250. This amount does not include benefits in kind. Under *ERA 1996, ss 123* and *124*, the compensatory award is such an amount as the employment tribunal considers just and equitable in all the circumstances, having regard to the loss sustained by the complainant, including loss of any pension benefit. The compensatory award is subject to a cap of the lesser of a year's gross pay or £78,335. The tribunal has discretion to reduce any award if it believes that the complainant has caused or contributed to his dismissal or has failed to mitigate his loss by securing suitable alternative employment. An additional award is payable where reinstatement or re-engagement orders have not been complied with. This latter award does not include allowance for loss of pension benefits.

In practice, an employee may suffer loss of pension rights if he fails to find new employment or if his new employer does not operate a pension scheme or operates a less beneficial scheme. Compensation for loss of pension rights is often difficult to quantify. In the majority of employment tribunal cases a starting point for calculation is a 'rough and ready' style of calculation found in guidelines ('Compensation for Loss of Pension Rights – Employment Tribunals'), originally prepared in 1990 by the Government Actuary's Department in consultation with three employment tribunal chairmen (as they were then known) and last updated in 2003. These guidelines are currently under review and in a consultation paper issued on 30 March 2016, the President of the Employment Tribunals proposed abandoning the current guidelines and replacing them with Presidential guidance. The consultation paper proposes that the new Presidential guidance should recommend the following approach:

(*a*)   Identifying simple cases and assessing pension loss on the basis of the employer's contributions over the period of loss. The working group anticipates that this will be the method used in most cases whether the claimants are members of defined contribution or defined benefit schemes.

(*b*)   Identifying complex cases which potentially involve large amounts at an early stage and holding a separate remedy hearing to assess pensions loss in such cases. In most instances the Tribunal would then assess loss on the basis of actuarial tables but, in some, it would consider expert actuarial evidence, ideally from a jointly instructed expert.

As this new guidance is in the consultation stage and has not yet been finalised, tribunals continue to use the current guidelines 'Compensation for Loss of Pension Rights' – Employment Tribunals, as summarised below.

In summary, using the 'simplified approach', the current guidelines require a loss to be viewed in three stages, namely:

(*a*)   between the date of the dismissal and the date of the hearing (being the actual loss sustained, for example, the difference between an old and a new employer's benefit provision or, if the complainant is unemployed, between the scheme benefits and State scheme benefits);

(*b*)   the loss of future pension rights to the date of retirement (which is essentially speculation on the part of the employment tribunal – it may even conclude that the employee's future earnings and benefits will never match his old package, thus the loss may continue over the remainder of his working life); and

(*c*)   the enhancement of accrued pension rights.

The guidance also explains how tribunals should reach a just and equitable sum for compensation and breaks down the calculation into three areas:

(i)   when attempting to calculate the loss of rights which would have accrued between the date of dismissal and the hearing, reference should be made to the contributions which the employer would have made during that period (although the report admits that this method is not technically correct);

(ii)   for the calculation of loss of future pension rights between the date of the hearing and the date of retirement, the employment tribunal should estimate how long it will take for the applicant to enter equivalent employment;

(iii)   when calculating the loss of enhancement of the pension rights accrued to the date of dismissal, no enhancement should be granted where the applicant is in any public sector scheme, where he is within five years of retirement or where the employment would have been terminated within one year. Otherwise a multiple (as set out in the report) will be used and the employment tribunal may also, at its discretion, apply a withdrawal factor, based on the likelihood of the complainant leaving service, being made redundant or fairly dismissed.

The guidance (*see paragraphs 4.13* and *4.14*) recommends the use of the 'substantial loss' approach where it is generally considered that the employee will suffer a quantifiable continuing loss in circumstances where: the employment had lasted a considerable period of time prior to termination; the employment was stable and unlikely to have been affected by economic cycle; and the employee had reached an age where he was less likely to seek new employment. This was confirmed by the Employment Appeals Tribunal (EAT) in *Sibbit v St Cuthbert's Catholic Primary School EAT0070/10/2005*.

The substantial loss approach involves using actuarial tables to assess the capitalised value of the pension rights which the employee would have accrued up to retirement. These tables use factors similar to those in the Ogden Tables for personal injury and fatal accident cases, although some of the assumptions used are different. Calculation under the substantial loss approach automatically includes compensation for loss of enhancement of accrued pension rights at the date of dismissal and for loss of pension rights from the date of dismissal to the date of the hearing, as well as for loss of future pension rights from the date of the hearing.

In *Chief Constable of West Midlands Police v Gardner UKEAT/0174/11/DA* the EAT stated that, whilst an employment tribunal is not to be encouraged to adopt a 'pick and mix' approach to calculating pension loss, it may do so provided that it does so for cogent and credible reasons and states what those reasons are. The Employment Tribunal had calculated pension loss on the basis of the approach set out in 'Compensation for Loss of Pension Rights' booklet but using multipliers taken from the Ogden Tables. This was because the Tribunal considered some of the financial assumptions underlying the booklet to be out of date. In coming to its decision, the EAT noted that most of the authorities support the use of the Ogden Tables where to use the booklet would produce an inequitable result. The judgment includes a useful discussion of the various approaches to pension loss and compensation.

Which calculation method is used is a crucial issue, as the different methods can produce different results and make a substantial difference to the amount of compensation awarded in respect of pension losses. Whilst the guidance suggests the ultimate decision as to the method of calculation to be used always rests with the Employment Tribunal. In *Griffin v Plymouth Hospital NHS Trust [2014] EWCA Civ 1240* where the circumstances of the case fell squarely within *paragraphs 4.13* and *4.14* of the guidance, Lord Justice Underhill held that the only conclusion open to the Employment Tribunal was to follow the substantial loss approach.

Loss of earnings may not always be the major component of any compensatory award, particularly where the absolute maximum cap applies. In some cases it will therefore be necessary for pension loss calculations to be precise. In *Clancy v Cannock Chase Technical College [2001] IRLR 331*, the EAT noted that the guidelines to calculating pension loss were drawn up at a time when the compensatory award was set at £10,000. In the EAT's opinion, the significant raising of the cap meant that an accurate calculation of compensation for loss of pensions will be relevant (rather than reliance on the guidelines) in many more cases in the future.

In *Aegon v Roberts [2009] EWCA Civ 932*, the Court of Appeal made it clear that the calculation of compensation should not involve any 'double counting'. Here, the former employee had, unusually, found a new job with a higher salary and membership of a money purchase scheme after she had been made redundant (and the Employment Tribunal had found that this was also an unfair dismissal). However, the EAT awarded her compensation for continuing loss of final salary pension benefits, on the basis that she was unlikely ever to be able to join a final salary scheme in future as so few are open to new members. The Court of Appeal overturned the EAT decision, holding that pension benefits were just one part of the remuneration package; the EAT should not have separated the issues of earnings and pensions; and the higher salary should offset the less favourable pension.

Wrongful dismissal

7.17   If an employer dismisses an employee without good cause in breach of an obligation to give notice (either statutory or contractual) and the employee suffers loss as a result, it will be liable to pay to that employee damages for wrongful dismissal. The primary remedy is damages, normally equal to loss of earnings and other contractual benefits up to the earliest date upon which the contract could have been lawfully terminated by the employer. The aim of damages is to put the employee in the same position as he would have been in had the contract been performed, although the employee is usually under a duty to mitigate his loss.

It is doubtful that an employer could successfully argue that it should not pay damages by reference to loss of pension rights on the grounds that it could have terminated the scheme at any time in accordance with the trust deed. In practice, most compensation payments will be negotiated between the employer and employee.

For example, if a fixed-term contract was terminated two years before it could lawfully have been terminated, this period will be the starting point for the assessment of loss of pay and other benefits. In the case of a final salary pension, the employee would have been entitled to two years' additional pensionable service, perhaps taking into account an assumed pay rise if provision for this was made in the contract. If pay increases were not provided for in the contract, these will not be taken into account (ie the actual salary at the date of termination will be used), nor will any element of discretionary increases. The following three methods can be used to calculate the loss:

(*a*)   The award of an additional two years' notional pensionable service to the employee under the rules of the scheme, dealing with the award under the augmentation provisions. The trustees would require payment of an additional contribution (generally a lump sum) by the employer to cover this. An actuary would be required to advise on the calculation of this contribution, and, depending on the employee's age, it may not be simply a case of using the general scheme contribution rate as the nearer an employee is to normal retirement date, the more costly this becomes.

(*b*)   The payment of a sum direct to the employee equivalent to the employer contribution rate over the two-year period. This method would not produce an accurate result (effectively younger employees may be over-compensated) and is more appropriate for money purchase arrangements. However, if it is used, it should be subject to grossing up and discounting for early receipt if it is paid directly to the employee.

(*c*)   Loss can also be calculated by reference to the difference in capital value of the benefits accrued to the effective date of dismissal and the capital value of the benefits which would have been accrued up to the end of the notice period. This is the most accurate method and actuarial advice will be required.

In a money purchase arrangement, the compensation will be calculated on the basis of the employer contributions which would have been made in the two-year period and an assumed investment return and (potentially) an allowance for salary increases. Similarly, discounting may apply.

Alternatively, it may be possible for the compensation to be paid as a contribution to the pension scheme. This may be advantageous to the employee, for example, if he is approaching retirement. It will be tax-deductible for the employer as an employer contribution to a registered pension if it is paid wholly and exclusively for the purposes of the trade (see HMRC Business Income Manual). It is likely that most contributions paid for this purpose will satisfy the test, but every case should be examined on its own facts. Care should be taken not to exceed the employee's annual allowance for tax relieved pension accrual (see **Chapter 17**).

It may be worth considering early retirement, to be funded by an additional amount of the damages being paid into the scheme, if the employee is over 55 (see **Chapter 17**). This can be tax-efficient from both an employer and employee viewpoint (although care has to be taken to ensure that the employee does not become liable to tax on the payment into the scheme as a benefit in kind or as a result of the annual allowance being exceeded). However, it may be less attractive if the amount does not compensate for the use of actuarial reduction factors. It would be necessary to involve the pension scheme trustees, as this would be an augmentation of the employee's pension benefits, and either trustee or employer consent to the early retirement is likely to be required. Actuarial advice on the scope of the augmentation will also be required. If the employee is entitled to pension benefits as of right under the trust deed (ie consent is not required) *Hopkins v Norcros [1994] PLR 27* confirmed that pension payments cannot be deducted from a wrongful dismissal award.

Exclusion in deed and rules

7.18   Many trust deeds contain a clause to the effect that an employer has no liability to compensate employees for loss of pension rights on termination of employment. There is some case law which suggests that the *Unfair Contract Terms Act 1977* (*'UCTA 1977'*) applies to contracts of employment (eg *Brigden v American Express Bank Ltd [2000] IRLR 94*) but, for an opposing view, see *Commerzbank v Keen [2007] IRLR 132*. In any event it is unlikely that such a clause will be effective, as either it is not a term of the contract of employment (being contained in the rules of the pension scheme only and not referred to in the employment contract) or, if it is part of the contract, it will fail the test of reasonableness under *UCTA 1977, s 3*.

In addition, *ERA 1996, s 203* provides that, subject to a number of exceptions, any agreement precluding an individual from making an unfair dismissal claim is void. The most important exception to this is where an employee enters into a valid settlement agreement following receipt of independent legal advice. This will be a valid way to 'sign off' the employee's rights, provided that the conditions set out in *ERA 1996, s 203(3)* are met.

Lump sum death-in-service benefits

7.19   Is an employer liable for the payment of a lump sum benefit if an employee dies following a dismissal which is wrongful or unfair? Providing death-in-service benefits can be costly and most insurance policies will lapse when an employee leaves service (although for larger schemes which self-insure, the provisions of the trust deed will apply).

In wrongful dismissal cases the employer would be liable if the employee died during the notice period, although it is likely that the duty to mitigate loss would apply. In certain cases the trustees of a scheme may also be liable, as the Ombudsman ruled in the complaint by *Mrs E Richards* in connection with the Merchant Navy Ratings Pension Fund (May 1999). Consequently, an employee should make his own arrangements (and be compensated for the cost of so doing in his damages award) unless he is uninsurable as a single life (for example, he may be unable to pass a medical). Any action would subsist for the benefit of the estate of the deceased.

The situation is less clear-cut in cases of unfair dismissal and discrimination. In such situations, a tribunal would normally make an award which it considered to be fair and reasonable, but bearing in mind that a wise employee would arrange his own life cover following dismissal. However, in *Fox v British Airways plc EAT/0033/12*, the EAT allowed the dependants of an employee who died a few days after being dismissed to recover the loss of the death in service benefit which would have been paid had he died during the employment. The EAT took the view that where the employee died shortly after dismissal, the loss amounted to the full sum which would have been payable on death, and not merely to the value of the premium required to ensure appropriate level of life assurance cover.

If an employee obtains a reinstatement or re-engagement order his employer should double-check the policy or rules to ensure that life cover continues and that the free cover limit is not breached.

Business reorganisations

Purchase of a company with its own scheme

7.20   If a company purchases the entire issued share capital of another company which is the sole employer in relation to a pension scheme, the employees' pension rights (if any) will not be affected, as the scheme will simply remain in place after the sale.

Purchase of a business

7.21   The situation is different if an employer purchases a business or part of a business, in circumstances where the *Transfer of Undertakings (Protection of Employment) Regulations 2006 (SI 2006/246)* ('*TUPE*') apply. *TUPE* came into force on 6 April 2006, replacing the *Transfer of Undertakings (Protection of Employment) Regulations 1981 (SI 1981/1794)* ('*TUPE 1981*') and was subsequently amended in January 2014. The provisions relating to occupational pensions in *TUPE* and *TUPE 1981* are substantially the same. As a result of the transfer of the business or undertaking (or part), the transferring employees become the employees of the purchasing (transferee) employer. Their employment contracts are not terminated, but are essentially novated to the purchasing employer.

Most rights under occupational pension schemes do not transfer as a result of an exclusion contained in *TUPE 1981, reg 7 (now TUPE, reg 10)*. However, since 6 April 2005, members and prospective members of occupational pension schemes have had some protection for their pension rights when their employment is transferred in circumstances where *TUPE* applies.

Tupe and occupational pension rights

7.22 *TUPE, reg 10* (previously *TUPE 1981, reg 7*) excludes 'so much of a contract of employment or collective agreement as relates to an occupational pension' from the automatic transfer effect of the regulations. *TUPE 1981* was intended to implement the *Acquired Rights Directive (Council Directive 77/187/EEC)* which states that protection will not be granted to supplementary company pension schemes but nevertheless expressly requires Member States to adopt 'the measures necessary' to protect the scheme members. This has been reinforced by an amending *Acquired Rights Directive (Council Directive 2001/23/EC)*, adopted on 12 March 2001, which effectively gives Member States the option of protecting pension rights under national legislation.

There have been a number of cases on the scope of *TUPE 1981*. In January 1992 in the case of *Warrener v Walden Engineering Co Ltd [1992] PLR 1*, the Hull Employment Tribunal was asked to consider employees' pension rights when, following a business sale, the new employer decided to discontinue all pension arrangements. The Tribunal stated that the benefits provided by the scheme had been 'part of the contract of employment' and that if a pension scheme is terminated, an employee has a contractual right to an equivalent scheme, providing benefits no less beneficial, being set up in its place. This case was based on the argument that, as the pension scheme was contracted out of the State earnings-related pension scheme, it was not a supplementary pension scheme for the purposes of the *Acquired Rights Directive,* as implemented in the UK by *TUPE 1981, reg 7*.

In December 1992 came the case of *Perry v Intec Colleges Ltd [1993] PLR 56* in the Bristol Employment Tribunal. The decision in that case was reached on a different interpretation of *TUPE*; the complainant argued that *TUPE 1981* had failed to translate the aims of the *Acquired Rights Directive* into UK law (ie the subsidiary aim to protect employees). After the transfer no pension provision was to be made for the employees. It was held that the complainant was entitled to pension provision at least as beneficial as that which he had received prior to the transfer. It was suggested that, to compensate the employee adequately, the employer should make an equivalent percentage contribution to a personal pension scheme and should also make a lump sum payment to compensate for lost opportunity to enhance accrued pension benefits. In effect, the Tribunal was advocating double recovery.

In June 1993 the EAT overturned the first instance decision in *Warrener* (*Walden Engineering Co Ltd v Warrener [1993] PLR 295*); meaning that an employer does not have to maintain the pension benefits enjoyed by employees prior to a business sale. The EAT stated that a contracted-out scheme is a supplementary scheme (ie supplementary to the basic State scheme) for the purposes of the *Acquired Rights Directive*, as implemented in the UK by *TUPE 1981*, and accordingly, the employer was protected under the *reg 7* exclusion. In January 1996 this approach was sanctioned by the High Court in the case of *Adams & Ors v Lancashire County Council & Ors [1996] IRLR 154*. It was held that *TUPE 1981* required protection to be given to accrued rights only (which are protected as deferred benefits in the transferor employer's scheme by the preservation requirements in *PSA 1993*). On 15 May 1997 the High Court decision was upheld by the Court of Appeal (*[1997] IRLR 436*).

In *Hagen v ICI Chemicals and Polymers Ltd [2001] 64 PBLR*, the High Court held that a transferor had made a negligent misrepresentation when persuading its employees to accept a *TUPE* transfer, when it stated that their pension rights after the transfer would be 'broadly comparable' to their pre-transfer rights. The court held that 'broadly comparable' meant no more than 2 per cent difference whereas, in practice, some claimants would have been 5 per cent worse off. Liability for misrepresentations normally passes from transferor to transferee under *TUPE 1981* (*reg 5(2)(a)*). However, since the misrepresentation related to pension entitlement, and was caught by *reg 7*, liability remained with the transferor only.

One important exception to the exclusion of pension rights from *TUPE* comes under *reg 10(2)* (*TUPE 1981, reg 7(2)*) which attempts to implement *Article 3(3)* of the *Acquired Rights Directive* (now *Article 3(4)* of the *Acquired Rights Directive 2001*). *Article 3(4)* excludes from the automatic transfer provisions 'employees' rights to old-age, invalidity or survivors' benefits under supplementary company or inter-company pension schemes ...'. *TUPE, reg 10* stipulates that contractual provisions relating to occupational pension schemes do not transfer from the transferor to the transferee, except that 'any provisions of an occupational pension scheme which do not relate to benefits for old-age, invalidity or survivors shall be treated as not being part of the scheme'. For many years, it was unclear whether certain benefits provided under occupational pension schemes (for example, enhanced redundancy terms on early retirement, life assurance etc) fall within *reg 10(2)*. This question has been dealt with, to some degree, by the ECJ in *Beckmann v Dynamco Whicheloe Macfarlane Ltd, Case C-164/00, [2002] All ER (EC) 865*. The ECJ ruled that the exceptions contained in *Article 3(4)* of the *Directive* ought to be interpreted narrowly so as to apply only to old age, invalidity or survivor benefits under occupational pension schemes falling due at the end of 'normal working life'. Other benefits, such as early retirement benefits and redundancy payments are excluded. The decision in *Beckmann* was subsequently approved in *Martin and others v South Bank University C 4/01, [2003] PLR 329* and considered further in *Procter & Gamble v SCA [2012] EWHC 1257 (Ch)*. This is dealt with in more detail in **Chapter 15**.

The Government has also made specific provisions regarding transfer of pension rights in the context of public sector transfers (see **Chapter 15**).

Given that *TUPE* derives from the *Acquired Rights Directive 2001*, the impact of the referendum vote for the UK to leave the EU (so-called Brexit) on *TUPE* is as yet unknown. There will be no immediate change.

Pension protection from April 2005

7.23   Following extensive consultation, the Government introduced new pensions provisions which give limited protection to employees where the transferring employer has an occupational pension scheme. The protection extends to both scheme members and those eligible to join (or in a probationary period to become eligible). Under *PA 2004, ss 257* and *258* and the *Transfer of Employment (Pension Protection) Regulations 2005 (SI 2005/649)* (as amended with effect from 6 April 2014), where *TUPE* applies to a transfer, transferee employers must offer transferring employees contributions or benefits as set out in the table below:

TUPE TRANSFERS AND MINIMUM PENSIONS OBLIGATIONS

Transferee scheme is not a money purchase scheme	Transferee scheme is a money purchase or stakeholder scheme
The member must be provided with: • benefits the value of which equals or exceeds six per cent of pensionable pay for each year of employment plus the value of any member contributions – and member contributions are not required to be more than 6 per cent of pensionable pay; or • 'relevant contributions'.	The employer must either: • make 'relevant contributions'; or • where immediately before the date of transfer the transferor had been required to make contributions which produced only money purchase benefits, the transferee must make contributions which are not less than those the transferor was required to make.
Relevant contributions are contributions made by the employer but **only where the member also contributes** at the following rates: • where the member's contributions are less than six per cent of remuneration, not less than the contributions made by the member; • where the member's contributions equal or exceed six per cent of remuneration, not less than six per cent of remuneration.	

(ie the employer must match member contributions of up to 6% of remuneration)

Remuneration for these purposes is gross basic pay (ie basic pay before deductions for tax, NI or pension contributions) and is not necessarily the same as pensionable pay under the scheme rules.

The transferee employer and employee can, however, agree that the above protections will not apply and that different pension arrangements will operate (subject to automatic enrolment). They can do this at any time after the employee becomes employed by the transferee.

Employers should always be cautious in situations where TUPE applies; if inferior pension provision is to be offered following a relevant transfer, providing the employees with alternative compensation may be the safest route and will go some way to forestalling industrial unrest. Transferor employers would be well advised to seek indemnity cover; although the judge in *Adams* confirmed that he did not believe that employees could claim against the transferor employer, this point has not yet been tested.

It is also important to remember that, under *TUPE*, transferors and transferees have onerous information and consultation obligations, and they are usually liable jointly for breach of these obligations. Proposed changes to the pension arrangements of the transferor's employees are likely to be 'measures' for the purposes of *TUPE, reg 13*, and the transferor will be obliged to consult with employee representatives about them. Although the transferor does not have to consult about measures envisaged by the transferee, the transferor is still required to inform employee representatives about the transferee's proposed measures. In practice, once information is provided, representatives will often start a discussion about the transferee's proposed measures (and a representative of the transferee may therefore attend meetings to answer questions). See **7.12** above for details of other information and consultation requirements.

The Court of Appeal in the case of *Whitney v Monster Worldwide Ltd [2011] Pens LR1* allowed employees to enforce their 'original ' pension rights as against the transferee employer. A 'no detriment' pension guarantee, which the transferor made some 18 years before the transfer, was held to amount to a binding commitment which passed on to the transferee under the legal doctrine of novation.

Purchase of a subsidiary participating in its parent's scheme

7.24   It the target company is a participating employer in the seller's multi-employer pension scheme then it may be allowed to continue to participate in the scheme on a temporary basis while arrangements are made for the employees to join the buyer's scheme and agreements are put in place for the treatment of the accrued pension liabilities relating to the target company's employees and former employees. This is a very complex area which is dealt with in more detail in **Chapter 15**. In practice if a new employer is unable to provide equivalent pension provision for future service, alternative methods of compensation (eg pay rises) should be considered.

Employer's lien

7.25   Many pension schemes permit a lien to be placed on benefits payable where the employee or ex-employee owes money to the employer or the trustees of a scheme resulting from criminal, negligent or fraudulent acts or omissions. Liens are governed by *PA 1995, ss 91–94* and are an exception to the general rule that pension benefits cannot be assigned or forfeited. However, a lien rule can only operate with the agreement of the employee unless a court or arbitrator has made an order or award in the employer's favour (*PA 1995, ss 91(5)(d), 93(3)*). As an employee can insist on his statutory rights to payment of a guaranteed cash equivalent (see **Chapter 6**), trustees may be forced to pay benefits out before a court or arbitrator has considered the lien issue unless they obtain a time extension for the payment of the cash equivalent.

It should be borne in mind that a lien cannot attach to benefits deriving from transfer credits (unless the transfer is attributable to employment with the same or an associated employer and the transferring scheme contained an appropriate lien rule) (*Occupational Pension Schemes (Assignment, Forfeiture, Bankruptcy etc) Regulations 1997 (SI 1997/785), reg 3*), and no part of a guaranteed minimum pension or protected rights may be subject to deduction. The amount that can be recovered is limited to the lesser of the actuarial value of the employee's actual or prospective benefits and the amount of the monetary obligation owed to the employer or trustees of a scheme (*PA 1995, s 91(6)*).

Owing to the restrictions referred to above, and in particular the need for consent or a court order or decision of an arbitrator, lien rules can often be difficult to operate in practice.

Maternity, paternity, adoption and parental absence

General

7.26   The requirements for the equal treatment of women on maternity leave, contained in the *Third Equal Treatment Directive 86/378/EEC*, led to the passing of the *Social Security Act 1989*, the relevant provisions of which came into effect on 23 June 1994. These provisions require benefits under occupational pension schemes to accrue for women on paid maternity leave in the same way as for women working normally, and by reference, therefore, to their full remuneration. Members pay contributions based upon their actual pay received, whether statutory or contractual, and pensionable service is treated as continuous notwithstanding the maternity absence.

Amendments to *Social Security Act 1989, Sch 5* have gradually extended these rights to employees on paid paternity leave (ordinary or additional), parental leave (see below) and adoption leave to bring them in line with paid maternity leave. Further amendments were made by the *Work and Families Act 2006* (*WFA 2006*), with effect from April 2007. Under the *Equality Act*, which came into force in October 2010, pregnancy and maternity are among the 'protected characteristics' which are subject to protection from discrimination, harassment and victimisation in specific areas, including pensions. The next paragraphs refer to maternity leave and pay, but similar provisions also apply to both adoption leave and pay and to paternity leave and pay.

The legislation distinguishes between 'ordinary' maternity leave (OML) and 'additional' maternity leave (AML). The maximum period for both is 26 weeks. Generally, all pregnant employees who satisfy certain conditions (mainly in relation to notifications) are entitled to a period of OML. This applies regardless of the number of hours a woman works. *WFA 2006* removed the former length of service qualification for AML (bringing it into line with OML), so that an employee who qualifies for OML now qualifies also for AML. In practice, however, an employee must give notice, and thus be employed, by the 15th week before the 'expected week of childbirth' (EWC) (see *ERA 1996, s 71* and the *Maternity and Parental Leave etc Regulations 1999 (SI 1999/3312)*).

Most employees will be entitled to statutory maternity pay (SMP) from their employer (depending on their earnings and period of continuous employment) or to maternity allowance, paid by the State. *WFA 2006* extended the period in respect of which SMP is payable from 26 to 39 weeks (ie for part of the period of AML as well as the whole of the OML period).

The *Children and Families Act 2014* (*CFA 2014*) inserts new provisions into *ERA 1996* which introduce a new entitlement for eligible employees who are parents to take shared parental leave (SPL) in the first year of their child's life or after the child's placement for adoption where the expected week of childbirth or placement date is on or after 5 April 2015. The new statutory provisions came into force on 1 December 2014. Parents are not obliged to take SPL; the default position will still be 52 weeks of maternity leave (39 weeks paid) including a two-week period of compulsory maternity leave from the child's birth unless SPL is requested. However, as additional parental leave and pay was abolished when SPL became available, the only other entitlement available to the child's other parent is ordinary paternity leave and pay.

Amendments to the *Sex Discrimination Act 1975* to remove the distinction between OML and AML were implemented by the *Maternity and Parental Leave etc and the Paternity and Adoption Leave (Amendment) Regulations 2008 (SI 2008/1966)*. However, the principle remains that remuneration is an exception to the requirement not to deprive an employee on maternity leave of the benefit of her terms and conditions of employment; and the definition of 'remuneration' is unchanged. In the absence in the 2008 regulations of any clarification of the benefits which have to be provided to employees on AML, it is our view that the consequences of the legislation set out in **7.28** to **7.30** below remain unchanged.

In the case of *Boyle & others v Equal Opportunities Commission (C-411/96) [1998] All ER (EC) 879* it was stated that a condition limiting accrual of pensionable service to periods of paid OML was contrary to *Article 12* of the *Pregnant Workers Directive (EU Directive 92/85/EEC)*. The court said that the Directive required the period of OML to be pensionable regardless of whether the woman concerned was in receipt of pay. This means that the pensionable service of any woman who is a pension scheme member but who is not entitled to either contractual or statutory maternity pay (perhaps because she has recently become an employee) must continue during this minimum period (see *ERA 1996, s 71(4)*).

Under the *Employment Relations Act 1999*, qualifying employees with one year's continuous service have a right to take up to 18 weeks' unpaid parental leave in respect of a child for whom they have parental responsibility. This right must be exercised before the child's 18th birthday or 18th anniversary of adoption. An employee on parental leave is entitled to accrue pension benefits on the basis of actual pay received (under *Maternity and Parental Leave etc Regulations 1999 (SI 1999/3312), reg 18A*.

Contractual remuneration

7.27   As noted in **7.26** above, SMP is payable for 39 weeks. The payment of contractual remuneration (ie payment under the employee's contract of employment) affects pension rights only in respect of maternity leave in excess of 39 weeks or if the contractual pay is higher than SMP.

Although the protection of pension rights during maternity absence can depend upon the payment of 'contractual remuneration', it is not clear what this includes. Employment legislation defines remuneration as comprising cash payments, whereas tax legislation includes benefits in kind within the definition. The safer approach is to treat remuneration as including all benefits in kind (eg a company car). *Gillespie v Northern Health & Social Services Board [1996] All ER (EC) 284* confirmed that bonuses or pay increases granted during paid maternity absence, but which are backdated to the relevant pre-absence period, are to be reflected in the remuneration of those on paid maternity leave. SMP will also have to be recalculated if a backdated pay increase affects the average earnings which underlie the calculation of SMP. Essentially, *Gillespie* underlines the requirement in the *Social Security Act 1989* that pension rights accruing during a period of paid maternity absence reflect any increase to 'normal pay'.

The UK and European courts have revisited the so-called 'contractual remuneration during leave' question and the cases have taken the issues much further than in *Gillespie*.

In relation to pay rises, the ECJ in *Alabaster v (1) Woolwich plc; (2) Secretary of State for Social Security Case C-147/02 [2005] All ER (EC) 490* ruled that any pay rise, awarded from the time a woman falls pregnant and up to the end of her maternity leave, must be reflected in her higher SMP rate, contractual maternity pay, and the rate of pay on which she returns to work. This is the case even if the pay rise takes effect after the end of the period during which the higher rate SMP is payable. This is provided for by *regulation 21(7)* of the *Statutory Maternity Pay (General) Regulations 1986/1960*.

Hoyland v Asda Stores Ltd [2005] IRLR 438 dealt with bonus entitlements during maternity leave. The EAT ruled that a woman must not be deprived of contractual bonus payments which are awarded to reflect work performance done at the time: (a) before the woman went on leave; (b) during which the woman was on a statutory compulsory maternity leave period (the two weeks period immediately following childbirth); and (c) after the woman returned to work following maternity leave. The decision was upheld by the Court of Session, which confirmed that it was lawful to reduce the bonus in respect of a period of absence on ordinary maternity leave because it fell within the exclusion in *Sex Discrimination Act 1975, s 6(6)*, which provides that the Act 'does not apply to benefits consisting of the payment of money when the provision of those benefits is regulated by the woman's contract of employment'. The bonus was a payment regulated by the employee's contract of employment notwithstanding that it was expressed to be discretionary because the bonus would not be paid but for the existence of the contract of employment. This decision should, however, be applied with caution owing to the varied nature and purpose of bonus provisions. The *Equality Act 2010*, which replaced the *Sex Discrimination Act 1975*, reflects the same position regarding contractual bonuses in *ss 73* and *74* and regarding discretionary bonuses in *s 76* and *paragraph 17* of *schedule 9*.

The ECJ decided in *North Western Health Board v McKenna [2006] All ER (EC) 455* that employers are not required to give full pay to women absent from work for a maternity-related illness, provided that they are treated in the same way as male employees on sick leave and that the level of pay they receive is not 'too low' so as to undermine the objective of protecting pregnant women. Here, the employee's sick pay was half her contractual pay; whether a lower level, including the current level of statutory sick pay, would be 'too low' is not clear.

Final salary schemes

7.28   As already noted, the *Social Security Act 1989* provides for periods of paid maternity absence to count as pensionable service as if the woman was working normally, and for the accrual of benefits to continue on the basis of the pre-absence level of remuneration. As the employee's contributions are based upon actual pay and full final salary benefits accrue during the periods of paid absence, the employer will incur an additional cost to fund those benefits to compensate for any reduction in the amount of contribution paid by the employee. It should be borne in mind, however, that the scheme rules may provide for better benefits than the statutory minimum, such as permitting members to purchase their 'lost' pensionable service, so the scheme rules should be checked in all cases.

Money purchase schemes

7.29   The position here is less clear, but money purchase schemes are not excluded from the scope of the legislation. Although the employee can only be required to contribute on the basis of actual pay received, the employer has to contribute at the full rate appropriate to the employee's pre-absence remuneration. It is also arguable that, as with the final salary schemes, the employer has to make good any shortfall in contributions (ie the difference between the contributions actually paid by the employee and those that would have been paid by her if she had been working normally) but this point is far from certain.

Death benefits

7.30   Benefits on death are treated in the same way as pension benefits, in that they must be continued during periods of paid maternity absence. On the death of an employee during such absence, death benefits will be calculated by reference to full pre-absence remuneration as if the employee had been working normally.

Additional changes

Time off for performance of duties and for training

7.31   Under *ERA 1996, s 58* (originally *PA 1995, s 42*), an employer must permit any employee who is a trustee of a scheme to take time off during working hours to allow him to perform all of his duties as a trustee or to undergo relevant training. The amount of time off, and any conditions imposed by the employer, must be reasonable having regard to the employer's business and the effect of the employee's absence. Any employee is entitled to be paid for any time taken off pursuant to this provision (*ERA 1996, s 59*).

An employee can bring a complaint to an employment tribunal if he believes that his employer has failed to give him time off and failed to pay him (*ERA 1996, s 60*). He has three months from the date when the failure occurred in which to present his complaint, but the tribunal will have the power to extend this period if it is satisfied that it was not reasonably practicable for the complaint to be presented within the period. If an employee's complaint is upheld, the tribunal can award such compensation at it considers just and equitable.

Right not to suffer detriment or to be unfairly dismissed

7.32   ERA *1996, s 46* (previously *PA 1995, s 46*) states that an employer is not permitted to victimise an employee simply on the ground that he performed or proposed to perform his functions as a trustee of a scheme which relates to his employment.

Further, if an employee is dismissed and the reason (or the principal reason) for the dismissal is that the employee performed or proposed to perform any functions as a trustee, the dismissal is to be regarded as automatically unfair and the employee may be entitled to compensation (*ERA 1996, s 102*).

Any provision in a contract of employment (or in any other agreement) which purports to exclude or limit the right not to suffer detriment or to be unfairly dismissed is void (*ERA 1996, s 203(1)*).

Conclusion

7.33   Up until October 2012, it was difficult to classify pension provisions or an entitlement to pension benefits as an employment 'right', as in most instances employers did not have to provide pension arrangements. The introduction of the automatic enrolment regime under the *PA 2008* will gradually change this position (see **Chapter 14**).

On becoming a member of a pension scheme, an employee does obtain rights and entitlements, but primarily against the trustees of the scheme. The only contractual 'right' of the employee is to join the pension scheme if eligible to do so. In the case of automatic enrolment, the rights are to be enrolled and re-enrolled onto a qualifying scheme, to receive certain employers' contributions, and to enjoy a range of statutory employment protections. These apart, it is easier to classify the rights of a member as being either statutory (eg not to be discriminated against on various grounds) or common law rights, for example, the *Imperial* duty of good faith. Some of the cases referred to in this Chapter clearly indicate the difficulties of differentiating between pension and employment issues. However, the basis of pension provision may, in time, move further towards a contractual as opposed to a trust based entitlement.

Chapter 8

Pensions and divorce

Introduction

8.1   Over the years there have been fundamental changes in the treatment of pension benefits in the context of divorce proceedings. These have arisen out of two different concepts for the treatment of pensions: earmarking and pension sharing, which were introduced by *PA 1995* and the *Welfare Reform and Pensions Act 1999* (*WRPA 1999*) respectively. This legislation has not only increased awareness of the comparatively high value that pension benefits may have in the context of the matrimonial assets as a whole, but has introduced flexibility designed to enable a fair settlement to be reached, whatever the divorcing parties' general and financial circumstances.

The family law courts generally had no jurisdiction over pension schemes in the context of divorce settlements until the introduction of *PA 1995* (*Brooks v Brooks [1995] 3 All ER 257* is the notable exception, although it is likely that this judgment is confined to its own facts and has now been superseded by legislation). That is not to say that the pension rights of parties to divorce proceedings were not taken into consideration prior to *PA 1995*, merely that the courts did not have the jurisdiction to make orders against pension scheme trustees or scheme members, in respect of their pension benefits, when deciding how the parties' assets were to be split. This lack of options in law for the treatment of pension rights on divorce had long been a cause for dissatisfaction and was the subject of various reports which, in essence, recommended that the courts should have the power to split the pension rights on divorce, thereby creating a separate entitlement for the ex-spouse.

Despite an obvious desire for change, it took a number of years for legislation to appear on the statute books. The reason for this lies in the nature of pension schemes themselves. The majority of pension schemes were designed to be eligible for tax approval (see **Chapter 17**). The requirements which applied before 6 April 2006 for obtaining exempt approved status, prevented benefits being paid to any person who was not a member or a 'dependent' (as defined in the Glossary to the Revenue's 'Practice Notes, IR12' (2001)) of a member, and specifically prevented pensions from being assignable (subject to certain statutory exceptions). This had proved the main obstacle for the courts in the past because the governing trust deed of an exempt approved scheme would always contain a specific provision that benefits cannot be assigned. There was no mechanism to assign benefits to an ex-spouse so that they would become payable to the ex-spouse as of right, nor to provide for the ex-spouse on the death of the scheme member unless, first, the ex-spouse fell within the definition of 'dependant' and, second, the trustees exercised their discretion to pay the benefits to him or her in that capacity. This position has not changed to any material extent under *FA 2004*.

These issues have been addressed in legislation. However, it may still be appropriate for parties in some circumstances to leave the pension benefits intact and it is, therefore, useful to look at the issues which were relevant prior to the introduction of *PA 1995* and the earmarking regime.

Position prior to PA 1995

8.2   Prior to the introduction of *PA 1995*, the treatment of property on divorce in England, Wales and Northern Ireland was governed by *Matrimonial Causes Act 1973, ss 21–25 (MCA 1973)*.

MCA 1973, s 25A(1) required the court to consider whether the financial obligations of each party towards the other could be terminated as soon after the grant of the decree as the court considered just and reasonable. This is known as a 'clean break'. It put the onus on the court to consider lump sum payments and property adjustment orders, rather than periodical payments orders (commonly known as maintenance payments) wherever possible and, if a periodical payments order was made, to limit its duration if appropriate. A clean break would usually be appropriate where the couple is young, both are working and have no children or where the couple's assets are sizeable enough that they can be split in such a way that the ex-spouse will have sufficient resources to live on.

Prior to amendment by *PA 1995*, *MCA 1973, s 25(2)* stated that the court should, when considering financial provision orders, have particular regard, amongst other matters, to the following:

'(*a*)   the income, earning capacity, property and other financial resources which each of the parties to the marriage has or is likely to have in the foreseeable future, including in the case of earning capacity any increase in that capacity which it would in the opinion of the court be reasonable to expect a party of the marriage to take steps to acquire;

  ...

(*h*)   in the case of proceedings for divorce or nullity of marriage, the value to each of the parties to the marriage of any benefits (for example, a pension) which by reason of the dissolution or annulment of the marriage, that party will lose the chance of acquiring.'

However, a problem of interpretation arose with the use of the words 'in the foreseeable future' in *MCA 1973, s 25(2)(a)*. The approach adopted by the courts resulted in consideration being given only to those assets which a party could expect to acquire in the next ten years. Consequently, where a party to the divorce was more than ten years away from retirement, the value of his pension entitlements was unlikely to be taken into account. In any event, the court had no power over either the trustees or the assets of a pension scheme and so could not make an order re-allocating assets or obliging the trustees to make a payment to an ex-spouse. Therefore, even where pension rights fell within the definition of matrimonial property their value could only be taken into account in relation to the distribution of non-pension assets.

Under *MCA 1973, s 25(2)(h)*, the court was required to have regard to the value of any pension that a party to a divorce loses the chance of acquiring. It was not clear, however, to which benefits these provisions referred (ie to the member's pension, any cash lump sum payable on retirement, a spouse's pension payable on the death of the member and/or lump sum on a member's death in service).

The courts' inability to divide pension assets was problematical, particularly where there were insufficient non-pension assets to provide for the ex-spouse's needs. A common result was that in the divorce settlement the ex-spouse would be allocated the matrimonial home whilst the scheme member retained the pension rights. This often created both long and short-term problems for both parties; the party with the matrimonial home had realisable assets but no income on retirement, whereas the scheme member retained pension rights, to which he could not gain access to set up a new home, but was guaranteed a certain level of future income. An even worse scenario was where the pension rights were the only or the largest asset and, consequently, the court was unable to make any order which would adequately compensate the ex-spouse. Therefore, in many cases, this was not satisfactory for either party. It was against this background that *PA 1995, s 166* was introduced.

Earmarking – impact of PA 1995

General jurisdiction

8.3   The concept of 'earmarking' was introduced by *PA 1995, s 166*. In general terms, earmarking introduced a means by which pension benefits could be used to pay either maintenance or a capital sum from the pension scheme direct to the ex-spouse on the member's behalf, but which would only become payable when entitlement arose under the pension scheme in respect of the member.

The powers of the courts regarding financial provision on divorce are still contained in *MCA 1973*, but s 25 was amended to introduce the concept of earmarking. *PA 1995, s 166* inserted new *ss 25B–25D* into *MCA 1973* with effect from 1 August 1996 which applied to petitions presented on or after 1 July 1996. *WRPA 1999* has subsequently made certain refinements to these sections which are reflected below. In essence, the earmarking provisions provide that the courts:

(*a*)   must have regard to pension benefits which either party has or is likely to have or stands to lose the chance of acquiring because of the divorce and must ignore the words 'in the foreseeable future' contained in *MCA 1973, s 25(2)(a)* for this purpose (*MCA 1973, s 25B(1)*). With effect from 1 January 2006 this includes any PPF compensation either party has or is likely to have or stands to lose (*MCA 1973, s 25E*);

(*b*)   have jurisdiction to make orders against the person responsible for the pension arrangement for payment of financial provision from a member's pension benefits to the other party when payment of those benefits becomes due to the member (*MCA 1973, s 25B(4)*). The term 'person responsible' was introduced by *WRPA 1999, s 46(2)* and means, in the case of occupational pension schemes or personal pension schemes, the trustees and managers of the scheme. In the case of a retirement annuity contract, it means the provider of the annuity and, in the case of an insurance policy, the insurer;

(*c*)   have power to require a member to commute his pension benefits, where such a right to commute exists under the arrangement, thereby reducing the pension benefits payable to him, and have power to order payment of any lump sum following commutation to be made to the ex-spouse (*MCA 1973, s 25B(7)*) – it is interesting to note that technically commutation is not applicable to defined contribution benefits;

(*d*)   can direct trustees to exercise their discretionary powers in the event of the death of a member or pensioner in favour of the ex-spouse in whole or in part, and can also, where the member has power to nominate, require a member to nominate his ex-spouse for all or part of a lump sum payable on his death (*MCA 1973, s 25C*).

Essentially, the type of order that the court is empowered to make was not changed by *PA 1995*, merely the source of the payment. The order is in the form of either a deferred periodical payments order or a deferred lump sum order. In the interim, the member's pension benefits remain in the scheme and are still attributable to the member, but a proportion becomes payable directly to the ex-spouse. No separate entitlement is created in the scheme for the ex-spouse so payments only become due to the ex-spouse when they become due to the member and pension payments will stop automatically on the death of the member. As with all periodical payments orders, either party can apply to the court to have the amount varied (*MCA 1973, s 31*) and payments will cease on the re-marriage or death of the ex-spouse.

The amount of pension payable to the ex-spouse must be expressed as a percentage of the total payment due to the member (*MCA 1973, s 25B(5)*). Such total amount can include the value of the member's GMP by virtue of the exclusion of the provisions relating to inalienability of GMPs (*PA 1995, s 91*) under *PA 1995, s 166(4)* and *(5)*. Any lump sum payment made by the persons responsible for the pension arrangement shall discharge them of any liability to the member to the extent of the amount of the payment (*MCA 1973, ss 25B(6)(a)* and *25C(3)*) and, in the case of pension payments, any payments made by the person responsible for the pension arrangement shall be treated as a payment made by the member towards the discharge of his liability under the court order (*MCA 1973, s 25B(6)(b)*).

The duty of the court to consider a clean break under *MCA 1973, s 25A(1)* was not affected by the changes introduced by *PA 1995*. In practice therefore, 'earmarking' orders against pension payments are likely only to be made where a clean break is not possible and a periodical payments order is appropriate. One example might be where the pension of the member is already in payment. Such an order, however, gives the ex-spouse additional comfort and security because, instead of obtaining a maintenance order payable by the member, the ex-spouse will instead receive payments directly from the pension scheme. This removes direct dependency on the member for financial support and avoids the potential problems caused by non-compliance with an order by the member.

The amendments to *MCA 1973* by *PA 1995* (and *WRPA 1999*) specified the schemes against which the court can make orders. These are referred to as 'pension arrangements', a term introduced by *WRPA 1999, s 46(1)*, meaning an occupational pension scheme, personal pension scheme, retirement annuity contract, an annuity or insurance policy which is to give effect to the rights of an occupational pension scheme or a personal pension scheme, or an annuity purchased for the purpose of discharging liability for a pension credit (*MCA 1973, s 25D(3)*).

MCA 1973, s 25E(3), introduced by *PA 2004* with effect from 1 January 2006, and the *Divorce etc (Pension Protection Fund) Regulations 2006 (SI 2006/1932)* provide that, where the Pension Protection Fund assumes responsibility for an occupational pension scheme after an order has been made in relation to pension payments or commutation of pension benefits payable from that scheme, then the Board of the PPF is required to give effect to that order in relation to the member's PPF compensation. See **8.29** below for more on pension sharing orders and the PPF.

332

Valuation of benefits for earmarking purposes

8.4   The question of the valuation of pension rights for earmarking is dealt with in the *Divorce etc (Pensions) Regulations 2000 (SI 2000/1123)* for divorce and nullity proceedings commencing on and after 1 December 2000. *Regulation 3* provides that, for the purposes of earmarking, benefits under a pension arrangement shall be calculated in the manner set out in *Pensions on Divorce etc (Provision of Information) Regulations 2000 (SI 2000/1048), reg 3*.

Pensions on Divorce etc (Provision of Information) Regulations 2000, reg 3 specifies that the basis of valuation depends on the category of member in question:

(*a*)   for active and deferred members of occupational pension schemes, members of personal pension schemes and a person with rights contained in a retirement annuity contact, the statutory cash equivalent transfer value basis ('CETV') must be applied. Generally, the effective date for calculating the CETV is the date on which the request for the valuation was received by the person responsible for the pension arrangement. However, it should be noted that, under *Divorce etc (Pensions) Regulations 2000, reg 3*, the court can specify another date, if it considers it appropriate, such date not to be earlier than one year before the date of the petition and not later than the date on which the court is exercising its powers. Trustees should therefore check they are using the correct date before running calculations.

(*b*)   in any other circumstances, eg pensions in payment, *reg 3* specifies that the value of benefits shall be calculated and verified in accordance with the *Occupational Pension Schemes (Transfer Values) Regulations 1996 (SI 1996/1847), regs 7–7C* and *7E(1)–(3)*, as amended.

Transfers of, and notices in relation to, earmarked benefits

8.5   Given that the courts' powers enable orders to be made for deferred maintenance payments, payable at some date in the future, it was necessary to make provisions permitting the transfer of the orders on the transfer of the member's accrued benefits to a new scheme (*MCA 1973, s 25D(1)(a)*). The *Divorce etc (Pensions) Regulations 2000 (SI 2000/1123)* provide for the person responsible for the transferring arrangement to give notice to the person responsible for the receiving arrangement in circumstances where an earmarking order is in force against a member who wishes to transfer his pension benefits. The effect of this notice is that the earmarking order will attach to the transfer credits granted in the receiving scheme and will be enforceable against the trustees of the receiving scheme.

8.5 *Pensions and divorce*

Divorce etc (Pensions) Regulations 2000, reg 4 sets out the content of the notices which must be given to the receiving arrangement and the ex-spouse and the period within which they must be given. Notice must be given within the period provided by *PSA 1993, s 99* for the person responsible for the transferring arrangement to effect a transfer (usually six months) and before the expiry of 21 days after the person responsible for the transferring arrangement has made all required payments to the person responsible for the receiving arrangement (*Divorce etc (Pensions) Regulations 2000, reg 4(5)*).

Regulation 4(3) provides that the notice to the person responsible for the new arrangement shall consist of:

(*a*)   every order made under *MCA 1973* imposing a requirement on the person responsible for the transferring arrangement in relation to the rights transferred;

(*b*)   any subsequent orders varying the original order;

(*c*)   all information or particulars supplied by the ex-spouse under the *Family Procedure Rules 2010 No 2955, r 9.33* and *r 9.34* (for example, address and bank details);

(*d*)   any notice given by the ex-spouse to the person responsible for the transferring arrangement relating to a change of personal details, remarriage or civil partnership; and

(*e*)   where the rights of a member under the transferring scheme derive from a transfer from a previous scheme, any notices to the person responsible for the previous arrangement on the former transfer.

Regulation 4(4) provides that the notice to the ex-spouse must contain the following particulars:

(*a*)   the fact that the pension rights of the member have been transferred;

(*b*)   the date on which the transfer takes effect;

(*c*)   the name and address of the person responsible for the new arrangement; and

(*d*)   the fact that the order made under *MCA 1973, s 23* is to have effect as if it had been made in respect of the person responsible for the new arrangement.

Under *Divorce etc (Pensions) Regulations 2000, reg 5*, notice is also required to be given by the person responsible for the arrangement to the ex-spouse, within 14 days of the occurrence of an event, when:

(*a*)   it is likely that there will be a significant reduction in the benefits payable under the scheme in respect of the member (save where a transfer of all benefits has been made or where market conditions have affected the value of the scheme's assets) (*Divorce etc (Pensions) Regulations 2000, reg 5(1)*); and/or

(*b*)   a partial transfer of the member's accrued benefits has been made (*Divorce etc (Pensions) Regulations 2000, reg 5(3)*).

This notice shall state the nature of the event which has occurred and the extent of the reduction in benefits and, in the case of a partial transfer, the name and address of the person responsible for the receiving arrangement.

It should be noted that in the event of a partial transfer the order will remain with the original scheme and this may therefore give the member scope for the avoidance of the order. Nevertheless, because notice is given to the ex-spouse by the scheme, this gives the ex-spouse an opportunity to apply to the court for a variation of the original order.

An ex-spouse is required to give notice (*Divorce etc (Pensions) Regulations 2000, reg 6*) within 14 days to the person responsible for the arrangement subject to a court order where the particulars supplied by her cease to be accurate; where the ex-spouse has remarried, entered into a civil partnership or where, for any other reason, the order has ceased to have effect. The person responsible for the arrangement will be discharged of any liability to the ex-spouse to the extent of a payment where, by reason of the inaccuracy of the particulars supplied by the ex-spouse or the ex-spouse's failure to give notice of a change in details, it is not reasonably practicable for the person responsible for the arrangement to make a payment as required by the order and a payment is therefore made to the member instead (*Divorce etc (Pensions) Regulations 2000, reg 6(4)*).

Charging for earmarking orders

8.6   Charges by pension arrangements in relation to earmarking orders are permitted pursuant to *WRPA 1999, s 24* and the *Pensions on Divorce etc (Charging) Regulations 2000 (SI 2000/1049), reg 10*. The charges which a person responsible for a pension arrangement may recover in relation to an earmarking order are those charges which represent the reasonable administrative expenses which have been incurred or are likely to be incurred by reason of the order.

The Pensions on Divorce etc (Charging) Regulations 2000, reg 3 deals with charges recoverable in respect of the provision of basic valuation information and provides that the person responsible for the pension arrangement may also recover the reasonable costs of providing such information to the extent that they would not have been required to provide such information in the ordinary course of disclosure in accordance with the *Occupational and Personal Pension Schemes (Disclosure of Information) Regulations 2013 (SI 2013/2734)*.

Disclosure

8.7 The provisions governing disclosure in relation to earmarking orders can be found in the *Pensions on Divorce etc (Provision of Information) Regulations 2000. Regulation 2* deals with the provision of the basic information which the person responsible for a pension arrangement can generally be required to disclose on request. These provisions apply equally to pension sharing and are set out in detail at **8.22** below.

Pensions on Divorce etc (Provision of Information) Regulations 2000, reg 10 deals with the provision of information after receipt of an earmarking order. The person responsible for the pension arrangement must, within 21 days of receipt of the earmarking order, issue to both parties to the marriage a notice that includes the following, as appropriate:

(*a*)   for an order in respect of pension rights that are not yet in payment, a list of the circumstances in respect of any changes of which the member or the ex-spouse must notify the person responsible for the pension arrangement;

(*b*)   where the pension is in payment:

    (i)   the value of the member's pension rights;

    (ii)   the amount of those pension rights after the order has been implemented;

    (iii)   the first date when a payment under the order is to be made; and

    (iv)   the circumstances in respect of any changes of which the member or the ex-spouse must notify the person responsible for the pension arrangement;

    plus, for the member, the amount of the pension currently in payment; and the amount of pension which will be payable to the member after the order has been implemented.

(*c*)   the amount of charges which remain unpaid by each party pursuant to *Pensions on Divorce etc (Charging) Regulations 2000, reg 3* (see **8.6** above) and in respect of complying with the order;

(*d*)   information as to how and when these charges will be recovered.

Pension sharing

Introduction

8.8 Pension sharing was introduced by *WPRA 1999* and is intended to facilitate a clean break approach towards dealing with pension rights. The aim is that the capital value of the pension will be divided between the parties with the effect that the rights of the member will be reduced by way of a 'pension debit' and the ex-spouse will be granted a 'pension credit' of the same amount. The primary advantage of pension sharing to an ex-spouse is that her rights are independent of those of the member and, in contrast with earmarking, will, therefore, continue beyond the death of the member and after the ex-spouse's remarriage. It is also easier for the ex-spouse to take advantage of the Government's new pension flexibilities *(Taxation of Pensions Act 2014)* where pension sharing has been ordered, rather than earmarking.

The relevant sections of *WRPA 1999* came into force on 1 December 2000 and were in the form of insertions and amendments to *MCA 1973*, the provisions of *WRPA 1999, Parts III* and *IV*, and a number of statutory instruments.

Pension sharing is only available in proceedings commencing on or after 1 December 2000, the effective date for the new legislation *(Welfare Reform and Pensions Act 1999 (Commencement No 5) Order 2000 (SI 2000/1116))*. The provisions only apply to proceedings for divorce or nullity of marriage, and do not extend to judicial separation *(MCA 1973, s 24B(1))*.

The effect of the amendments to *MCA 1973* is that the courts have the option to consider the possibility of granting a pension sharing order, if deemed appropriate, when considering ancillary relief *(MCA 1973, s 24B(1))* whether before or after the decree absolute. Whilst it is open to the courts to make more than one sharing order in relation to a given set of divorce proceedings, the courts cannot make a pension sharing order in relation to a pension arrangement which is already the subject of a pension sharing order in relation to that marriage *(MCA 1973, s 24B(3))*. Moreover, the court cannot make a pension sharing order in respect of pension benefits which are already subject to an earmarking order *(MCA 1973, s 24B(5))*.

MCA 1973, s 21A states that a pension sharing order involves the court ordering that the 'shareable rights' of the member be shared for the benefit of the ex-spouse, with the order specifying the value of those rights to be transferred as a percentage of the total rights attributable to the member. These can be shareable rights under a specified pension arrangement, or shareable state scheme rights. *MCA 1973, s 21B* also provides from 6 April 2011 for pension compensation sharing orders, which are orders in relation to a party's shareable rights to PPF compensation. PPF compensation is discussed further at **8.29** below.

WRPA 1999, s 27(2) sets out the definition of 'shareable rights' under a pension arrangement' as being any rights other than non-shareable rights of a description specified in regulations. Rights which are non-shareable are prescribed in *Pension Sharing (Valuation) Regulations 2000 (SI 2000/1052), reg 2*. As detailed at **8.3** above, the *WRPA 1999* definition of 'pension arrangement' *(s 46(1))* is broadly termed. Indeed, the only exceptions to date appear to be a small number of excepted public sector schemes (*WRPA 1999, s 27(1), (3)*) by reference to the *Pension Sharing (Excepted Schemes) Order 2001 (SI 2001/358)* (being the schemes relating to the Prime Minister and First Lord of the Treasury, Lord Chancellor and Speaker of the House of Commons).

With regard to state pensions *WRPA 1999, s 47* sets out the definition of 'shareable state scheme rights', the detail of which is beyond the scope of this chapter.

Pension debits and credits

8.9   The person responsible for a pension arrangement is not required to implement the pension debit and pension credit until the pension sharing order has taken effect (*WRPA 1999, s 28(1)*).

A pension sharing order cannot take effect unless the decree pursuant to which it has been made has been made absolute (*MCA 1973, s 24B(2)*). In addition, s 24C (by virtue of *Divorce etc (Pensions) Regulations 2000, reg 9*) provides that the order cannot come into effect earlier than seven days after the end of the period for filing notice of appeal against the order.

Once the pension sharing order has become effective, the member's shareable rights under the arrangement become subject to a 'debit' of the specified amount and the ex-spouse becomes entitled to a 'credit' of a corresponding amount, held as a right against the person responsible for the arrangement (*WRPA 1999, s 29(1)*).

Pension debits

8.10   The pension debit operates by reducing the member's current and future benefits under the pension arrangement by a specified percentage (*WRPA 1999, s 31*) on the transfer day (ie the date on which the order takes effect). The benefits to be reduced must be 'qualifying benefits' (*s 31(3)*). A benefit is a qualifying benefit if the member's cash equivalent includes an amount in respect of it.

When a benefit is reduced by a pension debit each part of the benefit is reduced equally. For example, the GMP benefits of a member are reduced by the same percentage as the excess over GMP. The debit is calculated as an amount of pension representing the specified percentage applied to the hypothetical deferred pension to which the member would have been entitled had he left pensionable service on that day. This so-called 'negative deferred pension' will attract revaluation under the scheme in accordance with the scheme's provisions. Given that the specified percentage is applied to the hypothetical deferred pension, the benefits of active members to be reduced by the pension debit therefore exclude any elements which would not be included in his deferred pension, such as a death-in-service lump sum.

Pension credits

8.11 The ex-spouse becomes entitled to a pension credit amount calculated by reference to the specified percentage of the cash equivalent of the relevant benefits on the valuation day, made up of the same elements and in the same proportions as the benefits of the scheme member (*WRPA 1999, s 29(2)*). The valuation day is such day within the implementation period for the credit under subsection as the person responsible for the relevant arrangement specifies (*WRPA 1999, s 29(7)*). An arrangement which is the subject of a pension sharing order may discharge its liability for the pension credit by conferring appropriate rights under that arrangement (an 'internal transfer') or by transferring the pension credit to another qualifying pension scheme or arrangement (an 'external transfer') (see **8.13** below).

Implementation period

8.12 The person responsible for the arrangement has a specified period within which to give effect to the provisions of the pension sharing order – this is known as the implementation period and is defined in *WRPA 1999, s 34(1)* as being a period of four months beginning with the later of the day on which the pension sharing order takes effect, and receipt by the person responsible for the arrangement of the relevant documents (eg the order itself and the order or decree of the divorce or annulment), and the information set out in *Pensions on Divorce etc (Provision of Information) Regulations 2000, reg 5* (this includes the names, addresses, dates of birth and National Insurance numbers of the divorcing couple). A further pre-condition of implementing the sharing order may be the payment of any charges due from the divorcing couple (see **8.23** below).

In the event that the order has not been implemented by the trustees of an occupational pension scheme within the implementation period they are required pursuant to *WRPA 1999, s 33(2)* to notify the Regulator within 21 days beginning with the day immediately following the end of the implementation period (*Pension Sharing (Implementation and Discharge of Liability) Regulations 2000, reg 2*). The Regulator may impose civil penalties under *PA 1995, s 10* if the trustees or managers failed to take all such steps as were reasonable to discharge liability for the pension credit before the end of the implementation period. On application by the trustees, the Regulator may extend the implementation period under certain circumstances (*WRPA 1999, s 33(4)*). These circumstances are set out in *Pension Sharing (Implementation and Discharge of Liability) Regulations 2000, reg 3* and provide that the application must be made to the Regulator before the end of the implementation period and the Regulator must be satisfied that:

- the scheme is being wound up or is about to wind up;

- the scheme has ceased to be contracted out within the previous 12 months or ceased as at 6 April 2016 and the scheme has not yet reconciled the GMP entitlement with HMRC;

- an extension is in the financial interests of the members of the scheme generally;

- the trustees have not been provided with such information as they reasonably require to properly discharge their liability within the implementation period; or

- there is a dispute by one of the parties as to the calculation of the cash equivalent transfer value that has been used to determine the pension debit and credit.

The Regulator's consideration of the application cannot be completed before the end of the implementation period, which may also be suspended or postponed where one of the parties has made an application for leave to appeal out of time (*reg 4*).

Discharging liability for the pension credit

General position

8.13   The main body of the pension sharing legislation is aimed at the means by which the liability of the person responsible for the pension arrangement which is subject to a pension sharing order can be discharged in respect of the pension credit. The relevant provisions can be found in *WRPA 1999, s 35* by reference to *Sch 5*, together with the *Pension Sharing (Implementation and Discharge of Liability) Regulations 2000*.

WRPA 1999, Sch 5 deals with funded schemes (*para 1*), unfunded schemes (*paras 2* and *3*) and 'other' pension arrangements (*para 4*). This chapter will concentrate on the position for 'funded' schemes in *Sch 5, para 1* (ie pension credits derived from a funded occupational pension scheme or a personal pension scheme).

WRPA 1999, Sch 5, para 1(2) states that the trustees or managers of these types of arrangements may discharge their liability in respect of the pension credit by conferring rights under the relevant scheme on the ex-spouse with his or her consent, or otherwise in accordance with regulations. The conferring right under the relevant scheme is known as the 'internal transfer' option. Alternatively, under *Sch 5, para 1(3)* the liability may be discharged by paying the amount of the pension credit to the person responsible for a 'qualifying arrangement' (defined widely in *Sch 5, para 6*) with the ex-spouse's consent or otherwise in accordance with regulations. This is known as the 'external transfer' option.

The *Pension Sharing (Implementation and Discharge of Liability) Regulations 2000* set out the detail of these procedures under *reg 7*. In summary, for internal transfers (*reg 7(1)*) the consent of the ex-spouse must be obtained unless the ex-spouse has failed to provide this consent and has also failed to specify a suitable recipient scheme under the external transfer route.

An external transfer (*reg 7(2)*) must be made with the ex-spouse's consent unless the ex-spouse fails to provide this consent and he or she has also failed to consent to an internal transfer or the trustees did not offer the internal transfer route as an option.

WRPA 1999, Sch 5, para 1(4) specifies that any consent to be given by the ex-spouse to an internal transfer will be invalid unless it is given after receipt of a written notice of an offer to discharge liability by way of an external transfer or, if given earlier, the consent is not withdrawn within seven days of receipt of such notice.

Death of ex-spouse prior to discharge of liability

8.14   *Pension Sharing (Implementation and Discharge of Liability) Regulations 2000, reg 6* specifies how a pension credit liability can be discharged when the ex-spouse dies after the liability has arisen but before it has been discharged. Essentially, where the rules of the scheme provide, any benefits the scheme provides must be in the form of a lump sum payment; payment of a pension; payment of both a lump sum and a pension and/or the purchase of an annuity contract or insurance policy with a 'qualifying arrangement' (defined in *reg 11*). Where the provisions of the scheme do not provide for such a benefit to be provided, liability in respect of the pension credit shall be discharged by retaining the value of the pension credit in the pension arrangement from which that pension credit was derived (*reg 6(4)*).

Pros and cons of internal v external transfer options

8.15   When pension sharing was first introduced there was much debate about which option trustees should adopt as their policy for securing pension credits. Arguments against internal transfers are the added costs and the administrative burdens of an extra membership category; extended ongoing disclosure requirements and the need for extensive rule amendments to incorporate a new benefit structure and category of member. Moreover, the external option sits more easily with the 'clean break' motivation that gave rise to the pension sharing legislation in the first place.

The majority of funded occupational pension schemes have expressed a preference for the external transfer option, which avoids the problems outlined above. Concerns were, however, raised about the ability of trustees who were not authorised under the *Financial Services and Markets Act 2000* to select a default external transfer destination without contravening the *Financial Services and Markets Act 2000 (Regulated Activities) Order 2001 (SI 2001/1544), art 37*. However, it is widely acknowledged that where trustees pay the pension credit to a designated default option provider, this will not amount to the purchasing of an investment which will be held for the purposes of the scheme and so falls outside the ambit of the definition of a specified activity for the purposes of the financial services legislation.

The question of the availability of a suitable 'qualifying arrangement' to receive external transfers (without the need for the ex-spouse's signature on a proposal form) has historically been a problem.

The Department for Work and Pensions ('DWP') has clarified a few points that had arisen regarding the type of vehicle available for the default option:

(*a*)   The default option should not be available until the former spouse has been given adequate opportunity to make his or her choice or to make a further choice where payment cannot be made in accordance with his or her wishes. Where the default option, nevertheless, comes into play the only options available are either an internal transfer or the purchase of an annuity or insurance policy.

(*b*)   This gives rise to the question as to the type of annuity and insurance policy available for this purpose. A deferred annuity can be purchased but it is not clear what other 'insurance policy' can be used. It is not possible to transfer the credit to a personal pension scheme or stakeholder schemes without the consent of the former spouse.

(*c*)   *Section 32* buy-out contracts would also seem not to be an option. This is because only pension *benefits* can be transferred to a *s 32* buy-out contract so it would only be in the event that an ex-spouse were to acquire a 'pension credit benefit' in the scheme that this could then be transferred out – and even in that case the consent of the ex-spouse would be required. In most cases there will be no pension credit benefit, only a pension credit liability to be discharged by the trustees. This appears to leave the purchase of an annuity as the only available external default option.

In practice this issue seems to have posed less of a problem than anticipated. An ex-spouse who agrees to a pension sharing order as part of the divorce settlement will have been notified of the trustees' policy and, where only an external transfer option is offered, is likely already to have made suitable arrangements before agreeing to such an order. There are however problematic cases where ex-spouses have failed or have refused to provide details of a provider, and where the amount of the pension credit is too small to be applied to purchase an annuity. The new pension freedoms introduced from 6 April 2015 make a pension credit even more attractive to the ex-spouse, given that they can be accessed more flexibly than previously, so a lack of engagement over the destination of the pension credit is even less likely going forward.

Pension credit benefits

General benefits and transfers

8.16   Where the trustees of a scheme choose to offer ex-spouses an internal transfer option, and the ex-spouse does not elect to transfer the pension credit to another arrangement, the ex-spouse will become an ex-spouse participant and will be entitled to pension credit benefits in the scheme.

Section 37 of WRPA 1999 inserted *ss 101A–101Q* into *PSA 1993*, which set out the requirements relating to pension credit benefits under occupational pension schemes. The protection given to ex-spouses with pension credit benefits broadly reflects the existing provisions for early leavers from occupational pension schemes, including similar transfer rights to those of a deferred member. This legislation is supplemented by the *Pension Sharing (Pension Credit Benefit) Regulations 2000 (SI 2000/1054)*.

Pension credit benefits are payable at 'normal benefit age', which means the earliest date at which a person who has a pension credit benefit is entitled to receive the benefit without adjustment for early or late payment (disregarding provisions as to early payment on grounds of ill-health). Normal benefit age must be between 60 and 65 and benefits cannot be taken in lump sum form before that age except in prescribed circumstances (*PSA 1993, s 101C*; *Pension Sharing (Pension Credit Benefit) Regulations 2000, Part II*). Essentially, this permits payment of a pension commencement lump sum, serious ill-health lump sum, trivial commutation lump sum or a winding-up lump sum.

Members with pension credit rights are entitled under *PSA 1993, s 101F* to request that their cash equivalent be transferred to another occupational pension scheme or personal pension scheme which satisfies the necessary criteria, or be used to purchase an annuity, subject to certain requirements and restrictions set out in *Pension Sharing (Pension Credit Benefit) Regulations 2000, Part III*.

Section *101H* of *PSA 1993* provides, in relation to salary-related schemes, that a statement of entitlement must be provided by the trustees or managers, on the application of an eligible member, following which the eligible member has three months within which to request a transfer (*s 101G(2)*). The exceptions to this general rule are that an eligible member may not take a transfer if a crystallisation event has occurred in relation to those rights (*s 101G(1)*) or, of the benefits are not flexible benefits, there is less than a year remaining before the member reaches normal benefit age (*s 101G(3)*).

Where the trustees receive a transfer notice (ie a request for transfer) from an eligible member, *PSA 1993, s 101J* requires the trustees to comply with the notice within six months of the valuation date for benefits other than money purchase benefits or, for money purchase benefits, within six months of the date on which the notice is given. *Pension Sharing (Pension Credit Benefit) Regulations 2000, reg 26* states that extensions may be applied for from the Regulator in similar circumstances to those referred to at **8.12** above in relation to the extension of the implementation period. Otherwise, failure to comply with the transfer notice must be reported to the Regulator within 21 days beginning with the day immediately following the end of the period for compliance (*reg 25*). The Regulator may then impose civil penalties under *PA 1995, s 10* if the trustees failed to take all such steps as were reasonable to ensure that the notice was complied with.

Indexation

8.17   *Pension Sharing (Pension Credit Benefit) Regulations 2000, regs 32–35* provide that occupational pension schemes must apply indexation to the pension credit benefit derived from post-April 1997 rights (other than money purchase benefits which come into payment after 6 April 2005). The indexation to be applied is 5 per cent per annum or the increase in the CPI, whichever is lower, in respect of pensions in payment prior to 6 April 2005 or where entitlement to the pension credit arose before that date, and 2.5 per cent per annum or the increase in the CPI, whichever is lower, where entitlement to the pension credit arose on or after 6 April 2005.

PA 1995, s 67

8.18   *PA 1995, s 67* (as amended by *PA 2004*) contains the 'Subsisting Rights Provisions' which apply to amendments to occupational pension schemes (see **Chapter 13**). Pension credit members of an occupational pension scheme benefit from the protections of *s 67* by virtue of their inclusion in the definition of 'member' (*PA 1995, s 124*) and the inclusion of 'pension credit rights' within the definition of 'subsisting right' (*PA 1995, s 67A(b)*).

Any amendment of a scheme's rules, however, to give effect to the trustees' pension sharing policy and enable the application of a pension debit is excluded from the ambit of *s 67* by virtue of *s 67(3)*, which excludes from the 'subsisting rights provisions' modifications for a purpose connected with pension debits under *WRPA 1999, s 29(1)*.

Treatment on winding up

8.19   In the case of a scheme to which *PA 1995, s 73* applies (see **Chapter 12**), the position of pension credits in the statutory order of priorities on winding up is referred to under *s 73(8)(b)*, where it is stated that benefits derived from pension credits are not to be treated as derived from voluntary contributions for the purposes of that section. In effect this means that pension credits are to be accorded the same treatment on winding up as any other scheme benefit and dealt with in accordance with the statutory priority order set out in *PA 1995, s 73*. Pension credits are to be accorded the same treatment on winding up as the rights of a pensioner member if they have come into payment and the rights of a deferred member if they have not come into payment (*WRPA 1999, s 38(2)*). This section overrides the provisions of the scheme to the extent that they conflict with it.

Valuation

8.20   In creating pension debits and credits under *WRPA 1999, s 29*, the pension sharing order is applied to the cash equivalent of the member's benefits. The specified percentage for reduction of a member's benefits is therefore the percentage of his or her cash equivalent of the relevant benefits on the valuation day (*WRPA 1999, s 29(2)*). 'Valuation day' is defined in *WRPA 1999, s 29(7)* as such day within the implementation period for the credit as the person responsible for the arrangement may specify by notice in writing to the member and ex-spouse.

For active members of occupational pension schemes, the cash equivalent is calculated in respect of the benefits to which the member would have been entitled to had his pensionable service been terminated on the day immediately prior to the transfer day (ie the day on which the pension sharing order takes effect (*WRPA 1999, s 29(4)*). *Section 30* provides for the calculation of the cash equivalent of these benefits to be carried out in accordance with the provisions set out in the *Pension Sharing (Valuation) Regulations 2000*.

Pension Sharing (Valuation) Regulations 2000, reg 4 provides that cash equivalents are to be calculated in accordance with *regs 7 to 7C and 7E(1)– (3)* of the *Occupational Pension Schemes (Transfer Values) Regulations 1996* on the basis of such assumptions as the trustees determine, having taken the advice of the scheme actuary. In the case of an active member, his cash equivalent is required to be calculated on the assumption that the member had made a request for a statement of entitlement (or a cash equivalent in the case of money purchase benefits) as if his pensionable service were to terminate on the valuation day.

With effect from 6 April 2016, *Occupational Pension Schemes (Transfer Values) Regulations 1996, reg 7D* has been disapplied so there is no longer the possibility of the cash equivalents being reduced at the valuation stage where an insufficiency report has been obtained from the scheme actuary or where the trustees are treating the actuary's last relevant GN11 report as an insufficiency report. A reduction for underfunding can still take place at the point a pension credit is discharged externally (*Pension Sharing (Implementation and Discharge of Liability) Regulations 2000, reg 16*).

Disclosure of information

8.21   *WRPA 1999, s 23(1)(a)* provides for regulations to impose requirements on the person responsible for a pension arrangement to supply information to certain parties in connection with the power to provide financial relief under *MCA 1973*. The *Pensions on Divorce etc (Provision of Information) Regulations 2000 (SI 2000/1048)* set out the details of these requirements.

At the beginning of the divorce process the person responsible for the arrangement must, on the request of a scheme member or spouse or pursuant to an order of the court, ensure that the following information is provided in connection with the divorce in accordance with *reg 2*:

(*a*)   a valuation of the pension rights or benefits accrued under the pension arrangement, if requested by the member or the court;

(*b*)   a statement that if the member requests or the court so orders, a valuation of the member's accrued benefits will be provided to the member or the court;

(*c*)   a statement summarising the way in which any such valuation of the benefits disclosed is calculated;

(*d*)   a statement of benefits included the valuation;

(*e*)   a statement as to whether the person responsible for the arrangement intends to offer membership of the scheme to a person entitled to a pension credit (ie internal transfer) and, if so, the type of benefits available;

(*f*)   a statement as to whether the person responsible for the arrangement intends to discharge liability for a pension credit other than by offering membership to a person entitled to a pension credit (ie external option only);

(*g*)   the schedule of charges to be levied by the person responsible for the arrangement; and

(*h*)   any other additional information relevant to the sharing order requested by the court.

Therefore only a member or the court can require the valuation of a member's accrued benefits to be provided by the arrangement. Once requested it must be provided within three months beginning with the date of receipt of the request; or within six weeks of the date of receipt of the request if the member has notified the trustees that it is required in connection with financial relief in divorce proceedings; or within a shorter period if so ordered by the court (*reg 2(5)*).

All the other items of information set out above (excluding a request for a valuation) must be supplied within one month of receipt of the request (*reg 2(6)*).

Regulation 4 sets out the information to be provided by the person responsible for a pension arrangement within 21 days of a notification that a pension sharing order or provision may be made (or such other date as the court orders), as follows:

(*a*)   the full name and address of the pension scheme;

(*b*)   whether the scheme is in winding up and, if so, the effective date of winding up, the contact details of the trustees dealing with the winding up and whether the benefits are likely to be reduced;

(*c*)   whether cash equivalents are subject to reduction;

(*d*)   whether the trustees are aware of any other relevant court orders;

(*e*)   any elements of the member's pension rights which are not shareable;

(*f*)   details of how charges are to be paid;

(*g*)   whether the member is a trustee of the scheme;

(*h*)   whether the scheme may request details of the member's health from the member, if the order were to proceed; and

(*i*)   whether the scheme requires any further information before implementation of the order.

Regulation 5 sets out the information required by the person responsible for the pension arrangement before the implementation period begins, as follows:

(*a*)   In relation to the member – all names and former names; date of birth; address; National Insurance number; name of scheme to which the order relates and membership/policy number.

347

(*b*)   In relation to the ex-spouse – all names and former names; date of birth; address; National Insurance number; if the ex-spouse is also a member of the scheme from which the pension credit is derived, the membership/policy number.

(*c*)   Where the ex-spouse is transferring to another arrangement – the full name and address of that arrangement; the membership or policy number; details of the person able to discharge liability for the pension credit; in the case of rights transferring from an occupational pension scheme which is in winding up with a deficit, whether the ex-spouse has indicated she wishes to transfer the pension credit rights; and any further information the receiving arrangement may require.

Regulation 6 sets out the information to be provided by the person responsible for the pension arrangement after the death of the ex-spouse prior to liability having been discharged with regard to discharge of liability for the pensions credit, recovery of charges and any further information they require.

Regulation 7 sets out the information to be provided by the person responsible for the pension arrangement after receipt of the pension sharing order or provision, and *reg 8* sets out the information to be provided by the person responsible for the pension arrangement in the notice of discharge of liability after the implementation of a pension sharing order.

Charging

8.22   *WRPA 1999, s 41* and the *Pensions on Divorce etc (Charging) Regulations 2000 (SI 2000/1049)* provide for persons responsible for pension arrangements to recover charges in respect of pension sharing costs.

Costs are not recoverable unless the divorcing parties have been informed in writing by the person responsible for the pension arrangement of the intention to recover costs and a written schedule of the charges has been provided. *Pensions on Divorce etc (Charging) Regulations 2000, reg 2* provides that charges cannot be recovered for the provision of basic information about pensions and divorce (pursuant to *Pensions on Divorce etc (Provision of Information) Regulations 2000, reg 2*), or for the provision of information in response to a notification that a pension sharing order may be made (*Pensions on Divorce etc (Provision of Information) Regulations 2000, reg 4*) unless that information has already been provided in the previous 12-month period, or the member has reached normal pension age or is within 12 months of normal pension age. Charges also cannot be recovered for the provision of a cash equivalent which is provided in accordance with *PA 1995, s 93A or 94* or for information provided in accordance with the *Disclosure Regulations*.

Where charges are recoverable they can only be for the reasonable administrative expenses the arrangement will incur in connection with the implementation of the pension sharing order or the provision of information in connection with the divorce proceedings and must be directly related to the individual case (*Pensions on Divorce etc (Charging) Regulations 2000, reg 5*). The legislation does not define, however, what is meant by 'reasonable'. The Pensions and Lifetime Savings Association ('PLSA') has issued guidance on this point to its membership (see **8.24** below).

MCA 1973, s 24D has been introduced to give the courts power to include a provision in the order relating to the apportionment of charges between the parties. To the extent that the court is silent on the issue, *WRPA 1999, s 41(3) (b)* provides that the charges shall be attributable to the scheme member.

Pensions on Divorce etc (Charging) Regulations 2000, reg 7 permits the postponement of the start of the implementation period for a sharing order until specified charges are paid, provided that appropriate notice has been given to the parties no later than 21 days after the person responsible for the pension arrangement has received the pension sharing order requiring the costs to be paid prior to implementation.

Regulation 9 provides for certain methods of recovery of the charges by the person responsible for the pension arrangement. Where the charges are not paid in cash, recovery can be by way of: deduction from the pension credit; deduction from the member's accrued rights; deduction from pension where the pension is in payment; and deduction from payments of pension credit benefits (subject to certain conditions having been satisfied).

Reference should be made to the *Pensions on Divorce etc (Charging) Regulations 2000* for full details of the conditions and restrictions relating to the charging for information and pension sharing activities.

In relation to earmarking orders, charges for the provision of information are dealt with as described above. In relation to the costs associated with the implementation of an earmarking order, *Pensions on Divorce etc (Charging) Regulations 2000, reg 10* provides that the person responsible for the pension arrangement may recover reasonable administrative expenses which have been or are likely to be incurred by reason of the order.

PLSA recommended scale of charges

8.23   The PLSA has produced a recommended scale of charges in relation to pension sharing (see table). The latest version, published in July 2011, is accompanied by a flowchart indicating when a scheme may charge for valuing members' rights. Broadly this would only be when the member is within 12

349

months of normal pension age and certain other conditions apply. No charge can be applied unless it has previously been disclosed to members in a schedule of charges. The full scale of charges and flowchart can be accessed through the PLSA website (www.plsa.co.uk) in the Policy and Research section.

Step	Suggested range	When chargeable	Notes
Produce CETV quotation (active or deferred)	£0–£250	Refer to flowchart	Member can only be charged if wouldn't otherwise be entitled to CETV free of charge.
Produce CETV quotation (pension in payment)	£600–£1,000	Refer to flowchart	
Provision of other information	£0–£500	At any time*	Information which does not have to be provided free may be charged for. Cost will depend upon the nature and complexity of the enquiry.
Processing a pension sharing order ('PSO') – internal transfer, DB scheme	£2,500–£3,000	At any time*	Includes allowance for future scheme admin costs of approximately £1,250.
Processing a PSO – internal transfer, DC scheme	£2,250–£2,750	At any time*	If trustees customarily pay for annuity purchase advice on retirement, it is recommended that an additional sum in the region of £500–£600 can be charged.
Processing a PSO – external transfer, DB scheme	£1,350–£1,950	At any time*	
Processing a PSO – external transfer, DC scheme	£1,300–£1,850	At any time*	

Step	Suggested range	When chargeable	Notes
Processing a PSO when pension already in payment	£250– £500 (in addition to the amount stated above)	At any time*	Includes allowance for recalculation of CETV and recovery of pension arrears if unreduced pension paid to member for a time after PSO effective.

* But only if previously disclosed to members in a schedule of charges

Safeguarded rights

8.24   As part of the measures introduced to simplify pension provision, *PA 2008, s 100* and related repeals in *Sch 11* removed the provisions relating to safeguarded rights in *PSA 1993, Part 3A*. Safeguarded rights were created where rights to future benefits under the scheme were attributable to a pension credit which included contracted-out rights. Safeguarded rights were treated broadly in the same way as contracted-out rights. Shared rights derived from contracted-out benefits are now treated in the same way as other shared rights.

Family Procedure Rules 2010

8.25   The *Family Procedure Rules 2010 (SI 2010/2955)* (which came into force on 6 April 2011) provide a new code of procedure for family proceedings in the various courts and replace the *Family Proceedings Rules 1991*.

Part 9 applies to applications for a financial remedy and sets out the obligations of the parties with regard to the provision of information relating to benefits which a party has or is likely to have under a pension scheme. When the court fixes a first appointment, within seven days after receiving notification of the date of that appointment, the member must request that the person responsible for the pension arrangement(s) under which the member has or is likely to have benefits provides basic information set out in *Pensions on Divorce etc (Provision of Information) Regulations 2000, reg 2(2)* (ie the valuation of the member's pension rights) (see **8.20** and **8.21** above).

Within seven days of receiving this information, the member shall send a copy of it to the other party together with the name and address of the person responsible for the pension arrangement(s). *Rule 9.30(4)* states that, where the member is already in possession of, or has requested, a relevant valuation of his benefits under the pension arrangement in question, then this request for disclosure need not be made (for these purposes a relevant valuation is one which has been provided to the member within the 12 months preceding the date fixed for the first appointment).

Where an application for financial relief includes a pension sharing order, the applicant must send a copy of the application to the person responsible for the pension arrangement (*r 9.31*). In the case of an application for an earmarking order the applicant must send the person responsible for the pension arrangement a copy of the application together with: an address for service of any notices on the applicant by the person responsible for the pension arrangement; an address to which payments can be remitted; and, if that address is a bank, sufficient details to enable payment to be made into the applicant's account (*r 9.33(1)*).

Within 21 days after service of a notice of application for an earmarking order under *r 9.33,* the person responsible for the pension arrangement has the right under *r 9.33(2)* to request the person with the pension rights to provide them with the information disclosed in the financial statement relating to the member's pension rights or benefits under that arrangement. The person responsible for the pension arrangement may, within 21 days of receipt of the financial statement, provide to the applicant, respondent and the court a statement in answer (*r 9.33(5)*). Where the person responsible for the pension does file a statement in answer, he will be entitled to be represented at the first appointment and the court must within four days (beginning on the date on which that person files the statement in answer), give the person notice of the date of the first appointment or other hearing, as may be the case (*r 9.33(6)*).

If the earmarking order is being applied for by way of consent order, the relevant information together with a copy of the draft order must be served on the person responsible for the pension arrangement and the order shall not be made until 21 days have elapsed since service without objections being made or the court has considered any objections (*r 9.34(2), (3)*).

Under *r 9.35*, any order for ancillary relief, whether by consent or not, which includes either a provision for pension sharing or for earmarking must:

(*a*)   in the body of the order state that there is to be provision by way of pension sharing or earmarking in accordance with the annex or annexes to the order; and

(*b*)   be accompanied by a pension sharing annex or an earmarking annex and if there is more than one pension arrangement, an annex must be attached for each arrangement.

8.26   *R 9.37 refers* to pension arrangements which are either in an assessment period for the purposes of the Pension Protection Fund '(PPF'), or where the PPF has assumed responsibility for the pension arrangement.

Where the party with the pension rights receives notification that the pension arrangement is in an assessment period for the purposes of the PPF, the member must send a copy of the notification and the valuation summary to the other party at the time when the valuation information is being sent, or within seven days of receipt (*r 9.37(2), (3)*). If the member subsequently receives notification that, following an assessment period, the PPF has assumed responsibility for the arrangement, the member must within seven days: (i) send a copy of that notification to the other party; and (ii) request from the PPF a forecast of his compensation entitlement and then send that on to the other party within seven days of receipt (*r 9.37(4), (5)*).

Overlap between earmarking and pension sharing

8.27   *MCA 1973, s 24B(5)* states that a pension sharing order may not be made in relation to the rights of a person under a pension arrangement if there is in force an earmarking order in relation to any of the member's benefits under the relevant schemes.

MCA 1973, ss 25B(7B) and *25C(4)* state, conversely, that the power to make an earmarking order may not be exercised in relation to a pension arrangement which is the subject of a pension sharing order in relation to the marriage in question or has been the subject of a pension sharing between the parties to the marriage.

Civil partnerships and same-sex marriages

8.28   The *Civil Partnership Act 2004* (*CPA 2004*) came into force on 5 December 2005 and provides the opportunity for same-sex couples to obtain legal recognition of their relationship by registering as civil partners. The general principles behind *CPA 2004* are that registered civil partners will have access to rights and responsibilities similar to those of married couples, including employment and pension benefits, the duty to provide maintenance for a civil partner, the duty to provide maintenance for children of the partnership, and recognition under intestacy rules.

A civil partnership is formed by signing a civil partnership document in the presence of witnesses and a civil partnership registrar, following which the civil partnership will end only on death, dissolution or annulment. *CPA 2004, Sch 5* makes provision for financial relief in connection with the dissolution of civil partnerships that corresponds to the financial relief available in connection with divorces after marriage under *MCA 1973*. *CPA 2004, Sch 5, Part 4* sets out full details in relation to pension sharing orders available on the dissolution or nullity of a civil partnership, and these provisions mirror in essence those set out in the preceding paragraphs of this chapter in relation to divorce. *CPA 2004, Sch 5, Part 6* sets out the provisions in relation to earmarking orders.

Consequential amendments have been made, therefore, to all relevant statutes and regulations referred to in the preceding paragraphs of this chapter to extend the provisions to apply on the dissolution of a civil partnership including, in particular, amendments to *MCA 1973* and *WRPA 1999*.

The Marriage (Same Sex Couples) Act 2013 (SSCA 2013) came into force on 13 March 2014, and provides that same sex couples may marry under the law of England and Wales. *SSCA 2013 s 11* and *Sch 3* modifies statutory references to 'marriage' so that the term also relates to individuals married to a person of the same sex, although this does not extend to survivors' benefits under occupational pension schemes (survivor's benefits of same sex spouses are to be treated in the same way as survivor's benefits for civil partners). However the effect of *SSCA 2013, s 11* is that with effect from 13 March 2014, the law on divorce will apply equally to same sex marriages as it does to opposite sex marriages. The provisions of the governing documentation of pension schemes which relate to pension rights on divorce should be reviewed and updated, if they have not been already, to reflect the new legal requirements in relation to same sex spouses.

Pension Protection Fund

8.29   *PA 2008, Part 3* extends the principle of pension sharing to apply to PPF compensation by the creation of pension compensation sharing orders. The provisions relating to the pension compensation payable on the discharge of a pension compensation credit are set out in *PA 2008, Sch 5*, and the necessary amendments to *MCA 1973* are set out in *PA 2008, Sch 6*. In summary, since 6 April 2011, the courts have been able to make an order requiring an individual's PPF compensation rights to be shared on divorce/ dissolution of civil partnership in the same way as ordinary pension rights. They cannot be made in relation to rights which have already been shared using a normal pension sharing order or earmarking order in relation to the same marriage/partnership. The mechanism is very similar to normal pension sharing, but it is the PPF Board which is required to implement the order. External transfers will not be permitted.

On 6 April 2011 the following two Regulations came into force which allow pension sharing orders and earmarking orders to be made in relation to PPF compensation:

• *Pension Protection Fund (Pension Compensation Sharing and Attachment on Divorce etc) Regulations 2011 (SI 2011/731)*. These regulations implement the provisions of *Chapter 1* and (in part) *Chapter 2* of *Part 3* of *PA 2008*, which permit the courts to make pension compensation sharing orders and attachment orders in relation to PPF compensation in proceedings related to divorce, dissolution of a civil partnership, or in cases of annulment.

- *Pension Protection Fund (Pensions on Divorce etc: Charges) Regulations 2011 (SI 2011/726)*. These regulations apply where a pension sharing or pension attachment order or provision was made before the PPF assumed responsibility for an occupational pension scheme and (in the case of a pension sharing order or provision) was not implemented by the trustees or managers of the scheme prior to the scheme's transfer to the PPF. The regulations set out the costs which may be charged to the parties to the order or provision and the circumstances in which the PPF may recover the costs of implementing a pension sharing order or provision, or complying with a pension attachment order or provision.

A third set of regulations, the *Divorce and Dissolution etc (Pension Protection Fund) Regulations 2011 (SI 2011/780)* also came into force on 6 April 2011. These regulations make provision relating to orders under the *MCA 1973* and the *Civil Partnership Act 2004*, including those made after proceedings overseas, made in connection with proceedings for divorce or dissolution of a civil partnership, nullity of marriage or nullity of a civil partnership or separation which relate to the pension compensation rights of a party to the marriage (described in *MCA 1973, s 25G(5)* as the 'party with compensation rights') or a party to a civil partnership (described in *PA 2004, Sch 5, para 37(1)* as the 'civil partner with compensation rights'). In particular, in so far as PPF compensation is concerned, they provide for:

(*a*) notices of a change of circumstances to be provided to the PPF by the 'other party' (defined in *reg 2(1)(d)* as the party to the marriage or the civil partnership (as the case may be) who is not the party with compensation rights or civil partner with compensation rights);

(*b*) the PPF to make a payment to the party with compensation rights where information or particulars provided by the other party under the *Family Procedure Rules 2010 (SI 2010/2955)* are inaccurate or the other party has not notified the Board about a change to that information or particulars such as a change of details of a bank account into which the payment is made;

(*c*) the PPF to be discharged of liability from a requirement in a relevant order (defined in *reg 3(1)*) to make a payment to the other party in the circumstances outlined in paragraph (*b*));

(*d*) the other party to make a payment to the party with compensation rights to the extent of the payment the other party has received from the PPF after the relevant order has ceased to have effect (eg because of the other party's remarriage or entering into a subsequent civil partnership), where the other party has failed to give the required notice to the PPF of that order ceasing to have effect; and

(e) the PPF to be discharged of liability to the party with compensation rights as a result of making a payment to the other party in the circumstances outlined in paragraph (d) above.

Chapter 9

Discrimination

Introduction

9.1   Much of the UK's anti-discrimination law comes from the European Union ('EU'). For example, the principle of equal pay for men and women is contained in *Article 157* of the *Treaty on the Functioning of the European Union ('TFEU')*, and the *Equal Treatment Framework Directive (2000/78/EC)* requires Member States to put in place legislation prohibiting discrimination in employment on a number of grounds including sexual orientation, age, disability and religious belief. This is a large and developing area of the law.

Domestic legislation reflecting EU requirements relating to age, disability, gender reassignment, marriage and civil partnership, pregnancy and maternity, race, religion or belief, sex and sexual orientation can be found in the *Equality Act 2010 (EqA 2010)*. The general provisions of *EqA 2010* are outlined in **9.2–9.5** below with the rest of this Chapter looking at the development of the law in different areas of discrimination in more detail.

On 23 June 2016, the UK voted to leave the EU. The consequences of the outcome of the referendum ultimately depend on the type of exit model adopted and any transitional provisions that are agreed in the meantime. Although the UK would no longer be bound by EU law following the withdrawal, it seems unlikely that provisions which are generally considered to be working reasonably well would be repealed. However, the UK will have the opportunity to deviate from EU requirements and adopt its own domestic direction. Over time we may see the UK Parliament repealing some existing provisions in an attempt to 'cut EU red tape'. In relation to discrimination and equal treatment there are unlikely to be major changes on policy grounds. There may be an opportunity to relax some of the age discrimination provisions in order to allow pension schemes to operate with more certainty and not have to rely on justification arguments.

Equality Act 2010

9.2   The sections of *EqA 2010* relating to pensions and employment law came into force on 1 October 2010. *EqA 2010* has two main stated purposes:

- to harmonise discrimination law; and

- to strengthen the law to support progress on equality.

The majority of the provisions which impact on pension schemes are covered by the first aim – essentially, it is a consolidation of discrimination law, with earlier statutes and regulations being repealed and a new statutory structure introduced.

EqA 2010 contains a list of 'protected characteristics' which are then subject to protection from discrimination, harassment and victimisation in specific areas – including occupational pensions.

Protected characteristics

9.3   The protected characteristics are:

- age – by reference to a particular age or to a range of ages;

- disability;

- gender reassignment – where someone is proposing to undergo, is undergoing or has undergone gender reassignment;

- marriage and civil partnership;

- pregnancy and maternity;

- race;

- religion or belief;

- sex; and

- sexual orientation.

Occupational pension schemes

9.4   An occupational pension scheme must be taken to include a non-discrimination rule (or a sex equality rule in relation to sex discrimination) by virtue of which the 'responsible person' must not discriminate (directly or indirectly) in the carrying out of any of his functions in relation to the scheme. 'Responsible persons' include trustees and employers.

Some points of interest not covered elsewhere in this chapter are:

- A non-discrimination rule does not apply in relation to pension credit members. They are excluded from protection because their rights are derived from orders of the court rather than employment rights (although the exclusion does not appear to apply to sex equality rules) (*EqA 2010, s 61(5)*).

- Non-discrimination rules were already in place in relation to age, disability, religion or belief and sexual orientation (and an equal treatment rule in relation to sex). *EqA 2010* adds a requirement for a non-discrimination rule in respect of gender reassignment and marriage and civil partnerships.

Trustees' power to amend

9.5   *EqA 2010, s 62* gives trustees an overriding power to modify their scheme rules by resolution to comply with the non-discrimination rule (a similar power is given in relation to a sex equality rule by *EqA 2010, s 68*). Trustees may use this power to eliminate discriminatory scheme rules where:

- they do not have power to amend; or

- the amendment procedure is 'liable to be unduly complex or protracted' or 'involves obtaining consents which cannot be obtained or which can be obtained only with undue delay or difficulty'.

Sex discrimination/equal pay

9.6   Prior to the 1990s, it was common for employers to offer different pension provision to men and women. The effect of EU law in prescribing requirements for equal treatment in pension schemes could no longer be ignored in the UK when the Court of Justice of the European Union ('CJEU') (previously the European Court of Justice ('ECJ')) confirmed in the *Barber* case (*Barber v GRE Assurance Group C-262/88 [1990] ECR I-1889*) that pensions were 'pay' for the purposes of the equal pay requirements of what was then *Article 119* of the *Treaty of Rome* (which is now referred to as the *TFEU*). *Article 119* was subsequently renumbered as *Article 141* by the *Treaty of Amsterdam* with effect from 1 May 1999, and is currently *Article 157* of the *TFEU* (from 1 December 2009 following the *Treaty of Lisbon*).

Article 157 of the *TFEU* provides that:

'1.   Each Member State shall ensure that the principle of equal pay for male and female workers for equal work or work of equal value is applied.

2.   For the purpose of this Article, 'pay' means the ordinary basic or minimum wage or salary and any other consideration, whether in cash or in kind, which the worker receives directly or indirectly, in respect of his employment, from his employer.

9.6 *Discrimination*

Equal pay without discrimination based on sex means:

(*a*) that pay for the same work at piece rates shall be calculated on the basis of the same unit of measurement;

(*b*) that pay for work at time rates shall be the same for the same job.'

The action in *Barber* was against the employer, not the pension scheme, as at that time there was no direct equal pay claim available against pension scheme trustees. In brief, Mr Barber was made redundant at the age of 52 and received various cash benefits, but was not entitled to take his pension. A woman in the same position as Mr Barber would have been entitled to an immediate retirement pension in addition to redundancy pay. Mr Barber claimed successfully in the CJEU that pensions should be treated as pay under *Article 157* and that, in consequence, he should be entitled to the same benefits as a woman of the same age. The CJEU's decision was not retrospective; claims were not permitted (unless legal proceedings had already begun) for entitlement to benefits accrued in relation to service prior to the date of judgment, 17 May 1990.

The *Maastricht Protocol* annexed to the *EU Treaty* (7 February 1992) formalised this by amending the then *Article 141* limiting its application in relation to pensions to benefits accrued on or after 17 May 1990.

Decisions of the CJEU are binding only upon those to whom they are addressed, but where EU law has direct effect (see *Article 288* of the *TFEU*) it will generally override UK law. The principle that *Article 157* has direct effect was established on 8 April 1976 by the *Defrenne (No 2)* case (*Defrenne v Sabena [1976] ECR 455*) which stated that the protections given under *Article 157* apply directly to the law of Member States without the need for any further national or European legislation. This was confirmed in the *Coloroll* case (*Coloroll Pension Trustees Ltd v Russell (C-200/91) [1995] All ER (EC) 23*), which also made it clear that *Article 157* can be relied upon by both employees and their dependants against pension scheme trustees who are also bound to observe the principles of equal treatment.

The general requirements for equal treatment in pension schemes are now incorporated in *EqA 2010* (see *ss 67–69*). These cover not only the terms on which scheme members are treated but also the terms on which employees are admitted to membership and the exercise of discretions under the scheme. *EqA 2010 s 67(2)* provides that in relation to a term which is less favourable to A than it is to B (someone of the opposite sex to A), the term is modified so as to be not less favourable. The requirements are overriding so schemes must comply with them, irrespective of the actual provisions in their governing documentation. *EqA 2010, s 68* empowers trustees of schemes with inadequate amendment powers to make whatever rule amendments are necessary to ensure compliance with the equal treatment requirements.

Employers or trustees will have a defence against an equal treatment claim if they can show that the difference in treatment is because of a material factor which is not the difference of sex (*EqPA 2010,s 69(4)*).

PA 2004 also contains equal treatment provisions. *Section 171*, which came into force on 6 April 2006, provides for the equal treatment of men and women in relation to the 'payment function' of the Board of the PPF. The Explanatory Notes to *PA 2004* state that *s 171* provides the mechanism to ensure that there is no discrimination between men and women arising from the use of the scheme rules when calculating entitlement to pension compensation (see **Chapter 5**).

It can be seen that there has been no clear policy or decision of principle underlying the development of UK law in this area. Indeed, it had been thought that the implementation of sex equality in pension schemes was simply not practicable. The cost issue alone was a significant deterrent to equalisation. Pension matters were expressly excluded from the equal pay and sex discrimination legislation passed in the 1970s and 1980s. Thus, the law has grown in fits and starts, very much in reaction to developments in the EU. It is an area of law in which most of the major issues have now been resolved, although a few anomalies remain.

Access/eligibility

General

9.7   The principle of equal access to pension scheme membership for men and women was first established in UK legislation by the *Social Security Pensions Act 1975*, with detailed provision contained in regulations (the *Occupational Pension Schemes (Equal Access to Membership) Regulations 1976 (SI 1976/142)*). These Regulations were superseded by the *Occupational Pension Schemes (Equal Treatment) Regulations 1995 (SI 1995/3183)* (the *'Equal Treatment Regulations'*). The relevant provisions of the *Social Security Pensions Act 1975* were re-enacted in *PSA 1993* (*s 118*) then in *PA 1995*, *ss 62–66* and now in *EqA 2010, ss 67–69*.

The CJEU, in the 1994 judgments of *Vroege v NCIV Instituut C-57/93 [1994] ECR I-4541* and *Fisscher v Voorhuis Hengelo BV C-128/93 [1994] ECR I-4583*, clearly stated that, as well as entitlement to benefits, the right to join an occupational pension scheme also falls within the scope of *Article 157* of the *TFEU*, and is therefore covered by the prohibition on sex discrimination laid down by that Article. This means that the direct effect of *Article 157* can be relied upon to claim (retrospectively) equal treatment from 8 April 1976 (the date of the *Defrenne* case when it was established that *Article 157* had direct effect). In these two judgments the CJEU confirmed the earlier decision in *Bilka-Kaufhaus GmbH v Weber von Hartz C-170/84*

[1986] ECR 1607 that indirectly discriminatory entry conditions which could not be objectively justified were in breach of *Article 157* (see **9.8** below).

Part-time employees

Exclusion from membership

9.8 The exclusion of part-time workers from scheme membership may infringe the equal pay requirements of *Article 157* if it can be shown that there has been indirect sex discrimination. *TFEU* does not itself outlaw different treatment of part-time workers although domestic law now does (see **9.11** below).

Direct sex discrimination occurs where, for example, women are denied entry to a pension scheme but men are not. Indirect sex discrimination occurs where, for example, the pension scheme eligibility requirements are such that they are to the detriment of a significantly greater proportion of women than men because fewer women can comply with them. By applying such restrictions the employer and/or trustees are indirectly discriminating against women unless they can either explain the difference by reason of a genuine material factor not related to sex or objectively justify the treatment.

It has generally been the case that considerably more women than men work part-time and, thus, may suffer indirect discrimination. In the *Bilka-Kaufhaus* case, the CJEU stated that there would be a breach of *Article 157* if the exclusion of part-time workers affected a much greater number of women than men (and could not otherwise be justified). Unfortunately, the CJEU did not expand on what it meant by 'a much greater number'.

In the case of *Regina v Secretary of State for Employment ex parte Seymour-Smith and Another Case C-167/97 [1999] ICR 447*, the CJEU considered among other questions the test for determining whether a measure adopted by a Member State had 'such a disparate effect as between men and women as to amount to indirect discrimination'. The CJEU stated that the best approach to this issue was to compare statistical evidence of the proportion of men and women able to satisfy the condition at issue and those unable to do so and to compare those proportions. If the statistics indicated that a 'considerably smaller percentage' of women than men were able to satisfy the condition, there was indirect sex discrimination unless the measure was justified by objective factors. In addition, a lesser but persistent and relatively constant disparity over a long period between men and women who satisfied the particular condition at issue could also amount to indirect sex discrimination. The question of whether the statistical difference is sufficient to establish a claim of indirect discrimination is one of fact in each individual case and the courts have been reluctant to set down any general guidelines.

Exclusion from membership with justification

9.9   Even if the workforce statistics suggest that there might be indirect discrimination, a scheme will not have to admit part-timers if the employer can demonstrate that the difference in treatment can be objectively justified on grounds unrelated to sex. In the *Bilka-Kaufhaus* case it was accepted that a rule that incidentally adversely affects more women than men may nevertheless be lawful. It is for national courts to decide whether a particular rule is or is not justifiable, but guidelines laid down by the CJEU suggest that the onus is on the employer to show that:

(*a*)   the grounds put forward do not relate to the employee's sex;

(*b*)   the grounds put forward relate to a real need of the employer; and

(*c*)   the measures taken are appropriate and necessary to achieve the desired end.

An employer who can show, for example, that there is a genuine need to encourage full-time working patterns because they increase productivity or that part-timers will gain very little or nothing by joining a scheme that is contracted out instead of remaining with the State second pension, may be able to exclude part-timers without infringement of *Article 157*.

Justification is considered in more detail in the context of age discrimination in **9.32** below.

Part-timers' claims – legal developments

9.10   The *Equal Treatment Regulations* came into force on 1 January 1996 to supplement the requirements for equal treatment relating to occupational pension schemes provided for in *PA 1995, ss 62–66* (now in *EqA 2010, ss 67–69*). The *Regulations* extended the scope of the *Equal Pay Act 1970* to cover pensions and consequently (in accordance with the then provisions of the *Equal Pay Act*) any claim had to be brought to the employment tribunal within six months of the end of the employment to which the claim related. Pensions claims were limited to two years' backdated membership. The *Equal Treatment Regulations* also imposed the full cost of funding the excluded employee's benefits after 31 May 1995 on the employer.

The CJEU reviewed the validity of these time limits in *Preston v Wolverhampton Healthcare NHS Trust [2000] All ER (EC) 714*. This was followed by a referral to the House of Lords (*Preston (No 2) [2001] IRLR 237, HL*). The House of Lords confirmed that national legislation was unlawful if it restricted claims to two years' service. Therefore, pension benefits payable after a successful claim had to be calculated by reference to all periods of service for which the employee should have been a scheme member (or, if later, from 8 April 1976

– the date of the *Defrenne* judgment (see **9.7** below)). The House of Lords upheld the requirement that a claim for membership of an occupational pension scheme must be brought to the employment tribunal within six months of the end of the employment to which the claim relates. It also made it clear that a series of short-term contracts can amount to a stable employment relationship and employment does not terminate at the end of each individual contract but at the end of the stable relationship. The EAT *(Preston v Wolverhampton Healthcare NHS Trust (No 3) [2004] IRLR 96)* decided that there was no continuing breach of *Article 157* by an employer failing to inform a part-time employee of his entitlement to join the pension scheme, unless that failure was itself on discriminatory grounds. However, employees may have a breach of contract claim in such circumstances on the basis of the employer's implied obligation to inform employees of advantageous contractual terms.

The *Occupational Pension Schemes (Equal Treatment) (Amendment) Regulations 2005 (SI 2005/1923)* implemented the rulings in the *Preston* case. They were repealed with effect from 1 October 2010 and the provisions relating to time limits can now be found in *EqA 2010, s 129* (which requires a claim to be brought to the employment tribunal within six months of the end of employment or of a stable working relationship) and to remedies in *EqA 2010, s 133* (which allows an order for pension scheme membership to be backdated to 8 April 1976 at the earliest).

The EAT held in the case of *Copple & Ors v Littlewoods Plc & Ors UKEAT/0116/10/ZT* that where a part-timer had been unlawfully excluded from an occupational pension scheme, but on the balance of probabilities she would never have joined it even if it had been open to her, there was no basis for awarding back-dated membership of the scheme. This decision was upheld by the Court of Appeal *([2011] EWCA Civ 1281)* which confirmed that if workers choose not to exercise their right to join the scheme when they are able to do so, they cannot later claim the right to be allowed to join it with retrospective effect.

It may be possible for employees who are outside the statutory time limits for bringing a claim to the employment tribunal to complain to the Pensions Ombudsman. The Ombudsman took this view in his determination of *Mrs D Copnall (Case No F00828, 28 September 2000)*. He determined that failure to admit part-timers retrospectively to a pension scheme was maladministration. However, this finding was overturned on appeal to the High Court in *Glossop v Copnall [2001] PLR 263* when Sir Andrew Morritt held that a trustee's failure to comply with the requirements of legislation is not of itself maladministration. The High Court held that trustees acted properly in waiting for the relevant decisions by the CJEU before granting backdated benefits.

The benefit of making a complaint to the Pensions Ombudsman is that the more generous limitation period of three years applies. The Ombudsman can also extend the three-year limitation period in exceptional cases where the complainant was unaware of the event giving rise to the complaint or if it was not reasonably practicable for the complaint to be made or referred within the three-year time limit. However, the Ombudsman is precluded from investigating complaints if proceedings have already been brought before the courts and this includes employment tribunal claims *(PSA 1993, s 146(6))*.

The Supreme Court has confirmed that breach of contract claims relating to equal pay can be brought in the High Court within six years of the breach complained of, even where the claimant is out of time for bringing a claim in the employment tribunal *(Abdulla v Birmingham City Council [2012] UKSC 47)*. This is subject to the inherent jurisdiction of the High Court to strike out a claim if it is an abuse of process (this leaves it open for the High Court to consider the reasons why the claim was not brought in the employment tribunal). The court would also be able to take into account all the circumstances when considering a costs order (were a claim to have claim been brought before the tribunal a costs order could only be made in certain limited circumstances – the implication being that the court should consider not making a costs order against the employer where a claim could have been brought to the tribunal but was not).

In the case of *National Pensions Office v Jonkman (C-231/06)* the CJEU confirmed that members can be required to make good contributions for the period of backdated membership but that:

(*a*) any interest payable must compensate for inflation only; and

(*b*) there can be no requirement for the payment to be made as a single sum where that condition makes the payment impossible or excessively difficult in practice, in particular where the sum exceeds the annual pension payable.

Where retrospective membership of a scheme has been granted, under the *FA 2004*, employees can make unlimited contributions to a registered pension scheme during a tax year but may only get tax relief on contributions up to the higher of their total UK earnings or £3,600 and tax charges will arise if the annual allowance is exceeded (see **Chapter 17**).

The Part-time Workers Regulations

9.11   The *Part-time Workers (Prevention of Less Favourable Treatment) Regulations 2000 (SI 2000/1551)* (the '*Part-time Workers Regulations 2000*') came into effect on 1 July 2000 implementing *Directive 97/81/EC* as extended to the UK by *Directive 98/23/EC (the 'Part-time Workers' Directive')*. The Regulations require employers to treat part-time workers no less favourably than they treat comparable full-time workers. In addition, employers may not treat less favourably an employee who, having worked full-time, returns to work on a part-time basis after absence, compared with the way the employee was treated when he or she worked full-time. This is subject to the defence of objective justification. It is therefore no longer necessary for a part-timer to prove indirect discrimination in order to claim entitlement to the same benefits as full-time workers. Employers must ensure that there are no restrictive conditions relating to access to, and benefits under, the pension scheme for part-time workers.

However, as referred to above, treating part-timers less favourably than full-timers can be justified on objective grounds provided that it can be shown that the less favourable treatment is:

(a)   to achieve a legitimate objective (for example, a genuine business objective);

(b)   necessary to achieve that objective; and

(c)   an appropriate way to achieve that objective.

To reflect the ruling in *Preston (No 3)* (see **9.10** above), the *Part-time Workers (Prevention of Less Favourable Treatment) Regulations 2000 (Amendment) Regulations 2002 (SI 2002/2035)* amended the *Part-time Workers Regulations 2000* from 1 October 2002 removing the restriction backdating a claim to two years from the date upon which the complaint was presented.

The first case under the *Part-time Workers Regulations 2000* to reach the Court of Appeal was *Matthews v Kent & Medway Towns Fire Authority [2004] EWCA Civ 844*. Mr Matthews worked as a part-time fire-fighter and complained that he was discriminated against compared to full-time fire-fighters, in particular by not being granted access to the pension scheme. The Court of Appeal found that the part-time fire-fighters were employed under the same type of contract as their full-time colleagues but that the full-time fire-fighters carried out additional job functions not carried out by the part-time workers and so were not relevant comparators. The part-time fire-fighters took their case to the House of Lords (*Matthews v Kent and Medway Towns Fire Authority [2006] All ER 171*). The fire-fighters' appeal was allowed and the case was sent back to the employment tribunal for reconsideration of the question whether part-time and full-time fire-fighters are engaged in the same or broadly similar work.

Following the House of Lords' decision, the tribunal reconsidered and upheld the part-time fire-fighters' claim (*Matthews and others v Kent & Medway Town Fire Authority and others 6100000/2001 (ET)*).

It was held that:

•   the part-time fire-fighters carried out the same or broadly the same work as full-time fire-fighters;

- the part-time fire-fighters were treated less favourably in terms of pension provision and sick pay; and

- the differences in treatment could not be justified.

The issue of the justification of less favourable treatment of part-timer workers was considered by the Supreme Court in 2013 in the case of *O'Brien v Ministry of Justice [2013] UKSC 6*. Mr O'Brien was a fee paid part-time judge (a recorder). On retirement he claimed a judicial pension but was declined one on the grounds that it was not open to recorders, only to full-time or salaried part-time judges. It was not in dispute that the *Part-time Workers' Directive* required that Mr O'Brien should be treated in a similar manner to a comparable full-time worker unless the difference could be objectively justified.

The Supreme Court considered the guidance given to it by the CJEU (*[2012] ICR 955*), which can be summarised as:

- the concept of 'objective grounds' ... requires the unequal treatment at issue to respond to a genuine need, be appropriate for achieving the objective pursued and be necessary for that purpose;

- budgetary considerations cannot justify discrimination ((*Schönheit (C-4/02 and C-5/02 [2003] ECR I-12575, para 85*) and *Tirol (C-486/08) [2010] ECR I-3527, para 46*));

- the unequal treatment at issue must be justified by the existence of precise, concrete factors, characterising the employment condition concerned in its specific context and on the basis of objective and transparent criteria for examining the question whether that unequal treatment responds to a genuine need and whether it is appropriate and necessary for achieving the objective pursued.

The three 'genuine needs' put forward by the Ministry of Justice were:

- 'Fairness' in the distribution of the State's resources that are available to fund judicial pensions. The court rejected this. Recorders were paid the same daily rate as full time judges minus the pension. Pensions are part of pay and it is not justifiable to pay a different daily rate to full and part-timers. The Ministry's argument was found to be in effect one of budget and not of fairness and this was not an argument which could succeed.

- Attracting a sufficiently high number of good quality candidates to salaried judicial office. This argument failed on the basis that giving or not giving recorders a pension would make no difference to those applying for full-time judge posts.

- Keeping the cost of judicial pensions within limits which were affordable and sustainable. The Ministry accepted that cost alone could not be a justification (see **9.32** below). The court concluded that: 'The European cases clearly establish that a Member State may decide for itself how much it will spend upon its benefits system, or presumably upon its justice system, or indeed upon any other area of social policy. But within that system, the choices it makes must be consistent with the principles of equal treatment and non-discrimination. A discriminatory rule or practice can only be justified by reference to a legitimate aim other than the simple saving of cost'.

Having rejected all three proposed justifications, the court directed that Mr O'Brien should be provided with a pension. The EAT subsequently confirmed that the pension should be back-dated only for service since 7 April 2000, the date on which the Part-time Workers' Regulations should have been transposed into UK domestic law (*UKEAT/0466/13*). Mr O'Brien made an made an unsuccessful appeal on this point to the Court of Appeal (*[2015] EWCA Civ 1000*), which confirmed that Mr O'Brien was only entitled to accrue pension from 7 April 2000. His rights fell to be determined on the basis of the EU rules which applied at the time of the period of service in relation to which those rights were acquired. Mr O'Brien appealed again to the Supreme Court (*UKSC 2015/0248*). On 7 July 2016 the Supreme Court, at a Permission to Appeal hearing, heard arguments as to whether the appeal should be dismissed or referred back to the CJEU. The Supreme Court's judgment on that issue is awaited.

Benefits

General

9.12   Although the matter of equal access to pension schemes has presented many difficulties, many more questions have been raised over the issue of equality in benefits and contributions. This arises, in the main, from the fact that benefit design and computation have been dictated by actuarial science which takes into account, among other matters, the differing mortality rates of the sexes. The *Barber* decision (17 May 1990) meant that immediate action had to be taken, and various measures were adopted to implement equalisation. Many, but not all, of the issues raised by the *Barber* decision were clarified in subsequent CJEU decisions (notably, the 1994 *Coloroll* decision (*Coloroll Pension Trustees Ltd v Russell C-200/91 [1994] ECR I-4389*)). It had been feared by employers that the equalisation of benefits would have to be fully retrospective. The CJEU in *Coloroll* confirmed that retrospection is only required in relation to benefits payable for periods of service from 17 May 1990.

The CJEU required employers and trustees to consider three time periods in respect of measures to equalise benefits under their schemes:

(*a*)   the period up to 17 May 1990, when benefits need not be equalised;

(*b*)   the period from 17 May 1990 to the date when scheme benefits are equalised, when benefits must be 'levelled up' (ie increased to the level enjoyed by the advantaged sex); and

(*c*)   the period after the date when scheme benefits are equalised. Although *Article 157* itself permits benefits to be 'levelled up' or 'levelled down' in respect of this period, the UK decision in the *Lloyds Bank* case should be noted at this point (*Lloyds Bank Pension Trust Corporation Ltd v Lloyds Bank plc [1996] OPLR 181*). In this case, the High Court decided that future accrual rates could not be reduced to meet equalisation objectives. However, this decision turns on the particular wording of the scheme amendment power. *Section 68* of *EqA 2010* allows trustees to modify their scheme to equalise benefits where they do not have power to do so under the scheme rules, or they do have that power but the procedure for doing so is liable to be unduly complex or protracted, or involves obtaining consents which cannot be obtained or which can be obtained only with undue delay or difficulty. It is not currently clear how this provision would interact with a Lloyds-type amendment power.

Derived rights

9.13   The requirement for equality in pay and pensions applies also to spouses, survivors, dependants and others who are entitled to claim benefits through an employee's membership of a scheme. In *Ten Oever v Stichting Bedrijfspensioenfonds voor het Glazenwassers-en Schoonmaakbedrijf C-109/91 [1993] ECR I-4879* the CJEU confirmed that a survivor's pension falls within the scope of *Article 157*. Thus, any scheme benefit provided for the wife of a male member must also be provided for the husband of a female member. The CJEU in *Coloroll* confirmed that, as for members' benefits, the requirement for equal treatment only applies in relation to service from 17 May 1990.

Transfers

9.14   Schemes which accept transfer payments in respect of benefits accrued since 17 May 1990 will bear the burden of equalisation as a consequence of any inadequacy in the transfer payments received. The CJEU considered (in *Coloroll*) that the rights accruing to an employee from *Article 157* cannot be affected by the fact that he changes his job and has to join a new scheme, with his accrued pension rights being transferred to the new scheme. However, in the event of an inadequate transfer payment being made, the CJEU envisaged the receiving scheme making a claim (under national law) against the transferring scheme for the additional sums required to equalise the benefits to be paid. In practice trustees of the receiving scheme should seek to obtain an indemnity from the transferring scheme to cover such additional sums as may be required.

9.15 *Discrimination*

Transferring employees may make a claim against both the trustees of the transferring scheme and of the receiving scheme. The *Acquired Rights Directive (77/187/EEC)* (replaced by *Directive 2001/23/EC*) was designed to safeguard employees' rights and ensure continuing employment following a transfer of a business undertaking. However, provisions contained in a contract of employment or collective agreement relating to an occupational pension scheme are specifically excluded. There have been a number of challenges to this pensions exclusion over the years (see **Chapter 15** for a discussion of the *Beckmann* and *Martin* cases).

The position of money purchase schemes which receive unequalised transfer payments is uncertain. Clearly, there would be serious practical difficulties in complying with the obligation to equalise, possibly entailing the re-allocation of funds in individual members' accounts. Arguably, the *Coloroll* decision does not encompass money purchase schemes (see **9.18** below) but pending clarification of the issue, the trustees of such schemes should act with caution.

Bridging pensions

9.15   Bridging pensions aim to achieve a form of equality between men and women, by taking into account the earlier date from which women are currently eligible to receive the State pension. In *Birds Eye Walls v Friedl M Roberts C-132/92 [1993] PLR 323*, the pension for a female ex-employee was reduced when she reached age 60 (the then State pension age for women), whereas a man would have received a full pension to age 65. The CJEU was asked whether bridging pensions where in breach of *Article 157*. The CJEU held that bridging pensions were not discriminatory because they were designed to remove an existing inequality arising as a consequence of the different ages that State pension commences for men and women. The *Equality Act 2010 (Sex Equality Rule) (Exceptions) Regulations 2010 (SI 2010/2132)* exclude bridging pensions paid in these circumstances from the ambit of the sex equality rule contained in *EqA 2010, s 67*. In addition, *FA 2004* (as amended by *FA 2013*) allows scheme pensions to be reduced at any time between the age of 60 and the date on which a member reaches State pension age by an amount not exceeding the rate of the State retirement pension (*Sch 28, para 2*). The *Pension Protection Fund and Occupational Pension Schemes (Miscellaneous Amendments) Regulations 2013 (SI 2013/1754)* came into force on 1 October 2013. They enable trustees to modify schemes by resolution, with employer consent, to bring bridging pensions in line with changing state retirement ages (or to fix them at a specified age between 60 and 65).

The decision in *Birds Eye* is difficult to reconcile with the decision in *Bestuur van het Algemeen Burgerlijk Pensioenfonds v Beune C-7/93 [1995] All ER (EC) 97*, where the CJEU held that it was unlawful for a scheme to make deductions in respect of the State pension where it had the effect of producing a lower pension for men but not women from the scheme.

Actuarial factors

9.16   The use of actuarial factors in funded final salary occupational pension schemes which vary according to sex was held by the CJEU in *Coloroll* not to fall within the scope of *Article 157*. This was so even though the amount of a transfer value for a man would be lower than for a woman in consequence of the actuarial factors used in the assessment of the capital sum transferred that are based on life expectancy which differs between men and women.

The issue of unequal transfer values had previously been considered in *Neath v Hugh Steeper Ltd C-152/91 [1993] ECR I-6935*. It considered that it is only the employer's commitment to the payment of a periodic pension at a particular level which constitutes pay within the meaning of *Article 157*. It decided that the funding arrangement by which the pension was to be secured falls outside the scope of *Article 157*. Although this was confirmed in the *Coloroll* decision, the CJEU has made the position clear only in relation to final salary schemes.

It was confirmed in *Neath* that as employees' contributions were deducted from salaries, employees' contribution rates must be the same for both men and women as they constitute an element of pay within *Article 157*. Thus, although contributions made by employees must be equal as between men and women, as these contributions are an element of their pay, employers' contributions are calculated to ensure the adequacy of the funds necessary to secure the future payment of periodic pensions and may be unequal due to the use of sex-based actuarial factors. Inequalities in the amounts of capital benefits or substitute benefits (for example, where a dependant's pension is payable in return for surrender of part of the member's annual pension or where a reduced pension is paid on early retirement) whose value can be determined only on the basis of the arrangements chosen for funding the scheme, were likewise considered to be outside the scope of *Article 157*.

Notwithstanding the above, the CJEU held on 11 September 2007 that the use by the Council of the European Union of different actuarial factors for men and women when calculating transfer values was unlawful sex discrimination (*Lindorfer v Council of the European Union C-277/04P [2009] All ER (EC) 569*). The *Lindorfer* case did not expressly overrule the decision in *Neath*, and UK schemes may still rely on the statutory exemptions relating to actuarial factors.

EqA 2010, Sch 7, part 2, paragraph 5 and the *Equality Act 2010 (Sex Equality Rule) (Exceptions) Regulations 2010, reg 4* expressly permit the use of actuarial factors which differ for men and women. It is stated that the sex equality rule does not operate in relation to actuarial factors which differ for men and women in respect of the differences in the average life expectancy of men and women and which are determined with a view to providing equal periodical pension benefits for men and women. The difference in treatment is permitted only in relation to certain prescribed benefits as set out in *regulation 4*.

The decision of the CJEU in the *Test-Achats* case (*Association Belge des Consommateurs Test-Achats ASBL, Yann van Vugt, Charles Basselier v Conseil des Ministres [2011] EUCJEU C-236/09*) on 1 March 2011 is another step towards the use of unisex actuarial factors in pension schemes. The court concluded that the derogation in *Council Directive 2004/113/EC* of 13 December 2004 (the 'Gender Directive') from the requirement not to discriminate on the grounds of sex in relation to insurance premiums had to be removed from 21 December 2012. With effect from that date, the UK government was required to ensure that the use of sex as a factor in actuarial calculations for the purposes of insurance and related financial services must not result in differences in individuals' premiums and benefits.

The *Test-Achats* ruling applies to insurance contracts under the *Gender Directive*, not to benefits provided under occupational pension schemes (which are subject to the *Equal Treatment Directive*). In order to comply with the *Test-Achats* ruling, the provision of *EqA 2010* which allowed sex-based actuarial factors to be used by the insurance and financial services industry (*Sch 3, para 22*) was repealed with effect from 21 December 2012 by the *Equality Act 2010 (Amendment) Regulations 2012/2992*. In addition, the *Registered Pension Schemes (Relevant Annuities) (Amendment) Regulations 2012 (SI 2012/2940)* come into force on 21 December 2012. These require pension providers to assume that the purchaser is male when calculating the 'annual amount' payable by a notional equivalent annuity for the purpose of draw-down pensions.

Occupational pension schemes remain subject to *EqA 2010* which allows both age and sex-based actuarial factors to be used in certain circumstances. *EqA 2010, s 29* prohibits discrimination in the provision of goods and services, including financial services but does not apply 'to the provision of a relevant financial service if the provision is in pursuance of arrangements made by an employer for the service-provider to provide the service to the employer's employees, and other persons, as a consequence of the employment'. This means that annuities purchased from insurance providers from 21 December 2012 are subject to the unisex requirement unless they fall within the *s 29* exemption (ie they are 'in pursuance of arrangements made by an employer'). The application of the *Test-Achats* ruling to pension schemes is still not entirely clear. In a response to consultation in July 2012, HM Treasury stated that 'the European guidelines on the Gender Directive [state] that the directive applies to annuity purchases where the employer is not involved' but goes on to say that further clarification of what this means can only be resolved by further EU law or by the courts.

What is clear is that those taking an annuity from a scheme which is not an occupational pension scheme from 21 December 2012 are subject to gender neutral actuarial factors. It is also settled that occupational pension schemes operating internal annuitisation or commutation may continue to use sex-based actuarial factors. What is less clear is the position of those purchasing annuities on retirement from occupational pension schemes. It is arguable (and HM Treasury seems to accept this) that an annuity purchased from an insurer using assets from an occupational scheme (even in the name of the member) could be subject to the exception in *EqA 2010, s 29* and so there would be no requirement for gender neutral actuarial factors to be used.

Under *FA 2004, s 234,* when calculating the annual allowance a single factor of 16:1 is used to value the annual increase in benefits regardless of the sex or age of the member. In addition, *FA 2004, ss 214–219* provide that, when valuing defined benefits against the lifetime allowance, a single factor is used regardless of the age or sex of the member (normally 20:1).

Additional voluntary contributions

9.17   Equality principles apply to all pension benefits under a scheme and it is irrelevant whether they are attributable to employers' or employees' contributions. However, where the scheme does no more than provide the necessary arrangements for the management of contributions and payments of the resulting benefits (in relation to money purchase additional voluntary contributions) those resulting benefits are not covered by *Article 157*. Consequently additional benefits deriving from contributions paid by employees on a voluntary basis are not covered by *Article 157*, as these additional contributions are to secure benefits over and above those which they are entitled to expect by reason of their employment and cannot, therefore, be regarded as pay within the meaning of *Article 157*.

Money purchase benefits

9.18   In money purchase schemes, the pension commitment of the employer is an obligation to pay a defined level of contribution. The CJEU has not directly decided how the principle of equal treatment is to be applied to money purchase schemes. What has been established is that the commitment or 'promise' to the employee, which must be equal between men and women, is to be distinguished from the funding considerations, which are not covered by *Article 157*.

It is generally accepted that, as the employer in a money purchase scheme does not promise any particular level of benefit, the commitment is the contribution, and as such these must be equal. In schemes which use sex-based actuarial factors, it is not possible to have both equal contributions and equal benefits. If the *Neath* case applies to money purchase schemes, women are most likely to be the disadvantaged sex. This is because the capital sum built up will not secure the same amount of pension for a woman as for a man. Her periodic pension will be lower as it will take account of the expectation that she will live longer. However, since 21 December 2012, gender-neutral actuarial factors may apply (see **9.17** above) resulting in equal benefits.

Retirement ages

State pension age and contractual retirement age

9.19   State pension age is being equalised at age 65 in the period to November 2018. It will then be increased to age 66 for both sexes by April 2020 and to 67 by March 2028 (*PA 1995, s 126, Sch 4* as amended *by PA 2007, PA 2011*, and *PA 2014*). *Section 27* of the *Pensions Act 2014* (which came into force on 14 July 2014) provides for the Secretary of State to review state pension age 'from time to time' to consider whether it remains appropriate having regard to life expectancy and other relevant factors. The results of the first review must be published before 7 May 2017 and thereafter a review must be published at least every six years (although the stated Government intention is that it should be once every parliament). In March 2016, John Cridland CBE was appointed to undertake the first review, looking at SPA from 2028. The terms of reference for the review provide that the recommendations should be affordable in the long term, fair to current and future generations of pensioners and consistent with supporting fuller working lives.

Ascertaining the contractual retirement age is not always straightforward. If the contract of employment is silent on the retirement age, the established custom and practice will be looked at to determine when employees have retired in the past in relation to that particular position. However, the contractual retirement age must not be different for men and women doing the same job.

Since 6 April 2011 employers cannot impose a contractual retirement age unless it can be objectively justified. See **9.35** below for commentary on retirement ages in the context of age discrimination.

Retirement age under the pension scheme

9.20   Although the *Barber* case established beyond doubt that pensions were 'pay' and, in consequence, that pensions had to be equal for men and women, the questions as to how and from what date equalisation was to be implemented were not answered until the later CJEU cases of *Coloroll* and *Smith v Avdel*. In *Smith v Avdel*, the employer proposed to implement the *Barber* decision by raising the retirement age of women to that of men from June 1991. The change was implemented in relation to benefits paid in respect of service both before and after June 1991. The CJEU held that until equalisation measures had been taken, the only proper method of compliance with *Article 157* was to confer upon the disadvantaged sex those advantages enjoyed by the favoured sex, in respect of service after 17 May 1990. In the *Smith v Avdel* case this meant that, for the period between May 1990 and June 1991, the pension rights of men were to be calculated on the basis of the same retirement age as women. This principle was followed in the *Harland and Wolff* case *(Harland and Wolff Pension Trustees Limited v Aon Consulting Financial Services Limited [2006] EWHC 1778 (Ch))*, even though the scheme's amendment power expressly allowed retrospective modification.

The High Court considered this issue again in *Safeway v Newton [2016] EWHC 377 (Ch)*, where it held that amendments to achieve equalisation (from 62 for women and 65 for men to 65 for all) could not be made retrospectively (following *Smith v Avdel* and *Harland v Wolff*). The main question in this case is whether the equalisation at 65 was effective from 1 December 1991 when a letter was sent to members announcing the change or from 2 May 1996 when the change was first included in a deed of consolidation. The court found that the change in retirement age would only take effect on the execution of a deed (although under domestic law, that deed could be retrospective to the date of the letter). The judge went on to hold that the general principle in *Smtih v Avdel* preventing retrospective levelling-down does not depend on the particular form of the scheme's amendment power and that under EU law the amendment could not be retrospective and the deed was effective to equalise retirement ages at 65 only from 2 May 1996.

Thus, from 17 May 1990 until the date of the equalisation of retirement ages, the pension rights of men must be enhanced to correlate with the lower retirement age of women. For the period prior to the date of the *Barber* decision, the CJEU determined that there was no requirement to equalise benefits. With regard to the period following the date of equalisation, *Article 157* does not preclude equalisation measures which have the effect of reducing the benefits of the (previously) advantaged sex but those measures cannot have retrospective effect. *EqA 2010, ss 67* and *68* (which aim to bring into statute the effect of *Barber* and the subsequent cases) do not preclude this either. However, neither *Article 157* nor *EqA 2010* overrides trustees' duties to act in their members' best interests (or an employer's duty of good faith).

Conclusions and practical issues

General

9.21   Although many of the equality issues raised by the *Barber* case have now been settled, there is still much case law dealing with equalisation. The main difficulty which has confronted many employers and trustees is how to implement the equal treatment requirement in their schemes.

Employers and trustees

9.22 It was unclear from the *Barber* decision whether *Article 157* imposed an obligation both on the trustees and the employer in respect of equal treatment. Whilst the primary obligation to implement equalisation falls upon the employer, the position of trustees was clarified by the CJEU in the *Coloroll* case. The CJEU confirmed that trustees in the exercise of their powers and in the performance of their obligations are also bound to observe the principles of equal treatment. Although *Article 157*, as interpreted by the decisions of the CJEU, is overriding, *EqA 2010* clearly envisages schemes being amended to comply with the sex equality provisions. *EqA 2010, s 68* empowers trustees or managers of occupational pension schemes to make amendments by resolution where either they do not have the necessary amendment powers to implement the sex equality rule, or they do have powers available but the procedure for implementation is 'liable to be unduly complex or protracted' or 'involves the obtaining of consents which cannot be obtained, or can only be obtained with undue delay or difficulties'.

Review of scheme documentation

9.23 Although the sex equality legislation is overriding, clarity and consistency in the day to day application of the principles can only be achieved if scheme documentation is brought into line with the current law. Most schemes have by now updated their documentation to reflect the sex equality requirements, but areas to look out for include:

(*a*) the definition of normal retirement age;

(*b*) equality in early retirement terms, survivors' benefits, and transfer arrangements; and

(*c*) allowing trustees the discretion to grant enhanced benefits in individual cases.

Scheme amendments

9.24 As stated above (see **9.12** and **9.20**), employers and trustees must consider three time periods in respect of measures to equalise benefits under their schemes:

(*a*) the period up to 17 May 1990, when benefits need not be equalised;

(*b*)   the period from 17 May 1990 to the date formal equalisation takes effect, when benefits must be 'levelled up'; and

(*c*)   the period after the date formal equalisation takes effect, when benefits can be levelled up or down.

Careful scrutiny of the power of amendment will be necessary to ensure that any changes made are a valid exercise of that power. Amendment powers often contain an express restriction that accrued rights cannot be reduced without members' consent. Even in the absence of specific wording to that effect, such a restriction is consistent with a trustee's fiduciary duty to act in the best interests of the members and it is generally accepted to be consistent with the employer's duty of good faith towards its employees. Further, *PA 1995, s 67* imposes restrictions on scheme amendments which affect 'subsisting rights'. In summary, subsisting rights are rights or entitlements which a member has accrued to or in respect of him to future benefits under the scheme rules. Schemes are not able to reduce the value of a member's subsisting rights (without member consent) but they are able to make changes to the nature of the rights, provided that the overall actuarial value of the affected person's subsisting rights is not reduced (see **Chapter 13**).

Following the decision in *Van den Akker v Stichting Shell PF C-28/93 [1994] ECR I-4527*, it is not possible to 'red circle' groups of members (ie to apply preferential benefits to a group of members who were exclusively women or men) unless the group delineation was objectively justified. More recently the EAT has considered the issue of red-circling in the context of transitional pay protection schemes in the *Bury* and *Sunderland* cases (*Bury Metropolitan Borough Council v Hamilton and others UKEAT 0413-5/09* and *Council of the City of Sunderland v Brennan and others UKEAT/024/09* upheld by the Court of Appeal in *[2012] EWCA Civ 413*). The EAT summarised the position as follows:

(*a*)   where the past discrimination was direct, continued discrimination in the form of transitional arrangements cannot be justified – the removal of the discrimination must be 'immediate and full' (*Smith v Avdel*);

(*b*)   the position is more flexible where the past discrimination was indirect. The continuation of the past indirect discrimination will not be unlawful if it can be justified. This would involve the employer doing 'all he could to minimise the effect of the continuing discrimination'.

There have been several cases concerning problems with the way pension schemes have sought to equalise benefits.

In *Betafence Limited v Veys and others [2006] EWHC 999 (Ch)*, the scheme provided men with a normal retirement age of 65 and women with a normal retirement age of 60. The scheme amendment power did not require amendments to be recorded in a formal document. In 1991 the employer issued an announcement to members stating that from 1 October 1991, the normal retirement age for both men and women would be age 65 but a member could retire from service from age 60 without incurring an early retirement reduction. Unfortunately for the company, this announcement was found by the High Court to have the unintended consequence of allowing male members to retire at age 60 without company consent, where previously consent had been required.

The case of *Trustee Solutions v Dubery [2006] 36 PBLR* considered whether a scheme amendment power had been validly exercised to change the normal retirement date (NRD) relating to female members. The Colour Processing Laboratories Pension Scheme was a final salary scheme with an NRD of 65 for male members and 60 for female members. In July 1992, the employer issued an announcement to female members informing them that, with effect from 1 October 1991, their NRD would be 65. In 2002, winding up of the scheme was triggered and the trustees sought directions from the court in relation to the following:

(*a*) whether the amendment power had been validly exercised in 1992;

(*b*) whether an estoppel arose so as to close the '*Barber* window'; and

(*c*) how the statutory priority order should be applied (see **9.26** below).

The scheme rules provided that amendments could be 'by any writing effected under hand by the Trustees and the Principal Company', provided that the amendments did not vary benefits already accrued.

Two documents were presented:

(*a*) a memorandum from the trustees to members setting out the options for equalising retirement ages for men and women and inviting members to a presentation; and

(*b*) an announcement from the principal employer to female members stating that the normal retirement date was being equalised at age 65.

The High Court held that there had been no valid amendment to the rules and no estoppel arose. It was held that 'under hand' meant a document that was signed. As neither of the documents met this requirement, the rules had not been validly amended and the *Barber* window remained open. In addition, it was stated that even if the documents had been signed, they were inadequate to amend the rules because the memorandum merely set out the options and the announcement did not come from the trustees. This case was the subject of an appeal but the High Court's findings in relation to the validity of the amendments stand (see **9.26** below).

In *Harland and Wolff Pension Trustees Limited v Aon Consulting Financial Services Limited [2006] EWHC 1778 (Ch)*, the trustees claimed that their advisers had failed to advise properly in relation to equalisation. The scheme rules provided different retirement ages for men and women (63 and 60 respectively). The rules were amended retrospectively in September 1993 so that, from 17 May 1990, the normal retirement age for female members would be 63. It was accepted that the rules of the scheme permitted retrospective amendments; however, the question before the court was whether the amendment satisfied the requirements of *Article 157*. The court held that although the amendment power was wide enough to permit the amendment in question, an amendment could not validly remove the free-standing rights granted by European law (ie following the *Smith v Avdel* case). Until equalisation measures are taken, the only proper method of compliance with *Article 157* is to confer upon the disadvantaged sex those advantages enjoyed by the favoured sex in respect of service after 17 May 1990 (ie levelling up). Therefore, the court held that, for the period between 17 May 1990 and September 1993, the normal retirement age for male members was age 60.

In *Hodgson and others v Toray Textiles Europe Limited and others [2006] EWHC 2612 (Ch)* the trustees and the employer had sought to equalise members' normal retirement ages at 65 by issuing an announcement in May 1994. Doubts about the validity of this amendment led to a deed of amendment being executed in 2004. Under the scheme amendment power, amendments had to be made by deed. However, the definition of normal retirement age itself provided that it could subsequently be altered, with no mention of a deed. The definition did not say who could amend members' normal retirement age, but all parties agreed that the consent of the employer, trustees and members was required. The court held that the 1994 amendment was ineffective and the announcements were not enough to alter the normal retirement age. Although the trustees and the employer might be said to have agreed the change, it would not be right to infer that members had consented to the change.

In *Capital Cranfield Trustees Ltd v Beck [2008] EWHC 3181 (Ch)*, the High Court held that an announcement by the employer was not effective to equalise retirement ages. This case focused on whether the announcement amounted to a valid exercise of the power of amendment and/or a power in the definition of NRD, allowing the employer to determine a member's NRD. It was held that the announcement did not comply with the strict requirements of the amendment power. Also, it was concluded that the power contained in the definition of NRD could not be exercised in relation to a class of member.

In *Capita Pension Trustees Ltd & others v Gellately & others [2011] EWHC 485 (Ch)*, the High Court ruled that an attempted equalisation had failed as, again, the formalities in the power of amendment had not been complied with. The Definitive Deed and Rules provided that the NRD was 65 for those joining on or after 1 January 1991 (65/60 for those before) 'except where otherwise stated or otherwise agreed by the Employers and the Trustees'. The amendment power required amendment by deed but also allowed the Rules to be amended by resolution. In 1995, an announcement was issued confirming that NRD would be 65 for all members.

It was argued that the wording of the NRD definition gave the Principal Employer and Trustees a freestanding right to alter the NRD without the formalities required by the power of amendment. Henderson J held that the power to agree a different NRD should not prevail over the formal requirements of the amendment power where the proposed change in NRD was of general application: 'Where a scheme-wide amendment to the rules is in issue, one expects to find that certain formalities have to be complied with, and it is to the amendment clause that one turns in order to find out what those formalities are'.

These cases emphasise the need for trustees and employers to ensure they follow the strict formalities of the amendment power when equalising benefits.

The recent case of *Premier Foods v RHM Pension Trust Ltd [2012] EWHC 447 (Ch)* may indicate a softening of the courts' approach to the formalities required for successful equalisation. In this case, the scheme's power of amendment allowed the trustee to amend the provisions of the scheme by deed. In November 1990 a 'Deed of Intention' was executed by the trustee. It recited that the trustee had decided to amend the scheme to reflect changes to the retirement age (NPA) which had already been announced to members and that it intended to amend the Trust Deed and Rules as soon as possible to reflect the change. On 18 February 1993 an amending deed was executed providing an NPA of 65 for all members. Warren J looked at cases concerning interpretation and concluded that:

'There is a well-established principle that in choosing between an interpretation which makes the instrument valid and effective and one which makes it invalid or ineffective, the court should lean towards the construction which saves the instrument'.

He went on to find that the alterations in the Deed of Intention were viewed by all parties as being substantive and effective and requiring the trustee to operate the scheme in accordance with the equalised NPA. The trustee would be in breach of trust if it operated the scheme other than in accordance with the governing documentation of the scheme so if the Deed of Intention did not make a successful amendment it would in effect be requiring the trustee to operate the scheme in a way inconsistent with the governing documentation. He therefore interpreted the Deed of Intention as being effective in amending the provisions of the scheme from November 1990.

Another recent decision which indicates a less rigid approach is the Scottish case of *Bett Homes Ltd v Wood [2016] CSIH 26* (decided on 15 April 2016), which contrasts with the decision in *Capita v Gellately*. In this case it was accepted by the employer and trustee that equalisation changes had not been made in accordance with the scheme's main amendment power. Instead, the employer sought to argue that the changes had been validly made under the 'special terms' power which provided:

> 'The Trustees may with the consent of the principal employer determine in relation to any Member that his Membership shall be on such special terms as are intimated to him.'

The court held that the special terms power was drafted in the widest possible terms and there was no restriction relating to the circumstances in which the trustees could operate it. However, the court found no evidence of a decision having been made by the trustees. The mere fact the trustees administered the scheme on the equalised basis was not sufficient to infer that a determination had been made by them.

In *Briggs v Gleeds [2014] EWHC 1178 (Ch)* the High Court (Newey J) ruled that the failure to witness the signatures of partners on various deeds (including one purporting to introduce *Barber* equalisation amendments) meant that the deeds were invalid as a result of failure to comply with statutory requirements for the valid execution of deeds.

Where there is no amendment power, or inadequate provision, the power conferred by *EqA 1995, s 68* may be used to implement the sex equality requirements. The exercise of the statutory power may place the employer in a vulnerable position, as it is a power to be used by the trustees alone.

Formerly contracted-out schemes/guaranteed minimum pensions (GMPs)

9.25 The issue of equalisation of GMPs (see **Chapter 4**) is fraught with difficulty. Neither the CJEU nor the Government has addressed all the difficulties that arise as a result of the fundamental design of GMPs correlating to the State scheme with its discriminatory pension ages. Specifically, the difficulties arise out of the methods of calculation and revaluation applied to the GMP element of a pension before and after state pension age is attained. The *Equality Act 2010 (Sex Equality Rule) (Exceptions) Regulations 2010* permit pension increases to be paid at different rates on GMPs and pensions in excess of GMPs, in so far as the difference does not exceed the increase on the State additional pension for the same period (although those regulations are yet to be amended to reflect the abolition of contracting-out from 6 April 2016).

The determination by the Pensions Ombudsman in *Williamson* dated 7 January 2000 *(No: H00177)* directed the trustee and the company to equalise GMPs in compliance with the equal treatment rule under the then *PA 1995, s 62*. However, he did not make any directions as to how this should be done and noted that:

> 'Parliament apparently concluded that salary-related schemes should have the flexibility and freedom to make their own arrangements as to how equalisation should be achieved.' (paragraph 37)

Furthermore, he expressed the view that the method of equalisation chosen should not be one that could lead to some members of the scheme being adversely affected.

The *Williamson* determination was subsequently overturned in the High Court in *Marsh Mercer Pension Scheme v Pensions Ombudsman [2001] 16 PBLR (28)* on the basis that the Ombudsman's jurisdiction did not extend to his making a decision on the question of equalisation of GMPs as this matter had an impact on other members of the scheme without allowing them the opportunity to put their case. Rimer J added that GMPs in isolation did not have to be equalised on the basis that they are not a distinct part of a pension scheme. However, the position as to whether total benefits should be equalised was undecided.

The rulings of the European Court in *Bestuur van het Algemeen Burgerlijk Pensioenfonds v Beune C-7/93 [1995] AII ER (EC) 97* and *Birds Eye Walls v Friedl M Roberts C-132/92 [1993] PLR 323* (see **9.16** above) appear contradictory in deciding whether a scheme may provide unequal benefits to men and women to remove an existing inequality as a result of the different ages that State pension commences for men and women. These two cases were considered by the High Court in *Uppingham School v Shillcock [2002] EWHC 641 (Ch)*, in its ruling that an LEL offset to integrate with the State scheme was not indirect sex discrimination and, had it been so, that it would have been objectively justified. This case would appear to support the argument that unequal GMPs are objectively justifiable if the intention is to integrate with the State scheme.

In the case of *Leadenhall Independent Trustees Limited v Welham [2004] All ER (D) 423 (Mar)*, the scheme was winding up with a surplus and the trustee sought directions from the court as to whether it had the power to allocate funds in such a way as to neutralise the gender discrimination of GMPs. The court said that the trustee could augment deferred benefits as there was express power in the governing documentation to do so. In the case of existing pensioners (for which there was no express power of augmentation) the court was not willing to say whether or not the trustee could augment benefits, nor was it prepared to state whether overriding EU equal treatment law could be applied. The court suggested that, if the trustee did decide to go ahead and augment benefits for pensioners, it should consider taking out trustee insurance.

PSA 1993, ss 24A–24H enable trustees of formerly contracted-out defined benefit schemes to convert GMPs into normal scheme benefits, provided that actuarial equivalence is maintained. This gives schemes more flexibility in the benefits they can provide and may make it easier for members to transfer out their benefits if they wish. There must, however, be some question as to how the actuary will be able to confirm actuarial equivalence when the question of the equalisation of GMPs for men and women has not been resolved. GMP conversion has been available since 6 April 2009 but few, if any, schemes have taken advantage of it. The DWP is currently 'exploring' whether changes can be made to the current provisions.

On 28 January 2010 the then Pensions Minister, Angela Eagle, issued a written ministerial statement to the effect that schemes should be equalising GMPs accrued from 17 May 1990. The Government received a number of representations from the pensions industry in response and took further legal advice on the points raised. In January 2012 the DWP issued consultation which includes draft legislation effectively requiring GMPs to be equalised (the *draft Occupational Pension Schemes and Pension Protection Fund (Equality) (Amendment) Regulations 2012*). The Government's view is that schemes are under an obligation to equalise GMPs accrued between 17 May 1990 and 5 April 1997 without the need for a comparator of the opposite sex. The draft Regulations, which the DWP states are intended to codify existing EU obligations into UK law, include amendments to *EqA 2010* effectively requiring the equalisation of GMPs. *EqA 2010, ss 64* and *67* are to be amended so that the sex equality rule operates without the need to find an opposite sex comparator, where any difference in treatment between men and women results from the application of the GMP provisions and *s 66* is to be amended so that, to the extent the sex equality clause applies, it also applies without the need to find an opposite sex comparator where the difference in treatment between men and women results from the application of the GMP provisions. The consultation also included draft guidance on a method of equalisation. The method, which is not intended to be compulsory, proposed a comparison of what each member actually gets and what that member would get if he or she were treated as being a person of the opposite sex. The member's entitlement is the higher of the two amounts. The comparison would be undertaken each time the amount of pension in payment is calculated (generally annually). The proposals have proved controversial within the pensions industry.

In February 2013, the Pensions Minister Steve Webb announced that the legislation would be delayed at least until the spring of 2014. Following on from that announcement, the DWP published an interim response to the 2012 consultation. The response confirmed that Government has not changed its view of the legal position but there had been some criticism of the complexity of the methodology set out in the consultation. The laying of the final regulations has been delayed so that the Government could give further consideration to providing statutory guidance for schemes on GMP conversion and including

GMP equalisation, as this 'could potentially offer schemes a simpler way to achieving equalisation'. As of April 2016, this is still awaited. In July 2016 the Pensions Ombudsman issued a determination in the case of *Kenworthy (PO-4579)* in which he noted the various statements from the DWP and the delay in enacting legislation requiring GMP equalisation and determined: 'In my opinion, the Respondent can continue to defer taking action to equalise GMPs until this issue has been resolved'.

The Government's view that GMPs must be equalised derives from EU law. It may therefore mean that the resolution of this issue may not come until after the UK has finalised its withdrawal from the EU.

Since November 2012, schemes entering a PPF assessment period have been required to equalise GMPs in accordance with the PPF's guidance (see **Chapter 5**).

Winding up and mixed retirement ages

9.26 *Cripps v Trustee Solutions Ltd and Dubery [2007] EWCA Civ 771* (the name on appeal of *Trustee Solutions v Dubery*, see **9.24** above) concerned the division of assets amongst different groups of members on winding up. This decision is of particular interest to trustees of defined benefit schemes which commenced winding up before 6 April 2005.

The question on appeal concerned which members fell into the priority pensioner category on winding-up, and for what portion of their benefits. The difficulty arose because male members of the scheme, who had been members since before May 1990, had accrued part of their benefits based on a retirement age of 65 and part on a retirement age of 60. The High Court had held that any member aged 60 or over as at the date winding-up commenced was in the pensioner priority category on winding-up for all his benefit (not just the tranche of benefit accrued with a retirement age of 60).

Mrs Cripps (a deferred member of the scheme who would have received a reduction in her benefit as a result of that decision) appealed. The Court of Appeal overturned the High Court judgment on this point and ruled that those members aged between 60 and 64 on the date winding-up commenced will be in the pensioner priority category only for that portion of their benefits accrued with a retirement age of 60. Consequently, they are to be treated as being in the deferred category with a lower priority in relation to benefits accrued with a retirement age of 65.

The decision in *Cripps* was distinguished by the Court of Appeal in *Foster Wheeler Limited v Hanley & Others [2009] EWCA Civ 651*. The facts of *Foster Wheeler* are fairly typical. Prior to May 1990, female members of the scheme had an NRD of 60 and male members 65. From May 1990 to August 1993, all members accrued benefits based on an NRD of 60. The scheme rules were amended from 16 August 1993, giving all members an NRD of 65. The High Court had held that all members could receive their benefits as a single pension from age 60, with no early payment reduction applied to the tranche of benefit accrued with an NRD of 65. This gave a significant windfall to those members with substantial benefits accrued with an NRD of 65, as they would have expected a reduction for early payment before age 65. The employer appealed the High Court decision. The Court of Appeal was asked to consider three options:

- **Option 1** – a single pension calculated on the basis that all the benefits had fallen due for payment on the date of retirement (no reduction for early payment). This is the decision which had been reached by the High Court in *Foster Wheeler*.

- **Option 2** – a single pension with benefits accrued with an NRD of 65 reduced for early payment.

- **Option 3** – split pensions (ie a separate pension payable from each NRD). This had been the decision in the Court of Appeal in *Cripps v Trustee Solutions*.

The Court of Appeal concluded that, in this case, Option 2 was the correct approach. This would result in each member obtaining a single pension from age 60 comprising the benefits accrued with an NRD of 60 in full plus the benefits accrued with an NRD of 65 reduced for early payment.

The facts of this case turn on the detailed provisions of the scheme rules, and so Option 2 will not always be the correct answer. The Court of Appeal did, however, set down some guiding principles:

- where possible, effect should be given to *Barber* rights by adhering to the scheme provisions;

- if some departure is required it should, so far as practicable, represent the minimum interference to both the substance and the form of scheme provisions;

- possible options should be compared, and consideration given in relation to each option as to whether effect can be given to *Barber* rights in some other way involving less interference with the rights of any party; and

- whether a particular option is appropriate will depend on the circumstances of the individual scheme.

Age discrimination

9.27   *Council Directive 2000/78/EC* 'establishing a general framework for equal treatment in employment and occupation' was adopted on 27 November 2000 (the *'Equal Treatment Framework Directive* '). The purpose of the *Equal*

Treatment Framework Directive (as stated in *Article 1*) is to 'lay down a general framework for combating discrimination on the grounds of religion or belief, disability, age or sexual orientation as regards employment and occupation'. Member States had until 2 December 2003 to implement its provisions into domestic law with the possibility of a three-year extension to 2 December 2006 for the age and disability aspects (*Article 18*).

The *Employment Equality (Age) Regulations 2006 (SI 2006/1031)* (the '*Age Regulations*') came into force on 1 October 2006 implementing the EU age discrimination requirements in the UK. Implementation of the requirements relating to pensions was delayed until 1 December 2006 to give the Government time to carry out a further consultation on the exemptions for pension schemes (the *Employment Equality (Age) (Amendment) Regulations 2006 (SI 2006/2408)*). The pension exemptions were finalised on 10 November 2006 (the *Employment Equality (Age) (Amendment No 2) Regulations 2006 (SI 2006/2931)*).

With effect from 1 October 2010 the relevant parts of the *Age Regulations* were repealed by the *EqA 2010*. The age discrimination requirements relating to pensions can now be found in the *EqA 2010* and the *Equality Act (Age Exceptions for Pension Schemes) Order 2010 (SI 2010/2133)* (as amended) (the '*Age Exceptions Order'*).

What is discrimination on grounds of age?

9.28 Direct discrimination on grounds of age occurs when trustees treat a member or prospective member, or an employer treats a worker, less favourably than he treats others on grounds of age. Indirect discrimination occurs when an apparently age-neutral provision is applied which in fact disadvantages members or workers of a particular age or age group (*EqA 2010, ss 4, 5, 13 and 19*). Unlike other strands of discrimination, both direct age discrimination and indirect age discrimination can be justified (*EqA 2010, s 13(2)*).

The discrimination, direct or indirect, must be between people where the relevant circumstances are the same or not materially different (*EqA 2010, s 23*). This means, for example, that employers could argue that the position of senior executives is not the same as, or is materially different to, the rest of the workforce, thus enabling them to be provided with better benefits.

In relation to pensions, *EqA 2010* applies only to rights accrued or benefits payable in respect of periods of pensionable service on or after 1 December 2006 (*Age Exceptions Order, art 3*). However, lump sum death-in-service benefits are not generally calculated based on a period of accrual, and the full amount of those benefits arising from a death on or after 1 December 2006 will be subject to the *EqA 2010*.

Exemptions from age discrimination requirements

9.29   There are a number of exemptions for pension schemes in the *Age Exceptions Order*. The exemptions allow some, but not all, common age-related rules and practices in pension schemes. Key exemptions are set out in the following table.

Exemption	Commentary
Age-related contributions to money purchase schemes (*Sch 1, para 4*).	The aim of the different rates of contribution must be to equalise or make more nearly equal resulting benefits in respect of comparable periods of pensionable service to which members of different ages will become entitled. In practice, this means that contributions for older members may be higher than for younger members, to reflect the fact that they will be subject to investment growth for a shorter period.
Maximum or minimum ages for admission including different ages for admission for different groups or categories of worker (*Sch 1, para 1*).	Schemes may set a minimum or maximum age for admission and to set different ages for different categories of worker.
Length of service requirement (*Art 6*).	In relation to admission to a scheme and the accrual of or eligibility for any benefit under the scheme, trustees and employers may impose a service requirement of up to five years. Any period of more than five years requires the employer to be satisfied that it is fulfilling a business need (eg by encouraging loyalty or motivation, or rewarding experience) and the trustees must obtain confirmation from the employer of this. The length of service can either be the actual length of service, or the length of service working at a particular level (eg the five-year period can run each time an employee is promoted).
Pension based on service (*Sch 1, para 17*).	Any difference in the amount of benefit attributable to differences in length of pensionable service is allowed as long as members in a comparable situation accrue a right to benefit based on the same fraction of pensionable pay.

Exemption	Commentary
Final pensionable salary *(Sch 1, para 25)*.	There is an express exemption allowing a cap to be placed on the salary to be taken into account when calculating a benefit (this could either be a cap equivalent to former HMRC limits, or a scheme-specific cap).
Maximum length of pensionable service *(Sch 1, para 21(2))*.	*Paragraph 21(2)* exempts any limitation on benefit where that limitation results from imposing a maximum number of years of pensionable service.
Targeted benefits *(Sch 1, para 18)*.	This exemption applies, for example, where an accrual rate is set so as to target a pension of two-thirds final pensionable salary at normal retirement date.
Closure to new entrants *(Sch 1, paras 26 and 27)*.	There is an express exemption allowing the closure of a scheme, from a particular date, to workers who have not yet joined it. There is also an exemption to allow sections of schemes to be closed from a particular date to new entrants. A section of a scheme means: (*a*) any group of members who became eligible to join, or who joined, the scheme on, after or before a particular date on the basis that particular benefits will be provided to or in respect of those members or that a particular level of contributions will be paid in respect of those members; or (*b*) any group of members who became eligible to join, or who joined, the scheme as a result of a block transfer.
Normal retirement date *(Sch 1, para 11)*.	Schemes may set a specific age as the earliest date at which a benefit becomes payable without consent and without actuarial reduction (other than in special cases such as ill health). This is referred to in the *Age Exceptions Order* as the early retirement pivot age ('ERPA').

Exemption	Commentary
Early retirement (*Sch 1, paras 8, 9* and *10*).	Schemes may include a provision setting a minimum age for the payment of or entitlement to benefits prior to ERPA (with or without consent).
	Any benefit paid between this minimum age and ERPA (other than on the grounds of ill health or redundancy) must be actuarially reduced and no added years awarded unless the practice can be objectively justified. The reduction must be on the basis that the aim is to reflect the fact that the benefit is paid before ERPA, which suggests that the aim should be cost neutrality.
	Existing enhanced early retirement rules may continue to apply in relation to members, or prospective members, as at 1 December 2006. This exemption also applies to members as at 1 December 2006 who are subject to a subsequent bulk transfer. The enhancement may be on the basis of potential future service to 'normal pension age' (which is the earliest age at which a member is entitled to receive benefits), a fixed number of years of future service or by reducing or removing the actuarial reduction. Enhancement on any other basis may need to be justified.
Enhancement of benefits on ill health (*Sch 1, para 12*).	There is an express exemption allowing benefits payable on retirement before ERPA (see above) on the grounds of ill health to be enhanced on the basis of potential future service to 'normal pension age' (which is the earliest age at which a member is entitled to receive benefits), a fixed number of years' future service or by reducing or removing the actuarial reduction.
Calculation of death benefits (*Sch 1, para 13*).	Death benefits may be enhanced by reference to prospective service to 'normal pension age' (which is the earliest age at which a member is entitled to receive benefits), a fixed number of years' future service or by reducing or removing the actuarial reduction. Enhancement on any other basis may need to be justified.
Bridging pensions (*Sch 1, para 14*).	Bridging pensions are exempt where they can be reduced at any time between the ages of 60 and 65, or at state pension age, by up to the level of State pension.

Exemption	Commentary
Requirements imposed by *FA 2004 (Sch 1, para 32).*	Paragraph 32 exempts any provisions relating to the entitlement to or payment of benefits under a registered pension scheme insofar as compliance is necessary to secure any tax relief or exemption available under *FA 2004, Part 4* or to prevent any charge to tax arising under that Part of that Act.

Which common practices are not exempt?

9.30   Many pension schemes require members to stop accruing benefits when they reach the scheme's normal retirement date (often age 60 or 65). There is no exemption allowing this and it may be difficult to justify. Consideration should be given to allowing those employees still in service after normal retirement date to continue as active members of the scheme. This issue became more important following the abolition of the default retirement age from 6 April 2011 (see **9.35** below).

There is no general exemption for schemes continuing to apply former HMRC limits. There is an exemption in relation to *FA 2004* requirements, but this is not wide enough to cover former HMRC limits. The exemption for 'sections' (*Sch 1, para 27* of the *Age Exceptions Order*) allows trustees to treat classes of members differently based on the date they joined the scheme, but any age discriminatory provisions within each class would have to be justified. The fact that it was a previous HMRC requirement is unlikely on its own to be sufficient justification for continuing the practice.

Do the exemptions comply with the Directive?

9.31   It has been suggested that some of the exemptions in the *Age Exceptions Order* go beyond those authorised by the *Equal Treatment Framework Directive*. If this is the case (and it would have to be decided by the courts), then the individual exemptions found to be outside the Directive will be struck down (for as long as the UK remains in the EU).

Article 2(2)(b)(i) of the *Equal Treatment Framework Directive* allows the justification of indirect discrimination generally where the particular 'provision, criterion or practice is objectively justified by a legitimate aim and the means of achieving that aim are appropriate and necessary'. In relation to age discrimination only, *Article 6(1)* allows Member States to 'provide that differences of treatment on grounds of age shall not constitute discrimination, if, within the context of national law, they are objectively and reasonably justified by a legitimate aim, including legitimate employment policy, labour market and vocational training objectives, and if the means of achieving that aim are appropriate and necessary'. This enables Member States to allow even direct differences in treatment as long as they can be justified.

Article 6(2) provides a general exemption which allows Member States to provide for 'the fixing for occupational social security schemes of ages for admission or entitlement to retirement or invalidity benefits, including the fixing under those schemes of different ages for employees or groups or categories of employees, and the use, in the context of such schemes, of age criteria in actuarial calculations, does not constitute discrimination on the grounds of age, provided this does not result in discrimination on the grounds of sex'. Essentially, this allows the Member State to authorise certain age related practices without any requirement for justification.

In the CJEU case of *Birgit Bartsch v Bosch und Siemens Hausgerate (BSH) Altersfursorge GmbH C-427/06 [2009] All ER (EC) 113* the Advocate General gave his opinion in relation to a young spouse provision of a German pension scheme which prevented a widow from receiving a pension because she was more than 15 years younger than the deceased member. The Advocate General found that as the period for implementing the *Equal Treatment Framework Directive* had not expired, there was no discrimination contrary to EU law. However, such a provision would now be in breach of EU age discrimination laws. It might be possible to objectively justify such discrimination (ie the Member State might be able to show that it was an appropriate and necessary means of achieving a legitimate aim) but, because this young spouse clause prevented any payment to the widow, it went beyond what was 'appropriate and necessary'. A sliding scale might instead be acceptable, or payments starting only when survivors reached a certain age. When the CJEU gave its judgment in *Bartsch* it held that the claim could not succeed as it was brought before the time limit for transposition of the age discrimination requirements of the *Equal Treatment Framework Directive* had expired. This means that the substantive issue remains undecided. The provision in question prevented any pension at all being paid to the spouse. The *Age Exceptions Order* allows for actuarial reduction in pension if a spouse is more than a specified number of years younger than the member. However, any scheme with a rule which could potentially allow for a reduction to zero might have to review its rules if future decisions of the CJEU follow the Advocate-General's opinion.

In *HK Danmark v Experian A/S [2013] EUECJ C-476/11*, the CJEU ruled that an employer can make age-related contributions to an occupational DC scheme as long as the difference in treatment can be objectively justified. It stated that age-related contributions cannot fall under the general exemption in *Article 6(2)* of the *Equal Treatment Framework Directive* (whereby Member States provide that the fixing of ages for admission or entitlement to retirement or invalidity benefits does not constitute discrimination on the grounds of age, provided this does not result in discrimination on the grounds of sex) as the

CJEU took a restrictive interpretation. *Article 6(2)* and can only apply to the fixing of ages or admission and entitlement and nothing else. Any exemption for age-related contributions would have to fall under *Article 6(1)* and must therefore be justified as an appropriate and necessary means of achieving a legitimate aim. This decision seems to cast some doubt on the general exemption for age-related contributions under the *Age Exception Order* and suggests that each employer may have to objectively justify its contribution rates even where they fall within the exemption.

If in future the domestic courts are no longer required to interpret the exemptions narrowly in line with EU law then, even without express amendments, the exemptions could be more widely applied.

Justification

9.32   If an age-related rule does not fall within one of the exemptions (or the exemptions are found to fall outside those allowed by the terms of *Article 6* of the *Equal Treatment Framework Directive*), it may be justified if it can be shown that it is a 'proportionate means of achieving a legitimate aim' (*EqA 2010, ss 13(2)* and *19(2)(d)*).

There are a number of decisions from the employment tribunal, EAT, Court of Appeal, Supreme Court and CJEU which deal with the issue of justification.

Justification was considered by the EAT in March 2005 in the case of *Cross v British Airways [2005] 26 PBLR*. The claim against British Airways was for unfair dismissal and sex discrimination (the case was brought before the *Age Regulations* were in force) where employees had a normal retirement age of 55 but wished to continue working until the age of 60. The appeal by the employees was dismissed. The EAT referred to various previous cases, and in particular *Hampson v Department of Education and Science [1989] ICR 179*, which said:

> 'In my judgment 'justifiable' requires an objective balance between the discriminatory effect of the condition and reasonable needs of a party who applies the condition.'

The key conclusion on justification in this case was that an employer/trustees seeking to justify a discriminatory practice cannot rely solely on considerations of cost.

Cost can however be taken into account, together with other justifications if there are any. This is referred to in later cases as a 'costs plus' justification. In *Woodcock v Cumbria Primary Care Trust UK EAT/0489/09/RN* concerning age discrimination, the EAT suggested that an employer should be allowed to justify a discriminatory measure on the basis of cost alone. The Court of Appeal (*[2012] EWCA Civ 330*) disagreed and confirmed that the saving of cost, on its own, cannot be a legitimate aim justifying discriminatory treatment.

In *Bloxham v Freshfields [2007] 53 PBLR* the ET found that there was less favourable treatment based on age in the restructuring of pension arrangements, but that it was justified. As an employment tribunal decision it has no formal precedent value; however, it includes some useful arguments on less favourable treatment and justification.

Key factors in the findings include:

- The arrangements as they stood discriminated against younger partners and it was legitimate to consider changing them – the question was whether the new arrangements were a proportionate response.

- There was a finite pool of money – if Mr Bloxham won, someone else of a different age would suffer.

- No one had put forward an alternative, less discriminatory, solution.

- Freshfields had tried to mitigate the effect of the change through transitional arrangements and there had been extensive consultation.

In *MacCulloch v Imperial Chemical Industries Ltd [2008] ICR 1334*, the EAT looked in some detail at the issue of justification in the context of age discrimination in a contractual redundancy scheme. Helpfully the EAT summarised some key principles with regard to justification:

- The classic test of justification is set out in *Bilka-Kaufhaus GmbH v Weber von Hartz C-170/84 [1986] ECR 1607* – the measures must 'correspond to a real need ... are appropriate with a view to achieving the objectives pursued and are necessary to that end' – but reference to 'necessary' means 'reasonably necessary' (*Rainey v Greater Glasgow Health Board [1987] IRLR 26*).

- The principle of proportionality requires an objective balance to be struck between the discriminatory effect of the measure and the needs of the undertaking. The more serious the impact, the more cogent the justification that is needed (*Hardys & Hansons v Lax [2005] IRLR 726*).

- It is for the tribunal to weigh up the reasonable needs of the undertaking against the discriminatory effect – there is no 'range of reasonable responses' test (*Hardys & Hansons*).

Of particular interest in a pensions context is the EAT's finding that, in a scheme where there is a standard set of rules, the aims must justify the scheme as a whole, not just the treatment of the individual claimant; but the extent to which an individual is disadvantaged compared to his or her comparators is highly relevant to proportionality.

9.32 *Discrimination*

In *Pulham & Others v London Borough of Barking and Dagenham [2009] UKEAT 0516/08/RN* the EAT considered age discrimination issues in relation to a pay protection scheme. Historically, LBB had had a pay scheme which rewarded long service and experience (from age 55 and with 25 years' service). LBB abolished the scheme and froze the benefits for those already in receipt of an increment. At the time the scheme was removed, Mrs Pulham had 25 years' service but had not reached age 55. Mrs Pulham's claim was that the transitional arrangements (applying only to those with a benefit already in payment) were discriminatory and could not be justified. Some interesting points on justification arose from the judgment:

- The elimination of a discriminatory scheme was a legitimate aim.

- Transitional arrangements could involve a degree of continuing discrimination (as long as it can be justified). This distinguishes *Smith v Avdel* which required 'immediate and full' elimination of discrimination.

- The fact that a justification is being produced long after the event may entitle a tribunal to treat it with some scepticism.

- The fact that the employer had 'used up' the budget it had allocated for eliminating discrimination was not an automatic justification but could be a relevant factor.

- The tribunal had to weigh the discriminatory impact of a particular measure against the cost of eliminating it.

The case of *R (on the application of Age UK) v Secretary of State for Business, Innovation and Skills [2009] EWHC 2336 (Admin)* (often referred to as the '*Heyday*' case) looks at the relevance of the *Equal Treatment Framework Directive* when considering justification. This case relates to compulsory retirement ages and is referred to in more detail in **9.35** below.

Two Supreme Court decisions in 2012 helped clarify the law on justification of both direct and indirect age discrimination. *Seldon v Clarkson Wright & Jakes [2012] UKSC 16* concerned a partner who was required to retire at 65. The partnership sought to justify its policy (as it did not employ Mr Seldon it could not rely on the statutory compulsory retirement age exemption then in place (see **9.35** below)). The Court of Appeal in *Seldon* had followed *Heyday* in finding that the UK Government's justification in adopting a compulsory retirement age to allow younger people to have a better chance of employment and better promotion prospects was a legitimate social policy objective (and so was allowed under the *Equal Treatment Framework Directive*). The Supreme Court concluded that, in the context of direct age discrimination, the UK government has chosen to give employers and partnerships the flexibility to pursue objectives (aims) as long as they:

- can count as legitimate objectives of a public interest nature;

- are consistent with the social policy aims of the state; and

- the means used are proportionate, that is both appropriate to the aim and reasonably necessary to achieve it.

The Supreme Court in *Seldon* found that the CJEU has through its case law identified two broad types of legitimate aim: intergenerational fairness and dignity. Once a particular aim has been identified as being capable of being legitimate it is necessary to establish that the aim is in fact being pursued. The aim need not have been articulated or even realised at the time when the measure was first adopted. Next, consideration must be given to whether it is legitimate in the particular circumstances of the employment concerned. The means chosen to pursue the aim have to be both appropriate and necessary and must be carefully scrutinised in the context of the particular business concerned in order to see whether they do meet the objective and whether there are other, less discriminatory, measures which would do so.

The Supreme Court remitted Mr Seldon's case to the ET for a decision on whether the retirement age was justified. In May 2013, the ET confirmed that the employer had established three legitimate aims – retaining younger staff (who had an expectation of future partnership), the long term planning of the business and collegiality (maintaining a co-operative relationship between colleagues). The ET had to decide whether a retirement age of 65 was 'appropriate and reasonably necessary' to achieve the aims at the relevant time (2006). It took into account a number of factors in concluding that 65 was proportionate – the balancing of the interests of partners and associates, the fact the partners had consented, the fact that at that time the statutory default retirement age for employees and the state retirement age for men was 65 and that the CJEU has upheld 65 as a mandatory retirement age in a number of cases. The ET made it clear that the decision might be different if it was deciding the question based on the position in 2013 rather than as things stood in 2006. This decision was upheld by the EAT in May 2014 (*UKEAT/0434/13*).

The second Supreme Court case, this time concerning indirect discrimination, is *Homer v Chief Constable of West Yorkshire Police [2012] UKSC 15*. The court found that the range of aims which can justify indirect discrimination is wider than that for direct as there is no requirement for a social policy objective. Mr Homer was a retired police officer who worked as a legal adviser for the Police National Legal Database (PNLD). The staff in PNLD were reorganised and graded into three levels. The highest of those required a law degree which Mr Homer did not have and would not be able to obtain before he reached retirement age of 65. The Supreme Court concluded that this was indirectly discriminatory on grounds of age unless it could be objectively justified as being a proportionate means of achieving a legitimate aim. The Supreme Court held that the range of aims which can justify indirect discrimination is not limited to the social policy or other objectives derived from the *Equal Treatment Framework Directive* (see **9.31** above), but can encompass a real need on the part of the employer's business.

The court approved the three-stage test:

- Is the aim sufficiently important to justify limiting a fundamental right (ie the right to not be discriminated against on the grounds of age)?

- Is the measure rationally connected to the aim?

- Are the means chosen no more than is necessary to accomplish the aim?

The aims in this case were identified as recruiting and retaining new staff and retaining existing high quality staff. The Supreme Court remitted the case to the ET for a decision on whether the employer's requirement for Mr Homer to have a law degree in order to gain the highest pay grade was justified. In March 2013, the ET found that the requirement was not justified. It was a legitimate aim for the employer to include a requirement for a law degree in its new pay structure (which was designed to recruit and retain good quality staff) but it was not 'appropriate or reasonably necessary' (ie proportionate) in this case to impose this requirement on existing staff.

The Court of Appeal in *Lockwood v DWP [2013] EWCA Civ 1195* found that a voluntary redundancy scheme providing higher payments for older employees was directly discriminatory. The Court found that the ET had properly applied the test for objective justification (as set out in *MacCulloch*). There was a limited pot of money and so some banding and disparate treatment would have to be adopted – the arrangements actually chosen were neither disproportionate nor inappropriate.

From a practical perspective the trustees/employer in considering any objective justification for a potentially age discriminatory practice, need to consider whether in the first instance there is a legitimate need for having this practice/rule. They should then consider if there is a way of achieving the aim with a lesser degree of discrimination and, if so, adapt the practice/rule to use the lesser degree of discrimination. However, if this cannot be done, and retention of the practice/rule is desired, then they would need to rely on the legitimate aim that they consider justifies the practice/rule and keep all records as evidence of the objective justification. This will be much harder if the practice/rule is directly discriminatory as it must be consistent with the social policy aims of the Government.

Effect of a non-discrimination rule

9.33   Where there is a discriminatory provision in a pension scheme which is not exempt or justified, a non-discrimination rule will be implied into the scheme, overriding the provision and requiring trustees to refrain from doing any act which is unlawful under the *EqA 2010*. Trustees have power to modify the scheme to secure conformity with the non-discrimination rule (*EqA 2010, s 62*).

The effect of the non-discrimination rule will be that until the discriminatory provision is eliminated, the less favoured group will be levelled up to the benefits of the more favoured group. For example, if a scheme provided accrual at 1/80ths for those under 40 and 1/60ths for those over 40, all the members would have to be granted 1/60th benefit accrual from 1 December 2006 onwards. It may be open to the trustees and employer to later modify the scheme to provide for 1/80ths accrual for all, but that change could only take effect in relation to accrual on or after the date of the modification.

Flexible retirement

9.34   Since the *FA 2004*, schemes may offer flexible retirement, whereby an individual may draw all or part of his pension and remain in employment with the same employer. Prior to 6 April 2006, most members had to leave pensionable service in order to draw their benefits. Many schemes which are considering this option may wish to require a member taking flexible retirement to cease accrual in that scheme (and possibly for the employer to offer DC accrual in another arrangement). This raises the possibility of an indirect age discrimination claim from the flexible retiree, who could argue that the requirement to cease accrual impacted unfairly on members of his age.

The alternative approach is not to offer flexible retirement at all, and continue with existing practice, which could itself be discriminatory. The argument in this case could be that requiring a member to cease working before drawing a pension would indirectly discriminate against older workers, who are more likely to want to draw all or part of their pension, perhaps in conjunction with reducing their hours as they move towards full retirement.

In September 2007, the DWP issued a consultation document on flexible retirement and pension provision. The DWP's response to this consultation and draft regulations ('Flexible Retirement and Pension Provision Government Response to the Consultation and Draft Regulations') were published on 16 December 2008. However, on 10 December 2009 the DWP announced that it was not going to proceed with the draft regulations but would consider further general guidance for occupational pension schemes on age discrimination issues. None has yet been forthcoming.

Age discrimination and retirement ages

9.35   Prior to 6 April 2011, the *EqA 2010* (and previously the *Age Regulations*) permitted employers to retire employees at the age of 65, provided they followed a specified statutory procedure, without needing to justify that decision. The provision allowing this was repealed with effect from 6 April 2011 by the *Employment Equality (Repeal of Retirement Age*

Provisions) Regulations 2011 (SI 2011/1069). Now an employer wishing to dismiss employees on the grounds of age must justify the decision.

The background to the removal of what was known as the default retirement age ('DRA') can be found in what is commonly referred to as the *Heyday* case. It began in 2007 when the National Council on Ageing (NCA) persuaded the High Court that it should ask the CJEU whether the provision in the *Age Regulations* which permitted enforced retirement at age 65 was lawful. The NCA argued that the *Equal Treatment Framework Directive*, on which the *Age Regulations* were based, had not been properly implemented by the UK.

On 5 March 2009, the CJEU gave its judgment *(R (on the application of) Age Concern England v the Secretary of State for Business Enterprise and Regulatory Reform (ECJ Case C-388/07)),* stating that it was for the UK court to determine whether legislation which permits employers to retire employees at age 65 is justified by legitimate social policy objectives, such as those related to employment policy, the labour market or vocational training. The CJEU held that the *Equal Treatment Framework Directive* gives Member States the option to provide, within the context of national law, for differences in treatment on the grounds of age if they are objectively and reasonably justified by a legitimate aim, and the means of achieving that aim are appropriate and necessary.

The case was referred by the CJEU back to the High Court which found in favour of the Government and confirmed that the decision to adopt a DRA was 'legitimate and proportionate' *(R (on the application of Age UK) v Secretary of State for Business, Innovation and Skills [2009] EWHC 2336 (Admin)).* On the issue of whether 65 was appropriate as the DRA, the court noted that the Government had announced that it was to undertake a review which should give 'particular consideration to whether the retention of 65 can conceivably now be justified'. The court also commented that, if the DRA had been adopted in 2009 instead of in 2006 or there had been no indication of an imminent review, it would have concluded that the selection of age 65 as the DRA would not have been proportionate because of the discriminatory effect on those who are able and willing to work longer.

As a result of the Government Review, the DRA was abolished with effect from 6 April 2011 (as mentioned above) with transitional provisions relating to retirements which had already been notified by that date. The practical result of this for pension schemes is the likelihood that more members will remain in service beyond NRD. Trustees will need to ensure that they do not unlawfully discriminate against these members. This may mean schemes having to offer continued accrual beyond NRD although an exemption does allow schemes to set a maximum period of pensionable service (many schemes will still have a 40-year maximum service provision as this was previously a HMRC requirement) *(Age Exceptions Order, Sch 1, para 21(2)).*

Employers wishing to retire employees on the grounds of age may still be able to do so if they can justify the practice (see **9.32** above and in particular the *Seldon* case).

The CJEU has considered compulsory retirement ages in other EU Member States and has, in general, found them to be legitimate. For example, in *Rosenbladt v Oellerking Gebaudereinigungsges mBh Case C-45/09 [2011] 1 CMLR 32* the CJEU considered a German law which allowed the termination of employment where either the employee could claim an immediate old-age pension or it was permitted by a collective agreement. Under a different German Code, the fact that an employee was entitled to an immediate pension could not be a ground for dismissal unless the employee was aged 65 or over. The effect of this was to allow a default retirement age of 65, for those entitled to an immediate pension. The CJEU held that a mechanism which strikes a balance between different generations and political, social, demographic and/ or budgetary considerations was a legitimate aim. The question was therefore whether the German system was 'appropriate and necessary'. Key factors in the CJEU's finding that the arrangements were 'appropriate and necessary' were that compulsory retirement was only applicable to those entitled to an immediate replacement income from pension and that, in this case, there was a collective agreement in place. The CJEU also found that where the national law does not specify the aim being pursued, other elements taken from the general context of the measure can be used to identify the underlying aim. In this case there was extrinsic evidence that the aim of the law was to facilitate the employment of younger people and to allow planned recruitment and balanced personnel management.

One case going the other way is *Prigge and others v Deutsche Lufthansa C-447/09*. Here the CJEU held that a compulsory retirement age of 60 for Lufthansa airline pilots required by a collective agreement recognised by German law, constituted age discrimination. International legislation, which German law has implemented, permits pilots aged up to 65 to fly commercial aeroplanes, subject to certain conditions in the case of those aged 60 to 65. The CJEU held that the compulsory retirement age of 60 was contrary to the age discrimination provisions of the *Equal Treatment Framework Directive* as it was not necessary for the protection of public security or health within the meaning of *Article 2(5)* of the *Directive* nor was it a genuine occupational requirement under *Article 4(1)*. Furthermore, it could not objectively justified under *Article 6(1)*. The non-exhaustive list in *Article 6* of possible legitimate aims which could justify direct discrimination includes employment policy, labour market and vocational training objectives but the ECJ decided that air safety does not constitute a legitimate aim for this purpose.

One issue connected with the abolition of the DRA which has yet to be fully resolved is the provision of death in service benefits for members aged over 65. The *Employment Equality (Repeal of Retirement Age Provisions) Regulations*

2011 (SI 2011/1069) amend the *EqA 2010* to provide that it is not unlawful discrimination for an employer to make arrangements for, or afford access to, the provision of insurance or a related financial service to or in respect of employees under the age of 65 (or State pension age if higher) (*EqA 2010, Sch 9, para 14*). This provision clearly exempts employers from any requirement to provide life cover for employees over age 65 but does not give similar protection to pension scheme trustees. Many pension schemes provide death in service benefits, backed by a group life policy held in the name of the trustees. Discrimination on the grounds of age in the provision of a financial service (which includes insurance) is exempt from the general prohibition of discrimination in the provision of goods and services in *EqA 2010, s 29* (*EqA 2010, Sch 3 part 5 para 20A*). Further, the provision of a financial service is exempt from *EqA 2010, s 29* if it is in pursuance of arrangements made by an employer for a service to be provided as a consequence of employment (*EqA 2010, Sch 3 part 5 para 20*).

It is arguable that as the law as it stands employers and insurers need not provide cover for those over 65 (or state pension age) but trustees may be required to do so by the scheme rules (as there is no equivalent exemption on which they can rely). This would leave the trustees having to objectively justify any difference in cover for older members. The Department for Business, Innovation and Skills ('BIS') has indicated that its view is that the employer exemption in *EqA 2010* (*EqA 2010, Sch 3 part 5 para 20*) is sufficiently wide to cover a policy in the name of the trustees where it forms part of the employee's overall pay and benefits package. However the legislation is not clear on this point and trustees should take reasonable steps to provide the level of cover required under the scheme rules. Where full cover cannot be obtained (or not obtained without substantial additional cost or onerous conditions) trustees may take some comfort from the BIS view but should keep a record of the attempts they have made to secure cover (to assist in any future objective justification defence).

Same-sex partners

Introduction

9.36   The legal position of same-sex partners was examined in the case of *Grant v South-West Trains Limited C-249/96 [1998] All ER (EC) 193*. This was an employment case involving the granting of travel concessions. South-West Trains refused to give travel concessions to Ms Grant's same-sex partner when she was promoted to a post at South-West Trains previously occupied by an employee whose opposite sex partner had obtained such concessions. The CJEU found that the refusal of the employer to grant the travel concessions in this case did not constitute discrimination prohibited by *Article 157* of the

TFEU or *Council Directive 75/117/EEC* of 10 February 1975, as the condition imposed by South-West Trains applied in the same way to female and male workers. The CJEU said that Community law as it stood at that time did not cover discrimination based on sexual orientation.

The *Equal Treatment Framework Directive (2000/78/EC)* requires Member States to enact legislation to prohibit discrimination on the grounds of sexual orientation by December 2003. In the context of sexual orientation discrimination, the Directive requires that pension schemes which recognise unmarried heterosexual partners must also recognise same-sex partners. The Directive allows pension schemes which recognise married couples only to continue to do so.

The *Employment Equality (Sexual Orientation) Regulations 2003 (SI 2003/1661)* ('*Sexual Orientation Regulations*') came into force on 1 December 2003 and were designed to implement the *Equal Treatment Framework Directive* in respect of sexual orientation discrimination. The Regulations prohibited direct discrimination (ie treating people less favourably than others on grounds of sexual orientation) and indirect discrimination (ie applying a provision, criterion or practice which disadvantages people of a particular sexual orientation and which is not justified in objective terms). The Regulations were revoked with effect from 1 October 2010 by the *EqA 2010* which makes similar provision against discrimination on the grounds of sexual orientation. *EqA 2010, s 61* makes provision for every occupational pension scheme to be treated as including a 'non-discrimination' rule prohibiting discrimination on the grounds of sexual orientation. As with other anti-discrimination legislation this extends to the field of occupational pensions. The primary target as it applies to pension schemes would seem to be to prevent discrimination in respect of dependant's pensions.

Originally, the Sexual Orientation Regulations provided that, if the scheme provides benefits to married partners but not unmarried opposite-sex partners, then there would be no discrimination. From 5 December 2005 the exemption was extended to cover benefits conferred on married people and civil partners to the exclusion of all others (see **9.37** below for more on civil partnerships). This is now found in *EqA 2010, Sch 9 para 18* which allows the provision of a benefit to married persons and civil partners (to the exclusion of all other persons) and also allows the exclusion of civil partners and same-sex married partners from benefits payable in relation to opposite-sex spouses which accrued before 5 December 2005. *EqA 2010* does not give non-married partners the right to the same benefits as married partners (*s 8(1)* requires that the less favourable treatment must be because someone is married or a civil partner, not because someone is not married or not a civil partner). In addition, *EqA 2010, s 23(3)* ensures that the status of a civil partner is comparable to that of a spouse (ie there is no 'material difference' between a spouse and a civil partner when considering discrimination on the grounds of sexual orientation).

The CJEU has ruled that the surviving registered life partner (the German equivalent of a UK civil partner) of a member of an occupational pension scheme was unlawfully discriminated against on grounds of sexual orientation where the national legislation had placed life partnership and marriage on an equal footing since 1 January 2005, but the scheme rules did not provide for survivor benefits for same-sex partners (*Tadao Maruko v Versorgungsanstalt der deutschen Bühnen C-267/06 [2008] All ER (EC) 977*). The CJEU refused to limit the period from which a registered partner had become entitled to survivors' benefits. This calls into question the UK's implementation of the *Equal Treatment Framework Directive*, now in *EqA 2010, Sch 9 para 18* which allows schemes to restrict survivors' benefits for civil partners to periods of service from 5 December 2005.

In *Innospec v Walker* the ET held that the provision of the *EqA 2010* limiting pension benefits for surviving civil partners to those relating to service since 5 December 2005 is in breach of the *Equal Treatment Framework Directive*. Mr Walker was employed by Innospec from 1980 until his retirement in 2003. He entered a civil partnership in January 2006. On his death, his partner will be entitled to a pension of about £500 pa (being a survivor's GMP) whereas, if they were a heterosexual married couple, the scheme rules would provide a pension of over £40,000 pa. The ET found that the failure to provide a survivor's pension equivalent to that which would be provided to a widow (ie for the full period of Mr W's pensionable service) was both directly and indirectly discriminatory on the grounds of sexual orientation. However this decision was overturned by the EAT (*UKEAT/0232/13/LA*) on the basis that the *Equal Treatment Framework Directive* is not retrospective and does not apply to pensionable service before the date on which the relevant provisions were required to be implemented into domestic law. Mr Walker had ceased to be in pensionable service before 3 December 2003 (the earliest date from which the Directive had to be implemented) and so none of his accrued benefits were subject to EU law against discrimination on the grounds of sexual orientation. In October 2015, the Court of Appeal (*[2015] EWCA Civ 1000*) refused Mr Walker's appeal, finding that the discriminatory treatment was not unlawful. It was held that conduct which was lawful when it occurred cannot be rendered unlawful by a change in law (unless expressly stated to do so) (this is referred to as the 'no retroactivity principle'). Mr Walker's entitlement to pension was fixed as and when he earned it. The right not to be discriminated on the grounds of sexual orientation did not become a fundamental principle of EU law until the expiry of the implementation period for the *Equal Treatment Framework Directive* (3 December 2003) and Mr Walker had already left pensionable service by then.

Section 16 of the *Marriage (Same Sex Couples) Act 2013* (see **9.40** below) required the Government to undertake a review of same sex survivors' benefits in occupational pension schemes, in particular looking at the exclusion of benefits relating to pensionable service before December 2005. The results of the review were published on 26 June 2014 but did not make any specific recommendations to change current legislation.

Civil partnerships

9.37   The parts of the *Civil Partnership Act 2004* (*CPA 2004*) relating to pensions came into force on 5 December 2005. The Act provides for same-sex couples to obtain legal recognition of their relationship by registering as civil partners. Registered civil partners have access to rights and responsibilities including, for example:

- employment and pensions benefits;
- the duty to provide maintenance for a civil partner;
- the duty to provide maintenance for children of the partnership; and
- recognition under intestacy rules.

There are certain eligibility requirements that must be satisfied before couples can register as civil partners. The couple must be of the same sex, both parties must be 16 years or over, neither party can be legally married or already a civil partner and the partner cannot be 'within prohibited degrees of relationship' (ie blood ties). There are also various formalities involved in registering a civil partnership. The register has to be signed by the couple in the presence of the civil partnership registrar and two witnesses (see *CPA 2004, Part 2, Chapter 1*).

In a similar way to divorce, a civil partnership can only be dissolved or nullified by a court order (see *CPA 2004, s 37*).

The Act impacts on pensions in a number of areas including:

- State pensions;
- survivor benefits;
- pension sharing; and
- *s 67* issues.

CPA 2004, s 255 contains an enabling power to allow a Minister of the Crown to amend, by statutory instrument, primary and secondary legislation relating to pensions in order to achieve the main purpose of the Act.

There are numerous statutory instruments that have been implemented in relation to the Act. In particular, the *Civil Partnership (Pensions and Benefit Payments) (Consequential, etc Provisions) Order 2005 (SI 2005/2053)* provides for a number of amendments to *PSA 1993*, *PA 1995* and *PA 2004*.

9.38 *Discrimination*

CPA 2004 makes a number of amendments to the *Social Security Contributions and Benefits Act 1992* so as to extend State pension rights to civil partners.

Occupational pension schemes

9.38 In formerly contracted-out schemes a civil partner must be entitled to an equivalent widow's/widower's pension on the death of a member if a legal spouse would be entitled to a GMP (post-5 April 1988) on the death of a member. It is also arguable that statutory reference scheme benefits should be provided but there is some dispute amongst pensions lawyers about this. The changes to the contracting-out legislation were made by the *Civil Partnership (Contracted-out Occupational and Appropriate Personal Pension Schemes) (Surviving Civil Partners) Order 2005 (SI 2005/2050)* and the relevant provisions are now in the *Occupational Pension Schemes (Schemes that were Contracted-out) (No 2) Regulations 2015 (SI 2015/1677)*. Formerly contracted-out schemes should have amended their rules to comply with the requirements.

Non contracted-out benefits for civil partners must be provided in respect of pensionable service from 5 December 2005 (see **9.36** above). The requirement to treat civil partners in the same way as spouses from 5 December 2005 is overriding although schemes may wish to amend their rules for clarity.

Where amending schemes to give effect to the *CPA 2004*, regard must be had to the provisions of *PA 1995, s 67* (restriction on the exercise of amendment powers). A change to include a new category of survivor could adversely affect subsisting rights. The *Occupational Pension Schemes (Modification of Schemes) Regulations 2006 (SI 2006/759)* exclude certain amendments from the ambit of *s 67* including modifications in relation to death benefits where a surviving civil partner is to be treated in the same way as a widow or widower, and where the rights of any other survivor of the member (eg children) are determined as if the surviving civil partner were a widow or widower. They also provide the power for trustees to modify a scheme by resolution to provide benefits for civil partners, with employer consent required if the proposal goes beyond the minimum statutory requirements.

Section 16 of the *Marriage (Same Sex Couples) Act 2013* (see **9.41** below) required the Government to undertake a review of same sex survivors' benefits in occupational pension schemes, in particular looking at the restriction to benefits relating to pensionable service since 2014. The results of the review were published on 26 June 2014 but did not make any specific recommendations to change current legislation.

Pension sharing

9.39 *CPA 2004, Sch 5, Part 4* provides the court with a power to make a pension sharing order on the dissolution or nullity of a civil partnership. This provides for one civil partner's 'shareable rights' under a 'specified pension arrangement' to be subject to pension sharing for the benefit of the other civil partner. A 'specified pension arrangement' includes occupational and personal pension schemes. There is also power for the court to make earmarking orders (*CPA 2004, Sch 5, Part 6*). See **Chapter 8** for more on pension sharing and earmarking orders.

Same-sex marriage

9.40   The relevant provisions of the *Marriage (Same Sex Couples) Act 2013 (M(SSC)A 2013)* came into force in England and Wales on 13 March 2014, with the first marriage ceremonies taking place on 29 March 2014.

Section 1(1) of the *M(SSC)A 2013* simply provides that 'Marriage of same sex couples is lawful' and *section 11* states that: 'In the law of England and Wales, marriage has the same effect in relation to same sex couples as it has in relation to opposite sex couples'.

Paragraph 1 of *Schedule 3* provides that in existing legislation, references to marriage is to be read as including a reference to marriage of a same-sex couple. This means that laws on intestacy, tax, divorce etc will all apply equally to same-sex and opposite-sex married couples, unless there is an express carve-out in the legislation.

Paragraph 1 of *Schedule 4* provides that 'Section 11 does not alter the effect of any private legal instrument made before that section comes into force'. Private legal instrument is defined as *including* 'an instrument which settles property' and 'an instrument which provides for the use, disposal or devolution of property'. It is widely accepted that existing pension scheme trust documents are covered by this provision, meaning that occupational pension schemes are not automatically required to provide full spouse benefits to widows/widowers of same-sex marriages. However, any amendments made to scheme rules after 12 March 2014 will not be subject to this exclusion so care must be taken not to unintentionally extend benefits to same-sex survivors.

The law on divorce applies equally to same-sex marriages. This may not automatically feed through to scheme rules on pensions on divorce because of *paragraph 1* of *Schedule 4* and so pension sharing schedules should be reviewed.

For state pension purposes, married same-sex couples are treated in the same way as men whose wives have died, irrespective of their gender.

Occupational pension scheme requirements

9.41   *Paragraph 17* of *Schedule 4* to *M(SSC)A 2013* amends *EqA 2010, Sch 9 para 18* effectively allowing schemes to discriminate on the grounds of sexual orientation in relation to benefits relating to service before 5 December 2005. This means that same sex spouses are to be treated in the same way as civil partners. In relation to service from 5 December 2005, schemes must provide the same benefits for same-sex spouses as they do for opposite-sex spouses. This provision is subject to the equality rule and so is overriding (see **9.36** above). It is open to trustees and employers to decide to provide benefits on a more generous basis.

There is an exemption in *EqA 2010, Sch 9 para 18* in relation to a 'relevant gender change case'. The effect of this means that the survivor of a marriage between a same-sex couple, where the deceased spouse had changed legal gender, will retain their expectation of survivor benefits as if their spouse had not changed legal gender. This provision is not yet fully in force.

As mentioned in **9.38** above, *section 16* of *M(SSC)A 2013* required a parliamentary review of survivor benefits under occupational pension schemes, particularly in relation to the December 2005 limit on backdating and there are regulation making powers to implement its proposals. However, the results of the review were published on 26 June 2014 but did not make any specific recommendations to change current legislation.

Amendments to *PSA 1993* mean that 'surviving same-sex spouses' should be treated as widowers for GMP purposes (this, again is similar to the treatment of civil partners set out in **9.38** above). GMP legislation is not overriding so this should be written into the rules.

Amendments made to the *Occupational Pension Schemes (Modification of Schemes) Regulations 2006 (SI 2006/759)* by the *Marriage (Same Sex Couples) Act 2013 (Consequential Provisions) Order 2014 (SI 2014/107)* exclude from the ambit of *PA 1995, s 67* any scheme amendments allowing, in relation to all or part of a member's subsisting rights, a same-sex spouse to be treated in the same way as an opposite-sex spouse. There is also provision (in *regulation 7ZA*) enabling trustees to modify schemes by resolution to allow a same-sex spouse to be treated in the same way as an opposite-sex spouse. Employer consent is required where the modification provides more than the statutory minimum benefit. These provisions are similar to those in relation to civil partners (see **9.38** above).

Gender reassignment

9.42   Case law and the *Gender Recognition Act 2004* have developed the law relating to gender reassignment. In the case of *Goodwin v United Kingdom [2002] IRLR 664*, the European Court of Human Rights held that UK law was in breach of the *European Convention on Human Rights* in not allowing Ms Goodwin to marry or enjoy the benefits and burdens of her new gender.

Ms Goodwin transitioned from male-to-female and had been required to pay National Insurance contributions until the age of 65 as if she were a man. In particular, it was held that Ms Goodwin was entitled to the pension rights available to members of her new gender.

In its judgment in *Bellinger v Bellinger [2003] 2 All ER 593,* the House of Lords considered the position of Mrs Bellinger, a transgender woman who had undergone a marriage ceremony to a man. The House of Lords held that the marriage was not a valid marriage but declared that the non-recognition of gender reassignment for the purposes of allowing transgender individuals to marry was incompatible with the right to respect for private and family life and the right to marry guaranteed by *Articles 8* and *12* of the *European Convention on Human Rights.*

In the *KB v National Health Service Pensions Agency C-117/01 [2004] All ER (EC) 1089,* the CJEU confirmed that national legislation which prevents marriage (and therefore the enjoyment of certain pension benefits) to individuals who have undergone gender reassignment was in breach of EU law.

The *Gender Recognition Act 2004* came into force on 4 April 2005. Under the Act, a person aged 18 or over may make an application to a Gender Recognition Panel for a gender recognition certificate on the basis of living in the other gender, or having changed gender under the law of a country or territory outside the UK. Where a gender recognition certificate is granted, the applicant's gender becomes for most purposes the acquired gender. The Act allows individuals, on acquiring a gender recognition certificate, to marry in their acquired gender and be given birth certificates that recognise the acquired gender. *Gender Recognition Act 2004, Sch 5* deals with benefits and pensions.

There have been a number of post-*Gender Recognition Act* cases dealing with pension rights. In the case of *Grant v United Kingdom (2007) 44 EHRR 1,* a complainant (G) (who transitioned from male to female) complained that the refusal by the Department of Social Security to pay her a State pension in 1997 at age 60 was in violation of her rights under the *European Convention of Human Rights.* The complaint was upheld, and it was stated that G was entitled to claim the lack of legal recognition from the date of the *Goodwin* judgment (see above). On 27 April 2006 the CJEU ruled in the case of *Richards v Secretary of State for Work and Pensions C-423/04 [2006] All ER (EC) 895.* In this case, R (who was born a male) underwent gender reassignment surgery in 2001. At age 60, R claimed State retirement pension but was denied on the basis that she had not reached the male retirement age of 65. The UK Government argued that national law was permitted to provide different State pension ages for men and women, and that EU law had not been breached because R's entitlement derived from national law. It was held that, although EU law allows Member States to discriminate in relation to State pension ages, the unequal treatment in question derived from R's gender reassignment, and not from the difference in State pension age.

In a further development in 2010 the Court of Appeal ruled in the case of *Timbrell v Department of Work and Pensions [2010] EWCA Civ 701* that an individual who had transitioned from male to female was entitled to claim a state retirement pension from age 60 despite the fact that she did not have a gender recognition certificate. This was on the basis that Ms T had made her claim for a pension in 2002, before the *Gender Recognition Act* was in force, and her rights fell to be considered under the European *Social Security Equal Treatment Directive (79/7/EEC)*. The Court of Appeal held that *Richards* clearly established that *Article 4(1)* of *Directive 79/7* precluded domestic legislation which denied a person who had undergone gender reassignment surgery entitlement to a pension because she had not reached the age of 65, when that person (who had become a woman) would have been entitled to that pension at the aged of 60 had she been held to be a woman as a matter of national law. This meant that Ms T had the right to a state pension from her 60th birthday as a result of the direct effect of *Directive 79/7*.

Temporary workers

9.43   Under the European Commission *Directive 2008/104/EC on Temporary Agency Work*, Member States had until December 2011 to ensure their own laws comply with the Directive. *The Agency Workers Regulations 2010 (SI 2010 No 93)* came into force on 1 October 2011.

In summary, the purpose of the Directive is to ensure the protection of temporary agency workers and to improve the quality of temporary agency work by ensuring that the principle of equal treatment is applied to temporary agency workers (*Article 2*).

Article 5 provides:

> 'The basic working and employment conditions of temporary agency workers shall be, for the duration of their assignment at a user undertaking, at least those that would apply if they had been recruited directly by that undertaking to occupy the same job.'

The phrase 'basic working and employment conditions' is stated to include pay. The Regulations exclude from the definition of pay 'any payment by way of a pension, gratuity or allowance ... in connection with retirement or loss of office'. BIS has indicated in guidance issued in May 2011 that occupational pensions are excluded from the scope of the Regulations. However, the wording referred to above is arguably not wide enough to exclude pension contributions, as it only refers to payments out.

In brief, the Regulations:

- require temporary employment agencies (and, ultimately, employers), after a 12-week qualifying period, to give temporary workers the same pay, working hours, rest breaks and holiday that they would have received if hired directly by the employer;

- require employers, from day one, to allow temporary workers equal access to information about vacancies at the hirer, as well as to canteen, childcare and transport services; and

- leave agencies and employers vulnerable to legal action by temporary workers, the outcome of which may be an order to pay 'just and equitable' compensation.

Notwithstanding the pension exclusion, agency workers are covered by the automatic enrolment regime and eligible agency workers will have to be enrolled into a qualifying pension scheme. See **Chapter 14** for more on automatic enrolment.

The right of access to a pension scheme for contract workers arose in the case of *Allonby v Accrington and Rossendale College [2001] IRLR 364 (CA)*. In 1996 the college terminated Mrs Allonby's part-time contract and employed her services through an employment agency instead. Mrs Allonby complained that she was no longer eligible for membership of the Teachers' Superannuation Scheme and that this amounted to discrimination on the grounds of sex. The Court of Appeal referred certain questions to the CJEU and, on 13 January 2004, the CJEU gave its judgment in *Allonby v Accrington and Rossendale College C-256/01 [2004] IRLR 224* as outlined below:

(*a*) The first question concerned whether Mrs Allonby could bring an equal pay claim identifying a male full-time employee as her comparator (Mr J). The CJEU held that Mr J could not be a comparator for Mrs Allonby. Mr J was paid by the college and Mrs Allonby by an employment agency. There was no basis on which the differences in pay between Mrs Allonby and Mr J could be attributable to a single source. There was therefore no single body responsible for the inequality.

(*b*) The CJEU considered whether Mrs Allonby was entitled to the right to equal pay conferred by *Article 157*. The CJEU held that the right extends to all 'workers' but does not cover an independent provider of services who is not in a relationship of subordination with the person who receives those services.

(*c*) Where an equal pay claim relates to a private occupational pension scheme a 'worker' must identify, in the same undertaking, workers of the opposite sex who perform or have performed comparable work.

(d)   Where the pension scheme is statutory, an equal pay claim could be pursued where the statistics support it, even in the absence of an actual comparator.

(e)   In order to succeed, Mrs Allonby would have to show that, among teachers who are 'workers' and fulfil all of the scheme's membership conditions except that of being employed under a contract of employment, there is a much higher percentage of women than men. It would be open for the college to objectively justify the difference in treatment.

In the case of *Dacas v Brook Street Bureau (UK) Ltd [2004] EWCA Civ 217*, Mrs Dacas worked for a local authority through an agency. She claimed unfair dismissal against both the agency (Brook Street) and the local authority. Brook Street appealed the EAT's decision that it was her employer. The Court of Appeal held that Brook Street was not Mrs Dacas' employer. It went on to say that there might be an implied contract of employment between Mrs Dacas and the local authority. If the local authority had been a party to the appeal then that question would have been remitted to the employment tribunal for decision. The importance of this decision for pensions is that the Court of Appeal is indicating that agency workers could be employees of the organisation they provide their services to. This is a move away from the previously generally held view that the individual's only contractual relationship was with the agency. If such workers can establish implied contracts of employment then they may well also, as employees, have rights to membership of pension schemes.

In *James v London Borough of Greenwich [2008] EWCA Civ 35*, the Court of Appeal upheld an EAT decision that an agency worker was not employed by the local authority to which she had been supplied by an agency. It held that the question of whether an agency worker is employed by the ultimate user must be decided in accordance with common law principles of implied contract and, in some extreme cases, by identifying sham arrangements. It is possible for the worker to have two legal arrangements, one with the agency and one with the end user. The Court of Appeal approved guidance given by the EAT (*UKEAT/00006/06/ZT*) in the earlier hearing as to how tribunals should approach the question of whether there was an implied contract.

The Fixed-term Employees Regulations

9.44   The *Fixed-term Employees (Prevention of Less Favourable Treatment) Regulations 2002 (SI 2002/2034)* came into force on 1 October 2002 implementing *EU Council Directive 1999/70/EC*. The Regulations require employers to treat fixed-term employees no less favourably than comparable permanent employees of the same employer, unless there is an objective justification for the difference in treatment. The Regulations also provide that, if a fixed-term employee is employed on a number of successive contracts for four years or more, the contract has the effect of a permanent contract unless the employer can objectively justify continuing employment on a fixed-term basis. The Regulations cover all employees under a fixed-term contract with the exclusion of apprentices, agency workers, the armed forces and those employed under a Government training scheme. The Regulations are addressed to employers and there is no direct claim against trustees.

The Regulations cover, in addition to other contractual terms, pay and occupational pension schemes and thus access to pension arrangements and the level of benefits offered. However, the Regulations do not require term-for-term equality, providing the overall package offered is broadly comparable. Therefore, whilst in principle employers are required to offer fixed-term employees the same rights of entry to the pension scheme and the same benefits under it as they do for permanent employees; it may, be possible, in certain circumstances, to offer access on different terms, providing that the overall package of rights is comparable.

If an employer does not wish to offer entry to the main pension scheme for employees on fixed-term contracts, it might consider offering to make equivalent contributions to a personal arrangement. However, there may be a difficulty in showing that this benefit is 'at least as favourable' as that offered to permanent employees. An alternative would be for fixed-term employees, whom the employer does not want to admit to the pension scheme, to be paid a salary bonus equivalent to the value of the scheme membership, although this could give rise to industrial relations problems where permanent employees then ask for the bonus instead of scheme membership.

Under the automatic enrolment requirements employers will have to enrol most fixed-term employees into a qualifying pension scheme (see **Chapter 14**).

Disability discrimination

9.45   The *Disability Discrimination Act 1995* (*DDA 1995*) made it unlawful for employers to discriminate without justification against disabled persons. The equivalent provisions are now in the *EqA 2010* which prohibits direct and indirect discrimination on the grounds of disability as well as discrimination arising from disability. Employers are under a duty to make reasonable adjustments for disabled employees and job applicants who are placed at a substantial disadvantage because of their disability.

Disability is defined in *EqA 2010, s 6* as a physical or mental impairment which has a substantial and long-term adverse effect on the individual's ability to carry out normal day-to-day activities. More detail on the meaning of disability is given in *EqA 2010, Sch 1*. In addition, the *Equality Act 2010 (Disability) Regulations 2010 (SI 2010/2128)* identify certain specific conditions which are deemed to be disabilities, as well as conditions which are excluded. Deemed disabilities include blindness, severe disfigurement, cancer, HIV infection and multiple sclerosis. Excluded conditions include substance addiction and hay-fever.

The *EqA 2010, s 61* implies an overriding 'non-discrimination rule' into occupational pension schemes. The trustees or managers and employer in relation to a scheme must refrain from discriminating against a disabled person in carrying out their functions in relation to the scheme (including in particular the admission of members to the scheme and the treatment of members of the scheme). Under the *DDA 1995*, the non-discrimination rule did not apply to rights accrued and benefits payable in respect of periods of service preceding 1 October 2004 however this restriction does not appear to have been carried forward into the *EqA 2010*.

Direct discrimination occurs where, because of someone's disability, A treats B less favourably than A treats or would treat others. Direct discrimination on the grounds of disability cannot be justified. Indirect discrimination occurs when A discriminates against B by applying to B a provision, criterion or practice which is discriminatory in relation to B's disability. Indirect discrimination can be justified if it can be shown to be a proportionate means of achieving a legitimate aim.

EqA 2010, s 15 introduces the concept of discrimination arising from disability. This occurs where A treats B unfavourably because of something arising in consequence of B's disability and A cannot show that the treatment is a proportionate means of achieving a legitimate aim.

Trustees and managers of occupational pension schemes have a duty to make reasonable adjustments in relation to provisions, criteria or practices (including scheme rules) which place a disabled member/prospective member at a substantial disadvantage compared with non-disabled members/prospective members. There is also a requirement to make any necessary reasonable adjustments to physical features of premises occupied by the trustees/scheme managers and to ensure that information is provided in an accessible format (*EqA 2010, s 20*).

Two areas where disability discrimination may commonly be an issue for pension schemes is where medical declarations are required before admission to membership or where conditions are placed on life cover benefits. In either case if the difference in treatment can be shown to be indirect discrimination, or discrimination arising from disability, then it would be open to the trustees or employer to justify the requirements.

412

Religion or belief discrimination

9.46   The *Employment Equality (Religion or Belief) Regulations 2003 (SI 2003/1660)* implemented the provisions of the *Equal Treatment Framework Directive (Council Directive 2000/78/EC)* on discrimination on grounds of religion or belief and came into force on 2 December 2003. The Regulations were repealed by the *EqA 2010* with effect from 1 October 2010 and the legislation outlawing less favourable treatment, victimisation and harassment, in the employment context, on grounds of religion or belief is now contained in that Act.

In the context of pensions, *EqA 2010* provides that it is unlawful for the trustees or managers of an occupational pension scheme to discriminate, on the grounds of religion or belief, against a member or prospective member of the scheme in carrying out any of their functions in relation to the scheme (*ss 4, 10, 13, 19 and 61*).

EqA, s 10 defines belief as 'any religious or philosophical belief'. In *Grainger plc and others v Nicholson [2010] IRLR 4* the EAT considered the criteria for identifying a 'philosophical belief'. It held that the belief must:

- be genuinely held;

- be a belief and not merely an opinion or viewpoint;

- must be as to a weighty and substantial aspect of human life and behaviour;

- must attain a certain level of cogency, seriousness, cohesion and importance; and

- it must be worthy of respect in a democratic society, be not incompatible with human dignity and not conflict with the fundamental rights of others.

In *Grainger* the belief in question was a belief in man-made climate change. Other cases have upheld beliefs in the higher purpose of public service broadcasting (*Maistry v BBC ET/1313142/10*) and anti-fox hunting (*Hashman v Milton Park (Dorset) Ltd t/a Orchard Park ET 3105555/2009*).

One area that trustees will need to consider in the context of religion or belief discrimination is the provision in DC schemes of investment options that comply with the requirements of different religions or philosophical beliefs. Also, prospective members may be prevented by religious requirements or philosophical beliefs from joining a DB scheme because of the way its assets are invested.

413

Race discrimination

9.47   The *EqA 2010* prohibits direct or indirect discrimination on the grounds of race:

(*a*)   in the arrangements made for determining who should be offered employment;

(*b*)   in the terms on which employment is offered;

(*c*)   by refusing or deliberately omitting to offer employment;

(*d*)   in the way he/she affords access to opportunities for promotion, transfer or training, or to any other benefits, facilities or services, or by refusing or deliberately omitting to afford access to them; or

(*e*)   by dismissing, or subjecting a person to any other detriment.

In a pensions context, the issue of race discrimination has been raised in a number of cases involving members and former members of the Gurkha regiments who challenged the Ministry of Defence's pension arrangements whereby members of the Gurkha Pension Scheme generally receive pensions which are lower than those available to others who retire from the British Army. The issues were most recently considered by the Court of Appeal in October 2010. Claims for race discrimination had been dropped by this stage and the case was argued solely under the European Convention on Human Rights. The Court of Appeal rejected the Gurkhas' claims on the grounds that the basis recruitment, service and discharge was not analogous with other members of the British Army and they could not compare themselves with them for the purposes of a discrimination claim (*British Gurkha Welfare Society v Ministry of Defence [2010] EWCA Civ 1098*).

Insurance

9.48   *EqA 2010, s 29* provides that a service provider must not discriminate in the terms on which it provides a service, and this includes insurance companies.

The provision of a financial service (which includes insurance) is exempt from *EqA 2010, s 29* generally if it is in pursuance of arrangements made by an employer for a service to be provided as a consequence of employment (*EqA 2010, Sch 3 part 5 para 20*). Discrimination on the grounds of age in the provision of a financial service is exempt from *EqA 2010, s 29* (*EqA 2010, Sch 3 part 5 para 20A*). (see **9.35** above).

There is also an exemption in relation to disability where the discrimination is relevant to the assessment of risk and in relation to sex, gender reassignment, pregnancy and maternity, an exemption allows insurers to rely on specified actuarial data. Any differences in treatment must be proportionate according to the data (*EqA 2010, Sch 3, paras 21* and *22*).

Table of relevant case law

9.49 The following table of cases lists some of the more important discrimination cases which affect pension schemes.

Cases

Decision	Date	Main issues decided
Defrenne v The Belgian State *Case No C-80/70 [1971] ECR 445*	1971	Distinguished between statutory pension provision and private occupational pension schemes, in that the former did not come within the scope of *Article 157*. Payments from the latter were not, in principle, to be excluded from the concept of 'pay' for the purposes of *Article 157*.
Defrenne v Sabena (No 2) *Case No C-43/75 [1976] ECR 455*	8 April 1976	Determination that *Article 157* had direct effect, and consequently could be enforced by individuals in Member States without the need for further legislation to implement it.
Bilka-Kaufhaus GmbH v Weber von Hartz *Case No C-170/84 [1986] ECR 1607*	1986	Exclusion of part-timers from scheme membership is unlawful where the reason for exclusion is indirectly discriminatory on grounds of sex. Here, the exclusion affected ten times as many women as men and could not be explained by any reason other than one based on sex discrimination (ie it was not 'objectively justified').

Decision	Date	Main issues decided
Barber v GRE Assurance Group *Case No C-262/88 [1990] ECR I-1889*	17 May 1990	A pension paid from a UK occupational pension scheme was 'pay' for the purposes of *Article 157*. The same retirement benefits 'package' available to a woman who is made compulsorily redundant, should also be available to a man in like circumstances, and that each element (as opposed to the totality) of a pay package must be equal.
Bullock v The Alice Ottley School *[1992] IRLR 564*	15 Oct 1992	Employers are permitted to have a variety of normal retirement ages for different types of workers, provided that the reason for the differences is not based upon direct or indirect sex discrimination.
Ten Oever v Stichting *Case No C-109/91 [1993] ECR I-4879*	6 Oct 1993	Temporal limitations of the *Barber* judgment clarified in that the direct application of *Article 157* can only relate to periods of employment on or after 17 May 1990, unless the claim is brought before that date.
Birds Eye Walls v Friedl M Roberts *Case No C-132/92 [1993] PLR 323*	9 Nov 1993	'Bridging' pensions do not infringe *Article 157*, as they are designed to remedy inequality (in this case, in taking into account the differing ages at which State pensions became payable).

Decision	Date	Main issues decided
Neath v Hugh Steeper Ltd *Case No C-152/91 [1993] ECR I-6935*	22 Dec 1993	Under a final salary scheme, it is the employer's commitment (ie the amount of pension promised) that must be equal, even though the use of sex-based actuarial factors may require unequal contributions from the employer to meet the funding requirements of the scheme.
Coloroll Pension Trustees Ltd v Russell *Case No C-200/91 [1994] ECR I-4389*	28 Sep 1994	Determined that: • both employees and their dependants may rely on the direct effect of *Article 157* against a scheme's trustees (who are required to observe the principles of equal treatment); • equal treatment may be implemented by the 'levelling down' of benefits (ie reduction of the advantages enjoyed by one group of members to the level received by a less advantaged group) from the date of scheme equalisation; • retrospection is only in relation to benefits (including survivors' benefits) for periods of service after 17 May 1990; • the receiving scheme must make good any inadequacy in respect of an unequalised transfer payment made to it; and • AVC's and single-sex schemes do not fall within the scope of *Article 157*.

Decision	Date	Main issues decided
Smith v Avdel Systems Ltd *Case No C-408/92 [1994]* *ECR I-4435*	28 Sep 1994	Retirement ages for women could not be raised to that of men for the period from 17 May 1990 to the date of equalisation, although this measure would not infringe *Article 157* in respect of service completed after the date of the change.
Van den Akker v Stichting Shell PF *Case No C-28/93 [1994]* *ECR I-4527*	28 Sep 1994	*Article 157* does not allow a uniform retirement age to be set whilst maintaining an advantage for women members (ie red-circling). Equality can only be achieved by the 'levelling up' of benefits (ie for men to enjoy the same advantages of women members, for service after *Barber* to the date of equalisation).
Algemeen Burgerlijk PF v Beaune *Case No C-7/93 [1994]* *ECR I-4471*	28 Sep 1994	Civil service pension schemes do come within the scope of *Article 157*.
Vroege v NCIV Instituut *Case No C-57/93 [1994]* *ECR I-4541*	28 Sep 1994	The right to join an occupational pension scheme is covered by *Article 157*, but falls outside the temporal limitations of the *Barber* judgment. This right continues to be governed by the *Bilka-Kaufhaus* judgment.

Decision	Date	Main issues decided
Fisscher v Voorhuis Hengelo BV *Case No C-128/93 [1994] ECR I-4583*	28 Sep 1994	As for *Vroege*, but also decided that administrators must comply with *Article 157*. Further, it confirmed that employees can claim retrospective membership although they cannot avoid paying backdated contributions.
Nolte v Landesversicherungsanstalt Hannover *Case No C-317/93 [1996] All ER (EC) 212*	14 Dec 1995	Exclusion of part-timers from membership is permissible, even where to do so affects more women than men, where the reason is to achieve a social policy unrelated to any discrimination.
Grant v South-West Trains Limited *Case No C-249/96 [1998] All ER (EC) 193*	17 Feb 1998	This was an employment case involving the granting of travel concessions. South-West Trains refused to give travel concessions to Ms Grant's same-sex partner. The CJEU held that EU law as it stood did not cover discrimination based on sexual orientation.
Regina v Secretary of State for Employment ex parte Seymour-Smith and Another *Case No C-167/97 [1999] ICR 447*	9 Feb 1999	The CJEU considered, among other questions, the test for determining whether a measure adopted by a Member State had 'such a disparate effect as between men and women as to amount to indirect discrimination'.

Decision	Date	Main issues decided
Preston v Wolverhampton Healthcare NHS Trust *Case No C-78/98 [2000] All ER (EC) 714 and [2001] IRLR 237* HL	16 May 2000 and 8 Feb 2001	Claims by part-timers in respect of unlawful exclusion from scheme membership have to be made within six months of leaving service as required under national UK law. Backdated benefits can be claimed going as far back as April 1976. However, Member States are permitted to require that individuals making a claim pay any past contributions.
Marsh Mercer Pension Scheme v Pensions Ombudsman *[2001] 16 PBLR 28*	23 Feb 2001	The Pensions Ombudsman could not make a direction relating to the equalisation of GMP's and compliance with equal treatment rules in *PA 1995, s 62* as the matter was too wide-ranging for determination in such a manner.
Allonby v Accrington & Rossendale College *[2001] IRLR 364*	23 Mar 2001	Claim brought by a part-time lecturer who was no longer eligible for membership of the scheme by virtue of change in employment status from being directly employed to being employed through an employment agency. It was held by the Court of Appeal that the part-time lecturer was in a contract of employment for occupational pension purposes. As there could be a possible conflict with *Article 157, Allonby* was referred to the CJEU.

Decision	Date	Main issues decided
Uppingham School v Shillcock *[2002] EWHC 641 (Ch)*	19 Apr 2002	The case overturned the decision of the Pensions Ombudsman and held that an LEL offset to integrate benefits with the State scheme was not indirect discrimination and, had it been so, it would have been objectively justified.
Goodwin v UK *[2002] IRLR 664*	11 Jul 2002	The European Court held that the UK was in breach of *Article 8* (right to respect for private and family life) and *Article 12* (right to marry and to found a family) of the *European Convention on Human Rights*. The UK had failed legally to recognise that Ms Goodwin who underwent gender re-assignment surgery was female. Ms Goodwin was therefore required to pay NICs until age 65. Had her sex change been legally recognised, NICs would have ceased at age 60.
Bellinger v Bellinger *[2003] 2 All ER 593*	10 Apr 2003	The House of Lords held that the marriage was not a valid marriage but declared that the non-recognition of gender reassignment for the purposes of allowing transsexuals to marry was incompatible with the right to respect for private and family life and the right to marry guaranteed by *Articles 8* and *12* of the *European Convention on Human Rights*.

Decision	Date	Main issues decided
Kutz-Bauer v Freie und Hansestadt Hamburg *Case No C-187/00 [2003] All ER (D) 327 (Mar)*	20 Mar 2003	Provisions allowing workers over 55 to work part-time applied only until the date on which the worker became entitled to a statutory old age pension. For most women this was 60 and for most men it was 65. It was held that this was capable of breaching the *Equal Treatment Directive* and it was for the national court to determine whether there was in fact indirect discrimination which could not be objectively justified.
Preston v Wolverhampton Healthcare NHS Trust (No 3) *[2004] IRLR 96*	19 Dec 2003	Decision of the Employment Appeal Tribunal on a number of part-timer issues raised by the 2002 *Preston* case.
KB v National Health Service Pensions Agency *Case No C-117/01 [2004] All ER (EC) 1089*	7 Jan 2004	The CJEU confirmed that national legislation which prevents marriage (and therefore the enjoyment of certain pension benefits) for individuals who have undergone a sex change is in breach of EU law.
Allonby v Accrington and Rossendale College *Case No 256/01 [2004] IRLR 224*	13 Jan 2004	The CJEU's judgment on matters referred to it by the Court of Appeal following the 2001 *Allonby* case.
Leadenhall Independent Trustees Ltd v Welham *[2004] All ER (D) 423 (Mar)*	19 Mar 2004	The trustee of a scheme in surplus sought directions as to whether it had the power to augment benefits to neutralise the gender discrimination of GMPs.

Decision	Date	Main issues decided
Matthews v Kent & Medway Towns Fire Authority *[2004] EWCA Civ 844*	2 Jul 2004	Case brought before the Court of Appeal under the *Part-time Workers (Prevention of Less Favourable Treatment) Regulations 2000 (SI 2000/1551).* The EAT had held that a part-time fire fighter had not suffered less favourable treatment than full-time fire fighters despite being excluded access from the pension scheme. The fire fighters' appeal to the Court of Appeal was dismissed.
Cross v British Airways *[2005] 26 PBLR*	23 Mar 2005	This case looked at the expense involved in allowing employees to work later. Cost alone could not be a justification.
Matthews v Kent and Medway Towns Fire Authority *[2006] All ER 171*	1 Mar 2006	Part-time fire-fighters case is remitted back to the employment tribunal.
Preston v Wolverhampton Healthcare NHS Trust (No 3) *[2006] UKHL* 13	8 Mar 2006	Decision of the House of Lords in relation to the point at which the time limit for a part-timer's claim begins to run following a TUPE transfer.
Richards v Secretary of State for Work and Pensions *Case No C-423/04 [2006] All ER (EC) 895*	27 Apr 2006	Case dealing with discrimination against transsexuals.
Grant v United Kingdom *(2007) 44 EHRR* 1	23 May 2006	It was held that G (a transsexual) was entitled to claim a lack of legal recognition from the date of the judgment in *Goodwin v UK (2002)*.

Decision	Date	Main issues decided
Harland and Wolff v Aon *EWHC 1778 (Ch)*	14 July 2006	Levelling down cannot be retrospective even where the scheme amendment power expressly allows it. Following *Smith v Avdel*.
National Pensions Office v Jonkman *[2005] All ER (D) 47 Case No C-231/06*	21 Jun 2007	Decision of the CJEU in relation to back-dated employee contributions following a successful claim for backdated membership of the scheme.
R (on the application of the Incorporated Trustees of the National Council for Ageing (Age Concern England)) v Secretary of State for Business, Enterprise and Regulatory Reform (Heyday') *Case No C-388/07*	24 Jul 2007	The National Council on Ageing (NCA) persuaded the High Court that it should ask the European Court of Justice whether the *Age Regulations*, which permit retirement at age 65, are lawful.
Bloxham v Freshfields *ET July 2007 [2007] PLR 375*	9–19 Jul 2007	Case before the employment tribunal looking at age discrimination and objective justification arguments.
Lindorfer v Council of the European Union *Case No C-277/04P [2009] All ER (EC) 569*	11 Sep 2007	Decision of the CJEU in relation to the use of sex based actuarial factors.
Betafence Limited v Veys and Others *[2006] EWHC 999 (Ch)* *Trustee Solutions v Dubery* *[2006] 36 PBLR* *Hodgson and Others v Toray Textiles Europe Limited and Others* *[2006] EWHC 2612 (Ch)* *Capital Cranfield Trustees Ltd v Beck [2008] EWHC 3181*(Ch)	2006–2008	Cases relating to equalisation and defective amendments.

Decision	Date	Main issues decided
Foster Wheeler Ltd v Hanley *[2009] EWCA Civ 651*	8 July 2008	This case looked at the correct way to treat members with mixed retirement ages as a consequence of *Barber*.
Matthews and others v Kent & Medway Town Fire Authority and others 6100000/2001 (ET)	2008	The employment tribunal reconsiders the case of the part-time fire-fighters following a successful appeal to the House of Lords.
Tadao Maruko v Versorgungsanstalt der deutschen Bühnen *Case No C-267/06 [2008] All ER (EC) 977*	1 April 2008	CJEU decision relating to discrimination on the grounds of sexual orientations. This case has implications for the implementation of the *CPA 2004* in the UK.
MacCulloch v ICI *Employment Tribunal*	22 July 2008	Decision of the EAT looking at the issue of age discrimination and justification.
Birgit Bartsch v Bosch und Siemens Hausgerate (BSH) Altersfursorge GmbH *Case No C-427/06 [2009] All ER (EC) 113*	23 September 2008	Consideration by the Advocate General of a young spouse provision of a German pension scheme which prevented a widow from receiving a pension because she was more than 15 years younger than the deceased member.
Pulham & Others v London Borough of Barking and Dagenham *[2009] UKEAT 0516/08/RN Bury Metropolitan Borough Council v Hamilton and Sunderland City Council v Brennan* *UKEAT/0413-5/09/ZT and* *UKEAT/0241/09/CEA*	2009–2011	EAT Cases considering discriminatory measures within pay protection schemes.

Decision	Date	Main issues decided
Martin & Others v Professional Game Match Officials *ET/2802438/09*	13 April 2010	ET decision concerning the test for justifying direct, as opposed to indirect, age discrimination.
Timbrell v Secretary of State for Work and Pensions *[2010] EWCA Civ 701*	22 June 2010	Court of Appeal ruling that a male to female transsexual was discriminated against by the DWP's refusal to pay her a pension at age 60 on the grounds that she lacked a full gender recognition certificate under the *Gender Recognition Act 2004.*
Association Belge des Consommateurs Test-Achats ASBL and Others v Conseil des Ministres *Case C-236/09 [2011] ECR 00*	1 March 2011	CJEU decision that the current permitted derogation from the requirement not to discriminate on the basis of sex in relation to insurance premiums will be abolished from 21 December 2012.
Woodcock v Cumbria Primary Care Trust [2012] EWCA Civ 330	22 March 2012	Court of Appeal case confirming that the saving of cost, on its own, cannot be a legitimate aim justifying discriminatory treatment.
Seldon v Clarkson Wright & Jakes [2012] UKSC 16	25 April 2012	Supreme Court ruling on the justification of direct age discrimination and the requirement for a social policy objective.
Homer v Chief Constable of West Yorkshire Police [2012] UKSC 15	25 April 2012	Supreme Court ruling on the justification of indirect age discrimination.
Abdulla v Birmingham City Council [2012] UKSC 47	24 October 2012	Supreme Court case confirming that it may be possible to bring equal pay claims (including pension claims) in the civil courts where they are out of time for the Employment Tribunal.

Decision	Date	Main issues decided
O'Brien v Ministry of Justice [2013] UKSC 6	6 February 2013	Supreme Court decision on the justification of less favourable treatment of part-time workers.
	6 October 2015	Court of Appeal decision confirms limit on backdating.
HK Danmark v Experian A/S [2013] EUECJ C-476/11	26 September 2013	CJEU decision on age-related contributions.
Innospec v Walker [2015] EWCA Civ 1000	6 October 2015	Court of Appeal decision that the restriction on benefits for civil partners in relation to service prior to 5 December 2005 is not in breach of EU law.

Chapter 10

Investment

Introduction

10.1 One of the fundamental duties of any trustee is to invest the monies under his control so as to produce a capital or income return for his trust. In doing so, a trustee must act within the boundaries imposed on him by the trust instrument, by statutory restrictions and by case law. The duties and obligations are onerous and, consequently, many trustees prefer to delegate their powers to professional fund managers. Trustees are in a fiduciary relationship with the beneficiaries of the scheme and therefore must exercise their powers of investment for the benefit of the beneficiaries of the scheme.

This chapter deals with the powers of trustees regarding the investment of the funds for which they are responsible and the duties imposed on them when exercising those powers. It considers how, and to whom, trustees may delegate their powers and briefly discusses the implications of (and recent amendments to) the *Financial Services and Markets Act 2000* (*FSMA 2000*). Finally, it examines the protection afforded to trustees in respect of investment decisions. Trustee duties generally are dealt with in **Chapter 3**.

The meaning of investment

10.2 The classic statement of the legal meaning of the words 'invest' and 'investment' was given in the case *Re Wragg* in which Mr Justice Lawrence said that:

> 'Without attempting to give an exhaustive definition of the words "invest" and "investment" I think that the words "to invest" when used in an investment clause may safely be said to include as one of its meanings "to apply money in the purchase of some property from which interest or profit is expected and which property is purchased in order to be held for the sake of the income which it will yield".' (*Re Wragg [1919] 2 Ch 58 at 64*)

On a strict interpretation, an asset purchased for some reason other than deriving an income would therefore not be an investment; for example, land

428

that is purchased for the financial gain it will produce when it is sold will not be an investment unless it is let for a rent or produces some other income.

In recent years there have been indications of greater flexibility in the definition of investment. In *Marson v Morton*, Sir Nicolas Browne-Wilkinson V-C recognised that in the modern financial arena 'new approaches to investment have emerged putting the emphasis in investment on the making of capital profit at the expense of income yield' (*Marson v Morton [1986] 1 WLR 1343* at 1350). He gives the purchase of short-dated stocks (which give a capital yield but no income) and works of art as examples of common ways of investing and concludes that the mere fact that land is not income-producing should not be decisive on the question of whether it was bought as an investment. In *Harries v Church Commissioners [1992] WLR 1241*, Sir Donald Nicholls V-C stated that 'the purposes of the trust will be best served by the trustees seeking to obtain therefrom the maximum return, whether by way of income or capital growth, which is consistent with commercial prudence'.

The Pension Law Review Committee used the term investment to mean 'any application of assets, whether or not investments in the technical sense, and thus (including), for example, stock lending and borrowing' (Report of the Pension Law Review Committee 1993, page 342). Unfortunately this approach was not adopted in *PA 1995*, which does not define 'investment'. Consequently there remains doubt as to the modern meaning of the term.

Trading or investing?

10.3 Broadly speaking, registered pension schemes are not liable for income tax or capital gains tax on the investments they make. However, in certain circumstances, HMRC may argue that trustees are not investing but are in fact trading. If a pension scheme is found to be trading, rather than investing, the transaction will fall outside the scope of the statutory tax exemptions and the trustees will be liable for the appropriate tax. It is, therefore, important to determine whether the proceeds of the sale of an asset constitute the realisation of an investment, or are the profits of a trade.

Badges of trade

10.4 The 1954 Royal Commission (Cmd 9474) identified 'six badges of trade' as being relevant in deciding whether a transaction is, or is not, to be treated as a trading transaction. These 'badges' have since been refined and enlarged to nine and are now included in HMRC's Business Income Manual (BIM20205), discussed in **10.5** to **10.16** below.

Profit-seeking motive

10.5   An intention to make a profit supports trading, but by itself is not conclusive. Evidence that the sole object of acquiring an asset was to re-sell it at a profit, without any intention of holding it as an investment, is a pointer to the conclusion that a trade is being carried on. However, the presence of a profit-seeking motive is not necessarily decisive to the existence of a trade. It is only one factor to be weighed along with all the other relevant factors.

The number of transactions

10.6   A single isolated transaction can amount to the carrying on of a trade for tax purposes, but it is generally not easy to show that that is the case. The systematic repetition of a transaction is a pointer towards trading. Where a number of transactions, each one not in itself constituting a trade, are carried out within a relatively short period of time, the series of transactions may amount to the carrying out of a trade.

In *Pickford v Quirke [1927] 13 TC 251*, Rowlatt J stated that 'it is very well known that one transaction of buying and selling a thing does not make a man a trader, but if it is repeated and becomes systematic, then he becomes a trader and the profits of the transactions, not taxable so long as they remain isolated, become taxable as items in a trade as a whole'.

The nature of the asset

10.7   The nature of the asset can be of great importance. Where assets are generally realised by way of trade (for example chemicals), transactions in those assets are almost always going to be a 'trade'. More difficult are assets which are generally bought as an investment that usually, but not necessarily, yield income (eg shares), are for personal use or enjoyment (eg paintings and classic cars) or are a fixed asset used by a business (eg plant and machinery).

The initial presumption is that these types of assets are acquired other than as the subject of trade (*CIR v Fraser [1942] 24 TC 498*) but that presumption can be overturned.

Existence of similar trading transactions or interests

10.8   Transactions that are similar to those of an existing trade may themselves be trading. In *Marson v Morton and Others [1986] 59 TC 381* the court asked 'is the transaction in question in some way related to the trade which the taxpayer otherwise carries on? For example, a one-off purchase of silver cutlery by a general dealer is much more likely to be a trade transaction than such a purchase by a retired colonel'.

Changes to the asset

10.9   Was the asset repaired, modified or improved to make it more easily saleable or saleable at a greater profit? These actions are typical of trading activities. However, expenditure on an asset after purchase and before sale is not always strong evidence of a trading motive. HMRC will have regard to the nature and scale of the expenditure. For example, insurance against loss may have little or no relevance when considering the question of trading as it is the sort of expenditure that any owner would incur, not just an owner intending trading the asset.

If land is purchased and then developed for sale, there is often a suggestion that the trustees are to sell the property and thus enter into a transaction in the nature of trade. However, this is not necessarily the case; trustees may well refurbish a property simply in order to retain its marketability in the long term, which most prudent investors would, and probably should, do.

The way the sale was carried out

10.10   If transactions are carried out in the same manner as those of an undisputed trader, this may indicate a 'trade'. In *CIR v Livingston and Others 11 TC 538*, Lord Clyde stated that 'I think the test, which must be used to determine whether a venture such as we are now considering is, or is not, 'in the nature of trade', is whether the operations involved in it are of the same kind, and carried on in the same way, as those which are characteristic of ordinary trading in the line of business in which the venture was made'.

The source of finance

10.11   Was money borrowed to buy the asset which could only be repaid by selling the asset? HMRC may examine the method of financing and consider whether the purchase was undertaken in the expectation that the asset would be paid for out of the proceeds of the sale.

For example, in *Wisdom v Chamberlain [1968] 45 TC 92* the taxpayer was held to be trading in relation to profits made from the purchase and sale of silver bullion. The purchase of the bullion was financed by loans at a high rate of interest in circumstances that made it clear that it was necessary to sell the asset in the short term, to repay the loan.

431

The interval of time between purchase and sale

10.12   There is an inference of trading where property is realised within a short time of acquisition. However, if trustees can show a good reason for their actions the presumption that the trustees are trading may be rebutted. There is no doubt, however, that a quick sale helps to support the finding of trading, especially where other indications of trading are present (*Turner v Last (1965) 42 TC 517*; *Eames v Stepnell Properties Ltd (1966) 43 TC 678*).

In *Marson v Morton and Others [1986] 59 TC 381*, it was asked 'What were the purchasers' intentions as to resale at the time of purchase? If there was an intention to hold the object indefinitely, albeit with an intention to make a capital profit at the end of the day, that is a pointer towards a pure investment as opposed to a trading deal. On the other hand, if before the contract of purchase is made a contract for resale is already in place, that is a very strong pointer towards a trading deal rather than an investment. Similarly, an intention to resell in the short term rather than the long term is some indication against concluding that the transaction was by way of investment rather than by way of a deal'.

The method of acquisition

10.13   The way in which an asset was acquired is relevant. If it is by gift or inheritance it will be difficult, although not impossible, to show that a subsequent sale is by way of trade. If the asset was acquired by purchase, the circumstance leading up to purchase may tend to show either that it was being bought for resale or that it was wanted for private use or as an investment.

If an asset acquired as a capital asset is later sold at a profit it will only be taxable as a 'trade' if it can be shown that, at some point before sale, the asset became trading stock. This is known as the concept of 'supervening trading'.

Application of the badges of trade

10.14   The 'badges of trade' are of general application to all types of transactions, where tax mitigation may be in question; they were not drawn up to apply solely to trustees or to pension schemes, and so may not always be relevant to dealings by pension scheme trustees. The onus of proving trading is, in reality, on HMRC, as far as occupational pension schemes are concerned (*Salt v Chamberlain (1979) 53 TC 143*) and there are presumptions to assist trustees who are accused of trading.

Presumption against trading

10.15 It is common practice for frequent changes to be made in a scheme's portfolio of securities. Normally no inference of trading would be drawn from such changes. However, if there is evidence of a large turnover of a scheme's holdings, which appears to have been carried out pursuant to a deliberate and organised plan of buying and selling with a view to profit-making, it may be possible to infer that trading has taken place (*Cooper v C & J Clarke Ltd (1982) 54 TC 670*).

In *Clark v British Telecom Pension Scheme [1999] 6 PBLR 21*, Lightman J overturned the earlier decision of the Commissioners of the Inland Revenue that profits received from the sub-underwriting of share issues by the trustees were not profits from trade rather than gains from investments and hence were not subject to tax. Lightman J found instead that the trustees had been involved in operations of a 'commercial character' for a period of years and the activity had all the hallmarks of trade being 'frequent (or habitual) and organised as well as extensive, business-like and for profit' (paragraph 31). However, the trustees of the British Telecom Pension Scheme appealed and the Court of Appeal (*[2000] 21 PBLR 13*) held that the sub-underwriting activities of the trustees were an integral and indissoluble part of their investment activities. Income from the sub-underwriting was not therefore trading income and was exempt from tax by virtue of *ICTA 1988, s 592*. Lightman J's decision was therefore reversed. Appeal to the House of Lords was refused.

Powers given under the trust instrument

10.16 The majority of trust deeds governing pension schemes contain wide powers permitting investments in many areas. Trustees may also be given power to trade, but when such a power is missing there is a very strong argument against any allegation of trading; it is unlikely that a trustee will knowingly commit a breach of trust in order to trade.

Power of investment

10.17 A trustee's power of investment will derive from two sources; statute and the trust instrument.

Statutory power to invest

10.18 Prior to 6 April 1997, statutory powers of investment were conferred on trustees by the *Trustee Investments Act 1961 (TIA 1961)* and, to a lesser extent, the *Trustee Act 1925*. Even before *PA 1995*, it was rare for a pension scheme to rely solely on the powers conferred by these Acts as they were very restrictive in the types of investments they permitted. So far as pension scheme trustees are concerned, the provisions of *TIA 1961* were largely replaced or superseded by the provisions of *PA 1995*.

PA 1995, s 34(1) confers a wide power of investment on trustees by providing that they have the same power to 'make an investment of any kind as if they were absolutely entitled to the assets of the scheme', subject to any restriction imposed by the scheme. The power is also subject to the provisions of *PA 1995, s 36(1)* and the *Occupational Pension Schemes (Investment) Regulations 2005 (SI 2005/3378)* (the '*2005 Investment Regulations*'). Taking effect as if it were contained in the scheme's governing documentation, *s 34(1)* was intended to aid trustees who were prevented from making some types of investment by an overly restrictive power of investment. However, the wording of the provision causes problems which were not intended. If the term 'investment' is narrowly construed, certain traditional assets including, arguably, group life policies, are not investments under *PA 1995*, and *s 34* alone would not permit trustees to purchase them. Consequently, trustees still need a carefully drafted investment power, allowing them specifically to undertake transactions, or to purchase assets, which fall outside the meaning of investment used in *Re Wragg [1919] 2 Ch 58* (see **10.2** above).

The Law Commission Report (see **10.24** below) led to the DWP issuing consultation on 'Reducing the Regulatory Burden', which also addresses its response to the February 2015 consultation on amending the *2005 Investment Regulations*.

The trust instrument

10.19   It is common for trustees to be given power to invest, or otherwise apply the monies under their control in any manner which they could do if they were absolutely and beneficially entitled to the assets of the scheme and in any manner which they could do as trustees of a pension scheme. The second limb is necessary to allow trustees to invest in those investments, such as exempt unit trusts which are only available to trustees of funds which are not liable for income or capital gains tax. The ability to 'apply' the fund is designed to permit trustees to purchase assets which are not technically investments.

Trustees will generally be given specific power to purchase certain assets such as traded options, financial futures, life assurance contracts and assets which are to be held for capital growth rather than for the income they produce. Trustees may also be given power to underwrite new issues on the stock market and possibly the power to engage in stock lending. Trustees are sometimes given specific power to trade, but this is less common (see **10.16** above).

Trustees may also be given the power to commingle the assets of their scheme with the assets of one or more other schemes in a common investment fund, which will usually be set up under an independent trust. In order to continue to benefit from the tax advantages available to 'registered pension schemes', all schemes participating in such a fund must themselves be registered schemes.

It is also advisable to have express power in the trust deed to lease, charge and otherwise deal in and conduct the management of real property, and to have a general power to give indemnities and guarantees (and perhaps express permission to use the assets of the scheme to pay sums due under any such indemnity or guarantee if inclusion of such a provision is possible having regard to the scheme's amendment power, *PA 1995 s 67* and general case law).

Notwithstanding the supposedly wide power of investment given in *PA 1995*, the investment provisions contained in most trust deeds will probably continue to spell out the powers of the trustees, since, if they do not, there is the possibility of the trustees exceeding their powers by inadvertently purchasing an asset which is not an investment and which cannot, therefore, be purchased under the power given by *PA 1995, s 34*.

Duties of trustees when exercising their investment power

10.20   When exercising their investment power, trustees must consider the duties imposed on them under the trust instrument, by statute and by case law. The main duties are set out in **10.21** to **10.25** below.

The duty to act in the best interests of the beneficiaries

10.21   One of the fundamental duties of a trustee is to exercise his powers in the best interests of the beneficiaries of the scheme and to act fairly between different classes of beneficiaries. In the context of an investment power, a beneficiary's best interests will generally mean his best financial interests. Consequently an investment power must generally be exercised so as to produce the best return possible, having regard to the level of risk involved (*Cowan v Scargill [1984] 2 All ER 750*).

The prudent man test

10.22   The basic duty of a trustee, when exercising his investment power, is to choose investments which are within the terms of his trust and, in selecting those investments, to 'take such care as an ordinary prudent man would take if he were minded to make (an investment) for the benefit of other people for whom he felt morally bound to provide' (*Re Whiteley (1886) 33 Ch D 347*).

The House of Lords' decision in *Learoyd v Whiteley* sets out the principles which trustees must consider when exercising their investment power as follows:

> 'As a general rule the law requires of a trustee no higher degree of diligence in the execution of his office than a man of ordinary prudence would exercise in the management of his own private affairs. Yet he is not allowed the same discretion in investing the money of the trusts as if he were a person *sui juris* dealing with his own estate. Business men of ordinary prudence may, and frequently do, select investments which are more or less of a speculative character; but it is the duty of a trustee to confine himself to the class of investments which are permitted by the trust, and likewise to avoid all investments of that class which are attended with hazard.'

(*Learoyd v Whiteley (1887) 12 AC 727,* Lord Watson at 733)

Sir Robert Megarry reiterated and clarified the standard required of a trustee in exercising his powers of investment, making it clear that, in addition to the above, the duty 'includes the duty to seek advice on matters which the trustee does not understand, such as the making of investments, and on receiving that advice to act with the same degree of prudence' (*Cowan v Scargill [1984] 2 All ER 750* at *762*).

PA 2004, ss 247 and *248* contain provisions concerning the 'requirement for knowledge and understanding' of trustees and impose more specific and onerous requirements for trustees of occupational pension schemes. This is dealt with in **Chapter 3**.

However wide the provisions of an express investment power may be, the trustees are not absolved from their duty to consider whether a proposed investment is such that it is prudent and right for them, as trustees, to make it. The mere fact that a certain type of investment is authorised by the trust instrument or by statute does not mean that it is necessarily proper to invest in it. Even though, under *PA 1995*, trustees have power to invest at their absolute discretion and as if they were absolute owners, they should remember that they must act as trustees in exercising that power. Moreover, *PA 2004* amended *PA 1995, s 36* to ensure compliance with *Article 18(1)* of the *Pensions Directive (2003/41/EC)*. This Directive requires investments to be carried out in accordance with the 'prudent person principle' as defined in the Directive. The detailed requirements are contained in the *2005 Investment Regulations*.

When exercising their investment powers, *PA 1995, s 36* requires trustees (and any fund manager to whom a discretion has been delegated) to do so in accordance with the *2005 Investment Regulations*. These Regulations require that the trustees of a trust scheme (and any fund manager to whom any discretion has been delegated) must exercise their powers of investment, in accordance with the provisions of *reg 4*:

- The assets must be invested in the best interests of members and beneficiaries and, in the case of a potential conflict of interest, in the sole interest of members and beneficiaries.

- The powers of investment, or the discretion, must be exercised in a manner calculated to ensure the security, quality, liquidity and profitability of the portfolio as a whole.

- Assets held to cover the scheme's technical provisions must also be invested in a manner appropriate to the nature and duration of the expected future retirement benefits payable under the scheme.

- The assets of the scheme must consist predominately of investments admitted to trading on regulated markets; investments in assets which are not admitted to trading on a regulated market must be kept to a prudent level.

- The assets of the scheme must be properly diversified in such a way as to avoid excessive reliance on any particular asset, issuer or group of undertakings and so as to avoid accumulations of risk in the portfolio as a whole. Investments in assets issued by the same issuer or by issuers belonging to the same group must not expose the scheme to excessive risk concentration.

- Investment in derivative instruments may be made only insofar as they:

    (*a*)   contribute to a reduction of risks; or

    (*b*)   facilitate efficient portfolio management (including the reduction of cost or the generation of additional capital or income with an acceptable level of risk),

    and any such investment must be made and managed so as to avoid excessive risk exposure to a single counter party and to other derivative operations.

Note that *reg 4* does not apply to a scheme that has fewer than 100 members but regard must still be had to the need for diversification of investments, in so far as appropriate to the circumstances of the scheme. *Regulation 9* of the *2005 Investment Regulations* also partially disapplies *reg 4* in respect of schemes being wound up.

PA 1995, s 36 requires 'proper advice' to be taken on the question of whether the investment is satisfactory taking into account the requirements of the *2005 Investment Regulations*, some of which are referred to above, so far as relating to the suitability of the investments and to the statement of investment principles (*s 36(3)*). In addition, in relation to retaining any investment, *s 36* requires the trustees to determine at what intervals, the circumstances and nature of the investment make it desirable to obtain 'proper advice' and then obtain and consider that advice (*s 36(4)*).

Broadly speaking, 'proper advice' is advice from a person authorised under *FSMA 2000* in relation to investments covered by that Act. In any other case proper advice must be obtained from a person whom the trustees reasonably believe to be qualified by his ability in, and practical experience of, financial matters and to have the appropriate knowledge and experience of the management of the investments of pension schemes (*s 36(6)*). Trustees must ensure that they obtain confirmation of the 'proper advice' given in writing in order to comply with the requirements of *PA 1995* (*s 36(7)*).

Civil penalties can be levied if trustees fail to take all reasonable steps to ensure compliance with the *2005 Investment Regulations* or do not obtain and consider proper advice (*s 36(8)*) (see **Appendix I**).

The duty to diversify

10.23   Trustees are required to exercise their powers of investment in accordance with the requirements of the *2005 Investment Regulations* and *PA 1995, ss 36(3) and (4)*. The trustees and any fund manager to whom any investment discretion has been delegated must exercise their investment powers in particular in accordance with the *2005 Investment Regulations, reg 4* which provides that '[t]he assets of the scheme must be properly diversified in such a way as to avoid excessive reliance on any particular asset, issuer or group of undertakings and so as to avoid accumulations of risk in the portfolio as a whole'.

In addition to the above requirements, *PA 1995, s 36A* restricts borrowing by trustees, or the fund manager to whom any discretion has been delegated under *PA 1995, s 34*. The *2005 Investment Regulations* provide that they cannot borrow money or act as a guarantor in respect of the obligations of another person where the borrowing is liable to be repaid, or liability under a guarantee is liable to be satisfied, out of the assets of the scheme. This is stated not to preclude borrowing made only for the purposes of providing liquidity for the scheme on a temporary basis.

The requirement imposed on the trustees to diversify is also important from the actuary's standpoint, particularly in mature schemes. Although the actuary does not advise between one investment and another he may, and frequently does, become involved in decisions on investment policy and asset allocation of the scheme. The actuary will ascertain the liabilities of a scheme and will advise on the short, medium and long-term liabilities. He should then be able to advise on the various types of investment and, for example, how they should be split to allow the trustees sufficient cash funds to provide lump sum and pension benefits for the beneficiaries as they fall due.

The trustees, or more likely the fund managers, will look at the strategy for the short, medium and long-term cash needs which the actuary has mapped out and should select investments that meet those needs. Not only must they look at diversification from that standpoint but they must also look at diversification on a second level. Therefore, if a certain percentage of the fund has to be put in short-term investments, they should not put the entire fund designated for such purpose into one investment; they should spread the risk amongst a group of investments.

Moral and ethical considerations

10.24   There has been much discussion on the ability of trustees legitimately to consider moral and ethical considerations in preference to financial return on any particular investment.

Decided case law indicates that trustees cannot invest other than on the usual criteria (financial returns, security and diversification). However, if, for example, trustees wish to make an ethically acceptable investment which will produce a financial return that is at least as good as that produced by any other suitable (although perhaps not so ethically sound) investment, there is no reason why they cannot do so. Essentially, they must act with the standard of care and prudence required by the law. What the trustees cannot generally do is subordinate the interests of the beneficiaries to ethical or social demands (see *Cowan v Scargill [1984] 2 All ER 750*; *Bishop of Oxford v Church Commissioners [1991] PLR 185*; *Martin v The City of Edinburgh District Council [1989] PLR 9*). In some circumstances, trustees 'may even have to act dishonourably (though not illegally) if the interests of their beneficiaries require it' (*Cowan v Scargill [1984] 2 All 750* at 761).

Although trustees cannot allow their own political, social and moral views to override financial considerations when making investments, they can, in some circumstances, be influenced by the views of the beneficiaries of the scheme. If all the beneficiaries are known to hold strong moral views on a matter '... it might not be for the "benefit" of such beneficiaries to know that they are obtaining rather larger financial returns under the trust by reason of investments in those activities than they would have received if the trustees had invested the trust funds in other investments' (*Cowan v Scargill [1984] 2 All ER 750* at 761). The circumstances where this principle could apply in relation to a pension scheme must be very limited, due to the inevitable divergence of opinions of a large number of beneficiaries.

10.24 *Investment*

Regulation 2 of the *2005 Investment Regulations,* requires the trustees to state in their statement of investment principles the extent (if at all) social, environmental or ethical considerations are taken into account in the selection, retention and realisation of investments and their policy (if any) in relation to the exercise of the rights (including voting rights) attaching to the investments.

These issues have recently been considered by the Law Commission which published its report on the Fiduciary Duties of Investment Intermediaries in July 2014 (the 'Report'). The Report particularly focussed on the investment duties of pension scheme trustees. It identifies that the primary purpose of pension trustee investment powers is 'to secure the best realistic return over the long term, given the need to control for risks' and concludes that trustees should take into account factors which are financially material to the performance of an investment. Where trustees think ethical or environmental, social or governance ('ESG') issues are financially material then they should take them into account. It also concluded that the law permits trustees to make investment decisions that are based on non-financial factors (including ethical or ESG factors), provided that:

- they have good reason to think that scheme members share the concern; and

- there is no risk of significant financial detriment to the fund.

The Report contains specific guidance on pension trustee investment duties and recommends that this should be disseminated to trustees, included by the Regulator in the trustee toolkit and in the longer term, included in a code of practice. The guidance raises the interesting issue of trustees consulting members on investment questions relating to non-financial factors in order to come to the view that members do share the concern. When considering whether or not to take into account a non-financial factor, trustees may make assumptions about the members' views in some circumstances (for example where activities contravene international conventions). Where members are consulted, there does not need to be 100 per cent agreement for the investment to be made. The guidance states that 'where a majority agree while the rest remain neutral, that may be enough'. There is no legal requirement for trustees to consider members' views but they should only take non-financial matters into account if they genuinely reflect the views of the members rather than the trustees.

The Report itself recommended three changes to legislation:

- widening the general investment duties in the *2005 Investment Regulations* to schemes with fewer than 100 members;

- revising the provisions in the *2005 Investment Regulations* on social, environmental or ethical considerations to take account of the Report's recommendations on financial and non-financial factors; and

- trustees should be encouraged to think about how they engage with the companies in which they invest – the Government should consider whether trustees should be required to state their policy (if any) on stewardship (see **10.55** below).

In February 2015 the DWP subsequently consulted on changes to the the law on investments in occupational pension schemes and issued its response to the consultation in November 2015. In summary, the DWP decided that amending the *2005 Investment Regulations* to distinguish between financial and non-financial factors would not necessarily lead to greater clarity for trustees and so no amendment will be made. Nor is it clear that requiring trustees to comply with the Stewardship Code (or explain why they have not) would be the most appropriate way to encourage trustees to engage.

Default fund requirements

10.25   In relation to DC investments, trustees need to ensure there is a default fund available where a member does not make a choice from the range chosen by trustees. A default option is compulsory for auto-enrolment (see **Chapter 14**).

The *Occupational Pension Schemes (Charges and Governance) Regulations 2015* introduced a charge cap for default funds used in certain pension arrangements. The charge cap is 0.75 per cent of funds under management within the default arrangement, or an equivalent combination charge. The cap applies to all scheme and investment administration charges, excluding transaction costs and a number of other specified costs and charges.

Duty to review investments

10.26   A trustee's responsibility does not stop once he has made an investment; trustees have a duty to review the investments of the scheme from time to time. Although this is a continuing duty it will be particularly relevant in a scheme which is close to winding up as it may be advisable to match the investments of the fund with the liabilities of the scheme. Even where a scheme is wholly insured, trustees should still review the position from time to time as it may be sensible for the trustees to consider changing the insurance company or to become self-administered.

Under *PA 1995, s 36*, trustees must consider at what intervals they should obtain 'proper advice' in respect of investments they retain and must then obtain and consider such advice accordingly (see **10.22** above regarding the meaning of 'proper advice'). In determining the appropriate intervals the trustees must consider the circumstances of the case and, in particular, the nature of the investment. It might, for example, be appropriate to review the scheme's gilt portfolio less frequently than its equity portfolio as equities are a more volatile investment than gilts.

Statutory obligations

Statement of investment principles

10.27   Under *PA 1995, s 35*, trustees must secure that a written statement of investment principles is prepared and maintained governing the decisions about investments for the purposes of the scheme and that that statement is reviewed and revised at intervals. Trustees (or the fund manager acting on their behalf) must exercise their investment power with a view to giving effect to the principles contained in the statement, so far as reasonably practicable (*PA 1995, s 36(5)*).

Section 35 should be read together with the provisions of *2005 Investment Regulations, reg 2*. Under these provisions, the trustees of the scheme must secure:

- that a statement of investment principles is prepared and maintained for the scheme (*PA 1995, s 35*); and

- that it is reviewed at least every three years and without delay after any significant change in investment policy (*2005 Investment Regulations, reg 2*).

The statement must cover, among other matters, the trustees' policy for securing compliance with *PA 1995, s 36* (see **10.22** and **10.23** above) and their policy about:

(*a*)   the kinds of investments to be held;

(*b*)   the balance between different kinds of investments;

(*c*)   risks (including the ways risks are to be measured and managed);

(*d*)   the expected return on investments;

(*e*)   the realisation of investments;

(*f*)   the extent (if at all) to which social, environmental or ethical considerations are taken into account in the selection, retention and realisation of investments; and

(*g*)   their policy (if any) in relation to the exercise of the rights (including voting rights) attaching to the investments.

The agreed investment strategy set out in the statement of investment principles must accord with the general law discussed in **10.20** to **10.26** above, and be devised to reflect the liability position of the scheme in question.

PA 1995, s 35 and the requirements relating to statements of investment principles under the *2005 Investment Regulations* do not apply to a scheme which has fewer than 100 members or a scheme which is established by an enactment and is guaranteed by a public authority (*2005 Investment Regulations, reg 6*). For wholly insured schemes, although a statement of investment principles is required, the requirements are modified and are less onerous (*2005 Investment Regulations, reg 8*).

Before a statement of investment principles is prepared or revised, trustees must:

(*a*)   obtain and consider the written advice of a person whom they reasonably believe to be qualified by his ability in, and practical experience of, financial matters and to have the appropriate knowledge and experience of management of the investments of pension schemes; and

(*b*)   consult the scheme's sponsoring employer.

(*2005 Investment Regulations, reg 2*)

Where a scheme has more than one sponsoring employer, the participating employers may nominate a person to represent them, in which case the trustees need only consult that person (*2005 Investment Regulations, reg 3*). Where the employers do not nominate a representative, each employer must be consulted individually unless all the employers notify the trustees to the contrary.

PA 1995 does not define what is meant by 'consult'. Consultation does not mean consent; in fact, *PA 1995* specifically prohibits the exercise of any investment power being subject to the consent of the employer (*PA 1995, s 35(5)*). To comply with their duty to consult, trustees should allow the employer sufficient time to make representations and should ensure that they consider suggestions put forward by the employer with an open mind. If the trustees are obliged to consult all the employers, they may specify a reasonable period (which cannot be less than 28 days) within which the employers must make representations regarding the statement of investment principles; any representations made after the specified date can be ignored by the trustees.

The extent of the requirement to consult was considered in the case of *Pitmans Trustees v the Telecommunications Group plc [2004] PBLR 32, [2004] All ER (D) 143*. The Vice-Chancellor ('V-C') confirmed that, to comply with the consultation requirements then contained in *PA 1995, s 35(5)(b)*, trustees must go further than simply giving notice to the employer of the proposed changes to the statement of investment principles. Although no timeframe was prescribed in *s 35(5)(b)*, it was held that it is necessary to give adequate time for the employer to obtain and consider advice of its own and to comment on the proposals. The V-C held that prior consultation is a pre-condition to the existence and exercise of the trustees' powers in *PA 1995, s 35* and, therefore, if prior consultation has not taken place, this pre-condition has not been satisfied, the power has not yet arisen and a purported exercise of it will be of no effect. The adoption of any revised statement of investment principles will be invalid as a result.

Trustees must confirm in their annual report whether they have produced a statement of investment principles in accordance with *PA 1995, s 35* and must also include a statement providing details of any investments which were not made in accordance with the statement of investment principles giving the reasons why and explaining what action has been or will be taken to resolve the position. A copy of the statement of investment principles must be provided to any member, prospective member or beneficiary who requests it (*Occupational and Personal Pension Schemes (Disclosure of Information) Regulations 2013 (SI 2013/2734), reg 11*).

A failure to take all reasonable steps to prepare or maintain a statement of investment principles or to take advice from an appropriately qualified person could result in a trustee being fined (*PA 1995, s 35(6)*). (See **Appendix I**.)

Restrictions on employer-related investment

10.28   Trustees are under a statutory duty to ensure that not more than 5 per cent of the current market value of the resources of the scheme is invested in employer-related investments. Furthermore, none of the resources of a scheme may be invested in any employer-related investment if it would involve the trustees entering into a transaction at an undervalue or in an employer-related loan (see *PA 1995, s 40* and the *2005 Investment Regulations, reg 12*).

In summary, employer-related investments are defined under *PA 1995, s 40* as:

(*a*)   shares or other securities issued by the employer or by any person who is connected with, or an associate of, the employer (for definitions of connected and associated employers, see *PA 1995, s 123*);

(*b*)   land which is occupied by, or used by, or subject to a lease in favour of, the employer or by any person who is connected with, or an associate of, the employer;

(*c*)   property (other than land) which is used for the purposes of any business carried on by the employer or by any person who is connected with, or an associate of, the employer;

(*d*)   loans to the employer or any person who is connected with, or an associate of, the employer;

(*e*)   other prescribed investments.

The *2005 Investment Regulations* contain the list of investments prescribed as employer-related investments at *reg 11*.

If any sums due and payable by a person (including, but not limited to, an employer) to the trustees of a scheme remain unpaid they are to be regarded, for the purposes of *PA 1995, s 40*, as a loan made to that person by the trustees and may consequently be treated as an employer-related investment.

Under *PA 1995, s 40*, if the resources of a scheme are invested in employer-related investments in excess of the maximum allowed, sanctions, in the form of a fine, could apply to any trustee who fails to take all reasonable steps to ensure compliance with the Act. Further, a trustee who agrees to make an employer-related investment is guilty of an offence and may be liable, in extreme cases, to imprisonment (see **Appendix I**).

The *2005 Investment Regulations* contain relaxations to the restrictions on employer-related investment at *reg 13*. *Reg 13* was amended with effect from 23 September 2010 by the *Occupational, Personal and Stakeholder Pensions (Miscellaneous Amendments) Regulations 2009 (SI 2009/615)* (the '*2009 Miscellaneous Amendments Regulations*'). This revoked the prior exceptions for investments such as qualifying insurance policies and authorised bank and building society accounts, as well as additional voluntary contributions invested in employer-related investments with the written agreement of the member who paid the contributions. The *Occupational Pension Schemes (Investment) (Amendment) Regulations 2010 (SI 2010/2161)* (the '*2010 Investment Amendment Regulations*') also revoked an exception relating to collective investment schemes (see below for more detail this issue). The *2009 Miscellaneous Amendments Regulations* also added a new *reg 15A* and amended *reg 12* so as to permit certain previously prohibited employer-related loans as long as they comply with the 5 per cent limit.

In November 2010, the Regulator issued a statement on employer related investments aimed at employers, trustees and advisers involved in funding negotiations and investment strategy. The Regulator expanded on that statement in November 2013 in its new guidance on 'asset backed contributions' for trustees and their advisers, in which it set out the risks involved and its expectations of trustees when considering such arrangements. Asset-backed contribution ('ABC') arrangements are increasingly used by pension schemes as a means of funding deficits otherwise than by direct cash contributions (ABC arrangements are discussed further in **Chapter 11**).

The Regulator's view is that some funding structures, including some ABC arrangements, could be classed as employer-related investment, and that investment in such arrangements could breach the statutory restrictions. The legislation on employer-related investments is very complex and will need to be considered on the facts of the particular ABC arrangement. Broadly, however, the relevant restriction on employer-related investments applies to owning 'shares' in a 'company' which is either connected or associated with an employer sponsoring or participating in the scheme. In an ABC arrangement, the Trustee will usually acquire a partnership interest in a Scottish Limited Partnership ('SLP'). As an unincorporated body constituted under the law of a country or territory *within* the UK (ie Scotland), an SLP falls outside the definition of 'company' for the purposes of the employer-related investment legislation. Therefore, the interest in the SLP is not a 'share' in an employer (or a person connected or associated with the employer) for the purposes of the employer-related investment legislation. Trustees will also need to ensure that the SLP does not constitute a collective investment scheme (this is discussed further below) and that no part of the transaction is at an undervalue.

The Regulator expects trustees to take specialist legal advice in relation to the risk of the arrangement being found to be in breach of the employer-related investment restrictions and 'void for illegality', and to ensure they properly understand the risks. In view of the employer-related investment risks, the Regulator expects ABC arrangements to include an 'underpin' to protect the scheme's position in the event it is found void for illegality or where there is a change in law. The 'underpin' must cover both any repayment to the scheme of monies previously received under the arrangement but returned, and future payments (reflecting that the scheme would lose the income stream and any security from the arrangement) (see further in **Chapter 11**).

Of more general concern for trustees is the position in relation to collective investment schemes. Since 23 September 2010, the employer-related investment provisions look through the collective investment scheme wrapper and at the investments themselves. Previously, as long as the collective investment scheme was established by a third party, it did not matter whether or not the underlying investments were employer-related investments. Now a scheme will be taken to hold an appropriate proportion of each underlying asset in the collective investment scheme – so if there are ten equal investors in the collective investment scheme each will (for employer-related investment purposes only) be taken to hold 10 per cent of each underlying asset.

The difficulty for trustees is accurately monitoring the underlying holdings given that many collective investment scheme structures will not allow the trustees any say in the underlying assets (and indeed there may be *FSMA 2000/ PA 1995* issues if they did). The guidance from the Regulator is that it expects trustees to have adequate internal controls in place to satisfy themselves that the scheme is being well managed in accordance with the law. Three examples are given as to how trustees might reduce the risk of breaching employer-related investment with a collective investment scheme:

- *The collective investment scheme is prevented from investing more than 10 per cent of its assets in shares from any one issuer. If Scheme A restricts its investment in the collective investment scheme to 50 per cent of scheme assets, its direct investment in any one company (including the sponsoring employer) will not exceed 5 per cent of scheme assets.*

This may not work in practice though as employer-related investment catches connected and associated companies, not just an investment in the sponsoring employer, so the collective investment scheme could have a 10 per cent holding in a number of associated connected companies. Also, the value of the shares in the collective investment scheme will fluctuate relative to each other, so an investment which is 10 per cent of collective investment scheme assets one day may be substantially more or less than 10 per cent the next day.

- *The collective investment scheme is well diversified and does not invest more than 5 per cent of assets in any one firm. This means the scheme will not invest more than 5 per cent of its assets in the sponsoring employer even if all its assets were invested in the collective investment scheme.* Again this only works provided there are no connected or associated employers also caught.

- *The collective investment scheme provider agrees to report on any investment holding in excess of 5 per cent of its assets. If the sponsoring employer appears on this list then the scheme can adjust its overall investment in the collective investment scheme accordingly.* Again, this focuses only on the sponsoring employer, not connected or associated employers, and assumes a level of flexibility in the investment into the collective investment scheme (ie that the trustees are not tied in to the investment for a particular period). It also might not actually stop the breach from occurring but just allows for it to be remedied.

An arrangement will not amount to a collective investment scheme where each of the participants is a body corporate in the same group as the operator (*paragraph 10 of the Schedule to the Financial Services and Markets Act 2000 (Collective Investment Schemes) Order 2001 (SI 2001/1062)*). Trustees entering into an ABC arrangement will need to ensure that the SLP partners are all in the same corporate group so that there is not look through to the underlying asset held by the SLP. This will usually require any individual trustees to be replaced with a corporate trustee in which the shares are owned by the employer company (ABC arrangements are discussed further in **Chapter 11**).

The Financial Services and Markets Act 2000

10.29 The *Financial Services and Markets Act 2000 (FSMA 2000)* provides for the regulation of the whole of the UK financial services and banking industry. *FSMA 2000* was radically overhauled by the *Financial Services Act 2012 (FSA 2012)* to introduce a new system of financial governance with effect from 1 April 2013. Ultimately, however, this change has had little immediate impact on the regulation of investments made by trustees of occupational pension schemes, the main change being the replacement of the Financial

Services Authority (*'FSA'*) in this context by the Financial Conduct Authority (*'FCA'*) (see **10.29** below).

Professional firms (solicitors, accountants and actuaries) who do not undertake FCA regulated activities such as providing investment advice are exempt from direct regulation by the FCA. Such firms are also exempt if they only carry out certain restricted activities arising out of, or incidental to, the provision of professional services.

The new regulatory structure

Financial Conduct Authority – FCA

10.30   The FCA replaced the FSA, taking over the majority of its existing roles and functions. The FCA has a strategic objective and three operational objectives under *FSMA 2000*:

(*a*)   The strategic objective is to ensure that the relevant markets function well;

(*b*)   The operational objectives are:

   (i)   securing an appropriate degree of protection for consumers (the consumer protection objective);

   (ii)   protecting and enhancing the integrity of the UK financing system (the integrity objective); and

   (iii)   promoting effective competition in the interests of consumers in the markets for regulated financial services and services provided by recognised investment exchanges (the competition objective).

The FCA will regulate the conduct of firms that are:

(*a*)   'dual-regulated' – by the FCA (for conduct) and the Prudential Regulation Authority ('PRA') (for prudence), such as banks, building societies, insurers and certain high risk investment firms; and

(*b*)   all other firms which were regulated by the FSA.

Prudential Regulation Authority – PRA

10.31   The PRA is a subsidiary of the Bank of England and is responsible for the prudential regulation and supervision of systematically important firms, such as banks, building societies, credit unions, insurers and major investment firms. The PRA sets standards and supervises financial institutions at the level of the individual firm. It has two statutory objectives: to promote the safety and soundness of these firms and, specifically for insurers, to contribute to the securing of an appropriate degree of protection for policyholders.

Financial Policy Committee – FPC

10.32 The FPC comprises five Executives of the Bank of England, the Chief Executive of the FCA, four external members and a non-voting HM Treasury member. It is responsible for macro-prudential regulation (which is concerned with the resilience and stability of the financial system as a whole). Its aim is to identify, monitor and take action to remove or reduce systematic risks.

Regulated activities

Investment managers

10.33 Most investment managers providing financial services to pension scheme trustees classify their trustee clients as 'Professional Clients' under FCA Handbook of rules and guidance made by the FCA Board (the '*FCA Rules*') and the Prudential Regulation Authority Handbook of rules and guidance made by the PRA Board (the '*PRA Rules*'). The *FCA Rules* and *PRA Rules* came into force on 1 April 2013.

Prohibited activities

10.34 It is a criminal offence under *FSMA 2000, s 24* to carry out a 'regulated activity', without authorisation or exemption from authorisation.

What constitutes a regulated activity?

10.35 *FSMA 2000* and specifically the *Financial Services and Markets Act 2000 (Regulated Activities) Order 2001 (SI 2001/544)* (the '*Regulated Activities Order*') specify a wide range of regulated activities which include the following activities, namely:

(*a*) dealing in investments;

(*b*) arranging deals in investments;

(*c*) managing investments;

(*d*) advising on investments;

(*e*) establishing, operating or winding up a stakeholder pension scheme;

(*f*)   establishing, operating or winding up a personal pension scheme;

(*g*)   safeguarding and administering investments; and

(*h*)   assisting in the administration and performance of a contract of insurance.

Specified investments, for the purposes of *FSMA 2000*, include shares and stocks, debentures, Government and public securities, certificates representing securities, units in collective investment schemes, rights under a stakeholder pension scheme or a personal pension scheme, options, futures, contracts for differences and rights under contracts of insurance (*Regulated Activities Order, Part III*). Land and cash are not investments for the purposes of *FSMA 2000*.

The position of the trustees

10.36   Ordinarily, where trustees deal, arrange deals or give advice in relation to investments, they are likely to benefit from the exclusions contained in the *Regulated Activities Order*. However, the *Financial Services and Markets Act 2000 (Carrying on Regulated Activities by Way of Business) Order 2001 (SI 2001/1177), art 4* (the '*Business Order*') provides that trustees will be treated as carrying out the activity of managing investments by way of business, where assets are held for the purposes of an occupational pension scheme. An exception to this is where all 'day-to-day' decisions in the carrying on of that activity (except for certain exclusions in *Business Order, art 4(6)*) relating to securities or contractually based investments are taken by an authorised or exempted person or an overseas person who does not require authorisation. Most commonly trustees seek to benefit from this provision by delegating investment management activities to duly authorised fund managers.

The *Business Order* also provides that certain decisions relating to pooled vehicles will not be categorised as 'day-to-day' decisions (see *Business Order, arts 4(1)(b) and (6)*).

The *Business Order* excludes decisions where trustees of occupational pension schemes are investing in pooled investment vehicles in general, if they have considered advice from a regulated person (as defined in the *Business Order*). Decisions to invest in such vehicles will not be caught by FCA regulation in those circumstances because the trustees in making these decisions will not be deemed to be managing investments by way of business.

Where a trustee undertakes investment management activities himself, he will need to be authorised under *FSMA 2000* and regulated by the FCA. The rules of the FCA are intended to ensure that those managing pension scheme assets are adequately trained and supervised and meet competence thresholds; that adequate records are kept; that proper investment contracts are entered into; and that adequate procedures exist to keep assets safe.

In supervising a fund manager (see **10.43** below), trustees must ensure that they do not inadvertently end up taking 'day-to-day' investment decisions which would require them to be authorised under *FSMA 2000*. Trustees entering into ABC arrangements (see **Chapter 11**) will also need to consider whether any ongoing decisions which may be made or consents needed under the partnership agreement during the life of the arrangement could amount to 'day-to-day' investment decisions.

There is no definition of 'day-to-day' in the *Business Order* but the FCA has issued guidance to trustees of pension schemes on the implications of *FSMA 2000* for them. The guidance is contained in the FCA's *Perimeter Guidance Manual, PERG 10 (Guidance on activities related to pension schemes).*

The fact that decisions may be taken only infrequently does not, of itself, prevent a decision from being a 'day-to-day' decision. The nature of the decision, not its frequency, is the important factor. The fact that a trustee might only occasionally make decisions about buying new, or selling existing, investments would not prevent those decisions being 'day-to-day' decisions. Similarly, frequent interventions outside scheduled review meetings with fund managers, or the making of recommendations to fund managers with a force amounting to a direction, might also amount to a 'day-to-day' decision. The guidance also makes it clear that 'day-to-day' decisions include decisions to 'buy, sell or hold particular investments'.

Trustees can make:

- strategic decisions (eg adopting a statement of investment principles; formulating general asset allocation policies; deciding the proportion of assets that should constitute particular investment categories; affecting the balance between income and growth; appointing new fund managers; deciding which pooled investment products to make available for members to choose from under a money purchase scheme);

- decisions that need to be taken in exceptional circumstances (eg where the manager has a conflict of interest; where an investment decision raises sensitive policy considerations such as investments in certain territories; or following a change in fund managers which results in the scheme holding investments which a new fund manager does not want to take on); and

- day-to-day decisions about investments in pooled investment products, provided that they have first taken advice from an authorised, exempt or overseas person or an exempt or professional firm.

PERG 10 also makes it clear that persons other than trustees involved in pension schemes, be they employers, administrators, etc, will also require authorisation in circumstances analogous to those of trustees.

Care should also be taken when investing in common investment funds because of the look through provisions since 23 September 2010 referred at **10.28** above. These are usually established where an employer operates more than one pension scheme and it is decided to place all of the schemes' investments in one vehicle. Usually such arrangements are established to enable the participant schemes to benefit from the additional purchasing power, reduction in costs and wider market exposure that a larger investment arrangement may offer.

The selection and supervision of investment advisers

10.37 Quite apart from the *FSMA 2000* implications discussed in **10.29** to **10.34** above, many trustees will lack either the time or skill to manage directly their scheme's portfolio and so will delegate their investment power to a professional fund manager. Although it is a fundamental rule of trust law that a trustee cannot delegate his powers and discretions, there are statutory exceptions to the rule and it can be overridden by the trust documents.

Position before PA 1995

10.38 *Trustee Act 1925, s 23* (now repealed) allowed trustees to employ and pay an agent to transact any business required in the execution of a trust. However, this provision did not allow a trustee to delegate the exercise of any discretion. The trustees still had to decide on the investments to be sold and purchased; the agent simply implemented the decisions made.

Trustee Act 1925, s 23 has now been replaced by *Trustee Act 2000, s 11*, which allows trustees to authorise any person to exercise any or all of their 'delegable functions' as their agent. Trustees may delegate any function other than:

(*a*) a function relating to the distribution of the assets of the trust;

(*b*) a power to decide whether payments from the trust funds should be made out of income or capital;

(*c*) a power to appoint trustees; or

(*d*) a power conferred by any other enactment or the trust instrument which permits the trustees to delegate their functions or to appoint a person to act as a nominee or custodian.

Trustee Act 2000, s 11 does not apply to the investment powers of trustees of occupational pension schemes (*Trustee Act 2000, s 36*) as this is dealt with in *PA 1995, s 34* (see **10.39** below).

Trustee Act 1925, s 25 allows trustees to delegate the exercise of their discretions for a period of up to one year under a power of attorney, but does not explicitly allow for the remuneration of the person to whom the discretion has been delegated.

Due to the constraints of the statutory power to delegate, trustees are generally given power to delegate investment decisions and to appoint and remunerate advisers and agents, including investment advisers and fund managers, in their scheme's documentation.

Position after PA 1995

10.39 The statutory power allowing trustees to appoint agents and delegate the exercise of their investment power was significantly extended from 6 April 1997 by *PA 1995*.

PA 1995, s 34 effectively permits delegation of investment decisions by the trustees where the delegation is:

(a)   to a fund manager who is authorised under *FSMA 2000*;

(b)   to a fund manager who is not authorised under *FSMA 2000* so long as any decisions made by that fund manager would not constitute activities of a specified kind under *FSMA 2000*;

(c)   to a sub-committee of two or more trustees;

(d)   in accordance with *Trustee Act 1925, s 25* (see **10.41** above).

Trustees cannot otherwise delegate any investment decision (*PA 1995, s 34(2) (b)*). As the provisions of *PA 1995* are overriding in this regard, even if the trust instrument permits delegation in other circumstances, it appears that the trustees cannot delegate outside the four situations referred to above. In the case of (c) and (d) above, the trustees' ability to delegate may be further restricted by the requirements of *FSMA 2000* (see **10.29** to **10.36** above).

PA 1995, s 34(2) permits trustees to delegate any discretion to make any decision about investments to a fund manager who is authorised under *FSMA 2000*. Provided that the trustees take all reasonable steps to satisfy themselves that the fund manager has the appropriate knowledge and experience for managing the investments of the scheme and is carrying out his work competently and complying with *PA 1995, s 36*, they will not be responsible for the acts or defaults of the fund manager. (See **10.22** above regarding the requirements of *s 36*, and see **10.43** below regarding supervision of a fund manager.)

PA 1995, s 34(5) provides that, subject to any restrictions imposed by the scheme, trustees may delegate investment decisions to a sub-committee of two or more of the trustees. However, in practice, the requirements of *FSMA 2000* may restrict the circumstances in which such a delegation would be appropriate. The trustees, or a person on their behalf, may also delegate decisions which do not constitute carrying on a regulated activity (within the meaning of *FSMA 2000*) to a fund manager who is not authorised under *FSMA 2000*. Trustees will remain liable for any acts or defaults of the sub-committee or the fund manager to whom the discretion has been delegated. However, if the trustees, or the person who delegated the discretion on their behalf, take all reasonable steps to ensure that such a fund manager has the appropriate knowledge and experience for managing the investments of the scheme and that he is carrying out this work competently and complying with *PA 1995, s 36*, the liability of the trustees for the acts and defaults of the fund manager can be excluded or restricted (see **10.55** below for discussion on restricting liability of trustees). The trustees may wish to make compliance with *PA 1995, s 36* and the *2005 Investment Regulations, regs 4* and *5*, a term of the appointment letter required under *PA 1995, s 47*.

Although *PA 1995, s 34* gives trustees a power to delegate investment decisions, it does not give them explicit authority to remunerate any fund manager to whom such decisions have been delegated. The cautious approach is to ensure that the trust instrument contains power to remunerate fund managers although, arguably, there is an implicit power to do so. Although the statutory power to delegate investment discretions has certainly been widened by *PA 1995*, most trust deeds will probably continue to include some form of express powers of delegation. The relationship between the trustees and the fund manager they appoint is, and will continue to be, governed to a large extent by the terms of the agreement entered into between them.

PA 1995, s 47 requires an individual or a firm to be appointed by or on behalf of the trustees as fund manager if the assets of the scheme consist of or include investments (within the meaning of *FSMA 2000*) (see **10.33** above). The appointment of the fund manager must be made in writing and must specify the date on which the appointment is due to take effect, to whom the fund manager is to report and from whom the fund manager is to take instructions (*Occupational Pension Schemes (Scheme Administration) Regulations 1996 (SI 1996/1715), reg 5*) (the '*Scheme Administration Regulations*'). The fund manager must also give certain declarations regarding conflicts of interest (see **10.50** below).

Neither *PA 1995, s 47* nor the *Scheme Administration Regulations* imposes any requirements or restrictions regarding the qualifications or experience required of a person to be appointed as a fund manager. He does not, for example, have to be authorised under *FSMA 2000*. In reality trustees are likely to appoint the person to whom they have delegated their investment decisions. Indeed, on a literal reading of *PA 1995*, a fund manager appointed under *PA 1995, s 47* need play no role in the scheme whatsoever.

Supervision of a fund manager

10.40   Trustees have a general duty to supervise and monitor the performance of a fund manager. In particular, trustees should ensure that the fund manager is carrying out his work competently and complying with the requirements of *PA 1995* if they wish to benefit from the statutory exoneration provision contained in *s 34(4)*, which is applicable where an FCA authorised manager is appointed. Supervising does not imply that the trustees should continually check up on their fund manager but it does impose an obligation to review his appointment from time to time. If the fund manager is regularly performing below the market performance or is outside the benchmark set by the trustees, the trustees should ask why this is and, if appropriate, consider whether they wish to continue their arrangement with that fund manager.

The liability of investment advisers

Duties arising from the agreement

10.41   As a matter of general contract law, a fund manager is obliged to act in accordance with the terms of his contract and must not exceed his authority or he will be liable for a breach of contract even if he acted in his client's best interests (*Fray v Voules (1859) 1 E&E 839*). A fund manager may be required to follow the trustees' instructions, but he cannot be obliged to commit an illegal act. It is not enough for the fund manager simply to follow the trustees' instructions and to observe to the letter the terms of his written agreement; he is in addition contractually bound to act with due care and skill. As a fund manager is remunerated for his services he must perform his duty exercising the care, skill and diligence which it is usual, necessary and proper for professional fund managers to employ.

FSMA 2000 has, to an extent, dictated the terms of the contractual relationship between fund manager and trustees. Under the *FCA Rules* a fund manager cannot generally manage the investments of trustees on a discretionary basis unless there is in place an investment management agreement regulating the rights and liabilities of the trustees and the investment manager. 'Standard' terms and conditions for discretionary fund management are now published by the Investment Management Association ('IMA'). Many fund managers do, however, prefer to use their own 'standard' terms and conditions. The fact that such contracts are described as 'standard' should not dissuade trustees from questioning their terms or seeking additional protections.

The agreement will also contain a schedule setting out specific investment policy, objectives and restrictions agreed upon by the fund manager and the trustees. The following provisions in the standard terms are examples of terms which could cause concern for trustees, particularly in light of *PA 1995*.

455

The investment management service and other services

10.42   The fund manager and the trustees must agree on any restrictions or objectives to be imposed on the fund manager. Trustees should consider supplying the fund manager with a copy of the investment power they are delegating to ensure that the fund manager does not inadvertently make an investment which is outside the scope of the power. Trustees may also wish to clarify the details of their statement of investment principles with the fund manager and to append it to the written agreement to seek to ensure that he exercises the investment power with a view to giving effect to the principles contained in the statement of investment principles (see **10.27** above and *PA 1995, s 36(5)*).

Liability

10.43   Typically, fund managers will attempt to limit their contractual liability. In particular, they will look to exclude liability for indirect or consequential loss (even where they have had prior notice of special circumstances concerning the possibility of such loss arising). It is not uncommon for managers to attempt also to avoid responsibility for the acts and omissions of delegates and agents. Trustees should be concerned to obtain protection in respect of these 'third parties', given that they will have little involvement in their selection and may have no direct contractual relationship with them.

Cash

10.44   If cash is to be held in a bank account, trustees should ensure that in doing so, the fund manager is obliged to comply with the requirements of *PA 1995* relating to the retention of money in a bank account (*PA 1995, s 49*; *Scheme Administration Regulations 1996, reg 11*). Consideration should also be given to the application of the 'FCA's Conduct of Business Rules' concerning the treatment of client money.

Voting

10.45   Trustees should consider whether they should impose any specific conditions on the fund manager in light of their possible duties to exercise voting rights (see **10.55** below).

Records, valuations and reports

10.46   Trustees will need to consider when they require reports to be made regarding the valuation of investments. In agreeing on a suitable time frame they should bear in mind their duty to supervise the fund manager and in particular whether the timing is appropriate to ensure that they are satisfied that the fund manager is carrying out his work competently and complying with *PA 1995, s 36* (see **10.19** above). They now also need to factor in the additional monitoring they need to carry out to ensure the employer-related investment restrictions are not breached (see **10.28** above). It may also be appropriate to require the fund manager to disclose other documents and information in his possession on the reasonable request of the trustees and to allow auditors or other advisers to inspect these documents. Trustees should also seek to resist clauses which provide that, following a specified period after the trustees have received a valuation or report, they may no longer bring an action against the manager for any breach which occurred during the period to which the valuation or report relates.

Custodianship

10.47   The IMA standard terms provide that the fund manager shall not provide custody services to the trustees and that the fund manager shall not at any time hold any assets belonging to the trustees. If the fund manager is to make use of the services of a custodian, the trustees should ensure that they have formally appointed that custodian in accordance with *PA 1995, s 47* and the *Scheme Administration Regulations, regs 4, 5*; otherwise they will not be able to rely on his skill or judgment without the risk of incurring sanctions in the form of a fine and/or removal (see **Appendix I**).

The debate as to whether trustees must also appoint sub-custodians was closed as a result of the publication of the *Occupational Pension Schemes (Scheme Administration) Amendment Regulations 1998 (SI 1998/1494)*, which relieved trustees of this obligation and enables them to rely on the skill and judgement of sub-custodians appointed by the custodian, provided that written disclosure of the extent to which (if any) the custodian accepts liability for its sub-custodians' actions is made in the custody agreement. Any changes to the liability position must be immediately notified to the trustees by the custodian. This can be a difficult area for trustees as sub-custodial arrangements can often be very complex and multi-layered. The trustees and their advisers need to be certain that they understand their position on liability and recovery in the event of a sub-custodian's default. The trustees should also check that the custodian they appoint has the appropriate *FSMA 2000* authorisation.

It is likely that there will be a separate 'global custody agreement' which will need to deal with a number of key areas in addition to core custody, including: settlement of transactions (contractual or actual); cash management; liability for sub-custodians; and foreign exchange transactions.

Investment management and custody agreements should always be carefully reviewed by trustees and their advisers before being entered into, as some of their terms (eg the extent to which the agreement seeks to exempt the fund manager or custodian from liability) can expose the scheme to significant liabilities.

Fiduciary duties

10.48 Because the fund manager is handling trust monies, it may be argued that his duties are not only contractual, but also fiduciary (ie they may have to be exercised in the best interests of the members). To the extent that the fund manager is a fiduciary, the following duties may be implied.

Duty not to delegate

10.49 The general duty not to delegate applies not only to trustees but also to their agents. An agency relationship is based on the confidence one person has in another, and so an agent is in principle prohibited from delegating his authority to another person or even appointing a sub-agent (see *Allam & Co Ltd v Europa Poster Services Ltd [1968] 1 All ER 826*). Delegation is, however, permitted in certain circumstances. For example, where the employment of a sub-agent is usual in managing a client's investments and is not unreasonable or inconsistent with the express terms of any written agreement; or where the act delegated is purely administrative and one which does not require or involve confidence or discretion.

Usually the investment management agreement will expressly permit a fund manager to delegate or appoint sub-agents, often without the consent of the trustees. Fund managers will often include a provision to the effect that they are not liable for the actions of their sub-agents unless they are 'connected companies'. As trustees may have no direct contractual relationship with the sub-agent it is advisable for them to ensure that, if the fund manager is to be allowed to delegate or appoint agents, he remains liable to the trustees for their acts or defaults.

The fund manager must not put himself in a position where his duties to the trustees conflict with his own interests

10.50 This is no more than the application of the equitable maxim that a person in a position of trust must not put himself in a situation in which his interest and his duty would be in conflict. An extreme example is where a fund manager seeks to buy an asset from the trustees. He would be attempting to achieve the impossible: trying to achieve the highest price for the trustees and at the same time endeavouring to pay the lowest possible price himself.

The IMA's standard terms specifically address potential conflicts of interest. They allow the fund manager to effect transactions where conflicts arise, but provide that the fund manager must ensure that such transactions are effected on terms which are not materially less favourable to the trustees than if the conflict or potential conflict had not existed. The agreement requires the fund manager to disclose 'promptly' to the trustees any conflicts which the fund manager is not able to manage effectively and it also refers to the fund manager's conflict of interest policy which provides detail of the types of actual or potential conflicts of interest which affect the fund manager's business and how these are managed. The agreement provides that, to the extent that any fiduciary or equitable duties arise as a result of the services to be provided under the agreement, these duties will not prevent or hinder the fund manager or associate in effecting customer transactions.

A fund manager appointed under *PA 1995, s 47(2)* must, on being appointed, confirm that he will declare any conflict of interest affecting his relationship with the trustees immediately he becomes aware of it or, if he is regulated under *FSMA 2000*, in accordance with the rules of the FCA. However, many managers will interpret the rules to allow them to give generic style disclosures in the investment management agreement, thus avoiding the impracticality of making prior disclosure on a case-by-case basis.

Duty not to accept bribes

10.51   This duty is self-explanatory. If a fund manager accepts a payment which could constitute a bribe and conducts himself in the way proposed by the person offering the bribe, it will be presumed that he has been influenced by the bribe and has breached his duty to the trustees. This presumption is not rebuttable and the trustees' loss is considered to be at least the amount of the bribe.

The person offering the bribe, as well as the fund manager who receives it, will be criminally liable. The fund manager will have to repay or forego any commission, profit or remuneration to which he would otherwise have been entitled from the trustees (*Andrews v Ramsay & Co [1903] 2 KB 635*). The trustees will be able to dismiss the fund manager without notice (*Bulfield v Fournier (1895) 11 TLR 282*) and claim for the amount of the bribe plus interest from the date upon which the bribe was received.

The fund manager has a duty not to take advantage of his position or the trustees' property in order to acquire a benefit for himself

10.52   An investment manager is liable to account to the trustees for any profits he makes using confidential information acquired in the course of his appointment (*Peter Pan Manufacturing Corporation v Corsets Silhouette Ltd [1963] 3 All ER 402*). The provisions relating to insider dealing contained in the *Criminal Justice Act 1993* may also be relevant. Broadly speaking, dealings in securities of a company by an individual who holds unpublished price-sensitive information in respect of that company by virtue of his connection with the company are prohibited. There are similar provisions with regard to advising others to deal in the shares or debentures of the company, and in respect of the communication of unpublished price-sensitive information to others where that person might reasonably be expected to make use of it for the purpose of dealing.

Ultra vires

10.53   If trustees make an investment which, under their investment power, is barred or outside its scope, they are acting *ultra vires*. *Hazell v Hammersmith and Fulham London Borough Council [1990] 2 WLR 17* raised the concept of *ultra vires* in connection with a local authority's funds as certain of the activities were beyond those permissible by the relevant Local Government Act. An act which is *ultra vires* is generally void and may not be ratified. Fund managers should be made aware of the powers of the trustees on whose behalf they are acting as otherwise they may enter into *ultra vires* arrangements. Equally, trustees are advised to ensure that they restrict fund managers from inadvertently acting outside the trustees' powers by ensuring that the investment management agreement contains appropriate investment restrictions. Trustees may seek to impose a condition that the manager shall not do anything which would breach the provisions of the trust deed and rules, however this is often resisted by managers who prefer to limit their liability to complying with their mandate with the trustees assuming responsibility for ensuring the mandate is compliant with the trust provisions.

Liability for breach of trust by agents

10.54   It is possible for an agent of trustees to be held liable in respect of a breach of trust committed by the trustees for whom he is acting, and which he, as agent, has facilitated. To be liable, the fund manager would have knowingly to commit a wrongful act in relation to the scheme's assets; in effect, he would have to know that the trustees did not have authority to give the instructions he followed or take the action he took. A fund manager may also be liable where he turns a blind eye to what is an obvious breach of trust where an honest and reasonable man would have considered it such.

Unless fund managers are either aware that a breach of trust is being committed by the trustees concerned, or the situation is such that it is, or should be, obvious to any competent fund manager that this is the case, they are entitled to assume that the instructions given are bona fide and within the powers of the trustees. If a fund manager follows an investment policy which he knows to be outside the powers of the trustees he renders himself liable to an action for breach of trust.

The most crucial factor on which liability of a fund manager depends is the precise terms of the investment powers given to the trustees and whether the fund manager is aware of them. Consequently trustees should ensure that the fund manager is fully apprised of any restrictions on their powers of investment and appropriate restrictions should be built into the investment management agreement.

Voting rights as a consequence of share ownership – is it a trust asset?

10.55   In the UK a high proportion of all shares in publicly quoted companies are held by pension funds. Trustees have traditionally exercised their voting rights only in exceptional cases but the sheer size of their voting power begs the question: are trustees and any fund managers to whom they have delegated their discretions in some way responsible for the actions of the companies in which they invest?

The Cadbury Committee recommended that institutional investors should make positive use of their voting rights and should also disclose their policies on the use of voting rights. The PLSA has recommended that trustees should decide on their voting policy and that voting policy should be made public. Trustees should then exercise their votes prudently and in the interests of scheme beneficiaries.

There is no doubt that this idea has progressed further in the US than in the UK. Pension funds in the US have been obliged to exercise their voting rights since 1988 in respect of US companies. This duty was extended in 1994 to include overseas companies.

The legislators in the UK have, to date, resisted attempts to impose a similar obligation on trustees. The previous Government successfully resisted an attempt by the then opposition to include such a duty in *PA 1995*. Although it was felt that imposing a mandatory duty to exercise voting rights was contrary to the general aim of deregulation and would be too difficult to enforce, it was accepted that trustees, or fund managers on their behalf, should be encouraged to exercise their voting rights.

Even in the absence of a statutory duty to exercise voting rights, there is a strong case for arguing that some form of duty exists. Trustees have a clear duty to act in the best interests of their members and this includes protecting the value of, and the income derived from, an investment. There may be circumstances where this can only be achieved by voting for or against certain proposals and in such situations trustees may be open to attack if they simply make no voting decision whatsoever. It should be remembered that positively abstaining from voting can be a legitimate voting decision. The duty is perhaps not necessarily to vote, but to consider whether, and if so how, to vote.

Arguably, fund managers to whom discretionary investment responsibilities have been delegated have fiduciary responsibilities similar to the responsibilities of trustees. Accordingly, if trustees have a duty to consider exercising voting rights, it follows that fund managers must also concern themselves with the running of those companies in which they invest trustees' monies.

In 2002, the Government gave its response to the Myners' Review in which it stated at Principle 6 on Activism:

> 'The mandate and trust deed should incorporate the principle of the US Department of Labor Interpretative Bulletin on activism. Trustees should also ensure that managers have an explicit strategy, elucidating the circumstances in which they will intervene in a company; the approach they will use in doing so; and how they measure the effectiveness of this strategy.'

In October 2002, the Institutional Shareholders Committee (which consisted of the Investment Management Association, the Association of British Insurers, the PLSA and the Association of Investment Trust Companies) unveiled the publication of a new Statement of Principles entitled, 'The Responsibilities of Institutional Shareholders and Agents – Statement of Principles'. It was updated in 2005 and again in June 2007. It develops the principles set out in its 1991 statement 'The Responsibilities of Institutional Shareholders in the UK' and expands on the Combined Code of Corporate Governance of June 1998.

In late 2009 the Committee published a 'Code on Responsibilities of Institutional Investors' and after consultation the Financial Reporting Council (FRC) adopted this code as the UK Stewardship Code in July 2010. The Stewardship Code was updated in September 2012 and the revised Stewardship Code came into effect from 1 October 2012.

The principles of the Stewardship Code are that institutional investors should:

- publicly disclose their policy on how they will discharge their stewardship responsibilities;

- have a robust policy on managing conflicts of interest in relation to stewardship and this policy should be publicly disclosed;

- monitor their investee companies;

- establish clear guidelines on when and how they will escalate their activities;

- be willing to act collectively with other investors where appropriate;
- have a clear policy on voting and disclosure of voting activity; and
- report periodically on their stewardship and voting activities.

The FRC encourages institutional investors to publish a statement of compliance and a list of organisations that have done so can be found on the FRC website.

Trustee liability and protection

10.56   The ultimate responsibility for investment decisions lies firmly with the trustees. The duties placed on trustees regarding investment are onerous, and becoming more so, not only in terms of the legal principles governing the propriety of their actions, but also in terms of the types of investment vehicles now available. It would be a foolish trustee who did not take specialist advice regarding the exercise of his investment power and, in any event, this is a statutory requirement (*PA 1995, s 36*). However, taking advice will not, on its own, necessarily protect the trustee; he/she must still act honestly with reasonable care and prudence. The requirement to have the required level of knowledge and understanding imposed by *PA 2004* should also be noted. The fiduciary duties and liability of fund managers are discussed at **10.43** and **10.48** above but the following particular points arise in relation to investment decisions.

Trustees will be liable for the acts or defaults of the fund manager if they fail to take reasonable care in choosing the fund manager or in fixing or enforcing the terms of his engagement (*Steel v Wellcome Custodian Trustees Ltd [1988] 1 WLR 167*).

Trustee Act 2000, s 23 gives trustees some protection by providing that a trustee is not liable for any act or default of an agent, nominee or custodian, or a permitted substitute, when entering into or reviewing the arrangements under which that person acts, unless the trustee has failed to comply with the applicable duty of care.

Case law considers 'wilful default' to include both positive acts and a 'want of ordinary prudence' (*Speight v Gaunt (1883) 22 Ch D 727*; *Re Chapman [1896] 2 Ch 763*). There have been cases to the effect that 'wilful default' should be interpreted in the company law context so that it includes a deliberate or reckless breach of duty but not a negligent breach of duty (*Re Vickery [1931] 1 Ch 572*). However, the safer and the generally more acceptable view of trustees' responsibilities is the former definition.

It is common sense that trustees should take care when selecting their advisers and agents, as would any man with common prudence, and further exercise reasonable and responsible supervision.

Many trust deeds attempt to mitigate trustees' responsibilities by widely drafted exoneration clauses. However, *PA 1995, s 33* limits the extent to which liability in respect of investment decisions may be excluded by providing that liability for breach of an obligation to take care or exercise skill in the performance of any investment functions exercisable by the trustees (or by a person to whom that function has been delegated under *PA 1995, s 34*) cannot be excluded or restricted by any instrument or agreement.

PA 1995 also offers some exoneration for trustees who delegate their investment discretion to a fund manager authorised under *FSMA 2000* in accordance with *PA 1995, s 34(2)*. The trustees will not be liable under *PA 1995* for the acts or defaults of such a fund manager provided they have taken all reasonable steps to satisfy themselves that he has the appropriate knowledge and experience and is acting competently and complying with the requirements of *PA 1995, s 36* (see **10.22** and **10.23** above) (*PA 1995, s 34(4)*).

In addition, *PA 1995, s 33* does not prevent trustees being exonerated under the provisions of the trust deed from liability for the actions of a fund manager to whom the trustees have delegated an investment discretion under *PA 1995, s 34(5)* (see **10.36** above).

Myners' Report: voluntary Code of Practice

10.57   The Myners' Report, published in March 2001, proposed a set of voluntary principles to be used by trustees of defined benefit schemes when taking investment decisions. There is a separate set of principles applicable to defined contribution schemes. The Government allowed schemes two years to comply with Myners (or explain why they could not). The PLSA agreed to undertake a review of compliance in 2007. The PLSA review concluded that overall standards of governance of UK pension schemes had improved, and that trustees' compliance with the principles had increased. The review made recommendations to bring the principles in line with best practice, and replace the original ten principles with six high-level principles.

The Government accepted the PLSA's principal findings and recommendations. In particular, it agreed that the principles would be more effective if Government and industry developed them to be more flexible and high level, rather than prescribing how pension funds should manage specific aspects of their business.

In March 2008, the Government consulted on proposals to update the Myners' Principles and establish a new industry-led framework for their application. The updated principles and framework include:

(A) *Principles*

A smaller number of higher-level principles to provide more flexibility for different types of schemes in terms of their size, financial position and strategy to explain their investment decision-making process to stakeholders. The consolidated principles are: effective decision-making; clear objectives; risk and liabilities; performance assessment; responsible ownership; and transparency and reporting.

(B) *Best practice guidance and trustee tools*

The principles are linked to comprehensive best practice guidance and trustee tools, which should ensure a thorough consideration of the issues relevant to investment decision-making.

(C) *Investment Governance Group (IGG)*

The IGG is a joint Government and industry body, chaired by the Pensions Regulator. The IGG is responsible for decisions on the nature, scope and development of the principles, best practice guidance and trustee tools. The IGG will formally 'own' the updated principles, monitor their effectiveness and the quality of reporting against them, and make recommendations for improvements to investment decision-making and governance.

The Government has identified four main issues for the IGG to address as a priority. These include: updating the Myners' Principles for DC schemes; drafting specific principles and associated guidance for smaller schemes; drafting brief and practical guidance on the location and content of reporting by trustees (without inhibiting trustees' flexibility to inform members in the manner they think most effective); and updating the guidance for the Local Government Pension Scheme.

On 4 November 2010, the IGG published a practical framework of principles and best practice guidance to help those running work-based DC schemes (ie trustees, employers, advisers, pensions providers and members) improve their investment decision-making and scheme governance. The framework recognises the growing importance of DC pension provision, particularly in light of the introduction of automatic enrolment from 1 October 2012 (see **Chapter 14**).

The six new DC principles are:

* *Clear roles and responsibilities* – clear processes and procedures need to be in place for investment governance.

- *Effective decision-making* – processes must be sound; decisions relating to investment governance must also be taken on a fully informed basis.

- *Appropriate investment options* – do the investment options take into account the range of risks and needs of the scheme membership?

- *Appropriate default strategy* – the default investment strategy made available to those who make no choice must be appropriately designed.

- *Effective performance assessment* – the performance of the chosen investment options must be monitored.

- *Clear and relevant communication* – members must be able to make informed decisions about where to invest based on clear, relevant and timely information.

The IGG's six new DC principles will be followed by guidance for small schemes and good practice case studies for DB schemes.

The principles themselves represent best practice. They are not legally binding. They are however designed to complement (as opposed to duplicate or substitute) existing legal requirements.

(D)   Enforcement

A more robust approach to disclosure and industry debate, within the voluntary 'comply or explain' framework. The Government believes that high-quality disclosure and thoughtful debate reinforce the development and dissemination of best practice, encourage self-assessment against the principles, and improve accountability to members.

Given the increasingly complex investment decisions which trustees are required to make, it seems entirely sensible that trustees should seek to increase their knowledge and understanding of how investment markets work and, in particular, how charges operate in relation to investment decisions made by the trustees.

However, it seems equally valid that, where investment managers with a full discretionary mandate involve pension scheme trustees in complex financial transactions or instruments, they should clearly communicate the value of entering into such transactions in relation to the trustees' particular circumstances.

The Government threatened to legislate to incorporate the Myners' Principles into trustees' investment decision-making. This has resulted in the 'trustee knowledge and understanding provisions' contained at *PA 2004, ss 247–249*, which set out the level of knowledge that the Government expects of trustees and which came into force in April 2006. Trustees and, where there is a trustee company, each individual who exercises any function which the company has as trustee of the scheme must be 'conversant with':

- the trust deed and rules of the scheme;

- any statement of investment principles;

- any statement of funding principles; and

- any other document recording policy for the time being adopted by the trustees relating to the administration of the scheme generally.

They must also have 'knowledge and understanding of':

- pensions and trust law; and

- principles relating to funding of occupational pension schemes and the investment of the assets of schemes.

The degree of knowledge and understanding required is that appropriate for the purposes of enabling the individual properly to exercise the function in question. This is considered in more detail in **Chapter 3**.

The Regulator's investment governance guide

10.58   In July 2016 the Regulator issued its Code No 13 'Governance and administration of occupational trust-based schemes providing money purchase benefits' together with six guides setting out practical guidance on how to meet the standards set out in the Code.

The guide on investment governance addresses delegation, financial and non-financial factors (reflecting the Law Commission Report), stewardship, designing investment arrangements, performance monitoring and review, changing investment funds and security of assets.

The section on designing investment arrangements includes suggestions on gathering information so that trustees can understand the needs of the membership (and therefore define their investment objectives). There is also a list of matters to take into account when implementing an investment strategy to achieve the objectives.

There is guidance on when a 'significant change in the demographic of the membership' should lead to a review of the SIP. These include:

- a bulk transfer;

- a significant increase in the proportion of members tending towards a particular method of accessing their benefits;

10.59 *Investment*

- a significant increase in contribution rates;
- a trend towards consolidation of pots.

It is stated that trustees should seek to carry of a full analysis of the demographics at least every three years (or without delay after any significant change).

In respect of changing investment funds, the guide provides that 'you should generally inform members before any fund transfer so that they can switch to a different fund if they do not want their investments to be automatically moved'.

Appendix 1 of the guide addresses default funds and mapping. The issue that is considered is whether a fund which a member originally selected can become a 'default fund' where the trustees have transferred them into equivalent new funds without consent. It can also arise in white-labelling where members choose the type of fund but trustees/managers select the actual fund.

Independent Governance Committees

10.59   With effect from 6 April 2015, the DWP introduced minimum quality standards to apply to all DC workplace pension schemes. At the same time the FCA introduced a requirement for the provider of such a scheme to set up an Independent Governance Committee ('IGC') and has been working with the Regulator and the DWP to ensure that its rules for IGCs and minimum quality standards are aligned. IGCs are required to act independently of the provider.

The FCA cannot directly regulate an IGC and so providers must set out the terms of reference contractually. These terms of reference must be publicly available.

The remit of an IGC is to:

(a)   ensure that such schemes act in the best interests of members; and

(b)   challenge the provider if they are not providing 'value for money'.

'Value for money' is not prescribed by the FCA, but it provides a non-exhaustive list of considerations including:

(a)   default investment strategies;

(b)   investment strategies;

(c)   scheme financial transactions;

(d)   level of charges;

(e)   costs.

Where an IGC raises a concern, a provider must take reasonable steps to address this and must provide written reasons where they choose to depart from the IGC recommended position.

IGCs must have a minimum of five committee members, with one acting as the provider representative. The remaining members must be independent (the FCA has set out specific requirements for 'independence') and, for example, cannot have been employed by the provider in the last five years. IGC members can only serve on the IGC for ten cumulative years.

Smaller providers with less complex pension schemes may establish a Governance Advisory Arrangement (GAA) instead whereby the provider appoints another independent provider to take on their IGC responsibilities. This third-party provider may be shared by multiple providers, but the GAA must perform the same functions as an IGC.

The FCA provides detailed guidance on both IGCs and GAAs.

Chapter 11

Funding, deficits and surpluses

Introduction

11.1   All but a handful of private sector occupational pension schemes in the UK are funded; assets are set aside in advance – legally and physically separate from the employer – to provide a fund to meet the benefits ultimately payable (although death-in-service benefits are commonly insured). Public sector schemes are often unfunded or partially funded as they are, instead, backed by the Government. Before the changes to pension scheme taxation introduced from 6 April 2006 by *FA 2004* (see **Chapter 17**), it was quite common for higher-paid employees to be provided with benefits by their employer from an unapproved top-up scheme (possibly unfunded), but these are less common now that unfunded schemes have lost the tax advantages they previously enjoyed.

The first part of this chapter deals with the legal requirements imposed on trustees and employers regarding funding of defined benefit schemes, in particular those contained in *PA 2004*. The second part of this chapter considers the implications of overfunding and discusses the ways in which a scheme's surplus can be reduced.

Pre-PA 1995 requirements relating to funding

11.2   Until *PA 1995* (ie prior to 6 April 1997), there was little legislation relating to funding and no legislation which specifically required an employer to fund a pensions promise in advance. An employer could, quite legitimately, promise a pension to an employee and then make no financial provision for that benefit until it became payable. The legislation that did have implications on funding included:

(*a*)   under the pre-6 April 2006 pensions tax regime, a Revenue requirement that an 'exempt-approved' occupational pension scheme have some employer contributions paid in respect of the member as a condition of discretionary approval (there are now no specific HMRC requirements for employers to contribute to registered pension schemes);

(*b*)   under that former tax regime, limits on the tax reliefs available in respect of overfunded schemes (which were replaced from 6 April 2006 by a tax charge of 35 per cent on any payment to an employer) (see **11.32** below);

(*c*)   a requirement for contracted-out defined benefit schemes to obtain an actuarial certificate at least triennially as to the scheme's ability to pay members' guaranteed minimum pensions in full if the scheme were to be wound up during the following three-and-a-half years; and

(*d*)   a requirement under the *Occupational Pension Schemes (Disclosure of Information) Regulations 1986 (SI 1986/1046)* for trustees of exempt-approved schemes to produce an annual report which had to include an actuarial statement on long-term funding (which is now superseded by the requirements of *PA 1995*, *PA 2004* and the *Occupational Pension Schemes (Disclosure of Information) Regulations 1996 (SI 1996/1665)*, as amended (see **11.24** below)).

Funding practice

11.3   Generally, it is preferable for individuals not to have to rely on their employer or former employer having the financial resources available to meet the pension commitment at the time benefits become payable. With an unfunded scheme, an individual could find that, when he comes to retire, the employer he worked for 20 years previously and who had promised him a pension has gone out of business. A properly funded scheme should ensure that members receive the pension due to them at retirement, irrespective of the employer's resources at that time.

From the employer's perspective, making provision for future benefits as they accrue (as opposed to only when they fall due for payment) means that the employer can budget for pension costs when running its business, and spreads the risk of funding the capitalised value of retirees' pensions at times it cannot control and when there is no guarantee of its ability to do so. Also, in the case of registered schemes (and exempt-approved schemes before them), the tax concessions for scheme assets (see **Chapter 17**) mean that the overall cost of providing benefits is reduced if funded over time.

Occupational pension schemes ought to be funded in a way that aims to ensure that, by the time each member reaches retirement, there are sufficient funds fully to provide the benefits that have been promised. A scheme's governing trust documentation will contain rules specifying how contributions payable by both the employer and the employees are to be determined. In most defined benefit schemes employees' contributions are fixed (as a percentage of pensionable pay), with the employer meeting the balance required to pay the benefits promised (a 'balance of cost' scheme). The provisions of the scheme's trust documentation about contributions need to be read in conjunction with the scheme-specific funding requirements contained in *PA 2004*, which override the provisions of scheme rules to the extent there is any conflict. These requirements are subject to modification depending on the exact provisions of the scheme rules and this is dealt with in more detail in **11.14** and **11.25** below.

Pensions Act 1995

The minimum funding requirement

11.4   *PA 1995, ss 56–61* introduced a requirement from 6 April 1997 (no longer in force – see **11.5** below) that the value of a scheme's assets should be not less than the amount of its liabilities assessed on a basis set out in that Act. This requirement, intended to increase the security of members' accrued pension rights, was referred to as the minimum funding requirement ('MFR').

The MFR was a cyclical process consisting of three components: triennial valuations, a schedule of contributions setting out the contributions payable and annual certification. It applied to most exempt-approved defined benefit occupational pension schemes, the main exemptions being broadly the same as the exemptions under the *PA 2004* funding regime (see **11.5** below).

Where the most recent MFR valuation showed funding at less than 100 per cent, the scheme actuary had to provide an 'annual certificate' stating whether or not, in his opinion, the contributions set out in the schedule of contributions were adequate for the purpose of securing that the MFR would continue to be met throughout the schedule period, or would be met by the end of the period. If the certificate expressed the opinion that the MFR would not be met in this way and the value of the scheme's assets was less than 90 per cent of its liabilities ('serious under-provision'), a new MFR valuation or a revised schedule of contributions was required and, broadly, the employer had to increase the value of the assets within a set period to the 90 per cent level.

The MFR was intended to prescribe only a minimum level of funding. Had the legislation based the MFR on the cost of securing benefits by the purchase of annuities, the funding requirement would have been considerably stronger, and would have provided members with greater security. Pending the introduction of the new statutory funding objective under *PA 2004*, the Government gradually changed the basis for valuing scheme assets in various circumstances where a share of the deficit was a debt on a departing employer (under *PA 1995, s 75*) from the MFR basis to the buy-out basis.

The MFR has now, in relation to valuations with an effective date on or after 22 September 2005, been replaced by the statutory funding objective (see

11.5 to **11.26** below). Schemes were permitted, under transitional provisions, to continue to operate under MFR valuations for effective dates up to 22 September 2008.

Pensions Act 2004

The statutory funding objective

11.5   The statutory funding objective ('SFO') is the funding standard that replaced the MFR for defined benefit schemes. In contrast to the 'one size fits all' approach adopted by the MFR, the SFO is intended to enable individual schemes to adopt a funding strategy that is appropriate to their specific circumstances. The provisions governing the SFO are set out in *PA 2004, ss 221–233* and the *Occupational Pension Schemes (Scheme Funding) Regulations 2005 (SI 2005/3377)* (the '*Scheme Funding Regulations*'). They apply to actuarial valuations with an effective date on or after 22 September 2005, but did not come into force until 30 December 2005. This was due to a delay in implementing (through *PA 2004*) certain provisions of *European Directive 2003/41/EC* on the Activities and Supervision of Institutions for Occupational Retirement Provisions ('IORP'), including those relating to scheme funding, investment and cross-border schemes – which IORP required to be transposed into national law by 22 September 2005. The statutory provisions are supported by the Regulator's Code of Practice No 3, 'Funding defined benefits', updated in July 2014. In May 2006 the Regulator issued its first statement on how it intended operating its powers in relation to scheme funding (see **11.16** below). It has since issued a number of statements and further guidance reminding trustees that prudent scheme funding requires trustees to keep the scheme's funding position and the employer covenant under constant review.

The SFO applies to all defined benefit schemes unless exempted by regulations. The main exemptions, listed in *Scheme Funding Regulations, reg 17* are:

- statutory schemes guaranteed by a public authority;

- pay-as-you-go schemes;

- certain schemes for overseas employees;

- an unregistered scheme with fewer than 100 members;

- a *s 615(6)* scheme with fewer than 100 members;

- a scheme with fewer than two members;

- a scheme with fewer than 12 members, where all the members are trustees of the scheme and either:

- the scheme rules require all trustee decisions to be made unanimously by the trustee/members; or

- the scheme has a trustee who is an independent trustee in relation to the scheme for the purposes of *PA 1995, s 23* and is on the Regulator's register;

- a scheme with fewer than 12 members, where a company is the sole trustee of the scheme and all the scheme members are directors of the company and either:

  - the scheme rules require all decisions made by the company as trustee to be made unanimously by the directors/members; or

  - one of the directors is a trustee who is independent in relation to the scheme for the purposes of *PA 1995, s 23* and is on the Regulator's register;

- a scheme under which the only benefits provided (other than money purchase benefits) are death benefits, if the death benefits are secured by insurance policies or annuity contracts;

- a scheme which is the subject of a PPF scheme failure notice under *PA 2004, s 122* or *130*; or

- a scheme which is being wound up (see **11.18** below).

The overriding statutory scheme specific funding requirement is set out in *PA 2004, s 222*. It requires that a scheme must have 'sufficient and appropriate assets to cover its technical provisions'. The term 'technical provisions' means the 'amount required, on an actuarial calculation, to make provision for the scheme's liabilities'. The technical provisions are made up of a set of actuarial assumptions including: inflation, longevity and the discount rate of future investment returns.

The *Scheme Funding Regulations* set out requirements as to how to value scheme assets and liabilities. The technical provisions are to be calculated in accordance with prescribed methods and assumptions. This must be an 'accrued benefits funding method', but it will be for the trustees to decide exactly which methods and assumptions are used for their scheme. In reaching this decision, the trustees will have to take into account certain matters. This will include taking advice from the scheme actuary and in most cases obtaining the employer's agreement (see **11.14** below).

The statutory funding documents (ie the statement of funding principles, actuarial valuation, any actuarial report, recovery plan and schedule of contributions) are documents that must be disclosed on request to certain people (see **11.24** below).

The statement of funding principles

11.6 Trustees are required to prepare, and from time to time review and if necessary revise, a statement of funding principles (SFP). This is a written statement setting out the trustees' policy for securing that the SFO is met.

Certain details to be included in the statement are set out in *PA 2004, s 223*. In particular, it must record any decisions by the trustees about the actuarial methods and assumptions to be used for calculating the scheme's technical provisions and the manner in which, and the period within which, any failure to meet the SFO is to be made good. *Scheme Funding Regulations, reg 6* lists further matters to be covered in the statement and sets out the timescales within which the statement has to be prepared, reviewed and if necessary revised (see **11.12** below).

Actuarial valuations and reports

11.7 *PA 2004, s 224* requires trustees either to obtain an actuarial valuation annually or, if they obtain an 'actuarial report' each year, they can obtain an actuarial valuation every three years (which is usual practice). An actuarial report is a written report from the scheme actuary 'on developments affecting the scheme's technical provisions since the last actuarial valuation was prepared'.

The trustees must ensure that they obtain an actuarial valuation or actuarial report within a prescribed period after its effective date. *Scheme Funding Regulations, reg 7* specifies 15 months in the case of the valuation (but see **11.12** below) and 12 months in the case of the report. The trustees must then ensure that a copy is made available to the employer within seven days of the trustees receiving it.

Certification of technical provisions

11.8 *PA 2004, s 225* requires that as part of the actuarial valuation process, the scheme actuary must certify that, in his opinion, the calculation of the technical provisions complies with the *Scheme Funding Regulations*. The certificate must include the actuary's estimate of the solvency of the scheme (*Scheme Funding Regulations, reg 7(4)*). This will usually be on a buy-out basis but, where this is not possible the actuary may substitute an alternative appropriate basis. The certificate should be included as part of the actuarial valuation document (see **11.7** above).

If the actuary cannot certify that the relevant legal requirements have been satisfied, he must report the matter in writing to the Regulator within a reasonable period following the date for receipt of the valuation by the trustees. The Code of Practice proposes ten working days as a reasonable period.

Recovery plan

11.9   Where an actuarial valuation shows that the SFO is not met on the effective date (ie that there is a funding deficit/shortfall), *PA 2004, s 226* requires the trustees to prepare a recovery plan or, if there is already a recovery plan in place, to review and revise the existing plan as necessary. The recovery plan must set out the steps to be taken to meet the SFO and the period within which this is to be achieved; and it must be 'appropriate having regard to the nature and circumstances of the scheme' (*PA 2004, s 226(3)*). The recovery plan must be reviewed, and if necessary revised, where the trustees or scheme manager consider that there are reasons that may justify a variation to it, or where the Regulator has given directions under *PA 2004, s 231* as to the period within which, and manner in which, a failure to meet the SFO is to be remedied.

Scheme Funding Regulations, reg 8 requires the trustees to take account of the following in setting the recovery plan:

- the asset and liability structure of the scheme;

- its risk profile;

- its liquidity requirements;

- the age profile of the members; and

- the recommendations of any person (other than the trustees) who determines employer contribution rates, where this is done without employer agreement.

The original February 2006 Code of Practice provided that when devising a recovery plan, trustees should aim to eliminate the shortfall as quickly as the employer can reasonably afford. The trustees should also ensure that the assumptions underlying the recovery plan are appropriate for the scheme. The Code of Practice listed matters the trustees should take into account, including:

- the employer's business plans and the likely effect any recovery plan would have on the employer's future viability;

- the scheme's membership profile (eg a shorter recovery period may be appropriate where most scheme members are pensioners);

- any proposed changes to the membership profile (eg a bulk transfer);

- the ability of the trustees to pursue the employer should the scheme wind up;

- the employer's expenditure commitments;

476

- the value of any contingent security provided by the employer (such as a parent company guarantee), bearing in mind both term and enforceability; and

- the likely outcome for members on the employer's insolvency.

The updated 2014 Code of Practice (which applies to schemes with valuation effective dates from 29 July 2014) sets out an integrated approach to risk management under which trustees should understand the interaction between employer covenant-related, investment-related and funding-related risks, and set parameters within which to balance these risks. The Regulator received a new statutory objective in July 2014 'in relation to the exercise of its functions under Part 3 [of *PA 2004*] only, to minimise any adverse impact on the sustainable growth of an employer'. *(PA 2004, s 5(1)(cza))* This is reflected in the new 2014 Code which states that in setting the recovery plan trustees should ensure that it is appropriately tailored to both the scheme and the employer's circumstances. The Code lists factors that trustees should take into account in considering the structure of a recovery plan and the affordability of deficit repair contributions.

The recovery plan must include the period within which the funding shortfall is expected to be eliminated *(PA 2004, s 226(2))*. The Code of Practice suggests that, except where the recovery period is less than one year, it should also include the date by which the amount of additional contributions to be made is half the amount of all the contributions due under the recovery plan (ie when half the shortfall will be eliminated). A copy of the recovery plan and prescribed information must, except in prescribed circumstances, be sent to the Regulator within a reasonable period (the Regulator suggests ten working days) after it is prepared or revised. The prescribed information is a summary of the information contained in the actuarial valuation and, where a recovery plan has been revised on the initiative of the trustees (ie not by the intervention of the Regulator), an explanation of the reasons for the revision (*Scheme Funding Regulations, reg 8(7)*).

Failure by trustees to take all reasonable steps to comply with the requirements for recovery plans can lead to civil penalties.

Schedule of contributions

11.10 Trustees must prepare, and from time to time review and if necessary revise, a schedule of contributions (*PA 2004, s 227*). This must be done within 15 months of the effective date of each actuarial valuation. The schedule of contributions must cover the period of five years from the date of its certification by the actuary, or the recovery plan period, if longer (*Scheme Funding Regulations, reg 10(2)*). The schedule of contributions has to show:

- the rates of contributions payable by the employer and active members of the scheme; and

- the due dates on or before which the contributions have to be paid.

The new 2014 Code of Practice sets out the principles for trustees to apply in preparing or revising a schedule of contributions. These include making the contents sufficiently clear that they can be monitored by the trustees and audited by the auditor, preferably without reference to other documents such as the scheme rules.

The actuary is required to certify that the schedule of contributions is consistent with the statement of funding principles and either:

- the scheme meets the SFO and can be expected to do so for the period covered by the schedule; or

- the scheme can be expected to meet the SFO by the end of the period specified in the recovery plan.

If the actuary is unable to give this certificate, he must report this to the Regulator within a reasonable period after the end of the period within which the schedule is required to be prepared or revised. The Code of Practice suggests ten working days would be reasonable.

The schedule must be signed by the trustees and make provision for signature by the employer in order to signify his agreement to the matters included in it. See **11.16** below for the role of the Regulator where the trustees and the employer cannot reach agreement on the schedule of contributions.

Where the actuary considers that because of the possibility of significant changes in the value of scheme assets or technical provisions since the effective date of the latest valuation, he is unable to certify the schedule as described above, he may sign a modified certificate (*Scheme Funding Regulations, Sch 2, para 12*).

Where the SFO was not met on the effective date of the most recent actuarial valuation, the trustees must send a copy of the schedule to the Regulator within a reasonable period of its completion. The Code of Practice suggests this should be within ten working days of the actuary certifying the schedule and that the recovery plan should be sent at the same time.

Again, failure by the trustees and the actuary to take all reasonable steps to comply with the requirements relating to schedules of contributions can lead to civil penalties.

Failure to make payments

11.11   The trustees must report late payment of contributions due under a schedule of contributions. *PA 2004, s 228* requires a report of late payment to be made to the Regulator and the members where the trustees have reasonable cause to believe that the failure to pay on time is 'likely to be of material significance in the exercise by the Regulator of any of its functions'. Appendix 2 to the 2014 Code of Practice sets out situations which are likely to be of material significance. These include where the employer appears to have been involved in fraudulent evasion, where there is an immediate risk to members' benefits and where contributions remain unpaid for 90 days. Situations unlikely to be of material significance include failures stemming from administrative lapses which have been remedied and cases where a claim has been made to the Redundancy Payments service. Reports to the Regulator should usually be made within ten working days, or earlier where an immediate report is required. Reports to members should be made within 30 days.

Similar reporting requirements and reasonable periods apply in the case of late payment of contributions to occupational money purchase schemes and to personal pensions (Codes of Practice Nos 5 and 6 respectively).

Any contributions that remain unpaid are to be treated as a debt due from the employer to the trustees (*PA 2004, s 228(3)*).

Civil penalties may be imposed on an employer who fails without reasonable excuse to make a payment of contributions and on a trustee who has failed to take all reasonable steps to report the late payment. Failure to pay contributions in accordance with the schedule of contributions may also be a breach of law requiring a report to the Regulator under *PA 2004, s 70* (see **Chapter 2**).

Timing

11.12   Under the *Scheme Funding Regulations* the trustees have a period of 15 months from the effective date of the actuarial valuation in which to obtain the actuarial valuation, produce a statement of funding principles, set a schedule of contributions and (if necessary) produce a recovery plan. It is possible for trustees to commission an ad hoc out-of-sequence actuarial valuation where they consider it unsafe to continue to rely on the current valuation.

Trustees should draw up a valuation action plan factoring in time for contingencies and to make allowance for taking actuarial advice, considering any recovery plan and reaching agreement with the employer, including bearing in mind that if agreement cannot be reached, it may be necessary to consider modification of future accrual of benefits, which would require the employer to consult with affected members under *PA 2004, ss 259–261* (see **Chapter 7**). If it is likely that the 15-month deadline will be breached, the trustees should as a matter of good practice inform the Regulator as soon as they are aware of this, explaining the reasons why and giving an estimated timeframe for completing and submitting the valuation.

Record keeping

11.13   Under *Scheme Funding Regulations, reg 11*, trustees are required to keep records of:

(*a*)   all contributions made to the scheme, showing separately:

(i)   the aggregate amounts of contributions paid by or on behalf of active members and the dates on which they were paid;

(ii)   the voluntary contributions (if any) paid by each member; and

(iii)   the aggregate of the contributions paid by or on behalf of each employer and the dates on which they were paid; and

(*b*)   any action taken by the trustees to recover:

(i)   any contributions which are not paid on the date on which they are due; and

(ii)   any debt which has arisen under *PA 1995, s 75(2)* or *(4)* (deficiencies in the assets).

Role of the employer

11.14   The intention behind the *PA 2004* scheme funding requirements is for there to be a partnership approach, with the trustees working openly and transparently with the employer to develop an appropriate funding strategy for the scheme, recognising also the employer's plans for sustainable growth (following the introduction of the Regulator's new statutory objective). A number of the requirements set out in the legislation are primarily the responsibility of the trustees. However, under *PA 2004, s 229*, trustees are (unless a modification applies, as set out below) required to obtain the consent of the employer in relation to the following key issues:

•   any decision about the methods and assumptions underlying the technical provisions;

•   the content of the statement of funding principles;

•   any recovery plan; and

•   the schedule of contributions.

This requirement for employer consent is modified where the existing scheme rules give the trustees a power to set contributions without the employer's agreement (*Scheme Funding Regulations, Sch 2, para 9*) as follows:

- where the trustees have sole power under the scheme rules to determine employer contribution rates (and no one else, other than the trustees, is permitted to reduce the rate or suspend contributions), the consent requirements set out above are replaced by a requirement for the trustees to *consult* with the employer only; and

- where the trustees have sole power, subject to conditions, to set the employer contribution rate (and no one else, other than the trustees, is permitted to reduce the rate or suspend contributions) then, provided the conditions are satisfied, the consent requirements set out above are replaced by a requirement for the trustees to *consult* with the employer only.

However, the Code of Practice recommends that, in either situation, the trustees should nevertheless seek to obtain the employer's agreement.

The *Scheme Funding Regulations* also impose the following additional conditions:

- Where the scheme rules provide for the contribution rate to be determined by or 'in accordance with the advice of' someone other than the trustees (eg by the scheme actuary), and without the agreement of the employer, then the trustees must take account of the recommendations of that other person on the methods and assumptions for calculating the technical provisions and on the preparation of any recovery plan (but not the schedule of contributions or the statement of funding principles) (*Scheme Funding Regulations, regs 5(3)* and *8(2)(e)*). It is not clear whether 'in accordance with the advice of' bites only where the trustees are bound by the scheme rules to follow the advice or where the trustees are obliged to take that advice into account but retain a discretion to make the determination themselves. In the latter case, the trustees may then be obliged only to consult with the employer (under *PA 2004, s 229*, as modified by *Scheme Funding Regulations, Sch 2, para 9*) and follow the recommendations of the other person.

- Where the scheme actuary has the power under the scheme rules to determine the contribution rate without the agreement of the employer, the trustees must determine the rate with the consent of the employer (in accordance with *PA 2004, s 229*) with an additional requirement that the scheme actuary may only certify the schedule of contributions if the contributions are no less than they would have been had the actuary determined the rate (*Scheme Funding Regulations, Sch 2, para 9(5)*). From 6 April 2009 this applies where, and to the extent that, the actuary has the sole power under the scheme rules to determine any (not just all) of the employer contribution rates without the employer's agreement, and applies only to the extent of that power (ie where the actuary has that power under the scheme rules only in certain circumstances, the balance of power is not shifted to the actuary in all other circumstances as well (*Occupational, Personal and Stakeholder Pensions (Miscellaneous Amendment) Regulations 2009 (SI 2009/615), reg 18*)).

In many schemes, the application of the above provisions may not be straightforward and legal advice may be required to establish which requirements the trustees are required to adopt.

Where it is necessary to obtain the consent of the employer, what happens where the employer does not agree? There are two consequences of failure to agree, which are set out in *PA 2004, s 229*:

- the trustees may modify future service accrual by resolution, with the employer's consent; and

- the trustees must report the failure to agree to the Regulator who has wide powers to intervene (see **11.16** below).

However, where modification for future accrual is being considered and the trustees have power under the scheme rules to fix contributions, they need only consult the employer with regard to the proposed changes (*Scheme Funding Regulations, Sch 2, para 9*). Any modification must not adversely affect subsisting rights. Modifications must be in writing and must be notified to the active members within one month of the modification taking effect. Where trustees have unilateral power of amendment under the scheme's governing trust documentation, this may not be diluted by the failure to agree provisions of *s 229* and, in those circumstances, the trustees could exercise the power of amendment without the consent of the employer. As noted in **11.12** above, modification of future accrual of benefits would require the employer to consult with affected members under the listed change provisions of *PA 2004, ss 259–261* (see **Chapter 7**).

Role of the actuary

11.15   *PA 2004, s 230* sets out the circumstances where trustees must obtain the advice of the scheme actuary. The trustees must obtain advice before:

- making any decision about the methods and assumptions to be used in calculating the scheme's technical provisions;

- preparing or revising the statement of funding principles;

- preparing or revising a recovery plan;

- preparing or revising the schedule of contributions; and

- modifying the scheme as regards future accrual of benefits in the event of failure to agree with the employer.

The *Scheme Funding Regulations* require the actuary to obtain relevant professional guidance or standards from time to time issued by the Financial Reporting Council.

Powers of the Regulator

11.16 The Regulator has a range of powers designed to ensure that the scheme funding requirements are complied with by trustees and employers. These powers are set out in *PA 2004, s 231* and include the ability to modify future service benefits and to impose a schedule of contributions, a statement of funding principles or a recovery plan where the trustees have failed fully to comply with the statutory requirements, the actuary has been unable to give a certificate, or the trustees and the employer have been unable to reach agreement where required.

The Regulator's 2014 Code of Practice provides guidance on the steps that it expects the trustees to take in order to reach agreement with the employer before reporting to the Regulator.

In May 2006 the Regulator issued a statement on how it intended to exercise its powers in relation to scheme funding. This statement, updated in September 2008 and February 2009, sets out the principles underpinning its regulatory approach and deals with how it might identify schemes which pose the greatest risk. Since 2012, the Regulator has also issued an annual DB funding statement setting out its views on acceptable approaches to the valuation process given the economic climate. Most recently, the Regulator consulted on a new DB regulatory strategy and issued new defined benefit regulatory strategy and defined benefit regulatory and enforcement policy with the new 2014 Code of Practice.

The Regulator has stated that it will implement its strategy by:

- assessing risk;
- setting policies and defining what good outcomes look like;
- deciding on appropriate interventions;
- setting a risk bar to determine where it should intervene;
- applying its regulatory tools; and
- measuring the effectiveness of its impact and reviewing its approach.

The Regulator believes that a strong, ongoing employer alongside an appropriate funding plan is the best support for a well-governed scheme.

11.17   *Funding, deficits and surpluses*

The Regulator's focus in future valuation cycles will be:

- encouraging trustees and employers to work collaboratively to use the flexibilities in the system appropriately to best suit their needs and those of the employer;

- ensuring that trustees reach appropriate funding outcomes that reflect a reasonable balance between the need to pay promised benefits and minimising any adverse impact on an employer's sustainable growth;

- ensuring that trustees understand and manage risks effectively through a proportionate application of an integrated approach to risk management;

- ensuring that trustees focus on the importance of understanding the employer's covenant and give full consideration to their employer's affordability, growth and investment plans;

- ensuring that we implement our regulatory approach to balance the needs of schemes and employers in an appropriate way.

In its 2014 *Defined benefit funding and regulatory and enforcement policy*, the Regulator recognises that risk is an inherent part of the DB funding regime and understanding this risk is key to it meeting its statutory objectives. In considering whether to intervene in the valuation process, the Regulator will test the scheme against its quantitative and qualitative risk indicators, including:

- funding risk;

- investment strategy risk;

- covenant risk;

- prudence of mortality assumptions;

- back end loading of contributions;

- reductions in contributions from the current recovery plan;

- any actions taken to weaken the employer covenant;

- risk to the PPF;

- over-reliance on investment outperformance in the recovery plan;

- governance;

- asset backed contributions;

- previous interaction with the scheme or employers.

Multi-employer schemes

11.17   The *Scheme Funding Regulations* modify *PA 2004* so that where there is a sectionalised multi-employer scheme, the SFO provisions apply to each section as if it were a separate scheme. A sectionalised scheme is one where contributions and assets are allocated to a particular section and cannot be used for the purposes of any other section.

Where a scheme or section has multiple employers, the Regulations enable a single employer (nominated by the other employers or under the scheme rules) to agree matters with the trustees. If no nomination has been made:

- the agreement of all participating employers must be sought to the matters referred to in *PA 2004, s 229(1)* (the methods and assumptions to be used in calculating the scheme's technical provisions, the statement of funding principles, any recovery plan, and the schedule of contributions) unless an employer has expressly waived its rights under that section; and

- in the case of a modification of the scheme as to future accrual, the agreement of all the employers must be obtained (*Scheme Funding Regulations, Sch 2, paras 1, 2*).

In *Hearn v Dobson [2008] EWHC 1620 (Ch)*, the High Court considered the interaction of the *SFO* and the meaning of 'employer' in the *Scheme Funding Regulations* in to a multi-employer sectionalised scheme. It held that 'employer' for this purpose did not include an employer that no longer employed active members. The court held that it was a single employer scheme for the purposes of the SFO and the trustees could not segregate the assets relating to each former participating employer and treat each separate fund as a separate scheme.

In *PNPF Trust Co Ltd v Taylor & Others [2010] EWHC 1S73 (Ch)* the High Court considered more widely the meaning of 'employer' for the purposes of the *PA 2004* funding regime (other than in the limited *Hearn v Dobson* circumstances). It held that that an employer is an 'employer' for the purposes of the SFO where it has active members and/or employees who are eligible to become members.

Funding and schemes in winding up

11.18 Schemes that commenced winding up before 30 December 2005 are not subject to the *PA 2004* scheme funding regime. Schemes that commence winding up on or after 30 December 2005 are required to obtain from the scheme actuary an annual estimate of the solvency position of the scheme as at the end of the preceding scheme year (*Scheme Funding Regulations, reg 18*). However, a relaxation was introduced on and from 6 April 2009 which provided that a segregated section of a multi-employer pension scheme which is winding up is exempt from *PA 2004* funding requirements where certain criteria are met (*Occupational, Personal and Stakeholder Pensions (Miscellaneous Amendments) Regulations 2009 (SI 2009/615), reg 18*).

Where an occupational pension scheme with a *PA 2004, s 226* recovery plan begins to wind up during the recovery period specified in the recovery plan, *PA 2004, s 231A* requires the trustees to prepare a winding-up project plan as soon as reasonably practicable and provide a copy to the Regulator. This must set out the actions and the estimated time to be taken to establish the scheme's liabilities, to recover assets and to discharge liabilities; and, to the extent that the trustees or scheme managers have sufficient information to do so, indicate which accrued rights or benefits (if any) are likely to be actuarially reduced (see further in **Chapter 12**).

Civil penalties apply to trustees who have failed to take all reasonable steps to comply with these requirements.

Schemes with fewer than 100 members

11.19   Domestic (as opposed to cross-border) (see **11.20** below) schemes with fewer than 100 members on the effective date of the most recent actuarial valuation made under the SFO are not required to obtain annual actuarial reports or issue annual funding statements (see **11.24** below) between their triennial valuations. But if the membership reaches 100 at any time during a year, then an annual actuarial report will be required. Members for this purpose include active, deferred, pensioner and pension credit members (*Scheme Funding Regulations, Sch 2, para 11*).

Cross-border schemes – European Economic Area

11.20   Stricter funding requirements apply to 'cross-border' schemes. IORP requires that a scheme operating cross border must be 'fully funded at all times'. The *Scheme Funding Regulations* require that such schemes must meet the SFO requirements (ie be 100% funded on this basis) at all times and have annual actuarial valuations; each such valuation must be signed by the actuary and received by the trustees within one year of its effective date. 'Cross-border' originally referred to EU Member States, but this was extended from 26 November 2007 to all EEA States once the three EEA Member States who were not also EU Member States (Norway, Iceland and Liechtenstein) had adopted IORP.

Application for authorisation and approval to operate a cross-border scheme must be made to the Regulator. The *Occupational Pension Schemes (Cross-border Activities) Regulations 2005 (SI 2005/3381)*, which came into force on the same date as the *Scheme Funding Regulations*, set out how the Regulator is to perform its functions in relation to cross-border schemes; and the Regulator has published guidance as well as an authorisation application form.

A new scheme must meet the SFO within two years of the date of application for authorisation. An existing scheme which is becoming cross-border for the first time must meet the SFO at the date of application. In both cases, this means without the use of a recovery plan, because a cross-border scheme is not permitted to rectify its underfunding through the use of a recovery plan. Note that the 'fully funded' requirement applies to the entire scheme and not only to the cross-border element of it (although the Regulator has power to order ring-fencing of assets in certain circumstances, (eg misappropriation)).

Regulatory own funds requirement (ROFR)

11.21   The *Occupational Pension Schemes (Regulatory Own Funds) Regulations 2005 (SI 2005/3380)* which came into force on 30 December 2005 require that where an occupational pension scheme itself – rather than an employer – covers any liability for risks linked to death, disability or longevity (biometric risk), guarantees any investment performance, or guarantees a level of benefits, then the scheme must have additional assets (free of foreseeable liabilities) above its technical provisions of at least 4 per cent of the scheme's technical provisions, plus 0.3 per cent of the amount by which the total amount that the scheme would be obliged to pay on the immediate death of all members of the scheme exceeds the technical provisions (calculated on the basis of the scheme's annual report and accounts). Actuarial valuations are required annually, and the scheme's statement of funding principles must include the policy for securing that the ROFR is met.

If the ROFR is not met as at the effective date of the actuarial valuation, the trustees must ensure it is met within two years and must send the Regulator a report of the steps to be taken to do this. The Regulator may modify the scheme as regards future accrual of benefits, give directions as to the calculation of the ROFR and may also impose a schedule of contributions. Penalties under *PA 1995, s 10* apply to trustees who fail to take all reasonable steps to ensure compliance with the requirements of the regulations.

Regulation 15 exempts certain kinds of schemes from the ROFR. These are broadly the same as the exemptions from the *Scheme Funding Regulations*. A scheme that begins winding up on or after 30 December 2005 will not be exempt from the ROFR unless the trustees ensure that they receive, before the end of each scheme year following the scheme year in which winding up began, the actuary's estimate of the solvency of the scheme as at the end of the preceding scheme year (*reg 16*).

Interaction between scheme funding obligations and s 75

11.22   In October 2013, the Regulator issued a statement on the correct way to approach the interaction between a scheme's funding obligations and the operation of *s 75* (see **Chapter 12**), which involves a two-stage process:

- Stage 1 – assess the impact of the departure of an employer and deal with any *section 75* debt; and

- Stage 2 – assess the net impact of the employer's departure and consider any ongoing funding obligations.

The Regulator considers attempts to double count to be reportable matters and, in some cases, notifiable events.

Reporting to the Regulator

11.23   The following information must be provided to the Regulator:

- The actuary must report if he is unable to certify that the calculation of technical provisions is made in accordance with the *Scheme Funding Regulations (PA 2004, ss 225(3))*. The Code of Practice suggests that this should be done within ten working days of the deadline for certifying the technical provisions.

- The actuary must report if he is unable to certify the schedule of contributions *(PA 2004, ss 227(9))*. Again, the Code of Practice suggests that this should be done within ten working days of the deadline for certifying the schedule.

- The trustees must provide a copy of any recovery plan (see **11.9** above) together with a summary of the information contained in the actuarial valuation (see **11.7** above) *(PA 2004, ss 226(6))*.

- Where the SFO was not met on the effective date of the actuarial valuation, the trustees must send a copy of the schedule of contributions (see **11.10** above) *(PA 2004, ss 227(7))*.

- The trustees must in certain circumstances report failure to pay in accordance with the schedule of contributions (see **11.11** above).

- The trustees must report failure to agree any matter with the employer (see **11.14** above). The Code of Practice suggests that this should be done within ten working days from the relevant deadline.

Failure to report could give rise to civil penalties.

Disclosure to members

11.24 The disclosure of information regime includes a requirement to disclose certain funding-related documents to any member, potential member, the spouse or civil partner of any member or potential member, any beneficiary or any recognised trade union who requests it, either by making them available to inspect physically or on a website or by providing copies (*Occupational and Personal Pension Schemes (Disclosure of Information) Regulations 2013 (SI 2013/2734), reg 13 (the 'Disclosure Regulations'*), as amended by the *Scheme Funding Regulations*). The trustees must disclose within two months of a request:

- the latest actuarial valuation and any more recent actuarial report;

- the schedule of contributions or payment schedule (for a money purchase scheme);

- the latest statement of investment principles;

- the statement of funding principles;

- any recovery plan; and

- any outline of the winding-up project plan prepared or revised under *PA 2004, s 231A*.

The trustees must also, as a matter of course, send an annual funding statement to all members and beneficiaries of schemes subject to the SFO. *Disclosure Regulations, reg 15* and *Sch 4* set out what the annual funding statement must contain for a defined benefit scheme:

- a summary, based on the most recent valuation and actuarial report, of the extent to which the assets were sufficient to cover the technical provisions;

- an explanation of any change in the funding position since the date of the last funding statement (or in the case of the first funding statement, since the last actuarial valuation);

- the actuary's estimate of solvency contained in the latest actuarial valuation;

- a summary of any recovery plan;

- information as to whether the scheme has been modified at the direction of the Regulator, or subject to directions of, or bound by a schedule of contributions imposed by the Regulator, together with an explanation of the circumstances in which this occurred; and

- whether any payment of surplus has been made to the employer and, if so, the amount of the payment.

The Code of Practice recommends that trustees consider including additional information such as an explanation of the operation of a defined benefit scheme, a summary of the scheme's investment policy, a reference to the Pension Protection Fund and a list of the funding and related documents available on request. The Regulator considers that the annual funding statement should normally be provided within three months from the date by which valuations or reports must be obtained.

Interplay between SFO and scheme rules

11.25   As noted in **11.14** above, the application of the SFO to the rules of many schemes may not be straightforward. This has already been demonstrated in two cases.

In *British Vita [2007] EWHC 953 (Ch)* the rules of the scheme, which had not yet had its first valuation under *PA 2004*, allowed the trustees to demand additional contributions from the employer. The trustees exercised this power. The employer argued that the scheme was subject to the statutory funding regime, and therefore the trustees and employer were required to agree a schedule of contributions. The High Court held that until the first schedule of contributions was produced under the SFO regime, the trustees' power to demand additional contributions under the scheme's rules remained valid. It was left open as to whether the employer contribution rule would survive once a *PA 2004* schedule of contributions was in place, until the judgment in *PNPF Trust Company Ltd v Taylor and others [2010] EWHC 1573 (Ch)*. This case confirmed that the *PA 2004* funding regime created an obligation on employers to pay any additional contributions needed if the scheme's employer contribution rule was inadequate to meet the SFO. So, a schedule of contributions or recovery plan can impose greater contributions on an employer than could be demanded under the scheme rules.

In *Allied Domecq (Holdings) Ltd v Allied Domecq First Pension Trust Ltd and another [2008] EWCA Civ 1084* the Court of Appeal upheld the judgment of the High Court that the scheme rules gave the scheme actuary unilateral power to set the contribution rate without the agreement of the employer. This power was unaffected by powers of the trustees under the scheme rules to apportion contributions among employers and to set the time period for past service deficit contributions; these were held to be separate limbs of the relevant rules. This case, of course, turns on the exact wording of the rules, but it gives a useful insight into the interaction between the legislation and individual scheme rules.

Other actuarial valuations

11.26   *PA 2004* introduced two new statutory actuarial valuations: (i) the 's 143 valuation' applies only to those schemes being considered for entry to the Pension Protection Fund ('PPF'), its purpose is to ascertain whether or not the scheme has sufficient assets to cover its liabilities for benefits at the PPF level and the expenses of winding up; and (ii) the '*s 179* valuation' which is required for all schemes eligible for the PPF for the purpose of calculating each scheme's risk-based levy (see **Chapters 2 and 4**).

Schemes in deficit

11.27   The position of deficits where a scheme is winding up is dealt with in **Chapter 12** and where an employer ceases to participate in a scheme this is dealt with in **Chapter 15**.

There are also a number of consequences for an ongoing scheme which is in deficit. The exact impact will depend on the basis upon which the deficit has been assessed. For example:

- (domestic) schemes in deficit on an SFO basis will be subject to a recovery plan (see **11.9** above) and may come under the scrutiny of the Regulator (see **11.16** above);

- schemes with a deficit on a PPF *s 179* basis are required to report more notifiable events to the Regulator than those that do not (see **Chapter 2**);

- schemes in deficit on a number of bases may be the subject of a clearance application for a Type A employer-related event under the Regulator's 'moral hazard' powers (see **Chapter 15**).

What is a surplus?

11.28   Although widely used, the expression 'surplus' is not a legally defined term. Surplus is generally said to exist when the actuarially assessed value of a scheme's assets at a certain date exceeds the actuarially assessed value of its liabilities at that date.

When a scheme is winding up, a surplus is easy to identify, as the cost of securing the liabilities of the scheme will ultimately be known, as will the value of the scheme assets. On a winding up, a surplus will exist if there are any funds left after all the benefits have been secured.

An ongoing defined benefit scheme, however, could be in deficit or in surplus on any given day depending on the actuarial methods and assumptions used for the valuation and the asset value on that day. A 'surplus' in an ongoing scheme is simply the actuary's prediction, based on a given method and on a certain set of assumptions, that the scheme will have more than sufficient assets to cover its liabilities over a certain period. Similarly when scheme liabilities are assessed for the employer's accounts at financial year end, the basis of the assessment (ie the accounting standard used such as FRS17 or IFRIC14) may reveal a surplus, even though the scheme is actually in deficit for statutory scheme funding purposes on that date.

An employer may regard a surplus in an ongoing scheme as representing past (or trapped) 'overfunding'. Trustees may see it as representing a reserve fund, providing security in the event of the cost of the benefits being more than the actuary anticipates or the investments of the scheme failing to perform at the assumed level. Members will sometimes regard a surplus in an ongoing scheme as 'spare' money that could be used for benefit improvements. However, arguably there can be no certainty of an actual surplus arising unless and until the scheme is wound up and all benefits secured. Any surplus in an ongoing defined benefit scheme is notional, as any number of events could happen which would eradicate it.

Why surpluses are an issue

11.29   During the 1980s a huge growth in the value of investments, coupled with a reduction in workforce numbers, led to many schemes having substantial surpluses. Sometimes, these were so large that even the suspension of contributions by employers and employees (a 'contributions holiday') was insufficient to eliminate them over a foreseeable period. Many employers began to look for ways to extract what appeared to be excess assets in their pension schemes.

At the same time, the Government became concerned that the tax advantages conferred on occupational pension schemes meant that it was losing valuable tax revenue from the assets in these overfunded schemes. *FA 1986* removed some of the tax advantages for exempt approved schemes, prompting some employers to take a contribution holiday or improve scheme benefits to use up the surplus funds. Some members and trustees of pension schemes became increasingly concerned that employers were unjustly appropriating part of their scheme's funds, resulting in the reduction in the security of members' benefits and the loss of any possibility of increased benefits.

In recent years, surplus funds in an ongoing scheme are a rare occurrence. Most defined benefit schemes are in deficit. This has resulted in the closure of many defined benefit schemes (either to future accrual or to new members) and their replacement with defined contribution schemes. However, surpluses can still arise in practice, so it is necessary to know how to deal with them if they do.

Who 'owns' a surplus?

Ongoing schemes

11.30 In most defined benefit schemes, the employer's contributions are the balance of the cost of providing the benefits promised. Therefore, one of the easiest ways of dealing with a surplus is simply to reduce the employer's contribution rate. However, trustees and beneficiaries may argue against this on the basis that the employer in question does not 'own' that surplus. In fact, a surplus will not necessarily have arisen because the employer has paid excessive contributions; it could be due to high investment growth on the assets purchased by both the employer's and members' contributions, or to members leaving the scheme at a faster rate than assumed by the actuary for the purposes of the scheme valuation. In such a situation the issue of who owns the surplus is inevitably raised.

The courts have been asked in a number of cases to consider the use of surplus and, in particular, the members' right to share in the surplus. These cases have generally recognised that, in a defined benefit scheme where an employer would be required to meet any deficit, it would be inequitable for the employer not to benefit at all from any surplus. This is consistent with treating the employer as a potential beneficiary under the scheme for trust fund purposes. There has, however, been a gradual shift away from the proposition that any surplus belongs solely to the employer while the scheme is ongoing.

In *Re Courage Group's Pension Schemes [1987] 1 All ER 528*, Millett J considered that, although members did not have an absolute legal right to share in the surplus in their scheme, they were entitled to have it dealt with by consultation and negotiation between them and the employer. He rejected the argument that members were entitled, as of right, to a contribution holiday, as any surplus arising from past overfunding in a balance of cost scheme arose primarily from the employer. However, he drew a distinction between the employer using a surplus to fund a contribution holiday and the employer requiring a payment out of the scheme assets. In the latter situation, the trustees could – and should – press for generous treatment of members (eg benefit enhancements) and the employer could be expected to be influenced by the desire to maintain good industrial relations with its workforce.

When considering how to deal with a surplus, it should be remembered that an employer can have regard to its own interests (financial and otherwise), but only to the extent that in doing so it does not breach the obligation of good faith to its employees and former employees (*Imperial Group Pension Trust Ltd v Imperial Tobacco Ltd [1991] 2 All ER 597*: see **Chapter 7**).

The issue of who owns a surplus continues to be subject to debate. The starting point should be the terms of the trust deed and rules of the particular scheme. The position would currently seem to be that members do not have an absolute right to any surplus, but may have a legitimate expectation of benefit improvements, particularly where the trustees have discretion as to the use of a surplus. When considering the use of a surplus the employer is, however, obliged to keep an open mind and consider arguments put forward on behalf of the members (see *Stannard v Fisons Pension Trust Ltd [1992] 1 PLR 27* and *LRT Pension Fund Trustee Co Ltd v Hatt [1993] PLR 227*). Much will depend on the respective powers of the trustees and the employer under the scheme's trust deed and rules and the relative bargaining position of the parties.

The courts have recognised that, if employers were to be prevented from taking contribution holidays, they might simply cease accrual or (if they can afford to do so) wind up the scheme, replacing it with one which is funded so as to avoid a surplus arising. This point was accepted by the judge in *The National Grid Company plc v Laws [1997] PLR 157*, which in 2001 progressed to the House of Lords. It was emphasised in the Court of Appeal that the treatment of surplus depends on the construction of the terms of the scheme, a view supported by the Court of Appeal in *Stevens v Bell (British Airways) [2002] PLR 247*.

Schemes which are winding up

11.31   A scheme's trust deed and rules will generally include a rule setting out how the scheme assets are to be distributed on a winding up. This rule should include a provision setting out how any assets remaining after all the liabilities have been secured are to be used. Usually there will be a power to increase benefits and/or make a payment to the employer. In some instances the rule will simply provide that all assets remaining should be paid to the employer.

If the rules do not contain provisions regarding the use of a surplus, the general principles of trust law will have to be considered. Essentially, where funds are transferred to a trust and it subsequently transpires that those funds are not needed for the purposes of the trust, the trustees hold those funds on a 'resulting trust' for the benefit of the person who provided them. However, a resulting trust does not arise where the person who provided the money never intended to receive any of it back. Therefore, if the rules of the scheme specifically provide that no payment can be made to an employer (on a winding up or otherwise) a resulting trust cannot arise.

How a surplus should be dealt with in the absence of a valid rule was considered by Scott J in *Davis v Richards Wallington Industries Ltd [1991] 2 All ER 563*. A resulting trust in favour of the members of the scheme was excluded largely on the grounds that, as the scheme provided salary-related benefits, two members who paid in the same monetary amount in contributions could be entitled to benefits of a different value; so a resulting trust was unworkable as between the different groups of beneficiaries. Consequently, any resulting trust had to be in favour of the employer. Again, the point was made that, in a balance of cost scheme, any surplus was to be treated as being provided first and foremost by the employer's contributions.

The issue of a resulting trust and the question of *PA 1995, s 69* was considered by the Determinations Panel in *Case C14920906 Wright Health Group Limited Superannuation & Life Assurance Scheme.*

Where a registered pension scheme lacks any power under its rules to distribute surplus on winding up, *PA 1995 s 69 (3)(b)* enables the trustees to apply to the Regulator for an order either authorising the modification of, or modifying, the scheme, with a view to enabling assets remaining after the liabilities have been fully discharged on winding up to be distributed to the employer. The Trustees could make such an application even where the amendment power prohibits the return of assets to the employer (*PA 1995, s 71(3)*). However, an order will not be granted unless all avenues have been exhausted to discharge the scheme's liabilities. In the *Wright Health Group* determination, this meant that the Trustees ought to have used the surplus to augment members' benefits on winding up using an explicit power to do so under the rules – being a 'liability' of the scheme in question. They had not done so, nor had they provided sufficient information to demonstrate that there would still be a residual surplus after doing so (for example because Revenue limits had been hit) and the Determinations Panel decided that, on the basis of the information it had been provided with, it was not able to make the order being sought.

HMRC requirements relating to the reduction of surpluses

11.32 Legislation restricts the tax advantages available to registered occupational pension schemes if they are in surplus (so that the Government does not lose potential tax revenue). The current restriction (since 6 April 2006) is in the form of by a tax charge of 35 per cent on payments to employers (*FA 2004, ss 177, 207*) combined with the requirements of *PA 1995, s 37* (see **Chapter 17** and **11.33** below).

Pensions Act 2004 – position from 6 April 2006

Ongoing schemes

11.33 *PA 1995, s 37* introduced, with effect on and from 6 April 1997, certain requirements which had to be satisfied before a repayment of surplus could be made to an employer. These included an increase in all pensions by 5 per cent LPI and a requirement to give advance notice to members.

11.33   *Funding, deficits and surpluses*

PA 2004, s 250 substituted a new *PA 1995, s 37* with effect on and from 6 April 2006 applying to ongoing schemes, not being wound up. The new *s 37* provides that, where power is conferred on the employer or any other person to make payments to the employer out of funds held for the purposes of the scheme, that power may be exercised only by the trustees and any restriction imposed by the scheme on the exercise of the power shall, so far as capable of doing so, apply to its exercise by the trustees. The power to repay surplus may only be exercised if:

- except in the case of a scheme subject to the regulatory own funds requirement (see **11.21**), the trustees have obtained a written valuation prepared and signed by an actuary (usually the scheme actuary);

- there is a certificate in force which meets prescribed requirements (see below) and specifies the maximum amount which may be paid to the employer;

- the payment does not exceed the maximum amount specified in the certificate;

- the trustees are satisfied that it is in the interests of the members that the power is exercised in the manner proposed;

- there is no freezing order in force under *PA 2004, s 23*; and

- notices have been given to members in accordance with prescribed requirements.

The *Occupational Pension Scheme (Payments to Employer) Regulations 2006 (SI 2006/802)* (the '*Payments to Employer Regulations*'), which also came into force on 6 April 2006, provide that valuation methods similar to those under the *Scheme Funding Regulations* should be adopted. Alternatively, trustees may rely on an SFO valuation (see **11.7** above) for 15 months from the effective date of the valuation. The maximum amount of any refund payment to the employer will be the amount by which the value of the assets exceeds the buyout liabilities, as shown in the actuary's certificate for this purpose (*Payments to Employer Regulations, reg 7*).

Where the trustees intend to make a payment to the employer, the prescribed requirements (*Payments to Employer Regulations, reg 10*) for the notice to members are:

- a statement that the trustees have decided to make a payment;

- the payment amount;

- the date the payment is to be made (at least three months from the date of the notice and not later than the last day on which the valuation certificate is valid for the purposes of *s 37(4)(e)*); and

- a statement that the member may, within one month of the date of the notice, request a copy of the relevant valuation certificate (which the trustees must then provide within one month of their receiving the request).

Where a payment is made, notice must be given to the Regulator within one week (*Payments to Employer Regulations, reg 11*).

Where the scheme is an insured money purchase scheme (also known as an 'earmarked scheme'), it is possible for a surplus payment to be made to the employer where all the liabilities in respect of the relevant member, beneficiary or estate have been satisfied by the purchase of an annuity or payment in full (*Payments to Employer Regulations, reg 8*).

The tax simplification provisions of *PA 2004* removed the requirement for excessive surplus to be removed as a condition of continued exempt-approval.

Transitional powers in *PA 2004, s 251* were designed to give trustees the ability to amend scheme rules by resolution to take account of the repeal of *ICTA 1988* and the substitution of *s 37*. *Section 251* requires trustees to pass a resolution stating how the power to return surplus to the employers may be exercised in accordance with new *PA 1995, s 37*. Any such resolution must have been made before 6 April 2016 (this date being a correction to the 6 April 2011 date in the section – this change being announced by the DWP in an open letter dated 14 October 2010). *Section 251* has been further amended by the *Pensions Act 2011* to clarify that the section does not apply to payments which trustees can make without having to satisfy the requirements in *s 37*. *PA 2011* also formally extended the transitional period during which *s 251* applied to 6 April 2016 from 6 April 2011. Trustees must be satisfied that it is in the interests of the scheme members to resolve to amend the scheme in the manner proposed (ie to revive, limit or allow their original power to return surplus to lie dormant). They may only make this decision once and must give written notice to the scheme members and the employers that they plan to change the scheme rules on payments to the employer.

Civil penalties apply to the trustees if they try to make a payment of surplus to an employer without following all the requirements of *s 37*.

Schemes in winding up

11.34 If a registered scheme commences winding up on or after 6 April 2006, any power conferred on the employer or the trustees to distribute surplus assets to the employer on a winding up cannot be exercised unless the requirements set out in *PA 1995, s 76* and *Payments to Employer Regulations, regs 15–17* are satisfied. These can be summarised as follows:

- the liabilities of the scheme must have been fully discharged;

- where there is any power under the scheme to distribute surplus assets to any person other than the employer, that power must have been exercised or a decision must have been made not to exercise it; and

- notice must have been given to scheme members, in accordance with the prescribed requirements, of the proposal to exercise the power.

Where the trustees or employer propose to exercise the power to make a payment, they must take all reasonable steps to ensure that each member is sent a written notice divided into two parts. The first part must:

- inform the member of: the trustees' estimate of the value of assets remaining and the persons or classes of person to whom, and in what proportions, it is proposed that they should be distributed; and whether the requirements of *PA 1995, s 76(3)* are satisfied;

- invite the member to make written representations before a specified date (not earlier than two months from the date the first part of the notice is given); and

- advise the member that the second part of the notice will be issued if they intend to proceed with the proposal and that no assets will be distributed until at least three months after the date on which the second part of the notice is given to him.

The second part of the notice must be given after the date specified (see second point above) and at least three months before the power is exercised and must:

- contain the information referred to in the first point above, including any modifications to the proposal; and

- advise the member that he may make written representations to the Regulator before a specified date (not earlier than three months from the date on which the second part of the notice is furnished to him) if he considers *PA 1995, s 76(3)* is not satisfied.

Where the Regulator receives written representations from a member before expiry of the second part of the notice, or obtains information from any other source sufficient to raise a doubt as to whether the requirements of *PA 1995, s 76(3)* have been met, the Regulator may notify the trustees or employer (as appropriate) that the power should not be exercised until the Regulator has confirmed in writing that it is satisfied. Where the three-month time limit has expired and the trustees or employer have heard nothing from the Regulator, they should ask the Regulator for written confirmation that it has not received any representations or information (*Payments to Employer Regulations, regs 16, 17*).

Schemes with more than one employer

11.35 Where a scheme has more than one employer and is divided into two or more sections, the requirements of *PA 1995* relating to payments to the employer for both ongoing schemes and schemes which are winding up apply as if each section of the scheme were a separate scheme (*Payments to Employer Regulations, reg 18*), but only if the provisions of the scheme are such that:

(*a*) contributions payable to the scheme by an employer or by its employees are allocated to that section; and

(*b*) a specified part or a proportion of the assets of the scheme is attributable to each section and cannot be used for the purposes of any other section (or cannot be used for those purposes except on a winding up).

Trust law requirements relating to the reduction of surpluses

Powers under the trust instrument

11.36 The ways in which a reduction of scheme assets can be achieved may be restricted by the terms of the scheme's trust deed and rules. Usually, these will be wide enough to let the employer and the trustees decide on benefit improvements or a contribution holiday. However, the trust deeds of many schemes established before 1970 include a restriction on the power of amendment to the effect that no amendment can be made which would permit scheme funds to be paid to the employer. It is debatable whether or not such a restriction can be validly removed; much will depend on the circumstances and the exact wording of the power of amendment. Accordingly, before agreeing to a payment to the employer, trustees should carefully check all previous trust deeds to ensure that the current power of amendment has not been invalidly amended in the past.

Even if an amendment is possible, trustees must consider whether, in agreeing to it, they are acting in the best interests of the beneficiaries. They may be offered benefit improvements for the beneficiaries in return for making the amendment to enable and subsequently make a payment to the employer. Trustees must balance the security of members' interests against the benefit improvements on offer when deciding whether or not to agree to the amendment. The potential availability (or otherwise) of excessive scheme assets to the employer is likely to affect its negotiating position for scheme funding purposes.

Exercise of trustees' powers

11.37 Before agreeing to a payment of surplus to the employer (or, where the trust deed requires their agreement, to an employer's contribution holiday), trustees should obtain independent legal advice and should also consider whether they are subject to any conflicts of interest. For example, a trustee who is also a director of the employer may have difficulty maintaining his impartiality and fulfilling his duties as a trustee. In some circumstances, it may be necessary to appoint an independent trustee (see **Chapter 3**).

In exercising their powers, trustees must act in the best interests of the beneficiaries and must act impartially between different groups of beneficiaries. If, for example, an agreement was reached between the employer and the employees' representatives, it would indicate that active members find the proposal satisfactory, but the trustees would still have to consider the interests of deferred members and pensioners. Trustees have a duty to negotiate the best bargain they can in the circumstances, taking into consideration the relative balance of power between themselves and the principal employer (see *Re Courage Group's Pension Scheme [1987] 1 All ER 528*). The employer also has obligations to the membership; it must ensure that it is not acting in breach of its implied obligation of good faith (see *Imperial Group Pension Trust Ltd v Imperial Tobacco Ltd [1991] 2 All ER 597* and *IBM United Kingdom Holdings v Dalgleish [2014] EWHC 980 (Ch)*). In practice, it is difficult to see how the trustees can justify making any payment to the employer unless they have also secured some clear advantage (usually benefit improvements) for the beneficiaries.

Asset-backed contribution arrangements

11.38   Asset-backed contribution arrangements ('ABC's) (also referred to as asset-backed funding arrangements) are being increasingly used by schemes as a means of funding deficits otherwise than by direct cash contributions. They may also be a means of alleviating trapped surplus risk and can improve the security of member benefits by providing the scheme with access to valuable assets that were previously out of reach. However, these structures raise risks for both trustees and employers and have been subject to increasing scrutiny by the Regulator.

Typical ABC structure

11.39   ABCs are arrangements under which the employer transfers group assets into a separate entity, usually a Scottish Limited Partnership ('SLP'). The SLP uses those assets to generate an income stream over a period of time. The trustees invest in the SLP and their investment entitles them the right to a share of the profits of the SLP.

The details of these arrangements will vary depending on the particular needs of the employer's business and/or the scheme but an ABC arrangement will usually involve the following steps (as illustrated in the diagram below):

- the employer (or another group company) establishes new entities to facilitate the ABC arrangement, including an SLP and a general partner to manage the SLP. An SLP is used to avoid a breach of the employer-related investment legislation (see further the discussion on employer-related investments in **Chapter 10**);

- the employer makes a cash contribution to the scheme;

- the trustees use the employer contribution to subscribe for a partnership interest in the SLP. The other partners of the SLP will normally be group entities;

- the SLP uses the funds received from the partners to acquire an asset (eg property, intellectual property or loan notes) from the employer/group company;

- the employer/group company makes payments to the SLP in return for the use of the asset (eg rents, royalties, or interest payments);

- the SLP uses the income received to pay distributions to the trustees (and other partners of the SLP), in accordance with the terms of the partnership agreement; and

- the arrangement continues for the duration agreed in the partnership agreement.

Typical ABC Structure

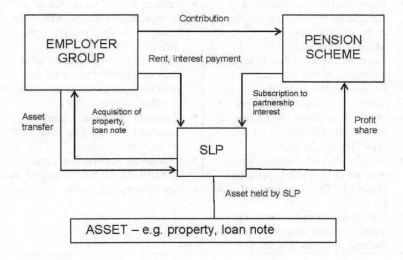

11.40   *Funding, deficits and surpluses*

The majority of ABCs implemented to date have involved real property. However, an increasingly wide range of underlying assets are being used, including intangible assets such as brand names, intellectual property and loan notes. Trustees would ideally want underlying assets that are of real value, so that if the employer becomes insolvent, the property reverts to the pension scheme and can be sold.

The trustees' limited partnership interest in the SLP is an asset of the scheme and is taken into account for scheme valuation purposes. The value of the trustees' interest in the SLP is normally the net present value of the future income stream due to the scheme under the ABC arrangement.

Reasons for using ABCs

11.40   The employer and the trustees may agree to enter into an ABC arrangement for the following reasons:

Employer reasons	Trustee reasons
• Immediate reduction in actuarial funding deficit and reduction in PPF levies • Improvement of the employer covenant – cash is retained in the business allowing it to develop economically and become stronger • Reduction (or avoidance of significant increase in) employer cash contributions • Manage trapped surplus risk, by including a facility to stop payments to the scheme • Payments due under the scheme's recovery plan may be reduced or spread over a longer period (the lifespan of an ABC is typically 15–20 years) • Accelerated tax relief on the upfront contribution, provided certain HMRC requirements are met • Retain use of the underlying asset, with the assets returned at the end of the arrangement	• Immediate reduction in actuarial funding deficit and reduction in PPF levies • Improvement of the employer covenant – cash is retained in the business allowing it to develop economically and become stronger • Higher overall contribution may be available with the ABC than under a standard recovery plan alone • Trustees may receive an asset they can sell for value on the event of an employer insolvency or other trigger event • Trustees receive a stream of income backed by an asset and/or another covenant • Increased security for members' benefits on the insolvency of the sponsoring employer

There are, however, a number of key risks and considerations that trustees and employers will need to consider when comparing ABCs with alternative funding arrangements (such as a standard cash recovery plan):

- *Impact on funding negotiations:* ABC arrangements may involve long payment periods, with the scheme locked into a fixed payment stream producing lower annual payments than under an appropriate recovery plan. This potentially exposes the scheme to a credit risk on the employer/ group company and a risk of underfunding if the employer or employer group fails.

- *Value of underlying asset:* trustees will need to consider how to value the underlying asset and will need to consider the value both at inception and on the insolvency of the employer or wider group. This can be particularly problematic with intangible assets. The value on insolvency is relevant because the SLP's ability to make the promised payments to the scheme will often be tied to the fortunes of the employer/group. The trustee will need to ensure that the asset is independently valued rather than relying solely on an audit valuation.

- *Legal claims to underlying asset:* trustees will need to consider the extent to which they are entitled to enforce their rights directly under the partnership agreement or whether are reliant on another party (eg the general partner of the SLP) to enforce their rights. Trustees will want to negotiate 'step-in' rights enabling them to access the value of the underlying asset quickly eg on company insolvency or on other 'early warning' triggers such as failure to make a payment to the SLP.

- *Weakened employer covenant:* this may arise due to the loss of control by the employer of key assets (ie where the asset transferred to the SLP was owned by the employer itself) or if the ABC requires payments from the employer for the use of the assets.

- *Risk of illegality / change of law:* if structured in the right way, these arrangements are currently considered to fall outside the statutory restrictions on employer-related investment (see **Chapter 10** for further details). However, these structures have not been tested by the courts and a change in law may render these arrangements commercially unviable or even disallow them entirely. The Regulator expects trustees to protect the scheme's position by ensuring that the ABC arrangements include a suitable 'underpin' to provide for what will happen if the courts find these structure void for illegality or there is a change of law (see further the discussion at **11.41** below).

- *Investment duties:* by subscribing for the partnership interest, the trustees are making an investment decision and must satisfy their statutory and trust law investment duties. Trustees will also need to ensure that they do not end up taking 'day-to-day' investment decisions under the partnership agreement (see **Chapter 10**).

- *Costs and complexity*: ABC arrangements can be costly and time-consuming to implement, especially where a more complex arrangement (eg using intangible assets) is being used.

The Regulator

11.41   In November 2013 the Regulator issued new guidance on asset backed contributions for trustees and their advisers, in which it set out the risks involved and its expectations of trustees when considering such arrangements. Whilst the Regulator would clearly prefer direct cash contributions, it recognises that ABC's '...*may help employers meet their obligations to schemes and can, in certain circumstances, improve a scheme's security by providing access to valuable assets which were previously out of reach.*'

The Regulator expects trustees to consider the risks involved in ABC arrangements as part of their assessment of any proposal by the employer, obtaining appropriate advice (including legal, actuarial, asset valuation and covenant advice) and considering available alternatives as appropriate (for example, a standard cash recovery plan). The Regulator identifies the following key risks of ABCs that the trustees should consider:

- inflexible schedule of payments delaying full funding;

- weak underlying assets or limited legal claims on those assets;

- masking the scheme's overall risk profile;

- weakened covenant;

- illegality of the structure;

- costs and complexity.

The Regulator is becoming increasingly active in ABC transactions and will challenge trustees' investment decisions where it considers there is concern. Ultimately, trustees will need to be able show '*how they have reached the conclusion that entering into an ABC is in the best interests of beneficiaries*'.

Trustees must report any investment in an ABC to the Regulator in the annual scheme return and should be prepared to respond to queries regarding the ABC, including details of the income stream and nature of the underlying asset. Trustees are also expected to inform scheme members of the ABC in the next available communication. The communication should be clear about funding implications, the extent to which the scheme remains reliant on the employer/group and why the ABC arrangement benefits the scheme.

Chapter 12

Winding up

Introduction

12.1   The winding up of a pension scheme consists of two key stages. The trigger, when the scheme is terminated and benefits cease to accrue; and the winding up process itself where its assets are used to secure the scheme's benefits through other means (typically, by purchasing annuities or making transfer payments to other schemes).

The circumstances in which schemes go into winding up are varied, but some examples are:

(*a*)   where the purpose of the winding up is to make a bulk transfer to another scheme;

(*b*)   where the employer can no longer afford to run the scheme. The employment law implications of this are considered in **Chapter 7**;

(*c*)   where a scheme (perhaps with few, if any, remaining active members) has become too small to justify the cost of continuing to operate it; or

(*d*)   the insolvency of the principal employer (see **Chapter 5**).

Winding up – general

Triggering events

12.2   The events which will trigger a winding up of a scheme will depend upon the scheme's governing trust deed and rules. These might typically provide for a winding up of the scheme to be triggered upon the earliest of:

(*a*)   the expiry of a notice to the trustees by the principal employer, requiring that the scheme be wound up;

(*b*)   the trustees resolving to wind the scheme up and notifying the principal employer accordingly;

505

(*c*)   the principal employer being in arrears in its contributions to the scheme and failing to rectify the position within a specified period of the trustees formally requesting it to do so;

(*d*)   the principal employer going into liquidation; and

(*e*)   the expiry of a specified period from the date on which the scheme was established.

Many trust deeds and rules will, in some of these circumstances, give the trustees a discretion to continue operating the scheme (with a new principal employer, where appropriate) rather than wind it up immediately; this is dealt with in **12.8** below.

Order of the Regulator

12.3   The Regulator may, under *PA 1995, s 11*, authorise or direct a winding up if:

(*a*)   the scheme (or any part of it) ought to be replaced by a different scheme;

(*b*)   the scheme is no longer required; or

(*c*)   it is necessary in order to protect the interests of the generality of the scheme members.

It should only rarely be necessary for the Regulator to intervene, and the Regulator is unlikely to make such an order without a compelling case being made to it. Alternatively, it may in exceptional circumstances be necessary to apply to the court for directions to wind up a scheme.

Effect of triggering winding up

12.4   Once winding up is triggered, the scheme ceases to be subject to the scheme specific funding provisions of *PA 2004* and is instead subject to the employer debt legislation of *PA 1995, s 75*. From the effective date of termination, no further benefits may accrue to or in respect of existing members and no new members may be admitted to the scheme (*PA 1995, s 73A(3)*). Members who were active members immediately before the winding up was triggered automatically become deferred members. No further employee contributions are due and, except for any debt due from the employers under *PA 1995, s 75* or outstanding contributions which are yet to be paid, no further contributions would normally be due from the employer(s).

The scheme's trust deed and rules may provide that the employer remains liable for the ongoing administrative expenses (including advisers' fees) during the winding up. If so, actuarial advice should be sought on the extent the employer may end up paying these expenses twice as a result of an expense allowance (determined by the trustees) which is also built into the calculation of any *PA 1995, s 75* debt on the employer.

Once the winding up has been triggered, it will also be possible for trustees to pay a winding up lump sum of up to £18,000 to a member (as an alternative to buying out the benefits) where the following conditions under *FA 2004, Sch 29, para 10 (FA 2004, s 166(1)(f))* are met:

(*a*)   the pension scheme is an occupational pension scheme;

(*b*)   any person by whom the member is employed at the time when the lump sum is paid, and who has made contributions under the pension scheme in respect of the member within the period of five years ending with the day on which it is paid:

   (i)   is not making contributions under any other registered pension scheme in respect of the member; and

   (ii)   undertakes to the Inland Revenue not to make such contributions during the period of one year beginning with the day on which the lump sum is paid;

(*c*)   it is paid when all or part of the member's lifetime allowance is available; and

(*d*)   the payment of the winding up lump sum extinguishes the member's entitlement to benefits under the pension scheme.

Section 75 debt

12.5   The employer debt legislation aims to ensure that solvent employers cannot walk away from their pension liabilities and must meet the annuity buy-out cost in full on the winding up of the scheme. It also provides a mechanism for trustees to calculate a debt which they can then seek to recover through the insolvency process of an insolvent employer (see **Chapter 5**). A debt can also be triggered on the withdrawal of an employer from a multi-employer scheme (see **Chapter 15**). In this section, only the impact of the employer debt legislation on the winding up of a scheme is considered. The legislation does not generally apply to money purchase schemes.

Broadly, under *PA 1995, s 75* if a scheme is wound up and the value of the assets of the scheme is less than the amount of the scheme liabilities an amount equal to the difference is treated as a debt due from the employer (*PA 1995, s 75(2)*).

12.5 *Winding up*

Any *s 75* debt has to be calculated and verified by the actuary (which will usually be the scheme actuary appointed under *PA 1995, s 47*). For the purposes of calculating any *s 75* debt the liabilities in respect of pensions and other benefits are calculated on the assumption that they will be discharged by the purchase of annuities (the *Occupational Pension Schemes (Employer Debt) Regulations 2005 (SI 2005/678)* (the *'Employer Debt Regulations'*), *reg 5*). The liabilities to be taken into account for *s 75* debt purposes include all expenses (except the cost of the annuities) which in the opinion of the trustees are likely to be incurred in connection with the winding up of the scheme (*Employer Debt Regulations, reg 5(3)*).

Assets and liabilities have to be calculated in accordance with *reg 5* of the *Employer Debt Regulations*.

Under *PA 1995, s 75(2)*, when a scheme is in winding up, the trustees must designate 'that time', being the date at which the assets and liabilities are to be calculated, before a 'relevant event' (broadly the insolvency of the employer) occurs in relation to an employer. The amount equal to the difference between the assets and liabilities on that date is then treated as a debt due from the employer to the trustees. This will apply as long as no 'relevant event' has already occurred during the period between 6 April 2005 and the date on which the scheme begins to wind up. Nevertheless, if a 'relevant event' has occurred during that period but it has been followed by a binding 'cessation notice' then the provisions set out above will still apply (trustees being able to designate the time for calculation of assets and liabilities). A 'cessation notice' is broadly a notice that scheme rescue has occurred or a notice that no insolvency event has occurred or is likely to occur.

The mechanics of how *s 75(2)* works in practice are best illustrated by the following timelines:

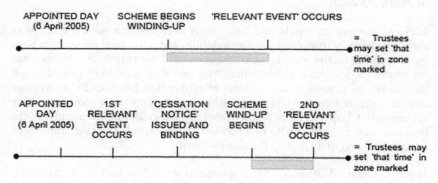

PA 1995, s 75(2) provides trustees with an opportunity to select the most advantageous date for calculation of the debt and as such they should keep themselves abreast of the employer's financial position and the funding position of the scheme once winding up has been triggered. Typically, in a wind-up where the employer is solvent, the trustees will delay designating a time for determining the *s 75* debt until near the end of the winding-up process when the cost of purchasing annuities and the total winding-up expenses are known.

If, for whatever reason, the trustees fail to designate 'that time' before a 'relevant event' occurs (or a 'relevant event' occurs before or at the same time as the winding up is triggered) then *PA 1995, s 75(4)* will apply and the date for the calculation of assets and liabilities is fixed as the time immediately before the insolvency event occurred (combined effect of *PA 1995, ss 75(2)(a)(ii)* and *75(4)(c)*).

In a multi-employer scheme *PA 1995, s 75(2)* is modified so that the trustees can designate any time from the commencement of the wind-up until the date 'relevant events' have occurred in relation to all the employers for the purposes of calculating the debt. All employers at the date of the commencement of the winding up with active members in the scheme will be liable to meet their share of the debt as will certain former employers (*Employer Debt Regulations, reg 6*). Each employer's share of the debt will generally be equal to its 'liability share' unless some form of apportionment or withdrawal arrangement has been entered into as detailed in the *Employer Debt Regulations*. The 'liability share' is an amount equal to the 'liability proportion' multiplied by the total difference between the value of the assets and the amount of the liabilities of the scheme (*Employer Debt Regulation, reg 2*); the 'liability proportion' is an amount equal to K divided by L where:

(*a*)   'K' equals the amount of a scheme's liabilities attributable to an employer in accordance with *Employer Debt Regulations, reg 6(4)*; and

(*b*)   'L' equals the total amount of the scheme's liabilities attributable to employment with all the employers.

The calculation and management of *s 75* debts in multi-employer schemes is dealt with in more detail in **Chapter 15**.

Disclosure requirements

12.6   There are a number of specific disclosure requirements which apply to occupational pension schemes in winding up:

(*a*)   the trustees must provide all members and beneficiaries on the commencement of winding up with certain information which includes:

    (i)   giving a statement that the scheme has begun winding up;

    (ii)   the reasons why winding up has commenced;

(iii)   where the scheme has active members, whether death benefits will continue to be payable;

(iv)   a summary of what action is being (or has been) taken to establish the scheme's liabilities and recover any assets;

(v)   an estimate of when the scheme's liabilities are likely to be established and any assets are likely to be recovered; and

(vi)   either giving an indication of the extent to which, if at all, the actuarial value of accrued rights or benefits to which such person is entitled are likely to be reduced, or, where the trustees do not hold sufficient information to provide such an indication, a statement to that effect.

(The *Occupational and Personal Pension Schemes (Disclosure of Information) Regulations 2013 (SI 2013/2734)* (the *'Disclosure Regulations'*, *reg 24(2)(a)*))

Where the scheme began winding up before 6 April 2014, the last three matters listed above must be provided within 12 months of 6 April 2014 and at least once every 12 months thereafter until the wind up is completed (*Disclosure Regulations, reg 24(4)*).

Where the scheme began winding up on or after 6 April 2014, the information listed above needs to be provided as soon as is reasonably practicable after, and in any event no later than one month from, the date on which the scheme commenced winding up. The last three matters listed above also need to be provided at least once every 12 months after the date on which the information was first given to the members and beneficiaries until the wind up is completed (*Disclosure Regulations, reg 24(3)*).

(*b*)   where the scheme is being wound up and the trustees have done what they can to discharge the scheme's liabilities for a particular member or beneficiary of the scheme, the following information must be given as soon as is reasonably practicable after and in any event no later than three months from that date:

(i)   whether the member or beneficiary's benefits are reduced because the scheme's resources are not sufficient to meet its liabilities;

(ii)   the amount of any reduction of the member's or beneficiary's benefits;

(iii)   who has or will become liable for the payment of the member's or beneficiary's benefits;

(iv)   where the member or beneficiary is for the time being entitled to the payment of benefits, the amount of the benefit that is payable and, if the benefit is payable periodically, any conditions for continuing to make the payments and/or any provisions which would allow the payments to be altered; and

(v) where the member of beneficiary for the time being has no entitlement to the payment of benefits (save for any money purchase benefits), an estimate of the amount of the member's and beneficiary's benefits that are expected to be payable from normal pension age or death.

Where a member only has rights to money purchase benefits then the above requirements are modified and only disclosure requirements (i), (ii) and (iv) will apply (*Disclosure Regulations, reg 25*).

(c) the trustees must notify the Regulator where a scheme has been in the process of winding up for more than two years (*PA 1995, s 72A* and *The Occupational Pension Schemes (Winding Up Notices and Reports etc) Regulations (SI 2002/459)* as amended (the '*Winding up Notices and Reports Regulations*'), reg 9).

(d) the trustees must update the Regulator in writing every subsequent 12 months about progress (including details of what steps remain to be completed and a time estimate for completion of those steps) (*PA 1995, s 72A(3)* and the *Winding Up Notices and Reports Regulations, reg 10(2)*);

(e) the trustees must provide a member (or a beneficiary) of the scheme with a copy of any report sent to the Regulator within two months of a request being made (*Disclosure Regulations, reg 24(5)*);

(f) the Regulator has the power to give directions in order to speed up the winding up process of a scheme, where it deems it appropriate (*PA 1995, s 72B*); and

(g) the trustees and the employer (if appropriate) must keep a written record of any decisions to wind up a scheme (*PA 1995, s 49A(1), Winding Up Notices and Reports Regulations, reg 13*).

The Regulator's two-year target

12.7 The Regulator has issued good practice guidelines for schemes winding up. It states that it expects certain 'key activities' of the winding up to be completed within two years of the date winding up is triggered. The key activities include:

(a) serving a debt on the employer;

(b) securing pensioner benefits;

(c) identifying the remaining members' (non-pensioners) share of the assets and obtaining terms from an insurer to secure a pension;

511

(*d*)   conducting a final actuarial valuation; and

(*e*)   issuing option letters to non-pensioners or details of insured benefits.

The Regulator considers that there are few exceptions to the two-year deadline (although it does list some 'unavoidable delays' including legal issues involving court action and avoiding detrimental early redemption charges on investments). Where the trustees have not complied with the requirements to wind up a scheme, they will have to provide reasons to the Regulator for not doing so. Trustees may be fined by the Regulator in the event of unjustified delays in winding up a scheme.

The Regulator recognises, however, that winding up an occupational pension scheme which provides Guaranteed Minimum Pensions ('GMPs') may hamper a scheme's ability to meet the two-year target. The Regulator believes that dealing with any contracting-out queries prior to wind up will help reduce the amount of time spent reconciling GMP liabilities during the two-year target because the cost and delay involved in reconciling members' GMP records may result in members receiving lower benefits.

In its updated guidance issued in October 2012, the Regulator has also sought to help trustees try to reconcile their scheme's GMP records with those held by HMRC. Trustees are encouraged to use HMRC's figures where a discrepancy is identified in a member's GMP records. Schemes should, however, consider adopting a £2 per week tolerance level. This is consistent with the tolerance level accepted by the Board of the Pension Protection Fund ('PPF') and used by schemes entering a PPF assessment period. Using a tolerance level is intended to avoid pension benefits being reduced because of 'disproportionate efforts to reconcile GMP calculations "to the penny"'. HMRC has established a Scheme Reconciliation Service ('SRS') to assist schemes in reconciling GMP data on the abolition of contracting-out (see **Chapter 4**).

Deferral of winding up by trustees

Power under scheme rules

12.8   Some scheme rules give the trustees power, even after the winding up has been triggered, to defer winding the scheme up. Examples of circumstances where the trustees might wish to defer winding up are:

(*a*)   where annuity rates are low at the time when the winding up rule is triggered and the trustees wish to wait for them to rise, so placing the fund in a better position to secure the benefits with an insurance company;

(*b*)   where the trustees are awaiting a clarification of the law without which winding up may prove risky (the initial uncertainty over the CJEU's *Barber* decision – see **Chapter 9** – being an example); or (*c*)   where the scheme's winding up rule has been triggered by the principal employer going into receivership and the trustees expect the business to be sold to a new owner who is committed to the continued funding and operation of the scheme.

A scheme rule enabling the trustees to defer winding up in these circumstances may or may not permit the trustees to take steps during the deferral period (eg requiring further employers' contributions) which would create further liabilities for the employers.

Deferral of the termination by the trustees will have the effect of postponing the calculation of any *s 75* debt and its payment by the employers because, although no further benefits would accrue for existing members, the scheme would not be treated as being in winding up (see *PA 1995, s 124(3C)*). The scheme would continue to be subject to the scheme-specific funding provisions of the *PA 2004*. In practical terms therefore, any deficit repair contributions continue to be payable, but the future service costs would fall away.

In exercising a power to defer winding up, the trustees would need to be satisfied that deferral is in the best interest of the members (which would include maximising the security of members' benefits). There are unlikely to be many situations where trustees would exercise a power to defer winding up given that the *s 75* debt must be calculated on a full- buy-out basis – particularly in (the relatively rare) circumstances where the employer is capable of meeting the *s 75* debt in full.

Statutory power

12.9   There is in some (limited) circumstances a statutory power to defer winding up for those trustees who do not have such a power under their scheme rules.

This statutory power is conferred by *PA 1995, s 38(1)* and is available only where:

(*a*)   there is no power to defer winding up in the scheme's trust deed and rules (*s 38(1)*);

(*b*)   it is not a money purchase scheme (*s 38(3)(a)*);

(*c*)   the scheme:

- has at least two members;

- is registered or a relevant statutory scheme; and

- is not a small self-administered scheme (*Winding Up Regulations, reg 10(1)*); and (*d*)   an 'insolvency event' has occurred in relation to any of the scheme's employers which triggers a winding up of the scheme. An 'insolvency event' is defined in *PA 2004, s 121*. If the scheme has no active members, anyone who was an employer in relation to the scheme when the scheme last had active members will count as an employer for this purpose (*Winding Up Regulations, regs 10(1)(a) and 10(2)*).

Where trustees exercise this power, they may not allow new members to join the scheme during the deferral period. However, *PA 1995, s 38(2)* does allow them to decide:

(i)   that contributions will not continue to be payable; or

(ii)   that benefits will not continue to accrue to or in respect of scheme members,

during deferment, but this will not stop increases to accrued rights.

The power under *s 38* does not apply to a scheme which is required to wind up under *PA 2004, s 154(1)* following a PPF assessment period (see **Chapter 5**).

Winding up priorities

12.10   Whilst winding up is being deferred, some active members are likely to become deferred pensioners, others to become pensioners, and so on. These changes of status (sometimes referred to as 'priority drift') are important because, should the scheme be wound up with insufficient assets to secure all the benefits, some membership categories (such as pensioners) may have preferential rights over others. This is less important since new statutory winding up priorities were introduced from 6 April 2005 (see **12.15** below).

Trustees who defer winding up have a limited degree of scope under *Winding Up Regulations, reg 5* to decide the date at which membership status (eg whether a person is an active member or a pensioner) is to be determined for this purpose.

Disclosure requirements

12.11   Any decision to defer winding up (whether reached under the scheme rules or under *PA 1995, s 38*) or to fix a date for determining winding up priorities (whether reached under the power referred to in **12.8** above or under any other power) must be recorded and members must be informed of the decision within one month (*Winding Up Regulations, reg 11*).

If the trustees do not defer winding up, or when any period of deferral comes to an end, the winding up process will start.

The winding up process

Overview – methods of securing the liabilities

12.12

(a)   Statutory power to secure benefits

Where the winding up of a scheme commences after 5 April 1997, *PA 1995, s 74* gives trustees of a registered defined benefits scheme, the power to secure members' benefits.

(b)   Options available

PA 1995, s 74 and the *Winding Up Regulations* provide that trustees are treated as having discharged any liability in respect of scheme benefits as long as they have arranged for the discharge of that liability in one or more of the following ways:

- by making a transfer payment to another occupational pension scheme (*PA 1995, s 74(3)(a)*);

- by making a transfer payments to a personal pension scheme (*PA 1995, s 74(3)(b)*);

- by purchasing an annuity from an insurance company (*PA 1995, s 74(3) (c)*);

- by transferring the benefits of an annuity contract or insurance policy to the member concerned (or his dependant) (*Winding Up Regulations, reg 8(4)*);

- in certain limited circumstances, relating to insolvent contracted-out schemes, paying sums to the Department for Work and Pensions (*Winding Up Regulations, reg 8(5)*); and/or

- by paying a trivial commutation or winding up lump sum (*Winding Up Regulations, reg 8(6)*).

(c)   Notice to members

When securing a member's benefits in accordance with *PA 1995, s 74* trustees must also give to the member to whom the liabilities relate (or if the member is deceased to his beneficiaries), a notice in writing of the proposed discharge (a 'discharge notice') (*Winding Up Regulations, reg 6(2)(a)*).

(d)   Statutory discharge

In order to be discharged when securing members' benefits, the *Winding Up Regulations* provide that the trustees must comply with the requirements relating to: (i) the contents of the discharge notice (*reg 7)* as mentioned above; and (ii) other prescribed requirements, such as whether the individual's consent is required (*regs 6, 8*).

Timing and order in which benefits are secured

12.13   The order in which the trustees must secure members' benefits when a scheme is being wound up varies according to when the winding up began. There are three main time periods to consider:

(*a*)   on or after 6 April 2005;

(*b*)   10 May 2004 to 5 April 2005; and

(*c*)   6 April 1997 to 9 May 2004.

Prior to 6 April 1997, there was no general statutory framework to govern how the assets of a pension scheme were to be allocated. Contracted-out defined benefit schemes were required to adopt an order of priorities which afforded higher priority to guaranteed minimum pensions over the non-guaranteed minimum pensions element of deferred pensioners' benefits. Most pension schemes had a winding up rule which included a list of priorities in accordance with which the assets of the scheme were to be distributed on a winding up.

A statutory priority order was introduced for the first time by *PA 1995*. The provisions of *PA 1995, s 73* and the *Winding Up Regulations* imposed a statutory overriding priority order for wind-ups commencing from 6 April 1997 (see **12.17** below).

A new transitional priority order was introduced for schemes that commenced winding up after 9 May 2004 (*Occupational Pension Schemes (Winding Up) (Amendment) Regulations (SI 2004/1140)*) (see **12.16** below).

PA 2004 introduced changes to *PA 1995, s 73* which apply to schemes where winding up starts on or after 6 April 2005 (see from **12.15**).

Time at which winding up starts

12.14   The *Winding Up Regulations, reg 2* and *PA 1995, s 124(3A)–(3E)* determine the time at which the wind up starts.

Scheme rules

If the winding up is triggered under the scheme rules, then it is necessary to consider whether the rules specify a time for the winding up to start. If they do not, the *Winding Up Regulations* provide that the time at which winding up starts is the later of:

(*a*)   the time when the trustees (or whoever has the power) decide that the scheme wind up starts; and

(*b*)   the earliest date when there are no members in pensionable service.

If the rules do specify a time and the trustees have decided not to defer the winding up of the scheme, the winding up starts on the later of:

(*a*)   the date as specified in the scheme rules; and

(*b*)   the earliest date when there are no members in pensionable service.

Order of the Regulator

If the winding up has been triggered by the Regulator, the time at which winding up starts depends on whether or not a time is specified in the relevant order. If a time is specified, this is the time for winding up to start. If the order is silent, the winding up will start on the effective date of the order (*PA 1995, s 124(3A)*).

PPF assessment period

If an assessment period has been triggered in relation to the scheme, the PPF rules set out in *PA 2004, ss 154 and 219* will apply in relation to the time at which winding up starts.

Priority order – winding up started on or after 6 April 2005

12.15   *PA 2004, s 270* replaced *PA 1995, s 73* with new *sections 73, 73A and 73B*. These provisions apply to schemes that start to wind up on or after 6 April 2005 and is supplemented by the *Occupational Pension Schemes (Winding Up etc) Regulations 2005 (SI 2005/706)* (the '*Winding Up Regulations 2005*').

The intention behind the requirements was to ensure that the winding up provisions work in harmony with the provisions of *PA 2004* and associated regulations that establish the PPF and its procedures (see **Chapter 5** for more on the PPF). Individual scheme members should be no worse off where their scheme winds up than they would be if the PPF were instead to assume responsibility for the scheme and pay compensation.

PA 1995, ss 73, 73A and 73B do not apply in relation to any liability for an amount by way of pensions or other benefits which a person became entitled to payment of, under the scheme rules, before the start of the winding up (*PA 1995, s 73B(6)*). Nor do they apply to liabilities for money purchase benefits (*PA 1995, s 73(10)*).

The statutory priority order now set out in *PA 1995, s 73(4)* is as follows:

12.16 *Winding up*

First priority – pre-6 April 1997 insurance contracts

This is a contract of insurance entered into before 6 April 1997 to secure certain scheme liabilities which cannot be surrendered, or the amount payable on surrender would be less than the liability secured by the contract (*PA 1995, s 73(5)*).

Second priority – liability for benefits to the amount of the corresponding PPF liability

This is the cost of securing the benefits that would be payable to a member under the pension compensation provisions if the PPF assumed responsibility for the scheme in accordance with *PA 2004 (PA 1995, s 73(5))*.

Third priority – additional voluntary contributions benefits

Under the post-2005 priority order additional voluntary contributions benefits have been demoted from their top priority position. This is linked to the compensation mechanism within the PPF. Only those voluntary contributions not already covered by the two preceding categories fall into the third priority level. Money purchase additional voluntary contribution liabilities are effectively 'ring-fenced' on winding up and are to be secured before any of the priority categories. This is because they are excluded from the assets of the scheme for the purposes of *PA 1995, s 73 (PA 1995, s 73(10))*. It is therefore arguably only benefits attributable to additional voluntary contributions granted on an 'added years' basis for those pensions above the PPF cap which have slipped down the priority order.

Fourth priority – any other liability in respect of pensions or other benefits

Once the PPF liabilities and AVCs have been given priority, all other remaining benefits of members of the scheme are secured in the fourth priority category on a pro-rata basis (*PA 1995, ss 73(3)(b) and 73(4)(d)*).

Any assets remaining after all benefits of the members of the scheme have been secured will fall to be distributed in accordance with *PA 1995, s 76*.

Winding up started from 10 May 2004 to 5 April 2005

12.16   A transitional priority order was introduced for schemes that commenced winding up after 9 May 2004. The main changes from the priority order that applied before 10 May 2004 is that: (i) increases on pensions in payment fell below deferred benefits; and (ii) no priority was given to contracted-out benefits.

The transitional priority order was as follows:

First priority – additional voluntary contributions benefits

Either in defined contributions form or added years. If added years, the benefits must be identified by the trustees as being accrued by reference to additional voluntary contributions.

Second priority – pre-6 April 1997 insurance policies

These are the liabilities secured where:

- the trustees are entitled to benefits under an insurance contract entered into:
  - before 6 April 1997; and
  - in order to secure all or part of the scheme's liability for any benefit payable in respect of an individual whose entitlement to payment of a benefit has arisen (and for any benefit which will be payable in respect of him on his death); and
- either:
  - the contract cannot be surrendered; or
  - the surrender value would be less than the liability secured (excluding liability for pension increases).

Where an insurance policy has been taken out after 5 April 1997, it may need to be surrendered in order to comply with *PA 1995, s 73*.

Third priority – liability for benefits to which entitlement to payment has arisen and benefits which will be payable in respect of the person so entitled upon his death (excluding pension increases)

This would cover pensions in payment from the scheme and should also cover postponed pensioners (where a member has postponed taking benefits after normal retirement age) and any lump sum death benefits that arose prior to the commencement of the winding up.

Fourth priority – deferred benefits, pension credits and contribution refunds

- liabilities for pensions or other benefits which have accrued to or in respect of any members of the scheme (excluding increases to pensions) and refunds of contributions;
- future pensions, or other future benefits, attributable (directly or indirectly) to pension credits (but excluding increases to pensions); and
- refunds of contributions for members with less than two years' service.

12.17 *Winding up*

Fifth priority – liabilities for increases to pensions referred to in the second and third priorities above

Where the increases to the pension arose prior to the date on which winding up started, then they form part of the benefit liability as at that date and enjoy higher priority than post-wind-up increases.

Sixth priority – liabilities for increases to pensions referred to in the fourth priority above

Winding up started from 6 April 1997 to 9 May 2004

12.17   The priority order for a scheme that started winding up at any time on and from 6 April 1997 to 9 May 2004 is set out in *PA 1995, s 73* (as it stood during that period), as modified by the *Winding Up Regulations*.

When considering the provisions of *PA 1995, s 73* and the associated provisions of the *Winding Up Regulations*, it is necessary to ignore the changes made to that section by *PA 2004, s 270*. This is because the *Pensions Act 2004 (Commencement No 2, Transitional Provisions and Consequential Amendments) Order 2005 (SI 2005/275)* confirms that *PA 2004, s 270* does not come into force for all purposes. The new wording is not effective to the extent that it affects *PA 1995, ss 73* and *74* as they apply immediately before 6 April 2005 to a scheme in winding up at that time. The question of whether or not a scheme was in winding up at that time is determined under *Winding Up Regulations, reg 2* or *PA 1995, s 124* (as appropriate).

PA 1995, s 73(2), as it applies to schemes in wind-up before 6 April 2005, requires that the assets of the scheme must be applied first towards satisfying the amounts of the liabilities mentioned in *PA 1995, s 73(3)*. If the assets are insufficient to satisfy the amounts in full, the earlier paragraphs of *PA 1995, s 73(3)* take priority over the later paragraphs.

Any assets remaining after allocating these amounts in this way must then be used to satisfy any remaining liabilities, in the order of priorities set out in the scheme's own rules *(PA 1995, s 73(4))*.

The priority order in *PA 1995, s 73(3)* is as follows:

First priority – additional voluntary contributions benefits

Either in defined contributions form or added years. If added years, the benefits must be identified by the trustees as being accrued by reference to additional voluntary contributions.

Second priority – pre-6 April 1997 insurance policies

These are the liabilities secured where:

- the trustees are entitled to benefits under an insurance contract entered into:
    - before 6 April 1997; and
    - in order to secure all or part of the scheme's liability for any benefit payable in respect of an individual whose entitlement to payment of a benefit has arisen (and for any benefit which will be payable in respect of him on his death); and
- either:
    - the contract cannot be surrendered; or
    - the surrender value would be less than the liability secured (excluding liability for pension increases).

Where an insurance policy has been taken out after 5 April 1997, it may need to be surrendered in order to comply with *PA 1995, s 73*.

Third priority – liability for benefits to which entitlement to payment has arisen and benefits which will be payable in respect of the person so entitled upon death (excluding pension increases)

This will cover pensions in payment from the scheme and should also cover postponed pensioners (where a member has postponed taking benefits after normal retirement age) and any lump sum death benefits that arose prior to the commencement of the winding up.

Fourth priority – contracted-out benefits and refunds of contributions

Fifth priority – liabilities for increases to pensions referred to in the second and third priorities above

Where the increases to the pension arose prior to the date on which the winding up started, then they form part of the benefit liability as at that date and enjoy higher priority than post-wind up increases.

Sixth priority – liabilities for increases to pensions referred to in the fourth priority above

Seventh priority – other liabilities for accrued benefits (including pension increases)

This category is mainly for the deferred pensioners (including those with pension credits). Where the scheme is contracted out, it will cover non-guaranteed minimum pension benefits (as the contracted-out benefits currently have higher priority). For schemes that are not contracted out, a much larger proportion of the benefits will fall into this priority.

It also covers future pensions or other future benefits attributable (directly or indirectly) to pension credits.

Moving down the priority order

12.18   Once it has been established which priority order applies when securing members' benefits, the trustees have to work down the priority order securing benefits until they run out of funds.

It is important to establish which category of membership applies to each individual member of the scheme – this is done by reference to the 'crystallisation date'. It is then necessary to decide how much to apply to each category. *PA 2004* has given the trustees powers to make adjustments to the benefits of certain members that have to be secured which in turn has an impact on the amount to be applied for those members.

There is some uncertainty as to how the pension rights of members who had been affected by the *Barber* decision who have benefits accrued based on two or more normal retirement dates (typically 60 and 65) (for more see **Chapter 9**) should be treated under *PA 1995, s 73* for schemes commencing wind-up between 6 April 1997 and 5 April 2005.

In *Cripps v Trustee Solutions Limited and Dubery [2007] EWCA Civ 771* the Court of Appeal held that members who had a lower normal retirement age (because of the *Barber* judgment) for part of their pension should receive priority under the 'third' priority (set out in **12.15** above) under *PA 1995, s 73* for this part of their pension if they were over that age at the crystallisation date and the remainder would be in the relevant lower priority. This 'splitting' was a change from established practice, which was largely based on the requirement of HMRC to pay a pension from a single date.

In *Foster Wheeler Ltd v Hanley & Ors [2008] EWHC 2926 (Ch)* the Court of Appeal held that there was a legal principle that any amendments to the scheme rules that were required to give effect to *Barber* rights should represent the 'minimum interference' with the scheme's provisions. In this case, all that was required to give effect to *Barber* was to disapply the requirement to obtain the company's consent to the early retirement pension, as the payment of a single pension would more closely track the scheme rules than split pensions would. The result in that case was that all benefits could be paid from age 60, but the portion of pension accrued based on a normal retirement date of 65 must be reduced for early payment.

The contrasting decisions in *Cripps* and *Foster Wheeler* leave it open as to whether a scheme should provide split benefits or a single pension. It will depend on the detail of the scheme rules and the manner in which *Barber* equalisation was effected.

Crystallisation date

12.19   The 'crystallisation date' is the date when the scheme starts to wind up; or if the trustees have determined to postpone winding up, such earlier date, prior to the actual winding up which is fixed by the rules of the scheme (*Winding Up Regulations, reg 4*).

How much to apply to each category

12.20   *Winding Up Regulations, reg 4* sets out how the liabilities are calculated under *PA 1995, s 73*. A number of amendments have been made to *Winding Up Regulations, reg 4* as the amount to be applied to each category has increased over time.

(a)   The sum needed to secure pensions in payment plus minimum funding requirement value of other benefits

This amount applies where the members' rights crystallised before 19 March 2002 and so is unlikely to apply to many schemes now in winding up.

It also applies where all of the participating employers in the scheme immediately before the start of the winding up were insolvent (for winding ups commencing before 15 February 2005).

The liabilities for benefits other than pensions in payment should be calculated in the manner specified in *Occupational Pension Schemes (Minimum Funding Requirement and Actuarial Valuations) Regulations 1996 (SI 1996/1536), regs 7(2), (3), (7)–(10)* and *8(2)*. The liabilities do not include the expenses involved in meeting them and therefore the actuary should include no allowance for the buy-out costs.

(b)   Buy-out costs for pensions in payment and future increases plus minimum funding requirement value of other benefits

This is the amount to apply to each category where:

- the rights crystallised on or after 19 March 2002, but before 11 June 2003; and
- the participating employers were not insolvent immediately before the start of winding up.

12.20   *Winding up*

The amount to apply for pensioners is calculated as the cost of buying annuities in the market. The calculation of other benefit liabilities is based on the minimum funding requirement liabilities as set out above but expenses are included. This is unlikely to apply to many schemes currently in winding up.

This also applies to schemes commencing winding up between 11 June 2003 and 14 March 2004 where the liabilities were calculated before 15 March 2004. This is not express in the *Winding Up Regulations* but is a consequence of the timing of the various amendments to the regulations.

If the employers were insolvent immediately before the start of the winding up then all liabilities are based on the minimum funding requirement (see **12.20**(*a*) above).

(c)   Buy-out costs for all benefits

This is the amount to apply to each category where:

- the winding up started on or after 11 June 2003;

- the date chosen for calculating the liabilities falls on or after 15 March 2004; and

- the participating employers were not insolvent immediately before the start of the winding up.

The buy-out cost for this purpose includes full winding up expenses.

This change was introduced in March 2004 but was made retrospective to June 2003 when the change to buy-out cost was first announced by the Government.

Further changes were made in February 2005, so that if the winding up commenced on or after 15 February 2005, the amount to apply is the buy-out cost for all benefits whether or not the employer participating in the scheme is solvent or insolvent.

(d)   Calculating the liabilities

The scheme actuary calculates the value of the liabilities for the purposes of *PA 1995, s 73*. For schemes that commenced winding up before 1 December 2008, guidance on the calculation of the scheme liabilities is provided in Actuarial Guidance Note GN19. In such cases, the actuary must certify that the calculation made of the liabilities is made in accordance with GN19.

GN19 has been withdrawn for winding ups commencing on or after 1 December 2008. The technical detail to enable the scheme actuary to calculate the value of the liabilities is contained on the *Winding Up Regulations*.

Powers for trustees to make adjustments

12.21   *PA 1995, ss 73A* and *73B* confirm that, during the winding up period, no benefits may accrue to or in respect of members under the scheme rules and no new members can be admitted to the scheme. The benefits to be secured are those that apply on the crystallisation date. However, the *Winding Up Regulations 2005* permit the trustees to make adjustments to certain scheme liabilities in limited circumstances. These powers are intended to prevent the amount of the scheme's liabilities being increased after the date on which the winding up starts. This is consistent with the PPF rules in *PA 2004*.

(a)   Early leavers

Members of the scheme who have completed more than three months' pensionable service but less than two years' pensionable service at the time that the scheme starts to wind up, are deemed to have chosen the contribution refund option on the day that winding up commenced (*PA 1995, s 73(9)*; *Winding Up Regulations 2005, reg 5*). The trustees must therefore provide benefits for them on this basis.

(b)   Discretionary awards

If someone has exercised a power under the scheme rules to pay a discretionary award to a member in the winding up period, the trustees can reduce the member's benefits if the effect of the discretionary award is to increase the scheme's liabilities. The adjustment will ensure that the total benefits for that member do not exceed the amount of their benefits immediately before the day that winding up commenced (*PA 1995, s 73A(7), (8)*; *Winding Up Regulations 2005, reg 6*). If the date of winding up is backdated because an assessment period has been triggered and a withdrawal notice given, the adjustment takes effect from the date that the award takes effect, rather than the date on which winding up is treated as having started.

Where a discretionary award takes effect during the winding up period, the trustees must provide the affected member with a notice in writing within one month explaining that the trustees may make an adjustment to the award at a future date.

(c)   Survivors' benefits

If a member dies during the winding up period and a survivor's pension comes into payment, the trustees can reduce the survivor's benefits if the effect of the payment is to increase the scheme's liabilities. The adjustment will ensure that the total benefits payable in respect of the member do not exceed the amount of the member's benefits immediately before the day that winding up commenced (*PA 1995, s 73A(7), (8)*; *Winding Up Regulations 2005, reg 7*). If the date of winding up is backdated because an assessment period has been triggered and a withdrawal notice given, the adjustment takes effect from the date that the entitlement to benefits arises, rather than the date on which winding up is treated as having started.

Where the entitlement to a survivor's benefit arises during the winding up period, the trustees must provide the affected beneficiary a notice in writing within one month explaining that the trustees may make an adjustment to the benefits at a future date.

(d)   Death benefits

Where a member dies before winding up commenced but the trustees do not confirm a beneficiary's entitlement to death benefits until after the start of the winding up, those benefits will be treated as having arisen before the commencement of winding up (*PA 1995, s 73B(8)*; *Winding Up Regulations 2005, reg 8*). This means that the lump sum and any pension instalments payable before the commencement of winding up will be excluded from the scheme liabilities for the purposes of the winding up provisions in *PA 1995, s 73 (PA 1995, s 73B(6))*.

(e)   Benefits discharged during an assessment period

The PPF rules in *PA 2004, Part 2* allow certain liabilities to be validly secured during an assessment period. Where this happens those liabilities will be excluded from the scheme liabilities for the purposes of the winding up provisions in *PA 1995, s 73 (PA 1995, s 73B(6)*; *Winding Up Regulations 2005, reg 10*).

Powers for trustees to secure benefits in tranches

12.22   The scheme rules may contain a power enabling the trustees to secure members benefits on winding up in two or more tranches. Even where the scheme rules do not contain such a power, case law demonstrates that the courts may be prepared to imply a partial discharge power in certain circumstances.

In the case of *Sarjeant & Ors v Rigid Group Limited* [2013] EWCA Civ 1174, the Court of Appeal gave a very flexible and broad interpretation of the trustees' power to secure benefits on winding up. The case involved two schemes and the rules of both allowed the trustees to secure the scheme liabilities by purchasing annuities which were 'as nearly as practicable the same' as the benefits under the schemes. There was, however, no express power to discharge the liabilities in two or more tranches.

The Court of Appeal held that the trustees' core duty was to wind up the schemes by purchasing annuities which were as near as practicable to the beneficiaries' entitlements under the schemes. If by carrying out that duty in two or three stages the trustees are able to increase the assets available to secure members' benefits, then the Court of Appeal considered that this was consistent with that duty. By implication, the trustees should be given maximum flexibility in carrying out their duty. Accordingly, the Court of Appeal held that unless the scheme rules restrict the trustees to a particular course of action, then terms should be implied which best enabled them to perform that duty. The trustees should still be discharged at the end of the initial buy out for the benefits secured by those annuities, even though the scheme rules did not expressly provide for a partial discharge.

Money purchase schemes

12.23   *PA 1995, ss 73, 73A, 73B* and *74* do not apply to money purchase schemes and they are not eligible for PPF protection. In normal circumstances, at retirement the trustees will have purchased for existing pensioners an annuity with their money purchase 'pot' and this will be transferred into the name of the member on winding up. Deferred members' 'pots' will then be applied to purchase an annuity or will be transferred to another approved arrangement. The issue of 'priorities' is therefore not strictly relevant. Assets and liabilities in respect of money purchase benefits are excluded from scheme assets and liabilities of mixed benefit schemes for the purposes of *PA 1995, s 73*. Typically, this will mean that additional voluntary contributions will fall outside the statutory priorities (*PA 1995, s 73(10)*).

A facility enabling the trustees to deduct winding up costs from members' defined contributions accounts prior to applying them for transfer/buy-out needs to be included in the scheme rules. Schemes where there is a defined benefits and defined contributions section should make it clear that defined contributions assets cannot be used to subsidise a deficiency in the defined benefits section. By the same token, defined contributions members may not necessarily expect to share in a defined benefits surplus.

The decision of the Supreme Court in *Houldsworth v Bridge Trustees and Secretary of State for Work and Pensions [2011] UKSC 42* on 19 July 2011 shed doubt on where the dividing line lies between money purchase and other occupational pension schemes. The key finding of the Supreme Court was that there is no absolute requirement that the assets must always equal the liabilities in order for a scheme to be a 'money purchase scheme'. This went against the interpretation previously understood by the DWP. Following the judgment, the DWP issued an announcement confirming its view that the judgment will result in schemes which may previously have thought they were not 'money purchase schemes' falling within the definition, placing them outside the scope of legislation protecting members including that governing scheme funding, employer debt and the PPF. In the view of the DWP, it also introduced uncertainty about how the trustees of some schemes should distribute assets on winding up.

As a result, the Government amended the definition of 'money purchase benefits' in *PSA 1993 (PA 2011, s 29)*. The effect of the change is that in order for a benefit to qualify as a 'money purchase benefit', the amount or rate of the benefit must be calculated only by reference to assets which must necessarily suffice to provide the benefit. If any other factor such as a guaranteed investment return or other guarantee of the amount is used to calculate the benefit, it is not a money purchase benefit. The aim is to ensure that only benefits which cannot develop a deficit in funding can be money purchase benefits. The changes to the definition came into force on 24 July 2014 with retrospective effect to 1 January 1997. This is to ensure that, broadly, all schemes that have wound up since *PA 1995* came into effect can be treated fairly and consistently.

Transitional provisions mean that, for most schemes commencing winding up before 24 July 2014, trustees will not be required to revisit the past where action was taken in good faith and in accordance with existing legislation at the relevant time.

Under the *Pensions Act 2011 (Transitional, Consequential and Supplementary Provisions) Regulations 2014 (SI 2014/1711)* and the *Pensions Act 2011 (Consequential and Supplementary Provisions) Regulations 2014 (SI 2014/1945)* (together, the *'Transitional Money Purchase Regulations'*), the impact of the new definition on schemes winding up will broadly depend upon (i) when the winding up commenced, (ii) the type of benefits provided for under the scheme and (iii) how the trustees treated the benefits at the relevant time.

Key to this is the use of the definition 'cash balance benefit' in *PA 1995, s 51ZB* (as introduced by *PA 2011*) and the *Transitional Money Purchase Regulations*. 'Cash balance benefits' are defined as being a benefit where Conditions 1 and 2 are met:

Condition 1 is that a sum of money ('the available sum') is available under the scheme for the provision of the benefit to or in respect of the member.

Condition 2 is that under the scheme—

(*a*)   there is a promise about the amount of the available sum, but

(*b*)   there is no promise about the rate or amount of the pension to be provided from the available sum.

The *Transitional Money Purchase Regulations* broadly protect decisions made before 24 July 2014 in relation to cash balance benefits (including scheme pensions secured with cash balance or money purchase benefits) and underpin or top-up benefits.

The general implications of the *Transitional Money Purchase Regulations* on schemes which provide cash balance benefits or scheme pensions derived from cash balance or money purchase benefits (referred to below as 'non-money purchase benefits) and are in winding up can be summarised as follows:

Applicable circumstances	Impact of Money Purchase Regulations
Scheme commenced winding up before 6 April 2005 and the trustees have proceeded on the basis that the scheme was a money purchase scheme (so *PA 1995, s 73* did not apply)	Scheme continues to be excluded from *PA 1995, s 73* (*reg 11*)
Scheme commenced winding up before 6 April 2005 and the trustees have proceeded on the basis that non-money purchase benefits were money purchase benefits	The assets and liabilities relating to those benefits will be excluded from *PA 1995, s 73* (*reg 12*)
Scheme commenced winding up on or after 6 April 2005 but before 24 July 2014 and the trustees have proceeded on the basis that the scheme was a money purchase scheme (so *PA 1995, s 73* did not apply)	Scheme continues to be excluded from *PA 1995, s 73* (*reg 13*)
Scheme commenced winding up on or after 6 April 2005 but before July 2014 and includes non-money purchase benefits which the trustees have treated as money purchase benefits	The assets and liabilities relating to those benefits will be excluded from *PA 1995, s 73* (*reg 14*)
PPF assessment period commenced before 24 July 2014 but the scheme does not then transfer to the PPF and immediately before the start of the PPF assessment period the trustees were treating non-money purchase benefits as money purchase benefits.	Trustees are entitled to treat these benefits as money purchase benefits for the purposes of winding up (*reg 15*)

Trustee protection

Section 27 of the Trustee Act 1925

12.24   As part of the process of obtaining statutory discharge under *PA 1995, s 74*, the trustees need to be satisfied that they have identified all the relevant members of the scheme both past and present who could have a potential claim to benefits in the future.

A 'section 27 notice' is a mechanism under *Trustee Act 1925, s 27* by which the trustees can protect themselves from further claims after completion of the winding up by unknown beneficiaries. Trustees seeking to rely on *s 27* must advertise in both the *London Gazette* and a newspaper local to the scheme, giving notice that they intend to distribute trust property and requiring people having an interest to make a claim within a specified period (of at least two months). After this, the trustees are not liable to anyone of whom they did not have notice. However, as seen in the case of *AON Pension Trustees Ltd v MCP Pension Trustees Ltd [2010] EWCA Civ 377*, liability will not be escaped if the trustees already had notice of beneficiaries, even if that was historical and the details have since been lost. This case highlights the value of obtaining missing beneficiaries insurance.

Indemnity insurance

12.25 Trust deeds and rules often contain protection for trustees so that they are indemnified as far as legally possibly from the scheme and/or the employer. Once the scheme has finally wound up, however, the underlying protection of the scheme assets is lost and trustees will need to find alternative means to ensure their personal position is protected.

Trustees often seek to negotiate an ongoing employer indemnity against future claims. The value of the indemnity will depend on the financial strength of the employer providing it and will be of little practical value if the employer were subsequently to dissolve. As a result, trustees will often seek to obtain 'run off' and 'missing beneficiary' insurance. Whilst it may be possible, subject to the provisions of the particular scheme's trust deed and rules, to obtain 'missing beneficiary' insurance from scheme assets, it is very unlikely (unless specifically authorised by the rules) that trustees could use scheme assets to purchase 'run off' cover for their own protection, as this would have no benefit for the scheme's beneficiaries. It would, therefore, be down to the trustees to negotiate purchase of this cover by the employer (assuming it is still solvent) on their behalf. This was considered in some detail in the case of *NBPF Pension Trustees Ltd. v Warnock-Smith & Anor [2008] EWHC 455 (Ch)*.

Member tracing

12.26 The protection afforded by 'section 27 notices' and the availability of run off and/or missing beneficiary insurance should not be seen by trustees as an alternative to taking all reasonable and proportionate steps to trace those members with benefits under the scheme, both past and present, when winding up an occupational pension scheme. The Regulator lists the following as the most common tracing tools and methods available to trustees:

(*a*) consulting the wider membership and former employer/ trustee if appropriate, asking if they can help trace members;

(*b*) advertising in appropriate local and national newspapers – for example, using local press around former employer locations;

(*c*) use of the National Fraud Initiative;

(*d*) use of a professional tracing agency;

(*e*) use of online directory enquiries for example, attempting a trace using 192.com; and

(*f*) use of social networking sites.

For a small fee, the DWP will also forward, where this is possible, any communication from a pension scheme that is addressed to an untraceable individual based on its National Insurance records. The DWP, however, expects trustees to have made every effort to have traced the individual(s) before the service is used.

Sanctions against trustees under *PA 1995*

12.27 Trustees who disregard the provisions of *PA 1995* as summarised in this Chapter may be subject to prohibition orders and civil penalties. Further details appear in the table set out in **Appendix I.**

Chapter 13

Amendments and scheme redesign

Introduction

General

13.1   In this chapter the word 'redesign' is used to denote some significant change in the nature or structure of an employer's pension arrangements. Such a redesign will typically involve:

(*a*)   a scheme amendment;

(*b*)   a bulk transfer of assets and liabilities between different schemes operated by the same employer (or by employers within the same group);

(*c*)   a scheme merger and/or

(*d*)   the buy-out of all or part of the benefits.

Amendments

13.2   Examples of scheme amendments which are significant enough to be regarded for the purposes of this chapter as redesigns include:

(*a*)   converting a defined benefit scheme into a defined contribution scheme;

(*b*)   closing a scheme to future entrants;

(*c*)   amending a scheme so that no further benefits accrue under it; or

(*d*)   amending a scheme as part of a wider exercise, to enable the parties to make bulk transfer payments to other schemes (see **13.3** below) and/or wind up the scheme.

Scheme amendments are dealt with further in **13.7–13.30** below and winding up in **Chapter 12**.

Bulk transfers and scheme mergers

13.3   Bulk transfers of assets and liabilities between schemes operating within the same group of employers have become increasingly common in recent years. Typical cases include:

(*a*)   bulk transfers from a defined benefit scheme to a defined contribution arrangement; or

(*b*)   bulk transfers between defined benefit schemes operating within the same group of employers, to replace two or more defined benefit schemes with a single, larger defined benefit scheme (often referred to as a scheme merger). Some of the advantages of having a single, larger scheme are that:

(i)   it avoids the inefficiency for employers of operating some overfunded schemes and some underfunded schemes;

(ii)   administrative costs for a single scheme should be lower owing to economies of scale;

(iii)   a single, larger fund may justify the trustees in pursuing some investment opportunities which might be considered too risky in relation to a smaller fund; and

(iv)   the overall time and resources which need to be spent on compliance with statutory requirements are reduced, as there will be only one scheme (rather than several) in relation to which these requirements need to be met.

Bulk transfers and scheme mergers are considered further in **13.31–13.54** below.

Key considerations

Powers

13.4   The trustees and the employers need to be certain that they have the necessary powers to carry out any proposed redesign. If, for example, the trustees were to accept a bulk transfer from another scheme in circumstances where they had no power under their trust deed to do so, they could subsequently be challenged by the members and held liable for resulting losses even though the trustees had at the time taken all available steps to ensure that the arrangement was in the members' best interests.

The question of whether the parties have the necessary powers will be determined primarily by the scheme's trust deed and rules. For instance, if it is intended to amend a scheme, the governing documentation should be checked to ensure that it does not impose restrictions on the power of amendment which the proposed alteration would infringe.

The *Pensions Act 1995* (*PA 1995*) and the *Pensions Act 2004* (*PA 2004*) have a further bearing on whether the parties have the necessary powers. The effect of the legislation in some areas is to restrict the exercise of certain powers which a scheme's rules (when read in isolation) appear to confer, and in other areas the effect is to give wider powers to the trustees. For instance:

(*a*)   *PA 1995, s 67* (as modified by *PA 2004, s 262*) places certain restrictions on the exercise of the power of amendment (see further **13.17** below); and

(*b*)   where a registered defined benefit scheme begins to be wound up after 5 April 1997, any power in the trust deed to apply the assets in respect of pensions or other benefits becomes exercisable by the trustees (even if the trust deed confers that power on another party, such as the employer) (*PA 1995, s 73A(9)*; and before 6 April 2005, *PA 1995, s 73(5)*).

It is not sufficient, however, for the employers and the trustees simply to have the necessary powers to carry out the redesign; they must ensure that in exercising those powers they act in a manner consistent with their duties as employers (see **13.5**) and trustees (see **13.6**) respectively.

Employers' duties

13.5   Many scheme redesigns are initiated by employers, often prompted by funding concerns. An employer should ensure that its proposals do not contravene its contractual commitments towards its employees in relation to pensions. These commitments will be set out primarily in employees' written terms and conditions of employment (although references to pensions in such documents are usually brief). There will, in addition, be written announcements or booklets issued to the employees explaining the terms of the scheme. The position as regards the interaction of all the scheme documentation, particularly as to which prevails, has been the subject of many cases over the years and, despite the Court of Appeal's ruling in *Steria Limited v Hutchison [2006] EWCA Civ 1551*, the matter may be far from settled for good. This is considered in more detail in **Chapter 7**.

Employers are also under an implied contractual duty of good faith (*Imperial Group Pension Trust Ltd v Imperial Tobacco Ltd [1991] 2 All ER 597*). The nature of this duty is that both employers and employees are obliged to act in a manner which is consistent with a relationship of mutual trust and confidence between them. Failure to do so can amount to a breach of contract.

This implied duty of good faith (unlike the more onerous duties placed on trustees) does not require the employer to act solely in the best interests of those to whom the duty is owed; an employer is also entitled to take its own commercial interests into account. One example is *Prudential Staff Pensions v Prudential Assurance [2011] EWHC 960*, where the court held that the employer had not breached the duty of good faith when it began to award discretionary pension increases on a less generous basis than previously. The scheme's funding position had worsened; the discretion was not subject to any express restrictions; members understood that Prudential had not guaranteed the award of pension increases; and 'Prudential was entitled to have regard to its own interests when deciding on increases'.

In *IBM United Kingdom Holdings v Dalgeish [2014] EWHC 980 (Ch)*, the court found that changes to the pension scheme rules amounted to a breach of the employer's duty of trust and confidence to members because they were contrary to reasonable expectations engendered in the members by the employer and, in those circumstances, the existence of a commercial objective was insufficient to justify changes.

It is not possible to give a definitive statement as to what would and would not amount to a breach of that duty. However, the following instances, which can be expected to amount to a breach of the duty of good faith, may be useful as guidelines:

(a)   a refusal by the employer even to consider (as opposed to considering and then rejecting) alternative proposals put forward by the trustees;

(b)   putting forward proposals which discriminate between employees (or groups of employees) without justification;

(c)   threatening to suspend contributions unless the trustees agree to the proposals (*Hillsdown Holdings plc v Pensions Ombudsman [1996] PLR 427*);

(d)   threatening never to grant further pension increases unless the parties agree to the proposals (*Imperial Group Pension Trust Ltd v Imperial Tobacco Ltd [1991] 2 All ER 597*); or

(e)   closing to future accrual and altering the operation of the employer's early retirement policy in breach of member's reasonable expectations which expectations the employer had engendered through its own past actions (*IBM United Kingdom Holdings v Dalgeish [2014] EWHC 980 (Ch)*.

Chapter 7 considers the duty of good faith in further detail.

Trustees' duties

13.6 Trustees' powers are of a fiduciary nature, which means that they must exercise them in the best interests of the persons for whose benefit those powers were conferred. In most cases, this will be the scheme's present and past members (and any of their family or dependants who may have an interest in the scheme as a consequence of their membership).

Trustees may also owe a duty towards the employer when exercising certain of their powers. For instance, if the scheme rules give the trustees the discretion to pay surplus assets to the employer on winding up, they must at least take the employer's interest into account. However, their duties towards scheme members are undoubtedly more onerous than an employer's duty of good faith towards its employees (described in **13.5** above).

This mismatch between the trustees' duties and those of the employer can give rise to a potential conflict of interests between the two sides and trustees should, therefore, seek separate advice wherever such a conflict exists. In the absence of separate advice, trustees may find themselves vulnerable to criticism if their decisions are subsequently called into question by scheme members; even if the trustees have acted entirely in their beneficiaries' best interests, it may be harder to convince the Pensions Ombudsman (or a court) of this if independent advice has not been obtained. In recent years, the Regulator has put particular focus on the appropriate treatment of conflicts of interest, and both trustees and employers should ensure they are aware of the Regulator's guidance on the subject and deal with situations that may potentially arise having regard to such guidance. Directors of corporate trustees must also comply with the provisions of *Companies Act 2006* on avoiding actual and potential conflicts between with the interests of the employer and the corporate trustee. For more on conflicts of interest, see **Chapter 3**.

Conflicts can arise not only as between employers and trustees but also as between the trustees of separate schemes. This may happen where a bulk transfer of assets and liabilities from one scheme to another is under consideration as part of a scheme merger, as the trustees of the two schemes will owe their duties to different groups of beneficiaries. Where there is a conflict, separate advice should be sought.

Amendments

General

13.7 Scheme redesigns very often involve amending a scheme, either because the redesign itself takes the form of a fundamental change to the scheme's rules, or because an amendment is required to enable the employers or the trustees to make (or receive) a bulk transfer and/or wind up the scheme.

The main ways in which an occupational pension scheme may be amended are:

(*a*)   in accordance with a power of amendment contained in the scheme's trust documents;

(*b*)   by a court order;

(*c*)   by means of a modification order granted by the Regulator; or

(*d*)   by a trustees' resolution passed under a specific provision in *PA 1995* or *PA 2004.*

The first of these methods is by far the most common, but it is worth summarising the others before considering the scheme's own power of amendment in more detail. In recent years a practice has developed whereby members' pension rights are modified by the employer using extrinsic contracts. This is considered at **13.30** below.

Court order

13.8   A court order to vary the terms of a trust may be available in the following limited circumstances:

(*a*)   On application by the trustees (or, less likely, a beneficiary) under *Trustee Act 1925, s 57.* The basis for any such application must be that the trustees do not have the necessary investment or administrative powers which they need to deal in some particular way with the trust property. The court will need to be convinced that the proposed transaction is expedient.

(*b*)   On application to the court under the *Variation of Trusts Act 1958.* This Act (which is not normally used in relation to pension schemes) enables the court to approve amendments on behalf of beneficiaries.

(*c*)   Under the court's inherent jurisdiction to vary trusts. The court will generally only exercise this jurisdiction in circumstances where some matter concerning the scheme has in any event come before the court.

Modification orders

13.9   The Regulator has powers under *PA 1995, ss 69–71* to grant orders for the modification of occupational schemes (other than public service schemes) in certain circumstances.

13.9 *Amendments and scheme redesign*

There are two purposes for which the Regulator may grant an order in this context (*PA 1995, s 69*), as illustrated in the following table:

	Who may apply for order	Orders which may be granted
Where the purpose, in the case of a registered scheme which is being wound up, is to enable assets remaining after the liabilities have been fully discharged to be distributed to the employer (and all other relevant requirements for that distribution have been met).	The trustees.	• Order authorising the trustees to modify the scheme; or • Order modifying the scheme.
Where the purpose is to enable the scheme, for the period from 6 April 1997 to 5 April 1999, to be so treated that an employment to which it applies may be contracted out (see **Chapter 4**).	The trustees, the employer or any person other than the trustees who has power to alter the rules of the scheme.	• Order authorising such persons (not restricted to parties to the application) as the Regulator thinks appropriate to modify the scheme; or • Order modifying the scheme.

One such order was made in May 2010 in respect of the *Liberal Headquarters 1924 Pension Fund*. The scheme's last member died in 1968 and no further potential beneficiaries had been identified, leaving a question mark over how to deal with the remaining assets (there being no power in the scheme's rules to pay any surplus to the principal employer, the Liberal Democrat party). The Regulator authorised the modification of the rules to allow the surplus to be refunded to the employer and ordered the scheme to go into immediate wind-up.

The Regulator may make such an order only if it is satisfied that the desired result cannot be achieved without one or can only be achieved in accordance with a procedure which is liable to be unduly complex or protracted (or involves the obtaining of consents which cannot be obtained without undue delay or difficulty) (*PA 1995, s 70*).

There is provision for such a modification to be retrospective. The modification order may be made or complied with even if the scheme rules or other legal requirements would otherwise prevent it (*PA 1995, s 71*).

Where an occupational scheme (other than a public service scheme or other prescribed type of scheme) is being wound up with an insolvent employer, the Regulator has powers under *PA 1995, s 71A* to grant the trustees an order modifying the scheme, with a view to ensuring that it is properly wound up. The order must be limited to what the Regulator considers to be the minimum modification necessary for that purpose; and the modification must not have a significant adverse effect on accrued rights or entitlements.

Where an application is made to the Regulator under *PA 1995, s 71A* and *Regulation 8* of the *Occupational Pension Schemes (Winding-up Notices and Reports etc) Regulations 2002 (SI 2002/459)*, it must:

(*a*)   set out the modification required and specify what effects (if any) it may have on benefits;

(*b*)   specify the reason for the modification;

(*c*)   identify any previous application for a modification order made to a court or to the Regulator;

(*d*)   confirm that the employer is subject to an insolvency procedure;

(*e*)   specify whether the modification order will reduce the value of the assets; and

(*f*)   contain a statement that notices have been given to members of the scheme and any other relevant persons together with the relevant date(s) on which notice was given.

A member of the scheme or other recipient of a notice has the right to make a representation to the Regulator within one month of any notice to make representations about the modification. Before the Regulator considers any application for a modification order it must consider any such representations, and it will require:

(i)   a copy of the documents which govern the scheme;

(ii)   a copy of any actuarial advice on the effect or otherwise of the modification order on the scheme's assets or on benefits;

(iii)   a copy of any legal advice in relation to the application for a modification order;

(iv)   a copy of any court determination in relation to the application for a modification order or any similar order; and

(v)   a copy of any determination by trustees or managers to wind up the scheme.

Trustees' statutory power to modify

13.10   Subject to limited exceptions (primarily public service schemes), trustees have power under *PA 1995, s 68* to modify a scheme by resolution with a view to achieving any of the following purposes:

(*a*)   (subject to the consent of the employer) to extend the class of persons who may receive benefits in respect of the death of a member;

(*b*)   to enable the scheme to conform with arrangements required by *PA 2004* in respect of the appointment of member-nominated trustees or member-nominated directors (see **Chapter 3**);

(*c*)   to enable the scheme to comply with requirements imposed by the Pension Protection Fund in relation to payments to be made by that body; or

(*d*)   to enable the scheme to conform with certain other specified provisions of *PA 1995, PA 2004* and other prescribed provisions.

The *Occupational Pension Schemes (Modification of Schemes) Regulations 2006 (SI 2006/759)* prescribe additional purposes for which trustees have the power to modify schemes under *PA 1995, s 68*. These include taking into account the provisions of *FA 2004*, adopting provisions relating to survivors' benefits for civil partners and same-sex marriages, and removing or amending scheme rules which have become obsolete as a result of the abolition of protected rights (see **Chapter 4**).

Alongside these provisions, sections within other acts and regulations may also enable trustees to modify a scheme by resolution for specific purposes. For example, *s 68* of the *Equality Act 2010* enables trustees to alter a scheme in line with sex equality requirements in *s 67* of that Act (see **Chapter 9**).

Scheme's own power of amendment – general

Need for power

13.11   An occupational pension scheme may well continue in operation for several decades. During that time, it will almost certainly need to be adapted to cater for circumstances which could not reasonably have been predicted at the outset. For this reason, it is essential that the documents governing the scheme contain a power of amendment.

If no amendment power is included in an interim deed, it may still be possible to adopt a suitable power in the scheme's definitive deed, to take effect retrospectively from the date of the interim deed (*Re Imperial Foods Ltd Pension Scheme [1986] 2 All ER 802*).

The consequences of omitting the power from the definitive deed will be more serious and render it unlikely that a power of amendment can validly be inserted into the documents at a future date. It may still be possible subsequently to adopt a power of amendment, if it can clearly be shown that it had always been intended to include the power but that it was omitted by mistake; however, this would involve a court application.

Exercise of power

13.12   The exercise of any power of amendment must be carried out by the persons, and in accordance with any requirements, specified in the provision conferring that power. The vast majority of amendment powers require some involvement by both the principal employer and the trustees before the scheme may be amended.

To the extent that an employer is involved in the exercise of the power, it must act in accordance with its implied duty of good faith towards its employees (see **13.5** above). In the rare cases where an employer has power to amend without requiring the agreement of the trustees, the courts can be expected to scrutinise the exercise of that power particularly strictly.

The trustees' duties are more onerous, as mentioned in **13.6** above. Some examples of the sorts of amendments which trustees may and may not properly agree to are considered in **13.22** to **13.29** below. At this point, however, it is enough to say that trustees must not, as a matter of trust law, agree to amendments which reduce benefits earned before the amendment power is exercised (whether or not immediately payable).

Whoever exercises the power of amendment must do so for the purpose for which it was conferred, namely (unless the trust deed indicates otherwise) to promote the purposes of the scheme. Any statement in the trust deed as to the scheme's main purpose may therefore be relevant to the validity of a subsequent amendment. Thus in *Dalriada Trustees Ltd v Faulds [2011] EWHC 3391* a purported amendment to allow for an arrangement of loans between unconnected schemes and members in order to give members early access to their pension savings was held to be invalid as an attempt to alter the main purpose of the scheme as a registered pension scheme.

However, the purpose of the scheme need not remain fixed indefinitely, and it has been recognised that a scheme's underlying purpose may change gradually as a scheme evolves over a period of time (*Re Courage Group's Pension Schemes [1987] 1 WLR 495*).

The *Courage* case itself provides an example of scheme amendments which were successfully challenged in court as not promoting the schemes' purposes.

There were three schemes involved, whose principal employer had recently been acquired by a new owner. The aim of the amendments was to enable the new owner (who had no genuine relationship with the members and was already negotiating to sell the existing principal employer) to be substituted as the schemes' new principal employer, and so gain some benefit from the schemes' surplus funds. This conflicted with the purpose for which the schemes had been established, which was the provision of retirement benefits. The judge specifically commented upon the fact that the new owner was not recognisably the successor to the business or workforce of the company for which it was intended to be substituted.

The case of *Harwood-Smart v Caws [2000] PLR 101* arose following the compulsory liquidation of the employer. The trustees asked the court to determine whether they had to use any surplus to increase benefits prior to making any repayment to the employers. The court found in favour of the beneficiaries rather than the employers. The original trust provisions on winding up had required any surplus to be used to enhance benefits prior to making any payment to the employers. The power of amendment contained a specific prohibition on paying any part of the fund back to the employers. However, the power of amendment had itself been subsequently altered and been used to amend the winding-up provisions to permit refunds to be paid to the employers without increasing members' benefits in excess of their entitlement. The court found that this power of amendment was invalid.

In *Bestrustees v Stuart [2001] PLR 283*, the BAI pension scheme amended its normal retirement age to 65 for all members following the case of *Barber v GRE [1990] 2 All ER 660* in 1990. This case concerned ambiguity in how and when the decision was made to amend the rules to effect equalisation. As the employer was also the trustee, the issue of consent by the other party did not arise. The amendment to the rules was found to be of limited effect.

In *Sovereign Trustees Ltd v Glover [2007] EWHC 1750 (Ch)*, the High Court emphasised the need to comply with the formalities in the scheme's power of amendment in order for amendments to be valid. The trust deed and rules included specific provisions regarding amendment. Following a review of the scheme by benefit consultants on the principal employer's instructions, the trustees wrote to all active members to inform them that the company was introducing changes to the scheme: from 1 April 1998, future service benefits would be provided on a money purchase basis. From that date, contributions and benefits were paid on the basis that the scheme had been amended. Two of the three trustees had passed a resolution that 'the Company's proposals be accepted in full'. The question for the court was whether the money purchase section of the scheme had been validly created. The court ruled that the resolution was not effective to amend the scheme; it merely recorded the adoption of a policy for implementation later by amendments made in accordance with the rules. Accordingly, the money purchase section of the scheme had not been validly created.

The outcome of this case is not surprising, but it reinforces the need to ensure that amendments are made in accordance with the scheme's power of amendment and that when resolutions are passed it is clear to all concerned precisely what the scope of that resolution is. Further, where employer consent is required to an amendment, that requirement is not satisfied merely by fact that the amendment was originally proposed by that employer.

In *Walker Morris Trustees Ltd v Masterson and another [2009] EWHC 1955 (Ch)* the trustees' failure to take actuarial advice, as required by the amendment rule, led to amendments made since 1974 being declared invalid. The power of amendment allowed the trustees, with the consent of the principal employer, to amend the definitive deed by deed and to amend the rules by deed or resolution. It also required a written opinion from the actuary that members' rights 'secured in terms of the Scheme prior to the [effective date of the amendment]' would not be substantially prejudiced. The main issue was that there was no evidence that the actuary's written opinion had been sought for any of the amendments.

The first question was whether the amendment rule required the trustees to seek the opinion of the actuary even in cases where there could not possibly be any prejudice to members' benefits. The judge looked at a number of cases on the interpretation of pension schemes. He found that the clause was clear and it did require the trustees to seek the opinion of the actuary in all cases. He accepted that this gave an unfortunate result but it did not arise out of an overly literal or technical interpretation of the deed, but rather from the trustees having ignored the clear provision. The consequence of this is that none of the amending deeds was valid.

The court went on to consider whether those amendments which were supported by a *s 67* certificate (see **13.17** below) could stand (on the basis that the actuary had been involved). It was held that *s 67* certificates are designed for a different purpose and could not be used to save the proposed amendments.

In *Capita ATL Pension Trustees v Gellately (Sea Containers) [2011] EWHC 485* the court held that failure to comply with the formal requirements of the power of amendment rendered the purported amendment invalid. Here again it was the requirement to amend a scheme by deed which was not satisfied. In consequence men's and women's normal retirement ages remained unequalised (the '*Barber* window' remained open: see **Chapter 9**).

More recently the courts have taken a slightly more flexible and purposive approach. In *HR Trustees v Wembley [2011] EWHC 2974* (Ch) the High Court held that non-compliance with the formal requirements of an amendment power was not fatal to the amendment. Here the requirement was for all the trustees to declare the amendment in writing under their hands, but only four out of the five trustees had done so. The court found, on the facts, that the fifth trustee, who had not been present at the relevant meeting, would have signed the declaration. It applied the equitable maxim that 'equity regards as done that which ought to be done' to cure the administrative error. Similarly, in *Premier Foods Group v RHM Pension Trust [2012] EWHC 447 (Ch)* the High Court held that a deed of intention to amend a scheme was effective as though it were the formal deed of amendment which the power of amendment required. It said that, in choosing between an interpretation which makes the instrument valid and effective and one which makes it invalid or ineffective, the court should lean towards the construction which saves the instrument.

The court took a different approach in the case of *Honda Motor Europe v Powell [2014] EWCA Civ 437* where the employer's application for permission to rely on the maxim 'equity regards as done that which ought to have been done' was refused. This case was an appeal from a High Court decision refusing the request by the employer that a deed of adherence should be construed to operate as amending the Scheme from the date of adherence so as to apply a lower scale of benefits to the employees then admitted to the Scheme. The court found that as the wording of the deed of adherence was clear and did not include the new lower benefit scale, despite the underlying agreement to provide lower benefits, the background and context were not relevant to the interpretation of the deed and its strict wording was to be applied.

More recently in *Bett Homes Ltd v Wood [2016] CSIH 26*, the Inner House of the Court of Session in Scotland took a more relaxed approach and found that use of a 'special terms' power had resulted in the valid amendment of the pensions increases provision despite the lack of detailed formal documentation. However, the court did not uphold an amendment relating to equalisation and found that the mere fact that the trustees administered the scheme on the equalised basis was not sufficient to infer that the trustees had given their consent to the change. The Scottish courts also took a more relaxed approach in the case of the *Scottish Solicitors Staff Pension Fund v Pattison & Sim [2015] CSIH 96*. In contrast to the more stringent approach that has tended to be demonstrated by the English courts, the judge warned against following an 'unduly technical or restrictive' approach towards amendment of Scottish pension schemes. In this case the trustees were unable to demonstrate full compliance with the amendment procedures on every occasion although they stated that they had followed proper procedure. The judge was satisfied that, as the amendments were so historic, there was a general presumption under Scottish law that all necessary procedures had been properly followed and the burden was on the challenger to prove that proper procedures had not been followed (which they were unable to do). The court upheld the validity of the amendments.

Despite this recent trend, however, it is arguable that these cases turn on their particular facts and might have been decided differently in even slightly different circumstances. Amending schemes in accordance with the formalities required in the power of amendment remains the proper and safest approach.

As a separate matter, parties to deeds must also ensure that the relevant execution formalities are followed. The decision of the High Court in *Gleeds Retirement Benefits Scheme [2014] EWHC 1178 (Ch)* concerned the serious consequences of the failure to follow the correct formalities for the execution of deeds. The court found that on account of partners' signatures not being witnessed, none of the deeds entered into in the period 1990 to 2012 were validly executed by the employer and were therefore ineffective, resulting in a multi-million pound cost to the scheme.

Effect of winding up

13.13   It is unlikely that a power of amendment can be exercised once winding up has started, unless the terms of that power and the other provisions of the scheme rules indicate a contrary intention (*Thrells v Lomas [1992] PLR 233*). However, a power of amendment can probably be exercised (unless the scheme rules indicate otherwise), after an employer has given notice to wind up a scheme, but before that notice has expired (*Municipal Mutual v Harrop [1998] PLR 149*).

Many trust deeds include wording to the effect that the trusts of the scheme will cease once winding up begins, and this can be taken to include any amendment power. Others include a provision to the effect that amendments may be made during the winding-up stage, in which case the power will continue to be exercisable.

If a scheme's winding-up rule has not been triggered, but the scheme has become closed to new entrants or benefits have ceased to accrue, the power of amendment remains exercisable unless the scheme rules suggest that it does not.

Retrospective amendments

13.14   A power of amendment may be worded so as to permit scheme amendments to take effect from a date earlier than the date on which they are made. Retrospective amendments may validly be made under such a power, although the requirements of *PA 1995, s 67* (as amended by *PA 2004, s 262*) will usually apply (see **13.17** below).

If the power of amendment does not expressly allow retrospective alterations, the position is less certain. In reality, a court's decision on the validity of a purportedly retrospective amendment in these circumstances may depend on the nature of the change. A retrospective amendment made simply to ensure compliance with some statutory requirement would probably be upheld; a more controversial alteration might not.

Not surprisingly, therefore, the judge in *Municipal Mutual v Harrop [1998] PLR 149* disallowed a retrospective amendment which would have taken away vested rights. He also decided that the amendment could not be upheld on the grounds that its purpose was to correct an error in the scheme rules.

In *Bank of New Zealand v Bank of New Zealand Officers Provident Fund [2003] 53 PBLR*, it was confirmed that there is a presumption against retrospective amendments unless the substance of what is proposed is within the power of amendment, in which case back-dating will not automatically invalidate the amendment. However, if retrospective amendments attempt to make an action valid that is outside of the power of amendment, the principles of trust law and fairness will invalidate the amendment.

In *HR Trustees v German (IMG Pension Plan) [2009] EWHC 2785 (Ch)*, the court rejected an argument that a retrospective amendment (by a deed executed in March 1992 but purporting to take effect from the preceding January) to amend the scheme from a defined benefit to a defined contribution scheme must be upheld on the basis that everyone involved with the scheme had expected it to have retrospective effect. The amendment was held to be 'an attempt to re-write history', not a validly back-dated amendment.

The power to make retrospective amendments is therefore subject not only to a general rule of fairness, but will depend largely on the nature of the change. Based on the most recent case law, it would appear that the courts are now taking a stricter line on such amendments.

Restrictions

13.15   An amendment will not be valid if it infringes restrictions written into the amendment power under which it is made. Some of the more common restrictions found in amendment powers are as follows:

(*a*)   That no amendment may be made which would alter the main purpose of the scheme. This reflects the general law on scheme amendments (see **13.12** above).

(*b*)   That no amendment may be made which would result in surplus assets being returned to the employers. Such restrictions were built into some older trust deeds in order to comply with requirements of tax approval which no longer apply. *PA 1995* introduced provisions to overcome restrictions of this nature in certain circumstances (see **13.9** above).

(*c*)   That no amendment may reduce pensions in payment or accrued benefits. This adds nothing to existing trust law principles; the position is reinforced by *PA 1995* (see **13.17** below).

(*d*)   That amendments (or amendments of a certain nature) may be made only with the members' consent. Sometimes the members concerned are simply not contactable; *PA 1995* helps to relieve this problem.

Of course, an amendment will not be valid if it infringes overriding legislation.

Amending a power of amendment

13.16   The presence of unwanted restrictions in an amendment power raises the question of whether those restrictions can be removed by amending the power of amendment.

If the trust deed permits amendment of the amendment power, then this should be possible in certain circumstances. However, if the restriction being removed is one which can only serve to protect members' interests, the change would be difficult to justify.

If changes to the amendment power do not fall within the scope of the governing trust deed and rules, it will generally not be possible (without a court order or modification order) to remove restrictions which have been there since the scheme was established; widening the amendment power in this way would be like introducing an amendment power where none had previously existed. This general position was reinforced by *HR Trustees v German [2009] EWHC 2785 (Ch)*, which confirmed that: 'Trustees could not achieve by two steps what they could not achieve by one' (following Lord Millett in *Air Jamaica v Charlton [1999] 1 WLR 1399*). In other words, the trustees here could not first remove the restriction in the amendment power and then make the amendments to benefits which had previously been prohibited.

At the heart of the case law precluding the removal of restrictions from the amendment power (or otherwise in the governing trust documentation) is a concern to protect members' interests. However, where a change is made that is technically within the scope of the power of amendment and which does not prejudice members' interests (for example, provision allowing members to consent to the disapplication of a protective fetter), this does not seem inconsistent with the case law. In that situation, a member can prevent (or allow) an amendment, if he so wishes.

In addition, removing a restriction which did not exist at the scheme's inception but was introduced at a later date may present less of a problem. The nature of the restriction being removed, how it arose, and how long it has been in place are likely to be relevant.

It is not usual for the parties to wish to introduce restrictions where none previously existed. Were the trustees to do so, they might be in breach of the general trust law duty not to fetter their own discretion (although it is possible for that duty to be excluded by an express provision in the trust deed).

Statutory protection of entitlements and accrued rights

General

13.17   From 6 April 1997, under *PA 1995, s 67*, any power conferred by an occupational pension scheme (other than a public service pension scheme or a prescribed scheme or a scheme of a prescribed description) to modify the scheme could not be exercised 'in a manner which would or might affect any entitlement, or accrued right, of any member of the scheme acquired before the power is exercised' unless the statutory requirements were satisfied. *PA 2004, s 262* substituted, from 6 April 2006, new *PA 1995, ss 67–671* (collectively referred to for convenience as *s 67*, unless otherwise indicated). The legislation is supported by the Regulator's Code of Practice No 10 'Modification of subsisting rights' (the 'Code of Practice').

Under the original provisions of *s 67*, consideration had to be given to whether an amendment would or might affect accrued rights or entitlements. Under the revised *s 67*, the question is whether the power to modify is being used to make a 'regulated modification'. A regulated modification is either:

(*a*)   a protected modification; or

(*b*)   a detrimental modification,

or is both.

A protected modification is a modification which would or might result in the reduction of any pension in payment and/or a modification which involves converting defined benefit rights into money purchase rights.

A detrimental modification is a modification that would or might adversely affect the 'subsisting rights' of any member of the scheme or any survivor of a member of the scheme, ie (broadly) a member's accrued rights or entitlements or a survivor's entitlements or rights to future benefits.

Any exercise of a power to make a regulated modification is voidable unless certain conditions are satisfied, and the Regulator may make an order declaring that the modification is void to the extent specified in the order. These conditions are as follows:

(*a*)   In the case of each 'affected member' (this includes an affected survivor of a member), for protected modifications the consent requirement must be satisfied and for detrimental modifications either the consent requirement or the actuarial equivalence requirement must be satisfied (see further **13.18** and **13.19**).

(*b*)   In respect of all regulated modifications the trustee approval requirement and the reporting requirement must be satisfied.

(i)   *The trustee approval requirement*

Before the trustees can exercise the power to modify the scheme, if the modification is a protected modification, the informed consent requirement must be satisfied and, in the case of a modification which is not a protected modification, either the informed consent requirement or the information and actuarial value requirements must be satisfied (see **13.18** and **13.19**). The trustees must not exercise the modification power more than a reasonable period after the first affected member has given consent. The Code of Practice suggests that a 'reasonable period' should normally be no more than six months.

(ii)   *The trustee reporting requirement*

Where the consent requirement applies, trustees must notify affected members of the decision taken regarding the modification within a reasonable period of it being made, and before the modification takes effect. Where the actuarial equivalence requirement applies, they must take reasonable steps to notify them. The Code of Practice suggests that a 'reasonable period' to notify members would be within one month of the decision.

(*c*)   In summary there are three pre-conditions to make a regulated modification which are the consent or actuarial equivalence requirements, the trustee approval requirement and the reporting requirement.

The Regulator's 2010 order declaring an alleged amendment to the *ELCB Staff Pension Scheme* to be void for failing to meet these requirements is an example of *s 67* being put into action. In this instance, an amendment purporting to reduce the accrual rate retrospectively was held to be a detrimental modification under *s 67* which had been made with neither the consent nor the actuarial equivalence requirements being satisfied beforehand. Consequently, the Regulator used its *s 67* powers to declare the amendment void to the extent that it applied retrospectively.

The consent requirement

13.18   The consent requirement is made up of two components: the informed consent requirement and the timing requirement.

The consent requirement is satisfied if the trustees give information in writing to affected members explaining:

(*a*)   the proposed modification and its effect;

(*b*)   that they may make representations to the trustees about the modification;

(*c*)   the reasonable opportunity they have to make such representations; and

(*d*)   that the consent requirements apply;

and the member then gives his consent to the proposed modification in writing.

Once the affected member has given his consent, the timing requirement is satisfied if the modification takes effect within a reasonable period after the giving of consent.

The actuarial equivalence requirement

13.19   The actuarial equivalence requirement applies in relation to a detrimental modification which is not a protected modification (ie a modification which would or might adversely affect subsisting rights but which does not involve converting defined benefit rights into money purchase rights or reducing pensions in payment) and where the trustees determine that this test is to apply.

The actuarial equivalence test has three aspects: the information requirement, the actuarial value requirement and the actuarial equivalence statement requirement.

(*a*)   *The information requirement*

Under this requirement, trustees must, before the modification is made, take all reasonable steps to provide affected members with information in writing that adequately explains:

- the nature of the modification;

- the effect on the members;

- that the members may make representations to the trustees and how to do so;

- that the actuarial equivalence requirement applies; what constitutes actuarial equivalence and how it will be achieved; and

- that the members should consider whether they need to take independent financial advice.

What constitutes taking 'all reasonable steps' to provide the above information will vary depending on the particular circumstances. The Code of Practice contains the following suggestions:

- Where the affected members are still employed by the employer, use of internal post or email may be appropriate.

- In the case of other members, the use of post will usually be appropriate, although where contact has been lost, the trustees should consider using the local newspapers to alert the deferred members to the proposals and invite them to get in contact.

The members must be given reasonable opportunity to make representations to the trustees about the proposed modifications. The Code of Practice contains guidelines on how trustees should manage this. The Regulator expects members to be given at least four weeks to make representations. However, this will vary according to the number and location of members and complexity of the modifications.

Members should be able to contact the trustees during this period and ask any questions they may have, and answers should be given as soon as is reasonably practicable.

- Once representations have been received, the trustees must take time to consider them, obtain any further advice and hold discussions with the employer to identify whether any changes to the proposals are necessary in light of the representations.

- If changes to the proposals are needed, the trustees must consider whether this renders the modifications materially different, and legal and actuarial advice might be sought on this. If the changes are deemed material, the information requirement will need to be recommenced so that members have an opportunity to comment on the amended proposals.

- If the changes are not deemed material, the trustees will have fulfilled the information requirement.

(b) *The actuarial value requirement*

This requirement is satisfied if the trustees have taken steps to secure that 'actuarial value' will be maintained. Actuarial value is maintained if the actuarial value of the member's subsisting rights, immediately after the time when the modification takes effect, is equal to or greater than the actuarial value of his subsisting rights immediately before that time.

(c) *The actuarial equivalence statement*

The final condition of the actuarial equivalence requirement is that trustees obtain an actuarial equivalence statement, ie a certificate in writing that actuarial value has been maintained, usually from the scheme actuary, within a reasonable period after the effective date of the modification. The Code of Practice specifies a 'reasonable period' to be one month in this instance.

Civil penalties

13.20   *PA 1995, s 67I* provides that, where a modification is held to be voidable (see **13.17**), then civil penalties under *PA 1995, s 10* may be applied to any trustee who has failed to take all reasonable steps to secure that the modification was not voidable.

Power exercisable by a person other than the trustees

13.21   *PA 1995, s 67* applies to any power conferred on any person by an occupational pension scheme to modify the scheme (other than an excluded scheme: see **13.17**). If that person is not the trustee body, the trustee approval requirement applies to the trustees' consent to the exercise of the power of amendment by the other person instead of their own decision to make the amendment. However, in all other respects, the duty of complying with *PA 1995, s 67* – for example, the information requirement – remains with the trustees.

Examples of scheme amendments

13.22   The following examples consider some of the scheme amendments which an employer might wish to make, and whether the trustees could properly agree to them.

It is assumed for this purpose that the scheme's amendment power is wide enough to allow the amendments proposed but that agreement between the employer and the trustees is required.

The employer's decision to make these amendments and whether such a decision accords with its contractual obligations will be governed by the principles outlined in **Chapter 7**. Many changes will also require consultation with affected employees; this is also covered in **Chapter 7**.

Reduction of past service benefits

13.23   Trustees should think carefully before agreeing to an amendment which reduces any benefit earned before the amendment power is exercised (whether payable immediately or from some time in the future). If the trustees were to agree to such an amendment, it would arguably be a breach of trust (quite apart from the requirements of *PA 1995, s 67*).

Sometimes an employer will propose a method of recalculating all past service benefits which appears to represent a general benefit improvement but, on closer examination, disadvantages a small number of members. The trustees should not agree to the proposals unless they are revised to remove that detriment; it is no defence to a breach of trust action brought by a disadvantaged minority that the arrangements benefit the majority.

Reduction of future service benefits

13.24 Trustees should not agree to a reduction in future benefit accrual without legitimate reason and should require the employer to provide a robust business case. In considering whether to agree to this type of change trustees must exercise their powers in a way which promotes the purposes of the trust ie to provide pension benefits for employees of the employer and other beneficiaries. Trustees do also owe a duty to the employer (see **Chapter 3**), and are not required to push the company into paying more than it can genuinely afford. This is also a matter which may need to be considered when negotiating scheme funding (see **Chapter 11**). There is always a difficult balance for trustees to strike between the protection of future service benefits and ensuring the security of benefits accrued to date. Consideration of the strength of the employer covenant can be particularly important in this context.

Amending the scheme so that no further benefits will accrue in the future

13.25 This is simply a more drastic version of **13.24** above, and so the same principles apply.

Closing the scheme to future entrants

13.26 The proposal here will be that an amendment is made to the scheme's eligibility rule so that no further members may join the scheme in the future. This will not necessarily cause the trustees significant problems as the main effect of the amendment will be to exclude individuals who have never belonged to the scheme and to whom the trustees will, therefore, not normally owe a duty.

Some schemes impose a 'waiting period' for membership, so that an employee has to complete a certain period of service before he is allowed to join the scheme (subject, in the case of automatic enrolment, to his opting in during the deferral period: see **Chapter 14**). Individuals currently serving this 'waiting period' can be regarded as being contingently entitled to benefits from the scheme, and the trustees would usually, therefore, be well advised (unless the scheme is seriously underfunded) to insist that the closure to new entrants does not affect these particular individuals.

Introduction of different benefits for future joiners

13.27   The concern here is very often that the new benefits package is (or is capable of being) less generous than the one for current members. The issues which this raises for trustees are similar to those in **13.26** above, in that the individuals to be affected by the amendment will not yet be scheme members, but age discrimination issues may arise. The same considerations as regards anyone serving a 'waiting period' will apply.

Conversion to defined contribution for future accrual

13.28   An employer may continue to operate its defined benefit scheme on the existing basis for current members, but decide that future joiners should be admitted to membership on a defined contribution basis only. This is an example of the sort of amendment described in **13.27** above.

The trustees will face harder decisions if they are asked to agree to an amendment which will convert the current defined benefit scheme members to a defined contribution basis for future accrual, in which case the considerations at **13.24** above apply.

The trustees, acting on actuarial advice, should not hesitate where appropriate to seek improvements from the employer in the defined contribution benefits being offered. This might take the form of, for example:

(*a*)   an increase in the employer's future contributions; or

(*b*)   possibly even some form of 'defined benefit underpin' for the members involved, so that their eventual benefits will not dip below a given level.

The employer may be prepared to compromise on at least some of these points in order to see the conversion go ahead. The improvements will also make the exercise easier for the employer to justify to its employees.

In some circumstances, the trustees may justifiably go further than this towards accommodating the employer's proposals (eg if the future service benefits offered are genuinely the best which the employer can afford). However, in no circumstances should the trustees allow a reduction in the value of a member's accrued benefits. The conversion of past service defined benefits to a defined contribution basis will be a protected modification and require consent under *PA 1995, s 67* (see **13.17** above) and is very rarely undertaken.

Conversion of future benefits to defined contribution (hence breaking the link with final salary for benefits already accrued) was considered in *HR Trustees v German [2009] EWHC 2785 (Ch)*. In that case, it was found that a restriction in the amendment power meant that final salary linkage had to be retained for benefits already accrued. Future benefits could accrue on a money purchase basis. Note that in *HR Trustees v German* the judge decided that it may be possible for a member to consent by the way of a contractual agreement (ie outside the trust deed and rules) to the breaking of final salary linkage (see **13.30** below); however, the requirements for valid consent are stringent and had not been met in this case.

Pension increase exchange

13.29   Some employers have sought to reduce future pension risk by offering members a pension increase exchange ('PIE'). In its simplest form a PIE involves the member giving up the right to future pension increases in excess of statutory requirements, in exchange for an increase in the current level of pension. This is achieved by the member consenting to the variation of his rights under the scheme, enabling an amendment to be made to the scheme rules which complies with *PA 1995, s 67*.

In June 2012, following Government concerns that members were not always being given appropriate information or advice when faced with a PIE offer, an industry voluntary code of practice on incentive exercises (the 'code') was adopted. The code covers both PIEs and enhanced transfer value exercises (see **Chapter 6**) and is directed primarily at employers, although all those involved in the PIE will be expected to follow it, or give clear reasons why not. An industry monitoring body will review the effectiveness of the code and consider how it may be improved and updated.

The code covers exercises where one objective of providing the offer is to reduce risk or cost for the pension scheme or sponsor and the offer is not ordinarily available to members of the scheme. The key objectives of the code are to enable members to make informed decisions by making sure incentive exercises are:

- carried out fairly and transparently;
- communicated in a balanced way and in terms that members can understand;
- available with appropriate financial advice (or in some limited circumstances, financial guidance) that is paid for by the party initiating the exercise (typically the employer);
- able to achieve high levels of member engagement; and
- provided with access to an independent complaints and compensation process.

The first principle of the code is that no cash incentive should be offered which is contingent on the member's decision to accept the offer. The second key principle is that, in a PIE, each member should either be provided with independent advice or, where the 'value requirement' is met, each member should be provided with guidance. All advice should be paid for by the employer. Where the value requirement applies it should be a requirement to take guidance before an offer can be accepted. The value requirement will be satisfied where the expected value of the members' additional (new) benefits is at least 100 per cent of the expected value of the benefits being given up. This is an aggregate calculation for all those involved in the exercise, not an individual test.

Other principles of the code include fair, clear, unbiased and straightforward communications with members, exercises should allow sufficient time for members to reflect on the issues and all parties must be aware of their roles and responsibilities and act in good faith.

Version 2 of the code was issued in January 2016. The principles behind the code remain the same, but it has been updated to reflect changes in practice. Under the updated code there is a new proportionality threshold which removes the requirement for advice for transfers or commutations of £10,000 or less in value or a modification of a pension of £500 per annum or less. New boundary guidance provides useful examples which can assist parties in determining whether an exercise is within the scope of the code.

Modifying pension rights through extrinsic contracts

13.30   In recent years, employers have sought to reduce pension liabilities by contractual agreement with employees. This practice can be used to avoid the requirements of *PA 1995, s 67* although may not be successful if the intention is to avoid a restriction in the power of amendment.

In *South West Trains v Wightman [1998] PLR 113* ('*SWT*'), the terms of a collective agreement between SWT and ASLEF, a recognised trade union, provided that part of the allowances incorporated into basic pay should not be pensionable. The High Court held that the collective agreement was contractually binding on individual members and incorporated into their contracts of employment and that it was implicit in the agreement enforceable by SWT that the drivers would not claim pensions at a higher level than agreed and therefore that the SWT would be able to prevent the drivers from claiming pensions based on their actual salary.

The judge went on to consider whether the trustees (who were not a party to the agreement) could refuse to pay the drivers' pension based on their actual salary. Whilst the judge did not have to decide the issue (he had already concluded that SWT could prevent the drivers from claiming a pension based on the higher rate) he thought it was 'well arguable' that *PA 1995, s 67* did not invalidate the agreement since: (i) it was reached before *s 67* came into force and; (ii) on the basis that, as a result of the binding agreement, drivers could not seek a pension on a higher basis or could be prevented from seeking a pension on that basis by SWT, the drivers did not have 'any entitlement or accrued right' to claim a pension on a more favourable basis than agreed. The trustees could, and probably should, execute an amending deed giving effect to the agreement between SWT and the members. In the judge's view such amending deed would be no more than an 'administrative', or 'tidying up' act which would make the position clear for the future.

In *NUS Superannuation Fund v Pensions Ombudsman [2002] PLR 93*, the High Court relied on *SWT* to reaffirm the effectiveness of pensionable pay agreements. The High Court emphasised that an employee cannot accept a payment other than on the terms on which it is offered – if a salary increase is offered to an employee on condition that it is non-pensionable, the employee is entitled to: (a) accept the non-pensionable increase; or (b) decline the increase altogether. However, he cannot claim to have received a pensionable increase as that was never offered to him by the employer.

In *HR Trustees v German (IMG Pension Plan) [2009] EWHC 2785 (Ch)* (*'IMG'*), the underlying issue was the closure by the principal employer of its final salary pension scheme, and the transfer of members into a new money purchase section. A key point was that the rules of the pension scheme contained an express restriction in the amendment power which required a link to final pensionable salary and there was no carve-out under which amendments otherwise prohibited could be made with member consent.

One of the issues raised was whether various documents signed by the active members constituted an extrinsic contract between employer and employee which precluded the employee from claiming past service rights on a final salary linked basis. The judge found that the extrinsic contracts relied on were not established on the facts and in any event was not persuaded that extrinsic contracts can override a restriction in the amendment power. The judge also found that:

- the purported contract conflicted with the terms of the trust (especially the protection for accrued rights);

- therefore the enforcement of the contract by the trustees would constitute a breach of trust;

- enforcement must be prohibited unless the relevant members had given their fully informed consent;

- fully informed consent had not been given because: (a) the members had no knowledge of the restriction in the amendment power; (b) they had received no (legal) advice in respect of it; (c) they had not been given any real choice whether or not to consent.

557

13.30 *Amendments and scheme redesign*

The judge distinguished *SWT* on the basis that, in that case, there had been no conflict between the terms of the trust and the contracts which the employer sought to enforce. The judge noted in particular that in *SWT* the extrinsic contract only affected the salary on which pension would be calculated; which salary the trustees would have to look for outside the terms of the scheme in any event.

In *IMG* the court also considered whether there had been a breach of *PA 1995, s 91* which renders unenforceable any right by which a member assigns, commutes or surrenders his rights under an occupational pension scheme. In summary, the court held that a compromise agreement constituted a 'surrender' of rights under that section. This was rejected by the Court of Appeal in *IMG v German [2010] EWCA Civ 1349* which held that *PA 1995, s 91* does not apply to a 'bona fide compromise under which a putative entitlement or right is waived in order to avoid the need for legal proceedings and for a judicial determination'. In reaching its decision, the Court of Appeal distinguished between an 'entitlement' or 'right' to a pension the existence of which was accepted or established, which was covered by *s 91*, and a putative entitlement or right that was claimed but whose existence was in dispute or doubt, which was not.

In *Bradbury v BBC [2012] EWHC 1369 (Ch)*, the BBC sought to introduce a pensionable pay cap contractually, by offering pay rises which were only partially pensionable, in reliance on the *SWT* and *NUS* cases. Mr Bradbury's appeal (backed by his union) raised three main issues:

Could a pensionable pay cap be introduced by contractual agreement?

The court accepted that an agreement by a member, under the *SWT* principle, to accept a pay rise on the basis that part only was pensionable, would (subject to the implied duty of trust and confidence) be binding on that member. Where a salary increase had been offered on terms that only part of it would be pensionable, the court's view was that this offer contained 'two integral and interdependent elements, namely an increase in salary and the provision about pension entitlement. The terms cannot be severed. It was not open to [Mr Bradbury] to accept one and not the other. He could not accept the increase without agreeing the terms as to its treatment for pension purposes.'

The judge distinguished *IMG* on the basis that the present case, like *SWT*, concerned a pensionable pay agreement. There were a number of other factors that were significant in the *IMG* case that were not present in the *BBC* case – including, an express restriction in the amendment power and lack of clear explanation and communication of the changes to members.

Did the pensionable pay cap infringe PA 1995, s 91?

The court confirmed that although *PA 1995, s 91* protects all benefits payable in future which arise as a result of both past and future service, an agreement to cap increases to pensionable pay should not constitute a surrender of a member's pension entitlement or right to a future pension for the purposes of *s 91*. The court considered that ' [Mr Bradbury's] right to a future pension based on the full amount of an anticipated pay rise was no right at all; and by agreeing to a pay increase only part of which would be treated as pensionable, he did not alienate anything to which he was even prospectively entitled.'

Was there a breach of the implied duty of trust and confidence?

This principle requires the BBC to deal with its employees in a manner which is consistent with a relationship of trust and confidence (see **Chapter 7**). Whilst the High Court's comments on this issue were obiter, the judge did express some sympathy for the arguments advanced by the BBC in justifying its actions, principally its concerns regarding the magnitude of the scheme's funding deficit and the impact on licence payers of taking such steps.

As a separate matter, following the Warren J's decision in *Bradbury,* Mr Bradbury complained to the Pensions Ombudsman in relation to whether the imposition of a pensionable pay cap was in breach of the employer's implied duty of trust and confidence. The Pensions Ombudsman found against him in his determination dated 23 December 2013, as in the Ombudsman's view, the BBC did not act in breach of its duties taking into account the BBC's resources, its overall obligations and the steps taken by it to address the problems faced in relation to the scheme. Amongst other issues, the Ombudsman found that there was no collateral purpose to drive out older employees as contended by Mr Bradbury and that the principal purpose of the imposition of the cap was to address the scheme's deficit.

Mr Bradbury appealed to the High Court against that decision on four main grounds, all of which were rejected by Warren J in his judgment (*Bradbury v BBC [2015] EWHC 1368 (Ch)*):

- Improper coercion – Mr Bradbury had not been improperly coerced into making a choice about his pay rises and pension.

- Collateral purpose – the pension changes were primarily a response to the scheme deficit, even if there was a collateral benefit of staff leaving this was not sufficient to make it a breach of the duty of trust and confidence.

- Age discrimination – even if the change did have a disparate impact on older employees, this was not sufficient to give rise to a breach of the implied duty.

- Manner of consultation – the Pensions Ombudsman was entitled to reach the decision he had that the manner in which the BBC consulted on the proposed changes did not in itself give rise to a breach of the implied duty.

Warren J then went on to consider whether the Pensions Ombudsman was right to conclude that, taken as a whole, these matters did not give rise to a breach of the implied duty. He concluded that: 'It seems to me that it would require a very strong case indeed for a number of disparate objections (even though they arise out of the same conduct) to give rise when taken together to a breach of the implied duties when none of the objections by itself gives rise to such a breach'. He held that the overall conduct of the BBC did not give rise to a breach of the implied duties.

In the *IBM* case (see **13.5** above), Warren J found in the particular circumstances of that case, where members' reasonable expectations were raised by the employer, that certain extrinsic contracts were imposed in breach of the employer's implied duty of good faith. Nevertheless, he held that extrinsic contracts, of themselves, are not objectionable.

Bulk transfers and scheme mergers – general

Background

13.31 Some of the reasons for scheme mergers and making bulk transfers of assets and liabilities between schemes operating within the same group of employers were outlined in **13.3** above. The matters that arise in relation to scheme mergers vary hugely depending on the nature of the schemes involved. Bulk transfers also vary to some extent according to whether or not the transferring scheme has begun to be wound up before the time of the transfer (see **13.48** to **13.53** below). In this section, some general issues are considered.

Members' consents to transfer

13.32 An advantage of obtaining members' consents to the transfer is that, if matters have been properly and clearly explained to the members, they are less likely to feel aggrieved about the transfer arrangements later on.

However, the fact that members' consents are being sought in no way relieves the trustees of the responsibility to ensure that the arrangements are in the members' interests. The consent form which members are asked to sign may contain a statement discharging the transferring trustees from any further liability, but it may not be possible for trustees to rely on this discharge if it is later shown that they did not take proper steps to protect their members.

In seeking consents, care should be taken not to give unauthorised investment advice contrary to the *Financial Services and Markets Act 2000* (explained further in **Chapter 10**) and members should be encouraged to seek independent financial advice before taking a decision.

In reality, however, obtaining the consent of the entire membership will often be impractical, particularly in relation to deferred pensioners, some of whom are likely to have moved house and not advised their former employer or the trustees of their new address. Transfers to other occupational pension schemes (but not to personal pension schemes) are therefore permissible without the need for members' consents, but only if:

(*a*)   either:

    (i)   the scheme rules expressly permit transfers to be made without consent; or

    (ii)   the transferring scheme is a registered defined benefit scheme, the transfer follows the commencement, after 5 April 1997, of the winding up of that scheme and the requirements dealt with in **Chapter 12** are met; and

(*b*)   either:

    (i)   both schemes apply to employment with the same employer; or

    (ii)   it is a bulk (as opposed to an individual) transfer, either resulting from a financial transaction between the employers or where the employers are 'connected' for the purposes of the legislation (*Occupational Pension Schemes (Preservation of Benefit) Regulations 1991 (SI 1991/167), reg 12(2)* (the 'Preservation Regulations'));

(*c*)   an actuarial certificate regarding the members' rights in the receiving scheme is produced and meets the following criteria:

    (i)   the certificate follows the format in *Schedule 3* of the *Preservation Regulations*;

    (ii)   the actuary sends the certificate to the trustees or managers of the transferring scheme;

    (iii)   the transfer takes place within three months of the date of the actuary's signing the certificate; and

    (iv)   there are no significant changes to the benefits, data and documents used in making the certificate by the date on which the transfer actually takes place (*Preservation Regulations, reg 12(3)*); and

(*d*)   In relation to formerly contracted-out arrangements the transfer is not of such a kind that members' consents are required as set out in **Chapter 4**.

13.33 *Amendments and scheme redesign*

Where a transfer is to be made without consent, information about the proposed transfer and details of the value of the rights to be transferred (including rights in respect of death in service benefits and survivors' benefits) must be given to each member affected not less than one month before the proposed transfer is due to take place (*Preservation Regulations, reg 12(4B)*).

In the case of *Pollock v Reed [2015] EWHC 3685 (Ch)*, one key issue that the court considered was whether or not in giving his certificate (*Preservation Regulations, reg 12*), the actuary can consider the relative security of the benefits between the transferring and the receiving schemes, or whether the actuarial certificate must be based solely on the value of the benefits. Asplin J held that:

> 'In my judgement … *Regulation 12(3)* construed in the light of the [*Preservation*] *Regulations* as a whole, *section 73 PSA 1993* from which it emanates and the admissible background does not include the security of benefits as a factor to be taken into account by the actuary in the certification process.'

The ability to transfer without consent in these circumstances applies only to past service benefits. Future service benefits cannot accrue without consent in the receiving scheme; this would amount to compulsory scheme membership contrary to *Pension Schemes Act 1993 (PSA 1993), s 160*. Although, where automatic enrolment applies (see **Chapter 14**), the consent of relevant jobholders would not be required.

Even where all the above conditions are met, the trustees may not exercise a discretion to make a transfer unless they are satisfied that it is in their members' best interests.

Issues for trustees to consider

13.33   The matters to be borne in mind by the trustees in deciding whether they are doing the best for their members will vary according to the circumstances, but the following issues are amongst those which will most commonly arise. It is assumed here that the trustees have some discretion as to whether the transfer takes place.

Benefits

13.34   The employers may offer benefit improvements in order to encourage the trustees to agree to the transfer in order to facilitate a bulk transfer or scheme merger. If improvements are not offered, the trustees should seek them (particularly if, without any, there is no advantage for their members in the transfer going ahead). This is potentially an issue for both the transferring and receiving trustees. If enhancements are being offered then the employer and trustees should consider whether the voluntary code referred to in **13.29** above should be followed.

The transferring trustees should examine closely the benefits which are offered in respect of the transfer and guard against the possibility of agreeing to proposals which result in any person's benefits being reduced. Trustees' duties in relation to changes in benefits were considered in **13.22** to **13.29** above in the context of scheme amendments. The same principles apply in relation to transfers, so that trustees will be in breach of trust if they agree to a transfer that reduces any person's past service benefits, and whether trustees can agree to a transfer which reduces future benefits will depend upon the circumstances – see, for instance, **13.24** above.

The transferring trustees should also consider the Revenue issues relating to loss of protection of tax-free cash amounts and loss of enhanced protection that may occur if certain requirements are not satisfied. See **Chapter 17** for more detail.

Funding disparity

13.35   Another issue is the comparative funding levels of the transferring and receiving schemes. This is a key factor for consideration by trustees as part of any scheme merger proposal. If, for example, the trustees of an ongoing scheme are considering whether to make a bulk transfer, they should seek advice as to the solvency of both the transferring and receiving schemes. If the transferring scheme is significantly better funded than the receiving scheme, the transferring trustees should question whether they can justify making a transfer which would, in effect, put their members into a worse funded scheme than the one to which they presently belong.

How much of an issue this is will depend not only on the extent of the funding disparity but also on other factors. For instance, both schemes might be well funded, but the receiving scheme only slightly less so than the transferring scheme. In these circumstances the transferring trustees could properly take the view that the modest funding disparity was outweighed by any more significant advantages of the transfer, such as:

(*a*)   better benefits to be provided by the receiving scheme;

(*b*)   provisions in the receiving scheme's rules creating greater scope than under the transferring scheme for surplus assets to be used for benefit improvements; or (*c*) a likelihood of the receiving scheme's future investment performance significantly outstripping that of the transferring scheme (perhaps because the receiving scheme is much larger – see **13.37** below).

If the funding disparity remains an issue, the transferring trustees should impose conditions upon the employers (and, where appropriate, the receiving trustees) before agreeing to make the transfer. These conditions might typically include one or both of the following:

(i) That a benefit improvement be granted in respect of the members to be transferred.

(ii) That any surplus to be transferred from the transferring scheme be subject to some measure of 'ringfencing' in the receiving scheme. The aim of ringfencing is to ensure that assets transferred from the transferring scheme are subject to safeguards for the benefit of the transferring members in the receiving scheme. This would be done by amending the rules of the receiving scheme, so as (in this context) to give the transferring members prior rights over other members as regards the transferred assets in relation to such matters as:

- any use of surplus assets to grant benefit improvements;

- the calculation of future transfer values paid from the receiving scheme; and/or

- the distribution of assets on a winding up of the receiving scheme. However, such an amendment may be partly or wholly ineffective if the receiving scheme subsequently goes into winding up with insufficient assets to meet all its liabilities. This is because of the winding-up requirements in *PA 1995* and *PA 2004* which (as explained further in **Chapter 12**) override the scheme's rules.

(iii) That the merger can only proceed as a sectionalised merger. The aim of a sectionalised merger is to have complete separation of the assets and liabilities of each merging scheme in the receiving scheme, to maintain the security of the benefits of the better funded scheme.

Each section of a properly sectionalised scheme (also sometimes referred to as a 'segregated scheme') is treated as a separate scheme for winding up, employer debt, PPF and scheme funding purposes. However, in order to be treated as a sectionalised scheme the statutory definitions must be satisfied, which can be found in the following regulations:

- *regulation 8, the Occupational Pension Schemes (Employer Debt) Regulations 2005*;

- *Schedule 2, paragraph 1, the Occupational Pension Schemes (Scheme Funding) Regulations 2005;*

- *regulation 12, the Occupational Pension Schemes (Winding Up) Regulations 1996*;

- regulation 16, the Occupational Pension Schemes (Investment) Regulations 2005; and

- regulation 1, the Pension Protection Fund (Multi- employer schemes) (Modification) Regulations 2005.

These definitions vary slightly between the regulations but the key characteristics of a sectionalised scheme are as follows:

- the scheme must be multi-employer;

- contributions payable by employers and members must be allocated to their section of the scheme;

- the assets of each section cannot be used for the purpose of another section;

- employers can participate in more than one section as long as there is more than one employer participating in the scheme as a whole.

The employer may well insist that any 'ringfencing' or sectionalisation provisions only remain effective for a specified period of time. In agreeing to a suitable period, the trustees should consider actuarial advice.

The transferring trustees are likely to have less negotiating power if their scheme has gone into winding up.

If, conversely, the receiving scheme is better funded than the transferring scheme, then similar considerations in reverse will have to be borne in mind by the receiving scheme's trustees before they exercise any discretion under the terms of their trust deed to accept the transfer.

Comparison of balance of powers

13.36   The trustees of an ongoing scheme ought also, before agreeing to make a transfer, to consider the 'balance of powers' (as between the employers, on the one hand, and the trustees, on the other) under the provisions of their own scheme and compare it with the corresponding balance in the receiving scheme. If the receiving scheme's overall balance of powers is less favourable towards the trustees (and therefore the beneficiaries) than under the transferring scheme, then the transferring trustees should again question whether they can properly make the transfer.

An unfavourable shift in the balance of powers may be compensated for by other factors; for instance, if the receiving scheme is significantly better funded than the transferring scheme, provides better benefits, or (as mentioned in **13.37** below) has better prospects for future growth. If this is not the case, however, then the trustees should consider obtaining from the employer some benefit or safeguard for their members before agreeing to the transfer. This might take the form of:

(*a*)   an immediate benefit improvement in respect of the transferring members; or

(*b*)   amendments to the receiving scheme to make its balance of powers more favourable to the trustees, at least in so far as that scheme will ultimately relate to the transferring members.

The issue will not be as acute for the transferring trustees if their scheme is already in winding up.

Long-term future of schemes and employer covenant

13.37   It is increasingly difficult to predict the long-term stability and growth of any pension scheme, but it is nevertheless an issue which trustees should bear in mind. The overall financial circumstances of a scheme's sponsoring employers may give a clue as to the scheme's future. Another factor is the scheme's size.

Many transfers of the sort discussed in this chapter are from smaller schemes to larger schemes. Larger funds tend to bear proportionately lower administrative costs (owing to economies of scale) and may be able to pursue a successful investment strategy which might not realistically be available to a smaller scheme. Additionally, it is sometimes the case that the receiving scheme has a principal employer that is higher up the corporate chain and may enjoy a better employer covenant than the transferring scheme's principal employer. This should theoretically provide better security of benefits for members. However, trustees should be wary of relying too heavily on the size of a scheme or an improved employer covenant to justify a transfer which would not otherwise be in their members' best interests.

It is comparatively rare for trustees to be asked to agree to a transfer to a smaller scheme within the same group of employers. The trustees should make certain that there is a clear advantage for their members should this happen.

Other ways of securing benefits on a winding up

13.38   If the transferring scheme is in the course of being wound up, some of the issues mentioned above may be less relevant, as members will not have the alternative of simply remaining in the transferring scheme. Instead, the transferring trustees should satisfy themselves that any bulk transfer will be on terms which serve their members at least as well as the other courses of action available (such as transfers to personal pension schemes or purchasing annuities).

Consulting with transferring scheme members

13.39　The transferring scheme trustees should consider whether the bulk transfer of its members to the receiving scheme requires a 'listed change' consultation to be carried out with scheme members. See **Chapter 7** for details of when the consultation requirements apply.

Formerly contracted-out schemes

13.40　Further requirements apply in relation to formerly contracted-out schemes. These requirements are dealt with in **Chapter 4**.

Transfer or merger agreement

13.41　It is advisable for the parties involved to enter into a formal transfer or merger agreement where the terms of the arrangement which has been entered into can be clearly set out. The parties will usually be the trustees of the two schemes and each scheme's principal employer. The terms of any such agreement will vary enormously depending on the circumstances, but **13.42** to **13.46** below describe the provisions which will most often be included.

Some of these are, in reality, scheme amendments. The parties could, as an alternative, deal with these areas in separate deeds of amendment relating to the two schemes, but it is often more convenient to deal with all matters relating to the transfer in a single document. However, it is not uncommon for a benefit harmonisation exercise to be carried out prior to the transfer exercise in an attempt to make the process run more smoothly. Care should be taken to ensure that, if the transfer agreement is to amend either of the schemes, it complies with all the relevant requirements of that scheme's power of amendment.

The agreement will typically cover the following areas.

Amendments to the transferring scheme

13.42　Amendments to the transferring scheme may be necessary to:

(*a*)　permit the parties to make the bulk transfer; and/or

(*b*)　grant any benefit improvements which the transferring trustees require as a condition of their making the transfer. Alternatively, there may be some form of augmentation of benefits carried out between the trustees and the employer immediately prior to transfer.

Transfer amount

13.43   This may be stated as a specific sum (subject to a market value adjustment and/or increase for late payment) or the agreement may simply set out the method by which the amount is to be calculated (perhaps by reference to an actuary's letter appended to the agreement). If the agreement provides for the transferring scheme's entire assets to be transferred, then the precise calculation of the amount becomes less of an issue.

Past service benefits

13.44   The benefits to be provided in the receiving scheme in relation to the transfer payment should be clearly stated.

Amendments to the receiving scheme

13.45   Amendments may be required in relation to the receiving scheme, for instance, to:

(*a*)   permit the receiving trustees to accept the transfer;

(*b*)   incorporate any amendments to the scheme's balance of powers that have been agreed;

(*c*)   incorporate any special future service benefits in relation to the transferring members which have been agreed;

(*d*)   grant any benefit improvements for the receiving scheme's existing members which the receiving trustees require as a condition of their accepting the transfer; and/or

(*e*)   incorporate any provisions to enable ringfencing or sectionalisation (as referred to in **13.35**(ii) and (iii) above) which have been agreed between the parties as a condition of the transfer being made.

Indemnity

13.46   The transferring trustees may seek an indemnity from the receiving trustees in relation to any claims which might be brought against them in relation to the transferring members. The receiving trustees should of course consider how this might affect their own members' interests. Any such indemnity will normally exclude matters where there has been an element of bad faith or dishonesty by the transferring trustees and be limited, for instance, to that part of the receiving scheme's assets which is attributable to the transfer payment.

To the extent that these assets may be insufficient fully to indemnify the transferring trustees, one or more of the employers may agree to indemnify the transferring trustees for the difference; however, care should be taken not to infringe the provisions of the *Companies Act 2006* regarding companies indemnifying their own officers (referred to in further detail in **Chapter 3**).

Steps to be taken post- transfer

13.47   After the transfer date, there will be a number of administrative tasks to be completed such as notifications to HMRC, the Regulator and the PPF.

The receiving scheme trustees will need to consider whether an event report has to be submitted to HMRC in respect of the transfer, such as in relation to the change in number of members of the receiving scheme.

It is also possible that the decision to transfer will also qualify as a 'notifiable event' but this depends on the value of the transfer being made (*PA 2004, s 69* and *the Pensions Regulator (Notifiable Events) Regulations 2005*). Trustees of both schemes should also consider whether any 'registrable information' has changed and, if so, notify the Regulator as soon as reasonably practicable (*PA 2004, ss 60* and *62*).

The 'block' transfer of assets from a transferring scheme to the receiving scheme also has to be reported to the PPF via the Exchange system. The purpose of this is to ensure that levy due from the transferring and receiving schemes to the PPF are adjusted to reflect the change in their assets and liabilities as a result of the transfer.

Bulk transfers – specific issues where winding up has not commenced

Background

13.48   When considering whether there is power to make a bulk transfer and how any transfer payment is to be calculated, the answer will depend on whether or not the transferring scheme has gone into winding up at the time of the transfer. The date on which a scheme commences to be wound up for this purpose is governed by *PA 1995, s 124(3A)–(3E)*.

Where winding up has not commenced (or is not even expected to happen), the position is as set out in **13.49** and **13.50** below. The corresponding position where winding up has commenced is dealt with in **Chapter 12**.

Power to make bulk transfers

13.49   Whether there is the power to make a bulk transfer out of a scheme which is not in winding up depends upon the terms of that scheme's trust deed and rules. If there is the power to make the transfer, much will depend on whether the trust deed and rules place that power primarily with the employers or with the trustees. For instance:

(*a*)   the principal employer might have the power to direct the trustees to make a transfer, with the trustees having no right of refusal;

(*b*)   the principal employer might have the power to request the trustees to make a transfer, with the trustees having a discretion as to whether or not they act on that request;

(*c*)   the trustees might have the power to initiate a transfer, subject only to the employer's consent; this gives the trustees a greater degree of control than in (*b*) above since, in putting their proposals to the employer, the trustees are effectively requiring the employer to consider those proposals in a manner consistent with its implied duty of good faith (see **13.5** above);

(*d*)   the trustees might have the power to make a transfer, subject only to consultation with the employer; as long as a genuine consultation procedure is carried out, this does not require the trustees actually to obtain the employer's consent; or

(*e*)   the trustees might have the power to make a bulk transfer without any form of reference to the employer being required.

Amount to be transferred

13.50   Similarly, the calculation of the transfer amount is governed by the trust deed and rules, subject to members' statutory entitlements to a minimum of the cash equivalents of their accrued benefits (although underfunding in the transferring scheme may justify a reduction of cash equivalents – see **Chapter 6** for further details).

Trust deeds vary considerably as to how the transfer amount is to be calculated. Some examples are as follows:

(*a*)   The matter might be left entirely to the discretion of either the principal employer or the trustees, often subject to the requirement that they first consider the advice of the actuary (which advice the trust deed may or may not require them to accept, but in practice may be hard to reject without good reason).

(*b*) More commonly, the deed will leave the decision as to the amount to one of the two parties – either the principal employer or the trustees – subject to the consent of the other.

(*c*) The trust deed might (particularly if it is an older one) have the effect of requiring that the transfer payment represent a share of the overall fund in respect of the members being transferred. In an underfunded scheme, this would mean the transferring members bearing the brunt of a proportion of any overall deficit in the transferring scheme. This would be subject to any statutory cash equivalent transfer value rights (see **Chapter 6**). In an overfunded scheme, by contrast, the transfer payment would have to include a share of any surplus.

(*d*) The trust deed might (especially if it is a relatively modern one), seek to give the employers maximum control in relation to active members by specifying that the transfer payment be the lesser of:

(i) their statutory cash equivalents; and

(ii) the amount which would be available to be applied in respect of them were the scheme to be wound up;

(which is, effectively, the minimum which the law will allow) subject to the principal employer's sole discretion to direct a greater amount.

Bulk transfers – specific issues where winding up has commenced

Preliminary

13.51   This section now addresses the questions of whether there is power to make a bulk transfer, and how any transfer payment is to be calculated, from a scheme that has begun to be wound up. (The corresponding position where the transferring scheme has not gone into winding up is dealt with in **13.48** to **13.50** above.)

Power to make bulk transfers on winding up

13.52   *PA 1995, s 74* gives the trustees of registered defined benefit schemes which commence winding up after 5 April 1997 the power to make bulk transfers even if there is no power to do so in the scheme rules. Previously, the existence of such a power and the question of who could exercise it would be governed by the trust deed and rules. Whether trustees have power to make a transfer from a scheme to which *PA 1995, s 74* does not apply will continue to depend upon the trust deed and rules.

Many schemes' rules give the principal employer a power to direct the trustees to make a bulk transfer. Any such power in a registered defined benefit scheme where winding up has started after 5 April 1997 needs to be considered in the context of *PA 1995, s 73A(9)*. If it amounts to a power 'to apply the assets of the scheme in respect of pensions or other benefits', as the power will no longer be exercisable by the principal employer; it will be exercisable by the trustees instead.

Amount to be transferred on a winding up

13.53   The position as set out in **13.50** above regarding amounts to be transferred where a winding up has not commenced will similarly apply to winding-up scenarios. However, where winding up commenced after 5 April 1997, the following additional considerations will also apply in relation to registered defined benefit schemes:

(*a*)   if the scheme is underfunded, the amount of the transfer payment in respect of any given person must be consistent with the sums required to be allocated towards the scheme's various liabilities under the statutory order of priorities (*PA 1995, s 73*, as amended); and

(*b*)   under *PA 1995, s 73A(9)* any power given by the scheme's rules to a person other than the trustees (the principal employer, for instance) 'to apply' scheme assets during winding up 'in respect of pensions or other benefits' will become exercisable by the trustees and not by that person.

Bulk transfers – overview

13.54   The following table provides an overview of the requirements governing bulk transfers (in the context of scheme mergers and otherwise) as described in this Chapter.

	1. Where the transferring scheme has not gone into winding up	*2. Where the transferring scheme has gone into a winding up which commenced after 5 April 1997*
A. Issues for trustees	Before exercising any discretion enabling the transfer to go ahead, issues which the trustees should consider may include: • the effect of the transfer on members' benefits (issue for transferring trustees and receiving trustees);	

	1. Where the transferring scheme has not gone into winding up	2. Where the transferring scheme has gone into a winding up which commenced after 5 April 1997
	• any disparity between the funding position of the transferring scheme and that of the receiving scheme (issue for transferring trustees and receiving trustees); • the 'balance of powers' in the receiving scheme as compared with that in the transferring scheme (issue for transferring trustees); • the long-term futures of the transferring and receiving schemes and employer covenant (issue for transferring trustees); and • if the transferring scheme is already being wound up, the comparative merits of other ways of securing benefits (issue for the transferring trustees). See **Chapter 12** for more details.	
B. Members' consents	Members' consents are required unless in summary: • scheme rules permit non-consent transfers; either: (*a*) both schemes relate to employment with the same employer; or (*b*) it is a bulk transfer either resulting from a financial transaction between the employers or where the employers are 'connected'; • actuarial certificate is given; • members are notified at least one month before transferring; and • contracting-out requirements do not require members' consents.	As for column 1. *Section 74(3)(a), PA1995* gives power to make a transfer on winding up, but this will require consent unless the requirements of column 1 are satisfied.

	1. Where the transferring scheme has not gone into winding up	*2. Where the transferring scheme has gone into a winding up which commenced after 5 April 1997*
C. Contracting-out	Further requirements may apply if either the transferring scheme or the receiving scheme has been contracted-out (see **Chapter 4**).	As for column 1.
D. Do trustees have power to make a bulk transfer?	Depends on scheme rules.	If transferring scheme is a registered defined benefits scheme, yes. Otherwise, depends on scheme rules.
E. Can the employer(s) require the trustees to make a bulk transfer?	Depends on scheme rules.	Depends on scheme rules except that, if any such power of the employer (in a registered defined benefits scheme) amounts to a power 'to apply the assets of the scheme in respect of pensions or other benefits', that power becomes exercisable by the trustees and not by the employer(s).

	1. Where the transferring scheme has not gone into winding up	*2. Where the transferring scheme has gone into a winding up which commenced after 5 April 1997*
F. How is the transfer payment calculated?	As set out in the scheme rules, but subject to G below where the transferring scheme is in deficit.	As set out in scheme rules, but subject to: • G below where the transferring scheme is in deficit; and • the fact that, if a registered defined benefits scheme's rules give to any person other than the trustees (eg the employers) power 'to apply the assets of the scheme in respect of pensions or other benefits', that power ceases to be exercisable by that person and becomes exercisable instead by the trustees.
G. Deficit: may the scheme rules provide for the transfer payment to be reduced to take account of underfunding in the transferring scheme?	Yes, so long as members are not denied their statutory cash equivalents. Some reduction of cash equivalents is, however, permissible in cases of underfunding (see **Chapter 6**).	Yes, subject (in relation to a registered defined benefits scheme) to complying with the statutory order of priorities (as explained in **Chapter 12**).

	1. Where the transferring scheme has not gone into winding up	*2. Where the transferring scheme has gone into a winding up which commenced after 5 April 1997*
H. Surplus: may the scheme rules provide for the transfer payment to include a share of any surplus in the transferring scheme?	Yes.	Yes, but subject to: <ul><li>the fact that, if a registered defined benefits scheme's rules give to any person other than the trustees (eg the employers) power 'to apply the assets of the scheme in respect of pensions or other benefits', that power ceases to be exercisable by that person and becomes exercisable instead by the trustees; and</li><li>*PA 1995, s 76* which governs the treatment of excess assets on winding up (see **Chapter 12**).</li></ul>
I. Transfers as part of wider commercial transactions and the Pensions Regulator	Defined benefit scheme trustees should consider the following issues: <ul><li>Scheme 'abandonment': in line with the Regulator's guidance on abandonment (published in December 2008), will the proposed transfer effectively allow a sponsoring employer to sever its links with a scheme without providing it with sufficient assets or funds to compensate for losing that employer's ongoing support?</li><li>Moral hazard: is the proposed transfer part of a transaction that may give rise to the Regulator exercising its contribution notice or financial support direction powers?</li></ul>See **Chapter 15** for more details.	

Chapter 14

Governance of defined contribution schemes and automatic enrolment

Governance of defined contribution schemes

Background

14.1   In recent years, and particularly since the introduction of automatic enrolment in 2012 (see from **14.9** below) and the new flexibilities for defined contribution ('DC') benefits in the 2014 Budget (see **Chapter 17**), the governance of DC schemes has become a priority both for the Government through legislation and for the Regulator.

The development of DC governance regulation

14.2   The Regulator's first key publication focussing on DC governance was a discussion paper in January 2011, 'Enabling good member outcomes in DC pension provision'. This highlighted six elements necessary to deliver adequate income in retirement. These are:

- appropriate decisions with regards pension contributions;
- appropriate investment decisions;
- effective and efficient administration;
- protection of assets;
- appropriate decisions on converting pension savings into a retirement income; and
- value for money.

In December 2011 the Regulator set out six principles for good design and governance of workplace DC schemes.

- **Principle 1: Essential Characteristics** – Schemes should be designed to be durable, fair and deliver good outcomes for members (including

577

features such as the provision of a suitable default fund and transparency of costs and charges).

- **Principle 2: Establishing Governance** – A comprehensive scheme governance framework should be established, with clear accountabilities and responsibilities. This should include identifying key activities which need to be carried out and who owns the activity.

- **Principle 3: People** – Those who are accountable for scheme decisions and activity should understand their duties and be fit and proper to carry them out.

- **Principle 4: On-going Governance and Monitoring** – Schemes should benefit from effective governance and monitoring throughout their lifecycle.

- **Principle 5: Administration** – Schemes should be well-administered with timely, accurate and comprehensive processes and records.

The first DC Code of Practice and regulatory guidance

14.3   The Regulator set out its overall framework for regulating governance and administration of occupational trust-based DC schemes in:

- Code of Practice 13: governance and administration of occupational defined contribution trust-based schemes (the 'Code'); and

- Regulatory Guidance for defined contribution schemes.

The Code (originally published in November 2013 and republished in April 2015) and associated regulatory guidance for DC schemes (originally in force in November 2013, updated in April 2014 and republished in April 2015) built on the six principles and six elements (see **14.2** above) by highlighting 31 'quality features' describing the activities, behaviours and control processes that the Regulator believed were more likely to deliver good member outcomes. Together the Code and guidance were designed to 'provide principles, examples and benchmarks against which trustees can consider whether or not they are reasonably complying with and have understood their duties and obligations rather than prescribe fixed processes that trustees must follow in any given scenario'.

In its document entitled 'Strategy for regulating defined contribution pension schemes' (originally published in October 2013, updated and republished in April 2015), the Regulator suggested that trustees could produce a voluntary governance statement explaining the extent to which their scheme complied with the 31 DC quality features.

The Code was withdrawn and replaced by a new code of practice, 'Governance and administration of occupational trust-based schemes providing money purchase benefits', on 28 July 2016. See **14.8** below.

The Charges and Governance Regulations

14.4   In March 2014 the DWP announced its intention to introduce new mandatory quality standards and charge-capping measures, launching a consultation: 'Command Paper: Better workplace pensions: Further measures for savers'. The DWP published its response to this and a further consultation in October 2014: 'Better workplace pensions: putting savers' interests first'. The response to this was published on 4 February 2015.

The changes are being delivered in a number of ways, including primary legislation (*PA 2014*), regulations and FCA regulations and rules for contract-based schemes.

The majority of the provisions of the *Occupational Pension Schemes (Charges and Governance) Regulations 2015 (SI 2015/879)* (the '*Charges and Governance Regulations*') came into effect on 6 April 2015. The Charges and Governance Regulations introduced the more wide-ranging aspects of the new governance regime through amendments to the *Occupational Pensions Schemes (Scheme Administration) Regulations 1996 (SI 1996/1715)* (the '*Scheme Administration Regulations*'). More specific requirements on charges and investments are in the *Charges and Governance Regulations* themselves.

The requirements in the amended *Scheme Administration Regulations* apply to a 'relevant scheme'. This is defined in the *Scheme Administration Regulations*, *reg 1* as 'an occupational pension scheme which provides money purchase benefits'. There are a number of exemptions listed including executive pension schemes, relevant small schemes and schemes where the only money purchase benefits are attributable to additional voluntary contributions.

The provisions which came into effect on 6 April 2015 can be summarised as follows:

- Trustees must not be constrained in their choice of providers for administrative, fund management, advisory or other services to the scheme. This will override scheme provisions (*Scheme Administration Regulations, reg 6A*).

- Trustees must appoint a chair of trustees where the scheme does not already have one in place (*Scheme Administration Regulations, reg 22*).

- Trustees must ensure that core financial transactions are processed promptly and accurately. The *Scheme Administration Regulations* include a non-exhaustive list of core financial transactions including investment of contributions and certain transfers (*Scheme Administration Regulations*, *reg 24*).

- Trustees must calculate the charges and, as far as possible, the transaction costs borne by members of the scheme and assess the extent to which they represent good value for members (*Scheme Administration Regulations*, *reg 25*).

- Trustees must prepare an annual statement, signed off by the chair (or someone appointed to do so by the trustees where there is no chair in post), to report on their compliance with the above requirements and how they have met requirements for trustee knowledge and understanding (see **Chapter 3**). The statement must also include information on costs and charges and the statement of investment principles relating to the scheme's default arrangement. A default arrangement for these purposes is an arrangement under which (at any time from 6 April 2015) member contributions are allocated without members having expressed a choice as to where those contributions are allocated (or, broadly, under which the contributions of 80 per cent or more of active members are allocated without them having expressed choice). A chair's statement must be produced within seven months of the end of each scheme year. This effectively replaces the voluntary governance statement (see **14.3** above) (*Scheme Administration Regulations*, *reg 23*).

The *Charges and Governance Regulations* give enforcement powers to the Regulator (*regs 24–33*). The annual scheme return notice issued by the Regulator will incorporate three additional questions, which will be used to identify the chair of the trustees, gather information on the completion of the chair's statement and confirm compliance with the charges and quality measures.

In the case of non-compliance with the requirement to prepare a chair's statement, the *Charges and Governance Regulations*, *reg 28(2)* requires the Regulator to issue a fine against the trustees, including officers of corporate trustees.

Default arrangements and the charge cap

14.5   The *Charges and Governance Regulations* set limits from 6 April 2015 on the charges which can be imposed on default arrangements in 'relevant schemes'. A relevant scheme for these purposes is an occupational pension scheme under which some or all of the benefits which may be provided are money purchase benefits other than a scheme with only one member, an executive pension scheme or a relevant small scheme (*reg 2(2)*). A default arrangement is an arrangement used by a qualifying scheme (ie a scheme which is being used to satisfy the employer's automatic enrolment obligations (see **14.23** below)) in relation to at least one member and satisfies one of three requirements:

- member contributions are directed to the fund without the member having to make a choice;

- at least 80 per cent of the employer's workers who are active members are contributing to the fund either on 6 April 2015 or on the employer's staging date (whichever is later); or

- the fund first receives contributions after 6 April 2015 or the employer's staging date (whichever is later) and at least 80 per cent of the employer's workers who are active members are contributing to that fund (*Charges and Governance Regulations, reg 3*).

If using either of the 80 per cent tests, only active members who were required to make a choice as to the arrangement should be counted and any scheme members only accruing non-money purchase benefits (or whose only money purchase contributions are AVCs) should not be counted. Identifying which of a scheme's investment fund options are default arrangements may not always be straightforward.

The charge cap will apply only to the funds of those members who contribute to a default arrangement on or after 6 April 2015 (or their employer's staging date, if later). If the cap is triggered in relation to a member's contribution to a default arrangement, then the whole of that member's benefit within the default arrangement will be subject to the cap (not just the benefits relating to contributions made on or after 6 April 2015 or the staging date).

An arrangement where the only money purchase benefits are derived from additional voluntary contributions will not be a default arrangement (*reg 3(6)* as amended by the *Occupational Pension Schemes (Charges and Governance) (Amendment) Regulations 2015 (SI 2015/889)*).

Where an arrangement is identified as being a default arrangement in relation to an employer, then any worker of that employer who contributes to that arrangement will be protected by the cap, including those who make an active choice to contribute to the arrangement.

There are three types of charging structure which can be used in default arrangements (so it is not necessarily just a straightforward percentage cap). The charge limits apply at individual member level and cannot be smoothed across the default arrangement as a whole. The three options are:

- a single percentage charge capped at 0.75 per cent of funds under management;

- a combination of a charge on contributions plus a percentage of funds under management; or

- a combination of a flat annual fee plus a percentage of funds under management (*Charges and Governance Regulations, reg 6*).

The detailed percentages are set out in the DWP guidance: 'The charge cap: guidance for trustees and managers of occupational schemes' as are the two methods by which trustees can assess charges to confirm compliance (the 'prospective method' and the 'retrospective method').

The charge cap applies to costs and charges associated with scheme and investment administration but certain charges are excluded including:

- transaction costs (variable costs incurred as a result of buying, selling, lending and borrowing of investments);

- winding-up costs;

- the costs of complying with court orders;

- charges associated with pension sharing on divorce; and

- the costs associated with providing death benefits (*Charges and Governance Regulations, reg 2*).

A member can agree in writing that the charge cap should not apply. Such an agreement must not be a condition of membership and must be entered into before any higher charges are imposed (*Charges and Governance Regulations, reg 9*).

Prohibition on member-borne commission and active member discounts

14.6   From 6 April 2016 further provisions of the *Charges and Governance Regulations* came into force, prohibiting member-borne commission and active member discounts.

The commission ban applies to new arrangements entered into from 6 April 2016 (and the variation or renewal of existing arrangements). The *Charges and Governance Regulations* do not actually refer to commission but to 'advice and service', which is not defined (*Charges and Governance Regulations, reg 11A*).

The requirements apply to:

- occupational pension schemes providing money purchase benefits which are used as qualifying schemes for automatic enrolment ('specified schemes');

- all members will be covered (not just those subject to automatic enrolment);

- AVCs (even where they are the only money purchase benefits in the scheme); and

- decumulation products offered by specified schemes.

Protection will continue even if the scheme ceases to be used for automatic enrolment. Executive schemes, relevant small schemes and schemes with one member are excluded.

Broadly, in specified schemes, it will be prohibited to impose or permit to be imposed on a member, a charge that is used to pay an adviser (directly or indirectly) or to reimburse the service provider for a payment made to an adviser. A service provider is defined as 'a person who provides an administration service directly to the trustees of a specified scheme'. In practice, service providers are likely to be someone providing a bundled administration service, such as an insurer or master trust provider. It will also include someone who provides unbundled administration services, such as third-party administrators and employee benefit consultants (*Charges and Governance Regulations, reg 11A*).

Trustees are required to notify the service provider that the scheme is a specified scheme within three months of the latest of:

- 6 April 2016 (ie by 5 July 2016);

- the date on which the scheme becomes a specified scheme; or

- the date on which the service provider is appointed.

On receiving notice, the service provider then has two months to confirm to the trustees whether the scheme is compliant (ie there are no prohibited charges). The trustees must then confirm this confirmation (or otherwise) on the scheme return (*Charges and Governance Regulations, reg 11B*).

Members can opt out of the new prohibition in writing and agree with an advisor to bear a commission charge for a particular advice or service. The member or adviser must copy this to the trustees and service provider. If the trustees think that this opt-out would take the member over the restrictions on charges generally, then they can require him to enter into a separate services agreement. The agreement will not take effect if the trustees believe (and notify the member, adviser and service provider) that there are not sufficient assets relating to the member to pay the charge (*Charges and Governance Regs, reg 11C*).

The ban on active member discounts prohibits trustees from imposing or permitting to be imposed, charges on a non-contributing member which are higher than that which would have been imposed had the member been a contributing member (*Charges and Governance Regs, reg 11*). This applies only to those members who are active members on or after 6 April 2016 (ie are contributing members at that date) and subsequently become deferred (non-contributing members).

The ban on active member discounts applies only to 'relevant schemes' for the purposes of the charges provisions (see **14.5** above) as modified by *Charges and Governance Regulations, reg 11(5)*. These are money purchase schemes or schemes where some but not all of the benefits are money purchase which are used for automatic enrolment in relation to at least one jobholder. It includes AVCs (even where they are the only money purchase benefits). Relevant small schemes, schemes with one member and executive schemes are excluded.

Master trusts and other relevant multi-employer schemes

14.7   Additional governance requirements apply to master trusts and other 'relevant multi-employer schemes'. Master trusts are money purchase occupational schemes in which non-connected employers participate. They are generally marketed as a convenient and cost-effective way for smaller employers to fulfil their automatic enrolment obligations.

Relevant multi-employer scheme is defined in the *Scheme Administration Regulations, reg 1* as a relevant scheme which is or has been promoted as a scheme where participating employers need not be connected employers, except where the scheme has distinct sections relating to employers which are not connected employers and each of those sections is governed by different trustees or managers (or, where the scheme does not currently have participating employers which are not connected employers, it will have such sections when there are participating employers which are not connected employers).

Relevant multi-employer schemes must have at least three trustees, a majority of whom, including the chair, must be independent of any entity providing administration, investment or advisory services to the scheme (*Scheme Administration Regulations, reg 27*) and appointed through an open and transparent process (*Scheme Administration Regulations, reg 28*). Independent trustees can only be appointed for a term of up to five years at a time, with a maximum total term of ten years (although an independent professional trustee body can remain a trustee for longer than ten years, but must be represented by a nominated individual who is subject to the same time limits as an individual trustee). In addition, the trustees must make arrangements to encourage members of the scheme, or their representatives, to make their views on matters relating to the scheme known (*Scheme Administration Regulations, reg 29*).

The chair's annual statement for a relevant multi-employer scheme must (in addition to the requirements listed in **14.4** above) set out how the requirements of the *Scheme Administration Regulations, regs 27–29* have been met during the year.

In the Queen's Speech in May 2016 it was announced that further safeguards will be introduced to provide greater protection for members of master trusts.

The new Code of Practice and guidance

14.8   The Regulator's Code of Practice on 'governance and administration of occupational trust-based schemes providing money purchase benefits' (the 'New Code') came into force on 28 July 2016, replacing the previous Code (see **14.3** above).

The New Code is much shorter than the Code, concentrating on the Regulator's expectations of trustees in complying with their legal obligations. It is supported by six sets of guidance on specific areas of good practice. The New Code applies to trustees of any occupational pension scheme holding money purchase benefits (other than certain very small schemes). This includes AVC sections of defined benefit (DB) schemes and money purchase benefits with a DB underpin, to the extent that the legislation applies to those sections or schemes.

The first section of the New Code sets out the requirements and expectations for the appointment and fitness of trustees and the chair of trustees. It also includes reminders on the member nominated trustees and knowledge and understanding requirements. There are also enhanced requirements for trustee selection and independence for master trusts and other relevant multi-employer schemes (see **14.7** above).

The New Code focuses on the requirement to process core financial transactions promptly and accurately. This should include the handling of all employer and member contributions and assets relating to those contributions. There is no clear definition of 'promptness'. The Regulator accepts that trustees will not always have control over all the processes but where they do they should regularly review them to see if they can be done more quickly. Electronic processes should be used wherever possible. Trustee board sign-off should not delay a transaction. Statutory longstop dates should be considered by trustees as the absolute maximum. As to accuracy, trustees are expected to carry out a data reconciliation exercise at least annually and that contributions and investments are reconciled at least monthly.

On investment, under the New Code trustees are expected to engage with members about how and when they intend taking their benefits and then to use this information to help determine investment options and strategies. When considering value for members (see **14.4** above), the Regulator expects trustees to make efforts to understand the characteristics of their members, their preferences and their financial needs. This may include demographic characteristics and salary profile.

The requirements for communicating with members are largely set out in regulations. However, in the New Code, the Regulator expects trustees to consider what additional information members might need in order to make informed decisions. This might include reminders about the right to transfer out or about flexible benefit options not offered by the scheme.

The six guides provide more detail and best practice in the following areas:

- trustee board;

- management skills;

- scheme administration;

- investment governance;

- value for members;

- communicating and reporting.

Automatic enrolment

Introduction

14.9   Since 1 October 2012, employers have been under a duty to comply with the requirements of the automatic enrolment regime which is set out in the *Pensions Act 2008* (*PA 2008*) (as amended by the *Pensions Act 2011* (*PA 2011*) and the *Pensions Act 2014* (*PA 2014*)) and secondary legislation made under it. The new regime obliges employers to make arrangements from a specific date (their 'staging date') to automatically enrol 'jobholders' aged between 22 and state pension age who meet a minimum earnings threshold into a pension scheme which meets certain requirements (an 'automatic enrolment scheme'). An automatic enrolment scheme can be an occupational or workplace personal pension scheme. Jobholders may opt out of the regime but employers must not offer them any inducement to do so. There will be automatic triennial re-enrolment. Those jobholders who are younger or older than the target age band, or who have earnings below the qualifying threshold, may choose to opt in to the regime.

Although the bulk of the detailed provisions regarding automatic enrolment were formalised in *PA 2008* and various regulations, some aspects were modified further by *PA 2011* and subsequent amending regulations. Further changes came into force with effect from 1 April 2015 which introduced exceptions to the employer duty for individuals:

- with tax protected status for existing pensions savings;

- who have given or been given notice of termination of employment; and

- who cancel membership of a qualifying scheme or opt out before automatic enrolment,

under the *PA 2014*. The Government also intends to introduce regulations in 2016 to provide the discretion for employers under automatic enrolment legislation to be exempt from the duties in relation to anyone with the new tax protected status from 6 April 2016. However, such regulations cannot be introduced until the *Finance Act 2016* becomes law (see **14.12** below).

The Regulator has also issued detailed guidance aimed mainly at employers on fulfilling their obligations under the legislation.

This chapter summarises some of the key elements of the regime that has been established for a number of years and which was was rolled out to the largest employers and will be extended to smaller employers over the next two years. The Government is committed to making automatic enrolment as simple as possible to minimise the burden on employers.

The automatic enrolment requirement

14.10   With effect from the 'automatic enrolment date' each employer must make arrangements to enrol a 'jobholder' aged between 22 and state pension age who has 'threshold earnings' into an automatic enrolment scheme (see **14.11** below). The 'automatic enrolment date' for each jobholder will be the earliest of:

(*a*)   the employer's staging date (see **14.13** below), if the jobholder meets the above criteria on that date;

(*b*)   the jobholder starting work and meeting the qualifying criteria; or

(*c*)   the jobholder meeting the criteria sometime after he starts work.

PA 2008, as amended by *PA 2011*, allows an employer to postpone the automatic enrolment of a jobholder for a maximum period of three months (a 'waiting period'). Employers who use a waiting period will need to give affected jobholders notice of the deferral within six weeks from the relevant date (either the employer's staging date, the workers first day of employment or the date a worker first qualifies as an eligible jobholder). Jobholders can still choose to opt in during this period.

The requirement to automatically enrol does not apply to those jobholders who at the automatic enrolment date are already active members of a 'qualifying scheme' (see **14.23** below) (*PA 2008, s 3(3)*), nor does it apply to those who are exempt under the *Occupational and Personal Pension Schemes (Automatic Enrolment) Regulations 2010 (SI 2010/772)* (the '*Automatic Enrolment Regulations*'), *Part 1A* (see **14.12** below).

Jobholders, qualifying earnings and threshold earnings

14.11   For the purposes of the automatic enrolment requirements, a 'jobholder' is defined as a worker who is working or ordinarily works in Great Britain under a contract (including temporary and agency workers), is aged at least 16 and is under 75 and is a person to whom 'qualifying earnings' are payable by the employer in the relevant pay reference period. Where a jobholder has more than one employer or a succession of employers, the requirement applies separately in relation to each employment (*PA 2008, s 1*).

Where the jobholder is an agency worker, the person responsible for automatic enrolment (and so the 'employer' for the purposes of compliance) will be the person responsible for paying the agency worker – in most cases this will be the employment agency rather than the end user (*PA 2008, s 89*).

Only those jobholders aged between 22 and State pension age who have 'threshold earnings' (£10,000 per annum for 2016/2017) are subject to the automatic enrolment requirement (*PA 2008, s 3*). This figure is subject to annual review. Only jobholders earning that amount or above need be automatically enrolled, but once enrolled, contributions will start at the lower qualifying earnings level (£5,824 pa for 2016/2017). The Regulator uses the term 'eligible jobholder' for someone satisfying these requirements.

'Qualifying earnings' is defined in *PA 2008, s 13* as being that part of a person's gross earnings in a pay reference period of 12 months that is more than £5,824 and not more than £43,000 (for 2016/17). These figures are subject to annual review by the Secretary of State and may also be altered in proportion to any change to the length of the pay reference period either above or below 12 months. 'Earnings' means sums of any of the following descriptions payable to an individual in connection with their employment:

(*a*)   salary, wages, commission, bonuses and overtime;

(*b*)   statutory sick pay under the *Social Security Contributions and Benefits Act 1992, Part 11*;

(*c*)   statutory maternity pay under *Part 12* of that *Act*;

(*d*)   statutory paternity pay under *Part 12ZA* of that *Act*;

(*e*)   statutory adoption pay under *Part 12ZB* of that *Act*;

(*ea*)   statutory shared parental pay under *Part 12ZC* of that *Act*; and

(*f*)   sums otherwise prescribed as earnings for these purposes.

Qualifying earnings and threshold earnings are assessed over the 'pay reference period'. Employers will be able to use a jobholder's normal pay cycle (eg weekly or monthly) as the pay reference period or a pay reference period equal in length to the usual interval between payments of the jobholder's regular wage or salary (or a period of a week, if less) (*Automatic Enrolment Regulations, reg 4* as amended by the *Automatic Enrolment (Miscellaneous Amendments) Regulations 2013 (SI 2013/2556)* (the '*Miscellaneous Amendments Regulations*')).

Exceptions to the duty to enrol

14.12   Under *sections 3, 5, 7* and *9* of *PA 2008*, employers are obliged to automatically enrol (and re-enrol) workers who satisfy age and earnings criteria into a qualifying workplace pension scheme (see **14.11** above). However, automatic enrolment and pension saving is not always appropriate.

PA 2008, s 87A (inserted by *PA 2014, s 38* from 11 September 2014) provides a general regulation-making power to create exceptions to the employer duties. Regulations made under *PA 2008, s 87A* may not provide for an employer to be excluded from the automatic enrolment duty on the basis of their size and it also includes a power to reinstate the automatic enrolment duty if the circumstances that triggered the exclusion change.

The *Automatic Enrolment Regulations, Part 1A* (inserted by the *Occupational and Personal Pension Schemes (Automatic Enrolment) (Amendment) Regulations 2015 (SI 2015/501), reg 5*) provides exceptions to the employer duty to enrol eligible jobholders. These exceptions came into force on 1 April 2015. As a consequence, the following jobholders will be excluded from the employer duty to automatically enrol (although the employer retains the power to do so if it wishes):

- those serving a notice period or where notice is given up to six weeks after the duty to enrol has arisen (ie during the joining window). This applies equally to resignation, dismissal or retirement. It does not apply to those on fixed-term contracts;

- those who have left a qualifying scheme at their own volition or request in the last 12 months;

- individuals with tax protected status. The employer must have 'reasonable grounds to believe' that the worker has tax protected status (see below for more detail); and

- individuals paid a winding up lump sum and then re-employed by the same employer within a 12-month period (this is quite a limited exception).

If a scheme member who is registered for certain types of fixed, enhanced or individual protection for the purposes of the lifetime allowance accrues rights under a registered pension scheme, he will lose that protection (see **Chapter 17** for more detail on lifetime allowance protections). Although it would be open to an affected member to opt-out following automatic enrolment, the safer course would be for him not to be enrolled at all. The problem for employers is that the registration for protection is an individual matter and not something the employee would necessarily inform his employer of. The exception in the *Automatic Enrolment Regulations, reg 5D* applies where the employer has 'reasonable grounds to believe' that the worker has relevant tax protected status. Employers may wish to consider flagging this point to employees and inviting individuals to provide proof of tax protection at the point of joining the employer and before any re-enrolment exercise (see **14.18** below).

Further exceptions were added with effect from 6 April 2016 in relation to partners in limited liability partnerships ('LLPs') (*Automatic Enrolment Regulations, reg 5EB*) and company directors *(Automatic Enrolment Regulations, reg 5EA)*.

The LLP exception arose following the case of *Clyde & Co LLP v Bates Van Winkelhof [2014] UKSC 32* where the Supreme Court held that a member of an LLP counted as a 'worker' for the purposes of *ERA 1996, s 230(3))*. The definition of 'worker' is substantially similar to the one used in *PA 2008* for the purposes of automatic enrolment. It had previously been generally assumed that LLP partners would not be subject to automatic enrolment. The new exemption in *Automatic Enrolment Regulations, reg 5EB* applies to members of an LLP who:

- have qualifying earnings; and

- are not treated for income tax purposes as being employed by the LLP under *Income Tax (Trading and Other Income) Act 2005, s 863A*.

In practice, this new exemption may not be of much assistance: if a partner is not treated for tax purposes as being employed by the LLP then it seems unlikely that he would be a 'worker' for the purposes of *PA 2008* (see **14.11** above).

Under the *Automatic Enrolment Regulations, reg 5EA*, the duty to enrol company directors is replaced with an option to enrol where the eligible jobholder 'holds office as a director of the company by which the jobholder is employed'. This means that no director has to be enrolled, but (where they have a contract of service and qualifying earnings) they can be automatically enrolled and they can still choose to opt in. Sole directors (where there are no other employees) are already totally exempt by virtue of *PA 2008, s 90*.

The duty to automatically does not apply where the employer is a 'european employer' in relation to that individual for the purposes of the *Occupational Pension Schemes (Cross-border Activities) Regulations 2005 (SI 2005/3381)* (*Automatic Enrolment Regulations, reg 5A*). This is to prevent an employer becoming obliged to enrol workers in a situation which would trigger the enhanced funding and regulatory requirements which apply to cross-border pension schemes under *PA 2004, Part 7*.

The staging process

14.13   The automatic enrolment regime is being phased in over a staging period which began on 1 October 2012 with the largest employers (based on the size of their PAYE scheme) and ending in February 2018. The full list of staging dates is set out in the *Employers' Duties (Implementation) Regulations 2010 (SI 2010/4)* (the '*Implementation Regulations*') (as amended).

Between 1 October 2012 and 6 April 2016, employers were able to opt to automatically enrol their relevant jobholders before their designated staging date by obtaining the consent of their scheme's trustees or manager and by giving the Regulator at least one month's notice (*Implementation Regulations, reg 3*). However, the *Occupational and Personal Pension Schemes (Automatic Enrolment) (Miscellaneous Amendments) Regulations 2016 (SI 2016/311)* have simplified the conditions so that:

- the requirement to obtain agreement from the pension schemes for those employers who have no one to enrol is removed;

- the condition to give the Regulator one month's notice is removed. Instead, the employer is required to notify the Regulator no later than the day before their chosen new staging date and will be able to declare its compliance at the same time; and

- employers with no one to enrol are able to bring forward the staging date to any date (and not just the first of the month, as was previously required).

Relationship with stakeholder requirements

14.14   In light of the automatic enrolment requirements, the duty on employers under the *WRPA 1999* stakeholder regime was removed by *PA 2008, s 87* with effect from 1 October 2012. Transitional provisions require employers to continue to operate a payroll deduction facility for existing stakeholder plan member contributions, but this obligation will end when the member chooses to end contributions or leaves the particular employment.

Many employers, who used an existing stakeholder scheme to satisfy the automatic enrolment requirements, are now seeking to transfer their existing arrangements to a new scheme. Such transfers are not necessarily straightforward and employers will need to ensure that the automatic enrolment requirements are still complied with (see **14.46** below).

Action from automatic enrolment date

14.15   In relation to occupational pension schemes, employers must within six weeks of the automatic enrolment date (see **14.10** above) take the necessary steps to complete the automatic enrolment process, as well as provide written enrolment information to the eligible jobholder and provide certain information about jobholders to the scheme. Active membership must be effected by the employer from the automatic enrolment date (*PA 2008, s 3* and *Automatic Enrolment Regulations, regs 2, 3* and *7* (as amended by the *Miscellaneous Amendments Regulations*)).

In relation to workplace personal pension schemes, employers must within six weeks of the automatic enrolment date (see **14.10** above) make arrangements with the provider to ensure that the eligible jobholder receives key information on the terms and conditions of the scheme, as well as to provide written enrolment information to the jobholder and certain information to the scheme about the jobholders. The jobholder is deemed to have entered into an agreement to become an active member of the personal pension scheme with effect from the automatic enrolment date on the later of the date on which the provider gives the jobholder the key information about the terms and conditions of the scheme and the date on which the employer gives the jobholder the enrolment information (*Automatic Enrolment Regulations, reg 6* (as amended by the *Miscellaneous Amendments Regulations*)).

Details of the information which must be made available are set out at **14.34** and **14.35** below.

Opting out

14.16   A jobholder who has been automatically enrolled may opt out by giving the employer an opt-out notice. A valid opt-out notice must include the wording set out in the *Automatic Enrolment Regulations, Sch 1* and:

- include the jobholder's name;
- include the jobholder's national insurance number or date of birth;

- include a statement from the jobholder to the effect that he or she wishes to opt out of pension saving and understands that, in doing so, the jobholder will lose the right to pension contributions from the employer and may have a lower income in retirement;

- be signed by the jobholder or, where the notice is in an electronic format, must include a statement confirming the jobholder personally submitted the notice; and

- be dated.

(*Automatic Enrolment Regulations, reg 9(6)* (as amended by the *Miscellaneous Amendments Regulations*)).

The opt-out notice must be available from the scheme in which the jobholder is an active member. It may not be provided by the employer, unless the employer is also the scheme administrator. In the case of an occupational pension scheme, the notice must be received by the employer within one month after the day on which the jobholder becomes an active member of the scheme or the day on which he receives the enrolment information (whichever is the later). In the case of a workplace personal pension scheme, the notice must be given within one month after the day on which the agreement is 'deemed' to exist (the *Automatic Enrolment Regulations, reg 9*).

Where the employer is given a valid opt-out notice, the employer must inform the relevant scheme that the notice has been received (*Automatic Enrolment Regulations, reg 10*). Where an opt-out notice is found to be invalid, the employer must inform the jobholder and explain the reason for the invalidity. In such circumstances, the opt-out period will be extended to six weeks, so the jobholder has an opportunity to resubmit the notice without losing the chance to opt out (*Automatic Enrolment Regulations, reg 9*).

Where an opt-out occurs, the employer must refund the jobholder's contributions within one month or by the second payday from and including the day the jobholder gives notice to opt out, whichever is the later. The scheme must refund any contributions it has received to the employer within the same period (*Automatic Enrolment Regulations, reg 11*).

PA 2008 prohibits employers from offering inducements which encourage workers to give up future membership of a qualifying pension scheme or to opt out of automatic enrolment (*PA 2008, s 54*). 'Inducement' is not defined, but the Regulator has stated that it considers an inducement to be 'any action taken by the employer, the sole purpose of which is to attempt to induce:

- a jobholder to opt out without becoming an active member of a qualifying scheme with effect from the date on which they originally became an active member (ie their automatic enrolment date or enrolment date)

- a jobholder or an entitled worker to cease active membership of a pension scheme without becoming an active member of another scheme with effect from the day after the original membership ceased.'

(The Regulator's 'Detailed guidance for employers: Safeguarding individuals' (no 8).)

There are certain clear examples of inducements, such as offering higher salaries, a one-off bonus payments or a promotion. However, employers should also consider whether flexible benefit packages could be considered inducements (see **14.43** below).

A jobholder may lodge a complaint with the Regulator about an unlawful inducement he or she encounters within six months of the contravention (although there will be a four-year 'look back' period) (*Employers' Duties (Registration and Compliance) Regulations 2010 SI 2010/5, reg 16* (the '*Compliance Regulations*')). If the complaint is upheld, the Regulator will be able to issue the employer with a compliance notice (see **14.39** below).

Automatic Enrolment Timeline

14.17

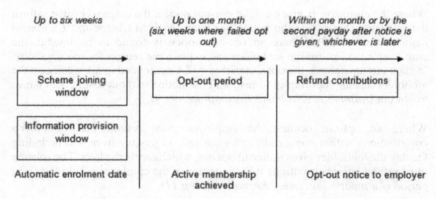

All contributions that are deducted in the first three months after the worker is automatically enrolled must be paid to the scheme by the employer by the 22nd of the fourth month if paid electronically (or the 19th of that month if not paid electronically) (*Occupational Pension Scheme (Scheme Administration) Regulations 1996 (SI 1996/1715), reg 16* (as amended by the *Miscellaneous Amendments Regulations*)). This position simplifies the previous position whereby pension contributions deducted from a jobholder's salary by an employer during the opt-out period after the jobholder had been automatically enrolled had to be paid to the scheme by the end of the second month after the month which included the jobholder's automatic enrolment date. This allows the employer to hold on to the contribution until after the opt-out period has ended saving the employer from having to go to the trouble of recouping the contributions from the trustees or provider when a refund has been made.

Re-enrolment

14.18   *PA 2008* requires employers to make arrangements for jobholders who have previously opted out to be automatically re-enrolled with effect from the automatic re-enrolment date (*PA 2008, s 5*). Jobholders must be automatically re-enrolled every three years during a six month window (the exact date being selected by the employer) if they continue to work for the same employer (*Automatic Enrolment Regulations, reg 12*), running from three months before the third anniversary of the employer's staging date to the end of three months after that date.

The same exceptions and exemptions apply on re-enrolment as on initial automatic enrolment (see **14.12** above).

PA 2014 has corrected a provision under the *PA 2008* in respect of the interaction between the statutory re-enrolment duty and the provisions which allow an employer to postpone automatic enrolment in respect of their DB or hybrid schemes for a period of three months on top of the five-year transitional period ending on 30 September 2017. From 11 September 2014, employers are no longer required to automatically re-enrol an eligible jobholder if auto-enrolment has been postponed for a period of up to three months or deferred to the end of the transitional period in the case of a DB or hybrid scheme (*PA 2014, s 37*).

Opting in

14.19   Jobholders who are not eligible to be automatically enrolled can give their employer notice requiring the employer to arrange for them to be opted into an automatic enrolment scheme.

Jobholders who will not immediately qualify for automatic enrolment but who have the right to opt in fall into three categories:

- they are a non-eligible jobholder because they either meet the earnings triggers but are under age 22 or above State pension age or because they earn less than the earnings trigger (£10,000 for 2016/2017) but more than the qualifying earnings threshold (£5,824 for 2016/2017);

- they are an eligible jobholder who opted out after being auto-enrolled or re-enrolled, but have changed their mind; and

- their employer is using a postponement period for automatic enrolment and were it not for the postponement they would qualify for automatic enrolment as an eligible jobholder (*PA 2008, s 4*, as amended by *PA 2011, s 6*).

Employers will be required to inform these individuals in writing that they have a right to join an automatic enrolment scheme, the process for opting in and how to get more information on pension saving. Where the jobholders inform their employers in writing that they want to join the scheme, employers will have a duty to treat them as jobholders eligible for automatic enrolment and will have to follow the normal automatic enrolment process. Jobholders may request to opt in once in a 12-month period. The information must be provided within six weeks of the date on which the right to opt in first applies to the jobholder (*Automatic Enrolment Regulations, reg 21*).

PA 2008, s 9 provides that workers who are aged between 16 and 74 but do not have qualifying earnings ('entitled workers') have the right to require their employer to arrange for them to be enrolled into a registered pension scheme but do not have the right to any employer contribution. Employers have a duty to inform these individuals in writing that they have the right to join a pension scheme, the process for applying and details as to where they can get more information about pension saving. Where a worker instructs the employer in writing that they wish to start saving in a pension, the employer must make arrangements for them to become an active member of a registered pension scheme. This need not be the same as the automatic enrolment scheme used for jobholders.

Options for employers

14.20   Options that employers might consider include:

Option one: NEST

14.21   The National Employment Savings Trust ('NEST') is a government-established trust-based occupational defined contribution scheme operated by a corporate trustee (the NEST Corporation) and is registered with HMRC under *FA 2004* and with the Regulator. NEST is governed by an order made under statute, the *National Employment Savings Trust Order (SI 2010/917)* (the '*Nest Order*') (as amended) and the *National Employment Savings Trust (NEST) Scheme Rules*, which supplement the Nest Order.

Some of the key features of NEST include:

- An annual contributions limit prescribed by order under *PA 2008, s 70*. This was initially set at £3,600 but it must be adjusted each year (*NEST Order, article 22*). The limit for the 2016/2017 tax year is £4,900. The contribution limit is expected to be abolished on 1 April 2017.

- Minimum levels of contributions by the employer and the jobholder are being phased in over the transitional periods which apply to other defined contribution schemes (see **14.24** below).

- There are severe restrictions on transfers into and out of NEST. These are expected to be lifted on 1 April 2017.

- An annual management charge of 0.3 per cent of a member's fund value is levied on members, and an initial charge of 1.8 per cent of the value of new contributions.

The use by an employer of NEST outsources much of the administrative burden. This could be an attractive option for employers, as their only responsibility would be to enrol employees and provide contributions. This option may not be appropriate for employers with a significant number of higher earners, given the current limit to annual contributions to the scheme and the restrictions on transfers out, although as noted above, these are due to be abolished in April 2017. Many employers may need to consider a top-up pension scheme in addition to NEST (see **14.31** below) in the interim period until the above changes come into force.

NEST may be attractive for both employers and jobholders in industries where there is a high mobility rate amongst workers as any employer can contribute to it, so for both employer and employee there will be minimum disruption when they move jobs. NEST could also be advantageous for those with more than one job as it can accept concurrent contributions from more than one employer.

Option two: using existing pensions arrangements

14.22   Where an employer decides to use its existing scheme, it must satisfy itself that it meets the statutory requirements for automatic enrolment and certify that the scheme meets the relevant quality requirement (see **14.23–14.27** below). In certain circumstances, quality requirement certification must be provided by the scheme actuary.

An increase in cost is likely with this approach, especially for employers who currently have a low take-up for their pension scheme, as the percentage of employees joining the scheme is likely to swell under an automatic enrolment system.

Scheme amendments are likely to be needed, so employers should be considering in advance how they will comply. There may be scope for levelling down contributions or accrual in an existing scheme whilst retaining 'qualifying scheme' status (see **14.29** below). Careful consideration of eligibility rules and joining arrangements will also be required.

Automatic enrolment schemes, qualifying schemes and the quality requirement

14.23   An 'automatic enrolment scheme' is a 'qualifying scheme' where no provision of the scheme prevents the employer from making arrangements for relevant jobholders to become active members of the scheme and no provision of the scheme requires the jobholder to express a choice in relation to any matter, or to provide any information, in order to remain an active member (*PA 2008, s 17*).

A pension scheme is a 'qualifying scheme' in relation to a jobholder (J) if:

(*a*)   the scheme is an occupational or a personal pension scheme;

(*b*)   the scheme is registered under *FA 2004, Part 4, Chapter 2*; and

(*c*)   while J is an active member, the scheme satisfies the 'quality requirement' in relation to J.

The quality requirements for different types of scheme are set out in *PA 2008, ss 20–28* and are summarised in **14.24** to **14.27** below.

UK money purchase schemes

14.24   *PA 2008, s 20* provides that a money purchase scheme that has its main administration in the UK satisfies the quality requirement in relation to a jobholder if, under the scheme:

(*a*)   the jobholder's employer must pay contributions in respect of the jobholder;

(*b*)   the employer's contribution, however calculated, must be at least 3 per cent of the amount of the jobholder's qualifying earnings in the relevant pay reference period; and

(*c*)   the total amount of contributions, however calculated, must be at least 8 per cent of the amount of the jobholder's qualifying earnings in the relevant pay reference period.

PA 2008, s 29 and the *Implementation Regulations* (as most recently amended by the *Employers' Duties (Implementation) (Amendment) Regulations 2016*

(*2016/719*) with effect from 1 October 2016) provide that contribution rates will be phased in over transitional periods as follows:

PHASED CONTRIBUTIONS: DEFINED CONTRIBUTION SCHEMES

Date	Employer minimum contributions	Total minimum contribution
Employer's staging date to 05/04/18	1 per cent	2 per cent (including 1 per cent employee contribution)
06/04/2018 – 05/04/19	2 per cent	5 per cent (including 3 per cent employee contribution)
06/04/2019	3 per cent	8 per cent (including 5 per cent employee contribution)

Employers can self-certify that their schemes meet the prescribed minimum requirements. The mechanism detailing how employers can do this is set out in *PA 2008*, *s 28*, *Automatic Enrolment Regulations, Part 7A* and the DWP's 'Automatic Enrolment: Guidance on certifying money purchase schemes' (published in 2012 and updated in 2013 and 2014).

The ability to self-certify was introduced following concerns that many employers would have problems in satisfying the relevant quality requirement, as pensionable pay as defined under the scheme might not have the same definition as 'qualifying earnings'. As a consequence, it made it difficult for employers to be certain that the appropriate level of contribution was being paid in relation to each relevant jobholder. A certification model was therefore included in *PA 2011*, allowing employers to certify that the quality requirement has been met or that one of the new alternative requirements are satisfied in relation to the scheme. They will then, for the purposes of *PA 2008*, *s 28* be taken to satisfy the quality requirement. The alternative tests are set out in the *Automatic Enrolment Regulations, reg 32E*:

Set 1 test:

• Employer contribution of at least 4 per cent of pensionable earnings;

• Total contribution of at least 9 per cent of pensionable earnings;

• Pensionable earnings must be at least 'basic pay'.

Set 2 test:

• Employer contribution of at least 3 per cent of pensionable earnings;

• Total contribution of at least 8 per cent of pensionable earnings;

• Pensionable earnings must be at least 'basic pay';

- The pensionable earnings of all 'relevant jobholders' constitute at least 85 per cent of the 'earnings' of those jobholders.

Set 3 test:

- Employer contribution of at least 3 per cent of 'earnings';
- Total contribution of at least 7 per cent of 'earnings'.

Reductions apply to these figures during the transitional periods.

For the definition of 'earnings', see **14.11** above. 'Pensionable earnings' are defined as the gross earnings of the jobholder on which contributions are payable to the pension scheme by the employer or the jobholder. 'Basic pay' is defined as the gross earnings of a jobholder, disregarding the gross amount of any commission, bonuses, overtime or similar payments; any shift premium pay; and other reasonable allowances (*Automatic Enrolment Regulations, reg 32K*).

Schemes operating a salary cap or a cap on contributions can still self-certify as long as the upper limit does not result in the payment of contributions that are less than those required by the quality requirement (ie based on qualifying earnings) (*Automatic Enrolment Regulations, reg 32E(5)*).

Certification is voluntary. Schemes which expressly provide for the required minimum contributions based on qualifying earnings do not need certification. Neither do schemes where employers undertake individual benefit checks on each member (which may be simpler and cheaper than certification for very small schemes or employers).

A certificate produced under the self-certification system can run for up to 18 months from its 'effective date' (normally no later than the automatic enrolment date) and must be signed within one month after the effective date. The employer must retain a certificate for six years after the end of the certification period and produce it on request by the Regulator, relevant jobholder or recognised Trade Union (*Automatic Enrolment Regulations, reg 32B*).

The certificate must state that:

- in relation to relevant jobholders of the employer who are active members of the scheme, the scheme is in the opinion of the person giving the certificate able to satisfy the relevant quality requirement throughout the certification period; or
- in relation to those jobholders, the scheme is in that person's opinion able to satisfy a prescribed alternative requirement throughout the certification period (*PA 2008, s 28(2)*).

A relevant jobholder is a jobholder to whom the certificate applies (*PA 2008, s 28(1A)*).

The detailed requirements regarding the form of the certificate are set out in the *Automatic Enrolment Regulations, reg 32C* (the DWP's Guidance also contains a template certificate, although its use is not obligatory). In particular, where a certificate does not apply to all the jobholders who are active members (ie there are some jobholders who are active members but do not satisfy the relevant quality requirement) then detailed information must be provided as to:

• the names and roles of those who are included (relevant jobholders);

• the name and role of any active member who has not been included because they have chosen to pay lower contributions; and

• the name and role of any active member who has not been included because, in the opinion of the employer, the quality requirement will clearly be met.

As set out in the DWP's Guidance, certificates expire automatically at the end of their effective periods. An employer cannot cancel a certificate once it has been issued. While a certificate is in force, if a significant change in circumstances occurs in relation to a scheme or an employer which means the scheme can no longer satisfy the certification test, the employer should amend the expiry date so that the certificate expires on a day after the change takes place but before the original expiry date (certificates cannot be retrospectively cancelled).

Examples of significant changes include:

• corporate transactions;

• changes to a scheme's benefit structure;

• changes to the contribution rate;

• changes to the pay and reward structure; and

• the winding up of a scheme.

In respect of mis-certification, the DWP's Guidance states that where the Regulator finds that there were not reasonable grounds for a certificate to be issued and that there was a shortfall between the contributions payable under the scheme and those payable under the statutory quality requirement, the Regulator may require the employer to make good the shortfall. If the employer fails to do so, the certificate will be treated as being of no effect and the employer will be exposed to enforcement action for failure to enrol its jobholders into a qualifying scheme.

UK defined benefits schemes

14.25   A DB scheme that has its main administration in the UK satisfies the quality requirement in relation to a jobholder if it satisfies the 'test scheme' standard in relation to that jobholder (*PA 2008, s 21–23* as amended by the *PA 2014, s 24, Sch 13, Pt 2, para 82* with effect from 6 April 2016).

A scheme satisfies the test scheme standard in relation to a jobholder where the pensions to be provided for the relevant members of the scheme are broadly equivalent to, or better than, the pensions which would have been provided to them under the test scheme.

The test scheme is a model scheme (*PA 2008, s 23*), allowing for a pension to be provided from age 65 (or state pension age, if higher) with an accrual rate of at least 1/120ths of average qualifying earnings in the last three tax years preceding the end of pensionable service, multiplied by the number of years of pensionable service, up to a maximum of 40 years. Pensions should be revalued in line with *PSA 1993, s 84*, and increased in line with *PA 1995, s 51* (*Automatic Enrolment Regulations, reg 37*). Contingent and ancillary benefits may not be taken into account.

Certifying that a scheme meets the test scheme standard must be done by the scheme actuary or by the employer (*Automatic Enrolment Regulations, reg 39*); however the employer may only certify where no calculation, comparison or assessment normally carried out by actuaries is required. In applying the test scheme standard, the pensions to be provided for relevant members must be considered as a whole. A scheme actuary or employer may not certify that a scheme meets the test scheme standard if the pensions to be provided for more than 10 per cent of relevant members are not broadly equivalent to the pensions which would be provided to them under the test scheme.

The test scheme standard is modified in the case of career average schemes. Under the *Automatic Enrolment Regulations, reg 36*, a career average scheme cannot be a qualifying scheme if, in relation to active members, it has any of the following features:

* it does not provide for the revaluation of accrued benefits;

* it provides for revaluation, but at a level which is below the 'minimum rate' (unless the scheme's funding is based on the assumption that accrued benefits would be revalued at or above the minimum rate and such funding is provided for in the scheme's statement of funding principles); or

* it provides for discretionary revaluation only (unless the scheme's funding takes the discretionary power into account (and this is noted in the scheme's statement of funding principles), on the basis that accrued benefits would be revalued at or above the 'minimum rate').

The 'minimum rate' is the lower of the annual increase in the Retail Prices Index and the Consumer Prices Index capped at 2.5 per cent.

PA 2008, s 23A (inserted by *PA 2014, s 39*) provides for two alternative quality requirements for DB qualifying schemes. These are:

- **Shared risk test.** This test is aimed primarily at shared risk schemes with money purchase-type structures but which offer. The test is satisfied if the scheme meets the money purchase quality requirement (see **14.24** above) (*PA 2008, s 23A(1)(a)* and *Automatic Enrolment Regulations, reg 32L*).

- **Cost of accruals test.** This test is satisfied where the cost of providing the benefits accruing for or in respect of the relevant members over a relevant period would require contributions to be made of a total amount equal to at least a prescribed percentage of the members' total relevant earnings over that period. The rate must be tested either at a scheme level, or with at least 90 per cent of relevant members meeting the required percentage. The rates set in the regulations depend on how the scheme determines pensionable earnings, ranging from nine per cent where all earnings are taken into account to 13 per cent where only basic pay over the LEL for National Insurance contributions is included in pensionable earnings. The relevant members for this purpose are the active members of the scheme. Where there is a material difference in the cost of accrual of benefits in relation to different groups of members then each group must be tested separately. A temporary easement was introduced with effect from 6 April 2016, allowing schemes which were contracted-out immediately before that date to apply the cost of accruals test across the membership as a whole even if there is a material difference in the cost of the benefits accruing for different groups of members. This is available until 5 April 2019 only in respect of jobholders who were in contracted-out employment on 5 April 2016 and where the scheme rules have not been amended after that date in a way that would mean that the contracting out requirements would not continue to be satisfied but for the abolition of contracting out (*PA 2008, s 23A(1)(b)* and *Automatic Enrolment Regulations, reg 32M*).

The DWP issued updated guidance on the alternative quality requirements for DB pension schemes in April 2016.

The transitional period for schemes with defined benefits (including hybrid schemes which provide defined benefits) allows employers to delay automatic enrolment until 30 September 2017. The start of the transitional period will be the jobholder's first automatic enrolment date (usually their staging date) up to and including 30 September 2017(*Implementation Regulations, reg 6*). The effect is that for such employees, their automatic enrolment date is delayed until after the end of the transitional period. Jobholders retain a right to join the scheme (ie to opt in) during this transitional period, and the employer must provide information to the jobholder outlining that right. If the jobholder ceases to be entitled to join the scheme, or the scheme ceases to be a qualifying scheme during this period (eg the scheme is closed to future accrual), the jobholder must be enrolled into another DB auto-enrolment scheme, or be enrolled as a member of a defined contribution scheme where the employer's contribution will need to be backdated to the original staging date.

Where a DB pension scheme or hybrid pension scheme is a qualifying scheme by virtue of satisfying the alternative quality requirement under the shared risk test (PA 2008, s *23A(1)(a)*) then the employer cannot defer automatic enrolment during the transitional periods. Instead the transitional arrangements in respect of money purchase pension schemes apply (*PA 2008, s 30*) (see **14.24** above).

UK hybrid schemes

14.26   A hybrid scheme that has its main administration in the UK will satisfy the quality requirement if it satisfies the relevant requirements for a money purchase scheme or a DB scheme, subject to any prescribed modifications (*PA 2008, s 24* and the *Automatic Enrolment Regulations, regs 40* and *43*).

In terms of how to apply this principle to hybrid schemes in practice, guidance is provided in the *Hybrid Schemes Quality Requirements Rules 2016* (taking effect on 4 July 2016).

The general rule is that when considering hybrid schemes, the provisions of the scheme relating to defined benefits and those relating to money purchase benefits should be dealt with separately, with the relevant DB quality requirements being applied to the DB provisions and the relevant money purchase quality requirements being applied to the money purchase provisions. Where one set of quality requirements is satisfied, it will generally be irrelevant whether the other set are also satisfied (*Hybrid Schemes Quality Requirements Rules, Rule 3*), although there are some variations.

Under the *Automatic Enrolment Regulations, reg 32G*, hybrid scheme employers can self-certify their schemes' compliance with either the standard or the alternative quality requirements in relation to the money purchase aspects of those schemes.

An employer can delay automatic enrolment during the transitional period where a DB pension is offered to a jobholder (whether offered under a hybrid scheme or a DB scheme) (*PA 2008, s 30*). There is an exception to this where the DB or hybrid scheme providing the pension is only a qualifying scheme by virtue of satisfying the alternative quality requirement provided by *PA 2008, s 23A(1)(a)* (ie one based purely on contribution rates). Employers offering money purchase benefits under a hybrid scheme will still be able to use the transitional arrangements under *PA 2008, s 29* which permit a gradual phasing in of the contribution requirements.

UK personal pension schemes

14.27   Personal pension schemes satisfy the quality requirement in relation to a jobholder if the following conditions are met:

(1)   The scheme must be subject to regulation under *FSMA 2000* and have its operations carried out in the UK by a person who is an authorised person or an exempt person under *FSMA 2000, s 19*.

(2)   All of the benefits that may be provided to the jobholder under the scheme are money purchase benefits.

(3)   In relation to the jobholder, there is an agreement between the provider of the scheme and the employer under which:

    (*a*)   the employer must pay contributions in respect of the jobholder;

    (*b*)   the employer's contribution, however calculated, must be equal to, or more than, three per cent of the amount of the jobholder's qualifying earnings in the relevant pay reference period;

    (*c*)   if there is a shortfall, there is an agreement between the provider of the scheme and the jobholder under which the jobholder must pay contributions which, however calculated, are equal to or more than the shortfall. 'Shortfall' for these purposes is the difference (if any) between the employer's contribution in respect of the jobholder, and eight per cent of the amount of the jobholder's qualifying earnings in the relevant pay reference period; and

    (*d*)   there are direct payment arrangements (within the meaning of *PSA 1993, s 111A*) between the jobholder and the employer

(*PA 2008, s 26* and the *Automatic Enrolment Regulations, reg 5*).

Minimum contribution levels are being phased in and the certification provisions and three sets tests also apply (see **14.24** above).

Other types of pension scheme

14.28   Employers may use a non-UK scheme with its main administration in an EEA state for automatic enrolment if the scheme meets certain requirements, which include:

- being an institute for occupational retirement provision within the meaning of *Article 6(a)* of the *Institute for Occupational Retirement Provisions (IORP) Directive*; or

- a personal pension scheme is regulated by a competent authority in its home state;

- the regulatory requirements applicable to the occupational pension scheme or personal pension scheme must provide for some of the accrued benefits to be used to provide an income for life.

(see *PA 2008, s 25* and *27* and the *Automatic Enrolment Regulations, regs 44–47*).

Levelling down

14.29   Employers may have the option of keeping employees in an existing scheme (altering it where necessary to become a 'qualifying scheme') but reducing the employer contributions to the minimum contribution level of 3 per cent, or levelling down benefits to the 'test scheme' standard.

The attraction of this option is clear: it could save employers significant amounts of money if they currently provide a more generous pension scheme to their employees.

The 'levelling down' of pension scheme benefits is a major concern that has been raised by critics of the automatic enrolment regime. Levelling down could create contractual and employee relations problems and would almost certainly trigger consultation requirements under the *Occupational and Personal Pension Schemes (Consultation by Employers and Miscellaneous Amendment) Regulations 2006 (SI 2006/349)* (see **Chapter 7**). Careful consideration must also be given to any restrictions in the scheme's power of amendment (see **Chapter 13**).

Option three: establish or select a new scheme for the purposes of automatic enrolment

14.30   An employer could decide to establish a new occupational pension scheme for the purpose of compliance with the automatic enrolment regime. Although this would have significant time and cost implications the advantage would be that the scheme would be specifically designed to comply and the contributions and benefits would exactly fit the quality requirements described in **14.24** to **14.27** above. Alternatively an employer could select a new personal pension arrangement into which it could enrol its relevant jobholders.

Option four: use NEST and provide a top-up

14.31   Employers who wish to outsource the administration of their pension scheme but aim to give employees higher contributions than three per cent could consider this option. An employer can enrol its employees in NEST and then contribute more than the minimum three per cent (although currently total contributions would be restricted to the applicable contributions limit under NEST. The contribution limit restriction is being abolished in April 2017).

In order to recruit and retain higher earners, it is likely that the employer would have to provide additional benefits outside NEST (in the short term), perhaps through offering to contribute to personal pension schemes for certain employees.

Option five: use a combination of schemes

14.32   Employers could provide a combination of Options one to four above, perhaps making different schemes available to different sections of the workforce. Traditionally it has not been uncommon for employers to have different schemes for, for example, manual workers and executives. This approach has its attractions in allowing an employer to provide workers with pension provision which suits their individual budgets and expectations. However, there is scope for this to give rise to employee relations problems as well as potential claims for unlawful discrimination.

Employer disclosure requirements

14.33   Employers have significant disclosure duties under the *Automatic Enrolment Regulations*. They will need to provide information to both the trustees/scheme manager and the members themselves, as set out below.

Information to be provided by the employer to the scheme

14.34   The employer must provide the following information ('jobholder information') relating to the jobholder to the trustees or manager of an occupational pension scheme or the personal pension scheme provider in writing within six weeks of the automatic enrolment date:

(*a*)   name;

(*b*)   date of birth;

(*c*)   postal residential address;

(*d*)   gender;

(*e*)   automatic enrolment date (or automatic re-enrolment date or enrolment date as the case may be);

(*f*)   national insurance number;

(*g*)   the gross earnings due to the jobholder in any applicable pay reference period;

(*h*)   the value, if any, of contributions payable to the scheme by the employer or the jobholder in any applicable pay reference period;

(*i*)   postal work address;

(*j*)   individual work e-mail address (where an individual work e-mail address is allocated to that jobholder); and

(*k*)   personal e-mail address (where the employer holds this information).

(*PA 2008, s 3* and the *Automatic Enrolment Regulations, regs 3* and *7(1)(b)*)

Enrolment information

14.35   The following information ('enrolment information') must be given to all relevant jobholders in writing within six weeks of their automatic enrolment date:

(*a*)   a statement that the jobholder has been or will be enrolled into a pension scheme;

(*b*)   the jobholder's automatic enrolment date (or automatic re-enrolment date or enrolment date as the case may be);

(*c*)   the value of contributions (as a fixed amount or as a percentage of qualifying earnings or pensionable pay in a pay reference period) that will be made into the scheme by the employer and the jobholder in any pay reference period, including any changes as a result of transitional provisions;

(*d*)   a statement that any contributions payable to the scheme by the jobholder have been or will be deducted from any qualifying earnings or pensionable pay due to the jobholder;

(*e*)   confirmation as to whether tax relief will be given on employee contributions;

(*f*)   a statement that the jobholder has a right to opt out of the scheme during the opt-out period;

(*g*)   a statement indicating the start and end dates of the opt-out period applicable to the jobholder if that information is known to the employer;

(*h*)   where the opt-out notice may be obtained;

(*i*)   a statement that opting out means the jobholder will be treated for all purposes as not having become an active member of the scheme on that occasion;

(*j*)   a statement that following a valid opt-out notice, any contributions paid by the jobholder will be refunded to the jobholder by the employer;

(*k*)   a statement that following an opt-out, a jobholder may opt in, in which case the employer must arrange for the jobholder to become an active member of an automatic enrolment scheme once in any 12-month period;

(*l*)   that after the opt-out period, the jobholder may cease to make contributions to their pension in accordance with scheme rules;

(*m*)   that a jobholder who opts out or who ceases active membership of an automatic enrolment scheme will normally be automatically re-enrolled into such a scheme by the employer every three years;

(*o*)   a statement that a written notice from the worker must be signed by the worker or, if it is given by means of an electronic communication, must include a statement that the worker personally submitted the notice.

(*PA 2008, s 3* and *Automatic Enrolment Regulations, regs 2, 7(1)(a)* and *Sch 2*)

Compliance and the role of the Pensions Regulator

14.36   The Regulator has been charged with policing the automatic enrolment regime. The statutory provisions setting out the Regulator's role are contained in *PA 2008, Pt 1, Ch 2* and the *Compliance Regulations*.

The *Pensions Regulator (Delegation of Powers) Regulations 2009 (SI 2009/1888)* enable the Regulator to outsource a number of its powers which are prescribed. This includes delegation of its enforcement powers under *PA 2008*.

Duty to register with the Pensions Regulator

14.37   Employers are obliged to register with the Regulator within five months of their staging date, providing the following information:

(*a*)   the employer's name, address, postcode and registered company number where one exists, or, where such a number does not exist:

   (*aa*)   the number under which the employer is registered as a registered society within the meaning given by *section 1(1)* of the *Co-operative and Community Benefit Societies Act 2014*;

(*bb*)   but if the number mentioned in sub-paragraph (*aa*) does not exist, the employer's registered charity number;

(*cc*)   but if the number mentioned in sub-paragraph (*bb*) does not exist, the employer's VAT registration number, if one exists;

(*b*)   the name, telephone number, ordinary working address and email address of the person providing information on behalf of the employer;

(*c*)   the capacity in which the person providing information works for, or is related to, the employer;

(*d*)   the number of jobholders who are automatically enrolled with effect from the staging date or the deferral date;

(*e*)   the number of jobholders who are subject to a transitional period for a defined benefit or hybrid scheme;

(*f*)   the number of workers on PAYE who were, before the staging date, enrolled in a qualifying scheme;

(*g*)   the number of workers not covered by (*d*) to (*f*) above;

(*h*)   Where the employer is required to provide an automatic enrolment scheme, the name and address of an occupational pension scheme or a personal pension scheme provider, and the employer pension scheme reference;

(*i*)   A declaration that the information is, to the best of the employer's knowledge and belief, correct and complete.

On re-enrolment and from 6 April 2016, employers must re-register and provide updated information within five months of the employer's first automatic re-enrolment date (beginning with the third anniversary of the employer's staging date) and in any other case, within the period of five months beginning with the third anniversary of the employer's previous automatic re-enrolment date (*Compliance Regulations, regs 2–4* as amended by the *Automatic Enrolment Amendments Regulations*). The time at which an employer provides this information is referred to as the 'point of re-registration'.

Duty to keep records

14.38   Employers, trustees and managers of pension schemes and pension providers are required to keep certain records to enable the Regulator to verify compliance with the requirements (*Compliance Regulations, regs 5–8*).

These records include details of:

- pension arrangements employers have made;
- the enrolment of jobholders;

- the opt-in and opt-out processes; and
- contributions made by the employer.

Records will need to be kept for a period up to six years (opt-out notices for four years). It has been indicated by the DWP that employers and schemes will not be required to keep separate sets of these records, provided that both have access to the information in them.

Contravention of employer duties and employee protection

14.39 The Regulator has specific enforcement powers to ensure compliance by employers with the automatic enrolment obligations.

In addition, workers may bring a claim before an employment tribunal after suffering a detriment as a result of non-compliance with the automatic enrolment requirements (*PA 2008, s 55–57*). The *Employment Rights Act 1996* gives workers the right not to be unfairly dismissed where the reason for dismissal relates to those requirements. Contractual terms which attempt to exclude or restrict the automatic enrolment requirements are void, unless they are included in a regulated compromise agreement (*PA 2008, s 58*).

An employer who 'wilfully' fails to comply with requirements relating to the right to opt in, automatic enrolment or re-enrolment, will be guilty of an offence, liable on conviction to imprisonment or a fine or both (*PA 2008, s 45*).

PA 2008, s 34 provides that no private right of action for breach of statutory duty arises against an employer who has failed to comply with requirements set out in the employer duty provisions (*ss 2–11*). Under *PA 2008* the Regulator is the sole body responsible for taking action against such breaches.

In the event of non-compliance by an employer, the Regulator has power to issue the following notices:

- compliance notices: directing the defaulting employer to take (or refrain from) specified actions to remedy the default (*PA 2008, s 35*);
- third-party compliance notices: directing a third party (eg trustees or advisers) to take specified steps where the employer has contravened one or more of the core employer duties and a third party contributed to a breach of those duties (*PA 2008, s 36*);
- unpaid contributions notices: directing an employer to pay contributions which have not been paid by their due date. The notice will require an employer to pay contributions by a specified date. The Compliance Regulations give the Regulator the power to add interest at a rate of 4.2 per cent plus the increase in the retail prices index. If contributions

remain outstanding three months after the date specified in the notice the employer can be required by the Regulator to pay both its own and the worker's contributions (*PA 2008, s 37–38* and *Compliance Regulations, reg 10*).

Where a breach is not remedied, the Regulator may order two categories of penalty against the employer:

- fixed penalty notices: these will provide for flat-rate penalties of £400 (*PA 2008, s 40* and *Compliance Regulations, reg 12*);

- escalating penalty notices: these will relate to more serious or persistent breaches of employer duties, and will vary according to employer size, ranging from £50 a day for employers with one to four workers to £10,000 a day for those with 500 or more workers (*PA 2008, s 41* and *Compliance Regulations, reg 13*).

The Regulator issued a report advising employers not to ignore penalty notices on 28 April 2016 (www.thepensionsregulator.gov.uk/press/pn16-22.aspx), which confirms that since 2012 the total number of compliance notices issued is 7,834, there have been 2,234 fixed penalty notices issued and 127 escalating penalty notices issued.

Prohibited recruitment conduct

14.40   *PA 2008, s 50* sets out examples of 'prohibited recruitment conduct' which will be subject to fixed penalties (from £1,000 for employers with one to four workers to £5,000 for employers with 250 or more workers) and relate to instances where employers make any statement or ask any questions which indicate that their acceptance of an application for employment would be conditional on whether or not the applicant chooses to opt out of the scheme (*PA 2008, s 50–53* and *Compliance Regulations, reg 14*).

Review of notices

14.41   Any person receiving a notice or penalty will be able to apply to the Regulator for a review within 28 days of the notice or penalty being issued, which may confirm, revoke or vary a notice. The Regulator may institute its own review of a penalty or notice issued within the previous 18 months. Right of appeal will then lie with the Upper Tribunal and then the Court of Appeal (PA 2008, s 43 and Compliance Regulations, reg 15).

Requiring information

14.42   The Regulator has been given power to require an employer to provide information or documents, and if necessary, inspect its premises to investigate whether an employer has contravened the core employer duties or prohibited recruitment conduct (*PA 2008, s 61*).

Automatic enrolment: some difficult issues

Flexible benefits and the prohibition on inducements

14.43   The issue here is that PA 2008 prohibits employers from offering inducements which encourage workers to give up future membership of a pension scheme or to opt out of automatic enrolment (see **14.16** above). An employer who offers a flexible benefit package could possibly be said to be inducing staff to opt out. Is the offer of a company car or extra holiday instead of a pension an inducement?

The Regulator's guidance 'Safeguarding Individuals' looks at potential inducements. It gives examples of 'clear cut' inducements, including where a worker is offered a one-off cash payment for opting-out. Flexible retirement is included under the heading 'Less clear-cut cases'. The Regulator states that:

> 'The intention of the legislation is to encourage pension saving at a minimum level, not to restrict flexible benefit packages that employers wish to offer their workers. The individual retains the right to choose the makeup of their flexible benefits. However, employers must be confident that, in offering such a package, their sole or main purpose is not to induce individuals to opt out of a qualifying scheme.'

It then suggests that employers who are not sure if the proposed package could amount to an inducement should seek legal advice.

The key to this is going to be what the sole or main purpose of the package offered is. It seems unlikely that a flexible benefits package would be seen as an inducement as long as the pension scheme was presented as part of a balanced offering and as no less valuable or attractive than the other benefits on offer. To avoid the problem altogether, a flexible benefits package could be structured so that employees are required to retain a pension at least up to the qualifying scheme level, with any flex options only applying to contributions or accrual in excess of that.

Another issue would be where an employee has signed up for a flex arrangement before his automatic enrolment date and opted for pension contributions below the minimum automatic enrolment level. He will then have to be automatically enrolled on the relevant date, which could mean a windfall benefit.

TUPE transfers

14.44 *PA 2004, ss 257* and *258* provide future service pension protection for members (or prospective members) of occupational pension schemes who are subject to a TUPE transfer.

Where an employee is a member of an occupational pension scheme immediately before the transfer (or was eligible to join one but did not), the transferee was (before 6 April 2014) required to provide a pension scheme (DB or money purchase) after the transfer with matching employer and employee contributions of up to 6 per cent. There was concern that this could leave the transferee employer having to pay much higher contributions than the transferor (if the transferor had been operating at the minimum level for automatic enrolment and if the employee elected for six per cent contributions) because the auto enrolment requirements and the pension protection afforded by the *Pensions Act 2004* run in parallel.

On 6 April 2014, the *Transfer of Employment (Pension Protection) Regulations 2005 (SI 2005/649)* (the '*Pension Protection Regulations*') were amended by the *Occupational Pension Schemes (Miscellaneous Amendments) Regulations 2014 (SI 2014/540)*) to provide that if a money purchase scheme is offered to the transferring employees on transfer, the transferee employer must pay contributions for a transferring employee which either:

- are not less than those paid by the transferor employer in respect of the employee immediately before the transfer (where the transferor employer was required to pay contributions); or

- match the contributions paid by the employee, up to a maximum of 6% of the employee's salary.

These changes addressed those concerns by allowing the transferee employer to pay the no more than the amount being paid by the transferor employer.

Where an employee is transferred from an employer who has reached its staging date to one which has not the automatic enrolment duties will not apply to the transferee employer until it reaches its own staging date.

Further guidance is available in the Pensions Regulator Guidance Note 2: Workplace Pensions Reform, Getting Ready, Section 4, which sets out how employers should deal with TUPE transfers.

A summary of the current position is set out below:

TUPE TRANSFERS AND MINIMUM PENSIONS OBLIGATIONS

Transferee scheme is not a money purchase scheme	Transferee scheme is a money purchase or stakeholder scheme
The member must be provided with: <ul><li>benefits the value of which equals or exceeds six per cent of pensionable pay for each year of employment plus the value of any member contributions – and member contributions are not required to be more than six per cent of pensionable pay; or</li><li>'relevant contributions'.</li></ul>	The employer must either: <ul><li>make 'relevant contributions'; or</li><li>where immediately before the date of transfer the transferor had been required to make contributions which produced only money purchase benefits, the transferee must make contributions which are not less than those the transferor was required to make.</li></ul>
Relevant contributions are contributions made by the employer **but only where the member also contributes** at the following rates: <ul><li>where the member's contributions are less than six per cent of remuneration, not less than the contributions made by the member;</li><li>where the member's contributions equal or exceed six per cent of remuneration, not less than six per cent of remuneration.</li></ul> (ie the employer must match member contributions of up to six per cent of remuneration) Remuneration for these purposes is basic pay (ignoring bonuses, commission and overtime) before deductions for tax, NI or pension contributions). It is not necessarily the same as pensionable pay under the scheme rules.	

Salary sacrifice

14.45 Under a salary sacrifice arrangement an employee will give up part of his salary in return for some other benefit from the employer, often an increased employer contribution into a pension scheme. Previously, HMRC required salary sacrifice arrangements to be in place for at least a year (subject to a lifestyle event happening, such as pregnancy or divorce). This would have created problems for a salary sacrifice member who wished to opt out as there would be no mechanism for his salary to revert to the pre-sacrifice level. HMRC confirmed that, in relation to contributions to registered pension schemes, the 12-month rule will not apply and salary sacrifice arrangements relating to pension contributions can be ended at any time.

Salary sacrifice cannot be a condition of automatic enrolment. Employers currently operating pension contributions only through salary sacrifice arrangements will have to change their arrangements to allow automatic enrolment for those eligible jobholders who do not want to enter into a salary sacrifice arrangement (ie by allowing them to contribute via direct pay arrangements).

A further issue with salary sacrifice is that an employee has to expressly agree to it. This may create timing issues for schemes not operating waiting periods as the member would have to sign up to salary sacrifice before he could be automatically enrolled. This could be built into the recruitment process to ensure a new employee has agreed to salary sacrifice in advance of his starting date.

Further guidance is available in the Pensions Regulator's Workplace Pensions Reform: detailed guidance number 4 which advises that employers should take one of the two following courses of action:

- put into place the salary sacrifice arrangements before the employee's automatic enrolment date (and use postponement to set up the salary sacrifice arrangement in advance); or
- automatically enrol the employees and deduct the first contribution via the direct payment method, before introducing salary sacrifice in the following month.

Transfers to new automatic enrolment arrangements

14.46   Many employers, having automatically enrolled their staff some years ago, are now reassessing and replacing their existing arrangements with a new scheme which offers employees a more modern platform.

Transferring from pension arrangement to another is not straightforward where the transferring scheme was used as the employer's qualifying scheme for automatic enrolment purposes. If a jobholder is an active member of a qualifying scheme the employer must not take any action or make any omission by which (without the jobholder ceasing to be employed by the employer) the jobholder ceases to be an active member of the automatic enrolment scheme (*PA 2008, s 2(1)*). This duty is not contravened if the jobholder remains an active member of another qualifying scheme (*PA 2008*, s *2(2)*). Neither is the duty contravened if the existing member becomes an active member of an automatic enrolment scheme with effect from the day after the cessation of active membership in the existing scheme (*PA 2008, s2(3)*) or where the action or omission is at the jobholder's request (*PA 2008, s 2(4)*).

This means that as long as the employer ensures that the member becomes an active member of another qualifying scheme or automatic enrolment scheme for the purposes of *PA 2008, s 2(2)* or *(3)* there will be no breach of *PA 2008, s 2(1)*.

There would also be no breach of the legislation if the member voluntarily asked to cease active membership of a qualifying scheme. The member would then be subject to re-enrolment in accordance with the usual three-year cycle (see **14.18** above).

Employers may find themselves in difficulty if they decide to make this change by consent rather than by using automatic enrolment for all relevant jobholders. If a member decides not to consent to join the new arrangement then the employer will be in breach of its obligations unless it automatically enrols them into a qualifying scheme. This means that non-consenting employees will be in the slightly strange position of asking not to join a pension scheme and then being enrolled into one anyway. They would then of course have the option to opt-out within the statutory period (see **14.16** above).

Chapter 15

Commercial transactions

Introduction

General

15.1   This chapter considers the pensions implications of buying or selling a company or business and gives an overview of both private sector and public sector transfers.

In the context of a commercial transaction, the value of the pension liabilities concerned can be very substantial and in some cases may exceed the value of the company or business itself, particularly where there is a defined benefit scheme involved. It is therefore essential that the main pensions issues arising from such a transaction are considered and addressed at an early stage in the negotiations. This introduction of the concept of 'moral hazard' in the *Pensions Act 2004 (PA 2004)* and the Regulator's anti-avoidance powers have made this even more important. Provisions in *PA 2004* and subordinate legislation specifically deal with this issue, including the clearance procedure with the Regulator, whereby parties to a transaction can seek the Regulator's confirmation that it will not issue a contribution notice or financial support direction as a result of the transaction in contemplation. Amendments made to the *Occupational Pension Schemes (Employer Debt) Regulations 2005 ('Employer Debt Regulations')* have also reinforced the obligations of employers to stand behind their pension schemes' obligations.

This chapter also looks at the implications of the *Transfer of Undertakings (Protection of Employment) Regulations 2006 (SI 2006/266) ('TUPE')* on business or asset sales from a pensions perspective. Following the British public's decision on 23 June 2016 to leave the EU, the future of *TUPE* has been called into question by many commentators because *TUPE* implements the requirements of the 1977 *Acquired Rights Directive (77/187/EEC)*. While it is possible that *TUPE* could be reformed or even repealed in the future, any such changes, if they took place, would take time to implement.

Type of scheme

15.2   Inevitably, much will depend upon the type of scheme involved. Pensions will tend to feature most prominently in the commercial negotiations where the employees affected by the sale belong to a defined benefit scheme. These schemes will predominantly be registered pension schemes under the *Finance Act 2004* (*FA 2004*), *Part 4* and, prior to 6 April 2016, would have frequently been contracted out (see **Chapter 4**).

This chapter therefore focuses on those transactions where the employees concerned belong to a registered, formerly contracted-out defined benefit occupational pension scheme. The implications for other types of scheme are considered at the end of the chapter (see **15.84** and **15.85**).

Type of sale

15.3   The course of the pensions negotiations will depend largely upon:

(*a*)   whether the sale is of shares or of assets (see **15.13** below); and

(*b*)   whether or not the sale will require a transfer of assets and liabilities between pension schemes. The circumstances which will typically give rise to such a transfer are described further in **15.18** below.

Funding

15.4   A preliminary point to establish, which will set the tone of subsequent negotiations, is the funding position of the scheme providing benefits for the employees of the company or business which is being sold.

Where employees' accrued benefits are to be transferred from the seller's scheme to the purchaser's scheme following completion (see **15.18** below), the funding level is likely to affect the sum which is transferred and consequently the level of past service benefits to be granted in the purchaser's scheme (unless the purchaser can negotiate a shortfall clause – see **15.43** below).

Where the purchaser is to take over the entire scheme (see **15.21** below), the funding level may impact on the profitability of the company or business being purchased. For example, a well-funded scheme may reduce future liability for the company to contribute (so boosting profits) but conversely, an underfunded scheme may require an immediate injection of cash to raise its funding level.

A crucial issue will be whether the transaction triggers a debt on the target company under the *Pensions Act 1995* (*PA 1995*), *s 75*. If the target company participates in a multi-employer pension scheme which is in deficit, an employment-cessation event may well occur, which could give rise to an immediate debt of that company's share of the deficit based on the full buy-out cost of benefits. This is considered in more detail from **15.61** below.

These situations are likely to affect the negotiation of the contract and the purchase price itself. In some instances, the funding level of the pension scheme may be of such concern to the purchaser that it is not prepared to acquire the target company unless the pension deficit has been addressed. Sometimes, the seller may try and sell the target company free of its defined benefit liabilities by using a flexible apportionment arrangement (see **15.68** below) to transfer those liabilities to another company within the seller's group prior to completion.

Warranties and indemnities

15.5   It is common in a sale and purchase agreement for both warranties and indemnities to be agreed to deal with specific issues of concern to the parties, often points which have arisen during the course of negotiations and the due diligence exercise.

A *warranty* is a statement of fact made by one party to the contract (usually the seller). An example of this may be that the benefits provided by the scheme have been fully equalised as between men and women as required by law (see **Chapter 9**). This statement may then be disclosed against in the disclosure letter (see **15.11** below) to negate the effect of the statement to some extent, for example, by the disclosure that guaranteed minimum pensions have not yet been equalised. In such a circumstance the purchaser may seek to obtain an *indemnity* to the effect that the seller will indemnify the purchaser for the costs of equalising benefits, should this cost be incurred by the purchaser after completion.

The main difference between a warranty and an indemnity is the level of protection given to the party for whose benefit it is given and the method by which each is enforced. To enforce a warranty, the party seeking to benefit must take steps to enforce the contract. Unless a breach of warranty is agreed by both the parties, this is likely to involve proceedings, incurring costs and delays.

By contrast, an indemnity requires the party who granted the indemnity to reimburse the other party for specified losses which have been incurred. There is no requirement for the indemnified party to mitigate his loss or to take steps to prove any wrongdoing by the indemnifying party. Consequently an indemnity offers not only more protection than a warranty to the purchaser but also considerably less inconvenience in obtaining a remedy. The primary purpose of a warranty is therefore usually to flush out any material risk areas so appropriate recourse can be documented in the sale and purchase agreement (eg indemnity protection).

Due diligence

15.6   Due diligence is the fact-finding exercise which takes place before and during negotiation of the contract. The purchaser will be concerned to find out as much information as possible about the company or business it is seeking to acquire, to ascertain not only what potential liabilities there are but also to ensure that these are quantifiable and that protection, in the form of warranties and indemnities, is sought from the seller where appropriate.

In the context of pensions, the purchaser will wish to see, for example, a copy of the trust deed and rules, the scheme's booklet, actuarial valuation and full details of employees (including salary details). Where a company with its own scheme is being purchased more extensive information will be sought, as the purchaser will effectively be inheriting the whole scheme. The results of the due diligence exercise may result in re-negotiation of the purchase price or the seeking of further warranties and indemnities. Due diligence is considered in further detail below.

The sale documents

The sale agreement

Parties

15.7   The distinction between share sales and asset sales is considered in **15.13** below, but in either case the main parties to the agreement will be the seller and the purchaser respectively. There may also be other parties including, for example, guarantors.

An important point to bear in mind is that the trustees of the respective pension schemes are unlikely to be parties to the agreement and consequently, there will be no contractual relationship between them. In any event, trustees may not under normal circumstances fetter a future exercise of their discretion and so making them a party to the agreement would be of little comfort to either the seller or the purchaser when the calculation of any transfer payment and the granting of past service benefits take place a few months after completion of the agreement (*Stannard v Fisons Pension Trust Ltd [1992] IRLR 27*).

This is relevant when the pensions schedule is negotiated. It may be impossible for a party to agree to procure that a certain event occurs because the scheme rules place that event in the hands of the trustees. An example of this would be where the rules of the purchaser's scheme provide that past service benefits are granted entirely at the trustees' discretion. Where this is the case, the purchaser cannot guarantee that a certain level of benefits will be granted. The most the purchaser is likely to agree to in such circumstances is that it will use its best endeavours to procure that the specified event will take place.

Warranties

15.8 The pensions warranties will usually appear in the part of the agreement which sets out all the warranties (not just those relating to pensions) being given by the seller. If they are in a separate schedule the seller should take care to ensure that any clauses limiting the scope of the warranties also extend to the pension warranties. The seller may also wish to restrict the warranties to matters of which it is aware, which in turn may lead to negotiations as to what extent of knowledge the contract should deem the seller to have. The purchaser, on the other hand, may seek to disapply any general limitations from the pension warranties schedule.

It is common for parties to enter into a 'disclosure letter' of the same date as the main agreement (see **15.11** below). To the extent that a warranty is disclosed against, this will negate the effect of the warranty. An example of this has already been given in **15.5** above.

The warranties that a purchaser requires will vary considerably according to the nature of and the circumstances surrounding the transaction and are dealt with later on in this chapter in the contexts in which they arise.

Pensions schedule

15.9 Where the transaction involves a transfer of assets and liabilities from a pension scheme operating within the seller's group to one to be set up (or already established) by the purchaser, its holding company or one of its subsidiaries, there will normally be detailed provisions specifying how this is to happen. These will usually be set out in a schedule to the agreement, dealing specifically with pensions.

Other provisions

15.10 Other provisions may be included either in the pensions schedule (where there is one) or in the main body of the agreement. These might include indemnities (see **15.5** above), for instance, in relation to equalisation issues (see **Chapter 9**) or as a consequence of obligations that may be inherited as a result of case law such as *Beckmann, Martin* and *Procter & Gamble* (see **15.14** below). Another example might be a provision which seeks to adjust the purchase price for any past overfunding or underfunding that may emerge where the purchaser is to inherit the scheme in its entirety (see **15.25** to **15.27** below) or for any employer debt or 'moral hazard' liabilities which may arise as a result of the transaction (see from **15.61** below).

Any action to be taken in connection with the transfer of benefits from one scheme to another will need to be carried out in accordance with the respective scheme's rules. It is therefore important that both parties are aware of the provisions in the schemes' rules governing each particular issue.

The disclosure letter

15.11 As mentioned briefly above, the disclosure letter documents the agreement between the parties on the information which has been provided during the due diligence exercise and acts to limit or negate the effect of the warranties given in the sale and purchase agreement. The disclosure letter is a letter from the seller to the purchaser which is likely to set out general statements of agreed information and will then go on to provide specific disclosures against specific warranties.

Purchasers should seek to ensure that the wording of disclosures is specific and to the point. From the perspective of the seller, by contrast, it will often be desirable to make general disclosures, or make reference to a bundle of documents (thereby making an effective disclosure without drawing attention to specific areas about which the purchaser should be concerned or, at least, aware). Any disclosure must, however, be full, clear and accurate (*Infiniteland v Artisan Consulting Ltd [2005] EWCA Civ 758*). From the purchaser's point of view, it is important to receive as much specific information as possible to ensure that it is informed of all potential and actual liabilities and can take these into account when negotiating the sale and purchase agreement.

Actuary's letter

15.12 Where the transaction involves a transfer payment from the seller's scheme, it may be necessary to agree a calculation method and assumptions for valuing the scheme's liabilities. This will usually be covered separately in a letter from the seller's actuary to the purchaser's actuary and countersigned by the purchaser's actuary by way of agreement. The letter should be clearly identified in the pensions schedule and attached as an Appendix.

Shares or assets

The distinction

15.13 For the purposes of this Chapter, a share sale takes place when the seller is selling all of the issued share capital of a company. In such a situation the identity of the company remains the same; it is the underlying ownership of the company which has changed. The purchaser inherits through its ownership of the company all the company's pre-existing contracts including (of particular relevance to pensions) contracts of employment and deeds which the company has entered into in relation to a pension scheme.

An asset sale takes place when all or part of a business is being sold to the purchaser. In such a transaction the purchaser will take on only specific contracts, premises and employees of the company selling the business and will only assume those liabilities specified in the agreement or, where applicable, under *TUPE* (see **15.14** below).

Practical implications

Employment aspects

15.14 Following a sale of shares there is no change in the employment relationship between the company and its employees. The employment contracts will stay intact and the employees therefore will enjoy the ongoing benefit of any contractual provisions, including any that relate to pensions.

This contrasts with the position of employees on an asset (or business) sale where their employment contracts are transferred to a new employer. *TUPE* contains provisions to transfer contractual employment rights to the purchaser but *reg 10* makes an exception in relation to 'so much of a contract of employment ... as relates to an occupational pension scheme ...'. Only those provisions of an occupational pension scheme which relate to benefits for old age, invalidity or survivors are treated as part of the pension scheme and therefore do not pass to a purchaser as a result of the *reg 10 exception*.

It is worth noting that schemes providing only death-in-service benefits are not included in the definition of 'occupational pension scheme' under *PSA 1993, s 1* and consequently, any contractual obligation to provide such benefits will not be covered by the occupational pension scheme exemption and will transfer under *TUPE*.

In *Beckmann v Dynamco Whicheloe Macfarlane Ltd, Case C-164/00 [2002] 64 PBLR, [2002] All ER (D) 05 (Jun)* the CJEU gave a ruling which considerably narrowed the previously understood ambit of the *reg 10* exception. Ms Beckmann was a former NHS employee whose employment transferred under *TUPE*. She was subsequently dismissed on redundancy grounds and claimed entitlement to an early retirement pension and other lump sum benefits, on the basis that these had transferred under *Article 3* of the 1977 *Acquired Rights Directive (77/187/EEC)* (now found at *Article 3* of *Council Directive 2001/23/ EC*). *Article 3* excludes the provision of 'employees' rights to old age, invalidity or survivors' benefits under supplementary company or inter-company pension schemes'. The CJEU decided that 'it is only benefits paid from the time when an employee reaches the end of his normal working life as laid down by the general structure of the pension scheme … that can be classified as old-age benefits, even if they are calculated by reference to the rules for calculating normal pension benefits'. As a result, the right to an early retirement pension on redundancy was held to transfer.

Following on from *Beckmann*, another case was subsequently referred to the CJEU in which additional questions were posed. In *Martin v South Bank University [2004] 1 CMLR 472, [2003] All ER (D) 85*, Martin and others transferred into a private pension arrangement following the transfer of their employment from the NHS to South Bank University. The claimants subsequently opted to take early retirement and an early pension. The CJEU ruled that early retirement benefits and benefits intended to enhance the conditions of such retirement, paid in the event of dismissal, did not relate to 'old age, invalidity or survivors' benefits' and the right did therefore transfer. This included circumstances where the early retirement was voluntary. It also held that an employee could not waive his rights by agreeing to a change in benefits going forward (if the transfer is the reason for the change).

Beckmann and *Martin* left a number of questions open:

(*a*)   Must benefits be replicated in a purchaser's scheme in all respects? *Mitie Management Services Limited v French [2002] IRLR 513, [2002] All ER (D) 150 (Sep)* provides some authority for not having to replicate unjust, absurd or impossible features. Replacement benefits, for example salary increases, may need to be offered instead.

(*b*)   When is the transfer going to be considered to be the reason for the change? Can it be argued that an employee agreeing to join the purchaser's scheme post transfer constitutes a variation of terms by mutual consent as opposed to a waiver?

(*c*)   Does it make a difference whether past rights are transferred? What happens if an employee is told that if his past service benefits are not transferred, will any benefits will be limited to future service?

(*d*)   Can *Beckmann/Martin* be distinguished in relation to private sector schemes? The *Beckmann* pension was only payable to normal retirement age – the rights under a private sector scheme may be payable for life.

The case of *Procter & Gamble Company v Svenska Cellulosa Aktiebolaget SCA and another [2012] EWHC 1257 (Ch)* (note that whilst leave to appeal had been given, the case was settled before any appeal) has clarified some (but not all) of the uncertainties. In 2007, Procter & Gamble ('P&G') sold its European tissue business to Svenska Cellulosa Aktiebolaget ('SCA') and P&G's Manchester employees transferred to SCA under *TUPE*. 129 of those employees were members of the P&G defined benefit pension scheme. The agreement provided for a valuation of the transferring pension liabilities in relation to those employees and a resulting adjustment to the purchase price. The dispute concerned which pension liabilities passed under *TUPE* and therefore what adjustment should be made to the purchase price.

The P&G scheme had an NRD of 65. It allowed early retirement with employer consent from age 55. The benefit consisted of a reduced pension (no reduction from age 60) and a bridging pension to state pension age. It was agreed that for the purposes of *TUPE*, the pension scheme is an arrangement arising from a contract of employment – and so (subject to the *reg 10* exemption) the rights and obligations would pass on transfer.

It was held that:

(*a*)   The *Beckmann* and *Martin* reasoning was potentially applicable to transfers from private sector occupational pension schemes (it had previously been argued not very convincingly that the principle was only applicable in relation to transfers from public sector schemes).

(*b*)   Discretionary rights can transfer by operation of *TUPE* (in this case the early retirement pension required the consent of the employer).

(*c*)   The right, in this case, which transferred under *TUPE* was for the employer to consider an application for early retirement, taking into account its own interests but subject to the employer's good faith obligation (ie not to act in a way which breaks down the relationship of trust and confidence between employer and employee).

(*d*)   *TUPE* should be interpreted in such a way as to achieve its objectives of safeguarding and maintaining employees' rights but not enhancing or duplicating them.

(*e*)   The only liability which transfers is in relation to the 'enhancements' (ie the right to ask to take the pension early and the unreduced element of that pension). The liability for the basic deferred pension remained in the P&G Scheme and did not transfer.

(*f*)   Instalments of pension payable after normal retirement age are 'old-age benefits' and therefore do not pass under *TUPE* even if the pension was triggered as an early retirement benefit.

This case may have given clarification to some of the unresolved issues in the *Beckmann* and *Martin* cases but it also raises unresolved issues of its own as no practical guidance was given on how the findings should work in practice. The case also does not:

(*a*)　provide any guidance directly on whether future service rights will pass under *TUPE* (as it did not need to consider the issue) although there seems no reason why they should not having regard to the reasoning in the case;

(*b*)　consider whether it could be argued in cases where employees were given the opportunity to transfer their past service rights but did not do so; or

(*c*)　consider whether in relation to past service rights if the revaluation granted in deferment is less than the final salary linkage which would have been granted in respect of past service, the employee is entitled to be compensated for this.

PA 2004 pension protection on the transfer of employment

15.15　Criticisms of the exclusion of occupational pensions from the ambit of *TUPE* (except in relation to *Beckmann* and *Martin*-type benefits) led to the introduction of limited protection for employees in *PA 2004*, introduced with effect from 6 April 2005. Where an employer acquires employees as a result of a business purchase governed by *TUPE*, the new employer will be required to provide a minimum level of pension protection (*PA 2004, ss 257, 258* and the *Transfer of Employment (Pensions Protection) Regulations 2005 (SI 2005/649 as amended)*).

To qualify for the protection, certain conditions must be met:

- there must be a relevant transfer within the meaning of *TUPE*;

- by virtue of that transfer, the employees cease to be employed by the transferor and become employed by the transferee;

- at the time immediately before the transfer, there is an occupational pension scheme in relation to which the transferor is the employer;

- the employees being transferred were either active members of the occupational pension scheme, were eligible to become members of such scheme, or were in a waiting period before becoming eligible; and

- if the transferor's scheme provided money purchase benefits: (i) for active members the transferor was required to make contributions to the scheme or elected to contribute, even though there was no requirement for it to do so; and (ii) for those who were not active members but were eligible to join or would have been eligible after completing a waiting period, the transferor would have been required to contribute if they had been active members.

If those conditions are met, the new employer is required to offer the transferred employees membership of a pension scheme which provides the contributions or benefits set out in the table below:

TUPE TRANSFERS AND MINIMUM PENSIONS OBLIGATIONS

Transferee scheme is not a money purchase scheme	Transferee scheme is a money purchase or stakeholder scheme
The member must be provided with: • benefits the value of which equals or exceeds six per cent of pensionable pay for each year of employment plus the value of any member contributions – and member contributions are not required to be more than six per cent of pensionable pay; or • 'relevant contributions'.	The employer must either: • make 'relevant contributions'; or • where immediately before the date of transfer the transferor had been required to make contributions which produced only money purchase benefits, the transferee must make contributions which are not less than those the transferor was required to make.
Relevant contributions are contributions made by the employer but **only where the member also contributes** at the following rates: • where the member's contributions are less than six per cent of remuneration, not less than the contributions made by the member; • where the member's contributions equal or exceed six per cent of remuneration, not less than six per cent of remuneration (ie the employer must match member contributions of up to six per cent of remuneration). Remuneration for these purposes is gross basic pay (ie basic pay before deductions for tax, NI or pension contributions) and is not necessarily the same as pensionable pay under the scheme rules.	

Unlike the position generally under *TUPE*, these protections can be disapplied in relation to a contract or contracts of employment if the employee(s) and the new employer agree alternative terms after the transfer (see *PA 2004, s 258(6)*).

Employer debt

15.16   We shall see later in this chapter (from **15.61** below) that, where the seller's scheme is underfunded, the sale may give rise to a statutory debt payable to the trustees by the purchaser or by the company that it is buying. There are mechanisms for dealing with this, including apportioning the debt or entering into a withdrawal arrangement. The extent of this problem will normally be less on an asset purchase than on a purchase of shares.

Deed of substitution

15.17 Circumstances may arise where an asset sale results in the employment contracts of all of the scheme's active members being transferred to the purchaser. In such a situation, it may be appropriate for the entire scheme to become the purchaser's responsibility. This will typically require the execution of a deed substituting the purchaser as the scheme's new principal employer.

A share sale is generally less likely to give rise to a deed of substitution. An example of where this might be appropriate would be where the seller is the scheme's principal employer but the subsidiary being sold employs all or the majority of the scheme's active members.

Any purchaser being asked to enter into a deed of substitution should first thoroughly investigate the liabilities it will be taking on in relation to the scheme and consider appropriate warranties and indemnities and/or a price adjustment.

Whether the sale will give rise to a transfer payment

General

15.18 The scope, nature and extent of the contractual provisions required in the sale and purchase agreement will generally depend on whether or not a transfer payment is anticipated. In most cases, the question of whether there is to be a transfer will be dictated largely by the structure of the pension arrangements and of the sale and the funding position of the scheme.

Even where the circumstances outlined in **15.19** below do apply, bulk transfer payments from defined benefit schemes have become much less common in recent years, largely because of funding deficits (so appropriate transfer payments may not be available) and the reluctance of the purchaser to establish or retain a suitable scheme to receive the transfer. It is now more usual for employees to leave their deferred benefits in the seller's scheme.

Circumstances involving a transfer

15.19 The following circumstances may give rise to a transfer payment:

(*a*)   where the company being sold is one of a number of companies which participate in the seller's scheme; or

(*b*)   on an asset sale, where some but not all of the scheme's active members are to have their employment transferred to the purchaser.

Transactions such as these are discussed further in **15.29** to **15.60** below.

Circumstances not involving a transfer

15.20   The following circumstances will not usually give rise to a transfer payment:

(*a*)   the sale of a company with its own scheme; or

(*b*)   an asset sale, where all of the scheme's active members are to have their employment transferred to the purchaser and the purchaser is to be substituted as the scheme's new principal employer.

In these cases, the purchaser will effectively be taking over the whole of the scheme, as it will be buying (or, alternatively, becoming) its principal employer. This is considered further in **15.21** below.

Also, as mentioned in **15.18** above, a transfer is unlikely where the seller's scheme is underfunded.

Transactions where the purchaser takes over the whole scheme

Protection of purchaser

General

15.21   Where the purchaser is to take over the whole of the seller's scheme its main concern will be to obtain as much protection as possible from any liabilities which arose prior to completion. This is especially the case because the scheme will relate not only to those current employees being acquired by the purchaser, but also to past employees with benefits (whether deferred or in payment) under the scheme. Protection will take the form of thorough due diligence, warranties and, in relation to areas of particular concern, indemnities. There may also be negotiation on payments into the scheme by the seller to address funding concerns, possibly as part of a clearance process (see **15.80** to **15.82** below).

It is not surprising that purchasers are becoming increasingly reluctant to acquire companies with defined benefit liabilities. This is a result of many factors, including unpredictability of costs, continually improving mortality rates and low inflation.

Due diligence

15.22   The purchaser should seek to ensure that its advisers have the opportunity to examine as much as possible of the scheme's documentation at an early stage.

At the very least, this should cover the scheme's governing trust documents, the latest actuarial valuation report (and any subsequent actuarial advice), booklets and announcements issued to members (as well as references to pensions in contracts of employment and service agreements), recent annual reports and accounts and sufficient membership data to enable the purchaser's advisers to take a view on the costs of the scheme's ongoing liabilities.

The purchaser should also seek to obtain proof of registration under the *FA 2004* requirements. Other relevant matters are trustees' minutes, copies of investment management agreements (and other advisers' appointment letters), insurance policies, transfer agreements with the trustees of other schemes, the statement of investment principles and any proposals to review or revise it, the schedule of contributions, the current statement of funding principles and any proposals to review or revise it, any recovery plan, details of PPF levy payments, documentation relating to member-nominated trustee arrangements and details of the scheme's internal dispute resolution procedure.

Additionally and pursuant to *PA 2004*, the purchaser should also be raising inquiries regarding whether any breaches of the law have been reported to the Regulator under *PA 2004, s 70* or if any notifiable events have arisen in relation to the scheme in accordance with *PA 2004, s 69*. Purchasers will also want to know if the seller has been the subject of a contribution notice or financial support direction (*PA 2004, ss 38, 43*), as such funding obligations could be inherited going forwards. Contribution notices and financial support directions are discussed in further detail from **15.74** below. A purchaser should also be making enquiries as to whether there are any withdrawal arrangements or apportionment arrangements in place in relation to the scheme, or whether there are any circumstances that might give rise to such arrangements (see **15.64** to **15.73** below).

The aim should be to build up a full picture of the scheme including funding levels, liabilities, the balance of powers between the employers and the trustees and compliance with *PA 1995* and *PA 2004*. This knowledge will all be important as part of the negotiation process, and also to enable the purchaser to operate the scheme going forwards post completion.

Warranties

15.23　The more comprehensive the warranties that the purchaser is able to obtain from the seller, the safer it will generally be. For maximum protection, the agreement may stipulate that the warranties apply not only as at the date of the agreement but also (if later) the date of completion. Even if the seller gives warranties but then discloses against them, the purchaser will at least be in a better position to know where any problems may lie.

Some examples of the warranties that a purchaser should seek are:

(*a*)　that there are no schemes or similar commitments (whether legally binding or not) relating to the employees, except those that have been disclosed;

(*b*)　that the documents provided to the purchaser are true and complete;

(*c*)　that the scheme is a registered scheme in accordance with *FA 2004, Pt 4* and there is no reason why the scheme should be de-registered;

(*d*)　that the scheme, its trustees and the employers have complied with all applicable legal and regulatory requirements, including with regards to automatic enrolment;

(*e*)　that the information contained in the latest actuarial valuation report is complete and accurate in all respects and that nothing has happened since its effective date which would have an adverse effect on its conclusions;

(*f*)　that no debt has arisen under *PA 1995, s 75*;

(*g*)　that all contributions due have been paid in accordance with the trust deed and rules and as required by the scheme's schedule of contributions and any recovery plan;

(*h*)　that no changes have been made (or proposed or announced) to the scheme's eligibility requirements, contribution rates or benefits;

(*i*)　that all risk benefits are appropriately insured;

(*j*)　that there are no court proceedings and no complaints (whether under the scheme's internal dispute resolution procedure or to the Pensions Ombudsman) in progress, pending, threatened or anticipated;

(*k*)　that no contribution notices or financial support directions have been issued by the Regulator in relation to the scheme or the seller;

(*l*)　that no employee has become employed by the seller as a result of a transfer pursuant to *TUPE*;

(*m*)   that no unauthorised payments under *FA 2004, Pt 4* have been made from the scheme; and

(*n*)   that the scheme is eligible for the Pensions Protection Fund and all applicable levies have been paid.

The purchaser may seek more extensive warranties than these, and the seller, conversely, will often aim to limit their scope. For instance, the seller may wish to restrict the warranties to matters of which it is aware, which in turn may lead to negotiations as to what extent of knowledge the contract should deem the seller to have. The seller will be particularly cautious with regard to any funding warranty, as a breach of this can prove extremely expensive.

Indemnities

15.24   Either party may seek indemnity protection from the other in respect of matters where there is some particular risk involved.

Purchasers frequently require indemnities against the costs of benefits not having been equalised as between men and women in respect of past service (see **Chapter 9**). Another area which may give rise to an indemnity is the possibility of an employer debt becoming payable under *PA 1995, s 75* (as amended) (see **15.61**) and claims relating to *Beckmann/Martin* type benefits where the transaction is subject to the provisions of *TUPE*.

Funding

General

15.25   Where the scheme is understood to be overfunded or underfunded on an ongoing basis it may be agreed that there should be some balancing payment between the parties following the sale (usually as an adjustment to the purchase price). Where this happens, the respective parties' actuaries will normally negotiate a method and assumptions for determining the amount of overfunding or underfunding; the calculation itself is then carried out after completion.

It is common for these issues to be dealt with at an earlier stage, as part of the purchase price negotiations. The most likely reason for dealing with the matter by means of a post-completion adjustment would be that there was insufficient information as to the scheme's funding position at the time of sale.

Underfunded scheme

15.26   Where the scheme is underfunded on an ongoing basis, the purpose of the compensating payment will effectively be to relieve the purchaser of the costs of bringing the funding up to that level.

The sum required will therefore be the amount by which the scheme's assets fall short of the value calculated in accordance with the agreed actuarial method and assumptions. The seller, however, will be reluctant to pay more than is necessary to achieve this, and so (instead of paying the sum directly into the scheme) may propose to pay it to the purchaser net of the standard rate of corporation tax, on the basis that corporation tax relief will become available to the purchaser's group when it is remitted to the trustees. The seller may be particularly concerned that the payment should be used to restore the scheme's funding position rather than to benefit the purchaser, and so expressly require that the purchaser pay the sum into the scheme as soon as it is received.

The purchaser will not necessarily be satisfied with this approach. For instance, the purchaser's group may prove not to be making profits when the time comes, in which case it will derive no benefit from the theoretical availability of corporation tax relief. Alternatively, even if the purchaser is making profits, the sum involved may be treated by HMRC as a special contribution, in which case the tax relief would have to be spread over a period of years.

A compromise position would be for the payment to be made to the purchaser gross of corporation tax, on condition that the purchaser takes steps to avail itself of corporation tax relief on paying the sum into the scheme and account to the seller for the value of that relief.

Overfunded scheme

15.27   Where the scheme has a surplus on an ongoing basis, the purpose of a compensating payment (which would be from the purchaser) is very different, as are the considerations affecting its calculation.

The payment would be a form of recognition that, before the sale, there was an overfunded scheme within the seller's group from which the seller might have gained some benefit in the future. Following the sale, the seller no longer has that opportunity, which has passed to the purchaser instead.

It would probably be inappropriate for the purchaser to pay to the seller the whole of this surplus. This would presume that it was open to the scheme's employers to acquire the full present value of the scheme's surplus, which is not the case for a number of reasons:

(*a*)   Only in exceptional cases may an employer receive a refund of surplus assets from its scheme, and even then the scheme rules may require that substantial benefit increases be granted first. Pursuant to *PA 1995, s 37*, as amended by *PA 2004, ss 250* and *251*, certain conditions will need to be satisfied before any refund of surplus can be made. For example, the scheme will need to show that it is funded at buy-out level on an actuarial basis; the trustees will need to have passed an appropriate resolution before 6 April 2016 (although no resolution needs to have been passed if the scheme is in winding up at the point the surplus is to be repaid) and confirmed that they are satisfied such a payment would be in the interests of the members; and the Regulator must not have issued a freezing order against the scheme which is in force. Any such refund would, in any event, be subject to a 35 per cent tax charge (see *FA 2004, s 207*).

(*b*)　It is more likely that the employer could benefit from the surplus by means of a reduction in its contributions or even a contributions holiday. However, it is by no means certain that the whole of the surplus could be used in this way.

(*c*)　Even if the employer is able to take a contributions holiday in respect of the entire surplus, the benefit of that holiday will only gradually be realised over a period of time. An immediate payment to the seller in lieu of that contributions holiday, therefore, ought not to be equal to the entire surplus, but should be discounted to take into account the fact that (unlike a contributions holiday) the benefit to the seller is immediate.

It can be seen from this that agreeing a suitable method for ascertaining the amount of the compensatory payment is likely to prove complex. Often the matter will instead be dealt with between the parties before the sale as part of the purchase price negotiations.

Change of trustees

15.28　Usually, the scheme's trustees will be directors, employees or a subsidiary company of the seller. If the trustees are to remain with the seller's group following completion, it will generally be appropriate for them to be replaced as trustees by individuals or by a company within the purchaser's group (and may well need to be in order to satisfy the member-nominated trustee requirements – see **Chapter 3**). The contract may expressly provide for this to be done, and may even require that a deed of removal and appointment of trustees be one of the completion documents.

Transactions involving a transfer payment

General

15.29　Where the transaction involves a transfer payment (see **15.19** above), the sale agreement may provide for the company being sold (or, in the case of an asset sale, the purchaser) to participate in the seller's scheme on a transitional basis for a temporary period after completion. This is not always the case, however, and the following paragraphs, from **15.30** to **15.49** below, assume that there is to be no such transitional period.

15.30 *Commercial transactions*

The further issues which will become relevant if there is to be a transitional period are considered later in this Chapter (see from **15.50** below).

Methods of calculating transfer payments

Past service reserve

15.30 There are several ways of calculating a bulk transfer payment. A 'past service reserve' calculation seeks to produce a sum which is sufficient to provide past service benefits which are equal overall to the benefits that the transferring members could otherwise have expected to receive in respect of their completed membership of the seller's scheme had there been no sale. It is calculated by reference to the length of past pensionable service of the members concerned, but with present pensionable salaries being increased by an actuarially assumed rate of future salary growth. The calculation will also require other assumptions to be made, for instance, in relation to the future mortality rates, inflation, rates of withdrawal by members from pensionable service and investment growth.

The assumptions should normally be agreed between the respective parties' actuaries before the contract is signed. Two very slightly differing sets of assumptions can produce vastly different results and consequently these negotiations are often hard fought.

The purchaser's actuary will normally wish to see a copy of the scheme's most recent actuarial valuation report, so that he can form a view as to whether the assumptions on offer are consistent with the way in which the scheme as a whole is funded. The seller may refuse to make the valuation report available, but the purchaser may still be able to obtain it through links with members or with trades unions to whom the trustees can be required by law to provide a copy in accordance with the *Occupational and Personal Pension Schemes (Disclosure of Information) Regulations 2013 (SI 2013/2734)* (see summary at **Appendix II**).

Past service reserve plus share of surplus

15.31 The purchaser may seek a transfer payment that is calculated on a past service reserve basis but which also includes a proportionate share of any surplus funding in the seller's scheme over and above that.

Although the scheme rules will be relevant, it has been widely accepted since *Re Imperial Foods Ltd Pension Scheme [1986] 2 All ER 802* that there is no reason in principle why a purchaser (or the receiving trustees) should expect the transfer payment to include a share of any surplus. The rationale for this view is that a surplus in the scheme as at a given time simply reflects the fact that the employers are temporarily ahead with their contributions. The so-called surplus does not represent 'spare' money that should necessarily be available to a receiving scheme.

Transfer payments including a share of a surplus are comparatively rare. However, they can still occur where, for instance, a very substantial proportion of the seller's scheme's liabilities is to be transferred in circumstances where the seller's scheme's rules will make it difficult for the trustees to justify not transferring a share of the surplus. Where this does happen, the seller can be expected to require an increase in the purchase price. The manner in which this should be calculated is complex, but it will be governed by the same considerations as have been mentioned in the context of **15.27** above.

Cash equivalents

15.32   We saw in **Chapter 6** that a member's 'cash equivalent' is the statutory amount which he may be entitled by law to require the trustees to transfer to another scheme. In most cases, cash equivalents will produce a lower figure than would a past service reserve. This is primarily because the cash equivalent calculation does not provide for future salary growth.

A seller may propose that the transfer payment be restricted to cash equivalents where the scheme is too precariously funded to be able to pay more. If this is so, the purchaser may request a shortfall payment from the seller representing the difference between the cash equivalents and the higher amount which a past service reserve calculation would have produced (see **15.46** below) or alternatively seek a reduction in the purchase price. If the seller is not prepared to accede to either of these requests, then there is likely to be an adverse impact on the past service benefits which the purchaser's scheme will be able to offer, unless the purchaser is prepared to make up the shortfall itself. The employment law and industrial relations of this will have to be considered (see **Chapter 7**). The most likely outcome in these circumstances is that the past service benefits will simply be left in the seller's scheme (rather than transferred).

Sometimes a seller will offer only cash equivalent transfer payments, even though its scheme can afford to pay more. The scheme rules are likely to be especially relevant in such cases; it may well be that they require or allow the trustees to pay more than the seller is offering.

Reduced cash equivalents

15.33   The trustees of the seller's scheme may decide to reduce the cash equivalent where they have received an insufficiency report from the scheme actuary (the *Occupational Pension Schemes (Transfer Values) Regulations 1996 (SI 1996/1847), reg 7D* (as amended by the *Occupational Pension Schemes (Transfer Values) (Amendment) Regulations 2008 (SI 2008/1050)*)).

Matters the trustees are likely to take into account when deciding whether it is appropriate to reduce cash equivalents include the degree of underfunding, the strength of the employer covenant and any recovery plan. The problems which this can raise for the purchaser are essentially the same as those mentioned in **15.32** above, only even more acute.

Other possibilities

15.34   There are, of course, other ways of calculating a transfer payment. For instance, it could be calculated as an agreed percentage of the amount needed to meet the statutory funding objective ('SFO') as explained more in **Chapter 11** in respect of the transferring members' past service benefits. So, a scheme which, being funded at 104 per cent of the scheme's SFO, could afford to pay more than the statutory cash equivalents but was unable to pay a reasonable past service reserve, might pay transfer payments equal to 104 per cent of the SFO in respect of the members concerned.

Timescales, mechanics and calculation adjustments

Timescales and mechanics

15.35   In the absence of a transitional period (see **15.50** onwards below), the mechanics of the transfer provisions will tend to revolve around two key dates.

The first of these is the date of completion of the sale which, for pension purposes, will be the date on which the relevant employees' pensionable service in the seller's scheme will terminate.

The second of these is the date on which the transfer payment becomes payable.

The length of time that is to pass between the completion date and the payment date will be determined by the sale agreement. In most cases the agreement will provide for certain steps to be taken between the two dates. In a typical agreement, these might include:

(*a*)   On the completion date, members are to be invited to join the purchaser's scheme for future service and advised that if they do elect to join they will have a right to transfer their past service benefits to the purchaser's scheme.

(*b*)   The members are to be given a period in which to decide whether to elect for such a transfer. This will normally involve their signing and returning a consent form. The information given to members should recommend that they obtain independent financial advice.

(*c*)   Once that period has expired, the parties know which members have elected to transfer. The parties then instruct their actuaries to liaise with a view to calculating the transfer payment in accordance with the method of calculation previously agreed between them. There will usually be a set timescale for this.

(*d*)   Once the calculation of the transfer payment has been agreed, there is a short further period allowed for, at the end of which the payment becomes due. If it has been agreed that the transfer be paid in cash, the transferring trustees may need to realise assets during this period. Alternatively, the parties and their actuaries may agree *in specie* transfers of assets.

Timing adjustment

15.36   A past service reserve transfer payment will usually be calculated as at the date of completion, as that will be the date on which pensionable service in the seller's scheme terminated. As the transfer payment will not actually become payable until some time after that, provision needs to be included in the agreement specifying how the transfer payment is to be adjusted in respect of the period from completion until the date on which it becomes payable.

An interest calculation can be used, but this may not take proper account of the effects of investment conditions during the period in question. The actuaries may therefore agree a market-related 'timing adjustment' in respect of this period. In effect, this means that the past service reserve figure is to be adjusted by a formula representing movements over the period in a notional portfolio. The actuaries will discuss and agree the formula to be used before the sale agreement is signed. The respective schemes' investment strategies can be expected to have some bearing on these discussions.

Interest

15.37   If the transfer payment is not paid until after it has fallen due, a further adjustment will be necessary in respect of the period of late payment.

This may be dealt with simply by continuing to apply the timing adjustment for that further period, but the purchaser may consider that the sale agreement should require a more punitive adjustment as payment by that stage will be overdue. One approach would be to continue to apply the timing adjustment, but to make the sum resulting from it subject to an agreed rate of interest in respect of the period of delay.

Voluntary contributions

15.38   The agreement should also provide for the transfer of assets arising from the payment of money purchase voluntary contributions by those members who elect to transfer their past service benefits. Because of the money purchase nature of these, this will be a simpler provision than those parts of the agreement dealing with the transfer of defined benefit liabilities.

Disputes clause

15.39   There may be circumstances in which, following the sale, the actuaries are unable to agree the calculation of the transfer payment as required by the sale agreement. Alternatively, the sale agreement may require that the past service benefits to be granted by the purchaser's scheme should be equal in overall value to the amount of the transfer payment; this is another area where the actuaries may fail to agree.

Most pension schedules therefore include a clause providing for disagreements of this nature to be referred to an independent actuary. The clause will normally provide for the independent actuary to act as expert (rather than as arbitrator) as this is generally suitable for disputes of this nature and is less formal than arbitration. The agreement should also make provision for who is to bear the expert's costs.

HMRC issues

Loss of protection of cash lump sum

15.40   Where a member of a scheme had a right as at 5 April 2006 to a tax-free cash lump sum which exceeded the 25 per cent pension commencement lump sum limit and this is preserved by the transitional protection contained in *FA 2004, Sch 36, para 31* (see **Chapter 17**), then a transfer to a new arrangement can cause such protection to be lost unless the transfer is a 'block transfer'.

A transfer is a 'block transfer' if it is a single transfer of all the assets of at least two members and either:

(*a*)   the member was not a member of the receiving scheme before the transfer; or

(*b*)   he has been a member of the receiving scheme but for no longer than 12 months.

Loss of enhanced or fixed protection

15.41 A condition of both enhanced and fixed protection (see **Chapter 17**) is that there can be no further benefit accrual in any registered pension arrangement (other than in strictly limited circumstances) so this consideration will only apply to a limited number of deferred scheme members. In relation to ensuring no loss of protection, it is necessary to consider the provisions of *FA 2004, Sch 36, para 12* which provides that, for protection to be retained on transfer, the transfer must be a 'permitted transfer'. A transfer is a permitted transfer if *sub-para (8)* applies and the aggregate of the amount of the sums and the market value of the assets is, applying normal actuarial practice, equivalent before and after the transfer.

Sub-paragraph (8) requires the transfer to satisfy one of the following:

(*a*) it is a transfer to a money purchase scheme;

(*b*) it is a transfer 'in connection with the winding-up of the pension scheme and the rights transfer to employment with the same employer;

(*c*) it is a transfer in connection with a relevant business transfer of all or part of the undertaking or business involving at least 20 employees and the transfer is not being made between entities within the same corporation tax group; or

(*d*) it is a transfer as part of a company's retirement benefit activities compliance exercise to comply with *Pensions Act 2004, s 255*.

Contracting-out

15.42 Separate requirements apply to the transfer of contracted-out benefits. The relevant law is summarised in **Chapter 4**.

Shortfall and excess clauses

Shortfall clause

15.43 As has been mentioned already, the trustees will not be a party to the sale agreement and so will not be bound by its terms. Consequently, except in those cases where the seller's scheme's rules enable the seller to direct the amount of the transfer payment, there can be no guarantee that the trustees of that scheme will in fact transfer the amount provided for in the sale agreement. The purchaser will have particular cause for concern if the funding position of the seller's scheme suggests that its assets may prove insufficient to justify the transfer payment which the parties have negotiated.

The purpose of a shortfall clause is to protect the purchaser (and the purchaser's scheme) from the possibility of the trustees transferring less than the amount which the seller and the purchaser have agreed. The clause will require a payment by the seller itself (or by a company in its group) to achieve this. Shortfall payments (including the tax considerations) have already been considered in **15.26** above.

Excess clause

15.44 An excess clause is essentially the converse of a shortfall clause. Whereas a shortfall clause requires a payment from the seller should the trustees of the seller's scheme pay less than the agreed transfer payment, an excess clause requires a payment from the purchaser should they pay more.

A seller might insist that any shortfall clause in the agreement should be accompanied by a mirror-image excess clause. The purchaser, however, may take the view that the seller's trustees will only exceed the negotiated transfer payment if they are satisfied that their scheme can afford it. Consequently, many excess clauses are expressed so as only to apply to the extent that the trustees have transferred the excess by mistake.

The purchaser's scheme

Type of scheme

15.45 The course of action which ought to create the least disruption to the continuing accrual of members' pension benefits will be a properly funded transfer payment to a defined benefit scheme of the purchaser, containing similar provisions to those of the seller's scheme.

Often, however, the purchaser will not have an existing defined benefit scheme and the number of employees to be transferred may simply not be enough to make the establishment of a defined benefit scheme financially viable. In these circumstances, the purchaser might instead offer membership of a money purchase scheme or agree to pay contributions to personal pension schemes in relation to the employees concerned.

The seller will normally require a commitment in the sale agreement that the receiving scheme should be registered under the *FA 2004*, so that the seller's scheme may properly make the transfer to it. The contracted-out status of the purchaser's scheme prior to 6 April 2016 will also need to be considered if it is to receive the transfer of members' benefits accrued while in contracted-out employment (see **Chapter 4**).

One related point concerns announcements which the seller may have made about the purchaser's scheme. When contemplating making announcements to members about an impending sale, sellers will need to bear in mind the case of *Hagen v ICI Chemicals and Polymers Ltd [2002] IRLR 31* where a seller was found liable in relation to inaccurate statements it made about the purchaser's scheme. In the light of this case, the seller may want to leave as much detail as possible to be explained by the purchaser, whilst still complying with any duty to provide disclosures under *TUPE*.

Past service benefits

15.46   If the sale agreement provides for a past service reserve transfer payment to a defined benefit scheme, the seller is likely to require some commitment as to what past service benefits the purchaser's scheme will provide. The seller may prefer that these be determined in the same manner as applies for the calculation of benefits under the seller's scheme, but this could prove impractical for the purchaser if its own scheme has a different benefit structure.

Instead, the purchaser may (if it is satisfied that the transfer payment will be sufficient) be prepared to agree to procure that the past service benefits will be broadly equivalent overall to those earned in the seller's scheme, or if the purchaser agrees to go further than that, at least equal in value; the seller, in turn, may consider that this should be tightened so as to apply separately in respect of each member. The agreement may have to make it clear how benefits are to be valued for this purpose.

A more stringent line that a seller could take would, in effect, be to insist that the whole of the transfer payment is used to provide past service benefits in respect of the employees concerned. This would prevent the purchaser from using any part of the sum to fund a reduction in employers' contributions or to provide benefits for other scheme members. Much will depend upon the trust deeds and funding positions of the respective schemes, but a purchaser may well be reluctant to accept such a suggestion on the ground that it places a more onerous obligation upon it than would previously have applied under the seller's scheme.

The purchaser may be reluctant to give any commitments as to the level of past service benefits at all if it has doubts about the adequacy of the transfer payment being offered.

Where the transfer is to be made to a money purchase scheme, the question of past service benefits is less controversial. These will normally be whatever the value of each member's portion of the overall transfer payment provides.

Future service benefits

15.47   Purchasers are generally reluctant to commit themselves in the sale agreement to a specific level of benefits in respect of future service. This is partly because to do so would in most cases be a more onerous obligation than the seller itself had ever assumed, but more particularly because it would fetter the future running of their business. This is subject to the protections afforded to those transferred under *TUPE* given by *PA 2004, ss 257* and *258* (see **15.15** above).

A purchaser which has decided initially to provide defined benefits might, therefore, be prepared to commit itself to a particular benefits structure as at the date when the employees join the scheme, but reserve the right to amend or discontinue the scheme at any time after that. In the comparatively rare cases where the purchaser agrees to maintain a particular benefit structure (perhaps because it is receiving a generous transfer payment), this will only normally apply for a limited period.

Transfer agreement

15.48   The nature of the purchaser's scheme and the benefits under it will generally tend to be of greater concern to the transferring trustees than they are to the seller itself. These trustees may even have adopted a practice of requiring receiving trustees to enter into a transfer agreement with them, dealing specifically with these issues, before they will agree to make a particular transfer payment. The ability of trustees to take such a stance will depend on the balance of powers in the transferring scheme.

However, where this is the case, the seller may require that a form of transfer agreement is attached to the sale agreement and that the seller's obligations in relation to any transfer are dependent upon the purchaser's scheme's trustees entering into such an agreement with the seller's scheme's trustees.

Transfer agreements, and examples of the matters that they will frequently cover, are considered in **Chapter 13**.

Due diligence, warranties and indemnities

15.49   Where the purchaser will not be inheriting the whole of the seller's scheme, it may not require the same level of warranty protection as described in **15.23** above but a key concern will be to establish whether the transaction triggers a debt under *PA 1995, s 75* and/or whether either party should be seeking clearance from the Regulator. These issues are discussed from **15.61** below.

The purchaser should request a complete copy of the scheme's trust deed and rules and obtain a warranty as to its accuracy. There are two main reasons for needing to see this. The first is to enable the purchaser to satisfy itself that its provisions will not be such as to prevent the agreed pensions schedule from being implemented. The second is to enable the purchaser to ascertain the contributions and benefits structure in the seller's scheme; with this in mind, the purchaser should also seek to obtain copies of members' booklets and should also require a warranty that no changes to the information shown have been proposed or announced. This (together with appropriate membership data) should enable the purchaser's actuary to assess the likely costs to the purchaser of providing the same benefits for future service and suggest what alternative approaches might be available. This information should also reveal any particular expectations the members may have that could prove expensive for the purchaser, such as generous early retirement provisions on redundancy.

The purchaser ought also to request a copy of the latest actuarial valuation report, schedule of contributions and any recovery plan. The purchaser should seek to obtain warranties to the effect that nothing has happened since the effective date of the valuation which might adversely affect its findings. An understanding of the scheme's funding position will help the purchaser to take a view as to how large a transfer payment it can realistically negotiate. Where there is an indication of underfunding, this will alert the purchaser to the possible need for a shortfall clause (see **15.43** above) and an indemnity in respect of any employer's debt that may arise (see **15.61** onwards below).

Warranties should also be sought as to the registered status of the seller's scheme (as, broadly, a transfer can be made without adverse tax consequences if it counts as a 'recognised transfer' (see **Chapter 17**).

Another area of concern is the equalisation of benefits as between men and women as required by law (see **Chapter 9**). The purchaser should seek a warranty that these requirements have been met, as a member who is entitled to bring a claim based on a scheme's failure to equalise can also sue the trustees of another scheme to whom the benefits in question have been transferred. It is common for purchasers also to seek an indemnity against this eventuality.

Transitional periods

General

15.50   In a transaction involving a transfer payment the purchaser may, if it has no suitable scheme in place to receive the transfer payment and requires a period of time in which to establish one, wish to have the benefit of a transitional period, where employees continue to be active members of the seller's scheme following the completion date.

In the context of a share sale, this will simply be a case of the company continuing to participate in the scheme for a temporary period after it has been sold out of the seller's group. In an asset sale, by contrast, it will mean the purchaser (or employer of the transferring employees) being admitted to the seller's scheme as a participating employer, but only for the agreed transitional period commencing on the completion date.

Transitional periods are now relatively rare as purchasers do not want to run the risk of inheriting any additional liabilities under the employer debt regime, or increasing the risk of being made subject to a contribution notice or financial support direction in relation to the seller's scheme (see from **15.74** below). However, this risk can be mitigated if a suitably worded indemnity can be obtained from the seller.

HMRC

15.51　Prior to 6 April 2006, any period of participation by an employer which was not (or had ceased to be) associated with the scheme's principal employer required the agreement of HMRC.

The position now is that non-associated employers are able to participate in a scheme and/or allow previously associated employers receiving a transfer of employees following a business transfer to participate for longer than the previously permitted period of 12 months on completion of the transaction. This may give rise to 'balance of power' issues and consideration will be required as to whether the participation of a non-associated employer would be consistent with the main purpose of the scheme (ie where the scheme in question has been established for the benefit of the employees and directors of the principal and associated employers).

Role of trustees

15.52　Before agreeing to a period of temporary participation, the seller should check the scheme rules to see if the trustees have a discretion as to whether or not to permit this (or, indeed, if it is permitted at all). If so, then the seller will not be in a position to *procure* a transitional period in the sale agreement, and should ensure that the level of commitment required of it under the sale agreement is consistent with those rules.

In most instances, the trustees should be amenable to the agreement of a transitional period of participation, but circumstances may arise where they are not (for instance, if the trustees consider that the temporary employer has a weak covenant, to the detriment of the scheme's funding position).

The sale agreement will normally seek to regulate the terms upon which the company or purchaser is to be permitted to participate.

Employers' contributions

15.53 The parties may leave the question of contributions during the transitional period to be determined in accordance with the scheme rules and current schedule of contributions. If they want to agree a different rate, the schedule of contributions may need to be revised, which will require input from the trustees (see **Chapter 11** for more on schedules of contributions).

If employers are all paying very high contributions (possibly under a recovery plan) then the purchaser can be expected to request a lower rate, taking into account only ongoing liabilities during the participation period.

If the seller's scheme is overfunded and the participating employers are enjoying a contributions holiday, the seller is likely to prefer to specify a fixed contribution rate, probably equal to the long-term contribution rate which the actuary would be recommending if the scheme was evenly funded on an ongoing basis.

Even where a specified rate of contribution is agreed, the seller's scheme's trustees will have to agree to the contribution rates (see **Chapter 11** for more detail on the setting of contribution rates). If, therefore, the parties have agreed a rate which tends to favour the purchaser, then the purchaser may also seek an indemnity from the seller against the possibility of the trustees requiring a higher rate.

Expenses

15.54 Expenses arising during the transitional period may take the form of:

(*a*) administrative expenses; or

(*b*) the cost of insuring risk benefits.

They may form part of the contribution rate required to be paid by the purchaser during the transitional period, or be specified in the agreement as an additional further sum to be paid.

Limit on salary increases

15.55 One of the actuarial assumptions by reference to which the seller's scheme is funded will relate to future salary increases. A transitional period presents some risk to the seller of the temporarily participating company granting salary increases during that period which significantly exceed this assumption.

Such an increase will inflate the seller's liabilities for deferred pensions in respect of those members affected by the transaction who elect not to transfer to the purchaser's scheme. It may also increase the amount of the transfer payment, depending on the circumstances. This, of course, will be detrimental to the funding of the seller's scheme.

The seller may therefore insert a provision requiring the purchaser to procure that pay increases do not rise by more than a certain percentage during the transitional period (often a percentage consistent with the scheme's assumptions). Whether this presents a problem for the purchaser will depend on whether it anticipates granting such increases. If not, then the purchaser may choose to accept the restriction, but with the qualification that the increases may be granted with the consent of the seller (usually not to be unreasonably withheld or delayed).

Other obligations of the purchaser during the transitional period

15.56   The sale agreement may also require the purchaser to procure that, during the transitional period, it (or, where appropriate, the participating employer owned by it):

(*a*)   will comply with all the provisions of the seller's scheme which apply to it as a participating employer;

(*b*)   will not exercise any discretion which it may have in relation to the seller's scheme without the seller's consent (usually not to be unreasonably withheld or delayed);

(*c*)   will not by any act or omission prejudice the scheme's registered status;

(*d*)   will not take any steps which might increase the transfer payment; and

(*e*)   will nominate the seller to act on its behalf in relation to its rights to be consulted and make decisions about scheme funding and investment.

Obligations of the seller during the transitional period

15.57   Obligations of the seller under the sale agreement in respect of the transitional period might be as follows:

(*a*)   to keep the scheme in full force and effect;

(*b*)   not to increase benefits in relation to the members concerned; and

(*c*)   not to take any steps which might reduce the transfer payment.

Date as at which past service liabilities are calculated

15.58   The date as at which the transfer payment should be calculated may be either:

(*a*)   the completion date; or

(*b*)   the end of the transitional period.

A number of issues will arise depending upon which of the two dates is to apply:

(*a*)   If the completion date is used, an addition should be made to the calculation of the transfer payment representing the contributions paid by the participating employer in respect of the transferring members, and by the transferring members themselves, during the transitional period (less any part of the employer contributions which relates to the expenses mentioned in **15.54** above).

(*b*)   If the end of the transitional period is used, then the issue of salary increases during the transitional period (see **15.55** above) becomes particularly relevant, as increases in excess of the assumptions will inflate the calculation of the transfer payment.

(*c*)   If the end of the transitional period is used, then the timing adjustment (which, in the absence of a transitional period, would operate from the completion date – see **15.36** above) should operate from the end of the transitional period.

Admission of new members during the transitional period

15.59   If during the transitional period the purchaser does not have any other scheme in place, it may wish to have new members employed by it (who were not members before completion) admitted to the seller's scheme during that period. The seller's views on this are likely to depend on the administrative implications.

It may be that the seller will draw a distinction between:

(*a*)   applicants who were employed by the company (or within the business) before completion but were at that time serving a 'waiting period' before they could become eligible to join; and

(*b*)   applicants who are recruited as employees by the new owners after completion,

and agree only to admit the first of these two groups.

Due diligence, warranties and indemnities

15.60   The purchaser should obtain the same information, and seek the same protections, as mentioned in **15.49** above.

In addition, the fact that there will be a temporary period of participation in the seller's scheme will necessitate a careful review of the participating employers' obligations under the scheme's trust deed and under statute. The issues in relation to employers' contributions have already been mentioned (see **15.53** above).

The purchaser should also check to see whether the trust deed (or any other document) contains an indemnity by the participating employers in favour of the trustees. If so, more extensive warranties may be necessary to satisfy the purchaser that there is no matter in respect of which it might become liable under that indemnity.

In participating in the seller's scheme, the purchaser is bringing itself clearly within the ambit of the Regulator's moral hazard powers (see from **15.74** below) and the end of the participation period is likely to trigger a *s 75* debt (see from **15.61** below). The purchaser should fully assess the related risks before embarking on a participation period.

Employer debt

Overview

15.61   We saw in **Chapter 12** that there are certain circumstances where *PA 1995, s 75* may render an employer liable for a debt to the trustees of an underfunded scheme.

Some of those circumstances are especially relevant in the context of this Chapter. The *Occupational Pension Schemes (Employer Debt) Regulations 2005 (SI 2005/678)* (the '*Employer Debt Regulations*'), were amended by the *Occupational Pension Schemes (Employer Debt and Miscellaneous Amendments) Regulations 2008*, which came into force on 6 April 2008, the *Occupational Pension Schemes (Employer Debt – Apportionment Arrangements) (Amendment) Regulations 2008* which came into force from 15 April 2008, the *Occupational Pension Schemes (Employer Debt and Miscellaneous Amendments) Regulations 2010 (SI 2010/725)*, which came into force on 6 April 2010 and the *Occupational Pension Schemes (Employer Debt and Miscellaneous Amendments) Regulations 2011 (SI 2011/2973)*, which came into force on 27 January 2012. The intention of the changes was to make the operation of the *Employer Debt Regulations* more flexible, particularly in relation to corporate restructurings, whilst at the same time encouraging employers to stand behind their pension liabilities.

Under the *Employer Debt Regulations* a statutory debt is triggered under *PA 1995, s 75* where an 'employment-cessation event' occurs. This occurs, in a multi-employer scheme, where an employer ceases to employ at least one person who is an active member of the scheme, and at least one other employer continues to employ at least one active member of the scheme. So, for example, where the target company which is sold outside the group is participating in a group pension scheme and ceases to participate on sale, there will be an employment-cessation event and if there is a deficit in the scheme an immediate debt, due from the target company to the scheme trustees, will be triggered. The default position is that the debt will be calculated on a full annuity buy-out basis plus 'cessation expenses' (unless one of the methods for dealing with the debt outlined below is adopted). Money purchase assets and liabilities are expressly excluded.

Clearly, the possibility of a *s 75* debt arising will have a significant impact on the viability and structure of a proposed transaction and the value of a withdrawing company. The *Employer Debt Regulations* are in themselves a complex piece of legislation and should be considered in detail in the event that the purchaser is acquiring a company which participates in a multi-employer scheme.

Under the *Employer Debt Regulations*, there are now a number of ways to deal with the debt (some of which stop it triggering, or stop it triggering for the full amount). These are summarised below.

Dealing with the debt

Liability share – default position (Employer Debt Regulations, regs 5, 6(4)–(7))

15.62   If no active steps are taken to adopt one of the alternatives outlined below, the 'liability share' will apply. The liability share is an amount equal to the liability proportion of the full buy-out debt. The liability proportion is a fraction K/L where:

K =   the amount of a scheme's liabilities attributable to an employer, and

L =   the total amount of the scheme's liabilities attributable to employment with all the employers.

Only liabilities arising during or as a result of pensionable service with that employer (including transfers in) and not as a result of pensionable service with any other employer under the scheme will be included. However, where the trustees are unable (or without disproportionate cost) to determine the exact liabilities attributable to an employer, all the liabilities will either be attributable to the most recent employer or they will be attributable in a reasonable manner to one or more employers. These are commonly known as 'orphan' liabilities.

Period of grace (Employer Debt Regulations, reg 6A)

15.63   An employer, on ceasing to employ active members, may on, before or within two months of the cessation date, give the trustees a period of grace notice. This is a notice in writing that the employer intends, during the period of 12 months from the employment-cessation event (unless agreed otherwise), to employ at least one person who will be an active member. The trustees may agree in writing before the 12-month period expires, to extend the period of grace to longer than 12 months but less than 36 months from the employment-cessation event. The trustees can consent to extending the period of grace on multiple occasions provided that the total period does not exceed 36 months. This defers the triggering of the debt, and the employer continues to be an employer in relation to the scheme. A debt will arise at the date of the original employment-cessation event if the employer:

(*a*)   does not employ an active member by the last day of the period of grace;

(*b*)   informs the trustees during the period of grace that it no longer intends to employ an active member during this period;

(*c*)   becomes insolvent; or

(*d*)   changes its intention to employ an active member during the period of grace, in which case it must notify the trustees.

Once the employer employs an active member (either before or after the notice is given), the period of grace comes to an end and the employer shall be treated as if the employment-cessation event had never occurred. Whilst this provision may assist where an employer's last employee leaves employment, it is difficult to see how it could be used in the context of corporate transactions.

Scheme apportionment arrangement (Employer Debt Regulations, reg 6B)

15.64   This is an arrangement under the scheme rules (it must be written into the rules) which satisfies the conditions below and to which the trustees, the exiting employer and/or any remaining employer(s) to whom all or part of the exiting employer's liability has been apportioned consent. Which employer will be required to consent depends on whether the exiting employer is paying more or less than the 'liability share'. If it is paying more, its consent will be needed. If it is paying less than the liability share (which is more likely), then it will be the remaining employer(s) to whom all or part of the exiting employer's liability has been apportioned who will need to consent. The other conditions to be met, apart from the consent requirements, are that the arrangement:

(*a*)   provides for the employer to pay a 'scheme apportionment arrangement share' instead of its liability share;

(*b*)   where that amount is less than the liability share, apportions all or part of the liability share to one or more of the remaining employers;

(*c*)   is entered into before, on or after the applicable time (being the date the employment-cessation event occurs);

(*d*)   sets out the amount of an employer's scheme apportionment arrangement share;

(*e*)   meets the funding test (unless one of the exceptions applies) – see **15.69** below; and

(*f*)   may set out when the 'amount apportioned' is to be paid (in practice, trustees will want to specify a time for payment).

Where scheme rules do not currently permit the trustees to enter into a scheme apportionment arrangement or a regulated apportionment arrangement (see **15.65** below), a rule permitting apportionment can be introduced, either by amendment of the deed and rules of the scheme or by resolution of the trustees. The *Employer Debt Regulations* give trustees power under *PA 1995, s 68*, after consulting such employers under the scheme as they think fit, to modify the scheme by resolution to achieve this, even if the scheme rules would enable them to modify the scheme in a different manner.

Clearance should usually be sought for scheme apportionment arrangements as they are generally classified as Type A events (see **15.80** onwards below). However, a scheme apportionment arrangement which is entered into after the event triggering the employer debt will always be a Type A event and clearance should be obtained. It will also be a notifiable event for the trustees (see **15.72** below).

Regulated apportionment arrangement (Employer Debt Regulations, reg 7A)

15.65   This is designed to be used in restructuring situations where the trustees consider that there is a reasonable likelihood of the scheme entering a Pensions Protection Fund ('PPF') assessment period in the next 12 months or where an assessment period has already commenced but not ended. It is an arrangement under the scheme rules which broadly:

- provides for the amount that would have been the employer's liability share to be changed;

- where the employer's liability share is reduced, apportions all or part of the amount that would have been the employer's liability share to one or more of the remaining employers;

- is entered into before, on or after the applicable time (being the date the employment-cessation event occurs);

- sets out the amount of an employer's regulated apportionment arrangement share;

- may set out when the amount apportioned is to be paid; and

- where a PPF assessment period has not already commenced, satisfies the following conditions:

  - the trustees and the employer/any remaining employer to whom all or part of the employer's liability has been apportioned consent to the arrangement;

  - the arrangement and any amendments to it are approved by the Regulator by a notice of approval (issued only if the Regulator considers it reasonable); and

  - the PPF does not object.

All the conditions are equivalent to those for a scheme apportionment arrangement, except that the funding test is replaced by Regulator approval and the requirement that the PPF does not object.

This arrangement allows apportionment of a smaller amount of debt in order to avoid employer insolvency, enabling the employer to continue to trade free of the pension liabilities. It will be used only where the potential recovery to the PPF is greater than putting the employer through an insolvency process.

In August 2010, the Regulator issued a statement on regulated apportionment arrangements and insolvency. The statement sets out how the Regulator would deal with applications for approval of regulated apportionment arrangements and what factors it would consider when granting approval, which are as follows:

- whether employer insolvency would otherwise be inevitable or whether there could be alternative solutions that could avoid it;

- whether the scheme may receive more on the employer's insolvency;

- whether other options might produce a better outcome for the scheme (including use of the Regulator's anti-avoidance powers);

- the position of the rest of the employer's group;

- the outcome for other creditors; and

- the independent financial advice obtained by the Trustees.

If the Regulator takes an initial view to support an application, it will then evaluate the 'mitigation' proposed in conjunction with the PPF. The PPF updated its guidance for insolvency practitioners, specifically relating to restructurings, in August 2016 and currently applies the principles set out in 'The PPF Approach to Employer Restructuring' and its guidance 'PPF General Guidance for Restructuring & Insolvency Professionals' to determine whether or not to object to a regulated apportionment arrangement (see **Chapter 5**).

The Regulator expects that any application for approval of a regulated apportionment arrangement is accompanied by a clearance application (see **15.80** below).

Withdrawal arrangement (Employer Debt Regulations, reg 6C, Sch 1A)

15.66   A withdrawal arrangement can be entered into before, on or after an employment-cessation event.

The cessation employer must pay an amount of at least the 'withdrawal arrangement share'. This is an amount that is:

- a cessation employer's share of the difference,

- equal to or, with employer agreement, greater than 'Amount A', and

- payable by the cessation employer pursuant to the withdrawal arrangement.

Amount A is broadly the employer's share of the shortfall on a scheme funding (not buy-out) basis. The guarantors are liable for amount B, a floating or a fixed amount payable on certain events occurring, including the agreed payment date, the scheme commencing winding-up, and a relevant event occurring in relation to the last employer.

The conditions are quite stringent: the trustees may enter into a withdrawal arrangement with the cessation employer and guarantor(s) only where they are satisfied that:

- the funding test is met (the same as the first limb of the funding test for a scheme apportionment arrangement) – see **15.69** below; and

- the guarantors have sufficient financial resources at the date the arrangement is entered into to be likely to pay amount B.

Withdrawal arrangements that do not require regulatory approval must contain certain statutory conditions (as set out in the *Employer Debt Regulations, Schedule 1A*). These statutory conditions must be fully included as failure to do so will mean that the withdrawal arrangement does not comply with the legislation and the departing employer may retain liability for the remainder of the *s 75* debt and would also remain an employer for the purposes of *PA 1995, s 75*.

On the face of it, withdrawal arrangements have costs and speed advantages; however, if clearance is required (see **15.80** below), some of those advantages will be lost.

Approved withdrawal arrangement (Employer Debt Regulations, reg 7, Sch 1A)

15.67 An approved withdrawal arrangement is entered into by the cessation employer, the trustees and a guarantor, with the approval of the Regulator, which may be given before or after the employment-cessation event. This is the only withdrawal arrangement option if the exiting employer wishes to pay less than the scheme funding basis shortfall.

A previous requirement, that the Regulator could approve an agreement only where the resources of the guarantors were such that the *s 75* debt was more likely to be met if the agreement was approved, has been removed. It has been replaced by new conditions which give the Regulator significant flexibility. The requirements are that:

- the amount the cessation employer proposes to pay as its approved withdrawal arrangement share must be less than amount A (broadly the employer's share of the shortfall on a scheme funding basis);

- the trustees have notified the Regulator that the funding test is met (the same test as for withdrawal arrangements under the *Employer Debt Regulations, reg 6C*); and

- the Regulator must be satisfied that it is reasonable to approve the arrangement, having regard to such matters as it considers relevant, including:

    - the potential effect of the employment-cessation event on the method or assumptions used to calculate the scheme's technical provisions;

    - the financial circumstances of the proposed guarantors;

    - the amount of the cessation employer's 'liability share';

    - the amount of the proposed approved withdrawal arrangement share and where there is likely to be a relevant transfer deduction, an estimate of the amount the cessation employer will pay if the transfer is completed; and

– the effect of the proposed arrangement on the security of members' benefits.

There is a practical problem if it cannot be established, before a withdrawal arrangement or approved withdrawal arrangement is entered into, whether the amount to be paid is above or below amount A, as it is then not possible to work out which option to choose.

Flexible apportionment arrangement (Employer Debt Regulations, reg 6E)

15.68   From 27 January 2012, it became possible to enter into a flexible apportionment arrangement. The arrangement can be put in place:

- if an employment-cessation event has occurred;

- if an employment-cessation event would have occurred, and in any event within 28 days, but for the operation of the *Employer Debt Regulations, reg 6ZA(7)*;

- if an employment-cessation event would have occurred in relation to a 'frozen scheme'.

Before the flexible apportionment arrangement can take effect, the following conditions must be satisfied:

- the funding test has been met (see **15.69** below);

- one or more of the replacement employers agree to take over responsibility under a legally enforceable agreement for all the liabilities of the leaving employer under the scheme;

- the trustees, the leaving employer and the replacement employer(s) consent in writing to the arrangement;

- the leaving employer is not in a period of grace (see **15.63** above);

- the scheme is not in a PPF assessment period or being wound up; and

- the trustees are satisfied that an assessment period is unlikely to begin within the period of 12 months beginning with the date on which a flexible apportionment arrangement takes effect.

In order for the arrangement to qualify as a flexible apportionment arrangement where a part payment is intended to be made regarding the leaving employer's *s 75* debt, then:

- the payment must be made to the trustees by or on behalf of the leaving employer;

- the payment must be in addition to any amount required to be paid under the schedule of contributions;

- the trustees must decide to reduce the scheme liabilities of the leaving employer as a result of that payment; and

- the reduction must relate to the amount of the payment made.

Unlike a scheme apportionment arrangement, a flexible apportionment arrangement is not defined in the *Employer Debt Regulations* as 'an arrangement under the scheme rules'. Instead it is 'an arrangement that takes effect in accordance with regulation 6E'. There is no need to insert a power into the scheme rules to allow the trustees to enter into a flexible apportionment arrangement, however, it may be best practice to do so, particularly if other amendments are being made to the scheme rules to facilitate the apportionment.

The funding test (Employer Debt Regulations, regs 2(4A) to (4D))

15.69 The funding test is designed to prevent an apportionment being used to abandon the scheme. The test is met if the trustees are reasonably satisfied that:

- when the arrangement takes effect, the remaining employers will be reasonably likely to be able to fund the scheme so that, after the applicable time (or, in the case of a flexible apportionment arrangement, after the time the arrangement takes effect), it will have sufficient and appropriate assets to cover its technical provisions, taking into account any change in those provisions which are necessary as a result of the arrangement; and

- the arrangement will not adversely affect the security of members' benefits as a result of any:

    - material change in legal, demographic or economic circumstances that would justify a change to the method or assumptions last used in calculating the scheme's technical provisions; or

    - material revision to any existing recovery plan.

The first limb of the funding test applies to scheme apportionment arrangements, withdrawal arrangements, approved withdrawal arrangements and flexible apportionment arrangements. The second limb applies only to scheme apportionment arrangements and flexible apportionment arrangements.

The *Employer Debt Regulations* expressly provide at *reg 2(4C)* that the first limb of the test may be satisfied if the trustees consider that the remaining employers are able to meet the relevant payments as they fall due under the statutory schedule of contributions (revised as necessary).

The funding test does not have to be met in the case of a scheme apportionment arrangement if:

- the proposed employer scheme apportionment share is greater than the liability share, ie above buy-out level (although few employers are likely to wish to pay more than buy-out); or

- the scheme has commenced winding up and the trustees are satisfied that it is likely that the employer would be unable to pay the liability share if it applied but will be able to pay the scheme apportionment share.

Group Restructuring

15.70 Since April 2010, the *Employer Debt Regulations, Reg 6ZB* introduced two easements from the employer debt requirements for employers undertaking group restructuring exercises: the 'general easement' and the '*de minimis* easement'. A corporate restructuring that falls within one of these easements does not qualify as an employment-cessation event and no employer debt will arise.

The 'general easement' applies to transactions where the assets of an exiting employer are transferred to a single receiving employer. The '*de minimis* easement' applies to small-scale restructurings. A detailed series of steps must be completed for an existing employer to take advantage of either easement. In practice, employers are likely to find it hard to surmount the necessary hurdles, meaning the easements have not been widely used. The introduction of flexible apportionment arrangements from 27 January 2012 (see **15.68** above) has also provided a less prescriptive alternative.

Business and asset sales

15.71 On a business and asset sale, no debt on the purchaser (or new employer depending on where the business assets and employees are transferred) is likely to arise as long as the purchaser (or new employer, where applicable) is not admitted to participate in the seller's scheme for a transitional period. If the purchaser (or new employer, where applicable) does participate it could be liable for a statutory debt when it ceases to participate.

Employer debt alternative arrangements – summary

15.72

Arrangement	Amount of debt to be paid	Applicable conditions	Is the Regulator's approval required?	Is clearance required?	Is it a notifiable event?
Liability share (default position)	Buy-out	N/A	No	No	No
Scheme apportionment arrangement ('SAA')	Any	Trustee and employer consent Must meet the funding test unless the SAA is greater than the liability share (or in certain circumstances when the scheme is winding up): (i) remaining employers reasonably likely to be able to fund to the technical provision level; and (ii) security of members' benefits not adversely affected	No	Yes, if entered into retrospectively Yes, if entered into in advance unless: (i) increases debt immediately payable by an employer who can afford it; or (ii) alternatives too costly or complex and actuary's best estimate of unmodified debt is immediately payable; or (iii) no net reduction of employer covenant	Yes, if entered into retrospectively (notifiable by trustees) No

Arrangement	*Amount of debt to be paid*	*Applicable conditions*	*Is the Regulator's approval required?*	*Is clearance required?*	*Is it a notifiable event?*
Regulated apportionment	Any	Trustee and employer consent PPF does not object	Yes	Yes, the Regulator's August 2010 statement indicates all applications for approval of a regulated apportionment arrangement should be accompanied by a clearance application.	No
Withdrawal arrangement	At least amount A (employer's share of liabilities on scheme funding basis)	Satisfies conditions in *Employer Debt Regulations, Sch 1A* Funding test met: remaining employers reasonably likely to be able to fund to technical provisions level Guarantors have, sufficient financial resources to be likely to pay amount B at the date the arrangement entered into	No	Yes, if detrimental to scheme's ability to meet its liabilities (eg if guarantee insufficient) or a type A event.	No, but certain events notifiable by guarantors

Arrangement	*Amount of debt to be paid*	*Applicable conditions*	*Is the Regulator's approval required?*	*Is clearance required?*	*Is it a notifiable event?*
Approved withdrawal arrangement	Less than amount A	Funding test met: remaining employers reasonably likely to be able to fund to technical provisions level	Yes	Yes, if it has a related type A event (eg if guarantee insufficient)	No, but certain events notifiable by guarantors
Flexible apportionment arrangement	Apportions scheme liabilities rather than share of the debt – no employer debt calculation required	Funding test has been met One or more of the replacement employers agree to take over responsibility for all the liabilities of the leaving employer	No	Yes, if there is a type A event. If the debt has already been triggered this will always be classified as a type A event	Yes, by the trustees

Arrangement	Amount of debt to be paid	Applicable conditions	Is the Regulator's approval required?	Is clearance required?	Is it a notifiable event?
		The trustees, the leaving employer and the replacement employer(s) consent in writing to the arrangement The leaving employer is not in a period of grace The scheme is not in a PPF assessment period or being wound up The trustees are satisfied that an assessment period is unlikely to begin within the period of 12 months beginning with the date on which a flexible apportionment arrangement takes effect			

Parties' positions

15.73   The purchaser should be concerned about the risk that he may be entering into a transaction which may give rise to a debt payable by him or by the company he is buying. Even if the purchaser can persuade the seller to indemnify him against any such debt, there remains the possibility that a considerable period of time might pass before the actuarial calculations are complete and the debt is notified to the purchaser. There is a risk that, by this stage, the seller may no longer be in a financial position to meet the indemnity. As well as an indemnity, therefore, the purchaser may ask the seller to procure that the scheme will be valued, and the amount of any debt notified, within a set timescale.

None of this is likely to appeal to the seller, especially if the scheme's funding is weak. The prospect of an indemnity will be particularly unattractive if the seller is promising a past service reserve transfer payment backed up by a shortfall clause (see **15.43** above).

The possibility of an employer debt arising may, therefore, present major issues for the parties, and this highlights the need for early due diligence in relation to the scheme's funding position. It may be possible to lessen the impact of the legislation by structuring the deal, for example, as an asset sale rather than a company sale, or to enter into one of the arrangements permitted by the *Employer Debt Regulations* (see **15.72** above), so that the purchaser has certainty over the amount of any debt that may arise as a consequence of the transaction. The following table sets out some of the options available to a purchaser, depending upon the structure of the transaction:

	Potential size of debt	*Reason*	*Options*
Company sale, no transitional period	Could be huge.	The purchaser acquires all the company's liabilities. The company may have participated in the seller's scheme for years and be responsible for a proportion of the overall debt (calculated on a full buy-out basis). This will relate not only to the company's present employees, but also to pensioners and deferred pensioners formerly employed by it.	Restructure the deal so it becomes an asset sale; Amend the trust deed and rules governing the scheme to introduce a scheme apportionment arrangement; Enter into a withdrawal arrangement; Request the seller make good the deficit prior to completion; or Adjust the purchase price to take into account the pension scheme liabilities that will be acquired on completion.
Company sale with transitional period	Larger still.	As above, except that the extra period of participation will increase any debt still further.	Same considerations as above, but the purchaser would want to ensure that it is only responsible, if at all, for any s 75 liabilities arising solely in relation to its period of participation.
Asset sale, no transitional period	Nil (assuming the seller of the assets continues to have some employees in the scheme following completion).	No employer will be ceasing to participate in the seller's scheme.	

	Potential size of debt	Reason	Options
Asset sale with transitional period	Smaller debt than for corresponding company sale (again, assuming the seller of the assets continues to have some employees in the scheme following completion).	The purchaser (or new employer, where applicable) will have participated in the seller's scheme only for a short time following completion, and so be responsible for a (probably small) proportion of any overall deficit.	Indemnification required from the seller that the purchaser (or new employer, where applicable) will only be liable for those debts arising whilst a participating employer. A review of the trust deed and rules also necessary to ensure that other debts cannot be apportioned to the purchaser (or new employer, where applicable). In practice, very few purchasers are likely to want to take up this option.

Moral hazard

Introduction

15.74   The Regulator has powers to prevent employers 'dumping' their defined benefit liabilities upon the Pensions Protection Fund and to increase member security. These 'moral hazard' provisions are of particular relevance to corporate transactions. The Regulator's powers include the ability to issue contribution notices, requiring specified persons to make contributions to pension arrangements, and to issue financial support directions ('FSDs'), requiring certain persons to put in place financial support arrangements for a pension scheme. These, together with the 'clearance procedure' for corporate transactions, are set out in further detail below.

These provisions apply to occupational pension schemes, other than money purchase schemes and certain other prescribed schemes (broadly public sector schemes, unregistered schemes and centralised schemes for non-associated employers) (*PA 2004, ss 38* and *43, The Pensions Regulator (Contribution Notices and Restoration Orders) Regulations 2005 (SI 2005/931)* and *The Pensions Regulator (Financial Support Directions etc) Regulations 2005 (SI 2005/2188)*). Any purchaser of the shares of a company participating in a defined benefits pension scheme needs to take great care to establish any potential risk of a contribution notice or FSD being imposed as a result of the transaction, and if appropriate seek clearance from the Regulator and/or an indemnity from the seller.

Contribution notices

15.75   The Regulator may, in accordance with *PA 2004, s 38* (as amended by *PA 2008* on 26 November 2008, with retrospective effect to 14 April 2008) issue a contribution notice to an employer or person *connected* with, or an *associate* of, the employer (see **15.78** below) where there is an act or failure to act and:

(*a*)   the 'material detriment test' is met (see **15.77** below); or

(*b*)   the main purpose, or one of the main purposes of the act or failure, was to:

  –   prevent the recovery of all or part of the statutory debt; or

  –   prevent the statutory debt becoming due, to compromise or otherwise settle or reduce that debt;

and the 'reasonableness test' is satisfied (see **15.76** below).

The contribution notice will require the person to pay a specified sum into the scheme, or to the PPF where the PPF has assumed responsibility for the scheme. This specified sum could be of an amount up to the total shortfall of any *s 75* debt (or even where there is no debt yet due, the total assessed shortfall as if a *s 75* debt were due (ie in practice this would mean the full buy-out cost)). Contribution notices can also be imposed against individuals personally.

A contribution notice may be issued in relation to a series of acts rather than requiring the test to be met in relation to a single act (*PA 2004, s 38(12), (13)*) and, where a transfer has been made from a scheme, the Regulator may issue a contribution notice in relation to the transferor scheme, the transferee scheme, or both (*PA 2004, s 39A*).

The legislation is retrospective and the Regulator can issue a contribution notice in relation to an act or failure to act which occurred on or after 27 April 2004 (limited overall to a six-year 'look back' period).

The Regulator has published guidance for employers involved in corporate transactions, available on its website, which reminds employers of the importance of understanding the effect any transaction may have on the pension scheme and on the sponsor's ability to meet the liabilities.

Purchasers should be seeking confirmation from the seller that no contribution notices have been issued by the Regulator and remain unpaid in relation to a pension scheme if acquiring the entire issued share capital of the target company and that no circumstances have occurred which could give rise to a contribution notice. See **15.23** above for further details on suggested warranties.

Reasonableness test

15.76   The Regulator can only impose a contribution notice if it considers that it is reasonable to do so. (*PA 2004, s 38(3)(d)*) states that when deciding what is reasonable, the Regulator must have regard to the extent to which it was reasonable for the person to act, or fail to act, in the way that the person did and have regard to such other matters as the Regulator considers relevant including those which fall under PA 2004, s 38(7):

- the degree of involvement of the person in the act or failure to act;

- the relationship which the person has or has had with the employer;

- any connection or involvement which the person has or has had with the scheme;

- if the act or failure to act was a notifiable event for the purposes of *PA 2004, s 69*, any failure to notify;

- all the purposes of the act or failure to act (including whether a purpose of the act or failure was to prevent or limit loss of employment);

- the value of any benefits which directly or indirectly the person receives, or is entitled to receive, from the employer under the scheme;

- the likelihood of relevant creditors being paid and the extent to which they are likely to be paid;

- the financial circumstances of the person; and

- such other matters as may be prescribed (which has not yet been brought into force under *PA 2004, s 38(7)(g)*).

The material detriment test

15.77 The material detriment test is met in relation to an act or failure to act if the Regulator is of the opinion that 'the act or failure has detrimentally affected in a material way the likelihood of accrued scheme benefits being received' (*PA 2004, s 38A(1)*).

In deciding whether an act meets the material detriment test, the Regulator must have regard to matters it considers relevant, including (*PA 2004, s 38A(4)*):

- the value of the assets or liabilities of the scheme or any relevant transferee scheme and the effect of the act or failure on the value of those assets or liabilities;

- the scheme obligations of any person and the effect of the act or failure on any of those obligations;

- the extent to which any person is likely to be able to discharge any scheme obligation in any circumstances and the extent to which any act or failure to act has affected or might affect that; and

- other matters which may be prescribed.

Under *PA 2004, s 38B* there is a statutory defence to the material detriment test where the person against whom the Regulator intends issuing a contribution notice can show *each* of the following:

- he gave due prior consideration (such that a reasonably diligent person would have done) to the extent to which the act or failure to act might have a materially detrimental effect on the likelihood that accrued scheme benefits would be received;

- as a result of that consideration, he took all reasonable steps to eliminate or minimise any potential detriment identified; and

- in all the circumstances prevailing at the time of the act or failure to act, it was reasonable for him to conclude that the act or failure to act would not detrimentally affect in a material way the likelihood of accrued scheme benefits being received.

When issuing a warning notice that it intends to issue a contribution notice under the material detriment test, the Regulator must inform the recipient that this defence is available.

The Regulator issued Code of Practice No 12 in June 2009 which sets out the circumstances in which it expects to issue contribution notices as a result of the material detriment test being met. The circumstances set out in Code are:

- the transfer of the scheme out of the jurisdiction;

- the transfer of the sponsoring employer out of the jurisdiction or the replacement of the sponsoring employer with an entity that does not fall within the jurisdiction;

- sponsor support is removed, substantially reduced or becomes nominal;

- the transfer of liabilities of the scheme to another pension scheme or arrangement which leads to a significant reduction of the:

  – sponsor support in respect of the liabilities; or

  – funding to cover the liabilities;

- a business model or the operation of the scheme which creates from the scheme, or which is designed to do so, a financial benefit for:

  – the employer; or

  – some other person,

  where proper account has not been taken of the interests of the members of the scheme, including where risks to members are increased.

The Regulator has helpfully provided examples of circumstances which would not normally give rise to a contribution notice under the material detriment test, which include:

- the payment of a routine annual dividend in the normal course of business where the employer is trading profitably and an appropriate recovery plan is in place to address the scheme deficit;

- buying out pensioner liabilities with a regulated insurer;

- the weakening of an employer covenant due to poor trading because of market conditions;

- granting security where proper mitigation is provided to the trustees; and

- agreeing an investment strategy which has been properly chosen, is compliant and has prudent assumptions taking into account the employer's ability to cope with adverse experience.

'Connected' and 'associated'

15.78 The Regulator can only issue a contribution notice to a person if that person was at any time in the relevant period:

(*a*)   an employer in relation to the scheme; or

(*b*)   a person connected with, or an associate of, the employer.

These are complex definitions. In summary, a person is 'connected' with a company if:

(i)   he is a director or shadow director of the company or an associate of such a director or shadow director, or

(ii)   he is an associate of the company (see *Insolvency Act 1986, s 249*).

'Associate' (as defined under *Insolvency Act 1986, s 435*) is widely drawn and includes corporate bodies and private individuals such as husbands, wives, civil partners and relatives. The definition is complex and includes as associates partners, trustees, employers and employees and companies if the person has control or if he and his associates have control of the company. For example, a person can be associated with a company if he and one or more of his associates jointly hold one third of the company's voting rights in that company or in another company which has control of it. A company can also be an associate of another company where a person controls one company and his associate (or he and his associate jointly) controls the other. For the purposes of the legislation, one person will also be regarded as having 'control' over another if, irrespective of any shareholding, the latter is accustomed to act in accordance with the directions or instructions of the former (eg under the terms of a secured lending or joint venture arrangement). Consequently, the definition could potentially catch a number of individuals or companies within a group structure – even unrelated companies could be treated as associated with each other and potentially brought into the scope of the Regulator's powers.

Financial support directions

15.79 A financial support direction ('FSD') is a direction which requires the person to whom it is issued to secure that financial support is put in place for the scheme within the period specified, that it remains in place while the scheme is in existence and that the Regulator is kept notified of prescribed events (*PA 2004, s 43(3)*). If there is non-compliance with an FSD, the Regulator may then issue a contribution notice under *PA 2004, s 47*. An FSD can be issued against an employer or a person connected or associated with an employer (see **15.78** above), save that an FSD can only be issued against an individual in very limited circumstances (*PA 2004, s 43(6)*).

The Regulator can issue an FSD where it is of the opinion that the employer in relation to the scheme is a 'service company' or is 'insufficiently resourced', or has been at any point during the period of 24 months immediately before the date on which the Regulator determines to issue the FSD (*PA 2004, s 43*). A 'service company' is one where it is part of a group and its turnover is solely or principally derived from amounts charged for the provision of the services of its employees to other members of that group. An employer is 'insufficiently resourced' if the value of its resources is less than 50 per cent of the estimated *s 75* debt in relation to the scheme, and there is another person or persons connected or associated with the employer to whom an FSD can be addressed whose resources (or combined resources) are not less than the relevant deficit (ie the difference between the value of the resources of the employer and 50 per cent of the estimated *s 75* debt) (*PA 2004, s 44* and *The Pensions Regulator (Financial Support Directions etc) Regulations 2005 (SI 2005/2188)* (as amended)).

A reasonableness test must also be satisfied (*PA 2004, s 43(5)*). It is slightly different to the test described in **15.76** above in relation to a contribution notice. The Regulator must be of the opinion that it is reasonable to impose the requirements of the FSD on the person concerned. When deciding whether it is reasonable, the Regulator must have regard to such matters as it considers relevant including, where relevant, the following (*PA 2004, 43(7)*):

(*a*)   the relationship which the person has or has had with the employer (including, where the employer is a company, whether the person has or has had control of the employer;

(*b*)   the value of any benefits received directly or indirectly by that person from the employer;

(*c*)   any connection or involvement which the person has or has had with the scheme;

(*d*)   the financial circumstances of the person; and

(*e*)   such other matters as may be prescribed (this has not yet been brought into force under *PA 2004, s 43(7)(e)*).

FSDs are considered in **Chapter 5** in the context of employer insolvency.

Clearance

History

15.80   As a consequence of the 'moral hazard' powers of the Regulator brought into effect by *PA 2004*, a statutory clearance procedure was introduced to give greater certainty to parties considering transactions involving companies with defined benefit schemes. Once issued, the clearance statement will bind the Regulator unless it transpires the application included materially incorrect information *(PA 2004, s 42(5))*.

According to the original guidance issued by the Regulator:

'Clearance was introduced with the underlying aims being:

– the protection of jobs, particularly where clearance is needed to prevent the employer becoming insolvent; and

– the continuation of appropriate deal activity involving employers with defined benefit schemes.'

Applications for clearance

15.81   The clearance guidance has been updated by the Regulator with the latest version being issued in March 2010 (the '2010 Guidance').

Given the complex nature of some corporate transactions, the 2010 Guidance is aimed at professional advisers working alongside trustees and employers in considering events that may have a detrimental impact upon the pension scheme.

Clearance applications are voluntary. The 2010 Guidance suggests the following practical steps should be taken to speed up the process when seeking clearance:

• involve trustees and share relevant information;

• ensure that any trustee conflicts have been dealt with;

• ensure advice has been taken and any opportunity to mitigate has been discussed;

• keep the Regulator informed of the likely application, providing an outline of the event and making them aware of any timescales and external deadlines;

• liaise with any parties making a related application;

• ensure that applicants and trustees are available to discuss the application; and

• provide the appropriate information to support the application.

Parties wishing to apply for clearance should complete the Regulator's standard application form (available on the Regulator's website) and provide the information requested or where not possible provide an explanation as to why, which includes but is not limited to:

- a copy of the family tree of the wider employer group and identifying the employers;

- a table showing an estimated outcome for creditors pre and post event both at group and employer level on an ongoing and an insolvent basis;

- the latest statutory accounts for all relevant entities;

- any relevant documents relating to the effect of the event on the scheme or actions taken to improve the position of the scheme;

- any independent reports that the trustees have commissioned in respect of the events described in the application;

- where the trustees have not taken independent advice, the document recording this decision together with the trustees' view of the events described in the application;

- a copy of the current and complete winding-up power and the power to set contributions from the scheme's trust deed and rules;

- a copy of the most recent actuarial valuation of the scheme, recovery plan and schedule of contributions;

- a copy of the assumptions used in assessing the scheme deficit on an FRS17/IAS19 basis; and

- copies of any withdrawal arrangements, any proposed rule amendments and existing apportionment rules.

The above documentation should be provided with all applications. There are other documents listed in the 2010 Guidance which should be provided where relevant.

The standard form issued by the Regulator for use for a clearance application invites the applicant to request that the Regulator issues one or more of the following statements:

'In the Regulator's opinion …:

- it would not be reasonable to impose any liability on the applicant under a contribution notice issued under *s 38*.

- it would not be reasonable to impose the requirements of a financial support direction, in relation to the scheme, on the applicant.'

In addition, the Regulator has a power to grant a clearance statement in relation to contribution notices which states that in its opinion and in the circumstances described in the application, the applicant would not be a party to an act or a deliberate failure to act. However, this would require significantly more evidence and, therefore, extensive due diligence, which would take much more time.

Type A events

The 2010 Guidance advises that, in line with its commitment to operate in a risk-based and proportionate manner, the Regulator expects a clearance statement to be sought only in relation to type A events. Type A events are those which are *materially detrimental* to the ability of the pension scheme to meet its liabilities. They fall into two categories: employer-related events and scheme-related events.

Employers and trustees should assess whether a detrimental event is a type A event. A detrimental event, including any type A event, will have one or more of the following effects, either immediately or in the near future:

- it prevents the recovery of the whole or any part of the employer's s 75 debt;

- it prevents the employer's s 75 debt becoming due or compromises the s 75 debt;

- it reduces the amount of the employer's s 75 debt which would otherwise become due; or

- it weakens the employer covenant, because it has an impact on the ability of the employer to meet or impacts on its ongoing funding commitments to the scheme or it reduces the dividend that would be available to the scheme in the event of employer insolvency.

Employer-related events

Broadly, an employer-related event is an event which weakens the employer covenant either because it has an impact on the ability of the employer to meet its ongoing funding commitments to the scheme or because it reduces the dividend that would be available to the scheme in the event of employer insolvency.

For employer-related events, there will need to be:

- a comparison of the employer covenant before and after the type A event;

- an assessment of whether any weakening in the employer covenant is to such a degree that the event could be considered to be materially detrimental to the ability of the scheme to meet its liabilities; and

- the identification of whether the scheme has a relevant deficit.

The 2010 Guidance suggests that it is important to carry out these three steps in this order, because the outcome of the first two steps may determine what basis should be used for the relevant deficit.

15.81 *Commercial transactions*

A type A event will not be an employer-related event unless the scheme has a relevant deficit, and the general rule is that it will usually be the highest of the scheme's deficits according to the following bases:

- FRS17/IAS19 (current accounting standards);

- *s 179* (PPF levy basis);

- technical provisions (scheme funding basis); and

- ongoing (following scheme valuation, where technical provisions are not yet available).

An exception to the general rule regarding the relevant deficit is where an employer-related event is significantly materially detrimental to the scheme's ability to meet its liabilities and in these circumstances the relevant deficit will be measured on a higher basis. Also, where there are 'going concern' issues, the scheme is in wind-up or there is scheme abandonment, the relevant deficit will be measured on the *s 75* full buy-out basis.

Examples of employer-related events provided in the 2010 Guidance include:

- a change in priority (eg the granting or extending of a fixed or floating charge over assets of the employer or the wider group);

- a return of capital (eg dividend payments; share buy backs; repayment of subordinated debt; and distributions in specie, including de-mergers);

- a change in group structure, including a change in control;

- a change to the employer in relation to a scheme;

- granting or repayment of inter-company loans;

- business and assets sales, particularly where these are not on arm's length terms, the sale proceeds are not retained within the business or where a substantial proportion of the operating business is being sold;

- sale and lease back transactions where there is a reduction of assets or the net cash available has been adversely affected;

- 'phoenix events' where the employer re-emerges as substantially the same entity following an insolvency event (but free of its defined benefit liabilities); and

- corporate events which reduce sustainable cash flow cover for the wider employer group's funding commitment to the scheme.

Scheme-related events

The 2010 Guidance states that although a scheme-related event may have a direct impact on the employer's legal obligations to a scheme, the detriment resulting from a scheme-related event cannot usually be assessed solely by reference to the employer covenant. The method for assessing whether a scheme-related event is a type A event will vary, depending on the specific event. In addition, some scheme-related events will be directly detrimental to members' benefits rather than to the ability of the **scheme** to meet its pension liabilities, and these may also be type A events, depending on the particular circumstances.

Examples of scheme-related events that could be type A events are set out in the 2010 Guidance and include:

- compromise agreements;

- apportionment of a scheme's deficit;

- non-payment of all or any part of a *s 75* debt for an unreasonable period (eg more than 12 months); or

- an arrangement that has the result of preventing a *s 75* debt from triggering.

In relation to both *employer-related* events and *scheme-related* events, where a type A event has been identified, the parties should consider and agree the most appropriate mitigation. Various different types of mitigation are listed in the 2010 Guidance, ranging from additional contributions through to more complicated parent and intra-group guarantees. The 2010 Guidance also advocates that trustees should generally adopt the approach of a bank that has advanced a large unsecured loan.

15.82 As mentioned above, the Regulator can issue a contribution notice to a person requiring an amount up to and including the *s 75* debt which is due from an employer, or the *s 75* debt which might become due on the winding up of a scheme, to be paid to the scheme or the PPF if the Regulator is of the opinion that a person was a party to an act or deliberate failure to act and:

- the material detriment test is met in relation to that act or failure to act; or

- the main purpose or one of the main purposes of the act or failure to act was:

  – to prevent the recovery of the whole or part of a *s 75* debt which was or might become due from an employer in relation to the scheme; or

  – to prevent such a debt becoming due, to compromise or otherwise settle such a debt, or to reduce the amount of such a debt which would otherwise become due.

Under the 2010 Guidance, it is clear that the material detriment test can still apply, whether or not the benefits accrued at the time of the relevant act or omission are still to be received from the scheme (ie where there has been a subsequent transfer or buy out), and the Regulator will disregard payments which might be received from the PPF. So, in the Regulator's opinion employers and trustees cannot use the PPF as an argument that members have not suffered a detriment.

There is a reminder in the 2010 Guidance that the material detriment test is not the same as a type A event. Therefore, even where the material detriment test is met, there may not always be a type A event (and so clearance may not always be available). For example, the material detriment test will apply whether or not there is a relevant deficit in the scheme.

Abandonment

15.83   The Regulator issued updated guidance on 'abandonment' in December 2008. According to the guidance, the abandonment of a pension scheme occurs where the sponsoring employer severs its links with the scheme without providing the scheme with sufficient funds or assets to compensate for the loss of ongoing support. This will include circumstances where trustees of a defined benefit scheme are asked by the employer to consider:

- the transfer of liabilities in whole, or in part, to another employer; and/or

- a change in control, or significant restructuring of the employer (or group of companies associated with the employer) that would result in the substantial reduction in the financial strength of the employer who will in future sponsor the scheme.

It is possible that such arrangements may be materially financially detrimental to the pension scheme, and the Regulator expects trustees to negotiate robustly and seek mitigation prior to agreement.

Commercial activities may give rise to issues of abandonment, for example, where the proposal results in the current employer severing its links with the pension scheme without meeting its obligations to the scheme, or the scheme is transferred to another employer that is unable to meet the scheme's liabilities. Trustees will need to be able to recognise that such arrangements may result in the abandonment of the scheme, exposing members to an increased risk that their benefits may not be provided in full and increasing the chances of the scheme entering the PPF.

The Regulator expects the trustees' starting point to be that any arrangement that breaks the link with the existing employer may not be in the best interests of the members unless the full *s 75* debt is paid, or unless the scheme remains supported by an employer of substance and the scheme is suitably compensated for any negative change in the strength of the employer's covenant.

The guidance is also stated to be applicable to all cases where an arrangement could result in the employer breaking the link with the scheme (or a significant proportion of the members of the scheme), without the payment of an appropriate proportion of the scheme's potential *s 75* debt or, where a debt has actually fallen due, without obtaining approval for a withdrawal arrangement. It is also applicable where there will be a restructuring of the employer, or group of companies associated with the employer, such that the scheme is no longer supported by an employer of substance.

The guidance recognises that any proposed arrangement will no doubt be very complex and that it is essential for trustees to obtain independent advice to obtain an analysis and explanation of the implications for the scheme. Trustees and employers are expected to report to and consult with the Regulator on any arrangement that may result in the abandonment of the pension scheme, at an early stage in the process. The Regulator has a number of powers at its disposal if it is felt that the proposed arrangement would result in the scheme being abandoned, including contribution notices and financial support directions (see **15.75** and **15.79** above) as well as powers to prohibit, suspend and appoint trustees of pension schemes, and to wind up a pension scheme.

The full guidance can be found on the Regulator's website.

Other types of scheme

Money purchase schemes

15.84 Where the seller's scheme provides money purchase benefits, the issues are considerably simpler.

In the context of a money purchase occupational scheme, the warranties will focus far less on the sufficiency of the scheme's assets and more on the extent of the liability to contribute (and whether all the contributions due have been paid). There may still, however, be some defined risk benefits (such as death-in service), and the purchaser should seek the necessary disclosures and warranty as to the insurance of these.

If the circumstances give rise to a transfer payment (see **15.19** above), the amount to be transferred will effectively be the realisable value of the transferring members' money purchase accounts, rather than involving complex valuation methods and assumptions.

If the purchaser is taking over the entire scheme (see **15.21** above), it will also require warranties to satisfy itself that the scheme complies with all relevant legal requirements. However, money purchase arrangements are less heavily regulated than defined benefit ones. Money purchase assets and liabilities are expressly excluded from the scope of *PA 1995, s 75* in the *Employer Debt Regulations* and the moral hazard provisions do not apply (see from **15.61** above).

If the scheme is a personal pension arrangement, the purchaser will want to see the documentation setting out the contribution promise. It will also need a warranty to the effect that all contributions due have been paid (and that there has been no proposal or announcement to pay higher contributions).

Unregistered schemes

15.85 The purchaser should seek to obtain as much information as it can about any unregistered schemes that there may be.

Much of the legislation that applies to other types of scheme does not apply to unregistered arrangements. This will to some extent lessen the level of warranty protection that the purchaser will require, although in assessing the costs of these arrangements it should be borne in mind that the early leaver legislation (see **Chapter 6**) may apply (even to unfunded arrangements).

Public sector transfers

15.86 Schemes such as the Principal Civil Service Pension Scheme, the NHS Pension Scheme and other public service pension schemes have separate requirements (see **15.87** below) if there is an outsourcing, re-organisation or privatisation from the public sector. This may involve a bulk transfer of past service benefits from the public sector scheme into a private sector scheme. However, given the changes to the Fair Deal guidance (see **15.87** below) these are likely to become fewer and fewer.

In order for the Government Actuary's Department ('GAD') to agree to the transfer of public service scheme benefits, the receiving scheme must satisfy prescribed criteria. These criteria relate generally to the level of benefits to be provided and the balance of powers in the receiving scheme. GAD will usually provide a standard pensions schedule setting out its requirements but its provisions can be negotiated to a limited extent, subject to the circumstances of a particular case. Some schemes may be required to make amendments to the scheme rules to satisfy GAD's criteria. If the necessary criteria are satisfied, GAD will issue either a 'certificate of broad comparability' or a 'passport'.

The distinction between the passport and the certificate of broad comparability is that the passport attaches to the receiving scheme and is valid for more than one transfer in, only ceasing to be of general application if GAD's requirements change. A passport is more usually applied for when a new scheme is being established specifically to receive public service transfers. By contrast, a certificate of broad comparability will be required for all schemes without a passport on each occasion on which it is proposed that a transfer be made.

Of course, not all outsourcing contracts lead to a transfer of benefits and this is now being phased out (see **15.87** below). The Local Government Pension Scheme (the 'LGPS') allows a new employer to participate in the scheme subject to meeting certain criteria as set out in *Part 3 of Schedule 2 of the Local Government Pension Scheme Regulations 2013 (SI 2013/2356)* (the *'LGPS Regulations'*). The new employer must enter into an admission agreement with the administering authority, and may also have to enter into an indemnity or bond or secure a parent company guarantee under *paragraphs 7 and 8 of Part 3 of Schedule 2 of the LGPS Regulations.*

Given the recent changes to the Fair Deal (see **15.87** below) other public sector schemes are in the process of being amended to allow private sector entities to participate in the relevant public sector scheme subject to satisfying certain criteria.

The Fair Deal

15.87   The HM Treasury 'Guidance to Departments and Agencies: Staff Transfers from Central Government: A Fair Deal for Staff Pensions' dated June 1999 as annexed to the Cabinet Office 'Statement of Practice – Staff Transfers and the Public Sector' dated January 2000 (the 'Old Fair Deal') provided a single unified framework which set out in general terms how pensions issues were to be handled when staff from Central Government departments and agencies or other public sector bodies were transferred to a new employer. The Old Fair Deal was then updated in June 2004.

Following a lengthy consultation process which began in March 2011, HM Treasury published revised guidance 'Fair Deal for Staff Pensions: staff transfers' (the 'New Fair Deal') in October 2013 which replaced the Old Fair Deal.

Interestingly, the New Fair Deal requires public sector bodies to request bidders for outsourcing contracts to offer transferring employees continued membership of the relevant public sector pension scheme or in limited circumstances membership of a broadly comparable pension scheme for future service as if *TUPE* applied, even though *TUPE* provides that occupational pension scheme benefits so far as they relate to 'old age, invalidity and survivor's benefits' do not pass. The New Fair Deal acknowledges that *TUPE* was failing to adequately protect the interests of public sector employees and their pension provision when the services they deliver are outsourced. The New Fair Deal is intended to deliver value for money for the taxpayer and remove barriers to plurality of service provision.

Under the Old Fair Deal, where staff were compulsorily transferred under TUPE from the public sector, their new employer had to give them access to an occupational pension scheme which was broadly comparable to the public service pension scheme they were leaving. Staff were also offered the choice of becoming a deferred member of their old public sector scheme or transferring accrued benefits into the new scheme through a bulk transfer agreement.

Under the New Fair Deal, first generation transfer and second generation transfers have been reformed in different ways with first generation transferees remaining in their current public-sector scheme and with second generation transferees returning to a public sector scheme or remaining in a broadly comparable pension scheme in certain circumstances. This opens up access to public sector schemes that were not previously open to private sector employers.

15.88 The New Fair deal applies to the NHS, central government departments, agencies, maintained schools (including academies) and other parts of the public sector under the control of Government ministers.

It does not apply to local authorities, or other best value authorities – alternative arrangements exist in respect of these bodies and these remain subject to the current best value guidance. However, the Department for Communities and Local Government ('DCLG') is currently reviewing this.

The New Fair Deal goes on to state:

> 'it is of course open to contracting authorities in other parts of the public sector to adopt approaches comparable to those set out here. It is also open to private sector bodies whose members participate in a public service pension scheme to seek to adopt a comparable approach, subject to the independent contractor to whom staff are being compulsorily transferred meeting the relevant requirements to participate in the scheme.'

15.89 The New Fair Deal applied from October 2013 with immediate effect. It applies when staff who are members of a public service pension scheme move from the public sector to a private sector contractor by way of TUPE transfer. It also applies where there is a non-voluntary transfer to a private service mutual or other new models of public sector delivery (regardless of whether TUPE applies or not).

Where a procurement was already at an advanced stage when the New Fair Deal came into effect, the contracting authority should consider whether it would be 'legitimate and desirable' to adjust the terms of the procurement to take account of this new guidance. There is no requirement for an advanced procurement to be terminated or delayed in order to apply the New Fair Deal. Where it is not practicable to apply this new policy, the previous policy, as set out in the Old Fair Deal should continue to be followed. However, as time moves on this will become less and less relevant.

15.90   In relation to first generation transfers, the contracting authority must make it clear at an early stage that the New Fair Deal will apply and that pensions are integral to the procurement process.

Those staff 'wholly or mainly' employed on the transferred service or function can remain in the scheme (or remain eligible if not an active member) – subject to them continuing to be employed in that way. If they cease to be employed on the transferred function then generally they will become a deferred member of the scheme as they will have ceased to be in qualifying employment. Those eligible to be a member but who had opted out previously should be enrolled into the public service scheme on the day the new employment commences. If an employee moves to be partially employed on the transferred function then they can remain a member of the scheme for that portion of their work (ie like a part-timer). It is up to the responsible authority to decide how to deal with partial employment and how they interpret 'wholly or mainly'. Where someone transfers from the transferred function into another employment which qualifies for membership of the scheme then they may be allowed to remain a member if they elect to do so and both the contracting authority and the employer consent.

On a first generation transfer the contracting authority needs to ensure the following:

- the contractor provides access to the relevant scheme. This must be set out in the contract;
- the contracts of employment give employees the right to continued membership of the scheme (these rights are enforceable by the employees);
- staff continue to be given access to the scheme – including on second generation and subsequent transfers;
- the contract expressly requires the contractor to comply with the Participation Agreement (which will be between the contractor and the responsible authority); and
- breach of the Participation Agreement is grounds for termination of the contract.

Continued membership need not be offered if there are exceptional circumstances giving rise to special reasons which mean that it would not be appropriate to provide continued access to a public service pension scheme. No examples are given in the New Fair Deal as to when this would be applicable. It does, however, say that the reasons should be 'tested rigorously' by the contracting authority and that trade unions or staff must be consulted with a view to reaching agreement.

In these circumstances the Old Fair Deal must be applied and staff provided with a broadly comparable pension scheme. However, in the event that is not appropriate to provide a broadly comparable scheme or continued access then the contracting authority would need to consider whether compensation should be offered to transferring staff and actuarial advice should be taken.

15.91   On a retender or second generation transfer, contractors should be required to provide the transferring staff with access to the appropriate public sector scheme. This will usually be the scheme the employee was a member of, or eligible to join, immediately before the original transfer had they not transferred out on the terms at the current time. Transferred staff will be able to re-join a scheme that is closed to new members if they would have remained in that scheme had they not been transferred out of the public sector. Where the scheme has been closed to future accrual and the staff would have been offered membership of a new public service pension scheme (had they not been transferred out) then they will be eligible to be members of that new or alternative scheme.

If the contracting authority, in the particular circumstances of a specific retender, would be unable to comply with their obligations under procurement law to treat economic operators equally if they were to require the incumbent to provide access to a public service pension scheme, the incumbent should have the option of providing either access to a public service pension scheme or to a broadly comparable pension scheme. In exceptional circumstances, both the incumbent and new bidders, can be required to offer a broadly comparable scheme rather than access to a public sector scheme.

There may be cases when an incumbent contractor has a contractual obligation to provide staff with a broadly comparable scheme, so is unable to provide access to a public service scheme instead. In such cases, the contracting authority should ensure that the incumbent contractor seeks to re-negotiate the employment contracts to provide for access to the appropriate public service pension scheme following the retender. Where, however, the incumbent contractor is unable to secure agreement to a change in employment contracts, it may provide ongoing access to the broadly comparable scheme. In these circumstances the contracting authority may have to consider whether all bidders should be allowed to tender on this basis.

Where a broadly comparable scheme is offered, this should wherever possible be broadly comparable with the scheme they would have been in had they not been transferred out of the public sector. This would be based on the current provisions of that scheme. Where there are contractual or other reasons why this cannot be done then broad comparability can be based on the provisions of the public sector scheme at the time they left it. Where the original contract pre-dates the Old Fair Deal (ie is pre-June 1999) the contracting authority must consider whether it was done on Fair Deal equivalent terms – if so New Fair Deal should apply (as long as the responsible authority agrees).

15.92   Where a second generation transfer takes place members will also have the option of requiring a bulk transfer of their accrued pension rights into the public sector scheme. As with other types of transfers, this will require a transfer payment by the transferor scheme to the receiving scheme to extinguish the transferor scheme's liability to the person transferring their accrued benefits.

All existing contracts should contain an enforceable obligation on the employer to allow for an onward bulk transfer agreement under which the onward terms are no less favourable than the inward terms for the bulk transfer. The contracting authority should provide details of these terms used to each of the other bidders in the procurement, along with the details of the service credits which each of their schemes will need to provide.

In this situation, there is a risk that the onward bulk transfer terms are insufficient to purchase year for year service credits in the new scheme. In those circumstances, bidders should indicate in their bid documentation whether they agree to the bulk transfer terms or whether any price adjustment is proposed to reflect the anticipated shortfall arising out of the bulk transfer payment.

If the contracting authority is satisfied that bulk transfer requirements of the New Fair Deal have been met, the contracting authority will meet the cost of any shortfall due to the termination of the existing pension arrangements.

Deferred pensions of former staff who left employment prior to the retender are generally not expected to be included in bulk transfers.

15.93   The contractor must enter a Participation Agreement with the responsible authority.

With regard to the level of employer contributions, these will normally be at the same rate applicable to other employers in the scheme and so subject to change during the period of the contract in line with actuarial valuations. The contracting authority and employer could agree in advance how any changes in the contribution rate are to be dealt with and scheme regulations may provide for differential rates for Fair Deal employers – this could, for example, be to take into account the higher risk of default associated with a particular employer.

15.94 *Commercial transactions*

Employers could also be required to enter into indemnities or bonds or secure a guarantee in order to protect the scheme from potential costs arising from their participation in the scheme. An example might be a bond to cover contributions owed to the scheme in the event of the employer's insolvency.

The Best Value Authorities Staff Transfers (Pensions) Direction 2007

15.94 *Local Government Act 2003, s 101* allows for the Secretary for the DCLG to issue directions to best value authorities in England and Wales to provide how employment and pensions matters will be treated in the contracting of services.

In 2007, the DCLG issued a direction under *s 101* called the Best Value Authorities Staff Transfers (Pensions) Direction 2007 ('2007 Direction') which applies to 'best value authorities' (ie those listed in *Local Government Act 1999, s 1*).

The 2007 Direction sets out the standard of pension protection with effect from 1 October 2007 by protecting the future service of former authority employees whose employment is transferred to a contractor and also to former authority employees who have already transferred to a contractor and are then transferring on again as a result of a re-let of the contract. Authorities are required under the 2007 Direction to ensure, via the contract governing the outsourced services, that the contractor will secure pension protection for the employees with pension rights that are 'the same as, or count as broadly comparable to or better than' the pension provision the employees had or had the right to acquire as an employee of the authority prior to transfer or before the change of contractor. In addition, the transferred employees must be given a direct right to enforce the pensions protection.

The cost involved with protecting the pensions of the transferring employees is often the key consideration for authorities negotiating with possible contractors. Experience has shown that whilst contractors have been willing to undertake to provide the agreed level of pensions protection going forward, in practice, they have not been willing to pay for this protection.

The 2007 Direction provides statutory protection for local authority employees who are compulsorily transferred to a new employer as part of an outsourcing or procurement project, whereas the Fair Deal is only guidance. However, *Local Government Act 2003, s 102* only protects the future service of the transferred employees. There is no statutory protection for the treatment of their past service benefits accumulated whilst an employee of the authority.

The two-tier requirements

15.95   Local authorities were subject to the 'Code of Practice on Workforce Matters' in Local Authority Service Contracts'. The Code prevented the emergence of a two-tier workforce in cases where local authority employees are contracted out to a service provider by ensuring that new recruits are employed on terms and conditions that are, overall, no less favourable than those transferred local authority public sector employees.

In pension terms, the Code required the contractor to offer new employees 'working alongside' former local authority employees 'reasonable pension arrangements' which can include:

- membership of the LGPS; or

- membership of the employer's contracted-out final salary pension scheme; or

- membership of an employer's defined contribution occupational pension scheme (or stakeholder scheme) to which the contractor must match contributions up to a maximum of six per cent.

The Code was revoked on 23 March 2011 with immediate effect, following the abolition on 13 December 2010 of the 'Code of Practice on workforce matters in public service contracts'. It was confirmed in a Ministerial Statement that the abolition of the Code is not retrospective and therefore existing contracts to which the Code applies will not be affected.

Admitted body status or broadly comparable scheme in respect of ex-local authority employees?

15.96   Prior to the Guidance entitled 'Admitted body status provision in the Local Government Pension Scheme when services are transferred from a local authority or other scheme employer' being issued in December 2009, there were increasing attempts to restrict the choice being offered to contractors. However, the 2009 Guidance clarified the position. It states that:

> 'It needs to be recognised that it is the Contractor who chooses whether they offer their employees membership of the LGPS or a pension scheme that can be certified as a broadly comparable pension scheme, when tendering for a local authority contract as part of an outsourcing exercise.'

Whilst the decision is open to the contractor, more and more contractors are going down the LGPS admission route and not opting for the broadly comparable scheme route. This echoes the recent changes made to the Fair Deal (see **15.87** above) in which private sector entities are now able to participate in the relevant public schemes.

The broadly comparable scheme route gives contractors greater control over the funding rate and investment strategy, but they will be responsible for the full annuity buy-out costs of any benefits accrued and the funding risk in the scheme. The LGPS route also exposes contractors to significant funding and investment risk, however, it avoids the cost of establishing a GAD-passported scheme where the contractor does not already have one in place. By law, contractors that become admitted bodies into the LGPS are required to accept onerous obligations to administering authorities, such as making contributions during the contract term to ensure that the 'notional fund' created on admission remains fully funded. At the end of the contract, there can be a significant 'exit debt' (see **15.97** below).

Risk allocation in the LGPS overview

15.97   Broadly, the way admission agreements work is that on the contractor being admitted to participation in the LGPS, a notional fund is set aside on a 'past service reserve' basis that is supposed to be sufficient to fund the past service liabilities of the employees being transferred. The legislative position is that the LGPS actuary will then set an ongoing employer contribution rate to the LGPS for the contractor (which may differ from the ongoing contribution rate to the scheme as a whole, to reflect differences in the membership). The contribution rate can be reviewed from time to time and will be reviewed in any event when there is an LGPS valuation. The actuary will then produce a 'rates and adjustment certificate' setting out any additional contributions needed to ensure that the contractor's section remains fully funded throughout the contract. At the end of the contract, the legislation states that the LGPS actuary carries out a valuation of the contractor's section and if there is a funding shortfall on the actuarial basis determined by the actuary, the contractor has to make a shortfall payment. If there is a surplus the LGPS keeps it.

The commercial reality is that most contractors will now only enter into an admission agreement if they bid on the basis that there will be a straight 'pass through' of pension costs (other than any redundancy costs under their control) or will bid on the basis that their pension costs should be fixed at a specified percentage of pensionable salary. The contractor will still have to pay the LGPS administering authority any sums due under the admission agreement but there will be an indemnity from the contracting authority to the contractor in the main outsourcing agreement. Clearly, given the volatility of pension contributions, this is a risk for the authority. The authority will need to seek actuarial advice to be able to estimate the potential costs involved, but it will depend to a degree on the number and profile of the staff transferring.

Other mechanisms for dealing with pensions risk include caps on the contractor's assumed contribution rate or agreeing a risk allocation matrix.

It is not unusual for the contractor to seek to cap its ongoing contributions to the fund when it becomes an admitted body. A cap on the contributions that the contractor has to pay to the LGPS will usually be expressed as a percentage of payroll. This will mean that any contributions that have to be made in excess of this amount are then deemed to be the authority's responsibility. For example, if the ongoing employer contribution to the LGPS is 20 per cent of pensionable pay, the contractor may propose a cap of 25 per cent in total throughout the contract term. Therefore the authority will pick up the cost of any pension contributions in excess of 25 per cent. This means that, in practice, the authority retains an ongoing liability in respect of the employees it has transferred to the contractor. Such clauses usually lead to protracted negotiation, unless the authority takes a clear stance from the outset.

Contractors often bid assuming a 'cap and collar' arrangement with ongoing contributions made at the level of the cap. If the authority is prepared to accept a cap in principle, then it may also impose a 'collar' mechanism. Under a collar mechanism, if the contribution rate falls below a specified level, then the contractor must pay the difference to the authority. For example, if the ongoing employer's contribution to the LGPS is 20 per cent of pensionable pay, a collar could be proposed at 15 per cent throughout the contract term. Therefore where the employer contribution level falls below 15 per cent, the contractor will continue to pay to the authority 15 per cent.

The effect of the above mechanisms is essentially to remove some of the pensions risk from the contractor and reallocate it to the authority. An authority will need to address whether it is willing to accept this in principle. The current market position is that many authorities are indeed accepting this sort of risk reallocation, subject to certain measures. The argument that the contractor will probably put forward is that it should not be required to accept liability for fluctuating contributions as it is not in control of LGPS investment or funding policies.

There is an argument that contractors should be building contingencies for the costs of becoming an admitted body in the LGPS into their financial models rather than seeking to reallocate the risk. Of course, the quid-pro-quo here is that there may be a financial impact on the costing for the outsourcing project in order to build in this risk. If the principle is generally agreed that the authority will retain some of the pensions costs, it may be better to indemnify the contractor for actual costs rather than estimated costs, which could prove to be higher.

Conclusion

15.98 This chapter is only an overview, but it should be sufficient to illustrate the complexity and the possible risks and cost implications of pension

689

arrangements in negotiations for the sale or purchase of a company or business. The potential impact of pension issues for both the seller and the purchaser should never be underestimated, and the sooner these are addressed the better the chances of the deal progressing to a successful conclusion for both sides. This has never been more so than since the introduction of the Regulator's powers to issue contribution notices and financial support directions by *PA 2004*, and the onerous level of debt calculation on the withdrawal of a participating employer in a multi-employer defined benefit arrangement.

The Regulator's clearance procedure can provide the parties to a transaction with greater certainty. Clearance provides the parties with assurance via the clearance statement that their proposed activities will not later be found to fall foul of the legislation. Similarly, the arrangements permitted under the *Employer Debt Regulations*, provide the parties to a transaction with a number of ways to deal with a *s 75* debt in the event that an employment-cessation event arises.

Chapter 16

Pensions dispute resolution and litigation

Introduction

16.1 Whilst there has always been scope for disputes to arise over pension schemes, there was a dramatic growth in this area from the early 1990s. The reasons for this include the increased regulation of pension schemes, the introduction of public bodies to police such schemes, the authority of the Office of the Pensions Ombudsman to adjudicate upon disputes, the introduction of internal dispute resolution procedures and increased public awareness.

The 1990s began with the high-profile *Maxwell* scandal, followed by disputes over large surpluses in various privatised industries. Equalisation, and failures correctly to document equalisation or other benefits changes in the course of the 1990s, also led to a significant body of litigation, including construction applications, professional negligence claims and, as most such negligence claims are now statute barred, loss of chance claims. The new millennium witnessed a slump in the stock market causing large pension deficits, the high-profile *Equitable Life* case, the increasing cost of annuities, the closure of final salary pension schemes and the widely publicised 'pensions crisis'. These events together served to increase public awareness about pension rights.

Pension disputes have also been affected by further legislation. The *Pensions Act 2004* saw the replacement of OPRA with the Pensions Regulator ('the Regulator'), with wider powers to regulate schemes. The Regulator's so-called 'moral hazard' powers, to seek contributions to underfunded pension schemes from entities other than the employer, and the actual or threatened exercise of such powers, have given rise to litigation both in the UK and overseas. The establishment of the Pension Protection Fund ('PPF'), and its funding by 'risk-based' levies on schemes, has also added to the existing field of litigation.

As a consequence, the management and resolution of disputes has become an increasingly important factor for both trustees and employers in the administration of pension schemes.

In addition to traditional 'hostile' litigation, 'non-hostile' litigation often arises in the context of the day-to-day administration of pension schemes. Trustees, in particular, can apply to court to resolve ambiguities or mistakes in pension scheme documents, and to seek approval of a proposed course of action which has certain consequences for the scheme.

This chapter is not intended to be an exhaustive survey of every type of dispute and procedure. Instead, it is intended to provide an overview of the principal forums for dispute resolution, and, in relation to litigation through the courts, to highlight some of the issues that may arise in pensions cases, including the use of alternative dispute resolution ('ADR') to settle disputes.

Non-court forums for dispute resolution

Internal dispute resolution procedure ('IDRP')

16.2 *PA 1995* introduced a requirement for trustees of occupational pension schemes to implement an IDRP to deal with disputes by members and other beneficiaries about matters concerning the scheme. The current IDRP requirements are set out at sections *50, 50A* and *50B* of *PA 1995*, supplemented by the *Occupational Pension Schemes (Internal Dispute Resolution Procedures Consequential and Miscellaneous Amendments) Regulations 2008* (the *'IDRP Regulations'*). IDRP is discussed in more detail in **Chapter 3**.

IDRP should be capable of resolving the majority of the common complaints made by members and beneficiaries against the trustees and managers (but is not the appropriate avenue for pursuing a complaint against an employer, as such complaints fall outside the scope of the procedure).

It should be noted that a complaint is exempted from the IDRP if proceedings have already been commenced in a court or other tribunal, or where the Pensions Ombudsman has already commenced an investigation. The Pensions Ombudsman will ordinarily require a complainant to have made full use of the IDRP before accepting a complaint for investigation. However, if the trustees do not implement any decision made under the IDRP, or the complainant is not satisfied with the decision, they may refer his complaint to TPAS (see below) and/or the Ombudsman.

Complaints to the Pensions Advisory Service ('TPAS')

16.3 TPAS (formerly known as OPAS) provides free advice and assistance to members of the public who have a complaint about their occupational or personal pension scheme and will seek to resolve a dispute by negotiation and correspondence between the parties. The success of this forum depends to a great extent on the willingness of the parties, as any suggested resolution proposed by TPAS is not directly enforceable. If TPAS cannot resolve the member's complaint, the complaint may then be submitted to the appropriate Ombudsman for resolution. The Pensions Ombudsman encourages individuals complaining to him to have consulted TPAS first.

Financial Conduct Authority ('FCA') and Financial Ombudsman Service ('FOS')

16.4   Where a person has a complaint about the sale and marketing of a pension arrangement, the complaint may be investigated by the FCA (which regulates the personal pension industry) or the FOS (which settles disputes between consumers and financial institutions). If the complaint involves a financial product or service, the FOS requires the complaint to be submitted first to the firm involved to be considered under its internal complaints procedure. If the complainant is unhappy with the firm's final response to the complaint, or eight weeks have elapsed from the date the complaint was submitted without a final response from the firm, the complainant has six months in which to submit the complaint to the FOS. The FOS will first seek to resolve the complaint through an informal process of mediation. If that is unsuccessful, the FOS will conduct a full investigation into the complaint and issue a written determination which is binding on the firm (to a limit of £150,000 plus interest and costs).

Further information, the relevant forms and contact details can be found on the FOS website: www.financial-ombudsman.org.uk

Complaints to the Pensions Ombudsman ('PO')

16.5   The role of the Pensions Ombudsman and Deputy Pensions Ombudsman, their jurisdiction and a summary of the applicable procedure are set out in **Chapter 2**. The PO is not permitted to investigate or determine a complaint if proceedings have already been commenced in any court or employment tribunal in connection with matters to which the complaint relates, unless the proceedings have been discontinued without a settlement binding on the complainant. The court has the power to stay court proceedings concerning matters which are the subject of a complaint or dispute before the PO (*PSA 1993, ss 146, 148*). The Pensions Ombudsman publishes several plain English guidance notes on its website, covering common cases such as overpayments and ill health.

Determination

16.6   A determination given by the PO is final and binding on the complainant and any person responsible for the management of the scheme to which the complaint relates (subject to being overturned, on appeal, by the court). The PO has the power to direct any person responsible for the management of the scheme to take, or refrain from taking, such steps as he may specify. Any determination of the PO is enforceable in a county court as if it were a judgment or order of that court (*PSA 1993, s 151(5)*).

The PO's determination or direction must be in writing and state the grounds upon which it is made. A dissatisfied party may ask for the court's permission to appeal the determination on a point of law. The appeal is heard in the High Court (*PSA 1993, s 151(4)*) (see **16.16** below).

PPF and FAS Ombudsman

16.7 *PA 2004, ss 209–218* make provision for a PPF Ombudsman ('PPFO') and one or more Deputies, who have jurisdiction over complaints of maladministration and 'reviewable matters' (set out in *PA 2004, Sch 9* including PPF entry and PPF levy assessments. The PO and Deputy PO fulfil these functions. Decisions of the PPFO are enforceable as judgments of the County Court. Appeal can be made to the High Court, and the PPFO may also refer points of law to the High Court. The PPFO and Deputy also have the role of FAS Ombudsman and Deputy under the *Financial Assistance Scheme (Appeals) Regulations 2005 (SI 2005/3273)*. These functions form a small part of the work of the Pensions Ombudsman.

Employment tribunals

16.8 Disputes concerning an employee's rights under an occupational pension scheme may also be dealt with during the course of employment tribunals. This is discussed in more detail in **Chapter 7**.

Divorce proceedings

16.9 Disputes over pension benefits also arise in the context of divorce proceedings. This is dealt with in more detail in **Chapter 8**.

Regulatory bodies

The Pensions Regulator

16.10 The Regulator does not directly determine disputes, but regulates work-based pension schemes using powers given to it by *PA 1995* and

PA 2004. A summary of those powers can be found in **Chapter 2**. Details of the penalties the Regulator can impose are summarised in **Appendix I**. In particular, where the Regulator considers that there has been a breach of the law it can require corrective action to be taken. Further, where it is believed that an employer is deliberately seeking to avoid its obligations to its pension scheme, the Regulator has powers to issue contribution notices, financial support directions and restoration orders for the purpose of restoring value to the pension scheme, thus reducing the exposure of the PPF to an underfunded scheme (see **Chapter 15**). The exercise of these powers by the Regulator can potentially be challenged, giving rise to possible areas for dispute. As such challenges are best considered in the context of the Regulator's powers rather than forum, we deal with them below, regardless of whether they were launched as freestanding challenges in the Upper Tribunal or as part of wider litigation in the High Court or overseas.

The final decision to issue a contribution notice or financial support direction is made by the Regulator's Determinations Panel, which is a body separate from the caseworker team investigating the scheme. The caseworker team (at arm's length) and, if they wish, the parties subject to a warning notice, make submissions to the Panel which then decides whether to issue the notice or direction, and in what terms. The Panel may hold an oral hearing (typically no more than two days in length), and, in effect, such hearings amount to a form of litigation.

The Upper Tribunal

16.11   *PA 2004* provides for references to the Pensions Regulator Tribunal (which on 6 April 2010 became part of the unified 'Upper Tribunal' of the Tax and Chancery Chamber of tribunals). The Tribunal is an independent judicial body, in order to comply with the requirements of *Article 6* of the *Human Rights Act 1998*. Right to refer is relatively wide, and is not restricted to points of law. The Upper Tribunal gave guidance about its jurisdiction in respect of a decision to issue an FSD in *Granada UK Rental & Retail Ltd v Pensions Regulator [2014] Pens LR17*. Its role was to consider the determination afresh, examining all the facts and circumstances which had been within the scope of the Pension Regulator's warning notice, even those which had not contributed to the decision of the determinations panel. The tribunal was also entitled to see evidence relevant to facts and circumstances which had not been before the Determinations Panel.

In addition, any party which is 'directly affected' by a determination can make a referral with the Tribunal's permission. The procedural rules of the Tribunal are contained in the *Tribunal Procedure (Upper Tribunal) Rules 2008 (SI 2008/2698)*. Appeal from the Tribunal lies to the Court of Appeal and can only be made on a point of law and by parties to a Tribunal reference.

Litigation involving the Regulator and PPF

References to the Upper Tribunal

16.12   Early decisions by the Regulator's Determination Panel typically involved appointment of independent trustees, delays in providing CETVs, and winding up orders. The Panel issued its first determination notices to impose financial support directions ('FSDs') on 15 June 2007 in schemes sponsored by Sea Containers Services Limited. However, despite an interim decision on disclosure, the substantive issue was not ultimately brought before the Tribunal.

On 14 May 2010, after an oral hearing, a contribution notice was confirmed by the Determinations Panel in respect of the Bonas Scheme. Further FSDs were confirmed in respect of various Nortel group companies on 25 June 2010 and in respect of a number of Lehman Brothers companies on 13 September 2010.

The Bonas contribution notice was referred to the Tribunal and an application was then made under the Tribunal rules to bar the Regulator from pursuing certain issues. The application was decided by Warren J as President of the Upper Tribunal on 11 January 2011 (*Michel Van De Wiele NV v Pensions Regulator 2011 WL 197294*). Warren J barred parts of the Regulator's case and gave a strong indication that the amount of the contribution notice (over £5m, calculated by reference to the scheme deficit on the PPF basis) was not reasonable and that the reasonable measure should be the amount of any undervalue in sale of employer assets, which was likely to be a much smaller sum.

The *Bonas* case settled in June 2011, with the Regulator issuing a contribution notice of £60,000. The Regulator issued a formal report under *PA 2004, s 89* rejecting the analysis of Warren J regarding the amount that should generally be specified in a contribution notice and stating that *Bonas* was a case that turned on its own facts.

The subsequent Upper Tribunal reference, *The Trustees of the Lehman Brothers Pension Scheme v The Pensions Regulator (FS/2012/0029 – 31)* held that trustees have standing to refer a determination to the Tribunal and that a decision not to issue an FSD could also be referred. The decision in regard to the standing of trustees has been affirmed by the Court of Appeal in *Trustees of the Lehman Brothers Pension Scheme v The Pensions Regulator [2013] EWCA Civ 751*.

High Court litigation

16.13   Litigation in the High Court has involved both the Regulator and the PPF. The PPF has no direct equivalent of the Upper Tribunal (for the

PPF Ombudsman see **16.7** above), but has been present in both High Court and international litigation.

In taking over the assets of a scheme, the PPF takes over the trustees' claims against the employers, including for instance *s 75* claims for lump sum deficit contributions. The PPF can therefore find itself the defendant in High Court actions brought by an insolvency practitioner, as in the case of *In re Federal-Mogul Aftermarket UK Ltd and others* (also known as *Gleave and others v Board of the Pension Protection Fund) [2008] EWHC 1099 (Ch),* where the court was asked to determine whether the supervisors of a CVA were bound to accept the actuary's certificate in respect of a *s 75* debt. In the *Federal-Mogul* litigation the PPF was effectively in the shoes of the scheme trustees.

Both the Regulator and the PPF have also intervened as third parties in litigation in the High Court. The Nortel and Lehman FSDs led to litigation in the Companies Court to determine what priority an FSD should take in the insolvency of the relevant companies. With both statutory bodies appearing, Briggs J held that the costs of complying with an FSD were, on the facts, expenses of the insolvency, with super-priority as against the claims of unsecured creditors (*Nortel GmbH, Re [2010] EWHC 3010 (Ch)*). This decision was initially affirmed by the Court of Appeal (*Bloom and others v Pensions Regulator and others [2011] EWCA Civ 1124*) but reversed by the UK Supreme Court (*Bloom v Pensions Regulator [2013] UKSC 52*) which held that an FSD issued against a company after it had entered insolvent administration was to be treated as a provable debt ranking pari passu with other unsecured debts.

In *Independent Trustee Services v Hope (2009) EWHC 2810 (Ch)* (concerning the Ilford Pension Scheme), again with both bodies appearing, the court held that it was not appropriate for trustees to take into account the benefits available through the PPF when making decisions regarding the assets of an occupational pension scheme. The Regulator supported and supplemented the arguments made by the PPF.

There was no consideration of the Regulators' intervention in that case. However, in the subsequent case of *Capita ATL Pension Trustees Ltd v Zurkinskas (2010) EWHC 3365 (Ch)* (part of the ongoing *Sea Containers* litigation) the court was asked to determine whether a compromise of certain equalisation issues constituted a 'rule change' which could later be disregarded by the PPF. The court accordingly required documents to be provided to the PPF, which replied by letter. The PPF declined to intervene, and indicated that its approach where a scheme is not yet in an assessment period 'is not to participate unless an issue of general application arises, for example such as that which arose in the case of *ITS v Hope'*.

International employers

16.14   Since the introduction of the Regulator's powers, there has been speculation as to the reach of those powers as against overseas companies. Barriers include the attitude of an overseas court to what is arguably a penalty imposed by a foreign government, and practical difficulties in overseas enforcement.

In the Carrington Wire investigation, in 2015 a settlement was reached with Russian former parent companies over prospective contribution notices. The settlement was £8.5 million, insufficient to make up the £27 million deficit, so that the scheme will still enter the PPF. The potential difficulties in enforcing a contribution notice in Russia may have informed the settlement. In this case the Russian parent had sold the UK employer to an English company for £1, with a working capital adjustment resulting in a payment of £400,000 to the purchaser. A contribution notice for £382,136 was also made against the company's sole director and shareholder, who was determined to have benefited in this amount.

There has been long-running litigation over Nortel in both the US and Canada as well as in the UK (where the PPF represented 93 per cent of the creditors by value of the UK company). In 2010, the Ontario Court of Appeal upheld the decision of the Superior Court that the issue of a warning notice was a breach of the stay of claims in the insolvency, and void in Canadian law (*Re Nortel Networks Ltd* 2010 ONCA 464). However, the trustees and PPF were permitted to prove in the Canadian parent company insolvency. In December 2014, the Ontario court (*Re Nortel Networks Corporation* 2014 ONSC 6973) made a number of decisions which may be persuasive in the UK, and also indicate the approach an overseas common law court may take. The Canadian court upheld one claim by the PPF, and rejected four others (one is subject to appeal). The case included both private law claims (chiefly claims under parent company guarantees) and a public law claim (to enforce an FSD). The FSD claim failed, but not on public international law grounds, which were not considered in detail. The PPF claimed that the FSD issued by the Regulator against Nortel in Canada would be followed by a non-compliance contribution notice for a specified amount and that this should be a provable debt to the PPF. The court ruled that this was too speculative (and commented that the FSD in this case was not reasonable). However, the court rejected arguments that the Trustee and PPF had no standing to pursue an FSD, that FSDs were void in Canada as acts of a foreign government, or that they sought to privilege one creditor over another. Despite this, the PPF was awarded £182 million under one of the parent company guarantees. While this illustrates the difficulties in enforcing orders of the Regulator overseas, it also shows that the PPF is willing to embark on such litigation where the stakes are high, and that it can be successful in absolute terms (even if recovery only partly makes up the scheme deficit).

Court proceedings

Introduction

16.15 Litigation through the courts has, traditionally, been regarded as costly, time consuming and relatively unpredictable. Costs and the risk of ancillary litigation have potentially been increased by the more 'robust' approach now taken to court deadlines, as exemplified by *Mitchell v News Group Newspapers Limited [2014] 1 WLR 795*. It is not surprising, therefore, that the PO and TPAS are attractive alternative forums in which beneficiaries of pension schemes may pursue their claims. However, court proceedings may be unavoidable in some circumstances, such as where a determination of the PO is appealed; where the trustees seek the court's directions on a pensions issue; or where the claimant has no other available forum in which to pursue the claim. Set out below is a summary of the most common types of applications that are made to the court in pensions disputes and a basic explanation of the various procedures under the *Civil Procedure Rules 1998 (SI 1998/3132)*, as amended (the '*CPR*') and Practice Directions to them ('*PDs*'), which govern the procedure in the civil courts.

Types of application to court

Appeals from the PO

16.16 *PSA 1993, s 151* provides a route for appeal to the High Court on a point of law arising out of a determination given by the PO. Permission is required from the High Court for an appeal (*CPR 52.21*). Such an appeal can extend to the way in which the Ombudsman has found on questions of fact: in *AF Blakemore & Son Ltd v Machin [2007] EWHC 963 (Ch)* the High Court found that the Ombudsman had made a determination of fact in the face of the evidence and remitted the decision to an oral hearing before the Ombudsman.

Any such appeal will be heard in the Chancery Division of the High Court. The procedure is set out in *CPR Part 52* and *Practice Directions 52, 52B and 52D*. The party lodging the appeal – the 'appellant' – must file a notice of appeal (known as the 'appellant's notice') at the High Court within 21 days after the date of the PO's determination (*CPR 52.4(2)(b)* following the deletion of paragraph 17.3 of the old *Practice Direction on Appeals*). A copy must also be served on the PO and any respondents (see *PD 52D 3.4*). The appellant's notice should be in a form prescribed by the *CPR* (Form N161) and set out the grounds for the appeal, the arguments in support of those grounds and the decision sought from the High Court on appeal. It should be accompanied by a skeleton argument (a summary of a party's submissions) and a bundle of relevant documents including a copy of the decision appealed and any evidence in support of the appeal.

The other parties to the appeal are referred to as 'respondents' (eg the Scheme trustees or other party originally complained against). A respondent can ask the appeal court to uphold the PO's determination for reasons different from or additional to those given by the PO, in which case that respondent must file a 'respondent's notice' within 14 days of being served with the appellant's notice. Like the appellant's notice, the respondent's notice should be in a prescribed form (Form N162), accompanied by a skeleton argument and bundle of relevant documents.

It is important to note that the time limits referred to above are strict and cannot be varied without the court's permission. This means that once the PO has issued a determination, the parties should take immediate steps to consider whether they wish to appeal and, if so, prepare the relevant documents. This should be considered with care, as a trustee or employer will not be able to appeal merely as a respondent without entering a notice of appeal (*Davies v Meadwestvaco Calmar Ltd (2008) EWCA Civ 8*). An appeal does not operate as an automatic stay of the determination of the PO unless the court or the PO permits otherwise.

The appeal will be limited to a review of the PO's determination unless the court considers that, in the circumstances, it would be in the interests of justice to hold a rehearing. Oral evidence and evidence which was not before the PO are not allowed to be introduced in the appeal unless the court orders otherwise. The court has power to affirm, set aside or vary any determination made by the PO; refer any claim or issue back to the PO for determination; order a new hearing before the PO; and make orders for the payment of interest on any monies awarded and the parties' costs.

In practice, whilst an employer may have the resources to fund the costs of an appeal, an individual complainant may be reluctant to pursue an appeal given the costs of mounting the appeal and the risk of being ordered to pay the respondent's costs if the appeal is lost. In such circumstances, the potential appellant may consider applying for a prospective costs order (which is discussed in more detail at **16.50** below) before pursuing an appeal. This should be set out when seeking permission (*PD 52D 3.8*).

While the PO is not properly speaking a respondent (he is rather the tribunal from which appeal is sought), in certain appeals the PO may decide that he wishes to participate, and the court is likely to allow such participation (*Moore's (Wallisdown) Ltd v Pension Ombudsman [2002] 1 All ER 737*). If the PO participates, he may expose himself to a risk that, if he loses, the court may order him to pay the costs of the appeal. For this reason, the PO has previously demonstrated a reluctance to participate in appeals, even where the issue is of wider public relevance, unless the appeal relates to the Ombudsman's jurisdiction. This approach was reflected in the 2003 case of *Legal & General Assurance Society Ltd v CCA Stationery Ltd [2003] EWHC 2989 (Ch)*, in which the court requested the PO's participation in the appeal but the PO declined because of the costs risk. The result was that the appeal hearing went ahead without the participation of the respondents. However, the PO has participated in certain recent appeals touching on jurisdiction including *Pensions Ombudsman v EMC Europe Ltd [2012] EWHC 3508 (Ch)*; *R (on the application of the Government Actuary's Department) v Pensions Ombudsman [2013] Pens LR 291 (CA)* and (the Deputy Ombudsman) in *NHS Business Services Authority v Wheeler [2014] EWHC 2155 (Ch)*. The new PO has indicated that he will be taking a more active role in appeals where it may be in the public interest.

The decision of the High Court may be appealed to the Court of Appeal. The court's permission is required and will only be granted if it is considered that the appeal would raise an important point of principle or practice, or there is some other compelling reason to hear it. The Court of Appeal's judgment may, with the court's permission, be appealed to the UK Supreme Court.

It is relevant to note that, in general, attempts to seek judicial review of the PO's determinations, as an alternative to pursuing an appeal under the procedure explained above, have failed. In those cases, the court referred to the appeal procedure as being the more appropriate means of determining the issues. The case of *R (on the application of Parish) v Pensions Ombudsman* (the two hearings are reported at *[2009] EWHC 32 (Admin)* and *[2009] EWHC 969 (Admin)* respectively) is an exception. There, the Ombudsman declined jurisdiction on the basis that the complaint was already the subject matter of a judicial review against the public sector employer. The claimant then issued a further application for judicial review against the Ombudsman, which was upheld.

Claims by/against a third party

16.17   These are claims which involve the trustees (and/or the employer) and third parties (ie parties external to the trust). For example, they may include claims by trustees against their professional advisers for professional negligence or a claim by trustees against a former trustee for breach of trust. They are usually hostile in nature and are usually brought under the *CPR Part 7* procedure (which is discussed in more detail in **16.25** below).

Non-hostile litigation

16.18   Litigation may also arise where trustees face a dilemma in exercising their powers or where there is an error or an ambiguity in the Scheme documentation or in legislation.

These types of application are not usually of a particularly hostile nature (unless the employer and/or the beneficiaries take strong exception to what is proposed) and may be distinguished from proceedings between the trustees and a third party, which are usually categorised as 'hostile' litigation.

Seeking directions from the court

16.19   The court has a wide jurisdiction to provide directions to trustees on matters relating to the administration of a pension scheme (see *CPR Part 64* and the *Practice Directions* to it). Applications to court for such directions usually concern issues arising out of the trustees' exercise of a discretion or a power under the pension scheme's trust deed or rules, or where the meaning of the scheme's trust deed or rules is unclear or ambiguous. For example, the trustees may seek the court's direction because:

(*a*)   they are uncertain whether or not a proposed course of action is within their powers;

(*b*)   they wish to seek the court's blessing to a proposed course of action which may have a significant impact on the scheme (for example, application for a *Beddoe* order – see **16.48** below); or

(*c*)   they wish to surrender the exercise of a discretion to the court because they are unable to arrive at a decision for some reason (for example, conflict of interest, deadlock).

Directions applications are usually brought under the simplified *CPR Part 8* procedure (which is discussed in more detail in **16.29** below).

Rectification and construction claims

16.20   Where an error is discovered in the drafting of a pension scheme document, such that the document does not accurately reflect the true common intentions of the trustees and the employer, and that error cannot be resolved completely by other means (for example, by the proper construction of the document, or by the use of any applicable amendment power which does not offend *PA 1995, s 67*), the trustees or employer may apply to the court to rectify the error.

To obtain rectification, the claimant trustees or employer have to provide credible evidence that the error did not accurately reflect the clear and common intentions of the trustees and employer when the wording in the document was drafted and executed. The mistake must also be of significant importance such that it justifies the court making an order for rectification and in all the circumstances it must be appropriate to grant rectification (eg there are no legal bars to rectification).

A key recent contractual rectification case is *Daventry DC v Daventry District Housing Limited* [2012] 1 WLR. Recent pension decisions include *Colorcon Ltd v Huckell [2009] EWHC 979 (Ch), Industrial Acoustics Company Ltd v Crawhurst and others [2012]* EWHC 1614 (Ch) and *IBM UK Pensions Trust Limited v IBM UK Holdings Limited and others [2012] EWHC 2276 (Ch).*

Since in most schemes both the trustees and the employer are involved in changes to the deed or rules, it is their common intention which is important. In *Daventry* at 1333, Etherton LJ (dissenting in the event but with whom Lord Neuberger LJ agreed in this respect) indicated that continuing common intention was to be judged objectively and that 'outward expression of accord' in this respect was the other side of the same coin. *Colorcon, Industrial Acoustics* and *IBM* have all followed this approach.

In *Colorcon* the court also confirmed that there are no special restrictions applying to rectification of pension documents. It also held that the behaviour of the parties following the execution of the deed could stand as evidence of the intention itself: this included administration of benefits on the intended basis, and scheme reports and member booklets published and circulated in subsequent years stating the intended benefits.

The *IBM* case provides a useful summary of the current state of the law on rectification of pension scheme documents. In *IBM* the Court upheld the trustee's claim for rectification of a trust deed executed in 1983. It also granted rectification of all subsequent deeds and rules containing the relevant error.

Given the importance to a rectification application of documentary and oral evidence, it is usually made using the *Part 7* procedure (see **16.30** below), unless there is no dispute on the facts, in which case the *Part 8* procedure may be more appropriate (see **16.29** below). The trustees and the employer will both be parties to the application and a representative beneficiary (see **16.35** below), or more than one where appropriate, is usually appointed to represent the beneficiaries of the scheme. As a result of the evidential burden on the claimant, rectification applications are not by their nature straightforward, particularly where another party objects to the proposed rectification. They are often made in conjunction with, and as an alternative to, an application for a declaration that the offending document can be properly construed to give effect to the parties' instructions, which, if successful, would mean that the trustees would no longer need to pursue the alternative rectification application.

Alternatively, a declaration may be sought as to the construction of a potentially ambiguous provision in a trust deed or in legislation. Such applications are commonly referred to as 'construction' applications. In principle, a construction application requires significantly less evidence, as it relates primarily to an issue of legal interpretation. However, where an ambiguity has been introduced in error, it may be that both construction and rectification remedies are potentially available. Claimants may therefore have to take a view as to whether they should claim both remedies (with the additional cost burden of preparing evidence for the rectification aspect of the claim) or whether they are sufficiently confident that the construction claim will succeed that they are prepared to claim on that basis alone, saving time and cost in preparation of evidence but with the risk of having to make a fresh claim for rectification if unsuccessful. Recent cases include *ICM Computer Group Limited v Stribley [2013] EWHC 2995 (Ch)* (decided by summary judgment) and *Dutton & Others v FDR Ltd [2015] EWHC 2946 (Ch)*. In *Sterling v Sterling [2015] EWHC 2665 (Ch)* (which may be subject to appeal) Nugee J granted in effect 'rectification by construction' (applying *Chartbrook* and 'the ability of the court to correct mistakes by construction') by construing a trust deed so as to remove a word inserted in error. In the *ICM* case Asplin J in effect added words by construction, to give effect to an intended equalisation.

Rectification and construction will only allow for the correction of a mistake or ambiguity in an existing document and so will not assist in cases where no document satisfying the relevant formalities has been put in place.

Administration of Justice Act, s 48

16.21 Where a question has arisen as to how the terms of a trust deed should be interpreted and the trustees have obtained a written opinion from counsel of at least ten years' standing, in the absence of a dispute over the issue, the *Administration of Justice Act 1985, s 48* allows trustees to apply to the High Court, without the need for a hearing, for an order authorising them to take the proposed steps in reliance on the opinion. This abbreviated procedure has the potential of providing a relatively speedy and cost-efficient resolution of the issue.

However, it is unlikely to provide sufficient comfort to trustees where there is significant scope for dispute, eg where the trustees' favoured construction would clearly reduce benefits or favour one category of member over another. Where there is, or is likely to be, a dispute, a full application to court will be required. In practice, therefore, this route is not often employed. *Section 48* was, however, successfully used in the case of *Re BCA Pension Trustees Ltd [2015] EWHC 3492*. The decision authorised the trustee to continue administering the Scheme on the basis that certain words had not been deleted on a consolidation exercise. This involved reading words into the trust deed, and is therefore a parallel case to the *ICM* construction case (see **16.20** above). The court made clear that *s 48* protects the trustee against any claim that it has acted in breach of trust by administering the scheme according to the order; however, it does not bind the beneficiaries, who can still argue for an alternative construction and seek benefits accordingly. It is also worth noting that the court did not in this case decide the application on paper, chiefly because the judge had concerns about the trustee's initial proposal not to inform members of the decision.

Compromise of a rectification or construction claim

16.22   Where the claim is not considered sufficiently strong to merit summary judgment (see below at **16.18**), it may be that seeking a compromise with the representative beneficiary is a less expensive option than proceeding to a full trial.

In a rectification or construction claim, it may be possible for the employer and representative beneficiary (with the agreement of the trustees) to agree a compromise between the higher and lower levels of benefits in dispute. For example, in a construction case where it is unclear whether pension increases in respect of a given period of service should be fixed three per cent or fixed five per cent, the parties might agree a rate of four per cent for the period.

See also the comments on compromises with a representative party below at **16.40** and on ADR at **16.51** to **16.54**.

Summary judgment in rectification and construction claims

16.23   The costs of a rectification action are typically high, and, in a number of recent cases, where the employer or trustee considered there was a clear case for rectification (or similarly for a declaration as to the construction of the scheme documents), they have used the *Part 7* procedure and have also then applied for summary judgment under *CPR Part 24*. This can reduce the costs and time required to obtain judgment by dispensing with a full trial and directions under *Part 7* (for which see **16.30**(*e*) below). In a rectification case, however, significant work in preparing evidence is still likely to be required in advance of issuing the claim and summary judgment application.

The test for summary judgment is a high one: that the representative beneficiary has no real prospect of successfully defending the claim at trial, and that there is no other compelling reason why the case should be disposed of at a trial. Rectification is in addition a remedy which requires convincing evidence.

This approach is therefore typically used where the claimant's counsel are confident there is a very strong case and anticipate that the representative beneficiary will accept on advice that there is no real prospect of a successful defence. The same mechanism of a confidential opinion from the representative beneficiary's counsel is used as in the case of a compromise (see **16.40** below).

Cases dealt with by summary judgment include *Pioneer GB Limited v Webb & Others [2011] EWHC 2683 (Ch), Industrial Acoustics Company Ltd v*

Crawhurst and others [2012] EWHC 1614 (Ch), Misys Limited v Misys Retirement Benefits Trustees Limited and Another [2012] EWHC 4250 (Ch) and *Hogg Robinson Plc v Brian Harvey & Others [2016] EWHC 129 (Ch)* (all rectification claims) and the *ICM* construction case (see **16.20** above). These claims were all unopposed (although in *Misys* there had been initial opposition from the representative beneficiary prior to seeing further documents). Where such an application has been made but the representative beneficiary ultimately concludes that the test for summary judgment is not met on the evidence provided, the claimant may decide to proceed to a contested summary judgment hearing (albeit that rectification may be a difficult remedy to obtain summarily in the face of opposition) and/or proceed to trial (where the case need only be proved on the balance of probabilities in the normal way).

Outline of procedure

Issues for consideration before commencing court proceedings

16.24 Before embarking on court proceedings, a claimant should consider, in particular, the following important factors:

(*a*) Is the claim being brought within any relevant limitation period prescribed by law? If not, the claim may be time barred.

(*b*) How will the costs of the proceedings be funded and paid? (Some relevant issues on costs are discussed in **16.43** below.)

(*c*) Who will be the parties to the proceedings?

(*d*) What remedy is sought and will it be an effective remedy?

(*e*) What are the merits of the application?

The answers to these questions will assist a claimant in determining not only whether to commence proceedings in the civil courts, but also the strategy to be adopted in progressing the claim, including whether to pursue alternative dispute resolution methods ('ADR', for which see **16.52** below). The decision to commence court proceedings should not be taken lightly, because once commenced, the claimant cannot unilaterally withdraw them without having to pay the other party's costs (unless the other party or the court agrees otherwise).

Trustees' obligations to disclose information to a beneficiary

16.25 Beneficiaries and trustees should be aware that the beneficiary may request disclosure by the trustees of certain 'trust documents', which the trustees may be legally obliged to disclose, without the need for litigation. This may assist a beneficiary's investigation into a matter. It is a common law principle that trustees are obliged to disclose 'trust documents' to beneficiaries who have a fixed (as opposed to discretionary) interest in a trust (including a pension scheme) (*O'Rourke v Darbishire [1920] AC 581, [1920] All ER Rep 1*). This obligation has been based on the principle that beneficiaries have the 'proprietary' right to the documents held by the trustees. Trust documents include the trust deed, rules, accounts and all documents relating to the trust, including minutes or trustee meetings. It may also extend to legal advice obtained by the trustees on behalf of the scheme, although not usually legal advice obtained in respect of the beneficiary's claim against the trustees or legal advice paid for by the trustees themselves rather than out of trust monies.

This disclosure obligation has not, however, extended to disclosing the trustees' deliberations on and reasons for exercising their discretionary powers under the scheme in a particular way. Therefore, trustees have not had to disclose any document evidencing their reasons and deliberations on that issue, unless there is evidence of improper conduct (*Re Londonderry's Settlement [1964] 3 All ER 855*; *Wilson v Law Debenture Trust Corporation plc [1995] 2 All ER 337*). If the trustees fail to disclose the disclosable trust documents, they may be ordered by a court to pay the costs of any application that the beneficiary may make to the court to compel such disclosure.

However, this obligation has been affected by two subsequent decisions.

(*a*) In *Schmidt v Rosewood Trust Ltd [2003] UKPC 26, [2003] 3 All ER 76* the Privy Council appeared to move away from the 'proprietary right' as the underlying rationale of the obligation and, instead, asserted the court's inherent power to supervise the administration of trusts, and right to order disclosure of any trust documents if it is considered appropriate in all the circumstances. This potentially widens the scope of the disclosure obligation not only in terms of the range of documents that could be disclosable but also the type of beneficiary who may be entitled to disclosure. As a Privy Council decision, it is not binding on the English court or the PO, but nonetheless is of highly persuasive authority, and appears to have been taken as such in *Blades v Isaac [2016] EWHC 601 (Ch)*. The PO has confirmed that he regards it as highly persuasive authority (see his determination in April 2005 in *Mr B Cameron (M00949)*).

(*b*) The PO indicated in a determination in 2002 (*Allen v TKM Group Pension Trust Ltd [2002] PLR 333*) that he considered it to be 'good administrative practice' for pension trustees to give reasons for their decisions and to make minutes of trustee meetings available to beneficiaries with a legitimate interest in the matter, even when exercising discretionary powers. Where he could see no good reason for trustees withholding disclosure of their reasons, he was prepared to determine that the trustees were guilty of maladministration. Given the above, trustees who receive a request for documents should consider it carefully, with appropriate advice, before deciding whether to reject it or the extent to which it should be complied with.

(See also a trustee's disclosure obligations pursuant to relevant pension statutes and regulations at **3.21** above and **Appendix II**.)

Pre-action protocols

16.26 The *CPR* set out steps that the court will expect the parties to undertake before proceedings are commenced. In particular, the court will expect all parties to have complied in substance with the terms of any applicable 'pre-action protocol' in the *CPR*. In practice the pre-action protocols are not generally followed in non-hostile litigation, where the parties have in any event jointly considered in advance how the proceedings should be dealt with. Whilst there is no specific protocol applicable to pension disputes in general, there is a protocol which applies specifically to professional negligence claims (eg a trustee's claim against his professional advisors for negligence).

Where there is no specific protocol that applies to the dispute in issue, the *Practice Direction on Pre-Action Conduct* (set out in the *CPR*) sets out a pre-action procedure that parties should seek to adhere to with the intention of avoiding litigation in so far as possible. The procedure specified includes the following, although this may be revised by the parties to suit their particular circumstances, provided that the revisions are reasonable:

(*a*) Each party should act reasonably in exchanging information and documents relevant to the claim and generally in trying to avoid the necessity for the start of proceedings.

(*b*) The claimant should write to the defendant setting out its claim. The letter should:

- give sufficient and concise details to enable the recipient to understand and investigate the claim without extensive further information;

- enclose copies of the essential documents which the claimant relies on;

- ask for a prompt acknowledgment of the letter, followed by a full written response within a reasonable stated period (for many claims, a normal reasonable period for a full response may be one month);

- state whether court proceedings will be issued if the full response is not received within the stated period;

- identify and ask for copies of any essential documents not in his possession which the claimant wishes to see;

- state (if it is so) that the claimant wishes to enter into mediation or another alternative method of dispute resolution; and

- if the recipient is not legally represented, refer to the Practice Direction and draw attention to the court's powers to impose sanctions for failure to comply with this practice direction.

(*c*)   The defendant should acknowledge the claimant's letter in writing within 14 days of receiving it and should state when the defendant will give a full written response. If this is longer than the period stated by the claimant, the defendant should give reasons why a longer period is needed.

(*d*)   The defendant's letter should, as appropriate, accept the claim in whole or in part and make proposals for settlement, or state that the claim is not accepted. If the claim is accepted in part only, the response should make clear which part is accepted and which part is not accepted.

(*e*)   If the defendant does not accept the claim, or part of it, the response should:

- give detailed reasons why the claim is not accepted, identifying which of the claimant's contentions are accepted and which are in dispute;

- set out details of any counterclaim or contention that the claimant is partly or wholly to blame for the problem complained of;

- enclose copies of the essential documents which the defendant relies upon;

- enclose copies of documents asked for by the claimant, or explain why they are not enclosed;

- identify and ask for copies of any further essential documents not in his possession which the defendant wishes to see; and

- state whether the defendant is prepared to enter into mediation or another alternative method of dispute resolution (and, if not, why not).

(*f*)   The claimant should provide requested documents within a reasonably short time or explain in writing why he is not doing so, and reply as defendant to any counterclaim.

(*g*)   If the claim remains in dispute, the parties should promptly engage in appropriate negotiations with a view to settling the dispute and avoiding litigation.

It should be noted that any documents disclosed by either party in accordance with the above procedure, may not be used for any purpose other than resolving the dispute, unless the other party agrees. Further, if the dispute requires the assistance of an expert, the Practice Direction suggests that the parties should, wherever possible and to save expense, engage a single agreed expert (eg if an actuary is required to provide a valuation). It should be noted that the court retains a power to refuse an expert's report sought by a party at this stage or refuse that party to claim the costs of an expert report in any subsequent proceedings.

It is important that a party to hostile litigation follows this procedure, or any agreed revised procedure, as the court has an express power to apply costs and other sanctions in the event of a party's non-observance. One potential exception is where there is a limitation issue: Paragraph 17 of the Practice Direction provides that 'If proceedings are started to comply with the statutory time limit before the parties have followed [the protocols], the parties should apply to the court for a stay of the proceedings while they so comply'. Paragraph 4.1 of the professional negligence protocol adds: 'The protocol does not alter the statutory time limits for commencing court proceedings. A claimant is required to start proceedings within those time limits. However, ... a claimant may commence court proceedings and invite the professional to agree to an immediate stay of the proceedings to enable the protocol procedures to be followed before the case is pursued'.

Whilst the above protocols provide for limited voluntary disclosure of documents, the *CPR* also provides a mechanism, in certain circumstances, for a potential claimant to apply to the court for an order obliging a potential defendant to anticipated proceedings to disclose documents before those proceedings are commenced (see *CPR 31.16*), although the party making the application will usually have to pay the other party's costs of the application and of complying with any order made.

Procedure in the civil court

16.27 Court procedure in civil cases is governed by the *CPR*. With the exception of appeals, court proceedings are initiated by the issue and service of a claim form (which replaced the 'writ' and 'originating summons'). There are two principal procedures under the *CPR* for issuing a claim (as opposed to an appeal) – the *Part 7* and *Part 8* procedures. They are discussed in more detail below. The *Part 7* procedure is the most commonly used procedure in claims involving third parties because such cases involve disputes of fact. The *Part 8* procedure is the standard procedure for directions applications by trustees.

Once proceedings have been commenced, the court will allocate the case to one of its three tracks. The *Small claims track* and *Fast Track* are the normal tracks for simple cases up to £10,000 or from £10,000 to £25,000 in value. Claims issued under the *Part 8* procedure are automatically allocated to the *Multi-track*, whereas *Part 7* claims will be allocated to the appropriate track, according to the value and complexity of the claim. Almost all pensions litigation will be High Court litigation allocated to the multi-track. However, in November 2013 *Professional Pensions* reported that a number of pensioners in the British Airways Pension Scheme had issued small claims following a change in the basis of inflation awards in the Scheme and that a pensioner had been awarded default judgment when attempts by BA's solicitors to obtain agreement to an extension of time for filing a defence were unsuccessful.

Case management powers

16.28   In all proceedings, the court has wide case management powers. When exercising any power under, or interpreting any rule in, the *CPR*, the court must give effect to what is known as the 'overriding objective'. The overriding objective stipulates that the court must deal with cases justly (see *CPR Part 1* for a full definition). This includes dealing with the case expeditiously and fairly, and in ways which are proportionate to the amount of money involved; the importance and complexity of the case; and to the financial position of each party. The parties themselves are also required to help the court to further the overriding objective.

The court also has wide powers to penalise parties for their conduct in the proceedings by, for example, disallowing all or any part of their costs, or ordering them to pay another party's costs or, in more serious instances, by striking out their case. As noted at **16.45** below, where there is a sanction for failing to meet a deadline in the *CPR* or in an order, the court will now use its powers to relieve the party in default from sanction more sparingly. As a result, parties should always meet time deadlines imposed by the court and conduct themselves appropriately.

Part 8 procedure

16.29   The *Part 8* procedure is designed to be more streamlined than the *Part 7* procedure. The *Part 8* procedure should be employed where the court's decision is required on a question which is unlikely to involve a substantial dispute of fact or where a Practice Direction permits or requires its use for that type of proceedings. In pension cases, a trustee's application for directions (see **16.19** above) is required to be brought under the *Part 8* procedure. Whilst third party claims (see **16.17** above) and claims for rectification (see **16.20** above) may also be brought under the *Part 8* procedure, such claims will often involve a substantial dispute of fact so the *Part 7* procedure is usually more appropriate. The *Part 8* procedure is sometimes also used tactically and aggressively by a claimant to seek to limit evidence from the Defendant or put the Defendant under a high degree of time pressure, where the parties have not agree to use of that procedure. The court may, at any time, direct that a claim brought under the *Part 8* procedure should proceed under *Part 7*. *Part 8* claims are automatically allocated to the multi-track. As *Part 8* is already a streamlined procedure, there is no provision under *Part 8* for summary judgment.

An outline of the *Part 8* procedure is as follows:

(*a*) *Issue and service of claim form*

The *Part 8* claim form is in a prescribed form and should set out, among other things, the question(s) for determination by the court, the remedy sought and the legal basis for that remedy. Any evidence upon which the claimant wishes to rely at the hearing of the claim should accompany the claim form (set out either in the claim form or in a witness statement, but in both cases verified by a signed statement of truth).

(*b*) *Acknowledgment of service*

The defendant must acknowledge service of the claim form within 14 days by filing at court, and serving on all parties, the prescribed form. In acknowledging service, the defendant should state whether the claim is contested, whether a different remedy is sought, or whether use of the *Part 8* procedure is itself disputed. Unlike under the *Part 7* procedure, the defendant does not have to serve a defence. Failure to acknowledge service will result in the defendant not being able to take part in the hearing of the claim without the court's permission.

(*c*) *Evidence*

If the defendant wishes to rely on evidence at the hearing, that evidence, in the form of a witness statement with any relevant documents exhibited to it, should be filed and served at the same time as the acknowledgment of service. The claimant then has 14 days in which to serve any evidence in reply, unless an extension of time can be agreed with the defendant(s) or is ordered by the court. The default deadline for evidence is therefore extremely short and opportunities to vary this by agreement are limited under the CPR. This makes Part 8 most suitable for non-hostile litigation where the parties can consider these matters in advance or seek tailored directions by agreement.

(*d*) *Case management directions*

The court may give case management directions when the claim form is issued. It is more usual, however, for the court to give directions after the defendant has acknowledged service or the time limit for acknowledging service has expired. The parties are encouraged to agree, so far as is possible, appropriate case management directions for the court's approval. The court may give such directions without a hearing or by calling a case management conference. Such directions may include the disclosure of documents (see **16.32** below), the exchange of further witness statements (see **16.33** below), the preparation and exchange of expert reports (see **16.34** below), and any other steps that may be necessary for the efficient management of the claim, although under *Part 8* these will not be ordered by default.

(*e*) *Hearing of claim*

The hearing of the claim will take place in open court before a judge, unless the court permits it to be held in private. Written evidence may not be relied on by a party at the hearing unless it has been served in accordance with the rules or the court gives permission. At the hearing, each party's legal representatives make their oral submissions to the judge. The judge may require or allow a party to give oral evidence at the hearing and may require a witness's attendance for cross-examination.

(*f*) *Judgment*

After hearing the parties' submissions, the judge will either hand down the judgment at the end of the hearing or may reserve judgment to a future date (in order to allow time for the judge to consider and draft the judgment).

In applications by trustees for directions in the administration of a pension scheme, the court's *Practice Direction B to CPR Part 64* provides additional guidelines, which include the following:

(i) *Confidentiality*

If the confidentiality of the directions sought is important (such as in a *Beddoe* application – see **16.48** below), the claim form should only give a general description of the remedy sought, with a more detailed explanation set out in the trustee's witness statement. The hearing will be in private and aside from the served claim form court documents will not be available for public inspection without the permission of the court.

(ii) *Representative parties*

As regards 'representative parties' (see **16.35** below) it may not be necessary for a representative of each class of beneficiary in the pension scheme to be joined as a party to the proceedings because the trustees may be able to present the arguments for or against the application on behalf of some classes of beneficiary. If the trustees are unable to decide which categories of beneficiaries to join as defendants (for example, where there are many members and categories of interest), the trustees may apply to issue the claim form without naming any defendants (under *CPR 8.2A*). At the same time, they may apply to the court for directions as to which persons to join as parties.

(iii) *No defendants required*

If the trustees consider that the court may be able to give the directions sought without hearing from any other party, again they may apply for permission for the claim form to be issued without naming any defendants (*CPR 8.2A*). However, see also the comments at **16.27** below regarding consultation with members.

(iv)   *Requirement for a hearing*

The court will always consider whether it can deal with the application on paper without the need for a hearing. If the trustees and/or the defendant(s) consider that a hearing is needed, they should state so, with reasons, in their evidence. If the court deals with the application on paper and refuses the application, the parties will be given an opportunity to request a hearing.

(v)   *Trustees' evidence*

The trustees' evidence, which is given by witness statement, should disclose fully any matters which are relevant to the application, failing which they may not be protected by the court's order. The duty of full disclosure of relevant matters exists even when the case proceeds with the participation of the beneficiaries as defendants. In addition to all matters relevant to the application the evidence should also include the latest actuarial valuation, a description of the membership profile; and if a deficit on winding up is likely, of the priority provisions and their likely effect.

The trustees need not serve their evidence on beneficiaries who are prospective defendants where the contents are privileged and there is potential prejudice in doing so, and other parties may be excluded from part of the hearing for the same reason.

(vi)   *Consultation with beneficiaries*

The trustees' evidence should also describe what, if any, consultation there has been with beneficiaries, and the results of that consultation. The Practice Direction states as general guidance that, unless the members are few in number, the court will not expect any particular steps by way of consultation with beneficiaries (including, where relevant, employers) or their representatives to have been carried out in preparation for the application. If no consultation has taken place, the court may direct that meetings of one or more classes of beneficiaries are held to consider the subject matter of the application, possibly as a preliminary to deciding whether a representative of a particular class ought to be joined as a defendant.

For judicial comments on consultation in representative actions more generally, see **16.38** below.

Part 7 procedure

16.30   The *Part 7* procedure is used if the *Part 8* procedure is inappropriate (for example, there is a substantial dispute of fact). The majority of third party claims (see **16.17** above) will therefore be brought under this procedure. The *Part 7* procedure usually requires more procedural steps prior to the trial than the *Part 8* procedure. An outline of the *Part 7* procedure is as follows:

(a)   *Claim form and particulars of claim*

The claimant issues and serves a claim form which sets out a basic summary of the claimant's claim. Unlike the *Part 8* procedure, the claimant's case is set out in a separate particulars of claim, which contains a detailed description of the claim and the facts on which the claimant relies.

(b)   *Acknowledgment of service*

Having been served with the claim form and particulars of claim, the defendant has 14 days to file an acknowledgment of service in the prescribed form, indicating whether it admits the claim, admits part of the claim but contests another part, or contests the entire claim. If the defendant fails to acknowledge service within the prescribed time limit and no extension of time has been agreed, judgment in default may be entered in the claimant's favour.

(c)   *Defence (and counterclaim if relevant)*

If the defendant contests all or part of the claim, unlike under the *Part 8* procedure, the defendant must prepare, file and serve a defence within 14 days after being served with the particulars of claim (if no acknowledgment of service has been filed) or 28 days after service of the particulars of claim (if an acknowledgment of service has been filed). If a defence is not filed within the prescribed time limit and no extension of time has been agreed, judgment in default may be entered in the claimant's favour. If the defendant wishes to make a counterclaim against the claimant, this should be served with the defence.

(d)   *Reply (and defence to counterclaim if relevant)*

If the claimant wants to allege facts to answer those alleged in the defence, the claimant may serve a reply. If the defendant has served a counterclaim, the claimant must, at the same time as serving the reply, serve a defence to the counterclaim, failing which judgment in default may be entered in the defendant's favour on the counterclaim.

(e)   *Case management directions*

The court will allocate the case to one of the three court tracks (see **16.27** above) and give case management directions. These typically involve the following (in chronological order):

(i)   disclosure and inspection of documents (see **16.32** below);

(ii)   exchange of witness statements (see **16.33** below); and

715

(iii)   exchange of expert reports (if necessary), followed by meetings of the experts in order to narrow the issues in dispute (see **16.34** below).

(*f*)   *Trial*

The trial of the claim takes place before a judge in open court, at which each party's advocate makes oral submissions, and the witnesses and experts give oral evidence and are cross-examined. At the conclusion of the trial the judge will hand down a written judgment (or reserve judgment as described at **16.21**(*f*) above) and will make any appropriate costs orders.

Summary judgment

16.31   Where a claim form has been issued under *Part 7*, and a party can show that their opponent has no real prospect of success at trial and that there is no other compelling reason why the case should be disposed of at a trial, the court can determine the case by way of summary judgment under *CPR Part 24*. An application for summary judgment can be made once service of the claim form has been acknowledged. Where such an application is made, the defendant need not file a defence. Instead, the parties serve and file evidence (in the form of witness statements and exhibited documents) in preparation for a hearing, which will typically be one or two days, and can be held without further directions, and without the need for a formal process of disclosure and the other steps noted above. Typically, no oral evidence is required at a summary judgment hearing. Summary judgment can significantly reduce the time and cost involved in litigation; however, the hurdle for summary judgment is high (if this test is not met, the matter must continue to trial in the normal way). An application for summary judgment can be used aggressively, or (as noted at **16.23** above) by prior agreement in non-hostile litigation.

Disclosure of documents in litigation

16.32   Disclosure in the context of court proceedings is the process by which each party discloses to the other parties to the claim relevant documents within that party's control and in respect of which privilege is not being claimed. The disclosure process aims to ensure that each party has sight of the material that is available to the other parties so that each party can prepare adequately before trial of the proceedings. Disclosure of documents is not always ordered under the *Part 8* procedure (see **16.29** above), whereas traditionally 'standard disclosure' is usually ordered under the *Part 7* procedure (see **16.30** above).

Standard disclosure requires a party to disclose those 'documents' on which it relies, as well as those which adversely affect its own case or another party's case or which support another party's case. The word 'documents' has a wide meaning and includes anything in which information of any description is recorded (for example, paper documents, computer files, film, video, photographs). It includes electronic documents, such as emails, databases, saved documents and other electronic communications, stored on a computer's hard drive or a server or a back-up system, or on other electronic devices and media. A party must conduct a reasonable search for, and disclose, documents within its control (ie where the party has or had a right to possess it, inspect it or take copies of it). Disclosure usually takes the form of the parties exchanging a list of documents in a form prescribed in *CPR Part 31*. There are now detailed guidelines in relation to electronic disclosure, which are set out in *Practice Direction B to CPR Part 31* introduced in October 2010. The Practice Direction indicates that electronic disclosure should be considered at the outset of proceedings.

A party is entitled to inspect and take copies of the documents disclosed by another party. However, a party giving disclosure may object to the inspection of certain documents on the grounds that they are legally privileged from inspection (an analysis of the various types of privilege that may be relied upon is outside the scope of the chapter). It should be noted that, as the duty to give disclosure continues to the end of the case, a party should take care when creating new documents in case they also need to be disclosed. A party who gives inadequate disclosure may be compelled by the court to give further disclosure. If a party fails to disclose a document, it may not rely on that document at the trial of the proceedings without the court's permission and, ultimately, if in breach of its obligations, a party may be held to be in contempt of court. (The rules of disclosure are set out in *CPR Part 31* and should be distinguished from trustees' obligations to disclose information to members under common law and under various pensions statutes and regulations, for which see **3.22** and **16.25** above and **Appendix II.**)

For claims issued on or after 1 April 2013, standard disclosure remains the default *(CPR 31.5(1)(a))*. However, the court, or the parties by agreement, may now dispense with or limit standard disclosure. This has the potential significantly to reduce the scope of disclosure in some cases, although where there are disputes of fact which might be informed by disclosure, and it would be proportionate to the matters in issue, parties may be slow to agree to dispense with or limit disclosure.

The court has a range of orders it may make, set out in *CPR 31.5(7)*, having regard to the overriding objective and the need to limit disclosure to that which is necessary to deal with the case justly:

(*a*)   an order dispensing with disclosure;

(*b*)   an order that a party disclose the documents on which it relies, and at the same time request any specific disclosure it requires from any other party;

(*c*)   an order that directs, where practicable, the disclosure to be given by each party on an issue by issue basis;

(*d*)   an order that each party disclose any documents which it is reasonable to suppose may contain information which enables that party to advance its own case or to damage that of any other party, or which leads to an enquiry which has either of those consequences;

(*e*)   an order that a party give standard disclosure;

(*f*)   any other order in relation to disclosure that the court considers appropriate.

The court can also give detailed directions as to searches to be undertaken and the manner of disclosure.

The revised disclosure rules are primarily driven by costs management, and there are also new budgeting requirements specifically for disclosure in addition to the new general costs budgeting rules (for which see **16.45** below). Not less than 14 days before the first case management conference each party must file and serve a report verified by a statement of truth, which:

(*a*)   describes briefly what documents exist or may exist that are or may be relevant to the matters in issue in the case;

(*b*)   describes where and with whom those documents are or may be located;

(*c*)   in the case of electronic documents, describes how those documents are stored;

(*d*)   estimates the broad range of costs that could be involved in giving standard disclosure in the case; and

(*e*)   states which of the orders above is sought.

Not less than seven days before the first case management conference, and on any other occasion as the court may direct, the parties must, at a meeting or by telephone, discuss and seek to agree a proposal in relation to disclosure that meets the overriding objective.

The disclosure report should include an estimate of the broad range of costs that could be involved in giving standard disclosure. At least seven days before the first CMC (or on any other occasion that the court directs), the parties must discuss and seek to agree a proposal for disclosure that meets the overriding objective (*CPR 31.5(5)*). At a CMC, the court will decide which of the above orders to make (*CPR 31.5(7)*).

Witness statements

16.33   A fact which needs to be proved by the evidence of a witness must, as a general rule, be proved at the trial of the case by the oral evidence of that witness under oath. At any other hearing (ie before the trial) the fact may be proved by the written evidence of the witness (ie in a witness statement). A witness statement is a written statement of a witness's evidence. It is signed by the witness and contains a statement that he believes the facts in it are true (a 'statement of truth'). If a witness makes a false statement without an honest belief in its truth, proceedings for contempt of court may be brought. Witness statements have largely replaced affidavits (a written sworn statement). There are strict rules governing the form and content of witness statements (see *CPR Part 32* and the *Practice Direction* to it).

Expert evidence

16.34   Expert evidence is frequently required in pension disputes to assist the court. For example, an expert actuary may be required to give an opinion on the valuation of the assets and liabilities of the pension fund or certain benefits under a pension scheme. The court has wide powers to control the use of expert witnesses in litigation because they are usually expensive and lengthen the proceedings. Expert evidence is restricted to that which is reasonably required to resolve the proceedings and a party may only call an expert with the permission of the court. A recent pensions case deciding on these questions is *British Airways PLC v Paul Spencer and Others [2015] EWHC 2477 (Ch)*. In certain circumstances, the court may direct that expert evidence on an issue is to be given by a single expert, jointly instructed by both parties. The expert's overriding duty is to the court and not to the instructing or paying party. Experts will usually give their evidence in the form of written reports, which the parties exchange. Often the court will direct the parties' experts, following the exchange of reports, to meet in order to identify the technical issues in the proceedings and, where possible, reach agreement on those issues. An expert may be called to give oral evidence and be cross-examined at the trial of the action. (See *CPR Part 35* and the *Practice Direction 35 – Experts and Assessors* for the rules and guidelines on the use of experts). In applications for directions, it is often the case that, where a party needs some analysis carried out in relation to the scheme, to save costs, the parties agree to instruct the scheme actuary to carry out this work as, in effect, an expert (although this may not be appropriate in all cases, in which case the parties will need their own independent actuary expert).

Representation orders

CPR Part 19

16.35   It is a basic rule under the *CPR* that, where the party making a claim is seeking a remedy to which another person is jointly entitled, every other person who is so jointly entitled to that remedy must be joined as a party to the proceedings, unless the court orders otherwise (*CPR 19.3*). There is no limit to the number of parties who may be joined to a claim (*CPR 19.1*). This rule is designed to prevent a multiplicity of proceedings for similar claims and is of particular relevance to litigation involving pension schemes (eg trustees' applications for directions). Whereas the number of trustees of a pension scheme will be small, the number of beneficiaries under the scheme, who may be entitled jointly to a remedy, can be large – often amounting to hundreds, thousands and even tens of thousands. However, for each member or beneficiary of a scheme to be a named party to the litigation in accordance with the basic principle described above would give rise to a procedural and logistical burden which would seriously impair the efficient resolution of the litigation. Similarly, an industry-wide pension scheme may have in excess of 50 separate employers, each independent of the others. That said, trustees require certainty that any order made by the court will be binding on all beneficiaries and employers. The practical solution, therefore, is to appoint a party to represent the interests of other similarly interested parties. That party is known as a 'representative party' and may be appointed under two alternative provisions of the *CPR*:

(*a*)   If more than one party has the same interest in a claim, the claim may be commenced, or the court may order the claim to be continued, by or against one or more of those parties as representatives of the other parties. Any judgment or order made by the court in the proceedings will bind all the persons represented in the claim (but may only be enforceable by or against a person who is not a party to the proceedings with the consent of the court) (see *CPR 19.6*).

(*b*)   In claims concerning the assets of a pension scheme or the meaning of a document or statute the court may appoint, prior to or after the claim has commenced, a party to represent persons who are (i) unborn, or (ii) cannot be found, or (iii) cannot be easily ascertained. It may also appoint a party to represent a class of persons who have the same interest in a claim and either one or more members of that class fall within (i), (ii) or (iii) above, or if the court considers that the appointment would further the overriding objective of dealing with the claim justly (see **16.28** above) (see *CPR 19.7*).

Interests represented

16.36   Given the frequently large membership of a pension scheme, representation orders provide a practical way for proceedings to be pursued in an efficient and timely manner, and provide certainty for the trustees that the judgment handed down will bind all affected beneficiaries.

Where there is more than one distinct category of beneficiaries with a separate interest, it may be necessary to join more than one representative party. As each representative party will require legal representation, the court will usually seek to keep to a minimum the number of representative parties to minimise the costs as much as possible, particularly where the costs are being borne by the pension fund.

Where it is unclear which beneficiaries may benefit from taking a particular position, 'interest-based' representation may be used. A representative party is said to represent all those in whose interest it is to argue for a positive (or negative) answer to a given question. This ensures that the arguments are made on each question even where the precise boundaries of each interest class may be difficult to set at the commencement of proceedings, and may also serve to reduce the number of necessary representatives. Representation orders were made on this basis by Warren J in *PNPF Trust Co Ltd v Taylor [2010] EWHC 1573 (Ch)*. Alternatively, there is precedent for the trustees and representative beneficiary to instruct one solicitor to act for both, but with separate barristers then retained for each (*Capital Cranfield v Beck [2008] EWHC 3181 (Ch)*).

Trustees should therefore give proper consideration, at an early stage, to the various interests and who should be an appropriate representative party. A proposed representative party should not have a conflict of interest and should have availability to provide proper instructions to his legal representatives throughout the expected length of the proceedings.

Parties objecting to representation

16.37   An additional factor is the question whether a person whose interests are represented in proceedings by a representative party may challenge the representation order or challenge a settlement approved by the court on the grounds that it is a breach of that person's right to a fair trial under *Article 6* of the *European Convention on Human Rights* or otherwise. *Article 6* could also be relevant where a settlement is approved by the court and is binding on a person represented in the proceedings by a representative party, without that person having had a chance to state his own case.

If a person objects to being represented in an action, a practical solution may be for that person to be joined as a party in his own right (although that person will run the risk that he will have to bear his own legal costs in the event that the court does not permit his costs to be paid from the pension fund). In *Re PD Teesport Limited [2009] EWHC 1693 (Ch)* (an interim application in the Pilots National Pension Fund litigation), the Trustee had put in place a proposed scheme of representative parties and for case management reasons argued that additional parties who were already represented should not be joined in their own right. The applicant sought joinder on several grounds including *Article 6* rights. The court, while granting joinder on other grounds, held that 'there is no

721

breach of *Article 6* merely because a person has no direct access to the Court but only access through a representative, even where that representative is not of his own choosing'. In limited circumstances, two classes of member with aligned interests may nevertheless be allowed separate representation and costs from the fund (*Re British Airways Pension Schemes (2000) Pens LR 311*).

Consultation with beneficiaries

16.38   Trustees should consider giving proper notice of the proceedings to all the persons represented (in so far as they can be ascertained). Such notice would typically set out the nature of the proceedings (and the terms of the proposed compromise if applicable), and invite the persons represented to write to the trustees or representative party to state any objections to the order proposed (which can then be drawn to the court's attention). Although this is likely to be most important in the case first of a compromise, and secondly of an unopposed application for summary judgment, trustees and representative beneficiaries will generally consider adopting the same approach in other cases.

In *Re Owens Corning Fibreglass (UK) Pensions Plan Ltd [2002] All ER (D) 191* where a trustee applied for the court's approval of a compromise without informing the beneficiaries, Neuberger J indicated that, in most such cases, it would be desirable that potential beneficiaries, or their representatives (for example, their union representatives or the pensions committee) be informed about the proposed arrangement and of any related application to the court to allow them to make their views known. The court indicated that, but for overriding considerations specific to that case, as the beneficiaries had not been informed, it would have adjourned the hearing to allow the beneficiaries to be told of the proposed compromise.

In *Smithson v Hamilton [2008] EWCA Civ 996*, taking a pragmatic view as to what was likely to prevent further dispute on the part of represented pension scheme members, the Court of Appeal took a step similar to that contemplated in *Owens Corning* and delayed the effective date of the order while members were informed of the proposed compromise.

The issue was considered in the context of an unopposed summary rectification claim in *Industrial Acoustics Company Ltd v Crawhurst and others [2012] EWHC 1614 (Ch)*. Vos J held that, where there was a properly briefed representative beneficiary, there was no legal requirement for the employer or trustees to inform all scheme members of a claim affecting them. However, it was desirable to do so and a good idea where possible.

Where a consultation has taken place, one or more scheme members may write to the trustees or representative beneficiary expressing their view. Such correspondence would typically be drawn to the attention of the court so that it can be taken into account, but is only likely materially to affect the outcome if it raises a relevant issue not already addressed in submissions.

Trustees or solicitor representing beneficiaries' interests

16.39   If the trustees are undecided as to who or how many representative parties should be appointed or cannot find a willing volunteer, they may issue the claim form without naming the defendant(s) and seek the court's directions – (see also (iii) in **16.29** above).

In some cases it may be sufficient for the trustees to be a party. Where proceedings are brought by or against trustees without joining any of the beneficiaries of the pension scheme, any judgment or order made in those proceedings will bind the beneficiaries, unless the court orders otherwise (see *CPR 19.7A*). The court may order otherwise if it considers that the trustees could not or did not in fact represent the interests of those persons in the proceedings. Trustees should therefore consider carefully whether they can and are properly representing the beneficiaries' interests in such proceedings, because, if not, it may be necessary to appoint an additional representative party.

Where it is not appropriate for the trustees to argue in a particular interest, and there is difficulty in identifying a member of the class to act; a solicitor may sometimes be appointed to represent that interest. For instance, in *Sovereign Trustees Limited & Another v Philip F Glover & Others (2007) EWHC 1750 (Ch)* it was unclear where the interests of the representative beneficiaries lay on a particular issue. A solicitor was therefore joined as a defendant to argue as a representative party on one side of the question. Similarly, in *Walker Morris Trustees v Masterson (2009) EWHC 1955 (Ch)* solicitors ('professional representative beneficiaries') were appointed as first and second defendants.

In *Alexander Forbes Trustees Limited v Doe and Roe [2011] EWHC 3930 (Ch)* the fictional defendants John Doe and Richard Roe appeared as representative parties on a question of pure law (thereby eliminating the possibility of additional expense in addressing fact-sensitive issues in relation to real individual beneficiaries). Representation orders were made at an interim hearing by District Judge Williams, sitting in the Birmingham District Registry. At trial, however, Purle J held that, although there was no mischief in this case, the use of fictional defendants was unnecessary and undesirable.

Compromise with a representative party

16.40   If a representative party has been appointed, the court must give its approval to any compromise of the proceedings, and will only do so where it considers that the compromise is for the benefit of all the represented persons. Any judgment or order made by the court will bind all represented persons unless the court orders otherwise, but can only be enforced by or against a person who is not a party to the claim with the court's consent.

When applying for the court's approval of a settlement, it is common practice for each representative party to obtain a written legal opinion on the merits of the compromise, the purpose of which opinion is to assist the judge in his consideration of whether the settlement is for the benefit of all the persons represented. The opinion will, by agreement with the other parties, be seen only by the judge, and it is customary for counsel for the representative beneficiary to address the court on the opinion in the absence of the other parties.

It is important in the case of a compromise also to consider consultation with the persons represented (see **16.38** above).

A compromise does not therefore eliminate the need for a claim to come before the court. However, it can typically be approved at a short half-day hearing; legal costs are likely to be comparable with or less than those of a summary judgment application and significantly less than the cost of going to trial. Recent compromises approved by the court include *Grolier International Ltd v Capital Cranfield Trustees Ltd [2015] EWHC 1832 (Ch)* (change from DB to DC benefits) and *Archer v Travis Perkins Plc [2014] EWHC 1362 (Ch)* (equalisation).

Appeals

16.41   Appeals can also raise difficult issues, as the wider class may find it convenient for the representative party (who had a prospective costs order in the proceedings below) to appeal, although this may be at his own risk as to costs and possibly against his own inclination or interests. In *Chessels v British Telecom (2002) 05 PBLR* an application by a representative party for a further prospective costs order for an appeal was rejected. By contrast, in *IMG Pension Plan, Re [2010] EWHC 321 (Ch)* such an order was granted. For more details, see **16.50** below.

Group litigation

16.42   Where there are a number of individual claims by separate persons which all give rise to common or related issues of fact or law (eg claims by individual members of a pension scheme against the trustees for a breach of trust that has caused each of them loss and which has arisen out of the same facts), the court may order each of the cases to be managed together under a group litigation order. This should be distinguished from a representation order, where each person represented has the same interest in the outcome of a claim. A group litigation order ('GLO') is a useful and efficient mechanism in circumstances where the claims are individually small, but collectively large. In principle, it allows for an efficient and cost-effective method of determining the claims. (The detailed provisions relating to group litigation orders can be found in *CPR 19.11* and the related *Practice Direction 19B*.) GLOs have been used in cases relating to pensions. In 2004 transferred employees secured a GLO in actions against BT Pensions Group Limited, alleging diminished pension benefits as a result of representations made when the joint venture was set up; a GLO was made in similar actions against Ford in 2013 (see *Varney v Ford Motor Co Ltd [2013] EWHC 1226 (Ch)* for a summary of the background in a judgment of Asplin J). However, the occasions where such an order is appropriate are limited compared with the use of representation orders in pension schemes.

In recent years there has also been a growth in interest particularly from larger schemes in more sophisticated investment vehicles. GLOs have also been made in this context: in 2004 pension funds obtained a GLO in a group action over foreign income dividends carrying no right to a tax credit. Such third-party claims are in the first instance investment funds litigation rather than pension litigation and lie outside the scope of this chapter. However, trustees contemplating involvement in such a claim should consider carefully whether there are pensions-specific issues for them to consider, including the possible need for *Beddoe* relief (see **16.48** below).

Costs in litigation

16.43   The issue of costs is central to the assessment of whether or not to pursue or defend a claim, what strategy to adopt, in which forum the matter should be pursued, settlement considerations, and whether alternative dispute resolution methods should be explored. It is also an important factor that the court considers when it exercises its case management powers.

General principles

16.44   The court has a broad discretion to award costs (*Senior Courts Act 1981, s 51*). In deciding what costs order (if any) to make, the court will take into account all the circumstances, including the conduct of the parties before and during the litigation, whether a party was only partly successful and any offers of settlement (*CPR 44.4(3)*). The court may penalise a party by denying it costs where it does not approve of that party's conduct or where the party has recovered a lesser amount than a previous offer of settlement which it rejected. Where the court orders a party to pay another party's costs, the amount of those costs will be assessed by the court, unless it can be agreed between the parties.

The court may assess those costs summarily at the hearing itself, or conduct a separate detailed assessment of those costs after the hearing. In small claims track cases the court will only award limited costs and will assess those costs at the hearing. In fast-track cases the trial costs of the advocate that are awarded are also limited. In multi-track cases, there is no prescribed limit on the costs that can be recovered and the amount of those costs will be assessed by the court.

When ordering a party's costs to be assessed, the court will state the basis on which those costs will be assessed. There are two bases:

(a) *Standard basis*: This is the usual basis ordered. On this basis the court will only allow costs which are proportionate to the matters in issue and will resolve any doubt which it may have over a specific cost incurred in favour of the paying party.

(b) *Indemnity basis*: The court will resolve any doubt it may have over a specific cost incurred in the favour of the receiving party.

The receiving party can expect to recover more of its costs under the indemnity, rather than standard, basis. However, it is important for parties to appreciate that on neither basis is the receiving party ever likely to recover 100 per cent of its costs. Indeed, under the standard basis, the receiving party may recover as little as 60 per cent of its costs (or even less). This should be borne in mind at the outset of litigation and when considering offers of settlement.

The general rule followed by the court is that the winner's assessed costs are paid by the loser. In pensions cases involving third parties (see **16.17** above), this rule will usually apply. However, there are special rules that apply to trustees' costs and the costs of applications for directions brought in relation to the administration of a pension scheme. These are discussed below, in **16.46** onwards.

Costs budgeting

16.45 The overriding objective of the *Civil Procedure Rules* stated at *CPR 1.1(1)* provides for the court to deal with cases justly *and at proportionate cost*. Proportionality of cost will therefore be considered as a thread running through the court's case management. Specifically, where costs are assessed on the standard basis, the court will only allow costs which are proportionate to the matters in issue, and 'costs which are disproportionate in amount may be disallowed or reduced even if they were reasonably or necessarily incurred' (*CPR 44.3(2)(a)*). Proportionality is defined at *CPR 44.3(5)*.

Subject to certain exceptions (for very large value claims and certain divisions of the High Court), parties are required to file costs budgets. The court may reduce a party's budget (typically by reducing individual elements of the budget for particular future stages of litigation, eg the amount estimated for disclosure of documents, or for preparation of witness statements). Parties are held to their revised budgets in that any overspend may not be recoverable by a winning party from the losing party (although this does not affect the winning party's own contractual obligations to pay its advisers).

Where a party fails to file a costs budget, they are not entitled to recovery of any costs beyond court fees for the period after the budget is made (ie a nominal amount). The Mitchell case (*Mitchell v News Group [2014] 1 WLR 795*) held that this sanction also applies where a budget has been filed late and application for relief is made after the due date. The *Mitchell* decision has attracted some comment as being overly restrictive; some subsequent cases on late or imperfect filing or service of documents have suggested that the court may continue to take a more flexible view. However, Richards LJ in *Durrant v Avon and Somerset Constabulary (2013) EWCA Civ 1624* at 38 held that 'it is vital that decisions… which fail to follow the robust approach laid down in that case should not be allowed to stand.'

These cost management powers apply specifically to costs incurred after submission of a costs budget. It is therefore worthwhile for claimants to consider how to structure work on the claim, as in some cases it may be advantageous to complete as much as possible of the necessary analysis and document review before issuing proceedings. There are similar tactical considerations for claimants arising from the use of 'Part 36' offers, which require a payment of the claimant's costs.

Trustees' costs

16.46   Where a trustee is a party to proceedings in his capacity as trustee, as a general rule he is likely to be entitled to be paid his legal costs out of the trust fund (which may include costs that the trustee is ordered to pay to another party) to the extent that they are not recovered from or paid by another person (*CPR 46.3*) and provided they are properly incurred (*Practice Direction 46 paragraph 1.1*). In such cases, those costs will be assessed on the indemnity basis. The court may order otherwise if it considers that the trustee has, in all the circumstances, acted improperly. By way of example, in *Mark Niebuhr Tod v Judith Cobb Lady Barton & Others [2002] 2 WTLR 469*, the court disallowed a proportion of a trustee's costs which related to an application made by him which the court considered to be unnecessary.

Indemnity and power in trust deed

16.47   A pension scheme's trust deed may contain an indemnity clause which indemnifies the trustees against any costs and liabilities incurred in taking certain action for the benefit of the pension scheme. It may also give the trustees a power to agree to pay from the pension fund the costs of certain other parties to litigation. In the event that the trustees have, and exercise, such a power by agreeing to pay the costs of another party to the litigation (for example, in an application to court for directions), it is prudent for the trustees to enter into a formal agreement with that party stipulating what costs may be payable under that agreement and a mechanism for the trustees to control the level of costs incurred. The trustees' prior approval to large items of proposed expenditure (for example, expert witness fees, counsel's fees) should also prudently be sought by that party.

In applications to court concerning the administration of a pension scheme, if the trustees have and exercise properly a power to agree to pay the costs of another party to that application, the court will presume, when assessing the amounts of costs payable under that agreement, that (unless the agreement states otherwise) the costs have been reasonably incurred and are reasonable in amount (see *CPR 44.5*). In such a case, a prospective costs order (see **16.50** below) is not required and the trustees are entitled to recover out of the pension fund any costs of another party which they pay pursuant to such agreement (*para 6.2* of *Practice Direction A* to *CPR 64*). By contrast, where there is no express power under the scheme's trust deed to pay the costs of third parties, representative beneficiaries will typically seek a prospective costs order (see **16.50** below).

Beddoe orders

16.48   The proviso to the general rule entitling a trustee to an indemnity out of the trust fund for its costs (see **16.46** above) is that the costs must have been 'properly incurred'. If they are improperly incurred, a trustee may incur personal liability for those costs. To determine what costs are properly incurred, the court will examine all the circumstances of the case including whether the trustee obtained the court's directions before bringing or defending proceedings, acted in the interests of the scheme or some other interest or conducted himself unreasonably. If trustees propose to commence or defend proceedings against or by a third party, they are able to protect themselves from this risk of personal liability by applying at an early stage for the court's directions on their proposed course of action (this is known as a '*Beddoe*' application, following the Court of Appeal judgment in *Re Beddoe, Downes v Cottam [1893] 1 Ch 547*). If the court sanctions the proposed action, the trustees can proceed in the comfort that the court regards their action as being proper and reasonable.

A *Beddoe* application is treated as a directions application under *CPR Part 64* (see **16.19** above). The application must be made in separate proceedings under the *Part 8* procedure (see **16.29** above). The trustees should be the claimant and a representative beneficiary should be put in place. In the event that a party will be party to the main proceedings and the *Beddoe* application and has an interest which conflicts with that of the trustees, the trustees should exercise care not to disclose to that party privileged information (for example, the legal advice of the trustees' lawyer), and that party may be excluded from all or part of any hearing of the *Beddoe* application.

In a *Beddoe* application, the court is asked to express its view on whether the action proposed by the trustees is proper. To enable the court to express a considered view, the trustees' application should be supported by evidence (in the form of witness statements) giving full disclosure of, among other things, the proposed course of action and the strengths and weaknesses of the trustees' case.

This means that the trustees must include in their evidence a statement as to whether there has been compliance with the pre-action protocols and proposals for ADR; the advice of an appropriately qualified lawyer on the prospects of success; estimates of the value of the issue and costs likely to be incurred for each stage in the proceedings and any potential costs liabilities to which the trustees may be exposed; any known facts concerning the means of the other parties to the proceedings, and other relevant matters to be taken into account, including a draft of any proposed statement of case (see *Practice Direction B to CPR Part 64*).

If the trustees fail to reveal in full to the court the strengths and weaknesses of their case, they may expose themselves to personal liability, even if the court grants the *Beddoe* order sought.

The *Beddoe* application will be dealt with on paper, without the need for a hearing where possible (*paragraph 7.8(2) of Practice Direction B to CPR Part 64*). If the court allows the trustees to pursue the litigation proposed, it may do so only up to a particular stage in the litigation, thereby requiring the trustees to make a further *Beddoe* application in order to proceed beyond that stage.

Lord Justice Jackson in his review of litigation costs questioned whether too many *Beddoe* applications are made from an abundance of caution. Trustees should consider carefully, with their legal advisers, the appropriateness of incurring the expense of making a *Beddoe* application. Equally, trustees should have regard to the uncertainties of litigation, even in the most apparently clear cut of cases, and the risk that if *Beddoe* consent is not sought prior to taking a step, the trustees may be held personally liable for their costs (unless they can prove to the satisfaction of the court that they were properly incurred). An assessment of the risk of proceeding without *Beddoe* protection must, therefore, be made by trustees with their legal advisers at the outset. One alternative to incurring the costs of a *Beddoe* application may be for the trustees to seek an indemnity from the employer, particularly if the employer is ultimately liable under the pension scheme's trust deed to make up any shortfall in the assets of the fund.

Beneficiaries' costs

16.49   The indemnity enjoyed by trustees (which is discussed in **16.46** above) is not shared by beneficiaries who are parties to proceedings. However, the court has traditionally sought to divide trust litigation into three categories when considering which party should pay the costs of those proceedings (following the decision in *Re Buckton, Buckton v Buckton [1907] 2 Ch 406*):

(*a*)   Proceedings brought by trustees for the court's guidance on the construction of the trust deed or a question arising in the course of the trust's administration. In such cases, the costs of all parties are usually treated as 'necessarily incurred for the benefit of the fund' and ordered to be paid out of the fund on an indemnity basis (such an application is usually brought under *CPR Part 64*).

(*b*)   Applications which are brought by someone other than the trustees, but which raise the types of issues as in (*a*) above and would have justified an application by the trustees. In this case, the costs are also usually treated as being 'necessarily incurred for the benefit of the fund' and ordered to be paid out of the fund on an indemnity basis (whilst such an application may be made under *CPR Part 64, Practice Direction B to CPR Part 64* only relates to applications made by trustees, and not other parties).

(*c*)   Proceedings in which a beneficiary is making a hostile claim against trustees or another beneficiary. The costs of such proceedings are usually treated in the same way as ordinary litigation and the winner's costs are usually paid by the loser, unless the winner has, in some way, conducted himself inappropriately in connection with the litigation or is only a partial winner or has failed to win more than a previous offer of settlement from the loser.

These are known as *Buckton* categories 1, 2 and 3 and the court still deems these general guidelines applicable, albeit that it now takes a more robust attitude towards costs (*D'Abo v Paget (No 2) [2000] WTLR 863*). There is a costs risk to both the trustees and the beneficiaries in the third category of claims, which is a principal reason why trustees generally seek *Beddoe* consent before pursuing or defending such proceedings, and why beneficiaries prefer to avoid such costs risk and pursue their complaints through the PO. It is often difficult, in practice, to assess whether a particular claim is a category 2 or 3 type claim, but given the costs consequences, it is important to reach a conclusion before embarking upon the litigation.

In the case of *Singapore Airlines Ltd and another v Buck Consultants Ltd [2011] EWCA Civ 1542* the Court of Appeal have added a fourth category to the *Buckton* categories. In that case, Singapore Airlines took a negligence action against Buck. A point of construction of the scheme rules was taken as a preliminary issue and was resolved in favour of Buck. The Court of Appeal held that, had it not been for the third party, the costs would have fallen in category 2. Where a third party and a beneficiary pursued an issue of construction, the principled approach was to share costs between the parties. Singapore Airlines should therefore pay Buck's costs on the standard basis, and half of the difference between standard and indemnity costs should also be paid to Buck from the scheme.

Prospective costs orders

16.50 Whilst the principles in *Buckton* provide a useful guide to what the likely costs order will be at the conclusion of the proceedings, a party may require greater comfort at the outset of the proceedings that its costs will be paid out of the fund no matter what the outcome of the proceedings. For example, a representative beneficiary may not wish to become a party in the proceedings if there is a risk that he will incur a personal liability for his, and other parties', costs of the proceedings. In applications to the court concerning the administration of a trust (ie under *CPR Part 64* – see **16.19** above), if the trustees do not have, or decide not to exercise, a power to agree to pay the costs of another party to the application, the trustees or the party concerned may apply to the court for an order that the costs of any party (including the trustees) shall be paid out of the assets of the pension scheme. These are known as 'prospective costs orders' (formerly as 'pre-emptive costs orders') and provide the applicant with the comfort that his costs of the proceedings will be paid, no matter what the outcome of the proceedings.

In *Buckton* category 1 and 2 cases (see **16.49** above) at the conclusion of the case the court will usually follow the general rule that the parties' costs (including those of any beneficiary) are paid out of the assets of the pension scheme. This makes the grant of a prospective costs order at an earlier stage in the case less problematic. A difficulty arises, however, in *Buckton* category 3 cases (hostile claims against the trustees). This is because in *Buckton* category 3 cases, the general rule is that the loser pays the winner's costs. This makes it difficult to make an assessment at any time prior to the full trial as to the likely outcome and therefore the likely costs order the court would make. In the leading case of *McDonald v Horn [1995] 1 All ER 961* the court overcame this difficulty by deciding that an action by a member of a pension scheme to compel the trustees or others to account to the fund was analogous to what is known as a 'derivative action' by a minority shareholder on behalf of a company. In those circumstances a minority shareholder was entitled to a prospective costs order under the principle in *Wallersteiner v Moir (No 2) [1975] 1 All ER 849*. On this basis, the court held that a member of a pension scheme could also be entitled, by analogy, to a prospective costs order in those circumstances. When deciding whether to exercise its discretion to make such an order, the court has in each case a duty, under the *CPR*, to give effect to the overriding objective of dealing with cases justly. This includes ensuring, so far as possible, that the parties are on an equal footing and dealing with the case in a way which is proportionate to the financial position of each party. Such factors are particularly relevant in the pensions context, as the beneficiary who is a party to the case can often be a pensioner with limited financial resources.

Further guidance was given by the court in *Laws v National Grid [1998] PLR 295* where it considered that a prospective costs order should be made where the amount of money in issue is large, the matter in issue affects a large number of persons, the case involves difficult issues of law or fact, and the person applying for the order has substantial support from others in a similar position. In the subsequent case of *Chessels & ors v BT plc & ors [2002] PLR 141*, the court refused to grant a prospective costs order to a beneficiary to whom it had granted permission to appeal the court's judgment. The court followed the principle that prospective costs orders indemnifying a third party should only be made where the court is satisfied that no other orders can properly be made by the court which is to hear the substantive proceedings. The appeal in this case would, if successful, only benefit a relatively small number of beneficiaries of the scheme, was not for the benefit of the scheme as a whole, and was hostile litigation of the *Buckton* category 3 type in which the court usually awards the winner his costs. The court also reiterated the principle that the fact that the pension scheme had substantial assets, and was in surplus, was not relevant to whether or not it should grant the prospective costs order. The case of *IMG Pension Plan, Re [2010] EWHC 321 (Ch)* shed doubt on the 'only order the court could make' test. In the *IMG* case, the court understood the decision in *McDonald* to mean that: 'a claim by a member of a pension fund to compel trustees or others to account to the fund was different to ordinary trust litigation ... Accordingly, in such a case the court had a discretion to make a prospective costs order even though such an order could not be justified on *Buckton* principles ...' This may open up the prospect of prospective costs orders in circumstances where, on *Chessels* principles, they would not be available.

Applications for prospective costs orders can be made at any time during the proceedings but are usually made at the outset, or before a hearing. An order may be made in favour of a prospective representative beneficiary before a representation order is made (*IBM United Kingdom Pensions Trust Ltd v Metcalfe [2012] EWHC 125 (Ch)*). In the witness statement supporting the application the trustees and the applicant (if different) must give full disclosure of the relevant matters which show that the case is one which falls within the category of cases where a prospective costs order can properly be made. Ordinarily, the court will seek to deal with such an application on paper, without the need for an oral hearing, but if the trustees or any other party think a hearing should be held, they should set out their reasons in the evidence that they file at court. A model form of prospective costs order for straightforward cases is set out in the court's *Practice Direction A* to *CPR Part 64*. It allows for a party's solicitor to request from the trustees monthly sums on account and for that party's costs to be subject to a detailed assessment by the court on the indemnity basis, unless agreed. It also indemnifies the party against any costs that it is ordered to pay to another party to the proceedings. When granting a prospective costs order the court may set a limit on the costs to be paid (as in *Re AXA Equity & Law Life Assurance Society plc (No 1) [2001] 2 BCLC 447*).

Alternative dispute resolution

Introduction

16.51   Alternative dispute resolution ('ADR') is the generic phrase used to describe alternative means of resolving a dispute other than by a trial in court. The use of ADR has developed rapidly in recent years and its importance is actively promoted by the courts. Under the *CPR*, the court is obliged when using its active case management powers to encourage parties to use an ADR procedure if it considers it appropriate and to facilitate the use of such procedure (*CPR 1.4(2)(e)*). Further, when trustees apply for *Beddoe* approval concerning actual or possible litigation, they are required to state, in the witness statement they prepare in support of their application, whether they have proposed or undertaken, or intend to propose, mediation by ADR, and if not why not (*paragraph 7.5 of Practice Direction B to CPR Part 64*).

In the case of *Halsey v Milton Keynes General NHS Trust [2004] EWCA Civ 576, [2004] All ER (D) 125*, the Court of Appeal provided some guidelines on the court's approach to ADR (mediation in particular) and to penalising parties who fail to agree to pursue ADR. In summary:

(*a*)   Although the court may encourage parties to seek to resolve a dispute through ADR in the strongest terms, it would not order parties to undertake ADR against their will.

(*b*)   As an exception to the general rule that the loser would be ordered to pay the winner's costs, the court may penalise a party, by making an alternative costs order, if that party has acted unreasonably in refusing to agree to ADR.

(*c*)   The burden is on the loser to show why the winner acted unreasonably.

(*d*)   In deciding whether a party had acted unreasonably in refusing to agree to ADR, the court will consider the following, non-exhaustive factors:

   •   Is the nature of the dispute suitable for ADR? Not every dispute is suitable for ADR, for example, a directions application concerning the construction of the pensions deed may be unsuitable for settlement.

- What are the merits of the case? A party, who reasonably believes that he has a strong case, may reasonably not wish to compromise his position through ADR.

- Have any other settlement methods been attempted before? A history of unsuccessful attempts at resolving the dispute may justify a decision not to agree to ADR.

- What are the likely costs of ADR? If the costs of ADR are likely to be disproportionately high, this may justify a party not agreeing to it.

- Will ADR cause unreasonable delay? Pursuing ADR will require the commencement or continuation of proceedings to be stayed which may cause unreasonable delay to the resolution of the dispute.

- Will ADR have a reasonable prospect of success? The more remote the prospect of ADR resulting in a settlement, the more reasonable a court is likely to regard a refusal by one party to agree to ADR.

(e)   All members of the legal profession should routinely consider with their clients whether their client's disputes are suitable for ADR.

These principles have been applied by the court in subsequent cases. For example, in *P4 Ltd v Unite Integrated Solutions plc [2006] EWHC 2924 (TCC)*, the court made a costs order in favour of a party which made only a nominal recovery, in part because of its opponent's unreasonable failure to mediate. Similarly, in *Garritt-Critchley v Ronnan [2014] EWHC 1774 Ch* the court ordered costs on the indemnity basis against the losing party as a result of their unreasonable failure to engage in mediation. By contrast, in *Daniels v Commissioner of Police for the Metropolis [2005] EWCA Civ 1312*, the Court of Appeal applied the *Halsey* decision and decided that where a defendant, particularly a public body, regularly faced unmeritorious claims which it chose to contest rather than settle, the court would be slow to view such conduct as being unreasonable. In *Re Midland Linen Services Ltd sub nom Chaudry v Yap & Ors [2005] EWHC 3380 (Ch)*, even though a party had offered mediation which was refused by the other party, the court viewed the refusal to mediate as not being unreasonable because it was questionable whether the party offering the mediation was sufficiently serious in pursuing it and, given the relationship between the parties, whether a mediation would have resulted in a resolution. These cases demonstrate that the court will consider the facts of each case in deciding whether there has been unreasonable conduct. The factors to be taken into account were considered further in *Corby Group Litigation v Corby DC [2009] EWHC 2109 (TCC)*.

Types of ADR

16.52 There are different forms of ADR, but the principal ones are as follows:

(*a*) *Mediation.* This is the most common form of ADR. It is a private, without prejudice process of negotiation between the parties, facilitated by an independent qualified mediator. It is non-binding so that a settlement can only be achieved if the parties agree. It is discussed in more detail below.

(*b*) *Conciliation.* This is a more formal form of mediation, and often involves the use of a formal conciliation service (such as Acas). The 'conciliator' will often take an active role (ie proffering his views) in the negotiations.

(*c*) *Expert determination.* This is where the parties agree to refer a (usually) technical issue in dispute for a binding determination by an independent expert. For instance, a pension scheme's trust deed or rules may provide for an actuarial issue to be determined by an independent actuary, or the pensions schedule in a sale and purchase agreement may provide for expert determination in the case of disputes.

(*d*) *Adjudication.* Like an expert determination, this usually involves the parties agreeing to submit the dispute for determination by a neutral third party (for example, a retired judge or experienced lawyer).

(*e*) *Arbitration.* The process of arbitration takes place in a statutory framework which sets out various rules of conduct. It is common for commercial contracts to contain 'arbitration clauses' which require all disputes to be referred to arbitration. The arbitrator is usually a suitably qualified independent third party who determines the dispute, acting as a judge. The procedure can closely mirror that of court litigation. It is designed to be flexible and less procedural than court litigation. However, it is often regarded as being as time consuming and expensive as court proceedings.

Mediation

16.53 Mediation is the most common formal ADR process adopted to settle disputes (in practice it is rare for a pensions dispute to be settled other than by mediation or informal negotiation). Once the parties to a dispute have agreed to mediation, the next step is to appoint a mediator. A number of traditional barristers' chambers, law firms and 'mediation chambers' arrange appointments for experienced mediators (typically QCs or current or former partners in law firms who are also accredited mediators).

The costs of the mediator(s) (there can be more than one if the parties wish) are usually borne equally by the parties. The costs of the mediation can be substantial as they may include the costs of the mediator, room hire and the costs of the parties' lawyers in preparing for and attending at the mediation. Before the mediation takes place, it is common for each party to exchange brief summaries of their case, if necessary accompanied by supporting documents. The mediation is usually attended by a senior person from each party who has the authority to negotiate and enter into a settlement agreement. The mediation often commences by each party giving an oral summary of its case to the other party in front of the mediator. The mediator may ask questions to clarify a point. Each party then retires to its own private room, and the mediator will visit each party in turn to discuss the structure of a possible settlement and the issues which each party should consider as part of the negotiations. Through this process of 'shuttle diplomacy' the mediator can gauge what possible terms of settlement may be agreeable to the parties and make appropriate suggestions to the parties to facilitate a settlement. As the process is without prejudice and non-binding, a settlement will only be achieved if both parties agree to it. A mediation can often lead to a settlement being signed on the day (in which case the parties may need to be prepared to remain at the mediation for a very long day). However, even where there is no agreement on the day, the mediation may lead to subsequent settlement, and a good mediator will try to keep in touch with the parties to help facilitate this.

Practical considerations

16.54   Pension disputes between trustees/employers and third parties are usually hostile and involve a claim for damages, and in such cases, ADR (specifically mediation) may provide an efficient means of resolving the dispute, thereby avoiding the costs and risk of litigation. As stated above, trustees who seek a *Beddoe* order are required to tell the court whether a mediation has been or will be proposed. This means that trustees must factor into their consideration from the outset the potential for a mediation (or other appropriate form of ADR) as the court is likely to be interested. Further, trustees who have the benefit of a *Beddoe* order (see **16.48** above), may wish or need to seek the court's approval of any settlement (although trustees have a power under *Trustee Act 1925, s 15* to enter into a settlement), in which case this should be made clear to the other parties and may affect the choice of ADR method.

Claims against trustees by individual members may also be amenable to ADR, even if those disputes have been referred to the PO rather than the court.

Some applications, by their nature, are not suitable to negotiated settlement. Directions applications (see **16.19** above) are not always suitable for resolution in this way as the trustees are requesting the court's approval of a proposed transaction or are surrendering their discretion to the court. Rectification and construction claims may be amenable to compromise depending on the nature of the relief sought. Where ADR is possible, there are a number of practical issues which will require consideration, including the following:

(*a*)   Trustees will usually want to avoid negotiating with all the beneficiaries under the pension scheme, not only for logistical reasons but also the difficulty of reaching agreement with all of them. To facilitate negotiations trustees may, therefore, seek the appointment of a representative party with whom they may negotiate. This necessitates the commencement of proceedings prior to ADR being commenced.

(*b*)   Where a settlement is agreed, the trustees may seek the court's approval to that settlement (for example, if a *Beddoe* order has been granted or is sought, or where a representative party has been appointed).

Whilst such factors may provide practical hurdles to be overcome in order for ADR to lead to a successful resolution of the dispute, the advantages of ADR (notably, the potential for a relatively quick, private and less costly settlement of the dispute at an early stage) may justify its use as a means of resolving the dispute. If a party is considering rejecting an offer of ADR, it should first consider the guidelines given by the court in *Halsey*. This may assist in an assessment of whether the rejection is likely to be considered unreasonable, as a refusal to agree to ADR could potentially expose that party to costs sanctions by the court.

Chapter 17

Taxation of registered schemes

Section A: Introduction

17.1   This chapter is intended to give an outline of the tax treatment of registered pension schemes, including both occupational and personal pension schemes. The tax treatment of non-registered pension schemes is considered from **17.116** below.

The previous eight pension taxation regimes were replaced by a single integrated pension tax regime from 6 April 2006 ('A-Day') which applies to all 'registered pension schemes'. The provisions are contained in *FA 2004* (as amended by subsequent Finance Acts and supplemented by regulations) and follow the proposals outlined in the joint HM Treasury and HMRC consultation paper, 'Simplifying the taxation of pensions; increasing choice and flexibility for all', published December 2002. The concept is simple. Tax relievable contributions can be made to build up benefits in a tax approved environment up to a lifetime allowance. There is nothing to stop tax relievable contributions being made to enable an individual to build up benefits with a value in excess of this allowance but, if it is exceeded, there is an additional tax charge on any excess when the benefits come into payment. All types of registered pension scheme are able to pay members any type of payment which is treated as an authorised member payment under *FA 2004*. If an unauthorised member payment is made there can be penal tax charges. Details of how HMRC operates the regime in practice can be found in the Pensions Tax Manual ('PTM'), available at www.hmrc.gov.uk. The PTM replaced the previous Registered Pension Schemes Manual ('RPSM') in December 2015.

Following an announcement in the Budget on 19 March 2014, an HM Treasury consultation paper, 'Freedom and choice in pensions' was published. This consultation paper, together with announcements made in the briefing notes accompanying the subsequent Queen's Speech on 4 June 2014, set out proposals for significant further changes to the taxation regime for registered pension schemes. These changes were made by amendments to *FA 2004* by the *Taxation of Pensions Act 2014* (*TPA 2014*). The most important changes are that, from 6 April 2015:

(*a*) individuals aged 55 or over with defined contribution pension savings are able to withdraw those savings as they wish, subject to their marginal rate of income tax and scheme rules;

(*b*) death benefits can now generally be paid tax-free either in lump sum or pension form on the death of a member before age 75 as long as they are paid within the permitted two-year period. Income tax (or in certain cases a freestanding 45 per cent tax charge) is generally payable at the recipient's marginal rate on lump-sum death benefit and annuity and drawdown payments on deaths on or after 75;

(*c*) there has been a further reduction in the lifetime allowance from £1.25 million to £1 million;

(*d*) there are also new restrictions on the amount of annual allowance available for higher earners and in cases where a member has accessed the new defined contribution flexibilities.

Treatment of former tax approved schemes

17.2 Pension schemes which were already tax approved before A-Day automatically became registered schemes from A-Day unless they took action to opt out (*FA 2004, Sch 36, paras 1, 2*). This included:

(*a*) Private sector defined benefits and defined contributions retirement benefit schemes that were previously approved on a discretionary basis under *Income and Corporation Taxes Act 1988, Part XIV, Chapter I ('ICTA 1988')*.

(*b*) Relevant statutory schemes (more commonly known as public sector schemes) defined in *ICTA 1988, s 611A*, such as the Local Government Pension Scheme.

(*c*) Certain deferred annuity contracts used to secure pension benefits under (*a*) and (*b*) that do not provide for the immediate payment of benefits. These deferred annuity contracts were not previously approved before A-Day.

(*d*) Retirement annuity contracts or retirement annuity trust schemes previously approved under *ICTA 1988, s 620* or *621* or a substituted contract within the meaning of *ICTA 1988, s 622(3)*. These were the only type of policy that could be taken out by the self-employed and individuals without access to an occupational pension scheme before personal pension schemes were introduced with effect from 1 July 1988.

(*e*) Personal pension schemes previously approved under *ICTA 1988, Part XIV, Chapter IV*, which includes most stakeholder pension schemes and group personal pension schemes.

(*f*) Former approved superannuation funds (often referred to as 'old code schemes'). These schemes were approved before 1970 but had not been re-approved as new code occupational pension schemes.

Application to become a registered pension scheme after A-Day

17.3 Any new pension scheme established on or after A-Day is required to make an application to HMRC to be registered (*FA 2004, s 153*). The application is made by the person who will become the scheme administrator.

An application to register must contain any information reasonably required by HMRC and must be accompanied by a declaration that the application is made by the scheme administrator and any other declarations reasonably required by HMRC (*FA 2004, ss 153(2), 270*).

Registration is made online through the completion of a form by the proposed scheme administrator.

HMRC has expressed its commitment to combatting pension liberation activity (see **Chapter 6**). From 21 October 2013, HMRC made the pension scheme registration process more robust by moving away from a 'process now, check later' approach. Scheme registration is no longer confirmed on successful submission of the online form. HMRC now conduct detailed risk assessment activity before deciding whether or not to register a pension scheme. As part of this risk assessment HMRC has, from 20 March 2014, taken into consideration whether or not it appears to them that the pension scheme has been established for the main purpose of providing authorised benefits. A new information power was inserted into *FA 2004* (by *FA 2014*) which allows HMRC to issue a notice to the scheme administrator or other person requiring them to provide to HMRC any information or document that is in the person's possession or power to provide, that HMRC may reasonably require to decide whether or not the pension scheme should be registered.

Additionally, from 1 September 2014, there is a requirement for the scheme administrator to be a fit and proper person (inserted as *FA 2004, s 159A*). If it appears to HMRC that the scheme administrator is not a fit and proper person, they may refuse to register a new pension scheme, or in the case of a registered pension scheme, de-register that scheme. HMRC also have information powers, including powers to inspect documents to enable HMRC to consider whether the scheme administrator is fit and proper version.

An application to register a pension scheme may be made only if the pension scheme is an occupational pension scheme or has been established by a person with permission under *FSMA 2000* to establish a personal pension or stakeholder scheme.

There is no longer a requirement in the tax legislation that the only type of occupational pension scheme that can be registered as a registered pension scheme is one set up under irrevocable trusts. However, this has been replaced by an equivalent requirement in *PA 2004* that if an occupational pension scheme has its main administration in the UK, the trustees or managers of the scheme cannot accept any payment to fund benefits for or in respect of its members unless the scheme is established under irrevocable trusts (*PA 2004, s 252*). The trustees or managers can be liable to penalties if they accept a funding payment to an occupational pension scheme in breach of this requirement.

An occupational pension scheme that does not restrict membership to its own employees can be a registered pension scheme and can include employees of other non-associated employers. Before A-Day the general rule was that a non-sectionalised occupational pension scheme had to restrict membership to employees of associated employers to obtain and retain exempt approved status.

The scheme administrator of a pension scheme that is registered on or after A-Day is the person or persons appointed in accordance with the rules of the pension scheme to be responsible for the discharge of the functions conferred or imposed on the scheme administrator of the pension scheme under *FA 2004, Part 4* (*FA 2004, s 270*). A person or persons can only become the scheme administrator if the person or one of the persons is resident in the UK or another EU member state, or a non-EU EEA member state and has made the required declaration to HMRC. The required declaration is that the person:

(*a*) understands that the person will be responsible for discharging the functions conferred or imposed on the scheme administrator of the pension scheme under *FA 2004, Part 4*; and

(*b*) intends to discharge those functions at all times, whether resident in the UK or another EU member state or a non-EU EEA member state.

Responsibilities of the scheme administrator

17.4   The scheme administrator is responsible for the discharge of certain functions under *FA 2004* (see from **17.76** below on scheme administration) and is liable to pay certain tax charges (*FA 2004, ss 270–274*). In certain circumstances, the trustees of the registered pension scheme or, failing that, certain other persons who fall next down a statutory priority order set out in *FA 2004, s 272* (including the sponsoring employer of an occupational pension scheme) can be liable as scheme administrator if:

(*a*) there is no scheme administrator; or

(*b*) the scheme administrator cannot be traced; or

(*c*) the scheme administrator is in serious default.

There are further default provisions under *FA 2004, s 273* which can make members of the pension scheme liable as scheme administrator in certain circumstances to pay the tax that was due under *s 239* (scheme sanction charge) or *s 242* (de-registration charge).

Finding your way round FA 2004

17.5 *FA 2004* was amended before it came into force by *FA 2005* and has been amended since by successive Finance Acts.

The main provisions relating to pensions in *FA 2004, Part 4* are as follows:

(*a*)   *Chapter 1* (Introduction) – defines some key concepts used in *FA 2004*, some of which are discussed below (*ss 149–152*);

(*b*)   *Chapter 2* – registration and deregistration of pension schemes (*ss 153–159D*);

(*c*)   *Chapter 3* –payments that may be made by registered pension schemes and related matters (*ss 160–185J*);

(*d*)   *Chapter 4* – tax reliefs and exemptions (*ss 186–203*);

(*e*)   *Chapter 5* – tax charges in connection with registered pension schemes (*ss 204–242*);

(*f*)   *Chapter 6* – schemes that are not registered schemes (*ss 243–249*);

(*g*)   *Chapter 7* – compliance (*ss 250–274*);

(*h*)   *Chapter 8* – interpretation and other supplementary provisions (*ss 274A–284*).

The schedules relating to the tax treatment of registered pension schemes are as follows:

(i)   *Schedule 28* – Registered pension schemes: authorised pensions – supplementary:

  • *Part 1* – Pension Rules;

  • *Part 2* – Pension Death Benefit Rules;

(ii)   *Schedule 29* – Registered pension schemes: authorised pensions – supplementary:

  • *Part 1* – Lump Sum Rule;

  • *Part 2* – Lump Sum Death Benefit Rule;

(iii)   Schedule 29A – Taxable Property held by investment-regulated pension schemes;

- *Part 1* – Investment-regulated pension schemes;

- *Part 2* – Taxable property;

- *Part 3* – Acquisition and holding of taxable property;

- *Part 4* – Amount and timing of unauthorised payment;

(iv) *Schedule 30* –Registered pension schemes: employer loans;

(v) *Schedule 31* – Taxation of benefits under registered pension schemes;

(vi) *Schedule 32* – Registered pension schemes: benefit crystallisation events – supplementary;

(vii) *Schedule 33* – Overseas pension schemes: migrant member relief;

(viii) *Schedule 34* – Non-UK schemes: application of certain charges;

(ix) *Schedule 35* – Pension schemes etc: minor and consequential changes;

(x) *Schedule 36* – Pension schemes etc: transitional provisions and savings:

- *Part 1* – Pre-commencement pension schemes;

- *Part 2* – Pre-commencement rights: lifetime allowance charge;

- *Part 3* – Pre-commencement benefit rights;

- *Part 4* – Other provisions.

Key definitions

17.6   *FA 2004* makes use of certain key definitions set out in *ss 150–152* that are, in the main, borrowed or adapted from pre-A-Day requirements. Other important *FA 2004* definitions can be found in *ss 275–280*, and are discussed later in the Chapter.

'Arrangement' in relation to a member of a pension scheme, means an arrangement relating to the member under the pension scheme (*FA 2004, s 152*). Arrangement is a concept borrowed from the regime that applied to personal pension schemes before A-Day and is now applied generally to all types of registered pension schemes. Typically personal pension schemes were set up before A-Day so that the funds invested on behalf of the member were divided into multiple arrangements so that the member could just vest part of his benefits at any one time. Under the current regime it is possible to have multiple arrangements under an occupational pension scheme that vest at different times. There are different types of arrangement, the main ones being 'money purchase arrangements' (which are sub-divided into 'cash balance arrangements' and 'other money purchase arrangements') and 'defined benefits arrangements'.

'Occupational pension scheme' means a pension scheme established by an employer or employers and having or capable of having effect so as to provide benefits to or in respect of any or all of the employees of:

(*a*)   that employer or those employers;

(*b*)   any other employer,

whether or not it also has or is capable of having effect so as to provide benefits to or in respect of other persons (*FA 2004, s 150(5)*).

The definition of 'occupational pension scheme' is extended to include a pension scheme:

(*a*)   established–

(i)   for the purpose of providing benefits to, or in respect of, people with service in the employment of a participating employer, or

(ii)   for that purpose and also for the purpose of providing benefits to, or in respect of, other people;

(*b*)   that has its main administration in the United Kingdom or outside the EEA states; and

(*c*)   the terms of which provide that each participating employer is a contributor to the scheme.

(The *Pension Schemes (Categories) Regulations 2005 (SI 2005/2401*)

There have been a number of cases brought by independent trustees where guidance has been sought on whether a pension scheme used for the purposes of 'pension liberation' was a genuine occupational pension schemes. In *Pi Consulting v Pension Regulator [2013] EWHC 3181 (Ch)* it was held that in determining whether a pension arrangement fell within the definition of occupational pension scheme, the issue is whether the scheme meets two tests: (i) a purpose test; and (ii) an establishment test.

In relation to the purpose test the court held that the purpose of the scheme was key, rather than the intention of those establishing the scheme. This had to be considered objectively, based on the scheme documentation. A scheme can meet the purpose test where the documentation is drafted with the purpose of providing benefits as envisaged by the legislation. In relation to the establishment test, the court must consider both whether the sponsor of the scheme needs to employ someone of the relevant description at the time the scheme is established; and also whether the sponsor did employ such a person at that time. The court held that if was not essential for the sponsor to have any actual employees in the conventional sense at the time the scheme is established. It was enough that the directors of the founding company themselves are 'employed' by the founding company, even where they were not remunerated.

'Pension scheme' means a scheme or other 'arrangements', comprised in one or more instruments or agreements, having or capable of having effect so as to provide benefits to or in respect of persons:

(*a*)   on retirement;

(*b*)   on death;

(*c*)   having reached a particular age;

(*d*)   on the onset of serious ill-health or incapacity; or

(*e*)   in similar circumstances (*FA 2004, s 150(1)*).

A pension scheme is a 'registered pension scheme' at any time if it is registered under *FA 2004, Part 4, Chapter 2* (*FA 2004, s 150(2)*).

'Personal pension scheme' is not defined in *FA 2004*. The term is not used as the provisions relating to registered pension schemes apply at an arrangement level. The definition of 'personal pension scheme' under *PSA 1993* provides that:

(*a*)   it is not an occupational pension scheme; and

(*b*)   it is established by a person with permission under *FSMA 2000* to establish a personal pension scheme (*FA 2004, s 154(1)*).

The lifetime allowance and benefit crystallisation events

17.7   The tax regime sets a personal lifetime allowance for all pension savings in registered pension schemes. The standard lifetime allowance was initially set at £1.5 million for the tax year 2006/2007 and that applicable to the following four tax years was contained in an order made by HM Treasury (*Registered Pension Schemes (Standard Lifetime and Annual Allowance Order 2007 (SI 2007/494)*). For the tax year 2010/2011 the standard lifetime allowance stood at £1.8 million and was set to be frozen at this amount for the following five years (*Registered Pension Schemes (Standard Lifetime and Annual Allowances Order 2010 (S1 2010/922)* – now revoked)). However, legislation was introduced to reduce the standard lifetime allowance to £1.5 million to with effect from the tax year 2012/2013 and to £1.25 million with effect from the tax year 2014/2015 (*FA 2004, s 218(2)*). *FA 2016* (which received royal assent on 15 September 2016) reduces the standard lifetime allowance to £1 million for the tax years 2016/2017 and 2017/2018, with the lifetime allowance being indexed in line with increases in the CPI in subsequent tax years.

17.7 *Taxation of registered schemes*

The lifetime allowance available to an individual can be increased in certain circumstances by multiplying the standard lifetime allowance by a lifetime allowance enhancement factor (see **17.10** and **17.11** below).

The amount of the individual's lifetime allowance available is tested on each 'benefit crystallisation' event occurring in relation to an individual (see **17.14** below). For money purchase arrangements the amount applied under a pension policy or under the member's account to provide pension or other benefits on a benefit crystallisation event will be tested against the individual's lifetime allowance (Benefit Crystallisation Event 4 – *FA 2004, s 216*). For defined benefits arrangements, a pension coming into payment is valued using a standard valuation factor of 20:1 (Benefit Crystallisation Event 2 – *FA 2004, ss 216, 276*), although a scheme specific factor can be used with the agreement of HMRC. For example, when a defined benefits pension of £25,000 comes into payment, it will be valued at £500,000 for the purpose of assessing how much of the lifetime allowance is available. On a benefit crystallisation event occurring, the member's lifetime allowance is then reduced by the percentage of the lifetime allowance used up. So, in the previous example, if the pension of £25,000 per annum came into payment in the tax year 2014/2015 when the standard lifetime allowance of £1.25 million was available, this will have used up 40 per cent of the member's standard lifetime allowance. 60 per cent of the lifetime allowance will still be available on future benefit crystallisation events.

When pension benefits come into payment, the member will need to be informed of the percentage of the lifetime allowance that is being used up. The member will then need to confirm whether he has sufficient lifetime allowance remaining after taking into account other pension benefits that have already come into payment. If the pension provided by the scheme takes the member over the lifetime allowance (or if the lifetime allowance has already been used up), then the benefits will be subject to a lifetime allowance charge (*FA 2004, s 214*). The lifetime allowance charge for sums in excess of the lifetime allowance will be 25 per cent, or 55 per cent if the excess funds are taken as a lump sum (*FA 2004, s 215*).

The scheme administrator and the member will generally be jointly and severally liable to pay the lifetime allowance charge (*FA 2004, s 217(1)*). However, when a benefit paid on the death of a member gives rise to a lifetime allowance charge, the person to whom the benefit is paid is liable (*FA 2004, s 217(2)*).

In practice (other than in death benefit cases), the scheme administrator of a registered pension scheme (assuming the scheme's governing documentation permits the scheme administrator to do so) should deduct the lifetime allowance charge and make net payments to the member or other recipient. The scheme administrator should account to HMRC for the tax due in the next quarterly return (see **17.82** below) and pay the tax within 45 days of the end of the quarter in which the charge arose. The scheme administrator then gives details of the lifetime allowance due, how the amount was calculated, and whether the amount due has been accounted by them within three months of the benefit crystallisation event.

The scheme administrator can, in certain circumstances, apply to HMRC to be absolved from any liability to meet the lifetime allowance charge where:

(*a*)   the scheme administrator reasonably believed that there was no liability to the lifetime allowance charge in respect of the benefit crystallisation event; and

(*b*)   in all the circumstances of the case, it would not be just and reasonable for the scheme administrator to be liable to the lifetime allowance charge (*FA 2004, s 267(2)*; PTM158000).

It is therefore important to keep documentary evidence of information requests made to the member and the responses received.

Lifetime allowance – transitional protection

17.8   Three main options enable rights accrued prior to A-Day to be protected from the lifetime allowance charge. Additional protections are available to protect against the reductions made to the standard lifetime allowance with effect from 6 April 2012, 6 April 2014 and 6 April 2016 (see **17.7** above).

(*a*)   Primary protection

Primary protection was available to individuals with pension benefits in excess of £1.5 million at 5 April 2006 (being the standard lifetime allowance for the 2006/07 tax year) (*FA 2004, Sch 36, paras 7–11*). Individuals claiming primary protection can continue to make tax relieved contributions to accrue further benefits under registered pension schemes after A-Day. The value of an individual's rights will be their individual lifetime allowance, expressed as a percentage of the standard lifetime allowance. This will then be indexed in line with the lifetime allowance. Following the reduction of the standard lifetime allowance from £1.8 million to £1.5 million for the tax year 2012/2013 and subsequent tax years, an 'underpinned lifetime allowance' of £1.8 million will apply for this purpose for so long as this is greater than the standard lifetime allowance (*FA 2004, s 218(5B)*). For example, a member with accrued benefits valued at £3 million on A-Day could register a figure of 200 per cent. If, when that member came to draw his benefits, the underpinned lifetime allowance of £1.8 million applied, his personal lifetime allowance would be £3.6 million (see PTM092300).

To claim primary protection, the individual must have notified HMRC of his intention to rely on this protection no later than 5 April 2009.

(b)   Enhanced protection

As an alternative to primary protection, an individual (whether his pension benefits were above or below the lifetime allowance at A-Day) could opt for enhanced protection (*FA 2004, Sch 36, paras 12–17A*). Enhanced protection fully protects the value of the individual's pension rights on A-Day. Such rights will not be subject to the lifetime allowance charge when they are brought into payment. Effectively this means that, if the value of the rights increases faster than the increase in the standard lifetime allowance, the individual will still be protected from the lifetime allowance charge (see PTM092400).

To take advantage of this option, there can be no further accrual of defined benefits or cash balance rights above a specified level of indexation, and no contributions can be paid to increase pension rights in other money purchase arrangements on or after A-Day. No benefits can be taken as a lifetime allowance excess lump sum while a claim to enhanced protection is in place.

Where an individual has made a valid notification of his intention to rely on enhanced protection, it will remain in force until he loses it because he fails to comply with the conditions for enhanced protection. If enhanced protection is lost the individual will revert to primary protection if he has claimed this as well (see below) or the standard lifetime allowance if he has not claimed primary protection.

To claim enhanced protection, an individual must have notified HMRC of his intention to rely on this protection no later than 5 April 2009.

(c)   Enhanced protection with primary protection

Individuals with pension rights valued at more than £1.5 million at A-Day may have notified HMRC that they wished to claim both enhanced protection and primary protection. If they did so, the claim for enhanced protection will take precedence. The protection will operate on an enhanced protection basis until it is lost (see PTM092000).

When enhanced protection ceases, the protection will default to primary protection for benefit crystallisation events after enhanced protection is lost. In some circumstances primary protection will apply to the benefit crystallisation event which causes enhanced protection to be lost.

(d)   Fixed protection (2012)

With effect from the tax year 2012/2013 the standard lifetime allowance was reduced to £1.5 million (from £1.8 million in the tax year 2011/2012).

Individuals with enhanced or primary protection were not affected by the change. Fixed protection was available to those who had pensions savings in excess of £1.5 million (or who thought they may have by the time they take their benefits) and who applied to HMRC by 5 April 2012 *(FA 2011, Sch 18, paras 14–17; Registered Pension Schemes (Lifetime Allowance Transitional Protection) Regulations 2011 (SI 2011/1752))*. The effect of fixed protection is to 'fix' the individual's lifetime allowance at £1.8 million. If in future the standard lifetime allowance exceeds £1.8 million then those with fixed protection will automatically become entitled to the higher standard lifetime allowance. Fixed protection is conditional on there being no further accrual of defined benefits or cash balance rights above a specified level of indexation and no contributions being paid to increase pension rights under other money purchase arrangements (see PTM093000).

(e) Fixed protection 2014

With effect from the tax year 2014/2015 the standard lifetime allowance was reduced to £1.25 million (from £1.5 million in the tax year 2013/2014). Individuals with enhanced protection, primary protection or fixed protection (2012) were not affected by the change. Fixed protection 2014 was available to those individuals who had pension savings in excess of £1.25 million (or who thought they might have by the time they take their benefits) and who applied to HMRC by 5 April 2014 *(FA 2013, Sch 22, paras 1–4; Registered Pension Schemes and Relieved Non-UK Pension Schemes (Lifetime Allowance Transitional Protection) (Notification) Regulations 2013 (SI 2013/1741))*. Fixed protection 2014 operates in a similar manner to fixed protection (2012) with its effect being to 'fix' the individual's lifetime allowance at £1.5 million. Subject to this, fixed protection 2014 is subject to similar terms and conditions as apply to fixed protection (2012) (See PTM093000).

(f) Individual protection 2014

FA 2014 (s 44 and *Sch 6)* introduces a personalised protection regime, individual protection 2014. This is available to individuals with pension rights valued at more than £1.25 million on 5 April 2014 who have not already claimed primary protection. Individuals claiming individual protection 2014 are able to continue to make tax-relieved contributions to accrue further benefits under registered pension schemes on and after 6 April 2014. Individual protection will give an individual a personalised lifetime allowance equal to the value of their pension rights on 5 April 2014, subject to a maximum of £1.5 million. If the standard lifetime allowance increases to a level above the personalised lifetime allowance, the standard lifetime allowance will then apply.

To claim individual protection 2014, an individual must notify HMRC of his intention to rely on this protection no later than 5 April 2017.

(g)   Fixed protection 2016

With effect from the tax year 2016/2017 the standard lifetime allowance is being reduced from £1.25 million to £1 million. Individuals with enhanced protection, primary protection, fixed protection (2012) or fixed protection 2014 are not affected. *FA 2016* contains provision for fixed protection 2016 to be available to those individuals who have pension savings in excess of £1 million (or who think they will have by the time they take their benefits). Fixed protection will operate in a similar manner to fixed protection (2012) and fixed protection 2014, with its effect being to 'fix' the individual's lifetime allowance at £1.25 million. Subject to this (and also there being no deadline for making an application to HMRC), fixed protection 2016 will be subject to similar terms and condition as apply to the earlier forms of fixed protection.

(h)   Individual protection 2016

FA 2016 also includes provision for a personalised protection regime, individual protection 2016. This will be available to individuals with pension rights valued at more than £1 million on 5 April 2015 who have not already claimed any of the earlier forms of lifetime allowance protection referred to above. Individuals claiming individual protection 2016 will be able to continue to make tax-relieved contributions to accrue further benefits under registered pension schemes on and after 6 April 2016. Individual protection will give an individual a personalised lifetime allowance equal to the value of their pension rights on 5 April 2016, subject to a maximum of £1.25 million. If the standard lifetime allowance increases to a level above the personalised lifetime allowance, the standard lifetime allowance will then apply. As with fixed protection 2016, there will be no deadline for making an application to HMRC.

Enhanced lifetime allowance when an individual acquires pension credit rights that relate to pensions that came into payment on or after 6 April 2006

17.9   If, following a divorce or dissolution, an ex-spouse or ex-civil partner of a scheme member acquires pension credit rights under a pension sharing order (see **Chapter 8**) that are derived from a pension that came into payment on or after 6 April 2006, that pension will have already been tested against the lifetime allowance. To avoid the same pension being tested again for lifetime allowance purposes the person who has acquired the pension credit rights is entitled to a lifetime allowance enhancement factor (*FA 2004, s 220*). Notice has to be given to HMRC of intention to claim the lifetime allowance enhancement factor.

Enhanced lifetime allowance where the member acquired pension credit rights before 6 April 2006

17.10 An individual who, prior to 6 April 2009, gave appropriate notification to HMRC may have increased the standard lifetime allowance by a 'pre-commencement pension credit factor'. This was an available option where the individual (other than an individual who had claimed primary protection) had acquired pension credit rights under the pension scheme as a result of a pension sharing order being made before 6 April 2006 (*FA 2004, Sch 36, para 18*).

Enhanced lifetime allowance where member is a relevant overseas individual

17.11 An individual may also be able to increase the standard lifetime allowance by a 'lifetime allowance enhancement factor' on a benefit crystallisation event if, during any 'active membership period' of a registered scheme, he is a 'relevant overseas individual' (see *FA 2004, s 221* and **17.75** below). Broadly this means that, if the individual did not receive tax relief on any contributions made to a UK registered scheme while he was accruing benefits in the scheme (other than tax relief on contributions of up to £3,600 where he has been resident in the previous five years), his lifetime allowance can be enhanced.

Reduction in lifetime allowance to reflect the value of pensions in payment before 6 April 2006

17.12 Pre-A-Day pensions are only considered for lifetime allowance purposes if there is a benefit crystallisation event on or after 6 April 2006. Broadly, on the first benefit crystallisation event occurring on or after 6 April 2006, it is assumed that a benefit crystallisation event occurred immediately before that date in relation to all the individual's pre-commencement pensions. The amount crystallised is the value of the individual's pre-commencement pension rights. Generally, this will be 25 times the annual rate or rates at which the relevant pension is, or pensions are, payable to the individual at that time. In the case of a drawdown pension (or, prior to 6 April 2011, an unsecured or alternatively secured pension), the value is the maximum amount that may be paid in the drawdown (or unsecured or alternatively secured) pension year calculated in accordance with the Pension Rules (*FA 2004, Sch 36, para 20*).

Reduction to lifetime allowance where member has a protected normal minimum pension age

17.13   If a member has a protected normal minimum pension age of below 55 (see **17.29** below) the amount of the member's lifetime allowance is generally reduced by 2.5 per cent for each complete year falling between the date of the benefit crystallisation event and the date he will reach his normal minimum pension age (*FA 2004, Sch 36, para 19*).

Benefit crystallisation events in more detail

17.14   The different types of 'benefit crystallisation event' are set out in a table contained in *FA 2004, s 216*. The table refers to various types of 'authorised payments' which are described in more detail in **17.22** to **17.57** below. The expressions used in the table are defined in *FA 2004, Sch 32*, which sets out details of how the amounts crystallised should be calculated. Reference should be made to PTM088000 for a comprehensive treatment of the subject.

	Benefit crystallisation event	*Amount crystallised*
1.	The designation of sums or assets held for the purposes of a money purchase arrangement as available for the payment of *drawdown pension* to the individual.	The aggregate of the amount of the sum and market value of the assets designated.
2.	The individual becoming entitled to a *scheme pension*.	$RVF \times P$ 'RVF' or the 'Relevant Valuation Factor' will generally be 20 but in certain circumstances a higher RVF can be agreed with HMRC by the scheme administrator. 'P' is broadly the amount of pension which will be payable to an individual in the 12 months from the date the individual becomes entitled to it.

	Benefit crystallisation event	*Amount crystallised*
3.	Pension increases which:	RVF × XP
	(*a*) exceed the threshold annual rate; and	'RVF' or the 'Relevant Valuation Factor' will generally be 20, but in certain circumstances a higher factor can be agreed with HMRC by the scheme administrator (see opposite).
	(*b*) exceed by more than the permitted margin the rate at which it was payable on the day on which the individual became *entitled* to it.	
	The 'threshold annual rate' is, in effect, an increase to the scheme pension, compared to the *scheme pension* a year ago, not exceeding the greatest of 5 per cent, RPI or £250. Where the Relevant Valuation Factor for converting the *scheme pension* is greater than 20:1, a higher figure than 5 per cent may be agreed with HMRC.	'XP' will be broadly the amount by which the increase in the pension exceeds the 'permitted margin'.
	The 'permitted margin' is a notional ongoing cost of living increase since the *scheme pension* came into payment and is measured as an annual rate of increase of the greater of 5 per cent (or higher figure agreed with HMRC) or RPI.	
	A registered pension scheme that has 50 or more pensioner members may increase some or all of those *scheme pensions* beyond the threshold rate and the permitted margin without triggering this benefit crystallisation event where:	
	(*a*) the same rate of increase is applied at the same time to all the *scheme pensions* that are in payment in respect of a particular class of pensioner members under the scheme; and	
	(*b*) there are at least 20 pensioner members in that particular class.	
	This is to allow schemes to award benefit augmentations to groups of members without triggering a benefit crystallisation event.	

	Benefit crystallisation event	Amount crystallised
4.	The individual becoming entitled to a *lifetime annuity* purchased under a *money purchase arrangement*.	The aggregate of the amount of such of the sums, and the *market value* of such of the assets, representing the individual's rights under the *arrangement* as are applied to purchase the *lifetime annuity* and any *relevant dependant's annuity* and any related *nominees' annuity*.
5.	The individual reaching age 75 when prospectively entitled to a *scheme pension* or a lump sum (or both) under a *defined benefits arrangement*.	(RVF × DP) + DSLS 'RVF' or the 'Relevant Valuation Factor' will generally be 20, but in certain circumstances a higher factor can be agreed with HMRC by the scheme administrator. 'DP' is broadly the annual rate of the scheme pension to which the individual would have been entitled if, at the date the individual reached age 75, he acquired an actual right to receive it. 'DSLS' is the amount of free-standing lump sum (ie not a commutation lump sum) the individual would have been entitled to at age 75 if he had taken the lump sum.

	Benefit crystallisation event	*Amount crystallised*
5A.	The individual reaching age 75 having designated sums or assets held for the purposes of a *money purchase arrangement* available for the payment of *drawdown pension*.	The aggregate of the amount of the sums and the market value of the assets representing the individual's drawdown pension fund under the arrangement (if any), plus the aggregate of the amount of the sums and the market value of the assets representing the individual's flexi-access drawdown fund under the arrangement (if any), less the aggregate of amounts crystallised by benefit crystallisation event 1 in relation to the arrangement and the individual.
5B.	The individual reaching age 75 when there is a *money purchase arrangement* relating to him.	The amount of any remaining unused funds.
5C.	The designation, on or after 6 April 2015 but before the end of the relevant two-year period, of *relevant unused uncrystallised funds* as available for the payment, to a *dependant* or *nominee* of the individual of (as the case may be) *dependants' flexi-access drawdown pension* or *nominee's flexi-access drawdown pension*.	The aggregate of the amount of the sums and the market value of the assets designated.
5D.	A person becoming entitled, on or after 6 April 2015 but before the end of the relevant two-year period, to a *dependants' annuity* or *nominees' annuity* in respect of the individual if – (a) the annuity is purchased using (whether or not exclusively) *relevant unused crystallised funds*, and (b) the individual died on or after 3 December 2014.	The aggregate of – (a) the amount of such of the sums, and (b) the market value of such of the assets, applied to purchase the annuity as are *relevant uncrystallised funds*.

	Benefit crystallisation event	Amount crystallised
6.	The individual becoming entitled to a *relevant lump sum.*	The amount of the lump sum paid to the individual.
7.	A person being paid a relevant lump sum death benefit. A *relevant lump sum death benefit* is a defined benefits lump sum death benefit or an uncrystallised funds lump sum death benefit.	The amount of the lump sum death benefit.
8.	The transfer of sums or assets held for the purposes of, or representing accrued rights under, any of the relevant pension schemes so as to become held for the purposes of or to represent rights under a *qualifying recognised overseas pension scheme* (see **17.60** below).	The aggregate of the amount of any sum transferred and the market value of any assets transferred.
9.	Any event prescribed in regulations made under *FA 2004, s 164(1)(f)*. This includes (among other events) certain payments which have been paid in error as prescribed by the *Registered Pension Schemes (Authorised Payments) Regulations 2009 (SI 2009/1171)* and certain payments of arrears of pension as prescribed by the *Registered Pension Schemes (Authorised Payments – Arrears of Pensions) Regulations 2006 (SI 2006/614)*.	An amount determined in accordance with the regulations. Under the regulations made, the amount crystallised is the amount of the payment which is deemed to be authorised for the purpose of *FA 2004, s 164(1)(f)*.

If an unauthorised member payment is made, this will not count as a benefit crystallisation event but there will be various adverse tax consequences (see **17.25** to **17.28** below).

Contributions and the annual allowance

Tax relief on employee contributions

17.15   Tax relief on employer and employee contributions is dealt with in PTM040000. Broadly, any member may make unlimited contributions to a registered pension scheme during a tax year. However, to qualify for tax relief on a contribution it must be a 'relievable pension contribution' made by a 'relevant UK individual' (see *FA 2004, s 188(1)* and PTM044100).

A 'relievable pension contribution' is broadly any contribution paid by or on behalf of a member of the pension scheme other than contributions made after age 75 and contributions made by employers (see *FA 2004, s 188(2)*). Transfers in and pension credits granted under a registered pension scheme do not count as relievable pension contributions (*FA 2004, s 188(4), (5)*).

An individual is a 'relevant UK individual' (*FA 2004, s 189*) if he:

(*a*)   has relevant UK earnings chargeable to income tax for that tax year;

(*b*)   is resident in the UK at some time during that tax year;

(*c*)   was resident in the UK both at some time during the five tax years immediately before the tax year in question and when he became a member of the pension scheme;

(*d*)   has for that tax year general earnings from overseas Crown employment subject to UK tax (as defined by *Income Tax (Earnings and Pensions) Act 2003, s 28* ('*ITEPA 2003*'); or

(*e*)   is the spouse or civil partner of an individual who has for the tax year general earnings from overseas Crown employment subject to UK tax (as defined by *ITEPA 2003, s 28*).

'Relevant UK earnings' are:

(i)   employment income such as salary, wages, bonus, overtime, commission providing it is chargeable to tax under *ITEPA 2003, s 7(2)*;

(ii)   income chargeable under *Income Tax (Trading and Other Income) Act 2005, Part 2 (ITTOIA 2005)*, that is income derived from the carrying on or exercise of a trade, profession or vocation (whether individually or as a partner acting personally in a partnership);

(iii)   income chargeable under *ITTOIA 2005, Part 3* derived from a UK or EEA furnished holiday lettings business;

(iv)   income arising from patent rights (*FA 2004, s 189(7)*).

Members will generally be given tax relief on the greater of £3,600 per annum or 100 per cent of their relevant UK earnings that are chargeable to income tax for the tax year on the individual's own contributions (*FA 2004, ss 188, 190*), subject to the annual allowance (see **17.17** below).

If relevant UK earnings are not taxable in the UK due to *s 2(1)* of the *Taxation (International and Other Provisions) Act 2010* (double taxation agreements), those earnings are not regarded as chargeable to income tax and will not count towards the annual limit for relief (*FA 2004, s 189(3)*).

A relevant UK individual under (*c*) above who has no *relevant UK earnings* in a tax year may still qualify for tax relief on contributions to a registered pension scheme up to the basic amount in any tax year (currently £3,600) (see *FA 2004, s 190(2)*). However, the individual will only be able to claim this if the arrangement operates the 'relief at source' system – tax relief cannot be given where the scheme operates the 'net pay system' (*FA 2004, s 191(7)*).

A transfer by an individual of shares that have been acquired under an SAYE option scheme or appropriated to the individual under a share incentive plan to a registered pension scheme can count as a tax deductible contribution in certain circumstances (*FA 2004, s 195*).

Tax relief on employer contributions

17.16 Employers will generally be able to claim a deduction in profits chargeable to UK tax in the year the contributions are made. Relief is not automatic; it will be considered in accordance with the normal rules in relation to deductibility of business expenses (see *Corporation Tax Act 2009, s 54* and *ITTOIA 2005, Part 2*). Pensions legislation amends the normal rules applying to allowable deductions (*FA 2004, s 196*). In particular:

(*a*) a pension payment is not treated as a capital payment if it otherwise would have been; and

(*b*) a deduction can only be given for the accounting period in which the contribution is paid.

The spreading of tax relief may occur on contributions in excess of £500,000 if the contribution to a registered scheme exceeds 210 per cent of the contribution paid in the previous chargeable period. The spread is generally as follows:

(i) £500,000 or over and less than £1 million – two years;

(ii) £1 million or over and less than £2 million – three years;

(iii) £2 million or over – four years (*FA 2004, s 197*).

If a contribution is made to discharge any liability of the employer under the employer debt provisions in *PA 1995, s 75*, this will be treated for tax purposes as if it were the payment of a contribution by an employer under a registered pension scheme (*FA 2004, s 199*).

Employees will not be taxed as a benefit in kind on any employer contributions (*FA 2004, ss 188(3)(b), 201; ITEPA 2003, ss 307, 308*).

FA 2008 introduced provisions intended to prevent the rules regarding the spreading of tax relief on employer contributions to be avoided by routing payments through another company. The provisions relating to indirect contributions are contained in *FA 2004, s 199A* and apply to payments made on or after 10 October 2007, except any made under a contract entered into before 9 October 2007. Essentially, where a large contribution is routed through another company it will still be caught by the spreading rules.

As a general rule contributions made by persons other than employers or members will be treated as member contributions and will not be tax deductible but there are exceptions (see PTM024200).

Employees may in certain circumstances be able to obtain tax relief on contributions to certain foreign pension schemes under the 'migrant member relief' provisions of *FA 2004* (see **17.75** below).

Annual allowance tax charge if contributions exceed the annual allowance

17.17   As explained above, there are no limits on the maximum amount of employee or employer contributions that can be made under a registered pension scheme but tax relief will not be granted above the annual limit for relief. There will be a tax charge (annual allowance charge) on the member if the combined member and employer contributions or the value of benefits that accrue, in any tax year exceeds the annual allowance for that tax year (*FA 2004, s 227*). The rate of the annual allowance charge is 40 per cent up to 5 April 2011 and the member's marginal tax rate for tax years from 2011/2012 (*FA 2004, s 227* as amended from 6 April 2011 by *FA 2011, Sch 17, para 3*).

The annual allowance was initially set at £215,000 for the tax year 2006/2007 and that applicable to the following four tax years was contained in an order made by the Treasury (*Registered Pension Schemes (Standard Lifetime and Annual Allowance Order 2007 (SI 2007/494)*). For the tax year 2010/2011, the annual allowance stood at £255,000 and was set to be frozen at this amount for the following five years (*Registered Pension Schemes (Standard Lifetime and Annual Allowance Order 2010 (SI 2010/922)* – now revoked). The annual allowance was reduced to £50,000 for the tax year 2011/2012 and to £40,000 with effect from the tax year 2014/2015 (*FA 2004, s 228*). There is a detailed description of how the Annual Allowance operates in PTM050000.

The following table summarises the changes in the general level of annual allowance since it was introduced in 2006/2007:

Tax year	Annual allowance
2016/2017	£40,000
2015/2016	£40,000
2014/2015	£40,000
2013/2014	£50,000
2012/2013	£50,000
2011/2012	£50,000
2010/2011	£255,000
2009/2010	£245,000
2008/2009	£235,000
2007/2008	£225,000
2006/2007	£215,000

Over time, changes to the rules relating to the annual allowance have also been made to introduce:

- a special annual allowance which applied to certain individuals for tax year 2009/2010;

- transitional provisions and general changes connected with the reduction of the annual allowance from £255,000 to £50,000 for tax year 2011/2012;

- from tax year 2015/16, a money purchase annual allowance for individuals who have flexibly accessed certain money purchase arrangements (see below);

- for tax year 2015/16, transitional arrangements relating to the alignment of the pension input periods with the tax year (see PTM05800);

- from tax year 2016/17
  - a tapered annual allowance for individuals with income for a tax year greater than £150,000. Those affected will broadly have their annual allowance for that tax year reduced on a tapered basis down to £10,000 once their income reaches £210,000;
  - the continued application of a money purchase annual allowance for individuals who have flexibly accessed certain money purchase arrangements; and
  - the alignment of the period of time over which pension savings are measured over a pension input period with the tax year.

For annual allowance purposes, pension contributions or accrual are tested over a 'pension input period' and then assessed for tax in the tax year in which the relevant pension input period ends.

The initial 'pension input period' will begin on the date of commencement of accrual in a defined benefits or cash balance arrangement or the date of commencement of contributions in a money purchase arrangement other than a cash balance arrangement. With regard to the end of the initial pension input period, and the timespan of subsequent pension input periods, the position immediately prior to 9 July 2015 depended upon whether or not there had been a 'nominated date'. On 8 July 2015, the Chancellor announced that all pension input periods would be aligned with the tax year. All existing pension input periods ended on 8 July 2015, with a new pension input period running from 9 July 2015 to 5 April 2016. All subsequent pension input periods start on 6 April and end on the next following 5 April (*FA 2004, ss 238–238ZB*).

For pension input periods ending up to and including the tax year 2010/2011, in a defined benefits arrangement the 'pension input amount' was the increase in the adjusted capital value of the individual's rights under the arrangement during that pension input period (*FA 2004, ss 234, 235, 236 and 238*). The value of the pension that accrued was generally calculated by multiplying the gross annual value of the pension at the beginning and the end of the pension input period by ten (*FA 2004, s 234(4), (5)*). Any free-standing lump sum was then added on. In a money purchase arrangement other than a cash balance arrangement, the 'pension input amount' was the amount of any employer and employee contributions paid in the pension input period that ended in the tax year (*FA 2004, s 233*). Any protected rights contributions were ignored (*FA 2004, ss 233(2), 238*). In a cash balance arrangement the 'pension input amount' was the adjusted amount of increase in the value of the individual's rights under the pension input period of the arrangement that ended in the tax year (*FA 2004, ss 230, 231, 232 and 238*). There was no test against the annual limit in the pension input period in which the individual died or became entitled to benefits under the arrangement (*FA 2004, s 229(3)*).

The detailed mechanism for calculating the annual allowance changed in relation to pension input periods ending in the 2011/2012 and subsequent tax years. Substantial amendments are made to *FA 2004* by *FA 2011, Sch 17*. The revised position is that benefits will not be tested against the annual allowance in the year of death, or on retirement in circumstances of severe ill-health. Deferred benefits will not be tested against the annual allowance as long as they do not increase by more than statutory revaluation or in accordance with scheme rules in place on 14 October 2010. In a defined benefits arrangement the 'pension input amount' is the increase in value of the individual's rights under the arrangement during the pension input period. The value of the pension is generally calculated by multiplying the gross annual value of the pension at the beginning and the end of the pension input period by 16. Adjustments are made for lump-sum entitlements and there is an allowance for an increase of CPI over the pension input period. Adjustments may also be made for transfer payments, pension debits and credits and any benefit crystallisation events. In a money purchase arrangement other than a cash balance arrangement, the 'pension input amount' is broadly the amount of any employer and employee contributions paid in the pension input period that ends in the tax year.

FA 2004, s 228A (introduced by *FA 2011, Sch 17, para 17*) provides for any unused annual allowance from the previous three tax years to be carried forward. This relaxation was introduced to allay fears that the £50,000 annual allowance introduced with effect from the tax year 2011/2012 would have an unintended impact on some moderately paid workers (eg if they received a large one off pension contribution as part of a redundancy package).

Transitional provisions were introduced for those who had a pension input period ending in the tax year 2011/2012 that had started before 14 October 2010 (when the reduction in the annual allowance to £50,000 was announced). For those individuals, the maximum tax relievable pension savings they could have in that pension input period was £255,000, but with a maximum of £50,000 in the period from 14 October 2010 until the end of the pension input period. The calculation was split so that the old rules applied to any accrual or contributions up to and including 13 October 2010, with any accrual or contributions from 14 October 2010 onwards being subject to the new rules (*FA 2011, Sch 17, para 28*).

From the tax year 2015/2016 onwards, individuals who flexibly access a money purchase arrangement will have to test their total pension input amount against the annual allowance and a 'money purchase annual allowance'. This change, introduced by *TPA 2014*, is intended to prevent individuals exploiting the new flexibilities by diverting their salary into a pension scheme with tax relief and then immediately accessing money purchase benefits (*FA 2004, s 227ZA*).

The money purchase annual allowance is triggered where an individual:

- draws down funds from a flexi-access drawdown fund (including payments from a short term annuity) (see **17.35** below);

- receives an uncrystallised funds pension lump sum (see **17.41** below);

- converts a pre-April 2015 drawdown fund to a flexi-access fund and then takes drawdown (see **17.35** below);

- takes more than the permitted maximum for capped drawdown (see **17.35** below);

- receives a 'stand-alone lump sum' from a money purchase arrangement where the individual was entitled to primary protection but not to enhanced protection (*Article 25C* of the *Taxation of Pension Schemes (Transitional Provisions) Order 2006 (SI 2006/572)*;

- has received a pre-6 April 2015 payment from a flexible drawdown fund (see **17.35** below); or

- has become entitled to a payment under a flexible annuity contract.

(*FA 2004, s 227G*)

For individuals who have triggered the money purchase annual allowance broadly, depending on the amount of their money purchase inputs:

- the annual allowance can either be £40,000; or

- a £10,000 money purchase allowance for 'money purchase inputs'; and

- the 'alternative annual allowance' for other inputs.

The 'alternative annual allowance' is found by subtracting £10,000 from the amount of the annual allowance for the tax year. For the tax year 2015/16 the alternative annual allowance is £30,000 (£40,000 less £10,000).

Where flexible access has occurred and 'money purchase inputs' do not exceed £10,000, the £30,000 alternative annual allowance will apply for other inputs. The amount of money purchase savings over £10,000 is added to any pension input amounts that exceed the alternative annual allowance to establish a chargeable amount potentially subject to the annual allowance charge (the 'alternative chargeable amount'). Any carry forward from previous years can only be used for non-money purchase savings. There can generally be no carry forward of unused money purchase annual allowance (except under transitional arrangements).

If the individual does not make money purchase inputs exceeding the £10,000 money purchase annual allowance in a tax year the annual allowance for all savings (including money purchase) will continue to be £40,000.

Individuals will be both assessed to a 'default chargeable amount' and the 'alternative chargeable amount'. The higher of these two amounts will be the 'chargeable amount' on which tax is paid. The default amount is the excess of all pension savings above £40,000.

Payments which will not trigger the money purchase annual allowance include:

- pension commencement lump sums (see **17.38** below);

- trivial commutation lump sums or small pots lump sums (see **17.44** and **17.47** below);

- scheme pensions (see **17.33** below);

- lifetime annuities (see **17.34** below);

- capped drawdown up to the permitted maximum (see **17.35** below).

A 'scheme pays' facility was introduced (*FA 2004, ss 237A–237F, inserted by FA 2011, Sch 17, Pt 1, para 15*) with effect from the tax year 2011/2012 and subsequent tax years. Individuals with an annual allowance charge above £2,000 can elect for the liability to be met from their future pension benefit. The immediate tax charge will be paid from scheme assets with an appropriate reduction being made to the member's benefit. Schemes are required to offer 'scheme pays' where a member's savings in that scheme exceed the annual allowance for the relevant year. Individuals with an aggregate annual allowance tax charge of more than £2,000 who have not exceeded the annual allowance in any one scheme, will be able to request that one of their schemes operates this facility but cannot require it. Schemes cannot charge for offering the facility. There is no prescription as to how schemes should manage the facility exactly nor what adjustment should be made to the pension rights of the individual but offsetting tax charges against benefits must be done on a just and reasonable basis having regard to normal actuarial practice. Amendments have been made to the *Occupational Pension Schemes (Assignment, Forfeiture, Bankruptcy etc) Regulations 1997 (SI 1997/785)* to allow adjustments to be made to benefits without breaching the provisions of *PA 1995, s 91* concerning the surrender of pension benefits. A scheme may be able to obtain an exemption from providing a 'scheme pays' facility if it can demonstrate to HMRC that 'to do so would be of substantial detriment to the members' interests or that it would not be just and reasonable'.

Annual Allowance for tax years 2016/2017 onwards – higher earners

17.18 From tax year 2016/2017 the amount of the annual allowance will generally be £40,000 per annum (plus any unused annual allowance from the previous three years), but may be reduced broadly if:

- the individual's 'adjusted income' is over £150,000 (and the individual's 'threshold income' is over £110,000 in the same tax year) and accordingly the tapered annual allowance applies; and/or

- the individual has flexibly accessed a money purchase arrangement (see **17.17** above).

Where the tapered annual allowance applies (but not the money purchase annual allowance), broadly the annual allowance of £40,000 is reduced by £1 for every £2 of adjusted income above £150,000 subject to a minimum reduced annual allowance of £10,000. This means that for individuals with income above £210,000 the annual allowance will generally be £10,000 per annum.

Adjusted income for purpose of calculating the tapered annual allowance

The manner in which adjusted income is calculated is explained with examples in PTM057100.

An individual's 'adjusted income' in relation to the tapered annual allowance is:

- the individual's 'net income' for the tax year as calculated under steps 1 and 2 of the *Income Tax Act 2007 (ITA 2007), s 23*; plus

- the amount of any relief under *FA 2004, s 193(4)* (a claim for excess relief under net pay, see PTM044240) and *FA 2004, s 194(1)* (relief on making a claim) deducted at step 2; plus

- the amount of any pension contributions made from any employment income of the individual for the tax year under net pay, under *FA 2004, s 193(2)*; plus

- where non-domiciled individuals make contributions to overseas pension schemes, any relief claimed under *ITEPA 2003, Chapter 2, Part 5* for the tax year; plus

- the value of any employer contributions for the tax year; less

- the amount of any lump sum death benefit mentioned in *ITEPA 2003, s 636A(4ZA)* that accrues to the individual in the tax year (*FA 2004, s228ZA(4)*).

In broad terms, 'net income' is an individual's taxable income left after deducting any reliefs due under *ITA 2007, s 24*. Taxable income for this purpose could include:

- earnings from employment;

- earnings from self-employment/partnerships;

- most pensions income (State, occupational and personal);

- interest on most savings;

- income from shares (dividend income);

- rental income; and

- income received by an individual from a trust.

The value of the employer contributions for a tax year is found by taking the individual's total pension input amount for the tax year less the total of any member contributions paid during the tax year.

The total of any member contributions paid during a tax year means any contributions paid by the individual or any contributions paid by a third party on behalf of the individual (excluding employer contributions) to:

- a registered pension scheme; or

- a currently relieved non-UK scheme, where the individual qualifies for relief in respect of the contributions due to being a currently relieved member of that scheme (see PTM113310).

Threshold income for the purpose of calculating the tapered annual allowance

An individual's threshold income for determining whether the tapered annual allowance applies is:

- net income for the tax year as calculated under steps 1 and 2 of *ITA 2007, s 23*; less

- the amount (before any deduction under *FA 2004, s 192(1)*) of any contribution paid in the year in respect of which the individual is entitled to be given relief under *FA 2004, s 192* (see PTM044220);

- the amount of any lump sum death benefit mentioned in *ITEPA 2003, s 636A(4ZA)* accruing to the individual in the tax year; plus

- the amount of any reduction of employment income for pension provision as a result of any 'relevant salary sacrifice arrangement', or 'relevant flexible remuneration arrangement' (*FA 2004, s228ZA(5)*).

An individual's taxable income is calculated in a similar manner as for the calculation of taxable income in the adjusted income calculation.

A 'relevant salary sacrifice arrangement' is where:

- an individual gives up employment income in exchange for pension contributions by an employer; and

- the salary sacrifice arrangement was made on or after 9 July 2015 (whether before or after the start of the employment concerned) (*FA 2004, s 228ZA(6)*).

A 'relevant flexible remuneration arrangement' is where:

- an individual and their employer agree that pension contributions will be made by the employer rather than the individual receiving some employment income; and

- the flexible remuneration arrangement was made on or after 9 July 2015 (whether before or after the start of the employment concerned) (*FA 2004, s 228ZA(6)*).

For the purpose of a relevant salary sacrifice or relevant flexible remuneration arrangement, 'a pension contribution by an employer' means an individual's employer or some other person:

- paying contributions (or additional contributions) to a pension scheme in respect of the individual or otherwise;

- to secure increased benefits under a pension scheme to which any of the following have an actual or prospective entitlement;

766

-   the individual,

-   a dependant of the individual, or

-   any person connected with the individual (*FA 2004, s 228ZA(7)*).

For individuals who have flexibly accessed a money purchase arrangement *and* the tapered annual allowance applies:

•   the annual allowance is the reduced annual allowance after the £1 reduction for every £2 of adjusted income over £150,000 is applied, subject to a minimum reduced annual allowance of £10,000;

•   a £10,000 money purchase annual allowance for 'money purchase inputs', and

•   the alternative annual allowance for 'other inputs'.

The 'alternative' annual allowance is found by subtracting £10,000 from the amount of the reduced annual allowance for the tax year. If the minimum reduced annual allowance of £10,000 applies, the alternative annual allowance is nil.

In practice it may be very difficult to know with certainty during a tax year how much annual allowance will be available to an individual. The only risk-free way to ensure that high earners do not trigger the annual allowance tax charge may be to restrict the maximum contributions in any tax year from 2016/2017 onwards to £10,000 and use the carry forward provisions where available to make use of any unused tax relief.

Different methods of obtaining tax relief

17.19   There are three methods of obtaining tax relief. The method that applies will depend on the type of pension scheme (*FA 2004, ss 192–194*, and see PTM044200).

Personal pension schemes must operate a 'relief at source' arrangement under which the individual makes his relievable pension contribution, after deducting a sum equivalent to basic rate tax, and the scheme administrator then claims back a sum equal to the basic rate of tax from HMRC. A higher rate taxpayer can also obtain tax relief at the higher rate by making a claim when he fills in his tax return or by way of adjustment to his PAYE code. Relief at source enables individuals who have earnings below £3,600 or no relevant UK earnings to claim tax back on contributions of up to £3,600 (*FA 2004, s 192*).

Occupational pension schemes can use a 'net pay arrangement' instead of 'relief at source' as long as the member is an employee of a sponsoring employer of the pension scheme and all the other contributing scheme members who are employees of the same employer are also receiving tax relief under the net pay arrangement (*FA 2004, s 191(3)*). A net pay arrangement allows the employer to give tax relief so employees are only taxed on their net pay after the pension contributions are deducted (*FA 2004, s 193*).

The third type of arrangement for obtaining tax relief on contributions is 'relief on making of a claim' (*FA 2004, s 194*). Broadly the member makes the contribution to the pension scheme and then claims tax relief from HMRC on his relievable pension contributions.

Authorised and unauthorised payments

Move from a discretionary to a mandatory tax regime

17.20   The majority of UK occupational pension schemes were approved before A-Day on a discretionary basis under *ICTA 1988, Part XIV, Chapter I*. The types of benefits that could be provided without jeopardising HMRC approval were set out in the Occupational Pension Scheme Practice Notes on Approval of Occupational Pension Schemes (IR12 (2001)), as amended (and are considered from **17.88** below). The types of benefits that could be provided under personal pension schemes before A-Day were set out (on a non-discretionary basis) in *ICTA 1988, Part XIV, Chapter IV*.

Under the post-A-Day regime, the types of 'authorised payments' that can be made by all registered schemes are set out in *FA 2004, Part 4*. If a registered pension scheme makes 'unauthorised member payments' or 'unauthorised employer payments' there can be adverse tax consequences for both the recipient and the scheme administrator (see below). In an extreme case if it appears to HMRC:

(*a*)   that the pension scheme has not been established, or is not being maintained, wholly or mainly for the purpose of making payments falling within *FA 2004, s 164(1)(a)* or *(b)* (authorised payments of pensions and lump sums);

(*b*)   that the person who is, or any of the persons who are, the scheme administrator is not a fit and proper person to be, as the case may be–

   •   the scheme administrator, or

   •   one of the persons who are the scheme administrator;

(*c*)   in any 12-month period the 'scheme chargeable payment percentage' (broadly most unauthorised payments) exceeds 25 per cent of the market value of the scheme's assets;

(*d*) the scheme administrator fails to pay a substantial amount of tax (or interest on tax) due from the scheme administrator by virtue of *FA 2004, Part 4*;

(*f*) that the scheme administrator fails to produce any document required to be produced by virtue of *FA 2004, Part 4* or *FA 2008, Sch 36, Part 1*;

(*g*) that any document produced to an officer of Revenue and Customs by the scheme administrator contains a material inaccuracy in relation to which at certain conditions are met;

(*h*) that any declaration accompanying the application to register the pension scheme, or otherwise made to an officer of Revenue and Customs in connection with the pension scheme, is false in a material particular;

(*i*) there is no scheme administrator; or

(*j*) that the scheme administrator has deliberately obstructed an officer of Revenue and Customs in the course of an inspection under *FA 2004, s 159B* or *FA 2008, Sch 36, Part 2*.

HMRC has the power to withdraw registration of the pension scheme (*FA 2004, ss 157, 158*). These are the only grounds on which deregistration can occur. There is an appeals procedure against deregistration (*FA 2004, s 159*). HMRC introduced a number of the above conditions from 20 March 2014 in an effort to combat pensions liberation (see **Chapter 6**). New powers were also given to HMRC to require information to be provided for the purposes of considering whether the administrator is a fit and proper person and to inspect a business or premises or documents at a business or premises for the purposes of determining whether the administrator is a fit and proper person to perform this role (*FA 2004, ss 159A, B*)).

HMRC only has the power to withdraw registration from an entire pension scheme and not from an arrangement or arrangements within a scheme (see PTM033000). It does, however, have the power to treat registered schemes as separate schemes in certain circumstances (*FA 2004, s 274A* and the *Registered Pension Schemes (Splitting of Schemes) Regulations 2006 (SI 2006/569)*). In practice, de-registration is unlikely to happen in a large occupational pension scheme, and HMRC is likely to enforce compliance through the tax charges that will fall on the scheme administrator and the member if unauthorised payments are made. The trustees of occupational pension schemes and scheme administrators of other registered pension schemes may, however, want to ensure that their existing rules or other scheme documentation do not provide for the payment of unauthorised payments. There are certain benefits or payments that were permitted under HMRC requirements for approval prior to A-Day that may be unauthorised under the *FA 2004* tax regime.

Activities of registered occupational pension schemes to be restricted to retirement-benefit activities

17.21   Under the pre-A-Day tax regime, for an occupational pension scheme to retain its status as an exempt approved scheme under *ICTA 1988, Pt XIV, Ch I*, it had to meet the 'sole purpose' test. HMRC required schemes to be bona fide established for the sole purpose of providing 'relevant benefits', and continued approval was dependent on maintaining the sole purpose. There is no sole purpose test under *FA 2004*, however, under *PA 2004*, the trustees or managers of an occupational pension scheme with its main administration in the UK have an obligation to secure that the activities of the scheme are restricted to 'retirement benefit activities' (*PA 2004, s 255*). Broadly, these are operations relating to retirement benefits and activities arising from operations relating to retirement benefits. 'Retirement benefits' are defined as:

(*a*)   benefits payable by reference to reaching, or expecting to reach, retirement; and

(*b*)   benefits that are supplementary to benefits within (*a*) and that are provided on an ancillary basis in the form of payments on death, disability or termination of employment or in the form of support payments or services in the case of sickness, poverty or need, or death.

Trustees of registered schemes can be fined by the Regulator if the scheme has activities that are not retirement-benefit activities and the trustee or manager has failed to take all reasonable steps to secure that the activities of the scheme are limited to retirement-benefit activities (*PA 2004, s 255(3)*).

Authorised member payments

17.22   The only authorised payments a registered pension scheme can make to or in respect of a person who is or has been a member are:

(*a*)   pensions permitted under the 'pension rules';

(*b*)   pensions permitted under the 'pension death benefit rules';

(*c*)   lump sums permitted by the 'lump sum rule';

(*d*)   lump sums permitted by the 'lump sum death benefit rules';

(*e*)   recognised transfers;

(*f*)   scheme administration member payments (ie payments made for the purposes of the scheme's management or administration, such as the payment of wages or salary or fees to persons engaged in administering the scheme);

(*g*)   payments made under a pension sharing order or provision; and (*h*)   other payments permitted under HMRC regulations (*FA 2004, ss 164–174A, Schs 28, 29*).

Included within (*h*) above are regulations which provide that certain payments to or in respect of members that would otherwise be unauthorised payments are regarded under the legislation as authorised payments (*FA 2004, s 164(1) (f); Registered Pension Schemes (Authorised Payments) Regulations 2009 (SI 2009/1171)*). These payments include (subject to the satisfaction of conditions) pensions and lump sums that have been paid in error by scheme administrators or insurance companies, 'stranded pots' which do not otherwise satisfy all of the conditions relating to the payment of trivial commutation lump sums and part refund payments relating to short service. In the case of payments in error, the 'deemed authorisation' has retrospective effect from 6 April 2006. In other cases, the payments are only to be regarded as authorised if made on or after 1 December 2009 or, in the case of part refund payments relating to short service, on or after 8 August 2012 (see **17.47** below).

Authorised and unauthorised employer payments

17.23   The only payments which a registered, private sector occupational pension scheme is authorised to make to or in respect of a sponsoring employer are:

(*a*)   authorised surplus payments;

(*b*)   compensation payments (ie payments made to an employer in respect of a member's liability to the employer arising from a criminal, fraudulent or negligent act or omission);

(*c*)   authorised employer loans;

(*d*)   scheme administration employer payments; and

(*e*)   other payments permitted under HMRC regulations (*FA 2004, ss 175–184*).

Employers can be treated as having made unauthorised employer payments in certain circumstances, eg in the case of 'value shifting' or if they engage in unauthorised borrowing (*FA 2004, ss 181, 182–185*).

Unauthorised member payments

17.24   Any payment or transfer made to or in respect of a member that is not an authorised member payment will be an unauthorised payment with the various tax consequences discussed below (*FA 2004, s 160(2)*). There are also provisions which may deem a payment to be an unauthorised member payment including where:

(*a*) value shifting of assets occurs (*FA 2004, s 174*);

(*b*) a member of a registered pension scheme (or the member's personal representatives) assigns or agrees to assign (or surrenders or agrees to surrender) any benefit to which they (or any dependant, nominee or successor) have an actual or prospective right to under the scheme other than in certain permitted circumstances, such as the making of a pension sharing order (*FA 2004, ss 172, 172A*);

(*c*) there is an increase in rights on death of a connected person (*FA 2004, s 172B*);

(*d*) an asset held for the purposes of a registered pension scheme is used to provide a benefit other than a payment to a member, or a member of his family or household. This can include loans to a member or connected party (*FA 2004, s 171(4)* and PTM 123300);

(*e*) unallocated contributions are allocated to a member who is connected with the employer or any other person connected with the employer above a certain permitted level (*FA 2004, s 172C*);

(*f*) the contributions made in respect of a member, or the capital value of the benefits that accrue in a pension input period in respect of a defined benefits arrangement, a cash balance arrangement or a hybrid arrangement relating to a member, exceed a certain amount where the member is connected with the employer or a person connected with a sponsoring employer (*FA 2004, s 172D*);

(*g*) direct or indirect investment in 'taxable property' (for example, residential property or fine wines or vintage cars) by an investment-regulated pension scheme (*FA 2004, s 174A*) (see **17.64** below).

Tax consequences of making unauthorised payments – unauthorised payments charge

17.25 Unauthorised payments can give rise to punitive tax charges and, in an extreme case, deregistration of the scheme.

If an unauthorised member payment is made to or in respect of a person before the person's death generally the person in respect of whom the payment was made will be liable to an 'unauthorised payments charge' of 40 per cent of the value of the payment (*FA 2004, s 208(2)(a)*). If the unauthorised member payment is made, in respect of a person after the person's death the recipient is subject to an 'unauthorised payment charge' of 40 per cent of the value of the payment (*FA 2004, s 208(2)(b)*).

If an unauthorised employer payment is made the person to or in respect of whom the payment is made is subject to an unauthorised payment charge of 40 per cent of the value of the payment (*FA 2004, s 208(2)(c)*).

Tax consequences of making unauthorised payments – unauthorised payment surcharge

17.26   An unauthorised member payment surcharge of 15 per cent may also be payable to or in respect of a person who has been a member where unauthorised payments in any 12-month period exceed 25 per cent of the value of that member's rights under the scheme (*FA 2004, s 210*).

An extra 15 per cent unauthorised employer payment surcharge may also be payable, broadly, where unauthorised employer payments in any 12-month period exceed 25 per cent of the value of scheme assets (*FA 2004, s 213*).

Tax consequences of making unauthorised payments – scheme sanction charge

17.27   The scheme administrator will generally become liable to pay a scheme sanction charge in relation to any unauthorised payment which qualifies as a 'scheme chargeable payment' (unless the payment falls within narrowly defined circumstances) (*FA 2004, ss 239–241*).

Potentially the scheme administrator could have to pay up to 40 per cent of the amount of the unauthorised payment that counts as a 'scheme chargeable payment'. However, there is a complicated formula which allows the scheme administrator to reduce its liability by part of any tax being paid by the member or recipient to meet the unauthorised payments charge. As long as the 40 per cent tax is paid by the member or recipient, this should result in the scheme only being liable for payment of an extra 15 per cent (*FA 2004, s 240*).

If the authorisation of a payment is conditional on matters which are known only by the member, schemes will need to ask the member to supply sufficient information so that the scheme is satisfied that those conditions are met.

Where a member gives a scheme inaccurate information or makes a false statement, so that a payment which a scheme considered to be authorised turns out not to be, the scheme can seek discharge from any resulting scheme sanction charge through the 'good faith' provisions in the legislation where it is reasonable to do so (*FA 2004, s 268* and PTM135400).

In order to show that a scheme had reasonable grounds for believing that an unauthorised payment was authorised schemes should retain documentary evidence of any member statement or information they have relied on.

Where schemes discover that a payment that they had believed to be authorised is not in fact so, they should report the unauthorised payment on the Event Report (PTM161100) (see **17.80** below).

Tax consequences of deregistration – deregistration charge

17.28   If the registration of the scheme is withdrawn, a deregistration charge is payable of 40 per cent of the value of any sums held by the pension scheme immediately before deregistration and the market value of any assets held at that time for the purposes of the pension scheme (*FA 2004, s 242*).

The Pension Rules (FA 2004, s 165)

Normal minimum pension age

17.29   Under Pension Rule 1, broadly benefits cannot be paid before the 'normal minimum pension age,' other than where the ill-health condition is met. The normal minimum pension age is age 55 (it was age 50 until 6 April 2010). Members who immediately prior to A-Day had an existing actual or prospective right under the rules of the pension scheme (as they stood at 10 December 2003) to draw any benefit before age 55 may, on and after 6 April 2010, retain those rights and have a 'protected pension age' (*FA 2004, Sch 36, paras 21, 22*).

The right to a protected pension age under an occupational pension scheme is lost if all the member's benefits payable under arrangements under the pension scheme are not paid at the same time. The protection may also be lost in certain circumstances where the member continues in employment or is re-employed (*FA 2004, Sch 36, para 22(7)–(7J)*). The right to a protected pension age can be preserved in certain circumstances on block transfers (*FA 2004, Sch 36, para 22(6)*).

Where, prior to A-Day, an individual had an actual or prospective right under a scheme to the payment of benefits before age 50 (because of a prescribed occupation), that right is also protected, subject to satisfying certain conditions (*FA 2004, Sch 36, paras 21, 23; Registered Pension Schemes (Prescribed Schemes and Occupations) Regulations 2005 (SI 2005/3451)*).

If a pension is paid to a member before the normal minimum pension age (or protected pension age) other than when the 'ill-health condition' is met (see **17.30** below), the instalments of pension paid prior to that age will be unauthorised member payments.

Ill-health retirement

17.30   The ill-health condition is met if:

(*a*)   the scheme administrator has received evidence from a registered medical practitioner that the member is (and will continue to be) incapable of carrying on the member's occupation because of physical or mental impairment; and

(*b*)   the member has in fact ceased to carry on his occupation (*FA 2004, Sch 28, Part 1, para 1*).

HMRC expects the medical evidence to be in writing and appropriate records should be kept to demonstrate that it has been received.

It is permissible to reduce or stop an ill-health pension if the member recovers (*FA 2004, Sch 28, Part 1, para 2(3), (4)*).

The ill-health condition is similar, but not identical, to the pre-A-Day definition of 'Incapacity' in IR12 (2001) (see **17.105** below). Care should be taken to ensure that the operation of pre-A-Day ill-health retirement rules do not result in the making of unauthorised member payments.

Flexible retirement

17.31   Under the pre-A-Day taxation regime, it was a requirement in most cases that, to take benefits from a tax approved occupational pension scheme, a member must retire from service. Benefits could not generally be taken in tranches unless the member transferred out his benefits to a personal pension scheme or, if the scheme rules permitted, took advantage of the opportunity to delay taking his AVC fund until a later date.

Under the *FA 2004* regime, there is nothing to prevent the member taking benefits from any type of registered pension scheme in tranches (whether still in employment or not) if the scheme rules permit. In certain circumstances, however, this can lead to the loss of transitional relief. For example, if a member has a protected pension age below age 55 this may be lost (see **17.29** above). Additionally, any protection relating to the maximum amount of tax-free lump sum relating to pre-A-Day rights where this exceeds the normal 25 per cent limit (see **17.39** below) can be lost if not all pensions are taken at the same time.

Pensions payable by defined benefits arrangements

17.32   Defined benefits arrangements can only pay 'scheme pensions' (Pension Rule 3). These are either pensions paid directly by the scheme out of its own resources or by an insurance company selected by the scheme administrator (*FA 2004, Sch 28, Part 1, para 2*).

Generally, scheme pensions must be payable (at least annually) until the date of the member's death or until the later of the member's death and the end of a fixed term of up to ten years.

FA 2004 does permit the pension to be reduced in certain circumstances. These circumstances include the situation when all scheme pensions payable to or in respect of the members are reduced or in relation to the payment of bridging pensions.

If a scheme pension is reduced in circumstances other than those permitted under the Pension Rules this will result in all subsequent pension payments being treated as unauthorised payments with the tax consequences discussed above.

Pensions payable by money purchase arrangements

17.33 Money purchase arrangements may, after 6 April 2015, be used to provide the member with pension income in the following ways:

- through the purchase of a lifetime annuity contract from an insurance company (see **17.34** below);

- as a scheme pension;

- by designating some or all of the fund to provide a drawdown pension (from a flexi-access drawdown fund) (see **17.35** below);

- as an uncrystallised funds pension lump sum or series of lump sums (see **17.37** below).

A scheme pension can only be provided if the member has first been given the opportunity to select a lifetime annuity (*FA 2004, s 165, Pension Rule 4*). The precise options available to a member depend on the scheme rules.

Major changes were made in relation to the manner in which money purchase arrangements could be applied from 6 April 2015 giving the individual far greater flexibility to access the value of his money purchase arrangement than was previously the case. This included introducing flexi-access drawdown and enabling members to take uncrystallised funds pension lump sums.

To assist members in making an informed decision about how best to access their money purchase arrangements the Government set up a new service called Pensions Wise offering free impartial guidance to members and introduced new disclosure requirements.

In the past, HMRC required money purchase funds (other than a proportion which could be taken as tax free lump sum) to be applied to provide a pension or annuity. It has also been possible for a number of years, as an alternative to paying a pension or annuity, to use a money purchase arrangement to take a drawdown pension subject to limits on the maximum pension which could be taken. These restrictions were gradually liberalised over time.

The broad structure of the drawdown regime that applied immediately before 6 April 2015 was introduced with effect from the 2011/12 tax year in the place of the earlier provisions for the payment of 'unsecured pensions' and 'alternatively secured pensions'. It permitted both:

• capped drawdown; and

• flexible drawdown (subject to a minimum income requirement).

Broadly, under capped drawdown there was a single annual withdrawal limit. This was originally set at 100 per cent of the equivalent of a comparable annuity. The percentage was increased to 120 per cent in relation to drawdown years beginning on or after 26 March 2013 and then to 150 per cent of the value of a comparable annuity for drawdown years beginning on or after 27 March 2014 (*FA 2014, s 41*). Individuals could choose how much, if anything, to draw down annually from their pension pot throughout their retirement, subject to the cap. GAD issued drawdown tables, available on the HMRC website, to be used to calculate the annual capped drawdown limit. There are transitional provisions relating to existing capped drawdown funds which apply from 6 April 2015 (see **17.35** below).

Flexible drawdown was also permitted from the 2011/2012 tax year. An individual could draw unlimited amounts from his designated drawdown fund, provided that he could demonstrate that he met a minimum income requirement (MIR) and satisfied various other requirements. Relevant income for the MIR is income in payment (ie not a deferred entitlement) and was guaranteed for life. This included scheme pension, lifetime annuity and state pension. When it was introduced in relation to the 2011/12 tax year the MIR was set at £20,000 but it was reduced to £12,000 with effect from 27 March 2014 (*FA 2004, Sch 28, para 14A* inserted by *FA 2011* and amended by *FA 2014, s 41*). Existing flexible drawdown funds automatically converted to flexi-access drawdown funds with effect from 6 April 2015 (see **17.35** below).

Lifetime annuity

17.34 Where the entitlement arises on or after 6 April 2015, the requirements for a lifetime annuity are that:

(*a*) it must be payable by an insurance company; and

(*b*) it is payable until the member's death or, if later, the end of a term certain (*FA 2004, Sch 28, para 3(1A)*).

Where the member became entitled to a lifetime annuity before 6 April 2015 then additional conditions applied including a requirement for the member to be given the opportunity to select the insurance company, a requirement that the amount cannot decrease other than in prescribed circumstances and any guarantee period could not be more than ten years (*FA 2004, Sch 28, para 3(1)*).

Drawdown and flexi-access drawdown

17.35   From 6 April 2015 a drawdown pension can be in either of the following forms:

- a short-term annuity (payable for no more than five years); or

- income withdrawal (*FA 2004, Sch 28, paras 4, 6* and *7*).

Income withdrawal from 6 April 2015 is generally only possible where an individual has designated funds for flexi-access drawdown. There will be a benefit crystallisation event at the point of designation for the purposes of the lifetime allowance (see **17.14** above). The individual will only become subject to the money purchase annual allowance once income is actually taken from the flexi-access drawdown fund (see **17.17** above). Amounts taken from a flexi-access drawdown fund will be taxed as pension income (*ITEPA 2003, s 579A*). The designation of funds for flexi-access drawdown also gives rise to the possibility of the member taking a tax-free pension commencement lump sum from any remaining undesignated funds (*FA 2004, s 166(1)(a)* and *Sch 29, para 1*) (see **17.38** below).

Flexible drawdown funds set up before 6 April 2015 (see **17.33** above) automatically converted to flexi-access drawdown funds on 6 April 2015 (*FA 2004, Sch 28, paras 7, 8, 8A(1)* and *(2)(b)*).

Transitional provisions apply where an individual had already designated funds for the purposes of capped drawdown before 6 April 2015 (see **17.33** above). Further funds can be designated into existing capped drawdown arrangements and income withdrawal can continue without making the individual subject to the money purchase annual allowance. If, however:

- a payment is made in excess of the capped drawdown amount in a tax year; or

- the individual flexibly accesses another money purchase arrangement,

then the money purchase annual allowance will be triggered (see **17.17** above).

In relation to a capped drawdown fund, where:

- a member receives a payment in excess of the capped drawdown amount;

- the scheme administrator agrees to a request for conversion; or

- certain transfers are made

then the fund will be converted into a flexi-access drawdown fund (PTM062750 and *FA 2004, Sch 28, paras 8B–8D*).

Guarantee periods

17.36 If a member dies before the end of the period of ten years beginning with the day on which he became entitled to a scheme pension (or an annuity to which the member became entitled before 6 April 2015), the payment may continue to be made (to any person) until the end of that period. Where the member became entitled to an annuity on or after 6 April 2015 then the payment may continue for a term certain which may be for any specified period (Pension Rule 2 – *FA 2004, s 165* as amended by *TPA 2014*).

It is permissible for a scheme pension or a lifetime annuity with a guarantee period to cease after the date of the member's death and before the end of the guarantee term if the annuitant marries, enters a civil partnership, reaches the age of 18 or ceases to be in full-time education (*FA 2004, Sch 28, paras 2(6), 3(2)*).

The lump sum rule (FA 2004, s 166)

17.37 Under the lump sum rule, no lump sum may be paid other than:

(a)   a pension commencement lump sum;

(b)   a serious ill-health lump sum;

(c)   an uncrystallised funds pension lump sum

(d)   a short service refund lump sum;

(e)   a trivial commutation lump sum;

(f)   a refund of excess contributions lump sum;

(g)   a winding-up lump sum;

(h)   a lifetime allowance excess lump sum (*FA 2004, s 166*).

If any lump sum other than those listed above is paid, it will count as an unauthorised payment unless it is covered by any of the transitional saving provisions or has been prescribed as an authorised payment by regulations made under *FA 2004, s 164(1)(f)*.

Pension commencement lump sums

17.38   A person becomes entitled to a pension commencement lump sum immediately before he becomes entitled to the pension in connection with which it is paid (or, if the person dies before becoming entitled to the pension in connection with which it was anticipated it would be paid, immediately before death) (*FA 2004, s 166(2)*).

A person is entitled to a pension commencement lump sum if:

(*a*)   the member becomes entitled to it in connection with becoming entitled to a relevant pension (or dies after becoming entitled to it but before becoming entitled to the relevant pension in connection with which it was anticipated that the member would become entitled to it);

(*b*)   it is paid when all or part of the member's lifetime allowance is available;

(*c*)   it is paid within the period beginning six months before, and ending one year after, the day on which the member becomes entitled to it;

(*d*)   it is paid when the member has reached normal minimum pension age (or the ill-health condition is satisfied); and

(*e*)   it is not an excluded lump sum (*FA 2004, Sch 29, Part 1, para 1*).

A relevant pension for the purposes of (a) above includes income withdrawal, a lifetime annuity or a scheme pension.

Generally, when a member becomes entitled to a scheme pension, a pension commencement lump sum can be paid of up to one-quarter of the value of the benefits that are crystallised for lifetime allowance purposes. Any lump sum paid in excess of the permitted maximum lump sum will count as an unauthorised payment.

The pension commencement lump sum is paid tax free (*ITEPA 2003, s 636A(1) (a)*, as inserted by *FA 2004, Sch 31, para 11*).

The pension entitlement giving rise to the pension commencement lump sum does not have to arise under the same arrangement paying the lump sum but may be calculated on a scheme wide basis. For example, as long as all benefits are taken at the same time as the scheme pension comes into payment, in a defined benefits scheme the member's additional voluntary contribution fund could be applied to provide all the lump sum rather than commuting scheme pension to provide the lump sum (if the scheme rules allow).

Pension commencement lump sum – transitional relief

17.39   A pension commencement lump sum in excess of the normal 25 per cent limit may be paid in certain circumstances where the member was entitled or prospectively entitled to a higher lump sum benefit on 5 April 2006.

In the case of a member who has primary protection and lump sum rights of more than £375,000 on 5 April 2006, the permitted maximum lump sum will be replaced by a higher figure. The manner in which this works is set out in the *Registered Pension Schemes (Enhanced Lifetime Allowance) Regulations 2006 (SI 2006/131)* and explained in RPSM03105135.

In the case of a member with enhanced protection and lump sum rights of more than £375,000 on 5 April 2006, the permitted maximum will broadly be the proportion of the fund which could have been taken as a lump sum benefit on 5 April 2006.

Members who do not have primary or enhanced protection and whose uncrystallised lump sum is less than £375,000 on 5 April 2006 may also be able to take a larger lump sum if the percentage of their benefits that could be taken as a lump sum as at 5 April 2006 under pre-A-Day HMRC requirements exceeded 25 per cent *(FA 2004, Sch 36, para 31)*. There is no need to register with HMRC to benefit from this protection, but scheme administrators will need to keep a record of the maximum permitted percentage tax-free cash that could be taken immediately before A-Day.

Pension commencement lump sums – recycling of lump sums

17.40   Anti-avoidance provisions were inserted into *FA 2004 (Sch 29, para 3A)* by *FA 2006* to target cases where a lump sum is taken with the sole or main purpose of reinvesting it through the pension scheme thus generating further tax relief on the amount reinvested.

Under the recycling provisions, a lump sum paid to the member that would normally be a tax-free pension commencement lump sum may be treated as an unauthorised payment (PTM133810).

Where a lump sum is an unauthorised payment due to recycling the member must tell the scheme administrator within 30 days of the unauthorised payment being made:

- the date on which the unauthorised payment is treated as made; and

- the amount of the payment.

(The *Registered Pension Schemes (Provision of Information) Regulations 2006, SI 2006/567, reg 11A*)

The recycling rule applies in respect of all pension commencement lump sums paid on or after 6 April 2006, where those lump sums are used as part of a recycling device, regardless of when the significantly increased contributions are actually paid. The recycling rule applies when all of the following conditions are met:

- the individual receives a pension commencement lump sum;

- because of the lump sum, the amount of contributions paid into a registered pension scheme in respect of the individual is significantly greater than it otherwise would be (PTM133830);

- the additional contributions are made by the individual or by someone else, such as an employer;

- the recycling was pre-planned. Guidance about determining whether the recycling was pre-planned is at PTM133820;

- the amount of the pension commencement lump sum, taken together with any other such lump sums taken in the previous 12-month period, exceeds;

  - £7,500 for events on or after 6 April 2015, or

  - 1 per cent of the standard lifetime allowance for events before 6 April 2015; and

- the cumulative amount of the additional contributions exceeds 30 per cent of the pension commencement lump sum (PTM133830).

There are a number of detailed examples of when recycling will and will not have occurred in PTM133950 and PTM133860.

Uncrystallised funds pension lump sums

17.41   From 6 April 2015 individuals who have reached age 55 (or their protected pension age, if they have one under the arrangement (see **7.29** below)), or who met the ill-health condition (see **7.30** below), can freely access their pension savings under money purchase arrangements as a lump sum, part of which will be tax-free. The payment must be made from uncrystallised rights (ie not from a drawdown fund). An uncrystallised funds pension lump sum can only be paid where some (age 75 or over) or all (under age 75) of the amount is within the available lifetime allowance (*FA 2004, Sch 29, Part 1, para 4A*) .

Generally, one-quarter of the amount taken as an uncrystallised funds pension lump sum will be tax-free with the remainder being taxed as income.

Where an individual over age 75 takes an uncrystallised funds pension lump sum which exceeds the individual's available lifetime allowance, the tax-free part will be 25 per cent of the available lifetime allowance with the remainder subject to income tax at the individual's marginal rate.

An uncrystallised funds pension lump sum is not available to certain members with enhanced or primary protection or, in some circumstances, to members entitled to a lifetime allowance enhancement factor.

Individuals taking an uncrystallised funds pension lump sum will be subject to the money purchase annual allowance (see **17.17** above).

Serious ill-health lump sum

17.42   A serious ill-health lump sum can be paid if:

(*a*)   the scheme administrator has received evidence from a registered medical practitioner that the member is expected to live for less than one year;

(*b*)   all or part of the member's lifetime allowance is available;

(*c*)   it is paid in respect of an uncrystallised arrangement; and

(*d*)   it extinguishes the member's entitlement to benefits under the arrangement (*FA 2004, Sch 29, Part 1, para 4*).

An uncrystallised arrangement is an arrangement in respect of which there has been no previous benefit crystallisation event (*FA 2004, Sch 29, Part 1, para 4(2)*).

There is no liability to income tax on a serious ill-health lump sum paid to a member who has not reached age 75 (*ITEPA 2003, s 636A(1)(b)*, as inserted by *FA 2004, Sch 31, para 11*). On or after 6 April 2011 a serious ill-health lump sum paid to a member aged 75 or older will be subject to a 55 per cent tax charge known as the serious ill-health lump sum charge (*FA 2004, s 205A inserted by FA 2011*).

If a member's pension is commuted on serious ill-health grounds, any GMP which has accrued must still be provided for the spouse. HMRC take the view that, in order to extinguish the member's entitlement, any attaching spouse's pension required by the contracting-out legislation must be provided following the member's death under a separate arrangement.

Short service refund lump sum

17.43   A short service refund lump sum allows for the return of a member's contributions in relation to a members of occupational pension schemes whose pensionable service is terminated in circumstances where they not entitled to short-service benefit under the scheme (*FA 2004, Sch 29, Part 1, para 5*). In broad terms, such a lump sum may become payable where a leaver has completed less than two years' qualifying service (or 30 days' qualifying service for those with money purchase contributions commencing on or after 1 October 2015) under the scheme and has not either been provided with deferred benefits under the scheme or elected for a transfer payment to be made to another scheme or arrangement (see **Chapter 6**). The lump sum must extinguish the member's entitlement to benefits under the scheme except to the extent that a provision under some enactment prohibits all of a member's entitlement from being extinguished by the payment of a lump sum.

The scheme administrator is liable to tax on the short service refund lump sum at the rate of 20 per cent on sums up to £20,000 and 50 per cent on any excess (*FA 2004, s 205* as amended by the *Taxation of Pensions Schemes (Rates, etc) Order 2010 (SI 2010/536)*). Tax should be deducted from any payment by the administrator where the rules of the scheme permit.

Where interest is paid on a short service refund lump sum it may be treated as a scheme administration member payment. Payments must be made on an arm's length commercial basis. If the interest paid exceeds a reasonable commercial rate of return, any excess will be treated as an unauthorised member payment and will be taxed in the manner described above (PTM045000). We understand that, to avoid making an unauthorised payment, where the total amount of the refund exceeds the amount of actual contributions made by the member to the scheme, HMRC require refunds to be treated as two distinct payments:

(*a*)   the amount of the contributions actually paid by the member (tax deductible and payable by the scheme administrator); and

(*b*)   the amount of any interest/investment growth (payable gross to the member, who must account for the tax on a self-assessment tax return).

Refund of excess contributions lump sum

17.44   A refund of excess contributions can be made where the member has paid relievable pension contributions in any tax year which are more than the maximum amount that can receive tax relief (see **17.15** above) (*FA 2004, Sch 29, Part 1, para 6*). The rules of a registered scheme would need to make provision for this payment to be made. Any repayment must be made before the end of six years following the end of the tax year in which the excess contributions were made. A refund of excess contributions lump sum is not subject to income tax (*ITEPA 2003, s 636A(1)(c)*, as inserted by *FA 2004, Sch 31, para 11*). If interest is paid, it may count as a scheme administration member payment. If the interest is not calculated at a reasonable commercial rate, the excess may be treated as an unauthorised member payment, with the resulting tax consequences (PTM045000).

Trivial commutation lump sum

17.45   A lump sum is a trivial commutation lump sum if:

(*a*)   no such sum has previously been paid to the member (by any registered pension scheme) or, if it has previously been paid, before the end of the commutation period;

(*b*)   it is paid in respect of a defined benefit arrangement;

(*c*)   on the nominated date, the value of the member's pension rights does not exceed the commutation limit;

(*d*)   all or part of the member's lifetime allowance is available;

(*e*)   it extinguishes any entitlement to defined benefits under the pension scheme;

(*f*)   the member has reached normal minimum pension age (or the ill-health condition is met) (*FA 2004, Sch 29, Part 1, paras 7–9*).

The commutation limit from 6 April 2006 was one per cent of the standard lifetime allowance. From 6 April 2012 the limit was fixed at £18,000 and then was increased by *FA 2014* to £30,000 with effect from 27 March 2014. The member's pension rights on the nominated date are all the member's crystallised and uncrystallised pension rights on that date under all registered arrangements. The benefits from the registered pension schemes that are going to be commuted have to be commuted within the trivial commutation period, which is the 12-month period beginning with the day on which a trivial lump sum is first paid to the member.

The opportunity to take a trivial commutation lump sum from a money purchase arrangement ceased on 5 April 2015 as it has been effectively replaced by the uncrystallised funds pension lump sum (see **17.41** above).

If a member receives a trivial commutation lump sum, he is treated as having taxable pension income for the tax year in which the payment is made equal to the amount of the lump sum (*ITEPA 2003, s 636B(2)*, as inserted by *FA 2004, Sch 31, para 11*). However, if the member has uncrystallised rights the amount of taxable income is reduced by 25 per cent of the value of the uncrystallised rights (*ITEPA 2003, s 636B(3)*).

When valuing the member's entitlement, the value of any spouse's or dependant's pensions should be taken into account. PTM063500 states that: 'Where specifically identifiable contingent dependant benefits/rights exist, these too must be commuted with the member's benefits. They must be included when valuing the member's pension rights.' Any trivial commutation lump sum must be paid to the member not the spouse (*FA 2004, s 166(1)*). The contracting-out legislation allows GMPs and *s 9(2B)* rights to be commuted on the grounds of triviality.

Winding-up lump sum

17.46   A lump sum is a winding-up lump sum if:

(*a*)   the pension scheme is an occupational pension scheme;

(*b*)   the pension scheme is being wound up;

(*c*)   any person by whom the member is employed at the time when the lump sum is paid, and who has made contributions under the pension scheme in respect of the member within the period of five years ending with the day on which it is paid, meets certain conditions);

(*d*)   all or part of a member's lifetime allowance is available; and

(*e*)   it extinguishes the member's entitlement to benefits under the pension scheme (*FA 2004, Sch 29, Part 1, para 10*, as modified by *FA 2007 and FA 2011*).

Since 6 April 2012 the commutation limit has been fixed at £18,000.

The employment conditions are that any employer of the member at the time the lump sum is paid who has made contributions under that scheme in the last five years in respect of the member:

(i)   is not making contributions under any registered pension scheme in respect of the member; and

(ii)   undertakes to HMRC not to make such contributions during the period of one year beginning with the day on which the lump sum is paid (*FA 2004, Sch 29, Part 1, para 10(3)*).

If a member receives a winding-up lump sum, he is treated as having taxable pension income for the tax year in which the payment is made equal to the amount of the lump sum (*ITEPA 2003, s 636B(2)*, as inserted by *FA 2004, Sch 31, para 11*). However, if the member has uncrystallised rights the amount of taxable income is reduced by 25 per cent of the value of the uncrystallised rights (*ITEPA 2003, s 636B(3)*).

Lifetime allowance excess lump sum

17.47   This is the lump sum which is paid when none of the member's lifetime allowance is available. A lifetime allowance excess lump sum is subject to the 55 per cent lifetime allowance tax charge. It cannot be paid before the member reaches normal minimum pension age (unless the ill-health condition is met) (FA 2004, Sch 29, Part 1, para 11). The payment has to be made before age 75 or it will count as an unauthorised payment.

It will be necessary for scheme rules to contain express provision for payment of a lifetime allowance excess lump sum.

Other authorised lump sums – small pots

17.48 The *Registered Pension Schemes (Authorised Payments) Regulations 2009 (SI 2009/1171)* (now amended) added a number of additional authorised lump-sum payments. These include:

(a)   a payment of up to £10,000 made after there has been a 'relevant accretion'. This is to cover a situation where a member's benefits have been transferred out or secured by an annuity and subsequently a payment is received into the scheme or an allocation made in respect of the member. It enables the scheme administrator to make a payment of this subsequent amount to the member;

(b)   a payment of up to £10,000 made by way of compensation under the Financial Services Compensation Scheme which extinguishes the member's entitlement to benefits under the pension scheme;

(c)   a payment which would be a trivial commutation lump sum but for the continuance after the payment of an annuity; and

(d)   payments of up to £10,000 which extinguish a member's entitlement to benefits under the pension scheme (occupational and public service schemes only).

The £10,000 limit in relation to the payments described in paragraphs (a), (b) and (d) above were increased from the previous limit of £2,000 with effect from 27 March 2014.

The regulations were amended with effect from 8 August 2012 to include provision for a part refund payment of a member's contributions relating to short service to be an authorised lump sum payment. One of the conditions for payment of a short service refund lump sum (see **17.43** above) is that the lump sum must extinguish the member's entitlement to benefits under the scheme except, in effect, where the scheme was required by statutory enactment to retain a liability to pay contracted-out protected rights benefits. Following the abolition of contracting-out on the protected rights test with effect from 6 April 2012 (see **Chapter 4**) there ceased to be any requirement for schemes to hold back protected rights when making refunds of contributions. However, some scheme rules will have been drafted in a way which prevents those funds which represented former protected rights from being refunded. Therefore, the regulations were amended to provide that part refund payments which satisfy prescribed requirements will be authorised lump sum payments.

Pension death benefit rules (FA 2004, s 167)

Dependants' pensions under defined benefits arrangements

17.49 The only type of dependants' pension that can be paid in respect of a defined benefits arrangement is a 'dependants' scheme pension' (Pension Death Benefit Rule 2 – *FA 2004, s 167*). A dependants' scheme pension is either a pension paid directly by the scheme out of its own resources or by an insurance company selected by the scheme administrator to a 'dependant' (*FA 2004, Sch 28, Part 2, para 16*).

The following persons qualify as a 'dependant':

(i)   A person who was married to, or the civil partner of, the member at the date of the member's death.

(ii) If the rules of the scheme so provide, a person who was married to, or the civil partner of, the member when the member first became entitled to a pension under the scheme.

(iii) A child of the member who:

  • has not reached age 23; or

  • has reached that age and, in the opinion of the scheme administrator, was at the date of the member's death dependent on the member because of physical or mental impairment.

(iv) A person who was not married to, or the civil partner of, the member at the date of the member's death and is not a child of the member who, in the opinion of the scheme's administrator, at the date of the member's death:

  • was financially dependent on the member;

  • was in a financial relationship with the member of mutual dependence; or

  • was dependent on the member because of physical or mental impairment (*FA 2004, Sch 28, para 15*).

In certain respects, this definition is more restrictive than that which applied under the pre-A-Day regime (as set out in IR12 (2001)), in particular the requirement that a child's pension must cease by age 23, whether or not the child is in full-time education. This means that if, under the *FA 2004* regime, a pension continues to be paid after the child has reached age 23, it is potentially an unauthorised payment. There are transitional provisions which, in limited circumstances, enable certain children's pensions to continue beyond age 23.

Dependants', nominees' and successors' pensions under money purchase arrangements

17.50 The types of pension that can be paid under money purchase arrangements after the member's death are summarised in the table below.

Under the pension death benefit rules, pension death benefits from money purchase arrangements can only be paid to 'dependants' (see **17.49** above) and, on and after 6 April 2015, to 'nominees' and 'successors' (*FA 2004, s 167, Pension Death Benefit Rule 1*). Dependants, nominees and successors are referred to collectively as 'beneficiaries'.

A 'nominee' of the member is an individual:

(*a*)   nominated by the member; or

(*b*)   nominated by the scheme administrator,

who is not a dependant of the member (*FA 2004, Sch 28, para 27A(1)*).

An individual nominated by the scheme administrator will not count as a nominee at any time when there is:

(*a*)   a dependant of the member; or

(*b*)   an individual, or charity, nominated by the member in relation to the benefits (*FA 2004, Sch 28, para 27A(2)*).

A 'successor' means an individual:

(*a*)   nominated by a dependant of the member;

(*b*)   nominated by a nominee of the member;

(*c*)   nominated by a successor of the member; or

(*d*)   nominated by the scheme administrator (*FA 2004, Sch 28, para 27F(1)*).

An individual nominated by the scheme administrator will not count as a successor at any time after the beneficiary's death when there is an individual, or charity, nominated by the beneficiary in relation to the benefits (*FA 2004, Sch 28, para 27F(2)*).

Where a successor of the member is an individual who is also a dependant of the member, the individual in the capacity of a successor is to be treated as not also being a dependant of the member (*FA 2004, Sch 28, para 27F(4)*).

789

References in the table to the 'relevant two-year period' is to a period within two years after the day on which the scheme administrator first knew (or could reasonably have been expected to know) of the member's, nominee's or successor's death.

Pension	Source/conditions	Tax treatment
Dependants' scheme pension	Payable by the scheme administrator or by an insurance company selected by the scheme administrator. The member or dependant must first have had the opportunity to select a dependant's annuity instead (*FA 2004, s 167(1), rule 3*). Where the member dies age over 75 then there may be limits on the amount of dependants' scheme pension which can be paid as an authorised payment (*FA 2004, Sch 28, paras 16A–16C* and PTM072120).	Taxed as income in the hands of the recipient (*ITEPA 2003, ss 579A–579C*).
Dependants' or nominees' annuity	Annuity must be purchased from an insurance company. This could be during the member's lifetime alongside the purchase of a lifetime annuity or from uncrystallised funds or unused drawdown funds following the death of the member. It may also be purchased from the drawdown fund of the dependant or flexi-access drawdown fund of the dependant or nominee (*FA 2004, Sch 28, paras 17, 27AA* and PTM07220).	Generally free of tax where the member died on or after 3 December 2014 and before age 75 and no payment was made under the annuity before 6 April 2015. Where the annuity was purchased using at least some uncrystallised funds then the entitlement to the annuity must have arisen within the relevant two-year period. Where the annuity was purchased from the recipients own drawdown funds then there must have been no income withdrawal from the fund before 6 April 2015 (*ITEPA 2003, ss 579A–579D, 646B, 646C* and *683*).

Pension	Source/conditions	Tax treatment
Successors' annuity	Annuity must be purchased from an insurance company using undrawn funds from a beneficiary's flexi-access drawdown fund immediately before their death. It may also be purchased from the flexi-access drawdown fund of the successor (*FA 2004, Sch 28, para 27FA* and PTM072200).	Generally tax free where the beneficiary died on or after 3 December 2014 and before age 75 and no payment was made under the annuity before 6 April 2015 (*ITEPA 2003, ss 579A–579D, 646B, 646C* and *683*).
Dependants' drawdown pension	Applies only where a dependant had designated funds for drawdown before 6 April 2015. Where a dependant had designated funds for flexible drawdown then this automatically converted to flexi-access drawdown on 6 April 2015. Where the dependant was taking capped drawdown then he can continue to take capped drawdown or convert the fund into a flexi-access drawdown fund (PTM072410 and PTM072310).	Income tax is generally payable under PAYE (*ITEPA 2003, ss 579A–579D* and *683*).

Pension	Source/conditions	Tax treatment
Beneficiaries' short-term annuity	Annuity purchased from funds designated for dependant's drawdown or beneficiary's flexi-access drawdown. It must be payable by an insurance company for a term not exceeding five years and ending before the death of the beneficiary (*FA 2004, Sch 28, paras 20, 27C* and *27H* and PTM072420).	Generally tax-free where the beneficiary died on or after 3 December 2014 and before age 75 and no payment was made under the annuity before 6 April 2015 (*ITEPA 2003, ss 579A* and *646C*).
Beneficiaries' income withdrawal	The beneficiary must designate sums and assets as being available for drawdown from unused drawdown funds or uncrystallised funds (*FA 2004, Sch 28, paras 21–22A, 27B–27E* and *27G–27K* and PTM072430).	BCE 5C (for lifetime allowance purposes) will be triggered where uncrystallised funds are used and the member died aged under age 75 and the designation occurs within the relevant two-year period (*FA 2004, s 216*). Income tax will not generally be payable where the member or relevant beneficiary dies before age 75. Where uncrystallised funds are designated after 6 April 2015, the member dies before age 75 and the designation does not occur until after the relevant two year period then there will be an income tax charge (*ITEPA 2003, ss 579A* and *579CZA*).

Lump sum death benefit rule (FA 2004, s 168)

Lump sum death benefits

17.51 Under the lump sum death benefit rule, no lump sum death benefits can be paid other than:

(*a*) a defined benefits lump sum death benefit;

(*b*)   a pension protection lump sum death benefit;

(*c*)   an uncrystallised funds lump sum death benefit;

(*d*)   an annuity protection lump sum death benefit;

(*e*)   a drawdown pension fund lump sum death benefit (which can be paid on the death of a member or dependant);

(*f*)   a flexi-access drawdown fund lump sum death benefit (which can be paid on the death of a member, dependant, nominee or successor);

(*g*)   a charity lump sum death benefit;

(*h*)   a trivial commutation lump sum death benefit; or

(*i*)   a winding-up lump sum death benefit (payable on or before 5 April 2015).

For this purpose 'lump sum death benefit' means a lump sum payable on the death of the member (*FA 2004, s 168* as modified by *FA 2007, FA 2011* and *ToPA 2014*).

References in the following paragraphs to the 'relevant two-year period' are to a period within two years after the day on which the scheme administrator first knew (or could reasonably have been expected to know) of the member's, nominee's or successor's death.

Defined benefits lump sum death benefit

17.52   A lump sum death benefit is a 'defined benefits lump sum death benefit' if:

(*a*)   it is paid in respect of a defined benefits arrangement;

(*b*)   where the member had not reached age 75 at the date of death and payment is before 6 April 2016, it is paid before the end of the 'relevant two-year period'; and

(*c*)   it is not a pension protection lump sum death benefit, a trivial commutation lump sum death benefit or a winding-up lump sum death benefit (*FA 2004, Sch 29, Part 2, para 13*, as modified by *FA 2007, FA 2011 and Finance (No 2) Act 2015*).

The requirement at (*b*) above does not apply to payments made on or after 6 April 2016 (but see below regarding taxation of a defined lump sum death benefit).

If a defined benefits lump-sum death benefit paid on or after 6 April 2016 is made in respect of a member who died before reaching age 75 and it is paid within the relevant two-year period, it will not be taxable (*ITEPA 2003, s 636A(4)*). The benefit will however be tested against the member's lifetime allowance under benefit crystallisation event 7 (see **17.14** above).

A defined benefits lump sum death benefit will be taxable in the following circumstances:

(*a*)   where, at the date of death, the member was aged 75 or more; or

(*b*)   where the member was under age 75 at the date of death but payment is not made within the relevant two-year period.

Where a defined benefits lump-sum death benefit is paid in the circumstances described above, the benefit will either be subject to tax as pension income (*ITEPA 2003, s 579A*), or it will be subject to the 'special lump-sum death benefits charge' of (currently) 45 per cent (*FA 2004, s 206*). The way in which the benefit is taxed will depend upon whether it is paid to a 'qualifying person' (when it will be taxed as pension income) or to a 'non-qualifying person' (when it will be subject to the special lump-sum death benefits charge). An explanation of the procedure for deducting income tax and for payment by the scheme administrator of the special lump-sum death benefits charge can be found at PTM073010. In broad terms, a 'qualifying person' is an individual or a bare trustee. Where payment is made to a non-individual (eg to personal representatives), the payment would be to a non-qualifying person (*ITEPA 2003, ss 636A(4ZA), 636AA*, as modified by *FA (No 2) Act 2015, ITEPA 2003, ss 636A(4)* and *FA 2004*, as modified by *FA (No 2) Act 2015*).

Taxable payments before 6 April 2016 were subject to the special lump sum death benefits charge of 45 per cent (55 per cent before 6 April 2015).

Pension protection lump sum death benefit

17.53   This benefit can be paid in respect of a scheme pension under a defined benefits arrangement where the member has specified that it is to be treated as a pension protection lump sum death benefit (instead of a defined benefits lump sum death benefit).

A lump sum death benefit is a pension protection lump sum death benefit if:

(*a*)   it is paid in respect of a defined benefits arrangement;

(*b*)   it is paid in respect of a scheme pension to which the member was entitled at the date of death; and

(*c*)   the member has specified that it is to be treated as a pension protection lump sum death benefit (instead of a defined benefits lump sum death benefit).

The maximum lump sum that can be paid is broadly the amount crystallised by reason of the member becoming entitled to a pension, less the amount of pension paid before the date of death and less the amount of pension protection lump sum death benefit previously paid in respect of the pension (*FA 2004, Sch 29, Part 2, para 14*).

A pension protection lump sum death benefit paid on or after 6 April 2016 will only be subject to tax if it is paid after the member has reached age 75. The tax position will depend upon whether the benefit is paid to a 'qualifying person' or to a 'non-qualifying person' on the same principles as those described above in relation to payment of a defined benefits lump sum death benefit (see **17.52** above).

Prior to 6 April 2015 an administrator was subject to tax on the payment of a pension protection lump sum death benefit at the rate of 55 per cent irrespective of the member's age at the date of death (*FA 2004, s 206* amended with retrospective effect from 6 April 2011 *(FA 2011)*; *ITEPA 2003, s 636A(4) (b)*, as inserted by *FA 2004, Sch 31, para 11*).

Trivial commutation lump sum death benefit

17.54   A trivial commutation lump sum death benefit can be paid to a dependant to extinguish his entitlement to a dependant's pension or, from 6 April 2015, to a surviving beneficiary to extinguish that beneficiary's entitlement to receive remaining pension or annuity payments due to the member under a guarantee. The amount of the lump sum cannot exceed £30,000 (increased from £18,000 from 6 April 2015) (*FA 2004, Sch 29, Part 2, para 20* as amended by *FA 2011* and *ToPA 2014*).

If a trivial commutation lump sum death benefit is paid, the person who receives it is treated as having taxable income for the tax year in which the payment is made equal to the amount of the lump sum (*ITEPA 2003, s 636C*, as inserted by *FA 2004, Sch 31, para 11*).

Lump sum death benefits from money purchase arrangements

17.55   Lump sum death benefits payable under money purchase arrangements are summarised in the table below.

The terms 'dependants', 'beneficiaries' and 'relevant two-year period' are as described in **17.50** above.

Lump sum	Source/conditions	Tax treatment
Uncrystallised funds lump sum death benefit ('UFLSDB')	Paid from relevant uncrystallised funds (ie funds not previously used to purchase an annuity or designated for drawdown) (*FA 2004, Sch 29, para 15*).	*Benefits paid on or after 6 April 2016:* If the member dies under age 75 and the UFLSDB is paid within the relevant two-year period, the lump sum will be tested against the lifetime allowance. Any sum in excess of the lifetime allowance will be taxed at 55 per cent (*FA 2004, Sch 32, para 2*). Subject to this, no tax will be payable on the UFLSDB. If the member dies age 75 or over, or under 75 and the payment is not made within the relevant two-year period, then either income tax will be payable or the special lump sum death benefits tax charge (depending on the recipient). *Benefits paid before 6 April 2016:* As above for members dying under age 75 where the UFLSDB is paid within the two-year relevant period. If the member died age 75 or over, or under 75 and the payment was not made within the relevant two-year period, then the lump sum was taxed at 45 per cent (55 per cent for payments made before 6 April 2015). (*ITEPA 2003, ss 636A and 636AA and FA 2004, s 206*)

Lump sum	Source/conditions	Tax treatment
Annuity protection lump sum death benefit	Paid in respect of a scheme pension or lifetime annuity to which the member was entitled at the date of the member's death. The amount payable is limited broadly to amount of scheme pension or annuity which crystallised for lifetime annuity purposes less the amount of payments made to the member (*FA 2004, Sch 29, para 16*).	If paid before 6 April 2015, a special lump sum death benefits charge of 55 per cent was payable. If paid between 6 April 2015 and 5 April 2016, tax-free if the member dies under age 75 and a special lump sum death benefits charge of 45 per cent if the member dies age 75 or over. For payments made from 6 April 2016, tax free if the member dies under age 75 and where the member dies age 75 or over either income tax will be payable or the special lump sum death benefits tax charge (depending on the recipient). (*ITEPA 2003, ss 636A and 636AA and FA 2004, s 206*)

Lump sum	Source/conditions	Tax treatment
Drawdown pension fund lump sum death benefit	Paid in respect of assets remaining in a member's or dependant's capped drawdown fund on the death of the member or dependant (*FA 2004, Sch 29, para 17* and PTM073500).	*For payments made on or after 6 April 2016:* If the member or dependant dies under age 75 and the lump sum is paid within the relevant two-year period then no tax will be payable. If the member or dependant dies age 75 or over, or under 75 and the payment is not made within the relevant two-year period, then either income tax will be payable or the special lump sum death benefits tax charge (depending on the recipient). *For payments made between 6 April 2015 and 5 April 2016:* If the member or dependant died under age 75 and the lump sum is paid within the relevant two-year period then no tax will be payable. If the member or dependant died age 75 or over, or under 75 and the payment is not made within the relevant two-year period, then a special lump sum death benefits tax charge of 45 per cent will be payable. *(ITEPA 2003, ss 636AA(4)* and *FA 2004, s 206)*

Lump sum	Source/conditions	Tax treatment
Flexi-access drawdown fund lump sum death benefit	Paid in respect of assets remaining in member's or beneficiary's flexi-access drawdown fund on the death of the member or beneficiary (*FA 2004, Sch 29, para 17A* and PTM073600).	For payments made on or after 6 April 2016: If the member or beneficiary dies under age 75 and the lump sum is paid within the relevant two-year period then no tax will be payable. If the member or beneficiary dies age 75 or over, or under 75 and the payment is not made within the relevant two-year period, then either income tax will be payable or the special lump sum death benefits tax charge (depending on the recipient). For payments made between 6 April 2015 and 5 April 2016: If the member or beneficiary died under age 75 and the lump sum is paid within the relevant two-year period then no tax will be payable. If the member or beneficiary died age 75 or over, or under 75 and the payment is not made within the relevant two-year period, then a special lump sum death benefits tax charge of 45 per cent will be payable. (*ITEPA 2003, ss 636AA(5)* and *FA 2004, s 206*)

Lump sum	Source/conditions	Tax treatment
Charity lump sum death benefit	Paid to a charity nominated by the member in respect of assets remaining in a member's capped drawdown fund or flexi-access drawdown fund on the death of the member where there are no dependants. Paid to a charity nominated by the member in respect of uncrystallised funds remaining on the death of the member where there are no dependants (for payments made before 16 September 2016 the member must have died age 75 or over). Paid to a charity nominated by the member, or if no nomination, one nominated by the beneficiary, in respect of assets remaining in a dependant's drawdown fund or a beneficiary's flexi-access drawdown fund on the death of the beneficiary where there are no dependants of the member. *(FA 2004, Sch 29, para 18* and PTM073900).	No tax payable.

Lump sum	Source/conditions	Tax treatment
Trivial commutation lump sum death benefit.	See **17.54** above.	

Winding-up lump sum death benefit

17.56   Prior to 6 April 2015, on the winding up of a pension scheme, a winding-up lump sum death benefit could be paid to a dependant to extinguish his entitlement to pension death benefit and lump sum death benefit in respect of the member. The amount of the lump sum paid could not exceed £18,000 (*FA 2004, Sch 29, Part 2, para 21* as amended by *FA 2011* and repealed from 17 December 2014 by *TPA 2014*).

If a winding-up lump sum death benefit was paid, the person who received it was treated as having taxable income for the tax year in which the payment was made equal to the amount of the lump sum (*ITEPA 2003, s 636C*, as inserted by *FA 2004, Sch 31, para 11*).

From 6 April 2015 a lump sum that would otherwise have satisfied the conditions for a winding-up lump sum death benefit will meet the conditions for payment as a trivial commutation lump sum death benefit (see **17.54** above).

Life assurance only members in occupational pension schemes

17.57   In most cases it is possible to retain life assurance only members in occupational pension schemes. As explained in **17.21** above, the trustees or managers of occupational pension schemes with their main administration in the UK have an obligation to secure that the activities of the scheme are restricted to 'retirement benefit activities' (*PA 2004, s 255*). Broadly, 'retirement benefit activities' are operations related to retirement benefits and activities arising from operations related to retirement benefits.

There is uncertainty whether the provision of life assurance benefits for members who are included in a scheme solely for such benefits fall within the definition of 'retirement benefits'. This will depend on what is meant by 'related to' as highlighted above. It would appear from the parliamentary debates that the relevant provisions in *PA 2004* were inserted to mirror the EU *Directive 2003/41/EC on the Activities and Supervision of Institutions for Occupational Retirement Provisions* ('*IORP Directive*') and were not intended to restrict existing activities of occupational pension schemes. However, on a narrow interpretation of *PA 2004* provisions, only members with full scheme benefits could have death benefits 'arising from' or 'supplementary to' them. But, on a wider view, the death benefits would be sufficiently 'related to' the retirement benefits provided to other members to be allowed. The Regulator's view is that, as long as there is a concrete and identifiable link between an individual's life assurance benefits and 'main' pension benefits, there will be no breach of this requirement. This may require the scheme providing the life assurance benefits to expressly provide that members entitled to those benefits are also entitled to pension benefits in another scheme made available by the employer.

Transfers

Transfers out

17.58   If the rules of the scheme permit, or there is a statutory right to transfer, a member will, generally, be able to transfer his benefits under the *FA 2004* regime without adverse tax consequences, subject to certain conditions (see PTM100010). Broadly, a transfer can be made without adverse tax consequences if it counts as a 'recognised transfer' – a type of authorised payment (*FA 2004, ss 164(1)(c), 169*). A 'recognised transfer' is a transfer of sums or assets held for the purposes of, or representing accrued rights under, a registered pension scheme so as to be held for the purposes of, or to represent rights under:

(*a*)   another registered pension scheme; or

(*b*)   a qualifying recognised overseas pension scheme (see **17.60** below),

in connection with a member of that pension scheme (*FA 2004, s 169*). Transfers from a registered pension scheme to an insurance company will also generally count as recognised transfers if the sums transferred are applied to provide a scheme pension or dependant's scheme pension (*FA 2004, s 169(1A)–(1C)*).

A recognised transfer will not be treated as a contribution (*FA 2004, s 188(5)*).

For lifetime allowance purposes:

(*a*)   a transfer to another registered pension scheme will not be a benefit crystallisation event; and

(*b*)   a transfer to a qualifying recognised overseas pension scheme will be tested under benefit crystallisation event 8 (see **17.14** above).

With regard to the annual allowance test, for defined benefits arrangements and cash balance arrangements, the test is performed by comparing the value of rights between the opening value and closing value in a pension input period. Any increase in the rights between the two will produce the pension input amount to be tested (see **17.17** above). Where a recognised transfer is made, it is necessary in the relevant pension input periods to make certain adjustments to the closing values of the arrangements under both the transferring and receiving schemes, so as to compare like with like. Therefore, in the case of a transfer-out, the amount of the reduction in benefits under the transferring arrangement is added back to the member's benefits for the purpose of calculating the closing value of the member's benefits under that arrangement. Conversely, in the case of a transfer-in, the amount of the increase in the member's benefits under the receiving arrangement is subtracted from the member's benefits for the purposes of calculating the closing value of the member's benefits under the receiving arrangement (*FA 2004, s 236(4)* and *(5)* as amended by *FA 2011*).

If a transfer is made which is not a recognised transfer, it will count as an unauthorised payment with the tax consequences described earlier in this chapter (see **17.25–17.27** above).

As part of a joint campaign with the DWP and Regulator to prevent pensions liberation (where individuals are encouraged to access their pension savings early, often by transferring them to sham arrangements), HMRC has introduced a new process to help trustees decide if the requested transfer is to a registered pension scheme. Under this new process HMRC will respond to requests for confirmation of the registration status of the receiving scheme without seeking consent from the receiving scheme. HMRC will provide confirmation where the receiving scheme is registered and the information held by HMRC does not indicate a significant risk that the scheme was set up, or is being used, to facilitate pension liberation. See **Chapter 6** for more on transfer payments and pensions liberation.

In the case of a transfer to an insured scheme (defined as meaning a pension scheme all the income and other assets of which are invested in policies of insurance), the administrator of the transferring scheme should ensure that any transfer is made directly to the scheme administrator or the insurance company which issues policies under the receiving scheme. Failure to do so can result in a fine of up to £3,000 (see *FA 2004, s 266* and PTM100010).

Care also needs to be taken to avoid any loss of lifetime allowance protection (see **17.8** above) on making a transfer.

Partial transfers

17.59 Under *FA 2004*, it is possible to make a partial transfer from any type of registered pension scheme as long as the rights under the arrangement being transferred are uncrystallised. Any transfer is also subject to relevant contracting-out transfer requirements and to the express provisions of the scheme.

From 6 April 2015 members who are no longer accruing benefits and, in the case of members with benefits that are not 'flexible benefits' who are below normal pension age, will generally have a separate transfer right in respect of their (a) money purchase benefits; (b) flexible benefits other than money purchase benefits; and (c) benefits that are not flexible benefits (*PSA 1993, s 93* as amended by *PSA 2015*) (see **Chapter 6**). In other situations, generally if a partial transfer is to be made from an occupational pension scheme, there will need to be a specific power in the scheme rules (independent of any statutory transfer right).

Transfers to qualifying recognised overseas pension schemes

17.60   A transfer out can be made to a qualifying recognised overseas pension scheme without adverse tax consequences. A qualifying recognised overseas pension scheme is a pension scheme which:

(a)   meets the conditions enabling it to be treated as an 'overseas pension scheme' under *FA 2004, s 150(7)*;

(b)   meets the additional conditions enabling it to be treated as a 'recognised overseas pension scheme' under *FA 2004, s 150(8)*; and

(c)   meets other conditions laid down in *FA 2004, s 169*.

The Pension Schemes (Information Requirements – Qualifying Overseas Pension Schemes, Qualifying Recognised Overseas Pensions Schemes and Corresponding Relief) Regulations 2006 (SI 2006/208) as amended with effect from 6 April 2012 and 14 October 2013, set out the information which a qualifying recognised overseas pension scheme must provide to HMRC.

HMRC has the power to exclude a scheme from being a qualifying recognised overseas pension scheme in certain circumstances. The following events can trigger an HMRC decision to exclude a scheme:

(a)   the scheme has no scheme manager;

(b)   there has been a significant failure to comply with a requirement imposed by the prescribed information requirements;

(c)   any information given when complying with the prescribed information requirements is false in a material respect; or

(d)   any declaration given when complying with the prescribed information requirements is false in a material respect (*FA 2004, s 169(5)*).

There is an appeal procedure against such a decision (*FA 2004, s 170*).

HMRC maintains a list of qualifying recognised overseas pension schemes that have consented to their details being published – not all qualifying recognised overseas pension schemes will necessarily feature on it. HMRC states that publication on the list should not be seen as confirmation that HMRC has verified all the information supplied by the scheme. If a scheme has been included on the list in circumstances where it should not have been included because it did not satisfy the conditions to be a recognised overseas pension scheme, any transfer made to that scheme could potentially give rise to an unauthorised payments charge liability (see PTM102000 and PTM1023000).

Retention of pre-A-Day rights – transitional protection post-transfer

17.61 If a member is entitled to a protected pension age, they may be able to retain this following the transfer if certain conditions are met (*FA 2004, Sch 36, paras 21, 22(5)* and *23(5)*) (see **17.29** above and PTM028000). Careful consideration needs to be given before making a transfer as to whether any of these protections could be lost as a result.

Transfers of pensions in payment or rights where there is already an entitlement to benefits

17.62 Generally under the pre-A-Day tax regimes, transfers could not be made once the member had reached normal retirement age. *FA 2004* permits the transfer of pensions in payment or rights where there is an entitlement to benefits subject to certain conditions being met.

The conditions relating to such transfers are described in PTM107000. Failure to meet the required conditions will result in the payment being an unauthorised payment with the tax consequences discussed previously. The rules or governing documentation of the registered pension scheme will generally need to make express provision for the making of such transfers.

Transfers in

17.63 A transfer in can be accepted from:

(*a*)   a registered pension scheme; or

(*b*)   a recognised overseas pension scheme; or

(*c*)   an unregistered pension scheme which does not count as a recognised overseas pension scheme (eg an employer financed retirement benefits scheme or a non-UK pension scheme that does not satisfy the requirements to count as a recognised overseas pension scheme).

A transfer in from any of these sources will not count as an unauthorised payment. Transfers in do not count as a contribution to the scheme so are not tax relievable (see *FA 2004, s 188(5)*). There will also be no benefit crystallisation event on a transfer in.

Contracting-out requirements relating to transfers in also have to be complied with (see **Chapter 4**).

As, generally, no UK tax relief will have been received on benefits transferred in from a recognised overseas pension scheme, special treatment is given in relation to the lifetime allowance. The individual's lifetime allowance can be enhanced by the amount of the transfer in if an application is made to HMRC (see *FA 2004, ss 224–226* and PTM095400). The enhancement will not apply in relation to any part of the transfer payment which is derived from tax relieved contributions to a qualifying overseas pension scheme.

On a transfer from a non-registered scheme that is not a recognised overseas pension scheme, again there is no tax relief on the transfer in, but the investment funds derived from the transfer will be free of income and capital gains tax. There will again be no benefit crystallisation event on the transfer in but, when the member takes his benefits, the amount crystallised that is derived from the transfer in will count towards the lifetime allowance.

Investment and scheme borrowing

17.64   *FA 2004* does not contain any general restrictions on investments for registered pension schemes. However some restrictions have been introduced to prevent people directing the scheme to acquire assets from which a personal benefit is derived, rather than acquiring assets for the purpose of building a fund for retirement. These provisions were introduced into *FA 2004* (as *Sch 29A*) by *FA 2006* in relation to 'investment-regulated pension schemes' ('IRPS's). These are schemes where a member, or person related to a member, is or has been able, directly or indirectly, to direct, influence or advise on scheme investment. The legislation applies to direct and indirect investment in residential property and most forms of tangible moveable property, which are collectively referred to as 'taxable property'.

FA 2004, s 174A provides that, where an IRPS acquires an interest in 'taxable property', and it is held for the purposes of an arrangement under the pension scheme relating to the member, then that pension scheme will be treated as having made an unauthorised payment to the member. Subsequent improvements to that property will also constitute an unauthorised payment, as will the conversion of non-residential property to residential use.

The provisions in *FA 2004, Sch 29A* provide the definitions and details required to operate *s 174A*, and relate to schemes that hold a direct or indirect interest in 'taxable property'. Taxable property includes 'residential property' (*FA 2004, Sch 29A, paras 7–10*) and 'tangible moveable property' (*FA 2004, Sch 29A, para 11*).

Residential property is defined in *FA 2004, Sch 29A, para 7* as:

(*a*)   a building that is used or suitable for use as a dwelling;

(*b*)   any land consisting of or forming part of the garden or grounds of such a building (including a building on any such land) which is used or intended for use for a purpose connected with the enjoyment of the building;

(*c*)   a hotel or similar accommodation, unless it is a whole hotel (*FA 2004, Sch 29A, para 13(2)*); or

(*d*)   a beach hut.

Building includes a structure and part of a building or structure (*FA 2004, Sch 29A, para 7*). PTM125200 provides that:

(*a*)   if a building includes a large number of separate flats, these are each treated as separate buildings;

(*b*)   if a building includes a shop with a wholly separate flat, these are separate buildings. A flat is wholly separate if it has a separate entrance and has no inter-connection with other parts (other than a communal hallway); and

(*c*)   if a building comprises part which is used for commercial purposes, such as a shop with an interconnected residential area such as a flat, then the whole will be treated as suitable for residential purposes.

The following are not considered to be residential property (*FA 2004, Sch 29A, para 8*):

(*a*)   a children's home;

(*b*)   a student hall of residence;

(*c*)   residential care homes for people by reason of old age, disability, past or present dependence on alcohol or drugs, or past or present mental disorder;

(*d*)   a hospital or hospice; or

(*e*)   a prison or similar establishment.

Furthermore, *FA 2004, Sch 29A, para 10* provides that residential property is not taxable property where 'Condition A' or 'Condition B' is met:

- *Condition A*: The property is, or is to be, occupied by an employee, who is not a member or connected with a member of the pension scheme, nor connected to the employer and is required as a condition of employment to occupy the property.

- *Condition B*: The property is, or is to be, occupied by a person, who is not a member or connected with a member of the pension scheme and is used in connection with business premises held as in investment of the pension scheme.

Land or a building in the process of development becomes residential property from the point when it is first suitable for use as a dwelling (PTM125200).

Tangible moveable property is not defined in *FA 2004, Sch 29A, para 11* and it does not appear to be defined anywhere else in tax legislation. PTM125100 describes it as 'things that can be touched and that are moveable rather than immovable property'. Examples given are 'art, antiques, classic cars and also plant and machinery'.

The *Investment-regulated Pension Schemes (Exception of Tangible Moveable Property) Order 2006 (SI 2006/1959)* specify particular items that are not to be regarded as taxable property for the purposes of *FA 2004, Sch 29A*. These include:

(*a*) gold bullion; and

(*b*) any item of tangible moveable property (whose market value does not exceed £6,000) that:

    (i) is held by a vehicle (within the meaning of *FA 2004, Sch 29A, para 20(2)*) solely for the purposes of the administration or management of the vehicle;

    (ii) in which the relevant IRPS does not hold an interest directly; and

    (iii) where a member of the pension scheme or a person connected with such a member does not occupy or use, or have any right to occupy or use, the property.

The provisions contained in *FA 2004, Sch 29A* apply where taxable property is held either 'directly' or 'indirectly'. *FA 2004* defines both terms.

Direct holdings are interests which are held jointly, in common or alone where the person:

(*a*) holds the property or any estate, interest, right or power in or over the property;

(*b*) has the right to use the property, or participate in arrangements relating to its use;

(c)   has the benefit of any obligation, restriction or condition affecting the value of any estate, interest, right or power in or over the property; or

(d)   is entitled to receive payments determined by reference to the value of or income from the property.

FA 2004, Sch 29A, para 15 goes on to specify a number of exceptions to the general principles of direct holding, related to holding assets through insurance products.

Indirect holdings are interests that are held jointly, in common or alone where the person holds an interest in a person who holds a direct or indirect interest in the property. It also includes circumstances where one person makes another a loan to acquire property.

Holding an interest includes participating in a collective investment scheme under *FSMA 2000, s 235* (*FA 2004, Sch 29A, para 18*) and holding an interest in a trust (*para 19*).

There are exceptions where a scheme will not be taken to have an indirect holding:

(a)   Holding through a 'trading vehicle' which must satisfy four conditions:

    (i)   the main activity is carrying on a trade, vocation or profession;

    (ii)   the pension scheme, alone or with associated persons, does not have control;

    (iii)   neither a scheme member nor person connected is a controlling director of the vehicle nor of any other vehicle which holds a direct or indirect interest in the vehicle; and

    (iv)   the pension scheme does not hold an interest for the purpose of enabling a member or connected person to occupy or use the property (*FA 2004, Sch 29A, para 21*).

(b)   A UK REIT within the meaning of *Part 12* of the *Corporation Tax Act 2010* (*FA 2004, Sch 29A, para 22*) and the conditions below are met.

(c)   Other vehicles meeting certain conditions. The conditions are that:

    (i)   the vehicle must hold at least £1 million of assets, or at least three assets which consist of an interest in residential property, and no asset held directly by the vehicle which consists of an interest in taxable property has a value which exceeds 40 per cent of the total value of the assets held directly by the vehicle;

    (ii)   if the vehicle is a company, it must be a non-close company; and

(iii) the vehicle must not have as its main purpose, or one of its main purposes, the direct or indirect holding of an animal or animals used for sporting purposes.

The additional conditions in relation to (*b*) and (*c*) above are that:

(i) the pension scheme's interest in the vehicle must not be for the purpose of enabling a member or a person connected with a member to occupy or use the property; and

(ii) where the scheme is not an occupational pension scheme, no arrangement under the pension scheme, either alone or together with one or more associated persons, directly or indirectly holds an interest of 10 per cent or more in the vehicle nor does the interest in the vehicle give rise to income or gains from a specific property (*FA 2004, Sch 29A, para 24*).

Where the interest increases without any new holding being taken (for example by another participant leaving), there will be no charge to tax unless the increase was as part of a deliberate device to avoid tax (*FA 2004, Sch 29A, para 29*).

Scheme borrowing is limited to 50 per cent of scheme assets at the time the loan is taken out. Any borrowing above that limit will count as an unauthorised payment with the tax consequences discussed above (*FA 2004, ss 182–185*). In practice, only trust-based occupational schemes with fewer than 100 members or certain categories of 'small schemes' will be able to take advantage of this flexibility as, generally, trust based schemes are not permitted to borrow money or act as a guarantor, other than for the purpose of providing temporary liquidity for the scheme and on a temporary basis (*Occupational Pension Scheme (Investment) Regulations 2005 (SI 2005/3378), reg 5* – see **Chapter 10**).

Restrictions on investment in the sponsoring employer and associated employers are limited to 5 per cent of the fund value (see **Chapter 10**).

Fund income

General

17.65 Investment income derived from investments or deposits held for the purposes of a registered pension scheme is exempt from income tax (*FA 2004, s 186*). This exemption does not apply, however, to investments or deposits held as a member of a property investment LLP (*FA 2004, s 186(2)*) or in relation to taxable property held by an investment-regulated pension scheme (*FA 2004, ss 185A–185H*).

Income from a trading activity of a registered pension scheme does not fall within the above exemption (see **17.66** below and **Chapter 10** for a discussion of what is meant by 'trading').

Underwriting commissions applied for the purposes of a registered pension scheme which are not relevant foreign income and which would otherwise be chargeable to income tax under *ITTOIA 2005, Part 5, Chapter 8* (income not otherwise charged) are exempt from income tax (*FA 2004, s 186(1)(b)*).

Stock lending fees received by a registered pension scheme from any investment held by a registered pension scheme will, generally, also be exempt unless they derive from investments in a property investment LLP (*FA 2004, s 186; ICTA 1988, s 129B*).

Futures and options contracts involving registered pension schemes are also defined as falling within the definition of investments and therefore fall within the exemption for income tax (*FA 2004, s 186(3)*).

Any gains realised by a person on a disposal of investments held for the purposes of a registered pension scheme are not chargeable to capital gains tax (*TCGA 1992, s 271(1A)*). However, a gain arising from the acquisition or disposal of assets held as a member of a property investment LLP will be a chargeable gain liable to capital gains tax (*TCGA 1992, s 271(12)*, as amended by *FA 2004, s 187(7)*).

Capital gains derived from dealing in financial futures or options are also exempt from capital gains tax (*TCGA 1992, s 271(10)*).

If a registered pension scheme invests directly in assets, the income and gain from that investment will benefit from tax relief. Registered pension schemes can also pay premiums to invest indirectly in assets through an insurance policy where the underlying assets are owned by the insurance company. These underlying investments do not benefit from the same tax exemptions. An insurance company can, however, apply the premiums it receives from registered pension schemes to its 'pension business' fund, which will enable them to benefit from a similar tax treatment to that which would apply if they were directly invested. *FA 2012, Part 2*.

An insurance company's life assurance business is 'pension business' if:

(*a*)   it consists of the effecting or carrying out of contracts entered into for the purposes of a registered pension scheme, or

(*b*)   it is the re-insurance of business within paragraph (*a*) (*FA 2012, s 58*).

Trading

17.66   Certain activities undertaken by pension scheme trustees may be classed as trading by HMRC. This does not prevent a pension scheme from being a registered pension scheme. However, tax is payable on the income derived from such activities. This is discussed in **Chapter 10**.

Tax treatment of payments to employers

Authorised surplus payments

17.67   If a repayment of surplus is made to an employer, this must be in accordance with the requirements of *PA 1995, s 37* (see **Chapter 11**). An authorised surplus payment will be an authorised employer payment if it meets the requirements prescribed under *FA 2004, s 177* (*Registered Pension Schemes (Authorised Surplus Payments) Regulations 2006, SI 2006/574*), which include compliance with *PA 1995, s 37*. There will be a 35 per cent tax charge on any authorised surplus payments to the employer (*FA 2004, s 207*). The scheme administrator is liable to pay the tax and should account for it by using the accounting for tax return (see **17.79** below and PTM145200).

Tax treatment of benefits paid to members

Pension benefits

17.68   Pensions paid under a registered pension scheme (other than any pension which gives rise to an unauthorised payments charge and certain pension death benefits payable after 6 April 2015 out of money purchase funds (see **17.50** above)) will be taxable as pension income (*ITEPA 2003, ss 566(4), 579A* and *579B*). The taxable pension income for the year is the full amount of the pension under the registered pension scheme that accrues in the year irrespective of when any amount is actually paid (*ITEPA 2003, s 579B*). The person liable for the income tax is the person receiving or entitled to the pension under the registered pension scheme (*ITEPA 2003, s 579C*).

Any unauthorised pension paid under a registered pension scheme will also be chargeable to income tax as pension income unless the unauthorised pension has been assessed to income tax as an unauthorised payment.

PAYE will apply to all pensions from registered pension schemes which are taxed as pension income. The payer of the pension must deduct PAYE in accordance with PAYE rules before paying the pension. There are transitional provisions for:

(*a*)   retirement annuity contracts;

(*b*)   pensions that were taxed before 6 April 2006 but accrued after 6 April 2006; and

(*c*)   annuities that were paid from a scheme that was formerly an approved scheme that does not become a registered scheme.

Lump sums free of income tax or partially free of income tax

17.69   No liability to income tax arises on a lump sum paid under a registered pension scheme if the lump sum is:

(*a*)   pension commencement lump sum;

(*b*)   a serious ill-health lump sum paid to a member who has not reached the age of 75;

(*c*)   a refund of excess contributions lump sum; or

(*d*)   a transitional 2013/14 lump sum (*ITEPA 2003, s 636A(1)*).

The first 25 per cent of an uncrystallised funds pension lump sum is tax free where the member takes it before age 75 (it can only be taken where the sum is equal to or greater than the member's available lifetime allowance). The remaining 75 per cent is taxed as pension income (*ITEPA 2003, s 636A(1A)*). Where an individual aged 75 or over takes an uncrystallised funds pension lump sum which exceeds his available lifetime allowance, the tax-free part will be 25 per cent of the available lifetime allowance with the remainder subject to income tax at the individual's marginal rate.

A lifetime allowance charge can still arise if the benefits crystallised on a benefit crystallisation exceed the remaining available lifetime allowance.

Lump sum death benefits

17.70   The tax treatment of death benefit lump sums in relation to money purchase arrangements are summarised in **17.55** above.

Where an annuity protection lump sum death benefit, or a pension protection lump sum death benefit, in relation to a defined benefits arrangement was paid before 6 April 2015 a special lump sum death benefits charge of 55 per cent was payable. If it was paid between 6 April 2015 and 5 April 2016 then it was tax free if the member was under age 75 at the date of death and a special lump sum death benefit charge of 45 per cent was payable if the member was aged 75 or over. Benefits paid on or after 6 April 2016 will be tax-free if the member was aged under 75 at the date of death. Where the member dies age 75 or over, either income tax will be payable or the special lump sum death benefits tax charge (depending on the recipient) (*FA 2004, s 206* and *ITEPA 2003, s 636A*).

Tax treatment of serious ill-health lump sums and short service refund lump sums

17.71   A serious ill-health lump sum which is paid under a registered pension scheme to a member who has reached the age of 75 is subject to income tax in accordance with *FA 2004, s 205A* (charge to tax on scheme administrator in respect of such a lump sum) but not otherwise (*ITEPA 2003, s 636A(3)*).

A short service refund lump sum under a registered pension scheme (see **17.43** above) is subject to income tax in accordance with *FA 2004, s 205* (charge to tax on scheme administrator in respect of such a lump sum) but not otherwise (*ITEPA 2003, s 636A(3A)*).

Tax treatment of trivial commutation and winding-up lump sums

17.72   If a trivial commutation lump sum or a winding-up lump sum is paid to a member of a registered pension scheme, he is treated as if he had received taxable pension income for the tax year in which the payment is made equal to the amount of the lump sum (*ITEPA 2003, s 636B*). However, if, immediately before the lump sum is paid, the member has uncrystallised rights (within the meaning of *FA 2004, s 212*) under any one or more arrangements under the pension scheme, the amount of the taxable pension income, if all his rights under the pension scheme are uncrystallised rights, is 75 per cent of the lump sum. Otherwise, it is reduced by 25 per cent of the value of the uncrystallised rights.

If a trivial commutation lump sum death benefit or a winding-up lump sum death benefit is paid to a person under a registered pension scheme, the person is treated as having taxable pension income for the tax year in which the payment is made equal to the amount of the lump sum (*ITEPA 2003, s 636C*).

Scheme administration member payment

17.73   A scheme administration member payment is a payment by a registered pension scheme to or in respect of a member, or former member, of a pension scheme that is made for the purposes of the administration or management of the scheme (*FA 2004, s 171*). This might include payment of wages to a person administering the scheme, payments made to purchase a pension scheme asset or a payment representing interest on a short service refund lump sum payment (see **17.71** above). If a scheme administration payment is made, normal tax rules would apply to each type of payment (see PTM143000).

Inheritance tax

17.74   There is no general inheritance tax exemption for registered pension schemes.

Most registered occupational pension schemes will be set up under trust. Trusts are a kind of settled property for inheritance tax ('IHT'). There are, however, a number of specific exemptions which take registered pension schemes outside the usual charges on this type of settlement for IHT purposes. This means that:

(*a*)   contributions by employers under registered pension schemes are not treated as chargeable transfers and not subject to IHT (*Inheritance Tax Act 1984, s 12(2)* (*IHTA 1984*)), and contributions made by members are not generally seen as transfers of value (*IHTA 1984, s 10*; IHTM17035);

(*b*)   property held for the purposes of a registered pension scheme is not subject to an IHT charge which would otherwise be levied on a discretionary trust every ten years (*IHTA 1984, s 58(1)(d)*; IHTM17038);

(*c*)   IHT charges do not generally arise on a distribution of capital from a registered pension scheme such as a payment of a lump sum on death or retirement, as it is not regarded as relevant property (*IHTA 1984, s 58(1) (d)*); and

(*d*)   the value of the IHT estate on death will not generally include any value representing a pension or annuity, but see below in relation to provisions introduced by *FA 2006* (*IHTA 1984, s 151*; IHTM17036).

HMRC is concerned that pension planning should not be used to avoid IHT. A discussion paper on IHT was issued by HMRC on 21 July 2005. This resulted in amendments being made to *IHTA 1984* by *FA 2006, Sch 22*. These provisions are revised with retrospective effect from 6 April 2011 by *FA 2011*.

The pre-6 April 2011 rules applied differently, depending on whether a scheme member died before age 75 or on or after his 75th birthday. Where the member died before age 75, the earlier IHT rules, found in *IHTA 1984, s.12,* continued to apply. An IHT charge could arise under *IHTA 1984, s 3(3)* if he did not exercise his right to take pension benefits. The charge applied at the latest time when the right could be exercised (ie immediately before death). For example, if he did not take his pension when he was seriously ill and this resulted in an enhanced death benefit, then IHT might apply. Where a member died on or after age 75 and he had an alternatively secured pension, any funds used to make a payment to an employer or provide benefits for anyone other than a spouse, civil partner or financial dependant, or transferred to a charity, would have been subject to an IHT charge as if the funds were part of the deceased member's estate. An IHT charge could also fall on the estate of a dependant where the dependant himself opted for an alternatively secured pension derived from benefits inherited from the original member. These provisions were *IHTA 1984, ss 151A–151C* but were repealed with effect from 6 April 2011 by *FA 2011*.

From 6 April 2011 the replacement of unsecured pensions and alternatively secured pensions with a drawdown pension means that a number of IHT charges no longer apply. In addition, the IHT charge that arose when a member did not exercise his right to take pension benefits is removed. *IHTA 1984, ss 151A–151E* were repealed and new *s 12(2ZA)* disapplies *s 3(3)* where a registered pension scheme member omits to exercise his pension rights (this includes unused funds designated for drawdown or flexi-access drawdown (*IHTA 1984, s 12A*, inserted by *FA 2016*)). The previous IHT charge was effectively replaced by a special lump sum death benefits tax charge of 55 per cent on drawdown pension fund lump sum death benefits, defined benefits lump sum death benefits, and uncrystallised funds lump sum death benefits paid in respect of a member who has reached age 75 by his date of death (*FA 2004, s 206,* as amended with retrospective effect from 6 April 2011 by *FA 2011*). *TPA 2014, s 2* reduced the rate of the special lump sum death benefits charge from 55 per cent to 45 per cent for lump sums paid during the 2015/2016 tax year following the death of a member who had attained age 75. No tax is payable in relation to a member who had not attained 75 provided payment has commenced within the relevant two-year period and, since 6 April 2016, *FA (No 2) 2015* provides the charge is generally payable by the recipient at his marginal rate of income tax rather than at 45 per cent (*ITEPA 2003, s 636AA*). See **17.50** and **17.55** above for more on the tax treatment of death benefits.

IHT charges will continue to apply to pension contributions and transfers of pension entitlement where contributions are made by the member or his employer within two years of death whilst the member was in ill health. HMRC are likely only to consider such a charge where an established pattern of contributions has been altered in the knowledge that the member would not survive to enjoy the retirement benefit, thus enhancing the death benefit, or there is a transfer of pension benefits within two years of the death by the member whilst in ill health (IHTM17043 and 17072).

IHT charges continue to apply on death where:

(*a*)   the deceased could, right up to his death, have signed a nomination which bound the trustees of the pension scheme to make a payment to a person nominated by the deceased, as this will be considered as a general power to dispose of property (*IHTA 1984, s 5(2)*; IHTM17052);

(*b*) payments under a pension scheme are guaranteed and continue to be paid to the estate after the deceased's death (IHTM17054); and

(*c*) pension scheme trustees have no discretion over the payment of lump sum death benefits where the benefits are paid to the deceased's estate.

The flexibility changes made in relation to money purchase arrangements from 6 April 2015, particularly the number of different payment options following a member's death, complicated the situation regarding the IHT treatment of pension benefits. The general rule was that death benefits were only treated as part of a member's estate for IHT purposes if the scheme provider could be bound to pay those benefits in accordance with the member's directions. HMRC has since clarified the situation regarding flexi-access drawdown funds. A member can make a binding nomination of a particular person to receive any flexi-access drawdown funds if: (a) the pension provider can choose the type of death benefit to pay; and (b) the member cannot also make a binding nomination of any lump sum death benefit. The proceeds of such nominations will fall outside the member's estate for IHT purposes (IHTM17052).

International benefit issues

17.75 The *FA 2004* regime relating to international benefits set out in *FA 2004, Schs 33* and *34* is complicated, and can only be described in outline in this Chapter. Reference should be made to PTM111000, which contains a detailed description. The main elements of the regime are as follows:

(*a*) a member of a registered pension scheme who is a 'relevant overseas individual' can apply to receive an enhancement to his lifetime allowance in respect of non-UK tax relieved contributions;

(*b*) a member of a registered pension scheme who receives a transfer from a recognised overseas pension scheme can apply for an enhancement to his lifetime allowance in respect of the transfer to the extent that it relates to non-UK tax relieved benefits;

(*c*) migrant member tax relief can be obtained from UK tax on contributions to a qualifying overseas pension scheme in certain circumstances;

(*d*) members of a qualifying overseas pension scheme may be subject to UK tax charges in certain circumstances even when they have ceased to be tax resident in the UK; and

(*e*) overseas members of a registered pension scheme receiving payments from a registered pension scheme can be subject to UK income tax unless exempted by virtue of a double tax agreement.

Administration

General

17.76 Guidance on the administration of registered pension schemes is contained in PTM. In addition to the duties imposed on scheme administrators, members and sponsoring employers of registered pension schemes, qualifying overseas pension schemes and qualifying recognised overseas pension schemes are also obliged to provide information in certain circumstances.

Tax relief and VAT recovery

17.77 If a pension scheme bears the costs of its administration itself, it will not be able to obtain tax relief on those costs as its income is not taxable (unless it is trading and the costs relate to the trading activity). The employer may obtain tax relief in respect of the costs of establishing and operating a pension scheme if the expenses concerned are wholly and exclusively incurred in running the employer's business (*Corporation Tax Act 2009, s 54)*). However, if the employer pays costs which are attributable to the trustees, for example, a valuer's fees incurred on property valuations, tax relief will not be given.

Value Added Tax ('VAT') incurred by the trustees is an expense of the pension scheme and may be recoverable in certain circumstances. HMRC practice is to allow employers to recover VAT incurred in relation to the administration expenses of an occupational pension scheme. The rationale being that this has a direct and immediate link with the employer's business activities. The current position on VAT treatment in relation to fund management costs is different, depending on whether the pension scheme is defined contribution (DC) or defined benefit (DB).

In relation to DC schemes, the CJEU judgment in *ATP Pension Service A/S v Skatteministeriet [2014] (C-464/12))* ('*ATP*') confirmed that, where certain conditions are met, pension scheme fund management fees will be exempt from VAT. The basis of the *ATP* decision was that the fund management services provided to the pension scheme were services supplied to a 'Special Investment Fund' ('SIF'). The provision of such services to a SIF are exempt from VAT under *Article 135* of the *EU VAT Directive (2006/112/EC)*. Prior to the *ATP* decision, HMRC had not considered pension funds to be SIFs and so had not allowed them to benefit from the relevant VAT exemption.

The key tests as to whether a particular fund is a SIF are as follows:

* Are they are solely funded by contributions made by or on behalf of members?

* Does the member bear the investment risk?

- Do the funds contain the pooled contributions of several members?
- Is the risk spread over a range of securities?

HMRC accepts (as set out in Revenue and Customs Brief 44(2014)) that this includes the pooled assets of DC occupational pension schemes and may also include the DC sections of hybrid schemes. Where fund management services are supplied to a scheme that has a number of funds, some which satisfy the requirements of a SIF and some which do not, then the VAT treatment will have to be split in accordance with HMRC guidance on multiple supplies. The exemption applies to those fund management and administration services which are integral to the operation of the pension scheme – this could include administering member accounts as well as wider fund management services. In practice, the HMRC change in practice following *ATP* may make little difference for most DC schemes (or schemes holding DC benefits) as many DC arrangements are set up as contracts of insurance with life insurers and as such already benefit from an insurance VAT exemption.

The position is more complex and uncertain in relation to fund management costs in DB schemes. The practice prior to 2014 had been that where the invoice was addressed to the employer, the VAT on administration expenses (but not fund management) costs was recoverable by the employer. HMRC operated a notional 70/30 split between fund management and scheme administration costs where a single VAT invoice had been issued (the '70/30 split').

Following the CJEU judgment in *Fiscale Eenheid PPG Holdings BV cs te Hoogezand [2013] (C-26/12)* ('*PPG*'), HMRC announced in November 2014 (in Brief 43 (2014)) that, in future, it would not differentiate between the administration of a pension scheme and the management of its assets for VAT purposes. HMRC confirmed that VAT incurred by an employer in relation to a pension scheme would only be recoverable where there was evidence that the services were provided to the employer and, crucially, the employer was a party to the contract for those services (and has in fact paid for them). The '70/30 split' would be allowed to continue on a transitional basis until 31 December 2015.

It was immediately identified that the suggested new practice could be problematic for trustees, as legislation requires them to appoint fund managers and other professional advisers in writing, on terms agreed by them (*PA 1995, s 47*). Following submissions made on behalf of scheme trustees and others in the pensions industry in response to Brief 43(2014), HMRC issued a further briefing on VAT on pension fund management costs in relation to DB schemes (Brief 8(2015)). This confirmed that, due to the unique nature of DB pension schemes, tripartite contracts (trustee/employer/provider) could be used to demonstrate that the employer is the recipient of the supply in relation to DB fund management services. The employer may be able to deduct VAT where, as a minimum, the contract with the provider evidences:

- the provider makes its supplies to the employer – even though for regulatory reasons it may have been appointed by the trustee;

- the employer pays for the services directly;

- the provider will pursue the employer for payment – and will only seek recovery from the scheme or trustees where the employer is unlikely to be able to pay;

- both employer and trustees have the right to seek redress in the event of breach;

- the provider will supply the employer with performance reports (subject to conflicts); and

- the employer is allowed to terminate the contract (this can be with trustee consent and can be in addition to any right of the trustees to terminate).

For many schemes this will not be a straightforward solution to the VAT issue. Entering into a tripartite contract can give rise to some quite major legal issues for trustees.

Subsequently, in October 2015, HMRC issued Brief 17(2015). This extended the transitional arrangements for the '70/30 split' to the end of December 2016. It also reconfirmed that trustees, employers and fund managers could adopt tripartite agreements as outlined in Brief 43(2014). However, even where the trustees, employer and fund manager have agreed a tripartite contract, this may not provide a complete solution, Brief 17(2015) states that only costs recognised in the profit and loss account or contributions to a pension scheme attract a deduction for corporation tax purposes. Direct payment by an employer of fund management costs do not clearly fall into either of those categories and so are unlikely to attract a corporation tax deduction for the employer. Brief 17(2015) also outlined options which trustees and employers might wish to consider. These include the trustees contracting with the employer to provide third-party administration – the VAT charged by the trustees to the employer could be deductible to the extent to which it relates to the taxable supplies of the employer. Another option is for a corporate trustee to be in the same VAT group as the employer. This could have implications for the VAT treatment of the group as a whole and detailed advice should be taken before adopting this route.

Most recently, in September 2016, in Brief 14(2016), HMRC confirmed that it has further extended the transitional period for the VAT treatment of pension costs (the '70/30 spilt') to 31 December 2017 with scope for further extensions after that. The reason given was: 'It's taking longer than expected to reconcile the court decision [PPG] with pension and financial service regulations, accounting rules and emerging case law. It's therefore been decided to extend the transitional period for a further 12 months'.

For those who have adopted new structures or contracts following earlier HMRC briefings, HMRC confirmed:

'Some taxpayers may have already made changes to their structure and/ or contractual arrangements to comply with the judgment. Provided the employer and pension scheme trustees agree and both apply the same treatment, these taxpayers may continue with those arrangements. If they wish, they may choose to revert back to the previous treatment during the transitional period.

'The guidance that HM Revenue and Customs was intending to publish on possible options for recovery has currently been put on hold whilst we fully consider the wider implications of the options being proposed. In the meantime, VAT can be recovered on fund management costs in line with the guidance laid out in the previous Revenue and Customs Briefs. Taxpayers are advised, however, that adopting alternative structures to comply with the VAT requirements could have wider implications, in particular in respect of regulatory requirements and Corporation Tax deductions.'

There also remain questions over the ability of trustees of DB schemes to reclaim VAT on administration fees (including actuarial or legal fees) going forward. In Brief 8(2015) HMRC confirmed that it would be issuing further guidance including on the VAT treatment of other types of service (such as legal, actuarial and accounting services) but none has yet been published.

Annual returns by scheme administrator

17.78   A scheme administrator is required to complete and submit an annual return in relation to any tax year if HMRC have served notice on him requiring him to file one (*FA 2004, s 250*). The return must be filed by 31 January next following the end of the tax year to which it relates. The return has to be submitted electronically. The notice from HMRC will specify the period to be covered by the annual return, which can be the whole or part of any tax year or, where audited accounts have been prepared which end in that tax year, the period or periods covered by those accounts.

Accounting for tax returns

17.79   The scheme administrator of a registered pension scheme must make returns to HMRC of the income tax to which they are liable for each period of three months ending 31 March, 30 June, 30 September and 31 December (*FA 2004, s 254*). A return is only required if a listed tax charge has arisen in a quarter (RPSM12301300).

An accounting for tax form is provided in electronic format and the return must be delivered electronically within 45 days of the end of the relevant three-month period. The income tax has to be paid within the same period without the need for an assessment to tax (*FA 2004, s 254(5)*).

Events reports to HMRC

17.80   The scheme administrator of a registered pension scheme has to provide specified information to HMRC in respect of any prescribed reportable events that have occurred in the scheme year to which the report relates (*Registered Pension Schemes (Provision of Information) Regulations 2006 (SI 2006/567), reg 3 as amended*). Reportable events include unauthorised payments, suspension of ill-health pensions, transfers to qualifying recognised overseas pension schemes and changes in the legal structure of the scheme.

Where a registered pension scheme is wound up, notice that the winding up has been completed must be given to HMRC by the person who, immediately before the scheme was wound up, was the scheme administrator (*Registered Pension Schemes (Provision of Information) Regulations 2006, reg 4 as amended*).

A person who has been, or has ceased to be, the scheme administrator must notify HMRC of the termination of his appointment, together with the date the termination took effect, within 30 days (*Registered Pension Schemes (Provision of Information) Regulations 2006, reg 6*).

The information requirements in relation to qualifying recognised overseas pension schemes (see **17.60** above) are not detailed in this Chapter.

17.81   Where a registered pension scheme makes an unauthorised employer payment to a company, that company must provide the following information to HMRC no later than the 31 January following the tax year in which the payment is made:

(*a*)   details of the scheme that made the payment;

(*b*)   the nature of the payment;

(*c*)   the amount of the payment; and

(*d*)   the date on which the payment was made (*Registered Pension Schemes (Provision of Information) Regulations 2006, reg 5*).

Any unauthorised borrowing by a money purchase arrangement must be reported to HMRC no later than the 31 January following the tax year in which the payment treated as having been made ((*Registered Pension Schemes (Provision of Information) Regulations 2006, reg 5A*)).

Information to be provided to the member or his personal representatives by the scheme administrator

17.82 Certain information must be provided by the scheme administrator to the member or the member's personal representatives. This is set out in the *Registered Pension Schemes (Provision of Information) Regulations 2006 (SI 2006/567)* (the '*Provision of Information Regulations*') and includes:

(*a*)   If a registered pension scheme has made an unauthorised payment to a member, the scheme administrator is required to give the member details of the nature of the benefit provided; the amount of the unauthorised payment which is treated as being made by the provision of the benefit and the date on which the benefit was provided. This information must be provided no later than the 7 July following the tax year in which the payment was made (*Provision of Information Regulations , reg 13*).

(*b*)   Generally, the scheme administrator has to provide to each member:

(i)   who has an actual (as opposed to prospective) entitlement to be paid a pension, at least once in each tax year; or

(ii)   in respect of whom a benefit crystallisation has occurred, within three months of that event,

a statement of the standard lifetime allowance expended by:

(i)   benefit crystallisation events in respect of the scheme, to the extent that the sums or assets subject to any such event have not been transferred to another registered pension scheme; and

(ii)   where the first-mentioned scheme has received (whether directly or indirectly) a transfer in respect of the member, any crystallisation event, prior to the transfer in connection with:

● the sums or assets represented by the transfer; and

● sums or assets replaced by the sums or assets mentioned in (i) above.

In broad terms, the information does not have to be provided if it has already been provided in compliance with certain other requirements of the *Provision of Information Regulations, reg 14*.

(*c*)   The scheme administrator must provide the personal representatives of a deceased scheme member with information regarding the percentage of the lifetime allowance crystallised by, and the amount and date of payment of a relevant lump sum death benefit in relation to, that member. This information must be provided within three months beginning with the date of the final payment of the benefit. Additionally, the personal representatives may request a statement of the total percentage of standard lifetime allowance expended, at the date of the statement, by:

(i)   any benefit crystallisation event in respect of the deceased member's rights under the scheme to the extent that:

- the sums or assets subject to any such event; and

- any sums or assets subsequently representing those sums or assets,

have not been transferred to another registered pension scheme; and

(ii)   where sums or assets have been transferred to the scheme from another registered pension scheme (whether directly or indirectly) in respect of the deceased member, any benefit crystallisation event in connection with:

- those sums or assets; and

- any other sums or assets held prior to the transfer which the sums and assets mentioned in (i) above represented,

but excluding from that percentage any amount in respect of any relevant lump sum death benefit payment in respect of the deceased member.

Where the personal representatives request this information, the scheme administrator must provide it within two months of the date on which the request is received (*Registered Pension Schemes (Provision of Information) Regulations 2006, reg 8*).

(*d*)   If the scheme administrator has made or intends to make a payment on account of his liability to tax in respect of the lifetime allowance charge on a benefit crystallisation event, he must provide the member with a notice giving details of the chargeable amount in respect of the benefit crystallisation event, how the chargeable amount has been calculated and the amount of the resulting tax charge and stating whether the administrator has accounted for the tax or intends to do so. The notice must be provided within three months after the benefit crystallisation event (*Provision of Information Regulations, reg 12*).

(*e*)   In relation to the money purchase annual allowance (see **17.17** above) the scheme administrator must inform the member that:

- the member has flexibly accessed his pension rights;

- if in any tax year the total of the pension inputs to money purchase arrangements, and certain hybrid arrangements, relating to the member exceeds £10,000, there will be an annual allowance tax charge on the excess, and the annual allowance for pension inputs to other arrangements relating to the member will be £10,000 less than it would otherwise be; and

- the member has duties under *reg 14ZB* and the circumstances in which the member will have to comply with them (*Provision of Information Regulations, reg 14ZA*).

(*f*)   The scheme administrator must provide active members (and in certain cases, other categories of member) with a statement of relevant pension inputs where the aggregate pension inputs in a pension input period in that registered pension scheme exceed the annual allowance (*Provision of Information Regulations, reg 14A*).

Information to be provided by the member and his personal representatives

17.83   The *Provision of Information Regulations* include detailed requirements in relation information which must be provided by members and their personal representatives. This includes the information summarised below.

If a member of a registered pension scheme wants to rely on entitlement to an enhanced lifetime allowance, enhanced protection or fixed protection, fixed protection 2014, individual protection 2014, fixed protection 2016 or individual protection 2016, he must give the scheme administrator the reference number issued by HMRC in respect of that entitlement (*Provision of Information Regulations, reg 11* as amended).

Where a registered pension scheme is treated as making an unauthorised member payment on the grounds that it constitutes a recycled lump sum under *FA 2004, Sch 29, para 3A*, the member must notify the scheme administrator, within 30 days of the date on which the unauthorised payment is treated as made of:

(*a*)   the date on which the unauthorised payment is treated as made; and

(*b*)   the amount of the payment (*Provision of Information Regulations, reg 11A*).

Where a registered pension scheme intends to pay a pension commencement lump sum to a member and *FA 2004, Sch 29, para 2(5)(a)* applies to determine the permitted maximum, and a benefit crystallisation event has occurred previously in relation to the member in respect of a scheme pension that crystallised under a money purchase arrangement, the member must provide such information as will enable the scheme administrator to calculate the available portion of the member's lump sum allowance (*Provision of Information Regulations, reg 11B*).

Where a scheme administrator needs an individual's national insurance number in order to complete an event report (see **17.80** above) other than in relation to a transfer to a qualifying recognised overseas pension scheme, the individual must provide the scheme administrator with this information within 60 days of the scheme administrator requesting it. Where the individual does not qualify for a national insurance number, the individual must provide the scheme administrator with confirmation of this in writing, together with his date of birth and address (*Provision of Information Regulations, reg 11C*). Separate requirements relating to information to be provided to a scheme administrator by members requesting transfers to qualifying recognised overseas pension schemes are not covered in this chapter.

If a relevant lump sum death benefit has been paid, a designation of relevant unused uncrystallised funds has been made or an entitlement to a dependant's or nominee's annuity has arisen in respect of a deceased member and the payment, together with any other relevant benefit crystallisation events, results in a lifetime allowance charge, the personal representatives of the deceased member (who will be liable for any tax due) have to provide HMRC with certain specified information about the deceased member and the payment (*Provision of Information Regulations 2006, reg 10*).

Information to be provided to and by insurance companies

17.84 If a registered pension scheme has provided an insurance company with funds (other than from a drawdown fund or flexi-access drawdown fund) to secure the payment of a scheme pension or a lifetime annuity, the scheme administrator is required to provide the insurance company with a statement of the total percentage of the standard lifetime allowance expended, and any pension commencement lump sum connected with that pension or annuity. This information has to be provided within three months of the date on which the recipient becomes entitled to the pension or annuity. The insurance company must then provide to each pensioner or annuitant, at least once in each tax year up to and including the tax year in which the pensioner or annuitant reaches age 75, a statement of the percentage of the standard lifetime allowance expended at the date of the statement by benefit crystallisation events in respect of that pension or annuity and any pension commencement lump sum paid in connection with that pension or annuity (*Provision of Information Regulations, reg 16* as amended).

Where an insurance company or other person has paid an annuity to a registered pension scheme member and the member to has died, the insurance company is required, within two months of a request, to provide to the personal representatives of the deceased member details of the cumulative total percentage of the standard lifetime allowance crystallised, at the date of the statement, by benefit crystallisation events in respect of the deceased member under the scheme or any scheme from which assets have been transferred to the scheme in respect of the deceased member's pension rights (*Provision of Information Regulations, reg 9*).

Retention of records

17.85   Any documents that are in the possession or control of the persons listed below relating to any of the following matters have to be preserved in relation to a registered pension scheme, namely:

(*a*)   any monies received by or owing to the scheme;

(*b*)   any investments or assets held by the scheme;

(*c*)   any payments made by the scheme;

(*d*)   any contracts to purchase a lifetime annuity in respect of a member of the scheme; and

(*e*)   the administration of the scheme.

(Provision of Information Regulations, reg 18(1))

The persons subject to this record keeping obligation are:

(i)   any person who is or has been the scheme administrator;

(ii)   any person who is or has been a trustee of the scheme;

(iii)   any person who provides or has provided administrative services to the scheme; and

(iv)   if the scheme is an occupational pension scheme, any person who is or has been a sponsoring employer or a director of an employing company.

(Provision of Information Regulations, reg 18(2))

The obligation to preserve the documents does not apply to a person who has ceased to act in relation to a scheme or has ceased to provide administrative services to a scheme if he has transferred all documents to another person who has succeeded him in acting in relation to the scheme or providing administrative services to the scheme (*Registered Pension Schemes (Provision of Information) Regulations 2006, reg 18(3)*).

The obligation to preserve the documents applies for the tax year to which they relate and the following six tax years (*Provision of Information Regulations, reg 18(4)*).

Information to be provided between scheme administrators

17.86   If a member's crystallised rights under one registered pension scheme ('Scheme A'), are transferred to another registered scheme ('Scheme B'), the scheme administrator of Scheme A must provide to the administrator of Scheme

B, within three months of the transfer, a statement of the total percentage of the standard lifetime allowance expended, at the date of the statement, by benefit crystallisation events in respect of Scheme A (and in respect of any scheme from which Scheme A had previously received a transfer) in connection with the sums and assets represented by the transfer (*Provision of Information Regulations, reg 15*).

Where a recognised transfer of sums or assets (or both) which represent a dependant's flexi-access drawdown fund, a nominee's flexi-access drawdown fund, a successor's flexi-access drawdown fund or a dependant's drawdown pension fund is made then the scheme administrator of the transferring scheme must provide specified information to the scheme administrator of the receiving scheme within three months of the transfer (*Provision of Information Regulations, reg 15A*).

Penalties

17.87   Penalties that can be levied include the following:

(*a*)   Failure to provide the registered pension scheme return in relation to any tax year where notice has been served requiring one to be submitted can give rise to a penalty of £100 on the scheme administrator. A further penalty not exceeding £60 a day for each day that the failure continues can also be levied (*FA 2004, ss 250, 257(1)–(2)*).

(*b*)   If the scheme administrator of a registered pension scheme fraudulently or negligently makes an incorrect registered scheme return in response to a notice from HMRC to provide one or delivers any incorrect accounts, statements or other documents with such a return the scheme administrator is liable to a penalty not exceeding £3,000 (*FA 2004, s 257(4)*).

(*c*)   If the scheme administrator fraudulently or negligently makes an incorrect accounting return he is liable to a penalty not exceeding the difference in the amount of tax shown in the form and the amount that should have been due (*FA 2004, s 260(6)*).

(*d*)   Any person who fraudulently or negligently makes a false statement or representation is liable to a penalty not exceeding £3,000 if as a result that person or any other person obtains relief from or repayment of tax chargeable under *FA 2004, Part 4* or a registered scheme makes a payment which is an unauthorised payment (*FA 2004, s 264(1)*).

(*e*)   Any person who assists in or induces the preparation of any document which the person knows is incorrect and will or is likely to cause a registered pension scheme to make an unauthorised payment is liable to a penalty not exceeding £3,000 (*FA 2004, s 264(2)*).

(*f*)   Failure to provide or make available any document or information required under the enhanced lifetime allowance regulations can result on a penalty not exceeding £3,000 on the individual (*FA 2004, s 262*).

(*g*)   Where an individual has claimed enhanced protection, failure to notify HMRC that relevant benefit accrual has occurred resulting in loss of protection within 90 days of its occurring can result in a penalty on the individual of up to £3,000 (*FA 2004, s 263*).

(*h*)   If HMRC considers that a scheme is being wound up wholly or mainly to facilitate the payment of winding-up lump sums or winding-up lump sum death benefits (or both) the scheme administrator is liable to a penalty of up to £3,000 in respect of each member to or in respect of whom such payments are made (*FA 2004, s 265*).

Section B: Pre-A-Day Revenue limits

17.88   Many occupational pension schemes which before A-Day were tax approved may have chosen to retain all or some of the pre-A-Day Revenue limits and have written similar requirements into their rules as scheme limits. Consequently, for a number of occupational pension schemes, the limits (or some of them) will have continued application. For reference purposes, this part of the Chapter outlines the key features of pre-A-Day Revenue limits on benefits provided under tax-approved occupational pension schemes.

Transitional arrangements

17.89   The *Registered Pension Schemes (Modification of the Rules of Existing Schemes) Regulations 2006 (SI 2006/364)* (the '*Modification Regulations*') gave schemes a transitional period of five years from A-Day in which to modify their scheme rules.

During the transitional period, the Regulations had the following effects:

(*a*)   any rule *requiring* trustees to make an unauthorised payment would be construed as conferring a *discretion* to make that payment;

(*b*)   if the scheme rules limited any benefit by reference to the permitted maximum, the permitted maximum would continue to apply;

(*c*)   if the scheme rules provided for the payment of a specified sum or rate of pension and refer to the possibility of that sum or rate being such greater amount as would not prejudice approval by HMRC, the rules were construed as authorising the trustees to make only those payments they could have made prior to A-Day;

(*d*)   if the scheme rules provided for benefits to be limited to those which would not prejudice approval of the scheme by HMRC, the rules would be construed as prohibiting the trustees from making payments that they would not have been authorised to make prior to A-Day;

(*e*)   scheme rules were modified to permit the trustees to reduce a member's benefits in respect of the administrator's liability for the lifetime allowance charge (see **17.7** above).

The net effect of the *Modification Regulations* was that, until the scheme rules were amended (and the provisions of the Regulations expressly disapplied), no additional liabilities were imposed on schemes as a result of the introduction of the A-Day taxation regime. In particular, the limits imposed on benefits in order for a scheme to obtain tax-approved status under the pre-A-Day regime continued to apply to a registered pension scheme during the transitional period. The transitional protection fell away on 6 April 2011 and any scheme which had not modified its rules by that date could incur significant additional liabilities.

Limits applicable to exempt approved schemes

17.90   Prior to A-Day, HMRC exercised its discretion under *ICTA 1988, s 591* to approve schemes in accordance with guidelines set out in an office manual which was summarised in Practice Notes, the last version of which was IR12 (2001). The requirements which a scheme had to meet in order to obtain approval related primarily to the maximum benefits which could be paid from the scheme. There were also limits on the contributions members could pay to the scheme. Further details of the pre-A-Day limits on benefits are summarised in **17.95** to **17.113** below.

It is important to note that HMRC's Practice Notes set out the maximum benefits that could be paid. Pension schemes were not obliged to pay maximum benefits and, in the vast majority of final salary schemes, the rules effectively limited the benefits payable to lesser amounts.

Remuneration and final remuneration

17.91   The maximum benefits a member could receive from an exempt approved occupational pension scheme and the maximum contributions he could make to such a scheme were calculated by reference to his 'final remuneration' and his 'remuneration' respectively. As the expression suggests, final remuneration was itself calculated by reference to 'remuneration'.

Remuneration

17.92   Remuneration included any emoluments chargeable to tax under *ITEPA 2003, ss 15* or *21*, except:

(*a*)   sums arising from the acquisition or disposal of shares or from a right to acquire shares; and

(*b*)   payments on the termination of office (eg redundancy payments and golden handshakes).

(ITEPA 2003, Part 6, Chapter 3; Glossary to IR12 (2001); ICTA 1988, s 612)

Remuneration was limited in certain circumstances by legislation.

For members generally known as 'high earners' joining pension schemes on or after 17 March 1987, but before 1 June 1989, the amount of remuneration which could be used to determine cash lump sum benefits could not exceed £105,600 (*ICTA 1988, Sch 23, para 6(2), Pensions Update 153*).

The level of remuneration which could be taken into account for the purposes of determining the maximum benefits payable was restricted to the 'permitted maximum' or, as it is colloquially known, the 'earnings cap' imposed by *ICTA 1988, s 590C*. The earnings cap was first introduced in 1989 and was set at £60,000 per annum for the tax year 1989/90. The legislation contained provision for the earnings cap to be increased annually in line with the retail prices index rounded up to the nearest multiple of £600 (*ICTA 1988, s 590C(5)*). The earnings cap for the tax year 2005/06 was £105,600. In relation to subsequent tax years up to the tax year 2010/2011, HMRC published an annual notional earnings cap. For the tax year 2010/11 this was £123,600. In future, schemes requiring this figure will have to calculate the notional earnings cap themselves by using the method in *ICTA 1988, s 590C*, or by any alternative method specified in scheme rules.

The earnings cap generally applied to all members of schemes established on or after 14 March 1989. It also applied to members of schemes established before 14 March 1989 who became members on or after 1 June 1989. However, it did not apply where employees were considered to have continuity of membership from before 1 June 1989 (*Retirement Benefits Schemes (Continuation of Rights of Members of Approved Schemes) Regulations 1990 (SI 1990/2101)*). For example, if a member moved from one pension scheme of an employer to another scheme of the same employer, he could be treated as if he had always been a member of the second scheme and so would not necessarily become subject to the earnings cap.

Final remuneration

17.93   The definition of final remuneration is set out in IR12 (2001) Appendix I. There are two basic definitions of final remuneration, depending upon the category of member involved. Broadly, these definitions are:

(*a*)   the highest remuneration liable to income tax under *ITEPA 2003, s 15* or *21* for any one of the five years preceding a member's date of retirement, leaving pensionable service or death (whichever is earlier), being the total of:

     (i)   the basic pay for the year in question ('the basic pay year'); and

     (ii)   the yearly average over three or more consecutive years ending with the expiry of the corresponding basic pay year of any fluctuating emoluments; or

(*b*)   the yearly average of the total remuneration liable to income tax under *ITEPA 2003, s 15* or *21* for any three or more consecutive years ending not earlier than ten years before the date of retirement, leaving pensionable service or death (whichever is earlier).

Whichever formula gave the best results could be used for most members but only the second formula could be used for controlling directors or other members whose remuneration after 5 April 1987 exceeded £100,000 per annum (subsequently £105,600 from 5 April 2005: see **17.92** above). The restriction was introduced because the directors of private companies are able to control the remuneration paid to them. Their ability to increase their remuneration just before they retire was therefore restricted by the imposition of the three-year averaging.

Normal retirement date

17.94   There was a requirement that the normal retirement date of any member must be specified in the rules of the scheme (IR12 (2001) PN 6.5 to 6.11). It could differ for different categories of member but had to be between the ages of 60 to 75. Lower ages were permitted in some employments (eg for sportsmen or those with hazardous occupations). Female members of occupational pension schemes who joined before 1 June 1989 were permitted to have a normal retirement date of 55. This HMRC distinction did not, however, override the requirements for equal treatment of men and women.

Maximum benefits

The three regimes

17.95   The maximum benefits in respect of a member were partly governed by his date of admission to membership of the pension scheme. There were three regimes in this respect:

(*a*)   admission to membership before 17 March 1987;

(b)   admission to membership of a scheme established before 14 March 1989, between 17 March 1987 and 31 May 1989 (inclusive); and

(c)   admission to membership from 1 June 1989.

In some circumstances, a member who would otherwise have fallen within categories (b) and (c) could be treated for these purposes as if he had joined the scheme on an earlier date, eg where a member moved between schemes following the sale of his employer.

Members who fell within categories (a) and (b) were said to have 'continued rights' (IR12 (2001) Appendix III). Such a member could elect to be treated as if he had been admitted to membership on or after 1 June 1989. An election could be made at any time before benefits commenced, were bought out or transferred, or attainment of age 75, whichever occurred first. Following such an election, the member's benefits would be based on HMRC's permitted maximum for members joining pension schemes on or after 1 June 1989, but they became subject to the earnings cap (see **17.92** above).

Pension at normal retirement date

Maximum total benefits

17.96   The maximum total benefits that could be provided on retirement under an approved scheme were calculated by reference to an employee's length of service with the employer and his final remuneration. Total benefits were measured in terms of an annual pension for the member payable for life, being the aggregate of any pension payable (including, where the member did not fall within the administrative easement described in **17.97** below (IR12 (2001) PN 7.7), any pension debit) and the pension equivalent of any non-pension benefits (IR12 (2001) PN 7.2). The maximum aggregate benefit payable without taking account of 'retained benefits' (see **17.113** below) was a pension (of which part could be taken in lump sum form as described in **17.100** below) of 1/60th of final remuneration for each year of service (up to 40 years) (IR12 (2001) PN 7.3). However, this was subject to special provisions relating to controlling directors (IR12 (2001) PN 7.10) and the aggregation of benefits with other approved schemes (IR12 (2001) PN 7.25 and 7.26).

Pension sharing easement

17.97   Under an administrative easement, pension debits could be ignored in calculating the member's maximum permissible total benefits (both pension and lump sum), under IR12 (2001) PN 7.2. With two important exceptions, the easement applied to members of schemes other than simplified defined contribution schemes. The first exception was a controlling director (within the meaning in *Retirement Benefits Schemes (Sharing of Pensions on Divorce or Annulment) Regulations 2000 (SI 2000/1085), reg 5(5))*. The second exception related to members whose earnings exceeded one quarter of the permitted maximum determined at its level for the year of assessment in which the marriage was dissolved. For this purpose, earnings meant those in respect of pensionable service to which the scheme related, and which were received during the year of assessment immediately preceding the year of assessment in which the dissolution or annulment of the marriage occurred, and from which tax was deducted under PAYE.

The test was applied as at the date of divorce and once it was satisfied, the pension debit could be permanently ignored, that is irrespective of subsequent employment changes (IR12 (2001) PN 7.7).

Pre-17 March 1987 member

17.98   For a member who became, or was treated as having become, a member prior to 17 March 1987, the maximum permissible pension of two-thirds of final remuneration could be accrued over a period of ten years' service, in accordance with the following table:

Years of service to normal retirement date	Maximum pension (before any commutation and including the annuity value of any lump sum entitlement) expressed as 60ths of final remuneration
1–5	1 for each year
6	8
7	16
8	24
9	32
10 or more	40

Regardless of the date on which the member joined the scheme, the pension (unless it did not exceed 1/60th of final remuneration for each year of service) could not, when aggregated with any 'retained benefits' (see **17.116** below), exceed two-thirds of final remuneration.

Post-17 March 1987 member

17.99   The maximum pension payable to a member on retirement at normal retirement date was, as indicated in **17.99** above, two-thirds of his final remuneration (IR12 (2001) Part 7). For a person who became, or was treated as having become, a member on or after 17 March 1987 (that is a person who was within either category (*b*) or (*c*) as described in **17.95** above), this was restricted to 1/30th of final remuneration for each year of service, subject to a maximum of 20 years.

Cash lump sum at normal retirement date

17.100 Members were allowed to commute some or all of their pension for a tax-free cash lump sum (IR12 (2001) Part 8). The lump sum was limited to no more than 3/80ths of final remuneration for each year of service, up to a maximum of 40 years. This allowed a cash lump sum of one and a half times final remuneration to be paid after 40 years of service. A higher accrual rate was permitted if the member had continued rights (see **17.95** above).

The actual accrual rate depended on when the member was treated as having joined the scheme, and was calculated in accordance with **17.101** to **17.103** below, as appropriate.

Pre-17 March 1987 member

17.101 If the member was treated as having joined the scheme before 17 March 1987, the following table applied:

Years of service to normal retirement date	Maximum lump sum expressed as 80ths of final remuneration
1–8	3 for each year
9	30
10	36
11	42
12	48
13	54
14	63
15	72
16	81
17	90
18	99
19	108
20 or more	120

17.102   *Taxation of registered schemes*

The limits described in this paragraph did not apply where a member's benefit entitlement in a scheme was permanently reduced following a pension sharing order and the member did not fall within the pension sharing administrative easement described in **17.97** above. The calculation of the maximum lump sum benefit depended on whether the lump sum was obtained by commutation of pension or whether the scheme rules provided for a pension and a separate lump sum rather than a commutable pension. In the former case the maximum lump sum benefit was the greater of:

(a)   2.25 times the initial annual rate of pension after reduction to take account of the pension debit; or

(b)   an amount determined in accordance with the scheme rules as if there had been no pension share, then reduced by 2.25 times the amount of pension from the pension debit calculated at the member's normal retirement date.

Where scheme rules provided for a pension and a separate lump sum as opposed to a commutable pension, the maximum lump sum benefit was the greater of:

(a)   three times the initial annual rate of the separate pension after reduction to take account of the pension debit; or

(b)   an amount determined in accordance with the scheme rules as if there had been no pension share, but then reduced by three times the amount of pension from the pension debit calculated at the member's normal retirement date (IR12 (2001) PN 8.26).

Post-16 March 1987 but pre-1 June 1989 member

17.102   If the member was treated as having joined the scheme between 17 March 1987 and 31 May 1989, then (except for schemes commencing on or after 14 March 1989 (see **17.103** below)) a more complex formula applied. The member could use the higher accrual rate set out in the table in **17.101** above, but only to the same proportionate extent that his pension from the scheme (before any part of it had been exchanged for a lump sum or given up to provide further pensions for dependants) fell within the range between 1/60th and 1/80th of final remuneration for each year.

These limits did not apply where a member's benefit entitlement in a scheme had been permanently reduced following a pension sharing order and the member did not fall within the administrative easement. In such circumstances, the maximum lump sum benefit was calculated in accordance with **17.101** above.

Post-31 May 1989 member

17.103 If the member was treated as having joined the scheme on or after 1 June 1989 (or before then if the scheme itself commenced on or after 14 March 1989), and his pension (before any part of it had been exchanged for a lump sum or given up to provide further pensions for dependants) exceeded 1/60th of final remuneration for each year of service, his lump sum could be increased to 2.25 times the annual amount of that pension.

However, in any of the above cases, the lump sum plus any 'retained benefits' (see **17.113** below) could not exceed one and a half times final remuneration.

For the purpose of calculating Revenue limits, commutation factors were set by the Inland Revenue to determine the cash value provided for each £1.00 of pension given up (IR12 (2001) Part 7). A commutation factor of 12:1 had to be used irrespective of age, sex or escalation rate for current members and those members with continued rights who opted for the post-31 May 1989 regime. For members with continued rights, commutation factors differed according to age. At age 60 a commutation factor of between 10.2 and 11.0 could be used; at age 65 the range was 9.0 to 9.8 (IR12 (2001) PN 7.59). It was possible to agree enhanced commutation factors with HMRC outside these ranges.

Early retirement and leaving service before normal retirement date

17.104 The rules of approved occupational pension schemes could permit members to draw early retirement benefits at any age after 50 (or earlier on grounds of incapacity), provided they actually retired or ceased pensionable service with the employer concerned (IR12 (2001) PN 10.8). A female member with continued rights could receive early retirement benefits from age 45 if she retired within ten years of her normal retirement date as such members were permitted to have a normal retirement date of 55.

The receipt of an early retirement pension did not preclude a member from taking up employment elsewhere although the early retirement benefits may have had to be taken into account as 'retained benefits' (see **17.113** below) if the member joined the subsequent employer's pension scheme. If a member was subsequently re-employed by the employer from whose scheme early retirement benefits had been, or were being, paid the rules of the scheme could permit the suspension of the early retirement pension (IR12 (2001) PN 7.32); if the member was to accrue further benefits under the scheme the early retirement benefits had to be suspended (IR12 (2001) Appendix IV).

Early retirement on grounds of incapacity

17.105 If a member retired early at any age on grounds of incapacity, his benefits could be calculated in the same manner as if he had retired at normal retirement date. Both his actual service and potential service (ie the service he would have completed had he remained a member up to his normal retirement date) could count towards the calculation. Final remuneration was calculated as at his date of actual retirement.

'Incapacity' was defined in the Glossary to IR12 (2001) as 'physical or mental deterioration which is sufficiently serious to prevent the individual from following his or her normal employment, or which seriously impairs his or her earning capacity. It does not mean simply a decline in energy or ability'.

Early retirement other than on grounds of incapacity

17.106 The maximum pension payable from an approved scheme on early retirement, other than on grounds of incapacity (IR12 (2001) PN 10.9 to 10.14), for a member without continued rights was the greater of:

(*a*)   1/60th of final remuneration for each year of service up to a maximum of 40 years; and

(*b*)   the lesser of:

     (i)   1/30th of final remuneration for each year of service up to a maximum of 20 years; and

     (ii)   2/3rds of final remuneration less 'retained benefits' (see **17.113** below).

Where the member had a pension debit in relation to the scheme and did not fall within the administrative easement described in **17.97** above, the maximum benefits were calculated in accordance with the requirements set out above but had to be reduced by the pension debit.

The maximum cash lump sum payable in such circumstances (IR12 (2001) PN 10.15 to 10.18) was 3/80ths of final remuneration for each year of service up to a maximum of 40 years or, if greater, an amount equal to 2.25 times the initial annual rate of pension to be paid (before any part of that pension had been commuted for the lump sum or given up to provide further pensions for dependants). However, (unless it did not exceed 3/80th of final remuneration for each year of service) the lump sum could not, when aggregated with any 'retained benefits' (see **17.113** below), exceed one and a half times final remuneration.

For members with continued rights (see **17.95** above), the maximum pension on early retirement was either 1/60th of final remuneration for each year of service up to a maximum of 40 years or, if more favourable, the amount calculated by the formula:

$$\frac{N}{NS} \times P;$$

where:

N is the number of actual years of service up to a maximum of 40 years;

NS is the number of actual years of service plus years of potential service to normal retirement date; and

P is the maximum pension the member could have received had he remained in service until normal retirement date calculated by reference to final remuneration as at the date of termination of pensionable service.

For members with continued rights (see **17.95** above) the maximum cash lump sum available on early retirement was either 3/80ths of final remuneration for each year of service up to a maximum of 40 years or, if more favourable, the amount calculated by the formula:

$$\frac{N}{NS} \times LS;$$

where:

N is the number of actual years of service with a maximum of 40 years;

NS is the number of actual years of service plus years of potential service to normal retirement date; and

LS is the maximum lump sum the member could have received had he remained in pensionable service until normal retirement date calculated by reference to final remuneration at the date of termination of pensionable service.

Leaving service benefits

17.107 If a member left service before reaching normal retirement date, several options were available regarding his accrued benefits (IR12 (2001) Part 10). If the member was at least age 50, retirement benefits could be paid immediately if the scheme's rules permitted it. If the member had not reached age 50, benefits could be left in the scheme and paid either after age 50 as early retirement benefits or at normal retirement date. The maximum benefits payable on leaving service in respect of pensions and cash lump sums were, broadly, the same as those payable on early retirement.

Alternatively, a deferred annuity could be purchased or a transfer value paid to another occupational or personal pension scheme.

Retirement after normal retirement date

17.108 In certain circumstances, a member could be permitted to postpone receipt of his benefits until after normal retirement date (IR12 (2001) PN 7.43 to 7.46). The calculation of the maximum pension permissible by HMRC on late retirement depended on whether the member had continued rights.

If the member had continued rights (see **17.95** above), his maximum pension was the greatest of:

(*a*) his maximum pension at normal retirement date, but substituting the date of actual retirement for normal retirement date;

(*b*) his maximum pension at normal retirement date plus 1/60th (up to a maximum of 5/60th) for each further year of service over 40 years after normal retirement date; and

(*c*) his maximum pension at normal retirement date increased by increases in the Retail Price Index or by actuarial increases (whichever produces the greater result) since normal retirement date,

except that the first two options were not available to controlling directors other than in respect of service after age 70.

If the member did not have continued rights (see **17.95** above), the maximum pension was the maximum pension he could have received if his date of actual retirement had been substituted for his normal retirement date.

Death benefits

Lump sums payable on death in service before normal retirement date

17.109 On a member's death in service before reaching normal retirement date (IR12 (2001) Part 11), a lump sum could be paid equal to the greater of:

(*a*)   £5,000; and

(*b*)   four times final remuneration less 'retained benefits' (see **17.113** below).

In addition, a refund of the member's own contributions could be paid with or without interest. Final remuneration on death could be:

(i)   the annual basic salary immediately before death; or

(ii)   the annual basic salary immediately before death plus the average of fluctuating emoluments during the three years up to the date of death; or

(iii)   the total remuneration, fixed and fluctuating, paid during any period of 12 months falling within the three years prior to death.

If a scheme's rules provided for a lump sum benefit on death that did not exceed twice the member's final remuneration, 'retained benefits' (see **17.113** below) did not need to be taken into account.

Spouses' and dependants' benefits

17.110   Following the death of a member in service or after retirement, a spouse's and/or dependant's pension could be provided. The maximum level of all such pensions could not exceed two-thirds of the maximum pension that could have been provided for the deceased member had he retired due to incapacity immediately before death, calculated as though there had been no lump sum commutation at retirement and as if the deceased had no 'retained benefits' (see **17.113** below) from earlier occupations.

Death of an early leaver

17.111   If a former active member died before age 50, having deferred benefits in the scheme, a cash lump sum could be paid. Spouse's and dependants' pensions could also be provided, calculated by reference to the deceased member's maximum approvable deferred pension.

Death in service after normal retirement date

17.112   Where a member died in service after normal retirement date, the maximum benefits that could be provided were on the basis of death in service (see **17.109** and **17.110** above). In the case of a member with continued rights, benefits could be provided on the basis that the member died in retirement having retired the day before the date of death.

Retained benefits

17.113   Retained benefits (IR12 (2001) Appendix I) generally were retained rights to relevant benefits and, where appropriate, pension debits built up in previous employments or periods of self-employment from schemes or contractual arrangements which had benefited from tax privileges.

Section C: Non-registered pension schemes

17.114   From 6 April 2006, pension schemes which are not registered pension schemes are employer-financed retirement benefit schemes ('EFRBS'). Essentially, all existing pre-A-Day unapproved pension schemes come under the tax regime applicable to EFRBS.

Former unapproved arrangements

17.115   Prior to A-Day, unapproved pension schemes were established by employers to top up benefits for employees whose benefits were limited by legislation. This applied, in particular, to employees subject to the so-called 'earnings cap' (see **17.92** above). There were two types of unapproved schemes: funded unapproved retirement benefit schemes ('FURBS'), and unfunded unapproved retirement benefit schemes ('UURBS').

FURBS

17.116   In broad terms, the pre-A-Day tax treatment of a FURBS can be summarised as set out below.

(*a*)   Contributions by the employer were allowable against corporation tax as soon as they were made.

(*b*)   The employee was taxed on the employer's contributions as a benefit in kind.

(*c*)   National Insurance contributions ('NICs') were payable on the contributions made.

(*d*)   Investment returns were subject to tax at the basic rate on income and capital gains were subject to capital gains tax (with tapering relief available).

(*e*)   Benefits payable to the employee were subject to income tax when paid as a pension; however, there was no liability to income tax if the benefits were paid as a lump sum (as long as the employer's contributions had been taxed on the employee as a benefit in kind when they were paid in).

In practice, all benefits paid from FURBS on an employee's retirement were paid as a tax-free lump sum in order to avoid the double tax charge. No NICs were payable on the lump sum.

(*f*) Lump sum benefits on the death of an employee were free from liability to income tax and also free from inheritance tax, provided that the benefits were paid under a discretionary trust and the FURBS qualified as a 'sponsored superannuation scheme'.

UURBS

17.117 The pre-A-Day tax treatment of an UURBS was considerably more straightforward than that of a FURBS, and can be summarised as set out below:

(*a*) Payments of benefit made to an employee were deductible for corporation tax when made.

(*b*) The employee was subject to income tax on payment of the benefit (whether paid as a lump sum or a pension).

(*c*) Lump sum benefits on the death of an employee were free from inheritance tax if they were provided from a 'sponsored superannuation scheme' under a discretionary trust; however, income tax was payable on the benefit (unless it was insured – ie 'funded').

EFRBS from A-Day

17.118 As EFRBS are not registered pension schemes, they are not subject to the *FA 2004* regime. Non-registered pension schemes are allowed to continue but they do not receive any particular tax-favoured status. In particular, it should be noted that the exemptions from inheritance tax previously afforded to 'sponsored superannuation schemes' no longer apply.

A summary of the tax treatment of EFRBS is set out below:

(*a*) The value of the individual's benefits is not taken into account for the purpose of testing against the lifetime allowance (see **17.7** above).

(*b*) Contributions are not subject to the annual allowance charge (see **17.17** above).

(*c*) All contributions are treated as if made to an employee benefit trust. This means that, when contributions are made, no income tax or NICs are payable, and no corporation tax relief is available to the employer on those contributions. When the benefits are paid, income tax will be charged and relief from corporation tax given (but see **17.119** below).

(*d*)   So long as the employment relationship between employer and employee has ceased, there is no National Insurance charge on the benefits paid from an EFRBS, provided that the benefits are within the limits of benefits that can be paid under a registered scheme. As registered pension schemes may only pay a lump sum retirement benefit of up to a maximum of (broadly) 25 per cent of the value of the scheme benefits (see **17.38** above), this means that, in order to avoid any National Insurance charge, the lump sum must not exceed 25 per cent of the fund.

(*e*)   The taxation of investment income has been aligned with the rates paid by higher rate taxpayers. Investment returns, whether income or capital gains, are taxed at 40 per cent (dividends at 32.5 per cent). Tapering relief continues to be available on capital gains tax.

(*f*)   There is no automatic relief from inheritance tax (see **17.121** below).

Unfunded EFRBS

17.119   It can be seen from the above summary that the tax treatment of EFRBS is similar to the tax regime to which UURBS were subject prior to A-Day. Consequently, there continues to be a place for unfunded EFRBS under the new regime. Indeed, if an employee already has, or is likely by retirement to have, benefits that exceed the lifetime allowance, an unfunded EFRBS could be a viable option for providing retirement benefits in excess of this amount. The rate of tax on benefits payable under the EFRBS (currently 40 per cent) is less than the 55 per cent applied to lump sums in excess of the lifetime allowance payable from a registered scheme.

How attractive an employee finds an unfunded EFRBS will depend upon his view as to security. An unfunded benefit promise is only of value to the extent that the employer remains in existence and is able to pay the benefit. One way of addressing this concern has in the past been to provide some form of security for the promise, such as a charge over certain assets. However, in the June 2010 Budget the Government announced it would be introducing new measures to tackle arrangements with employees (including EFRBS) which 'seek to avoid, defer or reduce tax liabilities'. *FA 2011, Sch 2* introduces a new *Part 7A* to *ITEPA 2003* which catches payments and transactions from 9 December 2010. There is an accompanying Treasury document called 'Disguised Remuneration'. The intention is that an immediate charge to income tax and National Insurance will occur when a third party makes provision for a reward in relation to an individual's employment. One area which will be caught is where a person earmarks a sum of money or asset with a view to it later being paid or transferred to the individual employee. This provision will catch contributions to funded EFRBS (see **17.120** below) and will affect unfunded EFRBSs where some form of security is given or particular assets ear-marked. In many cases there may no longer be any financial benefit in maintaining the EFRBS structure.

Funded EFRBS

17.120 The absence of any tax relief on contributions paid by an employer after 5 April 2006 makes funded EFRBS a less attractive option (at least for employers). Transitional protections allow benefits under an EFRBS that were accrued before 6 April 2006 to be paid as a tax-free lump sum, provided that the employee was taxed on the employer's contributions paid into the arrangement (see **17.116** above). However, any part of a lump sum attributable to contributions paid into an EFRBS after 5 April 2006 is taxable, so many employers will have ceased paying contributions into former FURBS (now EFRBS) after 5 April 2006 and investigated other options for compensating the employee. The changes made by *FA 2011, Sch 2* give an immediate charge to income tax and national insurance on contributions to EFRBS.

Inheritance tax

17.121 Pension schemes established under trust are settled property for inheritance tax ('IHT') purposes. A number of specific exemptions take registered pension schemes outside the usual charges on this type of settlement for IHT purposes (see **17.74** above). Prior to 6 April 2006, most FURBS were also able to obtain these exemptions by virtue of being 'sponsored superannuation schemes' (*IHTA 1984, s 151(1)*). In practice, this required the payment of a separately identifiable administration charge by the employer. However, the exemption for sponsored superannuation schemes has been repealed (by *FA 2004, s 203(4)*). This means that EFRBS will be subject to the periodic charge and exit charge applicable to settlements without interest in possession. Transitional IHT protection is available for pre-6 April 2006 funds.

Penalties under the Pensions Act 1995, Pensions Act 2004 and other legislation

Types of penalty

General

The Pensions Act 1995 (PA 1995) carries a number of sanctions for non-compliance, ranging from fines to, in extreme cases, imprisonment. Many failures to comply with the requirements of the *Pensions Act 2004 (PA 2004)* also give rise to penalties. The *Pensions Act 2008 (PA 2008)* includes civil and criminal penalties relating to breaches of the automatic enrolment obligations, the *Finance Act 2004 (FA 2004)* has civil penalties for non-compliance with some of its requirements and the *Pension Schemes Act 2015 (PSA 2015)* includes a penalty for failing to check that a member has received appropriate advice before transferring safeguarded benefits. The *Occupational Pension Schemes (Charges and Governance) Regulations 2015 (SI 2015/879)* provide for penalties for breaches of new requirements relating to charge restrictions on, and the governance of, money purchase benefits. Both civil and criminal sanctions may arise under *FSMA 2000* but are not covered in this Appendix.

Civil penalties

The Regulator may require a person to pay a penalty in respect of an act or omission in contravention of various requirements of *PA 1995* and *PA 2004* (*PA 1995, s 10*). The maximum amount of the penalty varies from £5,000 in the case of an individual and £50,000 in any other case (or such lower amount as may be prescribed). The time limit for payment is usually 28 days.

Where a penalty is recoverable from a corporate body, and the act or omission was done with the connivance or consent of an officer (or, in some cases, a managing shareholder) of the company, the Regulator may instead impose a penalty on that person (*PA 1995, s 10(5)*).

Criminal penalties

Certain transgressions carry criminal sanctions. Penalties for conviction of an offence are:

(*a*)   on summary conviction – a fine not exceeding the statutory maximum; and

(*b*)   on conviction on indictment – a fine or imprisonment or both.

Where an offence committed by a corporate body is proved to have been committed with the consent or connivance of an officer or purported officer of the company, that person is guilty of an offence and subject to the same punishment (*PA 1995, s 115*).

Appeals

The powers of the Regulator to impose penalties and prohibit trustees are 'reserved regulatory functions' exercisable by the Determinations Panel (*PA 2004, s 10*). Appeals against decisions of the Determinations Panel may be referred to the Upper Tribunal (*PA 2004, s 103*, as amended from 6 April 2010 by the *Transfer of Tribunal Functions Order 2010, SI 2010/22, art 5(1)*). The Tribunal must determine any reference to it and then must remit the matter to the Determinations Panel with any appropriate directions (which may include a direction to vary or revoke the original decision). A party to a determination of the Tribunal may, with permission, appeal to the court on a point of law (*Tribunals, Courts and Enforcement Act 2007, s 13*).

Summary of penalties

A brief summary of the main transgressions for which penalties may be imposed is set out in the table below. This is not an exhaustive list.

CRIMINAL PENALTIES	
IMPOSED ON:	**HOW THE PENALTY ARISES:**
Pensions Act 1995	
Trustee/manager	Agreeing to a determination to invest in employer-related investments in excess of the statutory limit (*PA 1995, s 40*)
Any person	Purporting to act as a trustee whilst prohibited or suspended (*PA 1995, s 6*)
	Purporting to act as a trustee whilst disqualified (*PA 1995, s 30*)
	Acting as an auditor or actuary whilst ineligible (*PA 1995, s 28*)
	Being knowingly concerned in the fraudulent evasion of the obligation to pay deductions from employees' earnings to the trustees within the prescribed time (*PA 1995, s 49*)
	Being knowingly concerned in the fraudulent evasion of direct payment arrangements (*PSA 1993, s 111A*)
Pensions Act 2004	
Trustee/manager	Accepting or permitting reimbursement for fines or civil penalties imposed under *PA 1995, PA 2004, PSA 1993* or *PA 2008 (PA 2004, s 256(4))*
Any person	Failure to provide information or produce a document when required under *PA 2004, s 72 (PA 2004, s 77(1))*
	Delaying or obstructing an inspector exercising any power under *PA 2004, s 73, 74* or *75;* neglecting or refusing to produce any document under *PA 2004, s 75;* or neglecting or refusing to answer questions or provide information when required by the inspector (*PA 2004, s 77(2)*)
	Intentionally and without reasonable excuse altering, suppressing, concealing or destroying a document required by the inspector (*PA 2004, s 77(5)*)
	Knowingly or recklessly providing false or misleading information to the Regulator (*PA 2004, s 80*)
	Disclosing restricted information received from the Regulator without authority (*PA 2004, s 82*)
	Failure following the issue of a summons to attend tribunal proceedings in relation to a decision of the Regulator or failure to give evidence (*PA 2004, s 102A(3)*)

Appendix 1

IMPOSED ON:	HOW THE PENALTY ARISES:
	Without reasonable excuse, altering, suppressing, concealing or destroying a document required to be produce for the purposes of proceedings before the tribunal; or refusing to produce a document when so required (*PA 2004, s 102A(5)*)
	Without reasonable excuse, intentionally delaying or obstructing a person appointed by the PPF Board exercising any power under *PA 2004, s 192;* neglecting or refusing to produce any document under *PA 2004, s 192;* or neglecting or refusing to answer questions or provide information when required (*PA 2004, s 193(2)*)
	Intentionally and without reasonable excuse altering, suppressing, concealing or destroying a document required by the PPF Board (*PA 2004, s 193(6)*)
	Knowingly or recklessly providing false or misleading information to the PPF Board (*PA 2004, s 195*)
	Disclosing restricted information received from the PPF Board without authority (*PA 2004, s 197*)
Any prescribed person	Failure to provide information or produce a document when required by the PPF Board under *PA 2004, s 191* (*PA 2004, s 193(1)*)
Pensions Act 2008	
Employer	Wilful failure to comply with the duty under *PA 2008, s 3(2)* (automatic enrolment), *s 5(2)* (automatic re-enrolment), or *s 7(3)* (jobholder's right to opt in) (*PA 2008, s 45*)
Officer of body corporate	An offence under *PA 2008, s 45* by body corporate was committed with the consent or connivance of an officer of that body corporate or is attributable to any neglect on his part (*PA 2008, s 46*)
CIVIL PENALTIES	
IMPOSED ON:	**HOW THE PENALITY ARISES:**
Pensions Act 1995	
Trustee/manager	Failure to comply with a direction of the Regulator to make payments to members, include a statement in the annual report and send a statement to members (*PA 1995, s 15*)

IMPOSED ON:	HOW THE PENALTY ARISES:
	Failure to give notice to the Regulator that a trustee appointed under *PA 1995, s 23* is no longer an independent person (*PA 1995, s 25*, amended by *PA 2004, s 36*)
	Failure to give notice of trustee meetings where decisions taken by majority (*PA 1995, s 32*) (unless the 'urgency'1 exemption in the *Scheme Administration Regulations 1996 (SI 1996/1715, reg 9* applies)
	Failure to prepare or maintain a statement of investment principles or failure to obtain and consider advice before preparing the statement or (where required) to consult the employer (*PA 1995, s 35*)
	Failure to obtain and consider proper advice before making an investment or failure to comply with the *Investment Regulations* (*PA 1995, s 36*)
	Failure to comply with requirements in relation to the payment of surplus to an employer (*PA 1995, s 37*)
	Failure to take reasonable steps to secure compliance with the statutory restrictions on employer-related investments (*PA 1995, s 40(4)*)
	Failure to disclose documentation and information when required to do so (*Disclosure Regulations (SI 2013/2734)* made under *PA 1995, s 41*)
	Placing reliance on the skill and judgment of legal or other specified professional advisers (as to which, see *Scheme Administration Regulations 1996 (SI 1996/1715), reg 2*) not appointed by the trustees (*PA 1995, s 47*)
	Failure to appoint a scheme auditor, scheme actuary or fund manager when required to do so or failure to comply with requirements prescribed regarding the appointment of professional advisers (*PA 1995, s 47*)
	Failure to keep money in a separate account and failure to maintain adequate records relating to trustee meetings and certain transactions as required by regulations (see, in particular, the *Scheme Administration Regulations 1996 (SI 1996/1715)*) (*PA 1995, s 49*)
	Failure to give notice to the Regulator and the member of the failure of the employer to pay deductions from the employee's earnings to the trustees within the prescribed time (*PA 1995, s 49*)

IMPOSED ON:	HOW THE PENALTY ARISES:
	Failure to comply with the statutory requirements to keep written records of any determinations or decisions in relation to the winding up of the scheme (*PA 1995, s 49A*)
	Failure to make and/or implement arrangements for the resolution of disputes (*PA 1995, s 50*)
	Failure to take all reasonable steps to ensure that a modification is not voidable (*PA 1995, ss 67(2) and 67I(2)*)
	Failure to comply with any requirement imposed by the Regulator under *PA 1995, s 67G(5)(a)* (*PA 1995, s 67I(4)*)
	Exercising a power to make a regulated modification in contravention of an order under *PA 1995, s 67H(2)(a)* (*PA 1995, s 67I(5)(a)*)
	Failure to comply with any requirement specified in an order under *PA 1995, s 67H(2)(b)*
	Failure to make a report regarding a scheme's winding up where required to do so (*PA 1995, s 72A*)
	Failure to comply with a direction given by the Regulator for facilitating winding up (*PA 1995, s 72C*)
	Failure to comply with the statutory order on a winding up (*PA 1995, s 73B*)
	Exercising a power to distribute excess assets on a winding up to an employer without having complied with the statutory requirements (*PA 1995, s 76*)
	Failure to comply with the requirements for the preparation, maintenance and revision of schedules of payments for defined contribution schemes (*PA 1995, s 87*)
	Failure to notify the Regulator and members within the required time where payments have not been made in accordance with the schedule of payments (*PA 1995, s 88*)
	Failure to comply with an improvement notice issued by the Regulator (*PA 2004, s 13*)
Employer	Failure to keep adequate records, as required by regulations (*PA 1995, s 49*)

IMPOSED ON:	HOW THE PENALTY ARISES:
	Deducting contributions from employees' earnings and failing to pay them to the trustees within required time with no reasonable excuse for doing so (*PA 1995, s 49*) (unless it is required to pay a penalty under *WRPA 1999, s 3(7)* for failures in respect of stakeholder schemes)
	Failure to make payments to a defined contribution scheme in accordance with the schedule of payments (*PA 1995, s 88*)
Person purporting to exercise power	Non-trustee purporting to exercise a power in relation to the payment of surplus to the employer (*PA 1995, s 37*)
Prescribed person	Failure to keep adequate records, as required by regulations (*PA 1995, s 49*)
Any person other than the trustees	Without reasonable excuse, exercising a power to modify a scheme without trustee consent or in breach of the timing requirement (*PA 1995, s 67I(3)*)
	Exercising a power to make a regulated modification in contravention of an order under *PA 1995, s 67H(2) (a) (PA 1995, s 67I(5)(b)*)
	Failure to comply with a direction given by the Regulator for facilitating winding up (*PA 1995, s 72C*)
	Exercising a power to distribute excess assets on a winding up to an employer without having complied with the statutory requirements (*PA 1995, s 76*)
Pensions Act 2004	
Trustee/manager	Failure to comply with the terms of a freezing order issued by the Regulator (*PA 2004, s 24*)
	Failure to comply with directions of the Regulator where a winding-up order is made when a freezing order is in force (*PA 2004, s 28*)
	Failure to comply with directions where the Regulator revokes a freezing order (*PA 2004, s 30*)
	Failure to take all reasonable steps to report the failure of the employer to comply with a requirement from the Regulator to make a contribution on the revocation of a freezing order (*PA 2004, s 30*)
	Failure to comply with a notification order issued by the Regulator in relation to a freezing order (*PA 2004, s 31*)

IMPOSED ON:	HOW THE PENALTY ARISES:
	Failure of trustees of a transferee scheme to comply with a direction from the Regulator where a contribution notice has been issued following a bulk transfer (*PA 2004, s 39A*)
	Failure to comply with a direction from the Regulator to suspend recovery of a *s 75* debt (*PA 2004, ss 41 and 50*)
	Failure of trustees of a transferee scheme to comply with a direction from the Regulator where a financial support direction has been issued following a bulk transfer (*PA 2004, s 43A*)
	Failure to provide the Regulator with information in relation to the register (*PA 2004, s 62*)
	Failure to provide a scheme return to the Regulator (*PA 2004, s 64*)
	Failure to notify the Regulator of a 'notifiable event' (*PA 2004, s 69*)
	Failure to report a breach of the law to the Regulator (*PA 2004, s 70*)
	Failure to comply with a report notice issued by the Regulator (*PA 2004, s 71*)
	Failure to comply with statutory requirements during an assessment period (*PA 2004, s 133*)
	Failure to comply with directions of the PPF Board during an assessment period (*PA 2004, s 134*)
	Failure to comply with statutory restrictions on winding up during an assessment period (*PA 2004, s 135*)
	Failure to reduce benefits to PPF level during an assessment period (*PA 2004, s 138*)
	Failure to decide pre-assessment date applications for ill-health pensions within six months of the assessment date (*PA 2004, s 140* and the *Pension Protection Fund (Reviewable Ill Health Pensions) Regulations 2005 (SI 2005/652)*)
	Failure to comply with statutory requirements for applying to the PPF for authority to continue as a closed scheme (*PA 2004, s 153*)
	Failure to comply with directions of the PPF Board to wind up the scheme (*PA 2004, s 154*)

IMPOSED ON:	HOW THE PENALTY ARISES:
	Failure to make an application to the PPF for it to assume responsibility for a closed scheme (*PA 2004, s 157*)
	Failure to comply with directions of the Regulator in relation to backdating the winding-up of a scheme (*PA 2004, s 219*)
	Failure to prepare, review and revise a statement of funding principles (*PA 2004, s 223*)
	Failure to obtain, receive and make available to the employer an actuarial valuation or report (*PA 2004, s 224*)
	Failure to comply with the requirements in relation to a recovery plan (*PA 2004, s 226*)
	Failure to comply with the requirements in relation to a schedule of contributions (*PA 2004, s 227*)
	Failure to report a failure to pay contributions where there are reasonable grounds to believe it may be of material significance to the Regulator (*PA 2004, s 228*)
	Failure to obtain the agreement of the employer where required (*PA 2004, s 229*)
	Failure to report failure to agree to the Regulator (*PA 2004, s 229*)
	Failure to obtain the advice of the actuary where required (*PA 2004, s 230*)
	Failure to comply with requirements for winding up procedure (*PA 2004, s 231A*)
	Failure to put in place or to implement arrangements for member-nominated trustees (*PA 2004, s 241*)
	Failure to put in place or to implement arrangements for member-nominated directors of corporate trustees (*PA 2004, s 242*)
	Accepting a funding payment if the scheme is not established under trust or does not have written benefit rules which are in force (*PA 2004, s 252*)
	Failure to limit the activities of a UK-based occupational pension scheme to 'retirement-benefit activities' (*PA 2004, s 255*)

IMPOSED ON:	HOW THE PENALTY ARISES:
	Failure to take steps to prevent the payment out of scheme assets for the purpose of reimbursing any trustee or manager in relation to fines or civil penalties imposed under *PA 1995, PA 2004, PSA 1993* or *PA 2008* (*PA 2004, s 256(3)*)
	Accepting contributions from a European employer in contravention of the cross-border requirements (*PA 2004, s 287*)
	Operating a scheme in relation to cross-border members in a way inconsistent with the social and labour law requirements of the host EEA state (*PA 2004, s 291*)
	Failure to comply with a ring-fencing notice issued by the Regulator (*PA 2004, s 292*)
Employer	Failure without reasonable excuse to repay contributions required under the terms of a freezing order issued by the Regulator (*PA 2004, s 24*)
	Failure without reasonable excuse to comply with a requirement from the Regulator to make a contribution on the revocation of a freezing order (*PA 2004, s 30*)
	Failure to notify the Regulator of a 'notifiable event' (*PA 2004, s 69*)
	Failure to report a breach of the law to the Regulator (*PA 2004, s 70*)
	Failure to comply with a report notice issued by the Regulator (*PA 2004, s 71*)
	Failure without reasonable excuse to pay contributions in accordance with the schedule of contributions or debt arising (*PA 2004, s 228*)
	Failure to comply with requirements regarding contribution payments to a scheme with its main administration outside the EEA states (*PA 2004, s 253*)
	Failure of a UK employer to comply with directions from the Regulator in relation to contravention of relevant legal requirements by a European pensions institution which receives contributions from the UK employer (*PA 2004, s 293*)

IMPOSED ON:	HOW THE PENALTY ARISES:
Any person to whom a third party notice is issued	Failure without reasonable excuse to comply with a third party notice issued by the Regulator (*PA 2004, s 14*)
Any deposit taker	Failure without reasonable excuse to comply with a pensions liberation restraining order issued by the Regulator (*PA 2004, s 20*)
	Failure to take all reasonable steps to comply with a pensions liberation repatriation order issued by the Regulator (*PA 2004, s 21*)
Any person other than the trustees	Failure without reasonable excuse to comply with directions of the Regulator where a winding-up order is made when a freezing order is in force (*PA 2004, s 28*)
Other prescribed person	Failure to notify the Regulator of a 'notifiable event' (*PA 2004, s 69*)
	Failure to report breaches of law to the Regulator (*PA 2004, s 70*)
Any other person issued with a report notice	Failure to comply with a report notice issued by the Regulator (*PA 2004, s 71*)
Any other person	Failure without reasonable excuse to comply with directions of the PPF Board during an assessment period (*PA 2004, s 134*)
	Failure without reasonable excuse to comply with directions of the PPF Board to wind up the scheme (*PA 2004, s 154*)
	Failure without reasonable excuse to comply with directions of the Regulator in relation to backdating the winding-up of a scheme (*PA 2004, s 219*)
Scheme actuary	Failure to report to the Regulator when no certificate of technical provisions can be given (*PA 2004, s 225*)
	Failure without reasonable excuse to report to the Regulator if the schedule of contributions cannot be certified (*PA 2004, s 227*)
Pensions Act 2008	
Any person	Failure to comply with a compliance notice, third party compliance notice, unpaid contributions notice or notice under *PA 2004, s 72* (provision of information) (*PA 2008, ss 40* and *41*) (fixed penalty and escalating penalty notices)

IMPOSED ON:	HOW THE PENALTY ARISES:
Finance Act 2004	
Scheme administrator (usually the trustees)	Failure to provide a registered pension scheme return (*FA 2004, s 257(1)-(3)*)
	Fraudulently or negligently making an inaccurate registered pension scheme return or providing incorrect accompanying documents (*FA 2004, s 257(4)*)
	Winding up wholly or mainly to facilitate the payment of lump sums (*FA 2004, s 265*)
	Transferring sums to insured schemes unless payment is made to the scheme administrator or relevant insurance company (*FA 2004, s 266*)
Person who fails to comply	Failure to provide information required by regulations (*FA 2004, s 258*)
The individual member	Fraudulently or negligently providing false information in relation to enhanced lifetime allowance or failing to provide information (*FA 2004, ss 261 and 262*)
	Failure to notify the HMRC within 90 days of relevant benefit accrual in relation to enhanced protection of lifetime allowance (*FA 2004, s 263*)
Person making the statement	Fraudulently or negligently making a false statement (*FA 2004, s 264*)
Welfare Reform and Pensions Act 1999	
Trustee/manager	Failure to secure that the conditions for registration of a stakeholder pension scheme are fulfilled while the scheme is registered (*WRPA 1999, s 2*)
	Failure to discharge liability in respect of a pension credit within the implementation period (*WRPA 1999, s 33*)
	Failure to notify the Regulator of a failure to discharge liability for a pension credit within the implementation period (*WRPA 1999, s 33*)
Employer	Failure to comply with duty to deduct employee's contributions on request and pay them to the trustees or manager (*WRPA 1999, s 3*)
Prescribed person	Failure to secure that the conditions for registration of a stakeholder pension scheme are fulfilled while the scheme is registered (*WRPA 1999, s 2*)

IMPOSED ON:	HOW THE PENALTY ARISES:
Pension Schemes Act 1993	
Trustee/manager	Failure to comply with the requirements for conversion of GMPs into other scheme benefits when amending scheme to effect this (*PSA, s 24H*)
	Failure to provide a statement of entitlement to members when applied for by a member (*PSA 1993, s 93A*)
	Failure to carry out what a member of the scheme requires within six months of the necessary date as regards the exercise of the option conferred by *PSA 1993, s 95* (*PSA 1993, s 99*)
	Failure to notify a member of his right to a cash transfer sum within a reasonable period (*PSA 1993, s 101AC*)
	Failure to carry out early leaver's request for a cash transfer sum or a contribution refund (*PSA 1993, s 101AG*)
	Failure on application of an eligible member of a salary related occupational pension scheme to provide him with a written statement of the amount of the cash equivalent of his pension credit benefit under the scheme (*PSA 1993, s 101H*)
	Failure to notify the Regulator of a failure to comply with a transfer notice before the end of the period for compliance (*PSA 1993, s 101J*)
	Failure to notify the Regulator and/or the employee or jobholder where contributions due under the direct payment arrangements had not been paid before the due date (*PSA 1993, s 111A*)
Employer	Failure to prepare/maintain a record for direct payment arrangements regarding contributions to personal pension schemes or to send a copy of the record to the trustees or managers (*PSA 1993, s 111A*)
	Failure to pay the contribution payable under direct payment arrangements to the trustee/managers of the scheme on or before its due date (*PSA 1993, s 111A*) (unless it is required to pay a penalty under *WRPA 1999, s 3(7)* for failures in respect of stakeholder schemes)

IMPOSED ON:	HOW THE PENALTY ARISES:
Pensions Schemes Act 2015	
Trustee/manager	Failure to check the member/survivor has received independent advice regarding subsisting rights in safeguarded benefits before: (*a*) converting any of the benefits into flexible benefits under the scheme; (*b*) making a transfer payment with a view to acquiring a right or entitlement to flexible benefits under another pension scheme; or (*c*) paying an uncrystallised funds pension lump sum in respect of any of the benefits (*PSA 2015, s 48(6)*).
Occupational and Personal Pension Schemes (Consultation by Employers and Miscellaneous Amendment) Regulations 2006 (SI 2006/349)	
Employer	Failure to comply with the employer consultation requirements made under *regs 6* to *16* (*reg 18A*)
Occupational Pensions Schemes (Requirement to Obtain Audited Accounts and a Statement from the Auditor) Regulations 1996 (SI 1996/1975)	
Trustee/manager	Failure without reasonable excuse to obtain audited accounts or an auditor's contribution statement within seven months of end of scheme year (*reg 2(3)*)
Occupational Pension Schemes (Preservation of Benefit) Regulations 1991 (SI 1991/167)	
Any person	Failure to provide information regarding transfer of accrued rights without consent (*reg 27B*)
Disclosure Regulations (SI 2013/2734)	
Any person	Failure to comply with any requirement of the *Disclosure Regulations* (*reg 5*)
Pensions on Divorce etc (Provision of Information) Regulations 2000 (SI 2000/1048)	

IMPOSED ON:	HOW THE PENALTY ARISES:
Trustee or Manager	Failure to provide specified information regarding pension sharing (*reg 9*)
Occupational Pension Scheme (Winding Up) Regulations 1996 (SI 1996/3126)	
Any person	Failure to issue appropriate notice in writing within one month following determination to defer winding up of scheme or as to when liabilities are to be determined (*reg 11*)
Occupational Pension Schemes (Charges and Governance) Regulations 2015 (SI 2015/879)	
Any person	Imposing charges on members exceeding the limits or of a prohibited description under *regs 4* to *13* (or not complying with a compliance notice regarding charges), or failure to comply with *Part V* of the *Scheme Administration Regulations* on the governance of schemes providing money purchase benefits (*reg 28*)
Occupational Pension Schemes (Power to Amend Schemes to Reflect Abolition of Contracting-out) Regulations 2015 (SI 2015/118)	
Trustee or Manager	Failure to take all reasonable steps to provide information reasonably requested by the employer/ principal employer regarding the use of the power under *PA 2014, s 24(2)* to amend occupational schemes to take account of increases in employer's national insurance contributions (*reg 12*)

Summary of the provisions of the Occupational and Personal Pension Schemes (Disclosure of Information) Regulations 2013 (SI 2013/2734) (the 'Disclosure Regulations'), and other requirements to disclose information in relation to registered occupational pension schemes

Unless otherwise stated, information or documents should be disclosed by the methods set out in *Disclosure Regulations, regs 26* to *28*. This is referred to in the table as the 'standard methods'. The information may be given by:

- sending it to the person's last known postal address;

- sending it to the person's last known electronic address; or

- making it available on a website.

When any information is given by the standard methods, it must be accompanied by the postal or electronic address to which a person should send requests for further information or any other enquiry.

The member can request that the information is not given electronically. Information may only be given electronically where the trustees are satisfied that the electronic communications have been designed so that the person will be able to get access and to store or print the information, and taking into account the requirements of disabled persons. Where a website is used for the first time to make the information available, a notification must be given to the recipient including:

- a statement that the information or document is available on the website;

- the website address;

- details of the place on the website where the information or document may be read; and

- an explanation of how the recipient may read the information or document on the website.

Each time the website is subsequently used to make information available then a notification must be given to the recipient (other than through the website) unless certain limited exceptions apply.

'Relevant person', for the purposes of the *Disclosure Regulations*, means a:

- member or prospective member of the scheme,

- spouse or civil partner of a member or prospective member,

- beneficiary of the scheme,

- recognised trade union.

'Excluded person', for the purposes of the *Disclosure Regulations*, means a member or beneficiary:

- whose present postal address and electronic address is not known to the trustees or managers of the scheme, and

- in respect of whom the trustees or managers of the scheme have sent correspondence to their last known;

  – postal address and that correspondence has been returned, or

  – electronic address and the trustees or managers of the scheme are satisfied that correspondence has not been delivered.

To be disclosed	Disclosure to	Form of disclosure	When
CONSTITUTION OF THE SCHEME (*Disclosure Regulations, reg 11 and Sch 3 Part 1*)			
The contents of: • the trust deed or other document constituting the scheme; • the scheme rules (if not in above document); • any documents amending, supplementing or superseding any of the above; • a document setting out the names, addresses and email address of participating employers, if not in the above documents.	Relevant person, where the information is relevant to the person's rights or prospective rights under the scheme	• Copy for inspection, free of charge at a place which is reasonable; or • Personal copy at a reasonable charge (ie cost of copying, postage & packaging) or, if publicly available, notice of where a copy may be obtained; or • On a website. (*reg 29*)	On request, within two months of the request being made. There is no information required to be given to a relevant person where that information has been given in the last 12 months, unless there has been a change to the information.
BASIC INFORMATION ABOUT THE SCHEME (*Disclosure Regulations, reg 6, Sch 2 Part 1, Sch 2 Part 3*)			
The conditions persons must meet to become members of the scheme and a summary of the categories of persons who are eligible to become members of the scheme.			

865

To be disclosed	Disclosure to	Form of disclosure	When
How persons who are eligible to be members of the scheme are admitted to it.	Prospective members.	Standard methods.	As of course, where practicable, to every prospective member and to members who have not already received it.
A summary of what can be done with a member's accrued rights where the member leaves pensionable service before normal pension age, including whether accrued rights can be transferred out of the scheme, converted into an annuity, designated as available for the payment of drawdown pension and commuted to a lump sum, whether a charge may be made and that further information is available on request.	Members who have not already been given the information.		If the information has not already been provided, it must be given:
	Relevant person if they make request and have not had the information in the last 12 months.		• where the trustees have received jobholder information about the member, within one month of their receiving it.
	Only information relevant to an individual need be disclosed to him or to his trade union.		• where no jobholder information has been received, within two months of individual becoming a member.
Where the member has flexible benefits, a statement explaining the circumstances in which the member may transfer accrued rights to flexible benefits out of the scheme.			Otherwise, on request, (unless the same information was provided in the 12 months prior to the request being made), as soon as practicable and in any event, within two months of the date of receipt of request.
Where the member has safeguarded benefits (except where the individual is a member of an unfunded public service defined benefits scheme), a statement that the member may be required to take independent advice before the member may:			

To be disclosed	Disclosure to	Form of disclosure	When
• convert any of the safeguarded benefits into different benefits that are flexible benefits under the scheme; • transfer safeguarded benefits to another pension scheme with a view to acquiring a right or entitlement to flexible benefits; and • withdraw an uncrystallised funds pension lump sum. Whether the scheme is a tax registered scheme or, if not, whether an application for the scheme to become a tax registered scheme is under consideration by the Commissioners for HMRC. A statement that explains whether transfers can be made into the scheme, including whether such transfers can be made in accordance with *Chapters 1 and 2 of Part 4ZA of PSA 1993*. The arrangements, if any, for the payment by members of additional voluntary contributions.			Otherwise, on request, (unless the same information was provided in the 12 months prior to the request being made), as soon as practicable and in any event, within two months of the date of receipt of request. Details of material alterations to the information disclosed must be drawn to attention of affected members and beneficiaries (but not excluded persons) before the change if practicable, but in any event, within three months after the change (*reg 8*).

To be disclosed	Disclosure to	Form of disclosure	When
A summary of how the contributions, if any, payable by the employer and the member are calculated.			
A statement that TPAS is available to assist members and beneficiaries with pensions questions, and issues they have been unable to resolve with the trustees or managers of the scheme.			
A statement that the Pensions Ombudsman may investigate and determine certain complaints or disputes.			
A statement that the Regulator may intervene in the running of schemes where trustees, managers, employers or professional advisers have failed in their duties.			
The postal and electronic address at which each of the bodies referred to above may be contacted.			
If a member of the scheme has to give a period of notice to terminate their pensionable service, the length of that period of notice.			

To be disclosed	Disclosure to	Form of disclosure	When
Whether, and if so on what conditions (if any), a member of the scheme, whose pensionable service has terminated before normal pension age, may re-enter pensionable service.			
Information about benefits payable under the scheme including what the benefits are, how benefits are calculated, how the scheme defines pensionable earnings (if appropriate), how and when benefits in payment are increased (if appropriate), the rate at which rights to benefits accrue (if appropriate), the conditions on which benefits are payable, when benefits (including survivor's benefits) are payable.			
Where the member has money purchase benefits, a statement that the value of the pension will depend on several factors including the amount of contributions paid, any cost of exercising any right to transfer the benefits, any charges payable, the age at which the member accesses the benefits, the performance of investments and any cost of converting benefits into an annuity.			

To be disclosed	Disclosure to	Form of disclosure	When
Where the member has cash balance benefits, a statement that the value of the pension will depend on several factors including the amount of contributions paid, any cost of exercising any right to transfer the benefits, any charges payable, the age at which the member accesses the benefits, any guaranteed interest or bonuses and any cost of converting benefits into an annuity.			
A statement that the annual report will be provided on request.			
The scheme's IDR arrangements and the address and title of the person who should be contacted.			
Where offered, a statement explaining lifestyling, its advantages and disadvantages.			
Any material change to basic information (*reg 8*).			

To be disclosed	Disclosure to	Form of disclosure	When
BENEFIT INFORMATION – NOT MONEY PURCHASE (*Disclosure Regulations, regs 16, 16A, Sch 5, Sch 6*)			
The amount of benefit which would be payable if the member were to die in service. An amount, chosen by the trustees, of the member's benefits and survivors' benefits calculated without regard to possible increases in the member's salary which is either: • the amounts that would be payable from the date benefits are payable if pensionable service were to end on a date specified, • the amounts that would be payable from the date benefits are payable if pensionable service were to end on the member attaining normal pension age, or • the amounts that would be payable from the date benefits are payable if pensionable service were to end on a date agreed between the member and the trustees. The amount of the member's pensionable remuneration on a date specified by the trustees or managers of the scheme.	Active members.	Standard methods.	On request from the member but only once every 12 months and only where a benefit information statement has not been provided in the past 12 months. Information must be given as soon as practicable and no more than two months after the request.

871

To be disclosed	Disclosure to	Form of disclosure	When
The date on which the member's pensionable service started. A summary of the method for calculating the member's and any survivor's benefits. Details of how any deduction from benefits is calculated.	Active and deferred members.	Standard methods.	On request from the member but only once every 12 months and, in relation to active members, only where a benefit information statement has not been provided in the past 12 months. Information must be given as soon as practicable and no more than two months after the request.
The date the member's pensionable service ended. The amount of the member's benefits and survivor's benefits payable from the date benefits are payable. The amount of the member's pensionable remuneration on the date pensionable service ended.	Deferred members.	Standard methods.	On request from the member but only once every 12 months. Information must be given as soon as practicable and no more than two months after the request.
The amount of the member's benefits and survivors' benefits payable from the date benefits are payable. A summary of the method for calculating the member's benefits and any survivors' benefits. Details of how any deduction from benefits is calculated.	Pension credit members.	Standard methods.	On request from the member but only once every 12 months. Information must be given as soon as practicable and no more than two months after the request.

To be disclosed	Disclosure to	Form of disclosure	When
Information listed above (as appropriate) plus: • an illustration of the amount of pension likely to be secured at normal pension age; • a statement that the information is given for illustration only; • a statement of how the member may obtain further details from the trustees about the information; • a statement that general assumptions have been made; • a statement that any amounts are expressed in today's prices; • the retirement date and illustration date used for the purposes of the information; • a statement that the amount of pension payable will depend on considerations which may be different from any assumptions made; and • a statement of any assumptions made in relation to future contributions, lump sums, increases and survivor's benefits and any changes from previous assumptions used.	Cash balance members.	Standard methods.	On request from the member but only once every 12 months. Information must be given as soon as practicable and no more than two months after the request.

To be disclosed	Disclosure to	Form of disclosure	When
BENEFIT INFORMATION – MONEY PURCHASE (*Disclosure Regulations, reg 17, Sch 6*)			
The amount of contributions credited to the member in the immediately preceding scheme year (occupational scheme).	Each member with rights to money purchase benefits, except excluded members.	Standard methods.	As of course, within 12 months of the end of each scheme year.
The value of the member's accrued rights under the scheme at a date specified by the trustees or managers of the scheme.			
Any cash equivalent in respect of the transfer of the member's accrued rights that would be different from the value specified above, calculated in accordance with *ss 97* and *101* of the *PSA 1993*.			
An illustration of the amount of the pension: • calculated as set out below • an entitlement to which would be likely to accrue to the member, or be capable of being secured by the member, at the member's retirement date, and • in respect of rights to money purchase benefits that may arise under the scheme.	Members, other than excluded persons and other than where *reg 17(6)* applies (in which case it may be given).	Standard methods.	As of course, within 12 months of the end of each scheme year.

To be disclosed	Disclosure to	Form of disclosure	When
The amount must be calculated by reference to relevant guidance, and the assumptions listed below and having regard to the value of the member's accrued rights to money purchase benefits under the scheme on the illustration date. It may take account of any lump sum.			
The assumptions are, where the calculation relates to the rights of a non-contributing member, that no contributions will be made to the scheme by the member, or on the member's behalf, after the illustration date, or in any other case, that until the member's retirement date contributions to the scheme will be made by the member or on the member's behalf, and the scheme will maintain its tax registration under *FA 2004, s153.*			
A statement that the information given is only for the purposes of illustration and that it does not represent any promise or guarantee as to the amount of benefit that may be receivable by the member or a beneficiary of the scheme under the scheme.			

Appendix II

To be disclosed	Disclosure to	Form of disclosure	When
A statement of how the person to whom the information given relates may obtain further details from the trustees about that information.			
A statement that general assumptions have been made.			
A statement that any amounts in the information are expressed in today's prices.			
The member's retirement date used for the purposes of the information.			
The illustration date used for the purposes of the information.			
A statement that assumptions have been made about the nature of the investments and their likely performance.			
A statement that the amount of any pension payable will depend on considerations which may be different from any assumptions made.			

To be disclosed	Disclosure to	Form of disclosure	When
A statement that the amount of any pension payable under the scheme to or in respect of the member will depend on considerations (including the cost of buying an annuity at the time the pension becomes payable) which may be different from any assumptions made. A statement of any: • assumptions made relating to future contributions to the scheme; • assumptions made relating to the lump sum, level of increases and survivors' pensions; and changes to those assumptions since the information was last given.			
ACCESSING BENEFITS *(Disclosure Regulations, regs 18, 19, 18A, 18B, 19A, 20, 21, Sch 7, Sch 10, Sch 2)*			
A statement explaining lifestyling, its advantages and disadvantages.	Members where the scheme contains provision for lifestyling.	Standard methods.	Between five and 15 years before the member's retirement date.

To be disclosed	Disclosure to	Form of disclosure	When
A statement of the options available to the member under the scheme rules. Where the member has the opportunity to transfer flexible benefits: • A statement that the member has an opportunity to transfer flexible benefits to one or more different pension providers. • A statement that different pension providers offer different options in relation to what the member can do with the flexible benefits, including the option to select an annuity. • A statement that different options have different features, different rates of payment, different charges and different tax implications. • Either a copy of the Money Advice Service leaflet 'Your pension: it's time to choose' or a statement that gives materially the same information.	Members with a right or entitlement to flexible benefits.	Standard methods.	At least four months before a specified retirement date or, where none, normal pension age. Where the period between the specified date and the date benefits will become payable is less than four months then the information must be given within 20 days of the date on which the retirement date is specified.

To be disclosed	Disclosure to	Form of disclosure	When
• A statement that pensions guidance is available to help the person to understand their options in relation to what they can do with their flexible benefits. • A statement that pensions guidance may be accessed on the internet, by phone, or face-to-face. • The phone number (0330 0330 1001) and website address (www.pensionwise.gov.uk) at which pensions guidance may be accessed and details of how the person may access pensions guidance face-to-face. • A statement that pensions guidance is free and impartial. • A statement that the person should access pensions guidance and consider taking independent advice to help them decide which option is most suitable for them.			

Appendix II

To be disclosed	Disclosure to	Form of disclosure	When
• An estimate of the value of any accrued rights to flexible benefits that the member may transfer out of the scheme under the scheme rules, in respect of which the cash equivalent is not required to be given. • The date by reference to which the cash equivalent or value (as appropriate) is calculated. • An explanation that the cash equivalent or value (as appropriate) is an estimate and may not represent the exact amount available to the member to transfer to another pension provider. • In relation to the member's accrued rights to flexible benefits in respect of which there is an opportunity to transfer, details of any guarantee to which the benefits are subject and details of any other features, restrictions and conditions that apply to the benefits that affect, or may affect, their value.			

To be disclosed	Disclosure to	Form of disclosure	When
• Where the member has a right or entitlement to benefits under the scheme that are not flexible benefits, that the member has that right or entitlement and how the member may access information about those benefits. • A statement that there may be tax implications associated with accessing flexible benefits, income from a pension is taxable and the rate at which income from a pension is taxable depends on the amount of income that the person receives from a pension and from other sources. • Where the member has accrued rights to flexible benefits that are not money-purchase benefits, has not reached normal pension age and does not satisfy the ill-health condition: – a statement that the value of the member's accrued rights to flexible benefits is likely to be lower if the member accesses the benefits before normal pension age; and – the age at which the member will reach normal pension age			

To be disclosed	Disclosure to	Form of disclosure	When
But, where the member has been given information on request in the 12 months before the date on which the above information is required to be given, the following information must be provided instead: • A statement that the member has been given information about the flexible benefits that may be provided to the member, the member's opportunity to transfer those benefits, and the options available to the member under the scheme rules. • A statement that pensions guidance is available to help the person to understand their options in relation to what they can do with their flexible benefits. • A statement that pensions guidance may be accessed on the internet, by phone, or face-to-face.			

To be disclosed	Disclosure to	Form of disclosure	When
• The phone number (030 0330 1001) and website address (www. pensionswise.gov.uk) at which the pensions guidance may be accessed and details of how the person may access the pensions guidance face-to-face. • A statement that pensions guidance is free and impartial. • A statement that the person should access pensions guidance and consider taking independent advice to help them decide which option is most suitable for them. • An estimate of the cash equivalent of any of the member's accrued rights to flexible benefits that are transferrable rights or would be transferrable rights if the member stopped accruing rights to some or all of the flexible benefits. • An estimate of the value of any accrued rights to flexible benefits that the member may transfer out of the scheme under the scheme rules, in respect of which an estimate of the cash equivalent is not required to be given.			

To be disclosed	Disclosure to	Form of disclosure	When
• The date by reference to which the estimate of the cash equivalent or value (as appropriate) is calculated. • An explanation that the cash equivalent or value (as appropriate) is an estimate and may not represent the exact amount available to the member to transfer to another pension provider.			
A statement of the options available under the scheme rules. A statement that the member has an opportunity to transfer flexible benefits to one or more different pension providers. A statement that different pension providers offer different options in relation to what the member can do with the flexible benefits, including the option to select an annuity. A statement that different options have different features, different rates of payment, different charges and different tax implications.	Members with an opportunity to transfer flexible benefits and who have reached normal minimum pension age (generally 55), are within four months of normal pension age or meet the ill-health condition.	Standard methods.	Within two months of the relevant member requesting information about what they may do with their flexible benefits or informing the trustees that they are considering or have decided what to do with their flexible benefits. Not required within 12 months of either this information or the information in the above section on accessing benefits being provided to the member.

To be disclosed	Disclosure to	Form of disclosure	When
Either a copy of the Money Advice Service leaflet 'Your pension: it's time to choose,' or a statement that gives materially the same information.			
A statement that pensions guidance is available to help the person to understand their options in relation to what they can do with their flexible benefits.			
A statement that pensions guidance may be accessed on the internet, by phone, or face-to-face.			
The phone number (030 0330 1001) and website address (www.pensionwise.gov.uk) at which pensions guidance may be accessed and details of how the person may access the pensions guidance face-to-face.			
A statement that pensions guidance is free and impartial.			
A statement that the person should access pensions guidance and consider taking independent advice to help them decide which option is most suitable for them.			

To be disclosed	Disclosure to	Form of disclosure	When
An estimate of the cash equivalent of any of the member's rights to flexible benefits that are transferrable rights or would be transferrable rights if the member stopped accruing rights to some or all of the flexible benefits.			
An estimate of the value of any accrued rights to flexible benefits that the member may transfer out of the scheme under the scheme rules, in respect of which the cash equivalent is not required to be given.			
The date by reference to which the cash equivalent or value (as appropriate) is calculated.			
An explanation that the cash equivalent or value (as appropriate) is an estimate and may not represent the exact amount available to the member to transfer to another pension provider.			
In relation to the member's accrued rights to flexible benefits in respect of which there is an opportunity to transfer: • details of any guarantee to which the benefits are subject; and			

886

To be disclosed	Disclosure to	Form of disclosure	When
• details of any other features, restrictions and conditions that apply to the benefits that affect, or may affect, their value. Where the member has a right or entitlement to benefits under the scheme that are not flexible benefits, that the member has that right or entitlement and how the member may access information about those benefits. A statement that: • there may be tax implications associated with accessing the flexible benefits; • income from a pension is taxable; and • the rate at which income from a pension is taxable depends on the amount of income that the person receives from a pension and from other sources.			

887

To be disclosed	Disclosure to	Form of disclosure	When
Where the member has accrued rights to flexible benefits that are not money-purchase benefits, has not reached normal pension age and does not satisfy the ill-health condition: • a statement that the value of the member's accrued rights to flexible benefits is likely to be lower if the member accesses the benefits before normal pension age; and • the age at which the member will reach normal pension age.			
A statement that pensions guidance is available to help the person to understand their options in relation to what can be done with their flexible benefits. A statement that pensions guidance is free and impartial. A statement that the person should access pensions guidance and consider taking independent advice to help them decide which option is most suitable for them.	Members with an opportunity to transfer flexible benefits and who have reached normal minimum pension age (generally 55), are within four months of normal pension age or meet the ill-health condition.	May be given verbally unless requested in writing by the member.	Within 20 days of the latter of: • the trustees contacting the relevant member or the relevant member contacting the trustees in connection with what the member may want to do with his flexible benefits; and • a request from the member that the information is given in writing.

To be disclosed	Disclosure to	Form of disclosure	When
Unless the above is given verbally and the trustees offer to give the member information about how he may access pensions guidance and that offer is declined, the following must also be provided: • A statement that pensions guidance may be accessed on the internet, by phone, or face-to-face. • The phone number (0330 0330 1001) and website address (www.pensionwise.gov.uk) at which pensions guidance may be accessed and details of how the person may access pensions guidance face-to-face. Where the member has not received information on request within 12 months before the date on which the above information is given then the following must also be provided:			Not required where the member has accessed Pension Wise or has received independent advice within the last 12 months or the information under *reg 18A* (immediately above) has been given in the previous two months or is required to be given in the following two months.

To be disclosed	Disclosure to	Form of disclosure	When
• A statement that the member may request information about the flexible benefits that may be provided to the member, the member's opportunity to transfer those benefits and the options available to the member under the scheme rules; and that the information may help the member to decide what to do with the flexible benefits.			
A retirement risk warning. • Must include the 'characteristic attributes and features' (ie those that have the potential to adversely affect retirement income) of an annuity, lump sum and drawdown pension but may be limited to the options that the member is being given a method of access to.	Members with an opportunity to transfer flexible benefits and who have reached normal minimum pension age (generally 55), are within four months of normal pension age or meet the ill-health condition.	In writing.	Where any of the above information on accessing benefits is being or has been sent along with an application form, online access, information or any other method that enables the member to require that flexible benefits are accessed. At the same time as providing the method of access to flexible benefits and before assets are applied by the trustees to purchase an annuity, pay a lump sum or designate assets for drawdown.

To be disclosed	Disclosure to	Form of disclosure	When
• Must include factors that have the potential to affect the appropriateness of an annuity, lump sum and drawdown pension for a member eg the impact of health status and lifestyle choices, whether a member has dependants, whether a member is in debt or in receipt of means tested benefits. • Must be generic in nature and not tailored to or based on the personal circumstances of any individual member. A statement asking the member to note the importance of reading the retirement risk warning and accessing pensions guidance or independent advice.			Not required where the same information has been given in relation to the same type of benefit within the previous 12 months. Not required if a timely appropriate risk warning (below) is provided instead.
An appropriate risk warning. • Must set out the risks associated with flexible benefit options that the member proposes to take that have the potential to adversely affect the retirement income of the member or their dependants.	Members with a right or entitlement to flexible benefits. Members with a right or opportunity to transfer flexible benefits and who have reached normal minimum pension age (generally 55), are within four months of normal pension age or meet the ill-health condition.	Either verbally or in writing.	Where a retirement risk warning would otherwise be required, but trustees have already asked the member whether they have received pensions guidance or independent advice and have encouraged a member to do so if they have not.

891

To be disclosed	Disclosure to	Form of disclosure	When
• Must be based on the characteristic attributes and features of an annuity, lump sum or drawdown pension as well as answers to questions the trustees have asked the member to identify the factors that increase the risks.			Before assets are applied by the trustees to purchase an annuity, pay a lump sum or designate assets for drawdown.
The amount of benefit that is payable. If the benefit is paid periodically: • any conditions for continuing to make the payments; • any provisions which would allow the payments to be altered. Any rights and options that persons have on the death of the member or beneficiary and the procedures for exercising them.	All persons where benefits have, or are about to, become payable.	Standard methods.	Where the benefit comes into payment on or after normal pension age, before it comes into payment if practicable and in any even within one month after it comes into payment. Where the benefit becomes payable before normal pension age, within two months of it becoming payable.
A statement that the person has an opportunity to select an annuity. A statement that the person has an opportunity to select the provider of the annuity.	All persons where benefits have, or are about to, become payable and the person has the opportunity to select an annuity under any rights and options in relation to the death of the member.	Standard methods.	Before the benefit becomes payable.

To be disclosed	Disclosure to	Form of disclosure	When
A statement that different annuities have different features and different rates of payment such as the same payments every year, increasing payments every year, payments only for the person, payments for the person's spouse or civil partner or a guarantee on the early death of the person.			
An explanation of the characteristic features of the annuities or a copy of guidance giving that explanation that has been prepared or approved by the Regulator.			
A statement that the person should consider taking advice about which annuity is most suitable for them.			
A statement that pensions guidance is available to help the person to understand their options in relation to what they can do with their flexible benefits. A statement that the pensions guidance may be accessed on the internet, by phone, or face-to-face.	All persons where benefits have, or are about to, become payable and the person, under any rights and options in relation to the death of the member, and the person has an opportunity to: • transfer accrued rights to flexible benefits out of the scheme rules;	Standard methods.	Before the benefit becomes payable.

To be disclosed	Disclosure to	Form of disclosure	When
The phone number (030 0330 1001) and website address (www. pensionwise.gov.uk) at which pensions guidance may be accessed and details of how the person may access pensions guidance face-to-face. A statement that pensions guidance is free and impartial. A statement that the person should access pensions guidance and consider taking independent advice to help them decide which option is most suitable for them.	• apply sums or assets held for the purpose of providing flexible benefits for purchasing an annuity; • take payment of a lump sum in respect of flexible benefits; or • designate sums or assets held for the purpose of providing flexible benefits as available for the payment of drawdown pension.		
Where the person has an opportunity to select an annuity: • any rights and options that persons have on the death of the member or beneficiary and the procedures for exercising them; • the provisions under which the pension payable to a survivor may or will be increased and the extent to which such increases are dependent on the exercise of a discretion.	A person who may be entitled to exercise rights or options on the death of a member or beneficiary, where that person is at least 18 years old and the trustees know their postal or electronic address. The personal representative of the member or beneficiary (on request).	Standard methods.	As soon as possible and within two months of the trustees becoming aware of the death or of a request from a PR.

To be disclosed	Disclosure to	Form of disclosure	When
A statement that pensions guidance is available to help the person to understand their options in relation to what they can do with their flexible benefits.	A person who may be entitled to exercise rights or options on the death of a member or beneficiary, where that person is at least 18 years old and the trustees know their postal or electronic address. The personal representative of the member or beneficiary (on request).	Standard methods.	As soon as possible and within two months of the trustees becoming aware of the death or of a request from a PR.
A statement that the pensions guidance may be accessed on the internet, by phone, or face-to-face.	Where the person has an opportunity to:		
The phone number (030 0330 1001) and website address (www.pensionwise.gov.uk) at which pensions guidance may be accessed and details of how the person may access pensions guidance face-to-face.	• transfer accrued rights to flexible benefits out of the scheme rules;		
A statement that pensions guidance is free and impartial.	• apply sums or assets held for the purpose of providing flexible benefits for purchasing an annuity;		
A statement that the person should access pensions guidance and consider taking independent advice to help them decide which option is most suitable for them.	• take payment of a lump sum in respect of flexible benefits; or		
	• designate sums or assets held for the purpose of providing flexible benefits as available for the payment of drawdown pension.		

895

To be disclosed	Disclosure to	Form of disclosure	When
CHANGES TO BENEFITS IN PAYMENT (*Disclosure Regulations, reg 22, Sch 7*)			
The amount of the benefit that is payable. Any rights and options that persons have on the death of the member or beneficiary and the procedures for exercising them.	A person in receipt of a benefit, the amount of which is to be altered, other than where the provisions allowing alteration have previously been disclosed.	Standard methods.	Where possible, before the date on which the decision to alter the benefit takes effect and in any event within one month of that date.
ANNUAL REPORT (*Disclosure Regulations, reg 12, Sch 3*)			
A document which contains (where applicable): • the audited accounts and the auditor's statement required under *PA 1995, s 41*; • the latest actuarial certificate obtained in accordance with *PA 2004, s 227*; • the names of the trustees, in the case of a scheme none of the trustees of which is an individual, the names of the directors of any company that is a trustee, during the relevant scheme year; • the provisions of the scheme (or articles of association in the case of a sole trustee company) in relation to appointing and removing trustees or directors;	Relevant person.	Standard methods for information relating to the most recent scheme year. Where the information is not in relation to the most recent scheme year then where it is requested in hard copy form, the trustees must send it in that form (and can charge for the costs of copying, postage and packing). Alternatively they can give details of where a hard copy is publically available. Were a request is made for it other than in hard copy form, the trustees can give details as to where it can reasonably be inspected or of a website.	On request within five years of the end of the scheme year to which the report relates and has not been given the document before. Must be given within two months of the request being made. The report must be prepared within seven months of the end of the relevant scheme year.

To be disclosed	Disclosure to	Form of disclosure	When
• the names of the professional advisers and others who have acted for the trustees during the year, with an indication of any change since the previous year; • the postal and electronic address to which enquiries about the scheme generally or about an individual's entitlement to benefit should be sent; • the number of active, deferred and pensioner members and beneficiaries as at any one date during the scheme year; • (except for a money purchase scheme), the percentage increases made during the year to pensions in payment and deferred pensions and a statement of the extent to which they are discretionary;			

To be disclosed	Disclosure to	Form of disclosure	When
• (except for an insured money purchase scheme) a statement, where applicable, explaining why any cash equivalents paid during the year were not calculated and verified in accordance with legislative requirements; why cash equivalents paid during the year were less than the amount for which legislation provides and when full values were or will be available; and whether, and if so how, discretionary benefits are included in the calculation of transfer values;			
• a statement as to whether the accounts have been prepared and audited in accordance with *PA 1995, s 41*, and if not, the reasons why not, and a statement as to how the situation has been or is likely to be resolved;			
• details of who has managed the investments during the year and the extent of any delegation by the trustees;			

898

To be disclosed	Disclosure to	Form of disclosure	When
• confirmation as to whether the trustees have produced a statement of investment principles in accordance with *PA 1995, s 35*, and that a copy is available on request; • a statement as to the trustees' policy on the custody of the scheme's assets (except in relation to a wholly insured scheme); • an investment report containing a statement by the trustees, or fund manager, with details of any investments which were not made in accordance with the SIP, giving the reasons and explaining what action, if any, has been or will be taken to resolve the position; a review of the investment performance during the year and a period of between three and five years previously, including an assessment of the nature, disposition, marketability, security and valuation of the scheme's assets; the trustees' policy (if any) in relation to the rights attaching to investments; and the extent (if at all) to which social, environmental or ethical considerations are taken into account in the selection, retention and realisation of investments;			

To be disclosed	Disclosure to	Form of disclosure	When
• a copy of any statement made on the resignation or removal of the auditor or actuary; • where the scheme has employer-related investments a statement as to the percentage of the scheme's resources invested in such investments at the end of the year; if that percentage exceeds 5%, as to the percentage of the scheme's resources which are not subject to the statutory restriction on employer-related investments is exceeded, the steps taken (or to be taken) to secure compliance, and when those steps will be taken; and • where the scheme is a relevant scheme within the meaning of the *Scheme Administration Regulations 1996*, the annual statement regarding governance which the trustees are required to prepare under *reg 23* of those regulations.			

To be disclosed	Disclosure to	Form of disclosure	When
SUMMARY FUNDING STATEMENT (*Disclosure Regulations, regs 15, Sch 7*)			
A summary explaining the extent to which the assets of the scheme are adequate to cover its technical provisions and is based on the last actuarial valuation and any subsequent report received under *PA 2004, s 244*. An explanation of changes in the funding position since the last actuarial valuation. The actuary's estimate of solvency contained in the last actuarial valuation. A summary of any recovery plan prepared under *PA 2004*. A statement explaining whether the scheme has been modified under *PA 2004, s 231(2)(a)*, whether the scheme is subject to directions by the Regulator under *PA 2004, s 231(2)(a)*, and whether the scheme is bound by a schedule of contributions imposed by the Regulator under *PA 2004, s 231(2)(a)*.	Members and beneficiaries of a scheme which where the trustees have obtained an actuarial valuation or report under *PA 2004, s 244*, other than excluded persons or those whose only entitlement is to money purchase benefits.	Standard methods.	On, before, or within a reasonable period after the date by which the trustees are required by *PA 2004, s 244* to ensure an actuarial valuation or report is received by them.

To be disclosed	Disclosure to	Form of disclosure	When
Where there has been a modification, directions or a schedule of contributions referred to above, a summary of the circumstances in which they were made. A statement explaining whether any payment to the employer under *PA 1995, s 37* has been made, in the case of the first summary funding statement issued in respect of the scheme, in the 12 months before the date on which that statement is prepared, and in the case of any subsequent summary funding statement issued in respect of the scheme, since the date of the last such statement. Where a payment referred to above has been made, the amount of that payment.			
MODIFICATION BY THE REGULATOR (*Disclosure Regulations, reg 9*)			
Any modification to the scheme by the Regulator under *PA 2004, s 231(2)(a)*.	Active members.	Standard methods.	Within one month of the modification taking effect.

To be disclosed	Disclosure to	Form of disclosure	When
DURING WINDING UP (*Disclosure Regulations, reg 24, Sch 8*)			
A statement that the scheme is being wound up.	Members and beneficiaries except excluded persons.	Standard methods.	As soon as practicable and no more than one month from the date winding up commenced.
The reasons why the scheme is being wound up.			
If the independent trustee requirements apply, notification that at least one of the trustees is required to be an independent person.			Within two months of a request from a member or beneficiary.
In the case of active members, whether death in service benefits will continue to be payable.			
A summary of the action that is being taken, and that has been taken, to establish the scheme's liabilities, and recover any assets.			
An estimate of when the scheme's liabilities are likely to be established and any assets are likely to be recovered.			
Either an indication of the extent to which (if at all) the actuarial value of accrued rights or benefits are likely to be reduced; or a statement that there is insufficient information to provide such an indication.			

To be disclosed	Disclosure to	Form of disclosure	When
Where a report has been made to the Regulator, under *PA 1995, s 72A*, a copy of that report.			
A summary of the action that is being taken, and that has been taken, to establish the scheme's liabilities, and recover any assets. An estimate of when the scheme's liabilities are likely to be established and any assets are likely to be recovered. Either an indication of the extent to which (if at all) the actuarial value of accrued rights or benefits are likely to be reduced; or a statement that there is insufficient information to provide such an indication. Where a report has been made to the Regulator, under *PA 1995, s 72A*, a copy of that report.	Members and beneficiaries except excluded persons.	Standard methods.	Within every 12 months from the date information was given above until the completion of winding up, or, where the scheme began to wind up before 6 April 2014, by 5 April 2015 and then within every 12 months thereafter until the completion of winding up. Within two months of a request from a member or beneficiary.

904

To be disclosed	Disclosure to	Form of disclosure	When
AFTER WINDING UP (*Disclosure Regulations, reg 25, Sch 7, Sch 8*)			
Whether the benefits are reduced because the scheme's resources are not sufficient to meet its liabilities. The amount of any reduction of the benefits. Who has or will become liable for the payment of the benefits.	Member or beneficiary with rights to benefits other than money purchase benefits, other than excluded persons.	Standard methods.	As soon as practicable and in any event no more than three months after the date that the trustees have done what they can to discharge the relevant liabilities.
Who has or will become liable for the payment of the benefits.	Member or beneficiary with rights to money purchase benefits, other than excluded persons.	Standard methods.	As soon as practicable and in any event no more than three months after the date that the trustees have done what they can to discharge the relevant liabilities.
The amount of benefit that is payable. If the benefit is paid periodically: • any conditions for continuing to make the payments; • any provisions which would allow the payments to be altered.	Member or beneficiary entitled to the payment of benefits, other than excluded persons.	Standard methods.	As soon as practicable and in any event no more than three months after the date that the trustees have done what they can to discharge the relevant liabilities.

To be disclosed	Disclosure to	Form of disclosure	When
An estimate of the amount of the benefits that are expected to be payable from normal pension age or death.	Member or beneficiary not entitled to the payment of benefits (other than money purchase benefits), other than excluded persons.	Standard methods.	As soon as practicable and in any event no more than three months after the date that the trustees have done what they can to discharge the relevant liabilities.
FORMER STAKEHOLDER SCHEMES *(Disclosure Regulations, reg 10)*			
A statement that the scheme: • has been removed from the stakeholder register; • is no longer a stakeholder scheme; and • is required to begin winding up.	Members other than excluded persons.	Standard methods.	Within two weeks of the trustees being notified that the scheme has been removed from the stakeholder register.
OTHER INFORMATION ABOUT THE SCHEME *(Disclosure Regulations, reg 13, Sch 3)*			
Statement of funding principles where required under *PA 2004, s 223*. Where *PA 2004, Part 3* applies to the scheme, the latest actuarial valuation under *PA 2004, s 224* received by the trustees and an actuarial report received by them under that section if more recent. Any recovery plan prepared under *PA 2004, s 226* which is currently in force.	Relevant person.	Where it is requested in hard copy form, the trustees must send it in that form (and can charge for the costs of copying, postage and packing). Alternatively they can give details of where a hard copy is publically available. Were a request is made for it other than in hard copy form, the trustees can give details as to where it can reasonably be inspected or of a website *(reg 29)*.	On request, within two months of the date the request is made.

906

To be disclosed	Disclosure to	Form of disclosure	When
Payment schedule where required under *PA 1995, s 87* or schedule of contributions where required under *PA 2004, s 227.*			
Latest statement of principles governing decisions about investments where required under *PA 1995, s 35.*			
A summary of the winding up procedure prepared or revised under *PA 2004, s 231A.*			
INFORMATION TO BE FURNISHED TO EARLY LEAVERS (*Occupational Pension Schemes* (*Preservation of Benefit*) *Regulations 1991* (*SI 1991/167*), *reg 27A*) (*all schemes*))			
Information relating to the rights and options available to a member whose pensionable service terminates before he attains normal pension age.	Member or prospective member.	In writing.	As soon as practicable and, in any event, within two months of the request being made (unless within 12 months of information being given following a similar request).
Information relating to the rights and options available to a member whose pensionable service terminates before he attains normal pension age.	Deferred member.	In writing.	As of course, as soon as practicable and, in any event, within two months of notification of termination of pensionable service.

To be disclosed	Disclosure to	Form of disclosure	When
Information whether a refund of contributions is, or would be, available in any circumstances together with an estimate of the amount of the refund and an explanation of the method of calculation.	Any person who has paid contributions to the scheme (which have not already been refunded).	In writing.	As soon as practicable and, in any event, within two months after request (unless he has already been told that there will be no refund or the request is within 12 months of information being given following a similar request).

TRANSFER OF MEMBER'S ACCRUED RIGHTS WITHOUT CONSENT (*Occupational Pension Schemes (Preservation of Benefit) Regulations 1991 (SI 1991/167), reg 12(4B)*)

To be disclosed	Disclosure to	Form of disclosure	When
Information about the proposed transfer and details of the value of the rights to be transferred including rights in respect of death in service benefits and survivors' benefits.	Those members being transferred.	In writing.	Not less than one month before the proposed transfer is due to take place.

CASH EQUIVALENTS AND TRANSFER VALUES (*Pension Schemes Act 2015 (Transitional Provisions and Appropriate Independent Advice) Regulations 2015 (SI 2015/742), regs 6, 8 and Occupational Pension Schemes (Transfer Values) Regulations 1996 (SI 1996/1847), regs 6, 11, Sch 1) (all schemes)*)

To be disclosed	Disclosure to	Form of disclosure	When
An explanation that the trustees are required to check that appropriate independent advice has been received by the member before the trustees are able to carry out the transfer, unless the total value of the member's safeguarded benefits is £30,000.	Member with safeguarded benefits who: • requests information on how to carry out a transfer; • requests information on how to apply for a statement of entitlement;	In writing.	Within one month of receiving the request or application.

To be disclosed	Disclosure to	Form of disclosure	When
A statement that: • confirmation that appropriate independent advice has been received by the member should be provided to the trustees before the end of a three-month period beginning with: (a) the day on which a statement of entitlement is provided; or (b) where no statement of entitlement, the day on which the trustees provide written confirmation that they agree in principle to carry out the transfer or, if later, the day on which the trustees provide the member with a valuation of his safeguarded benefits; and • unless the member confirms otherwise, the trustees will assume that the purpose of the transfer is to provide flexible benefits under another pension scheme.	• makes an application for a statement of entitlement; • otherwise requests a valuation of their safeguarded benefits.		

909

To be disclosed	Disclosure to	Form of disclosure	When
The information above is not required where trustees can satisfy themselves, within one month of the member's request or application, that the total value of the safeguarded benefits is £30,000 or less. In this case, the trustees are required to inform the member that there will be no requirement for the trustees to check that appropriate independent advice has been received before they are able to pay a transfer.			
A statement of entitlement setting out a separate cash equivalent in relation to each of the categories of benefits, unless the member's application relates to one of the categories of benefits only.	Members of any scheme who have transferrable rights in relation to the following categories of benefits: • flexible benefits other than money purchase benefits; and • benefits that are not flexible benefits.	In writing.	Within 10 days of the 'guarantee date', which must be within three months of the date of receiving the application for a statement of entitlement.

910

To be disclosed	Disclosure to	Form of disclosure	When
The *Sch 1* information, which is: Whether a cash equivalent is available or would be available if the conditions specified in *section 93(2) to (4) of the PSA 1993* were met and, if so: • an estimate of the amount calculated in accordance with *reg 7 or 7E* on the basis that the above conditions are met or were to be met on a particular date; • the accrued rights to which it relates; • whether any part of the estimated part of the cash equivalent is attributable to additional benefits (wholly or only to part) awarded at the discretion of the trustees or which will be awarded if their established custom continues unaltered; • if the estimated amount of the cash equivalent included a reduction of the initial cash equivalent under *Sch 1A*: – a statement of that fact;	Members of any scheme who are: • currently accruing rights to money purchase benefits, flexible benefits other than money purchase benefits or benefits that are not flexible benefits; and/or • who are no longer accruing rights to money purchase benefits unless, in respect of those benefits, a crystallisation event has occurred.	In writing.	As soon as reasonably practicable and, in any event, within three months of the member's request (such request not being one made less than 12 months since the last occasion when the information was provided).

911

To be disclosed	Disclosure to	Form of disclosure	When
– a statement of the amount of the reduction; – an explanation of the reason for the reduction which must refer to the paragraph of *Sch 1A* relied upon; – an estimate of the date (if any) by which an unreduced cash equivalent will be available; – a statement of the member's right to obtain further estimates. Whether any transfer value is available or would be so available if the member's pensionable service were to terminate and if so: • an estimate of its amount calculated on the basis that the member's pensionable service terminated or will terminate on a particular date; • the accrued rights to which it relates;			

912

To be disclosed	Disclosure to	Form of disclosure	When
• whether any part of the estimated amount of the transfer value is attributable to additional benefits (wholly or only to part) which have been or will be awarded at the discretion of the trustees; and • if the estimated amount of the transfer value in relation to the member's rights to benefits other than money purchase benefits has been reduced to an amount which is less than it otherwise would be because of an actuary's opinion that the scheme's assets are insufficient to meet its liabilities in full, then a statement of that fact and an explanation; an estimate of the date (if any) by which it will be possible to make available a transfer value the amount of which is not so reduced; and a statement of the member's rights to obtain further estimates. Where information is made available under *Sch 1* to a member of a salary related scheme, the information also includes:			

To be disclosed	Disclosure to	Form of disclosure	When
• a statement that the Financial Conduct Authority, the Regulator and TPAS provide information about transfers that may assist the member in deciding whether to transfer; • if the scheme is an eligible scheme as defined in *PA 2004, s 126*, confirmation that the Scheme is so eligible and that the PPF exists; • except where *section 48, Pension Schemes Act 2015* applies, a recommendation that the member should take financial advice before making decisions about transfers. The statement of entitlement shall be accompanied by: • *'Sch 1* information' in relation to any cash equivalent of or transfer value in relation to the member's money purchase benefits (if any) under the scheme calculated by reference to the guarantee date;			

To be disclosed	Disclosure to	Form of disclosure	When
• A statement as to:			
– whether, for what reasons and by what amount the member's initial cash equivalent in relation to money purchase benefits, flexible benefits other than money purchase benefits or benefits that are not flexible benefits has been reduced as well as the paragraph of *Sch 1A* which has been relied upon, together with an estimate of the date by which it will be possible to make available a cash equivalent shown in the statement of entitlement which is not so reduced;			
– an indication of the amount of the cash equivalent which is attributable to each of the categories of benefits included in the statement of entitlement;			
– the terms and effect of *reg 6(3)* (no right to make an application for a guaranteed statement of entitlement within 12 months of the last application);			

To be disclosed	Disclosure to	Form of disclosure	When
– an explanation of the member's right to take the cash equivalent shown in the statement of entitlement and the need for that member to submit a written application to do so within three months beginning on the guarantee date; – an explanation that in exceptional circumstances the cash equivalent shown in the statement of entitlement may be reduced and that member will be so informed if that is the case; and – where the scheme has begun to wind up, an explanation that the value of the member's cash equivalent shown in the statement of entitlement may be affected by the winding up and that a decision to take a cash equivalent shown in the statement of entitlement should be given careful consideration.			

To be disclosed	Disclosure to	Form of disclosure	When
Where a cash equivalent shown in the statement of entitlement is increased or reduced under *reg 9*, notification of that reduction or increase including: • the reasons for and the amount of the reduction/increase; • indication of the paragraph of *reg 9* which has been relied upon; • a statement explaining that the member has a further three months from the date on which the member was informed of the reduction/increase to make a written application to take the cash equivalent shown in the statement of entitlement as reduced/increased.	Relevant member.	In writing.	Within ten days of reduction/increase (excluding weekends, Christmas Day, New Year's Day and Good Friday).

WINDING-UP (*Occupational Pension Schemes (Winding Up) Regulations 1996 (SI 1996/3126), reg 11*)

To be disclosed	Disclosure to	Form of disclosure	When
Details of any determination made: • to defer winding-up the scheme; • as to the time when the priorities into which the liability in respect of any person falls under *PA 1995, s 73(4)* is fixed; or	Members and any other person whose entitlement to payment of a pension or any other benefit under the scheme has arisen.	In writing.	Within one month of the date that the determination is made.

917

To be disclosed	Disclosure to	Form of disclosure	When
• as to the time when the amounts or descriptions of liabilities of the scheme are to be determined for the purposes of any rule of the scheme setting out the scheme's winding-up priorities.			
MODIFICATION ON WINDING-UP (*PA 1995, s 71A; Occupational Pension Schemes (Winding Up Notices and Reports etc.) Regulations 2002 (SI 2002/459), reg 8*)			
Where the trustees or managers make an application to the Pensions Regulator to modify the scheme in accordance with *PA 1995, 71A*, a notice setting out: For all recipients: • the modification requested; • the effects, if any, which the modification would or might have: – on benefits under the scheme that are in payment at the time of the application, and – on benefits under it which are or may be payable at a later time; • the reason for requesting the modification;	Members for whom they have a current address. The insolvency practitioner or official receiver (as the case may be), if the modification would reduce the value of the assets which might otherwise be distributed to the employer on the winding-up.	In writing.	Before the trustees or manager make the application to the Pensions Regulator.

918

To be disclosed	Disclosure to	Form of disclosure	When
• whether the modification would reduce the value of the assets which might otherwise be distributed to that employer on winding up; • the date of the notice; and • an explanation that a member may make representations to the Regulator about the modification within one month from the date of the notice. In addition, for the insolvency practitioner or official receiver: • whether any previous application has been made to the court or to the Pensions Regulator for an order to make the modification requested by the application or any similar modification.			

BASIC INFORMATION ABOUT PENSIONS AND DIVORCE (*Pensions on Divorce etc. (Provision of Information) Regulations 2000 (SI 2000/1048), reg 2*)

To be disclosed	Disclosure to	Form of disclosure	When
A valuation of pension rights or benefits accrued under the member's pension arrangement.	Member.	In writing.	Where the member requests information that does not include a valuation of pension rights or benefits accrued, within one month of receiving the request.
A statement summarising the way in which the valuation is calculated.			Where the member requests information that does include a valuation of pension rights or benefits accrued:
The pension benefits which are included in the valuation.			• within three months of receiving the request;
Whether the trustees offer membership to a person entitled to a pension credit and, if so, the types of benefit available.			• within six weeks of receiving the request where the member has notified the trustees on the date of the request that the information is needed in connection with proceedings commenced under provisions referred to in *WRPA 1999, s 23(1) (a)*; or
Whether the trustees intend to discharge their liability for a pension credit other than by offering membership.			
A schedule of charges which will apply.			• within such shorter period as the court may specify.

To be disclosed	Disclosure to	Form of disclosure	When
A statement that on the member's request or pursuant to a court order a valuation of pension rights or benefits will be provided to the member or the court.	Member's spouse or civil partner.	In writing.	Within one month of receiving the request.
A statement summarising the way in which the valuation is calculated.			
The pension benefits which are included in the valuation.			
Whether the trustees offer membership to a person entitled to a pension credit and, if so, the types of benefit available.			
Whether the trustees intend to discharge their liability for a pension credit other than by offering membership.			
A schedule of charges which will apply.			
A valuation of pension rights or benefits accrued under the member's pension arrangement.	Court.	In writing. May be provided by electronic communication only where the court has given its permission (*reg 11*).	Where the court order for the provision of information does not include a request for a valuation of pension rights or benefits accrued, within one month of receiving the request.
A statement that on the member's request or pursuant to a court order a valuation of pension rights or benefits will be provided to the member or the court.			

921

To be disclosed	Disclosure to	Form of disclosure	When
A statement summarising the way in which the valuation is calculated. The pension benefits which are included in the valuation. Whether the trustees offer membership to a person entitled to a pension credit and, if so, the types of benefit available. Whether the trustees intend to discharge their liability for a pension credit other than by offering membership. A schedule of charges which will apply. Any other information relevant to any power relating to matters specified in *WRPA 1999, s 23(1)(a)* and *Schedules 2 to 7* of the *Disclosure Regulations*.			Where the court order for the provision of information includes a request for a valuation of pension rights or benefits accrued: ● Within three months of receiving the request; ● Within six weeks of receiving the request where the member has notified the trustees on the date of the request that the information is needed in connection with proceedings commenced under provisions referred to in *WRPA 1999, s 23(1) (a)*; or ● Within such shorter period as the court may specify.
At the same time as providing the information set out above, the trustees may supply information specified in *Pensions on Divorce etc: (Provision of Information) Regulations 2000, reg 4(2)*.	Court. Member's spouse or civil partner. Member.	In writing. May be provided by electronic communication to the court only where the court has given its permission (*reg 11*).	

922

To be disclosed	Disclosure to	Form of disclosure	When
DIVORCE *(Pensions on Divorce etc. (Provision of Information) Regulations 2000 (SI 2000/1048), reg 4)*			
The full name of the pension arrangement and address to which any order or provision should be sent.	To the member or the court.	In writing. May be provided by electronic communication to the court only where the court has given its permission *(reg 11)*.	Within 21 days of the date when the trustees received notification that a Pension Sharing Order or provision may be made or, if the court has specified a date which is more than 21 days, by that date.
Whether the scheme is winding-up and, if so, the date of commencement of the winding-up, the name and address of the trustees who are dealing with the winding-up and whether the member's rights to benefit are to be or are likely to be reduced in accordance with winding up provisions.			
Whether a cash equivalent of the member's rights would be reduced if calculated on the date the trustees received notification that a pension sharing order or provision may be made, if the member were to transfer the cash equivalent of those rights out of the scheme.			
Whether the person responsible for the pension arrangement is aware of the member's rights being subject to any of the following and, if so, to specify which: • any order or provision specified in *WRPA 1999, s 28(1)*;			

923

To be disclosed	Disclosure to	Form of disclosure	When
• an order under *Matrimonial Causes Act 1973, s 23* (so far as it includes provision made by virtue of *s 25B* or *25C*);			
• an order under *Family Law (Scotland) Act 1985, s 12A(2)* or *(3)* which relates to benefits or future benefits to which the member is entitled under the pension arrangement;			
• an order under *Matrimonial Causes (Northern Ireland) Order 1978, art 25* so far as it includes provision made by virtue of *art 27B* or *27C* of that order;			
• a forfeiture order;			
• a bankruptcy order;			
• an order of sequestration on a member's estate or the making of an appointment on his estate of a judicial factor under *Solicitors (Scotland) Act 1980, s 41*.			
Whether the member's rights under the pension arrangement include any rights which are not shareable.			

To be disclosed	Disclosure to	Form of disclosure	When
If not provided previously, whether the trustees require any charges to be paid and, if so, whether prior to the commencement of the implementation period those are required to be paid in full, or the proportion which is required.			
Whether the trustees may levy additional charges and, if so, the scale which is likely to be charged.			
Whether the member is a trustee of the pension arrangement.			
Whether the trustees may request information about the member's state of health if a pension sharing order or provision were made.			
Whether the trustees require information in addition to that specified in *Pensions on Divorce etc. (Provision of Information) Regulations 2000, reg 5* in order to implement the pension sharing order or provision.			

925

To be disclosed	Disclosure to	Form of disclosure	When
PROVISION OF INFORMATION AFTER THE DEATH OF THE PERSON ENTITLED TO THE PENSION CREDIT *(Pensions on Divorce etc (Provision of Information) Regulations 2000 (SI 2000/1048), reg 6)*			
Where the person entitled to the pension credit dies before the trustees have discharged their liability, the trustees must notify relevant persons: • how the trustees intend to discharge their liability; • whether the trustees intend to recover charges and, if so, a schedule of those charges; • a list of any further information required in order to discharge their liability.	Any person whom the trustees consider should be notified.	In writing. May be provided by electronic communication to the court only where the court has given its permission *(reg 11)*.	Within 21 days of receipt of the notification of death.

To be disclosed	Disclosure to	Form of disclosure	When
PROVISION OF INFORMATION AFTER RECEIVING A PENSION SHARING ORDER (*Pensions on Divorce etc. (Provision of Information) Regulations 2000 (SI 2000/1048), reg 7*)			
On receipt of a pension sharing order or a provision: • a notice of charges; • a list of information relating to the transferor or the transferee or where *Pensions on Divorce etc. (Provision of Information) Regulations 2000, reg 6(1)* applies a person other than the person entitled to the pension credit, which has been requested already, which the trustees need or which remains outstanding; • a notice of implementation; or • a statement of why the trustees are unable to implement the pension sharing order or agreement.	The transferor or transferee, or where *Pensions on Divorce etc. (Provision of Information Regulations 2000 reg 6(1)* applies, the person other than the person entitled to the pension credit (referred to in *Pension Sharing (Implementation and Discharge of Liability) Regulations 2000 (SI 2000/1053), reg 6*).	In writing.	Within 21 days of receipt of the pension sharing order or provision or, in the case of a notice of implementation, the later of the days specified in *WRPA 1999, s 34(1)(a)* and *(b)*.

To be disclosed	Disclosure to	Form of disclosure	When
PROVISION OF INFORMATION AFTER IMPLEMENTATION OF AN ORDER (*Pensions on Divorce etc. (Provision of Information) Regulations 2000 (SI 2000/1048), reg 8*)			
Notice of discharge of liability including: (where the transferor's pension is not in payment) • the value of the transferor's accrued rights on a cash equivalent basis; • the value of the pension debit; • any amount deducted by way of charges; • the value of the transferor's rights after the deductions of the pension debit and charges; • the transfer day; OR (where the transferor's pension is in payment) • the value of the transferor's benefits on a cash equivalent basis; • the value of the pension debit; • the amount of the pension which was in payment before the pension credit liability was discharged;	Transferor or transferee or the person entitled to the pension credit by virtue of *Pension Sharing (Implementation and Discharge of Liability) Regulations 2000 (SI 2000/1053), reg 6.*	In writing.	Within 21 days of the date of discharge of the pension credit liability.

To be disclosed	Disclosure to	Form of disclosure	When
• the amount of pension payable following the deduction of the pension debit; • the transfer day; • the amount of any unpaid charges; • how those charges will be recovered; OR (in the case of a transferee whose pension is not in payment and who will become a member) • the value of the pension credit; • the amount deducted by way of charges; • the value of the pension credit after deduction of charges; • the transfer day; • any periodical charges to be made including when and how those charges will be recovered; • information concerning membership of the pension arrangement which is relevant to the transferee; OR			

To be disclosed	Disclosure to	Form of disclosure	When
(in the case of the transferee who is transferring his pension credit rights out of the pension arrangement from which those rights were derived)			
• the value of the pension credit;			
• the amount of any charges deducted;			
• the value of the pension credit after the deduction;			
• the transfer day;			
• details of the pension arrangement including its name, address, reference number, telephone number and where available the business facsimile number and e-mail address to which the pension credit has been transferred: OR			
(in the case of a transferee who has reached normal benefit age on the transfer day and whose pension credit liability has been discharged)			
• the amount of pension credit benefit to be paid to the transferee;			
• the date when the pension credit benefit is to be paid to the transferee;			

To be disclosed	Disclosure to	Form of disclosure	When
• the transfer date; • details of any unpaid charges and how those charges will be recovered; OR (in the case of a person entitled to the pension credit by virtue of *Pension Sharing (Implementation and Discharge of Liability) Regulations 2000 (SI 2000/1053), reg 6*) • the value of the pension credit rights; • any amount deducted by way of charges; • the value of the pension credit after deduction of charges; • the transfer day; • details of any unpaid charges, including how and when those charges will be recovered.			
PROVISION OF INFORMATION AFTER RECEIPT OF AN EARMARKING ORDER (*Pensions on Divorce etc. (Provision of Information) Regulations 2000 (SI 2000/1048), reg 10*)			
If a member's pension is not in payment, a list of circumstances in respect of any changes which the member or spouse or civil partner must notify to the trustees.	Member. Member's spouse or civil partner.	In writing.	Within 21 days of receipt of the order.

Appendix II

To be disclosed	Disclosure to	Form of disclosure	When
(Except in Scotland) if the order is made in respect of a member whose pension is in payment the notice will include: • the value of the pension rights or benefit of the member; • the amount of the member's pension after implementation of the order; • the first date when a pension pursuant to the order is to be made; • a list of the circumstances which the member and spouse or civil partner must notify to the trustees; • (to member only) the amount of the member's pension currently in payment and the amount of the member's pension after the order has been implemented.			

932

To be disclosed	Disclosure to	Form of disclosure	When
In any event: • the amount of any charges not yet paid by the member or spouse or civil partner in respect of the provision of information and how those charges will be recovered including the date when payment is required in whole or in part, the sums payable by the member and spouse or civil partner respectively and whether the sum will be deducted from payments of pension to the member or from payments for the spouse or civil partner.			

To be disclosed	Disclosure to	Form of disclosure	When
DISCLOSURE OF INFORMATION TO MEMBERS (*Stakeholder Pension Schemes Regulations 2000 (SI 2000/1403), regs 18, 18A and 18B and Sch 3*)			
For as far as the below information relates to that statement year or to the part of that statement year beginning with the first day of that statement year (whether or not that day is earlier than the day on which he becomes a member) and ending with the time at which he so ceases: An illustration of the amount, calculated in accordance with *reg 18B*, of the pension an entitlement to which would be likely to accrue to, or be capable of being secured by, the member at his retirement date in respect of rights that may arise under the scheme. This calculation may take account of a lump sum. Statements: • that the information is provided only for the purposes of illustration; • how to obtain further information from the trustees;	Member (subject to certain exclusions) for all or part of a statement year.	In writing (by post or, in some cases and subject to certain conditions, electronically).	Within three months of the end of that statement year or, where he ceases during that statement year to be a member, from the time he ceases to be a member to within three months of the end of that statement year. Where the member has requested specified information, as soon as practicable, and in any event within two months of the date the request is received.

934

To be disclosed	Disclosure to	Form of disclosure	When
• that certain general assumptions have been made in relation to the information provided;			
• that the amount referred to is expressed in today's prices;			
• of the member's retirement date;			
• of the illustration date used for the purpose of calculating the amount referred to in the illustration;			
• assumptions have been made about the nature of the investments made for the purposes of the member's money purchase benefits and their likely performance, which may not correspond to the actual investments or their performance;			
• that the actual amount of any pension under the scheme will depend on considerations which may differ from the assumptions made for the purpose of providing the illustration;			
• specifying any assumptions made in relation to future contributions to the scheme;			

935

To be disclosed	Disclosure to	Form of disclosure	When
• of any assumptions made relating to the lump sum, the level of increases in the pension and the pension payable to the spouse or civil partner; • of any changes to the assumptions mentioned in above that were used for the previous information given under *reg 18A(2)*. The value of the member's rights under the scheme on the day before the first day of the statement year, being an amount which is not less than the cash equivalent of those rights on that date. The value of the member's rights on the last day of the statement year, being not less than the cash equivalent of those rights on that day or, where he ceases during the statement year to be a member, being not less than the cash equivalent of those rights at the time immediately before he so ceases.			

To be disclosed	Disclosure to	Form of disclosure	When
The value of the member's rights on the last day of the statement year, being not less than the cash equivalent of those rights on that day or, where he ceases during the statement year to be a member, being not less than the cash equivalent of those rights at the time immediately before he so ceases.			
In relation to any permitted reduction in the member's rights, the rate, expressed as an annual percentage rate, at which, and the period in relation to which, deductions giving rise to that reduction were made, or where such deductions were made in relation to different periods at different rates, each rate in relation to each period.			
Either (*Sch 3, para 2*): The amount of the value of the member's rights during the statement year (or immediately before he ceased to be a member during the statement year) that is attributable to investment gains or losses made or sustained.			

937

Appendix II

To be disclosed	Disclosure to	Form of disclosure	When
The amount of each contribution made by, on behalf or in respect of the member and the date on which it was received.			
The amount of each contribution made by any employer and the date on which it was received.			
Except where contributions are increased by the trustees or manager in anticipation of a payment to the scheme by the Inland Revenue by way of tax relief in respect of the member, the amount of each such payment by the Inland Revenue and the date on which it was received.			
The amount of any transfer payment made to the scheme in respect of the member, the name of the scheme or arrangement from which the payment was made and the date on which it was made.			
Any amount credited to the member's account in respect of a pension credit under *WRPA 1999, s 29.*			

938

To be disclosed	Disclosure to	Form of disclosure	When
Any reduction under *WRPA 1999, s 31* (pension sharing: reduction of benefit), or any corresponding provision in Northern Ireland, in the benefits or future benefits to which the member is entitled under the scheme.			
Any amount paid to the member in accordance with *FA 2004, Sch 28, para 7 or 21*.			
Any other amount deducted from the member's account, the nature of the deduction and the date on which it was made.			
The total amount of any part of any of the contributions and payments which has not been credited to the member's account and the manner in which that amount has been used.			
Where the whole or any part of the member's rights under the scheme is represented by rights in a with-profits fund;			
– the principles adopted in allocating rights under that fund, including the extent of any smoothing of investment returns and the levels of any guarantees;			

To be disclosed	Disclosure to	Form of disclosure	When
– the principles which will be adopted in allocating such rights if the member's rights under the scheme cease to be represented by rights in that fund. **Or (*Sch 3, para 3*):** The total amount of contributions made by an employer on behalf of or in respect of the member. The total amount of other contributions made by, on behalf of, or in respect of, the member. Except where contributions are increased by the trustees or manager in anticipation of a payment to the scheme by the Inland Revenue by way of tax relief in respect of the member, the total amount of such payments by the Inland Revenue. The total amount of any deductions or payments from the member's account. A statement that the member may request from the scheme any of the information listed in *Sch 3, para 2*.			

To be disclosed	Disclosure to	Form of disclosure	When
In all cases: Any change in the scheme's rules or practice as regards the extent to which or the circumstances in which any of the following may be used otherwise than to provide benefits for or in respect of the member: • any payment made to the scheme by or on behalf of a member; • any amount credited to the member's account in respect of a pension credit under *WRPA 1999, s 29*; • any income or capital gain arising from the investment of such a payment, or • the value of any rights under the scheme.			Within one month of the change.

941

To be disclosed	Disclosure to	Form of disclosure	When
INDEPENDENT TRUSTEES (*Occupational Pension Schemes (Independent Trustee) Regulations 2005 (SI 2005/703), reg 13*)			
The trustee and the independent trustee must provide: • their name and address; • the scale of fees chargeable; • details of amounts charged to the scheme by the trustees in the past 12 months	Every member and or relevant trade union (in relation to the first point, as of course, within a reasonable period of appointment). Every member, prospective member or relevant trade union (in relation to all three points) on request.	In writing.	As of course, within a reasonable period of appointment. Within a reasonable period following the request (unless the same information was provided to the same person or trade union in the 12 months prior to the request being made).
EARLY LEAVERS: NOTIFICATION OF RIGHT TO CASH TRANSFER SUM OR CONTRIBUTION REFUND (*PA 2004, s 264, inserting s 101AC into PSA 1993*)			
Information adequate to explain the nature of the right acquired by him to a cash transfer sum or contribution refund and how he may exercise the right and such other information as may be prescribed. The statement must specify, in particular in relation to the cash transfer sum to which the member acquires a right, its amount and the permitted ways in which the member can use it, the amount of the contribution refund to which the member so acquires a right, and the last day on which the member may exercise the right.	A member whose pensionable service has terminated before he reaches normal pension age.	A statement in writing.	Within a reasonable period after the termination. This should usually be within three months.

942

To be disclosed	Disclosure to	Form of disclosure	When
INFORMATION AND CONSULTATION OF EMPLOYEES (*Information and Consultation of Employees Regulations 2004* (*SI 2004/3426*))			
Provision of information on: • decisions likely to lead to substantial changes in work organisation or in contractual relations, eg introduction of, or a change to, compulsory retirement age or changes to an occupational pension scheme but only where there was a contractual right to participate in the scheme; • recent development of the undertakings' activities and economic situation; • the situation, structure and probable development of employment within the undertaking. *Reg 17A* excludes certain consultation where it is required under the *Occupational and Personal Pension Schemes (Consultation by Employers and Miscellaneous Amendment) Regulations 2006* (see below).	Information and consultation representatives in organisations with 50 or more employees (calculated in accordance with *reg 4*).	Ensure that the method and content of the consultation are appropriate. Consult on the basis of the information supplied to the information and consultation representatives and in such a way as to enable the information and consultation representatives to meet the employer at the relevant level of management depending on the subject under discussion and to obtain a reasoned response from the employer to any such opinion. The employer must notify the information and consultation representatives in writing that it is complying with its duty under the legislation.	Either in line with any existing information or consultation agreements, or a negotiated information and consultation agreements or, in default, with appropriate timing. Must be given at such time, in such fashion and with such content as are appropriate to enable, in particular, the information and consultation representatives to conduct an adequate study and, where necessary, to prepare for consultation.

943

To be disclosed	Disclosure to	Form of disclosure	When
CONSULTATION BY EMPLOYERS (*Occupational and Personal Pension Schemes (Consultation by Employers and Miscellaneous Amendment) Regulations 2006 (SI 2006/349)*)			
For employers with occupational pension schemes making listed changes (see **Chapter 7**).	An employer with 50 or more employees (calculated in the same way as under *SI 2004/3426*) must embark on a consultation process with one or more of the following: • a trade union representative recognised for collective bargaining purposes; • an elected information and consultation representative (elected under the *Information and Consultation of Employees Regulations 2004 (SI 2004/3426)*; or In the absence of the appointment of one of the above, the employer must consult with representatives elected under the pension consultation requirement specifically in relation to the proposed pension changes.	Consultation, but employer must provide written information about the proposed changes.	At least 60 days before the change takes effect.

To be disclosed	Disclosure to	Form of disclosure	When
	The employer must consult directly with affected members of the pension scheme (which includes employees who are not yet members of the scheme but who are or will become eligible to join) where there are no representatives in place for direct consultation.		
	A person proposing to make a listed change which requires consultation must give written notice of that change to each employer in relation to the scheme.		

ENROLMENT INFORMATION PROVIDED FOR THE PURPOSES OF AUTOMATIC ENROLMENT (*Occupational and Personal Pension Schemes (Automatic Enrolment) Regulations 2010 (SI 2010/772), regs 2, 7, Sch 2*)

To be disclosed	Disclosure to	Form of disclosure	When
The employer must give the enrolment information, being: • a statement that the jobholder has been, or will be, enrolled into a pension scheme; • the jobholder's automatic enrolment date;	Any jobholder being automatically enrolled into an automatic enrolment scheme. The trustee or manager of the occupational pension scheme or the personal pension scheme provider.	In writing.	Within six weeks beginning on the jobholder's automatic enrolment date.

To be disclosed	Disclosure to	Form of disclosure	When
• the value of employer and jobholder contributions and a statement that jobholder contributions will be deducted from the jobholder's earnings and paid to the scheme; • confirmation as to whether tax relief is or will be given on employee contributions; • a statement that the jobholder has a right to opt out of the scheme during the opt-out period; • the start and end date of the opt-out period applicable to the jobholder; • where the opt-out notice may be obtained; • a statement that opting out means that the jobholder will be treated as not having become an active member of the scheme on that occasion; • a statement that, after a valid opt out notice is given to the employer, any contributions paid by the jobholder will be refunded to the jobholder by the employer;			

To be disclosed	Disclosure to	Form of disclosure	When
• a statement that a jobholder who opts out may opt in, in which case the employer will be required to arrange for him to become an active member of an automatic enrolment scheme once in any 12-month period; • a statement that, after the opt-out period, the jobholder may cease to make contributions in accordance with scheme rules; • a statement that a jobholder who opts out or who ceases active membership of an automatic enrolment scheme will normally be automatically re-enrolled into such a scheme by the employer in accordance with regulations made under *PA 2008, s 5*; and • a statement that a written notice from the worker must be signed by the worker or confirm that the worker personally submitted the notice in the case of electronic communication.			

JOBHOLDER INFORMATION PROVIDED FOR THE PURPOSES OF AUTOMATIC ENROLMENT (*Occupational and Personal Pension Schemes (Automatic Enrolment) Regulations 2010, (SI 2010/772) regs 3, 7*)

To be disclosed	Disclosure to	Form of disclosure	When
The employer must give information about the jobholder's: • name • date of birth • postal residential address • gender • automatic enrolment, automatic re-enrolment, or enrolment, date, as applicable • national insurance number • the gross earnings due to the jobholder in any applicable pay reference period • the value of any contributions payable to the scheme by the employer and the jobholder in any applicable pay reference period where this information is available to the employer • postal work address • individual work email address where the jobholder has been allocated such an email address • personal email address where the employer holds this information	The trustees or managers of the occupational pension scheme or the personal pension scheme provider	In writing.	At any time before the end of a period of six weeks beginning with the automatic enrolment date unless the trustees or managers notify the employer that they do not require certain pieces of information. Where the jobholder's national insurance number is not available to the employer on the automatic enrolment date, the time limit is varied, in the case of that piece of information only, to six weeks from the date on which the employer receives details of the national insurance number.

To be disclosed	Disclosure to	Form of disclosure	When
INFORMATION ON WORKERS' RIGHT TO JOIN PENSION SAVING (*Occupational and Personal Pension Schemes (Automatic Enrolment) Regulations 2010, (SI 2010/772) reg 21, Sch 2*)			
The employer must give the following information: A statement that the jobholder may, by giving written notice, require the employer to make arrangements for the jobholder to become an active member of an automatic enrolment scheme and that the jobholder will be entitled to employer's contributions.	Jobholders with a right to opt in (*PA 2008, s 7*)	In writing.	Within six weeks of *PA 2008, s 7* first applying to the jobholder.
A statement that the worker may, by giving written notice, require the employer to make arrangements for the worker to become an active member of a pension scheme but (optional) that the worker will not be entitled to employer contributions.			
	Workers without qualifying earnings (*PA 2008, s 9*).	In writing.	Within six weeks of *PA 2008, s 9* first applying to the worker.

949

To be disclosed	Disclosure to	Form of disclosure	When
INFORMATION ON POSTPONEMENT OF AUTOMATIC ENROLMENT (*Occupational and Personal Pension Schemes*) (*Automatic Enrolment*) *Regulations 2010, (SI 2010/772) reg 24, Sch 2*)			
An employer giving notice under PA 2008, s 4 that it intends to defer automatic enrolment for the worker by a period of up to three months must give the following information: • a statement that, by written notice to the employer: – a jobholder with gross earnings of more than £5,824 (which must be specified in the statement) who is not an active member of a qualifying scheme may opt in to an automatic enrolment scheme and that the jobholder will be entitled to employer's contributions; and – a worker who earns £5,824 or less (which must be specified in the statement), and who is not a member of a registered pension scheme, may require the employer to make arrangements for him to become an active member of such a pension scheme and that the worker will not be entitled to employer's contributions;	All workers	In writing.	Within six weeks after the staging/starting date.

To be disclosed	Disclosure to	Form of disclosure	When
• a statement that the employer has deferred automatic enrolment until a specified deferral date; • a statement that the employer will automatically enrol the worker into an automatic enrolment scheme if, on the deferral date, the worker satisfies the conditions for automatic enrolment (which must be listed); and • a statement that a written notice from the worker must be signed by the worker or confirm that the worker personally submitted the notice in the case of electronic communication.			
A statement that the jobholder may, by notice in writing, require the employer to make arrangements for the jobholder to become an active member of an automatic enrolment scheme and that the jobholder will be entitled to employer's contributions; or	All jobholders who are not active members of a qualifying scheme	In writing.	Within six weeks after the staging/starting date.
A statement that the worker may, by notice, require the employer to make arrangements for the worker to become an active member of a pension scheme;	All workers who are not jobholders and who are not active members of a qualifying scheme	In writing.	Within six weeks after the staging/starting date.

To be disclosed	Disclosure to	Form of disclosure	When
INFORMATION ON DB OR HYBRID SCHEME DURING TRANSITIONAL PERIOD (*Occupational and Personal Pension Schemes (Automatic Enrolment) Regulations 2010 (SI 2010/772), reg 27, Sch. 2*)			
An employer giving notice that it intends to defer automatic enrolment until the end of the transitional period for defined benefits and hybrid schemes must give the following information: • a statement that the jobholder may, by notice in writing, require the employer to make arrangements for the jobholder to become an active member of an automatic enrolment scheme and that the jobholder will be entitled to employer's contributions on qualifying earnings; • a statement that the employer intends to defer automatic enrolment in respect of the jobholder until the end of the transitional period; • a statement that a written notice from the worker must be signed by the worker or confirm that the worker personally submitted the notice in the case of electronic communication.	Jobholders who qualify for automatic enrolment, who on the employer's first enrolment date are active members of the employer's qualifying DB or hybrid scheme and who remain so during the transitional period.	In writing.	Within six weeks after the employer's first enrolment date.

To be disclosed	Disclosure to	Form of disclosure	When
ON THE DEATH OF A MEMBER *Registered Pension Schemes (Provision of Information) Regulations 2006 (SI 2006/567), reg 8*			
The percentage of standard lifetime allowance expended by, and the amount and the date of payment of, a relevant lump sum death benefit by the scheme in relation to the member.	Personal representatives of the deceased scheme member.		No later than the last day of the period of three months beginning with the day on which the final lump sum death benefit payment is made.
The total percentage of standard lifetime allowance expended, at the date of the statement, by:			No later than the last day of the period of two months beginning with the day on which a request for it is received from the member's personal representatives.
• any BCE in respect of the deceased member's rights under the scheme to the extent that the sums and assets have not been transferred to another registered pension scheme; and			
• any BCE in connection with sums or assets that have been transferred to the scheme from another registered pension scheme in respect of the deceased member			
excluding any amount in respect of any lump sum death benefit payment, any designated, unused uncrystallised funds and any aggregate amount in respect of an entitlement to a dependant's or nominee's annuity.			

To be disclosed	Disclosure to	Form of disclosure	When
excluding any amount in respect of any lump sum death benefit payment, any designated, unused uncrystallised funds and any aggregate amount in respect of an entitlement to a dependant's or nominee's annuity.			No later than the last day of the period of three months beginning with the day on which the designation is made.
Where there is a designation of relevant unused uncrystallised funds as available to a dependent or nominee of the member: • the percentage of standard lifetime allowance expended by the designation; • the amount designated; and • the date of designation.			
Where the member was entitled to a dependants' or nominees' annuity: • the percentage of standard lifetime allowance expended; • the aggregate of the amount of such of the sums and the market value of such of the assets applied to the purchase of the annuity as are relevant unused uncrystallised funds; and • the date on which the person became entitled to the annuity.			No later than the last day of the period of three months beginning with the day on which the person became entitled to the annuity.

LIFETIME ALLOWANCE *Registered Pension Schemes (Provision of Information) Regulations 2006 (SI 2006/567), regs 12, 14*

To be disclosed	Disclosure to	Form of disclosure	When
If the scheme administrator has made or intends to make a payment in respect of his liability to account for a lifetime allowance charge on a benefit crystallisation event: • the chargeable amount in respect of the benefit crystallisation event; • how that chargeable amount has been calculated; • the amount of the resulting charge to tax; and • whether the scheme administrator has accounted for the tax or intends to do so.	Members subject to a lifetime allowance charge.		
The percentage of standard lifetime allowance expended by: • benefit crystallisation events in respect of the scheme, to the extent that the sums or assets subject to any such event have not been transferred to another registered pension scheme; and	Members (or if a member has died, their personal representatives) who have an actual (as opposed to a prospective) entitlement to be paid a pension or in respect of whom a benefit crystallisation event has occurred.		Regarding members with an actual right to be paid a pension, at least once in each tax year. Within three months after the benefit crystallisation event.

To be disclosed	Disclosure to	Form of disclosure	When
• where the scheme has received (whether directly or indirectly) a transfer in respect of the member, any benefit crystallisation event, prior to the transfer, in connection with the sums or assets represented by the transfer.			Not required if this information has already been supplied under *regs 16, 17 or 17A*; in a tax year following the tax year in which the member reaches the age of 75; or if a statement is required under *reg 8*.
UNAUTHORISED PAYMENTS *Registered Pension Schemes (Provision of Information) Regulations 2006 (SI 2006/567), reg 13*			
The nature of the benefit provided. The amount of the unauthorised payment which is treated as being made by the provision of the benefit. The date on which the benefit was provided.	Members to whom an unauthorised payment has been made.		Before 7 July following the tax year in which the payment is made.
FLEXIBLE BENEFITS *Registered Pension Schemes (Provision of Information) Regulations 2006 (SI 2006/567), reg 14ZA*			
The scheme administrator must inform the member that: • a relevant event has occurred in relation to the member and that, as a result, the member has flexibly accessed the member's pension rights (although may have first done so previously);	A member in relation to whom a 'relevant event' occurs: • a qualifying payment is made to the member from their flexi-access drawdown fund; • an uncrystallised funds pension lump sum is paid to the member;		Before the end of the 31 days beginning with the date of the relevant event. Not required if the information has already been provided to the member in respect of an earlier relevant event or if the scheme administrator is informed that the member has already flexibly accessed pension rights.

To be disclosed	Disclosure to	Form of disclosure	When
• if in any tax year the total of the pension inputs to money purchase arrangements, and certain hybrid arrangements, relating to the member exceeds £10,000, there will be an annual allowance tax charge on the excess, and the annual allowance for pension inputs to other arrangements relating to the member will be £10,000 less than it would otherwise be; and • the duties under *regulation 14ZB* and the circumstances in which the member will have to comply with them.	• the first payment of a lifetime annuity under a flexible annuity contract; • the first payment of the scheme pension where the member was entitled to the scheme pension after 5 April 2015, he became entitled at a time when fewer than 11 other individuals were entitled and it is not payable under an annuity contract; • a stand-alone lump sum is paid on or after 6 April 2015 to the member in circumstances where *article 25B(2) of the Taxation of Pension Schemes (Transitional Provisions) Order 2006* applies.		

To be disclosed	Disclosure to	Form of disclosure	When
ANNUAL ALLOWANCE *(Registered Pension Schemes (Provision of Information) Regulations 2006 (SI 2006/567), regs 14A, 14B*			
The aggregate of the pension input amounts for the relevant pension input period in respect of all arrangements relating to the member.	• Active members, and • deferred members of cash balance or defined benefit arrangements where the value of the member's rights does not increase during the PIP by more than the relevant statutory increase percentage;		No later than 6 October following the relevant tax year.
The annual allowance for the tax year in which the relevant pension input period ends ('the relevant tax year').	where the member is a member for all or part of a pension input period ending in a tax year; AND		
The aggregate of the pension input amounts for the relevant pension input period in respect of all arrangements relating to the member for each of the pension input periods ending in the three tax years immediately preceding the relevant tax year.	the aggregate of the pension input amounts for the relevant pension input period in respect of each arrangement under the registered pension scheme relating to the member exceeds the annual allowance for that tax year.		
The annual allowance for each of the three preceding tax years or where one or more of the three preceding tax years is the 2008/09, 2009/10 or 2010/11 tax year, the assumed annual allowance for that tax year pursuant to *para 30(3)(a) of Sch 17 to the Finance Act 2011*.			

To be disclosed	Disclosure to	Form of disclosure	When
The total of: • the pension input amounts for the relevant pension input period in respect of each money purchase arrangement relating to the member under the scheme, and • the pension input amounts for the relevant pension input period in respect of each hybrid arrangement under the scheme that relates to the member.	• Active members, and • deferred members of cash balance or defined benefit arrangements where the value of the member's rights does not increase during the PIP by more than the relevant statutory increase percentage; where the member is a member for all or part of a pension input period ending in a tax year; **AND**		No later than 6 October following the relevant tax year. If the member's employer does not provide the scheme administrator with PIP information, within three months of receiving that information, on or before 6 October following the relevant tax year.
The total of: • the pension input amounts for the relevant pension input period in respect of each defined benefits arrangement relating to the member under the scheme, and • the pension input amounts for the relevant pension input period in respect of each hybrid arrangement under the scheme that relates to the member, for which the pension input amount for the relevant pension input period is input amount C mentioned in section 237, and that is made before 14 October 2014 and has not become a hybrid arrangement (whether or not for the first time) on or after that day,	The scheme administrator has reason to believe that the member has first flexibly accessed pension rights for the purposes of sections 227B to 227F. **Condition E** That the overall total of the following amounts is more than £10,000: (a) for each money purchase arrangement relating to the member under the scheme, the pension input amount for the relevant pension input period in respect of the arrangement, and		

959

Appendix II

To be disclosed	Disclosure to	Form of disclosure	When
• for each hybrid arrangement relating to the member under the scheme that is made on or after 14 October 2014 or has become a hybrid arrangement (whether or not for the first time) on or after that day, and for which the pension input amount for the relevant pension input period is input amount C mentioned in section 237, which of input amounts A, B and C mentioned in section 237 is a relevant input amount for the purposes of section 237 for the relevant pension input period in the case of the arrangement, and the amount of each of those input amounts that in the case of the arrangement is a relevant input amount for those purposes for that period; • the unadjusted alternative annual allowance for the relevant tax year, and the fact the member's money-purchase input sub-total for the relevant tax year will be tested against a £10,000 allowance;	(b) for each hybrid arrangement relating to the member under the scheme, the greater of such of input amounts A and B mentioned in section 237 as are, for the purposes of section 237, relevant input amounts for the relevant pension input period in the case of the arrangement.		

960

To be disclosed	Disclosure to	Form of disclosure	When
• the unadjusted alternative annual allowance for each of the three preceding tax years, and the fact that the member's money-purchase input sub-total for each of those preceding years will be tested against a £10,000 allowance or, if any of those preceding years is earlier than the tax year 2015/6, the annual allowance for each such earlier year, and • for each of those three preceding years, the information given in the pension savings statement for the pension input period ending in that year under, as the case may be, sub-paragraphs (a) to (c) or paragraph (2)(a).			

To be disclosed	Disclosure to	Form of disclosure	When
A pension savings statement containing the pension input amount in respect of the pre-announcement period and post-announcement period.	Where a member's pension input period in the tax year 2011/12 begins before 14 October 2010 and the total pension input amount for that tax year exceeds £50,000.		
The aggregate of the pension input amounts for the relevant pension input period in respect of all arrangements relating to the member.			
The annual allowance for the tax year in which the relevant pension input period ends ('the relevant tax year').			
The aggregate of the pension input amounts for the relevant pension input period in respect of all arrangements relating to the member for each of the pension input periods ending in the three tax years immediately preceding the relevant tax year.			
The annual allowance for each of the three preceding tax years or where one or more of the three preceding tax years is the 2008/09, 2009/10 or 2010/11 tax year, the assumed annual allowance for that tax year pursuant to *para 30(3)(a) of Sch 17 to the Finance Act 2011*.			

To be disclosed	Disclosure to	Form of disclosure	When
The information requested by the member.	Members, on request.		Within three months following receipt of the written request from the member or, if later, on or before 6 October following the tax year in which the relevant pension input period ended.

Index

Index